Table Ib Percentiles of the Normal Distribution

This table gives values that have specified probabilities p to the left of them for the standard normal distribution.

p	.000	.005	.010	.015	.020	.025	.030	.035	.040	.045
.500	.000	.013	.025	.038	.050	.063	.075	.088	.100	.
.550	.126	.138	.151	.164	.176	.189	.202	.215	.228	.240
.600	.253	.266	.279	.292	.306	.319	.332	.345	.359	.372
.650	.385	.399	.413	.426	.440	.454	.468	.482	.496	.510
.700	.524	.539	.553	.568	.583	.598	.613	.628	.643	.659
.750	.675	.690	.706	.723	.739	.755	.772	.789	.806	.824
.800	.842	.860	.878	.897	.915	.935	.954	.974	.995	1.015
.850	1.036	1.058	1.080	1.103	1.126	1.150	1.175	1.200	1.227	1.254
.900	1.282	1.311	1.341	1.372	1.405	1.440	1.476	1.514	1.555	1.598
.950	1.645	1.695	1.751	1.812	1.881	1.960	2.054	2.171	2.326	2.576

Example: To find the number with area .735 to the left of it under the standard normal curve, locate the tabled entry at the intersection of the .700 row and the .035 column. This gives $P(Z < .628) = .735$. To find the number with .265 area to the left of it under the standard normal curve, use symmetry and the fact that $.265 = 1 - .735$ to obtain $P(Z < -.628) = .265$.

STATISTICS
for Business
and Economics

S. Christian Albright

INDIANA UNIVERSITY

STATISTICS
for Business and Economics

MACMILLAN PUBLISHING COMPANY
NEW YORK
COLLIER MACMILLAN PUBLISHERS
LONDON

Macmillan Publishing Company
866 Third Avenue, New York, New York 10022

Collier Macmillan Canada, Inc.

LIBRARY OF CONGRESS CATALOGING IN PUBLICATION DATA

Albright, S. Christian.
  Statistics for business and economics.

  Includes index.
  1. Commercial statistics.   2. Statistics.   I. Title.
HF1017.A43   1987   519.5   86-23751
ISBN 0-02-301620-5

Printing: 1 2 3 4 5 6 7 8   Year: 7 8 9 0 1 2 3 4 5 6

To My Parents

Preface

Due to the increasing use of data analysis in today's business world, the subject of statistics is now a required course in practically every undergraduate and graduate business program. Yet a great many students continue to dread this course, either because they believe the mathematics is too difficult, or they believe the subject is irrelevant, or both. Instructors know that neither of these beliefs is well founded. At the elementary level at least, the subject of statistics is intuitive and the various techniques can be mastered without too much difficulty if they are taught properly. As far as relevance is concerned, there is no doubt that statistics is used and is indeed a necessity in a wide variety of business areas, including quality control, marketing research, stock price analysis, and others. The fact of the matter is that statistics *can* be learned without too much pain and, more importantly, it does provide a set of very useful tools for the business world.

The purpose of this book is to convey this message. Specifically, I have written this book with the following broad goals in mind: (1) to present the main ideas and techniques of statistics in an intuitive and interesting manner, without allowing mathematical symbols to obscure these ideas; (2) to show how statistics can be used in a wide variety of business applications; and (3) to provide a large number of realistic examples and problems that help students to learn the material. This set of goals is by no means unique to my book; many authors have expressed the same goals. However, as I will discuss below, I believe I have incorporated a number of features into my book that will make it quite attractive relative to much of the competition.

1. The statistical ideas are presented in an intuitive manner whenever possible. Many statistics texts present a quick explanation of an idea or a technique, then give the relevant formula, and finish by working a numerical example or two. I also go through this sequence, but I try to provide more insight into what is behind the idea and why the technique works the way it does. For example, in Chapter 6, I explain the intuitive idea behind sampling distributions, rather than simply stating, for example, that the distribution of the sample mean is approximately normal with the appropriate mean and standard deviation. In this case and in many others, it is possible for students to learn techniques by rote and without much understanding, but they will certainly be more successful in applying these techniques and remembering them if they understand the underlying concepts.

2. I rely as little as possible on advanced mathematical knowledge and mathematical notation, and instead, concentrate more on statistical ideas. Of course, statistics is a quantitative subject, and some mathematics and mathematical notation are necessary. It certainly helps, for example, to use summation notation and subscripts. But for an introductory course in statistics, I do not believe calculus is a real necessity, and I have avoided it in all but several optional appendices. In this case the point is not that students have not had calculus—most of them probably have—but that just as many *statistical* ideas, even relatively advanced ones, can be learned without using calculus. In general, I have used mathematical techniques and notation only when they are necessary or aid the understanding of the statistical ideas. In addition, since many students need a "refresher course" even on basic mathematical knowledge, I have also included a *Mathematical Background* appendix to cover such topics as linear functions, exponential and logarithm functions, and summation notation.

3. There is an emphasis on probability throughout the text (except for Chapter 2 on descriptive statistics). Students must learn that probability is the key to statistical inference, and they must learn how to perform probability calculations. However, the traditional emphasis on counting formulas for applications such as flipping coins, rolling dice, and card games has been minimized. The only counting formulas introduced are those that help to motivate the binomial and hypergeometric distributions in the context of sampling.

4. Throughout the book, there are numerous realistic examples taken from business applications. These not only serve to illustrate the statistical techniques, but they also show how pervasive statistical applications are in the business world. At the end of most of these examples, there is a short explanation of what the results mean; the student is not simply left with a numerical answer.

5. There are approximately 60–70 problems per chapter. These occur within the chapters and at the ends of chapters, and they range from very straightforward exercises to those that require more complex reasoning and/or mathematical manipulation. (The more difficult problems are marked with an asterisk.) With very few exceptions these problems deal with business applications, and many of them draw on articles from business or news publications. Also, a large percentage of the problems have small or medium-sized data sets, so that the students must start the calculations from the raw data, as they would have to do in the real world.

6. There are several features in each chapter that make the book easier to use. These include a list of chapter objectives and a short table of contents at the beginning of each chapter, and a short summary, a glossary of important terms, and a list of important formulas at the end of each chapter. In addition, key formulas, terms, and results are boxed in as they appear throughout the chapters.

7. Whenever it is particularly applicable, as in the regression chapters and in the time series chapter, computer printouts from standard statistical packages are provided and explained. The particular packages used are SPSS (Statistical Package for the Social Sciences) and IDA (Interactive Data Analysis). No attempt is made to teach students how to use these packages; this is done better by the manuals that accompany the packages. Instead, I stress interpretation of the output, and I stress that the outputs from most of the available packages are very similar. This should allow instructors to use whatever packages are available at their schools without fear of inconsistency with the text.

8. Whenever possible, I stress the similarities among statistical techniques. For example, in the chapter on hypothesis testing I present all of the main ideas and formulas for a test of the population mean. Then I give a table (Table 9.2) that lists the forms of the other standard tests. This table reinforces the important idea, to be seen in subsequent chapters, that all tests can be performed by comparing a test statistic with a value from one of the statistical tables.

9. Recognizing that regression analysis is one of the most widely used topics in statistics, I have taken extra care to present a relatively complete treatment of simple and multiple regression. The regression chapters represent one of the main strengths of the book.

The features listed above are present to some extent in a large number of competing statistics texts. The features listed below, however, are much less prevalent in competing texts.

10. I have frequently used computer-generated random samples from a given population distribution to provide insight into sampling distributions and estimation problems. For example, in Chapter 7, I generate 40 random samples from a known distribution and use each of them to calculate a 90% confidence interval for the mean. By seeing that approximately 90% of these intervals include the true mean, the students gain an extra bit of insight into what a 90% confidence interval really means.

11. In terms of coverage, this book has all of the usual topics plus a few extras not usually seen in introductory texts. These extras include (1) a discussion of the estimation of the difference between two means when the population variances are not assumed to be equal; (2) a discussion of randomized block designs and two-way analysis of variance; (3) a treatment of dummy variables, nonlinear terms, and interactive terms in multiple regression analysis; (4) a discussion of Winters' exponential smoothing method for time series data; and (5) an entire chapter (Chapter 16) on survey sampling methods. With the possible exception of (1), any of these topics can easily be omitted without losing continuity.

12. Each chapter concludes with two or three *Applications*. These are discussions of real applications cited in business journals, magazines, or newspapers. They show specifically how statistics has been applied in such areas as marketing, accounting, economics, finance, and information systems. They are interesting in their own right, and they should furnish material for further class discussion. In addition, each chapter begins with a short discussion of one of these applications as a lead-in to the statistical topic of that particular chapter.

13. The final unique feature of this book (saving the best for last) is a statistical software package written in BASIC for use on IBM or IBM-compatible microcomputers. (A slightly scaled-down version is also available for Apple computers.) While this package is not nearly as complete as, say, SPSS or IDA, it does allow students to perform the vast majority of the statistical methods discussed in this book. Furthermore, it takes almost no time to learn, an important advantage over the more powerful packages. A short "mini-manual" is provided as an appendix to the text, but even without reading this manual, students should be able to follow the menu-driven programs with little difficulty. In addition, several data sets and "computer problems" have been included in each chapter to accompany the software. These data sets are listed in Appendix D and are stored on the computer disk for easy use with several of the programs in the package.

This book can be used in several ways. First, it can be used for undergraduate or graduate (particularly MBA) students. It is my belief that the main difference between these two groups is an appreciation and understanding of business problems, not mathematical ability. Therefore, it seems perfectly reasonable to use the same statistics text for both groups. I certainly had both groups in mind when I wrote this text.

Second, the book can be used for a one- or two-semester course in statistics. If the course lasts for one semester, then coverage should extend through Chapter 9. For a two-semester course, the second semester should cover at least Chapters 10, 11, 12, and 14. Beyond that, instructors can choose topics of most interest to them. In any case, Chapter 16 on survey sampling requires a bit of explanation. Some instructors believe survey sampling topics are a must; others never teach them. Because of the latter group, I did not place this chapter where it logically belongs, between Chapters 7 and 8. However, for those instructors who wish to cover this material, it fits nicely after Chapter 7 and should probably be covered at that stage in the course.

This text is accompanied by a complete supplementary package:

1. *Student Solutions Manual.* This item, of which I am the author, is for sale to students and contains completely worked-out solutions to the odd-numbered problems (the ones that are answered in the back of the text).

2. *Faculty Solutions Manual.* This item, also written by myself, is for instructors only and contains solutions to the even-numbered problems. These solutions are not available elsewhere, so the even-numbered problems can be used for quizzes and exams.

3. *Test Bank.* The test bank, developed by Michael Broida of Miami University at Oxford, Ohio, includes 1000 multiple-choice items.

4. *MICROTEST.* The test bank is available on Macmillan's microcomputer-based test generator system (for IBM, Apple II, and TRS 80 microcomputers).

5. *Student Study Guide.* The study guide, prepared by Ronald Coccari of Cleveland State University, stresses problem-solving by presenting a large number of solved and unsolved problems. It also provides a short summary of important concepts from each chapter of the text.

Acknowledgments

There are several people who helped a great deal to make this a quality book. Foremost among them is my editor, Jack Repcheck. Besides being a really nice and accessible person throughout the whole project, he was the one who kept pushing me to go one or two steps further. At times, I wondered whether I would have the energy to do everything Jack suggested, but now that the project is finished, I know he was right. Second, I would like to thank Susan Reiland. At first, her role was as a reviewer. Later I was fortunate that she agreed to become my production supervisor. In both roles, she brought an unbelievable perfectionism that would have been difficult to do without.

The manuscript for this book went through more rounds of reviewing than I would like to count. Among other things, I learned that everyone who teaches statistics has his or her own opinions on how it should be done, and a consensus is practically impossible to obtain. Therefore, I am certain that I was unable to incorporate all of the fine suggestions made by the reviewers. But their impact on the finished product was tremendous, and I would like to acknowledge their contributions: Larry M. Austin, Paul D. Berger, Michael Broida (Miami University), P. L. Claypool (Oklahoma State University), Ronald L. Coccari (Cleveland State University), James S. Ford (University of Southern California), D. H. Frank (Indiana University of Pennsylvania), Godfrey Ibom (Franklin University), Albert Kagan (University of Northern Iowa), Ronald S. Koot (The Pennsylvania State University), Vince LaRiccia (University of Delaware), Ralph H. Miller (California Polytechnic Institute and State University), David W. Pentico, Jackie Redder (Virginia Polytechnic Institute), Susan L. Reiland, Don R. Robinson (Illinois State University), Ernest M. Scheuer (University of California, Los Angeles), Mack C. Shelley II (Iowa State University), Michael G. Sklar (University of Georgia), Pamela H. Specht (University of Nebraska at Omaha), William R.

Stewart, Jr. (College of William and Mary), Luis G. Vargas (University of Pittsburgh), Richard Withycombe (University of Montana), and Mustafa R. Yilmaz (Northeastern University).

I would also like to make a couple personal acknowledgments. I am both appreciative and proud of my wife Mary and my son Sam for not complaining about the ordeal of living with a textbook writer. Many of my weekend and evening hours were spent at the computer terminal working on "the book," but neither of them ever nagged me about when I was ever going to finish. (Well, almost never.) Finally, I would like to thank all of my piano teachers over the years. After spending hours at the computer keyboard, the ability to relax at the piano keyboard was wonderful!

S. C. A.

Contents

Sampling Distributions   247

Large-Sample Estimation   301

CHAPTER *14*

Time Series Analysis, Forecasting, and Index Numbers   715

CHAPTER *15*

Decision Making Under Uncertainty   783

CHAPTER *16*

Methods of Survey Sampling   861

CHAPTER 1

Introduction to Data Analysis

Objectives

1. To classify the types of data that arise in statistical applications.
2. To learn the most important methods for obtaining data.
3. To learn the most important sources of errors in data analysis.
4. To gain an appreciation for the types of statistical applications we study in this book.

Contents

1.1
Introduction

The subject of statistics is the study of data analysis. The goal is to make sense out of data so that users in such diverse areas as marketing research, auditing, quality control, and economic forecasting can make intelligent conclusions. In this chapter we begin our study of statistics by giving a brief overview of four aspects of data. In Section 1.2 we describe the types of data that arise in statistical contexts. In Section 1.3 we discuss the sources of data that are available. In Section 1.4 we discuss the primary sources of errors in data analysis. Finally, in Section 1.5 we present several examples that illustrate typical statistical applications.

1.2
Types of Data

Suppose that a television ratings service mails a questionnaire to selected families requesting information about the family and its television-viewing habits. Let's consider the types of data the families will be asked to supply. We begin by distinguishing two basic types of data: qualitative data and quantitative data. Qualitative data are often referred to as categorical data, because the data specify which of several categories each observation is in. Quantitative data, on the other hand, are inherently numerical data. As we discuss below, this type of data arises from counting or measuring.

The simplest type of qualitative data is called *dichotomous* data. In this case there are only two possible categories. For example, if one of the questions is "Are you married?", the only possible responses are "yes" and "no." Other examples of dichotomous data are (1) whether a prospective employee is hired or not, (2) whether a customer purchases a company's product or not, (3) whether a manufactured item is defective or not, and (4) whether the price of a certain stock rises or does not rise. We discuss these and many other examples of dichotomous data throughout this book.

> Dichotomous data are categorical data with only two categories.

Suppose that the questionnaire asks us which brand of television we watch most often. The type of data requested here is also qualitative, but it is not dichotomous because there are more than two possible categories. Other examples of qualitative nondichotomous data are (1) the company from which a person has bought his car insurance, (2) the religion to which a person belongs, and (3) the type of energy a family uses to heat its home.

In contrast to qualitative data, consider the data required by the questions "How many television sets do you own?" and "How long has it been since you bought a television set?" Now the data requested are quantitative. As these two questions indicate, quantitative data generally arise in two ways: by *counts* and by *measurements*.

When we ask a person how many television sets he or she owns, the answer is obtained by counting the number of sets. For this reason the answer is an integer (a whole number), since an answer such as 3.7 obviously makes no sense. Whenever we ask for the *number* of something, such as the number of faculty members in a business school, the number of bonds included in an investment portfolio, or the number of brands of home computers on the market, we are asking for data that arise from counts and are therefore integer-valued.

On the other hand, when we ask a person how long it has been since he or she bought a television set, we are asking the person to measure a certain length of time. The answer could be any number greater than 0, such as 3 years, 3.25 years, or 3.2562 years. It is not likely that a person would answer with as much precision as 3.2562; in fact, there is a tendency to round the answer to a number such as 3 or 3.5. However, there is nothing impossible about the 3.2562 answer. This is because the answer to the question results from a measurement.

Other examples of measurement data are a company's net profit for the preceding year, the length of time between calls to a switchboard, and the fraction of time a bank teller is busy with customers on a given day. Admittedly, the data from any of these situations are often rounded to the nearest convenient unit, but conceptually these data can have *any* values, not just integers. This is the essential difference between count data and measurement data: the former are necessarily integer-valued, while the latter are not. (Roughly speaking, this is the distinction we will see when we discuss discrete and continuous random variables in Chapter 4. However, we postpone the terms "discrete" and "continuous" until then.)

Four Scales of Data

So far, we have divided data into two types, qualitative (or categorical) and quantitative (or numerical). We now categorize data in a slightly different way. We separate all possible data into four groups, often called *scales,* on the basis of their "quantitativeness." These types are called (1) nominal data, (2) ordinal data, (3) interval data, and (4) ratio data.

Nominal data represent a subset of qualitative data. Each piece of nominal data is a nonnumerical "name" of one of the possible categories. For example, if the categories are "have never been married," "am presently married," and "was married but am presently unmarried," each response indicates the category a particular person is in.

With nominal data there is no implication that the categories are ordered in any way. For example, we do not imply that the "never married" category is any better or worse than the "presently married" category. However, if the categories can be ordered in a natural way, the data are called ordinal data. A good example of ordinal data in business is a bond rating. The possible ratings are Aaa, Aa, A, and so on. The higher the rating, the safer the bond. Therefore, the ordering of the categories is based on safety.

There are many other examples of ordinal data. One example is when the possible responses to a question are "disagree strongly," "disagree slightly," "neither agree nor disagree," "agree slightly," or "agree strongly." Another example is when a marketing researcher asks respondents to rate a new product in relation to the brand they currently use: "worse than," "about the same as," or "better than." In these and similar examples, the data requested can be ordered in a natural way, but any numerical assignment to the categories is rather arbitrary.

> Nominal data occur when each piece of data falls into one of several "name" categories. Ordinal data are the same as nominal data, except that there is a natural ordering of the categories.

The last two scales of data, the interval and ratio scales, represent quantitative data. For the purposes of this book, we will not need to distinguish between these two scales; we will simply refer to *quantitative* data. For the sake of completeness, however, we provide a simple example that illustrates the basic difference between these two scales.

Consider temperature data. There are two common measures of temperature, Fahrenheit and Celsius. These are equally informative, and there are simple formulas for converting one to another. Suppose that we have observed the following temperatures in three cities on a given day: San Francisco, 68°F (20°C); New York, 50°F (10°C); Chicago, 32°F (0°C). The difference between San Francisco and New York is 18°F, and the difference between San Francisco and Chicago is 36°F. The corresponding Celsius differences are 10° and 20°. Notice that the *ratio* of these two differences is ½ for Fahrenheit *and* for Celsius. This is the important property of interval data: The ratio of two differences does not depend on the unit of measurement.

On the other hand, we cannot say that it was $^{68}/_{32}$ as warm in San Francisco as it was in New York, or that it was $^{68}/_{50}$ times as warm in San Francisco as it was in New York. When we say that one object is twice as warm (or large or expensive, etc.) as another, we mean that the first object is twice as far from a natural *zero* point as the second. But with interval data there is no natural zero point. Clearly, neither zero degrees Fahrenheit nor zero degrees Celsius indicates the lack of *any* temperature.

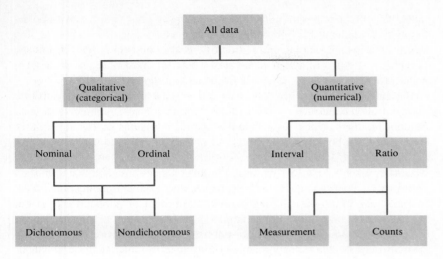

Figure 1.1
Data Classification

Quantitative data that satisfy the properties of interval data but have a natural zero point are called ratio data. Most of the quantitative data we encounter are of this type.

> Interval and ratio data are both quantitative data. The basic difference between them is that there is no natural zero point for interval data.

Figure 1.1 summarizes the types of data we have discussed. Notice that either scale of quantitative data, interval or ratio, can arise from measurements, but data that result from counts are always ratio data. Similarly, either scale of qualitative data, nominal or ordinal, can be dichotomous or nondichotomous. Most ordinal data, however, are nondichotomous because there are usually more than two ordered categories.

1.3
Sources of Data

Now that we know what types of data exist, we discuss the sources of data. This is an important topic for at least two reasons. The first is that no matter how well we understand statistical formulas or how sophisticated our techniques are, we cannot obtain good results if the data we collect are inaccurate or inappropriate. There is an important principle to remember here, the so-called GIGO (garbage-in-garbage-out) principle. This simply says that no amount of mathematical or computer magic can transform poor data into worthwhile results. The second reason data collection is important is that this is typically the part of a statistical study where the most time and money are spent. We certainly want to spend this time and money wisely.

Basically, there are three main sources of data: published data, surveys, and controlled experiments. We also list a fourth source, computer-generated random numbers, since we will have several occasions to use this source throughout this book.

Published Data

No matter what field we are interested in, the chances are good that published data about it exists somewhere. We can check government publications, trade journals, academic journals, and a wide assortment of publications put out by individual companies. For example, most companies publicize data on their financial positions, magazines publish data on television ratings, trade journals publish data on new manufacturing practices, medical journals publish data on the effects of new drugs, and so on.

A recent article by Vaughn (Reference: Ronald L. Vaughn, ''Demographic Data Banks: A New Management Resource,'' *Business Horizons,* Vol. 27, 1984, pp. 38–42) suggests that the number of published data sources is already larger than most people realize and is constantly growing. This is due primarily to the ability of computers to store large sets of data. Many private companies and nonprofit organizations are now in the business of selling data stored on computer tapes to companies that need the information. For example, The Roper Center, Incorporated, is a nonprofit organization that maintains a huge supply of public opinion data; it contains results from over 10,000 separate public opinion studies. Another example is Chase Econometrics, a private company that provides specialized services in forecasting population trends based on demographic models. Obviously, these types of companies are attractive sources of data because the data have already been compiled and are usually available at a reasonable cost.

Surveys, Polls, and Samples

When published data are unavailable or inappropriate, it may be necessary to conduct a survey to obtain data. (Frequently used synonyms for survey are poll, or opinion poll, and sample.) The population we survey usually consists of *people,* but this is not always the case. For example, we could sample a few manufactured items from a large batch of these items in order to measure the quality of the batch. Or we could sample several supermarkets throughout the country to discover whether food prices in some parts of the country are higher than in others.

There are two aspects of surveys (or polls or samples) that we will discuss. The first is certainly important but is not really the subject of this book. It concerns the techniques for obtaining data from the members of the population we decide to survey. We discuss this aspect only briefly. The second aspect plays a much more important role in our study of statistics: Which members and how many members of the population should we survey?

Suppose that a company has been marketing a new product in a relatively small region of the country, and it wishes to survey people's attitudes toward the product. Once it decides which people it is going to survey, how should it proceed? There are basically three possibilities: person-to-person interviews, telephone surveys, and questionnaires.

The most expensive and time-consuming technique is to interview the people in person. This technique generally results in a high response rate, and it allows the interviewer to obtain more complete answers than could be obtained through other techniques. The primary advantage of this approach, in fact, is the in-depth quality of the answers obtained.

A less costly and less time-consuming technique is to perform a telephone survey. Again the response rate is generally good, but the type of information obtained is generally not as complete as in a person-to-person interview. If the company marketing the new product decides to use this method, there are several considerations that it should keep in mind. On the one hand, it can obtain the desired data quickly and fairly inexpensively. On the other hand, however, it risks losing goodwill among potential customers because most people do not like to be bothered at home or at the office by telephone surveys.

The third and most common technique for performing a survey is to mail out questionnaires. This method is the least expensive technique and is not too time-consuming. Its drawbacks are that the response rate is often low and the data obtained are often not as complete as with the first two techniques. Despite these drawbacks, questionnaires are being used increasingly often to obtain data.

There are several guidelines for developing a good questionnaire. First, the questionnaire must be understandable and unambiguous to the people being surveyed. Second, it should be as short as possible to accomplish its purpose, because the response rate will almost surely decrease as the length of the questionnaire increases. Finally, the questionnaire must be designed so that the data obtained are appropriate for the particular study. The author of a poorly designed questionnaire will no doubt wish, *after* he receives the responses, that he had asked more questions or different questions. But by that time, it is too late. Respondents do not want to fill out two questionnaires from the same company or the same person, especially if they believe the second questionnaire is a follow-up to a poorly designed first one.

The other aspect of surveys is choosing the members of the population to be surveyed. This selection process is extremely important in the subject of statistics. Which members of the population should be surveyed, and how many members should be surveyed? In this chapter we only touch upon these issues, but in later chapters we study them in detail.

In practically any statistical study, the objective of the study is to learn about one or more characteristics of a population. Political pollsters try to discover how many voters will vote for the various candidates. Marketing surveys try to discover how a segment of the market feels about various products. Nielsen ratings measure the percentage of the viewing public who are watching a certain television show. An auditor examines the financial statements of a company to see whether the company has followed accepted accounting standards.

In each of these examples, the most thorough way to obtain the desired information is to survey every member of the population. Such a survey is called a *census*. But a census is almost never taken. Its most obvious drawback is the expense involved. There are other less obvious drawbacks. For example, a census might take so much time that its results would be outdated by the time they were available. Another drawback is that some surveys are inherently destructive to the members being surveyed. The automobile industry routinely does impact studies by crashing a small percentage of its automobiles into a wall at various speeds to see which models meet safety requirements. Clearly, a census is not practical in this situation! A final reason for not taking a census is that it might be impossible to identify each member of the relevant population. If the objective is to measure certain characteristics of people who have bought hand guns in the past five years, for example, it would be practically impossible to identify and locate each member of this population.

If we decide not to perform a census, then what do we do? The answer is that we survey a relatively small representative subset of the population. In later chapters we discuss in detail how we choose the size and makeup of this subset. For now we simply state that the subset is generally chosen by some type of random mechanism. The reason is that we can then use powerful results from probability theory to measure the *accuracy* of the conclusions drawn from the survey data.

Controlled Experiments

A third way to obtain data is through a controlled experiment. Here the experimenter deliberately controls selected aspects of the experiment so that valid inferences can be drawn from the data obtained. Usually, the form of control is that the experimenter holds one or more variables constant as the levels of other variables are manipulated. In a scientific laboratory this is usually fairly simple to do, but in business and economics (and in the social sciences in general), it can be practically impossible. Consider the following examples of controlled experiments.

Consider a farmer who wishes to measure the effects of four types of fertilizer on wheat yields. He divides the land available for experimentation into four equal parts and uses a separate fertilizer on each of the four sections. This experiment is controlled if the farmer attempts to minimize the influence of extraneous factors as much as possible. For example, if there are different types of soil in the available land, he should not use the first type of fertilizer exclusively on one type of soil, the second type of fertilizer on a second type of soil, and so on. If he does this, he will probably not be able to separate the influence of fertilizer types from the influence of soil types. The farmer should control for these differences in soil types by randomly assigning the fertilizers to the available land in such a way that the soil types get "averaged out" over the four fertilizers. Here a controlled experiment is possible and should be used.

Now consider a reading instructor who claims that she has discovered a superior technique for teaching reading to elementary school students. She decides to test her claim by using her method on one group of elementary school students and a traditional method on another group of elementary school students. Obviously, she must control for a wide variety of factors before she can claim that the results of her study are valid.

Her objective is fairly narrow: to compare the two different teaching methods. Therefore, the two groups of students should be as similar as possible. This means that the teachers in the two groups should be approximately equal in teaching abilities, the students in the two groups should have similar reading abilities and backgrounds, the facilities used by the two groups should be equally well suited to their purposes, and so on. Although it is practically impossible to control each of these factors completely, the instructor should try to do so if she wants to draw valid conclusions from her data.

In business and economics there are many situations similar to this reading example where we would like to test a theory while controlling for extraneous factors. The difficulty lies in trying to keep the extraneous factors constant. Suppose, for example, that a razor blade company wants to measure the effect on sales of its advertising policy. The company decides to retain the same media mixture it has traditionally used, but to vary the amount spent on advertising from month to month.

This experiment is controlled in the sense that the company is deliberately manipulating the variable of interest, advertising. However, there are factors that are difficult or impossible to control. Probably the most important of these are competitors' advertising and new products in the market. For example, if the company and its main competitor advertise "in phase" with one another, the effect on sales may be quite different than if they are out of phase. The point is that there is no way the company can control all extraneous factors that might affect its razor blade sales. These uncontrollable factors make it very difficult to interpret the effects of the company's own advertising strategy.

Computer-Generated Random Data

In statistical applications we usually make several assumptions about a particular population, and we then select a sample from this population in some random manner. If the assumptions are valid, we can use probability theory to infer the properties of the population from the observed sample data. It is frequently useful to ask what types of samples we would observe if our assumptions were perfectly valid. One convenient, inexpensive way to do this is to feed our assumptions into a computer and have the computer randomly generate samples that conform to these assumptions.

There are two primary uses for randomly generated data. First, they can be used instead of real data to help explain statistical concepts. This is the primary reason for their inclusion in this book. Second, randomly generated data often help researchers to understand the implications of policy decisions or experimental designs. This is particularly true when mathematical formulas are either too complicated or unavailable, and when physical experimentation is too expensive. In these cases we can *simulate* real systems, with the help of random number generators, on a computer. Since this type of simulation is not the subject of this book, however, we will not pursue it any further.

A simple application of randomly generated data is the following. Consider a population known to be 55% Democrat and 45% Republican. If we randomly sample 100 people from this population, what are we likely to see? For example, how likely is a sample with more than 65 or fewer than 45 Democrats? We can answer these questions by having a computer generate many samples of size 100 from a population with 55% Democrats and then observing the characteristics of these samples. (In later chapters we will see how to analyze sampling problems like this without resorting to computer simulation. Nevertheless, the computer results provide valuable insight.)

To generate a single person from a given sample, we have the computer generate a random number between 0 and 1. We call this person a Democrat if the random number is between 0 and .55; otherwise, we call the person a Republican. After generating 100 such numbers, we count the number who are Democrats. Then by repeating this procedure many times, we keep track of the fraction of samples with, say, more than 65 or fewer than 45 Democrats in them. The resulting fraction indicates the likelihood of drawing a *single* sample with more than 65 or fewer than 45 Democrats.

1.4

Sources of Errors

In most statistical studies we wish to learn about one or more characteristics of a population. Unless we take a census of the entire population, we are forced to settle for information from a subset, or sample, of the population. Then we attempt to infer population characteristics from the characteristics of the sample. Of course, we hope these inferences are as free of errors as possible. We now discuss the types of errors that are possible.

To be specific, suppose that we conduct a survey at a well-known university to discover the students' attitudes toward intercollegiate athletics. We select 100 students and ask them how they feel about the amount of money spent on athletics, the issue of male dominance in athletics, cheating in athletics, and so on. After tabulating the responses, we state the results and implicitly, if not explicitly, affirm that these results are true of the student body as a whole. What types of errors are possible when we make these statements?

One type of error is called *bias*. This usually occurs when the sampled group is not representative of the whole population in some systematic way. For example, suppose that part of the questionnaire attempts to discover whether students think women's sports should receive as much funding as men's sports. It would certainly be a mistake to sample disproportionately from the male or the female student populations, because an obvious bias could result. Sometimes, however, the sources of bias are not so obvious.

Consider the questions relating to the amount of funding appropriate for athletics. It is difficult to say ahead of time what type of sample is representative and what type is biased. Should we sample proportionately from students with different grade-point averages, or does this matter? Should we sample proportionately from students with different family income levels, or does this matter? Should we sample proportionately from undergraduate students and graduate students, or does this matter? The point is that the inclusion of too few or too many of any segment of the population can introduce a bias that is very difficult to detect.

A second source of error is *measurement error*. This can range from the obvious situation where questionnaire results are tabulated incorrectly to much more subtle situations. In the athletic questionnaire, suppose that we want to discover how many athletes are guilty of cheating in classes. One question on the survey might be, ''How many athletes are you aware of who have cheated in courses?'' Certainly, there are other ways of obtaining this information, and this question is probably not a very good one. But the problem is that on a sensitive issue like this one, it may be difficult to get respondents to answer truthfully to any such question. Therefore, we must be aware of possible measurement errors, in this case, less than truthful responses, when we analyze the results of the survey.

A prime example of measurement error occurs in national economic data. Measures such as the consumer price index, the national unemployment rate, and others are only approximations of quantities that are difficult to define, let alone measure. Probably no one will ever devise a method that adequately measures the national inflation rate or the national unemployment rate to everyone's satisfaction, so we should be aware of the measurement errors in these data.

Besides bias and measurement error, there is one other type of error that plays an especially important role in this book. This is called *sampling error*. Usually, we cannot predict ahead of time what a truly representative sample should consist of, so we choose the sample in some random manner. The reasons for doing this are that (1) we are more likely to obtain a sample free from biases, and (2) we are allowed to use the rules of probability to make inferences from the sample results. However, when we choose a sample randomly, there is always some chance that we will obtain an unrepresentative sample simply because of bad luck. In this case the difference between the true state of the population and our sample estimate of it is called *sampling error*.

> Sampling error is the difference between the true state of the population and our sample estimate of it.

In the athletic survey, suppose that 10,000 of the 20,000 students in the university believe that athletics receive too much funding and the other 10,000 believe the opposite. However, the 100 respondents selected randomly from the 20,000 students may not be representative of this 50–50 split in the population. At the extreme, we could be very unlucky and obtain a sample where all 100 students favor more funding for athletics. As we will see when we study probability, this extreme is very unlikely. But a 55–45 split or even a 60–40 split in favor of increased funding is not at all uncommon.

If we obtain either of these splits and then infer that the majority of the student population favor increased funding for athletics, we are committing an error. However, there is no way to avoid this type of error. The only way we can make it less probable is to choose a larger sample, but even then the possibility of sampling error still exists.

1.5

Uses of Data Analysis

In this section we discuss several typical statistical applications. Then in the remainder of this book, we will learn how to analyze these problems.

EXAMPLE 1.1

There have recently been many arguments that today's college students are not able to read and write as well as college students a generation ago. No matter which side of this argument one is on, there are ample data to support that side. For example, several studies have shown that the average verbal test scores from the SAT, a standardized college entrance exam, have been decreasing in recent years. But there is also statistical evidence that the average grade-point average in college courses is increasing. The point of this example is not to make a careful critique of the arguments and evidence supporting either side. Rather, it is to ask what type of analysis a statistician should perform on the existing data.

There are undoubtedly many sophisticated techniques a statistician could employ in order to "prove" one theory or another. The trouble is that most of these techniques are based on assumptions that are unlikely to hold. For example, we can probably *not* assume that the students taking the SAT exam today represent the same cross section of the United States as students who took it a generation ago. The reason is that more students from lower economic backgrounds, and often lower-quality academic backgrounds, are now applying for college, and this automatically tends to lower average SAT scores. On the other hand, we can probably not assume that college grades mean the same as they used to mean. The reason is "grade inflation." Therefore, higher college grades may be a result of easier grading rather than better reading and writing.

In a situation like this, the epitome of an *uncontrolled* experiment, we should probably regard sophisticated statistical analyses with skepticism. Nevertheless, it is certainly useful to present the data in an easily understandable form, such as a graphical display. It is also useful to calculate summary measures of the data, such as averages, variances, and correlations. This analysis simply exposes some of the properties of the data that might otherwise remain hidden. We will learn methods for doing this in Chapter 2 when we study *descriptive statistics*.

EXAMPLE 1.2

Suppose that a consumer agency conducts a survey to learn how the price of a pound of coffee varies from store to store in the state of New York. Since coffee is sold in thousands of different stores, a census is impractical, so the agency surveys a randomly selected sample of 50 stores. The price at these stores vary from a low of $2.79 to a high of $3.89, with an average price of $3.11.

Based on these data, the people in the agency would like to make inferences about the population of coffee prices throughout the state. For example, they would like to estimate the average coffee price for all stores in the state, and the proportion of all stores that charge more than $3.50 per pound. They would also like to know how accurate their estimates are. For example, is the estimate of the average price likely to be off by more than 10 cents?

This example illustrates the typical problems of statistical *estimation*. We use sample data to estimate a numerical characteristic of a population, such as an average or a proportion. We also want to measure the accuracy of the resulting estimates. Although problems of statistical estimation occur throughout this book, we study this important topic in detail in Chapters 7 and 8.

EXAMPLE 1.3

Suppose that a group of medical scientists believe they have discovered a drug that cures influenza faster than any other drug on the market. To test this drug, they administer it to a group of 150 patients who have the illness. Another group of 150 patients with the same illness are given the drug that has worked best in the past. Each patient is otherwise treated in precisely the same manner. The physicians observe that the average duration of the illness for the patients taking the new drug is 5.2 days. The corresponding average for patients taking the other drug is 7.3 days.

If this evidence is shown to a patient suffering from influenza, and this patient is given a choice of drugs to use, he or she will probably choose the new drug. The reason is that the sample evidence favors the new drug. However, the medical profession will probably require a careful statistical analysis of the experimental results before they accept the new drug as being superior.

In this example one group of physicians, who we will call the "doubters," argue that the new drug is no better than the existing drug unless there is strong evidence to the contrary. They challenge the claim of the scientists who have developed the new drug. Therefore, the experiment above is performed. The results of the experiment seem to favor the new drug, but the question is whether the evidence is strong enough to satisfy the doubters. The developers of the new drug can argue that if their drug were really no better than what already exists, they would not have obtained such favorable experimental results. The doubters can argue that the two averages obtained in the experiment are not really that far apart and that the difference between them can be attributed to chance.

This is a typical example of *hypothesis testing,* a topic we begin studying in Chapter 9. In any hypothesis-testing problem, there are two conflicting hypotheses, only one of which is true. Usually, one of the hypotheses represents the current thinking on a subject (the new drug is no better than what exists), and the other hypothesis represents a new theory (the new drug is better). After observing sample data, the statistician must decide whether the evidence from the data is strong enough to reject current thinking in favor of the new theory.

This drug example is one of many possible examples of *decision making under uncertainty.* If the evidence from the experiment is strong enough to support the new drug, its developers can go ahead with the manufacturing and marketing of the new drug. If the evidence in favor of the new drug is not strong enough, there will probably be continued testing. The estimation example, Example 1.2, is also an example of decision making under uncertainty. In that case the consumer agency will probably report its findings on coffee prices in a consumer journal. Therefore, it must decide what conclusions to report.

In fact, almost every problem we consider in this book can be viewed as an example of decision making under uncertainty. In many of these, we are content to report the probability that we have made an error. We then design our experiments so that these error probabilities are sufficiently small. The drawback to this approach is that we may ignore important monetary costs when we consider only probabilities of errors. That is, some types of errors may be much more costly than others, and we should take this into account when we make our decisions. Rather than minimize the error probabilities, we should really minimize the expected costs. The next example illustrates a problem where this type of analysis is useful.

EXAMPLE 1.4

Consider a cosmetics company that has recently developed a new type of lipstick. The new product has gone through the research and development phases that all products go through, and it is now ready for marketing. Because this is a new type of lipstick, the company must decide which marketing strategy to use. Its primary goal is to avoid large losses. One set of decisions concerns advertising strategy. How much money should be spent on advertising, and what media mixture should be used? Another set of decisions concerns the scale of the market in which the product is introduced. Should the product be introduced nationally right away, or should a regional test market precede national exposure?

When these decisions are made, the company knows many of the short-term costs that will result from its decisions. For example, it knows most of the advertising costs, production costs, shipping costs, and so on. But it does not know the medium- and long-term effects of its decisions on sales volume and profits. Given its marketing decisions, it can probably assess the probabilities of the possible outcomes, but it will not know the actual outcomes until after many of the decisions have been made.

In situations like this, it is important to realize that a good decision is one that considers all potential profits and losses, plus the probabilities of these potential profits and losses, and then attempts to maximize the expected profits or minimize the expected losses. Because there is uncertainty about the future, there is always the possibility of being unlucky and making less money (or losing more money) than was expected. This may lead others to "second-guess" the decisions that were made. But everyone has 20–20 hindsight. The job of the decision maker under uncertainty is to make the best decisions he or she can, given the information available *at the time of the decision*. We will learn systematic ways of doing this in Chapter 15.

EXAMPLE 1.5

Consider a company that is planning to build a new office building. Because it is located in the northeast, the company is particularly concerned with future heating bills. Therefore, it would like to estimate annual heating costs for the new building. It realizes that the heating costs depend on several variables: square footage, amount and type of insulation, type of fuel used, amount of glass in the outside walls, and others. From a sample of existing buildings, it attempts to relate annual heating costs to these variables. If it can find an appropriate relationship for the buildings in the sample, it can use this relationship to predict the annual heating cost for the new building.

The statistical method used to find the relationship is called *regression analysis*. The company uses sample data from existing buildings to estimate an equation that relates the variable of interest (annual heating cost) to the explanatory variables (type of fuel, square footage, and so on). The result, a *regression equation*, can then be used to predict the annual heating cost for the new building.

The subject of regression is one of the most important and widely applied methods in statistics. This is particularly true because of the widespread use of computers, which are capable of performing the many arithmetic operations required by regression analysis in a matter of seconds. Therefore, we devote two chapters, Chapters 11 and 12, to this important topic.

Example 1.5 illustrated a particular type of prediction. In the next example we consider a different type of prediction, usually called *forecasting*. In forecasting, we use historical data on a given variable to forecast future values of the variable.

EXAMPLE 1.6

Consider a toy company that is trying to plan its production schedule for the next 12 months. There are several uncertainties that affect the company's decisions, such as anticipated wage increases, competitors' marketing strategies, and others. However, the company believes that the most important variable is the demand for its product over the next 12 months. The company wants to make sure that it has plenty of inventory available if demand is high, but it does not want to overproduce and have a lot of toys left on the shelves if demand is low. Furthermore, the company wants to plan its inventory and work force appropriately if it knows the demand follows a seasonal pattern. Therefore, the crucial problem is to obtain accurate forecasts of the demand for the next 12 months.

To do this, the company looks at monthly records of past sales. These data are called *time series data*. Usually, time series data are shown on a *time series graph*, so that any past trends and seasonal patterns become more obvious. But it is still not an easy problem to look at a time series graph and be able to forecast *future* data. The problem is that trends or seasonal patterns are often obscured by relatively minor but frequent random fluctuations. The job of the forecaster is to sift through these random fluctuations and see the real patterns in the historical data.

Unfortunately, there are really two problems involved in forecasting. One problem is the problem discussed above. This is not an easy problem, but it is a technical problem that trained statisticians are generally able to solve. The second problem, however, is what makes forecasting such a risky business. Even if the properties of past data are known, we can never be certain that future data will continue to exhibit these properties.

Suppose the toy company concludes, on the basis of sales data from the past five years, that the demand for toys has been slowly rising at a 5% annual rate and that there are definite seasonal variations, particularly at Christmas time. Should the company infer that these characteristics will continue next year? Probably the best answer is that unless the company knows something has occurred that will change its demand pattern, its best forecast is to extrapolate past trends to the coming year. We will have more to say about this problem when we study time series analysis and forecasting in Chapter 14.

EXAMPLE 1.7

This final example treats the important problem of comparing several populations with respect to a given characteristic. Suppose that a city government agency wants to know how different neighborhoods in the city compare to one another with respect to average household income. A census would certainly answer their questions, but this is considered too expensive and time consuming. Instead, they send a questionnaire to 30 randomly selected households in each neighborhood. Each household in the sample is requested to provide its family income for the preceding calendar year. From these data the agency attempts to determine whether any neighborhoods have significantly higher average incomes than any others.

Suppose that the average household incomes in the four neighborhoods are $12,500, $13,600, $16,200, and $15,100. Based on these four numbers alone, the agency is likely to report that neighborhood 1 earns the least, neighborhood 3 earns the most, and the other two neighborhoods are in between. However, such a statement concerns the entire populations in these neighborhoods, not just the sampled members. Hence it may not be accurate. For example, the sample from neighborhood 3 may be much higher than the overall average in neighborhood 3. There may be similar distortions in the other neighborhoods as well. So the job of the agency is to decide whether the *apparent* differences are *real* differences.

For this type of problem, we use a statistical method called *analysis of variance*. In general, analysis of variance tests whether differences in sample averages are generalizable to the respective population averages. Analysis of variance is particularly useful in controlled experiments where we are attempting to determine whether different levels of one or more variables produce significantly different effects. Since there are many "experimental designs" available for these types of experiments, a trained statistician must be able to apply many versions of analysis of variance. In Chapter 10 we discuss the most basic aspects of this complex topic.

The examples above are merely a sample of the types of problems we will learn how to solve. The purpose of including them here is to convince the reader that there really are important problems in business and economics that can be solved by statistical methods. In short, we will see that the statistical methods in this book enable businesses to be conducted more intelligently and more profitably than would otherwise be possible.

Summary

This chapter has presented a brief summary of the types of data and the sources of data that are available. It has also described some of the most important sources of errors in data analysis. For our purposes the most important of these is called sampling error, which results from unluckily choosing an unrepresentative subset from a population and then making incorrect inferences about the population based on this subset. The examples in the last section of this chapter form a preview of the rest of this book. They illustrate some of the typical problems we will learn how to solve by statistical methods.

Applications

Application 1.1 In survey sampling there is an important type of bias called *nonresponse bias*. This occurs when the people who choose not to respond to a questionnaire have different characteristics than those who do. Naturally, any inferences from the sample (of respondents) to the population as a whole can be different in this case than if everyone in the sample had responded. Rosenthal and Rosnow, in a study of several hundred surveys, concluded that respondents, relative to nonrespondents, (1) are better educated, (2) have higher social-class status, (3) are more intelligent, (4) have a higher need for social approval, (5) are more social, (6) are more interested in the research topic, and (7) have higher expectations of being favorably evaluated by the investigator. (Reference: R. Rosenthal and R. L. Rosnow, *The Volunteer Subject,* John Wiley & Sons, New York, 1985.) When respondents have different demographic and social characteristics than nonrespondents, there is certainly a danger that their responses to the survey questions will be systematically different from those of the nonrespondents (if they had responded). This is the source of the nonresponse bias.

However, as Finn, Wang, and Lamb illustrated in a 1983 article, nonresponse bias is not inevitable even when respondents and nonrespondents differ demographically. (Reference: David W. Finn, Chih-Kang Wang, and Charles W. Lamb, "An Examination of the Effects of Sample Composition Bias in a Mail Survey," *Journal of the Market Research Society,* Vol. 25, 1983, pp. 331–338.) They sent a questionnaire to 500 people and coded the response sheets so that they could identify the respondents. They received 273 usable responses, for a 54.6% response rate. By comparing respondents and nonrespondents, they concluded that nonrespondents were older, poorer, more often nonwhite, more often male, and possessed less education and fewer occupation skills than respondents. These characteristics would indicate possible nonresponse bias. However, when a sample of the nonrespondents were telephoned in a follow-up study, they gave practically the same answers to the *survey questions* as the original respondents. Therefore, differences in demographic characteristics between respondents and nonrespondents do not necessarily imply that inferences drawn from survey results will be in error.

Application 1.2   The statistical methods that exist for manipulating, graphing, and interpreting data are practically endless. Furthermore, today's high-speed computers allow us to perform these statistical analyses quickly and easily. However, as Seymour points out, we should constantly be aware of the *sources* of the data used in statistical analyses. (Reference: Daniel Seymour, "Numbers Don't Lie—Do They?" *Business Horizons,* Vol. 27, 1984, pp. 36–37.) If the sources provide inaccurate data (garbage in), any computer analysis is bound to be inacccurate as well (garbage out). He gives several classic examples of studies where the conclusions would have been far from accurate if the researchers had not checked their data carefully.

For example, he cites a 1934 study by LaPierre, who watched the treatment of a Chinese couple as they crossed the United States. Of the

251 hotel and restaurant establishments they approached, every one but one accommodated them. However, a later questionnaire was sent to the establishments asking them, "Would you accept members of the Chinese race as guests in your establishment?" Only one response was positive. A more recent example is a 1969 study by Dannick. He interviewed people he had just observed crossing an intersection against a "don't walk" light. Most of these people responded that they never engaged in such behavior, and even more of them responded that they thought it was wrong for anyone to do it.

The point of these examples is that if only the questionnaire or interview data had been available, a very inaccurate impression would have been obtained. The fact is that people do not always respond truthfully, and we need to be aware of this when we interpret statistical findings. Seymour ends his article with a very appropriate quote by Josiah Stamp, a nineteenth-century official of the British Inland Revenue Department: "The government are very keen on amassing statistics. They collect them, add them, raise them to the Nth power, take the cube root and prepare wonderful diagrams. But you must never forget that every one of these figures comes in the first instance from the village watchman, who just puts down what he damn pleases."

Glossary of Terms

Four scales of data   nominal data (categorical data with no natural ordering of the categories), ordinal data (categorical data where the categories are ordered), interval data (quantitative data with no natural zero point), and ratio data (quantitative data with a natural zero point)

Primary sources of data   published data, survey data, data from controlled experiments, and randomly generated data (from a computer or a table of random numbers)

Census   a survey of an entire population

Three primary sources of errors in data analysis   bias, measurement, and sampling error

Sampling error   the difference between the true population characteristic and the sample estimate of it

CHAPTER 2

Descriptive Statistics

Objectives

1. To learn how to form and interpret frequency tables.
2. To learn how to draw and interpret frequency graphs, especially histograms.
3. To learn methods for describing data with more than one attribute, including cross-classification tables, scatter diagrams, and time series graphs.
4. To learn the most important measures of central tendency: the mean, the median, and the mode.
5. To learn the most important measures of variability: ranges, the mean absolute deviation, the variance, and the standard deviation.
6. To learn two measures of association for data with two numerical attributes: the covariance and the correlation.

Contents

Most of us spend a good deal of our spare time watching television, and as we do so, we are constantly being "educated" by various types of messages, ranging from product commercials, public service announcements, and news information, to shows with a "message." How much of the content of these messages do we viewers comprehend? One large study of 2700 randomly chosen viewers was performed to answer this question. The viewers were shown various types of 30-second television messages and were then given a six-question true–false quiz on each message they saw. Perhaps the most important single finding of the study was that about 30% of the answers on the quizzes were incorrect, indicating that we miscomprehend much of what we see.

However, in a study such as this, there is a large amount of data generated. Therefore, we need to analyze the data carefully and summarize the findings as clearly as possible. For example, the 30% figure given above, an average over the entire 2700 viewers, is an aggregate figure. There are several ways we could break it down. For example, we could look at the number of incorrect answers for each viewer. Some viewers got no incorrect answers, some got one incorrect answer, some got two incorrect answers, and so on. We could then tabulate the numbers of viewers in each of these categories, or we could display them graphically. We could also use these numbers to find the average number of incorrect answers per viewer. In this chapter we learn methods for summarizing the information from data sets such as this one. The purpose is always to highlight important characteristics of the data so that we are better able to make reasonable conclusions from the study.

2.1

Introduction

Most of the material in this textbook concerns the subject of statistical inference. The term statistical inference means that we use probability theory to generalize the characteristics of a population from the characteristics of a representative sample. The emphasis is often not on what the sample tells us about the specific members sampled but on how we can make inferences about the nonsampled members of the population.

This is certainly a worthwhile objective, but it is easy to become so involved with the methods of statistical inference that we forget to look carefully at the sample itself. Therefore, before we study probability and statistical inference, we will learn methods for describing and summarizing data. In this chapter we will *not* worry about generalizing from a sample to a population; that will come in future chapters. Instead, we will see how to describe and summarize a set of data so that its characteristics become evident. This topic is generally referred to as *descriptive statistics*.

2.2
Categorizing and Displaying Data

When data are presented in raw form, most of us have difficulty seeing the overall characteristics of the data. We need to see the data presented in a meaningful, transparent form. One useful way of doing this is to group the data into categories and then display them in a frequency table or a frequency graph.

The first step in forming a frequency table or a frequency graph is to divide the data into natural categories. Then by comparing the numbers of observations in the various categories, we are able to gain insight into the properties of the data. The categories themselves may be defined somewhat arbitrarily, but they must satisfy two conditions:

Categorizing Data

1. Each observation must fall into some category.
2. No observation can fall into two categories.

This means that the categories, taken together, must exhaust all possibilities, and they should not overlap one another.

How do we define the categories? For qualitative data, the definition of the categories is usually straightforward. For example, if the possible responses to a survey question are "strongly disagree," "slightly disagree," "neutral," "slightly agree," and "strongly agree," these five responses define the five categories. For quantitative data, however, the problem is more difficult to resolve. We need to know how many categories to choose and how to choose the "boundaries" of each category. This depends on the type and amount of data available.

Consider the data in Table 2.1 (p. 24), for example. These data represent the electricity bills in a given month for 60 randomly selected companies. (We continue to use this data set throughout this chapter.) There are 60 observations, all of which fall between $1314 and $1987. What we would like to do is to divide this range into several categories and then count the number of observations in each category to obtain a better understanding of this data set.

Table 2.1   Electric Bill Data

$1512	1543	1810	1421	1527	1487
1632	1725	1926	1581	1593	1314
1711	1803	1981	1725	1741	1561
1623	1499	1825	1603	1781	1752
1724	1653	1921	1810	1528	1501
1421	1722	1629	1318	1580	1625
1510	1811	1785	1625	1424	1640
1602	1943	1893	1683	1622	1524
1539	1640	1984	1527	1824	1656
1483	1843	1987	1662	1432	1720

The first issue is choosing the *number* of categories. If we use too few categories, most of the data get lumped together, and we gain practically no insight into their characteristics. As an extreme example, if we choose only two categories, below $1650 and $1650 or above, say, the only information we obtain is that 32 of the observations are in the first category and the other 28 observations are in the second category.

If we use too many categories, on the other hand, we are practically no better off than when we started. For example, if we divide the data into $20 ranges, say, from $1301 to $1320, from $1321 to $1340, and so on, most of the categories have only zero, one, or two observations. The problem now is that there are too few observations per category, so that no meaningful patterns emerge.

Therefore, we want to strike a balance between too few and too many categories. Some trial and error may be necessary, but a useful guideline is to choose somewhere between 5 and 15 categories. We try to do this so that most categories have at least five observations. (Some people suggest at least three observations per category.) Of course, it follows that if we have more observations, we can afford to have more categories.

> For quantitative data, a useful guideline is to define between 5 and 15 categories so that most categories have at least five observations.

Once we choose the number of categories, it is useful to divide the range of observations into this many *equal-width* categories. In the electric bill example, a convenient choice is to break the range from $1301 to $2000 into seven equal-width categories. These categories are $1301 to $1400, $1401 to $1500, and so on, up to $1901 to $2000. Notice that there is a small $1 gap between consecutive categories. However, this causes no problems because all observations are expressed in whole-dollar amounts; thus no observations fall into the gaps.

Given the choice of the categories, the next step is simple. We count the number of observations in each category and list these counts in a *frequency table*. The resulting counts are often called *frequencies*. If a frequency is divided by the total number of observations, the resulting proportion is called a *relative frequency*. The relative frequencies are often shown in a frequency table along with the frequencies.

The number of observations in any category is called the frequency of that category. The relative frequency for any category is the proportion of observations in that category. A table of the frequencies and possibly the relative frequencies is called a frequency table.

For the electric bill data and the $100-width categories discussed above, the frequencies are shown in Table 2.2. Below each frequency, we show the relative frequency, found by dividing the frequency by 60. In the second line of Table 2.2, we have used the familiar tallying device to count the frequencies. This is a particularly useful device when the data set is large.

Table 2.2   Frequency Table for Electric Bills

Category	$1301 –$1400	$1401 –$1500	$1501 –$1600	$1601 –$1700	$1701 –$1800	$1801 –$1900	$1901 –$2000
Tally	||	⊬⊬ ||	⊬⊬ ⊬⊬ |||	⊬⊬ ⊬⊬ ||||	⊬⊬ ⊬⊬	⊬⊬ |||	⊬⊬ |
Frequency	2	7	13	14	10	8	6
Relative Frequency	.033	.117	.217	.233	.167	.133	.100

A frequency table lets us see at a glance some of the important properties of a data set. For example, we see from Table 2.2 that almost half of the bills are between $1501 and $1700. Also, we see that very few of the bills, only 8 out of 60, are less than $1400 or more than $1900. In short, we obtain a good overall impression of the distribution of the data over the observed range of values.

Although a frequency table is certainly a useful and meaningful way to display data, we can gain even more insight by displaying the frequencies or relative frequencies in graphical form. There are many ways to do this. Some of the terms for these graphs are frequency graphs, histograms, bar charts, pie charts, and frequency polygons. The only difference between these is that they display the frequencies in slightly different graphical forms. Examples

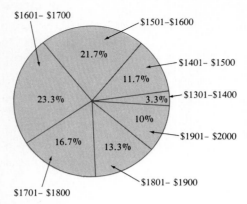

Figure 2.1
Pie Chart for Electric Bills

of the various possibilities are shown in Figures 2.1 through 2.4. Each of these graphs is based on the electric bill data from Table 2.1.

As the name implies, a *pie chart* is a circular representation of the frequencies, with each category getting "its share of the pie." A *frequency polygon* is a graph where the horizontal axis shows the categories and the vertical axis shows the frequencies (or relative frequencies). Generally, each category's frequency is represented by a point drawn above the midpoint of that category. Then these points are joined by straight lines. A *bar chart* is perhaps the most common type of frequency graph. Here each category's frequency is represented by a bar, the length of which is proportional to the frequency of that category. The bars are sometimes drawn horizontally (as in Figure 2.3) and sometimes vertically.

A particular type of bar chart is called a *histogram*. This is the type of frequency graph we focus on in this chapter and throughout the book. As with other types of frequency graphs, a histogram is simply a graphical display of the frequencies. On a horizontal axis, we show the possible values of the data, grouped by the possible categories. Above each category we draw a rectangle with height proportional to the frequency of that category. The *actual* height of each rectangle is irrelevant; only the *relative* heights are important. For example, if three categories have frequencies of 10, 8, and 6, the heights of the three corresponding rectangles must have the correct proportions. The first must be $^{10}/_8$ as high as the second, and the second must be $^8/_6$ as high as the third.

Because the relative heights are all that matter, the vertical axis of a histogram may be regarded in several equivalent ways. The most straightforward way is to let the vertical axis measure the frequencies themselves. Then if a category has frequency 10, its height along the vertical axis is 10. However, the vertical axis can also measure relative frequencies. Then if a category

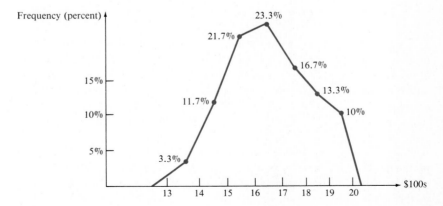

Figure 2.2
Frequency Polygon for Electric Bills

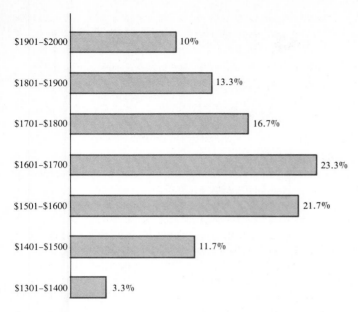

Figure 2.3
Bar Chart for Electric Bills

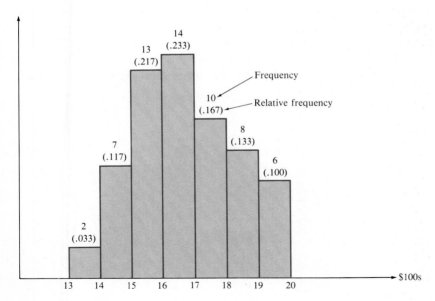

Figure 2.4
Histogram for Electric Bills

has 10 observations out of 60, its height along the vertical axis is its relative frequency, ⅙. The important point is that the *shape* of the histogram is the same regardless of the scale used for the vertical axis.

> A histogram is a graphical display of the frequencies in a frequency table. There is one rectangle for each category, with a height proportional to the frequency of that category.

The histogram of the electric bill data shown in Figure 2.4 illustrates these comments. Above each rectangle we show the frequency and the relative frequency for that category. Clearly, the vertical axis can measure either the frequency or the relative frequency, and the shape of the histogram remains the same.

There is one technical point we need to mention. So far, we have suggested using equal-width categories. Suppose, however, that we decide to collapse the categories $1301 to $1400 and $1401 to $1500 into a single category, $1301 to $1500. The reason for doing so may be that there are so few observations in the range $1301 to $1400. Then the new category has frequency 9, but its width is now $200, twice as large as the other widths. If we draw the revised histogram in the obvious way, as in Figure 2.5a, it may be misleading. This is because most of us tend to perceive *areas* of rectangles, not only their heights, when we look at such a graph.

If all the widths are equal, the areas bear the same relationship to one another as the heights (because area equals height times width), and we are not misled. But when one width is twice as large as the others and nothing is done to modify its height, the corresponding area is twice as large as it ought to be. So when we look at Figure 2.5a, we probably imagine that there

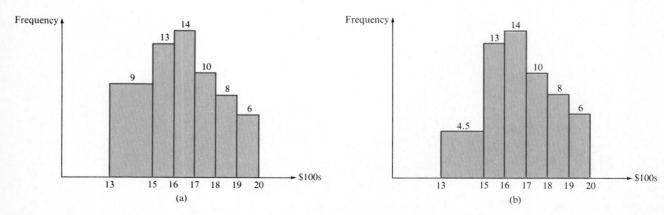

Figure 2.5

are more observations in the $1301 to $1500 category than there really are. To compensate for this, it is customary to reduce the height of this rectangle so that its area is in the correct proportion to the areas of the other rectangles. This means that we halve its height and produce the histogram in Figure 2.5b.

The best way to avoid the problem of unequal widths is very simple: Always define categories so that they have equal widths. This is why we suggested using equal-width categories in the first place. However, there is one special exception to this rule. This is when one or both ends of the data range are essentially open-ended.

As an example, consider annual income data. Ninety-five percent or more of the observations will probably be below $50,000, but a few of the observations may be above $50,000. In fact, some may be well above $50,000, possibly up to $1,000,000 and above. Based on the bulk of the data, we may decide to break the $0 to $50,000 range into 10 categories of width $5000 each. But it would not make sense to do this beyond $50,000. First, there would be too many categories, and second, most categories above $50,000 would contain very few observations. In a situation like this, it makes more sense to define an eleventh category as "above $50,000." An example of such a histogram is shown in Figure 2.6.

Many histograms and frequency tables have one or two open-ended categories for the relatively small and relatively large observations in the sample. The height of the rectangle for such an open-ended category is usually drawn proportional to the frequency of this category. This causes no problems of visual interpretation (of the type illustrated in Figure 2.5) because the percentage of observations in an open-ended category is usually very small.

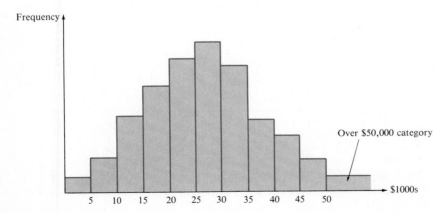

Figure 2.6
Histogram with an Unbounded Category

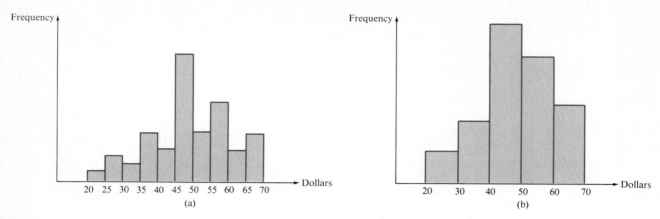

Figure 2.7

The following example suggests that the choice of categories can make a difference in the way we visualize the distribution of the data.

EXAMPLE 2.1

Suppose that we gather data on retail prices of portable cassette tape recorders. As we all know, prices tend to be of the form $49.99, $59.99, and so on. If we choose the categories as $40.00 to $44.99, $45.00 to $49.99, $50.00 to $54.99, and so on, the resulting histogram might appear as in Figure 2.7a. The bumpiness in this histogram obscures the distribution of prices that really exists. By redefining the categories as $10 intervals, we obtain the histogram in Figure 2.7b. The distribution of prices is now much clearer. There is nothing *wrong* with the first set of categories; the resulting histogram is simply not as informative as it could be.

2.3

Shapes

The most obvious quality of a histogram is its shape. In fact, this is the reason why a histogram is so useful. It gives us an immediate impression, through its shape, of how the data are distributed. We now briefly discuss the general types of shapes that occur. For this discussion we take the liberty of smoothing off the rough edges and minor hills and valleys inherent in most histograms. That is, we represent histograms by smooth curves. This helps us to see more clearly the basic shapes that exist.

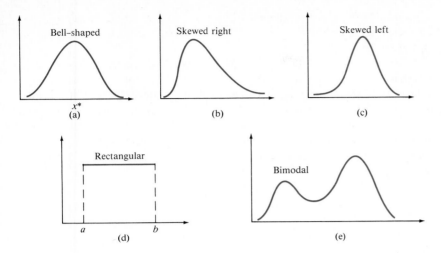

Figure 2.8

The most common shapes are shown in Figure 2.8. The shape in Figure 2.8a is the type we will see most often in this book. It has two properties of interest. The first is that it is symmetric about the point x^*; the curve to the left of x^* is a mirror image of the curve to the right of x^*. Also, this curve is *bell-shaped;* that is, it literally looks like a bell. It has a peak at x^* and tapers off quickly on both sides. As an example, if we draw a curve representing the distribution of heights of a large number of women, the result will probably be approximately symmetric and bell-shaped, with x^* around 5 feet 5 inches.

The curves in Figures 2.8b and 2.8c are *skewed* distributions. This means that they are not symmetric around any value. The distribution in Figure 2.8b is skewed to the right, and the distribution in Figure 2.8c is skewed to the left. (A simple way to remember which is which is to remember that the direction of the skew is the direction of the longer "tail.") A typical example of a distribution skewed to the right is the distribution of family wealth in this country. The majority of the families are not wealthy or are only moderately wealthy, but there are a few families who are very wealthy. These families contribute the long tail on the right of the curve. A typical example of a distribution skewed to the left is the distribution of scores on an exam where most students do well, but a small group of nonstudiers "pull down the curve."

The "curve" in Figure 2.8d is called a *rectangular* distribution. This curve does not represent a histogram with a single category; it represents a histogram with several categories, all of equal height. We obtain this type of distribution when there is a range where the data must fall (from a to b in Figure 2.8d), and the data are evenly distributed within this range. An example of this distribution occurs when we generate random numbers from a computer, as described in Chapter 1. Then $a = 0$ and $b = 1$, and a histogram of a large set of numbers generated this way would be approximately flat, as in Figure 2.8d.

The final curve, shown in Figure 2.8e, is *bimodal*. Generally, this type of distribution represents data from two separate populations. For example, suppose that a company began a major advertising campaign in 1980 in order to increase its sales. Assuming that the campaign was successful, a histogram of monthly sales data for the period 1977–1984 might be bimodal. The left part of the curve would represent sales before the advertising campaign, and the right part of the curve would represent the increased sales due to the advertising campaign.

2.4

Cumulative Frequency Distributions

Sometimes it is useful to convert a frequency table into a *cumulative frequency table*. For each category we list the number of observations in that category plus the number of observations in all categories to the left of it. In the electric bill data, for example, the cumulative frequency of the $1501 to $1600 category is the number of observations less than or equal to $1600, namely $2 + 7 + 13 = 22$. The complete cumulative frequency table for this example follows directly from the frequencies in Table 2.2 and is shown in Table 2.3. Notice how the cumulative frequencies increase from left to right, as they must from their definition.

Table 2.3 Cumulative Frequency Table for Electric Bills

Category	$1301 –$1400	$1401 –$1500	$1501 –$1600	$1601 –$1700	$1701 –$1800	$1801 –$1900	$1901 –$2000
Cumulative Frequency	2	9	22	36	46	54	60

We may also display these cumulative frequencies graphically as in Figure 2.9. This graph resembles a histogram except that each height is at least as high as the height to its left. Here we have followed the usual convention of omitting parts of the vertical lines in the rectangles. The resulting "staircase" graph is called an *ogive*.

> An ogive is a graph of the cumulative frequencies. It always appears as a staircase, with the steps rising from left to right.

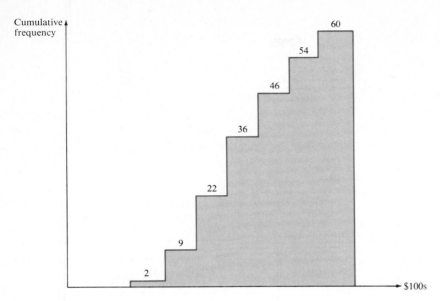

Figure 2.9
Cumulative Frequency Graph (Ogive) for Electric Bills

A frequency table and a cumulative frequency table are really equivalent in the sense that they both contain exactly the same information. Given a frequency table, we can derive the entries in the cumulative frequency table by addition, as we did for the electric bill data. Conversely, if we are given the cumulative frequency table, we can obtain the entries in the frequency table by subtraction. For example, to obtain the frequency of the $1501 to $1600 category from Table 2.3, we subtract the number of observations to the left of $1501 from the number of observations to the left of $1601: $22 - 9 = 13$. Similar calculations for the other categories are shown in Table 2.4 (p. 34).

Before leaving this section, we note that a frequency table makes sense for any type of data, qualitative or quantitative. A cumulative frequency table, on the other hand, makes sense only for data that are at least *ordinal* on the scale of "quantitativeness." This includes quantitative data and ordinal data, but not nominal data. For example, if the possible responses to a question are "disliked the product very much," "disliked the product a little," "was indifferent to the product," "liked the product a little," and "liked the product very much," both a frequency table and a cumulative frequency table make sense. A frequency table tells how many responses are in each of the categories, while a cumulative frequency table has entries such as "number of respondents who were at best indifferent to the product." But if the data are nominal, no natural ordering of the categories exists, and the concept of cumulative frequencies does not apply.

Table 2.4

Category	Frequency	Cumulative Frequency		Category	Cumulative Frequency	Frequency
$1301–$1400	2	⟶ 2		$1301–$1400	2 ⟶ 2	
$1401–$1500	7	2 + 7 = 9		$1401–$1500	9	9 − 2 = 7
$1501–$1600	13	9 + 13 = 22		$1501–$1600	22	22 − 9 = 13
$1601–$1700	14	22 + 14 = 36		$1601–$1700	36	36 − 22 = 14
$1701–$1800	10	36 + 10 = 46		$1701–$1800	46	46 − 36 = 10
$1801–$1900	8	46 + 8 = 54		$1801–$1900	54	54 − 46 = 8
$1901–$2000	6	54 + 6 = 60		$1901–$2000	60	60 − 54 = 6
(a) From frequencies to cumulative frequencies				(b) From cumulative frequencies to frequencies		

Problems for Sections 2.2, 2.3, 2.4

1. As an exercise, take the data in Table 2.1 and reverse the digits to obtain a new set of data. For example, 1512 becomes 2151, and 1580 becomes 0851 (or 851). Using a set of 10 equal-width categories of width 1000 each, record the frequency counts in a frequency table, and draw the associated histogram. Then repeat what you just did by using five equal-width categories of width 2000 each. How do the two histograms compare?

2. A study of U.S. college students showed the following data on parental incomes. Each figure shows the percentage of all incomes falling into that particular category.

Estimated Parental Income	Percent
Below $15,000	20.5
$15,000–$19,999	9.1
$20,000–$24,999	13.2
$25,000–$29,999	11.5
$30,000–$34,999	12.0
$35,000–$39,999	8.5
$40,000–$49,999	10.6
$50,000–$99,999	11.3
$100,000 or more	3.3

a. Draw a histogram of these incomes.
b. Draw the cumulative frequency graph for these incomes.

3. A study of two groups of travelers, one group over age 50 and the other under 50, compared the amounts spent on recent trips. (Reference: B. Anderson and L. Langmeyer, "The Under-50 and Over-50 Travelers: A Profile of Similarities and Differences," *Journal of Travel Research*, Vol. 20, 1982, pp. 20–24.) The data are shown below. There were 481 travelers in the under-50 group and 324 travelers in the over-50 group.

Amount Spent	Under 50 Frequency	Over 50 Frequency
$0	2	0
$1–$25	9	4
$26–$50	23	11
$51–$100	37	21
$101–$200	80	43
$201–$300	69	34
$301–$400	56	29
$401–$500	43	31
$501–$600	36	29
$601–$700	32	29
$701–$800	15	10
$801–$900	22	10
$901–$1000	22	19
$1001 or more	35	54

a. Draw histograms of the two groups and see if you can spot any obvious differences. Use the categories shown in the display of the data.

b. Compute the cumulative frequencies for the two groups and graph these.

c. Repeat part (a) but make the categories equal-width categories of $100 each (except for the over-$1000 category).

4. The following data represent the numbers of pairs of jeans of various waist sizes sold by a department store in a given week.

Waist Size (Inches)	Pairs Sold
30	12
31	35
32	40
33	56
34	43
35	25
36	27
37	15
38	12
39	5
40	1

a. Convert these numbers to percentages and graph them in a histogram.

b. Use the percentages from part (a) to draw a graph of the cumulative percentages.

5. A sample of 75 students in a large business school were asked how much they spent on their current hand calculators. The data are summarized in the following cumulative frequency table.

Price Range	Cumulative Frequency
$5–$9.99	12
$10–$14.99	33
$15–$19.99	48
$20–$29.99	64
$30–$49.99	72
$50 or more	75

a. What percentage of these students have a calculator that cost between $15 and $20?

b. Find a price such that at least 70% of all students sampled paid less than this price.

c. Find a price such that at least 40% of all students sampled paid at least this price.

* 6. The following data show how the total deposits of the 100 largest banks were distributed among these banks for several years. (Reference: "Size and Rank Stability, Largest Commercial Banks," *Journal of Economics and Business,* Vol. 34, 1982, p. 125.) For example, in 1925, 19% of the total deposits were accounted for by the top five banks. Calculate the average percentage in each category over the years from 1925 to 1943. Then do the same for the years after 1943. Draw histograms of these averages for the two time periods. Do you detect any obvious differences?

Percentage of the Largest 100 Banks' Deposits Accounted for by Different Groups

Year	Top 5	Top 6–10	Top 11–25	Top 26–50	Top 51–75	Top 76–100
1925	19	12	24	22	13	10
1928	23	14	23	20	12	8
1933	28	16	22	17	10	7
1938	30	15	23	15	10	7
1943	30	14	22	17	10	7
1948	30	13	22	16	11	8
1953	29	14	20	18	11	8
1958	31	13	20	17	11	8
1963	33	14	20	15	10	8
1968	33	14	20	16	10	7
1973	35	16	21	14	8	6
1978	38	16	19	14	7	6

7. Many new businesses fail fairly early if they are going to fail at all. One study showed the following statistics. (Reference: R. Dickenson, "Business Failure Rate," *American Journal of Small Business,* Vol. 6, 1981, pp. 17–25.) For example, these figures imply that 67% of all new businesses failed by the end of their fifth year.

Cumulative Discontinuances Each Year (Percent)

1st year	33	6th year	71
2nd year	51	7th year	74
3rd year	58	8th year	77
4th year	63	9th year	78
5th year	67	10th year	80

a. What percentage of the businesses in the study failed *during* their third year in operation?

b. Draw a histogram of the number of years these businesses continued to survive. (As an example, the category from 2 to 3 should show the percentage of all businesses that failed during their third year.)

8. a. The following histogram shows the manufacturing cost per unit of output for a sample of firms in the same industry. Draw the cumulative frequency graph that corresponds to this histogram. Label the heights on the cumulative frequency graph with frequencies and with percentages.

b. Draw the histogram that corresponds to the following cumulative frequency graph. (This graph also shows the distribution of costs per unit, but for firms in a different industry.) Label the heights on the histogram with frequencies and with percentages.

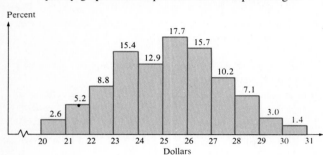

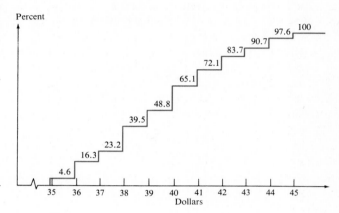

2.5

Contingency Tables (Cross-Tabs)

The electric bill data in Table 2.1 have only one attribute, the dollar amount of each bill. Often, however, we collect data with two or more attributes. Usually, we are interested in how these attributes are related to one another. As an example, suppose that we are interested in coffee consumption across a given population. If we are concerned only with the distribution of coffee consumption for the population as a whole, we can choose a sample of people from this population, ask each member of the sample how much coffee he or she drinks, and then draw a histogram to reflect the data from the sample.

Suppose, however, that our primary concern is the relationship between coffee consumption and age in this population. We wish to discover the differences, if any, between the various age groups with respect to coffee consumption. In this case we should gather data from each of the selected age groups and compare the resulting frequency tables or histograms.

The simplest and most enlightening way to present this type of data is by means of a *contingency table*. These tables are also called *cross-classification tables* or *cross-tabs* (short for cross-tabulations).

> A contingency table shows the number of observations in the various categories when a population is categorized by more than one attribute.

Suppose that we categorize each person in the coffee example as young, middle-aged, or older, and we categorize each person's coffee consumption as light, medium-light, medium-heavy, or heavy. Then each person sampled falls into exactly one of 12 ($= 3 \times 4$) possible categories, depending on his or her age and coffee consumption. In this case a contingency table is a rectangular array with three vertical columns, corresponding to the ages, and four horizontal rows, corresponding to the coffee consumption levels. The 12 numerical entries in this array are the numbers of respondents in the 12 possible categories. Table 2.5 shows a possible numerical example, based on a sample of 900 coffee drinkers.

The 12 numbers inside the 12 cells are sometimes called *joint frequencies*. For instance, 85 of the people fall *jointly* into the light coffee consumption category and the young age category. The 12 joint frequencies sum to 900, as they should, since each respondent falls into exactly one of the 12 joint categories.

The numbers in the lower margin and the right-hand margin are called *marginal frequencies*. They are found by summing down columns and across rows, respectively. The numbers in the lower margin show how many respondents are in the various age categories. The numbers in the right-hand margin show how many respondents are in the various coffee consumption categories. Notice that the three numbers in the lower margin sum to 900, as do the four numbers in the right-hand margin.

Table 2.5 Contingency Table

			Young (Y)	Age Middle-Aged (MA)	Older (O)	
	Light	(L)	85	45	95	225
	Medium-Light	(ML)	90	55	50	195
Coffee Consumption	Medium-Heavy	(MH)	90	115	30	235
	Heavy	(H)	135	85	25	245
			400	300	200	

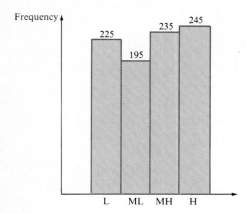

Figure 2.10
Coffee Consumption

This contingency table provides some interesting insights into the coffee consumption habits of the people sampled. If we look at the right-hand marginal totals, we see that the 900 people are fairly evenly distributed among the coffee consumption categories. This is illustrated by the graph in Figure 2.10.

However, this graph disguises the fact that coffee consumption is not evenly distributed in each of the separate age categories. This is illustrated in Figure 2.11. Obviously, if we are interested in the relationship of coffee consumption to age, the graphs in Figure 2.11 are much more informative than the single combined graph in Figure 2.10.

We may also exhibit data with *more* than two attributes in a contingency table. Now, however, at least two attributes must be combined across the top margin or down the left-hand margin. (This is because we must still exhibit the table on two-dimensional paper. Tables with three attributes are sometimes represented on paper as three-dimensional "cubes," with one dimension for each attribute. However, these are more for conceptual purposes. The "two-dimensional" tables shown here are much more useful for displaying the actual numbers.) To be specific, suppose that we classify the coffee drinkers as male or female, as well as by age and coffee consumption. Then there are 24 ($= 3 \times 4 \times 2$) joint categories, and each person falls into exactly one of these categories. This means that each of the 12 previous joint categories separates into two subcategories, male and female.

One way to exhibit these data is by means of the three-way contingency table shown in Table 2.6. The right-hand marginal totals are the same as in Table 2.5. However, the lower marginal totals are joint totals for age and sex attributes. For example, the first column total, 235, is the number of young males in the sample. Given these joint totals, we can easily obtain marginal totals for age or for sex separately. For example, the number of

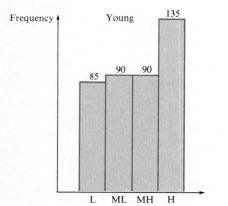
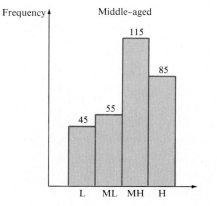
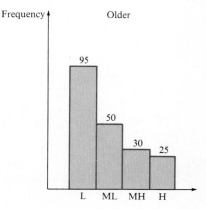

Figure 2.11
Coffee Consumption by Age

Table 2.6 Three-Way Contingency Table

		Male			Female			
		Y	MA	O	Y	MA	O	
	L	45	20	35	40	25	60	225
Coffee	ML	55	25	25	35	30	25	195
Consumption	MH	35	65	25	55	50	5	235
	H	100	50	20	35	35	5	245
		235	160	105	165	140	95	

males in the sample is $235 + 160 + 105 = 500$, and the number of young people in the sample is $235 + 165 = 400$.

Many frequency graphs can be drawn from the data in Table 2.6. For example, there are six age–sex combinations for which we could graph the coffee consumption distribution. These correspond to the six columns in Table 2.6. Also, by combining the sexes, we obtain the three distributions of coffee consumption by age category. (The reader may verify that these are identical to the graphs in Figure 2.11.) Finally, we may combine the ages to obtain the two coffee consumption distributions by sex. These graphs are shown in Figure 2.12. They indicate clearly that a difference exists between male and female coffee drinking habits for this particular sample.

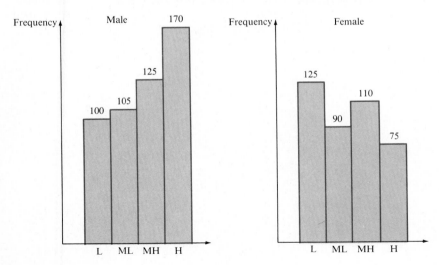

Figure 2.12
Coffee Consumption by Sex

2.6

Scattergrams and Time Series Graphs

Contingency tables are not the only way to present data with two or more attributes. We briefly mention two graphical methods that are often useful. These are called *scatter diagrams* (often abbreviated to *scattergrams*) and *time series graphs*. Scatter diagrams are appropriate when we are attempting to discover relationships between two attributes. Time series graphs are useful when one of the attributes of the data is time. We will have much more to say about both of these types of graphs in our chapters on regression analysis and time series analysis. The following simple examples illustrate the concepts.

EXAMPLE 2.2

Suppose that we survey a group of college seniors who have just accepted jobs in business. Each student is asked to supply his or her starting salary and cumulative grade-point average (GPA) in college. The purpose of the survey is to discover whether there is an observable relationship between salaries and GPA scores. If 20 students are sampled, we may summarize the data by the 20 pairs (X_1, Y_1), (X_2, Y_2), . . . , (X_{20}, Y_{20}), where X_i and Y_i are, respectively, the salary and the GPA for the ith student. We may graph each of these pairs as a point in the X-Y plane. For each point, the X coordinate is the salary and the Y coordinate is the GPA. The resulting graph is called a scatter diagram. Given the data in Table 2.7, the resulting scatter diagram is shown in Figure 2.13.

Table 2.7

Salary (Dollars per Week)	GPA
375	2.20
390	2.15
410	2.25
420	2.10
450	2.45
460	2.30
475	2.25
495	2.60
505	3.25
520	2.50
540	2.70
555	2.95
570	3.05
600	3.10
625	3.45
630	3.40
645	2.75
670	3.70
680	3.85
700	3.75

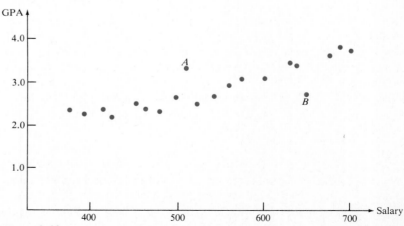

Figure 2.13
Scatter Diagram

This graph tends to confirm the plausible conjecture that high salaries and high GPAs go together, while low salaries and low GPAs also go together. This is because the points on the graph tend to rise from left to right. However, the graph also shows two points, labeled *A* and *B*, that do not fit the general pattern. Point *A* corresponds to a student with a low salary but a very high GPA, whereas point *B* corresponds to a student with a high salary but a low GPA. Each of these points is called an *outlier*, because each lies outside the general pattern. As we see from Figure 2.13, a scattergram not only identifies general patterns, but is also helpful in locating the outliers.

Now consider a set of data that measures a single attribute through time. Then a convenient way to display these data is by means of a time series graph. For time series data, there are really two attributes, one of which is time. Therefore, each observation may be written in the form (T_i, Y_i), where Y_i is the value of the ith observation and T_i is the time of the ith observation. (We have used the letter T, instead of X, to stand for time.) By plotting each of the (T_i, Y_i) pairs in the T-Y plane, we obtain a type of scatter diagram called a time series graph.

The usual situation is that there is exactly one observation per time period. The time period may be a month, a quarter, a year, or any other convenient unit of time. If the time periods are labeled in chronological order as 1, 2, 3, and so on, the points we plot on the time series graph are of the form $(1, Y_1)$, $(2, Y_2)$, $(3, Y_3)$, and so on. To make any possible patterns stand out more clearly, we usually join the successive points by lines.

EXAMPLE 2.3

Suppose that a manufacturing firm has collected monthly sales data for one of its products. The data cover the period from January 1985 to December 1986 and are given in Table 2.8. For any i between 1 and 24, Y_i represents the sales (in $1000s) in month i. A time series graph of these data appears in Figure 2.14 (p. 42). Such a graph clearly shows how the company's sales have been moving during these two years. In particular, it appears that there is some seasonal variation, with more sales in the summers than in the winters, and there is a slight upward trend in sales over the two years.

In later chapters on regression and time series analysis, we will learn some fairly complex methods for analyzing the types of data illustrated in Figures 2.13 and 2.14. It is worth emphasizing at this point, however, that in many applications, simple scattergrams and time series graphs provide as much information as we need to know. Further knowledge obtained through complicated mathematical analysis may merely confirm patterns that are already

Table 2.8

Month	i	Y_i
January 1985	1	57.5
February	2	64.2
March	3	58.9
April	4	65.2
May	5	70.3
June	6	85.2
July	7	95.1
August	8	88.4
September	9	75.1
October	10	54.2
November	11	58.1
December	12	60.4
January 1986	13	63.7
February	14	74.2
March	15	69.3
April	16	70.5
May	17	92.1
June	18	103.2
July	19	97.3
August	20	105.4
September	21	76.2
October	22	65.1
November	23	60.2
December	24	67.2

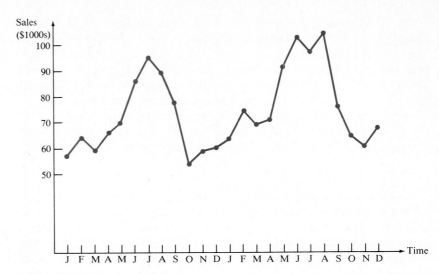

Figure 2.14
Time Series Graph

clear from the graphs. But even when more involved mathematical methods are necessary, a simple scattergram or time series graph is a good starting point for the analysis.

Problems for Sections 2.5, 2.6

*9. In a survey of n_1 men and n_2 women, each person was asked how many times he or she went shopping at a supermarket during the past month. The results are shown in the following two histograms. Draw a cumulative frequency graph for the combined group of men and women, assuming that $n_2 = 4n_1$.

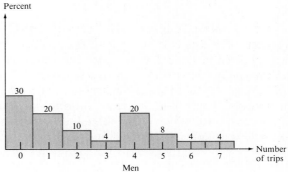

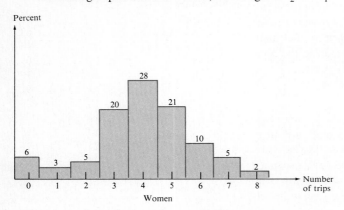

10. A group of 15 men were asked to give their age (X) and the average number of hours they sleep per night (Y). The results are shown at the top of p. 43. Draw a scattergram of these data. Does it suggest any relationship between age and amount of sleep?

Age	Hours of Sleep	Age	Hours of Sleep
21	6.5	24	5.5
35	6.0	58	6.0
54	6.5	46	6.5
25	8.0	33	8.0
32	7.5	29	7.0
39	8.5	38	7.5
45	7.0	63	6.5
36	7.5		

11. The following data represent a company's sales over the past 24 months. Draw a time series graph of these data. Are there any obvious trends or patterns visible?

Month	Sales ($1000s)	Month	Sales ($1000s)
January 1984	15.43	January 1985	16.88
February 1984	16.55	February 1985	20.56
March 1984	19.32	March 1985	23.31
April 1984	25.43	April 1985	27.65
May 1984	27.33	May 1985	32.53
June 1984	25.67	June 1985	30.61
July 1984	23.47	July 1985	31.55
August 1984	18.65	August 1985	25.76
September 1984	19.43	September 1985	22.12
October 1984	14.32	October 1985	17.67
November 1984	13.46	November 1985	18.77
December 1984	14.63	December 1985	19.49

12. A sample of 200 business managers found the following joint frequencies for age and amount of life insurance owned.

	Life Insurance Owned ($1000s)			
Age	0–50	51–100	101–250	251 or more
21–30	21	13	12	8
31–40	8	10	20	21
41–50	2	4	14	18
51–65	5	5	13	26

a. Draw a separate histogram of life insurance amounts for each age category. Are there any obvious differences among them?

b. Draw a histogram of life insurance amounts for the entire sample of 200 managers. How does it compare with the histograms from part (a)?

13. The following data on 25 blue-collar employees represent the number of days absent from work during the previous year and the number of years of seniority for each employee. Draw a scattergram of these data. Does there appear to be any relationship between the number of days absent and the number of years of seniority?

Days Absent	Years of Seniority	Days Absent	Years of Seniority
12	13	16	6
6	15	17	1
25	5	20	10
8	10	12	3
15	7	15	9
18	3	7	16
14	8	4	20
10	12	1	12
2	15	10	3
13	7	14	2
16	5	6	12
4	18	5	15
12	4		

14. The academic computer service at a university has been monitoring the execution times for the jobs run by faculty, graduate students doing research, and undergraduates enrolled in computer classes. The data on 300 jobs are summarized below. Draw a histogram of execution times for undergraduates only; for faculty and graduate students combined; for all 300 jobs combined.

	Execution Times (Seconds)				
	0–2	2–5	5–10	10–20	Over 20
Faculty	12	35	14	13	4
Graduates	30	41	20	10	6
Undergraduates	84	25	3	2	1

15. The data on p. 44 show the total value of all U.S. government bonds (in billions of dollars) from 1959 to 1980. (Reference: "The World Market Wealth Portfolio," *Journal of Portfolio Management*, Winter 1983, p. 11.) Draw a time series graph of these data. What patterns do you detect from this graph, if any?

Year	Government Bonds	Year	Government Bonds
1959	145.4	1970	195.6
1960	155.1	1971	207.4
1961	157.0	1972	221.4
1962	163.2	1973	233.9
1963	158.5	1974	247.2
1964	162.3	1975	302.3
1965	162.3	1976	373.0
1966	168.1	1977	428.9
1967	164.7	1978	481.0
1968	175.1	1979	537.4
1969	169.1	1980	594.0

16. The cumulative numbers of people in a particular community who bought a personal computer, as a function of time, are shown below. For example, there are 52 people who bought a personal computer by the end of 1981. Draw a time series graph of the number who bought a personal computer in each year, starting with 1979.

Year	Cumulative Number Who Bought by the End of This Year
1979	0
1980	14
1981	52
1982	88
1983	124
1984	205
1985	356
1986	434

2.7

Summary Measures

In this section we describe ways of summarizing sets of data by means of a few numerical summary measures. These summary measures seldom convey as much information about the data as the tables and graphs discussed above, but most of us find it easier to work with one or two summary measures than with an entire table or graph. Furthermore, a few well-chosen summary measures often convey more information about the data than we might expect.

We first make several general observations. As we have mentioned earlier, the principal role of statistics is to infer characteristics of a population from a sample selected from the population. When the population characteristic of interest is a single numerical summary measure, we refer to this number as a *population parameter*, or simply a *parameter*. When we calculate the same type of summary measure from sample data, the number is called a *sample statistic*, or simply a *statistic*.

> A population parameter is a numerical characteristic of the population as a whole. It can generally be calculated only by knowing the entire population.
>
> A sample statistic is a number that can be calculated from the data in the sample.

The usual situation is that the population parameter is unobservable (except perhaps through a census). Therefore, a statistic calculated from sample data is used to estimate the unknown parameter. For example, consider a population of executives and define p to be the fraction who smoke. After observing a sample of executives from this population, let $\hat{p}$ denote the proportion of the sample who smoke. Then p is the population parameter, and $\hat{p}$ is the sample statistic.

In this chapter we do not distinguish between population parameters and sample statistics. The point of view taken here is that the data can correspond to any sample, including a census. Given this point of view, the formulas for the summary measures given in this chapter are perfectly valid whether the data come from a subset of the population or represent the entire population.

The types of summary measures we usually consider in statistics fall into four general categories: (1) *proportions,* (2) measures of *central tendency,* (3) measures of *variability,* and (4) measures of *association*. We discuss each of these below.

The simplest type of summary measure, a proportion, requires little comment. If we consider any sample, and we are interested in any property A that members of this sample either have or do not have, the proportion having property A is what we should report. It is simply the number in the sample who possess property A divided by the number in the sample. Notice that a proportion and a percentage, while expressed differently, convey exactly the same information. To convert a proportion into a percentage, we simply multiply by 100.

The other three types of summary measures are not quite as simple to define as proportions, although their meanings are intuitive. The first of these, measures of central tendency, attempt to measure concepts such as the "average value," "middle value," or "most likely value" of a set of data. We discuss three important measures of central tendency: the mean, the median, and the mode. Each of these attaches a slightly different meaning to the term "central tendency," and we will see how each may be the most appropriate of the three in certain situations.

Any measure of central tendency tells us only where the "center" of the distribution is, but it does not measure the variability of the distribution. Therefore, we need measures of variability, or spread, to indicate whether the data are tightly packed or spread out over a large range. There are several measures that do this, including the variance and the standard deviation. We discuss these and other measures of variability below.

If a set of data has two or more attributes, we may be interested primarily in relationships between these attributes. For example, we may be interested in the relationship, if any, between salaries and years of schooling for the employees of a given company. Do they vary in the same direction, so that employees with more schooling tend to have higher salaries? Do they vary inversely, so that employees with less schooling tend to have higher salaries? Or is it possible that there is no relationship between salaries and years of schooling? These questions are concerned with measures of association. The two measures of association we will learn are called covariance and correlation.

2.8

Measures of Central Tendency

In this section we introduce the three primary measures of central tendency and examine their most important properties.

The Mean

The mean is the most important measure of central tendency. This does not imply that it is the most appropriate measure in every situation, but simply that it is used more frequently than any other measure. The mean is the average of the individual observations. As such, it applies only to *quantitative* data.

> The mean is the average of the observations. It applies only to quantitative data.

Let $X_1, X_2, \ldots, X_n$ be the values of the individual observations for the n members of a sample or a population. The mean, usually denoted by $\overline{X}$, is defined by the following formula. (The notation μ is also used for the mean. Generally, μ denotes the mean of a population, whereas $\overline{X}$ denotes the mean of a sample from a population. As indicated above, this distinction will not be necessary until later chapters.)

> *Formula for the Mean*
>
> $$\overline{X} = \frac{X_1 + X_2 + \cdots + X_n}{n} = \frac{\Sigma X_i}{n}$$

For example, to find the mean of the electric bills in Table 2.1, we add all 60 numbers and then divide by 60. The result is the mean electric bill:

$$\frac{1512 + 1543 + \cdots + 1720}{60} = \$1657.78$$

The definition of the mean as an average is probably familiar to all readers, so we now look at some of the possibly less obvious properties of the mean. First, in what sense is the mean a measure of central tendency? Consider the following four sequences of 10 observations: (3, 3, 3, 3, 3, 3, 3, 3, 3, 3), (1, 2, 2, 3, 3, 3, 3, 4, 4, 5), (1, 1, 1, 1, 1, 5, 5, 5, 5, 5), and (1, 1, 1, 1, 1, 1, 1, 1, 1, 21). Since the 10 numbers in each of these sequences sum to 30, each sequence has mean 3. For the first two sequences, the concept of central tendency seems appropriate. The numbers in the first sequence all equal 3, and the numbers in the second sequence vary symmetrically around 3. The symmetry around 3 is still present in the third sequence, but this sequence shows that the mean is not necessarily the "most likely value." The mean 3 never even appears in this sequence. The last sequence is even worse. Not only does the mean 3 not appear, but this sequence certainly does not vary around 3 in a symmetric way.

How can the mean be a measure of central tendency if the numbers are not symmetric about any number, as in the last sequence above? One possible answer to this question comes from physics. Consider a "weightless" narrow board with a number scale marked on it. For each observation X_i we put a 1-pound bag of sand on the board at the position equal to X_i. Then the mean is the position where we should place a fulcrum so that the board balances. This is shown in Figure 2.15 for the sequence (1, 1, 1, 1, 1, 1, 1, 1, 1, 21).

Figure 2.15
Physics Interpretation of Mean for Sequence (1, 1, 1, 1, 1, 1, 1, 1, 1, 21)

This property of the mean, although theoretically interesting, is not very useful in most business applications. However, it does show what can happen when we have a very skewed set of data, as in the sequence (1, 1, 1, 1, 1, 1, 1, 1, 1, 21). Because each observation plays the same role in the formula for the mean, outliers such as the 21 in this sequence exert a large influence on the value of the mean. Of course, this sequence has been devised to overstate the case, but the same type of phenomenon occurs in many sets of real-world data. Consider the following example.

EXAMPLE 2.4

A sample of yearly incomes from any population is likely to include a large number of incomes in the range $10,000 to $30,000. But a few incomes in the six-figure range will pull the mean up quite a lot. The effect may be that we believe the people of the city, on the average, are richer than they really are. This is exactly the type of conclusion we need to be wary of when we make statements based on the mean.

Despite its drawback in some situations, the mean does have several attractive properties. We discuss two of these. First, suppose that the data X_1, X_2, . . . , X_n have mean $\overline{X}$. Now we transform these data to Y_1, Y_2, . . . , Y_n by multiplying each X_i by a constant b and then adding a constant a. That is,

$$Y_i = a + bX_i \qquad \text{for each } i$$

(These Y's are called a *linear transformation* of the X's.)

Two Useful Properties of Means

To find the mean of the Y's, namely $\overline{Y}$, we could use the brute-force method of computing each Y, then summing the Y's, and finally dividing the sum by n. But we can save a lot of work by using the following rule:

> ### Mean of a Linear Transformation
> $$\overline{Y} = a + b\overline{X}$$

All we need to do is multiply the known mean $\overline{X}$ by b and then add a.

EXAMPLE 2.5

A manufacturing process produces an engine part in various batch sizes. Each batch requires a fixed cost of \$100, and the cost per part produced is 10 cents. If the mean batch size for a large number of batches is 5500 parts, what is the mean cost per batch?

SOLUTION

Let X_i be the number of parts in batch i, and let Y_i be the cost of batch i. Then Y_i equals $a + bX_i$, where $a = \$100$ (the fixed cost) and $b = \$.10$ (the cost per part). Since the mean number of parts per batch is 5500, $\overline{X} = 5500$. Therefore, from the rule above, the mean cost per batch is

$$\overline{Y} = a + b\overline{X} = 100 + .10(5500) = \$650$$

Another useful property of means is that we can easily "merge" several known subpopulation means into an overall population mean with very little arithmetic. Suppose that we have K subpopulations with means $\overline{X}_1, \overline{X}_2, \ldots, \overline{X}_K$, and that these are based on subpopulation sizes of $n_1, n_2, \ldots, n_K$. Then the mean $\overline{X}$ of the combined population is given by the following formula.

> ### Mean of a Merged Sample
> $$\overline{X} = \frac{n_1\overline{X}_1 + n_2\overline{X}_2 + \cdots + n_K\overline{X}_K}{n_1 + n_2 + \cdots + n_K} = \frac{\sum n_i\overline{X}_i}{\sum n_i}$$

This is *not* the same as the average of the K means, namely $(\overline{X}_1 + \overline{X}_2 + \cdots + \overline{X}_K)/K$, unless the subpopulation sizes $n_1, n_2, \ldots, n_K$ are equal. We illustrate the difference in the following example.

EXAMPLE 2.6

Suppose that the mean salaries per employee in three companies are $21,500, $25,400, and $22,250, and that these are based on 75, 125, and 45 employees, respectively. Find the mean salary for all three companies.

SOLUTION

The combined mean of these employees, taken as a single group, is given by

$$\overline{X} = \frac{75(21,500) + 125(25,400) + 45(22,250)}{75 + 125 + 45} = \$23,627.55$$

Notice that the numerator of the expression for $\overline{X}$ is the total of the salaries of the combined group of employees, while the denominator is the total number of employees. This explains why the formula for $\overline{X}$ is valid. Notice also that the answer is greater than the average of the three means, namely $(21,500 + 25,400 + 22,250)/3 = \$23,050$. The reason is simple. The company with the largest mean salary has the most employees, so its mean receives more weight in the formula for $\overline{X}$.

The Median

The median is a second measure of central tendency that is often reported along with, or instead of, the mean. The median is the "middle" observation of a set of data that have been arranged in increasing order. More precisely, the median is the number such that there are as many observations to the left of it as there are to the right of it. Therefore, to find the median, we first arrange the data from smallest to largest. The median is then the middle number if the number of observations is an odd number, and it is the average of the two middle numbers otherwise. For example, if the sequence of observations, in increasing order, is (1, 5, 8, 10, 16, 25, 32), the median is the fourth number, 10. If the sequence has an extra observation equal to 45, the median would then be the average of the fourth and fifth numbers, $(10 + 16)/2 = 13$.

> The median is the middle observation, or the average of the two middle observations, when the data are arranged in increasing order.

To find the median for a large set of data, a cumulative frequency table is useful. As an example, let's find the median of the electric bill data in Table 2.1. The cumulative frequency table for these data was shown in Table 2.3 and is repeated for convenience in Table 2.9 on p. 50.

Table 2.9 Finding the Median

Category	$1301 –$1400	$1401 –$1500	$1501 –$1600	$1601 –$1700	$1701 –$1800	$1801 –$1900	$1901 –$2000
Cumulative Frequency	2	9	22	36	46	54	60
Observations for "Median" Category			1602, 1603, ⟨1640,⟩ 31st	1622, 1623, 1640,	1625, 1653,	1625, 1656,	1629, ⟨1632,⟩ 30th 1662, 1683

The middle row in Table 2.9 allows us to find the vicinity of the median very quickly. There are 60 observations, so the middle two are the 30th and the 31st. Since 22 observations are less than 1600, and 36 observations are less than 1700, the 30th and 31st observations must be between 1600 and 1700. Therefore, we arrange the 14 observations between 1600 and 1700 in increasing order. This has been done at the bottom of Table 2.9. Then, starting with frequency count 23, we count until we get to 30 and 31. The 30th and 31st observations are found to be 1632 and 1640. Hence the median is (1632 + 1640)/2, or $1636.

The median and the mean are often equal or nearly equal. In the electric bill example, the mean is $1657.78 and the median is $1636. The difference of approximately $22 is probably not very significant, considering the sizes of the bills. If we want a simple answer to the question "How much do the company's electric bills tend to be?", either the median or the mean provides a reasonable answer.

However, in some data sets the median should be preferred to the mean. The reason is that the median is almost completely unaffected by extremely large or small observations, whereas the mean can be very sensitive to these values. If there are a few extremely large observations, for instance, and these are not offset by extremely small observations, we may decide to report the median as a more representative measure of the "center" of the data set. This is because the median is not affected by the values of these large observations, as is the mean.

Often, the decision on which measure to report depends on who is doing the reporting. A typical application concerns per capita income. As we mentioned earlier, the mean income in a population is likely to be larger than expected because a few rich people can pull up the average. But since these people have almost no effect on the median, the median is typically less than the mean. Now if one politician is trying to obtain government subsidies for his particular region, he will probably quote the median income of his region as an indication of its financial need. A politician arguing against subsidies for this region, however, will probably quote the mean income of the region as an indication that the people there do not need government money. Neither politician is deliberately lying, but neither is telling the whole truth.

Before discussing the mode, the other measure of central tendency, we briefly mention a group of summary measures, the principal one of which is the median. These measures are called the *percentiles,* or *fractiles,* of a distribution. The median has the property that no more than 50% of the data are on either side of it. Therefore, the median is also called the 50th percentile of the distribution. More generally, if R is any number between 0 and 100, the Rth percentile is defined to be any number P_R such that at most R percent of the data are less than it and at most $(100 - R)$ percent of the data are greater than it. Then the median is P_{50}.

> The Rth percentile is a number such that at most R percent of the observations are less than it and at most $(100 - R)$ percent of the observations are greater than it.

Percentiles are usually used to indicate a person's or company's ranking in a set of scores. For example, if a student's standardized test score is at the 85th percentile, she knows that 85% of the test scores in the population are less than hers and only 15% are above hers. If a steel company's return on investment is at the 32nd percentile of all steel companies, 32% of the steel companies have a lower return on investment and 68% have a higher return on investment.

A cumulative frequency table is useful for finding percentiles in the same way it was useful for finding the median. To find the 20th percentile of the electric bill data, we proceed as follows. Since there are 60 observations and 20% of 60 is 12, we know that P_{20} is any number such that 12 bills are less than P_{20} and the other 48 bills are greater than P_{20}. Referring to the cumulative frequency table in Table 2.9 and also to the original data in Table 2.1, we see that the 12th largest bill is \$1512 and the 13th largest bill is \$1524. Therefore, P_{20} is any value between these two numbers. For the sake of definiteness, we set P_{20} equal to the midpoint of these numbers, \$1518. As another example, if we want P_{80}, the 80th percentile of the electric bill data, we recognize that 80% of 60 is 48. Therefore, we locate the 48th and 49th largest bills. These are found to be \$1810 and \$1810, so that the 80th percentile, P_{80}, is equal to \$1810.

The third measure of central tendency is the mode. This is the value that occurs most often in a set of data. Unfortunately, if we interpret this definition in a strict sense, the mode often provides almost no information. For example, in the electric bill data, there are six numbers, 1421, 1527, 1625, 1640,

1725, and 1810, that appear twice in Table 2.1; all other numbers appear only once. So by the strict definition, there is a six-way tie for the mode. However, this information gives us no idea about the central tendency of the data. Therefore, it is useful to expand the definition of mode to the more typical case of *grouped* data. For data that have been grouped into categories, we refer to the mode (or modal category) as the category with the highest frequency. In the electric bill example, the mode then becomes the category between $1601 and $1700, based on the categories we defined earlier.

> For grouped data, the mode (or modal category) is the category with the most observations.

Since the concept of mode often makes more sense when it is applied to categories of data rather than to individual values, we may define a mode for qualitative data as well as for quantitative data. This makes the mode applicable in situations where the mean and median do not apply.

Even in some situations where all three measures make sense, however, the mode is occasionally the most relevant. For example, consider the problem of stocking women's dress sizes. The retailer can gather data and calculate the mean dress size demanded and the median dress size demanded, but she may be more interested in the modal dress size demanded. This is her best-seller, so she wants to make sure she does not run out of this size if possible.

In terms of a histogram, the modal category is the highest "peak" on the graph. See Figure 2.16a for an example. Sometimes there are two or more peaks. Such data sets are called *multimodal*, or *bimodal* if there are exactly two modes. A bimodal histogram appears in Figure 2.16b. As we mentioned earlier, a bimodal distribution usually indicates two distinct subpopulations in the data.

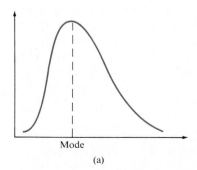
(a)

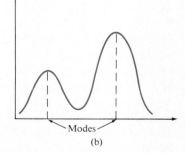
(b)

Figure 2.16

Measures of central tendency are intuitive concepts to most of us, especially since we are so used to seeing means, medians, and modes reported in magazines and periodicals. The concept of variability is somewhat different. Certainly, most of us have no trouble understanding the intuitive statement that one set of data has more variability than another set. So the *concept* of variability is not a mystery. The mystery arises when we attempt to *measure* variability. How do we translate the intuitive notion of variability into a numerical measure? In this section we provide several answers to this question.

Ranges

Let's first attack this problem from a naive point of view. Probably the simplest way to measure the variability of a data set is to calculate the difference between the largest and smallest numbers in the set. This difference is called the *range*.

> The range is the difference between the largest and smallest observations.

The range is certainly worth knowing, but it is sometimes too sensitive to extreme values to be of much use. For example, the sequence (1, 1, 1, 1, 1, 1, 1, 1, 1, 21) has range $21 - 1 = 20$, but is it fair to say that the data in this set are very spread out? Whatever we agree to say about the variability of this data set, the range seems to overstate its magnitude.

If the range is overly sensitive to extreme values, perhaps we should get rid of these values first and then calculate the range of what remains. A systematic way of doing this is to disregard the upper $R\%$ of the data and lower $R\%$ of the data, for some R, and then compute the range of the remaining data. This is commonly done for $R = 10$ or $R = 25$. If $R = 10$, we are computing the range of the middle 80% of the data; this is called the *interdecile range*. If $R = 25$, we are computing the range of the middle half of the data; this range is called the *interquartile range*.

> The interquartile range is the range of the middle 50% of the data.
> The interdecile range is the range of the middle 80% of the data.

These modified ranges are still not perfect measures of variability. The overall range is sometimes too sensitive to extreme values, but the modified ranges omit these extremes altogether. This omission may be unjustified, especially since a measure of variability ought to have something to do with extreme values. Also, these modified ranges ignore the actual *values* of the data in the middle of the distribution. These middle values could all be equal to one another or they could be fairly spread out within the ranges, and the ranges would be the same in either case. For example, the two sequences (1, 2, 5, 5, 5, 5, 5, 5, 9, 10) and (1, 2, 3, 4, 5, 6, 7, 8, 9, 10) have interdecile range $9 - 2 = 7$, but the variability within this range is quite different for the two sequences. Therefore, we need a measure of variability that is not overly sensitive to extreme values and takes into account the values of all the data. The measures we discuss next attempt to do this.

Mean Absolute Deviation

We define the *mean absolute deviation* (MAD) of a data set $X_1, X_2, \ldots, X_n$ to be the average distance from the observations to their mean. Here the distance from an observation X to the mean $\overline{X}$ is the absolute value $|X - \overline{X}|$.

> The mean absolute deviation is the average distance of the numbers from their mean.

The formula for the mean absolute deviation is given below.

> ### Formula for the Mean Absolute Deviation
> $$\text{MAD} = \frac{\Sigma \, |X_i - \overline{X}|}{n}$$

This measure of variability has several desirable properties. It equals 0 when all of the observations are equal, it uses the values of all of the observations, and it is generally larger for data sets that "look" more spread out than others. However, its drawback is that it is not particularly nice to work with from a mathematical point of view. In the next section we introduce a measure of variability that has all the nice properties of MAD but is easier to work with.

The Variance and Standard Deviation

A measure of variability similar to the mean absolute deviation can be obtained by averaging the *squared* deviations from the mean, rather than the absolute deviations from the mean. This measure is called the *variance* and is denoted by s^2.

> The variance is the average of the squared deviations of the observations from their mean. It is denoted by s^2.
>
> ### Formula for the Variance
>
> $$s^2 = \frac{\Sigma\,(X_i - \overline{X})^2}{n - 1}$$

This formula says to subtract the mean $\overline{X}$ from each observation, square these deviations from the mean, add these squared deviations, and finally, divide by one less than the number of observations.

Strictly speaking, s^2 as defined here is called the *sample* variance. It is not really an "average" because we divide by $n - 1$, not n. In contrast, the *population* variance, usually denoted by σ^2, is the same as s^2 except that we divide by n, not $n - 1$. When n is reasonably large, s^2 and σ^2 are practically equal. Because s^2 is the quantity used in later chapters, we prefer to work with it instead of σ^2 in this chapter. (Most hand calculators use $n - 1$ instead of n in the denominator when they calculate a preprogrammed variance. Some provide both options.)

The variance formula above entails a lot of work, particularly the calculation of the squared deviations from the mean. By manipulating the defining formula for s^2, however, we obtain a *computing formula* for s^2 that is much more efficient for hand calculation.

> ### Computing Formula for the Variance
>
> $$s^2 = \frac{\Sigma\,X_i^2 - n\overline{X}^2}{n - 1}$$

Now all we need to do is to square each observation, sum these squares, subtract n times the square of the mean, and finally divide by $n - 1$. This is certainly easier because no individual deviations from the mean need to be calculated.

EXAMPLE 2.7

Calculate the variance of the 10 numbers 8, 4, 3, 2, 7, 5, 4, 6, 2, 5. Use the defining formula and the computing formula for variance.

Table 2.10

X_i	X_i^2	$X_i - \overline{X}$	$(X_i - \overline{X})^2$
8	64	3.4	11.56
4	16	− .6	.36
3	9	− 1.6	2.56
2	4	− 2.6	6.76
7	49	2.4	5.76
5	25	.4	.16
4	16	− .6	.36
6	36	1.4	1.96
2	4	− 2.6	6.76
5	25	.4	.16
Totals 46	248		36.40
$\overline{X} = 4.6$			

SOLUTION

Table 2.10 presents the calculations in a systematic manner. From this table we obtain s^2 from the calculation

$$s^2 = \frac{\Sigma (X_i - \overline{X})^2}{n - 1} = \frac{36.40}{9} = 4.04$$

or from

$$s^2 = \frac{\Sigma X_i^2 - n\overline{X}^2}{n - 1} = \frac{248 - (10)4.6^2}{9} = 4.04$$

Notice that the $X_i - \overline{X}$ and $(X_i - \overline{X})^2$ columns are necessary only if we calculate s^2 the "hard" way. If we use the computing formula, we need only the X_i and X_i^2 columns. Furthermore, after a little practice it is not necessary to write all the calculations in a table. We just sum the X's and X^2's on a calculator and then do the necessary calculations on the resulting sums.

One problem with the variance is that its units are *squared* units. For example, if each X_i is expressed in dollars, s^2 is expressed in dollars squared. To convert this measure back to the original units, we take the square root of the variance. The result is called the *standard deviation* and is denoted by s.

The standard deviation s is the square root of the variance.

If each observation is expressed in dollars, s is also expressed in dollars. For example, if the X's in Table 2.10 are expressed in dollars, the standard deviation is \$2.01 because $\sqrt{4.04} = 2.01$.

The real appeal of using the variance or the standard deviation as a measure of variability is contained in the following two rules. The first rule is a mathematical result that holds for every conceivable data set. The second rule is a result that has been observed empirically for a wide variety of data sets.

Before stating these rules, consider the statement: "An observation is within k standard deviations of the mean." For a fixed positive number k (not necessarily an integer), this means that the distance from the observation to the mean $\overline{X}$ is less than k times the standard deviation s. Algebraically, if the value of the observation is X, this says that

$$|X - \overline{X}| < ks$$

or equivalently,

$$\overline{X} - ks < X < \overline{X} + ks$$

For example, if $\overline{X} = 100$, $s = 30$, and $k = 2$, then an observation is within k standard deviations of the mean if its value is in the interval from 40 to 160. This is shown geometrically in Figure 2.17.

(Chebyshev's inequality): For any set of data $X_1, X_2, \ldots, X_n$ and for any value of $k > 1$, the fraction of observations within k standard deviations of the mean is *at least* $1 - 1/k^2$.

RULE 2.1

As an example, if $n = 100$, at least $100 \times (1 - 1/k^2)$ of the observations are within k standard deviations of the mean. For $k = 1.5, 2, 2.5$, and 3, this yields approximately 55.6, 75, 84, and 88.9 observations, respectively. So if the mean is 100 and the standard deviation is 10, say, we know that at

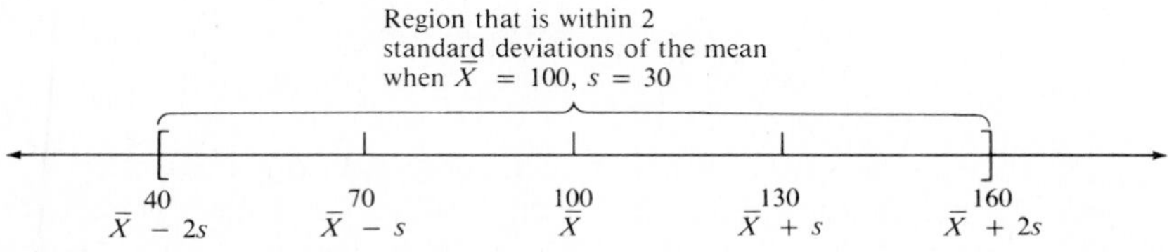

Region that is within 2 standard deviations of the mean when $\overline{X} = 100$, $s = 30$

Figure 2.17

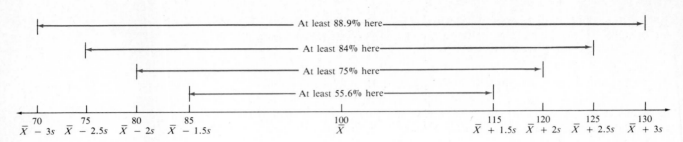

Figure 2.18
Illustration of Chebyshev's Inequality when $\overline{X} = 100$, $s = 10$

least 56 of the observations are in the interval 85 to 115 ($k = 1.5$), at least 75 are in the interval 80 to 120 ($k = 2$), at least 84 are in the interval 75 to 125 ($k = 2.5$), and at least 89 are in the interval 70 to 130 ($k = 3$) (see Figure 2.18). Furthermore, these statements are true for *any* set of 100 numbers with mean 100 and standard deviation 10.

If the histogram of the data is fairly symmetric and approximately bell-shaped, we can improve on Rule 2.1 as follows.

RULE 2.2

(Rule of thumb, or normal approximation): For any set of data X_1, X_2, . . . , X_n with an approximately symmetric and bell-shaped histogram, the following statements are approximately true.

1. 68% of the observations are within one standard deviation of the mean.
2. 95% of the observations are within two standard deviations of the mean.
3. Over 99% of the observations are within three standard deviations of the mean.

Notice how Rules 2.1 and 2.2 differ. Using $k = 2$, for instance, Chebyshev's rule says that for any 100 observations, at least 75 of them are within two standard deviations of the mean. If we have the additional information that the histogram of the data is approximately symmetric and bell-shaped, the rule of thumb improves on Chebyshev's rule. It says that approximately 95 of the 100 observations are within two standard deviations of the mean.

Chebyshev's rule is conservative in many numerical examples because it must hold for all kinds of strangely shaped distributions of data. The rule of thumb is much more specific (and informative) because it deals with more well-behaved distributions of data. The important point is that these rules show specifically how the standard deviation can be interpreted as a measure of variability.

Like the mean, the variance and standard deviation possess two nice mathematical properties. First, suppose that we transform the data $X_1, X_2, \ldots,$ X_n, with variance s_X^2, into $Y_1, Y_2, \ldots, Y_n$ by the formula $Y = a + bX$. Earlier we saw that the mean is transformed by the formula $\overline{Y} = a + b\overline{X}$. There is a similar transformation for the variance, as shown below.

Two Useful Properties of Variances and Standard Deviations

> *Variance of a Linear Transformation*
>
> $$s_Y^2 = b^2 s_X^2$$

Taking square roots, the corresponding transformation of standard deviations is

$$s_Y = |b| s_X$$

(In both of these formulas we use a subscript on s to indicate whether we are talking about the X's or the Y's.)

Since the constant b rescales the data and the constant a simply shifts each observation by a constant amount, it is not surprising that the variance, a measure of variability, is affected only by b, not by a.

EXAMPLE 2.5 (continued)

Recall that each batch of parts costs a fixed amount $100 plus 10 cents per part. In a large number of batches, suppose that the standard deviation of the number of parts per batch is 570. What are the variance and standard deviation of the cost per batch?

SOLUTION

As before, let X_i be the number of parts in batch i, and let Y_i be the cost of batch i. Then since $Y_i = a + bX_i$, with $a = 100$ and $b = .10$, the variance of the cost per batch is

$$s_Y^2 = b^2 s_X^2 = (.10)^2(570)^2 = 3249$$

This is not a very meaningful measure because its units are dollars squared. However, its square root is

$$s_Y = |b| s_X = (.10)(570) = 57$$

This tells us that the standard deviation of costs across the various batches is $57.

___

Next, suppose that we have data from K subpopulations with means $\overline{X}_1$, $\overline{X}_2, \ldots, \overline{X}_K$, variances $s_1^2, s_2^2, \ldots, s_K^2$, and subpopulation sizes $n_1, n_2, \ldots, n_K$. We know that the mean of the combined group of data is given by

$$\overline{X} = \frac{\Sigma \, n_i \overline{X}_i}{\Sigma \, n_i}$$

from Section 2.8. There is a similar formula for the variance of the combined group of data.

> ### Variance of a Merged Sample
>
> $$s^2 = \frac{\Sigma \, [(n_i - 1)s_i^2 + n_i \overline{X}_i^2] - n\overline{X}^2}{n - 1}$$
>
> where $n = \Sigma \, n_i$ is the total number of observations

___

EXAMPLE 2.6 (continued)

Recall that the mean salaries per employee in the three companies are $21,500, $25,400, and $22,250, and that these are based on 75, 125, and 45 employees, respectively. Now suppose that the standard deviations of the salaries for these three companies are $3250, $4750, and $2925. Find the standard deviation of the combined group of 245 employees.

SOLUTION

We already computed the combined mean $\overline{X}$; it is $23,627.55. So from the formula above, the variance of the combined group is

$$s^2 = \frac{[74(3250)^2 + 75(21,500)^2] + [124(4750)^2 + 125(25,400)^2] + [44(2925)^2 + 45(22,250)^2] - 245(23,627.55)^2}{244}$$

$$= 19,563,159$$

This means that the standard deviation of the combined group is

$$s = \sqrt{19,563,159} = \$4423$$

We now apply the measures of variability to the electric bill data in Table 2.1. (The cumulative frequency table in Table 2.3 is also useful for reference.) Since the largest bill is $1987 and the smallest bill is $1314, the range is $1987 − $1314 = $673. To find the interdecile range, we ignore the six largest bills and the six smallest bills (since 10% of 60 is 6). The range of the remaining bills is $1893 − $1483 = $410. Similarly, the interquartile range is found by ignoring the 15 largest bills and the 15 smallest bills (since 25% of 60 is 15). The range of the remaining bills is $1781 − $1528 = $253.

Next, recall that the mean electric bill is $1657.78. To find the mean absolute deviation, we must calculate

$$\frac{\Sigma |X_i - \overline{X}|}{60}$$

$$= \frac{|1512 - 1657.78| + |1543 - 1657.78| + \cdots + |1720 - 1657.78|}{60}$$

After a tedious calculation (which requires 60 absolute deviations from the mean since there is no "computing formula" for MAD), this turns out to be $132.99. But since there are no rules similar to Rules 2.1 and 2.2 for the mean absolute deviation, it is difficult to give an intuitive interpretation to this number.

To compute the variance s^2, we use the computing formula:

$$s^2 = \frac{\Sigma X_i^2 - n\overline{X}^2}{n - 1}$$

$$= \frac{(1512^2 + 1543^2 + \cdots + 1720^2) - 60(1657.78)^2}{59} = 26,926.98$$

The standard deviation is then

$$s = \sqrt{26,926.98} = \$164.09$$

Let's see what Rules 2.1 and 2.2 say about this set of data. (It appears that Rule 2.2 will apply, since the histogram in Figure 2.4 is approximately symmetric and bell-shaped.) Specifically, we will find the number of bills within k standard deviations of the mean for $k = 1$, $k = 2$, and $k = 3$. To be within 1 standard deviation of the mean, a bill must be inside the interval 1657.78 ± 164.09, that is, less than $1821.87 and greater than $1493.69. Similarly, the intervals within 2 and 3 standard deviations of the mean are from $1329.60 to $1985.96 and from $1165.51 to $2150.05, respectively. Counting the number of the 60 observations in each of these intervals and

Table 2.11

k	Interval	Number Predicted from Rule 2.1	Number Predicted from Rule 2.2	Number Counted from Data
1	1493.69–1821.87	Not applicable	$(.68)(60) = 40.8$	42
2	1329.60–1985.96	$\geq (1 - \frac{1}{4})(60) = 45$	$(.95)(60) = 57$	57
3	1165.51–2150.05	$\geq (1 - \frac{1}{9})(60) = 53.3$	$> (.99)(60) = 59.4$	60

comparing these numbers with the predictions from Rules 2.1 and 2.2, we see how conservative Rule 2.1 is and how accurate Rule 2.2 is for this data set. The results are summarized in Table 2.11.

2.10
Summary Measures for Grouped Data

Suppose that the original observations are unavailable, and we are given only the frequencies in a frequency table or a histogram. How do we compute the mean and variance? The answer is that we cannot do so, at least not exactly. Since the formulas for the mean and variance clearly depend on the values of the individual X's (which are unavailable), we can do no better than approximate $\overline{X}$ and s^2. However, the approximations are usually adequate if we assume that each of the observations in a given category equals the *midpoint* of that category. Under this assumption we can then substitute these midpoints into the formulas for $\overline{X}$ and s^2.

> To obtain the mean and variance for grouped data, substitute the midpoints of the categories for the observations.

The resulting formulas do simplify to a certain extent, since there are so many X's equal to one another. Let the subscript k stand for a typical category, let M_k be the midpoint of category k, and let f_k (f for frequency) be the number of observations in category k. Then the approximate values of $\overline{X}$ and s^2, denoted by $\overline{X}_g$ and s_g^2 (g for grouped), are shown below.

> *Mean and Variance Formulas for Grouped Data*
>
> $$\overline{X}_g = \frac{\Sigma f_k M_k}{n}$$
>
> $$s_g^2 = \frac{\Sigma f_k M_k^2 - n\overline{X}_g^2}{n - 1}$$

Table 2.12

Category	M_k	f_k	$f_k M_k$	$f_k M_k^2$
\$1301–\$1400	1,350	2	2,700	3,645,000
\$1401–\$1500	1,450	7	10,150	14,717,500
\$1501–\$1600	1,550	13	20,150	31,232,500
\$1601–\$1700	1,650	14	23,100	38,115,000
\$1701–\$1800	1,750	10	17,500	30,625,000
\$1801–\$1900	1,850	8	14,800	27,380,000
\$1901–\$2000	1,950	6	11,700	22,815,000
Total			100,100	168,530,000

We may apply these formulas to the electric bill example by using the frequencies in Table 2.2. For simplicity, we will use the numbers \$1350, \$1450, and so on, as the midpoints of the categories. (It does not matter if we use the *exact* midpoints of the categories since $\overline{X}_g$ and s_g^2 are only approximations to the true $\overline{X}$ and s^2 anyway.) The calculations are indicated in Table 2.12. The values of $\overline{X}_g$ and s_g^2 are

$$\overline{X}_g = \frac{100,100}{60} = \$1668.33$$

and

$$s_g^2 = \frac{168,530,000 - 60(1668.33)^2}{59} = 25,940.69$$

so that the approximate standard deviation is

$$s_g = \sqrt{25,940.69} = \$161.06$$

Obviously, the agreement between these values and the correct values found earlier, $\overline{X} = \$1657.78$ and $s = \$164.09$, is very good.

2.11

Measures of Association

If a set of data has a single numerical attribute, we usually construct a frequency table or draw a histogram and then calculate several summary measures, such as the mean and the variance. For a set of observations with two or more numerical attributes, there are more possibilities. If we concentrate on only one attribute at a time, we can again construct a frequency table, draw a histogram, or calculate a mean and a variance. However, we may be more interested in how the attributes are related than in the properties of each attribute taken individually. This is why we discussed contingency tables and scatter diagrams. We now discuss two summary measures that measure the relationship between two numerical attributes in a set of data. Essentially, these measures indicate (1) whether there is a linear (straight line) relationship between the two attributes, and (2) how successful we are likely to be when we attempt to predict one attribute as a linear function of the other.

Consider a set of data with two numerical attributes, labeled X and Y. Each member of the population has an X and a Y, so that the observations naturally come in pairs. If there are n pairs, we define the *covariance*, denoted by s_{XY}, as follows.

Formula for the Covariance

$$s_{XY} = \frac{\sum (X_i - \overline{X})(Y_i - \overline{Y})}{n - 1}$$

The numerator in this formula is the sum of the products, $(X_i - \overline{X}) \cdot (Y_i - \overline{Y})$, of deviations from means. Assume that the X's and Y's are related in a *positive* way; that is, large X's tend to go with large Y's, and small X's tend to go with small Y's. Then X's below $\overline{X}$ will tend to be paired with Y's below $\overline{Y}$, and X's above $\overline{X}$ will tend to be paired with Y's above $\overline{Y}$. In either case, the product $(X_i - \overline{X})(Y_i - \overline{Y})$ is positive, being a negative times a negative or a positive times a positive. So we expect the covariance to be positive. Similarly, if the X's and Y's are related in a *negative* way, with high X's paired with low Y's, and vice versa, we will tend to obtain mostly negative products $(X_i - \overline{X})(Y_i - \overline{Y})$. In this case, we expect the covariance to be negative. But if the X's and Y's are not related at all, the positive products will tend to cancel the negative products, and the covariance will be near 0.

The problem with the covariance is that although its *sign* determines the direction of the relationship between the X's and Y's, its *magnitude* does not tell us anything about the strength of that relationship. Therefore, it is useful to ''standardize'' the covariance so that its magnitude, as well as its sign, becomes meaningful. The standardized covariance is called the *correlation* and is denoted by r_{XY}. The defining formula for the correlation is given below.

Formula for the Correlation

$$r_{XY} = \frac{\sum (X_i - \overline{X})(Y_i - \overline{Y})}{\sqrt{\sum (X_i - \overline{X})^2} \sqrt{\sum (Y_i - \overline{Y})^2}}$$

This formula may be written more simply as

$$r_{XY} = \frac{s_{XY}}{s_X s_Y}$$

where s_X and s_Y are the standard deviations of the X's and Y's.

Because the formulas for r_{XY} and s_{XY} are not particularly convenient for hand use, we present computing formulas for each of them. As in the case of the variance, the advantage of these computing formulas is that no deviations from means need to be computed.

Computing Formulas for the Covariance and Correlation

$$s_{XY} = \frac{\sum X_i Y_i - n\overline{X}\,\overline{Y}}{n - 1}$$

$$r_{XY} = \frac{\sum X_i Y_i - n\overline{X}\,\overline{Y}}{\sqrt{\sum X_i^2 - n\overline{X}^2}\,\sqrt{\sum Y_i^2 - n\overline{Y}^2}}$$

EXAMPLE 2.8

The data in Table 2.13 represent the amount of driving (in thousands of miles) and the amount spent on car upkeep (in hundreds of dollars) for each of 10 drivers over a two-year period. Find the covariance and correlation between amount of driving (X) and amount spent on car upkeep (Y).

Table 2.13 Data for Example 2.8

Driver i	X_i	Y_i	X_i^2	Y_i^2	$X_i Y_i$
1	10.7	2.5	114.49	6.25	26.75
2	5.4	1.3	29.16	1.69	7.02
3	21.7	3.7	470.89	13.69	80.29
4	15.4	2.1	237.16	4.41	32.34
5	16.9	1.7	285.61	2.89	28.73
6	10.1	1.1	102.01	1.21	11.11
7	7.2	.7	51.84	.49	5.04
8	25.3	3.5	640.09	12.25	88.55
9	17.8	2.1	316.84	4.41	37.38
10	9.1	1.0	82.81	1.00	9.10
Total	139.6	19.7	2330.90	48.29	326.31

SOLUTION

The bulk of the work required has been done in Table 2.13. There we have calculated the sums of the X's and Y's, the sums of their squares, and the sum of the cross-products (X's times Y's). From these sums we obtain the means

$$\overline{X} = \frac{139.6}{10} = 13.96 \qquad \overline{Y} = \frac{19.7}{10} = 1.97$$

From the computing formulas, the covariance is

$$s_{XY} = \frac{326.31 - 10(13.96)(1.97)}{9} = 5.70$$

and the correlation is

$$r_{XY} = \frac{326.31 - 10(13.96)(1.97)}{\sqrt{2330.90 - 10(13.96)^2} \sqrt{48.29 - 10(1.97)^2}} = .852$$

The principal reason for preferring correlation to covariance is that correlations are unaffected by linear transformations of the data, whereas covariances are. In the example above, if we had expressed each X in miles (instead of thousands of miles) and each Y in dollars (instead of hundreds of dollars), the covariance would be inflated by a factor of 100,000 ($= 1000 \times 100$), but the correlation would not be affected at all. In fact, it can be shown that the correlation is a unitless quantity that is *always* between -1 and $+1$, whereas the covariance can be any number.

The sign of r_{XY} tells us whether the X's and Y's vary in the same direction

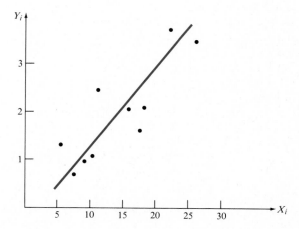

Figure 2.19
Scattergram for Example 2.8

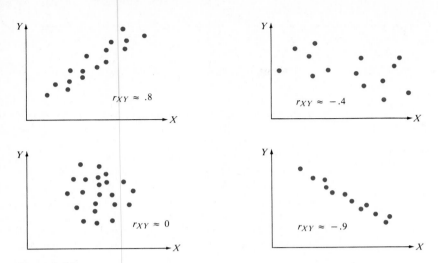

Figure 2.20
Selected Scattergrams and Approximate Correlations

($r_{XY} > 0$) or in the opposite direction ($r_{XY} < 0$). In this respect, the correlation is exactly like the covariance. But the magnitude of r_{XY} tells us how close the X's and Y's are to being *linearly* related. That is, the magnitude of r_{XY} tells us how well a single straight line fits the scattergram of the X's and Y's.

The scattergram of the data from Example 2.8 is shown in Figure 2.19. As we see, the 10 observations vary fairly tightly around the straight line shown in the figure. This could have been anticipated from the fact that the magnitude of the correlation, .85, is so close to 1. The fact that the correlation (and the covariance) are positive shows that the relationship between X and Y is positive. As the amount of driving increases, the amount spent on car upkeep also tends to increase. Geometrically, the relationship between these variables is a positive one because the points in the scattergram tend to rise from left to right.

If $|r_{XY}| = 1$, there is a perfect linear fit. This means there are constants a and b such that $Y_i = a + bX_i$ for each i. In this case the points on the scattergram lie exactly on a straight line. If $|r_{XY}|$ is fairly large, say, between .7 and 1, the points on the scattergram vary consistently around a straight line but do not all lie on any single straight line. If $|r_{XY}|$ is positive but not large, say, between 0 and .7, the points on the scattergram suggest a straight line but vary quite a lot around it. Finally, if r_{XY} is close to or equal to 0, the scattergram usually appears as a swarm of points with no linear trend at all. In the chapters on regression, we will have much more to say about this topic. Selected scattergrams with different correlations are shown in Figure 2.20.

Problems for Sections 2.7, 2.8, 2.9, 2.10, 2.11

17. The salaries of the employees in three separate departments of a company are shown below.

Salaries ($1000s)		
Department 1	Department 2	Department 3
18.66	15.56	20.45
17.32	17.43	23.65
19.65	18.17	32.47
21.32	21.61	28.65
24.12	15.32	25.45
20.44	18.66	23.18
17.32	15.23	
23.98	14.96	
17.63		
15.28		

a. Calculate the mean salary for each of the three departments separately.
b. Use the results from part (a) to calculate the mean salary of all the employees in the three departments combined.
c. The company has a special fund set aside for social events to which all employees are asked to contribute. Each employee is asked to give $10 plus .1% of his or her salary. Without going back to the original data, calculate the mean contribution per employee.

18. Repeat Problem 17, but now calculate standard deviations instead of means.

19. Consider the following scores from an aptitude test that was given to 60 prospective employees. Find the Rth percentile, P_R, for $R = 10$, $R = 25$, $R = 50$, $R = 75$, and $R = 90$.

76	65	89	57	64	47	95	55	77	58	68	81
68	73	89	92	53	48	66	88	84	82	36	59
59	85	43	61	74	69	96	89	79	49	72	57
91	84	79	72	69	75	82	58	52	49	66	61
68	83	81	76	79	98	92	56	73	89	73	56

20. A computer programmer ran the same FORTRAN program 16 times with different inputs on each run. The execution times for the 16 runs (in seconds) are shown below.

2.29	2.21	2.76	2.35	2.81	1.98	2.11	2.87
3.05	2.56	2.36	2.49	1.87	2.98	2.45	2.19

a. Find the mean absolute deviation and the interquartile range for these data.
b. Find the standard deviation of these data.
c. How many of the observations (at least) should be within 1.5 standard deviations of the mean as predicted by Rule 2.1? Confirm that this is the case.
d. How many of the observations should be within 1 standard deviation of the mean as predicted by Rule 2.2? Is this the case for these data?

21. Compute the standard deviation of the first 24 electric bills (the top four rows) in Table 2.1. Then compute the standard deviation of the last 36 electric bills. Finally, find the standard deviation of all 60 electric bills by "merging" the two separate standard deviations. Check that your answer agrees with the value found in the chapter.

22. The data in the following histogram show the high temperatures for each day in a two-month span in New York City. The data have been grouped into 5° intervals. Calculate the (approximate) mean and standard deviation of temperatures from the data that are given.

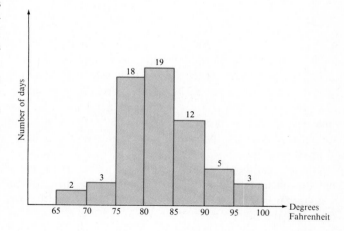

23. The following data represent the heights (in inches) of husbands and their wives for 10 selected families. Find the covariance between the husbands' heights and the wives' heights. Then find the correlation between these heights. Finally, draw a scattergram of the data. Does the appearance of the scattergram support the correlation value you found? Explain.

Husband	Wife
67	61
72	65
75	66
69	67
66	60
65	64
73	70
72	63
69	65
67	63

24. In Problem 23, convert each height to centimeters (1 inch equals 2.54 centimeters). Then answer the same questions asked in that problem. How is the covariance affected by the change in measurement units? How is the correlation affected? How is the appearance of the scattergram affected?

25. A study of one neighborhood in a suburban area of Chicago found the following data. Each observation shows the amount of unpaid principal on a given homeowner's mortgage. Find the 20th percentile; the 80th percentile; the median.

Unpaid Principal (Dollars)

65,123	56,342	32,410	57,891	43,270	21,150	33,900
54,190	31,198	25,782	21,189	13,890	5,392	26,774
14,154	86,743	66,720	44,642	27,684	13,254	59,832
15,632	76,432	47,843	27,421	37,683	28,683	85,341
93,266	37,563	69,832	105,326	34,768	10,325	66,882

26. One restaurant that advertises itself as a middle-priced place where families can get a good meal examined a sample of its customers' expenditures while eating there. Each of the observations below shows the size of the bill for a given family. Find the median food bill for the families observed. Also find the 25th percentile and the 75th percentile.

$25.67	$14.56	$16.74	$12.56	$20.35	$17.33
18.22	13.27	25.26	23.47	19.32	15.75
12.68	16.78	20.33	21.45	23.65	18.76
15.55	17.43	25.23	13.54	26.89	21.45
15.71	16.72	19.32	14.26	15.66	19.82
20.33	16.47	17.21	14.52	20.33	21.65

27. A sample of 60 families were asked to estimate the average amount spent per day during their most recent summer vacation. The accompanying data represent these expenditures.

$125	85	105	90	135	120	80	95	100	125
160	130	165	205	85	145	175	150	75	130
100	95	125	140	200	135	120	105	90	140
75	170	190	145	120	100	110	95	145	105
165	195	215	70	100	135	165	80	100	125
120	140	150	125	105	90	205	180	135	125

a. Draw a histogram of these data, using eight equal-width categories. Make the lower endpoint 60 and the upper endpoint 220.
b. Using the raw data, find the median vacation expenditure. Also find the 25th and 75th percentiles.

28. A study of 355 workers who retired voluntarily from their companies showed the number of years each had spent with his or her company. (Reference: George F. Dreher, "The Role of Performance in the Turnover Process," *Academy of Management Journal*, Vol. 25, 1982, pp. 137–147.) These data are shown below.

Years of Service	Frequency	Years of Service	Frequency
0	4	8	11
1	41	9	7
2	67	10	14
3	82	11	6
4	28	12	14
5	43	13	5
6	14	14	2
7	17		

a. Draw a cumulative frequency graph of these data.
b. Find the smallest number of years of service such that at least 50% of the workers had no more than this many years of service.
c. Calculate the 25th and 75th percentiles of years of service for this group of workers. (Look carefully at the definition of percentiles in the text.)

29. For the income data shown in Problem 2 (p. 34), use the formulas for grouped data to find the mean and standard deviation of the incomes shown. Use $125,000 as the "midpoint" of the category "$100,000 or more." Assume that the sample size is $n = 1000$.

30. The Commerce Department has predicted the following per capita incomes for the year 2000, as well as the percentage increases in per capita incomes from 1978 to 2000 for the 10 western states shown. (Reference: "States Where Incomes

Will Rise Fastest,'' *U.S. News & World Report*, Dec. 22, 1980, p. 50.) Find the mean and standard deviation of these percentage increases. Why are these measures possibly misleading?

State	Per Capita Income by Year 2000	Percentage Increase from 1978 to 2000
Alaska	17,006	57
Arizona	13,032	76
California	14,381	61
Colorado	13,857	71
Idaho	12,282	74
Montana	12,662	83
Nevada	14,432	54
Oregon	13,556	68
Utah	12,110	84
Washington	14,247	67

31. For the data in Problem 3 (p. 34), use the formula for the mean of grouped data to approximate the mean expenditure for the 481 under-50 travelers; for the 324 over-50 travelers; for the combined group of 805 travelers. Assume that the "midpoint" of the $1000-or-more category is $1100.

32. Even though all cars of a given model have the same estimated gas mileage on their window stickers, different cars experience different actual gas mileages, depending on the type of driver, the type of driving conditions, and other factors. Statistics on 50 cars of a particular model show the following miles per gallon (based on at least 1000 miles of driving).

23.5	24.6	26.3	27.5	23.0	24.2	25.1	27.6
21.7	25.0	23.6	21.7	19.7	26.3	21.5	22.9
24.1	25.1	23.7	18.5	22.1	20.9	23.5	24.3
23.6	21.8	23.0	23.6	21.6	24.3	20.8	29.8
25.0	23.6	22.4	21.6	21.8	25.2	18.4	20.7
24.3	22.7	28.7	23.1	25.3	29.5	20.1	22.2
22.3	19.2						

a. Draw a histogram of these mileages such that the bottom category starts at 18, the top category ends at 30, and there are six equal-width categories.

b. Suppose that the stickers on these cars predicted an average mpg of 28. Calculate the mean, median, and standard deviation of the 50 cars tested and comment on the accuracy of the 28-mpg claim.

33. Suppose that we want to convert the mean mpg from Problem 32 to mean kilometers per liter. Do this *without* converting each observation from mpg to kilometers per liter. Use the fact that 1 mile equals 1.609 kilometers and 1 gallon equals 3.785 liters.

34. There is a fairly wide variation in the interest rates that people are currently paying on their mortgage loans, due to the fact that these loans originated as long as 20 or more years ago. One savings and loan institution gathered data on 80 mortgage loans and found the following interest rates in force.

8.5	11.5	13.5	10.0	11.5	8.0	10.5	11.0
12.0	9.0	6.5	8.5	12.5	11.5	10.0	11.5
6.0	7.5	8.5	9.5	12.0	7.5	11.5	12.5
13.0	8.5	7.0	11.5	12.5	10.5	9.0	11.5
8.0	10.5	13.5	6.5	11.5	10.0	9.5	12.5
8.5	7.0	10.5	11.0	10.5	9.5	11.0	13.0
7.5	10.0	13.0	12.5	7.0	8.5	6.5	8.0
12.5	6.0	7.5	8.5	10.0	11.5	12.0	10.5
10.5	12.5	8.0	8.5	9.0	10.5	12.5	11.5
11.0	10.5	11.5	9.5	10.5	12.0	13.0	12.0

a. Draw a histogram of these interest rates. Use eight equal-width categories, a typical one of which is "greater than or equal to 11.0 and less than or equal to 11.5." (Notice that there will be gaps between the categories but that no observations will fall in these gaps.)

b. Find the approximate mean and standard deviation of these interest rates by using grouped data from the histogram in part (a).

35. In one study of audits, the numbers of accounting errors found per audit were tabulated. (Reference: J. Hylas and H. Ashton, "Audit Detection of Financial Statement Errors," *The Accounting Review*, Vol. 57, 1982, pp. 751–765.) The frequencies are shown below. Find the mean and standard deviation of the number of errors found per audit. Also, find the median number of errors found per audit.

Number of Errors	Number of Audits Reporting
0	57
1	28
2	20
3	10
4	9
5	25
6	1
7	0
8	2

36. A survey of 250 married women produced the following histogram for the number of trips taken to the supermarket per month. Calculate the mean and standard deviation of the number of trips to the supermarket per woman in this sample.

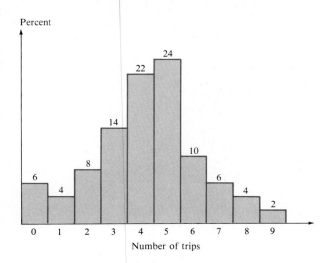

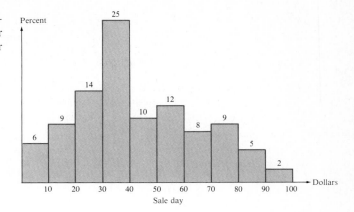

37. Consider the following yearly expenditures (in dollars) on medical care for a sample of 30 families.

834	145	246	379	85	1255	210	125
1452	96	218	853	105	365	520	140
149	65	241	652	126	420	135	416
223	142	185	478	80	1105		

a. Compute the mean and standard deviation of these data.
b. Now suppose that each observation is rounded to the nearest multiple of $50. For example, $379 and $395 would both be rounded to $400. Use the formulas for grouped data to find the mean and standard deviation of the rounded data. Compare your answers to part (a). (Round a multiple of $25 *up*. For example, round $375 up to $400.)

38. A clothing retailer kept track of purchase amounts on a day when a large end-of-month sale was in progress and on a day when no such sale was in progress. The following histograms show the results. The top histogram is based on 600 shoppers; the bottom one is based on 400 shoppers. Using the formula for grouped data, find the mean purchase amount on the sale day; on the nonsale day. Then find the corresponding standard deviations.

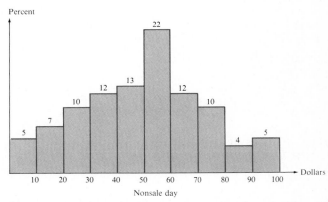

39. The following questions refer to the data from Problem 14 (p. 43).
a. Calculate the approximate mean execution time for each of the three groups of users separately. Use a midpoint of 25 for the "over-20" category.
b. Calculate the mean for the combined group of 300 users from the answers in part (a).

40. Repeat the preceding problem with "mean" replaced everywhere by "standard deviation."

41. The following questions refer to the data in Problem 27.
a. Calculate the mean, median, and standard deviation of expenditures per day.
b. Calculate the other measures of variability: the range, the interdecile range, the interquartile range, and the mean absolute deviation.

42. A company that regularly orders batches of parts recently ordered the following batch sizes (number of parts) in 10 separate orders.

55	25	175	30	100
125	75	60	120	45

a. Calculate the mean and standard deviation of these 10 batch sizes.

b. Assuming that each order costs a fixed $50 plus $3 per part ordered, use the answer from part (a) to calculate the mean and standard deviation of the costs for the 10 batches.

43. The following numbers between 0 and 1 were generated by a random number generator on a computer. They should have the following properties: (1) their mean should be close to .5, (2) their variance should be close to $\frac{1}{12}$; and (3) a histogram of them should be fairly flat. Check whether these properties hold, at least approximately. For the histogram, use five equal-width categories starting at 0 and ending at 1.

.114	.756	.159	.836	.011	.173	.868	.136	.243
.616	.854	.745	.262	.354	.432	.525	.853	.983
.105	.224	.241	.422	.376	.779	.996	.963	.896
.855	.289	.636	.094	.104	.071	.511	.024	.522
.071	.487	.542	.326	.293	.025	.150	.466	.484
.931	.400	.069	.729	.920	.143	.369	.696	.410
.940	.611	.973	.128	.214	.772			

44. The profits from the sale of a company's product over a 12-week period are shown below.

Week	Profit ($100s)	Week	Profit ($100s)
1	15.4	7	17.3
2	13.7	8	12.8
3	10.5	9	10.9
4	16.3	10	15.6
5	13.2	11	13.8
6	12.5	12	12.5

a. Find the variance and the mean absolute deviation of these observations.

b. What is the fundamental difference between the two measures above that makes them difficult to compare? (Think of units.) What should you do to the variance to make it comparable to the mean absolute deviation? Do it.

*45. Consider a distribution that is skewed to the right, as shown here. Then the positioning of the median m and the mean $\bar{X}$ are typically as shown in the figure. Why is this the case? That is, why are they both larger than the mode, and why is

m less than $\bar{X}$? Make up a set of data that is skewed to the right, and confirm that the positioning of the mode, median, and mean is as in the figure.

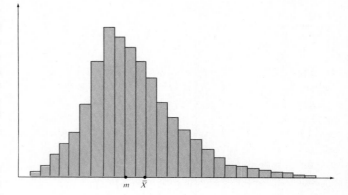

46. For the data in Problem 13 (p. 43), calculate the covariance and correlation between the number of days absent and the number of years of seniority.

47. The repair bills for 15 cars repaired on a particular day were compared to the ages of the cars (in years). The data are shown below.

Age of Car (Years)	Car Repair Bill	Age of Car (Years)	Car Repair Bill
4	$345	5	$445
2	125	6	255
4	130	1	150
6	250	3	190
1	95	7	355
8	305	4	205
3	185	5	265
2	145		

a. Draw a scattergram of these data to see whether there appears to be any relationship between repair costs and the ages of the cars.

b. Compute the covariance and the correlation between repair costs and the ages of the cars. Is the value of the correlation consistent with the scattergram in part (a)? Explain.

48. Suppose that the 50 families in Problem 27 are also asked how many days they spent on their most recent vacation. The

data for the first 20 families (the top two rows in the table) are shown below.

| 10 | 7 | 14 | 21 | 7 | 10 | 14 | 17 | 12 | 7 |
| 10 | 8 | 10 | 7 | 21 | 14 | 7 | 10 | 17 | 12 |

a. Draw a scattergram of the expenditure per day versus the number of vacation days for these 20 families. Put expenditure per day on the vertical axis.
b. Calculate the correlation between the expenditure per day and the number of vacation days for these 20 families.

Summary

In this chapter we have learned how to summarize data in several ways. These include (1) graphical methods, such as histograms, cumulative frequency graphs, scattergrams, and time series graphs; (2) tabular methods, such as frequency tables, cumulative frequency tables, and contingency tables; and (3) summary measures, such as the mean, median, standard deviation, variance, covariance, and correlation. The material in this chapter does not tell us how to make inferences about members of a population that were not included in the observed data set—that will come in later chapters—but it has taught us many descriptive measures of data sets that will be useful when we begin to learn about statistical inference.

Applications

Application 2.1   Are TV viewers able to comprehend what they are watching? This was the question addressed by Jacoby and Hoyer in a large 1979 study. (Reference: Jacob Jacoby and Wayne D. Hoyer, "Viewer Miscomprehension of Televised Communication: Selected Findings," *Journal of Marketing*, Vol. 46, 1982, pp. 12–26.) They taped 60 different 30-second TV messages, ranging from 30-second product commercials to 30-second public service announcements to 30-second segments from TV shows. These were then shown to 2700 viewers in such a way that each viewer saw two messages and each of the 60 messages was viewed by 90 viewers. Directly after each viewing, the viewer took a six-question true–false quiz on each message that he or she watched. The six statements on each quiz required only very basic understanding of the message just observed. The results are fairly surprising. Of the 32,400 quiz responses (2700 viewers $\times$ 2 messages per viewer $\times$ 6 true–false questions per message), 29.6% were incorrect. Each of the 60 quizzes (one for each message) had a certain overall percentage of wrong answers. These 60 percentages ranged from 11 to 50%, with a median of 28% and an interquartile range from 23 to 36%. Based on these figures, the researchers stated that "one might expect anywhere from one-fourth to one-third of the material information content contained in communications that are broadcast over commercial television to be miscomprehended."

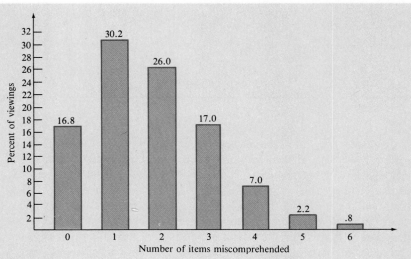

Figure 2.21

Jacoby and Hoyer also showed the distribution of the number of incorrect responses per quiz. This is based on the 5400 quizzes taken (two per viewer). The graph of this distribution is shown in Figure 2.21. For example, it shows that only 16.8% of the quizzes had zero mistakes. Notice that the mean of this distribution,

$$0(.168) + 1(.302) + \cdots + 6(.008) = 1.77$$

is the average number of wrong answers per quiz. Therefore, the average fraction of wrong answers per quiz is $1.77/6 = .295$, which agrees (aside from rounding error) with the statement above that 29.6% of all answers were incorrect.

Since each viewer was quizzed on two messages, those who did well on one of the quizzes may have missed questions on the other quiz. To highlight this, Jacoby and Hoyer also showed the distribution of the number of wrong answers over the 2700 viewers. The graph of this distribution is shown in Figure 2.22. Notice that only 3.5% of the viewers got perfect scores on both quizzes they took. Therefore, the 16.8% figure above may be misleading. Most viewers who achieved a perfect score on one quiz missed at least one question on the other. Also, notice that the mean of the distribution,

$$0(.035) + 1(.118) + \cdots + 12(.001) = 3.568$$

is the average number of mistakes per viewer. Therefore, the average fraction of mistakes per viewer, $3.568/12 = .297$, again agrees (aside

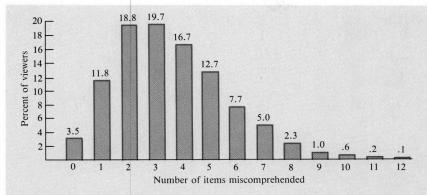

Figure 2.22

from rounding error) with the statement that 29.6% of all answers were incorrect.

Application 2.2   The problem of worker productivity in the United States has become very important, particularly in industries such as the automobile industry, where foreign imports are capturing a large share of the U.S. market. Productivity surely depends on technological improvements, but it also depends heavily on worker attitudes. Samiee performed a survey of 200 automobile workers in 1982 to measure their attitudes toward their work. (Reference: Saeed Samiee, "How Auto Workers Look at Productivity Measures: Lessons from Overseas," *Business Horizons,* Vol. 25, 1982, pp. 85–91.) The survey was a series of statements. For each statement the workers were asked to respond on the following six-point scale: 1, strongly disagree; 2, disagree; 3, mildly disagree; 4, mildly agree; 5, agree; 6, strongly agree. Selected results from the survey are shown in Table 2.14 (p. 76).

This study has two aspects in common with many survey studies. First, it uses a scale from "strongly disagree" to "strongly agree." Some studies use a five-point scale, whereas others use a seven-point scale, but the idea is always the same. Second, these studies almost always report means and often report standard deviations. The question we pose is whether it is appropriate to calculate means and standard deviations for this type of data. When we calculate means or standard deviations, we are tacitly assuming that the data are measured on an interval or ratio scale, not just an ordinal scale (refer to Section 1.2). This means that responses 1 through 6 are not only ordered in a natural way, but the difference between responses 3 and 2, say, is the same as the difference between responses 5 and 4. That is, the "gap" between the consecutive responses should remain constant. Only then are means and standard deviations appropriate.

Table 2.14

Statement	Mean	Standard Deviation
Production work is a satisfying occupation.	3.400	1.60
The job plays an important role in one's daily life.	5.418	.69
At work, the worker should really get involved with his job.	4.911	.72
Workers should not be too dedicated to their employers.	3.244	1.36
Every worker should belong to a union.	4.236	1.54
Producing a better product is not the aim of the average auto worker.	3.055	1.70
Workers could be more productive if they participated at different levels of management.	4.109	1.33

For this particular study it is hard to tell whether the difference between, say, "mildly disagree" and "disagree" is the same as the difference between "agree" and "mildly agree." This depends on how the respondents interpret these terms. However, to make any meaningful interpretations of the given means and standard deviations, we must assume that differences of this type are in fact equal.

Glossary of Terms

Frequency table   a listing of the numbers of observations (the frequencies) in the various categories

Frequency graphs   graphical methods for displaying information in frequency tables

Histogram   a frequency graph where a rectangle is drawn above each category with a height proportional to the frequency of that category

Cumulative frequency tables and graphs   displays of the number of observations to the left of and including any given category

Contingency table (or cross-tabs)   a tabulation of the joint frequencies for data with two or more attributes

Scatter diagram   a graphical means of showing data with two numerical attributes, where there is a point (X, Y) for every member of the data set

Time series graph   a graphical method for displaying data observed successively through time

Mean   the average of a set of observations

Median   the middle observation (or the average of the two middle observations) when the observations are arranged in increasing order

Mode   the most likely observation (or the category with the most observations)

Range   the difference between the largest and smallest observations

Interdecile and interquartile ranges the ranges of the remaining observations after 10% or 25% of observations at both extremes have been discarded

Mean absolute deviation (MAD) the average of the absolute deviations from the mean

Variance the average of the squared deviations from the mean

Standard deviation the square root of the variance; a measure of variability expressed in the same units as the original observations

Covariance a measure of the relationship between two attributes in a set of data

Correlation a unitless measure of the linear relationship between two attributes in a set of data, always between -1 and $+1$

Important Formulas

1. Formula for the mean

$$\overline{X} = \frac{\Sigma X_i}{n}$$

2. Formula for the mean absolute deviation

$$\text{MAD} = \frac{\Sigma |X_i - \overline{X}|}{n}$$

3. Computing formula for the variance

$$s^2 = \frac{\Sigma X_i^2 - n\overline{X}^2}{n - 1}$$

4. Computing formula for the covariance

$$s_{XY} = \frac{\Sigma X_i Y_i - n\overline{X}\,\overline{Y}}{n - 1}$$

5. Computing formula for the correlation

$$r_{XY} = \frac{\Sigma X_i Y_i - n\overline{X}\,\overline{Y}}{\sqrt{\Sigma X_i^2 - n\overline{X}^2}\ \sqrt{\Sigma Y_i^2 - n\overline{Y}^2}}$$

End-of-Chapter Problems

49. An article in a news magazine presented the following graphs. (Reference: "Medicine and Profits, Unhealthy Mixture?" *U.S. News & World Report,* Aug. 17, 1981, p. 50.) They show the trend in total U.S. medical costs and how these costs are divided into the various medical categories. The article also states that since 1940, costs of medical care have risen from 4% to nearly 10% of the nation's total output.

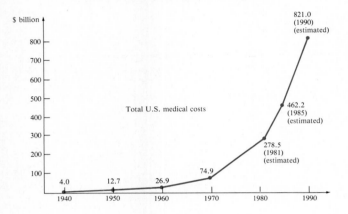

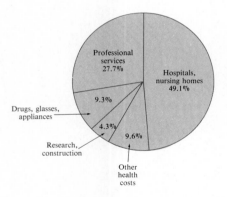

a. Assuming that the percentages in the pie chart have stayed relatively constant since 1940, draw a time series graph of the cost of hospitals and nursing homes since 1940.

b. Making the same assumption as in part (a), calculate the percentage of the nation's total output devoted to hospitals and nursing homes in 1940; in 1985.

50. The following cumulative frequency table shows a set of population figures from a group of 125 cities in the United States with fewer than 100,000 people. Calculate the (approximate) mean and standard deviation of these data by using the formulas for grouped data.

Population	Cumulative Frequency
10,000 or less	5
10,001–20,000	12
20,001–30,000	18
30,001–40,000	27
40,001–50,000	38
50,001–60,000	49
60,001–70,000	61
70,001–80,000	78
80,001–90,000	97
90,001–100,000	125

51. After an especially harsh winter in a midwestern city, there were many potholes throughout the city's streets. The department in charge of repairing streets discovered the following data from an examination of 100 blocks of streets with heavy traffic.

Number of Potholes	Number of Blocks with This Many Potholes
0	5
1	20
2	23
3	12
4	10
5	14
6	10
7 or more	6

a. Draw a histogram of these data.

b. If each pothole costs $50 to fix, find the approximate mean amount of money that must be spent per block to fix these potholes. In this part assume that each block in the "7-or-more" category has exactly 7 potholes.

52. An examination of the past 52 issues of *Time* showed an average of 84.2 pages per issue, and a corresponding standard deviation of 5.3 pages.

a. Using Rule 2.1, find an interval such that at least 75% of all 52 issues had a number of pages within this interval.

b. If the histogram of the number of pages is fairly symmetric and bell-shaped, find an interval such that approximately 49 or 50 of the issues had a number of pages within this interval.

53. In a study of the price ranges of 17 products, the following data were quoted in a consumer journal. (Reference: E. S. Maynes and T. Assum, "Informationally Imperfect Consumer Markets: Empirical Findings and Policy Implications," *The Journal of Consumer Affairs*, Vol. 16, 1982, pp. 62–87.)

Highest Price Exceeds Lowest Price by:	Number of Products	Percent of All Products
Less than 30%	4	23
30–49%	2	12
50–99%	4	23
100% or more	7	42

a. For what percentage of the products tested did the highest price exceed the lowest price by at least 50%?

b. As well as is possible from the data given, compute the mean percentage by which the highest price exceeded the lowest price. Assume that the "midpoint" of the "100% or more" category is approximately 125%.

54. For the data in Problem 7 (p. 35), consider only those businesses that failed before 10 years; that is, disregard the 20% that survived more than 10 years. Find the mean and standard deviation of the survival times of these businesses. (Treat the data as grouped data and assume that the study was based on 1000 small businesses total.)

55. Two neighborhoods were surveyed to discover the amount spent on lawn care during a typical summer season. In neighborhood 1, 50 families gave a mean response of $58 and a standard deviation of $19. In neighborhood 2, 85 families gave a mean response of $67 and a standard deviation of $27. Suppose that these two neighborhoods are pooled into one large sample.

a. Find the mean and standard deviation of the responses from the pooled sample.

b. Find an interval so that you are certain that at least 80% of the 135 families had an expenditure in this interval. (Use Rule 2.1.)

56. The following data represent frequencies on three attributes of 200 students in an MBA program: their sex, whether their undergraduate degree was in business, and their score on a standardized admission exam.

	Degree			
	Business		Nonbusiness	
	Sex			
	Male	Female	Male	Female
Test Score 401–500	9	8	13	5
501–600	23	17	19	30
601–700	8	8	14	15
701–800	5	2	11	13

a. Draw a histogram of the exam scores for each of the four sex–undergraduate degree categories.

b. Calculate the approximate mean exam score for all women; for all students with an undergraduate degree in business. Use the grouped data from the histograms in part (a).

*57. The daily high temperatures for 90 consecutive summer days in Indianapolis were recorded. These resulted in a mean high of 83.2°F and a standard deviation of 6.2°F. Also, the histogram of these temperatures was fairly symmetric and bell-shaped. Which of the following statements are necessarily true, and why?

a. At least 50 of the 90 days had a high temperature between 73.9 and 92.5°F.

b. About two or three days had a high temperature over 95.6°F.

c. About 20 of the 90 days had a high temperature lower than 77.0°F or higher than 89.4°F.

58. At a local supermarket the price of a 4-ounce jar of a popular brand of coffee was monitored over a 15-month period. The prices observed at the beginnings of these months are shown below.

Month	End-of-Month Price	Month	End-of-Month Price
1	$2.65	9	$2.76
2	2.67	10	2.83
3	2.74	11	2.85
4	2.70	12	2.89
5	2.75	13	2.89
6	2.79	14	2.93
7	2.85	15	2.87
8	2.79		

a. Graph these prices in a time series graph. What patterns, if any, do you observe?

b. Calculate the mean and median price over the 15-month period.

*59. Sometimes the standard deviation of a data set is approximated by the range divided by 4 (or possibly by 6). Can you provide any justification for this approximation? When do you believe this approximation would be very good; very bad? How does this approximation work for the data in Problem 27 (p. 69)? (Try both denominators, 4 and 6.)

*60. A radio report on the crime statistics for the previous year announced that the average criminal was a white male between 20 and 25. How would you criticize this report? What do you think it should have said?

*61. Show algebraically that the formula presented for merging the means from several populations into an overall mean is valid. That is, show that

$$\overline{X} = \frac{\sum_{i=1}^{K} n_i \overline{X}_i}{n}$$

where n is the total number of observations.

*62. Show algebraically that the formula for merging the variances from several populations into an overall variance is valid. That is, show that

$$s^2 = \frac{\sum_{i=1}^{K} [(n_i - 1)s_i^2 + n_i \overline{X}_i^2] - n\overline{X}^2}{n - 1}$$

where n is the total number of observations and $\overline{X}$ is the overall mean. (Show that the term in brackets is a sum of squared observations.)

63. The following data represent salaries from a selected subset of employees at a manufacturing company. This subset includes blue-collar workers as well as managers and executives. (The figures for workers on hourly pay have been converted to approximate yearly salaries.)

a. Draw a histogram of these salaries. Use intervals of length $5000 (starting with $15,000), plus an open-ended "over-$50,000" interval.

b. Calculate the mean and standard deviation of these salaries. (Use the facts that $\Sigma X_i = 1,492,390$ and $\Sigma (X_i - \overline{X})^2 = 2.7734683 \times 10^{10}$.)

c. Check that Rule 2.1 applies to these data for $k = 2$ and for $k = 3$.

d. Check whether Rule 2.2 applies to these data. Would you expect it to? Why or why not?

e. Find the median of these salaries. Which do you believe is a better measure of central tendency for these data, the mean or the median? Or is it possible that neither is a very good measure? Discuss.

*64. If we multiply each observation in a data set by a constant b and then add a constant a to the results, show algebraically that the mean is transformed to $a + b\overline{X}$ (where $\overline{X}$ is the mean of the original data), and the standard deviation is transformed to $|b|s_X$ (where s_X is the standard deviation of the original data).

*65. Calculate the standard deviation and the mean absolute deviation of the following 10 observations: 10, 20, 30, 40, 50, 60, 70, 80, 90, 100. Why do you suspect that the mean absolute deviation is smaller than the standard deviation? Do you think that this will usually be the case with any set of observations? Why or why not? Try to construct a set of data, symmetric about their mean, for which the mean absolute deviation is *larger* than the standard deviation.

*66. Consider a sequence of n observations $X_1, X_2, \ldots, X_n$. Then knowing the sums ΣX_i and ΣX_i^2 is equivalent to knowing $\overline{X}$ and s^2, because we can find $\overline{X}$ and s^2 from ΣX_i and ΣX_i^2, and we can find ΣX_i and ΣX_i^2 from $\overline{X}$ and s^2.

a. Show algebraically why this statement is true.

b. Illustrate this statement numerically using the data from Problem 65.

67. Retail stores obviously attract more business when they are running sales. It is not as clear what happens to business after the sales are over. One retail store measured the number of transactions on the 10 shopping days immediately following an end-of-month sale. The data are shown below.

Salaries (Dollars)

25,450	35,400	20,530	18,240	75,450	19,640	20,540
29,340	125,450	34,600	19,650	22,460	35,460	21,560
85,230	17,340	22,530	21,670	25,430	78,900	26,750
34,630	45,750	18,750	19,660	24,400	17,200	19,540
57,820	16,550	24,670	105,600	32,210	41,200	23,770
31,050	27,340	17,890	19,500	20,430	25,600	87,210

Day	Number of Transactions	Day	Number of Transactions
1	465	6	347
2	436	7	325
3	389	8	359
4	421	9	315
5	360	10	337

a. Graph these data in a time series graph. Is there any recognizable pattern?

b. Calculate the correlation between number of transactions and number of days since the sale was over.

*68. Consider any set of observations $X_1, X_2, \ldots, X_n$. For each observation X_i, let $Y_i = 2 + 3X_i$. Use algebra and properties of means and variances given in this chapter to show that the correlation between the X_i's and the Y_i's is 1. Next, let $Z_i = 2 - 3X_i$ for each i, and repeat your steps to show that the correlation between the X_i's and Z_i's is -1.

*69. Consider any set of observations $X_1, X_2, \ldots, X_n$. Let $\overline{X}$ and s be the mean and standard deviation of these observations. Now define the values $Z_1, Z_2, \ldots, Z_n$ by subtracting $\overline{X}$ from each X_i and then dividing the difference by s. That is, Z_i is given by $Z_i = (X_i - \overline{X})/s$.

a. Use the formulas for mean and variance to find the mean and variance of the Z's.

b. Illustrate that your answer from part (a) is correct by directly finding the Z's and their mean and variance for the following set of X's.

130	245	75	210	85
140	135	215	80	110

*70. Although we discussed only three measures of central tendency, there are other possible measures. For example, suppose that we calculate the mean $\overline{X}$ and standard deviation s. Then we ignore all observations that are more than 2 standard deviations away from the mean and calculate the average $\hat{X}$ of the remaining observations.

a. Why might $\hat{X}$ be a good measure of central tendency? What advantages might it have over $\overline{X}$? What disadvantages might it have compared to $\overline{X}$?

b. Calculate $\hat{X}$ for the data shown below.

55	43	56	51	57	49
46	68	53	42	68	63
67	78	43	5	53	57
8	35	10	65	57	9
53	47	57	73	38	42
52	38	59	52	46	71

71. According to the U.S. Bureau of the Census, the following table indicates the percentages of families in the various income brackets for the four regions of the country. (Reference: U.S. Bureau of the Census, *Current Population Reports*, Series

P-60, No. 137.) These are shown for 1975 and 1981. Also shown are the median incomes for these four regions. Use the formula for the mean of grouped data to approximate the mean family income for each region in each year. Compare these with one another and with the median incomes. For the "$50,000 and over" category, use a midpoint of $65,000 in your calculations. Use trial and error to see whether your answers would differ much if you used a midpoint other than $65,000 for this open-ended category.

1975 Distribution
(Percent in Constant 1981 Dollars)

Income	Northeast	North Central	South	West
Under $5,000	3.1	3.5	6.5	4.0
$5,000–$9,999	10.4	9.7	13.7	10.8
$10,000–$14,999	11.7	11.5	14.5	13.0
$15,000–$19,999	13.2	12.9	13.6	11.2
$20,000–$24,999	13.1	13.7	13.0	13.1
$25,000–$34,999	27.0	28.2	22.3	26.7
$35,000–$49,999	12.4	12.3	9.8	12.3
$50,000 or more	9.1	8.2	6.6	8.9
Median income	$24,470	$24,572	$20,677	$24,192

1981 Distribution
(Percent in Constant 1981 Dollars)

Income	Northeast	North Central	South	West
Under $5,000	5.2	5.1	7.2	4.9
$5,000–$9,999	10.1	10.5	13.6	10.5
$10,000–$14,999	12.5	13.5	14.5	13.2
$15,000–$19,999	12.4	12.3	13.1	12.2
$20,000–$24,999	13.0	13.1	12.4	11.7
$25,000–$34,999	20.8	21.8	18.8	19.8
$35,000–$49,999	16.5	15.9	12.3	16.6
$50,000 or more	9.5	7.8	8.1	11.1
Median income	$23,706	$23,118	$20,582	$23,873

72. In spite of the fitness craze in the United States, there are still large numbers of American workers who are not fit and whose living habits make them prime targets for coronary risk. Kreitner, Wood, and Friedman discuss one possible remedy for this problem, namely, company-financed coronary risk screening programs. (Reference: Robert Kreitner, Steven D. Wood, and Glenn M. Friedman, "Just How Fit

Are Your Employees?'' *Business Horizons,* Vol. 22, 1979, pp. 39–45.) In these programs employees are examined by doctors and are asked questions about their living habits, such as their smoking and exercise habits. As a result, employees receive a ''wellness'' score: the higher the score, the less they are prone to coronary disease. The authors report the distribution of wellness scores for 641 volunteer employees of a multinational electronics firm. This distribution is shown below.

Wellness Score	Frequency
10–19	1
20–29	4
30–39	25
40–49	73
50–59	122
60–69	167
70–79	164
80–89	81
90–99	4

a. Using the formulas for grouped data, calculate the approximate mean and standard deviation of the 641 wellness scores. (Use midpoints 14.5, 24.5, etc.)

b. As far as is possible, check how well the first statement in Rule 2.2 applies to this data set. What about the second statement in Rule 2.2?

73. Retailers who accept credit card payments would often rather receive cash. The reasons are (1) they have to pay a ''factoring fee'' to the company issuing the card, and (2) they do not receive the actual money from the sale for several days. Because of these drawbacks, Ingene and Levy have discussed the desirability of offering customers discounts, up to 7%, say, for cash purchases. (Reference: Charles A. Ingene and Michael Levy, ''Cash Discounts to Retail Customers: An Alternative to Credit Card Sales,'' *Journal of Marketing,* Vol. 46, 1982, pp. 92–103.) Such a discount could be beneficial for the retailer and the customer. To check how consumers would respond to such discounts, the authors performed a telephone survey of 248 respondents. A subset of 102 of these respondents were first asked whether they would use cash or a credit card for a $100 purchase. If they responded that they would use a credit card, they were then asked how large a discount for cash, in percentage terms, it would take before they would prefer a cash payment to a credit card payment. The same questions were asked of the other 146 respondents, but for a $25 purchase instead of a $100 purchase. The results are shown here. Graph the histogram of the percentage dis-

count for a $100 purchase required before a customer would prefer paying cash. Do the same for a $25 purchase. (Graph the histograms, not the cumulative distributions.) From your intuition and knowledge of consumer behavior, would you expect these two histograms to differ? Why or why not? Do they appear to differ substantially? If so, how? What does the rightmost category (for either group) represent?

Results for a $100 Purchase

Discount (Percent)	Cumulative Frequency Favoring Cash
0	12
2.5	28
3.0	51
3.5	59
4.0	61
4.5	73
5.0	84
5.5	88
6.0	90
6.5	92
7.0	94

Results for a $25 Purchase

Discount (Percent)	Cumulative Frequency Favoring Cash
0	50
2.5	73
3.0	92
3.5	96
4.0	107
4.5	118
5.0	126
5.5	130
6.0	134
6.5	138
7.0	140

74. Although all of us are aware that shoplifting is a major concern of retailers, the results of a large study conducted by the National Coalition to Prevent Shoplifting and reported by French, Crask, and Mader suggests that the problem may be larger than expected. (Reference: Warren A. French, Melvin R. Crask, and Fred H. Mader, ''Retailer's Assessment of the Shoplifting Problem,'' *Journal of Retailing,* Vol. 60, 1984, pp. 108–115.) In this study 670 retailers from 21 states responded to a questionnaire. The main objectives of the questionnaire were to detect the magnitude of the shoplifting prob-

lem, to learn how much was being done to deter shoplifting, and to see how the answers to these questions were related to the type of store involved. Selected results are shown below.

Type	Number	Retailers Saying They Have a Problem with Shoplifting (Percent)	Average Percent Loss
Food	115	71	6.1
Specialty	146	48	5.3
Department	98	91	7.4
Discount	49	83	8.5
Variety	34	93	8.2
Apparel	129	67	6.7
Drug	65	86	5.3
Hardware	34	93	5.8

a. Find the percentage of the 670 retailers sampled who say they have a problem with shoplifting.
b. Find the average percentage loss, taken over all 670 retailers sampled.

Computer Problems

(These problems are to be used in conjunction with the computer software package.)

1. a. Referring to the data on public school teachers in Table I of Appendix D, use the SUMMARY program to arrange the data on total number of elementary school teachers from lowest to highest. Do the same for the data on average salaries. What is the correlation (across the states) between the total number of elementary school teachers and the average salary per elementary school teacher?
   b. Repeat part (a) for secondary school teachers.
   c. Repeat part (a) for all school teachers.

2. Use program SUMMARY to find summary statistics for the projected percentage increases of personal income in Table V of Appendix D. Which five states are projected to have the smallest percentage increases? Which five are projected to have the largest percentage increases? State in words what the median for these data represents.

3. Referring to the data on grade point averages and test scores in Table II of Appendix D, choose any 30 students from the 100 listed. Then use the SUMMARY program to find summary measures (mean, median, variance, standard deviation, and mean absolute deviation) for the undergraduate and graduate GPA's of these students, and find the covariance and correlation between their undergraduate and graduate GPA's. Then repeat, substituting verbal and quantitative test scores for undergraduate and graduate GPA's.

4. Referring to the housing data in Table III of Appendix D, use the SUMMARY program to find the mean and standard deviation of appraised values and of selling prices for the first 40 homes listed. What is the correlation between appraised value and selling price for these homes?

References

HUFF, D. *How to Lie with Statistics*. New York: Norton, 1954.
KOOPMANS, L. H. *An Introduction to Contemporary Statistics*. Boston: Duxbury Press, 1981 (available from PWS Publishers, Boston).
TUKEY, J. W. *Exploratory Data Analysis*. Reading, Mass.: Addison-Wesley, 1977.

CHAPTER 3

Introduction to Probability

Objectives

1. To understand how probability measures uncertainty.
2. To understand the difference between objective and subjective probabilities.
3. To learn some of the basic terms used in probability, including sample space, event, mutually exclusive, complement, union, and intersection.
4. To learn the basic rules of probability, including the addition rule for unions of mutually exclusive events and the multiplication rule for intersections.
5. To learn how to work with conditional probabilities and how to recognize whether independence exists.
6. To learn how to solve equally likely (counting) problems that arise in sampling experiments.

Contents

One popular advertising strategy used by many companies is to have a contest where customers can win various prizes. For example, fast-foods companies frequently give their customers contest cards. By rubbing out the appropriate space or spaces, the customers can win hamburgers, soft drinks, or other food items, as well as possible cash prizes. Some of these contests, such as the one we discuss later in this chapter, allow the customers to rub out one or more of several possible spaces on the card. In this case every card is a potential winner of some prize, but the prize is actually won only if the customer rubs out the lucky spaces. This produces uncertainty not only for the customer, but also for the company. For instance, if they print 5000 cards with a potential prize of $100, how many of these will produce actual winners?

Clearly, the answer to this question cannot be known with certainty until the contest is over. It is conceivable that none of the 5000 cards will be winners, and it is also conceivable that all 5000 will be winners. However, neither of these outcomes is at all likely. Although the company cannot predict exactly how many winners there will be, it can use the results of probability theory to calculate how likely any particular outcome will be. For example, based on the rules of the contest and the form of the cards, it may be able to state that the chances of more than 200 winners are 1 out of 3, and the chances of more than 400 winners are 1 out of 10. Statements such as these obviously give the company useful information on how many prizes will be won. In fact, the ability to make these types of probability statements is what allows the company to design the contest in the first place.

3.1

Introduction

One aspect common to almost all statistical applications is the presence of uncertainty. This might be related to a characteristic of a given population, such as the percentage of blue-collar workers who have collected unemployment benefits during the past year, or it might be related to some future development, such as whether a new product will eventually be a success. If we refer to the examples in Chapter 1, we see how uncertainty plays a central role in each of them. The consumer agency in Example 1.2 does not know how the price of coffee varies from store to store in the state of New York, the cosmetics company in Example 1.4 does not know which marketing strategy will be most successful in promoting a new type of lipstick, the toy company in Example 1.6 does not know exactly what the demand for its product will be over the next 12 months, and so on. Unless the sole purpose of a statistical analysis is to describe a set of existing data (the subject of Chapter 2), the analyst will almost surely be forced to deal with uncertainty.

Probability theory is the branch of mathematics that teaches us how to measure uncertainty. Because statistical applications almost always involve uncertainty, it is absolutely essential that we learn the basic elements of probability before we proceed to the study of statistics. The subject of probability originated several centuries ago in order to study games of chance, and this is still the context many people think of when they think of probability. Interesting as games of chance are, however, we will instead shift our attention in this book to business applications, where probability applies equally well. In this chapter we learn the meaning of probability and some of the basic mathematical rules of probability. In later chapters we will apply these rules to statistical problems.

3.2

Quantifying Uncertainty: Objective and Subjective Probabilities

We say that a situation involves uncertainty if several outcomes are possible and we do not know which one will occur. For any particular outcome, we measure its likelihood by means of a numerical probability between 0 and 1. Relatively unlikely outcomes have probabilities near 0, whereas relatively likely outcomes have probabilities near 1.

> A probability is a number between 0 and 1 that measures the likelihood of any possible outcome. If p denotes the probability of the outcome, then $0 \leq p \leq 1$.

In this section we look at several examples to see how probabilities are measured. Before doing this, however, we first look at several alternative ways of expressing probabilities numerically. Most of us are accustomed to using ''odds,'' ''chances,'' or ''percentages'' to express likelihoods of possible outcomes. All of these alternatives provide equivalent information and can easily be converted to probabilities between 0 and 1.

For example, suppose the ''odds'' are 3 to 1 that a union will go on strike. This implies that a strike is three times as likely as no strike, which means

Table 3.1

Odds are a to b	$\longrightarrow$ Probability is	$\dfrac{a}{a+b}$
Chances are c out of d	$\longrightarrow$ Probability is	$\dfrac{c}{d}$
Percentage is $p\%$	$\longrightarrow$ Probability is	$\dfrac{p}{100}$

that the ''chances'' of a strike are 3 out of 4. Because 3 out of 4, expressed as a percentage, is 75%, we can also state that the chance of a strike occurring is 75%. Although all of these mean the same thing, in statistics we say that the probability of a strike is .75.

The information in Table 3.1 shows that it is easy to convert odds, chances, and percentages into probabilities.

The important issue is not how we express probabilities numerically, because all of the alternative ways provide the same information. Rather, the important issue is how to assess the probabilities of uncertain outcomes in the first place. This depends on the type of situation, as the following examples indicate.

EXAMPLE 3.1

Consider a manufacturing process that produces gears for automobiles. Each gear is then examined and classified defective or nondefective. If we choose a gear at random, we would like to know the probability p that it is defective. Assuming that the process generating gears does not change over time, it is reasonable to define p as the long-run proportion of gears that are defective. To find the value of p, we examine N gears (for some large number N), count the number N_D of them that are defective, and estimate p by the proportion N_D/N. Notice that this is only an estimate of p because another batch of N gears might yield another value of N_D and hence a different proportion N_D/N.

The important aspect of this example is that the ''experiment'' of choosing a gear, examining it, and classifying it as defective or nondefective can be repeated under nearly identical conditions as many times as we like. Therefore, it makes sense to define p as the long-run proportion of gears that are defective.

In general, if a situation can be repeated indefinitely under nearly identical conditions, the probability p that a given outcome E occurs can be estimated as in the gear example (Example 3.1). We observe N repetitions, count the number N_E of repetitions in which E occurs, and estimate p by N_E/N. This ratio is called the *relative frequency* of E, and this method is called the relative frequency approach for assessing probabilities.

> In the relative frequency approach, we estimate the probability p of any outcome E by the relative frequency N_E/N. Here N is the number of repetitions observed, and N_E is the number of these in which E occurs.

Any probability that can be estimated by a relative frequency approach is called an *objective probability*. The term "objective" means that any two people should agree on the value of p. Conceptually, they could both repeat the same experiment many times and, at least in the long run, observe practically the same relative frequencies.

> An objective probability is one that can be estimated by a relative frequency approach.

Not all situations involving uncertainty can be repeated indefinitely under identical conditions. In these cases we cannot resort to a relative frequency approach. Consider the following example.

EXAMPLE 3.2

Tasty Burger, a fast-foods chain, is trying to decide whether to build a new store in a particular location. This location appears to be attractive because there are currently no competitors in the immediate area. However, there is some chance that a prime competitor will also build a new store in this area in the near future. The management of Tasty Burger wants to know the probability of this occurring. Based on its information about the competitor and the desirability of the area, management assesses this probability to be .4.

The probability in this example is called a *subjective probability*. It cannot be found by a relative frequency approach because the problem involves a one-time situation: the competitor will either build a new store in this particular area or it will not. Therefore, Tasty Burger management must use whatever information it has, including the behavior of the competitor in past situations, plus its own subjective beliefs to assess the probability of any particular outcome.

> A subjective probability is one that cannot be found from a relative frequency approach, but instead uses an individual's subjective beliefs in the probability assessment.

In Example 3.2 it is possible, even likely, that another group with different information and/or beliefs than Tasty Burger management might assess a probability other than .4. This is a distinctive feature of subjective probabilities, namely, that different people or groups often make different subjective probability assessments. Furthermore, it is very difficult to say which assessment is better. In the Tasty Burger example, the competitor will make one of two possible decisions, build or not build, and neither will confirm that the .4 was a good or bad probability assessment.

This is an unsettling state of affairs. It appears to be saying that when we assess a subjective probability, we are obtaining a number that cannot be checked for accuracy. Does this mean that anyone's subjective probabilities are as good as anyone else's? Fortunately, the answer is no. By observing people's probability assessments, we *can* distinguish good probability assessors from poor ones, at least in the long run. Furthermore, an expert can help people make subjective probability assessments that are at least internally consistent with their own beliefs. This is particularly important because subjective probability assessments are a crucial ingredient in decision making under uncertainty, as we will see in Chapter 15. However, systematic methods for obtaining "good" subjective probabilities are outside the scope of this book.

The dividing line between objective and subjective probabilities is often not as clearcut as we have indicated above. There are many times when a one-time situation is in some respects unique but in other respects has precedents in the past. In this case we may use historical data via a relative frequency approach to obtain some idea of probabilities of future outcomes.

For example, suppose that Exxon is drilling for oil in a new location, and it wants to know the probability of success. On the one hand, there are probably similarities between this location and other locations that have already been explored, so that historical data are available for assessing the probability of success. On the other hand, there are probably unique aspects of this location that require Exxon to make subjective probability assessments.

We point out that most of the probabilities in this book, with the exception of Chapter 15, are objective probabilities. The reason is that they usually occur in the context of sampling experiments, where a relative frequency approach is physically possible. Fortunately, however, the mathematical rules of probability are the same regardless of whether we are dealing with objective or subjective probabilities. It is only our assessment and interpretation of these probabilities that differ.

In any applied probability problem, our first task is to define the set of all possible outcomes. This set is called the *sample space* and will be denoted by S. It is important that the "outcomes" in the sample space be defined in such a way that one and only one of them can occur in a given situation.

> The sample space S is the set of all possible outcomes, where the outcomes are defined so that exactly one of them will occur in any given situation.

The following examples illustrate several typical sample spaces.

1. Suppose that we observe two gears coming off a production line. If each gear can be classified as a defective (D) or a nondefective (N), the sample space is the set of pairs $\{(D, D), (D, N), (N, D), (N, N)\}$. The first member of each pair shows whether the first gear is defective or nondefective, and the second member does the same for the second gear.
2. Suppose that an appliance store is interested in the number of color television sets it will sell on each of the next two days. Then the sample space S is the set of all pairs (x_1, x_2) of nonnegative integers. Here x_1 is the number of sales on day 1 and x_2 is the number of sales on day 2.
3. Suppose that a company's personnel office gives an aptitude test to four prospective employees. The test consists of 100 multiple-choice questions. If the company is interested in the scores of the four people, the sample space S can be represented by the set of all sequences (x_1, x_2, x_3, x_4), where each x_i is an integer between 0 and 100. Here x_i represents the score for the ith prospective employee.
4. Suppose that an oil company drills for oil in a new location. If the company is interested in the amount of oil found, S is the set of all nonnegative numbers x. Any particular number x in S represents a possible amount of oil found at this location.

The description of a sample space S is not necessarily unique to a situation but may depend on the purposes of the investigation. In the second example above, the appliance store will favor the given sample space description if it is interested in the separate sales for each day. But if it is interested only in the total number of sales on both days combined, the appropriate sample space is the set of all nonnegative integers x, where $x = x_1 + x_2$. For example, the outcomes (0, 2), (1, 1), and (2, 0) in the previous sample space description all correspond to the combined outcome $x = 2$ in the new sample space description.

3.4

Events

In most applications we are interested not only in the individual outcomes in the sample space, but also in collections of these outcomes. In probability terminology, these collections of outcomes are called *events*. For example, if we select 50 families for a study on income levels, several events of interest are (1) the event that the average of the 50 incomes is less than $20,000, (2) the event that at least one of the families makes more than $50,000, and (3) the event that the difference between the largest and smallest incomes is at least $25,000. If an oil company drills in a location with an unknown amount of oil, events of interest include (1) the event that the location has no oil, (2) the event that the location has at least 3000 barrels of oil, and (3) the event that the location has no more than 8000 barrels of oil.

> An event is any subset of the sample space. Equivalently, an event is any collection of individual outcomes.

Usually, we denote typical events by capital letters such as E, F, and G, or by capital letters with subscripts, such as E_1, E_2, and E_3. We can describe any event E by listing the outcomes that comprise E. Conceptually, this can be done as follows. For each possible outcome in the sample space, we ask whether E occurs if that outcome occurs. If the answer is yes, we include that outcome in E, and we say that it is *favorable to E*. If the answer is no, we do not include that outcome in E, and we say that it is *unfavorable to E*. For example, if E is the event that an appliance store sells at least 50 television sets in the coming month, any sales figure of 50 or above is favorable to E, and any sales figure below 50 is unfavorable to E.

We may form new events from given events in the following three ways.

1. If E is any event, the *complement* of E, denoted by $\overline{E}$, is the set of outcomes unfavorable to E. (Some books prefer the notation E^c to $\overline{E}$.) Therefore, $\overline{E}$ occurs if and only if E does not occur.

2. If E and F are any events, the *union* of E and F, denoted by (E or F), is the event that at least one of these two events occurs. The union includes the set of all outcomes favorable to E but not F, the set favorable to F but not E, and the set favorable to both E and F.

3. If E and F are any events, the *intersection* of E and F, denoted by (E and F), is the event that E and F both occur. This is the set of outcomes favorable to both E and F. (Most books use the notation $E \cup F$ for unions and $E \cap F$ for intersections. However, this notation is usually dispensed with soon after the definitions are given, so we prefer not to use it at all.)

More generally, the union of the n events $E_1, E_2, \ldots, E_n$ is the event that at least one of these n events occurs; that is, it is the set of outcomes favorable to at least one of the E's. This event is denoted by (E_1 or E_2 or $\ldots$ or E_n). Similarly, the intersection of the n events $E_1, E_2, \ldots, E_n$ is the event that all n of the E's occur; that is, it is the set of outcomes favorable to all the E's. It is denoted by (E_1 and E_2 and $\ldots$ and E_n). Remember that union means *at least one*, whereas intersection means *all*.

> The union of events occurs if at least one of the events occurs. The intersection of events occurs only if all the events occur.

It is often helpful to use diagrams to show relationships between events. These diagrams are called *Venn diagrams*. The Venn diagrams in Figure 3.1 (p. 94) illustrate complements, unions, and intersections. In each case the large rectangle represents the sample space S, the set of all outcomes.

If $E_1, E_2, \ldots, E_n$ are any n events, we say that these are *mutually exclusive* if they have no outcomes in common. This means that if any one of the E's occurs, none of the others can occur.

> $E_1, E_2, \ldots, E_n$ are mutually exclusive if they have no outcomes in common.

In a Venn diagram, mutually exclusive sets have no overlap. Figure 3.2 (p. 94) illustrates several possibilities.

EXAMPLE 3.3

Consider a person who invests in two stocks, A and B. Let E be the event that his yearly return on investment (ROI) from stock A is at least 10%, and let F be the similar event for stock B. Interpret the union and intersection of E and F. Are E and F mutually exclusive?

SOLUTION

The union (*E* or *F*) occurs if at least one of the stocks has a yearly ROI of at least 10%. This includes the possibility that the yearly ROI from one of the stocks is less than 10%. The intersection (*E* and *F*) occurs if the yearly ROI from both stocks is at least 10%. Since this intersection is certainly possible, *E* and *F* are not mutually exclusive.

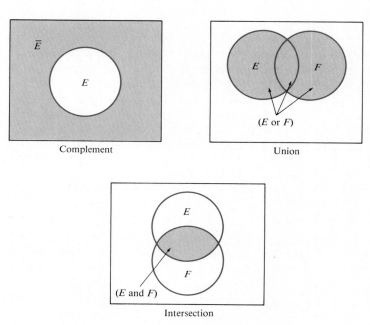

Figure 3.1
Venn Diagrams

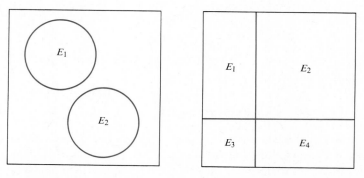

Figure 3.2
Examples of Mutually Exclusive Events

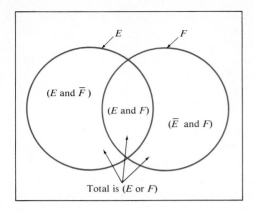

Figure 3.3

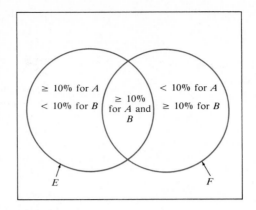

Figure 3.4

Suppose that two events are not mutually exclusive. Then it is always possible to write their union as a union of mutually exclusive events. This is often helpful when computing probabilities. For example, suppose that E and F are not mutually exclusive. From the Venn diagram in Figure 3.3, we see that $(E \text{ or } F)$ consists of three nonoverlapping parts: $(\overline{E} \text{ and } F)$, $(E \text{ and } \overline{F})$, and $(E \text{ and } F)$. These three events are the event where F occurs and E does not, the event where E occurs and F does not, and the event where E and F both occur.

To illustrate this, we refer to Example 3.3, with E and F defined as in that example. Then the union $(E \text{ or } F)$ can occur in one of three mutually exclusive ways: (1) the ROI from stock A is at least 10% and the ROI from stock B is less than 10%, (2) the ROI from stock B is at least 10% and the ROI from stock A is less than 10%, or (3) the ROI from each stock is at least 10%. These three events make up the union $(E \text{ or } F)$, as shown in Figure 3.4.

Problems for Sections 3.2, 3.3, 3.4

1. In a certain suburb 30% of the households subscribe to a particular news magazine. If a household is chosen at random from this suburb, what are the odds that this household does not subscribe to the magazine?

2. Which of the following two competitions would you rather enter (given that the prizes are the same for both): one where your chance of winning is ⅔ as large as your chance of losing, or one where the odds are 7 to 2 that you will lose? Answer by expressing the chance of winning each competition as a probability between 0 and 1.

3. Several competing companies are hoping to have the leading market share in the coming year. An outside expert assesses that the odds of company A not being the leader are 6 to 1. The odds against companies B and C being the leader are similarly assessed to be 12 to 5 and 8 to 3, respectively. Find the probability that company A will be the leader; that company B will be the leader; that company C will be the leader; that some other company will be the leader.

* 4. Professional oddsmakers often publish the odds that some type of sports event will occur. Suppose that there are four teams left in the competition for the Super Bowl, and an oddsmaker publishes the odds (p. 96) of the four teams not winning. Why are the oddsmaker's odds necessarily wrong? (Remember, there is only one winner.)

Team	Odds Against This Team Winning
Raiders	2 to 1
Redskins	5 to 2
Steelers	3 to 1
Cowboys	9 to 2

5. Below is a frequency distribution for weekly demands for classical records at a record store in the Motown Mall. Based on these historical frequencies, what is the probability that in a typical week, there will be a demand for (a) over 20 classical records; (b) between 11 and 50 classical records; (c) no more than 30 classical records?

Number of Records Sold	Frequency (Number of Weeks)
0–10	1
11–20	7
21–30	10
31–40	17
41–50	5
51 or more	4

6. A gambler makes five consecutive bets. On each bet he either wins or loses.
   a. If his betting strategy is such that his net winnings are determined solely by the *number* of bets he wins, what is the appropriate sample space of outcomes?
   b. Answer the question in part (a) if his net winnings are determined not just by the number of bets he wins but also by the *sequence* in which the wins and losses occur.

7. A number of calculator batteries are being tested. The experiment consists of using 100 batteries (simultaneously) for 30 consecutive hours. When a battery fails, the current time is recorded. After 30 hours, the number of batteries still functioning is also recorded. Describe the possible outcomes in the sample space.

8. A financial analyst "charts" the price movement of a given stock over a period of 30 consecutive trading days. He is interested in the number of days where the price is up by at least 1 point over the previous day, the number of days where it is down by at least 1 point from the previous day, and the number of days where its change is no more than 1 point from the previous day. Describe the possible outcomes in the sample space. Assume the analyst is concerned only with the *numbers* in the possible price movement categories.

9. The World Series in baseball is a sequence of games between the two best teams, say, the Yankees and the Cardinals. The series lasts until one of the teams wins 4 games. Since this means the series will never go past 7 games, it is usually called a "best of 7" series.
   a. Describe the possible outcomes of the sample space if all we want to know is how long the series lasts and which team wins.
   b. Describe the possible outcomes in the sample space if, in addition to the information requested in part (a), we also want to know the game-by-game sequence of winners.

10. Each employee at a production facility is scheduled to take a manual dexterity test, where a total of 10 tasks must be attempted. The company wants to know which of the tasks are done successfully. Describe the possible outcomes in the sample space. How many possible outcomes are there?

11. An agency that does TV surveys plans to run a telephone survey. The plan is to call 250 randomly chosen households and ask which, if any, of the three main networks' 6:00 news shows they usually watch. The responses could be any of the three networks or that they don't watch any of these news shows. It is also possible that the agency is not able to contact a given household by phone (in which case it will settle for information from less than 250 households). Describe the possible outcomes in the sample space for the survey as a whole.

12. From a group of three people named Smith, Jones, and Brown, we need to select a committee of two.
   a. If the only information we need is the identity of the two people selected, list the possible outcomes in the sample space.
   b. If one of the people selected is designated as the superior and the other is designated as the subordinate, list the possible outcomes in the sample space. Why is this different from part (a)?

13. A hand calculator manufacturer produces and sells two kinds of calculators. The first type costs $5 to produce and sells for $8. The second type costs $10 to produce and sells for $20. Let E be the event that the manufacturer makes at least $35,000 profit on the first type of calculator, and let F be the event that the manufacturer makes at least $20,000 profit on the second type of calculator.
   a. Describe the events E and F in terms of the *numbers* of calculators sold.
   b. What can be said about total profits if the union (E or F) occurs?

c. What can be said about total profits if the intersection (E and F) occurs?

d. Are $\overline{E}$ and $\overline{F}$ mutually exclusive? If so, why? If not, what are their common outcomes?

14. A questionnaire is sent to 30 companies. The questionnaire asks each company what percentage of its employees are women and what percentage are blacks. Let E_i be the event that at least 10% of company i's employees are women, and let F_i be the event that at least 5% of its employees are blacks. Describe the following events in words: (a) $\overline{E}_i$; (b) the complement of (E_i and F_i); (c) (E_1 and E_2 and . . . and E_{30}); (d) (F_1 or F_2 or . . . or F_{30})

*15. Continuing Problem 14, describe the following events in words.
  a. [(E_1 or F_1) and (E_2 or F_2) and . . . and (E_{30} or F_{30})]
  b. [(E_1 and F_1) or (E_2 and F_2) or . . . or (E_{30} and F_{30})]

16. Speedwear, a company that produces and markets running gear, plans to survey a randomly selected group of joggers. The company plans to ask the joggers how much they paid for their most recently purchased pair of running shoes. Let E be the event that no one paid more than $50 for a pair of shoes, let F be the event that the average price paid by the group was at least $28, and let G be the event that everyone paid somewhere between $20 and $45.
  a. Describe the three intersections (E and F), (E and G), and ($\overline{E}$ and G) in words.
  b. Describe the intersection (E and F and G) in words.
  c. Write the union (E or G) as the union of three mutually exclusive events and describe in words what each of these events represents. (Ignore event F for this part of the problem.)

*17. Continuing the preceding problem, does the union (E or F or G) represent the entire sample space? If so, why? If not, which outcomes in the sample space are not included in this union?

*18. Consider the following events that are related to a company's sales. E is the event that sales are at least $20,000, F is the event that sales are no more than $60,000, and G is the event that sales are between $15,000 and $30,000. Describe in words (as simply as possible) each of the following events: (a) (E and F and G); (b) (E or F or G); (c) the intersection of G and the complement of (E and F).

3.5

Basic Rules of Probability

Now that we know about sample spaces and events, we are ready to return to the role of probability. To each possible event E, we assign a probability $P(E)$ that reflects the likelihood of E. Of course, we want the probabilities to be consistent with what we observe in the real world, but we must also make sure that probabilities satisfy several mathematical rules. We discuss the most basic of these rules in this section.

Actually, there are three rules that imply all the others. If probabilities obey these three rules, they automatically obey all other rules of probability. These three basic rules are as follows.

If S is the set of all outcomes (the sample space), $P(S) = 1$.	*RULE 3.1*

$P(E)$ must satisfy $0 \leq P(E) \leq 1$ for any event E.	*RULE 3.2*

RULE 3.3

> If E and F are any mutually exclusive events,
>
> $$P(E \text{ or } F) = P(E) + P(F)$$

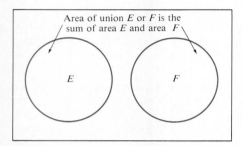

Figure 3.5
Venn Diagram of Rule 3.3

These rules are all intuitive. Rules 3.1 and 3.2 simply say that the probability of *some* outcome occurring is 1, and that all probabilities are between 0 and 1. Rule 3.3 is the rule that puts some real substance into probability theory. We may interpret it in terms of Venn diagrams as follows. In any Venn diagram it is useful to think of the probability of an event as the *area* of the associated set in the diagram, given that the area of the sample space S (the rectangle) is 1. Then Rule 3.3 says that the area of the union of two nonoverlapping sets is the sum of the two separate areas. Geometrically, this is obvious, as shown in Figure 3.5.

Rule 3.3 can also be interpreted from a relative frequency point of view. Suppose that the same experiment is repeated N times under identical conditions, with events E and F occurring N_E and N_F times, respectively. Then we know that $P(E)$ and $P(F)$ can be approximated by N_E/N and N_F/N. Now let $N_{(E \text{ or } F)}$ be the number of times the union (E or F) occurs. If E and F are mutually exclusive, the outcomes where E occurs are separate from those where F occurs, so that

$$N_{(E \text{ or } F)} = N_E + N_F$$

Therefore, the relative frequency approach gives us Rule 3.3:

$$P(E \text{ or } F) = \frac{N_{(E \text{ or } F)}}{N} = \frac{N_E + N_F}{N} = \frac{N_E}{N} + \frac{N_F}{N} = P(E) + P(F)$$

There are a number of other rules of probability that are implied by these three basic rules. Below we list several of the most important of these.

RULE 3.4

> If we denote the empty set (the set with no outcomes) by $\emptyset$, then $P(\emptyset) = 0$.

RULE 3.5

> For any event E, $P(\overline{E}) = 1 - P(E)$.

Rule 3.5 says that if we know the probability of an event E, we automatically know the probability of its complement $\overline{E}$. We simply subtract $P(E)$ from 1. Although this result is fairly obvious, it can be very useful. It implies that before we begin any probability calculation, we should always check whether the probability of the complement is easier to calculate than the probability of the event itself.

EXAMPLE 3.4

A magazine publishing company is about to undertake a campaign designed to gain new subscriptions. Company experts believe that there is 1 chance out of 4 that the increased number of subscriptions will be less than 1500, and there is 1 chance out of 3 that it will be between 1500 and 3000. What is the probability that the increased number of subscriptions will be less than 1500 *or* more than 3000?

SOLUTION

Define E, F, and G as follows:

E is the event that the increase is less than 1500
F is the event that the increase is between 1500 and 3000
G is the event that the increase is greater than 3000

We are given that $P(E) = \frac{1}{4}$ and $P(F) = \frac{1}{3}$ and we need $P(E \text{ or } G)$. Since E and G are mutually exclusive, Rule 3.3 states that $P(E \text{ or } G) = P(E) + P(G)$. To obtain $P(G)$, notice that G occurs when $(E \text{ or } F)$ does not occur, so that G is the complement of $(E \text{ or } F)$. By Rule 3.5,

$$P(G) = 1 - P(E \text{ or } F)$$

Then by Rule 3.3 and the fact that E and F are mutually exclusive, we have

$$P(G) = 1 - P(E \text{ or } F) = 1 - [P(E) + P(F)] = 1 - \left(\frac{1}{4} + \frac{1}{3}\right) = \frac{5}{12}$$

So the desired probability is

$$P(E \text{ or } G) = P(E) + P(G) = \frac{1}{4} + \frac{5}{12} = \frac{2}{3}$$

[An alternative solution method is to notice that $(E \text{ or } G)$ occurs only if F does not occur, so that $(E \text{ or } G)$ is the complement of F. This implies that

$$P(E \text{ or } G) = 1 - P(F) = 1 - \frac{1}{3} = \frac{2}{3}$$

the same answer as before.]

RULE 3.6

> For any events E and F (not necessarily mutually exclusive),
>
> $$P(E \text{ or } F) = P(E) + P(F) - P(E \text{ and } F)$$

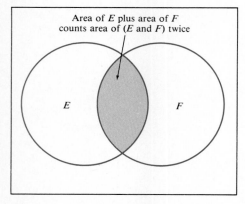

Area of E plus area of F
counts area of (E and F) twice

Figure 3.6
Venn Diagram for Rule 3.6

This rule is a generalization of Rule 3.3 to the case where E and F are not necessarily mutually exclusive. If we interpret probabilities as areas in Venn diagrams, then Rule 3.6 is easy to understand. If E and F overlap and we want the area of the union (E or F), then by summing the areas of E and F, we count the overlap (E and F) twice. Since it should count only once, we must subtract the area of the intersection (see Figure 3.6).

EXAMPLE 3.5

From historical records, the manager of the Prescription Drug Store knows that 50% of the customers entering the store buy prescription drugs, 65% buy over-the-counter drugs, and 28% buy both types of drugs. What is the probability that a randomly selected customer will buy at least one of these two types of drugs?

SOLUTION

Let E be the event that this customer buys prescription drugs. Define F similarly for over-the-counter drugs. We are given that $P(E) = .5$, $P(F) = .65$, and $P(E \text{ and } F) = .28$, and we need $P(E \text{ or } F)$. From Rule 3.6, the probability of the union is

$$P(E \text{ or } F) = P(E) + P(F) - P(E \text{ and } F) = .5 + .65 - .28 = .87$$

Notice that E and F are *not* mutually exclusive events, so that it would be wrong to use Rule 3.3 for this problem.

3.6

The Addition Rule

In this section we learn an extremely important rule that often allows us to calculate probabilities of complicated events from known probabilities of simpler events. It is called the *addition rule*.

> (Addition rule) For any mutually exclusive events $E_1, E_2, \ldots, E_n,$
>
> $$P(E_1 \text{ or } E_2 \text{ or } \ldots \text{ or } E_n) = P(E_1) + P(E_2) + \cdots + P(E_n)$$

RULE 3.7

The addition rule is another generalization of Rule 3.3. Now we allow more than two mutually exclusive events. In words, the addition rule states that if we can divide any event E into a union of mutually exclusive events $E_1, E_2, \ldots, E_n$, we can compute the probability of E as the sum of the probabilities of the individual events. Therefore, the trick is to carve E into nonoverlapping pieces with known probabilities. We illustrate this fundamental idea with several examples.

EXAMPLE 3.6

Suppose that 18% of the people in a given population are smokers, 57% are males, and 12% are male smokers. If we choose a person at random from this population, what is the probability that this person is a female smoker? What is the probability that this person is a female nonsmoker?

SOLUTION

First, let M, $\overline{M}$, S, and $\overline{S}$ denote that the chosen person is male, is female, is a smoker, and is a nonsmoker, respectively. Then the Venn diagrams shown in Table 3.2 are helpful for the solution of the problem.

Table 3.2

	S	$\overline{S}$			S	$\overline{S}$	
M	.12		.57	M	.12	.45	.57
$\overline{M}$				$\overline{M}$	.06	.37	.43
	.18				.18	.82	
	(a) Given data				(b) Completed table		

Table 3.2a contains the information given in the statement of the problem (with percentages replaced by probabilities). Notice that each person in the population is in exactly one of the four nonoverlapping categories: male smoker (M and S), female smoker ($\overline{M}$ and S), male nonsmoker (M and $\overline{S}$),

or female nonsmoker ($\overline{M}$ and $\overline{S}$). The proportion of the population in one of these categories, (M and S), is given as .12; this number appears in the upper left-hand cell.

The other given information concerns pairs of categories. For example, we know that .57 of the population are males. Because all males are either smokers (M and S) or nonsmokers (M and $\overline{S}$), the proportion of male smokers plus the proportion of male nonsmokers must be .57. This proportion is shown in the margin across from males. It implies that the proportion of male nonsmokers must be .57 − .12 = .45. Similarly, the proportion of smokers, .18, is shown in the margin below smokers. It implies that the proportion of female smokers is .18 − .12 = .06. Finally, since the four numbers inside the cells must sum to 1, the proportion of female nonsmokers must be .37. These results are shown in the diagram in Table 3.2b. We can now answer the original questions. The probability that a randomly chosen person is a female smoker is .06, and the probability that this person is a female nonsmoker is .37.

EXAMPLE 3.7

Suppose that the following information is found from a questionnaire of 200 middle-level managers. There are 66 managers who are labeled A's and 108 managers who are labeled B's. The A's are those who have been with their present company for at least five years, while the B's are those who plan to stay with their present companies for at least five more years. The questionnaire also shows that the number of A's who are not B's is twice as large as the number of A's who are also B's. If one of these managers is selected at random, what is the probability that he or she is either an A or B or both?

SOLUTION

We may solve this problem by first filling in a cross-classification table (as in Chapter 2) that shows the joint and marginal frequencies of the various categories. The data in Table 3.3a show what we know from the statement of the problem. The joint frequencies N_1, N_2, N_3, and N_4 are unknown except that they add up to the totals in the margins. For example, $N_1 + N_3 = 108$. We are also given that N_1 and N_2 satisfy $N_2 = 2N_1$. This is because the N_1 people are the A's who are also B's, and the N_2 people are the A's who are not B's. We substitute $2N_1$ for N_2 in the equation $N_1 + N_2 = 66$ to obtain

$$N_1 + N_2 = N_1 + 2N_1 = 3N_1 = 66$$

or $N_1 = 22$. The rest of the joint frequencies now follow easily. They are $N_2 = 44$, $N_3 = 86$, and $N_4 = 48$. These values are shown in Table 3.3b.

Table 3.3

	B	$\overline{B}$	
A	N_1	N_2	66
$\overline{A}$	N_3	N_4	134
	108	92	

(a)

	B	$\overline{B}$	
A	22	44	66
$\overline{A}$	86	48	134
	108	92	

(b)

Thus the probability that the selected person is an A or a B or both is

$$P(A \text{ or } B) = P(A \text{ and } B) + P(\overline{A} \text{ and } B) + P(A \text{ and } \overline{B})$$
$$= \frac{22}{200} + \frac{86}{200} + \frac{44}{200} = .76$$

Notice that we did not use Rule 3.6 to find the probability of the union. Rather, we divided the union into three mutually exclusive events and used the addition rule to find the required probability.

EXAMPLE 3.8

Consider a company about to market two new products. The company believes that the success or failure of these products depends to a large extent on whether the inflation rate goes up or down in the coming year. Let S_i be the event that product i is a success, for $i = 1, 2$, and let U be the event that the inflation rate goes up. Also, let F_i, $i = 1, 2$, and D be the complements of these events. That is, F_i is the event that product i is a failure, and D is the event that the inflation rate goes down or remains constant. The company is interested in the probabilities of S_1, S_2, $(S_1 \text{ or } S_2)$, and $(S_1 \text{ and } S_2)$. How should it proceed?

SOLUTION

The first thing to do is to draw a Venn diagram, as in Figure 3.7 (p. 104). Since any outcome can be written as an intersection of three events (what happens to product 1, what happens to product 2, and what happens to the inflation rate), we see that there are eight possible outcomes in the sample space: $(U \text{ and } S_1 \text{ and } S_2)$, $(U \text{ and } S_1 \text{ and } F_2)$, $(U \text{ and } F_1 \text{ and } S_2)$, $(U \text{ and } F_1$ and $F_2)$, $(D \text{ and } S_1 \text{ and } S_2)$, $(D \text{ and } S_1 \text{ and } F_2)$, $(D \text{ and } F_1 \text{ and } S_2)$, and $(D$

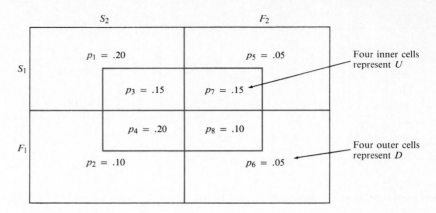

Figure 3.7

and F_1 and F_2). These are represented by the eight cells in the diagram. The upper four cells are outcomes where S_1 occurs, the four cells on the left are outcomes where S_2 occurs, and the four cells in the middle are where U occurs. We have labeled the probabilities of these cells p_1 through p_8, and we have assigned these probabilities values that sum to 1. (In Section 3.9 we discuss one method for assessing these eight probabilities in the first place. For now, we simply assume that they are given.)

Next we write the required probabilities in terms of p_1 through p_8. Since S_1 is composed of the four upper cells, we have

$$P(S_1) = p_1 + p_3 + p_5 + p_7 = .20 + .15 + .05 + .15 = .55$$

Similarly,

$$P(S_2) = p_1 + p_2 + p_3 + p_4 = .20 + .10 + .15 + .20 = .65$$

The intersection $(S_1$ and $S_2)$ contains only two outcomes, $(D$ and S_1 and $S_2)$ and $(U$ and S_1 and $S_2)$, so that

$$P(S_1 \text{ and } S_2) = p_1 + p_3 = .20 + .15 = .35$$

Finally, the union $(S_1$ or $S_2)$ occurs if neither $(U$ and F_1 and $F_2)$ nor $(D$ and F_1 and $F_2)$ occurs. Therefore,

$$P(S_1 \text{ and } S_2) = 1 - (p_6 + p_8) = 1 - (.05 + .10) = .85$$

EXAMPLE 3.9

In a consumer taste test, a blindfolded consumer is asked to make three taste comparisons of three brands of coffee, labeled brand *A*, brand *B*, and brand *C*. The first comparison is between *A* and *B*, the second is between *A* and *C*, and the third is between *B* and *C*. In each comparison the consumer must say which brand he or she prefers. Devise a method for finding the probability that a given consumer prefers no brand twice.

SOLUTION

An important aspect of this example is a proper definition of the "outcomes" of the experiment as a whole. Since we need to know which brand is favored in each comparison, an outcome is a listing of the winners of the three comparisons. For instance, the outcome (A, A, B) means that *A* is preferred to *B*, *A* is preferred to *C*, and *B* is preferred to *C*. There are eight possible outcomes: (A, A, B), (A, A, C), (A, C, B), (A, C, C), (B, A, B), (B, A, C), (B, C, B), and (B, C, C). Therefore, we need to assign eight probabilities (that sum to 1) to these eight outcomes. For the sake of illustration, we assume these eight outcomes are equally likely, which implies that each has probability $\frac{1}{8}$. Then the desired probability is

$$P(\text{no brand is preferred twice}) = P(A, C, B) + P(B, A, C) = \frac{1}{8} + \frac{1}{8} = .25$$

The addition rule states that the probability of a union of mutually exclusive events is the sum of the individual probabilities. If the events are *not* mutually exclusive, then the probability of the union is generally difficult to calculate. However, the following rule is a partial solution to the problem. It is called *Boole's inequality*.

An Inequality for Probabilities of Unions

For any events $E_1, E_2, \ldots, E_n$ (not necessarily mutually exclusive), we have

$$P(E_1 \text{ or } E_2 \text{ or } \ldots \text{ or } E_n) \leq P(E_1) + P(E_2) + \cdots + P(E_n)$$

RULE 3.8

This rule is another extension of Rule 3.3. It is most easily understood in terms of Venn diagrams, where probabilities are interpreted as areas (see Figure 3.8 on p. 106). If we approximate the area of the union (E_1 or E_2 or $\ldots$ or E_n) by the sum of the areas of the individual *E*'s, we clearly do a lot of multiple counting. Each pairwise intersection is counted twice, each three-

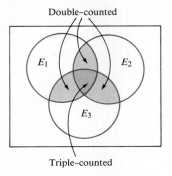

Double-counted

E_1 E_2

E_3

Triple-counted

Figure 3.8
Intersections Are Counted More Than Once
if Areas of Individuals E's Are Added

way intersection is counted three times, and so on. Therefore, the area of the union must be less than or equal to the sum of the individual areas.

The following example illustrates an important application of this rule in statistical inference.

EXAMPLE 3.10

Suppose that we survey a portion of a given population, and we wish to make several inferences about the population from the survey data. Since we have data for only a portion of the population, not for the entire population, there is a chance that any given statement we make might be wrong. Let C_i be the event that statement i is correct, and let $\overline{C}_i$ be the complement of C_i. We usually only make statements with a *small* probability of being incorrect, so that each $P(\overline{C}_i)$ is small. Let's suppose that $P(\overline{C}_i) = .02$ for each of 10 statements. Find the probability that at least 1 of the 10 statements is incorrect.

SOLUTION

Let E be the event that at least one of the statements is incorrect. Then

$$\begin{aligned} P(E) &= P(\text{at least one statement is incorrect}) \\ &= P(\overline{C}_1 \text{ or } \overline{C}_2 \text{ or } \ldots \text{ or } \overline{C}_{10}) \\ &\leq [P(\overline{C}_1) + P(\overline{C}_2) + \cdots + P(\overline{C}_{10})] = 10(.02) = .2 \end{aligned}$$

where the inequality follows from Rule 3.8. This calculation shows that although the probability of at least one incorrect statement is not known exactly, it can be no greater than .2. Equivalently, the probability that all 10 statements are correct is no less than .8.

Unfortunately, Rule 3.8 does not give us the exact value of $P(E_1 \text{ or } E_2 \text{ or } \ldots \text{ or } E_n)$. It provides only an upper bound for this value. The difference between the exact value and the upper bound depends on the overlap between the events E_1 through E_n. If there is no overlap, the inequality in Rule 3.8 becomes an equality, and Rule 3.8 coincides with Rule 3.7. If overlap does exist, however, it must be treated explicitly by taking into account the probabilities of the various intersections. A general discussion of this topic is beyond the scope of this book, but we discuss one special case in the next section.

Problems for Sections 3.5, 3.6

19. The police in a large metropolitan area have kept statistics on the people stopped for reckless driving over the past six months. Each person is classified in two ways: (1) whether he or she is at least 24 years old or under 24, and (2) whether

he or she has ever been stopped for reckless driving before. The data are shown below.

	Under 24	At Least 24
Previous offender	26	49
Not a previous offender	53	62

a. Convert these four frequencies into four probabilities of the four possible categories.

b. Assuming that the data above are appropriate for predicting future incidents of reckless driving, what is the probability that a person stopped for reckless driving will be: (a) at least 24; (b) a previous offender; (c) a previous offender or under 24 or both; (d) neither at least 24 nor a previous offender? (Answer each of these four parts separately.)

20. In a study designed to gauge women's increasing involvement in "nontraditional" roles, the following data are found from a sample of 750 randomly chosen married women in their thirties. Consider a woman chosen at random from this population.

	Has No Children	Has One Child	Has More Than One Child
Has a full-time job	98	126	83
Has a part-time job	39	59	80
Has no job outside the house	16	86	163

a. What is the probability that this woman has a job outside the house?

b. What is the probability that this woman has at least one child?

c. What is the probability that this woman has a full-time job and no more than one child?

d. What is the probability that this woman has a part-time job or at least one child or both?

21. Suppose that 8% of all people in a certain population are left-handed, 13% are over 6 feet tall, and 17% weigh over 200 pounds. A person is randomly selected from this population.

a. What can you say, in terms of an inequality, about the probability that this person has at least one of the three features?

b. What can you say about the probability that this person has none of the three features? Again use an inequality.

22. An automobile parts department has a stocking policy that assures it a probability .95 of not stocking out on any particular part on any particular day. If we look at five particular parts, what can be said about the probability of not stocking out on *any* of them on a particular day? What would the answer be if we looked at 25 parts instead of just five? Answer each question with an inequality.

*23. The readership of a certain magazine has the following characteristics: 25% are younger than 26, 25% are older than 45, 55% are males, 12% are males younger than 26, and 23% are females between 26 and 45. Suppose that a person is randomly selected from this population.

a. What is the probability that this person is a female over 45?

b. What is the probability that this person is neither male nor younger than 26?

c. What is the probability that this person is either female or at least 26 or both?

*24. A husband and wife are attempting to sell their present house and buy a new one. They assess that their chance of selling their house *and* finding a suitable new one, both within the next two months, is 1 out of 4. They also assess that their chance of being able to sell their house within two months is 2 out of 5, and their chance of finding a suitable new house within two months is 1 out of 3. If they find a new house they desire, but they cannot sell their current house (within two months), they will not be able to buy the new house. What is the probability of this unfortunate event occurring?

*25. The manager of a small supermarket is trying to decide whether to add a third checkout counter to the traditional two. To see whether this action is justified, the manager collects data at 10-minute intervals over several days during relatively busy parts of the day. At each observation point, he counts (1) the number of customers in the shorter of the two lines (whichever line this happens to be), and (2) the number of customers total in both lines. (Either of the two lines can be considered the "shorter" if there is a tie.) The following frequencies are observed for 125 observation points.

		Number of Customers in Shorter Line			
		0	1	2	3 or more
Number of	0	20	0	0	0
Customers in	1–7	12	12	17	11
Both Lines Total	8 or more	0	3	8	42

a. Why are there four cells with frequencies equal to 0? Is this just by chance, or is there a logical reason for it?

b. If a randomly selected customer arrives at the checkout counters during the relatively busy periods of the day (when these data were collected), what is the probability that this customer has to wait in line before beginning the checkout procedure? (Assume that customers always go to the shortest line.)

c. The manager will open a third checkout counter only if the probability of having at least eight customers total *and* at least three customers in each line is at least .33. Does it appear from these data that a third checkout counter will be added?

*26. Mr. Fallforit receives numerous pieces of mail where he is asked to submit his "lucky number" for a sweepstakes competition. In a given year he enters as many of these as possible—20 where his chances of winning are 1 out of 100,000, 10 where his chances of winning are 1 out of 10,000, and 5 where his chances of winning are 1 out of 1000. What can you say about the probability (a) that he will win at least once, and (b) that he will not win any? Give inequalities.

3.7

Conditional Probability

When we evaluate probabilities of events, we do so with the understanding that these probabilities are relative to the current sample space; that is, they are relative to the current set of possible outcomes. If we obtain new information that changes the sample space (by eliminating some of the possible outcomes), the probabilities may change. The following example illustrates this idea.

EXAMPLE 3.6 (continued)

We categorized people as males or females and as smokers or nonsmokers. The proportions in the joint categories are repeated in Table 3.4 for convenience. If we choose a person at random from this population, the probability is .57 that this person is male. However, if we are told that the selected person smokes and we want to know the probability that this person is male, the two nonsmoking cells on the right are irrelevant. That is, the relevant sample space now consists of male smokers and female smokers only. Since there are twice as many males as females in this subpopulation of smokers, the probability that the selected person is male is no longer .57; it is now ⅔.

Table 3.4 Data for Example 3.6

	S	$\bar{S}$	
M	.12	.45	.57
$\bar{M}$	.06	.37	.43
	.18	.82	

To formalize the ideas in this example, we introduce the extremely important concept of *conditional probability*. When we write $P(E)$ for the probability of an event E, we imply by this notation that all relevant information has been used to obtain the probability of E. If we learn that a related event F has occurred, we must explicitly use this information to revise the probability of E. The revised probability is called the conditional probability of E given F, and it is denoted by $P(E|F)$. The vertical bar means "given," the event to the right of the vertical bar is the event that is known to have occurred, and the event to the left of the vertical bar is the event that is still uncertain.

> *Conditional Probability of E Given F*
>
> $$P(E|F)$$
>
> uncertain event   given event

To calculate $P(E|F)$, we use the following probability formula. (This formula applies only when $P(F) > 0$.)

> *Conditional Probability Formula*
>
> $$P(E|F) = \frac{P(E \text{ and } F)}{P(F)}$$

The Conditional Probability Formula and the Multiplication Rule

A relative frequency argument shows the reasoning behind this formula. Suppose we repeat a given experiment N times. If the event E occurs N_E times, we approximate the probability of E by N_E/N. However, to obtain $P(E|F)$, we look only at those repetitions where F occurs. Let N_F be the number of repetitions where F occurs, and let $N_{(E \text{ and } F)}$ be the number of the N_F repetitions where E also occurs. Then we approximate $P(E|F)$ by $N_{(E \text{ and } F)}/N_F$. But we can write

$$\frac{N_{(E \text{ and } F)}}{N_F} = \frac{N_{(E \text{ and } F)}/N}{N_F/N}$$

where the numerator, $N_{(E \text{ and } F)}/N$ is the relative frequency approximation of $P(E \text{ and } F)$ and the denominator N_F/N is the relative frequency approximation of $P(F)$. Therefore, we obtain the conditional probability formula $P(E|F) = P(E \text{ and } F)/P(F)$.

The following example provides further intuition for the conditional probability formula. Suppose that computer technicians are searching for a hardware problem known to be in exactly one of four locations, labeled A, B, C, and D. They assess the probabilities of finding the problem at these four locations as .2, .3, .1, and .4. Now suppose that a thorough search of location D does not find the problem. Then the relevant sample space consists of locations A, B, and C. We want the conditional probabilities of these three locations to be proportional to what they were originally, but we want them to sum to 1. This means that we must divide .2, .3, and .1 by the probability of the given event (the problem is not at D), or .6. Therefore, the conditional probabilities of A, B, and C, given that D did not occur, are $\frac{2}{6}$, $\frac{3}{6}$, and $\frac{1}{6}$.

An equivalent way of expressing the conditional probability formula is to multiply through by the denominator $P(F)$. This gives us a *multiplication rule* for the intersection $P(E \text{ and } F)$.

RULE 3.9

> (Multiplication rule for an intersection) $P(E \text{ and } F) = P(E|F)P(F)$

The conditional probability formula and the multiplication rule for intersections provide equivalent information; the one we use in any problem depends on the probabilities we are given and the ones we need to calculate. For example, suppose the probability of a depression in the housing industry next year depends on the movement of the prime interest rate. Let E be the event that there is a depression in the housing industry next year, and let F be the event that the prime interest rate increases. If the probability of E and F *both* occurring is .6 and the probability of F is .75, the conditional probability of a housing depression, given a prime rate increase, is

$$P(E|F) = \frac{P(E \text{ and } F)}{P(F)} = \frac{.6}{.75} = .8$$

However, if we assess that $P(E|F)$ is .8 and $P(F)$ is .75, the probability of both a housing depression and a prime rate increase is

$$P(E \text{ and } F) = P(E|F)P(F) = (.8)(.75) = .6$$

Remember it this way. The conditional probability formula and the multiplication rule relate three pieces of a puzzle, $P(E|F)$, $P(E \text{ and } F)$, and $P(F)$. If any two of these are known, the third can be calculated from the appropriate formula.

It is important not to confuse the probability of the intersection $P(E \text{ and } F)$ and the conditional probability $P(E|F)$. We can explain the difference between them as follows. When we write $P(E \text{ and } F)$, we are not sure whether either event will occur, so there is uncertainty associated with both E and F. Also, the relevant sample space is still the original sample space S. However, when we write $P(E|F)$, there is no uncertainty about F; it has occurred. The only uncertainty concerns E. Now the relevant sample space is F, because all outcomes not favorable to F may be disregarded.

It is also important not to confuse $P(E|F)$ and $P(F|E)$. Referring to the smoking example (see Example 3.6), let E be the event that a male is chosen, and let F be the event that a smoker is chosen. Then $P(E|F)$ is the probability of choosing a male, given that we are choosing from the population of smokers, whereas $P(F|E)$ is the probability of choosing a smoker, given that we are choosing from the population of males. So if we know, for example, that 75% of the smokers are male, then $P(E|F) = .75$. But if we are told that 30% of the males are smokers, then $P(F|E) = .30$.

EXAMPLE 3.7 (continued)

Recall that managers are A's if they have been with the company for at least five years, and they are B's if they plan to stay with the company for at least five more years. Suppose that we choose a manager randomly from this population. What is the probability that this manager is an A, given that he is an A or a B or both?

SOLUTION

The information we need is repeated in Table 3.5 for convenience. For this problem we require the conditional probability $P[A|(A \text{ or } B)]$. That is, we are looking for the proportion of managers who are A's in the subpopulation who are A's or B's or both. Since there are 152 managers in the $(A \text{ or } B)$ category (everyone except the 48 who are neither A's nor B's), and there are 66 A's, the required proportion is $66/152$. This answer may also be found formally from the conditional probability formula. We have

$$P[A|(A \text{ or } B)] = \frac{P[A \text{ and } (A \text{ or } B)]}{P(A \text{ or } B)} = \frac{P(A)}{P(A \text{ or } B)} = \frac{66/200}{152/200} = \frac{66}{152}$$

The key here is to notice that the intersection of A and $(A \text{ or } B)$ is equal to the event A. The reason is that A is contained in $(A \text{ or } B)$. (Draw a Venn diagram to convince yourself of this.)

Table 3.5 Data for Example 3.7

	B	$\overline{B}$	
A	22	44	66
$\overline{A}$	86	48	134
	108	92	

3.8

Independent Events

It is conceivable that information about one event F will not affect the probability of another event E. In this case we say that E and F are *independent* events. For example, if E is the event that an elevator in one building needs repair tomorrow and F is the event that an elevator in the building next door needs repair today, it is reasonable to believe that $P(E)$ and $P(E|F)$ are equal. The operation of the first elevator is probably not at all related to the operation of the second. Therefore, we conclude that E and F are independent.

> *Definition of Independence*
>
> Events E and F are independent if $P(E|F) = P(E)$.

A common error in probability is to confuse the concepts of mutually exclusive events and independent events. These are definitely *not* the same. If E and F are independent, $P(E|F)$ equals $P(E)$, so that the knowledge about F does not affect the probability of E. But if E and F are mutually exclusive, $P(E|F)$ equals 0 because E and F cannot both occur. Therefore, $P(E|F)$ is certainly not equal to $P(E)$ (except in the trivial case when E has probability 0 anyway). When two events are mutually exclusive, they possess an extreme form of dependence: The occurrence of one implies that the probability of the other is 0.

The Multiplication Rule for Independent Events

In probability calculations we like to have independence because it is mathematically convenient. In particular, if E and F are independent events, then $P(E|F)$ equals $P(E)$, so that the multiplication rule for intersections reduces to $P(E \text{ and } F) = P(E)P(F)$. This special multiplication rule holds only for independent events.

RULE 3.10

> (Multiplication rule for independent events) $P(E \text{ and } F) = P(E)P(F)$

We may extend the definition of independent events to more than two events. We say that $E_1, E_2, \ldots, E_n$ are independent if knowledge about any of them is irrelevant for probabilities involving the others. The most important mathematical implication of independence is the following generalization of the multiplication rule.

RULE 3.11

> (General multiplication rule for independent events)
>
> $$P(E_1 \text{ and } E_2 \text{ and } \ldots \text{ and } E_n) = P(E_1)P(E_2) \cdots P(E_n)$$

EXAMPLE 3.11

Suppose that a marketing research firm sends questionnaires to 10 companies. Based on historical evidence, the firm believes that each company, independently of the others, will return the questionnaire with probability .7. What is the probability that all 10 questionnaires will be returned? What is the probability that none of them will be returned?

SOLUTION

Let E_i be the event that company i returns the questionnaire. Then we are given that E_1 through E_{10} are independent and each has probability .7. The event that all 10 companies return the questionnaire is the intersection of E_1 through E_{10}. By the multiplication rule for independent events, we have

$$P(E_1 \text{ and } \ldots \text{ and } E_{10}) = P(E_1) \cdots P(E_{10}) = .7^{10} = .028$$

On the other hand, the event that a given company does not return the questionnaire is .3. Since the E's are independent, their complements are also independent. (The reader is asked to verify this statement in one of the exercises at the end of this chapter.) Therefore, the probability of no returns is

$$P(\text{no returns}) = P(\overline{E}_1 \text{ and } \ldots \text{ and } \overline{E}_{10}) = P(\overline{E}_1) \cdots P(\overline{E}_{10}) = .3^{10} = .0000059$$

We conclude that there is a very small probability of getting all 10 returns, but the probability of no returns is practically zero.

3.9
Using Conditional Probabilities to Assess Probabilities

When we do not have independence, conditional probabilities can be very useful for assessing probabilities of intersections. This is often easier than assessing the probabilities of the intersections directly. Consider Example 3.8 again. Here a company plans to market two new products, and the success of these products depends on the rise or fall of the inflation rate. Again, we let S_i and F_i indicate success and failure of product i, and we let U and D indicate a rise and fall (or no change) in the inflation rate. The eight possible outcomes are the eight intersections (D and S_1 and S_2) through (U and F_1 and F_2), with probabilities p_1 through p_8 as shown in Figure 3.9 (p. 114).

Unlike Example 3.8, we do not assume that the values of the p's are given. Instead, it is the company's job to assess them. For most people it is quite difficult to estimate the probability of an intersection such as (D and S_1 and S_2). Most people find it easier to estimate a conditional probability such as $P(S_1 \text{ and } S_2|D)$, the probability of both products being successes, given a fall or no change in the inflation rate.

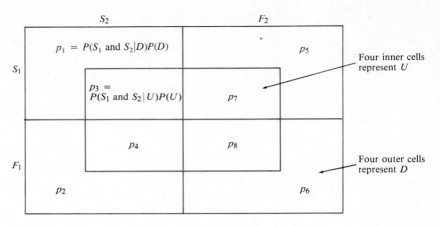

Figure 3.9

For example, suppose a company expert believes that the chance of both products succeeding is 1 out of 2 if the inflation rate falls or remains constant. That is, $P(S_1 \text{ and } S_2|D) = .5$. He also assesses that the chance of both products succeeding is only 1 out of 4 if the inflation rate increases. This means that $P(S_1 \text{ and } S_2|U) = .25$. Finally, he assesses $P(D) = .4$ and $P(U) = .6$. Then we can use the multiplication formula for conditional probability to fill in two pieces of the diagram in Figure 3.9. We have

$$p_1 = P(D \text{ and } S_1 \text{ and } S_2) = P(S_1 \text{ and } S_2|D)P(D) = (.5)(.4) = .2$$

and

$$p_2 = P(U \text{ and } S_1 \text{ and } S_2) = P(S_1 \text{ and } S_2|U)P(U) = (.25)(.6) = .15$$

By having the company expert give us more of his conditional probabilities of product success or failure, we can use the conditional probability formula to fill in the other p's in Figure 3.9.

Problems for Sections 3.7, 3.8, 3.9

27. The state highway department has conducted a study to see how the incidence of accidents on a certain set of highways is affected by weather conditions. Over a period of one year, the following data have been collected. Each observation corresponds to one day, so that the numbers in the cells indicate the numbers of days where the various conditions were observed. For the following questions, assume that you are pre- dicting the outcome on a particular road for a randomly selected day next year.

	Icy or Snowy Roads	Wet Roads	Dry Roads
No accidents	20	78	233
At least one accident	5	12	17

a. What is the probability that the road will not be dry?

b. What is the probability that there will be an accident?

c. What is the probability that there will be an accident *and* the road will not be dry?

d. What is the conditional probability that there will be an accident, given that the road is not dry?

e. Explain the difference between parts (c) and (d).

28. Department stores know that their total sales are higher in December than in any other month, but they also wish to know whether the average credit card purchase during December is higher than the average credit card purchase during the other months. The following data on 200 credit card purchases have been collected by one department store.

	Amount of Purchase	
	Less Than $50	More Than $50
December	45	35
Non-December	67	53

a. What is the probability that a given purchase made in December is for more than $50?

b. Answer part (a) for a non-December month.

29. A beer company sells two types of beer, a regular type and a light version with 30% fewer calories. The company's marketing people want to verify that their traditional approach of appealing to white-collar workers with light beer commercials and appealing to blue-collar workers with regular beer commercials is indeed a good strategy. A randomly selected group of 150 white-collar and 250 blue-collar workers are questioned about their beer-drinking preferences, and the following frequencies are obtained.

	Preference		
	Light	Regular	No Beer
White-collar	79	59	12
Blue-collar	111	122	17

a. If a blue-collar worker is chosen at random from this group, what is the probability that he prefers light beer (to regular beer or no beer at all)? Answer this question for a white-collar worker.

b. If we restrict the population to workers who do like beer, what is the probability that (i) a randomly selected blue-collar worker prefers light beer; (ii) a randomly selected white-collar worker prefers light beer?

c. Does the company's marketing strategy appear to be reasonable? Why or why not?

30. The following questions refer to the data in Problem 19 (p. 106).

a. What is the probability that a typical driver stopped for reckless driving is over 24 years old, given that he is a previous offender?

b. What is the probability that a typical driver stopped for reckless driving is a previous offender, given that he is under 24 years old?

c. What is the probability that a typical driver stopped for reckless driving is over 24 years old, given that he is over 24 years old or is not a previous offender or both?

31. Consider a married woman in her thirties selected at random from the population described in Problem 20 (p. 107).

a. What is the probability that this woman does not work outside the house, given that she has at least one child?

b. What is the probability that this woman has no children, given that she works part-time?

c. What is the probability that this woman has at least two children, given that she does not work full-time?

32. Suppose that we randomly select 2 people without replacement from a population consisting of 10 adult men, 10 adult women, and 10 children.

a. Let E be the event that the first person chosen is an adult man, and let F be the event that the second person chosen is an adult woman. Explain verbally why E and F are not independent events. Then show mathematically that they are not independent.

b. Now let E be the event that the first person chosen is an adult man, and let F be the event that the second person chosen is not a child. Decide one way or the other whether E and F are independent events.

33. Referring to Problem 25 (p. 107), consider a customer who arrives at the checkout counters and finds one customer in the shortest line. What is the probability that there are no more than six customers in the other line?

34. Referring to Problem 21 (p. 107), let E, F, and G be, respectively, the events that a randomly selected person is left-handed, is over 6 feet tall, and weighs over 200 pounds.

a. Would you expect E, F, and G to be independent events? Why or why not? (Give an intuitive answer.)

b. Assuming that E, F, and G are independent events, calculate the probabilities requested in Problem 21.

35. Answer the questions asked in Problem 26 (p. 108), assuming that the contests Mr. Fallforit enters have probabilistically

independent outcomes. Intuitively, is this independence assumption reasonable? Why or why not?

36. A business manager who needs to make many phone calls has estimated that when he calls a client, the probability is .6 that he will reach the client right away. If he does not reach the client on the first call, he believes the probability is .2 that he will reach the client with a subsequent call in the next hour.
    a. Find the probability that the manager will reach his client in no more than two calls.
    b. Find the probability that he will reach the client on the second call but not on the first.
    c. Find the probability that he will be unsuccessful on two successive calls.

37. Consider a population that can be categorized as (1) males or females, and (2) college graduates or not college graduates. The probability of a randomly chosen person being male is .4, and the probability of a randomly chosen person being a college graduate is .3. Fill in the probabilities of the four joint categories in the table below given that a person's sex is independent of whether the person graduated from college.

	College graduate	Not college graduate	
Male			.4
Female			
	.3		

3.10

Equally Likely Probabilities and Counting Rules

Earlier in this chapter we discussed two possible ways of assessing probabilities: a relative frequency approach and a subjective approach. In this section we learn another way of obtaining probabilities. This is called the *equally likely* approach. Consider a sample space with N_S possible outcomes. If we can argue that, by reason of symmetry, all N_S outcomes are equally likely, each outcome must have probability $1/N_S$. It follows that if E is any event such that N_E of the N_S outcomes are favorable to E, the probability of E must be N_E/N_S.

Equally Likely Probability Formula

$$P(E) = \frac{N_E}{N_S} \quad \text{where}$$

N_E = number of outcomes favorable to E

N_S = number of outcomes in the sample space S

In this section we discuss two important aspects of this simple formula. The first is how we recognize whether the possible outcomes are equally likely. The second is how we calculate N_E and N_S.

Clearly, not all sample spaces have equally likely outcomes. For example, the three events, no precipitation tomorrow, rain tomorrow, and snow tomorrow, are probably not equally likely. But even in situations where *some* assumption of equally likely outcomes is justified, we must be careful how we define the possible outcomes. Consider the following simple example.

Descriptions of Sample Spaces with Equally Likely Outcomes

EXAMPLE 3.12

A survey selects two executives from a large population of executives, half of whom are women. Find the probability of the event E that at least one of the two executives selected is a woman.

SOLUTION

One sample space description tells us the sex of each executive selected. The four possibilities are (F, F), (F, M), (M, F), and (M, M), where the first member of each pair is the sex of the first executive and the second member is the sex of the second executive. If these four possibilities are equally likely, each has probability $\frac{1}{4}$. In this case, three of the four outcomes are favorable to E, so that $N_E = 3$, $N_S = 4$, and $P(E) = \frac{3}{4}$.

However, we could let the sample space indicate the *number* of women selected for the survey. Then the three possible outcomes are 0, 1, and 2. If we assume that these outcomes are equally likely, each has probability $\frac{1}{3}$. Now two of the outcomes are favorable to E, so that $N_E = 2$ and $N_S = 3$, and $P(E)$ becomes $\frac{2}{3}$.

Which of these two sample space descriptions gives the right answer? We reason as follows. Let F_1 be the event that the first executive is a woman and define F_2 similarly for the second executive. Because the population is large, F_1 and F_2 are practically independent. (This is because the composition of the population is practically unchanged after the first draw. This means that the probability of F_2 is practically $\frac{1}{2}$ whether F_1 or $\overline{F}_1$ occurs.) Therefore,

$$P(E) = 1 - P(\text{no women}) = 1 - P(\overline{F}_1 \text{ and } \overline{F}_2) = 1 - P(\overline{F}_1)P(\overline{F}_2)$$
$$= 1 - \left(\frac{1}{2}\right)\left(\frac{1}{2}\right) = \frac{3}{4}$$

This implies that only the first sample space has equally likely outcomes. We are not saying that there is anything wrong with the second sample space; we are only saying that its outcomes are not equally likely.

In most situations we accept an assumption of equally likely outcomes because of some type of symmetry. When we flip a regular coin, we assume that the two outcomes "head" and "tail" are equally likely because the coin is presumably well balanced. When we deal a five-card poker hand from a well-shuffled deck of cards, we assume that all conceivable five-card hands are equally likely because the deck is well shuffled. If we randomly select a sample of 100 people from a population of 100,000 people, we assume that all possible groups of 100 people are equally likely because the sampling is done randomly.

Counting Formulas

Once we have settled on a sample space description and have decided that an assumption of equally likely outcomes is reasonable, there is really no more probability left to do. To calculate $P(E)$ for any event E, we simply count the number of outcomes favorable to E, N_E, and the number of outcomes in the sample space, N_S. We then set $P(E)$ equal to N_E/N_S. This means that our problem is really a counting problem. In this section we learn formulas for counting N_E and N_S.

If the sample space is small, the counting problem may be fairly simple. For example, suppose that a manufacturing process produces six machines on a given day and two of these are defective. If the company randomly chooses two of the six machines to ship to one of its customers, what is the probability of the event E that the customer receives at least one defective machine?

To solve this problem, we label the six machines by the numbers 1 through 6, where machines 5 and 6 are the defective machines. A typical outcome is a pair of numbers that identify the machines sent to the customer. For example, the outcome {4, 6} means that the customer receives machines 4 and 6. (This is the same as the outcome {6, 4}. In fact, we have used braces { } instead of parentheses to indicate that only the members in the set, not the ordering of these members, matters.) There are 15 such outcomes:

$$\{1, 2\} \quad \{1, 3\} \quad \{1, 4\} \quad \{1, 5\} \quad \{1, 6\}$$
$$\{2, 3\} \quad \{2, 4\} \quad \{2, 5\} \quad \{2, 6\} \quad \{3, 4\}$$
$$\{3, 5\} \quad \{3, 6\} \quad \{4, 5\} \quad \{4, 6\} \quad \{5, 6\}$$

Of these 15 outcomes, only nine are favorable to E—namely, those where a 5 or a 6 or both are included in the pair. Therefore, $N_S = 15$, $N_E = 9$, and $P(E) = \frac{9}{15} = .6$.

Although this example is simple, it indicates some of the difficulties that we face with larger problems. If the company instead produces 150 machines, 10 of which are defective, and the customer receives 15 machines, the probability that the customer receives at least one defective can be found by the same enumeration method as above, but the values of N_S and N_E are very large. In fact, a listing of the entire sample space is not practical; there are too many outcomes. What we need is a systematic way of calculating N_S and N_E without actually listing the outcomes. We now examine specific counting rules for doing this.

There are many counting formulas used in probability applications. Some of these are very simple and some are quite complex, but they are all based on the following principle. Suppose that any "task" can be divided into J "subtasks." Subtask 1 can be done in n_1 ways. Once subtask 1 has been done, subtask 2 can be done in n_2 ways. Once subtasks 1 and 2 have been done, subtask 3 can be done in n_3 ways, and so on. Then the number of ways the overall task can be done is the *product*, $n_1 n_2 \cdots n_J$. We will refer to this rule as the *product rule*.

Counting Rules for Sampling with and Without Replacement

(Product rule for counting)
   The number of ways of doing a task consisting of J subtasks is the product $n_1 n_2 \cdots n_J$. Here the n's are the numbers of ways the subtasks can be done, as described above.

RULE 3.12

The following two examples illustrate the product rule.

EXAMPLE 3.13

At an exclusive restaurant, a full-course dinner consists of an appetizer, an entrée, and a dessert. If the menu lists six appetizers, ten entrées, and five desserts, how many full-course dinners could be ordered?

SOLUTION

Here we may identify the "task" as the full-course dinner selection and the "subtasks" as the selections of the appetizer, the entrée, and the dessert. This means that $J = 3$. Also, n_1 equals 6 since there are six appetizers. Similarly, $n_2 = 10$ and $n_3 = 5$. So by the product rule, there are $6 \times 10 \times 5$, or 300, full-course dinners.

EXAMPLE 3.14

A company salesman has to visit seven cities in the state and then return home. He would like to visit the cities in an order that minimizes the amount of gasoline he uses, and he does not want to visit any city twice. Would you say that he has a hard problem?

SOLUTION

The answer depends on the number of orderings of the seven cities, since the salesman will presumably look at each ordering and choose the one that requires the fewest miles of driving. A typical ordering looks like (6, 3, 2, 1, 4, 5, 7), which means he visits city 6 first, city 3 next, and so on. To count the total number of orderings, notice that the first city visited can be chosen in seven ways. Once this city is chosen, there are six cities that he can visit next. Once the second city is chosen, there are five cities that he can visit next. This continues until there is only one city left to visit last. So there are seven subtasks and the numbers of ways of doing them are $n_1 = 7$, $n_2 = 6$, . . . , $n_7 = 1$. By the product rule, the total number of orderings is

$$7 \times 6 \times 5 \times 4 \times 3 \times 2 \times 1 = 5040$$

Evidently, the salesman's job of finding the best ordering will take him awhile!

There are many counting formulas based on the product rule. In fact, a quick glance at probability texts, particularly those published a good while ago, reveals large sections devoted to counting formulas in complicated problems, many of which relate to games of chance. Fortunately, we require only a few of these formulas for the statistical applications in this book. These applications usually arise when we are interested in a population of N members, N_A of which have a given characteristic A and N_B ($= N - N_A$) of which have the opposite characteristic B. To learn about the population, we randomly select n members from this population. Our interest then centers on the number of A's in the sample.

The sampling may be done with or without replacement. If it is done *without replacement,* no member of the population can be sampled more than once. Thus all n members of the sample must be different from one another. If sampling is done *with replacement,* we can think of the sample as being chosen one member at a time, where each of the N members in the population can be sampled at any draw, regardless of the members already sampled.

When sampling is done with replacement, it is convenient to define the outcomes of the sample space by the *ordered* sequences $(x_1, x_2, . . . , x_n)$. Here x_1 is the identity of the first member sampled, x_2 is the identity of the second member sampled, and so on. Since each x can have any of N values, regardless of the other x's, the product rule says that there are $N \times N \times \cdots \times N = N^n$ possible outcomes, so that $N_S = N^n$. Furthermore, these outcomes are equally likely, so each outcome has probability $1/N^n$.

When sampling is done without replacement, it is more convenient to define the outcomes of the sample space as *unordered* sets of the form $\{x_1,$

$x_2, \ldots, x_n$}. (We again use braces { } instead of parentheses to denote that order does not matter.) Each unordered set simply indicates which n members of the population are in the sample.

The number of these unordered subsets is the number of ways that we can choose n members from a total of N members. This number turns out to be very important in statistics. In fact, it is so important that it has been given a special name and a special notation. In general, the number of subsets of n objects that can be chosen from a total of N objects is called a *binomial coefficient* and is denoted by the symbol $\binom{N}{n}$, read "N choose n." (Be careful: This is *not* the same thing as N divided by n.) [Some books prefer the notation $_NC_n$ instead of $\binom{N}{n}$, where the "C" stands for "combinations." They then refer to this number as the number of combinations of N objects taken n at a time.]

A binomial coefficient, denoted by $\binom{N}{n}$, is the number of subsets of n objects that can be chosen without replacement from a total of N objects.

The following formula shows how to calculate a binomial coefficient.

Computing Formula for Binomial Coefficients

$$\binom{N}{n} = \frac{N!}{n!\,(N-n)!}$$

Here the symbol $n!$, read "n factorial," is the product of the first n integers for any positive integer n. By convention, we set 0! equal to 1.

Computing Formula for n Factorial

$$n! = n(n-1)(n-2) \cdots (2)(1) \qquad \text{for any integer } n \geq 1$$
$$0! = 1$$

The number $n!$ has an interesting interpretation in its own right. It is the number of ways n objects can be ordered from first to nth. These orderings are often called *permutations*. For example, the salesman in Example 3.14 has $7! = 5040$ permutations of the seven cities he needs to visit; each of these corresponds to a different route.

A permutation of n objects is any ordering of these objects. The number of permutations of n objects equals $n!$.

With this new notation, we can now specify the number of outcomes in the sample space when sampling is without replacement. Since each of the outcomes is one of the subsets of size n, there are $\binom{N}{n}$ possible outcomes. If sampling is done completely randomly, each of these outcomes is equally likely, so each has probability $1/\binom{N}{n}$.

EXAMPLE 3.15

A marketing research group plans to interview five randomly selected consumers from a population of 75 consumers. How many ways can these five consumers be selected, and what is the probability of each?

SOLUTION

Here sampling is done without replacement because the research group will not interview the same person more than once. Therefore, the sample space consists of all subsets of size 5 that can be chosen from 75 people. The number of outcomes is

$$\binom{75}{5} = \frac{75!}{5!\ 70!} = \frac{75 \times 74 \times 73 \times 72 \times 71 \times 70!}{5 \times 4 \times 3 \times 2 \times 1 \times 70!}$$

$$= \frac{75 \times 74 \times 73 \times 72 \times 71}{5 \times 4 \times 3 \times 2 \times 1} = 17,259,390$$

Each of these many subsets has a very small probability, $1/17,259,390 = .0000000579$, of being chosen.

This example illustrates two points: (1) the larger of the two factorials in the denominator of a binomial coefficient (here the 70!) can always be canceled with part of the numerator to simplify calculations, and (2) binomial coefficients are often extremely large numbers.

To complete our discussion, recall that we are sampling n members from a population with N_A A's and $N_B = (N - N_A)$ B's. Let E_k be the event that exactly k members of the sample are A's. This means there are exactly $(n - k)$ B's in the sample. For any possible value of k, we have the following formulas for sampling with and without replacement. (The reasoning behind these formulas is given in an appendix to this chapter.)

Sampling with Replacement

$$P(E_k) = \frac{\binom{n}{k} N_A^k (N - N_A)^{n-k}}{N^n}$$

Sampling without Replacement

$$P(E_k) = \frac{\dbinom{N_A}{k}\dbinom{N - N_A}{n - k}}{\dbinom{N}{n}}$$

In the sampling-with-replacement formula, we can make one important simplification. Let $p_A = N_A/N$ be the fraction of A's in the population. Then the formula above reduces to the following.

Alternative Formula for Sampling with Replacement

$$P(E_k) = \dbinom{n}{k}p_A^k(1 - p_A)^{n-k}$$

This alternative formula shows that $P(E_k)$ depends only on the *fraction* of A's in the population, not on N_A or N separately. We now present two applications of these formulas.

EXAMPLE 3.16

We begin by solving a problem mentioned earlier in this section. A manufacturing company produces 150 machines, 10 of which are defective. A customer receives a randomly selected 15 of these machines. What is the probability of the event E that the customer receives at least one defective machine?

SOLUTION

The population consists of 150 machines, 10 of which are A's (the defectives) and the other 140 of which are B's (the nondefectives). This means that $N = 150$, $N_A = 10$, and $N_B = 140$. When the customer receives 15 of these machines, this is the same as sampling $n = 15$ machines *without* replacement (because the customer cannot receive the same machine twice). Instead of finding $P(E)$ directly, we will find $P(\overline{E})$, the probability of no defective machines. In the notation above, we can write $\overline{E}$ as E_0 (zero defectives), so that

$$P(\overline{E}) = P(E_0) = \frac{\dbinom{10}{0}\dbinom{140}{15}}{\dbinom{150}{15}}$$

$$= \left(\frac{10!}{0!\ 10!}\right)\left(\frac{140!}{15!\ 125!}\right)\bigg/\left(\frac{150!}{15!\ 135!}\right)$$

$$= \frac{140 \times 139 \times \cdots \times 126}{150 \times 149 \times \cdots \times 136} = .337$$

Therefore, the desired probability is $P(E) = 1 - .337 = .663$.

EXAMPLE 3.17

Suppose that 60 people place long-distance phone calls during the next hour. We divide this hour into three 20-minute intervals and assume that each caller, independently of the others, is equally likely to place his or her call during any one of these intervals. What is the probability that exactly 20 of the calls will be placed during the first 20-minute interval?

SOLUTION

This problem is a sampling problem in the sense that each of $n = 60$ callers "samples" one of the $N = 3$ 20-minute intervals. That is, the three 20-minute intervals represent the "population" for this problem. Furthermore, sampling is done *with* replacement because any 20-minute interval can be chosen by more than one caller. Based on the question that has been asked, we let the A be the first 20-minute interval (there is only one A in this population), and we let the B's be the last two 20-minute intervals. This means that $N_A = 1$, $N_B = 2$, and $p_A = \frac{1}{3}$. We want the probability of 20 A's, that is, $P(E_{20})$. This is

$$P(E_{20}) = \binom{60}{20}\left(\frac{1}{3}\right)^{20}\left(\frac{2}{3}\right)^{40} = .1087$$

(A calculator with an "$n!$" and a "y^x" button was used to calculate this answer. We will have more to say about calculations such as this one in Chapter 5.) Although intuition says that about one-third of the calls should be placed during the first 20 minutes, the probability of *exactly* one-third of the calls occurring during this time is only slightly greater than 1 out of 10.

Before leaving this section, we again stress an important point. Not all sample spaces have equally likely outcomes. Even though we can count N_S possible outcomes, we cannot necessarily assign probability $1/N_S$ to each of them. Mathematically, there is nothing wrong with doing this, but practically, it may be nonsense. Unless there is some justification for an assumption of equally likely outcomes, whether it be symmetry or empirical evidence, the resulting probabilities have no relevance for the real world.

Problems for Section 3.10

38. a. If a given model car is distinguished by the color, the type of upholstery, the size of the engine, and the number of doors, how many versions of this model are there? Assume that there are 20 possible colors, three types of upholstery, and two engine sizes. Also, assume that all versions have two doors, with or without a hatchback, or four doors, again with or without a hatchback.
    b. How would your answer to part (a) change if the larger engine came only with the hatchback models (but every other combination were still available)?

39. In an Olympics race, there are eight runners in the finals and only three awards are given: a gold, a silver, and a bronze medal. In how many ways could the three medals be distributed to the eight runners? (For example, one way is that runner 3 gets gold, runner 1 gets silver, and runner 7 gets bronze.)

40. In a consumer panel for soap brands, each consumer is asked to rate six brands of soap from 1 (best) to 6 (worst). Assuming that no tied rankings are allowed, how many ways can the six brands be rated; that is, how many orderings are there?

41. Referring to Problem 40, suppose that two customers rate the six brands independently of one another. What is the probability that they will give identical ratings, given that each customer is equally likely to give any of the possible ratings?

42. In a very simple card game, a player chooses any 2 cards randomly from a well-shuffled deck of 40 cards. This deck has 10 red cards, 10 green cards, 10 blue cards, and 10 yellow cards. The red cards are numbered 1 to 10, as are the blue, green, and yellow cards.
    a. How many ways could the person choose the 2 cards?
    b. How many ways could the person choose 2 cards of the same color? (This color could be any one of the four colors.)
    c. What is the probability of the person choosing 2 cards of the same color?

*43. In the game of bridge, where each of the 4 players receives 13 cards from a deck of 52 cards (with 4 aces and 48 non-aces), one player claims that she is very unlucky because she receives no aces on approximately 3 out of every 4 deals. See how unlucky she really is by calculating the probability of no aces in a given 13-card hand.

*44. On an airline flight with 200 pieces of baggage, suppose that three of the pieces belong to you. If the baggage handlers misplace 10 pieces of baggage, what is the probability that at least one of yours has been misplaced? (Look at the probability of the complement.)

*45. At an appliance store, the people in charge of sales have come to the conclusion that whenever a sale takes place, it is equally likely to occur on any of the six days from Monday through Saturday. If six sales for a certain appliance occur in a given week, what is the probability that they occur on separate days of the week?

*46. Mr. Jones needs to find some information that is stored in various sources. In particular, he has eight possible sources to search, and it turns out that the identical information is stored in three of these. If he has time to search only two of the eight sources, and he chooses these two randomly, what is the probability he will find the information?

*47. Suppose that in a group of 100 smokers, 28 currently have some type of permanent respiratory ailment. In a study, 10 of these 100 people are chosen at random. The person conducting the study has decided she will report that smoking and respiratory ailments are related only if at least 4 of the 10 people selected have respiratory ailments. What is the probability of this occurring?

48. Calculate the following numbers.
    a. $10!$ b. $\dfrac{13!}{7!}$ c. $\dfrac{125!}{5!\,120!}$ d. $\dfrac{115!\,220!}{110!\,225!}$

49. Calculate the following numbers.
    a. $\dbinom{40}{20}$ b. $\dbinom{20}{15}\dbinom{15}{10}$
    c. $\dbinom{15}{12} \Big/ \dbinom{20}{12}$ d. $\dbinom{50}{10}\dbinom{40}{10} \Big/ \dbinom{90}{20}$

*50. For each of the following expressions, state what probability the expression represents in terms of sampling. Do not try to do any calculations.
    a. $\dfrac{\dbinom{n}{2}(3)^2(8)^{n-2}}{(11)^n}$
    b. $\dbinom{N}{2}\dbinom{M}{1} \Big/ \dbinom{N+M}{3}$
       for any integers $N \geq 2$ and $M \geq 1$
    c. $\dbinom{N}{n}\dbinom{M}{0} \Big/ \dbinom{N+M}{n}$
       for any integers n, N, and M, with $n \leq N$

*51. Calculate the following summations. Use cancellation whenever possible. Then interpret each of these as a probability in an appropriate sampling experiment.

a. $\displaystyle\sum_{k=0}^{3} \binom{5}{k}(200)^k(400)^{5-k}/(600)^5$

b. $\displaystyle\sum_{k=0}^{6} \binom{8}{k}\bigg/ 2^8$

c. $\displaystyle\sum_{k=1}^{3} \binom{8}{k}\binom{7}{4-k}\bigg/\binom{15}{4}$

d. $\displaystyle\sum_{k=2}^{3} \binom{996}{k}\binom{4}{3-k}\bigg/\binom{1000}{3}$

*52. Consider a population with 12,000 members, 5000 of whom are under 30 years old. A sample of size 2000 is chosen from this population. For each of the following events, write an expression (a summation involving binomial coefficients) for the probability of the event, first assuming that sampling is done without replacement and then assuming that sampling is done with replacement. (Do not attempt to evaluate these probabilities.)

a. At least 700 people in the sample are under 30.

b. The number of people in the sample under 30 is between 601 and 900 (inclusive).

c. At least 1200 people in the sample are not under 30.

Summary

This chapter has introduced some of the basic elements of probability theory that will be so important in our study of statistical inference. First, we saw how probabilities are numbers between 0 and 1 that encode our uncertainty about possible outcomes. These probabilities can be assessed objectively, via a relative frequency approach, if we have access to relevant historical data, or subjectively, if historical data are unavailable or irrelevant. In either case the probabilities must satisfy several mathematical properties.

To learn the mathematical theory of probability, we first defined the sample space as the set of all possible outcomes and then considered events that are subsets of the sample space. Three important ways of forming events from other events are by taking complements, unions, and intersections. The probability of the complement of an event is 1 minus the probability of the event. If the events are mutually exclusive, the addition rule states that the probability of their union is the sum of the probabilities of the individual events.

We then defined conditional probabilities, which are used to update probabilities as new information becomes available. If the information about one event does not affect the probability of another event, these events are independent. We saw that the conditional probability formula is equivalent to a multiplication formula for the probability of an intersection.

Finally, in the last section we saw that if the outcomes in a sample space are equally likely, probabilities can be calculated by counting outcomes. Two particular quantities that are useful in these counting problems are binomial coefficients, the number of subsets of a certain size that can be formed from a given set, and factorials, the number of permutations of the members of a set. These were used to provide important probability formulas in the context of sampling with and without replacement from a finite population.

Application 3.1 The results we obtain when we work with conditional probabilities can be quite unintuitive, even paradoxical. The following example is similar to one described in an article by Blyth and is usually referred to as Simpson's paradox. (Reference: Colin R. Blyth, "On Simpson's Paradox and the Sure-Thing Principle," *Journal of the American Statistical Association,* Vol. 67, 1972, pp. 364–366.) Essentially, Simpson's paradox says that even if one treatment has a better effect than another on *each* of two mutually exclusive and exhaustive subpopulations, it can have a *worse* effect on the population as a whole.

Suppose that the population is the set of managers in a large company. We categorize the managers as those with an MBA degree (the B's) and those without an MBA degree (the $\overline{B}$'s). These categories are the two "treatment groups." We also categorize the managers as those who were hired directly out of school by this company (the C's) and those who worked with another company first (the $\overline{C}$'s). These two categories form the two "subpopulations." Finally, we use as a measure of effectiveness those managers who have been promoted within the past year (the A's).

Imagine choosing a manager at random. Then the following conditional probabilities are assumed to be given:

$$P(A|B \text{ and } C) = .10 \qquad P(A|\overline{B} \text{ and } C) = .05$$
$$P(A|B \text{ and } \overline{C}) = .35 \qquad P(A|\overline{B} \text{ and } \overline{C}) = .20$$
$$P(C|B) = .90 \qquad P(\overline{C}|B) = .10$$
$$P(C|\overline{B}) = .30 \qquad P(\overline{C}|\overline{B}) = .70$$

Each of these can be interpreted as a proportion. For example, the first probability implies that 10% of all managers who have an MBA degree and were hired by the company directly out of school were promoted last year. Similar explanations hold for the other probabilities.

From the top two probabilities, if we consider only the subpopulation of managers who were employed directly out of school, MBA graduates are more successful at being promoted than non-MBAs. From the next two probabilities, the same statement is true if we consider only the subpopulation of managers who were hired from another company. Again, the MBAs are more successful than non-MBAs. However, it can be shown that

$$P(A|B) = P(A|B \text{ and } C)P(C|B) + P(A|B \text{ and } \overline{C})P(\overline{C}|B)$$

Using the given probabilities, we obtain

$$P(A|B) = .10(.90) + .35(.10) = .125$$

Similarly, substituting $\overline{B}$ for B and doing a similar calculation, we obtain

$$P(A|\overline{B}) = .05(.30) + .20(.70) = .155$$

Therefore, $P(A|B)$ is less than $P(A|\overline{B})$, which means that MBA graduates are *less* successful in getting promoted than non-MBAs. This is the paradox, namely, that MBA graduates are more successful in each of the two subpopulations but are less successful in the population as a whole.

The calculations above are correct, and the given probabilities are not inconsistent with one another. That is, there are no tricks. As with all "paradoxes," there is a logical explanation. Looking at the population of MBA graduates, we see that the C's are much more successful at getting promoted than the $\overline{C}$'s (.35 versus .10). Furthermore, there are many more C's among the MBAs than $\overline{C}$'s [since $P(C|B) = .90$]. Putting these two facts together, we see why MBAs do not tend to be very successful on the average. On the other hand, if we consider only the non-MBAs, we again see that the $\overline{C}$'s are more successful than the C's (.20 versus .05). But for non-MBAs, the C's are in the minority [since $P(C|\overline{B}) = .30$]. This is why the non-MBAs, although still fairly unsuccessful, are more successful than the MBAs on the average.

Application 3.2   Several years ago one of the large fast-foods companies ran a campaign where it gave game cards to its customers. These game cards made it possible for customers to win hamburgers, french fries, soft drinks, and other fast-food items, as well as cash prizes. The game cards were as follows. Each card had 10 covered spots that could be uncovered by rubbing them with a coin. Below three of these spots were "zaps." Below the other seven spots were names of prizes, two of which were identical. (Some cards had other variations of this pattern, but we'll use this type of card for purposes of illustration.) For example, one card might have two pictures of a hamburger, one picture of a coke, one of french fries, one of a milkshake, one of $5, one of $1000, and three zaps. For this card the customer could win a hamburger. To win on any card, the customer had to uncover the two matching spots (which showed the potential prize for that card) before uncovering a zap; any card with a zap uncovered was automatically void. Assuming that the two matches and the three zaps are arranged randomly on the cards, what is the probability of a customer winning?

Let's label the two matching spots M_1 and M_2, and the three zaps Z_1, Z_2, and Z_3. Then the probability of winning is the probability of uncovering M_1 and M_2 before uncovering Z_1, Z_2, or Z_3. In this case the relevant sample space is the set of all orderings of M_1, M_2, Z_1, Z_2, and Z_3, shown in the order they are uncovered. As far as the outcome of the game is concerned, the other five spots on the card are irrelevant. Then an outcome such as

$(M_2, M_1, Z_1, Z_3, Z_2)$ is a winner, whereas $(M_2, Z_1, Z_3, M_1, Z_2)$ is a loser. Actually, the first card would be declared a winner as soon as M_1 were uncovered, and the second card would be declared a loser as soon as Z_1 were uncovered. However, we show the whole sequence of M's and Z's so that we can count outcomes correctly. We find the probability of winning by an equally likely argument. There are 5! orderings of the five M's and Z's, and each is equally likely. The winners are exactly those orderings that have both M's to the left of the three Z's. For these winning sequences, there are 2! ways of ordering the M's and 3! ways of ordering the Z's. So we have

$$P(\text{winning}) = \frac{2!3!}{5!} = \frac{1}{10}$$

This calculation is obviously important to the fast-foods company. It shows that on the average, 1 out of 10 cards will be winners. Actually, this only provides an upper bound on the fraction of cards where a prize is awarded. The fact is that many customers throw their cards away without playing the game, and even some of the winners neglect to claim their prizes. So, for example, the company knows that if they make 50,000 cards where a milkshake is the winning prize, somewhat less than 5000 milkshakes will be given away.

Glossary of Terms

Probability a number between 0 and 1 that measures the likelihood of a possible outcome

Objective probabilities probabilities that can be estimated by a relative frequency approach

Subjective probabilities probabilities that cannot be estimated objectively because historical data is unavailable or irrelevant

Sample space the set of all possible outcomes

Event any collection of outcomes

Complement of an event the set of outcomes unfavorable to the event

Union of events the set of outcomes favorable to at least one of the events

Intersection of events the set of outcomes favorable to all the events

Mutually exclusive events events with no outcomes in common

Independent events events where the probability of any of the events is unaffected by information related to the others

Binomial coefficient the number of subsets of a certain size that can be chosen (without replacement) from a given set

Factorial the number of permutations (or rearrangements) of the members of a set

Important Formulas

1. Relative frequency formula

$$\text{Estimate of } P(E) = \frac{\text{number of repetitions where } E \text{ occurs}}{\text{number of repetitions}}$$

2. Addition rule for mutually exclusive events

$$P(E_1 \text{ or } E_2 \text{ or } \ldots \text{ or } E_n) = P(E_1) + P(E_2) + \cdots + P(E_n)$$

3. Conditional probability formula

$$P(E \text{ given } F) = P(E|F) = \frac{P(E \text{ and } F)}{P(F)} \qquad \text{provided that } P(F) > 0$$

4. Multiplication rule for intersections of events (independent or otherwise)

$$P(E \text{ and } F) = P(E|F)P(F)$$

5. Multiplication rule for the intersection of independent events

$$P(E_1 \text{ and } E_2 \text{ and } \ldots \text{ and } E_n) = P(E_1)P(E_2) \cdots P(E_n)$$

6. Equally likely probability formula

$$P(E) = \frac{N_E}{N_S}$$

where N_E is the number of outcomes favorable to E and N_S is the number of outcomes in the sample space S

7. Formula for a binomial coefficient

$$\text{``}N \text{ choose } n\text{''} = \binom{N}{n} = \frac{N!}{n! \, (N - n)!}$$

8. Formula for n factorial

$$n! = n(n - 1)(n - 2) \cdots (2)(1) \qquad 0! = 1$$

9. Formula for the probability of k A's out of n when sampling is with replacement

$$P(E_k) = \binom{n}{k} p_A^k (1 - p_A)^{n-k}$$

where p_A is the fraction of A's in the population and n is the sample size

10. Formula for the probability of k A's out of n when sampling is without replacement

$$P(E_k) = \frac{\binom{N_A}{k}\binom{N - N_A}{n - k}}{\binom{N}{n}}$$

where N_A is the number of A's in the population, N is the population size, and n is the sample size

End-of-Chapter Problems

*53. An automobile insurance company that has issued a $200 deductible insurance policy to Ms. Smith has assessed the probabilities of her various driving possibilities as follows. The probability that she will have no accidents is 15 times as large as the probability that she will have an accident involving more than $200 worth of damage. The probability of her having an accident involving more than $200 worth of damage is four times as great as the probability of her having an accident involving less than $200 worth of damage. Are the odds that she will have no accident at all greater or less than 20 to 1? Answer by finding the probability of each of her three possible driving records described above.

54. Let $E_1, E_2, \ldots, E_n$ be any n events. State in words what each of the following equalities says and why it is true. (Interpret each side of each equality as an appropriate event.)

a. Complement of $(E_1$ and E_2 and $\ldots$ and $E_n) = (\overline{E}_1$ or $\overline{E}_2$ or $\ldots$ or $\overline{E}_n)$

b. Complement of $(E_1$ or E_2 or $\ldots$ or $E_n) = (\overline{E}_1$ and $\overline{E}_2$ and $\ldots$ and $\overline{E}_n)$

55. To increase productivity, the management of an industrial plant divides its workers into three teams, team A, team B, and team C. Each month the three teams compete to see which can produce the most. (The monthly winner receives a bonus.) Let A_i be the event that team A wins in month i. The events B_i and C_i are defined similarly for teams B and C. In terms of these events, write the following events by using complements, unions, and/or intersections.

a. Team A wins at least once in the next three months.

b. Team B does not win all three of the next three months' competitions.

c. Each team wins exactly once in the next three months.

56. Referring to Problem 55, let $P(A_i) = .5$, $P(B_i) = .3$, and $P(C_i) = .2$ for each month i, and assume that the competi-

tions in different months are probabilistically independent. Find the probabilities of the events in parts (a), (b), and (c) of Problem 55.

57. Using the same assumptions from Problems 55 and 56, suppose it is given that team B wins next month's competition. Now find the (conditional) probabilities of the events in parts (a), (b), and (c) of Problem 55.

*58. This problem again refers to the competition in Problem 55, but now we drop the independence assumption from Problems 56 and 57. Instead, assume that $P(A_1) = .5$, $P(B_1) = .3$, $P(C_1) = .2$, and assume the probabilities of future winners are given by the following table of conditional probabilities. For example, this table implies that if team A wins in month 2, team B has probability .25 of winning in month 3. Now find the probabilities of the events in parts (a), (b), and (c) of Problem 55.

| | | Winner in Month $i + 1$ | | |
		A	B	C
Winner in Month i	A	.55	.25	.20
	B	.30	.40	.30
	C	.25	.35	.40

*59. In a large accounting firm, the percentage of accountants with MBA degrees and at least five years of experience is ¾ as large as the percentage of accountants with no MBA degree and less than five years of experience. Also, 35% of the accountants have MBA degrees, and 45% have less than five years of experience. If one of the firm's accountants is selected at random, what is the probability that this accountant has an MBA degree or at least five years of experience but not both?

*60. Consider a piece of equipment that is composed of two modules. Both modules must work for the equipment to work. Usually, equipment failure is caused by exactly one of the modules failing, but in some cases an outside shock can cause both modules to fail simultaneously. A large number of these pieces of equipment are put on test. After 400 hours, it is observed that 85% of the test units are still working, that module 1 has not failed on 87% of the test units, and that module 2 has not failed on 93% of the test units. What percentage of the test units have failed because of a simultaneous failure of both modules?

61. Consider a baseball player who comes to bat five times during a game.
   a. Is it reasonable to assume that the outcomes (success or no success) of his five successive at-bats are independent? Why or why not?
   b. Assuming that the successive outcomes *are* independent and that this batter has a .275 batting average (so that the probability of a success on any at-bat is .275), find the probability that (1) he gets five straight hits; (2) he gets no hits; (3) he gets at least one hit; (4) he gets no hits in his first two at-bats but gets at least two hits in his last three at-bats. (Assume that the only possibilities are a hit and an out.)

*62. Referring to Problem 61, assume that the successive outcomes are not independent. In particular, assume that the player is successful on his first at-bat with probability .275. From then on, if his previous at-bat was a success, his next at-bat will be a success with probability .325, but if his previous at-bat was not a success, his next at-bat will be a success with probability .245. Now calculate the probabilities requested in part (b) of Problem 61.

*63. In a certain population of college professors, 23% of the professors with tenure own some type of computer equipment. The similar figure for nontenured professors is 37%. Also, 45% of the professors are tenured.
   a. What is the probability that a randomly selected professor has tenure and some computer equipment?
   b. What is the probability that a randomly selected nontenured professor has some computer equipment?
   c. What is the probability that a randomly selected professor has some computer equipment?
   d. If E is the event that a randomly selected professor is tenured and F is the event that this professor has some computer equipment, are E and F independent events? Why or why not?

*64. In the airline industry, many flights are overbooked, that is, more tickets are sold than the number of available seats, with the expectation that some ticketed passengers will make last-minute cancellations. Let E_i be the event that passenger i (who has a ticket) does not cancel at the last minute. Assume that the passengers act independently of one another, so that the E_i's are independent events. If 176 tickets are sold for a 175-seat flight, and if each ticketed passenger shows up with probability .97, what is the probability that there will not be enough seats for all the passengers who show up? Answer this same question if 177 tickets are sold.

*65. Referring to Problem 64, suppose that 1% of all overbooked flights find themselves in the embarrassing position of having more passengers at flight time than seats. Suppose that 59% of these occur with short flights (less than 500 miles), and the other 41% occur with long flights.
   a. Find the probability that a randomly selected flight is a short flight *and* that it will run out of seats because of overbooking.
   b. Find the probability that a randomly selected flight is a long flight *and* that it will run out of seats because of overbooking.
   c. If it is known that 77% of all flights are short flights, what is the probability that a randomly selected short flight will run out of seats because of overbooking? What is the probability that a randomly selected long flight will run out of seats because of overbooking?

66. A nationwide department store chain has the following data on a randomly selected group of credit card purchasers. Each purchaser is categorized as (1) male or female, (2) over 30 years old or under 30, and (3) purchasers of at least $500 (with the credit card) within the past year or less than $500. The numbers below represent the percentages in the various categories. For a typical person randomly selected from this population, let E be the event that the person is male, let F be the event that the person is over 30, and let G be the event that the person purchased at least $500 of merchandise with a credit card.

| | Purchase Amount ||
	Less Than $500	At Least $500
Male over 30	20	15
Male under 30	17	4
Female over 30	18	7
Female under 30	15	4

a. Find $P(E$ and F and $G)$ and $P(E$ or F or $G)$.

b. Find $P(E$ or $F|G)$ and $P(E$ or $F|\overline{G})$.

c. Find $P(E|(F$ or $G))$ and $P(E|(F$ and $G))$.

d. Are E and F independent? What about E and G? What about F and G?

*67. Suppose it has been observed that it is twice as likely for the price of a certain stock to go up in a month when inflation rises as in a month when inflation falls. Let E be the event that the stock price rises in a given month, and let F be the event that inflation rises in this month.

a. Write a probability statement that reflects the information given.

b. Would you conclude that there are twice as many months when $(E$ and $F)$ occurs as when $(E$ and $\overline{F})$ occurs? Why or why not? (Use only the information given.)

c. If you are also told that inflation rises in 75% of all months, how would you answer part (b)?

*68. A high school math teacher has discovered through many years of experience that students are 1.5 times as likely to make a mistake on a "word" problem than on a "nonword" problem, even though each problem requires the same algebraic techniques. Let E be the event that a randomly selected student makes a mistake on a typical problem, and let F be the event that the problem is a word problem. The teacher typically gives 30% word problems and students typically do 25% of all problems incorrectly. Find $P(E$ and $F)$ and $P(E$ and $\overline{F})$.

*69. Let E be any event, and let F_1, F_2, ..., F_n be any events that "partition" the sample space S, that is, the F's are mutually exclusive and their union is S. State which of the following are true and which are false. If a statement is true, show why it is true. If a statement is false, give a numerical example to support your claim that it is false. (You might want to start by looking at the case when $n = 2$.)

a. $P(E) = P(E|F_1) + P(E|F_2) + \cdots + P(E|F_n)$

b. $P(E) = P(E$ and $F_1) + P(E$ and $F_2) + \cdots + P(E$ and $F_n)$

c. $P(E) = P(E|F_1)P(F_1) + P(E|F_2)P(F_2) + \cdots + P(E|F_n)P(F_n)$

d. $P(F_1|E) = \dfrac{P(E|F_1)P(F_1)}{P(E|F_1)P(F_1) + P(E|\overline{F_1})P(\overline{F_1})}$

*70. The definition of independence says that E and F are independent if $P(E|F) = P(E)$. Using this definition, show that if E and F are independent, their complements $\overline{E}$ and $\overline{F}$ are independent. [You must show that $P(\overline{E}|\overline{F}) = P(\overline{E})$.]

71. In an attempt to cut down on drunken driving on New Year's Eve, police initiate a system of stopping every tenth car passing a certain intersection for a spot check. If 8% of all drivers that night have had more than the legal limit to drink, what is the probability that the first 15 spot checks will catch at least three drunken drivers? (Formulate this as a sampling with replacement problem, since it is conceivable that the same person could be stopped more than once.)

72. A company that markets a certain brand of deodorant sends 1000 coupons to a randomly selected group of households in a large city, hoping that the recipients will go out and buy this brand at least once. If 60% of the population are loyal to another brand and would not try the company's brand with or without the coupon, find an expression for the probability that at least 450 of the coupons go to customers who might try the company's brand. (This expression should be a summation of terms involving binomial coefficients; do not try to evaluate it.) Do this under two different assumptions, as explained below.

a. Assume that the population size is 5000 households, and use the sampling without replacement formula.

b. Assume that the population size is extremely large, so that it is possible to act as if sampling is done with replacement.

73. In an attempt to discover how many fish are in a lake, a number of fish are caught, are "marked" in some way, and are then thrown back in. Later in the year, a second catch takes place and the number of marked fish is counted. Suppose that there are really 1000 fish in the lake, 40 of them are marked on the first catch, and 25 fish are caught in the second catch.

a. Find the probability of at least two marked fish in the second catch if each fish is kept (not thrown back in) on the second catch.

b. Find the probability requested in part (a) if each fish on the second catch is immediately thrown back in after it is caught. (This means that the same fish could be caught more than once.)

*74. A professor gives a difficult true-false test with 20 questions to a class of 15 students. From the results of the test—126 wrong answers out of a possible 300—the professor suspects that the students are really just guessing, that is, marking true or false randomly on each question. Given an expression (a summation involving binomial coefficients) for the probability of 126 or fewer wrong answers if all the students are in fact guessing. (Do not try to evaluate this expression.) If this expression turns out to have a fairly small value, say, less than .10, what might the professor conclude?

*75. In a certain population of 10,000 voters, suppose that 3000 plan to vote for the Republican in the upcoming election. Two polling agencies take *independent* polls of 100 voters each without replacement. For the questions below, do not do any calculations; just write the expressions requested.

  a. Write an expression (involving binomial coefficients) for the probability that 31 of those polled by the first agency plan to vote for the Republican *and* that 25 of those polled by the second agency plan to vote for the Republican. (This event is an intersection.)

  b. Write an expression (again involving binomial coefficients) for the probability that at least 35 of those polled by the first agency plan to vote for the Republican *and* that no more than 25 of those polled by the second agency plan to vote for the Republican.

  c. Find expressions that approximate the expressions in parts (a) and (b) by assuming that sampling is done with replacement. Do you suspect that these approximations are very accurate? Why or why not?

*76. Two researchers recently conducted a survey of approximately 100 female graduates of MBA programs. (Reference: Brooke Banbury-Masland and Daniel J. Brass, "Careers, Marriage, and Children: Are Women Changing Their Minds?" *Business Horizons,* May–June 1985, pp. 81–86.) Their purpose was to investigate attitudes and priorities concerning careers, family, and marriage. Of the respondents, 73% had graduated within the past five years, their average age was 30 years, 60% were married, 8% were divorced, and 22% had children. In one question, they were asked to rank the importance of having children, having a successful marriage, and having a successful career. They were asked to provide their current rankings and the rankings they would have given before they received the MBA degree. The results are shown below.

Before Receiving MBA (Percent)

Item	Ranked 1st	Ranked 2nd	Ranked 3rd
Children	6.0	12.6	81.4
Marriage	31.0	65.5	3.5
Career	63.0	21.9	15.1

Currently (Percent)

Item	Ranked 1st	Ranked 2nd	Ranked 3rd
Children	8.8	29.5	61.7
Marriage	60.0	29.6	10.4
Career	31.2	40.9	27.9

  a. Which percentages in the table above, if any, must logically add to 100? Why?

  b. If a female MBA is chosen randomly from this group, find the following probabilities, if possible, from the information given: (1) the probability that she doesn't currently rank having children third; (2) the probability that she ranked either having children or marriage first before receiving her MBA; (3) the probability that she currently ranks having children first, marriage second, and career third; (4) the probability that she ranked career first before receiving the MBA degree but currently ranks marriage first. If any of these probabilities cannot be found, indicate what further information is necessary.

*77. In the survey referenced in Problem 76, Banbury-Masland and Brass found the percentages of female MBA graduates in various categories who currently rank having children, marriage, or career as most important. These percentages are shown below. (Here "single" means not married and not divorced.)

Percent of Respondents, by Status, Who Ranked Each Item First

Item	Single	Married Without Children	Married with Children	Divorced
Children	3.1	2.4	27.2	25.0
Marriage	43.8	76.4	62.4	25.0
Career	53.1	21.2	10.4	50.0

  a. Now what percentages must logically add to 100? Why is this different from the answer to Problem 76a?

  b. If a female MBA is randomly selected from this group, what is the probability that she is single and ranks career most important? What is the probability that she ranks career most important, given that she is single? (Refer to the data from Problem 76.)

  c. For the randomly selected female MBA in part (a), find the probability that she ranks career most important. Assume that 55% of the married women have children.

*78. The results of a survey published in a 1980 issue of *Marketing News* indicate that many husbands are doing a significant amount of the household duties. (Reference: *Marketing News*, Oct. 3, 1980.) For example, the survey showed that 32% of the husbands shop for food, 47% cook for the family, and 29% do the laundry. However, husbands' attitudes toward their wives' place in the home versus the workplace were often conflicting. As an example, 62% said "the family is stronger if husband and wife share responsibilities, including providing income for the family,'' but 70% agreed that ''unless it's an economic necessity, a family is better off if the woman of the house does not work.'' Suppose that you randomly selected a husband from the group surveyed. Why is it impossible, given the percentages above, to find the probability that he would agree with *both* of these seemingly inconsistent statements? Nevertheless, explain why this probability must be between .32 and .62. Use the figure shown here.

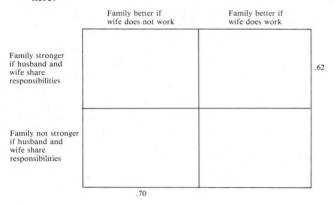

*79. There is a new word in the television vocabulary, zapping. This is the practice of not watching commercials. It can occur by switching channels or ''racing through'' a commercial on videotape. In studies of over 1500 adults and 400 children, Heeter and Greenberg found that most viewers can be categorized as ''zappers,'' those who frequently zap commercials, and ''nonzappers,'' those who almost never zap commercials. (Reference: Carrie Heeter and Bradley S. Greenberg, ''Profiling the Zappers,'' *Journal of Advertising Research*, Vol. 25, 1985, pp. 15–19.) They found that males are more

likely to zap, in the sense that 65% of all zappers are males, while only 37% of nonzappers are males. They also found that viewers with remote controls are more likely to zap, in the sense that 34% of zappers have remote controls, while only 27% of nonzappers own them. Although it is not stated in the article, let us assume that 40% of all viewers are zappers, 34% of the male zappers have remote controls, and 27% of the male nonzappers have remote controls.

a. Given the data, fill in the figure below; that is, find proportions p_1 through p_8 in the various joint categories that add to 1.

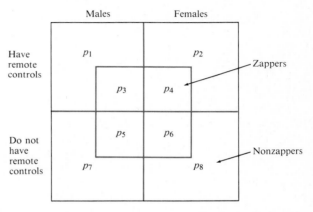

b. Suppose that we choose a viewer at random. Find the probability that this viewer is a zapper, given that the viewer is a male. Find the probability that this viewer is a zapper, given that the viewer has a remote control.

c. Which are more indicative of the fact that males and remote control owners are more likely to zap: the percentages given above or the probabilities from part (b)? For example, should we be looking at $P(\text{male}|\text{zapper})$ or $P(\text{zapper}|\text{male})$? Discuss.

APPENDIX 3A:

A Rationale for the With and Without Replacement Formulas

The reasoning behind the sampling with and without replacement formulas in Section 3.10 is enlightening. These formulas are repeated below.

Sampling With Replacement

$$P(E_k) = \frac{\binom{n}{k} N_A^k (N - N_A)^{n-k}}{N^n}$$

Sampling Without Replacement

$$P(E_k) = \frac{\binom{N_A}{k}\binom{N - N_A}{n - k}}{\binom{N}{n}}$$

First, notice that the denominator in each expression is N_S, the number of possible outcomes in the sample space. For sampling with replacement, $N_S = N^n$; for sampling without replacement, $N_S = \binom{N}{n}$. Therefore, by the formula for equally likely outcomes, we only need to verify that each numerator is the number of outcomes in the sample space with exactly k A's. We denote this number by N_k and calculate it below for each type of sampling.

For sampling with replacement, N_k can be found as follows. Any outcome with exactly k A's, being an ordered sequence, must have these k A's in k specific positions of the sequence. By the definition of binomial coefficients, these k positions can be chosen in $\binom{n}{k}$ ways. Once the k positions are chosen, there are N_A A's that can be put in each of the A positions, and there are $(N - N_A)$ B's that can be put in each of the B positions. By the basic product formula, we have

$$N_k = \binom{n}{k} N_A^k (N - N_A)^{n-k}$$

which is indeed the numerator of the ''with replacement'' formula for $P(E_k)$.

For sampling without replacement, we can think of ''building'' any outcome with exactly k A's in two stages. First we choose a subset of k A's from the N_A A's in the population. There are ''N_A choose k'' ways to do this.

Then we choose a subset of $(n - k)$ B's from the $(N - N_A)$ B's in the population. There are "$N - N_A$ choose $n - k$" ways to do this. Then the product rule says that the number of ways these two subsets can be put together is the product:

$$N_k = \binom{N_A}{k}\binom{N - N_A}{n - k}$$

Again this is what we wanted since it is the numerator of the "without replacement" formula.

References

BREIMAN, L. *Probability and Stochastic Processes: With a View Toward Applications*. Boston: Houghton Mifflin, 1969.

INGRAM, O., GLESER, L. J., and DERMAN, C. *Probability Models and Applications*. New York: Macmillan, 1980.

ROSS, S. *A First Course in Probability*, 3rd ed. New York: Macmillan, 1984.

Random Variables and Probability Distributions

Objectives

1. To learn what random variables represent.
2. To learn how to work with probability distributions.
3. To learn how the cumulative distribution function (cdf) of a random variable expresses its left-hand tail probabilities.
4. To learn the relationship between joint, marginal, and conditional distributions.
5. To learn the meaning of independent random variables.
6. To learn summary measures of a probability distribution, particularly the mean, the variance, and the standard deviation.
7. To learn how the covariance and correlation measure the relationship between two random variables.
8. To learn several rules of expected values.

Contents

When researchers attempt to study a system that has inherent uncertainty, they often build a "probability model" of this system. This is a mathematical representation of the system that can be analyzed (often with the aid of a computer) in order to provide valuable insights into the system. One type of system that has been studied extensively is a queueing, or waiting line, system. A perfect example of a queueing system occurs when we wait in one or more lines in a bank. In this queueing system, as in most others, there are two random quantities, the random times between customer arrivals to the bank, and the random times it takes the tellers to "serve" the customers once they are in the bank. These random times are considered inputs to the system. Once we know these inputs, we can derive important outputs, such as the average number of customers in the bank at any given time or the average amount of time a typical customer spends in the bank.

The keys to formulating a probability model of any such system are "probability distributions," which indicate how likely the possible values of the random quantities are. For example, the probability distribution of a typical customer service time might indicate that the probability of a customer service lasting longer than 5 minutes is only .1. The usual strategy in developing a probability model is to choose probability distributions for the random inputs (the times between customer arrivals and the customer service times) and then use the rules of probability to derive the probability distributions of the required outputs. Once these results have been obtained mathematically, they should be compared with observations from a real system. If the mathematical results do not match the observations adequately, then the mathematical analysis can be repeated with new probability distributions for the random inputs. Once there is an adequate match between mathematical results and actual observations, the probability model can be used to predict the effects of changes in the system, such as adding an extra teller when the waiting lines become sufficiently long.

4.1

Introduction

In this chapter we continue our discussion of probability in a very important direction. Recall that the sample space lists all the possible outcomes of any experiment. Often, we assign a numerical value to each outcome. For example, if the outcomes are sequences of defective and nondefective gears from a production line, we may be interested in the *number* of defective gears produced. If the outcomes are the identities of people selected in a survey, we may be interested in the *number* of women selected in the survey. If the outcomes indicate the direction of movement (up, down, or no change) of a stock price on several consecutive days, we may be interested in the *number* of days on which the price goes up. In each of these examples, the numerical value of interest is called a random variable. The probability distribution of a random variable specifies the probabilities of all its possible values. These two concepts, random variables and probability distributions, are the focus of study in this chapter.

There is a strong resemblance between the terminology used in this chapter and the terminology used in Chapter 2. Although the ideas are similar, they are not the same. In Chapter 2 we discussed descriptive measures for a specific set of numerical data. For example, we saw how to construct a frequency table, how to draw a histogram, and how to calculate summary measures such as means, variances, and covariances. All of this pertained to a set of existing data.

In this chapter we attempt to describe the properties of an entire population of data. Because the entire population of data is probably not available, we will approximate, or idealize, some of its characteristics. In the language of mathematics, we will build a *mathematical model* of the population. This model is usually not a perfect mirror image of the population, but it is usually a reasonable approximation. More important, this model enables us to study the characteristics of the population by using probability theory.

4.2

Random Variables

We begin our discussion with the extremely important concept of random variables. Consider any sample space. If we have a rule that assigns a numerical value to each outcome in this sample space, we obtain a random variable. Once any outcome has occurred, the value of the random variable is the number the rule assigns to this particular outcome.

> A random variable is a rule that assigns a numerical value to each outcome in a sample space.

The "random" in random variable implies that the value of the random variable is unknown until the outcome is observed; the "variable" implies that the value is numerical. Usually, a random variable is denoted by a capital letter near the end of the alphabet, such as X, Y, and Z, although other letters are certainly allowed. If there are many related random variables, it is convenient to label these by the same letter but to distinguish them with subscripts, such as X_1, X_2, and X_3.

When we make a statement such as "Let X be the random variable that represents the demand for refrigerators in the coming week," we imply that the value of X is not yet known. In this way, X is a variable just like ordinary variables in algebra. For example, in high school algebra, we learned the meaning of statements such as "Let x be the length of fence Mr. Jones needs for his yard." Here the variable x represents the length of fence Mr. Jones needs for his yard. We may manipulate the variable x according to the rules of algebra, and eventually we will find its value. Then we will make a statement such as "x equals 150 feet."

Precisely the same statements apply to random variables. The random variable X above represents the number of refrigerators that will be demanded in the coming week. We may manipulate X, using the rules of algebra, exactly as we manipulate algebraic variables. For example, if 50 refrigerators are demanded in the current week, $X - 50$ is the change in demand from this week to next week, and $X/50$ is the ratio of next week's demand to this week's demand. Eventually, after next week's demand has been observed, we can make a statement such as "X equals 65." At this point, X is no longer random; its value is 65.

The main difference between random variables and ordinary algebraic variables is that with random variables, we usually want to know the probabilities of their possible values *before* their values are observed. For example, we may wish to find the probability that fewer than 65 refrigerators will be demanded, $P(X < 65)$, or the probability that exactly 50 refrigerators will be demanded, $P(X = 50)$. To find the probabilities such as these, we must examine the "probability distribution" of X, the subject of the next section.

4.3
Probability Distributions of Random Variables

Let X be a random variable with possible values in a given set S. We know that X must equal *some* value in S, but we do not know which one. The probability distribution of X measures this uncertainty. It assigns probabilities to the possible values of X to reflect their relative likelihoods.

> The probability distribution of a random variable X specifies the probabilities of the possible values of X.

There are two types of random variables, discrete random variables and continuous random variables. A discrete random variable has only a finite number of possible values, whereas a continuous random variable has a continuum of possible values. (A discrete random variable may have a "countably infinite" number of possible values, such as *all* the nonnegative integers, but we will usually disregard this possibility. The only exception is the Poisson distribution in Chapter 5.)

> A discrete random variable has a finite or countably infinite number of possible values. A continuous random variable has a continuum of possible values.

The following example illustrates the difference between discrete and continuous random variables.

EXAMPLE 4.1

Consider customer arrivals to a bank, and let X be the random length of time between the 12th and 13th arrivals. Since X can have any positive value, it is a continuous random variable. However, if we let Y be the random number of arrivals in the first 15 minutes, Y is a discrete random variable. Its only possible values are the nonnegative integers 0, 1, 2, and so on.

Usually, the distinction between discrete and continuous random variables is the same as we discussed for quantitative data in Chapter 1. That is, discrete random variables usually arise from "counts," such as the *number* of arrivals, whereas continuous random variables usually arise from "measurements," such as the *time* between two arrivals.

The probability distributions corresponding to discrete and continuous random variables are called *discrete distributions* and *continuous distributions*. Both types of probability distributions provide the same information: they tell us how the total probability of 1 is assigned to the possible values of a random variable. However, in the discrete case we assign probabilities only to a finite set of values, whereas in the continuous case we need to spread the total probability over a continuum. The result is that discrete and continuous distributions are quite different mathematically. For this reason we discuss each type separately.

4.4
Discrete Distributions

If X is a discrete random variable, it has a finite or countably infinite set of possible values. We denote these values by $x_1, x_2, \ldots, x_N$. Then X must equal exactly one of the N values, x_1 through x_N. If we wish to refer to a typical possible value, we may omit the subscript and simply write x. (We are following the standard convention of denoting a random variable by a capital letter, such as X, and a typical possible value by a lowercase letter, such as x.)

It is conceptually very simple to specify the probability distribution of a discrete random variable. All we need to do is specify the probability of each possible x. The resulting probabilities are labeled $P(x_1), P(x_2), \ldots, P(x_N)$. We sometimes refer to this set of probabilities as the *probability mass function* of X, since $P(x)$ indicates how much "mass" of probability is assigned to the value x. Since the N probabilities must sum to 1, we have the following definition.

> The probability distribution (or probability mass function) of a discrete random variable X assigns a probability $P(x)$ to each possible value x so that
>
> $$\sum P(x) = 1$$

The notation $P(x)$ is really just shorthand for the probability that X equals the value x. Therefore, we often write $P(X = x)$ instead of $P(x)$. Also, we sometimes place a subscript such as X on $P(x)$, so that it becomes $P_X(x)$. This subscript is used only to remind us which random variable's probability distribution we are discussing. If there is no chance for confusion, this subscript will be omitted. (Similar comments apply to subscripts on other quantities, such as means and variances, that we will see later.)

Once we have specified the probability distribution of X, we can obtain the probability of any event E related to X. We simply sum the probabilities corresponding to the values of X that are favorable to E.

> *Probability of Any Event E*
>
> $$P(E) = \sum_{x \text{ in } E} P(x)$$

The "x in E" below the summation sign says to sum over those x's (and only those x's) favorable to E.

For a discrete random variable, this is all there is to it. We first list the possible values of X, we then assign a probability to each possible value, and finally, we sum the appropriate probabilities to calculate probabilities of events. The following examples illustrate this procedure.

EXAMPLE 4.2

Consider a population with three men and two women. We randomly select three people from this population and let X be the number of men in the sample. Find the probability distribution of X when sampling is done without replacement and when it is done with replacement.

SOLUTION

Although the required probabilities can be found from the formulas in Section 3.10, it is more instructive to start from scratch. First, assume that sampling is done without replacement. We label the three men M_1, M_2, and M_3 and the two women W_1 and W_2. Then any outcome indicates which three people are chosen. For example, the outcome $\{M_1, M_2, W_2\}$ says that the first two men and the second woman are chosen; hence $X = 2$. There are 10 outcomes altogether. These outcomes and the corresponding values of X are listed below.

$$\underbrace{\{M_1, W_1, W_2\}, \{M_2, W_1, W_2\}, \{M_3, W_1, W_2\}}_{X = 1}$$

$$\underbrace{\{M_1, M_2, W_1\}, \{M_1, M_2, W_2\}, \{M_1, M_3, W_1\}, \{M_1, M_3, W_2\}, \{M_2, M_3, W_1\}, \{M_2, M_3, W_2\}}_{X = 2}$$

$$\underbrace{\{M_1, M_2, M_3\}}_{X = 3}$$

Since these 10 outcomes are equally likely, $P(X = 1) = 3/10$, $P(X = 2) = 6/10$, and $P(X = 3) = 1/10$.

For sampling with replacement, we let the outcomes show the sampled members in the order they are chosen. For example, the outcome (M_1, M_2, M_1) indicates that man 1 is chosen first, man 2 is chosen second, and man 1 is chosen last. (Remember that when sampling is done with replacement, the same person can be chosen more than once.) There are $5^3 = 125$ such outcomes (each of three selections can be made in five ways). By listing these outcomes, we find that $X = 0$ for 8 outcomes, $X = 1$ for 36 outcomes, $X = 2$ for 54 outcomes, and $X = 3$ for 27 outcomes. (As an exercise, the reader should list the eight outcomes where $X = 0$.) Since the 125 outcomes are equally likely, $P(X = 0) = {}^{8}\!/_{125}$, $P(X = 1) = {}^{36}\!/_{125}$, $P(X = 2) = {}^{54}\!/_{125}$, and $P(X = 3) = {}^{27}\!/_{125}$.

It is often useful to graph a probability mass function. This lets us see at a glance which possible values are most likely, which are least likely, and in general how the total probability is assigned to the possible values. The usual method is to draw a line, or "spike," at each possible value, with a height proportional to the probability of that value. The graphs of the probability mass functions in Example 4.2 are shown in Figure 4.1.

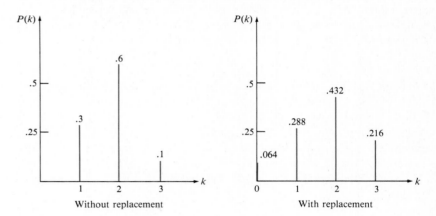

Figure 4.1

EXAMPLE 4.3

The Perfect Picture Camera Company has decided to launch an extensive advertising campaign. The cost of this campaign, exclusive of normal advertising costs, is estimated to be $2.5 million. Management estimates that this campaign will produce an extra X percentage points of the total market share and that each percentage point is worth $1.75 million in the short run. Although X is really a continuous random variable (because it has a continuum of possible values), management decides to treat it as a discrete random variable with possible values and probabilities shown in Table 4.1. Let Y be the net profit the company will obtain from this advertising campaign. Find the probability distribution of Y. Then find the probability that the increase in market share will offset the cost of the advertising campaign.

SOLUTION

Since X is a random variable and Y depends on X, Y is also a random variable. In fact, if Y is measured in millions of dollars, then $Y = 1.75X - 2.5$. This follows because each percentage point is worth $1.75 million and the adver-

Table 4.1

Possible Values of X	Probabilities of These Values
0	.05
.5	.07
1	.08
1.5	.15
2	.20
2.5	.20
3	.15
3.5	.05
4	.05

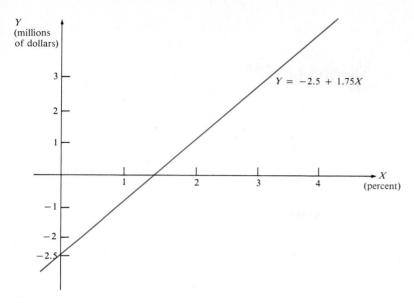

Figure 4.2

tising costs $2.5 million (see Figure 4.2). For example, when $X = 1.5$, the value of Y is

$$Y = 1.75(1.5) - 2.5 = .125 \text{ (or } \$125,000)$$

and the probability of this value is $P_Y(.125) = P_X(1.5) = .15$. (Notice that there is a subscript on each P in this example because there are two random variables involved.) Similarly, when $X = 3.5$,

$$Y = 1.75(3.5) - 2.5 = 3.625 \text{ (or } \$3,625,000)$$

and the probability of this value is $P_Y(3.625) = P_X(3.5) = .05$. Continuing in this way, we obtain the entire probability distribution of Y, as shown in Table 4.2.

Notice that a negative value of Y means a net loss for the company. In the cases where X equals 0, .5, or 1, the extra market share the company gains is not worth the advertising expense. The probability of a net loss is

$$P(Y < 0) = P_Y(-2.5) + P_Y(-1.625) + P_Y(-.75)$$
$$= P_X(0) + P_X(.5) + P_X(1)$$
$$= .05 + .07 + .08 = .20$$

So the probability that the company will make a profit is $1 - .20 = .80$.

Table 4.2

Possible Values of Y	Probabilities of These Values
−2.5	.05
−1.625	.07
−.75	.08
.125	.15
1	.20
1.875	.20
2.75	.15
3.625	.05
4.5	.05

Problems for Sections 4.2, 4.3, 4.4

1. A fair coin (heads and tails equally likely) is tossed twice. Let X be the number of heads observed. Find the probability distribution of X.

2. In Problem 1, suppose that two players observe the coin tosses. Competitor A wins \$1 (from competitor B) for every head and loses \$2 (to competitor B) for every tail. Let Y be competitor A's net winnings, which is negative if he loses. Find the probability distribution of Y.

3. A manuscript proofreader counted the number of typographical errors on each of 130 pages. The following data summarize the findings.

k	0	1	2	3	4
Number of pages with k errors	39	45	32	10	4

   a. Let X be the number of errors on a randomly selected page. Use a relative frequency approach to find the probability distribution of X.
   b. What is the probability of the event that X is less than 3?

4. Consider a random variable X with the following probability distribution: $P(0) = .1$, $P(1) = .3$, $P(2) = .2$, $P(3) = .1$, $P(4) = .3$. Find the probabilities of the following events: (a) $1 < X \leq 3$; (b) the intersection of $X < 2$ and $X \geq 3$; (c) the union of $X > 2$ and $X \leq 1$; (d) $X < 2$, given that $X < 3$.

5. A construction company has to complete a project no later than four months from now or there will be cost overruns. The people involved believe that there are four possible values for the random variable X, the number of months it will take to complete the project. These are 3, 3.5, 4, and 4.5 (all expressed in months). It is believed that the probabilities of these four possibilities are in the ratio 1 to 2 to 4 to 3. That is, $X = 3.5$ is twice as likely as $X = 3$, $X = 4$ is twice as likely as $X = 3.5$, and $X = 4.5$ is ¾ as likely as $X = 4$.
   a. Find the probability distribution of X.
   b. What is the probability that the project will be completed late?

6. a. An executive is attempting to arrange a meeting of his three top people for Wednesday afternoon. If he believes that each of these three people, independently of the others, has a .8 probability of being able to attend the meeting, find the probability distribution of X, the number of the three top people who attend the meeting.

   b. If the meeting will be held on Wednesday afternoon only if everyone can be there, what is the probability of this occurring?

7. At a checkout counter in a department store, a study has shown that the probability distribution of X, the number of customers in line (including the one being serviced, if any), is given by $P(0) = .3$, $P(1) = .25$, $P(2) = .2$, $P(3) = .15$, $P(\geq 4) = .1$. Here $P(\geq 4)$ represents the probability of at least four customers in line. Consider a newly arriving customer to the checkout line.
   a. What is the probability that this customer will not have to wait behind anyone?
   b. What is the probability that this customer will be behind at least two customers?

* 8. Based on anticipated demands, an appliance store stocks six humidifiers for the coming month. No regular orders for more humidifiers will be made until next month. The consumer demand for humidifiers has the following distribution:

Number Demanded	Probability
0	.02
1	.03
2	.05
3	.10
4	.25
5	.20
6	.15
7	.10
8	.05
9	.05
10 or more	.00

   a. Let X be the number of humidifiers left at the end of the month (if any), and let Y be the number of emergency shipments required (if any), assuming that an emergency shipment is required each time there is a demand and no unit is in stock. Find the probability distributions of X and Y.
   b. Assume that the company makes a \$30 profit on each unit sold from available stock, but it loses \$5 for each unit sold on an emergency order basis. Let Z be the profit the company makes this month. Find the probability distribution of Z.

Continuous Distributions

For discrete random variables, the conceptual idea behind a probability distribution is very simple. All we need to do is to distribute the total probability of 1 to a finite set of possible values. For continuous random variables, the procedure is not so simple. In this case the possible values represent a continuum, usually an interval such as all numbers between 0 and 100. Since there are infinitely many decimal numbers in any continuum, it is not feasible to assign a positive probability to each of them as we did in the discrete case. Therefore, we approach the problem in a somewhat indirect way.

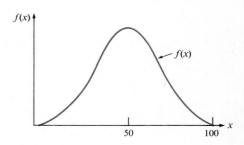

Figure 4.3
Typical Density Function

Instead of assigning a finite number of individual probabilities, we spread the total probability of 1 over the continuum of possible values in such a way that the more likely values receive more of the total probability. The function that accomplishes this is called the *probability density function* of the random variable X. It is usually denoted by $f(x)$, where x is any possible value of X.

This concept is illustrated graphically in Figure 4.3. In this figure the set of possible values is the interval from 0 to 100. Then the density function $f(x)$ is represented by a curve that lies above the horizontal axis on the interval from 0 to 100. The higher $f(x)$ is, the more likely x is. In this figure the values around 50 are most likely, while the values around 0 and around 100 are least likely.

> A density function $f(x)$ specifies the probability distribution of a continuous random variable X. The higher $f(x)$ is, the more likely x is.

In order to associate probabilities with the density function, we proceed as follows. We first scale the overall height of the curve so that the *area* between the curve and the horizontal axis is 1. This area represents the total probability of the sample space, which is 1. Then the probability that X is in any given interval, such as the interval from a to b, is the area under the curve between a and b. We illustrate this area in Figure 4.4.

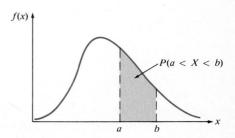

Figure 4.4
Probability as an Area Under the Density Function

> *Probability Formula for Continuous Random Variables*
>
> $P(a < X < b)$ = area under the density function between a and b

It is important to realize that the height of the curve at any point x, namely $f(x)$, is *not* a probability. We require $f(x)$ to be nonnegative, but we do not require $f(x)$ to be less than or equal to 1. The density values simply measure

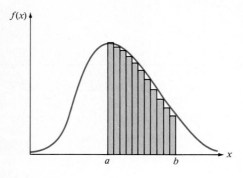

Figure 4.5
Approximating the Area Under the Curve
from *a* to *b*

relative likelihoods. This means that if $f(15)$ is twice as large as $f(20)$, then $P(15 - \Delta < X < 15 + \Delta)$ is approximately twice as large as $P(20 - \Delta < X < 20 + \Delta)$ for very small values of Δ. That is, the probability of X being "close" to 15 is approximately twice as large as the probability of X being "close" to 20.

Since probabilities of events are areas under the density function, we now look at methods for calculating these areas. The first method is to approximate the area under the curved region by many thin vertical rectangles, as shown in Figure 4.5. The reason we use rectangles is that the area of a rectangle is easily calculated as base times height. By summing the areas of these rectangles, we approximate the area of the curve. Although this method is certainly possible, it is very tedious to do by hand.

The second method is to use *calculus*. One branch of calculus, integral calculus, is designed precisely to find the area under a curve. In calculus terminology, the area under $f(x)$ between a and b is called the *definite integral* of $f(x)$ from a to b. Since calculus is not a prerequisite for this book, we will not pursue this method any further. However, for those readers with a calculus background, the appendix to this chapter shows how calculus can be used for continuous distributions.

The third method provides the simplest way to find areas under curves. Since the same density functions keep arising in statistical applications, mathematicians have numerically tabulated the areas we will need. These tables appear in Appendix B in the back of the book. (The method mathematicians use to construct these tables is essentially the approximation method illustrated in Figure 4.5.) In future chapters, whenever we want to find a probability for a continuous random variable, we will look up the appropriate area in the appropriate table in Appendix B. We postpone a discussion of these tables until later chapters, when we study the specific densities involved.

Three Ways of Finding Areas Under Curves

1. Approximate by summing areas of many thin rectangles (see Figure 4.5).
2. Use calculus (see the appendix to this chapter).
3. Use the tables in Appendix B.

A Note About Inequalities

If X is a continuous random variable and x is a possible value of X, the probability $P(X = x)$ must be set equal to 0. This does not mean that the event $X = x$ cannot occur. It simply means that there is no *mathematical* way to assign positive probabilities to these events. The reason is that there are too many possible values of X.

The fact that $P(X = x)$ equals 0 for each x does have one nice implication.

It means that when events are defined in terms of inequalities, it does not matter whether these inequalities are "weak" inequalities ($\leq$ or $\geq$) or "strict" inequalities ($<$ or $>$). For example, if X is a continuous random variable,

$$P(2 < X < 5) = P(2 \leq X < 5) = P(2 < X \leq 5) = P(2 \leq X \leq 5)$$

Remember, though, that this applies only to continuous random variables. With discrete random variables, we need to be more careful.

4.6
Cumulative Distribution Functions

In this section we discuss another method of specifying probability distributions. This method is applicable to discrete *and* continuous random variables. We do so by means of a *cumulative distribution function*, abbreviated *cdf*, and usually denoted $F(x)$. For any random variable X, discrete or continuous, we define the cdf $F(x)$ by $F(x) = P(X \leq x)$, where x is any specified number. This probability is called a left-hand tail probability, since we want X to have a value to the left of x on a number line.

> The cumulative distribution function (cdf) of a random variable X specifies all left-hand tail probabilities of X. The formula for the cdf is $F(x) = P(X \leq x)$.

If X is a discrete random variable, the definition of $F(x)$ reduces to the following formula.

> *Discrete CDF Formula*
> $$F(x) = \sum_{x_i \leq x} P(x_i)$$

That is, we sum the probabilities of all values less than or equal to x. (This x value does *not* have to be one of the possible values of X.)

EXAMPLE 4.2 (continued)

Again let X be the number of men in a sample of size 3 when sampling is done without replacement. Find the cdf of X.

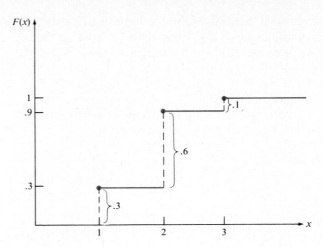

Figure 4.6
Cdf for Example 4.2

SOLUTION

Recall that the distribution of X is given by $P(1) = .3$, $P(2) = .6$, and $P(3) = .1$. This implies that the cdf can be expressed in four "pieces": (1) if $x < 1$, $F(x) = P(X \leq x) = 0$; (2) if $1 \leq x < 2$, $F(x) = P(X \leq x) = .3$; (3) if $2 \leq x < 3$, $F(x) = P(X \leq x) = .3 + .6 = .9$; and (4) if $x \geq 3$, $F(x) = P(X \leq x) = .3 + .6 + .1 = 1$. Notice that when x is a possible value of X, the value of $F(x)$ includes the probability of x. For example, $F(2)$ includes the probability of 2 because $F(2) = P(X \leq 2)$. The graph of $F(x)$ for this example is shown in Figure 4.6.

If X is a continuous random variable, $F(x)$ is the area under the density function to the left of x. We illustrate this graphically in Figure 4.7.

Continuous CDF Formula

$F(x)$ = area under the density function to the left of x

It is important to realize that the cdf contains exactly the same information as the probability mass function or the probability density function. If we know the cdf, we can find the probability mass function or the density function; if we know the probability mass function or the probability density function, we can find the cdf.

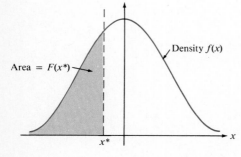

Figure 4.7

Let's see how this works in the discrete case. Let X be a discrete random variable with possible integer values 0 through n. For any value x, $F(x)$ can be calculated from the individual probabilities by summation. (We did this in the example above.) Conversely, if the cdf is given, we can find $P(k)$, for any k, from

$$P(k) = P(X = k) = P(X \le k) - P(X \le k - 1) = F(k) - F(k - 1)$$

[Notice that this formula is valid even when $k = 0$, because $F(-1) = 0$ for any nonnegative random variable.] The following example illustrates the procedure numerically.

EXAMPLE 4.4

Suppose that an automobile insurance company's records show the fraction of all policyholders who have had k or fewer accidents for each possible value of k. This information is listed in Table 4.3. (For simplicity we assume that none of the policyholders has had more than five accidents.) Let X be the number of accidents a typical customer has had. Then the cdf of X follows from the table: $F(x) = 0$ for $x < 0$, $F(x) = .32$ for $0 \le x < 1$, $F(x) = .58$ for $1 \le x < 2$, $F(x) = .67$ for $2 \le x < 3$, $F(x) = .85$ for $3 \le x < 4$, $F(x) = .96$ for $4 \le x < 5$, and $F(x) = 1$ for $x \ge 5$. The graph of $F(x)$ is shown in Figure 4.8. Now we can find the individual probabilities for X by subtraction:

$$P(0) = F(0) - F(-1) = .32 - 0 = .32$$
$$P(1) = F(1) - F(0) = .58 - .32 = .26$$
$$P(2) = F(2) - F(1) = .67 - .58 = .09$$
$$P(3) = F(3) - F(2) = .85 - .67 = .18$$
$$P(4) = F(4) - F(3) = .96 - .85 = .11$$
$$P(5) = F(5) - F(4) = 1.0 - .96 = .04$$

Table 4.3

k	Proportion with No More Than k Accidents
0	.32
1	.58
2	.67
3	.85
4	.96
5	1.0

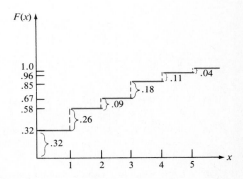

Figure 4.8
Cdf for Example 4.4

If X is a continuous random variable, we are usually interested in finding probabilities of intervals, such as $P(0 < X < 5)$, $P(X < 7)$, or $P(X \ge 10)$. We claimed earlier that these can usually be found in tables. This is where the cdf is relevant. The tables in statistics texts are usually tables of left-hand tail probabilities (or their complements, right-hand tail probabilities). So when we use these tables in future chapters, we will actually be finding cdf values.

Problems for Sections 4.5, 4.6

9. For the probability density function of X shown below, find the value of c required. Then find the probability that the random variable X is between 15 and 30.

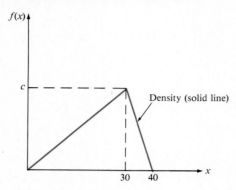

10. The number of miles a certain type of tire can be driven under normal driving conditions is a random variable X with a density function as shown below. The numbers inside the curve are specified areas.

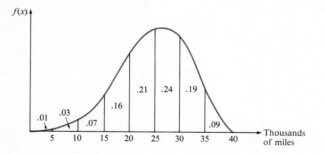

   a. What is the probability that a typical tire will wear out before 20,000 miles of driving?
   b. Is it fair to say that about 90% of these tires last between 15,000 and 35,000 miles of driving? Why or why not?

11. In a large batch of manufactured items, the fraction X of defective items is unknown and is treated as a random variable. Its density function is shown at the top of the next column, with areas indicated.

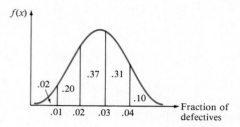

   a. What is the probability that no more than 3% of the items are defective?
   b. What can you say about the probability that at least 2.5% of the items are defective? (Find an upper and a lower bound for this probability.)

12. The cdf of a discrete random variable X is given as follows: $F(0) = 0$, $F(1) = .4$, $F(2) = .6$, $F(3) = .7$, $F(4) = 1$.
   a. Find the probability mass function of X.
   b. Find the probability of the event $1 < X < 4$ directly from the cdf values.

13. A study of U.S. population characteristics reveals the following divorce data for 3000 men in their 60s:

Number of Divorces	Number of Men with This Many Divorces
0	1506
1	1121
2	322
3	43
4	8
5 or more	0

   If one of these men is chosen at random, and X is the number of divorces he has had, list and graph the cdf of X.

14. Consider the following left-hand tail probabilities $P(X \le k)$ for a discrete random variable X. (The only possible values of X are multiples of 5 between 0 and 25.)

k	0	5	10	15	20	25
$P(X \le k)$	.20	.60	.60	.75	.80	1.0

a. Construct a similar table of the right-hand tail probabilities $P(X \geq k)$.
b. Construct a similar table of the individual probabilities $P(X = k)$.

15. Given the density function for the fraction of defective items

in Problem 11, find each of the following cdf values. Also interpret them as probabilities of appropriate events: (a) $F(.02)$; (b) $1 - F(.01)$; (c) $F(.04) - F(.02)$.

4.7

Joint Distributions

The discussion to this point has dealt with the distribution of a *single* random variable. Often we have a situation that involves two or more related random variables. Each of these has a probability distribution of the type we have already discussed. But we may be more interested in events that involve several random variables simultaneously. Then it is not enough to know how the random variables behave individually; we need to know how they behave *jointly*. This joint behavior of several random variables is specified by their *joint probability distribution*.

> The joint distribution of several random variables specifies the probabilistic relationship between these random variables.

We will discuss only the joint distribution of *two* random variables. This is called a *bivariate* distribution. (Although the same ideas carry over to joint distributions of more than two random variables, the notation becomes quite complex.) Furthermore, we will assume that both random variables are discrete.

> A bivariate distribution is the joint distribution of two random variables.

Let X and Y be discrete random variables with possible values $x_1, x_2, \ldots, x_M$ and $y_1, y_2, \ldots, y_N$, respectively. (Again, we may omit the subscripts on the x's and y's if we want to talk about a typical pair.) To specify the joint distribution of X and Y, we need to assign $M \times N$ *joint probabilities*. These probabilities, denoted by $P(x, y)$, are probabilities of intersections. That is, $P(x, y)$ is the probability that $X = x$ *and* $Y = y$.

> *Joint Probability Distribution of X and Y*
>
> $$P(x, y) = P(X = x \text{ and } Y = y)$$
>
> for each possible pair (x, y)

If M and N are not too large, it is customary to list the joint probabilities in a rectangular array. As an example, let X and Y represent the number of IBM and Apple personal computers sold in the coming year at a local computer store. For simplicity, assume that the possible values of X are 30, 35, 40, and 45, and the possible values of Y are 25, 30, and 35. Then $M = 4$ and $N = 3$, and we have the joint probability distribution illustrated in Table 4.4. The 12 probabilities inside the rectangle have been chosen arbitrarily, subject to the provision that they sum to 1. (In any actual situation, these probabilities would probably be assessed subjectively, as discussed in Chapter 3.) Table 4.4 gives us the joint probability of any possible pair. For example, it shows that the probability of 40 IBM sales and 25 Apple sales is .08.

Table 4.4   Joint Distribution of X and Y

		\multicolumn{4}{c}{IBM Sales (X)}		
		30	35	40	45	
Apple	25	.03	.05	.08	.09	.25
Sales	30	.10	.15	.15	.10	.50
(Y)	35	.08	.09	.05	.03	.25
		.21	.29	.28	.22 ←	Marginal distributions

Marginal Distributions

In addition to joint behavior, we may want to know the distribution of each random variable separately. This information is found by summing the appropriate joint probabilities. Referring to Table 4.4, we can find $P(X = 35)$ by summing down the $X = 35$ column. This gives $P(X = 35) = .29$. Similarly, we can find $P(Y = 30)$ by summing across the $Y = 30$ row. This gives $P(Y = 30) = .50$. By similar calculations we can find $P(X = x)$ for each possible x and $P(Y = y)$ for each possible y. The results are shown in the right-hand and lower margins of Table 4.4. These probabilities specify the *marginal distributions* of X and Y. In general, we have the following formula and definition. (Only the formula for the marginal distribution of X is given; the marginal distribution of Y is found similarly.)

> $P(X = x) = \sum P(X = x \text{ and } Y = y)$, where the sum is over all y's
>
> A marginal distribution is the probability distribution of a single random variable (in a context where there are several random variables).

The marginal probabilities can be found from the joint probabilities, but the opposite is not true. To illustrate this, imagine that we had omitted the joint probabilities in Table 4.4 and had given only the marginal totals. Then we could not calculate the joint probabilities from the marginal probabilities in a unique way. There are many sets of joint probabilities that yield the *same* marginal totals. We show two possibilities in Table 4.5.

Table 4.5   Joint Distributions with the Same Marginals

		IBM Sales (X)							IBM Sales (X)				
		30	35	40	45				30	35	40	45	
	25	.09	.08	.05	.03	.25		25	.0525	.0725	.07	.055	.25
Apple Sales (Y)	30	.08	.16	.16	.10	.50	Apple Sales (Y)	30	.105	.145	.14	.11	.50
	35	.04	.05	.07	.09	.25		35	.0525	.0725	.07	.055	.25
		.21	.29	.28	.22				.21	.29	.28	.22	
		(a)							(b)				

Conditional Distributions

We now discuss a third type of probability distribution, the conditional probability distribution of one random variable given the value of another.

> A conditional distribution specifies the probability distribution of one random variable, given the value of the other.

If we are given the value of Y, say $Y = y$, the conditional distribution of X specifies all conditional probabilities of the form $P(X = x \mid Y = y)$. By the conditional probability formula from Chapter 3, this probability is

$$P(X = x \mid Y = y) = \frac{P(X = x \text{ and } Y = y)}{P(Y = y)} = \frac{P(x, y)}{P_Y(y)}$$

Similarly, the conditional probability of Y, given $X = x$, is

$$P(Y = y \mid X = x) = \frac{P(x, y)}{P_X(x)}$$

Table 4.6   Conditional Distributions

		IBM Sales (X)						IBM Sales (X)		
		30	35	40	45			30	35	40	45
Apple Sales (Y)	25	.12	.20	.32	.36	Apple Sales (Y)	25	.143	.172	.286	.409
	30	.20	.30	.30	.20		30	.476	.517	.536	.455
	35	.32	.36	.20	.12		35	.381	.311	.178	.136

(a) Distribution of X, given Y (b) Distribution of Y, given X

In words, the conditional probability of one random variable given the other is the joint probability divided by the marginal probability of the given random variable.

We illustrate these formulas in Table 4.6. Table 4.6a lists the conditional probabilities of IBM sales (X) given Apple sales (Y); Table 4.6b lists the conditional probabilities of Apple sales (Y) given IBM sales (X). These conditional probabilities are derived from the joint probabilities in Table 4.4. Two of the calculations are shown below:

$$P(X = 35 \mid Y = 30) = \frac{P(X = 35 \text{ and } Y = 30)}{P(Y = 30)} = \frac{.15}{.50} = .30$$

and

$$P(Y = 35 \mid X = 40) = \frac{P(X = 40 \text{ and } Y = 35)}{P(X = 40)} = \frac{.05}{.28} = .178$$

The other calculations are similar.

In Table 4.6a, notice that the probabilities in any row sum to 1. This follows because some IBM sales value must occur, no matter how many Apples are sold. For an analogous reason, the probabilities in each column of Table 4.6b sum to 1.

4.8

Independent Random Variables

The probabilities in Table 4.6 (or Table 4.4) show that sales of IBMs and sales of Apples are related in a probabilistic way. For example, if 25 Apples are sold, the IBM sales figure with the highest probability is 45. But if 30 Apples are sold, the IBM sales figure with the highest probability is 35 (or 40). This means that knowledge of one variable influences our thinking about the other variable.

Table 4.7 Distribution of X, given Y, with Independence

| | | IBM Sales (X) | | | |
		30	35	40	45
Apple Sales (Y)	25	.21	.29	.28	.22
	30	.21	.29	.28	.22
	35	.21	.29	.28	.22

Now consider the joint probabilities given in Table 4.5b. The associated conditional probabilities of IBM sales given Apple sales are shown in Table 4.7. Notice that the rows in this table are not only identical, but they are the same as the *marginal* probabilities for IBM sales. For each possible sales figure x, we have

$$P(X = x) = P(X = x \mid Y = 25) = P(X = x \mid Y = 30) = P(X = x \mid Y = 35)$$

The random variables X and Y in this example are said to be *independent*. More formally, X and Y are independent (discrete) random variables if $P(X = x) = P(X = x \mid Y = y)$ for every x and y. If this is true, it is also true that $P(Y = y) = P(Y = y \mid X = x)$ for every x and y. Therefore, X and Y play symmetric roles in the definition of independence.

X and Y are independent (discrete) random variables if

$$P(X = x) = P(X = x \mid Y = y) \qquad \text{for each } x \text{ and } y$$

The concept of independence can be extended to more than two random variables in a natural way. Intuitively, any collection of random variables are independent if information about any of them is irrelevant for predicting the others.

Independence of two or more random variables is an extremely important concept in statistics. Many statistical results begin with the statement: "Assume that $X_1, X_2, \ldots, X_n$ are n independent random variables." Therefore, we ask two important questions. First, why do we want random variables to be independent, and second, how do we know (or check) whether random variables are independent?

The answer to the first question is simple. We want random variables to be independent because calculations are much easier when they are independent. To see why this is true, consider the joint probability $P(X = x, Y = y)$. By using the multiplication rule for intersections, we have

$$P(X = x, Y = y) = P(X = x \text{ and } Y = y) = P(X = x \mid Y = y)P(Y = y)$$

But if X and Y are independent, $P(X = x \mid Y = y) = P(X = x)$. Therefore, we obtain the important formula that the joint probability *factors* into the product of the marginals.

Multiplication Formula for Independent Random Variables

$$P(X = x, Y = y) = P(X = x)P(Y = y)$$

when X and Y are independent

This multiplication formula can be generalized as follows. Suppose that $X_1, X_2, \ldots, X_n$ are n independent random variables. Also, suppose that $A_1, A_2, \ldots, A_n$ are any events with the property that A_i depends *only* on the value of X_i (and not on the values of the other X's). Then we have the following multiplication formula (which applies to any set of independent random variables, discrete or continuous):

$$P(A_1 \text{ and } A_2 \text{ and } \ldots \text{ and } A_n) = P(A_1)P(A_2) \cdots P(A_n)$$

This multiplication formula is extremely important. It says that probabilities of intersections (where each individual event depends on only a single random variable) can be calculated as the product of the individual probabilities. The reason this is convenient is that each probability in the product can be found from the *marginal* distribution of the corresponding random variable.

EXAMPLE 4.5

Assume that the sales of IBMs and the sales of Apples are independent random variables with the joint distribution given in Table 4.5b. Find the probability of selling no more than 35 IBMs and at least 30 Apples.

SOLUTION

Here we need the joint probability $P(X \leq 35 \text{ and } Y \geq 30)$. This could be found directly from Table 4.5b by summing all joint probabilities that lead to this event, namely, $.105 + .145 + .0525 + .0725 = .375$. But because of independence, the required probability can also be found from the multiplication formula:

$$P(X \leq 35 \text{ and } Y \geq 30) = P(X \leq 35)P(Y \geq 30)$$
$$= (.21 + .29)(.50 + .25) = .375$$

This approach requires only marginal, not joint, probabilities.

In the following example, we illustrate the multiplication formula when each random variable is continuous with a *uniform* density on the interval from 0 to 1. This density, shown in Figure 4.9, is very simple to use because it is flat. It is also useful because tables of "random numbers," as well as random numbers generated on a computer, have this density.

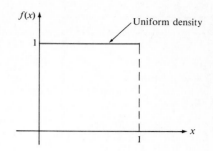

Figure 4.9

EXAMPLE 4.6

Suppose that we use a computer to generate 20 random numbers on the interval from 0 to 1. Find the probability that all of them are between .05 and .95.

SOLUTION

Let $X_1, X_2, \ldots, X_{20}$ be the 20 numbers generated. Then it can be shown that these 20 X's are independent and that each has the marginal density shown in Figure 4.9. For any i from 1 to 20, let A_i be the event that X_i is between .05 and .95. We are interested in the joint probability that *all* 20 A's occur. By independence, this joint probability is

$$P(A_1 \text{ and } A_2 \text{ and } \ldots \text{ and } A_{20}) = P(A_1)P(A_2)\cdots P(A_{20})$$
$$= P(.05 < X_1 < .95)\cdots P(.05 < X_{20} < .95)$$

For each i, $P(.05 < X_i < .95)$ is the area under the uniform density from .05 to .95, and this area is clearly .9 (see Figure 4.10). Therefore,

$$P(A_1 \text{ and } A_2 \text{ and } \ldots \text{ and } A_{20}) = .9^{20} = .122$$

This means that there is about 1 chance in 8 of generating 20 consecutive random numbers between .05 and .95. Alternatively, it means the chances are about 7 out of 8 that at least 1 of the 20 random numbers will be less than .05 or greater than .95.

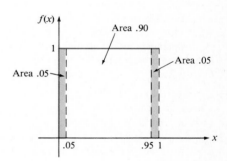

Figure 4.10

How do we know whether random variables are independent? In some applications the answer may be obvious. For example, we probably cannot assume independence of a store's sales of IBM and Apple computers; the sales of one probably occur at the expense of the other. On the other hand, if X is the sales level of IBMs in 1987 and Y is the sales level of Apples in 1997, we can probably assume independence of X and Y. Whatever effects 1987 IBM sales have on 1997 Apple sales are probably negligible.

In many cases, however, the answer to our question is not obvious. Fortunately, if we observe data related to X and Y, there are statistical methods for determining whether independence is a reasonable assumption. One test for independence is covered in Chapter 13.

Problems for Sections 4.7, 4.8

16. By examining past weather data for many years, the weather forecaster in a midwestern city estimates the joint distribution of X_1 and X_2, where X_1 is the number of "heavy" snowfalls in a typical year, and X_2 is the number of heavy snowfalls in the next year. That is, X_1 and X_2 are measured in consecutive years. The joint probabilities are shown below. The following questions pertain to the next two years in the future, referred to as year 1 and year 2.

			X_1		
		0	1	2	3 or more
	0	.03	.04	.02	.01
X_2	1	.04	.16	.10	.10
	2	.02	.10	.12	.06
	3 or more	.01	.10	.06	.03

a. What is the probability there will be at least two heavy snowfalls in year 1; in year 2?
b. What is the probability that neither year 1 nor year 2 will experience more than one heavy snowfall?
c. What is the probability there will be at least three heavy snowfalls in the next two years combined?

17. A supermarket has one regular checkout line and one express line. (Six or fewer items are required to join the express line.) Let X_1 and X_2 be the numbers of customers in the two lines at a typical point in time, with the joint distribution given below. Notice that X_1 and X_2 include the persons being served, if any, as well as those waiting in line.

			X_1 (express)		
		0	1	2	3 or more
	0	.10	.05	.02	.03
X_2	1	.05	.05	.04	.16
(regular)	2	.06	.05	.03	.10
	3 or more	.09	.05	.01	.11

a. What is the probability that no one is waiting in the regular line; in the express line? (Interpret "waiting" to mean "not yet being served.")

b. What is the probability that no more than one customer is waiting in both lines combined?
c. Consider an arriving customer who is eligible to go into either line, that is, with six items or less. What is the probability that this customer will be able to go into service immediately with no waiting?

18. Consider two identical electronic games. Each requires three batteries to operate, but right now neither is working on account of dead batteries. In game 1, the number of dead batteries is a random variable X_1 with probability distribution: $P(X_1 = 1) = .5$, $P(X_1 = 2) = .3$, $P(X_1 = 3) = .2$. An identical statement can be made about the number of dead batteries, X_2, in game 2. Also, X_1 and X_2 are assumed to be independent random variables.
a. Fill in a table of the joint probabilities for X_1 and X_2.
b. If you are told that game 1 has two dead batteries, what can you say about the number of dead batteries in game 2?

19. In Problem 18, what is the probability that there are enough (at least three) working batteries left to make one of the games operate?

20. Again referring to Problem 18, let Y be the number of batteries we would need to buy to make both games operate, that is, to obtain six good batteries total. Find the probability distribution of Y.

21. In a competitive industry, the price and demand for an item are both unknown quantities. Suppose that the manufacturer of a highly competitive product assesses the joint distribution of price (per unit) P and demand D for its product for the next year as follows.

		Price		
		$25.00	$27.50	$30.00
Demand	15,000	.05	.30	.08
	16,000	.07	.15	.07
	17,000	.08	.15	.05

a. How can you tell from the table that P and D are not independent random variables?
b. Find the probability that price is no more than $27.50 and demand is less than 17,000 (the intersection).

c. Find the probability that total revenue (price times demand) is at least \$440,000. (*Hint:* In which of the nine joint categories is total revenue at least this high?)

22. The following table shows the conditional distribution of the daily number of accidents on a given highway, X_2, given the amount of rainfall (in inches) for the day, X_1. The marginal distribution of X_1 is also shown in the bottom margin.

		X_1			
		0	.5	1.0	1.5
	0	.80	.76	.72	.60
X_2	1	.13	.12	.10	.14
	2	.05	.06	.08	.10
	3	.02	.06	.10	.16
		.70	.25	.03	.02

a. How can you tell from the table that X_1 and X_2 are not independent random variables?
b. Fill in a table of joint probabilities for X_1 and X_2.
c. What is the probability of at least one accident on a given day?

23. A store sells two competing brands of electronic video games. Let X_1 and X_2 be the numbers of the two brands sold on a typical day. From historical data, the joint probability distribution of X_1 and X_2 is assessed as follows.

		X_1			
		0	1	2	3
	0	.01	.03	.06	.09
X_2	1	.02	.06	.12	.09
	2	.03	.12	.06	.09
	3	.04	.09	.06	.03

a. Are X_1 and X_2 independent random variables? Why or why not?
b. Convert this table into a table of conditional probabilities of X_1 given X_2.
c. Convert this table into a table of conditional probabilities of X_2 given X_1.
d. Considering the tables in parts (b) and (c), would you accept or refute the claim that brand 2 sales are often made at the expense of brand 1 sales, and vice versa? Why?

24. Two side-by-side elevators service a three-story building. At any point in time when both elevators are stationary, let X_1 and X_2 be the floor numbers at which elevators 1 and 2 are currently stationed. The joint probability distribution of X_1 and X_2 is given below.

			X_1	
		1	2	3
	1	.20	.10	.20
X_2	2	.10	.03	.07
	3	.20	.07	.03

a. Are X_1 and X_2 independent random variables? Why or why not?
b. What is the probability that both elevators are stationed at the same floor?
c. What is the probability that elevator 1 is at floor 1, given that elevator 2 is not there?
d. What is the probability that a person arriving at the top floor elevators will find one available there?

25. Consider a sample of size 500 chosen from a population of men and women. Let X_1 be the number of men in the sample, and let X_2 be the number of women in the sample. Why is it impossible for X_1 and X_2 to be independent?

26. Consider the demand–price probabilities given in Problem 21. Which joint probabilities result in the same *marginal* probabilities for P and D as given earlier but make P and D independent random variables?

27. In a certain section of a large city, the police department has experimented with the number of police cars patrolling the neighborhood to see whether the number of robberies is affected. The following table shows the data that have been collected. Each day has had (1) either zero, one, two, or three robberies reported; and (2) either one, two, or three patrol cars in the neighborhood. The numbers in the table represent the numbers of days in the various joint categories.

		Number of Robberies			
		0	1	2	3
Number of Patrol Cars	1	25	15	7	3
	2	40	20	8	2
	3	20	8	1	1

a. Convert the frequency table into a table of conditional probabilities of X_1, the number of reported robberies on a typical day, given X_2, the number of patrol cars used that day.

b. Do these data suggest that X_1 and X_2 from part (a) are independent random variables? Why or why not?

28. A study on alcoholic beverage purchases in supermarkets revealed the following data. Each of 20 consumers was monitored for 12 consecutive weeks, for a total of 240 observations. Each observation included the number of bottles of wine and the number of six-packs of beer purchased. The frequencies of the possible joint categories are shown below.

		Number of Six-Packs of Beer		
		0	1	2 or more
	0	56	12	7
Number of	1	42	38	25
Bottles of Wine	2	12	10	13
	3 or more	5	5	15

a. Based on these relative frequencies, find the probability of the event that $X_1 \geq 1$ and $X_2 \geq 1$, where X_1 and X_2 are, respectively, the number of six-packs of beer and the number of bottles of wine purchased by a typical consumer.

b. What is the probability that a typical consumer buys some beer or some wine, but not both?

29. Suppose that four tires of the type discussed in Problem 10 (p. 154) are put on four separate cars. Let X_1, X_2, X_3, and X_4 be the number of miles the tires last under normal driving conditions.

a. Why is it reasonable to assume that X_1 through X_4 are independent? (Give an intuitive reason.)

b. Referring to the graph in Problem 10 and assuming independence of the X's, what is the probability that all four of the tires will last at least 20,000 miles? What is the probability that none of the tires will last more than 30,000 miles?

30. Assume that the household incomes in a city are distributed as in the graph below, where the numbers in the graph indicate areas. This means that if a household is chosen randomly from this city and X is its income, this graph represents the probability density of X.

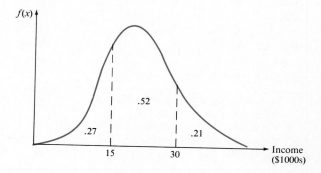

a. Consider three households chosen at random from this city and let X_1, X_2, and X_3 be their incomes. Why is it reasonable to assume that X_1, X_2, and X_3 are independent random variables? (Give an intuitive reason.)

b. Assuming independence of X_1, X_2, and X_3, find the probability that at least one of the households has an income between $15,000 and $30,000.

c. Again assuming independence of X_1, X_2, and X_3, find the probability that none of the households has an income over $15,000.

4.9
Summary Measures
of Probability Distributions

We often wish to summarize a probability distribution by means of one or two numbers. In this section we look at several of the more important summary measures: the mean, variance, standard deviation, covariance, and correlation. For simplicity, we discuss only discrete distributions. Readers with a sufficient calculus background may refer to the appendix at the end of this chapter for a brief account of summary measures of continuous distributions.

The summary measures in this chapter are obviously related to the measures in Chapter 2 since they have the same names. However, it is important to understand how the measures here differ from those in Chapter 2. In Chapter 2 we were dealing with a set of existing data. All the formulas for the summary measures were then expressions involving these data. In this chapter we do not have a set of data. All we have now is a probability distribution. Therefore, the summary measures in this chapter must be expressed entirely in terms of these probability distributions. To distinguish the measures in Chapter 2 from those discussed here, we often prefix the former by the adjective "sample" since they are computed from sample data.

The Mean

As in Chapter 2, there are three principal measures of central tendency of a probability distribution: the mean, the median, and the mode. For statistical purposes the mean is by far the most frequently used of these three, so we limit our discussion to the mean in this chapter.

Let X be a discrete random variable with probability distribution $P(x)$. Then the mean of this probability distribution, denoted by μ, is an average of the possible values of X, weighted by their probabilities. (It is common to refer to μ as "the mean of X" rather than the mean of the probability distribution of X.)

Formula for the Mean

$$\mu = \sum xP(x)$$

The mean of a probability distribution has many of the same characteristics as the sample mean from Chapter 2. In particular, if the graph of the probability distribution is symmetric about some point $x*$, then μ is equal to $x*$. Also, μ is very sensitive to extreme values. If the probability distribution is skewed with a long tail to the right, say, μ is pulled to the right by these large values (see Figure 4.11).

How do we interpret the mean of a random variable? To answer this, we again consider Examples 4.2 and 4.3.

EXAMPLE 4.2 (continued)

In this example X is the number of men in a sample of size 3 from a population of three men and two women. When sampling is done without replacement, we saw that $P(1) = .3$, $P(2) = .6$, and $P(3) = .1$. Therefore, the mean of X is

$$\mu = \sum xP(x) = 1(.3) + 2(.6) + 3(.1) = 1.8$$

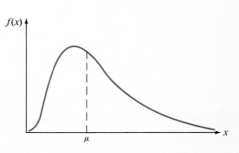

Figure 4.11
Mean of a Distribution Skewed to the Right

If sampling is done with replacement, the distribution of X is: $P(0) = {}^{8}/_{125}$, $P(1) = {}^{36}/_{125}$, $P(2) = {}^{54}/_{125}$, and $P(3) = {}^{27}/_{125}$. Now the mean of X is

$$\mu = \sum xP(x) = 0\left(\frac{8}{125}\right) + 1\left(\frac{36}{125}\right) + 2\left(\frac{54}{125}\right) + 3\left(\frac{27}{125}\right) = 1.8$$

(The fact that μ is 1.8 for both types of sampling is no coincidence. In general, let X be the number of A's in a sample of size n from a population of A's and B's. If p is the fraction of A's in the population, then $\mu = np$ when sampling is done with or without replacement.)

This example shows that the mean of X is not necessarily a *possible* value of X because we know that the sample cannot contain 1.8 men. However, we may interpret μ as follows. Suppose that we take repeated samples of size 3 (with or without replacement) from the same population of five people. We let X_1 be the number of men in sample 1, X_2 be the number of men in sample 2, and so on. Then the long-run average of these X's will be approximately 1.8.

The foregoing interpretation of the mean is very important. We state it in general below.

> When it is possible to obtain repeated observations of a random variable from a given probability distribution, the mean of this distribution can be interpreted as the long-run average of these observations.

EXAMPLE 4.3 (continued)

This example presents several new ideas. Now the random variable X, the number of percentage points in market share gained from the camera company's advertising campaign, arises from a one-time situation. We calculate the mean of X, μ_X, by the same formula as before. (Because there are two random variables X and Y in this example, we use subscripts on μ to avoid any possible confusion.) The value of μ_X is

$$\mu_X = \sum xP_X(x) = 0(.05) + .5(.07) + \cdots + 4(.05) = 2.065$$

In this example there is a related random variable, Y, the profit gained from advertising. Using the probability distribution of Y, we obtain

$$\mu_Y = \sum yP_Y(y) = (-2.5)(.05) + (-1.625)(.07) + \cdots + (4.5)(.05)$$
$$= 1.11375 \text{ (or } \$1,113,750)$$

Since the profit Y is related to the increase in market share X by the formula $Y = 1.75X - 2.5$, we might expect that $\mu_Y = 1.75\mu_X - 2.5$. This turns out to be true, since

$$1.75\mu_X - 2.5 = 1.75(2.065) - 2.5 = 1.11375$$

This result is no coincidence. It follows directly from one of the "rules of expected values" we discuss later in this chapter.

The mean profit μ_Y in this example is somewhat difficult to interpret because it pertains to a one-time situation. But in Chapter 15 we see that this mean can be used as a criterion for decision making. In particular, if there is an alternative advertising campaign for gaining market share, and its mean profit is *more* than \$1,113,750, the second campaign is probably preferred because its mean profit is higher.

Expected Values

The mean of a random variable X is often called the *expected value* of X and is often denoted by $E(X)$, or simply EX.

> The expected value of X, denoted by $E(X)$, equals the mean of X.

Often we are interested in the expected value of a function of X rather than the expected value of X itself. We denote a typical function of X by $h(X)$. This function could be of the form $h(X) = a + bX$, $h(X) = 3X^2$, $h(X) = e^X$, or any other conceivable form. In this book the usual situation is that $h(X)$ represents the total cost or profit associated with an outcome X. In the camera example (Example 4.3), X is the increase in market share and $Y = 1.75X - 2.5$ is the profit associated with X. In this case we have $h(X) = 1.75X - 2.5$. We denote this profit by $h(X)$ and not simply by Y to emphasize that the profit is *determined* by the value of X.

For any function $h(X)$, we denote its expected value by $Eh(X)$. It is defined as the average of all possible values of $h(X)$, weighted by their probabilities. In particular, if X is a discrete random variable, we compute $Eh(X)$ as follows.

> *Formula for the Expected Value of a Function of X*
> $$Eh(X) = \sum h(x)P(x)$$

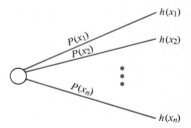

$Eh(X)$ = sum of probabilities on branches times $h(x)$ values at tips of branches

Figure 4.12
Tree Diagram for Finding $Eh(X)$

One way to conceptualize this expected value is by means of a *tree diagram,* as in in Figure 4.12. (Similar diagrams will be used extensively in Chapter 15.) In this diagram there are "branches" leading out of a central "node" (the circle on the left). Each branch corresponds to a possible value of X. We label each branch with the probability $P(x)$ of this branch's value x, and we put the function value $h(x)$ at the tip of this branch. Then the expected value $Eh(X)$ is the sum of the products of the $P(x)$'s and the $h(x)$'s.

The tree diagram for Example 4.3 is shown in Figure 4.13. Summing probabilities times profits gives $E(Y) = Eh(X) = 1.11375$, or \$1,113,750, the same as before.

One particularly important function of X is $h(X) = (X - \mu)^2$, the squared deviation of X from its mean μ. The expected value of this function is called the variance of X. It is denoted by σ^2 or $\text{Var}(X)$.

> *Definition of the Variance*
>
> $$\text{Var}(X) = \sigma^2 = E[(X - \mu)^2]$$

As in Chapter 2, the variance measures variability, in this case the variability of the probability distribution of X. In particular, σ^2 indicates the likelihood of X being far from its mean. If σ^2 is fairly small, X is likely to be close to μ. But if σ^2 is fairly large, values of X far from μ are not uncommon.

We illustrate the role of σ^2 in Figure 4.14. In Figure 4.14a, σ^2 is relatively small, so that the resulting graph is fairly "peaked." In Figure 4.14b, however, σ^2 is relatively large, so that this graph is much more spread out.

The Variance and Standard Deviation

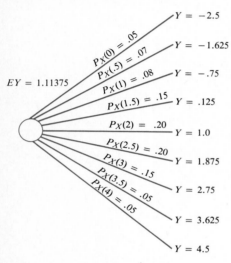

Figure 4.13
Tree Diagram for Example 4.3

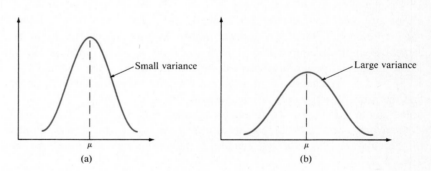

Figure 4.14

If X is a discrete random variable, the formula for the variance is as follows.

$$\sigma^2 = \sum (x - \mu)^2 P(x)$$

As in Chapter 2, however, this formula is inconvenient because it requires squared deviations from μ. An equivalent formula that is more convenient for hand use is given below.

Computing Formula for the Variance

$$\sigma^2 = E(X^2) - (EX)^2 = \sum x^2 P(x) - \mu^2$$

To remember this formula, remember that the variance is "the expected value of the squares minus the square of the expected value."

As an example, the variance of the gain in market share in Example 4.3 is

$$\sigma_X^2 = \sum x^2 P_X(x) - \mu_X^2$$
$$= [0^2(.05) + .5^2(.07) + \cdots + 4^2(.05)] - 2.065^2 = .9833$$

In the same example, the variance of the profit is

$$\sigma_Y^2 = \sum y^2 P(y) - \mu_Y^2$$
$$= [(-2.5)^2(.05) + (-1.625)^2(.07) + \cdots + 4.5^2(.05)] - 1.11375^2 = 3.0113$$

One drawback to the variance is that it is expressed in *squared* units. In contrast, the square root of the variance is measured in the same units as the original variable. This square root is called the *standard deviation* and is denoted by σ or StdDev(X). For example, if X is measured in dollars, both μ and σ are measured in dollars, whereas σ^2 is measured in dollars squared.

The standard deviation of X is the square root of the variance of X. It is denoted by σ or StdDev(X).

The following two rules show specifically how the standard deviation measures variability. As in Chapter 2, the first of these rules is always true, regardless of the distribution of X. For this reason, it is on the conservative side. That is, it provides a lower bound that is sometimes too low to be useful. In contrast, the second rule holds only for specific types of distributions, but for these specific types it is much more informative than the first rule.

Two Useful Rules

(Chebyshev's inequality)   Let X be any random variable with mean μ and variance σ^2. Then for any $k > 1$ (not necessarily an integer),

$$P(|X - \mu| < k\sigma) \geq 1 - \frac{1}{k^2}$$

RULE 4.1

RULE 4.2

(Rule of thumb, or normal approximation)   Let X be a random variable with mean μ and variance σ^2. If the distribution of X is approximately symmetric and bell-shaped, then

$$P(|X - \mu| < \sigma) \approx .68$$
$$P(|X - \mu| < 2\sigma) \approx .95$$

and

$$P(|X - \mu| < 3\sigma) \approx .997$$

where $\approx$ means "is approximately equal to."

Although these two rules are very similar to their counterparts in Chapter 2, there is an important difference between them. The rules in Chapter 2 specify the fraction of observations within a certain number of *sample* standard deviations from the *sample* mean. In this case the data have already been collected, and the sample mean and sample standard deviation are computed from these data. In contrast, the rules in this chapter deal with a *single* random variable X whose value has not yet been observed. The probability distribution of this random variable has mean μ and variance σ^2. The rules then specify the probability that X will be within a certain number of standard deviations of its mean.

As an example, let X be the revenue a company will earn during the coming month. Suppose that all we know about the distribution of X is that its mean is \$5400 and its standard deviation is \$350. Then the interval that extends 2 standard deviations on either side of the mean is from \$4700 to \$6100. By Chebyshev's inequality, the probability is at least $1 - (½)^2 = .75$ that the actual revenue will be between \$4700 and \$6100, regardless of the shape of the distribution of X. But if this distribution is approximately symmetric and bell-shaped, the probability of a revenue between \$4700 and \$6100 is approximately .95.

The Covariance and Correlation

In this section we discuss two measures of association for two random variables X and Y. These measures are called the *covariance* and the *correlation*. As we will see, they convey the same type of information as we discussed in Chapter 2.

We define the covariance of two random variables X and Y to be the expected value of the product $(X - \mu_X)(Y - \mu_Y)$, where μ_X and μ_Y are the means of X and Y. This covariance is denoted by σ_{XY} or $\text{Cov}(X, Y)$.

> The covariance of X and Y is the expected value of
>
> $$(X - \mu_X)(Y - \mu_Y)$$

The following formula shows how to compute the covariance when X and Y are discrete random variables.

> *Covariance Formula for Discrete Random Variables*
>
> $$\text{Cov}(X, Y) = \sigma_{XY} = \sum_x \sum_y xyP(x, y) - \mu_X\mu_Y$$

In words, we first calculate the weighted average of the products xy, weighted by their joint probabilities. We then subtract the product of the individual means μ_X and μ_Y.

As in Chapter 2, the covariance is a measure of the relationship between the random variables X and Y. If we expect a relatively high X to be accompanied by a relatively high Y, and we expect a relatively low X to be accompanied by a relatively low Y, the covariance is positive. If we expect the reverse to occur, so that X and Y vary in opposite directions, the covariance is negative. However, if X and Y are *independent* random variables, we do not expect X to provide any information about Y (or vice versa), and the covariance equals zero.

The problem with the covariance as a measure of association is that its magnitude depends on the units in which X and Y are measured. For example, if X and Y are originally measured in yards and are then converted to feet, their covariance is increased by a factor of 9. To produce a measure of association that is *not* dependent on the measurement units of X and Y, we "standardize" the covariance. This is done by dividing the covariance by the product of the standard deviations of X and Y. The result is called the correlation of X and Y and is denoted by ρ_{XY} or $\text{Corr}(X, Y)$.

> *Formula for the Correlation*
>
> $$\text{Corr}(X, Y) = \rho_{XY} = \frac{\text{Cov}(X, Y)}{\sigma_X\sigma_Y}$$

The correlation is always between -1 and $+1$. When $\text{Corr}(X, Y)$ is close to -1 or $+1$, X and Y are nearly related in a linear way; that is, Y is nearly equal to $a + bX$ for some constants a and b. If $\text{Corr}(X, Y)$ is close to 0, X and Y are usually close to being independent. (There are also cases when random variables with a *nonlinear* relationship can have a zero correlation.)

EXAMPLE 4.7

Calculate the covariance and correlation between IBM sales and Apple sales from the joint distribution in Table 4.4, shown again in Table 4.8 for convenience.

Table 4.8   Joint Distribution of X and Y

		IBM Sales (X)				
		30	35	40	45	
Apple	25	.03	.05	.08	.09	.25
Sales	30	.10	.15	.15	.10	.50
(Y)	35	.08	.09	.05	.03	.25
		.21	.29	.28	.22 ←	Marginal distributions

SOLUTION

We first find the means μ_X and μ_Y and the variances σ_X^2 and σ_Y^2. These are found from the marginal distributions as follows.

$$\mu_X = 30(.21) + 35(.29) + 40(.28) + 45(.22) = 37.55$$
$$\mu_Y = 25(.25) + 30(.50) + 35(.25) = 30$$

and

$$\sigma_X^2 = [30^2(.21) + 35^2(.29) + 40^2(.28) + 45^2(.22)] - 37.55^2 = 27.7475$$
$$\sigma_Y^2 = [25^2(.25) + 30^2(.50) + 35^2(.25)] - 30^2 = 12.5$$

To find Cov(X, Y), we need to sum the 12 possible products of X and Y times the corresponding joint probabilities. Then we subtract the product $\mu_X\mu_Y$. This leads to

$$\text{Cov}(X, Y) = [30(25)(.03) + 35(25)(.05) + \cdots + 45(35)(.03)]$$
$$- 37.55(30) = -5$$

This negative covariance shows that IBM sales and Apple sales vary in opposite directions. But to see how *strong* this negative relationship is, we calculate the correlation. This is given by

$$\text{Corr}(X, Y) = \frac{\text{Cov}(X, Y)}{\sigma_X\sigma_Y} = \frac{-5}{\sqrt{27.7475}\,\sqrt{12.5}} = -.268$$

This correlation is not particularly large (in absolute value), but it does show that IBM sales and Apple sales are definitely not independent. (The correlation would be zero if they were independent.)

Unlike the situation in Chapter 2, there is no scattergram available to measure the existence of a possible linear relationship between X and Y. This is because there are no sample observations to plot. All we have are the possible values of X and Y and their joint probabilities.

Problems for Section 4.9

31. A typical consumer buys a random number of shirts when he shops at a men's clothing store. The distribution of X is given by the probability mass function: $P(0) = .5$, $P(1) = .2$, $P(2) = .15$, $P(3) = .1$, $P(4) = .05$.
    a. Find the mean, variance, and standard deviation of X.
    b. Assuming that each shirt costs \$15, let Y be the total amount of money spent by a typical customer. Find the mean, variance, and standard deviation of Y.

32. A construction job has to be done no later than eight weeks from now or there will be problems. The remaining time (in weeks) to complete the job is a random variable X with probability distribution: $P(X = 6) = .1$, $P(X = 7) = .2$, $P(X = 8) = .4$, $P(X = 9) = .2$, $P(X = 10) = .1$. Let Y be the number of weeks the job is late, where Y is defined to be 0 if the job is not late. Find the mean, variance, and standard deviation of Y.

33. Referring to the data in Problem 3 (p. 148), find the mean, variance, and standard deviation of the number of errors on a randomly selected page.

34. The cdf of a discrete random variable X is as follows: $F(0) = 0$, $F(1) = .3$, $F(2) = .4$, $F(3) = .7$, $F(4) = 1$. Find the mean, variance, and standard deviation of this random variable.

*35. Consider a sample of three people selected randomly from a population of 50 people, 10 of whom smoke. Let X be the number of smokers in the sample. (For both parts below, refer to the sampling with and without replacement formulas in Chapter 3.)
    a. Find $E(X)$ and $Var(X)$ if sampling is done with replacement.

    b. Find $E(X)$ and $Var(X)$ if sampling is done without replacement.

36. For the data on divorces in Problem 13 (p. 154), find the mean, variance, and standard deviation of the number of divorces a typical man from this population has had.

37. For the demand–price data in Problem 21 (p. 162), find the mean demand, the mean price per unit, and the mean total revenue. Then use these answers to find the covariance between price per unit and demand.

38. For the data on sales of video games in Problem 23 (p. 163), again let X_1 and X_2 be the numbers of brand 1 and brand 2 video games sold on a typical day. Find $E(X_1)$ and $E(X_2)$. Then find $Var(X_1)$ and $Var(X_2)$. Finally, find $Cov(X_1, X_2)$ and $Corr(X_1, X_2)$.

*39. For the data on sales of video games in Problem 23, suppose that the profit on each video game of brand 1 is \$2.50 and the profit on each video game of brand 2 is \$3.50. Let Y_1 and Y_2 be total profits generated by brand 1 and brand 2 sales on a typical day. Find $E(Y_1)$ and $E(Y_2)$. Then find $Var(Y_1)$ and $Var(Y_2)$. Finally, find $Cov(Y_1, Y_2)$ and $Corr(Y_1, Y_2)$.

40. For the data displayed in Problem 24 (p. 163), find the covariance and correlation between X_1 and X_2, the positions of the two elevators at a random point in time when both elevators are stationary.

41. For the data in Problem 27 (p. 163), find the mean and standard deviation of the number of robberies on a typical day when there is one patrol car in the neighborhood. Do the same for a day when there are two patrol cars; for a day when there are three patrol cars. Explain intuitively why the three answers are not the same.

4.10

Rules of Expected Values

In this section we discuss several very useful rules for finding expected values of sums of random variables. These rules enable us to compute expected values of sums if we are given (or can compute) the expected values of the individual terms in the sums. Most of these rules are true for any random variables, although some require independence. We will be careful to point out when the independence assumption is required.

RULE 4.3

> For any constant c,
> $$E(c) = c \text{ and } \text{Var}(c) = 0$$

Because c is a constant, there is no uncertainty about its value. Therefore, the expected value of c must be c itself, and the variance is zero.

RULE 4.4

> For any constants a and b,
> $$E(a + bX) = a + bE(X) \text{ and } \text{Var}(a + bX) = b^2 \text{Var}(X).$$

The expression $a + bX$ is a linear function of X. The rule says that the expected value of this linear function is found by substituting $E(X)$ for X in the expression $a + bX$. The variance of $a + bX$, on the other hand, depends only on the constant b. Notice that we must square b, so that it loses its minus sign if it is negative. For example, $\text{Var}(1 + X)$ and $\text{Var}(1 - X)$ are both equal to $\text{Var}(X)$ since $(1)^2 = (-1)^2 = 1$.

RULE 4.5

> For any integer $n \geq 1$, any random variables $X_1, X_2, \ldots, X_n$, and any constants $a_1, a_2, \ldots, a_n$,
>
> $$E\left(\sum_{i=1}^{n} a_i X_i\right) = \sum_{i=1}^{n} a_i E(X_i)$$
>
> The X's do *not* need to be independent.

This rule is probably the most important rule in this section. It says that the expected value of a weighted sum $\Sigma a_i X_i$ is found by substituting $E(X_i)$ for each X_i in this sum. Special important cases of this rule are as follows.

The expected value of a sum equals the sum of the expected values:

$$E(X_1 + X_2 + \cdots + X_n) = E(X_1) + E(X_2) + \cdots + E(X_n)$$

The expected value of a difference equals the difference between the expected values:

$$E(X_1 - X_2) = E(X_1) - E(X_2)$$

For any integer $n \geq 1$, any *independent* random variables $X_1, X_2, \ldots,$ X_n, and any constants $a_1, a_2, \ldots, a_n$,

$$\text{Var}\left(\sum_{i=1}^{n} a_i X_i\right) = \sum_{i=1}^{n} a_i^2 \text{Var}(X_i)$$

This rule is not quite as general as Rule 4.5 because it requires independence of the X's. (If the X's are not independent, the variance of the sum depends on covariances as well as variances.) Special important cases of Rule 4.6 are given below.

Given independence, the variance of a sum equals the sum of the variances:

$$\text{Var}(X_1 + X_2 + \cdots + X_n) = \text{Var}(X_1) + \text{Var}(X_2) + \cdots + \text{Var}(X_n)$$

Given independence, the variance of a difference equals the sum of the variances:

$$\text{Var}(X_1 - X_2) = \text{Var}(X_1) + \text{Var}(X_2)$$

Notice that the variance of the difference is *not* the difference between the variances, as we might expect; it is the sum of the variances.

The following example illustrates several of these rules.

EXAMPLE 4.8

Consider a door-to-door salesman who works on commission. He estimates that his weekly earnings can be represented by a random variable with mean

[Handwritten margin notes:]

10 trials
$E(1)$ = expected value on 1 trial
$E(10) = 10\, E(1)$
$\text{Var}(10) = 10\, (\text{Var}(1))$
but
RULE 4.6 $\text{std}(10) = \sqrt{10}\; \text{std}(1)$

var (sum) = sum of variances
but
std (sum) $\neq$ sum of std

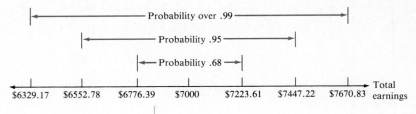

Figure 4.15

$350 and standard deviation $50. What are his expected earnings over a 20-week period? If his earnings in different weeks are independent random variables, what is the standard deviation of his total earnings over a 20-week period? Again assuming independence, what does Rule 4.2 (the rule of thumb) say about the total earnings for a 20-week period?

SOLUTION

Let X_i be his earnings in week i, and let X be his total earnings over a 20-week period. Then $X = X_1 + X_2 + \cdots + X_{20}$. To obtain the expected value of X, we use Rule 4.5. It says that

$$E(X) = E(X_1) + E(X_2) + \cdots + E(X_{20}) = 350 + 350 + \cdots + 350 = \$7000$$

This result does *not* require independence of the X's. However, if the X's are independent, Rule 4.6 implies that

$$\text{Var}(X) = \text{Var}(X_1) + \text{Var}(X_2) + \cdots + \text{Var}(X_{20})$$
$$= 50^2 + 50^2 + \cdots + 50^2 = 50,000$$

Since the square root of 50,000 is 223.61, the standard deviation of the salesman's total earnings for 20 weeks is $223.61.

Now that we have $E(X) = \$7000$ and $\text{StdDev}(X) = \$223.61$, we can use Rule 4.2 to predict how far the actual 20-week total is likely to be from its expected value, $7000. Assuming that the distribution of X is approximately symmetric and bell-shaped, Rule 4.2 states that X has approximate probability .68 of being between $7000 - \$223.61$ and $7000 + \$223.61$. Furthermore, it has approximate probability .95 of being between $7000 - 2(\$223.61)$ and $7000 + 2(\$223.61)$, and it has probability greater than .99 of being between $7000 - 3(\$223.61)$ and $7000 + 3(\$223.61)$. These three intervals are shown in Figure 4.15. (In Chapter 5 we will see why the distribution of X is likely to be symmetric and bell-shaped.)

Problems for Section 4.10

42. A retailer buys a batch of 5000 fluorescent light bulbs from a wholesaler for $2 apiece. The wholesaler agrees to replace each defective bulb with a guaranteed good one for a charge of 10 cents per bulb. The retailer sells the bulbs for $2.40 per bulb and gives his customers free replacements if they bring defectives back to the store. Let X be the number of defectives in the batch, and assume that the mean and standard deviation of X are 50 and 10, respectively.
    a. Use the rules of expected values to find the mean and standard deviation of the profit the retailer makes from the batch.
    b. Using Rule 4.2 and the results from part (a), find an interval with the property that the retailer can be approximately 95% sure that his profit will be in this interval.

43. Suppose that the number of puppies a dog has in a given litter is a random variable X with the following probability mass function: $P(3) = .1$, $P(4) = .2$, $P(5) = .3$, $P(6) = .2$, $P(7) = .2$.
    a. Find the mean, variance, and standard deviation of the number of puppies in a litter.
    b. If a dog has three litters of puppies, and their sizes are independent random variables, each with the distribution above, find the mean, variance, and standard deviation of the total number of puppies the dog has.
    c. Would you agree with the independence assumption in part (b)? Why or why not?

44. In a gambling casino, the "house" usually has only a very small edge on any given play. In particular, suppose that the house has a .503 probability of winning any bet.
    a. Let X be the house's winnings (or losings, if negative) on a $10 bet. Find $E(X)$ and $\text{Var}(X)$. (Note that X equals $10 or $-$10.)

    b. If the house makes 1000 independent $10 bets, find the mean and standard deviation of the house's net winnings (or losings, if negative) by using the rules of expected values.

45. An investor puts $1000 into each of two stocks, labeled A and B. The mean returns for the stocks are $\mu_1 = .15$ and $\mu_2 = .12$. That is, a dollar put into stock A, say, is expected to grow into $1.15. The standard deviations of returns are $\sigma_1 = .05$ and $\sigma_2 = .03$. Find the mean and standard deviation of X, the total amount the investor earns in one year, assuming that the two returns are independent random variables.

46. A company has a prediction scheme that predicts sales in the next three months will be $80,000, $85,000, and $70,000, respectively. The errors in these three predictions are random variables X_1, X_2, and X_3. These will be observed only when actual sales are observed. A positive error means a prediction overestimates sales; a negative error means a prediction underestimates sales. Assume that the means of the errors are each 0, and the standard deviations of the errors are $\sigma_1 = 4000, $\sigma_2 = 6000, and $\sigma_3 = 7000. Find the mean and standard deviation of the cumulative error X, where X is the sum $X_1 + X_2 + X_3$. Assume that the individual errors are independent random variables.

47. Suppose that you make 25 consecutive independent bets. On each bet, you either win $5, with probability .48, or you lose $4.90, with probability .52. Let X be your net winnings (or losings, if negative) on the 25 bets. Find the mean and standard deviation of X. Would you participate in such bets? Why or why not?

Summary

This chapter has specialized the study of probability to the case where numerical values are assigned to outcomes. This is done by means of a random variable, which assigns a specific numerical value to each outcome of an experiment. Of particular interest is the probability distribution of a random variable. This specifies the probabilities of all possible values of the random variable. We saw that there are two basic types of random variables, discrete and continuous. These must be treated differently mathematically, and in fact, calculus is needed to treat the continuous case adequately. Nevertheless, much of our study of statistical inference in later chapters will involve continuous distributions, and tables of the required probabilities appear in the back of this book. Therefore, we will be able to use continuous distributions without requiring calculus.

In case there are two or more related random variables, joint distributions are required. These describe how the random variables are related probabilistically. If we want to focus on one of the random variables, we can deduce its marginal distribution from the joint distribution. We can also deduce the conditional distribution of one random variable, given the other, by using the conditional probability formula. If the conditional distribution of one random variable, given another, is the same as this random variable's marginal distribution, the random variables are independent. The independent case is important because it implies that the joint distribution factors into the product of the individual marginals.

We also studied the most important summary measures of probability distributions. For a single distribution these are the mean and the variance (or the standard deviation). For a joint distribution we are often more interested in the covariance and the correlation. We stressed that although these measures have the same names as those in Chapter 2, there is an important distinction. The measures in this chapter are population measures calculated from probability distributions, whereas those in Chapter 2 are sample measures calculated from observed data. Finally, we learned several important rules of expected values, the two most important of which are that the mean of a sum is the sum of the means, and the variance of a sum of independent random variables is the sum of the variances.

Applications

Application 4.1   In an article on the risk of new product development, McIntyre and Statman reported that between 60 and 90% of all new products are failures by the end of their first year, at which time they are either totally withdrawn or left unsupported. (Reference: Shelby H. McIntyre and Meir Statman, "Managing the Risk of New Product Development," *Business Horizons*, Vol. 25, 1982, pp. 51–55.) With percentages such as these, many companies may be hesitant to introduce new products. However, one way to manage the risk of new product development is to diversify into different types of products.

Using the example by McIntyre and Statman, suppose that a company has a certain amount of money to invest. It can invest all this money in a new kind of yogurt, it can invest all of it in a new kind of ice cream, or it can invest half of the money in the yogurt and the other half in the ice cream. Assume that the percentage return, X_1, from the yogurt investment is 70% or -20% (a loss), with probability .5 each, regardless of the amount invested. Assume that the percentage return, X_2, from the ice cream investment, is also 70% or -20% with probability .5 each. Finally, assume that X_1 and X_2 are independent random variables if the company invests in yogurt and ice cream. Then the percentage return, X_3, from the joint investment in yogurt and ice cream has the following distribution, due to independence.

$$P(X_3 = -20\%) = P(X_1 = -20\%)P(X_2 = -20\%) = .25$$
$$P(X_3 = 25\%) = P(X_1 = -20\%)P(X_2 = 70\%)$$
$$+ P(X_1 = 70\%)P(X_2 = -20\%) = .25 + .25 = .50$$
$$P(X_3 = 70\%) = P(X_1 = 70\%)P(X_2 = 70\%) = .25$$

From a risk point of view, this joint investment is probably preferable because its probability of a 20% loss has been reduced to .25.

This analysis hinges on the assumption that X_1 and X_2 are independent. (Actually, diversification is a good idea as long as X_1 and X_2 are not perfectly correlated. Independence is certainly one case of this.) Is this assumption defensible? McIntyre and Statman believe it is. According to them: "Analysis of the case histories of new product failures leads us to believe that the correlation between new product introductions within the same firm is generally low; a large degree of the explanation of new product failures can be traced to idiosyncratic aspects of the particular introduction and not to systematic factors such as the state of the economy or the characteristic of the firm. These data indicate that the assumption of independence is defensible, and that the model is therefore valid when applied to reduce the total risk of several product innovations introduced by a single company."

Application 4.2   In many real-world systems, uncertainty is inherent and must be dealt with explicitly. For example, consider a small branch office of a bank that has a single teller. When customers enter the bank, they obtain service immediately if no one else is in the bank, or they wait in line if other customers are already there. There are two random "inputs" to this system: (1) the random times between customer arrivals, called interarrival times; and (2) the random times it takes for the teller to service the customers, called service times. These inputs produce "outputs" that are of interest to the bank manager, such as the number of customers in line and the time customers spend in the bank.

To study systems such as these, it is common to assume well-known probability distributions for the inputs, and then to deduce the probability distributions of the outputs by using probability theory. A possibility for the bank example is the following. We assume that the successive inter-arrival times are independent random variables $X_1, X_2 \ldots$, and that they have a common "exponential" probability distribution with mean 3 minutes. That is, the average time between successive arrivals is 3 minutes. The cdf of this distribution is

$$F_X(x) = 1 - e^{-x/3} \qquad \text{for any } x > 0$$

Similarly, we assume that the successive service times are independent random variables $Y_1, Y_2, \ldots$, and that they also have a common exponential probability distribution, now with mean 2 minutes. The cdf of this distribution is

$$F_Y(y) = 1 - e^{-y/2} \qquad \text{for any } y > 0$$

These exponential probability distributions are chosen because (1) they make probability calculations relatively easy, and (2) they produce relatively good fits to actual interarrival times and service times in many applications.

Once we assume the foregoing probability distributions for the inter-arrival and service times, it is possible to deduce the probability distributions of important output measures. For example, consider the probability distribution of the amount of time W a typical customer spends in the bank. It can be shown that W also has an exponential probability distribution, now with mean 6 minutes. Its cdf is

$$F_W(w) = P(W \le w) = 1 - e^{-w/6} \qquad \text{for any } w > 0$$

This cdf allows us to calculate more than the mean of W. For example, the probability that a typical customer spends more than 10 minutes in the bank is

$$P(W > 10) = 1 - P(W \le 10) = 1 - (1 - e^{-10/6}) = e^{-10/6} = .189$$

whereas the probability that a typical customer spends no more than 6 minutes in the bank is

$$P(W \le 6) = 1 - e^{-6/6} = 1 - e^{-1} = 1 - .368 = .632$$

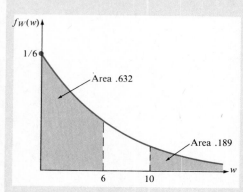

Figure 4.16
Exponential Density of Total Time in the System

The latter calculation shows that the distribution of W is definitely skewed to the right. This is because well over half of the total probability (of 1) lies to the left of the mean of W. The density function of W with the probabilities from above is shown in Figure 4.16.

Glossary of Terms

Random variable a rule that assigns a numerical value to each outcome of an experiment

Probability distribution a function that specifies the probabilities of a random variable's possible values

Probability mass function the probability distribution of a discrete random variable

Probability density function a function that specifies the probability distribution of a continuous random variable

Cumulative distribution function (cdf) a function that specifies all left-hand tail probabilities for a random variable

Discrete bivariate distribution the probability distribution that specifies how two random variables behave jointly

Marginal distribution the probability distribution of a single random variable (in a context where there are several random variables)

Independent random variables random variables where information about any of them is irrelevant for predicting the values of the others

Mean (or expected value) of a random variable weighted average of the possible values of the random variable, using the probabilities as weights

Variance of a random variable expected value of the squared difference between the random variable and its mean

Standard deviation the square root of the variance

Covariance a measure of association between two random variables

Correlation a measure of association between two random variables that is always between -1 and $+1$

Important Formulas

1. Probability of an event for a discrete random variable

$$P(E) = \sum_{x \text{ in } E} P(x)$$

where "x in E" means all x's favorable to E

2. Probability of an interval for a continuous random variable

$$P(a < X < b) = \text{area under the density function between } a \text{ and } b$$

3. Formula for the marginal distribution (of X) in the bivariate case

$$P(X = x) = \sum_{y} P(X = x \text{ and } Y = y)$$

4. Conditional distribution of X given Y

$$P(X = x \mid Y = y) = \frac{P(X = x \text{ and } Y = y)}{P(Y = y)}$$

5. Multiplication rule for independent random variables

$$P(X = x \text{ and } Y = y) = P(X = x)P(Y = y)$$

6. Formula for the mean (discrete case)

$$\mu = \sum xP(X = x)$$

7. Expected value of a function of a random variable (discrete case)

$$Eh(X) = \sum h(x)P(X = x)$$

8. Computing formula for the variance (discrete case)

$$\sigma^2 = \sum x^2 P(X = x) - \mu^2$$

9. Computing formula for the covariance between random variables X and Y (discrete case)

$$\sigma_{XY} = \text{Cov}(X, Y) = \sum \sum xyP(X = x \text{ and } Y = y) - \mu_X\mu_Y$$

where the double summation is over all pairs of x's and y's

10. Formula for the correlation between X and Y

$$\rho_{XY} = \text{Corr}(X, Y) = \frac{\text{Cov}(X, Y)}{\sigma_X\sigma_Y}$$

11. Expected value of a sum of random variables

$$E(X_1 + X_2 + \cdots + X_n) = E(X_1) + E(X_2) + \cdots + E(X_n)$$

12. Variance of a sum of independent random variables

$$\text{Var}(X_1 + X_2 + \cdots + X_n) = \text{Var}(X_1) + \text{Var}(X_2) + \cdots + \text{Var}(X_n)$$

End-of-Chapter Problems

48. If the density function in Problem 30 (p. 164) is changed to the one shown below, answer questions (b) and (c) from Problem 30. (You must first find the height c that makes this a density.)

49. Medical scientists wish to model the number of years, X, a patient lives after he or she has had a heart transplant. They decide on an approximate distribution that has the following form:

$$P(k) = P(X = k) = .5^k$$

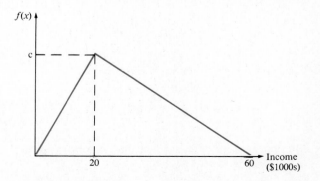

for any integer $k \geq 1$. (The event $X = k$ means the patient dies during the kth year after the operation.)

a. Graph the first few terms of this distribution, that is, $P(1)$, $P(2)$, and so on.

b. What is the probability that a patient will die within four years of the operation, $P(X \leq 4)$?

c. What is the probability that a patient will live at least five years after the operation, $P(X > 5)$?

50. To generalize Example 4.8, suppose that the salesman's earnings in week i is a random variable with mean μ_i and variance σ_i^2. We are interested in X, the total earnings in n weeks.

a. Assuming that the earnings in the successive weeks are independent random variables, find an expression for the mean and standard deviation of X.

b. Simplify the expressions in part (a) when all the μ_i's equal a common value μ and all the σ_i^2's equal a common value σ^2.

*51. The Smiths know that they are going to have a large income tax payment due on April 15, but they are not yet sure how large it will be. They assess the following probabilities for X, the amount of the payment: (1) X will be at least \$1000 with probability .6; (2) X will be no more than \$3000 with probability .9; (3) X will be between \$500 and \$2000 with probability .7.

a. Let $F(x)$ be the cdf of X. Translate the probability statements above into equations concerning F.

b. Which of the following are necessarily true, and why: (1) $F(1000) > .5$, (2) $F(500) < .4$, (3) $F(2000) > .6$?

52. For the "rectangular" density shown below, find the appropriate value of b, and then find a formula for the cdf $F(x)$ for each x between 0 and b.

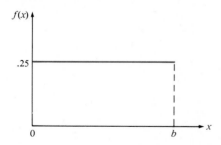

*53. Two basketball teams are about to play a "best of 3" series, which means that the series is played until some team wins two games. Let X_1 be the number of games team one wins, and let X_2 be the number of games team two wins. Find the joint distribution of X_1 and X_2 (in table form), assuming that the teams are evenly matched and that the outcomes of successive games are independent.

*54. A company is considering three types of advertising campaigns, labeled A, B, and C. These can be ranked from 1 to 3, 1 being best and 3 being worst. For example, the ranking $A2$, $B1$, $C3$ means that B is ranked best, A is ranked second, and C is ranked last. Since the actual effectiveness rankings of the campaigns are not known for certain, the following probabilities are assigned to the six possibilities:

$$P(A1, B2, C3) = .10$$
$$P(A1, B3, C2) = .20$$
$$P(A2, B1, C3) = .15$$
$$P(A3, B3, C1) = .25$$
$$P(A3, B1, C2) = .10$$
$$P(A3, B2, C1) = .20$$

Let X_1 be the ranking (1, 2, or 3) that A receives, let X_2 be the ranking B receives, and let X_3 be the ranking C receives.

a. Find the marginal distribution of X_1; of X_2; of X_3.

b. Find the joint distribution of X_1 and X_2 (in table form).

c. Why are X_1 and X_2 not independent? Given an intuitive reason as well as a mathematical one.

55. Three shoppers enter a department store. They purchase dollar amounts X_1, X_2, and X_3 independently of one another, where X_1, X_2, and X_3 each have the probability density function shown below (with the areas indicated).

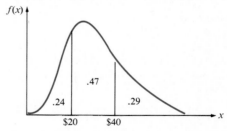

a. Find the probability that each of the three shoppers spends less than \$40.

b. Find the probability that none of the three spends between \$20 and \$40.

c. Find the probability that at least one of the three spends over \$40.

*56. In a manufacturing plant, workers frequently have to go to a parts department to get a special tool. The persons in charge of parts must search for the required part, so that the workers requesting parts often spend their time waiting for the requested parts. There are currently two people working in parts. With this setup, the probability distribution of X, the number of workers waiting for parts at a typical point in time, is $P(X = 0) = .2$, $P(X = 1) = .2$, $P(X = 2) = .3$, $P(X = 3) = .2$, $P(X = 4) = .1$. The company is thinking of hiring an extra person in parts. It believes that the probability distribution of X would then be $P(X = 0) = .4$, $P(X = 1) = .4$, $P(X = 2) = .1$, $P(X = 3) = .08$, $P(X = 4) = .02$. Assume that parts workers earn \$9.50 per hour and lost production time due to waiting in line is valued at \$7 per hour per worker. Based on expected costs, would you favor hiring the extra worker in parts? (Back up your answer with appropriate expected values.)

57. Consider a sample of size 2 taken with replacement from a population consisting of 40% brand A users and 60% brand B users. Let X_1 and X_2, be, respectively, the number of brand A users and brand B users in the sample. Find the table of joint probabilities for X_1 and X_2, and use it to verify that $\text{Corr}(X_1, X_2)$ equals -1. How can you explain this result intuitively?

*58. Consider the same situation as in Problem 57, except that the population now consists of 40% brand A users, 50% brand B users, and 10% brand C users. Again, let X_1 and X_2 be the numbers of brand A users and brand B users in the sample of size 2. Find the table of joint probabilities for X_1 and X_2, and use it to find $\text{Corr}(X_1, X_2)$. Intuitively, why is $\text{Corr}(X_1, X_2)$ not equal to -1 in this case? (*Hint:* List all joint possibilities for X_1, X_2, X_3.)

*59. An insurance company is trying to decide whether to insure a \$500,000 building against fire. The company believes there are only four possibilities. These are listed below, together with their probabilities. The insurance company decides to charge a yearly premium equal to the expected amount of any claim, plus \$150.

Damage Amount	Probability
\$ 0 (no fire)	.995
5,000	.003
50,000	.001
500,000	.001

a. If the policy is the type that pays for all damages, what should the company charge for it?

b. If the policy is of the \$10,000-deductible type (the building owners pay the first \$10,000 worth of damage, the insurance company pays the rest), what should the premium be?

c. Find the expected out-of-pocket cost (including the premium) to the building owners if they purchase the policy in part (a); if they purchase the policy in part (b).

60. On a given night, 7 out of 15 families in a certain neighborhood are watching the hottest new show, "Houston." Suppose that a television rating agency calls a random 3 of the 15 families after the show. Let X be the number called who are watching the show. Find the probability distribution of X. (Remember the sampling-without-replacement formula from Chapter 3.)

*61. A person carrying a \$200-deductible car insurance policy has an accident. (With this type of policy, the company pays for all damages except the first \$200.) Before getting formal estimates of the amount of damage, the person assesses the possible amounts of damage and their probabilities, as listed below. Find the individual probability distributions of the random variables X and Y, defined as

X = amount the person collects from the insurance company
Y = amount the person pays out of his own pocket

Amount of Damage	Probability
\$150	.1
200	.3
250	.4
300	.2

62. The completion time for a certain project (measured in weeks) is thought to have a "triangular" density, as shown below. The idea is that the earliest possible completion time is 10 weeks from now, the latest possible completion time is 18 weeks from now, and the "anticipated," or most likely, completion time is 12 weeks from now.

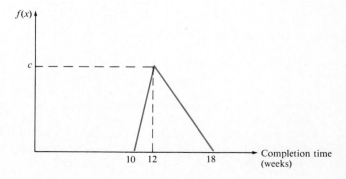

a. Find the value of c that makes this a density function. (Remember that the area of a triangle is $bh/2$, where b is the base and h is the height.)

b. Find the probability that the completion time is no later than 13 weeks from now.

63. A drugstore has recently begun giving points to its customers in the following way. For every \$10 of merchandise the customer buys, he or she receives 1 point. For example, if a customer spends a total of \$67 in one month, this customer receives 6 points. (The extra \$7 purchased does not count.) These points are then redeemable later for cash or merchandise. The density for the amount spent by a typical customer in a given month is shown below, where the numbers in the graph indicate areas. Assume for simplicity that no one spends more than \$100 in a month. If X is the number of points a typical customer earns in a month, find the probability distribution of X. (Notice that the amount spent is a continuous random variable, whereas X is a discrete random variable.)

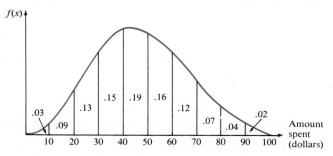

64. For the distribution in Problem 10 (p. 154), let $F(x)$ be the corresponding cdf.
a. Interpret $F(25,000)$ in words.
b. What probability does $F(30,000) - F(15,000)$ represent?
c. Evaluate the probabilities in parts (a) and (b).

65. The service department at an automobile dealership does most of its service for customers who make an appointment ahead of time. However, there are occasional "walk-ins," customers who require service that day but do not have an appointment. Their names are put on a list, and they are serviced only when an appointment cancellation occurs. Assume that the number of walk-ins on a given day, X_1, has the following probability distribution: $P(X_1 = 0) = .3$, $P(X_1 = 1) = .4$, $P(X_1 = 2) = .2$, $P(X_1 = 3) = .1$. The number of appointment cancellations, X_2, is also random with the following probability distribution: $P(X_2 = 0) = .5$, $P(X_2 = 1) = .4$, $P(X_2 = 2) = .1$. Assume that X_1 and X_2 are independent random variables.

a. Fill in the table of joint probabilities for X_1 and X_2.
b. What is the probability of a "one-for-one exchange," that is, exactly one cancellation and exactly one walk-in?
c. What is the probability of at least one walk-in being serviced that day?

*66. Consider a sample of two people chosen without replacement from a population consisting of two adults, two teenagers, and one child. Let X_1 and X_2 be, respectively, the number of adults and the number of teenagers in the sample.
a. Find the table of joint probabilities of X_1 and X_2.
b. Are X_1 and X_2 independent random variables? Why or why not?

*67. Each of five firms submits a bid for a government contract. If the bid amounts, labeled X_1, X_2, X_3, X_4, and X_5, are independent random variables with the density function shown below, and the winning bid is the lowest of the five bid amounts, what is the probability that the winning bid will be greater than \$45,000? (Notice that the lowest of five bids is greater than \$45,000 only if each bid is greater than \$45,000.)

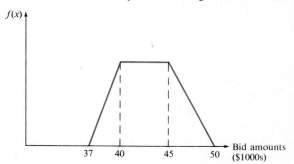

68. Find the mean, variance, and standard deviation of the random variables X and Y defined in Problem 61. How can you interpret the sum $E(X) + E(Y)$ for this problem?

*69. Consider the data on the demand for humidifiers in Problem 8 (p. 148). As in that problem, let X, Y, and Z be, respectively, the number of humidifiers left at the end of the month, the number of emergency shipments required, and the company's profit this month. Find $E(X)$, $E(Y)$, and $E(Z)$.

*70. Show algebraically that the computational formula for variance,

$$\text{Var}(X) = \sum k^2 P(k) - \mu^2$$

follows from the definition of variance,

$$\text{Var}(X) = \sum (k - \mu)^2 P(k)$$

71. Consider a motorcycle dealer who sells a random number of motorcycles each week. Assume that the expected number of sales in a given week is 7 and the standard deviation is 2.9. Assume also that the sales in separate weeks are independent random variables.
    a. Find the mean and standard deviation of the total number of motorcycles sold in 15 weeks.
    b. Can you conclude that the total number of motorcycles sold in 15 weeks is between 90 and 120 with probability at least .4? (Answer by referring to Rules 4.1 and 4.2.)

*72. A film processing store charges its customers 20 cents per print, but customers may refuse to accept any of the prints. There is no charge for prints refused. The number of prints refused per 24-print roll is a random variable with mean 1.7 and standard deviation 1.1.
    a. What are the mean and standard deviation of the amount actually paid for the development of a typical 24-print roll?
    b. If the company processes 195 24-print rolls in a given week, and if the numbers of refused prints on these rolls are independent random variables, find an interval with the property that the company is approximately 95% sure that its total revenue will be inside this interval. (Assume that Rule 4.2 applies.)

*73. In an extensive study Star and Massel examined the survival rate of various types of retail businesses. (Reference: Alvin D. Star and Michael Z. Massel, "Survival Rates for Retailers," *Journal of Retailing*, Vol. 57, 1981, pp. 87–99.) This rate is defined as the length of time a business operates before discontinuing or going bankrupt. They found that the following distribution applies to retail businesses as a whole. (Although their study is based only on Illinois businesses starting in 1974, we will assume that this distribution applies to all U.S. retail businesses begun in any year.)

Years Surviving	Probability
Less than .5	.196
.5–1.5	.199
1.5–2.5	.118
2.5–3.5	.080
3.5–4.5	.056
4.5–5.5	.019
More than 5.5	.332

Let X be the number of years a typical U.S. retail business survives.
a. Find $P(X > 1.5 \mid X > .5)$, $P(X > 2.5 \mid X > 1.5)$, $P(X > 3.5 \mid X > 2.5)$, $P(X > 4.5 \mid X > 3.5)$, and $P(X > 5.5 \mid X > 4.5)$. Interpret these probabilities in words. Do your answers exhibit any trends?
b. Explain how $E(X)$ is related to the result of the following calculation:

$$0(.196) + .5(.199) + 1.5(.118) + 2.5(.080) + 3.5(.056) + 4.5(.019) + 5.5(.332)$$

Is is possible to put a bound on the difference between $E(X)$ and this number? Why or why not?

Computer Problems

(These problems are to be used in conjunction with the computer software package.)

1. The probability distribution of the monthly demand (in 100s) for cartons of a particular brand of milk at a supermarket is shown here. Use the PROBDIST program to find the mean and standard deviation of this distribution. Then find the probability that the monthly demand will be (a) at least 1 standard deviation below the mean; (b) at least 1 standard deviation above the mean.

Demand	Probability
10	.05
11	.10
12	.14
13	.16
14	.21
15	.13
16	.11
17	.04
18	.03
19	.02
20	.01

2. Continuing Problem 1, the joint probability distribution of monthly demand for two brands of milk is shown below. Use the PROBDIST program to find the mean and standard deviation of monthly demand for each brand separately. What is the correlation between monthly demands for the two products? What is the probability that the monthly demand for each brand will be at least 1 standard deviation below its mean? What is the probability that at least one of the two monthly demands will be at least 1 standard deviation above its mean?

			Demand for Brand 1 (100s)				
		10	11	12	13	14	15
	10	.0075	.0125	.0175	.0150	.0075	.0075
	11	.0150	.0375	.0525	.0300	.0100	.0100
Demand for	12	.0300	.0625	.1050	.0525	.0175	.0200
Brand 2	13	.0450	.0625	.0875	.0300	.0075	.0075
(100s)	14	.0300	.0500	.0525	.0150	.0050	.0025
	15	.0225	.0250	.0350	.0075	.0025	.0025

3. One discrete probability distribution that is sometimes useful is given by the formula $P(X = k) = C/k^{\alpha+1}$, for $1 \leq k \leq K$, where α and K are numbers (greater than 1) that specify the particular form of the distribution, and C is the constant that makes these probabilities sum to 1. (This distribution is sometimes called the "zeta" distribution. It was first used by Pareto to describe the distribution of family incomes in a given country.) If $\alpha = 1$ and $K = 15$, then it can be shown that $C = 1.58044$. Use the PROBDIST program to find the mean and standard deviation of this particular zeta distribution. (Be careful not to have too much rounding error in your individual probabilities. The PROBDIST program will give you an error message if the sum of your probabilities is not between .9999 and 1.0001.) Then repeat, using $\alpha = 2$ and $K = 12$. (You have to find C this time.)

APPENDIX 4A

Continuous Distributions and Calculus

Probably the most important use of calculus in statistics and probability is dealing with continuous random variables. Here we require integral calculus for two purposes: (1) for calculating probabilities as areas under density functions; and (2) for calculating means, variances, and other expected values. In this appendix we illustrate some of the basic operations for readers with a suitable background in integral calculus.

Recall that the density function $f(x)$ of a continuous random variable X measures the relative likelihoods of the possible values of X. All density functions have two properties: $f(x) \geq 0$ for all x, and

$$\int f(x)\, dx = 1$$

(In this integral, and in all other integrals where bounds of integration are not shown, the integral extends over all possible values of X.) For any density function, probabilities can be found by integrating $f(x)$ over the appropriate regions. In particular,

$$P(a < X < b) = \int_a^b f(x)\, dx$$

for any numbers a and b.

The expected value of any function $h(X)$ can be found by integrating the product of $h(x)$ and the density $f(x)$.

> ### Expected Value of $h(X)$
>
> $$Eh(X) = \int h(x)f(x)\, dx$$

Two functions of special interest are $h(X) = X$ and $h(X) = (X - \mu)^2$. If $h(X) = X$, we obtain the formula for the mean:

> ### Mean of X
>
> $$\mu = E(X) = \int xf(x)\, dx$$

If $h(X) = (X - \mu)^2$, we obtain the formula for the variance:

> ### Variance of X
>
> $$\sigma^2 = \text{Var}(X) = \int (x - \mu)^2 f(x)\, dx$$

As with discrete random variables, there is a computational formula for σ^2 that usually simplifies the calculations.

> ### Computational Formula for σ^2
>
> $$\sigma^2 = E(X^2) - \mu^2 = \int x^2 f(x)\, dx - \mu^2$$

Again, remember this as "the variance equals the expected value of the squares minus the square of the expected value."

To illustrate the formulas above, let X be a continuous random variable with possible values from 0 to 1 and density function $f(x) = 12x^2(1 - x)$ over this interval. This density is shown in Figure 4.17. We see that the most likely values of X are in the neighborhood of $\frac{2}{3}$, and that the distribution of X is skewed to the left.

First, we check that $f(x)$ is a proper density function. By the graph, it is clear that $f(x) \geq 0$ for all x, so we only need to check that it integrates to 1. We have

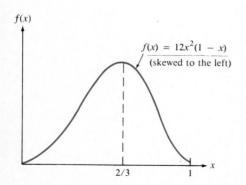

$f(x) = 12x^2(1 - x)$
(skewed to the left)

Figure 4.17

$$\int_0^1 f(x)\, dx = \int_0^1 12x^2(1 - x)\, dx = \left.\frac{12x^3}{3}\right|_0^1 - \left.\frac{12x^4}{4}\right|_0^1 = 4 - 3 = 1$$

Therefore, $f(x)$ is indeed a density function.

Next let's find the probability that X is between 0 and .5. This is the area under the density from 0 to .5, or

$$P(0 < X < .5) = \int_0^{.5} f(x)\, dx = \int_0^{.5} 12x^2(1 - x)\, dx = \left.\frac{12x^3}{3}\right|_0^{.5} - \left.\frac{12x^4}{4}\right|_0^{.5}$$
$$= 4(.125) - 3(.0625) = .3125$$

Actually, since X cannot be negative in this example, $P(0 < X < .5)$ equals $P(X < .5)$, a cdf value. That is, if $F(x)$ is the cdf of X, we have shown that $F(.5) = .3125$. Other cdf values can be calculated in a similar way.

Finally, we can calculate the mean and variance of X as follows. The mean is

$$\mu = \int_0^1 xf(x)\, dx = \int_0^1 12x^3(1 - x)\, dx = \left.\frac{12x^4}{4}\right|_0^1 - \left.\frac{12x^5}{5}\right|_0^1 = 3 - 2.4 = .6$$

and the variance is (from the computing formula)

$$\sigma^2 = \int_0^1 x^2 f(x)\, dx - \mu^2 = \int_0^1 12x^4(1 - x)\, dx - .6^2 = \left.\frac{12x^5}{5}\right|_0^1 - \left.\frac{12x^6}{6}\right|_0^1 - .6^2$$
$$= 2.4 - 2 - .6^2 = .04$$

This implies that the standard deviation is .2.

Unfortunately, most densities encountered in statistics are not nearly as simple to integrate as the one we have illustrated here. This is why tabulated probabilities (as well as means and variances) will be supplied for all the continuous distributions encountered in later chapters.

References

BREIMAN, L. *Probability and Stochastic Processes: With a View Toward Applications*. Boston: Houghton Mifflin, 1969.

INGRAM, O., GLESER, L. J., and DERMAN, C. *Probability Models and Applications*. New York: Macmillan, 1980.

ROSS, S. *A First Course in Probability*, 3rd ed. New York: Macmillan, 1984. Chapters 3–5.

CHAPTER 5

Normal, Binomial, and Poisson Distributions

Objectives

1. To learn the basic properties of the normal distribution and why it is so widely applicable.
2. To learn how to standardize normal random variables and how to use the standard normal tables.
3. To practice doing typical applications requiring normal probability calculations.
4. To understand the meaning and power of the Central Limit Theorem.
5. To learn when the binomial distribution is applicable and how it is useful in sampling problems.
6. To learn how to do binomial probability calculations and how to use the binomial tables.
7. To learn the normal approximation to the binomial.
8. To learn the basic properties of the Poisson distribution.

Contents

*I*n most manufacturing environments quality control is of utmost importance. In order to judge quality, a common strategy is to measure relevant dimensions of randomly selected items as they come off a production line. By seeing whether the average of these measurements is close to the desired level, the company can decide whether the process is "in control" or "out of control." In the latter case, adjustments can be made to bring the process back into control. Quality control is basically a statistical problem. For example, suppose that the item in question is a cylindrical rod that must have a particular diameter. We can imagine the population of diameters of all possible rods if they were produced by the machinery under current conditions. This population distribution has an overall shape, as well as a mean and a variance. However, we see only a sample from this distribution when we examine several specific rods. What can we infer about the population from the sample? In particular, is the mean diameter too small or too large?

One thing that would make our statistical job easier is if we could conclude that the population distribution is a special bell-shaped distribution called the normal distribution. This is because the normal distribution has very desirable properties, and probabilities based upon it are tabulated in all statistics books. Fortunately, the normal distribution is also a very good approximation for many real-world phenomena. This means that the population distribution of diameters in the manufacturing example above has an excellent chance of being normal or very close to normal. If this is the case, the statistical problem of judging the quality of the sample becomes fairly straightforward. In this chapter we study the basic properties of the normal distribution that make it so attractive. In Chapter 13 we will see how to test whether a sample of data could have come from a normal distribution.

5.1

Introduction

In this chapter we learn three specific distributions that occur constantly throughout the study of statistics. The first of these is a continuous distribution called the normal distribution. It is characterized by a symmetric, bell-shaped density and is the cornerstone of statistical theory. The other two distributions are discrete distributions called the binomial and Poisson distributions. The binomial distribution is relevant when we sample from a population with only two types of members or when we perform a series of independent, identical experiments with only two possible outcomes per experiment. The Poisson distribution is usually relevant when we are interested in the number of events that occur over a given interval of time, such as arrivals to a bank or calls to a telephone switchboard.

Our main objectives in this chapter are to list the properties of these three distributions, to give some examples of when they apply, and to learn how to calculate probabilities involving them. In accomplishing this last objective, we will learn how to use the normal, binomial, and Poisson tables in Appendix B. We will also learn how the normal, binomial, and Poisson distributions are related to one another. In particular, we will see how the normal approximation to the binomial greatly simplifies binomial probability calculations.

We cannot overemphasize the importance of the distributions introduced in this chapter. Almost all of the statistical results we will learn in future chapters are based on either the normal distribution or the binomial distribution or both. (The Poisson distribution plays a less important role in this book, but it is nevertheless extremely important in many applied probability settings.) Therefore, it is essential that we familiarize ourselves thoroughly with these distributions before continuing.

5.2

The Normal Distribution

The single most important distribution in statistics is called the normal distribution. All of the other continuous distributions we will use in later chapters are related to the normal distribution. Even the important discrete distributions we will use, especially the binomial, can often be approximated by the normal distribution.

The normal density function is the familiar symmetric, bell-shaped curve. This means that whenever we have a histogram of observed data that is at least approximately symmetric and bell-shaped, a normal density is a natural candidate for the population distribution. Furthermore, the normal density has two adjustable parameters. These allow us to shift the normal density to the right or the left and to make it more or less spread out. Therefore, there are really many normal densities, and one of them is likely to be appropriate in a given application.

If X is a random variable with a normal distribution, then X is a continuous random variable with the density function shown below.

> *Normal Density Function*
>
> $$f(x) = \frac{1}{\sqrt{2\pi}\,\sigma} e^{-(x-\mu)^2/(2\sigma^2)}$$

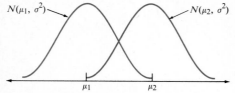

Two normal densities with the same variance but different means

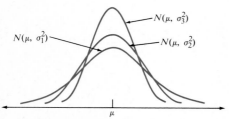

Three normal densities with the same mean but different variances $(\sigma_1^2 > \sigma_2^2 > \sigma_3^2)$

Figure 5.1

Here μ and σ^2 are parameters that must be specified in any particular application, and e and π are the two special constants, $e = 2.718...$ and $\pi = 3.14...$. The possible values of X extend infinitely far in both directions, but for all practical purposes the possible values lie within the interval from $\mu - 3\sigma$ to $\mu + 3\sigma$. This is because the probability of X being to the left of $\mu - 3\sigma$ or to the right of $\mu + 3\sigma$ is extremely small.

> A normal random variable has almost no probability of being outside of the interval from $\mu - 3\sigma$ to $\mu + 3\sigma$.

The graph of $f(x)$ is always symmetric and bell-shaped, but its exact position and shape depend on the parameters μ and σ^2. In particular, the graph of $f(x)$ is symmetric about the vertical line at $x = \mu$, and the value of σ^2 determines how peaked the bell-shaped curve is. The larger the value of σ^2, the more spread out the graph of $f(x)$ is; the smaller the value of σ^2, the more peaked the graph is. Several normal densities are shown in Figure 5.1.

It is no coincidence that the parameters of the normal density are denoted by μ and σ^2. It can be shown that these are the mean and the variance of X, which implies that σ is the standard deviation of X. Given these facts, we see why the graph of $f(x)$ is centered at μ and why its spread is determined by σ.

Because we obtain a different normal density for each possible μ and σ^2 combination, it is not really correct to refer to *the* normal distribution. Rather, we refer to the normal *family* of distributions, where each member of this family is determined by a specific pair μ and σ^2. When X has a normal distribution with mean μ and variance σ^2, we say that "X has a $N(\mu, \sigma^2)$ distribution," or simply that "X is $N(\mu, \sigma^2)$." For example, if X is $N(3, 4)$, then X has a normal distribution with mean 3, variance 4, and standard deviation 2.

> The notation "X is $N(\mu, \sigma^2)$" means that X is normally distributed with mean μ and variance σ^2.

5.3

Standardizing and Using the Normal Table

We now learn how to calculate probabilities involving normal random variables. The general procedure is probably easier to understand if we look at a typical example. Suppose that X is the net income of a restaurant in the next month, measured in thousands of dollars. We will assume that X is normally distributed with $\mu = 3$ and $\sigma = 2$. (These are also measured in thousands of dollars.) Let's calculate the probability that the restaurant's net income is between \$4000 and \$5000, namely $P(4 < X < 5)$. The relevant probability is shown as an area in Figure 5.2.

In Chapter 4 we said that probabilities for continuous random variables can be found in tables in the Appendix to this book. But imagine all the tables that we would require. For the restaurant problem we would need a table of $N(3, 4)$ probabilities. But for a second problem we might need a table for a $N(2, 5)$ random variable, for a third problem we might need a table for a $N(-2, 7)$ random variable, and so on. If we had to include a table for each conceivable normal distribution, our task would be hopeless. Fortunately, this is not necessary. We only need a table for one particular normal distribution. This is the $N(0, 1)$ distribution, often called the *standard normal distribution*.

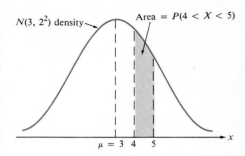

Figure 5.2

> The standard normal distribution is the $N(0, 1)$ distribution, with mean 0 and variance (and standard deviation) 1.

The procedure for finding $P(4 < X < 5)$ can now be broken down into two steps:

1. Write $P(4 < X < 5)$ as an equivalent probability involving a $N(0, 1)$ random variable.
2. Look up the latter probability in the $N(0, 1)$ table.

To carry out the first step, we need to *standardize* the random variable X. In general, if X is a $N(\mu, \sigma^2)$ random variable, we standardize it by (1) subtracting its mean μ, and then (2) dividing the difference $X - \mu$ by the standard deviation σ. The result is a $N(0, 1)$ random variable and is usually denoted by Z.

> *Standardizing a Normal Random Variable*
>
> Define $Z = (X - \mu)/\sigma$.
>
> If X is $N(\mu, \sigma^2)$, then Z is $N(0, 1)$.

In the restaurant example, $\mu = 3$ and $\sigma = 2$, so the standardized random variable is

$$Z = \frac{X - 3}{2}$$

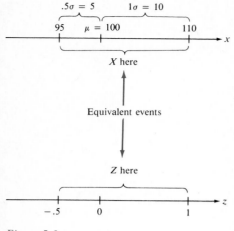

Figure 5.3

We will use this transformation many times in our study of statistical inference. In each case we will continue to use the letter Z to represent a standardized $N(0, 1)$ random variable. In fact, this usage is so common that many people refer to the $N(0, 1)$ distribution as the "Z distribution."

> The $N(0, 1)$ distribution is often called the Z distribution because it is common to denote a $N(0, 1)$ random variable by the letter Z.

We may interpret the value of Z in a very useful way. It tells us how many standard deviations X is from its mean. For example, if $Z = 1$, this means that X is 1 standard deviation above its mean. If $Z = -.5$, then X is ½ standard deviation below its mean. (The minus sign implies that X is *below* its mean.) The inequality $-.5 < Z < 1$ means that X has a value no more than ½ standard deviation below its mean and no more than 1 standard deviation above its mean. This event is illustrated in Figure 5.3, with $\mu = 100$ and $\sigma = 10$.

> A value of Z represents the number of standard deviations X is to the right or left of its mean.

Now we return to our probability calculation. The restaurant's net income X is normal with mean 3 and standard deviation 2, and we want to find $P(4 < X < 5)$. Since 5 is 1 standard deviation to the right of the mean, and 4 is ½ standard deviation to the right of the mean, X between 4 and 5 is equivalent to Z between .5 and 1. In probability notation, we have

$$P(4 < X < 5) = P\left(\frac{4 - 3}{2} < \frac{X - 3}{2} < \frac{5 - 3}{2}\right) = P(.5 < Z < 1)$$

This completes step 1 of the procedure, namely, converting a probability involving X into one involving Z. Now we learn how to calculate a probability involving Z. First consider the left-hand tail probability $P(Z < z)$. Here capital Z is a random variable and small z is any possible value of Z (see Figure 5.4).

The standard normal table, Table Ia in Appendix B, lists the probabilities $P(Z < z)$ for positive values of z (with no more than two digits to the right of the decimal point). The tabulated values of z are found from the left-hand and top margins of the table. The associated probabilities $P(Z < z)$ appear in the body of the table. A portion of Table Ia is shown in Table 5.1. For example, to find $P(Z < 1)$, we locate 1.0 along the left and .00 along the top (since $1 = 1.00$). The resulting probability is .8413. Similarly, to find $P(Z < .5)$, we locate .5 along the left and .00 along the top to obtain .6915.

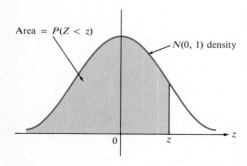

Figure 5.4

Table 5.1 Portion of Normal Table (Table Ia)

z	.00	.01	.02	.03	.04	.05	.06	.07	.08	.09
.										
.	$P(Z < .5)$									
.										
0.5	.6915	.6950	.6985	.7019	.7054	.7088	.7123	.7157	.7190	.7224
.	$P(Z < 1)$									
.										
1.0	.8413	.8438	.8461	.8485	.8508	.8531	.8554	.8577	.8599	.8621
.										
.										
.										

Table Ia allows us to finish the calculation for the restaurant problem. To find the probability $P(.5 < Z < 1)$, we subtract the area to the left of .5 from the area to the left of 1. This gives us the area between .5 and 1. The result is

$$P(4 < X < 5) = P(.5 < Z < 1) = P(Z < 1) - P(Z < .5)$$
$$= .8413 - .6915 = .1498$$

Often we need $P(Z < z)$ for a value of z that has more than two significant digits to the right of the decimal. For example, suppose that we need $P(Z < 1.3425)$. There are two ways to proceed, depending on the accuracy required. The simplest way is to round 1.3425 to the nearest tabulated value, 1.34, and then approximate $P(Z < 1.3425)$ by $P(Z < 1.34) = .9099$. (Here we located 1.3 along the left and .04 along the top.) A better (but still not exact) method is to interpolate the tabulated values. However, this method frequently leads to arithmetic errors, so we do not recommend it unless greater accuracy is absolutely required. For all the problems in this book, the rounding method is sufficiently accurate.

Notice that Table Ia contains values of $P(Z < z)$ for *positive* values of z only. However, if we need $P(Z < -z)$ for a negative value $-z$, we use the symmetry (around the mean 0) of the standard normal density. For example, $P(Z < -2.1)$, the area under the curve to the left of -2.1, is the same as the area under the curve to the *right* of 2.1, which in turn is 1 minus the area to the left of 2.1. Therefore, we can find $P(Z < -2.1)$ as follows.

$$P(Z < -2.1) = P(Z > 2.1) = 1 - P(Z < 2.1) = 1 - .9821 = .0179$$

In general, the following formula holds (see Figure 5.5).

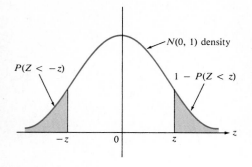

Figure 5.5

> *Formula for $P(Z < -z)$ When $-z$ Is Negative*
>
> $$P(Z < -z) = 1 - P(Z < z)$$

This formula shows why a table of $P(Z < z)$ for positive values of z is indeed sufficient.

EXAMPLE 5.1

Find the probability that the net income of the restaurant owner discussed above is less than $1500.

SOLUTION

We know that the net income X, measured in $1000s, is normal with mean 3 and standard deviation 2. Since the required probability is $P(X < 1.5)$, we have

$$P(X < 1.5) = P\left(\frac{X - 3}{2} < \frac{1.5 - 3}{2}\right) = P(Z < -.75)$$
$$= 1 - P(Z < .75)$$
$$= 1 - .7734 = .2266$$

Therefore, the restaurant owner's chance of failing to net at least $1500 is slightly less than 1 out of 4.

EXAMPLE 5.2

Suppose it is known that the distribution of purchase amounts by customers entering a supermarket is normal with mean $45 and standard deviation $10. Find the probability that a typical customer spends between $35 and $60.

SOLUTION

Let X be the amount this customer spends. Then we know that X is $N(45, 10^2)$, and we want to find $P(35 < X < 60)$. First we standardize each side of this inequality: 35 becomes $(35 - 45)/10 = -1$, 60 becomes $(60 - 45)/10 = 1.5$, and X becomes $(X - 45)/10 = Z$. Therefore,

$$P(35 < X < 60) = P(-1 < Z < 1.5) = P(Z < 1.5) - P(Z < -1)$$
$$= P(Z < 1.5) - [1 - P(Z < 1)]$$
$$= .9332 - (1 - .8413) = .7745$$

This says that the chance is slightly greater than 3 out of 4 that the customer will spend between \$35 and \$60 (see Figure 5.6).

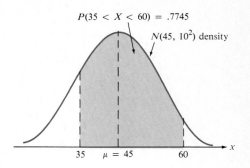

$P(35 < X < 60) = .7745$

$N(45, 10^2)$ density

Figure 5.6

After some practice, normal probability calculations such as these become routine. However, at first we strongly advise *drawing a graph* for each example to aid the calculations. This graph should contain the standard normal density, with the required area shaded. Graphs such as these usually eliminate careless mistakes, such as confusing an event with its complement. For example, consider $P(Z > 1.4)$. If we look up $z = 1.4$ in Table Ia, we find the value .9192. At this point it is tempting to write $P(Z > 1.4) = .9192$. But if we draw the graph in Figure 5.7, we see that the right-hand tail probability, $P(Z > 1.4)$, cannot possibly be as large as .9192. Therefore, we correctly subtract .9192 from 1 to obtain $P(Z > 1.4) = .0808$.

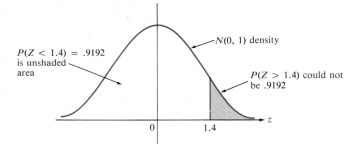

$P(Z < 1.4) = .9192$ is unshaded area

$N(0, 1)$ density

$P(Z > 1.4)$ could not be .9192

Figure 5.7

5.4
Finding z Values from Probabilities

So far, we have used Table Ia in only one way: to find a probability $P(Z < z)$ for a given value of z. However, the table may be used in the opposite direction just as well. For example, suppose that we want to know the number z such that 5% of the area under the $N(0, 1)$ density is to the right of z. Then we must solve the equation $P(Z > z) = .05$ for z. Since $P(Z > z)$ equals $1 - P(Z < z)$, $P(Z > z) = .05$ is equivalent to $P(Z < z) = .95$. That is, if there is .05 area to the right of z, there must be .95 area to the left of z (see Figure 5.8 on p. 200).

The procedure in this case is to locate the probability value .95 (or a probability value as close to .95 as possible) in Table Ia and then read to the left and up to find the associated z value. Alternatively, we can use Table

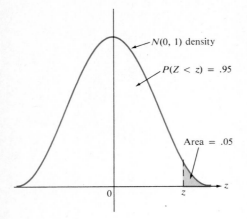

Figure 5.8

Ib, which has been supplied for precisely this type of problem. In this table the probability $P(Z < z)$ is listed along the left and the top margins (to three decimal places). The corresponding z values are shown in the body of the table. So to find the z value with .95 area to the left of it, we locate .95 along the left and .000 along the top. The appropriate z value is seen to be 1.645.

Since the problem of finding the appropriate z value for a given (usually small) right-hand tail probability occurs so often, we use a special notation for the required z value. If α is a given probability, we let z_α denote the value with probability α to the right of it. (Alternatively, z_α is the value with probability $1 - \alpha$ to the left of it.) For example, we just saw that $z_{.05} = 1.645$. The general definition of z_α follows.

Definition of z_α

For any probability α, z_α satisfies $P(Z > z_\alpha) = \alpha$.

By the symmetry of the $N(0, 1)$ density, if we want the z value with a small probability α to the *left* of it, this must be $-z_\alpha$ (see Figure 5.9). Several particular z values we will see many times are listed in Table 5.2.

Table 5.2 Frequently Used z Values

α	.10	.05	.025	.02	.01	.005	.001
z_α	1.282	1.645	1.960	2.054	2.326	2.576	3.090

EXAMPLE 5.2 (continued)

Recall that the purchase amounts for supermarket customers are normal with mean \$45 and standard deviation \$10. Find a dollar amount such that 90% of all customers spend no more than this amount.

SOLUTION

Let x be the desired amount. Then x satisfies $P(X < x) = .90$, where X is $N(45, 10^2)$. Standardizing X and x, we obtain

$$P\left(Z < \frac{x - 45}{10}\right) = .90$$

In words, there must be .90 area to the left of $(x - 45)/10$ under the $N(0, 1)$ density. But this means that there must be .10 area to the right of $(x - 45)/10$ (see Figure 5.10). From Table 5.2 (or Table Ib), we know there

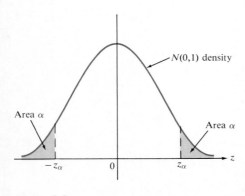

Figure 5.9

is .10 area to the right of $z_{.10}$, and that $z_{.10} = 1.282$. Therefore, we set $(x - 45)/10$ equal to 1.282 and solve for x. The result is $x = \$57.82$. That is, 90% of all customers spend no more than \$57.82; only 10% spend more.

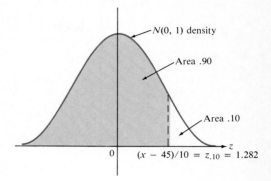

Figure 5.10

A somewhat more difficult problem is to find two z values such that the area between them is a specified probability, say .95. For now, we denote these two z values as z_1 and z_2. Then z_1 and z_2 must satisfy $P(z_1 < Z < z_2) = .95$. The difficulty here is that there is not a unique answer. If we do find one pair z_1 and z_2 with area .95 between them, we can shift both z_1 and z_2 to the left or to the right (by different amounts) and keep the area between them equal to .95. For example, the reader can check that $z_1 = -2.19$ and $z_2 = 1.80$ do the job, as do $z_1 = -1.71$ and $z_2 = 2.50$.

One way to obtain a unique answer to our question is to look for the pair z_1 and z_2 that are *closest* to one another and have area .95 between them. It can be shown that this occurs when $z_1 = -z_2$, that is, when the resulting interval from z_1 to z_2 is symmetric around 0. From now on, this is the type of interval we will find in these types of problems. Because of its symmetry around 0, the resulting interval cuts off an equal area in each tail. Since the area between z_1 and z_2 is required to be .95, the area in each tail must be .025. Therefore, z_2 must be $z_{.025} = 1.96$ (from Table Ib or Table 5.2) and z_1 must be $-z_{.025} = -1.96$.

In general, if $1 - \alpha$ is any probability and we want numbers z_1 and z_2 that satisfy $P(z_1 < Z < z_2) = 1 - \alpha$, we solve the problem by putting $\alpha/2$ area in each tail and letting $z_1 = -z_{\alpha/2}$ and $z_2 = z_{\alpha/2}$. This is shown graphically in Figure 5.11.

The same calculations can also be done with any normal random variables. As usual, the trick is to standardize the random variable, do the calculations on a Z random variable, and finally, convert the answer back to the original units. The following example illustrates the procedure.

EXAMPLE 5.2 (continued)

For the supermarket example, find two dollar values such that 90% of all customers' purchase amounts are between these values.

SOLUTION

Let x_1 and x_2 be the required values. We want $P(x_1 < X < x_2) = .90$, where X is $N(45, 10^2)$. By standardizing each of the quantities, we obtain

$$P(x_1 < X < x_2) = P\left(\frac{x_1 - 45}{10} < Z < \frac{x_2 - 45}{10}\right) = .90$$

Since the values $\pm z_{.05} = \pm 1.645$ cut off .05 in each tail of the $N(0, 1)$ density and therefore leave .90 in the middle, we set $(x_1 - 45)/10$ equal to

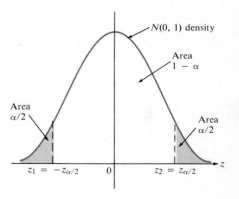

Figure 5.11

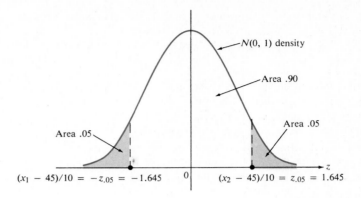

$(x_1 - 45)/10 = -z_{.05} = -1.645$ 0 $(x_2 - 45)/10 = z_{.05} = 1.645$

Figure 5.12

-1.645 and $(x_2 - 45)/10$ equal to 1.645, and solve for x_1 and x_2 (see Figure 5.12). The results are $x_1 = \$28.55$ and $x_2 = \$61.45$. In words, 90% of the customers spend between $28.55 and $61.45, 5% spend less than $28.55, and the other 5% spend more than $61.45.

All the calculations we will do are variations of the examples discussed to this point. There are three prescriptions for doing these problems both quickly and accurately.

Tips for Doing Normal Probability Calculations

1. Know exactly what information is available in Tables Ia and Ib and how to extract it. Use Table Ia when a z value is given and a probability is required. Use Table Ib when a probability is given and one or more z values are required. Do not try to be more accurate than what is shown in the table. For classroom problems and most real-world applications, greater accuracy than this is not necessary.
2. Draw graphs to see which areas are required. This makes the ideas in the problems much clearer, and it helps to eliminate careless mistakes.
3. Interpret a z value as the number of standard deviations from the mean, where a negative z value indicates it is to the left of the mean and a positive z value indicates it is to the right of the mean. This interpretation of a z value is valid regardless of the original values of μ and σ.

5.5

Rules 2.2 and 4.2 Revisited

We now look at one set of probability calculations where the results should be familiar. Let X be $N(\mu, \sigma^2)$ and let k be any positive number. We will find the probability that X has a value within k standard deviations of its mean. This is

$$P(\mu - k\sigma < X < \mu + k\sigma) = P(-k < Z < k)$$

When $k = 1$, $P(-k < Z < k)$ equals .6826. Similarly, when $k = 2$, $P(-k < Z < k) = .9544$, and when $k = 3$, $P(-k < Z < k) = .9974$.

These calculations are the basis for Rules 2.2 and 4.2 presented in Chapters 2 and 4. They show that normal random variables are within 1 standard deviation of the mean about 68% of the time, within 2 standard deviations of the mean about 95% of the time, and within 3 standard deviations of the mean well over 99% of the time. In fact, the probability of a normal random variable being outside the interval from $\mu - 3\sigma$ to $\mu + 3\sigma$ is only .0026. So for all practical purposes, a normal random variable has a value between $\mu - 3\sigma$ and $\mu + 3\sigma$. These facts are illustrated in Figure 5.13.

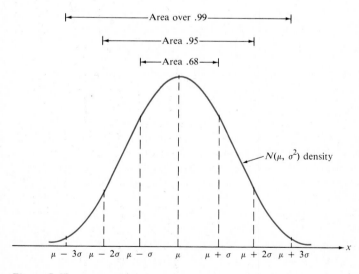

Figure 5.13
Graphic Illustration of Rule 4.2

5.6

Applications of the Normal Distribution

We now look at several practical examples involving the normal distribution.

EXAMPLE 5.3

Suppose a health insurance company finds that the annual medical expense per household is normally distributed with mean \$335 and standard deviation \$115. (This counts only those households that do not spend any time in hospitals.) Each household pays an annual premium of \$600 per year and is reimbursed 80% of its medical expenses after the first \$100 in expenses is paid. (The first \$100 is called the deductible amount.) For example, a household with \$300 of medical expenses pays all of the first \$100 but gets reimbursed 80% of the last \$200, or \$160. For a typical household, find (1) the probability that it incurs at least the deductible amount of expenses, and (2) the probability that the insurance company makes less than \$200 net from this houshold for the year.

SOLUTION

Let X be the amount of this household's medical expenses. We are given that X is $N(335, 115^2)$. To find the probability that the family incurs at least \$100 of expenses, we find $P(X > 100)$. This is

$$P(X > 100) = P\left(Z > \frac{100 - 335}{115}\right) = P(Z > -2.04) = P(Z < 2.04) = .9793$$

(Here we used Table Ia with $z = 2.04$.) So approximately 98% of these households do meet the deductible amount.

For the second question, notice that the profit the insurance company makes from a given household is the premium, \$600, minus the amount of reimbursement. If the household's expenses are less than \$100, there is no reimbursement, and the company certainly makes more than \$200. If X is greater than \$100, however, the reimbursement is 80% of (expenses $-$ \$100), or $.80(X - 100)$. In this case the net profit to the insurance company is $600 - .8(X - 100)$, or $680 - .8X$. This amount is less than \$200 if $680 - .8X$ is less than 200, which is equivalent to $X > 600$. The probability of this event, again using Table Ia, is

$$P(X > 600) = P\left(Z > \frac{600 - 335}{115}\right) = P(Z > 2.30)$$

$$= 1 - P(Z < 2.30) = 1 - .9893 = .0107$$

The implication is that the company makes at least $200 net profit from approximately 99% of these households.

EXAMPLE 5.4

Consider an investor who invests $10,000 of his money in a certain stock on January 1, 1988. By examining past movements of this stock and consulting with his broker, the investor estimates that the annual rate of return from this stock, X, is a $N(.10, .04^2)$ random variable. Here X is the amount of profit the investor receives per dollar invested. It means that on December 31, 1988, the investor's $10,000 will have grown to $10,000(1 + X)$. Because this investor is in the 40% tax bracket, he will then have to pay the IRS 40% of his profit. Calculate (1) the probability that he will have to pay the IRS at least $500, and (2) the dollar amount such that the investor's after-tax profit is 90% certain to be less than this amount.

SOLUTION

The investor's before-tax profit is $10,000X$, so the amount he pays the IRS is $(.4)10,000X$, or $4000X$ dollars. We want the probability that this is at least $500. Using Table Ia, this is

$$P(4000X > 500) = P\left(X > \frac{500}{4000}\right) = P(X > .125)$$

$$= P\left(Z > \frac{.125 - .10}{.04}\right) = P(Z > .63) = 1 - P(Z < .63)$$

$$= 1 - .7357 = .2643$$

So the chances are about three out of four that his IRS bill will be less than $500.

For the second question, we notice that the after-tax profit is 60% of the before-tax profit, or $6000X$ dollars. Therefore, we want the dollar value x such that $P(6000X < x)$ equals .90. This leads to

$$.90 = P(6000X < x) = P\left(X < \frac{x}{6000}\right) = P\left(Z < \frac{x/6000 - .10}{.04}\right)$$

From the graph shown in Figure 5.14 (p. 206), we see that the standardized value $(x/6000 - .10)/.04$ must equal $z_{.10}$, which is 1.282 (see Table 5.2 or

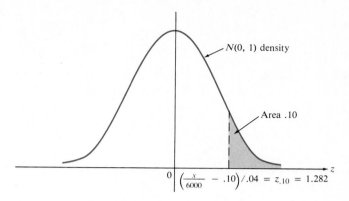

Figure 5.14

Ib). So we set $(x/6000 - .10)/.04$ equal to 1.282 and solve for x. The result is $x = \$907.68$. In words, the investor is 90% certain that his after-tax profit will be less than $\$907.68$.

EXAMPLE 5.5

The personnel department of a large company is reconsidering its hiring policy. Each applicant for a job must take a standard exam, and the hire or no-hire decision depends largely on the results of this exam. The scores of all applicants have been examined closely. They show that the scores are normally distributed with a mean score of 525 (out of a possible 800) and a standard deviation of 55. The current hiring policy occurs in two phases. The first phase separates all applicants into three categories: automatic accepts, automatic rejects, and "maybes." The automatic accepts are those whose test scores are 600 or above. The automatic rejects are those whose test scores are 425 or below. All other applicants (the "maybes") are passed on to a second phase where their previous job experience, special talents, and other factors are used as hiring criteria.

The people in charge of personnel want to calculate the probability that a typical applicant will be an automatic accept or reject, given the current standards. They also want to know how to change the standards in order to automatically reject 10% of all applicants and automatically accept 15% of all applicants.

SOLUTION

Let X be the test score of a typical applicant. Then X is $N(525, 55^2)$. The probability that this applicant is automatically accepted is

$$P(X > 600) = P\left(Z > \frac{600 - 525}{55}\right) = P(Z > 1.36)$$

$$= 1 - P(Z < 1.36) = 1 - .9131 = .0869$$

Similarly, the probability that the applicant is automatically rejected is

$$P(X < 425) = P\left(Z < \frac{425 - 525}{55}\right) = P(Z < -1.82)$$

$$= 1 - P(Z < 1.82) = 1 - .9656 = .0344$$

In words, the company automatically accepts about 8.7% and automatically rejects about 3.4% of all applicants.

For the second question, let x_1 and x_2 be the new standards for automatic accepts and rejects. These are to be set so that the percentages in these categories increase to 15% and 10% (see Figure 5.15). To find x_1, we set the standardized x_1 value equal to $z_{.15}$, which is 1.036 (from Table Ib). That is,

$$\frac{x_1 - 525}{55} = 1.036$$

The solution (rounded to the nearest integer) is $x_1 = 582$. Similarly, to find x_2 we set $(x_2 - 525)/55$ equal to $-z_{.10}$, which is -1.282. (We need a minus sign because we want area .10 to be in the *left-hand* tail.) The solution is $x_2 = 454$. These answers imply that if the people in personnel want more automatic accepts and rejects, they must lower the automatic accept score from 600 to 582 and raise the automatic reject score from 425 to 454.

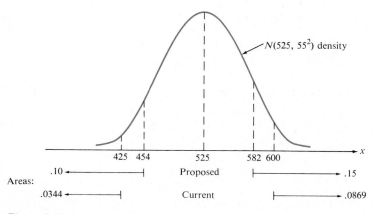

Figure 5.15

EXAMPLE 5.6

Consider a manufacturing facility that produces a paper product. The fiber content of this product is supposed to be 20 pounds per 1000 square feet. (This is typical for the type of paper used in grocery bags, for example.) Because of random variations in the inputs to the process, however, the fiber content of a typical 1000-square-foot roll varies according to a normal distribution with mean μ and variance σ^2. The value of μ can be set to any desired level by adjusting an instrument on the machine. The value of σ is .1 pound when the machine is "in control," but it sometimes increases to .15 pound when the machine goes "out of control." A given roll of this product must be rejected if its actual fiber content is less than 19.8 pounds or greater than 20.3 pounds. Calculate the probability that a given roll is rejected, for a setting of $\mu = 20$, when the machine is in control and when it is out of control.

SOLUTION

Let $\mu = 20$ and let X be a $N(20, \sigma^2)$ random variable. Here X represents the fiber content of a typical 1000-square-foot roll. The probability of a reject when the machine is in control ($\sigma = .1$) is the sum of two probabilities:

$$P(\text{reject when } \sigma = .1) = P(X < 19.8 \text{ or } X > 20.3)$$
$$= P(X < 19.8) + P(X > 20.3)$$

The first of these probabilities is

$$P(X < 19.8) = P\left(Z < \frac{19.8 - 20}{.1}\right) = P(Z < -2) = 1 - P(Z < 2) = .0228$$

Similarly, the second probability is

$$P(X > 20.3) = P\left(Z > \frac{20.3 - 20}{.1}\right) = P(Z > 3) = 1 - P(Z < 3) = .0013$$

So the probability of a reject is .0228 + .0013, or .0241.

When the machine is out of control, $\sigma = .15$. In this case the standardized values of 19.8 and 20.3 are -1.33 and 2, respectively. By imitating the calculations above, we obtain

$$P(\text{reject when } \sigma = .15) = .0918 + .0228 = .1146$$

Therefore, a 50% increase in the standard deviation (from .1 to .15) increases the probability of a reject by a factor of almost 5.

The Central Limit Theorem

In this section we discuss a mathematical result of fundamental importance to statistical theory. This result is called the *Central Limit Theorem*. Essentially, it says that sums and averages of many random variables from *any* distribution, normal or nonnormal, are normally distributed. This fact accounts for the widespread use of the normal distribution in so many real-world applications. It means that any time we gather observations that can be considered sums or averages of many small "components," these observations have a good chance of being normally distributed.

Actually, there are several versions of the Central Limit Theorem. Basically, they all say that sums or averages of many random variables from any distribution are normally distributed, although they all make slightly different assumptions. The version we present below is the simplest and most familiar version of this result. We do mention, however, that most of the assumptions in this version can be relaxed to some extent, and the conclusion remains valid.

The Central Limit Theorem

Suppose that $X_1, X_2, \ldots, X_n$ are n independent random variables, all with the same probability distribution. Also assume that the mean and variance of this common distribution are μ and σ^2. Then if n is sufficiently large, the distribution of the sum $X_1 + X_2 + \cdots + X_n$ is approximately normal with mean $n\mu$ and variance $n\sigma^2$, regardless of the distribution of the individual X's.

Let's examine what this result says. Since each of the X's is a random variable, each has a probability distribution. This common distribution is often called the *parent distribution*. We are given that the mean and variance of the parent distribution are μ and σ^2. The conclusion of the theorem concerns the probability distribution of the sum $X_1 + X_2 + \cdots + X_n$. By the rules of expected values and the independence assumption, we know (see Rules 4.5 and 4.6) that

$$E(X_1 + X_2 + \cdots + X_n) = E(X_1) + E(X_2) + \cdots + E(X_n)$$
$$= \mu + \mu + \cdots + \mu = n\mu$$

and

$$\text{Var}(X_1 + X_2 + \cdots + X_n) = \text{Var}(X_1) + \text{Var}(X_2) + \cdots + \text{Var}(X_n)$$
$$= \sigma^2 + \sigma^2 + \cdots + \sigma^2 = n\sigma^2$$

Therefore, it should come as no surprise that the mean of the sum is $n\mu$ and the variance of the sum is $n\sigma^2$.

The surprising part of the Central Limit Theorem is that the distribution of the sum is *normal*. Although the exact distribution of the sum can be derived mathematically from the parent distribution by using the rules of probability, the derivation is usually extremely difficult. This is where the Central Limit Theorem is useful. It says that the probability distribution of the sum becomes more symmetric and bell-shaped as n, the number of terms in the sum, becomes large.

EXAMPLE 5.7

Suppose that 150 customers enter a department store on a given day. Each customer spends a random amount. All that is known about the distribution of these expenditures is that its mean is $7.50 and its standard deviation is $3.40. Find the mean and standard deviation of the total amount spent during the day, and find the probability that this amount is at least $1200.

SOLUTION

We really do not need the Central Limit Theorem to answer the first question. Assuming that the individual expenditures are independent random variables, Rules 4.5 and 4.6 imply that the total amount purchased has mean $n\mu = 150(7.50) = \$1125$ and variance $n\sigma^2 = 150(3.40^2) = 1734$, so that the standard deviation is $41.64. To answer the second question, however, we do require the Central Limit Theorem. It tells us that the total amount spent, the sum of the 150 individual expenditures, is approximately *normally* distributed with mean $1125 and standard deviation $41.64. Therefore, letting X denote the total amount spent, we have

$$P(X > 1200) = P\left(Z > \frac{1200 - 1125}{41.64}\right) = P(Z > 1.80) = 1 - .9641 = .0359$$

In words, there is only about 1 chance in 30 that the total amount spent will be larger than $1200.

The conclusion of the Central Limit Theorem is true "if n is sufficiently large." How large must n be? This depends on the parent distribution. If the parent distribution is very nonnormal (extremely skewed or bimodal, for example), n may have to be quite large for the distribution of the sum to be approximately normal. If the parent distribution is already symmetric and somewhat bell-shaped, however, the distribution of the sum is approximately normal for n quite small, say, 5 to 10. In the extreme, if the parent distribution is normal itself, the distribution of the sum is *exactly* normal for *all* values of n.

In statistical problems, we usually require $n \geq 30$ before we conclude that the Central Limit Theorem applies. But for many "nice" distributions, the conclusion of the theorem is true even when n is quite a bit less than 30. Conversely, for extremely nonnormal distributions, $n = 30$ may not be enough. We will have more to say about this in Chapter 6, where we use the Central Limit Theorem to find the probability distribution of the sample mean.

Problems for Sections 5.2, 5.3, 5.4, 5.5, 5.6, 5.7

1. For each of the following, a normal distribution is given and next to it, several observations are given. Transform these observations into z values; that is, standardize them.
   a. $N(2, 16)$; 5, 4, and -1
   b. $N(-3, 2)$; .5, -4.2, and -4
   c. $N(0, 25)$; -4, -1, and 5.5
   d. $N(3, 3)$; 6, -1, and 0

2. Use the appropriate normal table to find $z_{.06}$, $z_{.27}$, $-z_{.40}$, and $-z_{.17}$. How much area is to the left of each of these?

3. For each of the following, find the probability for the given normal distribution.
   a. $P(X > 2)$ if X is $N(5, 25)$
   b. $P(X < 3)$ if X is $N(1.5, 9)$
   c. $P(0 < X < 7)$ if X is $N(-1, 40)$
   d. $P(1 < X < 10$ or $13 < X < 15)$ if X is $N(12, 200)$

4. Find the following normal probabilities.
   a. $P(8 < X < 12)$ if X is $N(10, 25)$
   b. $P(-2 < X < 4)$ if X is $N(1, 5)$
   c. $P(100 < X < 150)$ if X is $N(125, 400)$
   d. $P(-10 < X < -6)$ if X is $N(-8, 20)$

5. Find the following probabilities. In each, Z is a standard normal random variable.
   a. $P(Z < -1)$ b. $P(Z > -.45)$ c. $P(-2 < Z < 1)$
   d. $P(Z > .95)$ e. $P(-3 < Z < 0)$
   f. $P(-.27 < Z < .48)$

6. Find the following probabilities without resorting to any normal tables. (Remember the meaning of z_α for any α between 0 and 1.)
   a. $P(Z < z_{.1})$ b. $P(Z > z_{.3})$ c. $P(-z_{.3} < Z < z_{.4})$
   d. $P(Z < -z_{.4})$ e. $P(Z < z_{.05}$ or $Z > z_{.005})$
   f. $P(Z < -z_{.005}$ or $Z > z_{.5})$

7. For each of the following, a normal distribution and a probability are given. Find an interval symmetric about the mean with this probability.
   a. $N(0, 1)$; .92   b. $N(-3, 1)$; .90   c. $N(10, 100)$; .95
   d. $N(15, 20)$; .80   e. $N(-6, 10)$; .99   f. $N(100, 25)$; .70

8. For each of the following, a normal distribution and two probabilities are given. Find the endpoints of an interval that cuts off the first probability in the left-hand tail and the second probability in the right-hand tail.
   a. $N(6, 8)$; .01, .005   b. $N(20, 49)$; .10, .15
   c. $N(0, 15)$; .07, .025   d. $N(100, 27)$; .005, .05

9. Find six z values that divide the $N(0, 1)$ density into seven equal-area sections, as shown below.

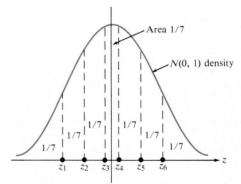

10. Given a normal random variable with mean 10 and variance 100, find values x_1 and x_2 that divide the $N(10, 100)$ density into three equal areas. That is, they should satisfy

$$P(X < x_1) = P(x_1 < X < x_2) = P(X > x_2) = \frac{1}{3}$$

11. If X is a $N(3, \sigma^2)$ random variable and $P(X < 6) = .95$, what must the value of σ be?

12. If X is normally distributed with standard deviation 5, and the event $X > 105$ has probability .97, what must the mean be?

13. The price per gallon of unleaded gasoline varies according to a normal distribution throughout the midwest. The mean and standard deviation of this distribution are $1.20 and $.04.

a. What is the probability that a given gas station charges less than $1.21 for its unleaded gasoline; more than $1.25?

b. Find two prices so that 95% of all gas stations charge between these prices for unleaded gasoline. (Make these two prices symmetric about the mean.)

14. The daily demand for a certain brand of cereal at the local supermarket varies according to a normal distribution with mean 45 and standard deviation 10. Let X be the number of boxes demanded on a typical day.

a. Find the probability that X is between 34 and 56.

b. Find the number of boxes such that this day's demand is 75% certain to be at least this amount.

c. Find the mathematical probability that X is less than 0. Keeping in mind that negative demand is physically impossible, is the assumption of a normally distributed demand realistic? Why or why not?

15. Assume that the length of a typical baseball game, including all the commercial timeouts, is normally distributed with mean 2.45 hours and standard deviation .37 hour. Consider a televised baseball game that begins at 2:00 in the afternoon. The next regularly scheduled broadcast is at 5:00.

a. What is the probability that the game will cut into the next show, that is, go past 5:00?

b. If the game is over before 4:30, another half-hour show can be inserted into the 4:30-to-5:00 slot. What is the probability of this occurring?

16. The amount of a soft drink that goes into a typical 12-ounce can varies from can to can. It is normally distributed with an adjustable mean μ and a fixed standard deviation of .05 ounce.

a. If regulations require that cans have at least 11.9 ounces, what is the *smallest* mean μ that can be used so that at least 99% of all cans meet the regulation?

b. If the mean setting from part (a) is used, what is the probability that a typical can has at least 12 ounces?

17. A family is considering a move from a midwestern city to a city in California. The distribution of housing costs where the family currently lives is normal with mean $75,000 and standard deviation $12,500. The distribution of housing costs in the California city is normal with mean $110,000 and standard deviation $16,400. The family's current house is worth $85,000.

a. What percentage of houses in the family's current city cost less than theirs?

b. If the family buys an $85,000 house in the new city, what percentage of houses there will cost less than theirs?

18. Referring to Problem 17, what price house would the family have to buy in California to remain in the same percentile

(that is, have the same percentage of houses cost less than theirs) that they are currently in? If they wish to increase their percentile ranking by five percentage points, what price house will they have to buy in California?

19. The number of traffic fatalities in a typical month in a given state has a normal distribution with mean 125 and standard deviation 31.

a. If a person in the highway department claims that there will be at least x fatalities in the next month with probability .95, what value of x makes this claim true?

b. If the claim is that there will be no more than y fatalities in the next month with probability .98, what value of y makes this claim true?

20. After many years of recording weather data, weather forecasters in an eastern city know that the yearly snowfall is normally distributed with mean 25 inches and standard deviation 8 inches.

a. How probable is the event that there will be no more than 10 inches of snow next year?

b. If the amounts of snow in successive years are independent random variables, how probable is the event that the next two years will *each* experience less than 15 inches of snow?

21. Consider the investor in Example 5.4. Suppose that he invests $15,000 instead of $10,000, and his return is still normally distributed with mean .10 and standard deviation .04. Also, assume that he is still in the 40% tax bracket.

a. Find the amount x such that he is 90% sure of not having to pay more than x dollars to the IRS.

b. Find two numbers x_1 and x_2 (symmetric about the mean) such that he is 95% certain that his before-tax profit will be between x_1 and x_2 dollars.

*22. A fast-foods restaurant sells hamburgers and chicken sandwiches. On a typical weekday, the demand for hamburgers is normally distributed with mean 313 and standard deviation 57; the demand for chicken sandwiches is normally distributed with mean 93 and standard deviation 22.

a. How many hamburgers must the restaurant stock to be 98% sure of not running out on a given day?

b. Answer part (a) for chicken sandwiches.

c. If the restaurant stocks 400 hamburgers and 150 chicken sandwiches, what is the probability that it will run out of hamburgers or chicken sandwiches (or both) on a given day? Assume that the demand for hamburgers and the demand for chicken sandwiches are independent random variables.

d. Do you believe that the independence assumption in part (c) is realistic? Why or why not?

*23. Consider a record collector who buys 155 records over a two-year period. The distribution of record prices during this period has mean $8.45 and standard deviation $.78, but it is not necessarily normal. Answer the following questions, using the Central Limit Theorem where necessary.

  a. What are the mean and standard deviation of the total amount the collector spends for records during this period? (Assume that the prices of the individual records are independent random variables.)

  b. What is the probability that the collector spends at least $1300 for records during this period?

  c. What value x has the property that we are 95% certain the collector spends no more than x during this period?

*24. Claims arrive at random times to an insurance company. The daily amount of claims is a random variable with mean $356 and standard deviation $156. Daily claims are independent of one another, but due to very large claims that occur now and then, the distribution of daily claims is skewed to the right.

  a. Using the Central Limit Theorem, find the (approximate) probability that the sum of the claims for 100 consecutive days totals at least $36,000.

  b. If the company receives premiums of $45,000 for the 100-day period, what is the probability that it will net at least $10,000?

5.8

The Binomial Distribution

The normal distribution is undoubtedly the most important probability distribution in statistics. Not far behind in order of importance, however, is the binomial distribution. The binomial distribution is a discrete distribution that can occur in two situations: (1) whenever we sample from a population with only two types of members, and (2) whenever we perform a sequence of identical experiments, each of which has only two possible outcomes.

Imagine any situation or "experiment" that can be repeated many times under identical conditions. We will refer to each repetition of the experiment as a *trial*. We assume that the outcomes of successive trials are probabilistically independent of one another and that each trial has only two possible outcomes. For now, we will label these two possibilities as A's and B's. (In specific contexts we will call the two possibilities whatever they happen to be, such as defectives or nondefectives, increases or decreases in stock prices, and so on.) On each trial, the probability of an A is labeled p, and the probability of a B is $1 - p$.

If there are n trials altogether, let X be the number of A's in these n trials. Then we say that X is a *binomial* random variable with parameters n and p. For example, if $n = 100$ and $p = .4$, then X is the number of A's in 100 trials when the probability of an A on each trial is .4.

A binomial random variable with parameters n and p is the number of A's in n independent trials when p is the probability of an A on any given trial.

The probability distribution of X is given as follows. First, the possible values of X are the integers 0, 1, 2, . . ., n. Now let k be any such integer. Then the probability of observing exactly k A's (and hence $n - k$ B's) is given by the following formula:

> *Binomial Formula*
>
> $$P(X = k) = \binom{n}{k} p^k (1 - p)^{n-k} \qquad \text{for } k = 0, 1, 2, . . ., n$$

To understand why this formula is correct, we use the following reasoning with $n = 8$ and $k = 3$. Each sequence of outcomes of the eight trials can be written as a list of A's and B's, where the ith member of this list is an A or a B depending on whether the ith trial results in an A or a B. For example, the sequence (A, B, A, B, A, B, B, B) indicates that A's occur on trials 1, 3, and 5. We know that X equals 3 if any sequence with exactly three A's and five B's occurs. (One of the many possibilities is the sequence above.) Since the outcomes of the individual trials are independent, the multiplication rule for independent events implies that

$$P(A, B, A, B, A, B, B, B) = P(A)P(B)P(A)P(B)P(A)P(B)P(B)P(B) = p^3(1 - p)^5$$

But by similar reasoning, the probability of *any* sequence with three A's and five B's is $p^3(1 - p)^5$.

Now all we need to do is multiply the number of sequences with three A's and five B's by $p^3(1 - p)^5$ to obtain $P(X = 3)$. Since any sequence with three A's and five B's can be formed by choosing the three trials where the A's occur from a total of eight trials, we know from Chapter 3 that there are $\binom{8}{3}$ such sequences. Therefore,

$$P(X = 3) = \binom{8}{3} p^3(1 - p)^5$$

This reasoning is perfectly general, so the binomial formula given above follows. This formula is not difficult to remember if we understand what it says. To obtain exactly k A's in n trials, we need k A's (this gives the p^k term) and $n - k$ B's [this gives the $(1 - p)^{n-k}$ term]. The $\binom{n}{k}$ term indicates the number of possible orderings of k A's and $n - k$ B's.

EXAMPLE 5.8

Many machines are structured as "k-out-of-n" systems. This means the machine is composed of n identical components and will continue to function as long as at least k of its components function. Consider a machine with a

2-out-of-4 structure. If the components work independently of one another (in a probabilistic sense), and each functions successfully with probability .85, what is the probability that the machine functions successfully?

SOLUTION

Let X be the number of components that function successfully. Then the probability that the machine functions successfully is $P(X \geq 2)$, which equals $P(X = 2) + P(X = 3) + P(X = 4)$. We find each of these individual probabilities from the binomial formula. For example,

$$P(X = 2) = \binom{4}{2}(.85)^2(.15)^2 = 6(.85)^2(.15)^2 = .0975$$

Similarly,

$$P(X = 3) = \binom{4}{3}(.85)^3(.15)^1 = 4(.85)^3(.15) = .3685$$

and

$$P(X = 4) = \binom{4}{4}(.85)^4(.15)^0 = (.85)^4 = .5220$$

Therefore, the probability that the machine functions successfully is

$$P(X \geq 2) = .0975 + .3685 + .5220 = .9880$$

The Binomial Table

Although binomial probabilities are fairly straightforward to calculate on many hand calculators, Table II in Appendix B lists cumulative binomial probabilities. For the values of n and p listed, the table gives $P(X \leq k)$ for each k between 0 and n. To locate one of these probabilities, we first locate the relevant values of n and p, and then we locate the specific value of k. For example, suppose that we need $P(X \leq 6)$ when $p = .4$ and $n = 10$. We first locate $n = 10$ and $p = .4$ and then read down the k column until we get to $k = 6$. The desired probability is $P(X \leq 6) = .9452$. If, instead, we want an individual probability such as $P(X = 6)$, we only need to subtract cumulative probabilities:

$$P(X = 6) = P(X \leq 6) - P(X \leq 5) = .9452 - .8338 = .1114$$

Table 5.3 (p. 216), a partial reproduction of Table II, illustrates these calculations.

Although Table II is useful in many examples, it is incomplete. If we have a value of n or p that is not tabulated, the table cannot be used, except possibly as an approximation. However, we will see in Section 5.10 how to deal with binomial probabilities when n is large.

Table 5.3   Portion of Binomial Table

k	$p \cdots .35$	$n = 10$ .40	$.45 \cdots$
0		.0060	
1		.0464	
2		.1673	
3		.3823	
4		.6331	
5		.8338	difference = .1114
6		.9452	
7		.9877	
8		.9983	
9		.9999	
10		1.0000	

EXAMPLE 5.9

As part of a promotional campaign for its new computer model, the Bigger Byte Computer Company is raffling away eight new computers. However, these prizes are given only if the people with the lucky numbers claim them. Assume that each winner, independently of the others, claims his or her computer with probability .40. Find the probability that at least six of the computers will be given away.

SOLUTION

Let X be the number of winners who claim their computers. Then X is binomially distributed with $n = 8$ and $p = .40$. We need $P(X \geq 6)$, or equivalently, $1 - P(X \leq 5)$. Using the binomial table, we obtain

$$P(X \geq 6) = 1 - P(X \leq 5) = 1 - .9502 = .0498$$

So even though the company is claiming that eight computers will be given away, there is about a 95% chance that five or fewer computers will actually be given away.

The Mean and Variance of the Binomial Distribution

Suppose that X is a binomial random variable with parameters n and p. Then the mean and variance of X are as follows.

Mean and Variance of a Binomial Random Variable

$$E(X) = np, \qquad \mathrm{Var}(X) = np(1 - p)$$

The formula for the mean of X is quite intuitive. Suppose that we sample 600 people (with replacement) from a large population, one-sixth of whom earn at least $30,000 per year. We label these people the A's. This is a binomial experiment with $p = \frac{1}{6}$ and $n = 600$. Naturally, we would expect approximately $\frac{1}{6}$ of the 600 people to be A's. This is exactly what the formula for the mean gives, since

$$E(X) = np = 600\left(\frac{1}{6}\right) = 100$$

The variance (or standard deviation) of X is also a very useful piece of information. It tells us how far an actual observation is likely to be from the mean. In the example above, our best guess for the number of A's in the sample is 100. However, we do not really expect to observe *exactly* 100 A's; in fact, the probability of exactly 100 A's is less than .05. We really only expect somewhere *near* 100 A's out of 600. How near? Would we be surprised, for example, if we saw as few as 60 A's out of 600? What about 180 or more A's out of 600?

The standard deviation of X, together with Rule 4.2, allows us to answer these questions. Rule 4.2 says that X is within 1 standard deviation of the mean with approximate probability .68, within 2 standard deviations of the mean with approximate probability .95, and within 3 standard deviations of the mean with probability greater than .99. (Rule 4.2 applies here because the distribution of X is fairly symmetric and bell-shaped when n is large.) In the example, $n = 600$ and $p = \frac{1}{6}$, so the standard deviation is

$$\text{StdDev}(X) = \sqrt{np(1 - p)} = \sqrt{600\left(\frac{1}{6}\right)\left(\frac{5}{6}\right)} = 9.13$$

Therefore, the interval within 1 standard deviation of the mean is 100 ± 9.13, or approximately from 91 to 109. For 2 and 3 standard deviations from the mean, the approximate intervals are from 82 to 118 and from 73 to 127, respectively. So we would be very surprised to see fewer than 73 or more than 127 A's out of 600.

5.9

The Binomial Distribution in the Context of Sampling

Before we look at more numerical examples of the binomial distribution, we discuss how the binomial distribution applies to sampling from a population with two types of members. (The reader may wish to review Section 3.10

before reading this section.) This is especially important for our study of statistics because the binomial distribution often arises in sampling contexts. Consider a population with two types of members, labeled A's and B's. We assume that the population size is N and that N_A of these are A's; the other $N_B = N - N_A$ members are B's. If we randomly sample n members of this population, each sampled member can be considered a trial. We let X be the number of A's in the sample.

If sampling is done with replacement each of the N members is equally likely to be chosen on each trial, regardless of the outcomes of the previous trials. That is, the population from which we sample remains *constant* from trial to trial. In this case the probability of an A on any trial is always $p = N_A/N$, so that X is a binomial random variable with parameters n and $p = N_A/N$.

> ### *Distribution for Sampling with Replacement*
>
> $$P(X = k) = \binom{n}{k} p^k (1 - p)^{n-k}, \qquad \text{where } p = \frac{N_A}{N}$$

This formula is exactly the same as the "with replacement" formula given in Chapter 3. In Chapter 3 we used an argument based on equally likely outcomes to produce the result; here we use the binomial formula and obtain the same result.

The Hypergeometric Distribution and Its Relationship to the Binomial

Sampling in the real world is usually done *without* replacement. When this is the case, the number of A's in a sample of size n does *not* have a binomial distribution. The reason is that the composition of the population keeps changing as the sampling progresses. Therefore, the binomial distribution does not apply because it assumes that p remains constant. Instead, the relevant distribution is called the *hypergeometric* distribution with parameters n, N_A, and N.

> The hypergeometric distribution applies when sampling is done without replacement from a population with only two types of members.

In this case the probability of exactly k A's out of n members is as follows.

> ### *Distribution for Sampling Without Replacement*
>
> $$P(X = k) = \frac{\binom{N_A}{k} \binom{N - N_A}{n - k}}{\binom{N}{n}}$$

Notice that this hypergeometric formula is the same formula as we gave in Chapter 3 for sampling without replacement. As we saw in Chapter 3, it is very tedious to use, due to the many binomial coefficients. Also, although tables of hypergeometric probabilities have been published, they are extremely bulky. The problem is that a set of probabilities has to be given for each combination of N, N_A, and n. Therefore, we have not tabulated hypergeometric probabilities in this book.

However, the mean and variance of the hypergeometric distribution are simple to calculate, as shown below.

Mean and Variance of Hypergeometric Distribution

$$E(X) = np, \qquad \text{Var}(X) = \left(\frac{N - n}{N - 1} \right) np(1 - p), \qquad \text{where } p = \frac{N_A}{N}$$

These are exactly the same as the "with replacement" formulas except for the factor $(N - n)/(N - 1)$ in the variance. This factor is often called the "finite population correction factor." Since this factor is necessarily less than 1 (when $n > 1$), we see that the variance is slightly smaller when sampling without replacement than when sampling with replacement.

Fortunately, in most sampling problems we may act as if sampling is done *with* replacement. This means that we may *approximate* hypergeometric probabilities with binomial probabilities, using $p = N_A/N$. Basically, this is a valid approximation any time the sample size n is a small percentage of the population size N. To be on the safe side, we usually require that the sample size be no more than 10% of the population size. But even when n/N is greater than .10, the approximation is often quite good.

5.10

The Normal Approximation to the Binomial

Suppose again that we sample 600 people from a large population, $\frac{1}{6}$ of whom (the A's) earn at least $30,000 per year. If X is the number of A's we observe, then X is a bnomial random variable with parameters $n = 600$ and $p = \frac{1}{6}$. A typical event of interest is the event that there are no more than 90 A's in the sample. The probability of this event is given by a sum of binomial probabilities, $P(X = 0) + P(X = 1) + \cdots + P(X = 90)$. In this section we learn how to calculate this type of probability (a summation of many binomial probabilities) without having to do a lot of arithmetic.

It can be shown that a binomial random variable X can be written as a sum $X_1 + X_2 + \cdots + X_n$, where a particular X_i equals 0 or 1 depending on whether the corresponding trial results in a B or an A. These X_i's are independent, and each has mean p and variance $p(1 - p)$. Therefore, the Central Limit Theorem says that if n is fairly large, the binomial distribution of the sum X is approximately normal with mean np and variance $np(1 - p)$.

> The binomial distribution with parameters n and p can be closely approximated by a normal distribution with mean np and variance $np(1 - p)$, provided that $np(1 - p) \geq 5$.

The reason for the $np(1 - p) \geq 5$ requirement is that the usual $n \geq 30$ requirement for the Central Limit Theorem is sometimes too much and sometimes not enough. This depends on p. If p is close to .5, the binomial distribution is approximately symmetric and bell-shaped even for small values of n. But if p is near 0 or 1, the binomial distribution is quite skewed to the right or the left unless n is quite large. By requiring $np(1 - p) \geq 5$, we require n to be quite large when p is close to 0 or 1; otherwise, n can be quite small. For example, if $p = .01$, then $p(1 - p) = .0099$, and $np(1 - p) \geq 5$ only if $n \geq 505$. But when $p = .4$, $np(1 - p) \geq 5$ when $n \geq 21$. So when $p = .01$, we might not trust the approximation unless n is 505 or above; when $p = .4$, we can trust it when n is as small as 21.

Even when n is sufficiently large, there is one small correction we can make to the normal approximation to improve its accuracy. This is often called the *continuity correction*. Let X be a binomial random variable with parameters n and p, and let X_N be the associated normal random variable with mean np and variance $np(1 - p)$. (We will continue to use this subscript N in this section to remind us that it refers to a normal random variable.) The fundamental difference between X and X_N is that X is discrete and X_N is continuous. To emphasize this, suppose that k is any integer. Then the binomial probability $P(k < X < k + 1)$ is 0 because there are no integers between k and $k + 1$. However, the normal probability $P(k < X_N < k + 1)$ is clearly nonzero, as shown in Figure 5.16.

> A continuity correction is useful when approximating the binomial by the normal because the binomial is discrete and the normal is continuous.

For the continuity correction, we associate half of $P(k - 1 < X_N < k)$, namely $P(k - 1 < X_N < k - .5)$, with the binomial probability $P(X = k - 1)$, and the other half, $P(k - .5 < X_N < k)$, with the binomial probability $P(X = k)$. The effect of this correction is that we always *expand* the interval

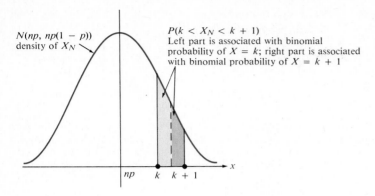

$N(np, np(1 - p))$
density of X_N

$P(k < X_N < k + 1)$
Left part is associated with binomial
probability of $X = k$; right part is associated
with binomial probability of $X = k + 1$

np k $k + 1$

x

Figure 5.16

on X by .5 unit to the left or to the right (or both) in order to obtain the interval for X_N. A prescription for doing this is given below.

Prescriptions for Using the Continuity Correction

1. Binomial $P(X \leq k)$ becomes normal $P(X_N < k + .5)$
2. Binomial $P(X \geq k)$ becomes normal $P(X_N > k - .5)$
3. Binomial $P(k_1 \leq X \leq k_2)$ becomes normal $P(k_1 - .5 < X_N < k_2 + .5)$
4. Binomial $P(X = k)$ becomes normal $P(k - .5 < X_N < k + .5)$

EXAMPLE 5.10

Suppose that we sample 30 people randomly (with replacement) from a population, 55% of whom favor the ERA (Equal Rights Amendment). Use the normal approximation to the binomial, with and without the continuity correction, to approximate the probability that between 15 and 18 (inclusive) of the 30 people favor the ERA. Compare these answers to the exact binomial probability.

SOLUTION

If X is the number in the sample who favor the ERA, then X is binomially distributed with $n = 30$ and $p = .55$. The exact answer to the problem is

$$P(15 \leq X \leq 18) = \binom{30}{15}(.55)^{15}(.45)^{15} + \cdots + \binom{30}{18}(.55)^{18}(.45)^{12} = .5364$$

To obtain the normal approximation, we use a normal random variable X_N

with mean $np = 16.5$ and variance $np(1 - p) = 7.425 = 2.725^2$. Without the continuity correction, the approximation is

$$P(15 \leq X \leq 18) \approx P(15 < X_N < 18) = P\left(\frac{15 - 16.5}{2.725} < Z < \frac{18 - 16.5}{2.725}\right)$$
$$= P(-.55 < Z < .55) = .4176$$

With the continuity correction, we expand the interval from 15 to 18 to the interval from 14.5 to 18.5 (as in prescription 3 above). Then the approximation is

$$P(15 \leq X \leq 18) \approx P(14.5 < X_N < 18.5)$$
$$= P\left(\frac{14.5 - 16.5}{2.725} < Z < \frac{18.5 - 16.5}{2.725}\right)$$
$$= P(-.73 < Z < .73) = .5346$$

Not only is the second approximation much better than the first, but it is also very accurate.

5.11
Applications of the Binomial Distribution

The following examples illustrate several applications of the binomial distribution. They also illustrate the normal approximation to the binomial, together with the continuity correction. In some cases the exact binomial answer and the normal approximation are both given, so that a comparison can be made.

EXAMPLE 5.11

Consider a manufacturing plant that produces various types of electronic components. The components are usually produced in large batches because of the setup time involved in tooling up for any particular type of component. Suppose that the company receives a special order for 500 components of a particular type. This is the only outstanding order for this type of component, so the company needs to run a special batch just to meet this order. Since it wants to tool up only once for this order, it wants to make sure that it produces a large enough batch to ensure 500 nondefective components. On the other hand, it does not want to produce too large a batch, because orders for this type of component are rare and storage of extra components is quite costly.

We assume that the number of nondefective components in a batch of size n is a binomial random variable with parameters n and $p = .97$. That is, each component, independently of the others, has probability .03 of being a defective. Management wants to know the probability of producing at least 500 nondefectives if a batch of size $n = 515$ is produced.

SOLUTION

To answer this question, we set $n = 515$ and let X be the number of non-defectives obtained in the batch. Then X has a binomial distribution with parameters $n = 515$ and $p = .97$. The probability of producing at least 500 nondefectives is the sum of the binomial probabilities $P(X = 500)$ through $P(X = 515)$. After a tedious calculation, we find that this binomial probability is .5214.

Since $np(1 - p)$ equals 14.99, the normal approximation applies. If X_N is a normal random variable with mean $np = 499.55$ and variance $np(1 - p) = 14.99 = 3.872^2$, we have

$$P(X \geq 500) \approx P(X_N > 499.5) \quad \text{(continuity correction)}$$

$$= P\left(Z > \frac{499.5 - 499.55}{3.872}\right) = P(Z > -.01)$$

$$= P(Z < .01) = .5040$$

Although this answer differs slightly from the exact answer of .5214, it does tell management that with a batch size of only 515, there is close to a 50–50 chance that the number of nondefectives will fall short of 500.

EXAMPLE 5.12

This example examines a problem common to most airlines. When airlines take reservations for a particular flight, they know from past experience that some fraction of the ticketed passengers will cancel their reservations (and obtain a refund) at the last minute. This is obviously not good for the airlines because it means empty seats and lost profit. One way the airlines counteract this problem, at least for flights with high demand, is to "overbook" on these flights. That is, they accept a few more reservations than the number of available seats, and then they hope there will be a few cancellations. Of course, if every ticketed passenger does show up, there will not be enough seats available, and the airline will be in an embarrassing position. Therefore, the airlines want to have an overbooking policy that has a very small probability of running out of seats. But they also want to overbook enough seats so that their flights will be filled close to capacity.

To be specific, consider a popular flight with a maximum capacity of 175 passengers. This flight has lately experienced a 5% no-show rate. In probabilistic terms, each ticketed passenger, independently of the others, cancels his or her reservation with probability .05. If the airline tickets n passengers and X is the number of passengers who keep their reservations, X has a binomial distribution with parameters n and $p = .95$. Find the maximum number of tickets the airline can issue and still be 99% sure of not running out of seats.

SOLUTION

If the airline wants to be 99% certain of not running out of seats, it needs the largest value of n such that $P(X \geq 176)$ is no greater than .01. To find the required value of n, we evaluate this probability for various values of n and quit when it is just less than .01. Using the normal approximation with mean $np = .95n$ and variance $np(1 - p) = .0475n$, we have

$$P(X \geq 176) \approx P(X_N > 175.5) = P\left(Z > \frac{175.5 - .95n}{\sqrt{.0475n}}\right)$$

We show the evaluation of this probability for several values of n in Table 5.4. These calculations indicate that the airline should use $n = 177$. Then it knows that the probability of running out of seats is approximately $1 - .9943 = .0057$ (see Figure 5.17).

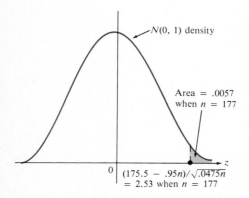

$N(0, 1)$ density

Area = .0057 when $n = 177$

0 $(175.5 - .95n)/\sqrt{.0475n}$
$= 2.53$ when $n = 177$

Figure 5.17

Table 5.4

n	176	177	178	179
$(175.5 - .95n)/\sqrt{.0475n}$	2.87	2.53	2.20	1.87
P(running out of seats) (normal)	.0021	.0057	.0139	.0307
P(running out of seats) (binomial)	.0001	.0012	0059	.0197

Notice that $np(1 - p) = .0475n$ is only slightly greater than 5 for each value of n in Table 5.4. For example, when $n = 176$, $np(1 - p)$ is only 8.36. Therefore, we check the accuracy of the normal approximation by calculating the exact binomial probability $P(X \geq 176)$ for each value of n. For example, when $n = 177$, we have

$$P(X \geq 176) = \binom{177}{176}(.95)^{176}(.05)^1 + \binom{177}{177}(.95)^{177}(.05)^0$$
$$= 177(.95)^{176}(.05) + (.95)^{177} = .0012$$

The results of all the binomial calculations are also shown in Table 5.4. As we see, the airline can really afford to sell 178, not just 177, tickets and still keep the probability of running out of seats under .01. This example illustrates that if we need a small tail probability such as $P(X \geq 176)$, and $np(1 - p)$ is not much larger than 5, it is a good idea to find the exact binomial probability rather than to rely on the normal approximation.

EXAMPLE 5.13

A problem that fascinates (or infuriates) many of us on election night is how the television networks can predict the winner of an election after a relatively small number of votes have been tabulated. Although the actual statistical analysis is much more complicated than we can do here, the present example will shed some light on the issue.

Assume that there are N voters in the population. N_R of these will vote for the Republican candidate, and $N_D = N - N_R$ will vote for the Democratic candidate. (We assume that no one votes for a third-party candidate.) Although N is known (at least approximately), N_R and N_D are obviously not known until all the votes are counted. Of course, the Republican wins if N_R is greater than N_D, and the Democrat wins otherwise. Let's suppose that a random 1% of the votes have been tabulated and at this point, the Republican and Democrat have 1500 and 900 votes, respectively. On what basis can the television networks claim that the Republican will be the eventual winner?

SOLUTION

Let $n = 2400$ be the total number of votes that have been tabulated. If X is the number of Republican votes so far, we are given that $X = 1500$. If we were not given this information, however, we would expect X to have a hypergeometric distribution with parameters N, N_R, and n. Also, we know that a binomial distribution with parameters n and $p = N_R/N$ closely approximates this hypergeometric distribution because only 1% of the population have been sampled so far.

Now we ask the crucial question. *If* the Democrat were going to be the eventual winner, that is, if $N_D > N_R$, how likely is it that the Republican would be so far out in front right now? To answer this, we require the binomial probability $P(X \geq 1500)$. But before we can evaluate this, we need a value of $p = N_R/N$, the fraction of Republicans in the population. Assuming that the Democrat will eventually win, the largest p can be is .5, so this is the value we will use to evaluate $P(X \geq 1500)$. (Look at it this way. If p is *less* than .5, the event $X \geq 1500$ is even more unlikely than if $p = .5$. So setting p equal to .5 will give us a conservative estimate of the required probability.) To obtain $P(X \geq 1500)$, we use the normal approximation to the binomial, with $np = 2400(.5) = 1200$ and variance $np(1 - p) = 2400(.5)(.5) = 600$. This gives

$$P(X \geq 1500) \approx P(X_N > 1499.5) = P\left(Z > \frac{1499.5 - 1200}{\sqrt{600}}\right)$$

$$= P(Z > 12.23) \approx 0$$

The implication is that if the Democrat is going to be the eventual winner, even by a very slim majority, there is almost no chance of the Republican being ahead by at least 1500 to 900 on the basis of 1% of the vote. But since it is *known* that the Republican is ahead by 1500 to 900, the television networks can feel safe in declaring the Republican the eventual winner.

Actually, the Republican's lead does not even have to be this large for television to declare him the winner. As the reader can check, a mere 1300 to 1100 lead is probably enough, because $P(X \geq 1300)$ is less than .0001 when $p = .5$. (In this example we have made the assumption that the first 2400 voters are selected randomly from the voting population. This assumption is probably not justified in an actual election, and this complicates the analysis tremendously.)

Problems for Sections 5.8, 5.9, 5.10, 5.11

25. Let X be a binomial random variable with parameters n and p. Find the following probabilities from the binomial table.
    a. $P(X = 5)$ when $n = 10$, $p = .4$
    b. $P(X = 10)$ when $n = 30$, $p = .3$
    c. $P(X = 7)$ when $n = 8$, $p = .9$
    d. $P(X = 35)$ when $n = 50$, $p = .7$

26. Let X be a binomial random variable with parameters n and p, and let p_0 be a given probability. For each of the following, use the binomial table to find the integer k such that $P(X \leq k) \leq p_0$ but $P(X \leq k + 1) > p_0$.
    a. $n = 20$, $p = .3$, $p_0 = .2$
    b. $n = 10$, $p = .8$, $p_0 = .9$
    c. $n = 50$, $p = .1$, $p_0 = .8$
    d. $n = 100$, $p = .5$, $p_0 = .95$

27. In terms of an appropriate binomial random variable, tell what probability each of the following represents. Then calculate it.
    a. $\binom{10}{4}(.763)^4(.237)^6$ b. $\binom{25}{2}(.1)^{21}(.9)^{23}$
    c. $(.995)^{10}$ d. $40(\frac{1}{9})(\frac{8}{9})^{39}$ e. $\binom{10}{8}(.011)^2(.989)^8$

28. In terms of an appropriate binomial random variable, state what probability each of the following represents. Then calculate it or, if possible, look it up in the binomial table.

    a. $\displaystyle\sum_{k=0}^{2} \binom{10}{k}(.2)^k(.8)^{10-k}$ b. $\displaystyle\sum_{k=5}^{10} \binom{20}{k}(.3)^k(.7)^{20-k}$

    c. $\displaystyle\sum_{k=45}^{50} \binom{55}{k}(.9)^k(.1)^{55-k}$ d. $\displaystyle\sum_{k=1}^{4} \binom{25}{k}(\frac{1}{3})^k(\frac{2}{3})^{25-k}$

29. A binomial random variable X results from 20 trials. Each trial results in a "success" or a "failure," and the probability of a success on each trial is .7. Write an expression for each of the following probabilities, and use the binomial table to evaluate them.
    a. The probability of exactly 15 successes.
    b. The probability of exactly 7 failures.
    c. The probability of no more than 18 successes.
    d. The probability of at least 5 failures.

30. If two evenly matched teams play a series of 10 games, and the results of the successive games are independent, what is the probability that either one of the teams wins at least eight games?

31. An airport has five runways that can be used for large jets. During an ice storm, the airport officials believe that each of the runways, independently of the others, has probability p of remaining serviceable.

a. If $p = .3$, what is the probability distribution of the number of serviceable runways? Calculate the required probabilities and graph the resulting probability mass function.

b. If $p = .5$, what is the largest value of k such that the probability of at least k serviceable runways is at least .9?

c. Would you criticize the independence assumption here? Explain.

32. A publishing company publishes 25 books by well-known novelists in a given year. If each of these books, independently of one another, has a 25% chance of selling at least 100,000 copies, find (a) the probability that no more than 10 of the books sell more than 100,000 copies, and (b) the probability that at least 3 but no more than 8 of the books sell more than 100,000 copies.

33. A questionnaire is sent to each of 50 companies. The response rate to such questionnaires has generally been 60%. This means that each company, independently of the others, responds with probability .6.

a. What is the probability (1) that at least 50% of the companies respond, and (2) that no more than 80% respond?

b. What are the mean and standard deviation of the number of companies that respond?

c. Using the answers to part (b) and Rule 4.2, find an interval such that the probability is approximately .68 that the actual number of companies responding is within this interval.

34. Assume that 45% of all cars in a particular city are "small" cars. Of these, 65% are of foreign makes. Consider a typical parking lot in this city where 20 cars are parked. Assume that these 20 cars are randomly drawn from the city's population of cars.

a. Find (1) the expected number of small cars in the parking lot, (2) the expected number of small American cars, and (3) the expected number of small foreign cars.

b. What is the probability that at least half of the cars in the parking lot are small cars?

c. What is the probability that at least 25% of the cars in the parking lot are small foreign cars?

35. An advertiser expects that each family with a television set, independently of all other families, has probability .2 of seeing at least one of its television ads shown on a given night. Consider a neighborhood of 15 families (all with television sets).

a. Find the mean μ and the standard deviation σ of X, the number of the 15 families who see at least one of the company's ads.

b. Find $P(\mu - \sigma \le X \le \mu + \sigma)$ exactly. (Remember that X must be an integer.) How does this answer compare to the approximation from Rule 4.2?

36. A questionnaire is given to 20 consumers who have just been exposed to a proposed advertisement. The key question asks the consumers to rate the effectiveness of the ad. The possible responses are "very ineffective" (VI), "mildly ineffective" (MI), "mildly effective" (ME), and "very effective" (VE). Each consumer, independently of the others, has the following probabilities of making the various responses.

$$P(\text{VI}) = .1, \qquad P(\text{MI}) = .3, \qquad P(\text{ME}) = .4, \qquad P(\text{VE}) = .2$$

a. Find the mean and standard deviation of the number of the 20 consumers who respond that the ad is effective (ME or VE). Do the same for the number who respond that the ad is ineffective (VI or MI).

b. How probable is it that at least half of the 20 consumers respond VI or VE?

37. Consider four people chosen at random (without replacement) from a population with 100 people, 25 of whom have never been married.

a. Find the exact (hypergeometric) distribution of the number of people chosen who have never been married. That is, find $P(X = k)$ for each k from 0 to 4. Then approximate this distribution by binomial probabilities, and compare the two distributions. Are they very close to one another?

b. Find the mean and variance of the two distributions found in part (a) by using the formulas for mean and variance in Chapter 4.

38. In the current tax year, suppose that 5% of the over 100,000 tax returns from a given city are fraudulent. That is, they contain errors that were purposely made in order to cheat the government. Although these errors are often well concealed, a thorough audit by an IRS person will uncover them. If a random 50 of the returns are audited thoroughly, find the probability that at least three cases of fraud will be uncovered. Why is it permissible to use binomial probabilities for this question?

39. In a city election 50,000 people vote for one of three candidates: the Republican, the Democrat, or the Independent. Assume that the final tally will be 22,000 Republican, 24,000 for the Democrat, and 4000 for the Independent. Before the final tally is known, however, let X_1, X_2, and X_3 be the numbers of votes for the Republican, the Democrat, and the Independent, respectively, after the first 1000 votes have been counted.

a. Find the mean and standard deviation of X_1. (Note that when we are considering X_1, the population can be split into Republicans and non-Republicans.)

b. Repeat part (a) for X_2; for X_3.

c. What can you say about the probability of the event that X_1 will be between 400 and 480? Use Rules 4.1 and 4.2 only.

40. For each of the following, X is a binomial random variable with the parameters shown. Use the normal approximation, with and without the correction factor, to calculate each probability.
    a. $P(X \leq 40)$ when $n = 100$, $p = .35$
    b. $P(X \geq 75)$ when $n = 200$, $p = .4$
    c. $P(20 \leq X \leq 70)$ when $n = 100$, $p = .6$
    d. $P(500 \leq X \leq 700)$ when $n = 1000$, $p = .5$

41. For each of the following, X is a binomial random variable with the parameters shown. Calculate the exact binomial probability requested and the normal approximation with the correction factor.
    a. $P(X \leq 2)$ when $n = 20$, $p = .1$
    b. $P(X \geq 5)$ when $n = 10$, $p = .4$
    c. $P(X \geq 98)$ when $n = 100$, $p = .99$
    d. $P(X = 17)$ when $n = 30$, $p = .5$

42. Consider a population of 100 people, 12 of whom smoke. A random 10 of these are chosen without replacement, and X is defined as the number chosen who smoke.
    a. Find the exact (hypergeometric) probability of the event $X \leq 1$.
    b. Find the binomial approximation to the probability in part (a).

43. A large discount store has estimated that on the average, 1 out of every 30 personal checks for more than $25 worth of

merchandise bounces. Suppose that 80 checks for more than $25 are written in a given week.
    a. Find the exact probability that no more than two of the 80 checks bounce.
    b. Is the normal approximation (with correction factor) appropriate here? Try it.

*44. Consider a population of two types: A's and B's. A sample of n members is chosen with replacement. The probability that any chosen member is an A is p. The probability that any chosen member is a B is $q = 1 - p$. For each of the following, fill in the missing parts so that the probabilities in (1) and (2) are the same. Then use the binomial table to evaluate them.
    a. (1) The probability of at least five A's when $n = 10$, $p = .3$; and (2) the probability of ? B's when $n = 10$, $q = ?$.
    b. (1) The probability of between three and seven A's (inclusive) when $n = 12$, $p = ?$; and (2) the probability of between ? and ? B's (inclusive) when $n = 12$, $q = .2$.
    c. (1) The probability of no fewer than six A's when $n = 15$, $p = .2$; and (2) the probability of no more than ? B's when $n = 15$, $q = ?$.

45. One of the major automobile manufacturers is afraid it may have to recall a certain model car because of a possible brake defect. Assume that the true proportion of cars of this model with the defect is .025. In doing a study to determine whether the recall is necessary, the manufacturer tests a randomly selected 500 cars. It decides to announce a total recall if at least 25 of these cars have the defect. What is the probability that a recall will be announced? Use the normal approximation. How does this compare with the probability of a recall if the manufacturer examines 100 cars and announces a recall if at least five of them have the defect?

5.12

The Poisson Distribution

The final distribution in this chapter is called the Poisson distribution. In most statistical situations, including those in the rest of this book, the Poisson distribution plays a much less important role than either the normal or the binomial distribution. For this reason we will not describe its properties in much detail. However, in many applied probability models that pertain to business and economics, the Poisson distribution is as important as any other distribution, discrete or continuous. For example, the entire study of inventory models, waiting line (or queueing) models, and reliability models relies heavily on the Poisson distribution.

The Poisson distribution is a discrete distribution. In particular, if X is a Poisson random variable, its possible values are *all* of the nonnegative integers, 0, 1, 2, ... This is the first discrete distribution we have encountered with an *infinite* number of possible values. However, this generally causes no difficulties because the probability of X falling outside some finite range is essentially zero. That is, for sufficiently large values of k, we can approximate the probability $P(X \geq k)$ by 0. The typical graph of a Poisson distribution, as illustrated in Figure 5.18, shows that the Poisson probabilities first increase from left to right until a modal value is reached; then they tail off to the right of the mode and eventually become negligible for large values of k.

The Poisson probabilities are found from the following formula.

Poisson Probability Formula

$$P(X = k) = \frac{e^{-\lambda}\lambda^k}{k!} \qquad \text{for all integers } k \geq 0$$

Here λ (the Greek letter lambda) is a positive number that defines any particular Poisson distribution. By adjusting the value of λ, we are able to produce different Poisson distributions, all of which have basically the same shape as in Figure 5.18, except that their modes are shifted. (An exception occurs when λ is small. Then it is possible for the mode to be 0.) Furthermore, it can be shown that the mean of the Poisson distribution is equal to λ. In fact, λ is also the variance of X, so that $\sqrt{\lambda}$ is the standard deviation of X.

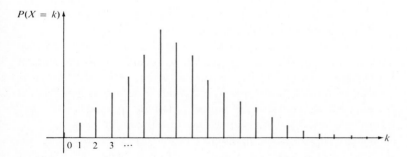

Figure 5.18
Typical Poisson Mass Function

> *Mean and Variance of a Poisson Random Variable*
> *with Parameter λ*
>
> $$E(X) = \text{Var}(X) = \lambda$$

The Poisson probabilities given by the formula above are somewhat complicated for hand calculation. Although some hand calculators have an "e^x" button (for $e^{-\lambda}$), a "y^x" button (for λ^k), and an "$n!$" button (for $k!$), many do not have all of these. Therefore, we have included a table of cumulative Poisson probabilities (Table VI) in Appendix B. Table VI is very straightforward to use. We locate the appropriate λ value and the desired value of k and then read across to find $P(X \le k)$. To find an individual probability such as $P(X = 5)$, we simply subtract the tabulated cumulative probabilities: $P(X = 5) = P(X \le 5) - P(X \le 4)$.

For example, suppose that X is a Poisson random variable with $\lambda = 5$. Then the mean of X is 5, and its standard deviation is $\sqrt{5} = 2.236$. By locating $\lambda = 5$ in Table VI, we find the probabilities shown in Table 5.5. Notice that beyond $k = 15$, the cumulative probabilities (rounded to four decimal places) are all equal to 1. Therefore, there is practically no chance of X being larger than 15.

Table 5.5   Cumulative Poisson Probabilities for $\lambda = 5$

k	0	1	2	3	4	5	6	7	8	9	10	11	12	13	14	15	16	...
$P(X \le k)$	.0067	.0404	.1247	.2650	.4405	.6160	.7622	.8666	.9319	.9682	.9863	.9945	.9980	.9993	.9998	.9999	1.000	...

The usual situation where Poisson random variables arise is when we are interested in the number of "events" that occur in some amount of time or space. Here are several typical examples.

1. A bank manager is studying the arrival pattern to the bank. Then the "events" are customer arrivals, the Poisson random variable is the number of arrivals in some unit of time, say an hour, and λ represents the mean number of arrivals per hour.
2. An engineer is interested in the lifetime of a type of battery. A device that uses this type of battery is operated continuously. When the first battery fails, it is replaced by a second, when the second fails, it is replaced by a third, and so on. The "events" are battery failures, the Poisson random variable is the number of failures in some unit of time, say a week, and λ is the mean number of failures per week.
3. A retailer is interested in the number of units of a product demanded in a given unit of time, say a week. Then the "events" are customer demands, the Poisson random variable is the number of units demanded in a week, and λ is the mean number of units demanded per week.

The examples above are representative of the many situations where the Poisson distribution occurs. Why does the Poisson distribution, rather than some other distribution, apply in examples like these? Although a complete explanation is beyond the scope of this book, the reason is basically that the Poisson distribution provides a close approximation to the binomial distribution under certain circumstances. In particular, consider an experiment that consists of n independent, identical trials. Each trial results in an "event" (such as an arrival to a bank) with probability p and "no event" with probability $1 - p$. Then the number of events, X, has a binomial distribution with parameters n and p. However, if n is very large and p is very small, it can be shown that the binomial distribution of X is closely approximated by a Poisson distribution with λ equal to np.

> When n is large and p is small, binomial probabilities can be closely approximated by Poisson probabilities, using $\lambda = np$.

As an example, if $n = 100$ and $p = .02$, we calculate the first few binomial probabilities and their Poisson approximations, with $\lambda = np = 2$. These are shown in Table 5.6. Obviously, the agreement is excellent.

Table 5.6 Poisson Approximation to the Binomial, when $n = 100$, $p = .02$

k	0	1	2	3	4	5	6
$P(k)$ (Binomial)	.1326	.2707	.2734	.1823	.0902	.0353	.0114
$P(k)$ (Poisson)	.1353	.2707	.2707	.1804	.0902	.0361	.0120

The following example shows how a manager (or consultant) might use the Poisson distribution.

EXAMPLE 5.14

Consider a department store that sells various brands of color television sets. One of the manager's biggest problems is to decide on an appropriate inventory policy for stocking television sets. On the one hand, he wants to have enough in stock so that customers receive their requests right away. On the other hand, he does not want to tie up too much money in inventory that is sitting on the storeroom floor.

Most of the difficulty results from the unpredictability of customer demand. If this demand were constant and known, the manager could decide on an appropriate inventory policy fairly easily. But the demand varies widely from month to month in a random manner. All the manager knows is that the historical average demand per month is approximately 17. Therefore, the manager decides to call in a consultant. The consultant immediately suggests using a probability model. Specifically, he lets X be the random demand in a given month, and he attempts to find the probability distribution of X. How might he go about doing this?

SOLUTION

The consultant knows that there are many possible values of X. For example, if historical records show that monthly demands have always been between 0 and 40, the consultant knows that almost all the probability should be assigned to the integers 0, 1, . . . , 40. However, he does not relish the thought of finding 41 probabilities, $P(X = 0)$ through $P(X = 40)$, that sum to 1 and reflect historical frequencies. Instead, he discovers from the manager that the histogram of demands from previous months has a shape like that shown in Figure 5.19. That is, it rises from left to right, with a modal value in the interval from 15 to 19, and then falls off at higher demand levels.

Knowing that a Poisson distribution has this same basic shape, the consultant decides to use a Poisson distribution for the monthly demand X. To choose a particular Poisson distribution, all he has to do is choose a value of λ, the mean demand per month. Since the historical average is approximately 17, he chooses $\lambda = 17$.

Now he can test the Poisson model by calculating probabilities of various events and asking the manager whether these probabilities are a reasonable approximation to reality. For example, the probability that no more than 20 television sets are demanded is $P(X \leq 20)$. From Table VI (with $\lambda = 17$),

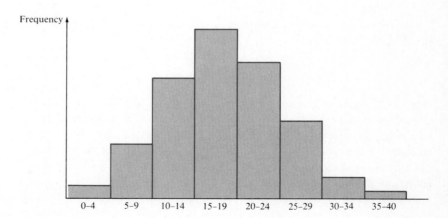

Figure 5.19
Histogram of Monthly Demands for Televisions

this probability is .8055. Similarly, the probability that demand is between 10 and 15 is

$$P(10 \le X \le 15) = P(X \le 15) - P(X \le 9) = .3453$$

If the manager believes these probabilities and probabilities of other similar events are reasonable, the statistical part of the consultant's job is finished. (The consultant's overall job is not yet finished because he still must recommend a good stocking policy. However, this is an optimization problem that we will not tackle in this book.) Otherwise, he must try a different Poisson distribution (a different value of λ) or perhaps a different type of distribution altogether.

Problems for Section 5.12

46. A Poisson random variable X has mean $\lambda = 2.2$. Find the following probabilities. Use your calculator or the Poisson table in Appendix B.
    a. $P(X = 0)$ b. $P(X > 3)$ c. $P(X < 4)$
    d. $P(1 < X < 6)$

47. Identify each of the following as an appropriate Poisson probability and then calculate it.
    a. $\dfrac{e^{-5}5^4}{4!}$

    b. $\dfrac{e^{-1/2}(\frac{1}{2})^2}{2!}$

    c. $\displaystyle\sum_{k=0}^{3} \dfrac{e^{-2.4}(2.4)^k}{k!}$

    d. $\displaystyle\sum_{k=6}^{9} \dfrac{e^{-10}10^k}{k!}$

48. Find the probability that a Poisson random variable X with parameter λ is no more than 2 standard deviations from its mean. Do this for $\lambda = 3$, $\lambda = 7$, $\lambda = 1$, and $\lambda = 2.6$. (Use the Poisson table, and remember that X is a *discrete* non-negative random variable.)

49. For a binomial random variable X with $n = 20$ and $p = .03$, find $P(X = k)$ for $k = 0$, $k = 1$, $k = 2$, and $k = 3$. Then compare these probabilities with the approximating Poisson probabilities, using an appropriate value of λ.

50. Consider a person who loves to bet on the real "long shots." In the course of several years, he places 150 bets at the race track on horses that each have 1 chance out of 100 of winning.
    a. Why does the number of bets he wins have a binomial distribution? Why is it possible to approximate this binomial distribution accurately by a Poisson distribution?

    b. Use the Poisson approximation to the binomial to find the probability that the person wins none of his 150 bets; that he wins no more than 2 of the 150 bets.
    c. Recall that the standard deviation of a binomial distribution is the square root of $np(1 - p)$ and the standard deviation of a Poisson distribution is the square root of λ. Compare these numerically for this example.

51. The number of incoming calls to a telephone switchboard can be modeled successfully as a Poisson random variable. (This has been shown in several studies.) Suppose that the mean number of incoming calls in a given 5-minute interval is 10.
    a. Find the probability that no more than seven calls are received during this 5-minute interval.
    b. Find the probability that at least 12 calls are received during this 5-minute interval.
    c. Find the smallest integer k such that we are at least 90% certain there will be no more than k calls during this 5-minute interval.

52. The local credit union estimates that the number of new car loans granted per month is a Poisson random variable with mean 8.5.
    a. Find the probability that there are no more than six new car loans granted next month.
    b. If the credit union knows the probability is at least .95 that no more than k loans will be granted next month, what can you say about k? Be as specific as possible.

Summary

This chapter introduced two distributions, the normal and the binomial, that will appear continually throughout this book in a variety of statistical applications. The normal distribution is a continuous distribution associated with the famous bell-shaped curve. By standardizing a typical normal random variable, we obtain a Z random variable, for which probabilities are tabulated in Appendix B. This allows us to perform probability calculations involving normal distributions very easily. The binomial distribution is a discrete distribution that occurs most frequently when we sample from a large population composed of two types of members. Although binomial probabilities are also tabulated in Appendix B, it is often more convenient, particularly when the sample size n is large, to use the normal approximation to the binomial when performing binomial probability calculations.

We also learned two other distributions in this chapter. The hypergeometric distribution is appropriate when we sample without replacement from a dichotomous population. However, hypergeometric probabilities are difficult to work with, and they may be approximated by binomial probabilities when only a small percentage of the population is sampled. The Poisson distribution is a discrete distribution that is often appropriate for describing the number of "events" that occur in some segment of time or space. Although we will not see many applications of the Poisson distribution in this book, it is one of the most important distributions in applied probability studies.

Applications

Application 5.1   A very important area where statistics is used is quality control of manufacturing processes. Here the objective is to check whether the parts being manufactured fall, on the average, within specified tolerance limits. Grant and Leavenworth provide the example of a rheostat knob produced by plastic molding. (Reference: Eugene L. Grant and Richard S. Leavenworth, *Statistical Quality Control,* McGraw-Hill, 1980, pp. 14–15.) A particular dimension determines how well the knob fits into a completed assembly. The engineering department specifies that this dimension must be within .003 inch of .140 inch, that is, .137 to .143 inch. To see how well the process is doing, five knobs are randomly selected and inspected each hour for 27 consecutive hours. The 135 measurements, as well as summary statistics, are shown in Table 5.7. (These data have been modified slightly from Grant and Leavenworth's data.)

The question we explore here is whether these data could come from a normal population. Unfortunately, we can never answer this question with assurance, although we will introduce one of several possible statistical

Table 5.7

Hour	Measurement on Each Item of Five Items per Hour (Inches)					Sum	Sum of Squares
1	.1401	.1434	.1372	.1345	.1353	.6905	.09541175
2	.1387	.1439	.1430	.1451	.1466	.7173	.10293947
3	.1395	.1334	.1472	.1488	.1390	.7079	.10038609
4	.1436	.1413	.1371	.1387	.1404	.7011	.09833291
5	.1421	.1425	.1458	.1359	.1366	.7029	.09888467
6	.1363	.1445	.1434	.1410	.1411	.7063	.09981171
7	.1426	.1474	.1372	.1420	.1388	.7080	.10031480
8	.1435	.1372	.1457	.1376	.1383	.7023	.09870523
9	.1411	.1423	.1474	.1405	.1409	.7122	.10147832
10	.1426	.1374	.1453	.1402	.1321	.6976	.09743206
11	.1413	.1472	.1421	.1412	.1356	.7074	.10015074
12	.1375	.1466	.1424	.1428	.1400	.7093	.10066741
13	.1424	.1422	.1391	.1413	.1427	.7077	.10017639
14	.1376	.1454	.1443	.1371	.1400	.7044	.09929382
15	.1445	.1422	.1431	.1354	.1444	.7096	.10076322
16	.1402	.1329	.1445	.1450	.1417	.7043	.09930259
17	.1374	.1374	.1422	.1431	.1416	.7017	.09850653
18	.1378	.1429	.1425	.1457	.1433	.7122	.10147888
19	.1426	.1424	.1432	.1405	.1353	.7040	.09916510
20	.1360	.1421	.1407	.1395	.1376	.6959	.09687891
21	.1424	.1443	.1404	.1381	.1439	.7091	.10059123
22	.1395	.1466	.1434	.1402	.1390	.7087	.10049241
23	.1401	.1455	.1423	.1397	.1374	.7050	.09944240
24	.1341	.1470	.1433	.1419	.1428	.7091	.10065415
25	.1382	.1455	.1413	.1374	.1417	.7041	.09919283
26	.1401	.1455	.1436	.1444	.1383	.7119	.10139747
27	.1452	.1450	.1378	.1389	.1409	.7078	.10024290
Total						19.0583	2.69209399

tests for normality in Chapter 13 that can help to answer the question. For now, we will be content to look at several descriptive measures. First, a histogram of the data is shown in Figure 5.20 (p. 236). Although this is not exactly symmetric and bell-shaped, it is certainly suggestive of the normal curve.

Next we calculate the mean and variance of the given data. From the summary columns we have

$$\overline{X} = \frac{19.0583}{135} = .1412 \text{ inch}$$

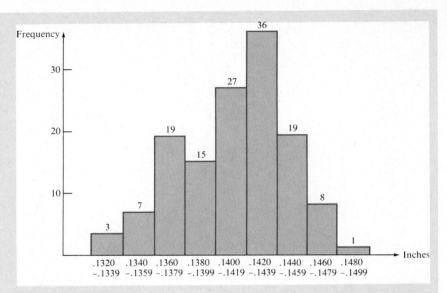

Figure 5.20

and

$$s^2 = \frac{2.69209399 - 135(.1412)^2}{134} = .0034^2.$$

If these data come from *any* normal population, it is a good guess that they come from a normal population with $\mu = .1412$ and $\sigma^2 = .0034^2$. To explore this one step further, we will find the proportion of all measurements that would fall within .137 and .143 inch, the tolerance limits, if the population were really $N(.1412, .0034^2)$. This is

$$P(.137 \leq X \leq .143) = P\left(\frac{.137 - .1412}{.0034} \leq Z \leq \frac{.143 - .1412}{.0034}\right)$$
$$= P(-1.24 \leq Z \leq .53) = .5944$$

If the normal assumption is correct, this proportion should be close to the observed proportion falling between .137 and .143 inch, namely $^{79}/_{135}$ = .585. Obviously, the agreement is excellent. (This agreement is almost *too* good. In later chapters we will learn how large a discrepancy between observed and theoretical proportions we should expect.) Therefore, we have two confirming pieces of evidence, the histogram and the agreement between proportions, that these data may come from a normal population.

In terms of quality control, these data would certainly be disturbing to the engineers. Due to the large variance, there is a fairly high proportion of items that fall outside the tolerance limits. At this point the engineers could take one of two actions. First, they could set the tolerance limits further apart. Perhaps the knob will work well for any dimension within .005 inch of .140, for example. Second, they could attempt to reduce the variance in the process itself, so that a higher proportion of items fall within the current tolerance limits. Clearly, this is an engineering problem. Although we as statisticians can *measure* variance, we do not necessarily have the engineering expertise to *reduce* it.

Application 5.2   When an airplane goes through its final inspection, a team of inspectors search for errors in alignment. Grant and Leavenworth report the results from an inspection of 50 airplanes. (Reference: Eugene L. Grant and Richard S. Leavenworth, *Statistical Quality Control,* McGraw-Hill, 1980, pp. 204–205.) Table 5.8 shows the frequency distribution of the number of alignment errors found on these planes. For example, seven planes had eight errors apiece. Is it possible that the number of alignment errors on a randomly selected plane is Poisson distributed? To answer this question, we compare the observed proportions of planes in the various categories with the proportions we would expect if the population distribution were Poisson.

Table 5.8

Number of Errors	Frequency	Number of Errors	Frequency
0	0	10	2
1	0	11	5
2	0	12	2
3	1	13	3
4	4	14	1
5	3	15	2
6	6	16	1
7	7	17	0
8	7	18	1
9	5		

First, we need a value of λ. Since λ is the mean of the distribution, we find the average number of errors per plane. This is given by

$$\text{average} = \frac{\text{total number of errors}}{50} = \frac{1(3) + 4(4) + \cdots + 1(18)}{50} = 8.72$$

This is the value of λ we will use. Then the proportion of all planes with exactly k errors, assuming a Poisson distribution, is the probability that a typical plane has k errors:

$$P(X = k) = \frac{e^{-8.72}(8.72)^k}{k!}$$

Table 5.9

k	$P(k) = e^{-8.72} (8.72)^k/k!$	Proportion of Planes with k Errors
0	.0002	0
1	.0014	0
2	.0062	0
3	.0180	.02
4	.0393	.08
5	.0686	.06
6	.0997	.12
7	.1242	.14
8	.1354	.14
9	.1312	.10
10	.1144	.04
11	.0907	.10
12	.0659	.04
13	.0442	.06
14	.0275	.02
15	.0160	.04
16	.0087	.02
17	.0045	0
18	.0022	.02

This probability cannot be found in the Poisson table because $\lambda = 8.72$ is not listed there. However, we can use a hand calculator to evaluate this probability for any k. The results appear in Table 5.9, where they are compared with the observed proportions. Although the agreement is not perfect, it is sufficiently good that we cannot rule out the Poisson assumption. (A formal test of whether the observed data "fit" a Poisson distribution will be given in Chapter 13. If this test were run, it would indicate that the fit above is quite good.)

Glossary of Terms

Normal distribution   a symmetric, bell-shaped distribution that appears in a wide variety of realistic situations

Meaning of "X is $N(\mu, \sigma^2)$" X has a normal distribution with mean μ and variance σ^2

Standard normal distribution (or $N(0, 1)$ distribution)   the normal distribution with $\mu = 0$ and $\sigma^2 = 1$

Standardized value of a random variable X   represents the number of standard deviations a value is to the right or left of the mean

Notation z_α   the number with area α to its right under a standard normal density

Central Limit Theorem   a mathematical result that says the sum or average of many independent random variables, all with the same distribution, is approximately normally distributed

Binomial distribution the distribution of the number of A's in a sequence of independent, identical trials when the probability of an A remains constant on each trial

Hypergeometric distribution the exact distribution of the number of A's in a sample when sampling is done without replacement

Normal approximation to the binomial a binomial random variable is approximately normal with mean np and variance $np(1 - p)$ when $np(1 - p) \geq 5$

Poisson distribution a discrete distribution often used to describe the number of "events" that occur in a given amount of time or space

Poisson approximation to the binomial a binomial random variable is approximately Poisson distributed with $\lambda = np$ when n is large and p is small

---

Important Formulas

1. Formula for standardizing a normal random variable

$$Z = \frac{X - \mu}{\sigma}$$

2. Formula for binomial probabilities

$$P(X = k) = \binom{n}{k} p^k (1 - p)^{n-k}$$

3. Formulas for the mean and variance of a binomial distribution

$$E(X) = np \qquad \text{Var}(X) = np(1 - p)$$

4. Formula for Poisson probabilities

$$P(X = k) = \frac{e^{-\lambda} \lambda^k}{k!}$$

5. Formulas for the mean and variance of a Poisson distribution

$$E(X) = \text{Var}(X) = \lambda$$

End-of-Chapter Problems

53. Suppose that the typing speeds of all secretaries in a large organization are normally distributed with mean 65.3 words per minute and standard deviation 9.5 words per minute. Find five nonoverlapping intervals such that 20% of the typists' speeds fall in each interval.

54. A company gives all its prospective clerical employees a standardized test. Traditionally, the females have obtained scores that are normally distributed with mean 285 and standard deviation 27. The males' scores have been normally distributed with mean 263 and standard deviation 18. The minimum

passing grade for the test is L points. Suppose that the test is considered discriminatory (on the basis of sex) if the percentage of one sex passing is at least 5 percentage points higher than the percentage of the other sex passing. If $L = 240$, is the test discriminatory?

*55. Parts are being manufactured by two adjacent production lines. Each part from the first line is acceptable with probability .95, independently of the others. The same is true of parts from the second line except that the probability there is .97. Consider a batch of $2n$ parts randomly selected from the two lines, where n parts are from each line.
a. If X is the number of acceptable parts in the batch, is X binomially distributed? Why or why not?
b. Find $P(X \geq 7)$ when $n = 4$.

*56. A company that stocks a certain item has the following costs associated with its inventory. It stocks 400 units of the item for the coming season. If X units are demanded and X is less than 400, the excess supply, $400 - X$, must be stored at a cost of $20 per unit. If X is greater than 400, the excess demand, $X - 400$, must be ordered separately at an extra cost of $30 per unit. The demand X is normally distributed with mean 400 and standard deviation 30. What is the probability that the company's cost due to excess demand or excess supply will be less than $1500?

*57. Mr. Smith is involved in an automobile accident. To collect his insurance, he is required to obtain three estimates of the amount of damage. If the estimates he would obtain from the available automobile repair shops are independent and normally distributed with mean $450 and standard deviation $50, and if he chooses three of these shops randomly, what is the probability that the lowest estimate is greater than $400? (Notice that the lowest is greater than $400 only if all three are greater than $400.)

*58. Two groups of people, one younger and one older, participate in a taste test for a new type of soft drink. Each participant is asked to rate the drink on a scale from 0 to 100. The younger group's ratings are normally distributed with mean μ_1 and variance σ_1^2. The older group's ratings are also normally distributed, but with mean μ_2 and variance σ_2^2. Assume that $\sigma_1 = \sigma_2$. It turns out that there is a rating x with the property that 30% of the younger group are below this rating and 30% of the older group are above this rating (see the figure at the top of the next column). If $\mu_1 = 65$, $\mu_2 = 61$, and $x = 63$, find the common variance of each group's ratings.

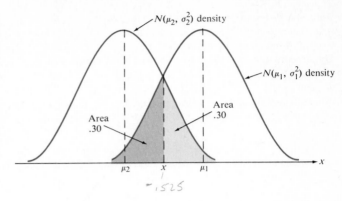

*59. It is commonly known that many, if not most, of the drivers on interstate highways do not obey the 55-mph speed limit. Suppose that the actual speeds driven by drivers are normally distributed with mean μ and standard deviation 5 mph. (Each of the parts below is separate from the other parts.)
a. If 8% of all drivers are clocked at 65 mph or more, what is the mean μ?
b. If only 2% of all drivers are clocked at 50 mph or less, what is the mean μ?
c. Suppose that μ and σ are both unknown, and it is observed that 2% of all drivers go slower than 50 mph and 8% of all drivers go faster than 65 mph. What must μ and σ be? (Solve two equations in two unknowns.)

*60. A government regulation states that the number of children per classroom in elementary schools must be normally distributed with a mean μ no greater than 27 and no less than 23. (There is no stipulation on the standard deviation σ.) For each of the following, assume that the actual distribution of students per classroom is normal, and tell whether the situation described is consistent with the regulation.
a. 10% of all classrooms have 30 or more students, and $\sigma = 4$.
b. 2% of all classrooms have 35 or more students, and $\sigma = 5$.
c. 3% of all classrooms have 15 or fewer students, and 12% of all classrooms have 30 or more students. (Find μ and σ.)

61. An appliance company has a complaint department for handling unsatisfied customers. The number of complaints in a given week is a random variable with mean 15.8 and standard

deviation 6.5, independent of the number of complaints in other weeks.

  a. Find the probability that the company receives at least 800 complaints during the next 52 weeks.

  b. Can the company be at least 95% certain that it will receive between 700 and 900 complaints during the next 52 weeks? Answer by calculating an appropriate probability.

*62. A so-called clairvoyant claims she can correctly predict the outcome of at least 15 out of 20 flips of a fair coin. Of course, she may have no "powers" but may simply get lucky.

  a. Find the probability that a pure guesser would, simply by luck, guess at least 15 out of 20 correctly.

  b. Using your answer to part (a), find the probability that a pure guesser would do what she claims (predict at least 15 out of 20 correctly) on at least three out of five separate occasions.

63. Many space vehicles have a great deal of built-in redundancy. This means that spare parts are included so that if one or more parts fail, the backup parts will assure the success of the vehicle. Suppose that one particular "module" is duplicated n times. Each of these functions, independently of the others, with probability .95. The vehicle as a whole is successful if at least two of these n modules function.

  a. Find the probability of a successful vehicle if $n = 3$ modules are included.

  b. What is the minimum number n of modules that must be included to ensure at least a .999 probability of vehicle success? (Keep trying values of n until you get one that does the job.)

*64. The daily gross sales of 50 auto supply stores from a certain chain are normally distributed with mean $702 and standard deviation $151.

  a. Find the probability that a given store in the chain grosses more than $1000 on a given day.

  b. Find the probability that at least 3 of the 50 stores gross more than $1000 on a given day, provided that the sales from different stores are independent random variables.

*65. An automobile insurance company uses historical data to estimate the probability distribution of yearly claim amounts by its customers. This distribution is approximated by the discrete distribution shown at the top of the next column. For example, the probability that a typical customer has no claims during the year is .8.

Claim ($100s)	Probability
0	.80
1	.03
2	.02
5	.02
10	.02
20	.03
50	.03
100 or more	.05

  a. If 25 customers are chosen at random, what is the probability that at least three of them have claims for at least $10,000? What is the probability that at least three of them have claims for at least $1000?

  b. For the 25 customers in part (a), find the mean and standard deviation of the number with claims no greater than $500.

*66. The price of a loaf of regular white bread varies from store to store in a given city according to a normal distribution with mean 86 cents and standard deviation 8 cents. Twenty stores are selected at random and their bread prices are observed.

  a. Find the mean and standard deviation of the number that charge at least 95 cents for a loaf of bread.

  b. Find the probability that at least four of the 20 stores charge at least 95 cents for a loaf of bread.

*67. Suppose that we simulate 10 independent uniform random variables on a computer. Each of these is a continuous random variable with the "rectangular" density shown below.

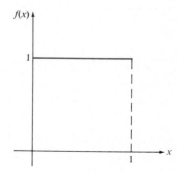

  a. Find the mean and standard deviation of the number of these 10 random numbers that are between .25 and .65.

  b. Find the probability that at least two of the 10 random numbers are greater than .9.

*68. A production process produces items with weights that are normally distributed with mean 4.98 pounds and standard deviation .03 pound. An item is labeled defective if its weight is less than 4.92 pounds or greater than 5.06 pounds. Currently, an order for 95 items is required. Just to be on the safe side, the company produces 100 items, expecting that a few of these will be defective. Find the probability that at least 95 of the 100 items will not be defective and hence the order will be satisfied. (Do not use the normal approximation to the binomial.)

*69. A peanut butter company believes that if customers are given a choice between the company's brand and the main competitor's brand, at least 55% will choose the company's brand. To test this, 15 randomly chosen people are blindfolded and asked to taste both brands of peanut butter.

a. If exactly 55% of the entire population would prefer the company's brand in such a test, find the probability that no more than five people in the test prefer the company's brand.

b. If the company is incorrect and only 45% of the entire population would prefer the company's brand in such a test, find the probability requested in part (a).

*70. A regular deck of cards has 52 cards, 12 of which are "face cards." Suppose that five cards from a well-shuffled deck are dealt to a poker player, and consider the event E that the player receives no more than two face cards.

a. Explain why $P(E)$ is given exactly by

$$P(E) = \sum_{k=0}^{2} \frac{\binom{12}{k}\binom{40}{5-k}}{\binom{52}{5}}$$

but may be approximated by

$$P'(E) = \sum_{k=0}^{2} \binom{5}{k}\left(\frac{12}{52}\right)^{k}\left(\frac{40}{52}\right)^{5-k}$$

b. Calculate the two expressions in part (a) to see how well they compare.

*71. Consider a population of 400 people, 10 of whom have been hospitalized in the past year. We sample n of these people without replacement and let X be the number in the sample who have been hospitalized in the past year. Let E be the event that X equals 0.

a. If $n = 10$, explain why $P(E)$ is given exactly by

$$P(E) = \frac{\binom{390}{10}}{\binom{400}{10}}$$

but may be approximated by $P'(E) = (.975)^{10}$. Then calculate each of these probabilities.

b. Consider the probabilities in part (a) for any value of n, not just $n = 10$. Let the percentage error in the approximation be

$$\frac{P'(E) - P(E)}{P(E)} \times 100\%$$

Calculate the percentage error when $n = 5$; when $n = 10$; when $n = 15$. Why do you suspect the percentage error is larger for larger values of n?

72. Digital watches have become popular within a fairly short period of time, and by now a sizable proportion of the population wear them. If $\frac{1}{3}$ of all the people in a given city wear digital watches, what is the probability that in a randomly selected group of 300 people from this city, less than $\frac{1}{4}$ wear digital watches? Use the normal approximation. Try the calculation with and without the correction factor to see how much difference it makes.

73. Suppose that scientists discover a new treatment for the common cold which, according to their claim, will significantly reduce the time required to recover from a cold. In particular, they claim that with the new treatment, the probability of getting rid of a cold in less than a week will increase from the current level of .25 to .55. (The .25 level results from today's usual treatments, such as taking aspirin, drinking liquids, and getting plenty of rest.) To test the scientists' claim, 300 people with colds are separated into two groups of 150 each. Group A receives the new treatment, while group B receives a traditional treatment.

a. Find the probability that at least 40 people in group B recover within a week. [Use the normal approximation in this part and in part (b).]

b. Find the probability that at least 80 people in group A recover within a week, given that the .55 claim for the new treatment is correct.

74. Everyone knows that it is difficult to make a long-distance call on a busy holiday, particularly on Christmas day. Assume

that on the average, only one out of every seven long-distance calls gets through on this day.

a. Use the normal approximation to find the probability of at least 25 of 200 calls getting through on Christmas day. Repeat the calculation for at least 250 of 2000 calls getting through.

b. The telephone company suspects that on the average, *more* than one out of seven long-distance calls get through on Mother's Day, another of the busiest days of the year. If they observe that 750 out of 4000 long-distance calls get through on Mother's Day, does this tend to confirm their suspicion? (Answer by finding the probability of at least 750 out of 4000 if only one out of seven gets through on the average.)

*75. Let $P(k)$ be the binomial probability of k A's in n trials when the probability of an A on each trial is p and the probability of a B on each trial is $q = 1 - p$.

a. Show that $P(k)$ satisfies the following equation for each integer k from 1 to n.

$$P(k) = \frac{(n - k + 1)p}{kq} \cdot P(k - 1)$$

b. Use the formula in part (a) to find the binomial probabilities $P(k)$ for each k from 0 to n when $n = 6$ and $p = .472$. Check that these add to 1. [First find $P(0)$ from $P(0) = q^6$. Then use the formula above to calculate the rest.]

*76. One of the major television networks recently ran a miniseries designed to capture a large portion of the viewing audience. Suppose that (unknown to the network) 37% of all television viewers actually watched this show. To discover this percentage, the network sampled a random 250 television viewers. Later, believing this sample was not large enough, the network sampled 100 more television viewers.

a. Find the probability that at least 135 of the total 350 people sampled watched the show. (Use the normal approximation for each part of this problem.)

b. Find the probability that at least 95 of the first 250 people sampled *and* at least 40 of the last 100 people sampled watched the show.

c. Find the *conditional* probability that at least 135 of the total 350 people sampled watched the show, given that exactly 95 of the first 250 people sampled watched the show.

77. A restaurant chain has been trying to increase its business. Recently, it put coupons in the local newspapers that were good for a free meal with every regularly priced meal ordered. The restaurant's business did increase. In fact, the chain suspects that at least 60% of its customers in the week following the introduction of the coupons were there because of the coupons.

a. If this suspicion is correct, find the probability that at least 65% of a randomly selected group of n customers will say they are at the restaurant because of the coupons. Do this when $n = 50$; when $n = 100$; when $n = 500$. Use the normal approximation.

b. If only 50 out of 100 customers say that they are there because of the coupons, what would you say about the restaurant's suspicion? Answer by finding the probability of 50 or less out of 100 if the restaurant's 60% figure is correct.

*78. A study finds that the distribution of driving speeds on interstate highways in Tennessee is as shown below.

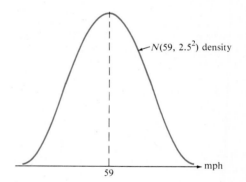

$N(59, 2.5^2)$ density

a. If the police monitor a randomly selected 500 drivers on Tennessee interstates, how probable is it that at least 95% of them are going over the speed limit of 55 mph?

b. Given that 470 of the 500 drivers in part (a) are going over the speed limit, find the conditional probability that at least 5 of these 470 are going over 65 mph. (First find the conditional probability of a typical driver going over 65 mph, given that he or she is going over 55 mph.)

79. Hotels often have an overbooking policy similar to airlines. Assume that the no-show rate at a hotel is 10%. That is, each customer with a reservation, independently of the others, cancels the reservation at the last minute (or simply does not show up) with probability .10. There are 200 available rooms in this hotel. Use the normal approximation for each of the following parts.

a. If the hotel makes 215 reservations for a given night, find the probability of at least 10 empty rooms.

b. If the hotel makes 215 reservations for a given night, find the probability that at least one customer with a reservation will not get a room.

*80. Let $P(k)$ be the probability that a Poisson random variable with mean λ equals k.

a. Show that $P(k)$ satisfies the following equation for every integer $k \geq 1$.

$$P(k) = \left(\frac{\lambda}{k}\right)P(k - 1)$$

b. Use the formula in part (a) to calculate $P(k)$ for k from 1 to 10 when $\lambda = 5.78$. [Start with $P(0) = e^{-5.78} = .0030887$.]

81. It can be argued that the number of babies born with birth defects in a given unit of time is a Poisson random variable. The reasoning is that there are a large number of births, but each one has a very small probability of resulting in a birth defect. If the mean number of babies born with defects in a given month in a given city is 5.7, find the probability of having no more than three babies born with birth defects during this month.

*82. According to a recent newspaper article, women exert a strong influence on men when men shop for clothes. (Reference: *Wall Street Journal,* Feb. 28, 1985.) In fact, 61% of the men interviewed said women exert a major influence on their purchase decisions, 20% said women exert some influence, and only 19% said women exert no influence. Consider five randomly selected men shopping for clothes. Find the following probabilities.

a. The probability that at least three of them are strongly influenced in their purchase decisions by women.

b. The probability that at least two of them are not influenced at all by women.

c. If it is observed that exactly 2 of the 5 are strongly influenced by women, what is the conditional probability that none of the other 3 are influenced at all by women?

*83. Recall from Chapter 2 that the interquartile range captures 50% of a distribution; 25% of the distribution falls to the left of this range and the other 25% falls to the right of it. For a normal distribution with mean μ and standard deviation σ, the interquartile range extends from $\mu - k\sigma$ to $\mu + k\sigma$ for an appropriate value of k. Find this value of k and explain why it is the same for *every* normal distribution, that is, why its value does not depend on μ or σ.

*84. The development of a computerized business application system usually goes through a prescribed sequence of phases. These include analysis (what is the system supposed to do?), design (how will the system perform its function?), coding (writing the required computer programs), testing (does the system perform as it should?), and implementing (teaching users how to use the system). McKeen performed a study of 32 typical business application systems to see how much effort had been expended on these five phases. (Reference: James D. McKeen, ''Successful Development Strategies for Business Application Systems,'' *MIS Quarterly,* Vol. 7, 1983, pp. 47–61.) For each system in the study, he found the percentage of total development effort devoted to each phase. Some of his findings concerning the distributions of these percentages are shown below. Consider the population distribution (taken over all application systems) of the percentage of total development effort spent on analysis. Keeping in mind the result of Problem 83, do McKeen's data suggest that this distribution is normal or nonnormal? What would you expect of these data if the population distribution were normal? Answer the same questions for the design phase and for the coding phase.

Phase	Mean (Percent)	Standard Deviation (Percent)	Interquartile Range (Percent)
Analysis	21	12	10–31
Design	18	7	10–22
Coding	42	17	36–57

*85. Referring to Application 2.1, viewers were shown 30-second commercials or 30-second segments from a TV show. For each 30-second message the viewer then answered a six-question true–false quiz. Each quiz had two true statements and four false statements. Consider a viewer who comprehends little, if anything, from a given message and then guesses on the quiz.

a. If the person guesses equally likely true or false on each of the six questions, what is the probability that he will answer at least four of the questions correctly?

b. Suppose the viewer believes that quiz-makers tend to put true statements on this type of quiz. In particular, he assumes that on the average, $\frac{2}{3}$ of all questions on such a quiz are true, so he answers each question true with probability $\frac{2}{3}$, independently of his answers to the other questions. (For example, he might roll a die for each question and answer true only if the die shows 1, 2, 3, or 4.) Now what is the probability that the viewer answers at least one of the true statements correctly and at least three of the false statements correctly?

*86. It is no secret that many business people have one or more drinks during a typical business lunch. Beeman suggests that these can have just as bad an effect on the ability of managers to make good decisions as they have on the much more publicized probability of having a fatal accident. (Reference: Don R. Beeman, ''Is the Social Drinker Killing Your Company?'' *Business Horizons*, Vol. 28, 1985, pp. 54–58.) With regard to this probability, Beeman cites the following data.

Blood Alcohol Level	Probability of a Fatal Accident on a Given Trip
.08	4 times that of a sober person
.10	7 times that of a sober person
.20	25 times that of a sober person
.25	100 times that of a sober person

Let p be the probability of a sober person being involved in a fatal accident on any single car trip. Also let $P(n)$ be the probability that a sober person is involved in a fatal accident in any of n successive car trips. Define $P(n, x)$ similarly for a person whose blood level on n successive trips is always x. In terms of p (whose value is not specified), find an expression for $P(n)$ and for $P(n, x)$ when $x = .08$, $x = .10$, $x = .20$, and $x = .25$. By what factor does $1 - P(n)$ exceed $1 - P(n, x)$ when $n = 10$ and $x = .10$; when $n = 20$ and $x = .25$? Answer this question when $p = .001$; when $p = .0001$. Interpret your findings in words.

87. According to a 1985 *Wall Street Journal* article, the crucial problem of obtaining TV ratings, particularly at the local level, is done primarily during a few ''sweeps'' periods each year. (Reference: *Wall Street Journal*, Feb. 28, 1985.) At these times (in November, February, May, and July), the stations compete for ratings by pitting their best ''blockbusters'' against one another. Of course, the higher the ratings, the higher the advertising dollars obtained. To measure these ratings, two companies, Nielsen and Arbitron Ratings Co., independently send seven-day diaries to a number of households scattered throughout 211 TV markets. Since there is a fairly high nonresponse rate, each company sends out 200,000 diaries, with the expectation that at least 100,000 diaries will be returned. Suppose that each household contacted responds with probability p, independently of what the other households do.

a. Nielsen hopes that it will receive at least 100,000 responses out of 200,000 mailings with probability at least .99. Using the normal approximation to the binomial, check if this will happen when $p = .505$; when $p = .503$; when $p = .501$.

b. Now find the probability that Nielsen and Arbitron will each receive at least 100,000 responses when $p = .503$; when $p = .501$.

*88. A device uses a single battery. When one battery fails, it is replaced by a new one. It is assumed that the number of consecutive battery failures that result in 400 hours of continuous use is a Poisson random variable with mean 7.5. Suppose that the device is left on for 400 hours of continuous use (with a new battery at the beginning of the 400-hour period).

a. Find the mean and standard deviation of the number of batteries that will be required *in addition* to the one originally in the device.

b. Let X be the number of batteries required for the 400-hour period in addition to the original battery in the device. Find the probability that X is at least 10.

Computer Problems

(These problems are to be used in conjunction with the computer software package.)

1. Suppose that a particular commercial flight has room for 175 second-class passengers. However, because of the high no-show rate, the airline does a substantial amount of overbooking. In particular, assume each ticketed passenger is a no-show, independently of the others, with probability .25. Use the BINOMIAL program to find (by trial and error) the largest number of tickets the airline can issue and still have at least .97 probability that everyone who shows up will have a seat. Then given that this many tickets are issued, use the BINOMIAL program to find (i) the probability that at least 170 of the seats will be occupied; (ii) the probability that less than 160 of the seats will be occupied.

2. Assume that the number of arrivals to a department store for each of the next four half-hour periods is a Poisson random variable with mean 20. Also assume that these four random variables are independent. This implies that the number of

arrivals during the next 2-hour period is also a Poisson random variable with mean 80.

a. Use the POISSON program to find (i) the probability that at least 25 customers arrive in at least one of the next four half-hour periods; (ii) the probability that at least 25 customers arrive in each of the next four half-hour periods. (The POISSON program will solve only part of this problem; the rest you must do by hand.)

b. Find the probability that between 75 and 85 customers arrive during the next 2 hours.

c. Consider the probability $P(X \geq k)$, where X is the number of arrivals in the next 2 hours, and k is a specified integer. What is the largest value of k that makes this probability at least .95? (Use the POISSON program, and think in terms of complements.)

3. Assume that each part that comes off a manufacturing line is defective with probability .03, independently of all other parts. If 300 parts are manufactured, and X is the number of defectives, we want the following probabilities: $P(X \geq 285)$, $P(280 \leq X \leq 290)$, and $P(X < 295)$.

a. Find each of these probabilities exactly by using the BINOMIAL program.

b. Approximate each of these probabilities by using the NORMAL program (with the appropriate mean and standard deviation). Use the continuity correction.

c. Approximate each of these probabilities by using the POISSON program (with the appropriate mean).

4. Consider a population of 500 people, 150 of whom have used marijuana. Suppose we randomly sample 50 of these people (without replacement), and we let X be the number in the sample who have used marijuana. We would like to find the probabilities $P(X \leq 18)$ and $P(14 \leq X \leq 20)$.

a. Find these probabilities by using the WOREPLCE program.

b. Approximate these probabilities by using the BINOMIAL program.

c. Approximate the binomial probabilities in part (b) by using the NORMAL program. Use the continuity correction.

5. An experiment that can result in "success" or "failure" is repeated 200 times under identical conditions. The probability of success each time is .01. Let X be the number of successes in the 200 repetitions.

a. Use the BINOMIAL program to calculate $P(X = k)$ for each integer k from 0 to 10.

b. Use the POISSON program to approximate the probabilities in part (a).

6. A microcomputer user has gathered 50 floppy disks, but only 20 of these have any useful information. (The information on the others is either outdated or irrelevant.) Suppose the user searches the contents of a randomly selected 10 of these disks. Let X be the number of the searched disks that have useful information.

a. Use the WOREPLCE program to find the probability distribution of X. Then use the PROBDIST program to find the mean and standard deviation of X.

b. Repeat part (a), but now use the BINOMIAL program to approximate the probability distribution of X. Then use these probabilities in PROBDIST to approximate the mean and standard deviation of X.

References

HOGG, R. V. and CRAIG, A. T. *Introduction to Mathematical Statistics*, 4th ed. New York: Macmillan, 1978.

INGRAM, O., GLESER, L. J., and DERMAN, C. *Probability Models and Applications*. New York: Macmillan, 1980.

ROSS, S. *A First Course in Probability*, 3rd ed. New York: Macmillan, 1984.

CHAPTER 6

Sampling Distributions

Objectives

1. To understand the concept of sampling distributions.
2. To learn the primary sampling distributions that are normal or approximately normal. These include the sampling distributions of the sample proportion, the difference between two sample proportions, the sample mean, and the difference between two sample means.
3. To see typical applications of these sampling distributions.
4. To see how computer-generated random variables can be used to find the sampling distribution of a sample statistic.
5. To learn about sums and differences of independent normal random variables.

Contents

One of the most important quantities to any company that produces retail goods is brand share, defined as the percentage of all product sales that are of the company's brand. To measure this quantity, a company typically hires a marketing research firm to perform audits at several typical retail stores. The audits themselves can be done in several ways. Basically, the more thorough the audit, the better information it provides but the more expensive it is. The question is whether a less expensive form of audit might produce practically the same results as a traditional but more expensive type. If so, the less expensive form would clearly be favored.

One way to answer this question is to perform the less expensive form of audit at several stores over a given time period. Over the same time period, the traditional type of audit is also performed, either at the same set of stores or perhaps at a different set of stores. Each type of audit produces an average company brand share, where the average is taken over all stores audited. If these averages are practically the same, we can conclude that they are measuring the same thing, and hence that the two auditing methods are essentially equivalent. The crucial statistical question is the following. How close would we expect the two averages to be if the two methods were really equivalent? This depends on the "sampling distribution" of the difference between two sample averages. In this chapter we learn what sampling distributions represent, and we learn several of the most important sampling distributions, including the sampling distribution of the difference between two sample averages.

6.1

Introduction

Chapters 3 to 5 have presented general material that can serve as a starting point for the study of statistics or more advanced probability. In this chapter we begin to learn what sets statistics apart from the general area of probability. In this sense it is probably accurate to say that our study of statistical *inference* really begins in this chapter. Specifically, we begin to learn what to expect of a random sample taken from a population with given characteristics.

There are two aspects of the material in this chapter we wish to stress. The first of these is technical. It concerns the various formulas, specific distributions, and tables we will learn now and use throughout the rest of this book. Obviously, it is important for any practitioner of statistics to know the technical details behind statistical methods so that he or she can make accurate calculations and correct inferences. Fortunately, there are not too many such details to learn, and after some practice they can be applied to a wide variety of problems fairly quickly and easily.

But there is more to the subject than simply learning rules and applying them in cookbook fashion. We also want to stress the intuitive meaning of the material. For example, we need to know what it means to say that the sample mean and the sample proportion are random variables with distributions of their own, and that these distributions have means and variances. This concept remains a mystery to many people even after they have mastered the numerical details. These people may obtain the correct answers to numerical problems, but they often do not really understand what they have done. In this chapter, therefore, we stress not only the technical details but also an overall understanding of the concepts.

6.2
Basic Ideas Behind Sampling Distributions

The basic situation common to all the material in this chapter is as follows. Each member of a given population has a numerical characteristic that can be measured. The characteristic may be a person's height, a family's income, a company's sales level, a city's pollution level, or many other possibilities. If we could take a census of the population, we could learn everything we want to know about this numerical characteristic. But because of cost, time, or other considerations, a census is not possible. Therefore, we choose a sample from this population, measure the numerical characteristic for the members of the sample, and then attempt to generalize from the sample to the population as a whole.

Before we can do this, however, we need to answer the following questions. If we *knew* what the population looked like and we then took a random sample from this population, what would we expect the sample to look like? The answer to this question involves *deductive reasoning,* whereas the problem posed in the paragraph above, generalizing from the sample to the population, involves *inductive reasoning.* Deductive reasoning is necessary when we want to go from the general to the specific (from the population to the sample), whereas inductive reasoning is necessary when we want to go from the specific to the general (from the sample to the population). Although our ultimate interest is in generalizing from the sample to the population, we first need to learn how to go in the opposite direction. The following example illustrates these ideas.

An Example

Consider a population of 10,000 light bulbs that have just come off the production line. Each bulb is either defective or nondefective, where a defective bulb is defined as one that will not last at least 300 hours of continuous use. Unfortunately, the only way to tell whether a light bulb is defective is to put it on test and see whether it lasts at least 300 hours. Clearly, the manufacturing company cannot test each of the 10,000 light bulbs in this way because of the destructive nature of the test. However, it does want to know how many of the 10,000 bulbs are defective. Therefore, it randomly selects 100 of the 10,000 light bulbs, puts these 100 on test for 300 hours each, and counts the number that burn out before the test is over.

We now pose the typical statistical problem. Suppose that exactly 13 of the 100 test bulbs burn out before 300 hours. What can we say about the proportion of the 10,000 light bulbs that are defective? For example, is it reasonable to conclude that at least 10% of the 10,000 bulbs are defective? Is it reasonable to conclude that no more than 15% of them are defective? These questions involve inductive, or inferential, reasoning since we must infer what is true about the population from the observed sample data.

Before we can answer these questions in an intelligent manner, however, we must first know what type of sample results we would expect if we *knew* how many of the 10,000 light bulbs in the population were defective. For example, if we knew that 15% (or 1500) of the bulbs were defective, how likely would it be to see as *few* as 13 defectives in a sample of 100? Or if we knew that 10% (or 1000) of the bulbs were defective, how likely would it be to see as *many* as 13 defectives in a sample of 100? These questions involve deductive reasoning and will be answered by the probabilistic methods in this chapter.

But why do we ask, for example, for the probability of 13 or more defectives from a population with 10% defectives? After all, we do not know that 10% of the population are defectives. The key here is to think of the description of the population (10% are defectives) as describing one possible population scenario. If this scenario turns out to be the correct one, deductive reasoning shows us how likely the observed sample result is. By performing this deductive reasoning on many different population scenarios, we can find which of these scenarios is most compatible with the observed sample data. Then we make the *inductive* conclusion. Namely, we assert that the population scenario most likely to be the true one is the one most compatible with the sample data (see Figure 6.1).

The argument above explains *why* we perform deductive reasoning. Now we see *how* to perform it. Again we refer to the light bulb example. Let's assume that 1400 of the 10,000 light bulbs are defective, so that the proportion of defectives in the population, labeled p, is .14. What characteristics do we expect a randomly selected 100 of these light bulbs to have?

To answer this, let X be the number of defectives in the sample, and let $\hat{p} = X/100$ be the proportion of defectives in the sample. Since the sample is drawn randomly, we cannot be sure of the value of X or $\hat{p}$ until the sample

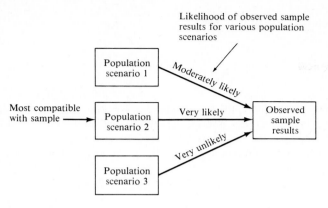

Figure 6.1

results are observed. Until that time, X and $\hat{p}$ are random variables. The distributions of these random variables are called *sampling distributions* because they arise in a sampling context. The sampling distribution of $\hat{p}$, say, can be explained as follows. Imagine listing *every* possible sample of 100 light bulbs from the population of 10,000 light bulbs. For every such sample, we could record the value of $\hat{p}$, the proportion of defectives in that sample. Then the sampling distribution of $\hat{p}$ is simply the histogram of all $\hat{p}$'s we would obtain from this list. Equivalently, we can define the sampling distribution of $\hat{p}$ as follows.

The sampling distribution of $\hat{p}$ lists, for each possible value of $\hat{p}$, the fraction of all possible samples with this value.

This listing procedure for deriving the sampling distribution of $\hat{p}$ is not very practical when the population size is 10,000 and the sample size is 100; there are too many samples to count. But to illustrate the idea, suppose that the population size is 4, with 1 defective, and the sample size is 2. Then we can easily illustrate the sampling distribution of $\hat{p}$. Suppose we number the four light bulbs 1, 2, 3, 4, with number 1 being the defective. Then we can list the six possible samples, with the corresponding $\hat{p}$ values, by listing which light bulbs are in a sample. They are: $(1, 2) \rightarrow \hat{p} = \frac{1}{2}$; $(1, 3) \rightarrow \hat{p} = \frac{1}{2}$; $(1, 4) \rightarrow \hat{p} = \frac{1}{2}$; $(2, 3) \rightarrow \hat{p} = 0$; $(2, 4) \rightarrow \hat{p} = 0$; $(3, 4) \rightarrow \hat{p} = 0$. Since three of the six samples result in $\hat{p} = \frac{1}{2}$, and the other three result in $\hat{p} = 0$, the sampling distribution of $\hat{p}$ is given by $P(\hat{p} = 0) = \frac{3}{6} = .5$ and $P(\hat{p} = \frac{1}{2}) = \frac{3}{6} = .5$. The mean and standard deviation of this sampling distribution are

$$E(\hat{p}) = .5(0) + .5\left(\frac{1}{2}\right) = .25$$

and

$$\text{Var}(\hat{p}) = \left[.5(0)^2 + .5\left(\frac{1}{2}\right)^2 \right] - (.25)^2 = .0625$$

In general, the sampling distribution of $\hat{p}$ cannot be obtained as simply as stated above because larger population sizes and sample sizes make a complete listing of all possible samples impractical. In the next two sections we provide methods for finding the sampling distribution of $\hat{p}$. But first we need to define several terms that are extremely important in the study of sampling distributions.

Statistics, Parameters, and Random Samples

In this chapter we describe the sampling distributions of the most important quantities that arise in practical applications. In particular, we investigate the sampling distributions of (1) $\hat{p}$, the sample proportion of A's in a sample from a population of A's and B's; (2) $\overline{X}$, the sample mean; (3) $\hat{p}_1 - \hat{p}_2$, the difference between two sample proportions; and (4) $\overline{X}_1 - \overline{X}_2$, the difference between two sample means.

Each of these quantities is called a *sample statistic,* or simply a statistic. This means that its value can be calculated from the sample data. Most statistics have a natural counterpart called a *population parameter,* or simply a parameter. For example, the statistic $\hat{p}$ corresponds to p, the proportion of A's in the population, and the statistic $\overline{X}$ corresponds to μ, the population mean. In these cases the population parameters are p and μ. We repeat the following definitions from Chapter 2.

> A population parameter is a characteristic of the population as a whole. It can generally be calculated only by knowing the entire population. A sample statistic is a random variable that can be calculated from the sample data.

(Notice that we now use the term "random variable" in the definition of sample statistic. This implies that the value of the statistic is not known until the sample is observed.)

Every sample statistic, including those mentioned above, has a sampling distribution. In general, a sampling distribution is defined exactly as we defined the sampling distribution of $\hat{p}$.

> The sampling distribution of any sample statistic lists, for each possible value of the sample statistic, the fraction of all possible samples with this value.

One other very important aspect of sampling is how we choose the members of a sample. In this chapter and in most of the rest of this book, we will assume that the samples chosen are *random samples*, where this term has the precise meaning given below. (Strictly speaking, this type of random sample is usually called a *simple* random sample. We discuss other types of random samples in Chapter 16.)

> A random sample of size n is a subset of the population chosen in such a way that every possible set of n members has the same chance of being chosen.

The motivation behind choosing *random* samples is that we tend to avoid unintentional bias and therefore tend to select "typical" samples from the population. We also sample in this way so that we can use probability theory to make valid inferences.

6.3
Computer-Generated Sampling Distributions

Let's take another look at the sampling distribution of $\hat{p}$ in the light bulb example. Again, we assume that the population proportion of defectives is $p = .14$. How can we obtain the sampling distribution of $\hat{p}$? For example, how can we find the mean of $\hat{p}$, the standard deviation of $\hat{p}$, and the probability that $\hat{p}$ has a value between .11 and .17?

From the definition of sampling distribution, we need to imagine many random samples of size 100, each drawn from the same population of size 10,000 with 1400 defectives. For the ith sample of size 100, we let $\hat{p}_i$ be the proportion of defectives in that particular sample. After obtaining M samples, we would have M $\hat{p}$'s, labeled $\hat{p}_1, \hat{p}_2, \ldots, \hat{p}_M$. If M is sufficiently large, the histogram of these M $\hat{p}$'s should give us a good idea of the sampling distribution of $\hat{p}$.

The only problem with this idea is that it is physically impossible to draw M samples of size 100 from the same population of 10,000 light bulbs. This is because the sampling is destructive to the light bulbs. Fortunately, there is a simple way to accomplish the sample results we desire. We let a computer do the work for us. As explained in Chapter 1, it is fairly simple to have a computer draw one random sample or many random samples of size 100 from a population of size 10,000 with 14% defectives. As the computer does

Table 6.1   Empirical Sampling Distribution of $\hat{p}$

$\hat{p}$	Number of Samples with This $\hat{p}$	$\hat{p}$	Number of Samples with This $\hat{p}$
.00	0	.16	99
.01	0	.17	78
.02	0	.18	64
.03	0	.19	36
.04	3	.20	32
.05	0	.21	24
.06	5	.22	4
.07	16	.23	4
.08	29	.24	2
.09	46	.25	2
.10	64	.26	0
.11	84	.27	0
.12	91	.28	0
.13	113	.29	0
.14	113	.30	0
.15	91		

this, we have it count the number of defectives generated in each sample, so that the computer's output includes the values of $\hat{p}_1$, $\hat{p}_2$, . . . , $\hat{p}_M$ directly. For our purposes, it is not necessary to know exactly how the computer does this; it is enough to know that the computer sampling is merely a quick, electronic replica of the experiment we are physically unable to perform.

We illustrate the results of such a computer program in Table 6.1. We had the computer draw 1000 samples of size 100 from a population with 14% defectives. In each sample we kept track of the sample proportion of defectives, $\hat{p}$. Rather than listing the 1000 observed values of $\hat{p}$, the table shows the number of the 1000 samples that resulted in the possible values of $\hat{p}$. For example, the most common values of $\hat{p}$ were .13 and .14 (13 and 14 defectives out of 100). These occurred in 113 samples each. The table also shows that none of the 1000 samples contained fewer than 4 defectives or more than 25 defectives.

The numbers in Table 6.1 give an *empirical* sampling distribution of $\hat{p}$. The word "empirical" means that we got these numbers by sampling many times to obtain many values of $\hat{p}$. The theoretical distribution of $\hat{p}$, on the other hand, is what we would obtain if we could observe *every* possible sample of size 100 (and there are more than 10^{100} of these).

We may use the results in Table 6.1 to provide approximate answers to the questions raised in the first paragraph of this section. First, consider the probability that $\hat{p}$ has a value between .11 and .17 (inclusive). Since 669 of the 1000 samples had $\hat{p}$'s between .11 and .17, we approximate the probability that a *single* $\hat{p}$ will be between .11 and .17 by $669/1000 = .669$.

For the mean and variance of $\hat{p}$, we treat the data in Table 6.1 as grouped data and apply the formulas from Chapter 2:

$$\text{mean of } \hat{p}\text{'s} = \sum \frac{(k/100)f_k}{n} = .1404$$

and

$$\text{variance of } \hat{p}\text{'s} = \sum \frac{(k/100)^2 f_k - n(.1404)^2}{n-1} = .001232$$

(Here f_k is the number of samples where $\hat{p}$ was equal to $k/100$, and $n = 1000$ is the number of samples drawn.) These values, .1404 and .001232, approximate the mean and variance of the $\hat{p}$'s we would observe if we could observe all possible samples of size 100 from this population.

6.4

Sampling Distribution of the Sample Proportion

In this section we formalize the ideas from the light bulb example by finding the theoretical sampling distribution of a sample proportion. Consider any population with two types of members. We refer to these types as A's and B's, and we let p be the proportion of A's in the population. To learn about p, we draw a sample of size n from this population and count the number of A's in the sample. Often, we refer to the sampling of a single member as a *trial*. Then the sample proportion, denoted by $\hat{p}$, is defined as the proportion of trials that result in A's. Notice that p is the population parameter and $\hat{p}$ is the sample statistic.

Definition of Sample Proportion

$\hat{p}$ = proportion of A's in the sample

The notation $\hat{p}$ suggests that the sample proportion of A's is a natural estimate of the population proportion of A's, p. Often when we wish to estimate a population parameter such as p, we label the sample estimate of that parameter by the same letter with a "^" above it. (When we do not use a "^", as when we use the notation $\overline{X}$ instead of $\hat{\mu}$ for the sample mean, it is to conform to standard notation found in the majority of statistical literature.)

There are three types of applications we will consider. The first is when we sample *with* replacement from a population of size N with N_A A's. Then p is the fraction of A's in the population, N_A/N. The second case is when we sample *without* replacement from this same type of population. In this case we assume that n/N, the fraction of the population sampled, is small, say less than .10. Again, the value of p is N_A/N.

The third type of application is not really "sampling" as we usually think of sampling. It occurs when we perform a sequence of n independent trials where each trial results in an A or a B. An example of this is when we examine successive parts coming off a production line (A = nondefective, B = defective). Although a sequence of n trials in this example could be considered a sample from a population, the population has no fixed, finite size N. In this type of application, p should be interpreted as the probability of an A on a given trial rather than the fraction N_A/N of A's in the population.

For the applications above, it is relatively easy to deduce the sampling distribution of $\hat{p}$ *without* performing a computer experiment as in Section 6.3. These applications all have two important properties in common: (1) as the sampling proceeds, the probability of sampling an A remains constant at value p, and (2) the results of the successive trials are probabilistically independent. These are exactly the properties required to use the binomial distribution. In particular, if X is the number of A's in n trials, X has a binomial distribution with parameters n and p. But since $\hat{p} = X/n$, we can immediately deduce the sampling distribution of $\hat{p}$.

Sampling Distribution of $\hat{p}$

$$P\left(\hat{p} = \frac{k}{n}\right) = \binom{n}{k} p^k (1 - p)^{n-k} \qquad \text{for } k = 0, 1, 2, \ldots, n$$

From Chapter 5 we know that X has mean np and variance $np(1 - p)$. By the rules of expected values from Chapter 4,

$$E(\hat{p}) = E\left(\frac{X}{n}\right) = \frac{E(X)}{n} = \frac{np}{n} = p$$

and

$$\text{Var}(\hat{p}) = \text{Var}\left(\frac{X}{n}\right) = \frac{\text{Var}(X)}{n^2} = \frac{np(1 - p)}{n^2} = \frac{p(1 - p)}{n}$$

We also know that when $np(1 - p) \geq 5$, the binomial distribution of X can be approximated closely by a normal distribution. The same applies to the distribution of $\hat{p}$.

> *Approximate Sampling Distribution of $\hat{p}$ When $np(1 - p) \geq 5$*
>
> $\hat{p}$ is approximately normal with mean p and variance $\dfrac{p(1 - p)}{n}$

The graphs in Figure 6.2 illustrate the distribution of $\hat{p}$ when $n = 100$ and $p = .14$ (as in the light bulb example). Figure 6.2a shows the exact (binomial)

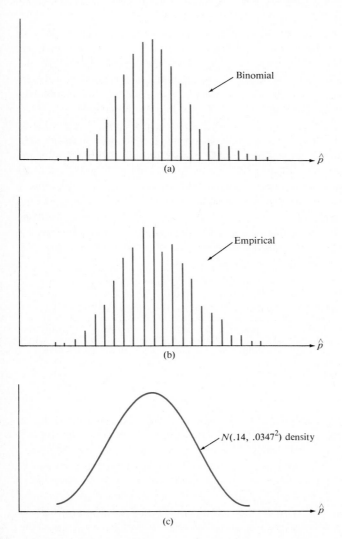

Binomial

(a)

Empirical

(b)

$N(.14, .0347^2)$ density

(c)

Figure 6.2
Binomial Probabilities for $\hat{p}$, Empirical and Normal Approximations

distribution of $\hat{p}$. Figure 6.2b illustrates the empirical distribution of $\hat{p}$ found from the computer simulation in Section 6.3. It is a result of the frequencies listed in Table 6.1. Finally, the continuous function graphed in Figure 6.2c is the normal approximation to the binomial. Clearly, the graphs in Figures 6.2b and c are close approximations to the graph in Figure 6.2a.

Provided that the sample size is sufficiently large, either the binomial probabilities or the normal approximation can be used in problems involving $\hat{p}$. As we saw in Chapter 5, the advantage of the normal approximation is that it is much easier to use when n is large. Fortunately, it is also quite accurate when $np(1 - p) \geq 5$.

The most intuitive information about the sampling distribution of $\hat{p}$ is contained in its mean p and its standard deviation $\sqrt{p(1 - p)/n}$. Since the mean of $\hat{p}$ is p, our ''best guess'' for $\hat{p}$, before the sample results are observed, is the population proportion p. For example, if 55% of a population are Democrats and we take a random sample of any size from this population, our best guess is that there will be 55% Democrats in the sample.

The standard deviation of $\hat{p}$, on the other hand, tells us how far a particular sample proportion is likely to be from its mean, p. As a rule of thumb (see Rule 4.2), the value of $\hat{p}$ has about a 68% chance of being within 1 standard deviation of p and a 95% chance of being within 2 standard deviations of p. Also, since the standard deviation of $\hat{p}$, namely $\sqrt{p(1 - p)/n}$, decreases as n increases, the interval that is ± 1 standard deviation from the mean keeps shrinking as n increases. If $p = .55$, for example, the interval is from $.55 - .497/\sqrt{n}$ to $.55 + .497/\sqrt{n}$. For selected values of n, this interval is shown in Table 6.2. Clearly, $\hat{p}$ is much more likely to be close to $p = .55$ when $n = 10,000$ than when $n = 10$.

Table 6.2 Interval That Is ± 1 Standard Deviation from the Mean ($p = .55$)

n	10	50	100	1000	10,000
$\sqrt{p(1 - p)/n}$	.157	.070	.050	.016	.005
Interval	.393–.707	.480–.620	.500–.600	.534–.566	.545–.555

We now present several numerical examples. There are two basic points we wish to illustrate in these examples. First, we show how to perform typical probability calculations involving $\hat{p}$ when the sample size n is fixed. Second, we illustrate how the sample size affects the difference between $\hat{p}$ and p. Notice that in Examples 6.1 and 6.3, we use the exact binomial probabilities. This causes no computational difficulties because n is relatively small in these examples. (Indeed, the normal approximation would not be appropriate in these examples.) In the other examples, however, we take advantage of the normal approximation.

EXAMPLE 6.1

Suppose that a company hires 20 new employees. These employees are required to go through a fairly rigorous six-month training program. Based on past experience, the company expects that each employee, independently of the others, will survive the training program with probability .7. (The others will quit.) What is the probability that between 70 and 80% of the new employees will survive the training program?

SOLUTION

Let $\hat{p}$ be the fraction of employees who survive the training program. We want the probability that $.7 \le \hat{p} \le .8$. Since $\hat{p} = X/20$, where X is the number who make it through, we want the probability that $14 \le X \le 16$. We can calculate this probability by using the binomial tables with $n = 20$ and $p = .7$:

$$P(.7 \le \hat{p} \le .8) = P(14 \le X \le 16) = P(X \le 16) - P(X \le 13) = .5009$$

This means there is about a 50–50 chance that between 70 and 80% of the employees will make it through the program.

EXAMPLE 6.2

In a gambling casino there is a game called "craps." The rules of this game are such that the casino has a .507 probability of winning on a given play. What are the mean and standard deviation of the proportion of plays the casino wins if it plays 10,000 times? What is the probability that the casino will win at least half of these plays?

SOLUTION

For this example we are given the probability of the casino winning on a given play. This is $p = .507$. If the casino plays 10,000 times and wins on X of these, $\hat{p} = X/10,000$ is the fraction of plays it wins. The mean of $\hat{p}$ is $p = .507$ and its standard deviation, denoted by $\sigma_{\hat{p}}$, is

$$\sigma_{\hat{p}} = \sqrt{\frac{p(1 - p)}{n}} = \sqrt{\frac{.507(.493)}{10,000}} = .005$$

The probability that the casino is ahead is $P(\hat{p} > .5)$. Using the normal approximation (which is justified because $np(1 - p)$ is much greater than 5), we have

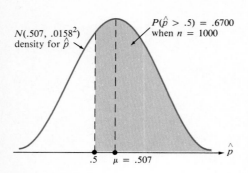

$$P(\hat{p} > .5) = P\left(Z > \frac{.5 - p}{\sigma_{\hat{p}}}\right) = P\left(Z > \frac{.5 - .507}{.005}\right)$$

$$= P(Z > -1.4) = P(Z < 1.4) = .9192$$

[A slightly more rigorous way to calculate this probability is to work with X, the number of wins, and to use the continuity correction discussed in Chapter 5. That is, $P(\hat{p} > .5)$ equals $P(X \geq 5001)$. Using the continuity correction, this probability becomes $P(Z > -1.39)$, practically the same as above. In general, this more rigorous approach is not necessary when the sample sizes are very large.]

Therefore, after 10,000 plays the casino is over 90% certain of being ahead. For the sake of comparison, a similar calculation for $n = 1000$ plays yields a probability of approximately .67. So there are only about 2 chances out of 3 that the casino will be ahead after 1000 plays (see Figure 6.3).

Figure 6.3
Probability Casino Is Ahead After 1000 Plays

EXAMPLE 6.3

Consider a chain of discount stores with many branches across the country. Although the various branches carry essentially the same brands of merchandise, their prices vary considerably. In particular, assume that the distribution of prices for a store brand of color television set is normal with mean \$379 and standard deviation \$25. Consider a random sample of 20 of these branch stores. Find the mean and standard deviation of the proportion of these branches that charge at least \$400 for the television set. Also, find the probability that less than 4 of the 20 stores sampled charge at least \$400.

SOLUTION

This example also concerns a proportion, the proportion of branches that charge at least \$400 for the television set. Our first task is to find the population proportion p. We can find p from the fact that the distribution of prices is $N(379, 25^2)$. If X is the price a randomly selected store charges, $p = P(X \geq 400)$, so that

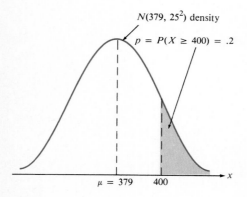

Figure 6.4
Value of p for Example 6.3

$$p = P(X \geq 400) = P\left(Z \geq \frac{400 - 379}{25}\right) = P(Z \geq .84) = .2005$$

(see Figure 6.4). This is the only place in the problem where we need to use the fact that prices are normally distributed. Now that we have the population proportion p (which we round off to .2 for convenience), we proceed as in Examples 6.1 and 6.2.

In this example, $\hat{p}$ is the proportion of the 20 stores sampled that charge at least \$400. Its mean is $p = .2$ and its standard deviation, using $n = 20$, is $\sqrt{p(1 - p)/n} = .089$. To find $P(\hat{p} < \frac{4}{20})$, we do *not* use the normal approximation to the binomial. Since $np(1 - p)$ is only 3.2, we obtain a more accurate value if we use the binomial table directly. Since $\hat{p} < {}^4\!/_{20}$ is equivalent to 3 or fewer stores out of 20, we look in the binomial tables under $k = 3$ to obtain

$$P\left(\hat{p} < \frac{4}{20}\right) = P\left(\hat{p} \leq \frac{3}{20}\right) = .4114$$

EXAMPLE 6.4

The IRS is well aware that a large percentage of taxpayers who prepare their own tax forms make arithmetic mistakes. Based on the examination of many tax returns from previous years, the IRS believes that the proportion of all taxpayers who make arithmetic mistakes is $p = .17$. Even though this figure is based on returns from previous years, there is no reason to believe that it will be any different in the current year. If the IRS thoroughly checks 15,000 self-prepared tax forms for arithmetic accuracy, how likely is it that more than 17.5% of these will contain errors?

SOLUTION

Let $\hat{p}$ be the proportion of the sampled returns with arithmetic mistakes. When $n = 15,000$, the mean of $\hat{p}$ is .17 and the variance is $p(1 - p)/n = .17(.83)/15,000 = (.003067)^2$. That is, the standard deviation of $\hat{p}$ is .003067. So the probability of errors on at least 17.5% of the 15,000 returns is

$$P(\hat{p} > .175) = P\left(Z > \frac{.175 - .17}{.003067}\right) = P(Z > 1.63)$$
$$= 1 - P(Z < 1.63) = .0516$$

[The normal approximation is justified because $np(1 - p)$ is much greater than 5.]

The point of the following example is that if we want the difference between $\hat{p}$ and p to be small, we must use a very large sample size n.

EXAMPLE 6.5

Consider any binomial experiment with n trials, where the probability of an A on each trial is p. If $\hat{p}$ is the sample proportion of A's, we will say that $\hat{p}$ and p are "close" if the absolute difference between $\hat{p}$ and p is no greater than some prescribed number B. (1) Find the probability of $\hat{p}$ and p being close when $B = .01$ and $p = .5$. Do this when $n = 100$; when $n = 1000$; when $n = 5000$. (2) Repeat the calculations (for the same sample sizes) when

$B = .01$ and $p = .1$. (3) Repeat the calculations (again for the same sample sizes) when $B = .005$ and $p = .5$.

SOLUTION

For any values of p, B, and n, we know $\hat{p}$ and p are "close" if $|\hat{p} - p| \leq B$. If we divide each side of this inequality by the standard deviation of $\hat{p}$, on the left side we obtain $|Z|$, the absolute value of a standard normal random variable. Therefore, the probability of $\hat{p}$ and p being close is

$$P(|\hat{p} - p| \leq B) = P\left[|Z| \leq \frac{B}{\sqrt{p(1 - p)/n}}\right] = P\left[|Z| \leq \frac{B\sqrt{n}}{\sqrt{p(1 - p)}}\right]$$

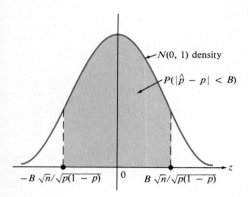

Figure 6.5

This probability, shown in Figure 6.5, can be calculated easily for any given values of n, p, and B. The results are shown in Table 6.3.

Table 6.3   Table of $P(|Z| \leq B\sqrt{n}/\sqrt{p(1 - p)})$

n	$B = .01$ $p = .5$	$B = .01$ $p = .1$	$B = .005$ $p = .5$
100	.1586	.2611	.0796
1000	.4729	.7081	.2481
5000	.8427	.9816	.5205

We can gain some important insight by studying Table 6.3 carefully. First, by comparing the first and second columns, we see that for a fixed B, the probability that p and $\hat{p}$ are close is higher when $p = .1$ than when $p = .5$. (In general, it can be shown that the farther p is from .5, the larger this probability is.) Second, by comparing the first and third columns, we see that, for a fixed p, the probability that p and $\hat{p}$ are close decreases as B decreases from .01 to .005. Finally, we see from all three columns that for fixed values of p and B, the probability that p and $\hat{p}$ are close increases as n increases.

Problems for Sections 6.2, 6.3, 6.4

1. It is known that 30% of the cars of a particular model and year have a defect in their exhaust systems. If a random 500 owners of these types of cars bring their cars in to be checked, what is the probability that at least 35% of them will have defective exhaust systems?

2. In Problem 1, what is the probability that the sample proportion of the 500 owners with defective exhaust systems will be within .025 of the population proportion? How does this probability change if 1500, not 500, owners bring their cars in to be checked?

3. One news magazine publishes a list of the best-selling books each week. This list is based on the magazine's data from approximately 1000 bookstores. Suppose that 20% of these bookstores report that the new book, *The Days of September,* is their best-selling book. If a random sample of 80 of these bookstores are polled, what is the probability that at least 25% of them will say that *The Days of September* is their best-selling book?

4. Planned Parenthood reported in 1983 that 25% of teenage girls who currently obtained contraceptives said they would stop using contraceptives if, as proposed by a new government regulation, their parents were informed of them buying the devices. (Reference: *Time,* Feb. 7, 1983, p. 41.) Assuming that this is true and the government regulation goes into effect, find the probability that at least 28% of a randomly selected group of 500 girls discontinue the use of the contraceptives because of the new regulation.

5. One magazine claimed in 1982 that 15% of the people in the United States believe in astrology. (Reference: P. E. Hammond, ''Up and Down with the National Faith: Implications for the Survival of a Nation,'' *Business Horizons,* Vol. 25, 1982, pp. 11–16.) Assuming that this is true, how likely is it to obtain no more than 13% astrology believers in a random sample of size n? Answer this for $n = 200$ and $n = 1000$.

6. Counting government jobs, approximately 70% of all jobs in the United States in 1980 were classified as ''service'' jobs. (Reference: F. Bateman, ''Industrial America: A Glance at the Past, a Guess at the Future,'' *Business Horizons,* Vol. 25, 1982, pp. 17–23.) Consider a random sample of 500 workers taken in 1980.
   a. What is the probability that at least 67% of the workers in the sample had service jobs?
   b. Let $\hat{p}$ be the sample proportion of workers having service jobs in the sample above. Find the value p_0 such that the event $\hat{p} < p_0$ has probability .75.

7. Suppose that 46% of all adults in a certain population wear glasses. We randomly sample 230 people and are interested in X, the number of people in the sample who wear glasses, and $\hat{p}$, the proportion of people in the sample who wear glasses.
   a. Use the sampling distribution of X to find the probability of the event $X \leq 104$. Do this as in Chapter 5, using the normal approximation to the binomial together with the continuity correction.
   b. In terms of $\hat{p}$, write the event that is equivalent to $X \leq 104$. Then use the sampling distribution of $\hat{p}$ to find the probability of this event. Do this calculation as in Section 6.4, without using a continuity correction. Then compare your answer with the (more exact) answer from part (a).

8. Consider a city where 3% of the people are left-handed. We are interested in the proportion $\hat{p}$ of left-handers in a random sample of 100 people taken from this city.
   a. Find the probability that $\hat{p} < .02$ by using binomial probabilities.
   b. Find the normal approximation of the probability requested in part (a). (Work with X, the number of left-handers in the sample, instead of $\hat{p}$, and use a continuity correction as in Chapter 5.)

9. By 1976 the percentage of American workers with government jobs was at its all-time high of 17%. (Reference: A. L. Kalleberg, ''Work: Postwar Trends and Future Prospects,'' *Business Horizons,* Vol. 25, 1982, pp. 78–84.) Consider a random sample of 500 workers taken in 1976.
   a. Find the probability that at least 18% of the sampled workers had government jobs.
   b. Let $\hat{p}$ be the proportion of the sampled workers with non-government jobs. Find a value p_0 such that the event $\hat{p} < p_0$ has probability .65.

10. In 1978 it was estimated that 11.4% of all Americans were living below the poverty line. (Reference: J. R. Wood, ''Poverty in America,'' *Business Horizons,* Vol. 25, 1982, pp. 85–90.) Consider a random sample of 500 Americans taken in 1978. How unusual would it be if at least 11.6% of the people in this sample were living below the poverty line?

6.5

Sampling Distribution of the Sample Mean

In this section we learn the sampling distribution of the sample mean, the average of the observations from a sample. In many applications we are interested in a numerical characteristic of a given population. This numerical characteristic could be the earnings per share of a stock, the price of an automobile, the pollution count in a city, or many others. In many such cases we may be primarily interested in the population mean. For example, we may be interested in the mean price of all automobiles of a certain make, or in the mean pollution count (averaged over many days) in a particular city. A natural way to estimate this population mean is to take a random sample from the relevant population and compute the sample mean. Our objective in this section is to study the distribution of the sample mean. This will tell us what to expect of the sample mean from a typical random sample.

For the following discussion we assume that the population is a population of school teachers and the numerical characteristic is yearly salary. Our discussion will focus on the population mean μ and the sample mean $\overline{X}$. The population mean μ is a population parameter, the average of all salaries in the population. The sample mean $\overline{X}$, on the other hand, is the average of the salaries in a random sample.

If we could examine all possible samples (of a fixed sample size) from the population, we could deduce the sampling distribution of the corresponding sample means. Our purpose in this section is to learn the properties of this sampling distribution. We first examine the sampling distribution of a *single* observation from the population. We will then use this to find the sampling distribution of $\overline{X}$.

Sampling Distribution of a Single Observation

Let X be the salary of a *single* randomly chosen school teacher. Then X has a probability distribution. We denote the mean and variance of the distribution by μ_X and σ_X^2. The principal result from this section is that the distribution of X is *identical* to the population distribution. In particular, μ_X equals the population mean μ, and σ_X^2 equals the population variance σ^2.

Sampling Distribution of a Single Observation X

The distribution of a single observation X is the same as the population distribution, so that $\mu_X = \mu$ and $\sigma_X^2 = \sigma^2$, where μ and σ^2 are the population mean and variance.

We interpret μ_X and σ_X^2 as follows. Suppose that we randomly choose a single school teacher from the population and let X be his or her salary. Then our best guess for the value of X is μ_X, which equals the mean of all teachers' salaries. The standard deviation σ_X indicates how far our best guess is likely to be from the value we observe. For example, if the population is approximately normally distributed, the probability is about ⅔ that the difference between X and μ will be less than σ_X. (This is because of Rule 4.2.)

EXAMPLE 6.6

The histogram of salaries for the 1312 school teachers in a given city is shown in Figure 6.6. (The numbers above the categories are frequencies.) Assume that the mean and standard deviation of salaries were calculated from the raw data (not shown) and are $17,700 and $4210, respectively. If we randomly choose one teacher from this population and let X be his or her salary, find the expected value and standard deviation of X. Then find the probability that this teacher's salary is between $16,000 and $20,000.

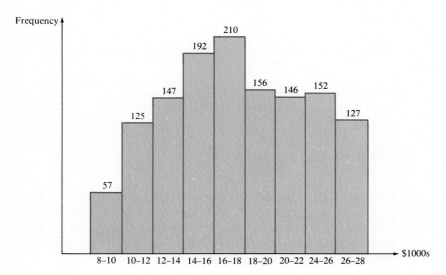

Figure 6.6
Histogram of Teachers' Salaries

SOLUTION

The expected value and standard deviation of X are the population mean and standard deviation, $17,700 and $4210. The probability that X is between $16,000 and $20,000 is the population proportion of all teachers with salaries between $16,000 and $20,000. From the histogram, this proportion is $(210 + 156)/1312$, or .279.

Now suppose that we randomly sample n school teachers. We denote their salaries by $X_1, X_2, \ldots, X_n$. Then the average of these X's is called the *sample mean* and is denoted by $\overline{X}$.

The Mean of the Sample Mean

Definition of Sample Mean

$$\overline{X} = \sum \frac{X_i}{n}$$

We now show that our best guess for the sample mean, its expected value, is the same as the population mean. Let $\mu_{\overline{X}}$ or $E(\overline{X})$ denote the expected value of $\overline{X}$. By the rules of expected values from Chapter 4, we have

$$\mu_{\overline{X}} = E(\overline{X}) = E\left(\sum \frac{X_i}{n}\right) = \sum \frac{E(X_i)}{n} = \frac{\mu + \mu + \cdots + \mu}{n} = \frac{n\mu}{n} = \mu$$

Here we have used the fact that the expected value of any single observation is equal to the population mean μ.

Expected Value of the Sample Mean

$$\mu_{\overline{X}} = \mu$$

where μ is the population mean

There are two ways to interpret the expected value of $\overline{X}$. The interpretation we have seen above is that $\mu_{\overline{X}}$ is our best guess for the value of a *single* sample mean $\overline{X}$. For example, if the population of teacher salaries has mean $17,700 and we take a single random sample of size n from this population, our best guess for the value of $\overline{X}$ is the population mean, $17,700.

A second interpretation of $\mu_{\overline{X}}$ is as follows. Suppose that we take M repeated random samples of size n, each from this same population. We label the sample mean of the ith sample by $\overline{X}_i$. Because the members included in the samples will vary from sample to sample, the values of the $\overline{X}_i$'s will vary also. However, the average of the $\overline{X}_i$'s will be close to $\mu_{\overline{X}}$ if M is large. Some sample means will be below $\mu_{\overline{X}}$ and some will be above $\mu_{\overline{X}}$, but the average of the M sample means will be close to $\mu_{\overline{X}}$.

Variance of the Sample Mean

Since $\overline{X}$ is a random variable, it has a variance, denoted by $\sigma_{\overline{X}}^2$. This variance indicates how $\overline{X}$'s from different samples vary from one another. We now show that this variance equals the population variance divided by the sample size. Assume that the individual observations $X_1, X_2, \ldots, X_n$ are *independent* random variables. (When samples are chosen without replacement from a finite population, these random variables are not quite independent. Therefore, a "finite population correction factor" is required for the variance of $\overline{X}$. We discuss this in Chapter 16. For now, we ignore the correction factor, which is a perfectly acceptable practice when the sample size is no greater than 5% of the population size.) Then the rules of expected values from Chapter 4 imply that

$$\sigma_{\overline{X}}^2 = \text{Var}(\overline{X}) = \text{Var}\left(\sum \frac{X_i}{n}\right) = \frac{1}{n^2} \sum \text{Var}(X_i)$$

We saw earlier in this section that the variance of a single observation equals the population variance σ^2, so we have

$$\sigma_{\overline{X}}^2 = \frac{\sigma^2 + \sigma^2 + \cdots + \sigma^2}{n^2} = \frac{n\sigma^2}{n^2} = \frac{\sigma^2}{n}$$

Taking square roots to obtain standard deviations, we have $\sigma_{\overline{X}} = \sigma/\sqrt{n}$. These important results are listed below.

Variance and Standard Deviation of $\overline{X}$

$$\sigma_{\overline{X}}^2 = \frac{\sigma^2}{n} \quad \text{and} \quad \sigma_{\overline{X}} = \frac{\sigma}{\sqrt{n}}$$

where σ^2 is the population variance

EXAMPLE 6.6 (continued)

Again assume that the population of teacher salaries has mean $17,700 and standard deviation $4210. Explain the difference between predicting the salary of a single teacher and predicting the mean salary for a random sample of 25 teachers.

SOLUTION

If we select a single teacher at random from this population and denote his or her salary by X, our best guess for X is $17,700. If we can assume that the population is approximately normal, Rule 4.2 implies that this best guess has about a ⅔ chance of being within 1 standard deviation of its actual value. Here the standard deviation is the population standard deviation σ, or $4210. The intuitive reason that our best guess for X is likely to be so inaccurate is that there are a few members of the population with salaries fairly far from the mean; if we take a sample of size 1, we might just be unlucky enough to obtain one of these members.

In contrast, if we sample $n = 25$ teachers and form the sample mean $\overline{X} = \sum X_i/25$, our best guess for the value of $\overline{X}$ is still $17,700. But since $\sigma_{\overline{X}} = \sigma/\sqrt{25} = \$842$, our best guess is now likely to be much more accurate than the best guess for a single X. The reason is simple. The relatively large X's in the sample are likely to offset the relatively small X's in the sample. The resulting average of the 25 observations is therefore likely to be close to the population mean \$17,700. In particular, the probability is about ⅔ that our best guess for $\overline{X}$ will be off by no more than \$842.

Approximate Normality of the Distribution of the Sample Mean

So far we know only the mean and variance of $\overline{X}$. To obtain the complete sampling distribution of $\overline{X}$, we use the Central Limit Theorem. If the individual observations $X_1, X_2, \ldots, X_n$ are independent random variables, we know from the Central Limit Theorem that for large values of n ($n \geq 30$ is usually sufficient), the sum $X_1 + X_2 + \cdots + X_n$ is approximately normally distributed, regardless of the population distribution. Since $\overline{X}$ is simply the sum $X_1 + X_2 + \cdots + X_n$ divided by n, it is also approximately normally distributed. In particular, $\overline{X}$ is approximately normal with mean μ and variance σ^2/n.

> *Central Limit Theorem for the Sample Mean*
>
> For any population distribution with mean μ and variance σ^2, and for any $n \geq 30$, $\overline{X}$ is approximately normal with mean μ and variance σ^2/n.

The population distribution is often called the *parent* distribution. The result above says that $\overline{X}$ is approximately normally distributed for *any* parent distribution, as long as n is fairly large. If the parent distribution happens to be normal itself, however, we can do even better than approximate normality. In this case, $\overline{X}$ is *exactly* normal for every $n \geq 1$.

> When the population distribution is normal with mean μ and variance σ^2, then $\overline{X}$ is exactly normally distributed with mean μ and variance σ^2/n for every sample size.

These facts are illustrated in Figure 6.7. In Figure 6.7a, the parent density is nonnormal (skewed to the right), but the density of $\overline{X}$ is approximately normal when $n \geq 30$. In Figure 6.7b, the parent density and the density of $\overline{X}$ are both normal. In each case the distribution of $\overline{X}$ is more peaked than the parent distribution, due to its smaller variance, σ^2/n.

EXAMPLE 6.6 (continued)

Consider again the population of 1312 teachers whose salary histogram is shown in Figure 6.6. Suppose that we randomly sample 35 of these teachers

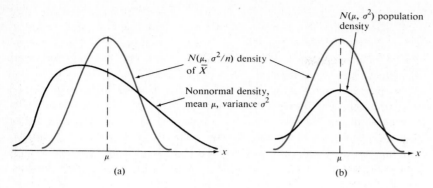

Figure 6.7

and let $\overline{X}$ be the resulting sample mean. What are the mean and standard deviation of $\overline{X}$? What is the probability that the sample mean is between $16,000 and $20,000?

SOLUTION

The mean of $\overline{X}$ is the population mean, $17,700. The standard deviation of $\overline{X}$ is $\sigma/\sqrt{n} = 4210/\sqrt{35}$, or $712. Finally, since the sample size is greater than 30, we may use the Central Limit Theorem to find $P(16{,}000 < \overline{X} < 20{,}000)$. We perform the usual normal calculation, using mean 17,700 and standard deviation 712:

$$P(16{,}000 < \overline{X} < 20{,}000) = P\left(\frac{16{,}000 - 17{,}700}{712} < Z < \frac{20{,}000 - 17{,}700}{712}\right)$$
$$= P(-2.39 < Z < 3.23)$$

From Table Ia, this probability is approximately .99. Comparing this answer with the population histogram (Figure 6.6), we see that the probability is slightly greater than .25 that a *single* randomly chosen teacher will have a salary between $16,000 and $20,000, but the probability is approximately .99 that the average of 35 teachers' salaries will be in this range.

6.6

Computer Simulation of the Distribution of the Sample Mean

We know from Section 6.5 that the approximate sampling distribution of $\overline{X}$ is normal when n is large. However, unless the population distribution is normal, the *exact* distribution of $\overline{X}$ is not normal, especially when n is small.

In fact, the exact distribution of $\overline{X}$ is typically very difficult to obtain even if we know the population (parent) distribution. However, we can get an idea of its shape by looking at computer-generated random samples of size n from a given parent population. For each random sample, we have the computer calculate $\overline{X}$; then we examine the $\overline{X}$ values obtained.

This process is useful for two reasons. First, it gives us a better understanding of the sampling distribution of $\overline{X}$. In particular, it shows us how the distribution of the $\overline{X}$'s generated differs considerably from the parent distribution. Second, this computer exercise helps to verify that the sampling distribution of $\overline{X}$ is indeed normal when n is sufficiently large.

To perform this computer simulation, we chose three parent distributions from which to sample. The first parent distribution is discrete, with possible values and probabilities given in Table 6.4. This distribution has mean 4, variance 1.6, and standard deviation 1.265. Also, its graph is quite skewed to the left. The second parent distribution is a continuous distribution with density function

$$f(x) = e^{-x} \qquad \text{for } x > 0$$

(This distribution is called the exponential distribution. Here e is the special number 2.718. . . .) It can be shown that the mean, variance, and standard deviation of this distribution are all equal to 1. The third parent distribution is normal with mean 10 and standard deviation 4. The graphs of these three parent distributions are shown in Figure 6.8.

For each of these three distributions, we generated 1000 samples of size $n = 3$, 1000 samples of size $n = 10$, 1000 samples of size $n = 30$, and 1000 samples of size $n = 100$. This may sound like a formidable task, but it is not at all difficult for a computer. The only conceptually difficult aspect is how we program the computer to generate random numbers from a given population distribution. Without going into the details, we merely state that this can be done so that the histogram of the resulting random numbers resembles the parent distribution. The rest is straightforward. For any population and any value of n, we have the computer generate n random numbers

Table 6.4   Parent I Distribution

k	$P(X = k)$
0	.02
1	.04
2	.06
3	.18
4	.20
5	.50

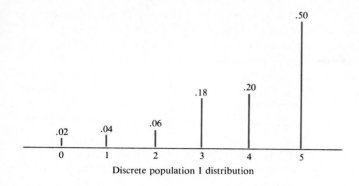

Discrete population I distribution

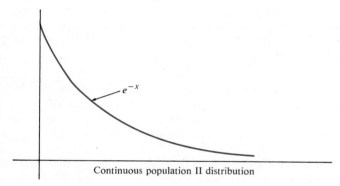

Continuous population II distribution

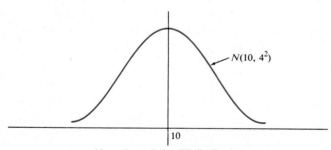

Normal population III distribution

Figure 6.8

from this population. We then have it average these n numbers to obtain a *single $\overline{X}$*.

The reason we generate a large number (1000) of sample means for each population and each sample size n is that we gain insight into the sampling distribution of the sample mean by seeing how a large number of "typical" sample means are distributed. For example, we can draw a histogram of the

1000 sample means and see if it is approximately bell-shaped. Also, we can check whether the sample means have the correct mean and variance. To do this, let $\overline{X}_i$ be the sample mean of the ith sample (for a given population and given sample size n). Then by considering the 1000 sample means $\overline{X}_1$, $\overline{X}_2$, . . . , $\overline{X}_{1000}$ as an ordinary collection of 1000 numbers, we can use the formulas in Chapter 2 to obtain the mean, labeled $\overline{\overline{X}}$, and the variance, labeled $s_{\overline{X}}^2$, of these 1000 sample means. If our theory is correct, then $\overline{\overline{X}}$, an estimate of $\mu_{\overline{X}}$, should be close to the population mean μ, and $s_{\overline{X}}^2$, an estimate of $\sigma_{\overline{X}}^2$, should be close to σ^2/n.

The results from the computer are shown below. We summarize the data from all the computer runs in Figure 6.9 (pp. 273–275). The graphs in Figure 6.9 are histograms of the sample means for each population and each sample size. In Table 6.5 we show the number of the sample means that fall into each of eight categories. These categories are symmetric around the mean μ and, except for the tail categories, have length $\sigma/\sqrt{n}$ each. This is done for each parent distribution and each sample size. The right-hand column of this table shows the number of sample means we would expect to see in each category if the distribution of the sample means were *exactly* normal. Finally, in Table 6.6 (p. 276) we show the theoretical mean μ and standard deviation $\sigma/\sqrt{n}$ of $\overline{X}$, together with the observed sample mean $\overline{\overline{X}}$ and sample standard deviation $s_{\overline{X}}$ of the simulated $\overline{X}$'s. Again, this is done for each population and each sample size.

The graphs in Figure 6.9 and the data in Tables 6.5 and 6.6 are quite interesting for several reasons. First, from Table 6.6 we see that the sample means really do center around the population mean μ. This follows because $\overline{\overline{X}}$ is very close to μ for each population and each sample size. Also, for each population and sample size, the individual sample means vary as we would expect, since $s_{\overline{X}}$ is close to $\sigma/\sqrt{n}$ in each case.

Table 6.5 Observed Frequencies of $\overline{X}$'s and Theoretical (Normal) Frequencies

	Population		I				II				III				
Interval	n	3	10	30	100	3	10	30	100	3	10	30	100	Theoretical
$\leq \mu - 3\sigma/\sqrt{n}$		2	3	1	3	0	0	0	0	0	1	1	1	1
$\mu - 3\sigma\sqrt{n}$ to $\mu - 2\sigma/\sqrt{n}$		32	18	30	18	0	5	8	14	21	21	15	20	22
$\mu - 2\sigma/\sqrt{n}$ to $\mu - \sigma/\sqrt{n}$		86	111	131	138	128	159	145	138	132	131	125	140	136
$\mu - \sigma/\sqrt{n}$ to μ		240	283	310	320	463	380	365	362	337	351	345	344	341
μ to $\mu + \sigma/\sqrt{n}$		497	396	358	352	257	301	331	323	351	335	356	344	341
$\mu + \sigma/\sqrt{n}$ to $\mu + 2\sigma/\sqrt{n}$		143	177	155	144	99	119	114	128	141	138	136	129	136
$\mu + 2\sigma/\sqrt{n}$ to $\mu + 3\sigma/\sqrt{n}$		0	12	15	24	38	29	27	31	18	21	22	21	22
$\geq \mu + 3\sigma/\sqrt{n}$		0	0	0	1	15	7	10	4	0	2	0	1	1

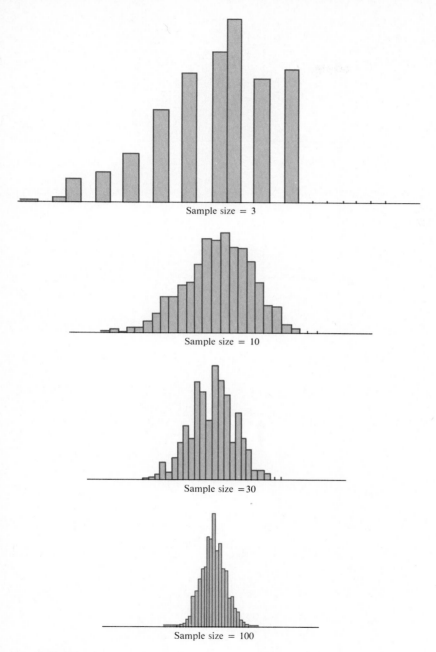

Figure 6.9a
Histograms for Discrete Population (Population I)

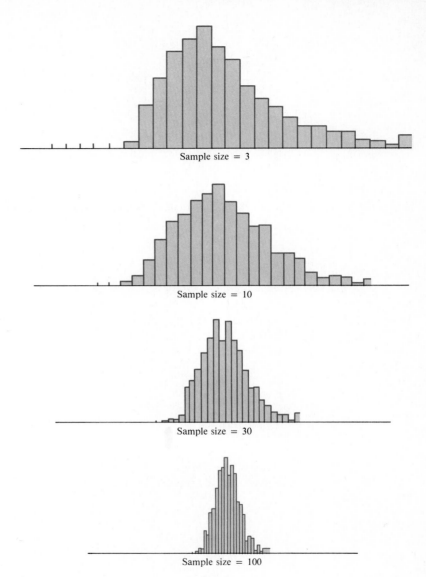

Figure 6.9b
Histograms for Exponential Population (Population II)

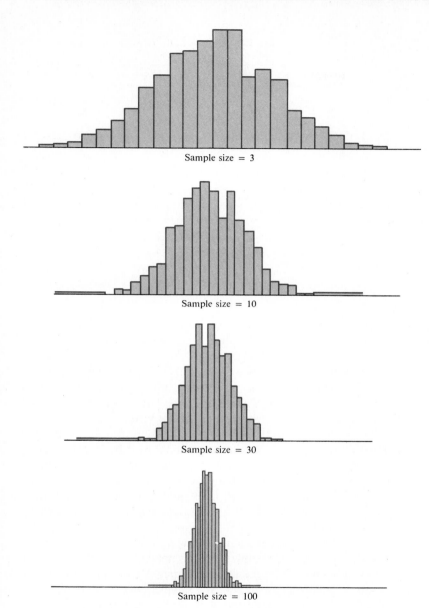

Figure 6.9c
Histograms for Normal Population (Population III)

Table 6.6   Theoretical and Observed Means and Standard Deviations of $\overline{X}$'s

Population	I				II				III			
n	3	10	30	100	3	10	30	100	3	10	30	100
μ (theoretical)	4	4	4	4	1	1	1	1	10	10	10	10
$\overline{\overline{X}}$ (observed)	4.029	4.004	3.996	4.002	1.009	1.001	1.002	1.002	10.014	10.013	10.020	9.995
$\sigma/\sqrt{n}$ (theoretical)	.730	.400	.231	.126	.577	.316	.183	.100	2.309	1.265	.730	.400
$s_{\overline{X}}$ (observed)	.711	.390	.223	.128	.599	.318	.186	.101	2.244	1.250	.710	.400

The frequencies in Table 6.5 and the histograms in Figure 6.9 give us additional information about the sampling distributions of the sample mean. They show us the *shapes* that can occur. For a nonnormal parent distribution, the shape of the sampling distribution of $\overline{X}$ can also be quite nonnormal unless n is fairly large. In particular, the population I histograms for $n = 3$ and $n = 10$ have far more observations ($\overline{X}$'s) to the left of the mean than we would expect of a symmetric distribution. Similarly, the population II histograms for $n = 3$ and $n = 10$ are significantly skewed to the right, as is the parent density itself. Only when $n = 30$ and $n = 100$ do the sampling distributions of $\overline{X}$ for populations I and II approach normality. Of course, this is exactly what is predicted by the Central Limit Theorem. The histograms for population III, on the other hand, are almost exactly symmetric and bell-shaped for *each* sample size n. Again, this is what we expect, because we know that the sampling distribution of $\overline{X}$ is exactly normal for any sample size when the parent distribution is normal.

To summarize, this computer experiment has not really taught us anything we did not already know from the theory. Its purpose has been to provide insight into the sampling distribution of the sample mean $\overline{X}$. In doing so, it has confirmed the most important properties of this sampling distribution. Namely, $\overline{X}$ is approximately normal with mean μ and standard deviation $\sigma/\sqrt{n}$ for $n \geq 30$, regardless of the parent distribution. This normal approximation works for even smaller values of n if the parent distribution is approximately symmetric and bell-shaped, and it is exact if the parent distribution is normal.

Applications of the Distribution of the Sample Mean

Now that we know the sampling distribution of the sample mean, we look at several examples.

EXAMPLE 6.7

At a large university, all freshmen planning to major in engineering must take the first-year course in calculus. There are many sections of this course, and students randomly select a section depending on their course schedules. All of these sections are taught in a standardized way so that no section tends to have higher scores than any others. In fact, the course is taught so that the distribution of all scores for the course has a mean of 83 and a standard deviation of 7. This distribution of scores is skewed to the left, as shown in Figure 6.10, because a few "stragglers" in the course always tend to pull down the curve. If Mr. Cabot's section has 25 students, (1) find the probability that a randomly selected student from his class scores below 76, and (2) find the probability that the average of the scores in his class is between 80 and 85.

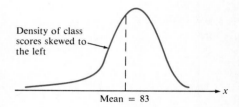

Figure 6.10
Population Density for Example 6.7

SOLUTION

For this problem we can consider Mr. Cabot's class to be a random sample of size $n = 25$ chosen from the population of all students taking the course. If we choose one student from his section and let X be his or her score, X has the same distribution as the population of all scores. In particular, $E(X) = \mu = 83$ and $\text{Var}(X) = \sigma^2 = 7^2 = 49$. However, the density function of X is skewed to the left. Therefore, we cannot use the normal approximation, Rule 4.2, to find the probability that X is less than 76. In fact, from the information given, this probability cannot be found.

The average of the 25 scores in Mr. Cabot's class is the sample mean $\overline{X}$. Since the population distribution is not extremely nonnormal, it is reasonable to conclude that $\overline{X}$ is approximately normally distributed, with mean $\mu = 83$ and standard deviation $\sigma/\sqrt{n} = 7/5 = 1.4$. Using this fact, we have

$$P(80 < \overline{X} < 85) = P\left(\frac{80 - 83}{1.4} < Z < \frac{85 - 83}{1.4}\right) = P(-2.14 < Z < 1.43)$$
$$= P(Z < 1.43) - P(Z < -2.14)$$
$$= P(Z < 1.43) - [1 - P(Z < 2.14)] = .9074$$

That is, the chances are slightly greater than 9 out of 10 that the average of the 25 scores will be between 80 and 85.

EXAMPLE 6.8

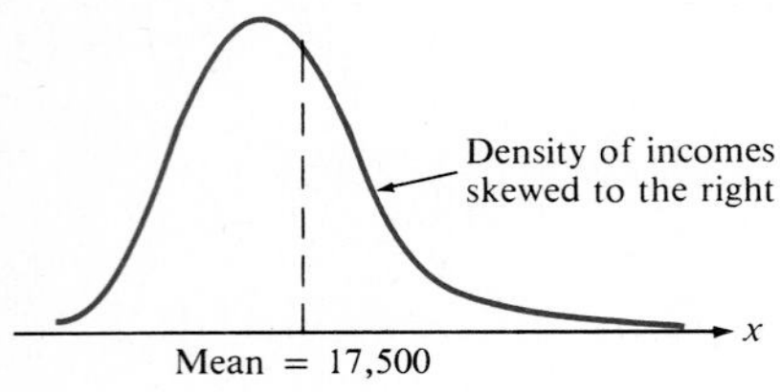

Consider a typical city with 75,000 working adults. Assume that the distribution of yearly gross incomes for these working people has mean $17,500 and standard deviation $5230. Also assume that it is skewed to the right as in Figure 6.11, due to the relatively few people in the very high income brackets. If we randomly survey n people from this population, what is the probability that the average income of these n people will exceed $18,000? How large must n be so that this probability is less than .01?

SOLUTION

To answer these questions, we need the distribution of $\overline{X}$, the average income in the sample. Although the population distribution is slightly skewed, we know that $\overline{X}$ is approximately normally distributed when $n \geq 30$, and n will almost surely be this large for any realistic survey. Furthermore, the mean of $\overline{X}$ is 17,500 and the standard deviation of $\overline{X}$ is $5230/\sqrt{n}$. The probability that $\overline{X}$ exceeds $18,000 is then found from

$$P(\overline{X} > 18,000) = P\left(Z > \frac{18,000 - 17,500}{5230/\sqrt{n}}\right) = P(Z > .0956\sqrt{n})$$
$$= 1 - P(Z < .0956\sqrt{n})$$

This probability can be evaluated once n is specified. For example, if $n = 100$, then $P(\overline{X} > 18,000) = 1 - P(Z < .96) = .1685$; if $n = 500$, then $P(\overline{X} > 18,000) = 1 - P(Z < 2.14) = .0162$. To find an n so that $P(\overline{X} > 18,000)$ equals .01, we set .01 equal to $1 - P(Z < .0956\sqrt{n})$ and solve for n. As Figure 6.12 indicates, $.0956\sqrt{n}$ must equal $z_{.01}$, or 2.326. From this we obtain $.0956^2 n = 2.326^2$, or $n = 592$. This means that if the sample size is at least 592, there is no more than 1 chance out of 100 that the average income in the sample will exceed $18,000.

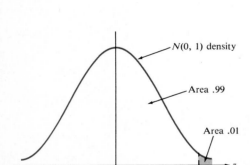

Figure 6.11
Population Density of Incomes for Example 6.8

Density of incomes skewed to the right

Mean = 17,500

Figure 6.12

$N(0, 1)$ density

Area .99

Area .01

$0 \quad .0956\sqrt{n} = z_{.01} = 2.326$

The Sum Versus the Sample Mean

In many examples it is important to notice that the calculation can be done in terms of the sample mean or the *sum* of the n observations. According to the Central Limit Theorem, each of these is approximately normal when n is large. The difference between them is that $\overline{X}$ has mean μ and standard deviation $\sigma/\sqrt{n}$, whereas the sum has mean $n\mu$ and standard deviation $\sqrt{n}\sigma$.

> The sum of n observations has mean $n\mu$ and standard deviation $\sqrt{n}\sigma$. In contrast, the sample mean of n observations has mean μ and standard deviation $\sigma/\sqrt{n}$.

The following example illustrates how the sum is sometimes more natural to use than the sample mean.

EXAMPLE 6.9

An elevator has a capacity of 2000 pounds. Suppose that the distribution of the weights of people using this elevator is normal with mean 155 pounds and standard deviation 35 pounds. Find the probability that 12 randomly chosen people will exceed the capacity.

SOLUTION

Let $X_1, X_2, \ldots, X_{12}$ be the weights of the 12 people. Then their combined weight exceeds the elevator's capacity only if $X_1 + X_2 + \cdots X_{12}$ is greater than 2000. Alternatively, this is true only if their average weight, $\overline{X}$, exceeds 2000/12. However, using $\overline{X}$ is not a very "natural" way to work this problem, so we use the sum instead. The mean and standard deviation of the sum are $n\mu = 12(155) = 1860$ and $\sqrt{n}\sigma = \sqrt{12}(35) = 121$. Also, the distribution of the sum is normal because the population distribution is normal. Therefore,

$$P(X_1 + X_2 + \cdots + X_{12} > 2000) = P\left(Z > \frac{2000 - 1860}{121}\right)$$
$$= P(Z > 1.16) = .1230$$

In words, there is approximately 1 chance out of 8 that 12 people will exceed the elevator's capacity.

The choice between using the sample mean $\overline{X}$ and the sum $X_1 + X_2 + \cdots + X_n$ is usually a matter of convenience. If the problem can be conceptualized more naturally in terms of the sum than the sample mean, as in the elevator example, we recommend doing probability calculations in terms of the sum.

Problems for Sections 6.5, 6.6, 6.7

11. A study of n randomly selected daytime television commercials shows that the average number of times a commercial actually says the name of the product is 4.1. Let μ and σ be the mean and standard deviation of the number of times the product's name is spoken, taken over all daytime television commercials.

a. Find the probability of this large a sample mean (4.1) if $\mu = 3.8$, $\sigma = 1.3$, and $n = 35$. Repeat the calculation for $n = 95$.

b. Suppose that the sample size in the study is $n = 45$. How compatible is the observed sample mean (4.1) with $\mu = 4.4$ and $\sigma = 1.1$? Back up your answer with an appropriate probability calculation.

12. During the recession in the early 1980s, there were an estimated 50,000 steelworkers laid off in Pittsburgh, many of whom were unable to keep up with their mortgage payments. (Reference: *Time*, Jan. 10, 1983.) Assume that the distribution of the amount a typical laid off worker is behind in mortgage payments has mean $6500 and standard deviation $1200. For a random sample of 100 of these workers, let $\overline{X}$ be the average amount these workers are behind in their mortgage payments.

a. Find the probability that $\overline{X}$ is between $6400 and $6700.

b. Find an amount x such that $\overline{X}$ is greater than x with probability .90.

*13. The following data represent a sample of paperback book prices offered by a national book club. (Reference: *Time*, Jan. 17, 1983, p. 26.) The original hardcover prices are also listed.

Softcover Price	Hardcover Price
$ 7.95	$22.95
7.95	15.50
7.50	16.95
8.95	19.95
4.95	12.95
6.95	12.95
8.50	16.95
6.95	14.95
7.95	17.95
4.95	12.95
8.50	17.95
10.95	27.95
7.95	13.95
9.95	19.95
4.95	10.95

Assume that the *differences* between hardcover and softcover prices for all books offered by the book club are normally distributed with mean $10 and standard deviation $3. Find the probability that as large an average difference between hardcover and softcover prices as observed in this sample would be observed in a typical random sample of 15 books. (Work only with differences.)

14. As anyone even remotely acquainted with sports knows, salaries for professional athletes are extremely high (and are increasing). Take baseball, for example. Suppose that the distribution of Major League baseball salaries in the current year has mean $340,000 and standard deviation $80,000.

a. Why might you suspect that these salaries are not normally distributed?

b. Given a random sample of 40 baseball players, what is the probability that their average salary is at least $360,000?

c. Again for a sample of 40 players, find a salary level x such that the probability of a sample average at least as large as x equals .95.

15. Cigarette manufacturers are required to list in their advertisements the number of milligrams of nicotine per cigarette. Suppose that the distribution of milligrams per cigarette, taken over the population of all cigarette brands, is normally distributed with mean .65 milligram and standard deviation .25 milligram. What is the probability of seeing a sample mean, based on a sample size of 10, at least as small as the sample mean from the sample shown below? Why is your calculation valid, even though the sample size is small?

Brand	Milligrams per Cigarette
1	.5
2	.7
3	.5
4	.2
5	.6
6	.2
7	.3
8	.6
9	.7
10	1.2

16. The *New York Times* has a very well known food critic. (Reference: *Time*, Jan. 17, 1983, p. 66.) Her column is so highly thought of, in fact, that the newspaper is willing to pick up her large food bills at the many fine restaurants she critiques. The distribution of monthly bills, according to a magazine article, has a mean of about $5800! Assume that this distribution is normally distributed with standard deviation $300. If we consider a random sample of six months, what is the probability that the total of the food bills she submits for these months is between $34,000 and $35,000? (Use the distribution of the sum, not the sample mean, of six observations.)

17. The following data represent the ages at death of the people whose obituaries appeared one day in a local newspaper: 73, 89, 46, 75, 80, 67, 39, 91, 65, 70, 76, 45, 57, 69, and 72. Suppose that the ages at death of all people in this community who die over a several-year span are normally distributed with mean 71 and standard deviation 10. What is the probability that a typical day's obituary page shows an average age as low as the one above (for the same sample size)?

18. A trucker loads 300 boxes of fruit on his truck. These boxes are a random sample from the production line that packs these boxes. The mean weight per box from the production line is 50 pounds and the standard deviation of the weight per box is 1.2 pounds.
    a. Find the mean and standard deviation of the total weight of the fruit on the truck.
    b. Find the mean and standard deviation of the average weight per box on the truck.
    c. Find the probability that the total weight of the boxes on the truck exceeds 15,025 pounds. Answer this in two ways: (1) by using the sampling distribution of the sum and the answer to part (a), and (2) by using the sampling distribution of the sample mean and the answer to part (b).

19. One of the large life insurance companies introduced a plan in the early 1980s whereby its policyholders could modify their policies and increase their dividends by close to 40%. Since the actual increase for any particular policyholder depends on that policyholder's type of policy and its loan status, the company could only claim that the mean increase in dividends, taken over all policyholders, was 39%. Suppose that the corresponding standard deviation was 4%. For a random sample of 55 policyholders who took advantage of this modification, find the probability that the average of their dividend increases was at least 40%.

20. In early 1983 the average interest rate on mortgages was 14%, the lowest rate in several years. (Reference: *Time*, Feb. 21, 1983, p. 16.) Suppose that the standard deviation was .7%. For a random sample of 100 newly obtained mortgages, find two numbers x_1 and x_2 (symmetric about 14%) such that the probability of the sample mean of the 100 mortgage rates falling between these two numbers is .95.

21. The average television repair bill for a typical week at a repair shop, based on 25 bills, is $78.30. Let μ be the mean of all television repair bills at this shop, taken over a long period of time, and let σ be the corresponding standard deviation.
    a. If $\mu = \$83.50$ and $\sigma = \$10.30$, find the probability of observing as small a sample mean (based on 25 bills) as the one observed.

    b. If $\sigma = \$10.30$, find the value of μ such that the probability of seeing a sample mean as small as the one observed is .95.
    c. If $\mu = \$83.50$, find the value of σ such that the probability of seeing a sample mean as small as the one observed is .05.

22. In all manufacturing firms, return on sales during the 1970s stayed fairly constant, with a mean of 5% and a standard deviation of .3% (taken over the population of all such firms). (Reference: F. Bateman, "Industrial America: A Glance at the Past, a Guess at the Future," *Business Horizons*, Vol. 25, 1982, pp. 17–23.)
    a. For a random sample of 40 of these firms, find the probability that the average return on sales is at least 4.9%.
    b. For the sample in part (a), find the value x such that the probability of a sample average at least as large as x percent is .95.

23. At a fruit-packing plant peaches are grouped into various sizes and then put into boxes. For example, a "50-box" has 50 peaches, all of roughly the same size. Assume that the mean weight of a peach that goes into a 50-box is 7.7 ounces, and the standard deviation of these weights is .3 ounce. Let X be the total weight of the peaches in a 50-box.
    a. Find the probability that X is less than 24.2 pounds by writing this event in terms of the sample mean and using the sampling distribution of the sample mean.
    b. Find the probability that X is less than 24.2 pounds by recognizing X as the sum of 50 weights and using the sampling distribution of the sum.

24. One thing that executives often complain about is the amount of time they have to spend in meetings. Suppose that the average time spent by all executives in meetings is 15 hours per week, and the corresponding standard deviation is 4 hours per week. If we randomly sample 35 executives, find the probability that they spend a total of at least 510 hours in meetings during the current week.

25. Assume that the population distribution of the number of children in a typical family is given by $P(X = 0) = .15$, $P(X = 1) = .2$, $P(X = 2) = .45$, $P(X = 3) = .15$, $P(X = 4) = .05$. (Assume for simplicity that no families have more than four children.)
    a. Find the mean and standard deviation of the number of children in a typical family chosen randomly from this population.
    b. Let $\overline{X}$ be the average number of children in a random sample of n families from this population. Find the mean and standard deviation of $\overline{X}$ when $n = 75$.

c. Find the probability that $\overline{X}$ is greater than 1.65 when $n = 75$. State explicitly how the Central Limit Theorem is useful in this calculation.

26. At an indoor jogging track, an observer watches 30 joggers and records that they run an average of 1.63 miles. Is this figure unusually low if the mean and standard deviation of the distances run by *all* joggers are 1.7 and .34 miles, respectively? Answer by calculating an appropriate probability.

27. From a random sample of 20 U.S. cities, the following data on student/teacher ratios in public schools as of 1977 were obtained. Each observation represents the average of the stu-

dent/teacher ratios in all classrooms of a given city: 11.99, 18.22, 16.57, 15.09, 19.11, 14.88, 18.02, 16.48, 18.34, 19.05, 16.75, 19.52, 16.97, 16.95, 17.68, 16.99, 15.73, 13.89, 13.42, and 14.61. Suppose that the distribution of these averages, taken over *all* U.S. cities, is approximately normal with mean μ and variance σ^2.

a. Find the probability of seeing as large a sample mean as the one from the data above (for the same sample size) if $\mu = 16.2$ and $\sigma = 2.1$.

b. Find the value of μ so that the probability of seeing a random sample of size 20 with a sample mean as large as the one above is .65. Again use $\sigma = 2.1$.

6.8

Sums and Differences of Independent Normal Random Variables

(This section and the next may be bypassed temporarily if readers wish to go immediately to Chapter 7, on estimation. However, these sections should be read before reading Section 7.5.)

In this section we learn one of the very attractive properties of normal random variables. We will see that the sum or difference of normal random variables is also a normal random variable. This topic represents a temporary digression from our discussion of sampling distributions. We do this now so that we can study differences between sample proportions and differences between sample means in Section 6.9.

Assume that $X_1, X_2, \ldots, X_n$ are independent random variables and that X_i has a $N(\mu_i, \sigma_i^2)$ distribution for each i. That is, each X is normal, but they may have different means and variances. Also, let $a_1, a_2, \ldots, a_n$ be any n numbers. Then the main result from this section is that the *weighted sum* $a_1X_1 + a_2X_2 + \cdots + a_nX_n$ has a normal distribution.

Distribution of a Weighted Sum of Independent Normal Random Variables

$\Sigma \, a_i X_i$ is normal with mean $\Sigma \, a_i\mu_i$ and variance $\Sigma \, a_i^2\sigma_i^2$.

EXAMPLE 6.10

Consider an investor with $10,000 to invest in three possible securities. Because the one-year returns on these securities are not known with certainty at the present time, they are regarded as random variables, X_1, X_2, and X_3. If one of these X's takes on a value such as .12, the interpretation is that this security returns \$1.12 for each dollar invested. We assume that X_1, X_2, and X_3 are independent normal random variables with the following means and standard deviations: $\mu_1 = .13$, $\mu_2 = .10$, $\mu_3 = .06$, $\sigma_1 = .05$, $\sigma_2 = .02$, and $\sigma_3 = .01$. Suppose that the investor puts \$5000 of his money into security 1, \$3000 into security 2, and \$2000 into security 3. Find the probability that his investments will earn him a profit of at least \$1000 during the next year.

SOLUTION

Let X be the amount of profit the investor makes in one year. Since his \$5000 in security 1 earns $5000X_1$ dollars in one year, his \$3000 in security 2 earns $3000X_2$, and his \$2000 in security 3 earns $2000X_3$, his total profit is

$$X = 5000X_1 + 3000X_2 + 2000X_3$$

Therefore, X is a weighted sum of X_1, X_2, and X_3, with weights $a_1 = 5000$, $a_2 = 3000$, and $a_3 = 2000$. This means that X is normal with mean $\Sigma\, a_i\mu_i$ and variance $\Sigma\, a_i^2\sigma_i^2$. Doing the required arithmetic, we have

$$\sum a_i\mu_i = 5000(.13) + 3000(.10) + 2000(.06) = 1070$$

and

$$\sum a_i^2\sigma_i^2 = 5000^2(.05)^2 + 3000^2(.02)^2 + 2000^2(.01)^2 = 66{,}500 = 258^2$$

That is, X is normal with mean \$1070 and standard deviation \$258. The rest is exactly as we have done before. The probability of earning at least \$1000 profit is

$$P(X \geq 1000) = P\!\left(Z \geq \frac{1000 - 1070}{258}\right) = P(Z \geq -.27)$$
$$= P(Z \leq .27) = .6064$$

In words, the investor's best guess for his yearly profit is \$1070, and the chances are about 3 out of 5 that he will make at least \$1000.

We know that $\Sigma\, a_iX_i$ is normal with mean $\Sigma\, a_i\mu_i$ and variance $\Sigma\, a_i^2\sigma_i^2$ for every value of n and every set of constants $a_1, a_2, \ldots, a_n$. We now look at several important special cases of this rule. [Throughout, we continue to assume that the X's are independent and that each X_i is $N(\mu_i, \sigma_i^2)$.]

1. If the weights all equal 1, the weighted sum $\Sigma\, a_iX_i$ is simply the sum of the X's. Then the general result says that $\Sigma\, X_i$ is normal with mean $\Sigma\, \mu_i$

and variance $\Sigma\ \sigma_i^2$. In particular, if all the μ_i's are equal to a common mean μ, and all the σ_i^2's are equal to a common variance σ^2, then $\Sigma\ X_i$ is normal with mean $n\mu$ and variance $n\sigma^2$. (We used this result in Example 6.9.)

2. If the weights all equal $1/n$, the μ_i's equal a common mean μ, and the σ_i^2's equal a common variance σ^2, then

$$\sum a_i X_i = \frac{\sum X_i}{n} = \overline{X}$$

Also,

$$\sum a_i \mu_i = \frac{\mu + \mu + \cdots + \mu}{n} = \frac{n\mu}{n} = \mu$$

and

$$\sum a_i^2 \sigma_i^2 = \frac{\sigma^2 + \sigma^2 + \cdots + \sigma^2}{n^2} = \frac{n\sigma^2}{n^2} = \frac{\sigma^2}{n}$$

This leads to the result stated earlier in this chapter: If the population is $N(\mu, \sigma^2)$, then $\overline{X}$ is $N(\mu, \sigma^2/n)$.

3. (This is the special case we will need for Section 6.9.) If $n = 2$, $a_1 = 1$, and $a_2 = -1$, then $\Sigma\ a_i X_i$ equals $X_1 - X_2$, the difference between two normal random variables. In this case,

$$\sum a_i \mu_i = \mu_1 - \mu_2$$

and

$$\sum a_i^2 \sigma_i^2 = 1^2(\sigma_1^2) + (-1)^2(\sigma_2^2) = \sigma_1^2 + \sigma_2^2$$

That is, the mean of the difference is the difference between the means, $\mu_1 - \mu_2$, but the variance of the difference is the *sum* of the variances, $\sigma_1^2 + \sigma_2^2$. We illustrate this special case in the following example.

EXAMPLE 6.11

Consider a population of discount stores that sell stereo sets. The mean of monthly stereo sales (across all stores) is $\mu = 115$, and the corresponding standard deviation is $\sigma = 15$. If two stores are chosen randomly from this population, find the probability that their stereo sales for a given month differ by less than 20.

SOLUTION

Let X_1 and X_2 be the sales for the two stores. Because each store is chosen randomly from the same population, X_1 and X_2 are independent and each has a $N(115, 15^2)$ distribution. Therefore, the difference $X_1 - X_2$ is normal with mean $115 - 115 = 0$ and variance $15^2 + 15^2 = 450$. The event that the two sales totals differ by less than 20 is the same as the event that $-20 < X_1 - X_2 < 20$. The probability of this event is

$$P(-20 < X_1 - X_2 < 20) = P\left(\frac{-20 - 0}{\sqrt{450}} < Z < \frac{20 - 0}{\sqrt{450}}\right)$$
$$= P(-.94 < Z < .94) = .6528$$

Before going on, we emphasize that the normal random variables in this section are assumed to be *independent*. If they are not independent, the mean of $\Sigma\, a_i X_i$ is still $\Sigma\, a_i \mu_i$, and the distribution of $\Sigma\, a_i X_i$ is still normal, but the variance of $\Sigma\, a_i X_i$ is *not* $\Sigma\, a_i^2 \sigma_i^2$. Instead, there are covariance terms present. In many applications, such as the example on investment portfolios (Example 6.10), independence is a poor assumption, and the covariances turn out to play a very important role. We will not pursue the nonindependent case in this book, however.

6.9
Sampling Distributions of Differences

In this section we make use of the result from Section 6.8 to generalize our findings about $\hat{p}$ and $\overline{X}$. In many applications we are more interested in the *difference* between the parameters of two populations than in the individual parameters themselves. Examples can be found in practically any area where statistics is used. If two drugs are administered to two groups of allergy patients, we may be interested in the difference between the cure rates of the two groups. If two types of tires are used on a sample of automobiles, we may be interested in the difference between the average mileage of the two types. If we examine two different areas of the country, we may be interested in the difference between the percentages of people living below the poverty level in the two areas.

The common element in all these examples is that there are two populations that differ in some way, and we are interested in the difference between specified parameters of these populations. There are two ways we usually encounter two populations. The first is when the populations can be distinguished in some natural way. For example, we may be comparing the populations of Los Angeles and New York, or we may be comparing women and men in management positions. The second way is when we divide one population into two parts, which are then treated differently. This is the case in the allergy example above where one group of allergy patients receives one drug and the other group receives a second drug. Here the two "treatment" groups are regarded as the two populations.

No matter how we encounter the two populations, we assume for right now that the observations obtained from one population are *independent* of the observations obtained from the other population. That is, the observations from population 1 are not at all useful for predicting the observations from population 2, and vice versa. In many applications this is a reasonable assumption. The only exception we will see is when the observations come in "matched pairs." This topic is studied in later chapters.

Sampling Distribution of the Difference Between Two Sample Proportions

In this section we study the sampling distribution of the difference between two sample proportions. We assume that in each of two populations, the members can be classified as A's and B's. In population 1 we let the population proportion of A's be p_1. In population 2 we let it be p_2. Then our interest centers on the difference between these two proportions, $p_1 - p_2$.

Suppose that we collect samples of sizes n_1 and n_2 from the two populations and calculate the sample proportions $\hat{p}_1$ and $\hat{p}_2$. We know from Section 6.4 that if $n_1 p_1(1 - p_1) \geq 5$, then $\hat{p}_1$ is approximately normal with mean p_1 and variance $p_1(1 - p_1)/n_1$. A similar statement applies to $\hat{p}_2$. But if $\hat{p}_1$ and $\hat{p}_2$ are approximately normally distributed, then from the preceding section we know that $\hat{p}_1 - \hat{p}_2$ is also approximately normally distributed. Its mean is the difference between the individual means, and its variance is the sum of the individual variances. Therefore, the approximate sampling distribution of $\hat{p}_1 - \hat{p}_2$ is as follows.

Approximate Sampling Distribution of $\hat{p}_1 - \hat{p}_2$

[when $n_1 p_1(1 - p_1) \geq 5$ and $n_2 p_2(1 - p_2) \geq 5$]

$\hat{p}_1 - \hat{p}_2$ is normal with mean $p_1 - p_2$ and

variance $\dfrac{p_1(1 - p_1)}{n_1} + \dfrac{p_2(1 - p_2)}{n_2}$

EXAMPLE 6.12

The percentage of people in a given population who consider brand A the best brand of hand calculator on the market was 22%. But after an extensive advertising campaign by brand A to improve its image, this percentage increased to 29%. If a random sample of 150 people was taken before the advertising campaign, and another random sample of 200 people is taken after the campaign, what is the probability of observing at least a 5-percentage-point increase from the first sample to the second?

SOLUTION

We are told that the population proportion favoring brand A before advertising is $p_1 = .22$. After advertising, it becomes $p_2 = .29$. However, all we observe are the corresponding sample proportions, $\hat{p}_1$ and $\hat{p}_2$, based on sample sizes of $n_1 = 150$ and $n_2 = 200$. The question asks us for the probability that $\hat{p}_2 - \hat{p}_1$ is at least .05. The mean of $\hat{p}_2 - \hat{p}_1$ is $.29 - .22 = .07$, and its variance is

$$\text{Var}(\hat{p}_2 - \hat{p}_1) = \frac{.22(.78)}{150} + \frac{.29(.71)}{200} = .047^2$$

Since $n_1 p_1 (1 - p_1)$ and $n_2 p_2 (1 - p_2)$ are both considerably larger than 5, we can calculate the desired probability as

$$P(\hat{p}_2 - \hat{p}_1 \geq .05) = P\left(Z \geq \frac{.05 - .07}{.047}\right)$$
$$= P(Z \geq -.43) = P(Z \leq .43) = .6664$$

Based on the population parameters, we would expect to see an increase of seven percentage points ($p_2 - p_1 = .07$). Because of sampling variation, we may not see this large an increase in the samples, but we are approximately 67% certain of seeing an increase of at least five percentage points.

EXAMPLE 6.13

A drill bit manufacturer has two types of production processes for manufacturing drill bits. The first is somewhat slow but is quite precise; it produces 97.1% nondefectives on the average. The second process is faster but produces only 95.8% nondefectives on the average. If we randomly sample 1000 bits from each of the two processes, what is the probability that there will be a smaller proportion of nondefectives from the first process than from the second? How does this probability change if the sample sizes are only 500 instead of 1000?

SOLUTION

We are given the population proportions of nondefectives, $p_1 = .971$ and $p_2 = .958$. If $\hat{p}_1$ and $\hat{p}_2$ are their sample counterparts, based on $n_1 = $

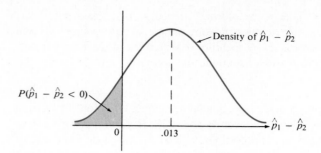

Figure 6.13

$n_2 = 1000$ observations, we want the probability that $\hat{p}_1$ is less than $\hat{p}_2$ (see Figure 6.13). Since the mean of $\hat{p}_1 - \hat{p}_2$ is $.971 - .958 = .013$ and its variance is

$$\text{Var}(\hat{p}_1 - \hat{p}_2) = \frac{.971(.029)}{1000} + \frac{.958(.042)}{1000} = .00827^2$$

we have

$$P(\hat{p}_1 < \hat{p}_2) = P(\hat{p}_1 - \hat{p}_2 < 0) = P\left(Z < \frac{0 - .013}{.00827}\right)$$
$$= P(Z < -1.57) = 1 - P(Z < 1.57) = .0582$$

[Again, a normal probability calculation is justified because each $np(1 - p)$ is considerably larger than 5.] In words, the chance that the more accurate process produces a *greater* proportion of defective bits, for such large samples, is only slightly greater than 1 out of 20.

If n_1 and n_2 are only 500 instead of 1000, then the standard deviation of $\hat{p}_1 - \hat{p}_2$ increases to .0117, and we have

$$P(\hat{p}_1 - \hat{p}_2 < 0) = P\left(Z < \frac{0 - .013}{.0117}\right) = P(Z < -1.11) = .1335$$

As we see, an unexpected event such as $\hat{p}_1 < \hat{p}_2$ (unexpected because the first process is *supposed* to be more precise) is more improbable for larger sample sizes.

Sampling Distribution of the Difference Between Sample Means

The problem we discuss in this section is undoubtedly one of the most important problems in statistics, especially in practical applications. We wish to compare two population means, μ_1 and μ_2. In particular, we study the difference $\mu_1 - \mu_2$. Since we have already seen that $\overline{X}$ is a natural estimate of μ for a single population, the natural estimate of $\mu_1 - \mu_2$ is $\overline{X}_1 - \overline{X}_2$. In this section we learn the sampling distribution of $\overline{X}_1 - \overline{X}_2$. This will enable us to make probability statements about $\overline{X}_1 - \overline{X}_2$, given that the difference between the population means, $\mu_1 - \mu_2$, and the population variances, σ_1^2 and σ_2^2, are known. (Actually, we do not need to know the individual means μ_1 and μ_2; all we really need to know is the difference $\mu_1 - \mu_2$.)

To obtain the sampling distribution of $\overline{X}_1 - \overline{X}_2$, we put together two facts that were presented earlier in this chapter. The first is that the sampling distribution of $\overline{X}_i$, for $i = 1$ or 2, is approximately normally distributed with mean μ_i and variance σ_i^2/n_i. Recall that this approximation is valid when the sample size n_i is large ($n_i \geq 30$) or when population i is normal (in which case the "approximation" is exact). We will always assume that at least one of these two conditions holds. The second fact is that the difference between two independent normal random variables is normal. Its mean is the difference between the two means, and its variance is the sum of the two variances. These facts lead directly to the sampling distribution of $\overline{X}_1 - \overline{X}_2$.

Sampling Distribution of $\overline{X}_1 - \overline{X}_2$

(when the sample sizes are large or the populations are normal)

$\overline{X}_1 - \overline{X}_2$ is normal with mean $\mu_1 - \mu_2$ and variance $\dfrac{\sigma_1^2}{n_1} + \dfrac{\sigma_2^2}{n_2}$

EXAMPLE 6.14

Consider two communities, labeled 1 and 2. Assume that the average household income in community 1 is \$15,900 and the standard deviation of incomes is \$6200. For community 2, the average income is \$17,100 and the standard deviation of incomes is \$4300. If random samples of $n_1 = 150$ and $n_2 = 100$ households are taken from these communities, what is the probability that the two sample means will differ by less than \$500?

SOLUTION

We are given that $\mu_1 = 15,900$, $\mu_2 = 17,100$, $\sigma_1 = 6200$, and $\sigma_2 = 4300$. Since $n_1 = 150$ and $n_2 = 100$, we know that the mean of $\overline{X}_1 - \overline{X}_2$ is $\mu_1 - \mu_2 = -1200$ and its variance is

$$\text{Var}(\overline{X}_1 - \overline{X}_2) = \frac{\sigma_1^2}{n_1} + \frac{\sigma_2^2}{n_2} = \frac{6200^2}{150} + \frac{4300^2}{100} = 441,167 = 664^2$$

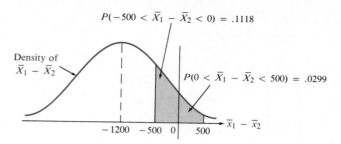

$P(-500 < \bar{X}_1 - \bar{X}_2 < 0) = .1118$

Density of $\bar{X}_1 - \bar{X}_2$

$P(0 < \bar{X}_1 - \bar{X}_2 < 500) = .0299$

-1200 -500 0 500 $\bar{x}_1 - \bar{x}_2$

Figure 6.14

If the two sample means differ by less than \$500, we must have $-500 < \bar{X}_1 - \bar{X}_2 < 500$. The probability of this event is

$$P(-500 < \bar{X}_1 - \bar{X}_2 < 500) = P\left[\frac{-500 - (-1200)}{664} < Z < \frac{500 - (-1200)}{664}\right]$$
$$= P(1.05 < Z < 2.56)$$
$$= P(Z < 2.56) - P(Z < 1.05) = .1417$$

Notice that the event $-500 < \bar{X}_1 - \bar{X}_2 < 500$ can occur by having $-500 < \bar{X}_1 - \bar{X}_2 < 0$ or $0 < \bar{X}_1 - \bar{X}_2 < 500$. In either case $\bar{X}_1$ and $\bar{X}_2$ are within 500 of one another. The only difference is that in the first case $\bar{X}_2$ is larger, and in the second case $\bar{X}_1$ is larger. The reader can verify that the individual probabilities of these two events are $P(-500 < \bar{X}_1 - \bar{X}_2 < 0) = .1118$ and $P(0 < \bar{X}_1 - \bar{X}_2 < 500) = .0299$. These two probabilities sum to the original answer, .1417, as they should. But they also give us additional information. They show that $0 < \bar{X}_1 - \bar{X}_2 < 500$ is much less likely than $-500 < \bar{X}_1 - \bar{X}_2 < 0$. This is reasonable, of course, since the population mean in community 2 is considerably larger than the mean in community 1 (see Figure 6.14).

EXAMPLE 6.15

Two car insurance companies, labeled 1 and 2, tend to insure two different groups in the population. Company 1 tries to insure only those drivers with good driving records and only those young people who have had a driver training course in high school. Company 2 is far less particular about its customers. Of course, company 1 does not charge the high premiums that company 2 is forced to charge, because it typically receives fewer claims from its customers. We assume that the distribution of yearly claims by company 1 customers has mean \$435 and standard deviation \$90. The distribution of yearly claims by company 2 customers has mean \$625 and standard deviation $175. Also, we assume that all company 1 customers pay a yearly premium of $475 and all company 2 customers pay a yearly premium of $700. If random samples of $n_1 = 35$ and $n_2 = 45$ customers are chosen from companies 1 and 2, what is the probability that the average company profit per customer is higher for the company 1 customers than for the company 2 customers?

SOLUTION

If $X_1, X_2, \ldots, X_{35}$ are the yearly claims for the 35 company 1 customers, the 35 individual company profits (or losses, if negative) from these customers are $475 - X_1, 475 - X_2, \ldots, 475 - X_{35}$. Adding these and dividing by 35, we see that the average company 1 profit per customer is $475 - \overline{X}_1$, where $\overline{X}_1$ is the sample mean of the 35 claims. Similarly, the average company 2 profit per customer is $700 - \overline{X}_2$. Therefore, the average company 1 profit per customer is larger if $475 - \overline{X}_1$ is greater than $700 - \overline{X}_2$, that is, if $\overline{X}_2 - \overline{X}_1 > 225$. Since the mean of $\overline{X}_2 - \overline{X}_1$ is $625 - 435 = 190$ and its variance is

$$\mathrm{Var}(\overline{X}_2 - \overline{X}_1) = \frac{90^2}{35} + \frac{175^2}{45} = 912 = 30.2^2$$

we have

$$P(\overline{X}_2 - \overline{X}_1 > 225) = P\left(Z > \frac{225 - 190}{30.2}\right) = P(Z > 1.16)$$
$$= 1 - P(Z < 1.16) = .1230$$

So with probability .123, the sample results will indicate that company 1 is making larger profits per customer than company 2.

Problems for Sections 6.8, 6.9

28. It was reported that the national unemployment percentage increased from 10.7% in November 1982 to 10.8% in December 1982. (Reference: *Time*, Jan. 10, 1983.) For random samples of 200 employable people taken in November and again in December, let $\hat{p}_1$ and $\hat{p}_2$ be the sample proportions of unemployed people.
    a. Find the mean and standard deviation of $\hat{p}_1$ and of $\hat{p}_2$.
    b. Find the probability that $\hat{p}_1$ is greater than .11. Do the same for $\hat{p}_2$.
    c. Find the probability that $\hat{p}_1$ is greater than $\hat{p}_2$.

29. By the early 1980s, Miami's police force had the following breakdown: 44.2% white, 39.2% Hispanic, and 16.6% black. The entire population of Miami, on the other hand, was 15% white, 58% Hispanic, and 27% black. (Reference: *Time*, Jan. 17, 1983, p. 18.) Consider two random samples, one (sample 1) of size 50 from the Miami police force, and one (sample 2) of size 200 from the population of Miami as a whole.
    a. Find the probability that the proportion of non-Hispanics in sample 1 minus the proportion of non-Hispanics in sample 2 is at least .25.

b. Find the probability that the proportion of blacks in sample 1 minus the proportion of blacks in sample 2 is less than $-.15$.

30. Toward the end of 1982, President Reagan predicted a 10.0% unemployment rate for 1984 and a 6.6% rate for 1988. Consider random samples of 300 people from the labor market in 1984 and another 300 in 1988.
   a. Assuming that Reagan's prediction is correct, would it be surprising to find at least 10.3% of the 1984 sample unemployed?
   b. Again assuming that Reagan is correct, would it be surprising to see less than 6.3% of the 1988 sample unemployed?
   c. Find the probability that the sample proportion unemployed in 1984 minus the sample proportion unemployed in 1988 is at least .04.

31. It is estimated that from 1974 to 1979, the percentage of teenagers who smoked dropped from 15.6% to 11.7%. (Reference: *Time*, Feb. 7, 1983, p. 61.) Consider random samples of 150 teenagers in 1974 and another 150 teenagers in 1979. Let $\hat{p}_1$ and $\hat{p}_2$ be the proportions of smokers in these two samples.
   a. What is the probability that $\hat{p}_1$ is greater than $\hat{p}_2$?
   b. What is the probability that the difference $\hat{p}_1 - \hat{p}_2$ is at least .03?

32. Between 1980 and 1983, the percentage of television viewers tuned to PBS (public broadcasting) doubled from 2.7% to 5.4%. Suppose that the results of a random sample of 200 television viewers taken in 1980 and a random sample of 300 television viewers taken in 1983 are compared.
   a. Find the probability that the sample proportion watching PBS in 1983 is at least .056.
   b. Find the probability that the sample proportion watching PBS in 1980 is no more than .025.
   c. Find the probability that the sample proportion watching PBS in 1983 minus the similar proportion in 1980 is between .025 and .03.

33. According to a recent article, the percentage of women in the workforce has increased from 28% at the end of World War II to 41% now. (Reference: A. L. Kalleberg, "Work: Postwar Trends and Future Prospects," *Business Horizons*, Vol. 25, 1982, pp. 78–84.) If we had the results of two random samples of American workers, each of size 150, one taken at the end of World War II and the other taken recently, what is the probability that the increased percentage of women would be no more than 12%? That is, what is the probability

that the more recent sample proportion minus the post–World War II sample proportion would be no greater than .12?

*34. Referring to Problem 13 (p. 280), suppose that a sample of n books such as the one listed is chosen from the population of all books offered. Let $\overline{X}_1$ be the average of the hardcover prices, and let $\overline{X}_2$ be the average of the softcover prices. Assume that the mean and standard deviation of *all* hardcover prices are μ_1 and σ_1. For the softcover books these quantities are μ_2 and σ_2.
   a. What is the mean of $\overline{X}_1 - \overline{X}_2$?
   b. Why is the standard deviation of $\overline{X}_1 - \overline{X}_2$ probably *not* equal to $\sqrt{\sigma_1^2/n_1 + \sigma_2^2/n_2}$, the formula from Section 6.9?

35. As inflation started to ease in the early 1980s, average interest rates from banks on new car loans went from 17.25% in one year (year 1) to 16% in the following year (year 2). (Reference: *Time*, Jan. 17, 1983, p. 35.) Assume that the standard deviation of the interest rates was .125% in year 1 and .25% in year 2. For random samples of 25 banks in year 1 and 35 banks in year 2, find the probability that the sample mean interest rate in year 1 is at least one percentage point higher than the sample mean in year 2.

36. The rental car agencies are engaged in fierce competition, as is evident from their frequent ads and marketing gimmicks. Assume that the distribution of the number of rental customers for company A cars, taken over all company A locations and all weekdays, has mean 50 and standard deviation 15. For company B, the similar quantities are 65 and 25. If 25 company A locations and 40 company B locations are sampled randomly on a given weekday, find the probability that the company B average is at least 10 customers higher than the company A average.

37. In 1980 the average salary for all school teachers was \$17,250. In contrast, the average *starting* salary for engineers was \$20,000. (Reference: H. D. Mehlinger, "Quality vs. Equality in American Education," *Business Horizons*, Vol. 25, 1982, pp. 24–30.) Assume that the population standard deviations were \$2200 for school teachers and \$2400 for starting engineers. Consider random samples of 75 school teachers and 50 starting engineers, both taken in 1980.
   a. Find the probability that the average salary of the 75 school teachers is greater than the average salary of the 50 starting engineers.
   b. Find the probability that the average salary of the 75 school teachers is no less than \$1500 lower than the average salary of the 50 starting engineers.

38. We have all heard that average college entrance (SAT) scores have been decreasing, but an even more alarming statistic is the following. For education majors the average SAT verbal score dropped from 418 in 1972 to 339 in 1980, and the average SAT quantitative score dropped from 449 to 418 during the same period. (Reference: H. D. Mehlinger, "Quality vs. Equality in American Education," *Business Horizons*, Vol. 25, 1982, pp. 24–30.) Assume that the standard deviation of all verbal and of all quantitative scores stayed level at 45 and 55, respectively, over this time interval. Consider two random samples of 50 education majors, one (sample 1) taken in 1972, and the other (sample 2) taken in 1980. Let $\bar{X}_1$ and $\bar{X}_2$ be the mean verbal scores for the two samples, and let $\bar{Y}_1$ and $\bar{Y}_2$ be their mean quantitative scores.

   a. Find the probability that $\bar{X}_1$ is at least 75 points higher than $\bar{X}_2$.

   b. Find the probability that $\bar{Y}_1$ is at least 35 points higher than $\bar{Y}_2$.

   c. Is it reasonable to assume that $\bar{X}_1$ and $\bar{Y}_1$ are independent random variables? Why or why not?

39. By the early 1980s the average life expectancy for men was 69 years, and for women it was 77 years. (Reference: G. J. Stolnitz, "Our Main Population Patterns: Radical Shifts, Cloudy Prospects," *Business Horizons*, Vol. 25, 1982, pp. 91–99.) Assume that the standard deviation of life expectancy is 11 years for men and 9 years for women. For random samples of 50 men and 60 women, find the probability that the average life span of the women is at least 7 years longer than that of the men.

Summary

The purpose of this chapter has been to introduce the concept of sampling distributions, as well as the most important sampling distributions that will be used in later chapters. Sampling distributions are the probability distributions of sample statistics, such as the sample mean and the sample proportion, that are used to make inferences about the corresponding population parameters. Before we can make intelligent inferences about an unknown population parameter, based on an observed sample, we must know what to expect from a typical random sample if we *knew* the characteristics of the population. This information is provided by sampling distributions.

By definition, the sampling distribution of a sample statistic such as the sample proportion is the distribution we would observe if we could observe *every* possible sample, and its corresponding sample proportion, from a given population. We saw how this distribution can be approximated by simulating many sample proportions on a computer and drawing the resulting histogram. However, we also saw that, at least in the case of large sample sizes, several of the most important sample statistics have normal or approximately normal sampling distributions because of the Central Limit Theorem. These sample statistics include the sample proportion, the sample mean, the difference between two sample proportions, and the difference between two sample means. For these statistics, computer simulation of the sampling distributions is not necessary; we know from theoretical arguments that their sampling distributions are approximately normal. This fact is what makes the normal distribution play such a key role in statistical inference.

Applications

Application 6.1   An important quantity of interest to companies that produce retail products is brand share, defined as their percentage of a product's total sales. To measure brand share, companies regularly employ marketing research firms to perform audits of retail stores' sales. The traditional retail store audit can be quite costly. Over a given period, say a month, auditors visit many retail stores. On these visits they count each store's inventory at the beginning of the period and at the end of the period. They also obtain the number of store purchases (additions to inventory) made during the period. Then they estimate retail sales as beginning inventory plus store purchases minus ending inventory. By obtaining retail sales from many stores for each brand, brand share can be calculated easily.

As Prasad, Casper, and Schieffer point out, a less costly alternative to the traditional retail audit is the weekend sell-down audit. (Reference: V. Kanti Prasad, Wayne R. Casper, and Robert J. Schieffer, "Alternatives to the Traditional Retail Store Audit: A Field Study," *Journal of Marketing,* Vol. 48, 1984, pp. 54–61.) Under the assumption that no store purchases arrive during the weekend, the weekend sell-down audit measures retail sales as inventory on Friday minus inventory on the following Monday. The main advantage of this type of audit is that store purchases do not need to be measured. The savings in cost can be 20% or more. However, the important question is whether the two types of audits tend to produce equivalent estimates of brand share.

Let's suppose that two marketing research firms are employed by a company to measure its brand share for a particular product. The first firm uses the traditional auditing method, while the second firm uses the weekend sell-down method. For each of n consecutive months, each firm estimates the company's brand share. Denote the difference between the two estimates in month i by X_i, and denote the average of these differences by $\overline{X}$. If the population of differences, taken over all months, is normally distributed with mean μ and standard deviation σ, what would we expect of $\overline{X}$? In particular, if $\mu = 0$, the two auditing methods tend to give equal estimates of brand share, and we would expect $\overline{X}$ to be no greater than $2\sigma/\sqrt{n}$ in magnitude. For example, if $n = 20$ months and $\sigma = 2$ percentage points (remember, this is the standard deviation of the *differences*), then $2\sigma/\sqrt{n} = .89$, and we would expect $\overline{X}$ to be within the interval from $-.89$ to $.89$ with approximate probability .95. The implication is that if we observe an $\overline{X}$ much larger in magnitude than .89, it would cast doubt on the assumption that μ equals 0. In this case we might be led to believe that the two auditing methods are really measuring different quantities.

Application 6.2 The quality control data in Application 5.1 of Chapter 5 offer us a perfect opportunity to compare the distribution of individual observations with the distribution of the sample mean. Recall that five measurements were taken each hour for 27 consecutive hours. In Chapter 5 we saw that the mean and variance of all 135 observations are .1412 and $.0034^2$. From the table in Chapter 5, we can also obtain the averages of the five measurements taken each hour. These 27 averages are shown in Table 6.7.

Table 6.7

Hour	Average of Five Observations
1	.13810
2	.14346
3	.14158
4	.14022
5	.14058
6	.14126
7	.14160
8	.14046
9	.14244
10	.13952
11	.14148
12	.14186
13	.14154
14	.14088
15	.14192
16	.14086
17	.14034
18	.14244
19	.14080
20	.13918
21	.14182
22	.14174
23	.14100
24	.14182
25	.14082
26	.14238
27	.14156
Total	3.81166

Each of these averages can be considered an $\overline{X}$ from the population of all $\overline{X}$'s that are based on $n = 5$ measurements. The mean of these $\overline{X}$'s is the average of the 27 averages:

$$\text{mean of } \overline{X}\text{'s} = \frac{(.13810 + .14346 + \cdots + .14156)}{27} = .1412$$

As expected, this is equal to the average of all 135 observations. On the other hand, the variance of the $\overline{X}$'s is found from the formula for variance in Chapter 2, except that now the "observations" are the 27 $\overline{X}$'s:

$$\text{variance of } \overline{X}\text{'s} = \frac{(.13810^2 + \cdots + .14156^2) - 27(.1412)^2}{26} = .0011^2$$

As predicted by theory, this is smaller than the variance of the individual observations, $.0034^2$. This means the 27 $\overline{X}$'s should cluster tighter around their mean than the 135 observations cluster around their mean. A visual comparison of the table of original observations in Chapter 5 and the table of $\overline{X}$'s shown above indicates that this is true.

Glossary of Terms

Sampling distribution the probability distribution of a sample statistic, such as the sample mean or the sample proportion

Population parameter a number associated with an entire population

Sample statistic a random variable that can be calculated from the sample data

Simple random sample a sample selected from a population in such a way that every sample (of the given sample size) has the same chance of being selected

Central Limit Theorem for the sample mean the sampling distribution of $\overline{X}$ is approximately normal when n is large ($n \geq 30$ is usually sufficient)

Important Formulas

1. Formulas for the mean and variance of $\hat{p}$

$$E(\hat{p}) = p \qquad \text{Var}(\hat{p}) = \frac{p(1 - p)}{n}$$

2. Formulas for the mean and variance of the sample mean

$$E(\overline{X}) = \mu \qquad \text{Var}(\overline{X}) = \frac{\sigma^2}{n}$$

3. Formulas for the mean and variance of the weighted sum $\Sigma\, a_i X_i$ of independent normal random variables

$$E(\Sigma\, a_i X_i) = \Sigma\, a_i \mu_i \qquad \text{Var}(\Sigma\, a_i X_i) = \Sigma\, a_i^2 \sigma_i^2$$

4. Formulas for the mean and variance of $\hat{p}_1 - \hat{p}_2$

$$E(\hat{p}_1 - \hat{p}_2) = p_1 - p_2 \qquad \text{Var}(\hat{p}_1 - \hat{p}_2) = \frac{p_1(1 - p_1)}{n_1} + \frac{p_2(1 - p_2)}{n_2}$$

5. Formulas for the mean and variance of $\overline{X}_1 - \overline{X}_2$

$$E(\overline{X}_1 - \overline{X}_2) = \mu_1 - \mu_2 \qquad \text{Var}(\overline{X}_1 - \overline{X}_2) = \frac{\sigma_1^2}{n_1} + \frac{\sigma_2^2}{n_2}$$

End-of-Chapter Problems

*40. In a large housing development the square footage per house is normally distributed with mean 1810 square feet and standard deviation 130 square feet. A random sample of 90 of these houses is selected.
   a. Find the probability that the sample mean is between 1790 and 1820 square feet.
   b. Find the probability that the proportion of the houses in the sample with at least 1900 square feet is at least .3.

*41. It has been reported that by the beginning of the 1980s, there were approximately ½ million illegal aliens entering the United States per year. (Reference: *Time*, Jan. 10. 1983.) Assuming that the numbers entering in different weeks are independent random variables with the same distribution, find the probability that the average number of illegal immigrants entering per week on 25 randomly selected weeks is at least 10,000. Assume that the standard deviation of the *yearly* rate is 40,000. (First find the implied μ and σ for a given week. Remember that the variance of a sum of independent random variables is the sum of the variances.)

*42. Although the EPA mileage estimate is listed on the sticker of each new car, most drivers soon discover that the average mileage they experience is less than the number on the sticker. Assume that the distribution of the *difference* between what is on the sticker and what drivers actually experience, taken over all new cars, is normal with mean 4 mpg and standard deviation 2 mpg. The accompanying data are from a random sample of drivers with new cars. What is the probability of

seeing such an unusual sample (unusual in the sense that the actual mpg's average so much less than the sticker mpg values)?

Actual	Sticker	Actual	Sticker
21	23	20	25
23	31	35	39
12	17	24	30
19	25	16	23
25	29	25	32
31	37	22	27
29	32	19	26
27	28		

*43. An elevator in an office building has a weight capacity of 3000 pounds. If the distribution of the weights of people working in the building has mean 154 pounds and standard deviation 15 pounds, find the largest number of people that can get on the elevator and still have at least a .98 probability of not exceeding its capacity. (Use trial and error.)

*44. Let X_1 and X_2 be any two independent normal random variables and let c be any constant. If the means of X_1 and X_2 are μ_1 and μ_2, and their variances are σ_1^2 and σ_2^2, find the distribution of $X_1 - cX_2$.

*45. Consider two types of batteries, labeled 1 and 2. Type 1's cost more than type 2's, but they last a lot longer. Assume that the mean lifetime of type 1 batteries is 4.2 months, and the standard deviation of these lifetimes is .8 month. The mean and standard deviation of type 2 batteries are 1.5 months and .2 month. Let $\overline{X}_1$ and $\overline{X}_2$ be the sample means of the lifetimes for 45 type 1 batteries and 35 type 2 batteries. Use the result from Problem 44 to find the probability that $\overline{X}_1$ is at least 3 times as large as $\overline{X}_2$.

*46. In Problem 25 (p. 281), let *PE* denote the percentage error between $\overline{X}$ and μ, defined as

$$PE = \left(\frac{\overline{X} - \mu}{\mu}\right) \times 100\%$$

   a. Find the probability that *PE* is less than 10% when $n = 75$ (using the data from Problem 25).
   b. Why might we be more interested in the percentage error *PE* than in the difference $\overline{X} - \mu$?

*47. An exponential random variable with parameter θ is a positive random variable with mean $1/\theta$ and variance $1/\theta^2$. (Here θ is a given positive constant.) Suppose that we have a computer generate 90 independent exponential random variables, each with $\theta = .2$.

   a. Find the probability that the average of the 90 numbers generated is at least 5.1. Explain how the Central Limit Theorem helps in this calculation.
   b. Find an interval (symmetric about the mean) such that the probability of the average of the 90 numbers being inside this interval is .99.

48. In 1978 the rate of arrests of foreigners for being in the United States illegally was approximately 20,400 per week. (Reference: A. J. Lizotte, "Crime in America: Why It Went Up, Why It's Going Down," *Business Horizons*, Vol. 25, 1982, pp. 60–65.) Assume this means that the distribution of arrests from week to week had mean 20,400. Also, assume that the standard deviation of this distribution was 1300 and the numbers of arrests in different weeks were independent. If a sample of 20 weeks from the current year has a sample mean of 20,900 arrests per week, is this strong evidence that the mean number of arrests has changed since 1978? Answer by seeing how unlikely such a large sample mean would be if the 1978 figures were still valid.

*49. When banks first introduced money-market savings accounts with check-writing privileges, the average rate, taken over all banks, was approximately 10%. (Reference: *Time*, Jan. 17, 1983, p. 34.) Assume a corresponding standard deviation of .7%. Consider a random sample of 25 banks across the country taken at that time.

   a. Find the probability that the sample mean rate offered by these banks was at least 9.8%.
   b. If the distribution of rates over the country was *normally* distributed with the mean and standard deviation given above, find the probability that all 25 of the banks sampled offered between 8.8 and 12% on their money-market savings accounts. Then find the probability that the sample mean rate offered by these 25 banks was between 8.8 and 12%. Intuitively, why are these two probabilities so different?

*50. One of the fiercest rivalries in the newspaper business is between the *Free Press* and the *News,* both from a large metropolitan U.S. city. Their circulations, as of 1982, were 632,000 and 643,000, respectively. (Reference: *Time*, Jan. 17, 1983, p. 44.) Both of these circulations come from the same pool of approximately 2,000,000 potential readers. Suppose that each company takes a random sample of 150 of these 2,000,000 people to see how the *other* company is doing. Let $\hat{p}_1$ be the proportion of *Free Press* buyers in the sample collected by the *News*. Similarly, let $\hat{p}_2$ be the proportion of *News* buyers in the sample collected by the *Free Press*. Find the probability that $\hat{p}_1$ is larger than $\hat{p}_2$.

*51. Carpet prices can vary widely from discount carpet stores to more-exclusive furniture stores. Suppose that the distribution of carpet prices, taken over all carpet stores, for a "medium-priced" type of carpeting is normal with mean $13.50 per square yard and standard deviation $1.30 per square yard. Mr. and Mrs. Hancock like this carpet, and they figure they need 35 square yards for their living room. They obtain estimates from 15 stores selected randomly.

   a. What are the mean and standard deviation of the total price of 35 square yards of this type of carpet (taken over the population of all carpet stores)?
   b. What is the probability that the average of the total prices quoted by the 15 stores is between $460 and $485?
   c. What is the probability that the Hancocks get at least one estimate for a total price of no more than $400? (This is a binomial probability.)

52. A business article recently claimed there has been a switch from optimism to pessimism among Americans in the past two decades. (Reference: P. E. Hammond, "Up and Down with the National Faith: Implications for the Survival of a Nation," *Business Horizons*, Vol. 25, 1982, pp. 11–23.) Specifically, in 1965 more than half the American people believed that the present was superior to the past, whereas by 1978 more than half believed the opposite. Assume that the true proportion in 1965 who believed the present was

superior to the past was $p_1 = .55$, and assume that the similar proportion in 1978 was $p_2 = .45$. For random samples of size 100 from 1965 and size 100 from 1978, find the probability that more people believed the present to be superior to the past in the 1978 sample than in the 1965 sample.

*53. A population of families is divided into three categories: (1) those who own no foreign cars, (2) those who own one foreign car, and (3) those who own at least two foreign cars. Let p_1, p_2, and p_3 be the proportions of the families in the three categories. A random sample of n families is chosen, where n is large. Let $\hat{p}_1$, $\hat{p}_2$, and $\hat{p}_3$ be the sample proportions in the three categories. State whether each of the following statements is true or false, and give a reason in each case.

a. $n\hat{p}_1$ is approximately normal, with mean np_1 and variance $np_1(1 - p_1)$.

b. $\hat{p}_2$ is approximately normal, with mean p_2 and variance $p_2(1 - p_2)$.

c. $\hat{p}_1 - \hat{p}_3$ is approximately normal, with mean $p_1 - p_3$ and variance $p_1(1 - p_1)/n + p_3(1 - p_3)/n$.

d. $\hat{p}_1 + \hat{p}_2$ is approximately normal, with mean $p_1 + p_2$ and variance $p_3(1 - p_3)/n$.

e. $\hat{p}_1 + \hat{p}_2 + \hat{p}_3$ is approximately normally distributed.

*54. The following data represent the average household incomes for a random sample of southeastern cities and a random sample of northeastern cities. (Reference: *Places Rated Almanac*, 1982.) Let μ_1 and μ_2 represent the true mean incomes of all northeastern and southeastern cities, respectively, and let $\sigma_1 = \$2200$ and $\sigma_2 = \$2500$ be the corresponding population standard deviations. Find the probability of two sample means differing as much as the sample means from the data above (for the same sample sizes) if $\mu_1 - \mu_2$ is really equal to $\$2000$.

Southeastern		Northeastern	
$20,099	$20,947	$23,682	$24,125
18,878	23,479	24,127	21,295
18,868	23,725	28,853	23,134
20,966	20,172	20,104	26,465
21,813	18,392	25,210	27,702
25,310	25,040	26,090	25,186
19,305	20,928	27,702	22,280
23,231	22,991	23,749	25,067
20,936	22,580	23,518	27,672
		21,033	24,456

55. In a recent study 27% of 108 companies said they offer their employees incentives for taking early retirement. (Reference: *Time,* Feb. 21, 1983, p. 56.) How unusual would this result be (a) if the percentage of *all* companies offering incentives for early retirement was only 23%, and (b) if it was 32%? (For both questions, see how far the 27% figure is in the appropriate tail of the appropriate distribution, given a sample size of 108.)

*56. In jury selection the defense and the prosecution are each allowed to rule out any prospective jurors (up to a certain limit) who are thought to be prejudiced one way or the other. Assume that in the entire population of potential jurors, 31% would be ruled out by the prosecution, 35% would be ruled out by the defense, and 6% would be ruled out by both. Also, suppose that a random sample of 30 of these potential jurors are interviewed, and let $\hat{p}$ be the sample proportion who are judged acceptable by both the prosecution and the defense.

a. Find the mean and standard deviation of $\hat{p}$.

b. Find the probability that $\hat{p}$ is greater than or equal to .3.

*57. In 1980 a census showed that 37% of people considered themselves Democrats, 28% considered themselves Republicans, and the other 35% considered themselves neither Democrats nor Republicans. (Reference: K. O'Lessker, "Political Parties and the Political System," *Business Horizons,* Vol. 25, 1982, pp. 53–59.) Assume that the people in the latter category are as likely to vote for the Democrat as for the Republican in any given election. If a random sample of 300 voters is taken before a given election, find the probability that at least 55% of the sample will vote for the Democrat. (Assume that everyone votes for the Democrat or the Republican.)

58. In a city with a population of 1,347,289, there are 287,391 people who weigh over 160 pounds. If 350 of these people are sampled randomly, what is the probability that the sample proportion and the population proportion of people who weigh over 160 pounds will differ by no more than .01?

*59. If we generate 10 independent uniform random variables on a computer, it is not difficult to show that the probability of all 10 of these being between .05 and .95 is .3487. (A similar example was done in Chapter 3. Recall that a uniform random variable of this type has a flat density function between 0 and 1.) Suppose that we replicate the experiment of generating 10 of these random numbers 500 times. Find the probability that all 10 of the random numbers are between .05 and .95 on at least 37% of the replications.

*60. At the same jogging track as in Problem 26 (p. 282), another observer watches 25 female joggers and 40 male joggers. The females average .7 mile less than the males. If the mean and standard deviation of the distances run by *all* female joggers are 1.45 and .36 mile, and the similar figures for all male joggers are 2.00 and .45 mile, would you say that the observed difference in the sample means is unusually high? Back up your answer with an appropriate probability calculation.

61. In an article about poverty in the United States, Wood reported that the percentage of white families living below the poverty line in 1976 was 7.3%. (Reference: James R. Wood, "Poverty in America," *Business Horizons,* Vol. 25, 1982, pp. 85–90.) The similar percentage of black families was 16.1%. These figures are based on income after taxes and after all types of transfer payments. Assume that these percentages remain valid today, and random samples of 500 white families and 500 black families are taken. Find an interval (symmetric about the mean) such that there is probability .99 that the sample proportion of white families below the poverty line will be in this interval. Do the same for the sample of black families.

References

BREIMAN, L. *Statistics: With a View Toward Applications.* Boston: Houghton Mifflin, 1973.

CANAVOS, G. C. *Applied Probability and Statistical Methods.* Boston: Little, Brown, 1984.

HOGG, R. V. and CRAIG, A. T. *Introduction to Mathematical Statistics,* 4th ed. New York: Macmillan, 1978.

MOOD, A. M., GRAYBILL, F. A., and BOES, D. C. *Introduction to the Theory of Statistics,* 3rd ed. New York: McGraw-Hill, 1974.

NETER, J., WASSERMAN, W., and WHITMORE, G. A. *Applied Statistics,* 2nd ed. Boston: Allyn & Bacon, 1982.

CHAPTER 7

Large-Sample Estimation

Objectives

1. To learn the properties of ''good'' estimates.
2. To learn what it means for estimates to be unbiased and efficient.
3. To see how confidence intervals indicate the accuracy of point estimates.
4. To learn how to compute confidence intervals for proportions and means.
5. To see how sample size and confidence interval length are inversely related, and to determine the sample size needed to achieve a given level of accuracy.

Contents

Since many supermarket goods come in various sizes and shapes, the price per package can be misleading for the price-conscious shopper. This is the reason most supermarkets have been using "unit pricing" for the past 10 to 20 years. This information states how much an item costs per pound, per fluid ounce, or per some other convenient unit. It is natural for marketing researchers to ask what proportion of consumers are aware of unit pricing and what proportion of those who are aware actually use this information in making purchasing decisions. It is also natural to ask how (or whether) these proportions have been changing through time.

This is an estimation problem, where the proportions or changes in proportions are the quantities to be estimated. It is impossible to estimate these quantities exactly, for this would require a census of all consumers, a physically infeasible task. But by selecting random samples of shoppers at various points in time, it is possible to estimate a proportion or a change in proportions, and to quantify the precision of these estimates. After we study general problems of estimation in this chapter, we examine a recent comparative study of consumer use of unit pricing in 1970 versus 1980 and see how statistical estimation was a key ingredient in this study.

7.1

Introduction

In this chapter and the next two chapters, we use our knowledge of sampling distributions to study the two primary areas of statistical inference: estimation and hypothesis testing. Each of these topics is concerned with the same basic problem, a problem we have already discussed several times. Consider a population with an unknown parameter such as a mean or a proportion. We take a random sample from this population and use the information from this sample, together with the rules of probability, to make inferences about the unknown population parameter.

The feature that distinguishes this chapter and Chapter 8 from Chapter 9 (on hypothesis testing) is whether we have any preconceived theories, referred to as hypotheses, about the values of the unknown parameters. If we do not, we essentially let the sample information "speak for itself" and use it to find estimates of the unknown parameters. If we have already formed hypotheses, we use the information in the sample to decide whether the data support or refute these hypotheses. The former topic is called estimation and is the subject of Chapters 7 and 8. The latter topic is called hypothesis testing and is the subject of Chapter 9.

Since we have already referred to estimates of several population parameters in previous chapters, it may appear unnecessary to study this topic any further. For example, we have already used $\hat{p}$, the sample proportion, to estimate a population proportion p, and we have used $\overline{X}$, the sample mean, to estimate the population mean μ. In both cases these estimates are "natural" ones, and they may appear to be the only sensible ones. So what more needs to be said about the issue if choosing estimates is always this straightforward?

There are two answers to this question. First, it is *not* always this straightforward to find a good estimate of a population parameter. For example, in Chapters 11 and 12 we will study "regression equations" which have several unknown parameters. Although these parameters have very meaningful interpretations, there are no obvious estimates of them. In such cases we need general guidelines for choosing estimates of the unknown parameters, and we need criteria for assessing the quality of these estimates.

A second reason why estimation is not straightforward is that we want more out of estimation than a single numerical estimate. We also want a measure of the *accuracy* of this estimate. Suppose, for example, that the executives of NBC want to know the proportion of families in the country who watch a particular show. They randomly survey a group of families and find that 13% of these families watch the show. Then .13 is a reasonable estimate of the proportion of *all* families who watch the show. However, the executives are aware that the .13 figure may contain sampling error. Therefore, they would also like to have an estimate of the accuracy of this estimate. Could it be off by as much as .03; by as much as .05? And how likely are these types of errors?

The usual way to measure the accuracy of an estimate is by means of a *confidence interval*. First, we prescribe a level of confidence, interpreted as the probability of being correct, and then we find an interval that includes the unknown population parameter with this prescribed level of confidence. In the example above, NBC may be able to conclude with 95% confidence that the proportion of the population who watch the show is between .115 and .145. Now they have two pieces of information. The first is a best guess, called a *point estimate*, that 13% of the population watch the show. If they had to put all their money on a single value of the unknown population proportion, they would probably choose this value, .13. But they also have a measure of the accuracy of this estimate. They are 95% confident that the difference between the point estimate and the actual population proportion is no more than .015 (see Figure 7.1 on p. 304).

This chapter is essentially divided into two parts. The first part discusses the issues involved in choosing good point estimates. In particular, it addresses the nontrivial issue of what we mean by a "good" estimate. The second part of the chapter discusses confidence intervals for means and proportions. Included in this part of the chapter is a discussion of sample size

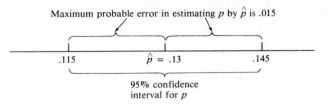

Figure 7.1

selection, a topic of particular concern to the investigator who wishes to balance sampling costs and accuracy of estimation. Throughout this chapter we assume that the relevant sample sizes are large ($n \geq 30$ is a rough guideline). In Chapter 8 we study the necessary modifications for smaller sample sizes.

7.2

Desirable Properties of Estimates: Unbiasedness and Efficiency

In this section we discuss the topic of estimation in a fairly general setting. Consider a population with an unknown parameter θ. This parameter might be the mean, the variance, a proportion, or any other unknown population parameter. We use the Greek lowercase letter theta (θ), rather than letters with specific meanings such as μ or p, to indicate that the following discussion is quite general and includes estimation of means, variances, and proportions as special cases.

To estimate θ, we observe a random sample $X_1, X_2, \ldots, X_n$ from the population. As usual, X_i is the observation on the ith member of the sample, and n is the sample size. By performing appropriate arithmetic on these X's, we transform them into a numerical estimate of θ. This estimate is denoted by $\hat{\theta}$ and is called a *point estimate* of θ. (It is customary in statistics to distinguish between an "estimator" and an "estimate." An estimator is the random variable $\hat{\theta}$, whereas an estimate is a particular value of this random variable, obtained from a particular sample. We will not make this terminology distinction in this book but will, instead, use the term "estimate" to denote both the random variable and its possible values.)

> A point estimate is a rule for converting the sample data into a single numerical estimate of an unknown population parameter.

For example, suppose that θ is the population mean μ. Then one estimate of μ is

$$\hat{\mu}_1 = \sum \frac{X_i}{n} = \overline{X}$$

(There is a subscript on $\hat{\mu}_1$ because we will discuss other estimates of μ below.) This formula for $\hat{\mu}_1$ says to sum X_1 through X_n and then divide by the sample size n. Of course, this results in the sample mean $\overline{X}$. Another sensible estimate of μ, especially if the population distribution is symmetric, is

$$\hat{\mu}_2 = \text{the sample median of the } X\text{'s}$$

The arithmetic implied by $\hat{\mu}_2$ is to order the X's from smallest to largest and let $\hat{\mu}_2$ be the middle value (if n is odd) or the average of the two middle values (if n is even). Still another sensible estimate of μ is

$$\hat{\mu}_3 = \text{the average of the middle half of the } X\text{'s}$$

Here we order the X's from smallest to largest, discard the lower 25% and upper 25% of the X's, and let $\hat{\mu}_3$ be the average of the remaining $n/2$ X's. (We assume for simplicity that n is a multiple of 4, so that $\hat{\mu}_3$ is defined unambiguously.) The following example illustrates these three estimates.

EXAMPLE 7.1

Suppose that we are interested in the mean monthly mortgage payment made by all homeowners in a given city. A random sample of 20 homeowners is chosen, and their monthly mortgage payments are shown in Table 7.1. (These have been arranged in increasing order to simplify the calculations.) Calculate the three estimates of μ discussed above.

Table 7.1

Homeowner i	X_i	Homeowner i	X_i
1	225	11	570
2	315	12	575
3	345	13	615
4	395	14	690
5	465	15	710
6	470	16	760
7	480	17	845
8	520	18	850
9	530	19	965
10	540	20	980

SOLUTION

The sample mean $\hat{\mu}_1$ (or $\overline{X}$) is given by

$$\hat{\mu}_1 = \sum \frac{X_i}{n} = \frac{225 + 315 + \cdots + 980}{20} = \$592.25$$

To obtain the sample median $\hat{\mu}_2$, we take the average of the 10th and 11th largest observations. This is

$$\hat{\mu}_2 = \frac{540 + 570}{2} = \$555$$

Finally, to find $\hat{\mu}_3$ we ignore the five lowest observations and the five highest observations, and form the average of the remaining 10 observations:

$$\hat{\mu}_3 = \frac{470 + 480 + 520 + 530 + 540 + 570 + 575 + 615 + 690 + 710}{10}$$
$$= \$570$$

Unfortunately, we cannot say which of these estimates is closest to the population mean μ because the value of μ is still unknown.

The situation is exactly the same for a general parameter θ. The point estimate $\hat{\theta}$ prescribes a set of arithmetic operations to be done on the X's in order to calculate a single number $\hat{\theta}$. Our objective is to find an estimate $\hat{\theta}$ that will be close to θ for most random samples. But since θ is unknown, how can we tell which arithmetic rules produce "good" estimates?

We answer this question by considering the sampling distribution of any particular $\hat{\theta}$. As usual, this sampling distribution has a mean and a standard deviation, which we denote by $\mu_{\hat{\theta}}$ and $\sigma_{\hat{\theta}}$. Because the mean and expected value of $\hat{\theta}$ are synonymous, we sometimes write $E(\hat{\theta})$ instead of $\mu_{\hat{\theta}}$. Also, in the context of estimation (and hypothesis testing), the standard deviation of $\hat{\theta}$ is often called the *standard error* of $\hat{\theta}$ and is denoted by $\text{StdErr}(\hat{\theta})$.

> The standard error of an estimate is the standard deviation of the estimate. If $\hat{\theta}$ is the estimate, its standard error is denoted by $\text{StdErr}(\hat{\theta})$ or $\sigma_{\hat{\theta}}$.

As in our previous discussions of means and standard deviations, the mean of $\hat{\theta}$ measures the central tendency of $\hat{\theta}$, whereas the standard error measures its variability. More specifically, if we take *many* random samples from this population and compute the value of $\hat{\theta}$ for each sample (always using the same arithmetic rule), the average of the $\hat{\theta}$'s will be close to $E(\hat{\theta})$, and StdErr$(\hat{\theta})$ will measure the variability of the $\hat{\theta}$'s around $E(\hat{\theta})$.

For example, suppose that θ is the population mean μ and $\hat{\theta}$ is the sample mean $\overline{X}$. Then we know from Chapter 6 that $E(\overline{X}) = \mu$ and StdErr$(\overline{X}) = \sigma/\sqrt{n}$. So if we observe many samples of size n from this population and calculate $\overline{X}$ for each of them, we expect the average of the $\overline{X}$'s to be close to μ, and we expect a high percentage of the $\overline{X}$'s to be no further than 2 standard errors, or $2\sigma/\sqrt{n}$, from μ.

Now we are in a position to discuss desired properties of "good" estimates. The first requirement of a good estimate $\hat{\theta}$ is that its expected value should be close to the true value θ, preferably equal to θ. Then if we observe many random samples of size n from this population, we know that the *average* of the resulting $\hat{\theta}$'s will be close to θ. Admittedly, some of the $\hat{\theta}$'s will be on the low side and some will be on the high side, but we have no reason to believe that any *particular* $\hat{\theta}$ will be too low or too high.

If $E(\hat{\theta}) = \theta$, we say that $\hat{\theta}$ is an *unbiased* estimate of θ; otherwise, $\hat{\theta}$ is said to be *biased*. Usually, we prefer unbiased estimates to biased estimates, and in most of the estimation problems we will study, the resulting estimates will be unbiased. However, good biased estimates do exist, and we will see them from time to time. If $\hat{\theta}$ is a biased estimate of θ, we define the *bias* of $\hat{\theta}$ to be the difference $E(\hat{\theta}) - \theta$. Notice that if this difference is positive, $\hat{\theta}$ tends to overestimate θ, whereas if it is negative, $\hat{\theta}$ tends to underestimate θ.

> If $E(\hat{\theta}) = \theta$, $\hat{\theta}$ is called an unbiased estimate of θ. Otherwise, the bias of $\hat{\theta}$ is defined to be the difference $E(\hat{\theta}) - \theta$.

Figure 7.2 (p. 308) shows the sampling distributions of three possible estimates of θ, labeled $\hat{\theta}_1$, $\hat{\theta}_2$, and $\hat{\theta}_3$. The density of $\hat{\theta}_1$ (on the left) has a negative bias, so we say that it is *biased downward*. Similarly, the density of $\hat{\theta}_3$ (on the right) shows that $\hat{\theta}_3$ is *biased upward*. Only $\hat{\theta}_2$ is unbiased, because the mean of its sampling distribution is equal to θ.

A second requirement of a good estimate $\hat{\theta}$ is that its standard error should be small. We not only want the *average* of a large number of $\hat{\theta}$'s (each from a separate sample) to be close to the true θ, but we also want most of the $\hat{\theta}$'s to be close to θ. That is, we do not want the $\hat{\theta}$'s to vary widely from sample to sample. The reason is simply that if the $\hat{\theta}$'s vary widely, the particular $\hat{\theta}$ we happen to observe from a single sample has a good chance of being far from θ.

This implies that if we are comparing two unbiased estimates $\hat{\theta}_1$ and $\hat{\theta}_2$ (derived from two different arithmetic rules), we prefer the one with the smaller standard error. In fact, many statisticians believe the ideal estimate is the one that among the set of all unbiased estimates has the minimum

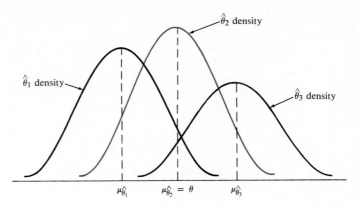

Figure 7.2
Biased and Unbiased Estimators of θ

variance. This estimate is called the *minimum variance unbiased estimate,* or simply the *MVUE.* Many of the estimates we use in this book are the MVUEs for their respective parameters.

One way of comparing two competing estimates $\hat{\theta}_1$ and $\hat{\theta}_2$ is by means of the *ratio* of their variances. This ratio is called the *relative efficiency* of one estimate with respect to the other.

$$\text{Relative efficiency of } \hat{\theta}_2 \text{ with respect to } \hat{\theta}_1 = \frac{\text{Var}(\hat{\theta}_2)}{\text{Var}(\hat{\theta}_1)}$$

As an example, suppose that the relative efficiency of $\hat{\theta}_2$ with respect to $\hat{\theta}_1$ is 1.5. Then it can be shown that in order for $\hat{\theta}_2$ to provide the same level of accuracy as $\hat{\theta}_1$, the sample size for $\hat{\theta}_2$ must be approximately 1.5 times as large as the sample size for $\hat{\theta}_1$. Since samples typically cost money, we clearly get more for our money when we use efficient estimates.

To illustrate these concepts of unbiasedness and efficiency, let θ be the population mean μ for a symmetric (not necessarily normal) population. Earlier in this chapter we proposed three possible estimates of μ:

$\hat{\mu}_1$ = sample mean $\overline{X}$
$\hat{\mu}_2$ = sample median
$\hat{\mu}_3$ = average of the middle 50% of the observations

By the symmetry of the population distribution, each of these three estimates is unbiased, that is, $E(\hat{\mu}_1) = E(\hat{\mu}_2) = E(\hat{\mu}_3) = \mu$. So in terms of bias, they are equally good. But they are not equally efficient, and their relative efficiencies depend on the particular population distribution involved.

As an example, suppose that the population distribution is normal with mean μ and variance σ^2. Then we know that the variance of $\overline{X}$ is σ^2/n. (This fact does not even require the normality assumption.) Furthermore, it can be shown that the variance of $\hat{\mu}_2$ is approximately $1.57\sigma^2/n$, and that the variance of $\hat{\mu}_3$ is approximately $1.20\sigma^2/n$. Therefore, the relative efficiencies of $\hat{\mu}_2$ and $\hat{\mu}_3$ with respect to $\hat{\mu}_1$ are approximately 1.57 and 1.20. This says that the sample mean is more efficient than the sample median or the average of the middle 50% of the observations when the population is normal.

To illustrate the statements above, we used the computer to generate 1000 samples of size $n = 36$ from a $N(10,1.5^2)$ population. For each sample we calculated the sample mean, the sample median, and the average of the middle 18 observations. According to theory, the standard deviation of the 1000 $\overline{X}$'s should be approximately $\sigma/\sqrt{n} = 1.5/\sqrt{36} = .25$. The standard deviations of the 1000 sample medians should be $\sqrt{1.57}\ \sigma/\sqrt{n}$, or approximately .313, and the standard deviation of the 1000 averages of the middle 18 observations should be $\sqrt{1.20}\ \sigma/\sqrt{n}$, or approximately .274. The actual standard deviations of the three estimates were close to what we expected, namely .248, .304, and .270. As the theory predicts, the sample means are indeed less spread out than the sample means or the averages of the middle 18 observations. We can also see this in Figure 7.3 (p. 310), where the histograms of the computer-generated estimates are shown. Notice that the center of each histogram is near the true mean, 10. This is because each estimate is unbiased. (The histograms in Figure 7.3 *are* drawn to scale. Even though the standard deviations vary from .248 to .304, there does not appear to be as much difference in variability among the three graphs as we might expect.)

For another example, consider a $N(\mu, \sigma^2)$ population where the unknown parameter is the variance σ^2. As we will see in Chapter 8, the sample variance s^2 has the property that $E(s^2) = \sigma^2$, so that s^2 is an unbiased estimate of σ^2. However, consider the more "natural" estimate $\hat{\sigma}^2$ defined by

$$\hat{\sigma}^2 = \sum \frac{(X_i - \overline{X})^2}{n}$$

(We say that $\hat{\sigma}^2$ is more natural because it is really the *average* of the squared deviations from the sample mean.) Because $\hat{\sigma}^2$ and s^2 are related by

$$\hat{\sigma}^2 = (n - 1)s^2/n$$

the rules of expected values imply that

$$E(\hat{\sigma}^2) = [(n - 1)/n]\sigma^2$$

which is less than σ^2 for any value of n. This means that the more natural estimate $\hat{\sigma}^2$ is always biased downward (it tends to underestimate σ^2), although the amount of bias decreases quickly as n increases.

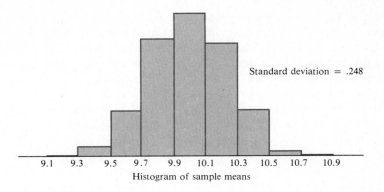

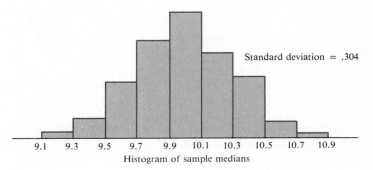

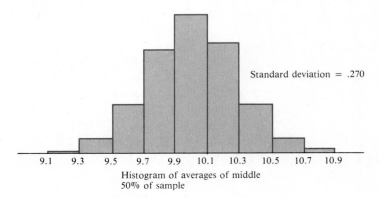

Figure 7.3

As a final example, consider s, the sample standard deviation. Since s^2 is an unbiased estimate of σ^2, it is reasonable to expect that s is an unbiased estimate of σ. However, this is not true! Instead, it turns out that

$$E(s) < \sigma$$

so that s is always biased downward. Nevertheless, s is almost always used to estimate σ.

Confidence Intervals: Qualitative Properties

In Section 7.2 we discussed only point estimates of unknown population parameters. Because a point estimate is based on a sample from the population, not on the entire population, it is not a perfect estimate of θ. That is, unless we are very lucky, $\hat{\theta}$ will not be equal to θ. Realizing this, it is natural to ask how far off $\hat{\theta}$ is likely to be. The answer to this question is provided by a confidence interval for θ. Roughly speaking, a confidence interval is an interval, computed from the sample data, that is very likely to include the true value of θ. It is a measure of the accuracy of a point estimate.

As an example, recall NBC's problem discussed earlier in this chapter. They wish to know the proportion p of the viewing public who watch a particular show. Suppose that they randomly sample 300 families and find that 13% (or 39) of these families watch the show. Then .13 is a point estimate of p. To judge the accuracy of this point estimate, they use the sample results to form a confidence interval for p. In a later section we will see that a 95% confidence interval for p extends from .092 to .168. This means that NBC executives can be 95% confident that the population proportion watching the show is between .092 and .168.

To generalize from this example, we typically specify a *level of confidence* $1 - \alpha$, where $1 - \alpha$ is a fraction close to 1. In the NBC example, we chose $1 - \alpha = .95$. We interpret $1 - \alpha$ as the fraction of all confidence intervals (formed from different samples) that would include the true value of θ. Then we observe a sample $X_1, X_2, \ldots, X_n$ and calculate not only a point estimate $\hat{\theta}$, but also the endpoints of an interval around $\hat{\theta}$. We denote these endpoints by $\hat{\theta}_L$ and $\hat{\theta}_U$ (L for lower, U for upper). In the NBC example, we had $\hat{\theta} = .13$, $\hat{\theta}_L = .092$, and $\hat{\theta}_U = .168$. Finally, we state with confidence level $1 - \alpha$ that the true value of θ is between $\hat{\theta}_L$ and $\hat{\theta}_U$.

In the best of all worlds, we would like the length of the confidence interval, $\hat{\theta}_U - \hat{\theta}_L$, to be small and we would like the level of confidence, $1 - \alpha$, to be high. For example, NBC executives obviously prefer the statement "We are 99% confident that the true population proportion is between .125 and .135" to the statement "We are 95% confident that the true proportion is between .09 and .17." The former confidence interval is much shorter and the level of confidence is higher.

Unfortunately, we do not obtain narrow confidence intervals easily. Basically, the length of a confidence interval is controlled by two numbers, the level of confidence $1 - \alpha$ and the sample size n, as we see in the following example.

EXAMPLE 7.2

Consider a fast-foods chain that wishes to know the proportion p of the consumer population who intend to try its new chicken sandwich. In a survey of n consumers, the company finds that 35% of the people surveyed intend to try the new sandwich. In Table 7.2 we show four confidence intervals for the unknown proportion p. These depend on the choice of the confidence level $1 - \alpha$ and the sample size n. (We will see how to compute these confidence intervals in Section 7.6.) The confidence intervals in this table illustrate two ways of reducing the length of a confidence interval: (1) by increasing the sample size n (from 100 to 400), and/or (2) by decreasing the level of confidence $1 - \alpha$ (from .95 to .90).

Table 7.2

Sample Size n	100	100	400	400
Confidence Level $1 - \alpha$	.90	.95	.90	.95
Confidence Interval for p	.272–.428	.257–.443	.311–.389	.303–.397
Length of Confidence Interval	.156	.186	.078	.094

In general, the effect of the sample size n is fairly obvious. The larger n is, the more information we obtain about the population and hence the narrower the confidence interval tends to be. However, to obtain a significant decrease in the length of a confidence interval, we usually have to increase n considerably. For example, notice from Table 7.2 that we needed to quadruple the sample size (for either confidence level) in order to halve the length of the confidence interval. We will see why this is so when we study confidence intervals in more detail.

For any given sample size n, we may also change the confidence level $1 - \alpha$. This is usually not done to a great extent, because $1 - \alpha$ is almost always set equal to one of the values .90, .95, or .99. There is no rule saying that $1 - \alpha$ *must* be one of these values, but in practical applications one of these values is almost always used. Notice that when $1 - \alpha$ is large, say .99, we want to be very confident that the true parameter is within the confidence interval we calculate. This means that the confidence interval has to be relatively wide. But for a smaller value of $1 - \alpha$, say .90, we can

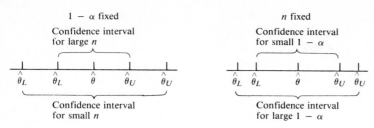

Figure 7.4
Effects of n and $1 - \alpha$ on Confidence Interval Length

achieve the desired level of confidence with a relatively narrow confidence interval.

The important ideas from this discussion are summarized below in words and graphically in Figure 7.4.

> To decrease the length of a confidence interval, we must increase the sample size n and/or decrease the level of confidence $1 - \alpha$.

Problems for Sections 7.2, 7.3

1. We know that the sample mean $\overline{X}$ is an unbiased estimate of μ. Does this imply that if we obtain 30 samples of size n and compute the sample mean of each sample, the average of the 30 $\overline{X}$'s will be exactly equal to μ? Why or why not?

2. It is known that the sample standard deviation s is a biased estimate of the population standard deviation σ. In fact, the expected value of s is *less* than σ. Does this mean that if we calculate the sample standard deviation s for a particular random sample, s will necessarily underestimate σ? Why or why not?

3. Let $\hat{\mu}_1$ and $\hat{\mu}_2$ represent any two reasonable arithmetic rules for converting sample data into estimates of μ. If $\hat{\mu}_1$ is unbiased and $\hat{\mu}_2$ is biased, and if $\hat{\mu}_1$ has a smaller variance than $\hat{\mu}_2$, explain why $\hat{\mu}_1$ is preferable to $\hat{\mu}_2$ for estimating μ. For a given sample, is it necessarily true that the difference between $\hat{\mu}_1$ and μ will be less than the difference between $\hat{\mu}_2$ and μ? Why or why not?

4. One reasonable way of estimating the population mean μ is the following. First, calculate the sample mean $\overline{X}$ and the sample standard deviation s from the observed data. Then discard all observations that are more than k sample standard

deviations from $\overline{X}$ (for some k), and let $\hat{\mu}$ be the average of the remaining observations.
   a. Why is this $\hat{\mu}$ a reasonable estimate of μ? Discuss how it might be better than $\overline{X}$ in some situations.
   b. Calculate $\hat{\mu}$ for the following data. Use $k = 1.6$.

23	45	76	89	64	10	65	57	87	64	37	59
35	8	95	37	65	58	74	46	86	44	79	45
46	42	13	47	87	99	66	57	73	62	35	95

5. Let X_1, X_2, X_3, and X_4 be a random sample of four independent random variables from a $N(\mu, \sigma^2)$ distribution. Find the bias and variance of the following estimates of μ. (Use the rules of expected values from Chapter 4.)
   a. $\dfrac{2X_1 + 2X_2 + X_3}{5}$
   b. $\dfrac{4X_1 - X_2 - X_3}{2}$
   c. $\dfrac{10X_1 + 10X_2 + 10X_4}{31}$
   d. $\dfrac{X_2 + 2X_3 + X_4}{4}$

6. Suppose that you collect $2n$ observations from a $N(\mu, \sigma^2)$ population and you wish to use these to estimate the mean μ. Let $\hat{\mu}_1$ be the sample mean of all $2n$ observations, and let $\hat{\mu}_2$ be the sample mean of the first n observations only.

a. Intuitively, why would you prefer $\hat{\mu}_1$ to $\hat{\mu}_2$ as an estimate of μ?

b. Calculate the relative efficiency of $\hat{\mu}_2$ with respect to $\hat{\mu}_1$.

c. Calculate the relative efficiency of $\hat{\mu}_2$ with respect to the sample median of all $2n$ observations. Which of these two estimates has the smaller variance? (The variance of the sample median is given in Section 7.2.)

7. Show that the following estimates are unbiased estimates of the population mean. Assume that $X_1, X_2, \ldots, X_{10}$ are independent observations from this population.

a. $\hat{\mu}_1 = \dfrac{X_1 + X_2 + \cdots + X_9}{9}$

b. $\hat{\mu}_2 = \dfrac{3X_1 + 2X_2}{5}$

c. $\hat{\mu}_3 = \dfrac{2X_1 + X_2 + X_3 + \cdots + X_{10}}{11}$

d. $\hat{\mu}_4 = \dfrac{19X_1 - X_2 - X_3 - \cdots - X_{10}}{10}$

8. Find the variances of the four estimates in Problem 7. Which of them is the most efficient (smallest variance)? What are their relative efficiencies with respect to the sample mean $\overline{X}$ of the 10 observations? (Use the rules of expected values from Chapter 4.)

9. Are there any populations or sample sizes for which $\overline{X}$ is not an unbiased estimate of μ? In particular, is $\overline{X}$ unbiased when the population is skewed and the sample size is small? Why or why not?

10. If we are computing a confidence interval for an unknown parameter and we wish to increase the level of confidence from 95% to 99%, is it true that we must increase the sample size n? Explain.

*11. Consider the following three confidence intervals for a proportion p: .485 to .715, .520 to .680, and .504 to .696. These intervals are the results of three settings of α and n: (1) $\alpha = .90$, $n = 100$, (2) $\alpha = .95$, $n = 100$, and (3) $\alpha = .95$, $n = 70$. Which confidence intervals necessarily go with which settings? Explain. (Do not do any calculations; none are necessary.)

*12. In our discussion of confidence intervals, we said that the real meaning of a 90% confidence interval for μ, for example, is that if we calculate this interval for each of many samples from the same population, approximately 90% of these intervals will contain μ. Suppose that we obtain 200 samples from the same population and compute a 90% confidence interval for the mean μ from each sample. Find the probability that between 170 and 185 of these intervals will contain μ. (*Hint:* Do the same type of "binomial" calculation as in Chapter 6 with an appropriate value of p.)

13. A pollster wishes to estimate the proportion of a given population who favor increased merit pay for high school teachers. He collects data from a random sample of people and decides to report the results as a 99% confidence interval for the population proportion. Actually, he decides to report a 99% confidence interval, rather than a 90% or 95% confidence interval, because he believes that the 99% level conveys more "preciseness." How would you support or criticize his reasoning?

7.4

Large-Sample Estimation of the Population Mean

In this section we focus on the population mean μ. As we mentioned in Section 7.2, there are several sensible point estimates of μ. These include the sample mean $\overline{X}$, the sample median, the average of the middle 50% of the observations, and others. Although any of these could be the preferred point estimate, depending on the population distribution, we will continue to use $\overline{X}$ as the point estimate of μ. (We point out, however, that many statisticians prefer not to use $\overline{X}$ to estimate μ. They argue that $\overline{X}$ is too influenced by extreme observations. A discussion of the relative merits of $\overline{X}$ and other possible estimates of μ can be found in a more advanced statistics book.)

Turning now to confidence intervals for μ, suppose that we set the level of confidence, $1 - \alpha$, equal to .95. To derive a 95% confidence interval for μ, starting with the point estimate $\overline{X}$, we proceed as follows. We know that the mean of $\overline{X}$ is μ and the standard deviation (or standard error) of $\overline{X}$ is $\sigma/\sqrt{n}$. Because of the large-sample-size ($n \geq 30$) assumption, we also know from the Central Limit Theorem that the sampling distribution of $\overline{X}$ is approximately normal, regardless of the population distribution. Therefore, Table Ib says that $\overline{X}$ will be no further than $1.96\sigma/\sqrt{n}$ from the mean μ with probability .95. [This follows because $P(-1.96 < Z < 1.96) = .95$.] In probability notation, this implies that

$$P\left(\frac{-1.96\sigma}{\sqrt{n}} < \overline{X} - \mu < \frac{1.96\sigma}{\sqrt{n}}\right) = .95$$

By manipulating the inequalities inside this probability, we can also write

$$P\left(\overline{X} - \frac{1.96\sigma}{\sqrt{n}} < \mu < \overline{X} + \frac{1.96\sigma}{\sqrt{n}}\right) = .95$$

Thus we use the endpoints $\overline{X} - 1.96\sigma/\sqrt{n}$ and $\overline{X} + 1.96\sigma/\sqrt{n}$ to form a 95% confidence interval for μ. Since the value of σ is usually unknown, we substitute the sample standard deviation s for σ when necessary. (The confidence level may not be exactly 95% when s is used instead of σ, but for large sample sizes, the discrepancy will be small.)

If we desire a confidence level other than 95%, the only necessary change is to use the appropriate tabulated z value in place of 1.96. In particular, if $1 - \alpha$ is the desired confidence level, we use $z_{\alpha/2}$, as indicated below.

Confidence Interval for μ
with Confidence Level $1 - \alpha$ ($n \geq 30$)

$$\overline{X} \pm z_{\alpha/2}\,\text{StdErr}(\overline{X}), \qquad \text{where StdErr}(\overline{X}) = \frac{\sigma}{\sqrt{n}}$$

(s may be used in place of σ if σ is unknown)

Notice that the endpoints of this confidence interval vary from sample to sample because they depend on $\overline{X}$ (and on s if σ is unknown). The confidence interval will always be centered at the observed value of $\overline{X}$ and its length will always be 2 times $z_{\alpha/2}\,\text{StdErr}(\overline{X})$. Also, because we are confident that $\overline{X}$ will be no further than $z_{\alpha/2}\,\text{StdErr}(\overline{X})$ from μ, the "half-length" of the interval,

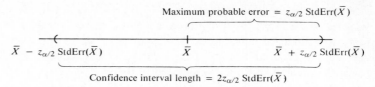

Figure 7.5

$z_{\alpha/2}$ StdErr($\overline{X}$), can be regarded as the maximum error we are likely to commit when we estimate μ by $\overline{X}$. It is important to realize that we could obtain a very unlucky sample and commit a larger error than $z_{\alpha/2}$ StdErr($\overline{X}$). However, this is the largest error we are *likely* to commit. Therefore, we will call this the *maximum probable error* in future discussions. Thus we have the important relationship shown below (see Figure 7.5).

Maximum probable error of estimation = half-length of confidence interval

---

EXAMPLE 7.3

Long-playing records vary fairly widely in the amount of music they contain. Some LPs contain as little as 30 minutes of music, whereas others contain as much as 60 minutes or more. Suppose that a random sample of 40 classical LPs has an average playing time of 53.6 minutes and a sample standard deviation of 6.2 minutes. Find a 95% confidence interval for the mean playing time of all classical LPs.

SOLUTION

We are given that $\overline{X} = 53.6$, $s = 6.2$, and $n = 40$. (The population standard deviation σ is not given.) This means the (approximate) standard error of $\overline{X}$ is $s/\sqrt{n} = .980$. Since we want a 95% confidence interval, we use $1 - \alpha = .95$ and $z_{\alpha/2} = z_{.025} = 1.96$. The required confidence interval is

$$\overline{X} \pm z_{\alpha/2} \text{ StdErr}(\overline{X}) = 53.6 \pm 1.96(.98) = 53.6 \pm 1.92$$

or from 51.68 to 55.52 minutes. In words, we are 95% confident that the average playing time of all classical LPs is between 51.68 and 55.52 minutes. Equivalently, we are 95% confident that the point estimate 53.6 differs by no more than 1.92 minutes from the (still unknown) population mean μ.

The following example illustrates how confidence intervals for the mean depend on the level of confidence required.

EXAMPLE 7.4

Suppose that the soft-drink industry wishes to estimate the mean amount of soft drinks consumed per week per person in a given population. We let μ and σ be the mean and standard deviation of the amount consumed per person per week over the entire population, and we assume that $\sigma = 16$ ounces. If a random sample of 50 people shows an average weekly consumption of 37.3 ounces, find a 90% confidence interval, a 95% confidence interval, and a 99% confidence interval for the mean μ.

SOLUTION

For each level of confidence, we must compute

$$\overline{X} \pm z_{\alpha/2} \, \text{StdErr}(\overline{X}) = 37.3 \pm z_{\alpha/2} \frac{16}{\sqrt{50}} = 37.3 \pm 2.26 \, z_{\alpha/2}$$

The three required z values are found from Table Ib. They are $z_{.10/2} = z_{.05} = 1.645$, $z_{.05/2} = z_{.025} = 1.96$, and $z_{.01/2} = z_{.005} = 2.576$. These give the following confidence intervals:

$$90\%: 37.3 \pm 2.26(1.645) = 37.3 \pm 3.72 \text{ (from 33.58 to 41.02)}$$
$$95\%: 37.3 \pm 2.26(1.96) = 37.3 \pm 4.43 \text{ (from 32.87 to 41.73)}$$
$$99\%: 37.3 \pm 2.26(2.576) = 37.3 \pm 5.82 \text{ (from 31.48 to 43.12)}$$

As we stated earlier, when we require more confidence that the true mean be within the limits of a confidence interval, we must push these limits farther apart.

The form of a confidence interval for μ is typical of most of the confidence intervals we will discuss. (The confidence interval for the variance, presented in Chapter 8, is the only exception.) We first find a point estimate of the unknown parameter, in this case $\overline{X}$ for μ. Then the endpoints of the confidence interval are plus or minus a certain constant, here $z_{\alpha/2}$, times the standard error of the point estimate, here $\sigma/\sqrt{n}$. The number of standard errors we add to and subtract from the point estimate is usually between 1.5 and 2.5, but this depends on the sampling distribution of the point estimate and the level of confidence $1 - \alpha$. In any case, this number is always a tabulated number from Appendix B.

> Most confidence intervals are of the form: a point estimate plus or minus a multiple of the standard error of the estimate. This multiple is usually between 1.5 and 2.5.

Sample Size Selection

In applied situations it is often important to find an appropriate sample size n. Since sampling is usually expensive, we do not want to make n any larger than it needs to be to achieve a prescribed level of accuracy. On the other hand, we want to guarantee that n is large enough to achieve this accuracy. Therefore, we usually proceed as follows. We first choose the maximum probable error B we are willing to tolerate and the desired confidence level $1 - \alpha$. That is, we want the difference between $\overline{X}$ and μ to be no greater than B with probability $1 - \alpha$. Then we find the smallest value of n that will achieve this goal. Notice that the resulting confidence interval for μ will have length $2B$ because the "half-length" of a confidence interval is the largest error likely to be committed. (Refer again to Figure 7.5.)

We know that the half-length of a confidence interval for μ is $z_{\alpha/2}\sigma/\sqrt{n}$. If we want this length to be no greater than a given value B (when $1 - \alpha$ and σ are fixed), we set B equal to $z_{\alpha/2}\sigma/\sqrt{n}$ and solve for n. This leads to the following formula for n.

Required Sample Size

$$n = \frac{(z_{\alpha/2})^2\sigma^2}{B^2}$$

Because this formula does not usually lead to an *integer* value of n, we always round the value *up* to the next higher integer to ensure that it is sufficiently large to achieve its purpose.

In many situations the population standard deviation σ is unknown, so that n cannot be found from the formula above. This time we cannot use s in place of σ because no sample has been taken prior to choosing n. To estimate σ and thereby estimate the required n, one of the following procedures can be used.

1. Take a small sample of size n_0 and calculate the sample standard deviation from this small sample. If its value is s_0, calculate n from the above sample size formula, using s_0 in place of σ. Then collect $n - n_0$ *more* observations, for a total of n observations altogether.
2. As a rule of thumb, we know that almost all of a population lies within 2 or 3 standard deviations of the mean. This means the range in the population (where range is the difference between the largest and smallest possible observations) is approximately 4σ to 6σ. So if we can estimate the range, we use

$$\text{estimated } \sigma = \frac{\text{range}}{4} \quad \left(\text{or } \frac{\text{range}}{6}\right)$$

This estimated σ can then be used in place of σ in the formula for n.

The formula for n illustrates a very important general property of estimation. The maximum probable error B typically varies inversely with the *square root* of the sample size n. Equivalently, the sample size varies inversely with the *square* of the maximum probable error. This means that to halve the maximum probable error, we must quadruple the sample size; to reduce the maximum probable error to ⅓ of its previous value, we must multiply the sample size by 9; and so on.

EXAMPLE 7.4 (continued)

In the soft-drink example, how many people must be sampled to reduce the length of a 95% confidence interval for μ to 5 ounces? If this sample size is chosen and a sample mean of 37.3 ounces is again observed, find the resulting 95% confidence interval for μ, and check that its length is as desired.

SOLUTION

Since we want the confidence interval to have length 5, we use $B = 2.5$. Then the required value of n, again using $1 - \alpha = .95$ and $\sigma = 16$, is

$$n = \frac{(z_{\alpha/2})^2\sigma^2}{B^2} = \frac{(1.96)^2(16)^2}{2.5^2} = 157.4$$

Since n must be an integer, we round this up to $n = 158$. Then the 95% confidence interval for μ, given a sample mean of 37.3, is

$$\overline{X} \pm z_{\alpha/2}\, \text{StdErr}(\overline{X}) = 37.3 \pm \frac{1.96(16)}{\sqrt{158}} = 37.3 \pm 2.49$$

or from 34.81 to 39.79 ounces. The length of this interval, 4.98, is slightly less than the desired value of 5. This is because we had to round n up to an integer value. Notice that once the confidence level $1 - \alpha$ and the sample size n have been set, the only information the sample gives us is where to *center* the confidence interval; its length has already been predetermined. (This is the case only when σ is known.)

The next example illustrates sample size selection when σ is not known.

EXAMPLE 7.5

An electrical supply company has designed a new type of high-intensity light bulb for movie projectors that company experts believe is better than any light bulb on the market. They would like to estimate the mean lifetime per light bulb, and in particular, they would like a 99% confidence interval for this mean to have a length of approximately 20 hours. Because the testing of these bulbs is relatively expensive, they want a sample size n that is not excessively large but is large enough to produce the desired accuracy. Based on a preliminary sample of 25 light bulbs, they have observed a mean lifetime of 432 hours and a sample standard deviation of 127 hours. How many more light bulbs should they test? Also, what is the resulting confidence interval for μ if the sample mean of the *combined* sample is 447 hours and the sample standard deviation of the combined sample is 116 hours?

SOLUTION

In the notation above, the "preliminary" sample has $n_0 = 25$ and $s_0 = 127$. For the accuracy required, we set $B = 10$. Since $1 - \alpha = .99$, the approximate total sample size required, using s_0 in place of σ, is

$$n = \frac{(z_{.005})^2 s_0^2}{B^2} = \frac{(2.576)^2(127)^2}{10^2} = 1070.28$$

which we round up to 1071. Since this number includes the original sample of size 25, the company needs to sample 1046 more light bulbs. (In a realistic situation, the company might conclude that this sample size is too large. Then it could lower the confidence level $1 - \alpha$ and/or increase the value of B, both of which would decrease the required sample size.)

If 1046 more bulbs are tested and the sample mean and sample standard deviation for the combined sample are $\overline{X} = 447$ and $s = 116$, the resulting 99% confidence interval for μ is

$$\overline{X} \pm z_{\alpha/2} \, \text{StdErr}(\overline{X}) = 447 \pm \frac{2.576(116)}{\sqrt{1071}} = 447 \pm 9.13$$

Notice that the length of the final confidence interval, 2(9.13), is very close to the desired length of 20.

Computer Simulation of Confidence Intervals for the Mean

Now that we know how to calculate confidence intervals for the mean, we illustrate these confidence intervals in a slightly different way. As in previous chapters, we make use of the computer to generate many samples of a given sample size, $n = 30$, all from the same $N(\mu, \sigma^2)$ population. For each sample we have the computer calculate $\overline{X}$ and s^2, and then we use these to calculate a 90% confidence interval for the population mean μ. Because σ is a parameter read in to the computer, its value may be used to obtain the confidence interval for μ with σ known. Alternatively, we may assume that σ is unknown and obtain the confidence interval for μ with the simulated s used in place of σ. For the sake of comparison, we compute both of these confidence intervals for each sample.

Since μ is also a parameter read in to the computer, its value is actually known. Therefore, we can check the number of the simulated confidence intervals that include μ. We simply see whether the true value of μ is within the limits of any given confidence interval. If the confidence intervals we obtain are really 90% confidence intervals, approximately 90% of them will include the true μ, while 10% will not. In practice, of course, if we unluckily obtain one of the confidence intervals that does not include μ, we will be fooled into thinking that the true μ is inside it, when in fact it is not. But at least we have the comfort of knowing that this will happen only about 10% of the time.

The graphs in Figure 7.6 (p. 322) illustrate the results of the computer simulation. For each of 40 samples of size 30, we computed the 90% confidence intervals

$$\overline{X} \pm z_{.05} \frac{\sigma}{\sqrt{n}} \quad (\sigma \text{ known})$$

and

$$\overline{X} \pm z_{.05} \frac{s}{\sqrt{n}} \quad (\sigma \text{ unknown})$$

We used $\mu = 100$ and $\sigma = 10$ as the true mean and standard deviation.

Each horizontal bar corresponds to the confidence interval for a single sample. When one of these bars intersects the vertical line positioned at $\mu = 100$, the corresponding confidence interval includes the true μ; otherwise, it does not. For each side of Figure 7.6 (with σ known and σ unknown), we expect 90%, or 36 out of 40, of the horizontal bars to cross the vertical line. Although this did not happen precisely as expected, the simulated results are very close to what the theory predicts: 35 out of 40 covered the true mean with σ known, and 37 out of 40 covered the true mean with σ unknown. Notice that each of the confidence intervals on the right has the same length. The lengths on the left vary slightly from sample to sample because the value of s varies from sample to sample.

The graphs in Figure 7.6 illustrate the precise meaning of a statement such as "The interval from 97.6 to 105.8 represents a 90% confidence interval for μ." Strictly speaking, we do *not* mean that μ is between 97.6 and 105.8 with probability .90. Because μ is a fixed (although unknown) number, it is either between 97.6 and 105.8 or it is not. Therefore, the probability of μ being between 97.6 and 105.8 is either 0 or 1. The confidence interval statement really means that if we use the same *procedure* to calculate 90% confidence intervals for μ from many different samples, approximately 90% of them will contain the true μ, and the other 10% will not. Since we do not know beforehand which confidence intervals will contain μ and which will not, we say we are 90% confident that any *particular* interval will be one of the "good" ones.

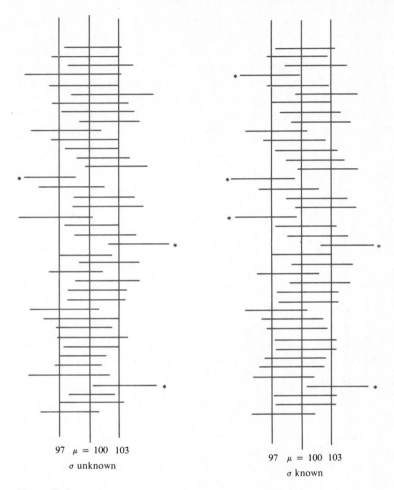

Figure 7.6
Computer-Generated Confidence Intervals for μ (''Bad'' Intervals Marked
with ''*'')

7.5

Large-Sample Estimation of the Difference Between Two Means

(Readers who skipped Sections 6.8 and 6.9 should go back and learn that
material before proceeding.)

Consider two populations with unknown means μ_1 and μ_2 and variances

σ_1^2 and σ_2^2. In this section we study the difference $\mu_1 - \mu_2$. The point estimate we use is the difference between the sample means, $\overline{X}_1 - \overline{X}_2$. We assume that these are based on *independent* samples of sizes n_1 and n_2, respectively. If these sample sizes are large ($n_1 \geq 30$, $n_2 \geq 30$), we know from Chapter 6 that the sampling distribution of $\overline{X}_1 - \overline{X}_2$ is approximately normal with mean $\mu_1 - \mu_2$. That is, $\overline{X}_1 - \overline{X}_2$ is an unbiased estimate of $\mu_1 - \mu_2$. We also know that the variance of $\overline{X}_1 - \overline{X}_2$ is $\sigma_1^2/n_1 + \sigma_2^2/n_2$. Since the standard error of $\overline{X}_1 - \overline{X}_2$ is simply another name for its standard deviation, we may write

$$\text{StdErr}(\overline{X}_1 - \overline{X}_2) = \sqrt{\frac{\sigma_1^2}{n_1} + \frac{\sigma_2^2}{n_2}}$$

As in Section 7.4, we may substitute the sample variances, s_1^2 and s_2^2, for σ_1^2 and σ_2^2 if σ_1^2 and σ_2^2 are unknown.

To obtain a confidence interval for $\mu_1 - \mu_2$, we proceed exactly as in Section 7.4. Since $\overline{X}_1 - \overline{X}_2$ is approximately normal, its value will differ by no more than $z_{\alpha/2}$ standard errors from the mean $\mu_1 - \mu_2$ with probability $1 - \alpha$. This implies the following result.

Confidence Interval for $\mu_1 - \mu_2$
with Confidence Level $1 - \alpha$ ($n_1 \geq 30$, $n_2 \geq 30$)

$$\overline{X}_1 - \overline{X}_2 \pm z_{\alpha/2} \, \text{StdErr}(\overline{X}_1 - \overline{X}_2),$$

$$\text{where } \text{StdErr}(\overline{X}_1 - \overline{X}_2) = \sqrt{\frac{\sigma_1^2}{n_1} + \frac{\sigma_2^2}{n_2}}$$

(s_1^2 and s_2^2 may be used in place of σ_1^2 and σ_2^2 if σ_1^2 and σ_2^2 are unknown)

This confidence interval is very similar to the confidence interval for a single mean. It is centered at the point estimate $\overline{X}_1 - \overline{X}_2$ and extends $z_{\alpha/2}$ standard errors of this point estimate on either side. The maximum error likely to be committed is the half-length of the interval, $z_{\alpha/2}\text{StdErr}(\overline{X}_1 - \overline{X}_2)$.

EXAMPLE 7.6

Suppose that the Labor Department is conducting a survey to discover whether the average monthly welfare check is different in Pennsylvania than in California. Random samples of 80 California people and 60 Pennsylvania people on welfare are selected. These samples show mean monthly welfare checks of $473 and $438, respectively. If it is known that the standard deviations of all welfare checks in California and Pennsylvania are $85 and $57, find a

95% confidence for the mean difference between the amounts of all California and Pennsylvania welfare checks.

SOLUTION

We let subscripts 1 and 2 stand for California and Pennsylvania, respectively. Then we are given that $\overline{X}_1 = 473$, $\overline{X}_2 = 438$, $\sigma_1 = 85$, $\sigma_2 = 57$, $n_1 = 80$, and $n_2 = 60$. The point estimate of the difference $\mu_1 - \mu_2$ is

$$\overline{X}_1 - \overline{X}_2 = 473 - 438 = 35$$

and the standard error of this point estimate is

$$\text{StdErr}(\overline{X}_1 - \overline{X}_2) = \sqrt{\frac{\sigma_1^2}{n_1} + \frac{\sigma_2^2}{n_2}} = \sqrt{\frac{85^2}{80} + \frac{57^2}{60}} = 12.02$$

Therefore, the 95% confidence interval for the difference between population means is

$$\overline{X}_1 - \overline{X}_2 \pm z_{\alpha/2} \, \text{StdErr}(\overline{X}_1 - \overline{X}_2) = 35 \pm 1.96(12.02) = 35 \pm 23.56$$

or from \$11.44 to \$58.56. In words, we are 95% confident that the average person on welfare in California receives between \$11.44 and \$58.56 more than his or her counterpart in Pennsylvania. Equivalently, we are 95% confident that the difference between the estimate, \$35, and the true mean difference, $\mu_1 - \mu_2$, is no greater than \$23.56.

Sample Size Selection

If we want the maximum probable error in estimating $\mu_1 - \mu_2$ to be a specified value B, there are two sample sizes to choose, n_1 and n_2. We will only examine the case where these are chosen to be equal, and in this case we let n denote the common sample size. That is, we assume that $n = n_1 = n_2$. In terms of n, the maximum probable error is given by

$$z_{\alpha/2} \, \text{StdErr}(\overline{X}_1 - \overline{X}_2) = z_{\alpha/2} \sqrt{\frac{\sigma_1^2}{n_1} + \frac{\sigma_2^2}{n_2}} = z_{\alpha/2} \frac{\sqrt{\sigma_1^2 + \sigma_2^2}}{\sqrt{n}}$$

Then the procedure is to set this expression equal to B and solve for n. The result is shown below.

Required Sample Sizes $(n_1 = n_2 = n)$

$$n = \frac{(z_{\alpha/2})^2(\sigma_1^2 + \sigma_2^2)}{B^2}$$

If σ_1^2 and σ_2^2 are unknown, we have the same problem that was discussed in the preceding section. Again, we suggest estimating σ_1^2 and σ_2^2 by taking small "preliminary" samples and using the resulting sample variances, or by using the "range" approximation for each σ. In either case the estimated σ's are used in the formula for n above.

EXAMPLE 7.6 (continued)

For the comparative study of welfare checks in California and Pennsylvania, how many people from Pennsylvania and California must be sampled to reduce the length of the confidence interval for $\mu_1 - \mu_2$ to \$20?

SOLUTION

Since B is the half-length of the confidence interval, we set $B = 10$. Then n, the number who must be sampled from *each* state, is given by

$$n = \frac{(z_{\alpha/2})^2(\sigma_1^2 + \sigma_2^2)}{B^2} = \frac{(1.96)^2(85^2 + 57^2)}{10^2} = 402.4$$

which we round up to $n = 403$. Notice that when $n_1 = 80$ and $n_2 = 60$ people were sampled, the maximum probable error was \$23.56. To reduce this to \$10, we must sample slightly over 400 people from each state. Obviously, narrow confidence intervals do not come cheaply!

Problems for Sections 7.4, 7.5

14. An educator is interested in the mean IQ in a given population of students.
    a. If a sample size of $n = 50$ is chosen, find a 95% confidence interval for the mean μ when the sample mean is 112 and the sample variance is 121.
    b. Suppose that the educator wishes to determine the sample size such that the width of a confidence interval for μ will be no greater than 5. By considering the sample in part (a) as a preliminary sample, how many more observations are needed? [Use the sample variance in part (a) to estimate the population variance σ^2.]

15. An article in a news magazine reported that Americans average 42 quarts of popcorn per year. (Reference: *Time*, March 14, 1983, p. 79.) If this claim is based on a random sample of 40 people, and if the sample standard deviation for this sample is 12 quarts of popcorn per person, find a 95% con-

fidence interval for the mean amount of popcorn consumed per person over the whole population.

16. A standardized writing test is given to 45 randomly chosen freshmen and 30 randomly chosen seniors at a given university. The sample mean and standard deviation of the freshmen scores are 120 and 14, while these quantities for the seniors are 125 and 11. Calculate a 95% confidence interval for $\mu_1 - \mu_2$, the difference between the mean senior score and the mean freshman score, taken over the entire population.

17. A sample of regular gasoline prices at 30 gas stations across the country was taken in early 1981. A similar but independent sample of regular gas prices was taken at another 30 gas stations in early 1983. The 1981 sample had mean \$1.27 and standard deviation \$.06. The 1983 sample had mean \$1.10 and standard deviation \$.05. Find a 90% confidence interval

for the mean change in price from 1981 to 1983, where the mean is taken over all gas stations.

18. Suppose that a sample of 35 commercial airline pilots shows a mean salary of $62,720 per year. If a resulting 90% confidence interval for the mean salary of all such pilots has length $5230, what can you say about the sample standard deviation of salaries? (Assume that the confidence interval was formed from the *sample* standard deviation.)

19. A recent survey of 98 firms showed that employee benefits averaged 37% of the company payroll. (Reference: J. H. Foegen, "The Creative Flowering of Employee Benefits," *Business Horizons*, Vol. 25, 1982, pp. 9–13.) Assume that the sample standard deviation was 6.2%. (This standard deviation shows the spread of the percentages of payrolls devoted to employee benefits across the sampled firms.) Find a 95% confidence interval for the mean percentage of payroll paid out in employee benefits by all firms in the population.

20. A secretary keeps track of the times between incoming phone calls to her department. She does this during a typical morning and during a typical afternoon. The times between 50 successive morning calls (in minutes) have mean 2.53 and standard deviation .72. For 45 successive afternoon calls, the figures are 3.78 and .82.
    a. What are the relevant sample sizes? (They are not quite 50 and 45.)
    b. Find a 95% confidence interval for $\mu_1 - \mu_2$, where μ_1 is the mean time between all morning calls and μ_2 is the mean time between all afternoon calls.

21. College students are continually concerned about how time-consuming a course is. (Presumably, the more time-consuming a course is, the less attractive it is!) Suppose that we sample 30 students from course *A* and 35 other students from course *B*. Each student is asked to estimate the time that he or she spends on the course per week (on the average). The sample mean and standard deviation of the responses for the class *A* students are 9.2 hours and 3.7 hours. The similar figures for the class *B* students are 8.1 and 1.7 hours. Find a 95% confidence interval for the difference between the mean time per week spent on class *A* and class *B*.

22. A credit union wishes to know the mean loan balance for all customers who are currently carrying loans. A small sample of 15 loans shows a sample mean of $575 outstanding and a corresponding sample standard deviation of $165.
    a. How many *more* accounts have to be sampled so that the resulting 95% confidence interval for the mean outstanding amount on all loans has length approximately equal to $50?
    b. If the resulting total sample (including the original 15) has sample mean $593 and sample standard deviation $143, find a 95% confidence interval for the population mean. Why is the length of this confidence interval not $50, as desired?

23. An automobile insurance company usually recommends that people in car accidents take their cars to two particular body shops for estimates of damage. Recently, however, it appears that body shop 2 has been giving higher estimates on average than body shop 1. Consider a random sample of 35 cars that have received recent damage estimates from both shops. The mean difference for these cars, where each difference is shop 2's estimate minus shop 1's estimate, is $35.40. The standard deviation of these differences is $15.75. Find a 95% confidence interval for the population mean difference taken over all cars. Why is the material from Section 7.4, not Section 7.5, relevant here?

24. A waterproofing company orders a sealant from a chemical manufacturer. The sealant comes in drums marked "50 gallons." Recently, the company has begun to suspect that there is less than 50 gallons of sealant in the average drum. Therefore, it measures the contents of 30 randomly selected drums. These show a sample mean of 49.64 gallons and a standard deviation of .35 gallon. Find a 95% confidence interval for the mean number of gallons in all of the drums. What conclusions should the company draw?

25. The waterproofing company in Problem 24 believes, based on the sample in that problem, that it is not getting its money's worth and switches to a different supplier. It then measures the contents of a randomly selected 30 "50-gallon" drums from the new supplier. Now the sample mean is 49.72 gallons and the sample standard deviation is .25 gallon. Find a 95% confidence interval for the difference between the mean amount per drum from the new supplier and the old supplier. Can you conclude with 95% confidence that the new supplier is really more honest in its claim? Why or why not?

7.6

Large-Sample Estimation of a Population Proportion

We now consider the problem of estimating the proportion p of A's in a population composed of A's and B's. We will continue to use the sample proportion $\hat{p}$ as a point estimate of p, and we will learn how to form a confidence interval for p that is based on $\hat{p}$.

Recall that the approximate sampling distribution of $\hat{p}$ is normal with mean p and variance $p(1 - p)/n$ [as long as $np(1 - p) \geq 5$]. This means that the standard error of $\hat{p}$ is

$$\text{StdErr}(\hat{p}) = \sqrt{\frac{p(1 - p)}{n}}$$

Proceeding as in Sections 7.4 and 7.5, we are tempted to conclude that the confidence interval for p is $\hat{p} \pm z_{\alpha/2} \, \text{StdErr}(\hat{p})$. The only problem, however, is that the formula for $\text{StdErr}(\hat{p})$ involves the unknown value of p. The usual way of getting around this problem is to substitute $\hat{p}$ for p in the expression for $\text{StdErr}(\hat{p})$. That is, we use the appropriate value $\sqrt{\hat{p}(1 - \hat{p})/n}$ for $\text{StdErr}(\hat{p})$ to form a confidence interval for p. The result is shown below.

> ### Confidence Interval for p
> ### with Confidence Level $1 - \alpha$ $(n\hat{p}(1 - \hat{p}) \geq 5)$
>
> $$\hat{p} \pm z_{\alpha/2} \, \text{StdErr}(\hat{p})$$
>
> $$\text{where } \text{StdErr}(\hat{p}) = \sqrt{\frac{\hat{p}(1 - \hat{p})}{n}}$$

[Notice that we require $n\hat{p}(1 - \hat{p}) \geq 5$. This is because we cannot check whether $np(1 - p) \geq 5$; we do not know the value of p.]

EXAMPLE 7.7

Suppose that a large company polls a random sample of 150 employees in order to estimate the proportion of all employees who have invested in Individual Retirement Accounts (IRAs). The poll shows that 45 of these 150 employees have invested in IRAs. Find a 95% confidence interval for the proportion of all the company's employees who have invested in IRAs.

SOLUTION

We first find the sample proportion $\hat{p}$ and the (approximate) standard error of $\hat{p}$. These are $\hat{p} = {}^{45}/_{150} = .3$ and

$$\text{StdErr}(\hat{p}) = \sqrt{\frac{\hat{p}(1 - \hat{p})}{n}} = \sqrt{\frac{.3(.7)}{150}} = .0374$$

Then the 95% confidence interval for p is given by

$$\hat{p} \pm z_{\alpha/2}\,\text{StdErr}(\hat{p}) = .3 \pm 1.96(.0374) = .3 \pm .073$$

In words, the company is 95% confident that between 22.7 and 37.3% of its employees have invested in IRAs. Equivalently, we conclude with 95% confidence that the maximum error in the estimate of p is .073.

Sample Size Selection

From the discussion above, we see that the maximum probable error in estimating p is $z_{\alpha/2}\sqrt{\hat{p}(1 - \hat{p})/n}$. Because this expression depends on $\hat{p}$, we cannot predict its value exactly until *after* we have observed the sample and have calculated $\hat{p}$. However, it is not difficult to show that for any $\hat{p}$ between 0 and 1, $\hat{p}(1 - \hat{p})$ is no greater than $\frac{1}{4}$, and that $\hat{p}(1 - \hat{p})$ *equals* $\frac{1}{4}$ only when $\hat{p}$ equals $\frac{1}{2}$. Therefore, we know that the maximum probable error is no greater than the value we obtain when we substitute $\frac{1}{2}$ for $\hat{p}$. This value is as follows.

Upper Bound for Maximum Probable Error in Estimating p

$$z_{\alpha/2}\sqrt{\frac{.5(.5)}{n}} = \frac{z_{\alpha/2}}{2\sqrt{n}}$$

If we want to find a sample size n so that the maximum probable error is no greater than a prescribed value B, we set $z_{\alpha/2}/(2\sqrt{n})$ equal to B and solve for n. The result is that $n = (z_{\alpha/2})^2/(4B^2)$. With this value of n, we have confidence level $1 - \alpha$ that the maximum error will be no greater than B, regardless of the value of $\hat{p}$ observed.

Sample size that guarantees a maximum probable error no greater than B

$$n = \frac{(z_{\alpha/2})^2}{4B^2}$$

EXAMPLE 7.7 (continued)

Suppose that the company interested in employee IRAs is not satisfied with the length of the confidence interval for p found earlier. It would like the length of a 95% confidence interval to be no larger than .04 (which we can interpret as plus or minus 2 percentage points). How many employees must it sample to guarantee this?

SOLUTION

Using $B = .02$, the required value of n is

$$n = \frac{(z_{.025})^2}{4B^2} = \frac{1.96^2}{.0016} = 2401$$

This large a sample size is not unusual. When we want the level of accuracy for a proportion to be very high, the sample size must be very large.

The point of the following example is that we can sometimes find a value of n considerably smaller than $(z_{\alpha/2})^2/(4B^2)$ that will still achieve the required accuracy. This is particularly important in situations where sampling is expensive and/or time-consuming. In general, we know that the maximum probable error in estimating p is $z_{\alpha/2}\sqrt{\hat{p}(1-\hat{p})/n}$. We found the sample size formula above by setting $\hat{p}$ equal to ½ and solving for n. As long as $\hat{p}$ is fairly close to ½, this is a reasonable procedure, because the expression $p(1-p)$ is fairly insensitive to the value of p for p close to ½ (see Figure 7.7). Now, however, suppose we know that one of the following two (mutually exclusive) possibilities will hold: either (1) $\hat{p}$ will be no larger than some value $p*$ close to 0, or (2) $\hat{p}$ will be no smaller than some value $p*$ close to 1. Then we may set $\hat{p}$ equal to $p*$ in the formula for B and solve for n. For $p*$ close to 0 or 1, this will result in a much smaller sample size.

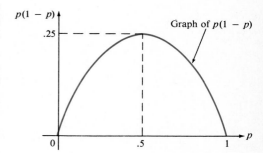

Figure 7.7

Modified Sample Size Formula

$$n = \frac{(z_{\alpha/2})^2 p*(1 - p*)}{B^2}$$

EXAMPLE 7.8

Assume that a certain type of battery is classified as defective if it does not function successfully for at least 1000 hours of continuous use. If the company that produces these batteries wishes to estimate the proportion p of defectives it produces, how many batteries must it put on test to ensure with

95% confidence that the maximum error in estimating p will be no greater than .02? Assume the company is certain that no more than 5% of the batteries will be defective. Then find the resulting 95% confidence interval for p if 2.4% of the sampled batteries fail to function for at least 1000 hours, and check that its length is as short as desired.

SOLUTION

For this example, we have $z_{\alpha/2} = 1.96$, $p* = .05$, and $B = .02$, so that the required sample size is

$$n = \frac{(1.96)^2(.05)(.95)}{.02^2} = 456.2$$

which we round up to 457. (Contrast this with the value required by the formula $n = (z_{\alpha/2})^2/(4B^2)$, namely $n = 2401$. The savings in sampling costs is certainly substantial.) If the company puts 457 batteries on test and 2.4% (or 11) of these fail before 1000 hours of use, then $\hat{p} = .024$ and the standard error of $\hat{p}$ is

$$\text{StdErr}(\hat{p}) = \sqrt{\frac{\hat{p}(1 - \hat{p})}{n}} = \sqrt{\frac{.024(.976)}{457}} = .00716$$

The resulting 95% confidence interval for p is

$$\hat{p} \pm z_{\alpha/2} \, \text{StdErr}(\hat{p}) = .024 \pm 1.96(.00716) = .024 \pm .014$$

As we predicted, the maximum probable error, .014, is indeed less than the required value, .02.

7.7

Large-Sample Estimation of the Difference Between Two Proportions

In this section we learn how to estimate the difference between two population proportions, $p_1 - p_2$. As the examples in this section indicate, this problem occurs in many realistic situations and is often at least as important as the estimation of a single proportion p. For example, suppose that we poll a random group of men and women to find the proportion of them who smoke. Then we might be at least as interested in the *difference* between the proportions of male and female smokers as we are in the individual proportions p_1 and p_2.

The point estimate of $p_1 - p_2$ we use is the difference between the sample proportions, $\hat{p}_1 - \hat{p}_2$. From Chapter 6 we know that if the sample sizes n_1 and n_2 are reasonably large $[n_1 p_1 (1 - p_1) \geq 5$ and $n_2 p_2 (1 - p_2) \geq 5$ are sufficient], the sampling distribution of $\hat{p}_1 - \hat{p}_2$ is approximately normal with mean $p_1 - p_2$ and variance $p_1(1 - p_1)/n_1 + p_2(1 - p_2)/n_2$. This means that the standard error of $\hat{p}_1 - \hat{p}_2$ is

$$\text{StdErr}(\hat{p}_1 - \hat{p}_2) = \sqrt{\frac{p_1(1 - p_1)}{n_1} + \frac{p_2(1 - p_2)}{n_2}}$$

When we try to obtain a confidence interval for $p_1 - p_2$, we run into the same problem that we encountered in the preceding section, namely, that the standard error of $\hat{p}_1 - \hat{p}_2$ contains the unknown values p_1 and p_2. We solve this problem in the same way as before. We substitute $\hat{p}_1$ for p_1 and $\hat{p}_2$ for p_2 in the expression for $\text{StdErr}(\hat{p}_1 - \hat{p}_2)$. The resulting confidence interval is as follows.

Confidence Interval for $p_1 - p_2$ with Confidence Level
$1 - \alpha$ $[n\hat{p}_1(1 - \hat{p}_1) \geq 5, \ n\hat{p}_2(1 - \hat{p}_2) \geq 5]$

$$\hat{p}_1 - \hat{p}_2 \pm z_{\alpha/2} \, \text{StdErr}(\hat{p}_1 - \hat{p}_2)$$

where $\text{StdErr}(\hat{p}_1 - \hat{p}_2) = \sqrt{\dfrac{\hat{p}_1(1 - \hat{p}_1)}{n_1} + \dfrac{\hat{p}_2(1 - \hat{p}_2)}{n_2}}$

If we want to guarantee that the maximum probable error in estimating $p_1 - p_2$ is no greater than a prescribed value B, there are a number of different ways we can choose the sample sizes n_1 and n_2. As in Section 7.5, we consider only the choice where n_1 and n_2 are set equal to a common value n. Then it can be shown that the following value of n will do the job, regardless of the $\hat{p}_1$ and $\hat{p}_2$ values actually observed.

Sample Sizes That Guarantee a Maximum Probable Error
No Greater than B $(n_1 = n_2 = n)$

$$n = \frac{(z_{\alpha/2})^2}{2B^2}$$

EXAMPLE 7.9

Suppose that a consumer information magazine tests two models of cars, labeled 1 and 2, to discover the proportions of these models that have major engine difficulties during the first 30,000 miles of driving. The numbers of cars tested are $n_1 = 50$ and $n_2 = 80$. If 8 of the model 1 cars and 10 of the model 2 cars develop major engine difficulties during the first 30,000 miles of driving, find a 90% confidence interval for the difference $p_1 - p_2$ between the proportions of all such cars that develop these problems.

SOLUTION

The sample proportions are $\hat{p}_1 = \frac{8}{50} = .16$ and $\hat{p}_2 = \frac{10}{80} = .125$, which implies that the point estimate of $p_1 - p_2$ is $\hat{p}_1 - \hat{p}_2 = .035$. The (approximate) standard error of $\hat{p}_1 - \hat{p}_2$ is

$$\text{StdErr}(\hat{p}_1 - \hat{p}_2) = \sqrt{\frac{.16(.84)}{50} + \frac{.125(.875)}{80}} = .064$$

Therefore, a 90% confidence interval for $p_1 - p_2$ is

$$\hat{p}_1 - \hat{p}_2 \pm z_{.05} \text{ StdErr}(\hat{p}_1 - \hat{p}_2) = .035 \pm 1.645(.064) = .035 \pm .105$$

or from $-.070$ to $.140$. [Notice that $n_1 \hat{p}_1 (1 - \hat{p}_1)$ and $n_2 \hat{p}_2 (1 - \hat{p}_2)$ are both slightly greater than 5, so that our procedure is valid.]

Because this confidence interval includes negative numbers and positive numbers, we are far from certain whether $p_1 - p_2$ is negative or positive. That is, in spite of the fact that $\hat{p}_1$ is greater than $\hat{p}_2$, we cannot be certain that the *population* proportion p_1 is greater than p_2. This is primarily because of the relatively "small" sample sizes involved. But since these types of sample sizes are typical of (or even greater than) those from real studies, we should learn to be wary of statements such as "This model has a higher proportion of breakdowns than that one." The experiment that produces such a statement may contain a considerable amount of sampling error.

EXAMPLE 7.10

Suppose that the Food and Drug Administration (FDA) wishes to test the claim of a drug company that its new cold tablets really help cold sufferers get rid of their colds faster. To do this, the FDA chooses $2n$ people at random. Half of these people, labeled group 1, are told to start taking the new medicine as soon as they get their next cold. The other half, labeled group 2, are given a placebo when they get their next cold. (The placebo is a pill of worthless medical value, but the group 2 people are not told this.) For each group, the proportion who recover within seven days is observed. These proportions, $\hat{p}_1$ and $\hat{p}_2$, estimate the proportions p_1 and p_2 of *all* people who would recover within seven days with and without the new medicine. How large must n be to ensure with 95% confidence that the maximum error in estimating $p_1 - p_2$ is no greater than .03? Then with this value of n, suppose that 45%

of the group 1 people recover in seven days or less, while only 37% of the group 2 people recover this quickly. Find the resulting 95% confidence interval for $p_1 - p_2$.

SOLUTION

Since we want the maximum probable error to be no greater than .03, we set $B = .03$ and calculate the required value of n from

$$n = \frac{(z_{.025})^2}{2B^2} = \frac{(1.96)^2}{2(.03)^2} = 2134.22$$

which we round up to 2135. Again we find that a huge sample size is needed to obtain the required level of accuracy.

If 2135 people take the new medicine and another 2135 people take the placebo, and if the sample proportions who recover within seven days are $\hat{p}_1 = .45$ and $\hat{p}_2 = .37$, then a 95% confidence interval for $p_1 - p_2$ is

$$\hat{p}_1 - \hat{p}_2 \pm z_{.025} \, \text{StdErr}(\hat{p}_1 - \hat{p}_2)$$

$$= .45 - .37 \pm 1.96 \sqrt{\frac{.45(.55)}{2135} + \frac{.37(.63)}{2135}}$$

$$= .08 \pm .0294$$

or approximately from .05 to .11. Therefore, we can conclude with 95% confidence that an extra 5 to 11% of the population will get over their colds within seven days by taking the new medicine.

To reiterate one of the main results that emerges from these examples, confidence intervals for proportions tend to be surprisingly wide unless the sample sizes are very large. This often leaves the investigator with two options, neither very appealing. On the one hand, he can collect the necessary sample sizes in order to obtain narrow confidence intervals, but the expense of doing so may be very large. On the other hand, he can use smaller sample sizes, but this leads to relatively wide confidence intervals. Therefore, he must find a trade-off between sampling costs and sampling error. Fortunately, the sample size formulas given in these sections are conservative. If we know that the proportions involved are either close to 0 or close to 1, as in Example 7.8, significantly smaller sample sizes can be used.

Problems for Sections 7.6, 7.7

26. A large population of people can be classified as two types: those who currently own a Japanese car and those who do not. A random sample of 80 people from this population shows that 42 own Japanese cars. Find 99%, 95%, and 90% confidence intervals for the proportion of Japanese car owners in this population.

27. How large a sample of people should we take in Problem 26 to be 95% confident that the true proportion of Japanese car owners does not differ from the sample proportion by more than .05?

28. In baseball a player's "batting average" is the number of successful times at bat divided by his total times at bat. Assume that a given player's number of successful times at bat follows a binomial distribution with parameters n and p, where n is his total times at bat.

   a. If p is known to be .270 (based on several past years), find two numbers, p_1 and p_2, such that the player's batting average next year will fall between p_1 and p_2 with probability .95. Assume that he will go to bat 400 times next year.

   b. For a player whose value of p is unknown and who is successful 26 out of 100 times at bat during a given month, find a 95% confidence interval for his value of p.

   c. If the 100 at bats in part (b) are consecutive at bats, what assumption (or assumptions) used for the confidence interval calculation might be questionable? Explain.

29. It is well known that a higher percentage of people enlisting in the military today have high school diplomas than in 1973 (when the draft was discontinued.) (Reference: *Time*, Mar. 7, 1983, p. 68.) Consider two random samples of 100 military enlistees each, one in 1973 and one today. The 1973 sample includes 57 people with high school diplomas, while today's sample includes 80 people with high school diplomas. Find a 95% confidence interval for the difference between the proportion of all military enlistees with high school diplomas in 1973 and the similar proportion today.

30. Referring to Problem 29, how large would the samples need to be (assuming that they are of equal size) to make the requested confidence interval no longer than .02? If the samples were this large and the sample proportions were the same as in Problem 29, what would the resulting confidence interval be?

31. In the 1980s many U.S. universities saw a significant increase in the percentage of freshmen electing business as their intended majors. Suppose that a random sample of 500 freshmen from U.S. universities reveals that 176 intend to major in business.

   a. Find a 90% confidence interval for the proportion of all U.S. university freshmen who intend to major in business.

   b. Find a 90% confidence interval for the proportion of all U.S. university freshmen who do not intend to major in business. How is this confidence interval related to the one in part (a)? Could you deduce it from the one in part (a) without doing any calculations?

32. A significant proportion of the food and drug products introduced between 1964 and 1979 are no longer on the market. (Reference: T. P. Hustad and T. J. Mitchell, "Creative Market Planning in a Partisan Environment," *Business Horizons*, Vol. 25, 1982, pp. 58–65.) Suppose that you obtain a list of 85 products that were introduced during that time. If you find that only 61 of these are still available, what is the resulting 90% confidence interval for the proportion of all such products still on the market? What is a 90% confidence interval for the proportion of all such products that are *not* still on the market?

33. Suppose it is known that the proportion of all U.S. children who have had chicken pox in the past two years is no greater than .25, but that the exact proportion is not known.

   a. How large a sample of children is needed to form a 90% confidence interval for this proportion that has length no greater than .02? (Keep the sample size as low as possible.)

   b. If a sample of the size from part (a) shows that 15.3% of the children have had chicken pox in the past two years, find the resulting 90% confidence interval for the population proportion. Check that its length is no longer than .02.

34. In one study it was found that 3% of U.S. companies pay their workers not to smoke, and the similar percentage for Canadian companies was 6%. (Reference: "Smoking Policies," *Industry Week*, Feb. 22, 1982, p. 101.) Let p_1 and p_2 be the population proportions of all U.S. and Canadian companies that pay these incentives. If we are interested in obtaining a 95% confidence interval for $p_1 - p_2$, approximately how large would the sample sizes in the study have to be before we could legitimately use the large-sample procedure from this chapter?

35. Following the night when the President gives a televised speech, a pollster wishes to sample a random number of people in order to estimate the population proportion who reacted favorably to the speech. If this proportion is p, the pollster would like to make a statement of the form: p is in the interval from $\hat{p} - .01$ to $\hat{p} + .01$ (for some $\hat{p}$) with 95% confidence.

   a. How many people must be sampled?

   b. Using the sample size from part (a), what will the resulting 95% confidence interval be if 41% of the sampled people reacted favorably? Why is the length of this confidence interval slightly less than what was required?

36. Suppose that we wish to find a 90% confidence interval for $p_1 - p_2$, where p_1 is the proportion of families in state 1 who earn at least $20,000 per year, and p_2 is the similar proportion for state 2.

a. If we decide to sample n families from each state, how large must n be to ensure a confidence interval of length no longer than .04?

b. If we use the value of n from part (a) and then observe $\hat{p}_1 = .392$ and $\hat{p}_2 = .351$, what is the resulting confidence interval for $p_1 - p_2$?

37. We have heard much about the effectiveness of the Japanese workers in comparison to U.S. workers. But one recent study concluded that Japanese blue-collar workers are not necessarily *happier* at their work than their U.S. counterparts. Suppose that the study sampled n Japanese and n U.S. workers.

a. If p_1 and p_2 are the two population proportions, how large must n be to ensure with 90% confidence that the error in estimating $p_1 - p_2$ is no greater than .05?

b. How does the answer to part (a) change if we change the confidence level to 95%?

c. If we observe $\hat{p}_1 = .632$ and $\hat{p}_2 = .681$ for the Japanese and U.S. samples, respectively, with the sample sizes from part (a), what is the resulting 90% confidence interval for $p_1 - p_2$? Answer the same question if these $\hat{p}$'s are based on the sample size from part (b) and we want a 95% confidence interval. Comment on the results.

38. The telephone company would like to know the proportion p of all residential (non-business) long-distance phone calls that are made during times when the lowest rates are in effect. In each of n randomly selected residential phone bills, the company inserts a small questionnaire asking whether the family's most recent long-distance phone call was made when the lowest rates were in effect. How large must n be so that the resulting estimate of p will be off by no more than .01 from the true p with probability .95? (Assume that all people who receive questionnaires respond.) What is the maximum length of the resulting 95% confidence interval for p?

7.8

Summary of Confidence Interval Formulas

In Table 7.3 we summarize the formulas for the confidence intervals we have learned in this chapter.

Table 7.3

1. Parameter to be estimated: μ
   Assumptions: Population is normal or sample size is large ($n \geq 30$).
   Point estimate: $\bar{X}$
   Standard error of point estimate: $\text{StdErr}(\bar{X}) = \sigma/\sqrt{n}$ (Use s for σ if σ is unknown.)
   Confidence interval: $\bar{X} \pm z_{\alpha/2} \, \text{StdErr}(\bar{X})$

2. Parameter to be estimated: $\mu_1 - \mu_2$
   Assumptions: Populations are normal or sample sizes are large ($n_1 \geq 30$, $n_2 \geq 30$); observations from two populations are independent.
   Point estimate: $\bar{X}_1 - \bar{X}_2$
   Standard error of point estimate: $\text{StdErr}(\bar{X}_1 - \bar{X}_2) = \sqrt{\sigma_1^2/n_1 + \sigma_2^2/n_2}$
   (Use s_1^2 for σ_1^2 and s_2^2 for σ_2^2 if σ's are unknown.)
   Confidence interval: $\bar{X}_1 - \bar{X}_2 \pm z_{\alpha/2} \, \text{StdErr}(\bar{X}_1 - \bar{X}_2)$

3. Parameter to be estimated: p
   Assumptions: Sample size is large ($n\hat{p}(1 - \hat{p}) \geq 5$).
   Point estimate: $\hat{p}$
   Standard error of point estimate: $\text{StdErr}(\hat{p}) = \sqrt{\hat{p}(1 - \hat{p})/n}$
   Confidence interval: $\hat{p} \pm z_{\alpha/2} \, \text{StdErr}(\hat{p})$

(*continued*)

Table 7.3 (*continued*)

4. Parameter to be estimated: $p_1 - p_2$
   Assumptions: Sample sizes are large ($n_1\hat{p}_1(1 - \hat{p}_1) \geq 5$ and $n_2\hat{p}_2(1 - \hat{p}_2) \geq 5$);
   observations from two populations are independent.
   Point estimate: $\hat{p}_1 - \hat{p}_2$
   Standard error of point estimate:
   $$\text{StdErr}(\hat{p}_1 - \hat{p}_2) = \sqrt{\hat{p}_1(1 - \hat{p}_1)/n_1 + \hat{p}_2(1 - \hat{p}_2)/n_2}$$
   Confidence interval: $\hat{p}_1 - \hat{p}_2 \pm z_{\alpha/2} \text{StdErr}(\hat{p}_1 - \hat{p}_2)$

Summary

This chapter has introduced one of the two main areas of statistical inference, estimation. (The other area is hypothesis testing.) When a population parameter is unknown and we attempt to estimate it from the information in a random sample, we generally obtain two types of results. The first is called a point estimate, or a best guess, for the value of the unknown parameter. The second is called a confidence interval. The latter is probably the more useful of the two because it indicates how accurate the point estimate is. If the confidence interval is narrow, we know that the point estimate is quite accurate. But if the confidence interval is wide, the probability of a fairly large difference between the point estimate and the true parameter value is substantial.

So far, we have assumed that the sample sizes are relatively large ($n \geq 30$). In this case the sampling distributions for the parameters discussed in Chapter 6 are approximately normal, which allows us to compute confidence intervals for the population parameters quite easily from the normal tables. We are also able to calculate the sample size required to reduce the length of a confidence interval to a specified value. This is obviously important when sampling is expensive. Unfortunately, we saw that narrow confidence intervals do not come cheaply. For example, to reduce the length of a confidence interval by a factor of 2, we must typically increase the sample size by a factor of 4. This simply points out the inevitable trade-off that must be made between sampling cost and accuracy in any estimation problem.

Applications

Application 7.1   Television advertisers are becoming increasingly concerned about the amount of time viewers spend watching their videocassette recorders (VCRs). Whether they watch prerecorded films or shows they recorded themselves, the chances are that they will not watch any commercials. Just how prevalent is this practice of watching VCRs? Yorke and Kitchen did a survey of VCR owners in 1983. (Reference: David A. Yorke and Philip J. Kitchen, "Channel Flickers and Video Speeders," *Journal of Advertising Research*, Vol. 25, 1985, pp. 21–25.) They sampled owners from four types of residential areas that differed with respect to key demographic variables. The VCR owners in each area were asked how many hours of recorded commercial TV they watched per week and also how many hours of prerecorded films they watched per week. The results for each area are shown in Table 7.4 as means and 95% confidence intervals. The lengths of these confidence intervals are also shown. Although Yorke and Kitchen did not report sample sizes, they did imply that the sample sizes in the four areas were equal. From this we can conclude that the standard deviations (as well as the means) were different among the four areas. These different standard deviations are the cause of the differences in confidence interval lengths.

Table 7.4

	Hours of Commercial TV per Week		
Area	Mean	95% confidence interval	Length
1	2.263	1.785–2.741	.956
2	2.945	1.988–3.901	1.913
3	2.177	1.400–2.953	1.553
4	2.840	2.248–3.432	1.184
	Hours of Prerecorded Films per Week		
Area	Mean	95% confidence interval	Length
1	2.947	1.990–3.904	1.914
2	2.945	1.846–4.043	2.197
3	3.295	2.092–4.497	2.405
4	3.200	2.374–4.026	1.652

The data in Table 7.4 show the separate amounts of time viewers in the four areas watch recorded commercial TV and prerecorded films. But what can we say about the *total* amount of time they watch their VCRs? To find the *mean* total time, we simply add the separate means. This is because the mean of a sum is always the sum of the means. For example, the mean total for area 1 is 2.263 + 2.947, or 5.21 hours per week. However, we cannot do the same type of addition for confidence intervals. That is, again using area 1, we cannot say that a 95% confidence interval for total hours of VCR viewing is from 1.785 + 1.990 to 2.741 + 3.904. Although the mathematical reason is slightly beyond the level of this book, the basic problem is that the standard deviation of a sum is not the sum of the standard deviations. In fact, from the information given, there is no way to find a 95% confidence interval for the total number of hours watched in any particular area.

Application 7.2   Unit pricing information was introduced to many supermarkets in the late 1960s. This is information posted on products that allows consumers to compare prices per unit. For example, the information might show price per pound or price per fluid ounce. Aaker and Ford report results of studies performed in 1970 and 1980 that measured consumers' awareness and use of unit pricing. (Reference: David A. Aaker and Gary T. Ford, "Unit Pricing Ten Years Later: A Replication," *Journal of Marketing,* Vol. 47, 1983, pp. 118–122.) The 1970 study was based on a sample of 878 shoppers; the 1980 study had a sample size of 481. These studies suggest that approximately 59.7% of 1970 suburban shoppers were aware of unit pricing in the store where they shopped, and of those who were aware, approximately 63.0% used this information in their shopping decisions. The similar percentages in 1980 were 90.4% and 66.2%.

From these data we can find several confidence intervals. Let $p_{1,1970}$ be the proportion of all suburban shoppers who were aware of unit pricing in 1970. Of the subpopulation who were aware of unit pricing in 1970, let $p_{2,1970}$ be the proportion who actually used this information. Define $p_{1,1980}$ and $p_{2,1980}$ similarly for the 1980 population. Then a 95% confidence interval for $p_{1,1970}$ is

$$.597 \pm 1.96 \sqrt{\frac{.597(.403)}{878}} = .597 \pm .032$$

or from .565 to .629. To obtain a confidence interval for $p_{2,1970}$, notice that the relevant sample size is $.597(878) = 524$, for this is the number in the 1970 sample who were aware of unit pricing. Therefore, a 95% confidence interval for $p_{2,1970}$ is

$$.630 \pm 1.96 \sqrt{\frac{.630(.370)}{524}} = .630 \pm .041$$

or from .589 to .671. Similar 95% confidence intervals can be calculated for $p_{1,1980}$ and $p_{2,1980}$. The results are (1) from .878 to .930 for $p_{1,1980}$, and (2) from .618 to .706 for $p_{2,1980}$. Finally, we can also calculate a 95% confidence interval for the difference between the proportions aware of unit pricing in 1980 and in 1970, that is, $p_{1,1980} - p_{1,1970}$. This confidence interval is

$$(.904 - .597) \pm 1.96 \sqrt{\frac{.597(.403)}{878} + \frac{.904(.096)}{481}} = .307 \pm .042$$

or from .265 to .349. This means that we can be 95% confident that the increased percentage of suburban shoppers aware of unit pricing from 1970 to 1980 was between 26.5 and 34.9%.

Glossary of Terms

Point estimate   a rule for converting the sample data into a single numerical estimate of an unknown population parameter

Confidence interval   an interval, with endpoints calculated from the sample data, that is likely to include the unknown population parameter

Standard error of an estimate   the standard deviation of the estimate

Bias of an estimate   the difference between the expected value of the estimate and the parameter being estimated

Unbiased estimate   an estimate with zero bias

Relative efficiency of one estimate with respect to another   the ratio of their variances

Maximum probable error in estimating a parameter   the half-length of the corresponding confidence interval; measures the maximum difference that is likely to occur between the point estimate and the parameter

Important Formulas

1. Formula for the bias of $\hat{\theta}$

$$\text{Bias}(\hat{\theta}) = E(\hat{\theta}) - \theta$$

2. Formulas for the confidence intervals discussed in this chapter—see Table 7.3

3. Sample size required to produce a maximum probable error for μ equal to B

$$n = \frac{(z_{\alpha/2})^2 \sigma^2}{B^2}$$

4. Sample size required from each population to produce a maximum probable error for $\mu_1 - \mu_2$ equal to B

$$n_1 = n_2 = \frac{(z_{\alpha/2})^2(\sigma_1^2 + \sigma_2^2)}{B^2}$$

5. Sample size required to guarantee that the maximum probable error for p will be no greater than B

$$n = \frac{(z_{\alpha/2})^2}{4B^2}$$

6. Sample size required from each population to guarantee that the maximum probable error for $p_1 - p_2$ will be no greater than B

$$n_1 = n_2 = \frac{(z_{\alpha/2})^2}{2B^2}$$

End-of-Chapter Problems

39. The mean and standard deviation of the diameters of a sample of 250 rivet heads manufactured by a company are .73595 inch and .00049 inch, respectively. Find 99%, 95%, and 90% confidence intervals for the mean diameter of all the rivet heads manufactured by this company.

40. The purchase amounts of 30 randomly selected customers at a department store are shown below. Assume that the distribution of all purchase amounts has mean μ and standard deviation σ. Find a 95% confidence interval for μ. Is your result valid even if the distribution of all purchase amounts is somewhat skewed to the right? Explain.

Purchase Amounts (Dollars)

13.57	24.64	22.78	15.26	75.42	26.43	45.89
12.32	16.75	64.23	25.67	41.76	31.24	26.77
18.34	7.44	20.66	10.45	8.44	65.22	19.42
47.32	16.78	25.38	27.32	31.44	87.23	6.71
62.30	17.26					

41. In Problem 40, how many customers would have to be sampled to reduce the length of the 95% confidence interval for μ to $4? (Use the sample standard deviation from Problem 40 to estimate σ.)

42. Consider a required calculus course at a large university. In one particular semester 1000 students take this course. They are divided randomly into 20 discussion sections of 50 students each. Each discussion section leader calculates a 95% confidence interval for the population mean of all 1000 students, based upon the 50 students in that section. Let X be the number of the 20 confidence intervals that include the true population mean.

a. Find the mean and standard deviation of X.
b. Find the probability that X is at least 17. (Use the binomial table.)

43. Consider 10 observations, $X_1, X_2, \ldots, X_{10}$, from a $N(\mu, \sigma^2)$ population. Show that $(X_1 + X_2 + X_3)/3$ and $(X_1 + X_2 + \cdots + X_8 + 2X_9)/10$ are both unbiased estimates of μ, but that neither is as efficient as $\bar{X}$, the sample mean of all 10 observations. (Use the rules of expected values in Chapter 4.) Explain this result intuitively.

*44. In a recent television program on income tax cheating, the following result of an opinion poll was quoted: 36% of those people questioned believe that cheating on income taxes is becoming more common. In a parenthetical remark, the program stated that the poll was based on a sample of 1008 registered voters, and "the sampling error is plus or minus 3%." Based on what you have learned in this chapter, explain what the statement in quotes means. Is it correct?

45. A random sample of 20 U.S. cities shows the following average household incomes.

Household Incomes (Dollars)

21,426	19,457	18,571	20,216	22,612	16,784	17,324
25,425	17,562	19,742	23,652	27,402	17,342	19,880
23,773	27,832	21,935	17,362	19,320	25,621	

a. Find a 95% confidence interval for the proportion of all U.S. cities with an average household income between $23,000 and $27,000.
b. Find a 95% confidence interval for the mean average household income, where the mean is taken over all U.S.

cities. Assume the population of incomes is normally distributed.

c. Based on this sample, approximately how many more cities would have to be included in the sample to reduce the length of the confidence interval for the mean in part (b) to $1500?

46. A large shipment of electronics parts is received from a supplier, and the parts are sampled in order to estimate the mean weight per part.

a. On the basis of past experience, the standard deviation of the weights is known to be 15 grams. How large a random sample should be drawn if the maximum difference between the actual mean weight and the sample mean weight is required to be 2 grams with 90% confidence?

b. Assume that the standard deviation of weights in the population is unknown, and a random sample of 60 parts yields a sample mean of 260 grams and sample standard deviation of 13.5 grams. Find a 95% confidence interval for the mean weight in the entire population.

47. The number of fluid ounces in successive soft-drink bottles from a production line is being measured. A random sample of 40 soft-drink bottles shows a mean $\overline{X}$ of 11.863 ounces and a standard deviation s of .020 ounce.

a. Use this information to find a 99% confidence interval for the population mean μ.

b. How many more bottles should be examined in order to have 99% confidence that the error in estimating the population mean is no more than .002 ounce?

*48. In a large study of male managers, 31.8% agreed with the statement that "people are reluctant to work for females." (Reference: A. S. Baron, "What Men Are Saying About Women in Business," *Business Horizons*, Vol. 25, 1982, pp. 10–14.) If the resulting 90% confidence interval for the proportion of all male managers who agree with this statement does not include the value .35, what is the smallest the sample size could have been?

49. Suppose that we want to estimate the mean amount of money families have spent on stereo equipment in the past five years. Specifically, we want a 95% confidence interval for this mean to have length approximately equal to $20. A small sample of 15 families shows a mean of $245 and a standard deviation of $75.

a. How many *more* families should be sampled to obtain the required confidence interval?

b. If the sample mean and sample standard deviation of the entire sample, based on the sample size in part (a), turn

out to be $273 and $96, what is the resulting confidence interval for the mean?

*50. Suppose that we are attempting to find a confidence interval for the difference between two population means, $\mu_1 - \mu_2$, that has a given length L. We gave a formula for the required sample sizes when it was assumed that $n_1 = n_2$. But assume now that we decide to sample twice as heavily from population 1 as from population 2; that is, $n_1 = 2n_2$. Find the values of n_1 and n_2 that make $L = 25$ when $\sigma_1 = 100$, $\sigma_2 = 50$, and the confidence level is 95%. [*Hint:* Use the formula for the confidence interval for $(\mu_1 - \mu_2)$.]

*51. In Section 7.6 we found an approximate confidence interval for a population proportion p by substituting $\hat{p}$ for p in the expression for the standard error of $\hat{p}$. A more rigorous approach yields the following confidence interval for p:

$$\frac{\hat{p} + k/2}{1 + k} \pm \frac{\sqrt{k\hat{p}(1 - \hat{p}) + k^2/4}}{1 + k}$$

where $k = (z_{\alpha/2})^2/n$. Suppose that a sample of size 1000 from a population of smokers and nonsmokers reveals 200 smokers. Find the approximate 95% confidence interval for p, the population proportion of smokers, from the formula given in the chapter. Then find the more exact 95% confidence interval for p from the formula above. Compare the two confidence intervals you obtain. Do they have the same length? Are they both centered at $\hat{p}$?

*52. Start with the inequality

$$-z_{\alpha/2} \le \frac{(\hat{p} - p)}{\sqrt{p(1 - p)/n}} \le z_{a/2}$$

and manipulate it algebraically to obtain the confidence interval for p given in Problem 51. That is, you should end up with the inequality

$$\frac{\hat{p} + k/2}{1 + k} - \frac{\sqrt{k\hat{p}(1 - \hat{p}) + k^2/4}}{1 + k} \le p$$

$$\le \frac{\hat{p} + k/2}{1 + k} + \frac{\sqrt{k\hat{p}(1 - \hat{p}) + k^2/4}}{1 + k}$$

where again $k = (z_{\alpha/2})^2/n$. [*Hint:* The quadratic formula says that if $ax^2 + bx + c = 0$, then

$$x = \frac{-b \pm \sqrt{b^2 - 4ac}}{2a}$$

From this and the graph of the parabola $y = ax^2 + bx + c$, it follows that if $ax^2 + bx + x \leq 0$ and if $a > 0$, then x is between

$$(-b - \sqrt{b^2 - 4ac})/2a \text{ and } (-b + \sqrt{b^2 - 4ac})/2a.]$$

*53. As in Section 7.2, let θ by any unknown parameter, and let $\hat{\theta}$ be an estimate of θ.
   a. Why is $E[(\hat{\theta} - \theta)^2]$ not necessarily the variance of $\hat{\theta}$?
   b. Let $\mu_{\hat{\theta}}$ be the mean of $\hat{\theta}$. Use the rules of expected values from Chapter 4 to show that

$$E[(\hat{\theta} - \theta)^2] = E[\hat{\theta} - \mu_{\hat{\theta}})^2] + (\mu_{\hat{\theta}} - \theta)^2$$

   [*Hint:*   Write $(\hat{\theta} - \theta)^2$ as $[(\hat{\theta} - \mu_{\hat{\theta}}) + (\mu_{\hat{\theta}} - \theta)]^2$; then multiply out this square and take expected values.]
   c. Interpret the two expressions on the right of the equation in part (b) in terms of variance and bias.

*54. Suppose that we use samples of size 200 to build what we hope are 90% confidence intervals for a population proportion p. Each sample is drawn independently from the same population. If 100 such samples are drawn and we verify that 84 of these include the true value of p, find a 95% confidence interval for the proportion of all possible samples of size 200 that would include the true value of p. Given your answer, do you seriously doubt that your method is producing "90% confidence intervals" for p? Why or why not?

55. In the analysis of queueing (waiting-line) systems, it is often convenient to "simulate" the system on a computer several times, using different random numbers each time. Suppose that we do this to estimate the mean wait per customer at a bank during a typical 9-to-5 day. (The wait for any customer lasts from the time the customer enters the bank until the customer's service begins.) On 35 independent simulations of the bank's 9-to-5 day, the following data are obtained, where each number represents the average wait per customer for all customers served during a day. Find a 95% confidence interval for the mean of all such numbers we would find if we simulated an extremely large number of 9-to-5 days.

Average Waiting Times (Minutes)

3.25	4.92	2.93	3.57	4.13	3.21	2.51	4.69	5.01
3.61	2.98	4.07	3.14	4.57	2.75	2.89	3.15	3.54
2.68	2.75	4.01	3.64	3.11	3.25	2.56	2.78	2.95
4.76	4.11	3.57	3.26	2.76	3.78	3.10	2.54	

*56. Assume that the data from Problem 55 are obtained when there are five tellers at the bank. To see whether the bank could afford to employ only four tellers, the simulation is run 35 more times, now with only four tellers available. The 35 simulated average waits per customer are shown below. Find a 95% confidence interval for the *difference* between the mean wait per customer in the four-teller and five-teller systems.

Average Waiting Times (Minutes)

4.75	4.92	4.93	3.57	4.13	5.21	4.99	4.69	5.01
3.78	5.25	4.35	3.47	3.86	3.95	4.25	4.96	5.25
4.76	4.52	4.01	3.74	5.10	4.14	3.68	3.51	3.94
5.50	4.28	3.66	3.06	5.31	5.20	4.76	3.89	

*57. Suppose that we want to obtain a confidence interval for a population mean when the population standard deviation is $\sigma = 10$. Specifically, we want α to be no larger than .1, and we want the confidence interval to be of length 1. Find 10 pairs (α, n) that will accomplish this objective. Make sure that each α is between .005 and .10, and that each n is at least 30. (There are an infinite number of such pairs—just choose any 10 of them.) Then graph these pairs on an α, n set of axes. (Let the vertical axis be the α-axis and let the horizontal axis be the n-axis.) Join the resulting points with a curve as well as possible.

58. A supermarket is considering adding one or more checkout lines because some customers have been complaining of excessive waiting times in the lines. Before taking any action, the store gets an employee to gather data on the times customers wait in line. For 50 randomly selected customers, the employee observes a mean waiting time of 3.75 minutes and a standard deviation of 1.2 minutes.
   a. Find a 95% confidence interval for the mean of all customers' waiting times.
   b. Your answer in part (a) is correct only if the 50 customers are selected randomly (throughout the day). Why would your answer be incorrect if the 50 customers selected were 50 *consecutive* customers arriving at the checkout lines? (Why would you suspect the independence assumption to be violated? Intuitively, how might this affect the accuracy of the confidence interval statement?)

*59. Consider a distribution of salaries in a large population that is skewed to the right. If many samples, each of size 3, are taken from this population and the sample means for these samples are computed, does the Central Limit Theorem state that if we have taken enough (at least 30) such samples, the resulting group of $\bar{X}$'s will be approximately normally distributed? Explain.

*60. In terms of reducing the length of a confidence interval for μ (with σ known), which has the greater effect: (1) quadrupling the size of n and leaving the confidence level at 99%, or (2) leaving n the same and changing the confidence level from 99% to 95%? Why?

*61. The president of a salespeople training company wrote in a 1981 *Marketing News* article that "the art of personal selling has reached an all-time professional low in the United States," with a success rate (proportion of calls that lead to sales) as low as 10% nationally. (Reference: Robert Evans, "Training, Employee Orientation Hike Sales Rep Performance," *Marketing News*, Nov. 13, 1981.) He cited various reasons for the failure of salespeople to make sales: They fail to follow-up on a deal properly, they lack empathy with the buyer, they treat all buyers equally, they sell price rather than product quality, and others. But in Evans's eyes, these are all the results of poor training programs. Suppose that we track two groups of salespeople, trained by two different types of training programs but practically equivalent in other aspects, such as college training, age, and type of product being sold. After n sales attempts, we observe that the first group is successful on 11.5% of its n calls. Similarly, the second group is successful on 8.6% of its n calls. If $p_1 - p_2$ is the difference between the population proportions of successful calls for the two groups, how large must n be before a 95% confidence interval for $p_1 - p_2$ does *not* contain the value 0?

62. A 1985 *Wall Street Journal* article reported that a vaccine to prevent chickenpox is now being tested. (Reference: *Wall Street Journal*, Jan. 16, 1985.) Although there is still some concern about the safety of the vaccine, it does appear to be effective. In a controlled experiment the vaccine was given to 468 children in the Philadelphia area, while a placebo (a drug of no value) was given to 446 of their brothers and sisters. Nine months later, 39 of those receiving the placebo had contracted chickenpox, whereas none of the vaccinated children did so.
   a. Assuming that taking the placebo is equivalent to taking no medicine, and also assuming that the children who took the placebo are a representative sample of all children, find a point estimate and a 90% confidence interval for the proportion of all unvaccinated children who will contract chickenpox in the next nine months.
   b. Suppose that an unknown proportion p of all children would

contract chickenpox within nine months even if they received the new vaccine. What is the probability that none of 468 such vaccinated children would contract chicken pox, assuming that p is equal to the lower endpoint of the confidence interval in part (a)? Repeat the calculation if p is only $\frac{1}{10}$ this large. Intuitively, what can you conclude from these calculations?

63. With the large number of people trying to get degrees in business and eventually obtain managerial jobs, we can infer that there must be something attractive about being a manager. Perhaps the attraction is simply pay, but it could also be the quality of the job itself. Baucus and Near reported the findings of a 1977 University of Michigan study that compared managers' and nonmanagers' attitudes toward their jobs. (Reference: David A. Baucus and Janet P. Near, "Managers and the Good Life: Fact or Fiction?" *Business Horizons*, Vol. 26, 1983, pp. 20–23.) The study included a random sample of 185 managers and 1819 nonmanagers. Their attitudes toward five important aspects of their jobs are listed below. Treating each of these five aspects separately, find a 95% confidence interval for the difference between the population proportions of managers and nonmanagers who respond affirmatively to a given statement. That is, find a 95% confidence interval for $p_1 - p_2$, where p_1 is the proportion of all managers who respond affirmatively to a given statement, and p_2 is defined similarly for nonmanagers.

Statement	Percentage Responding Yes	
	Managers	Nonmanagers
1. I get to do a number of different things.	98	83
2. People are affected by my work.	94	88
3. I have freedom to decide what I do.	81	55
4. My supervisor or co-workers let me know how I'm doing.	70	72
5. I am satisfied with my job.	92	87

*64. Referring to Application 7.2 (the Aaker and Ford study of unit pricing), let $p_{3,1970}$ be the proportion of all shoppers in 1970 who were aware of unit pricing *and* used this information in their shopping decisions. Define $p_{3,1980}$ similarly for the 1980 population.

   a. Find a 95% confidence interval for $p_{3,1970}$. Do the same for $p_{3,1980}$. How do these proportions differ from the proportions $p_{2,1970}$ and $p_{2,1980}$ defined in Application 7.2?

   b. Find a 95% confidence interval for $p_{3,1980} - p_{3,1970}$.

65. Since World War II there has been an increasing demand for education by the business world. The MBA degree is now more popular than ever. For example, Swinyard and Bond conducted a study of 11,000 executives newly promoted to a vice-presidency or presidency and found that the percentage having a master's degree increased from 18% to 25% between 1967 and 1976; approximately 45% of these degrees were in business. (Reference: A. Swinyard and F. Bond, "Who Gets Promoted?" *Harvard Business Review,* 1980, pp. 12–18.) Similarly, a more recent study reported by Runde found that nearly half of the upper-level executives under the age of 40 at large and medium-sized companies possessed an MBA degree. (Reference: R. Runde, "Does an MBA Still Pay?" *Money,* 1982, pp. 126–130.) Suppose that we conduct a similar study of 85 upper-level executives in 1986 and find that 53 of these possess an MBA degree. Find a 95% confidence interval for the proportion of all upper-level executives in 1986 who possess an MBA degree given this sample information.

66. In a study of the relationship between sales force turnover and job satisfaction, Futrell and Parasuraman questioned a sample of 263 salespeople from a large pharmaceutical organization. (Reference: Charles M. Futrell and A. Parasuraman, "The Relationship of Satisfaction and Performance to Salesforce Turnover," *Journal of Marketing,* Vol. 48, 1984, pp. 33–40.) To measure the turnover, or "propensity to leave,"

the people were asked: "To what extent are you presently seeking to change jobs?" All respondents answered on a 5-point scale, ranging from "to no extent" to "to a very great extent." For job satisfaction, the authors used the Job Descriptive Index, a well-known questionnaire that uses 72 descriptive adjectives relating to the worker's promotion, pay, supervision, work, and co-workers. In addition, the supervisors of these 263 salespeople were asked to rate their job performances. On the basis of these ratings, the salespeople were split into two groups: the 130 "low performers" and the 133 "high performers." Summary measures on job satisfaction and propensity to leave for these two groups are shown below. Find a 95% confidence interval for the mean difference between the high and low performers for each of the six measures shown.

Measure	High Performers		Low Performers	
	Mean	Standard Deviation	Mean	Standard Deviation
Satisfaction with pay	28.34	11.14	27.99	13.55
Satisfaction with promotion	34.57	15.80	34.86	16.45
Satisfaction with co-workers	46.74	8.01	44.16	9.48
Satisfaction with work	38.77	8.60	37.68	9.25
Satisfaction with supervision	45.04	9.02	44.95	9.15
Propensity to leave	1.55	.90	1.76	1.11

Computer Problems

(These problems are to be used in conjunction with the computer software package.)

1. Consider a population of families where 35% have one car, 45% have two cars, 15% have three cars, and 5% have four cars. We are interested in the sampling distribution of the sample mean number of cars per family when this sample mean is based on a random sample of n families.

   a. Use the SIMULATE program to approximate this sampling distribution when $n = 3$.

   b. Repeat part (a) when $n = 6$. (Be prepared to wait awhile for the computer results.)

   c. Does the Central Limit Theorem suggest that the sampling distribution in part (b) should be closer to normal than the sampling distribution in part (a)? Is it closer to being normal?

2. The cost of living indices for the 232 cities listed in Table VII of Appendix D are all relative to a "base" index of 100 for each category. Therefore, for any given category, we would

expect about half the cities to have an index above 100 and about half to have an index below 100. Use the PROPORTN program to find a 99% confidence interval for the proportion of all cities (including those not listed) that have a housing cost index less than or equal to 100.0. Does this confidence interval include the value .5? Repeat with the health care index and with the utilities index.

3. Repeat Problem 2, except that now you must find a 99% confidence interval for the mean housing (or health care or utilities) index over all cities. Use data from only 50 of the 232 cities listed, and use the RNSAMPLE program to select the 50 cities in the sample. (Imagine the cities are listed from 1 to 232. Then RNSAMPLE will tell which 50 of these numbers to use.) Does the confidence interval include the value 100?

Maximum Likelihood Estimation

In Section 7.2 we described desirable properties of estimates, but we did not suggest a systematic method for *finding* good estimates. For some population parameters there are "natural" estimates. Examples include the sample mean $\overline{X}$ for the population mean μ and the sample proportion $\hat{p}$ for the population proportion p. Fortunately, these natural estimates also have the desirable properties we discussed in Section 7.2. But what do we do when there is no obvious estimate of an unknown parameter θ? In this appendix we at least partially answer this question by discussing a very powerful method for deriving good estimates. This is called the *method of maximum likelihood*. (In the chapters on regression, we discuss a second method, the method of least squares.)

The method of maximum likelihood is based on a very simple idea. Suppose that we observe a random sample $X_1, X_2, \ldots, X_n$ from a population with one unknown parameter θ. We do not know the value of θ, but for any specific value of θ, we can imagine the sample having been generated from a population with this value. For some values of θ, the observed sample would be a very unlikely sample; for other values of θ, it would be a fairly typical sample. The method of maximum likelihood simply chooses the estimate that makes the observed sample most likely.

> The maximum likelihood estimate is the estimate that makes the observed sample values most likely.

To clarify the maximum likelihood procedure, suppose that we are interested in a population with an unknown proportion p of consumers who buy brand A and a proportion $1 - p$ who buy competing brands. If we observe a random sample of 100 consumers, 32 of whom buy brand A, why do we use $\hat{p} = {}^{32}\!/_{100} = .32$ as an estimate of p? The maximum likelihood reason is that the observed value of $\hat{p}$ (32 brand A buyers out of 100) is more likely if the population p is .32 than if p is any value other than .32. We can verify this from the binomial table, which shows the probability of 32 A's out of

Table 7.5

p	P(32 out of 100, given p)
.28	.0579
.285	.0636
.29	.0688
.295	.0735
.30	.0776
.305	.0809
.31	.0833
.315	.0848
.32	.0853 (maximum)
.325	.0848
.33	.0834
.335	.0810
.34	.0779
.345	.0741
.35	.0698
.355	.0650
.36	.0599

100 for various values of p. The relevant probabilities are shown in Table 7.5 for selected values of p.

Although Table 7.5 lists only a few values of p, we could conceivably calculate the probability of 32 A's out of 100 for every value of p between 0 and 1. The resulting graph of these probabilities is shown in Figure 7.8. As Table 7.5 and Figure 7.8 indicate, the maximum probability, or likelihood, of observing 32 A's out of 100 does indeed occur when p equals .32. Therefore, .32 is the maximum likelihood estimate of p.

In general, the idea behind maximum likelihood estimation is much simpler than the actual use of the method. The idea is that we express the likelihood

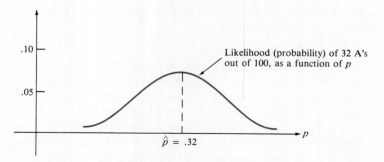

Figure 7.8

of the random sample $X_1, X_2, \ldots, X_n$ in terms of any unknown parameters. Then we maximize this expression with respect to these parameters. Both of these operations may be difficult to perform. First, it is not always easy to express the likelihood in terms of a nice formula. Second, it is often difficult to find the values of the parameters that maximize this formula. At the very least, this usually requires calculus, as indicated by the following important example.

Consider a normal population with mean μ and variance σ^2, and assume that both of these parameters are unknown. The likelihood function $L(\mu, \sigma^2)$ is the joint density of observing the sample values $X_1, X_2, \ldots, X_n$. This turns out to be

$$L(\mu, \sigma^2) = K(\sigma^2)^{-n/2} e^{-1/2 \sum (X_i - \mu)^2 / \sigma^2}$$

where K is a constant that does not involve μ or σ^2. To find the maximum likelihood estimates of μ and σ^2, we need to maximize $L(\mu, \sigma^2)$ with respect to μ and σ^2 (for fixed values of the X's). It turns out that we obtain the same estimates if we instead maximize the logarithm of $L(\mu, \sigma^2)$, which is an easier calculus problem.

The logarithm of $L(\mu, \sigma^2)$ is

$$\ln L(\mu, \sigma^2) = \ln(K) - \frac{n}{2} \ln(\sigma^2) - \frac{1}{2} \sum \frac{(X_i - \mu)^2}{\sigma^2}$$

To maximize this logarithm with respect to μ and σ^2, we take its two partial derivatives, set them equal to 0, and solve for μ and σ^2. (It can be shown that this operation does indeed produce a maximum.) The partial derivative with respect to μ is

$$\frac{\partial}{\partial \mu} [\ln L(\mu, \sigma^2)] = \sum \frac{(X_i - \mu)}{\sigma^2}$$

Setting this equal to 0 and multiplying through by σ^2 gives

$$\sum (X_i - \mu) = 0$$

This simplifies to

$$n\mu = \sum X_i$$

or

$$\mu = \frac{\sum X_i}{n} = \overline{X}$$

Therefore, the maximum likelihood estimate of μ is the sample mean $\overline{X}$.

To find the maximum likelihood estimate of σ^2, we take the partial derivative with respect to σ^2. This is

$$\frac{\partial}{\partial \sigma^2} [\ln L(\mu, \sigma^2)] = -\frac{n}{2\sigma^2} + \frac{1}{2} \sum \frac{(X_i - \mu)^2}{(\sigma^2)^2}$$

We set this equal to 0 and multiply through by $2\sigma^2$ to obtain

$$n = \sum \frac{(X_i - \mu)^2}{\sigma^2}$$

which simplifies to

$$\sigma^2 = \sum \frac{(X_i - \mu)^2}{n}$$

But since the maximum likelihood estimate of μ is $\overline{X}$, we substitute $\overline{X}$ for μ in this expression to obtain the following result.

For a $N(\mu, \sigma^2)$ population, the maximum likelihood estimate of μ is the sample mean $\overline{X}$, and the maximum likelihood estimate of σ^2 is the average of the squared deviations, $\sum (X_i - \overline{X})^2/n$.

Notice that the maximum likelihood estimate of σ^2 is not quite the sample variance s^2, because s^2 has denominator $n - 1$, not n. Therefore, the maximum likelihood estimate of σ^2 is slightly biased (downward), because s^2 is unbiased. However, the difference between these two estimates becomes negligible when n is reasonably large.

References

BREIMAN, L. *Statistics: With a View Toward Applications*. Boston: Houghton Mifflin, 1973.

CANAVOS, G. C. *Applied Probability and Statistical Methods*. Boston: Little, Brown, 1984.

HOGG, R. V. and CRAIG, A. T. *Introduction to Mathematical Statistics*, 4th ed. New York: Macmillan, 1978.

MOOD, A. M., GRAYBILL, F. A., and BOES, D. C. *Introduction to the Theory of Statistics*, 3rd ed. New York: McGraw-Hill, 1974.

NETER, J., WASSERMAN, W., and WHITMORE, G. A. *Applied Statistics*, 2nd ed. Boston: Allyn & Bacon, 1982.

CHAPTER 8

Small-Sample Estimation

Objectives

1. To learn how to make small-sample inferences about the population mean.
2. To learn the role of the t distribution in estimating population means.
3. To learn how to make small-sample inferences about the difference between two population means.
4. To learn how to make inferences about the population variance.
5. To learn the role of the chi-square distribution in estimating the population variance.
6. To learn the role of the F distribution in estimating the ratio of two population variances.

Contents

When a business wants to know how a new or newly revised system will operate, it often resorts to computer simulation. This is particularly true when the system has several unpredictable aspects that interact in a complicated manner. Each "run" of the simulation generates random numbers to quantify the unpredictable aspects of the system, and these are then used to provide a "snapshot" of how the system might evolve through time. The output from one run, for example, might indicate the system's total cost per day over a three-month span. By averaging the outputs from several runs, we can then estimate the mean cost per day over the three-month span. Each run essentially provides one "observation" for estimating this mean.

This is a statistical estimation problem much like the problem studied in Chapter 7. The main difference is that because each run of the simulation can be expensive in terms of computer time, the number of runs is often kept small, say, from 10 to 15. Therefore, the large-sample theory from Chapter 7 is not valid; instead, we require small-sample methods. These small-sample methods, explained in this chapter, will be exploited when we examine the simulated results from a realistic inventory management system.

8.1

Introduction

In Chapter 7 we learned how to estimate population means and proportions when the sample sizes are large. The reason for requiring large sample sizes is that we can then invoke the Central Limit Theorem to justify the use of the normal distribution. But in many applications large sample sizes are either too expensive or are physically unavailable. Then the relevant sampling distributions depend heavily on the population distribution. In this chapter we make the rather strong assumption that the population distributions are normal. This normality assumption leads to several new sampling distributions, called the t distribution, the chi-square distribution, and the F distribution. Fortunately, these new sampling distributions are tabulated in Appendix B and are no more difficult to use than the normal distribution. More important, they are valid even for small sample sizes as long as the population distributions are normal. (Since many populations are *not* normal, we test the "robustness" of this normality assumption in Appendix 8A. That is, we will see how accurate the new distributions are if the populations are not normal.)

The population parameters of primary interest in this chapter are the mean, the difference between two means, the variance, and the ratio of two variances. One omission is small-sample estimation of proportions. This may indeed be done by using the binomial tables in the appropriate way. However, we have chosen not to discuss this topic, for two reasons. First, most surveys used for estimating proportions have large sample sizes. Second, if the sample sizes are small, the resulting estimates contain such a large amount of sampling error (evidenced by extremely wide confidence intervals) that they are practically useless.

8.2

Small-Sample Estimation of the Population Mean

In this section we learn how to estimate the population mean μ when n is small, say, less than 30. We assume that the population distribution is normal and that both the mean μ and the variance σ^2 are unknown. We will again use $\overline{X}$, the sample mean, as a point estimate of μ. However, when we attempt to measure the accuracy of $\overline{X}$, we run into difficulties. As in Chapter 7, we would like to claim that $\overline{X}$ is approximately normal with mean μ and approximate standard error $s/\sqrt{n}$, where s^2 is the sample variance. However, because of the small sample size, the relevant sampling distribution of $\overline{X}$ is no longer normal. Instead, it is a new distribution called the *t distribution with n − 1 degrees of freedom*, as stated below.

> ### Small-Sample Sampling Distribution of $\overline{X}$
>
> $\dfrac{\overline{X} - \mu}{s/\sqrt{n}}$ has a *t* distribution with $n - 1$ degrees of freedom

We now examine the properties of this new distribution.

The t Distribution

The *t* distribution, sometimes called the Student *t* distribution, is a very close relative of the $N(0, 1)$ distribution. (Student was the pseudonym of the statistician Gosset, who discovered this distribution in the early 1900s.) In fact, to the naked eye, their densities are very similar. As we stated above, the *t* distribution is the sampling distribution of $(\overline{X} - \mu)/(s/\sqrt{n})$ when the population is normal. In contrast, we know that the $N(0, 1)$ distribution is the sampling distribution of $(\overline{X} - \mu)/(\sigma/\sqrt{n})$ when the population is normal.

(This is true even for small sample sizes.) So under the normal population assumption, we see that the only difference between the t and $N(0, 1)$ sampling distributions is the use of s in place of σ. The effect of using the random variable s instead of the constant σ is that an extra source of variability is introduced. Hence the t distribution has a slightly larger variance than the $N(0, 1)$ distribution.

Actually, there are many t distributions, one for each sample size n. In general, the feature that distinguishes one t distribution from another is a parameter, often denoted by the Greek letter ν (nu), called the *degrees of freedom* of the t distribution. Each t density looks very similar to a $N(0, 1)$ density. In particular, each t density is symmetric around 0, is bell-shaped, and has a variance close to 1. However, the exact variance of a t distribution with ν degrees of freedom is $\nu/(\nu - 2)$.

> *Variance of the t Distribution with ν Degrees of Freedom*
>
> $$\mathrm{Var}(t) = \frac{\nu}{\nu - 2}$$

For any value of ν (greater than 2), we see from the formula above that $\mathrm{Var}(t)$ is slightly greater than 1. In other words, the t distribution is slightly more spread out than the $N(0, 1)$ distribution. As ν gets larger, the variance of the t distribution decreases to 1, and in this case the t and $N(0, 1)$ distributions are practically identical. (This fact will be seen more clearly when

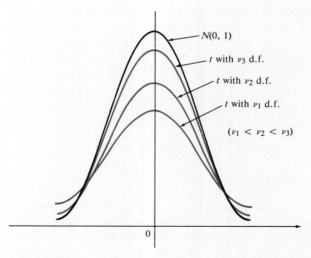

Figure 8.1
Comparison Between Normal and t Densities

we discuss the t table.) For example, if $\nu = 5$, $\text{Var}(t) = \frac{5}{3} = 1.67$; if $\nu = 20$, $\text{Var}(t) = \frac{20}{18} = 1.11$; and if $\nu = 100$, $\text{Var}(t) = \frac{100}{98} = 1.02$. Several t densities, superimposed on the $N(0, 1)$ density, are shown in Figure 8.1.

Recall that the distribution of $(\overline{X} - \mu)/(s/\sqrt{n})$ has $n - 1$ degrees of freedom. The reason we subtract 1 degree of freedom from the sample size n is that σ is unknown. In this context, σ is sometimes called a "nuisance parameter" because we need to estimate it in spite of our primary interest in μ. In general, the number of degrees of freedom (for the t distribution and for other distributions in this chapter) equals the sample size minus the number of nuisance parameters that have to be estimated.

The relevant aspects of the t distribution are tabulated in Table III of Appendix B. There are several important things to notice about Table III. First, only *right-hand* tail probabilities are given explicitly, as indicated in Figure 8.2 and in the diagram accompanying Table III. Because of the symmetry of the t density, however, left-hand tail probabilities can be found easily. Second, there are only a few right-hand tail probabilities listed. These are the ones usually required in applications, so they are sufficient for our purposes. For probabilities not listed in Table III, it is perfectly acceptable to interpolate from the values listed in the table. Finally, a separate set of t values must be given for *each* value of the degrees of freedom parameter ν. However, for large values of ν ($\nu > 60$, say), these t values are practically independent of ν and are very nearly equal to the "z values" found in the $N(0, 1)$ table. For convenience, the corresponding z values are shown at the bottom of Table III. These show that for all practical purposes, the t distribution with a large degrees of freedom parameter is identical to the $N(0, 1)$ distribution.

Suppose that we are given a probability value α and a value of ν. Then Table III gives us the number, denoted by $t_{\alpha,\nu}$, such that area α is to its right under the t density with ν degrees of freedom (see Figure 8.2).

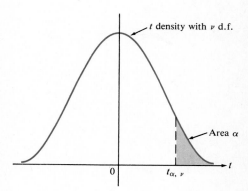

The t Table

Figure 8.2
Graphical Definition of $t_{\alpha,\nu}$

Defining Formula for $t_{\alpha,\nu}$

$$P(t > t_{\alpha,\nu}) = \alpha$$

Here t (without a subscript) is a random variable, whereas $t_{\alpha,\nu}$ is the number that cuts off area α in the right-hand tail of the t density. The defining probability statement for $t_{\alpha,\nu}$ implies several additional probability statements. For example, it implies that (1) area $1 - \alpha$ is to the left of $t_{\alpha,\nu}$, (2) area α is to the left of $-t_{\alpha,\nu}$ (by symmetry), and (3) area $1 - 2\alpha$ is between $-t_{\alpha,\nu}$ and $t_{\alpha,\nu}$. The key to using this table correctly is to draw a diagram and label the appropriate areas. We illustrate a typical calculation in the following example.

EXAMPLE 8.1

Find the probability that a t random variable with 20 degrees of freedom is outside the range -2.05 to 2.05.

SOLUTION

Let t denote a t random variable with 20 degrees of freedom. Then t is outside the range -2.05 to 2.05 if it is positive and $t > 2.05$, or if it is negative and $t < -2.05$. So the required probability is the shaded area in Figure 8.3.

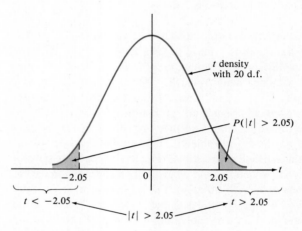

Figure 8.3

From Table III (a portion of which is shown in Table 8.1), we see that $P(t > 1.725) = .05$ and $P(t > 2.086) = .025$. Therefore, $P(t > 2.05)$ is between .025 and .05 (and is certainly closer to .025 because 2.05 is closer to 2.086). By symmetry, $P(t < -2.05$ or $t > 2.05)$ is twice as large as

Table 8.1   Portion of t Table (Table III)

	Right-Hand Tail Probability α			
d.f.	.10	.05	.025	.01
.				
.				
.				
20	1.325	1.725	2.086	2.528
.				
.				
.				

2.05 between these values

$P(t > 2.05)$, so the required probability is between .05 and .10, and is closer to .05. Given the limits of Table III, this is the best answer we can give.

The example above not only illustrates the use of Table III, but also indicates the typical kinds of information we obtain from the t table. The primary result so far in this chapter is that the random variable $(\overline{X} - \mu)/(s/\sqrt{n})$ has a t distribution with $n - 1$ degrees of freedom. Exactly as in Chapters 5 and 6, this t random variable is a standardized random variable. That is, starting with $\overline{X}$, we subtract its mean μ and then divide by an estimate, $s/\sqrt{n}$, of its standard deviation $\sigma/\sqrt{n}$. Therefore, a t value indicates how many estimated standard deviations $\overline{X}$ is from its mean. This is why the tabulated t values, $t_{\alpha,\nu}$, are almost all less than 3; there is almost no probability of $\overline{X}$ being more than 3 standard deviations from its mean.

> A t value is the number of estimated standard deviations $\overline{X}$ is to the right or left of its mean.

Using the t Distribution as the Sampling Distribution of $\overline{X}$

When we are interested primarily in the mean μ of a population and we use $\overline{X}$ to estimate μ, we usually want to know how likely it is to obtain values of $\overline{X}$ "far" from μ. For example, if $\mu = 100$, we may ask for the probability of obtaining an $\overline{X}$, based on $n = 20$, greater than 106. But this probability depends heavily on the population variance σ^2. The larger σ^2 is, the more likely it is to observe this large a difference between μ and $\overline{X}$.

If we do not know σ^2, we find the required probability by calculating $s/\sqrt{n}$ from the sample and then seeing how many estimated standard deviations 106 is above 100. For example, if we observe $s = 12$, then $s/\sqrt{n} = 12/\sqrt{20} = 2.68$, so that 106 is $(106 - 100)/2.68 = 2.24$ estimated standard deviations larger than 100. We then find the probability of obtaining a t value at least as large as 2.24 when there are $n - 1 = 19$ degrees of freedom. From Table III, this probability is slightly smaller than .025 (because $P(t > 2.093) = .025$ and $P(t > 2.539) = .01$). So we conclude that such a large $\overline{X}$ is quite unlikely. More precisely, we say that it is quite unlikely to see an $\overline{X}$ this many estimated standard deviations to the right of its mean.

There is one subtle point we wish to raise. Suppose that the real σ equals 24, but we are unaware of this. Then the probability of the event $\overline{X} > 106$ is found exactly as in Chapter 6:

$$P(\overline{X} > 106) = P\left(Z > \frac{106 - 100}{24/\sqrt{20}}\right) = P(Z > 1.12) = .131$$

So if σ is known to be 24, we conclude that an $\overline{X}$ as large as 106 will occur in approximately 13 out of every 100 samples of size 20. But if we do not know that σ equals 24 and we observe a sample with an abnormally small s equal to 12, the t calculation above implies that an $\overline{X}$ as high as 106 will occur in approximately 2 out of every 100 samples. This apparent paradox can be resolved by noticing that the poor estimate, $s = 12$, of the standard deviation σ misleads us into thinking that 106 is an abnormally high value of $\overline{X}$, when in fact it is not. In other words, the misleading inference about $\overline{X}$ is caused by an unlucky value of s.

The following example illustrates a typical application of the t distribution in its role as the sampling distribution of $\overline{X}$.

EXAMPLE 8.2

A new model car has an estimated miles per gallon (mpg) rating of 36.0 for highway driving. We will assume that this rating is correct, so that a large population of these cars should average 36.0 miles per gallon on the highway. Now suppose that a random sample of 15 cars produce the mpg values in Table 8.2. (These are based on 20,000 miles of highway driving.) Show that the sample mean is smaller than expected. Then find the probability of observing such a small average mpg from a random sample of size 15.

SOLUTION

To solve this problem, we first find $\overline{X}$ and s^2. Letting X_i be the mpg for car i, the two sums we need are

$$\sum X_i = 34.2 + 37.1 + \cdots + 34.9 = 523.8$$

and

$$\sum X_i^2 = 34.2^2 + 37.1^2 + \cdots + 34.9^2 = 18,344.66$$

These yield

$$\overline{X} = \frac{523.8}{15} = 34.92$$

and

$$s^2 = \frac{18,344.66 - 15(34.92)^2}{14} = 1.96^2$$

Since $\overline{X} = 34.92$ and $\mu = 36.0$, we have indeed obtained a smaller than expected $\overline{X}$. To see if it is abnormally small, we calculate the "observed t value," that is, the standardized value of $\overline{X}$:

$$\frac{\overline{X} - \mu}{s/\sqrt{n}} = \frac{34.92 - 36.0}{1.96/\sqrt{15}} = -2.13$$

Table 8.2

Car	Mpg
1	34.2
2	37.1
3	35.1
4	31.3
5	32.4
6	38.0
7	36.1
8	32.4
9	33.5
10	34.2
11	35.1
12	37.5
13	36.1
14	35.9
15	34.9
Total	523.8

From Table III, the probability of a t random variable with 14 degrees of freedom being to the left of -2.13 is slightly larger than .025. [This follows because $P(t > 2.145) = .025$ from the table, and $P(t < -2.145) = P(t > 2.145)$ by symmetry (see Figure 8.4).] In other words, an observed t value as low as -2.13 would occur in slightly more than 1 out of every 40 samples of size 15. So it is fair to say that the observed sample mean is an unusually low one.

The example above is typical. If we wish to see whether an observed $\overline{X}$ is unusually small or large, and we do not know the value of σ, we first calculate the observed t value, $(\overline{X} - \mu)/(s/\sqrt{n})$. Then we use the t table to see whether this observed t value is unusually small or large.

To obtain a confidence interval for μ when σ is unknown and n is small, we proceed exactly as in Chapter 7. We add and subtract a multiple of the standard error of $\overline{X}$ to the point estimate $\overline{X}$ to obtain the confidence interval. The only changes are that (1) we substitute s for σ and (2) we substitute $t_{\alpha/2,n-1}$ for $z_{\alpha/2}$. Notice that this is the appropriate tabulated t value because the numbers $\pm t_{\alpha/2,n-1}$ cut off area $\alpha/2$ in each tail of the t distribution with $n-1$ degrees of freedom.

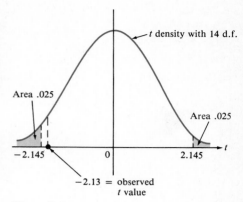

Figure 8.4

Confidence Intervals for the Population Mean

> *Small-Sample Confidence Interval for μ*
> *with Confidence Level $1 - \alpha$*
>
> $$\overline{X} \pm t_{\alpha/2,n-1}\, \mathrm{StdErr}(\overline{X})$$
>
> where $\mathrm{StdErr}(\overline{X}) = \dfrac{s}{\sqrt{n}}$

EXAMPLE 8.3

An automobile manufacturing company would like to estimate the average amount of damage caused to its newest model car when it hits a wall at 30 miles per hour. Because of the obvious expense involved, the company decides to crash only a small number of cars. For each of 12 cars, the estimated damage (in dollars) is shown in Table 8.3. Find a point estimate and a 95% confidence interval for the mean amount of damage that would occur to all such cars if they crashed at 30 miles per hour.

SOLUTION

The point estimate of the mean μ is the sample mean $\overline{X}$:

$$\overline{X} = \frac{2530 + 1790 + \cdots + 2130}{12} = \$2326.67$$

Table 8.3

Car	Damage X	X^2
1	2,530	6,400,900
2	1,790	3,204,100
3	3,050	9,302,500
4	2,470	6,100,900
5	2,640	6,969,600
6	1,980	3,920,400
7	1,620	2,624,400
8	2,850	8,122,500
9	2,320	5,382,400
10	2,690	7,236,100
11	1,850	3,422,500
12	2,130	4,536,900
Total	27,920	67,223,200

To calculate a confidence interval for μ, we first need the sample variance s^2. It is given by

$$s^2 = \frac{\Sigma \, X_i^2 - n\overline{X}^2}{n-1} = \frac{67{,}223{,}200 - 12(2326.67)^2}{11} = 205{,}680 = 453.52^2$$

This means that the standard error of $\overline{X}$ is

$$\text{StdErr}(\overline{X}) = \frac{s}{\sqrt{n}} = \frac{453.52}{\sqrt{12}} = \$130.92$$

and the 95% confidence interval for μ is

$$\overline{X} \pm t_{.025,11} \, \frac{s}{\sqrt{n}} = 2326.67 \pm 2.201(130.92) = 2326.67 \pm 288.15$$

or approximately from \$2039 to \$2615. Notice that the only assumption we are making is that the distribution of damage amounts for all such cars is normal.

Let's contrast confidence intervals for μ when σ is known with those when σ is unknown. First, confidence intervals for μ when σ is unknown tend to be *longer* than when σ is known (for fixed values of α and n). This is because $t_{\alpha/2,n-1}$ is greater than $z_{\alpha/2}$ for any values of α and n. For example, suppose that $1 - \alpha = .95$. Then $z_{\alpha/2} = 1.96$, and for $n = 10$, 20, and 30, $t_{\alpha/2,n-1}$ equals 2.262, 2.093, and 2.045, respectively. Clearly, the t values are always greater than the z value, although the difference between them is negligible for large values of n. So the confidence intervals in this chapter add and subtract a larger multiple of the standard error of $\overline{X}$.

A second difference is that we no longer use $\sigma/\sqrt{n}$, the true standard error of $\overline{X}$, but $s/\sqrt{n}$, an estimate of the standard error of $\overline{X}$. Since the value of s is not known until *after* the sample is taken, we cannot predict ahead of time how long the confidence interval will be. If we obtain an unusually small value of s, the confidence interval will be unusually short; if s is unusually large, the confidence interval will be unusually long. In contrast, if σ is known, confidence intervals from different samples (again for fixed α and n) all have exactly the same length.

We again stress that the small-sample confidence intervals for the mean developed in this section are valid only when the population distribution is normal. Fortunately, as we illustrate in Appendix 8B, the t distribution produces fairly accurate results even when the population distribution is not exactly normal. But if it is far from normal, the procedure in this section will produce a confidence level different from that desired. For example, a

"95% confidence interval" might really be an 85% confidence interval. In this case a nonparametric estimation procedure should be used instead. Nonparametric procedures are discussed in Chapter 13.

Problems for Section 8.2

1. For a t density with ν degrees of freedom, find two numbers (symmetric about 0) with area $1 - \alpha$ between them when (a) $\alpha = .10$, $\nu = 12$; (b) $\alpha = .05$, $\nu = 25$; (c) $\alpha = .02$, $\nu = 4$.

2. Find an approximate value for the following probabilities when t in each probability statement has a t distribution with ν degrees of freedom and t_0 is the number specified.
   a. $P(t > t_0)$ when $t_0 = 1.7$, $\nu = 15$
   b. $P(t < -t_0)$ when $t_0 = 2.4$, $\nu = 5$
   c. $P(-t_0 < t < t_0)$ when $t_0 = 2.1$, $\nu = 10$
   d. $P(|t| > t_0)$ when $t_0 = 1.8$, $\nu = 25$

3. For each of the following values of α and ν, find $t_{\alpha,\nu}$. (If α and/or ν is not in the t table, approximate $t_{\alpha,\nu}$ as well as possible.)
   a. $\alpha = .025$, $\nu = 20$ b. $\alpha = .05$, $\nu = 26$
   c. $\alpha = .04$, $\nu = 5$ d. $\alpha = .04$, $\nu = 120$
   e. $\alpha = .09$, $\nu = 15$ f. $\alpha = .07$, $\nu = 50$

4. Consider a sample of size 10 from a normal population with mean 25.
   a. How likely is a sample mean of at least 30 if it is known that the population standard deviation is $\sigma = 8.6$?
   b. If the observed sample mean and sample variance are 30 and 9.7^2, what is the associated t value of the sample mean?
   c. What is the probability of observing as large a t value as the one calculated in part (b)? How is this probability related to the probability in part (a)?

5. The large-sample 95% confidence intervals for the mean of a normal distribution are formed by the z values ± 1.96. What are the corresponding t values for small-sample-size confidence intervals when the sample size is (a) $n = 5$; (b) $n = 14$; (c) $n = 25$?

6. Five measurements of the reaction time of an individual to certain stimuli are recorded as .28, .30, .27, .33, and .31 second. Assume that these observations represent a random sample from the distribution of all possible reaction times that could be observed for this individual, and assume that this distribution is normal. Find 95% and 90% confidence intervals for the mean reaction time of this distribution.

7. The relatively new practice of time-sharing resort condominiums, where each owner owns a condominium for a specified week each year, has been accepted enthusiastically by the not-terribly-rich. Ten time-share owners are sampled at random and their annual incomes are as follows (in $1000s): 35, 47, 32, 56, 68, 25, 41, 30, 27, and 53.
   a. Compute $\overline{X}$ and s for this sample. Is the resulting t value for the mean abnormally low if the mean annual income of all time-share owners is $47,000? Answer by finding the probability of such a low t value if the population mean is $47,000. (What do you need to assume about the distribution of incomes of all time-share owners?)
   b. Find a 95% confidence interval for the mean annual income of all time-share owners.

8. It is increasingly difficult for unemployed people to locate new jobs. In fact, it has been reported that the average job search requires twice as much time now as it did in 1969. Consider a random sample of 12 people who were laid off and searched for new jobs. The search times (until they were successful) are as follows: 5.1, 3.2, 2.7, 8.2, 1.6, .5, 7.1, 4.1, 3.0, 2.1, 2.9, and 1.6. (Each number is expressed in months.)
   a. Compute the sample mean and sample standard deviation of these data. Is the resulting t value for the mean abnormally small if the mean search time for all unemployed people is 5.6 months? Answer by assuming that the search-time distribution is normal and calculating an appropriate probability for a t random variable.
   b. Does a 95% confidence interval for the mean search time include the value 5.6 months?

9. In 1979 the average moving cost for transferring an employee from one section of the country to another was approximately $30,000. Assume that the distribution of costs for all such employees is approximately normal. If a sample of 15 randomly selected home-moving employees in 1983 had a sample mean moving cost of $34,200 and sample standard deviation of $7300, would you strongly suspect that the mean had increased since 1979? Answer by performing an appropriate probability calculation.

10. Many companies are moving their production plants to the Far East because wages are much lower there. Assume that 15 production workers in 15 randomly selected electronics companies in Hong Kong are sampled. The sample mean of their wages is $1.35 per hour and the sample standard deviation is $.12 per hour. A similar sample of 15 workers in Taiwan has a sample mean of $1.45 per hour and a sample standard deviation of $.15 per hour. Assuming that the distribution of hourly wages in each of these populations is normal, find a 95% confidence interval for the mean hourly wage of all such workers in Hong Kong. Do the same for Taiwan.

11. Restaurant owners estimate that Americans spend, on the average, 25% of their household food expenditures in restaurants. Consider the following sample of 10 families. For each family the percentage of its food expenditures spent in restaurants is shown: 28, 32, 18, 15, 29, 27, 35, 31, 30, and 27. Assume that the distribution of these percentages across all families is normal. Find a 90% confidence interval for the mean of this distribution. Does it include the value claimed, namely, 25%?

12. The unemployment rate for 18- to 19-year-olds in 1983 was approximately 18%. Assume that a random sample of 10 U.S. cities (of approximately the same size) taken in 1983 showed an average unemployment rate for 18- to 19-year-olds of 16.8% and a standard deviation of 2.3%. Find the probability of observing a t value for the mean unemployment percentage per city as small as the one observed if 18% was the true mean over all cities.

13. Because of cars and plants equipped with the latest in clean-air equipment, there has been a definite improvement in smog control. One sample of 14 cities reported an average percentage decrease in smoggy days of 32.5% over the past decade. The standard deviation of their percentage decreases was 4.7%.
   a. Assuming that the distribution of percentage decreases across all cities with smog problems is normally distributed, is the given sample mean abnormally small if the mean percentage decrease across all cities was 36%? Back up your answer with an appropriate probability calculation.
   b. Based on the sample data, calculate a 90% confidence interval for the mean percentage decrease across all cities with smog problems.

14. A weight-reduction plan claims an average weight loss per person of at least 10 pounds in the first month. A random sample of 13 overweight people try the plan and experience the following reductions (in pounds) during the first month: 8.5, 10.1, 4.2, 5.6, 9.1, 11.3, 5.9, 9.0, 10.6, 7.3, 8.7, 12.0, and 4.7. Do these data tend to invalidate the plan's claim? Answer by finding the probability of as small a t value in a sample of size 13 as the observed t value if the true average weight loss over all dieters is really 10 pounds in the first month. Assume that the distribution of all weight losses in the first month is normal.

8.3

Small-Sample Estimation of the Difference Between Two Means

Suppose that we are interested in estimating the difference $\mu_1 - \mu_2$ between two population means. If the population variances σ_1^2 and σ_2^2 are unknown and we are unable to obtain large sample sizes, we cannot use the results of Chapter 7. As in Section 8.2, there are really two problems. First, even if the σ's were known, the small sample sizes prevent us from invoking the Central Limit Theorem to obtain a normal sampling distribution of $\overline{X}_1 - \overline{X}_2$. In fact, the only situation where we know that the sampling distribution of $\overline{X}_1 - \overline{X}_2$ is normal is when the population distributions are normal. Therefore, we will continue to make this assumption in this section. The second problem is that the σ's are unknown. If we estimate them from the sample data, then the appropriately standardized $\overline{X}_1 - \overline{X}_2$, using the estimated σ's, no longer has a $N(0, 1)$ distribution. Instead, it has a t distribution.

Actually, the sampling distribution of $\overline{X}_1 - \overline{X}_2$ depends on whether the population variances σ_1^2 and σ_2^2 are equal. We will treat the equal and unequal variance cases separately. First, we assume that σ_1^2 equals σ_2^2, and we let σ^2 denote the common variance. Then the variance of $\overline{X}_1 - \overline{X}_2$ becomes

$$\text{Var}(\overline{X}_1 - \overline{X}_2) = \frac{\sigma_1^2}{n_1} + \frac{\sigma_2^2}{n_2} = \frac{\sigma^2}{n_1} + \frac{\sigma^2}{n_2} = \sigma^2\left(\frac{1}{n_1} + \frac{1}{n_2}\right)$$

This value may be estimated by $s_p^2(1/n_1 + 1/n_2)$, where s_p^2 is an estimate of the common variance σ^2. (The subscript p means that s_p^2 is a "pooled" estimate from both samples.) Letting s_1^2 and s_2^2 be the separate sample variances from the two samples, the appropriate pooled estimate s_p^2 is given by the following formula.

> *Pooled Estimate of the Common Variance* σ^2
>
> $$s_p^2 = \frac{(n_1 - 1)s_1^2 + (n_2 - 1)s_2^2}{n_1 + n_2 - 2}$$

For example, if the sample variances are $s_1^2 = 173$ and $s_2^2 = 219$, and these are based on sample sizes of $n_1 = 23$ and $n_2 = 29$, the pooled estimate of the common population variance is

$$s_p^2 = \frac{22(173) + 28(219)}{23 + 29 - 2} = 198.76$$

In this case the variance of $\overline{X}_1 - \overline{X}_2$ is estimated by

$$s_p^2\left(\frac{1}{n_1} + \frac{1}{n_2}\right) = 198.76\left(\frac{1}{23} + \frac{1}{29}\right) = 15.5$$

so that the estimated standard error of $\overline{X}_1 - \overline{X}_2$ is $\sqrt{15.5} = 3.94$.

Using the pooled estimate s_p, it can be shown that the appropriately standardized $\overline{X}_1 - \overline{X}_2$ has a t distribution with $n_1 + n_2 - 2$ degrees of freedom. This result is listed below.

> *Sampling Distribution of* $\overline{X}_1 - \overline{X}_2$
> *with* σ_1^2, σ_2^2 *Unknown but Equal*
>
> $$\frac{(\overline{X}_1 - \overline{X}_2) - (\mu_1 - \mu_2)}{s_p\sqrt{1/n_1 + 1/n_2}}$$
>
> has a t distribution with $n_1 + n_2 - 2$ degrees of freedom.

In some applications, we may have good reason to believe that σ_1^2 and σ_2^2 are *not* equal. Then the procedure above is not valid. Instead, we simply substitute s_1^2 for σ_1^2 and s_2^2 for σ_2^2 in the standard error of $\overline{X}_1 - \overline{X}_2$. In this case the appropriately standardized $\overline{X}_1 - \overline{X}_2$ is approximately t distributed, but its degrees of freedom parameter, labeled $\overline{n}$, requires some computation. The value of $\overline{n}$ is the integer nearest the expression

$$\overline{n} \approx \frac{(s_1^2/n_1 + s_2^2/n_2)^2}{(s_1^2/n_1)^2/(n_1 - 1) + (s_2^2/n_2)^2/(n_2 - 1)}$$

Sampling Distribution of $\overline{X}_1 - \overline{X}_2$ with σ_1^2, σ_2^2 Unknown and Not Assumed Equal

$$\frac{(\overline{X}_1 - \overline{X}_2) - (\mu_1 - \mu_2)}{\sqrt{s_1^2/n_1 + s_2^2/n_2}}$$

is approximately t distributed with $\overline{n}$ degrees of freedom.

For example, when $s_1^2 = 173$, $s_2^2 = 219$, $n_1 = 23$, and $n_2 = 29$, the value of $\overline{n}$ is

$$\frac{(173/23 + 219/29)^2}{(173/23)^2/22 + (219/29)^2/28} \approx 49$$

Now the estimated variance of $\overline{X}_1 - \overline{X}_2$ is

$$\frac{s_1^2}{n_1} + \frac{s_2^2}{n_2} = \frac{173}{23} + \frac{219}{29} = 15.07$$

so that its standard error is $\sqrt{15.07} = 3.88$. Notice that both the degrees of freedom and the estimated standard error of $\overline{X}_1 - \overline{X}_2$ are practically the same as when we assumed *equal* population variances. This is not always the case, however, especially when s_1^2 and n_1 differ significantly from s_2^2 and n_2. Of course, when s_1^2 and s_2^2 are quite different, we have strong evidence that σ_1^2 and σ_2^2 are indeed not equal.

The following example illustrates the t distribution in its role as the sampling distribution of $\overline{X}_1 - \overline{X}_2$.

EXAMPLE 8.4

Assume that the executives of a large company are interested in whether their management people in the production division have (on the average) been with the company longer than their counterparts in the marketing division.

They take a random sample of 10 marketing managers and 20 production managers and look up the number of years each has been with the company. The sample means and variances are $\overline{X}_1 = 15.7$, $\overline{X}_2 = 11.4$, $s_1^2 = 8.6^2$, and $s_2^2 = 5.2^2$, where the subscripts 1 and 2 stand for marketing and production, respectively. What is the probability of observing this large a difference between $\overline{X}_1$ and $\overline{X}_2$ if $\mu_1 - \mu_2$, the difference between means for the whole company, is 0?

SOLUTION

To answer this question, we assume that $\mu_1 - \mu_2$ is 0 and then calculate the corresponding t value. First, we assume that the population variances σ_1^2 and σ_2^2 are equal. In this case the pooled estimate of the common variance σ^2 is

$$s_p^2 = \frac{9(8.6)^2 + 19(5.2)^2}{28} = 42.12 = 6.49^2$$

This implies that the observed t value, assuming that $\mu_1 - \mu_2 = 0$, is

$$\frac{(15.7 - 11.4) - (0)}{6.49 \sqrt{1/10 + 1/20}} = 1.71$$

From Table III of Appendix B, we find that the probability of observing a t value this large when the degrees of freedom is $n_1 + n_2 - 2 = 28$ is slightly less than .05. Therefore, we conclude that it is quite unlikely to see such a large difference $\overline{X}_1 - \overline{X}_2$ if $\mu_1 - \mu_2$ is really 0.

Next we answer the question without assuming that σ_1^2 and σ_2^2 are equal. The relevant degrees of freedom parameter $\overline{n}$ is

$$\frac{(8.6^2/10 + 5.2^2/20)^2}{(8.6^2/10)^2/9 + (5.2^2/20)^2/19} \approx 12$$

Notice that $\overline{n}$ is much less than the previous degrees of freedom, 28. Now the observed t value, assuming that $\mu_1 - \mu_2 = 0$, is

$$\frac{(15.7 - 11.4) - (0)}{\sqrt{8.6^2/10 + 5.2^2/20}} = 1.45$$

The probability of a t random variable with $\overline{n} = 12$ degrees of freedom exceeding 1.45 is about halfway between .05 and .10 (again from Table III). Again, we conclude that such a large difference between $\overline{X}_1$ and $\overline{X}_2$ is not very likely if $\mu_1 - \mu_2$ is 0. (However, it is not as unlikely as when we assumed equal population variances.)

Small-Sample Confidence Intervals for the Difference Between Population Means

Now that we know the sampling distribution of $\overline{X}_1 - \overline{X}_2$, it is straightforward to obtain confidence intervals for the difference $\mu_1 - \mu_2$. The two cases, depending on whether we assume equal population variances, are shown below.

Small-Sample Confidence Interval for $\mu_1 - \mu_2$ with Confidence Level $1 - \alpha$

(σ_1 and σ_2 assumed equal)

$$\overline{X}_1 - \overline{X}_2 \pm t_{\alpha/2, n_1 + n_2 - 2} \ \text{StdErr}(\overline{X}_1 - \overline{X}_2)$$

where $\text{StdErr}(\overline{X}_1 - \overline{X}_2) = s_p \sqrt{\dfrac{1}{n_1} + \dfrac{1}{n_2}}$

and $s_p^2 = \dfrac{(n_1 - 1)s_1^2 + (n_2 - 1)s_2^2}{n_1 + n_2 - 2}$

Small-Sample Confidence Interval for $\mu_1 - \mu_2$ with Confidence Level $1 - \alpha$

(σ_1 and σ_2 not assumed equal)

$$\overline{X}_1 - \overline{X}_2 \pm t_{\alpha/2, \bar{n}} \ \text{StdErr}(\overline{X}_1 - \overline{X}_2)$$

where $\text{StdErr}(\overline{X}_1 - \overline{X}_2) = \sqrt{\dfrac{s_1^2}{n_1} + \dfrac{s_2^2}{n_2}}$

and $\bar{n}$ is the integer closest to the expression

$$\bar{n} \approx \frac{(s_1^2/n_1 + s_2^2/n_2)^2}{(s_1^2/n_1)^2/(n_1 - 1) + (s_2^2/n_2)^2/(n_2 - 1)}$$

The two confidence intervals for $\mu_1 - \mu_2$ above are similar in that they are both centered at the point estimate $\overline{X}_1 - \overline{X}_2$, and they both add and subtract a *t* value times the (approximate) standard error of $\overline{X}_1 - \overline{X}_2$. Unless s_1^2 and s_2^2 are quite different from one another (an indication that σ_1^2 and σ_2^2 are *not* equal), the two confidence intervals for $\mu_1 - \mu_2$ above will usually be nearly the same. We illustrate this in the following example.

EXAMPLE 8.5

A bank manager of two branch banks several miles apart would like to estimate the difference between the average number of customers served over the noon hour for the two branches. On 10 randomly selected days, he has an employee at each branch count the number of customers served over the noon hour. The observed data are shown in Table 8.4. Calculate a 95%

confidence interval for the difference between the mean numbers of customers served at the two branches.

Table 8.4

Day	Branch 1		Branch 2	
	X_1	X_1^2	X_2	X_2^2
1	65	4,225	56	3,136
2	42	1,764	72	5,184
3	71	5,041	64	4,096
4	52	2,704	49	2,401
5	37	1,369	58	3,364
6	62	3,844	61	3,721
7	43	1,849	72	5,184
8	57	3,249	50	2,500
9	81	6,561	59	3,481
10	70	4,900	65	4,225
Total	580	35,506	606	37,292

SOLUTION

The preliminary calculations in Table 8.4 show that

$$\overline{X}_1 = \frac{580}{10} = 58 \qquad \overline{X}_2 = \frac{606}{10} = 60.6$$

so that a point estimate for $\mu_1 - \mu_2$, the difference between means, is $\overline{X}_1 - \overline{X}_2 = 2.6$. The sample variances are

$$s_1^2 = \frac{35,506 - 10(58)^2}{9} = 207.33 = 14.40^2$$

and

$$s_2^2 = \frac{37,292 - 10(60.6)^2}{9} = 63.16 = 7.95^2$$

If we assume that the population variances are equal (probably a poor assumption considering the large discrepancy between s_1^2 and s_2^2), then the pooled variance is

$$s_p^2 = \frac{9(207.33) + 9(63.16)}{18} = 135.25 = 11.63^2$$

This means that the estimated standard error of $\overline{X}_1 - \overline{X}_2$ is

$$\text{StdErr}(\overline{X}_1 - \overline{X}_2) = 11.63 \sqrt{\frac{1}{10} + \frac{1}{10}} = 5.20$$

and the 95% confidence interval for $\mu_1 - \mu_2$ is

$$-2.6 \pm t_{.025,18}(5.20) = -2.6 \pm 2.101(5.20) = -2.6 \pm 10.93$$

or from -13.53 to 8.33.

If we do not assume equal population variances, the estimated standard error of $\overline{X}_1 - \overline{X}_2$ is

$$\text{StdErr}(\overline{X}_1 - \overline{X}_2) = \sqrt{\frac{207.33}{10} + \frac{63.16}{10}} = 5.20$$

(This is no coincidence. If the sample sizes are equal, the estimated standard error of $\overline{X}_1 - \overline{X}_2$ will be the same whether we assume equal or unequal population variances.) Now the degrees of freedom, $\overline{n}$, is given by

$$\overline{n} = \frac{(207.33/10 + 63.16/10)^2}{(207.33/10)^2/9 + (63.16/10)^2/9} \approx 14$$

Therefore, the 95% confidence interval is

$$-2.6 \pm t_{.025,14}(5.20) = -2.6 \pm 2.145(5.20) = -2.6 \pm 11.15$$

or from -13.75 to 8.55.

There are two points to notice in this example. First, the confidence intervals are very nearly the same whether we assume equal or unequal population variances. This is despite the large difference between the sample variances. The reason is primarily that the sample sizes are equal. In general, if the sample sizes are equal or nearly equal, our results will usually be valid if we make the equal variance assumption. (Realizing this, many authors do not even present the procedure for the unequal-variance case.) However, if the sample variances are far apart *and* the sample sizes are far apart also, the two confidence intervals can differ significantly.

The second point is that both confidence intervals in this example are quite wide. This is because of the small sample sizes. Because both confidence intervals extend from a fairly large negative number to a fairly large positive number, the bank manager cannot be at all certain which of the two branches serves more customers on the average. To obtain more accuracy, he must gather more observations.

---

15. Gasoline prices for unleaded gas decreased considerably from early 1982 to early 1983. (Reference: *Time,* Feb. 14, 1983, p. 58.) Consider a random sample of 16 gas stations in early 1982 that showed an average price of $1.27 per gallon and a standard deviation of 3.6 cents per gallon. A similar sample of 12 gas stations in early 1983 showed an average price of $1.20 per gallon and a standard deviation of 3.2 cents per gallon.
   a. Assuming equal population variances in the two time periods, find an estimate of this common variance.
   b. Assuming equal population variances and normally distributed prices, calculate a 90% confidence interval for $\mu_1 - \mu_2$, the mean difference between all unleaded gas prices in the two years. (Here μ_1 refers to 1982 and μ_2 refers to 1983.)

16. Referring to the data in Problem 15, consider the claim that the mean difference $\mu_1 - \mu_2$ between 1982 and 1983 is 0. If this claim is true, find the probability of observing as large a t value as the t value observed. (Again assume equal population variances and normal distributions of prices.)

17. As anyone who has ever studied German knows, German words tend to be longer than English words. In two comparable books, one in English and one in German, the numbers of words on a random sample of pages are given below. Find a 95% confidence interval for the difference between the mean number of German words per page and the mean number of English words per page. (Assume equal variances and normal distributions of words per page.)

Number of German Words		Number of English Words	
305	296	312	322
289	278	345	310
315	299	363	287
324	305	315	318
301	337	298	348
		343	361

18. Two independent samples of sizes n_1 and n_2 are taken from two normal populations. The resulting sample means and standard deviations are

$$\overline{X}_1 = 93.2$$
$$\overline{X}_2 = 77.5$$
$$s_1 = 5.9$$
$$s_2 = 10.3$$

Find a 95% confidence interval for $\mu_1 - \mu_2$ when $n_1 = n_2 = 15$. Do this by (a) assuming equal population variances, and then (b) not assuming equal population variances. Then repeat the calculations when $n_1 = 5$ and $n_2 = 25$. What can you conclude, if anything, about having equal sample sizes versus unequal sample sizes?

19. A large university has many faculty and students with computer research account numbers. The computer usage committee wishes to estimate the mean usage (hours per month on a terminal) for all faculty and student users. Independent random samples of eight faculty members and 15 students with research account numbers have sample means of 4.3 hours for faculty and 3.6 hours for students. The corresponding sample standard deviations are 1.3 hours for faculty and 1.0 hour for students. Find a 95% confidence interval for the difference in mean usage between faculty and students. Assume equal population variances and normally distributed usages.

20. A department store wishes to know whether women or men tend to have higher purchase amounts at this store. A random sample of 15 women are asked how much they spent on their most recent visit to the store. The mean and standard deviation for this sample are $36.29 and $11.21. A similar sample of 10 men has mean $25.54 and standard deviation $8.21.
   a. Assuming that the male and female populations have normally distributed purchase amounts, find a 95% confidence interval for the mean difference between purchase amounts for women and men. Assume equal population variances.
   b. Is the observed t value unusually large if the true mean difference is 0?

8.4

Estimation of the Variance

Until now we have focused attention on the mean of the population, reasoning that the mean, a measure of central tendency, is usually the parameter of primary interest. However, we now shift our attention to the variance, not for the role it plays in helping us to study the mean, but for its own sake. The following examples illustrate applications where the variance is probably at least as important as the mean.

Consider the problem of quality control. Specifically, consider a manufacturing process that produces sheets of various kinds of paper products. These sheets must have a uniform thickness, where the required thickness depends on the type of paper product being produced. By means of machine controls, it may be relatively easy to keep the *mean* thickness within the proper limits, but the variance might be more difficult to control. In this case it does us little good to have the correct mean if the *variance* is too large. Therefore, in most quality control settings, the variance is the parameter of primary interest.

As a second example, consider daily trading of a stock on the stock exchange. If the quantity of interest is the daily price of the stock, the variance of this quantity, which measures the *volatility* of the stock, is very useful to traders of the stock. It tells them whether the stock price tends to move in relatively smooth patterns or in bumpy, irregular patterns.

In this section and the next, we study estimation problems involving one or more variances. We first look at a single population with variance σ^2. In this case the relevant sampling distribution is a new distribution called the chi-square distribution. In Section 8.5 we compare two populations with variances σ_1^2 and σ_2^2. Basically, we try to determine how close these two population variances are to one another. In this case the relevant sampling distribution is again new; it is called the F distribution.

The point estimate we will continue to use to estimate a population variance σ^2 is the sample variance s^2. This is defined by

$$s^2 = \frac{\sum (X_i - \bar{X})^2}{n - 1}$$

or by the computing formula

$$s^2 = \frac{\sum X_i^2 - n\bar{X}^2}{n - 1}$$

Like $\overline{X}$, the sample variance depends on the random observations X_1, X_2, . . . , X_n, so that it varies from one sample to the next. Actually, it varies more than we might expect. To show this empirically, we again utilize computer simulation.

To illustrate how the sample variance varies from sample to sample, we simulated 10,000 samples of size 30, each from a $N(100, 10^2)$ population. For each sample we computed the sample mean $\overline{X}$ and the sample variance s^2. We know that the $\overline{X}$'s should center around their mean of $\mu = 100$, with a standard deviation of $\sigma/\sqrt{n} = 10/\sqrt{30} = 1.83$. Therefore, most of the $\overline{X}$'s should be in the range 95 to 105 (plus or minus approximately 3 standard errors). On the other hand, the s^2's, each being an estimate of $\sigma^2 = 100$, should also vary around 100, but how much should they vary? Is it surprising, for example, to see an s^2 value as low as 60 or as high as 140? The results from 100 of the 10,000 samples are shown in Table 8.5. These show that such seemingly extreme values of s^2 are not exactly likely but that they do occur once in a while. For the sake of comparison, Table 8.5 also includes the simulated $\overline{X}$'s and the s values (the sample standard deviations). Below each column we show the average of the 100 numbers in that column. [Notice that the average of the s^2's (101.28) is *not* equal to the square of the averages of the s's (9.87^2). This is no mistake. In general, an average of s^2's is not equal to the square of the average of the individual square roots, the s's.]

Table 8.5   Simulated Means, Variances, and Standard Deviations

100 $\overline{X}$ Values		100 s^2 Values		100 s Values	
98.25	100.61	121.53	128.63	11.02	11.34
98.72	101.54	53.34	88.45	7.30	9.41
100.04	101.25	127.15	68.78	11.28	8.29
99.50	98.32	105.56	134.37	10.27	11.59
102.17	100.03	151.90	109.47	12.33	10.46
104.90	98.30	115.20	122.75	10.73	11.08
102.90	98.99	60.00	85.08	7.75	9.22
98.67	100.94	109.17	123.28	10.45	11.10
102.60	99.47	168.00	54.68	12.96	7.39
97.79	104.45	111.41	74.92	10.56	8.66
99.24	101.24	99.08	99.35	9.95	9.97
98.53	100.30	70.97	126.42	8.42	11.24
99.87	99.30	112.94	60.97	10.63	7.81
100.25	101.73	67.90	125.50	8.24	11.20
99.16	101.46	85.63	94.72	9.25	9.73
99.57	100.41	82.14	144.18	9.06	12.01
99.70	98.27	74.81	86.04	8.65	9.28
97.90	97.28	69.08	113.83	8.31	10.67

(continued)

Table 8.5   Simulated Means, Variances, and Standard Deviations (*continued*)

100 $\overline{X}$ Values		100 s^2 Values		100 s Values	
99.84	99.20	89.56	66.87	9.46	8.18
98.21	98.70	91.47	86.93	9.56	9.32
97.03	99.84	121.79	119.49	11.04	10.93
102.25	100.81	50.92	155.20	7.14	12.46
99.16	102.70	118.44	88.02	10.88	9.38
100.54	98.32	96.54	125.81	9.82	11.22
99.05	98.90	89.79	107.10	9.48	10.35
100.87	100.74	99.31	83.07	9.97	9.11
101.27	102.64	139.65	60.61	11.82	7.79
100.44	100.65	103.56	86.43	10.18	9.30
98.34	101.39	159.13	105.85	12.62	10.29
101.39	101.39	96.54	100.09	9.83	10.01
99.35	101.72	92.64	90.48	9.63	9.51
98.46	96.14	73.58	94.54	8.58	9.72
99.36	99.46	126.60	70.81	11.25	8.42
100.50	101.21	122.46	104.26	11.07	10.21
100.15	98.55	89.29	172.11	9.45	13.12
101.11	101.11	103.07	88.55	10.15	9.41
99.15	97.02	52.13	131.25	7.22	11.46
99.47	100.09	97.35	72.87	9.87	8.54
99.50	100.16	59.03	75.25	7.68	8.68
98.57	98.48	110.05	113.97	10.49	10.68
100.63	98.53	114.47	134.43	10.70	11.59
100.12	100.39	87.89	135.83	9.38	11.66
103.25	99.45	111.53	100.00	10.56	10.00
100.12	99.54	159.61	95.50	12.63	9.77
102.98	100.01	122.34	107.54	11.06	10.37
99.83	101.54	109.63	94.77	10.47	9.74
95.36	102.72	110.77	80.49	10.53	8.97
98.42	101.48	66.32	86.93	8.14	9.32
99.23	99.03	136.06	100.26	11.66	10.01
101.87	98.00	92.64	71.90	9.63	8.48
Mean	99.99		101.28		9.98

In Figure 8.5 we show the histogram of the 10,000 sample variances from the computer simulation. This graph represents the empirical sampling distribution of s^2. Notice that it is skewed to the right and that it does not extend to the left of the vertical axis (since the s^2's must be nonnegative). This empirical sampling distribution (except for a change of scale) approximates the theoretical sampling distribution of s^2, which is called the chi-square distribution.

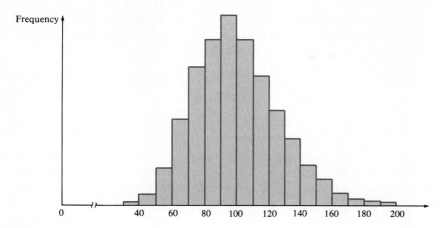

Figure 8.5
Histogram of 10,000 Sample Variances

Like the *t* distribution, there are many chi-square distributions, one for each sample size. We index each chi-square distribution by a numerical parameter ν, again called the degrees of freedom. Several chi-square densities are shown in Figure 8.6. We see from the figure that as the parameter ν increases, two things occur. First, the density becomes more symmetric and "normal-looking," and second, it shifts to the right. So unlike a *t* distribution that always has mean 0, a chi-square distribution's mean, variance, and whole shape change as the parameter ν changes.

Let χ^2 be a random variable with a chi-square distribution with ν degrees of freedom. (χ is the Greek lowercase letter chi.) The formulas for the mean and variance of χ^2 are given below.

> *Mean and Variance of the Chi-Square Distribution with ν Degrees of Freedom*
>
> $$E(\chi^2) = \nu \qquad \text{Var}(\chi^2) = 2\nu$$

We will use these results sparingly, but they do show that the mean and the variance of a chi-square distribution both increase as ν increases.

To obtain probabilities for the chi-square distribution, we refer to the chi-square table, Table IV of Appendix B. Table IV is very similar to the *t* table, Table III, with one important difference. Because the chi-square density is not symmetric, both extreme left-hand and right-hand tail probabilities must be supplied. Table IV does this as follows.

The Chi-Square Distribution

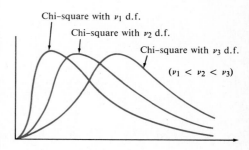

Figure 8.6
Comparison of Chi-Square Densities

The Chi-Square Table

Let χ^2 be a chi-square random variable with ν degrees of freedom, and let α be any number between 0 and 1. Then $\chi^2_{\alpha,\nu}$ is the number with area α to the *right* of it under the appropriate chi-square density.

Defining Formula for $\chi^2_{\alpha,\nu}$

$$P(\chi^2 > \chi^2_{\alpha,\nu}) = \alpha$$

We find $\chi^2_{\alpha,\nu}$ numerically by looking up the number listed under α and across from ν in Table IV. Notice that this is a *right-hand* tail probability, as illustrated in Figure 8.7, no matter how large or small α is. That is, the first subscript in $\chi^2_{\alpha,\nu}$ always denotes the probability to the *right* of this number. But also notice in Table IV that there are two sets of α values, large values (close to 1) and small values (close to 0). Therefore, if we want an extreme left-hand tail probability, we look up the right-hand tail probability for a large value of α. The following example illustrates the use of Table IV.

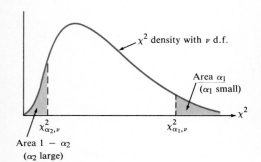

Figure 8.7
Graphical Definition of $\chi^2_{\alpha,\nu}$

EXAMPLE 8.6

Given a chi-square random variable χ^2 with ν degrees of freedom, find (1) the number such that χ^2 is larger than this number with probability .05, (2) the number such that χ^2 is smaller than this number with probability .05, and (3) two numbers such that χ^2 is between them with probability .90. Do this for $\nu = 10$ and for $\nu = 25$.

SOLUTION

For any ν, the diagram in Figure 8.8 shows us what is required. (*Always* get in the habit of drawing such a diagram for these types of problems.) By the definition of $\chi^2_{\alpha,\nu}$ in general, $\chi^2_{.05,\nu}$ has area .05 to its right. On the other hand, $\chi^2_{.95,\nu}$ has area .95 to its right, so it must have area .05 to its left. Finally, with area .05 in each tail, there must be area .90 in the middle. So the diagram in Figure 8.8 solves all three parts of the problem. Now all we need to do is look up these chi-square values in Table IV. For $\nu = 10$, we have $\chi^2_{.95,10} = 3.940$ and $\chi^2_{.05,10} = 18.307$; for $\nu = 25$, we have $\chi^2_{.95,25} = 14.611$ and $\chi^2_{.05,25} = 37.653$. Table 8.6, a portion of Table IV, illustrates how these numbers were found.

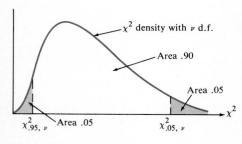

Figure 8.8

How do we find chi-square values when the appropriate values of α and/or ν are not tabulated in Table IV? Unless the value of ν is larger than 100, the answer is to interpolate from the tabulated values as well as possible. Usually,

Table 8.6 Portion of Chi-Square Table (Table IV)

	Right-Hand Tail Probability α							
d.f.	.99	.975	.95	.90	.10	.05	.025	.01
.								
.								
.								
10	2.558	3.247	3.940	4.865	15.987	18.307	20.483	23.209
.								
.								
.								
25	11.524	13.120	14.611	16.473	34.382	37.653	40.647	44.314
.								
.								
.								

extreme accuracy is not needed. If ν is larger than 100, interpolation is not possible. Instead, we use the following approximation for $\chi^2_{\alpha,\nu}$.

Approximate Chi-Square Value for $\nu > 100$

$$\chi^2_{\alpha,\nu} \approx \nu\left(1 - \frac{2}{9\nu} + z_\alpha\sqrt{\frac{2}{9\nu}}\right)^3$$

For example, if $\nu = 150$ and $\alpha = .05$, then $z_\alpha = 1.645$ and $\chi^2_{.05,150}$ is approximately

$$150\left(1 - \frac{2}{1350} + 1.645\sqrt{\frac{2}{1350}}\right)^3 = 179.58$$

Notice that the relevant z_α values used in the approximation are shown at the bottom of Table IV.

Sampling Distribution of the Sample Variance

Now we state specifically how the chi-square distribution is the sampling distribution of the sample variance s^2. In our previous discussions of the sample statistics $\hat{p}$ and $\bar{X}$, we first "standardized" these by subtracting their means and dividing by their standard deviations. In each case this operation produced a random variable with a known distribution (the standard normal or the t). This does not work with s^2, however. Instead, the "standardized" s^2 is a *multiple* of s^2, namely, $(n - 1)s^2/\sigma^2$. This statistic has a chi-square distribution with $n - 1$ degrees of freedom.

Sampling Distribution of s^2

$\dfrac{(n-1)s^2}{\sigma^2}$ has a chi-square distribution with $n-1$ degrees of freedom.

We note that the degrees of freedom parameter is $n-1$, not n. This is because we used an *estimate* of μ, namely $\overline{X}$, in the formula for s^2. This causes the loss of 1 degree of freedom.

Letting $\chi^2 = (n-1)s^2/\sigma^2$, we can easily find the mean and variance of s^2 from the formulas for $E(\chi^2)$ and $\mathrm{Var}(\chi^2)$ and the rules of expected values. The results are listed below.

Mean and Variance of the Sample Variance

$$E(s^2) = \sigma^2 \qquad \mathrm{Var}(s^2) = \frac{2\sigma^4}{n-1}$$

As we see, the expected value of the sample variance is the population variance σ^2. This is why we choose s^2 (with the $n-1$ in the denominator) as the "sample variance"; it provides an unbiased estimate of σ^2.

The formula for $\mathrm{Var}(s^2)$ indicates why the simulated values of s^2 in Table 8.5 vary so widely around σ^2. There we had $n = 30$ and $\sigma^2 = 100$, so that the standard deviation of s^2 is

$$\sqrt{\frac{2\sigma^4}{n-1}} = 100\sqrt{\frac{2}{29}} = 26.3$$

In this case it is not terribly unlikely to see s^2 values as low as 60 or as high as 140 since these values are less than two standard deviations (of s^2) away from their mean of $\sigma^2 = 100$.

To illustrate the sampling distribution of s^2, suppose that we sample 25 observations from a population with $\sigma^2 = 10$. Then we may find, for example, the probability that s^2 is at least 50% larger than expected, that is, at least 15. Letting χ^2 be a chi-square random variable with $25 - 1 = 24$ degrees of freedom, we have

$$P(s^2 \geq 15) = P\left[\frac{(n-1)s^2}{\sigma^2} \geq \frac{(n-1)15}{\sigma^2}\right] = P\left[\chi^2 \geq \frac{24(15)}{10}\right] = P(\chi^2 \geq 36)$$

This shows that to transform an inequality for s^2 into an equivalent inequality for a chi-square random variable, we multiply each side of the inequality by $(n-1)/\sigma^2$. From Table IV we find that $P(\chi^2 \geq 33.2) = .10$ and

$P(\chi^2 \geq 36.42) = .05$. Therefore, $P(\chi^2 \geq 36)$ is slightly greater than .05. (This level of accuracy is all that is usually required.) So there is slightly greater than 1 chance in 20 of observing this large an s^2 value.

We point out that this is also the probability of observing a sample standard deviation (an s value) at least as large as $\sqrt{15}$ when the population standard deviation σ is $\sqrt{10}$. So we simultaneously obtain a probability statement about the sample variance and a probability statement about the sample standard deviation.

EXAMPLE 8.7

Consider a technician at a manufacturing plant whose job is to make sure that the manufacturing process is "in control." The plant is currently manufacturing steel rods, each of which should have a length of 3 meters, plus or minus 1 millimeter. The lengths of rods vary randomly according to a normal distribution, and the process is said to be in control if the standard deviation σ of rod lengths is no greater than .25 millimeter. (This implies that most rods will meet specifications even if the mean μ differs from the desired value of 3 meters.) If the technician senses that the standard deviation is higher than .25 millimeter, he can make an adjustment or perform maintenance in order to bring the process back into control. Suppose that the technician observes a sample of 20 rod lengths (measured in meters) with a sample mean of $\overline{X} = 3.00085$ and a sample standard deviation of $s = .00033$. If the process is currently on the borderline of being out of control, that is, σ currently equals .00025 meter, is the observed sample standard deviation unusually large?

SOLUTION

Here the technician observes a value of s that indicates the process may be out of control. But he realizes, particularly because of the small sample size, that the large observed value of s could be due to sampling error. So we answer the question above by finding how probable an s value of at least .00033 is if the true value of σ equals .00025. This probability is

$$P(s > .00033) = P(s^2 > .00033^2)$$

$$= P\left[\frac{(n-1)s^2}{\sigma^2} > \frac{(n-1)(.00033)^2}{\sigma^2}\right]$$

$$= P\left[\chi^2 > \frac{19(.00033)^2}{(.00025)^2}\right]$$

$$= P(\chi^2 > 33.11)$$

where χ^2 has a chi-square distribution with 19 degrees of freedom. Notice that the first inequality on s had to be squared. This is because the chi-square distribution is relevant for s^2, not s. From Table IV we see that the probability of a chi-square random variable with 19 degrees of freedom being greater than 33.11 is between .01 and .025. At this point the technician can conclude that the process is in control and he got an unusual value of s, or he can conclude that the true σ is really *larger* than .00025 and his sample s was not so unusual after all. The latter conclusion is probably more realistic. Notice that the value of $\overline{X}$ never entered the calculations (except when the technician calculated the value of s in the first place.)

The following example is important in that it shows how much, in percentage terms, a sample standard deviation and the corresponding population standard deviation are likely to differ.

EXAMPLE 8.8

A well-known speed-reading program makes the claim that people taking the course will observe a significant percentage increase in their reading speeds, although this percentage increase will vary from person to person according to a normal distribution. The standard deviation of these percentage increases, for all people who take the course, is claimed to be σ percentage points. If 30 people take this course, and s is the sample standard deviation of the percentage increases in reading speeds for these 30 people, find the probability that s will be at least 20% larger than σ; that it will be at least 50% larger. How do the answers depend on the value of σ?

SOLUTION

Here we are interested in the event $s > C\sigma$ for two specific values of C: $C = 1.2$ (20% larger) and $C = 1.5$ (50% larger). For any value of C, the event $s > C\sigma$ is equivalent to $s^2 > C^2\sigma^2$, so we have

$$P(s > C\sigma) = P(s^2 > C^2\sigma^2) = P\left[\frac{(n-1)s^2}{\sigma^2} > \frac{(n-1)C^2\sigma^2}{\sigma^2}\right] = P(\chi^2 > 29C^2)$$

Since the σ^2's cancel, this probability does not depend on the value of σ at all, only on the value of C. If $C = 1.2$, then $29C^2 = 41.76$. Referring to Table IV with $n - 1 = 29$ degrees of freedom, we see that $P(\chi^2 > 41.76)$ is between .05 and .10. If $C = 1.5$, then $29C^2 = 65.25$, and Table IV shows that $P(\chi^2 > 65.25)$ is much less than .01 (see Figure 8.9). We can summarize these results by stating that for a sample of size 30, a sample standard deviation more than 20% higher ($C = 1.2$) than the population standard deviation is moderately unlikely—about 1 chance out of 20. But a sample standard deviation more than 50% higher ($C = 1.5$) than the popu-

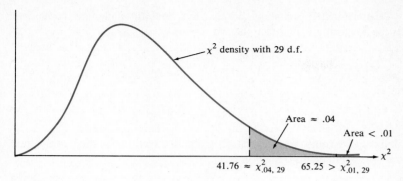

Figure 8.9

lation standard deviation is very unlikely—well less than 1 chance out of 100. Furthermore, these statements are valid regardless of the value of σ.

Now we develop a confidence interval for σ^2. Since $(n - 1)s^2/\sigma^2$ has a chi-square distribution with $n - 1$ degrees of freedom, we can write the probability statement

$$P\left(\chi^2_{1-\alpha/2,n-1} < \frac{(n - 1)s^2}{\sigma^2} < \chi^2_{\alpha/2,n-1}\right) = 1 - \alpha$$

Here $\chi^2_{1-\alpha/2,n-1}$ and $\chi^2_{\alpha/2,n-1}$ are the tabulated chi-square values that cut off area $\alpha/2$ in the left-hand and right-hand tails of the relevant chi-square density. (Recall that the first subscript on a χ^2 value indicates the area to its *right*.) These chi-square values are chosen so that area $1 - \alpha$ remains in the middle, as illustrated in Figure 8.10.

Confidence Intervals for the Population Variance

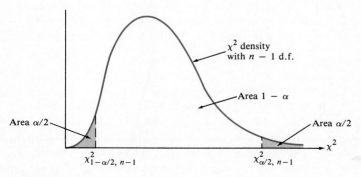

Figure 8.10

By transforming the inequality inside the probability statement above, we obtain the following confidence interval for σ^2.

> ### Confidence Interval for σ^2 with Confidence Level $1 - \alpha$
>
> σ^2 is between $\dfrac{(n-1)s^2}{\chi^2_{\alpha/2, n-1}}$ and $\dfrac{(n-1)s^2}{\chi^2_{1-\alpha/2, n-1}}$

By taking square roots, we automatically obtain the corresponding confidence interval for the standard deviation σ.

> ### Confidence Interval for σ with Confidence Level $1 - \alpha$
>
> σ is between $\dfrac{\sqrt{n-1}\, s}{\sqrt{\chi^2_{\alpha/2, n-1}}}$ and $\dfrac{\sqrt{n-1}\, s}{\sqrt{\chi^2_{1-\alpha/2, n-1}}}$

The confidence intervals above are different from the others we have seen. So far, every confidence interval has been a point estimate plus or minus a multiple of the standard error of this point estimate. In particular, all the confidence intervals have been symmetric about the point estimate. However, confidence intervals for σ^2 and σ do not have this property. The reason is basically that the chi-square sampling distribution is not symmetric. Therefore, these confidence intervals are *not* centered at the point estimate s^2 (or s), but instead appear as in Figure 8.11.

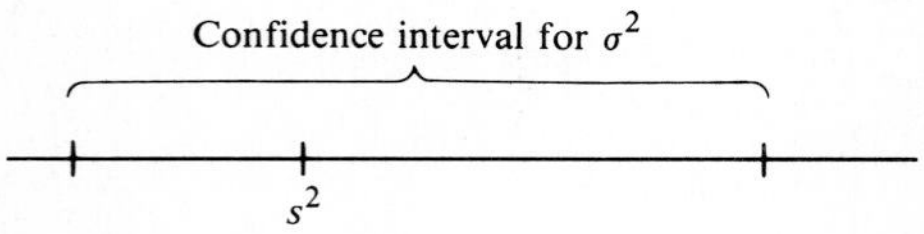

Figure 8.11
Confidence Interval for σ^2 Not Symmetric About s^2

EXAMPLE 8.9

Consider a manufacturing plant with an assembly line that produces a continuous stream of completed assemblies. The manager of the plant wants to investigate the amount of variation in the amount of output that occurs from one hour to the next. Therefore, he counts the number of assemblies completed during 25 randomly selected one-hour periods over a three-week interval. The results are shown in Table 8.7. Use these data to compute a 95%

Table 8.7

Period	1	2	3	4	5	6	7	8	9	10	11	12
Completed Assemblies	59	64	53	61	69	59	57	54	61	63	60	52

Period	13	14	15	16	17	18	19	20	21	22	23	24	25
Completed Assemblies	57	58	64	55	60	60	57	59	55	63	61	58	59

confidence interval for the variance of the number of completed assemblies per hour. Do the same for the standard deviation. Assume that the distribution of hourly output varies according to a normal distribution.

SOLUTION

To compute confidence intervals for σ^2 and σ, we first need to find (1) the tabulated chi-square values, $\chi^2_{1-\alpha/2,n-1} = \chi^2_{.975,24}$ and $\chi^2_{\alpha/2,n-1} = \chi^2_{.025,24}$, and (2) the sample variance s^2. From the chi-square table, we have $\chi^2_{.975,24} = 12.40$ and $\chi^2_{.025,24} = 39.36$. The sample variance s^2 is found in the usual way. We first find the preliminary sums,

$$\sum X_i = 59 + 64 + \cdots + 59 = 1478$$

and

$$\sum X_i^2 = 59^2 + 64^2 + \cdots + 59^2 = 87,732$$

These give

$$\overline{X} = \frac{\sum X_i}{n} = \frac{1478}{25} = 59.12$$

and

$$s^2 = \frac{\sum X_i^2 - n\overline{X}^2}{n-1} = \frac{87,732 - 25(59.12)^2}{24} = 14.69$$

Then the 95% confidence interval for σ^2 is

$$\text{from} \quad \frac{24(14.69)}{39.36} \quad \text{to} \quad \frac{24(14.69)}{12.40}$$

or from 8.96 to 28.43. Taking square roots, we see that the 95% confidence interval for σ is from 2.99 to 5.33. The meaning of this is that if we observe the number of completed assemblies for a very large number of hourly periods, we have 95% confidence that the standard deviation of these quantities will be between 2.99 and 5.33. Notice that in these confidence intervals for σ^2 and σ, the point estimates s^2 and s (14.69 and 3.83) are both closer to the left-hand endpoints than to the right-hand endpoints. This is exactly what is predicted in Figure 8.11.

Problems for Section 8.4

21. For a chi-square density with ν degrees of freedom, find two numbers with area $1 - \alpha$ between them, area α_1 in the left-hand tail, and area α_2 in the right-hand tail, for the following parameters.
    a. $\alpha = .05$, $\alpha_1 = \alpha_2 = .025$, $\nu = 10$
    b. $\alpha = .06$, $\alpha_1 = .05$, $\alpha_2 = .01$, $\nu = 30$
    c. $\alpha = .035$, $\alpha_1 = .01$, $\alpha_2 = .025$, $\nu = 5$
    d. $\alpha = .20$, $\alpha_1 = \alpha_2 = .10$, $\nu = 100$

22. Find an approximate value for the following probabilities when χ^2 has a chi-square distribution with ν degrees of freedom and χ_0^2 is the number specified.
    a. $P(\chi^2 > \chi_0^2)$ when $\chi_0^2 = 22$, $\nu = 14$
    b. $P(\chi^2 < \chi_0^2)$ when $\chi_0^2 = 11$, $\nu = 24$
    c. $P(\chi^2 > \chi_0^2)$ when $\chi_0^2 = 43$, $\nu = 20$
    d. $P(\chi^2 < \chi_0^2)$ when $\chi_0^2 = 2.3$, $\nu = 10$

23. For each of the following values of α and ν, find $\chi^2_{\alpha,\nu}$. (If α and/or ν is not in the chi-square table, approximate $\chi^2_{\alpha,\nu}$ as well as possible.)
    a. $\alpha = .025$, $\nu = 20$ b. $\alpha = .99$, $\nu = 10$
    c. $\alpha = .025$, $\nu = 120$ d. $\alpha = .04$, $\nu = 10$
    e. $\alpha = .03$, $\nu = 5$ f. $\alpha = .07$, $\nu = 150$

*24. Given a normal population distribution, consider the estimate of σ^2 defined by $\hat{s}^2 = \sum (X_i - \bar{X})^2/n$. Is it true that $\hat{s}^2$ is a biased estimate of σ^2, and that the amount of the bias, $E(\hat{s}^2) - \sigma^2$, depends only on the values of n and σ^2, not on the value of μ? Explain.

25. Consider the following three possible estimates of a population variance σ^2:

$$\hat{\sigma}_1^2 = \frac{\sum (X_i - \bar{X})^2}{n - 1}$$

$$\hat{\sigma}_2^2 = \frac{\sum (X_i - m)^2}{n}$$

$$\hat{\sigma}_3^2 = \frac{(\text{interdecile range})^2}{16}$$

(Here m is the sample median, and the interdecile range is as defined in Chapter 2.) Calculate these three estimates for the data at the top of the next column. Can you tell which of these three estimates is closest to the true value of σ^2? Explain.

| 25 | 43 | 39 | 65 | 41 | 37 | 63 | 22 | 46 | 13 |
| 26 | 14 | 82 | 30 | 34 | 67 | 32 | 28 | 43 | 55 |

*26. The variance of a given normal population is $\sigma^2 = 10$. Let α be the probability that the sample variance s^2 from a sample of size n is at least 15. How large must n be so that α is no greater than .05? (Use trial and error on n, together with the chi-square table.)

27. For the population in Problem 26, find two numbers so that the observed sample variance s^2 will be between these two numbers with probability .95 when $n = 20$. (Choose the numbers so that there is an equal probability in each tail.)

28. In Example 8.7 assume that a sample of 25 rod lengths is taken when the process is out of control, with $\sigma = .00030$. How unlikely is a sample standard deviation of .00023 or less? Will such a sample standard deviation convince us that the process is *not* out of control? Explain.

29. For a normal population with standard deviation σ, find the probability that the sample standard deviation s will be no less than $.75\sigma$ for the following sample sizes: (a) $n = 25$; (b) $n = 50$; (c) $n = 100$.

*30. For a normal population with standard deviation σ, which is more likely: obtaining a sample standard deviation s at least 25% below σ or a sample standard deviation s at least 25% above σ? Answer this question for $n = 50$.

31. A set of 14 randomly selected pro basketball games is chosen and the attendance figures for these games are as follows: 7,643, 3,125, 4,152, 23,745, 10,565, 5,730, 12,851, 15,470, 3,291, 5,549, 2,143, 12,154, 14,270, and 16,125. Find the probability of observing as large a sample standard deviation as the one observed if the population of all attendance figures is normally distributed with standard deviation 4,220.

32. For Problem 31, find a 95% confidence interval for the standard deviation of attendance figures across all pro basketball games.

33. The standard deviation of the lifetimes of a random sample of 25 light bulbs manufactured by a particular company is 113.56 hours. Find 95% and 90% confidence intervals for the standard deviation of the lifetimes of all light bulbs manufactured by this company. Assume that the distribution of all lifetimes is normal.

stop

8.5

Comparison of Two Population Variances

In some applications we are interested in comparing two population variances, σ_1^2 and σ_2^2. For example, a foreman of two parallel assembly lines may wish to know whether the variances of a specific quality measure such as weight are equal for the two lines. Another application arises when our primary concern is in estimating the difference between two means, $\mu_1 - \mu_2$. Recall from Section 8.3 that the relevant sampling distribution of $\overline{X}_1 - \overline{X}_2$ depends on whether the associated variances, σ_1^2 and σ_2^2, are equal. Therefore, our first task in this estimation problem is to compare the two variances; then we can turn our attention to the difference between means.

In this section we assume that the two populations are normally distributed with means μ_1 and μ_2 and variances σ_1^2 and σ_2^2. Independent samples of sizes n_1 and n_2 are obtained from these populations, and the two sample variances, s_1^2 and s_2^2, are calculated. To compare the two population variances, we focus our attention on the *ratio* σ_1^2/σ_2^2, and we estimate this ratio by the sample ratio s_1^2/s_2^2. Clearly, if the two population variances are similar, σ_1^2/σ_2^2 is close to 1, and we expect the ratio s_1^2/s_2^2 to be close to 1 also. But if the population variances are not similar, we expect to see a ratio s_1^2/s_2^2 either close to 0 ($\sigma_1^2 < \sigma_2^2$) or larger than 1 ($\sigma_1^2 > \sigma_2^2$). To learn how close to 0 or how much larger than 1 this ratio tends to be, we need to learn the sampling distribution of s_1^2/s_2^2.

The F Distribution

The relevant sampling distribution when we are comparing two population variances is called the F distribution. Specifically, we have the following result.

Sampling Distribution of s_1^2/s_2^2

$\dfrac{s_1^2/\sigma_1^2}{s_2^2/\sigma_2^2}$ has an F distribution with $n_1 - 1$ and $n_2 - 1$ degrees of freedom

---

Notice that in the special case when $\sigma_1^2 = \sigma_2^2$, the σ^2's in the ratio above cancel, and we can state that s_1^2/s_2^2 has an F distribution.

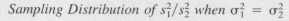

$$\textit{Sampling Distribution of } s_1^2/s_2^2 \textit{ when } \sigma_1^2 = \sigma_2^2$$

$\dfrac{s_1^2}{s_2^2}$ has an F distribution with $n_1 - 1$ and $n_2 - 1$ degrees of freedom

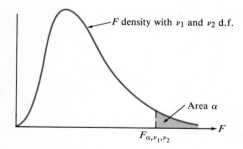

Figure 8.12
Typical F Densities

The F Table

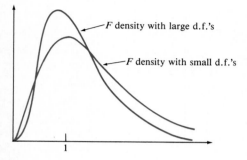

Figure 8.13
Graphical Definition of F_{α, ν_1, ν_2}

Actually, there are many F distributions, one for each pair of sample sizes n_1 and n_2. In shape, their densities resemble chi-square densities. In particular, they are skewed to the right, they do not extend to the left of the vertical axis (since the ratio of two squares must be positive), and their most likely values are around 1 (since we expect both s_1^2/σ_1^2 and s_2^2/σ_2^2 to be close to 1). Two typical F densities are shown in Figure 8.12.

In general, each F distribution is characterized by two parameters, ν_1 and ν_2, again called degrees of freedom. The first of these is associated with the numerator of the ratio, the second with the denominator. The usual terminology is that "the ratio has an F distribution with ν_1 degrees of freedom in the numerator and ν_2 degrees of freedom in the denominator." More simply, we say that "the ratio has an F distribution with ν_1 and ν_2 degrees of freedom." Each pair ν_1 and ν_2 produces a specific F distribution.

For many pairs ν_1 and ν_2, the areas under the corresponding F densities are listed in Table V of Appendix B. Because *two* parameters are needed to determine a given F distribution, a fairly complete listing of F values takes many pages. Therefore, we have listed only a few of the most frequently used F values in Table V. In particular, we have tabulated only right-hand tail values for the right-hand tail probabilities $\alpha = .10$, $\alpha = .05$, $\alpha = .025$, and $\alpha = .01$.

The F values in Table V are denoted by F_{α, ν_1, ν_2}. This is the number with area α to its right under the appropriate F distribution. Figure 8.13 depicts this graphically.

$$\textit{Defining Formula for } F_{\alpha, \nu_1, \nu_2}$$

$$P(F > F_{\alpha, \nu_1, \nu_2}) = \alpha$$

where F (without a subscript) has an F distribution with ν_1 and ν_2 degrees of freedom

Table V gives us F values for small values of α only. To find a number such as $F_{.95,10,15}$, the value with area .95 to its right when there are 10 and 15 degrees of freedom, we use the fact that the reciprocal of an F ratio is also an F ratio, but with the degrees of freedom reversed. If the original F

ratio is in the right-hand tail, its reciprocal is in the left-hand tail (and vice versa). Therefore, we have

$$F_{.95,10,15} = \frac{1}{F_{.05,15,10}} = \frac{1}{2.85} = .35$$

where the 2.85 was found in Table V.

The following two examples show how the F distribution can be used as a sampling distribution. In each case we assume equal population variances and then see how far apart s_1^2 and s_2^2 are likely to be.

Using the F Distribution as a Sampling Distribution

EXAMPLE 8.10

If two samples of sizes 20 and 15 are taken from populations with equal population variances, what is the probability that one of the sample variances will be at least three times as large as the other?

SOLUTION

Let s_1^2 be the sample variance for the sample of size 20, and let s_2^2 be the sample variance for the sample of size 15. Then s_1^2/s_2^2 has an F distribution with 19 and 14 degrees of freedom, and s_2^2/s_1^2 has an F distribution with 14 and 19 degrees of freedom. If one of the sample variances is at least three times as large as the other, then either $s_1^2 > 3s_2^2$ or $s_2^2 > 3s_1^2$. Because these events are mutually exclusive, the probability of the required event (a union) is

$$P\left(\frac{s_1^2}{s_2^2} > 3\right) + P\left(\frac{s_2^2}{s_1^2} > 3\right)$$

For the first of these probabilities, we find from Table V that $F_{.025,19,14} = 2.86$ and $F_{.01,19,14} = 3.53$. This means that $P(s_1^2/s_2^2 > 2.86) = .025$ and $P(s_1^2/s_2^2 > 3.53) = .01$. Therefore, $P(s_1^2/s_2^2 > 3)$ is approximately equal to .02 (see Figure 8.14a on p. 384). (This approximation is only a rough interpolation of the tabulated values, but it is sufficiently accurate for our purposes.) Similarly, for the second probability, Table V shows that $F_{.025,14,19} = 2.65$ and $F_{.01,14,19} = 3.19$. In this case, 3 is closer to $F_{.01,14,19}$, so we approximate $P(s_2^2/s_1^2 > 3)$ by .015 (see Figure 8.14b). The combined probability is then approximately equal to $.02 + .015 = .035$.

Usually we are interested in one tail only. Then it suffices to put the larger sample variance in the numerator. The following example is typical.

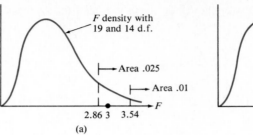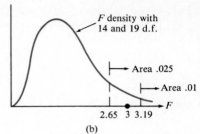

Figure 8.14

EXAMPLE 8.11

In each of two different residential areas of Indianapolis, a random sample of 15 houses is chosen, and the assessed valuation of each house is observed. The data in Table 8.8 show the results (in thousands of dollars). Find the sample variances for these two samples and verify that the second sample variance is larger. Then compute the probability of obtaining a sample variance for sample 2 this much larger than the sample variance for sample 1 if the population variances are equal.

Table 8.8

Home	Sample 1	Sample 2
1	67.5	79.4
2	78.4	81.7
3	89.2	85.9
4	64.3	61.3
5	77.1	107.3
6	81.4	105.2
7	87.3	97.1
8	66.1	110.2
9	83.2	65.2
10	59.2	73.5
11	76.1	69.1
12	81.5	57.1
13	77.3	98.2
14	65.1	101.3
15	60.7	69.2

SOLUTION

The sample means are

$$\bar{X}_1 = \frac{67.5 + 78.4 + \cdots + 60.7}{15} = 74.29$$

and

$$\overline{X}_2 = \frac{79.4 + 81.7 + \cdots + 69.2}{15} = 84.11$$

From these, we compute the sample variances as

$$s_1^2 = \frac{(67.5^2 + 78.4^2 + \cdots + 60.7^2) - 15(74.29)^2}{14} = 94.32$$

and

$$s_2^2 = \frac{(79.4^2 + 81.7^2 + \cdots + 69.2^2) - 15(84.11)^2}{14} = 323.20$$

Forming the ratio $323.20/94.32 = 3.43$, we see that the second sample variance is 3.43 times as large as the first. To see how improbable this is, we find $P(F > 3.43)$, the probability of observing an F ratio at least as large as 3.43 when there are 14 and 14 degrees of freedom. From Table V, $F_{.025,14,14} = 2.98$ and $F_{.01,14,14} = 3.70$. Therefore, a rough interpolation shows that $P(F > 3.43)$ is approximately equal to .015 (see Figure 8.15). In words, the probability of residential area 2 having this much larger a sample variance than residential area 1 if both residential areas have the same population variance is about .015, or 1 chance out of 67.

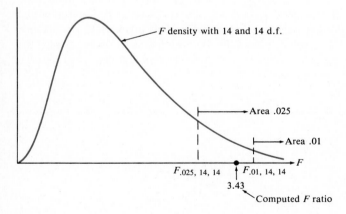

Figure 8.15

We have phrased all the quantities in this section in terms of ratios of two sample *variances*. By taking square roots, however, we can just as easily talk about ratios of sample *standard deviations*. For example, it is just as likely to have s_1^2 at least four times as large as s_2^2 as it is to have s_1 at least two times as large as s_2.

Confidence Intervals for σ_1^2/σ_2^2

We now see how to form a confidence interval for the unknown parameter σ_1^2/σ_2^2. Using the fact that $(s_1^2/\sigma_1^2)/(s_2^2/\sigma_2^2)$ has an F distribution with $n_1 - 1$ and $n_2 - 1$ degrees of freedom, we can obtain the following confidence interval.

Confidence Interval for σ_1^2/σ_2^2 with Confidence Level $1 - \alpha$

$\dfrac{\sigma_1^2}{\sigma_2^2}$ is between $\dfrac{s_1^2/s_2^2}{F_{\alpha/2,n_1-1,n_2-1}}$ and $(s_1^2/s_2^2)\, F_{\alpha/2,n_2-1,n_1-1}$

Notice that for the left-hand endpoint, s_1^2/s_2^2 is divided by an F value; for the right-hand endpoint, s_1^2/s_2^2 is multiplied by an F value.

EXAMPLE 8.11 (continued)

For the data in Table 8.8, find a 95% confidence interval for the ratio σ_1^2/σ_2^2.

SOLUTION

The point estimate of σ_1^2/σ_2^2 is the ratio of sample variances: $s_1^2/s_2^2 = 94.32/323.20 = .292$. To find the left-hand endpoint of the confidence interval, we divide .292 by $F_{.025,14,14} = 2.98$ to obtain .098. The right-hand endpoint is found by multiplying .292 by 2.98. This gives .870. (Notice that the *same* tabulated F value is used for both endpoints; this is because the sample sizes are equal.) Therefore, we are 95% confident that σ_1^2 is between 9.8% and 87% as large as σ_2^2.

Problems for Section 8.5

34. For an F density with v_1 and v_2 degrees of freedom, find the number with area α to the right of it for the following parameter values.
   a. $\alpha = .025,\ v_1 = v_2 = 15$
   b. $\alpha = .01,\ v_1 = 1,\ v_2 = 20$
   c. $\alpha = .05,\ v_1 = 10,\ v_2 = 15$
   d. $\alpha = .10,\ v_1 = 5,\ v_2 = 25$

35. For each of the following values of α, v_1, and v_2, find F_{α,v_1,v_2}. (If α, v_1, and/or v_2 is not in the F tables, approximate F_{α,v_1,v_2} as well as possible.)

   a. $\alpha = .05,\ v_1 = v_2 = 10$
   b. $\alpha = .025,\ v_1 = 1,\ v_2 = 25$
   c. $\alpha = .01,\ v_1 = 97,\ v_2 = 108$
   d. $\alpha = .10,\ v_1 = 57,\ v_2 = 10$
   e. $\alpha = .01,\ v_1 = v_2 = 10$
   f. $\alpha = .04,\ v_1 = 1,\ v_2 = 8$

36. For an F density with v_1 and v_2 degrees of freedom, find two numbers with area $1 - \alpha$ between them and equal areas in each tail for the following values.
   a. $\alpha = .05,\ v_1 = 5,\ v_2 = 15$

b. $\alpha = .02$, $\nu_1 = \nu_2 = 20$
c. $\alpha = .20$, $\nu_1 = 1$, $\nu_2 = 10$
d. $\alpha = .10$, $\nu_1 = 10$, $\nu_2 = 30$

*37. Consider two independent sample variances, s_1^2 and s_2^2, based on sample sizes $n_1 = 10$ and $n_2 = 25$, from two normal populations with common variance σ^2. Which is more likely: that s_1^2 is at least twice as large as s_2^2, or that s_2^2 is at least twice as large as s_1^2? Answer by finding the probabilities of these two events.

38. Explain why only right-hand tail F values need to be tabulated. What do we do if we need a left-hand tail F value? Be specific.

*39. A random sample of salaries of 16 pro basketball players has a sample standard deviation of $53,250. A similar random sample of 25 pro football players' salaries has a sample standard deviation of $44,350. Is this very convincing evidence that the variance of all basketball players' salaries is larger than that of football players? Answer by finding the probability of the basketball sample standard deviation being this much larger than the football sample standard deviation if the two population standard deviations are equal. Assume normal distributions of the players' salaries.

40. Given the sample data in Problem 39, find a 95% confidence interval for the ratio of the basketball salary variance to the football salary variance.

*41. In two undergraduate statistics classes, one with 10 students and one with 25 students, an identical exam is given. One class has a sample standard deviation 1.6 times as large as the sample standard deviation of the other class, but we are not told which class has the larger of the two standard deviations. If these two classes are samples from a large (normally distributed) population of undergraduates with a single σ^2, how likely is this large a discrepancy between the two sample standard deviations?

8.6

Summary of Confidence Interval Formulas

In Table 8.9 we summarize the confidence interval formulas from this chapter. Recall that these are used when the sample sizes are small and the population distributions are normal.

Table 8.9

1. Parameter to be estimated: μ
   Assumptions: Population is normal; sample size is small ($n < 30$).
   Point estimate: $\overline{X}$
   Standard error of point estimate: $\text{StdErr}(\overline{X}) = s/\sqrt{n}$
   Degrees of freedom: $n - 1$
   Confidence interval: $\overline{X} \pm t_{\alpha/2, n-1} \, \text{StdErr}(\overline{X})$

2. Parameter to be estimated: $\mu_1 - \mu_2$
   Assumptions: Populations are normal; sample sizes are small ($n_1 < 30$, $n_2 < 30$); population variances are equal; observations from two populations are independent.
   Point estimate: $\overline{X}_1 - \overline{X}_2$
   Standard error of point estimate: $\text{StdErr}(\overline{X}_1 - \overline{X}_2) = s_p\sqrt{1/n_1 + 1/n_2}$, where

   $$s_p^2 = [(n_1 - 1)s_1^2 + (n_2 - 1)s_2^2]/(n_1 + n_2 - 2)$$

   Degrees of freedom: $n_1 + n_2 - 2$
   Confidence interval: $\overline{X}_1 - \overline{X}_2 \pm t_{\alpha/2, n_1+n_2-2} \, \text{StdErr}(\overline{X}_1 - \overline{X}_2)$

   (*continued*)

Table 8.9   *(continued)*

3. Parameter to be estimated: $\mu_1 - \mu_2$

    Assumptions: Populations are normal; sample sizes are small ($n_1 < 30$, $n_2 < 30$); population variances are not equal; observations from two populations are independent.

    Point estimate: $\overline{X}_1 - \overline{X}_2$

    Standard error of point estimate: $\text{StdErr}(\overline{X}_1 - \overline{X}_2) = \sqrt{s_1^2/n_1 + s_2^2/n_2}$

    Degrees of freedom: $\overline{n}$, where $\overline{n}$ is the integer closest to the expression

$$\overline{n} \approx \frac{(s_1^2/n_1 + s_2^2/n_2)^2}{(s_1^2/n_1)^2/(n_1 - 1) + (s_2^2/n_2)^2/(n_2 - 1)}$$

    Confidence interval: $\overline{X}_1 - \overline{X}_2 \pm t_{\alpha/2, \overline{n}} \,\text{StdErr}(\overline{X}_1 - \overline{X}_2)$

4. Parameter to be estimated: σ^2

    Assumptions: Population is normal.

    Point estimate: s^2

    Degrees of freedom: $n - 1$

    Confidence interval: from $(n - 1)s^2/\chi_{\alpha/2, n-1}^2$ to $(n - 1)s^2/\chi_{1-\alpha/2, n-1}^2$

5. Parameter to be estimated: σ_1^2/σ_2^2

    Assumptions: Populations are normal; observations from two populations are independent.

    Point estimate: s_1^2/s_2^2

    Degrees of freedom: $n_1 - 1$, $n_2 - 1$

    Confidence interval: from $(s_1^2/s_2^2)/F_{\alpha/2, n_1-1, n_2-1}$ to $(s_1^2/s_2^2)F_{\alpha/2, n_2-1, n_1-1}$

Summary

This chapter continues the discussion of estimation, but it does not assume large sample sizes. The effect is that the sampling distributions are no longer normal, even when the population distribution is normal. Therefore, we have introduced three new distributions that are necessary when estimating means and/or variances. These are the t distribution, the chi-square distribution, and the F distribution. All of these distributions depend on parameters called degrees of freedom, all are tabulated in Appendix B, and all are relatives of the normal distribution in the sense that they apply (exactly) only when the population distribution is normal.

The t distribution is very similar to the standard normal distribution, except that it has a slightly larger variance. It is used to estimate a single mean or the difference between two means when the sample sizes are small and the population variances are unknown. The chi-square and F distributions are skewed distributions that are useful for estimating variances. In particular, the chi-square distribution is used to estimate a single variance, whereas the F distribution is used to compare two variances. By using these new distributions (and their tabulated values) appropriately, we have seen how to form confidence intervals for a mean, the difference between two means, a variance, and the ratio of two variances. However, it does not end here. We will see in later chapters that these new distributions are useful in a variety of different settings.

Application 8.1   Most of us dislike waiting in shopping lines so much that we overestimate the time we wait. This is the conclusion of a recent study done by Hornik. (Reference: Jacob Hornik, ''Subjective vs. Objective Time Measures: A Note on the Perception of Time in Consumer Behavior,'' *Journal of Consumer Research,* Vol. 11, 1984, pp. 615–618.) He and his assistants watched a random sample of 281 people checking out of a supermarket, a department store, and a bank. These people were classified by sex and by the type of line they waited in: multiserver (several cashiers, each of whom serves a separate line), snake (several cashiers working one line of customers with the first in line approaching the next available server), and express (a separate line to a cashier who handles a limited number of purchases). The people were timed from the instant they joined a line until they were finished being serviced. Then in a subsequent interview, they were asked how long (to the nearest minute) they thought they had waited in line. The means and standard deviations for the *difference* between estimated and actual times are shown below. From these we can calculate 95% confidence intervals for the mean difference between the estimated and actual waiting time, taken over the entire population for each category. For example, the confidence interval for males in express lines is

$$2.02 \pm 2.03\left(\frac{3.91}{\sqrt{35}}\right) = 2.02 \pm 1.34$$

Table 8.10

	Sample Size	Mean	Standard Deviation	95% Confidence Interval
Multiserver				
Men	62	2.79	5.59	1.37–4.21
Women	86	2.91	5.77	1.68–4.14
Snake				
Men	20	2.83	5.79	.13–5.53
Women	30	3.07	5.93	.86–5.28
Express				
Men	35	2.02	3.91	.68–3.36
Women	48	2.05	3.90	.92–3.18

or from .68 minute to 3.36 minutes. This confidence interval and others are shown in Table 8.10. (The t value for 34 degrees of freedom is 2.03. This and other exact t values, rather than z values, were used by Hornik to produce the results in Table 8.10.) From the data in this table, we can conclude that most shoppers, regardless of sex or the type of waiting line, *think* they are waiting in line longer than they actually wait.

Application 8.2   To study complex probabilistic systems, researchers often resort to computer simulation. The system is "modeled" by means of a computer program that simulates the system through a given period of time. As simulated time progresses in the computer program, we are able to see how the system evolves, and we are able to keep track of the simulated operating characteristics of the system. When there are random elements in the system, they are simulated by means of a computerized random number generator. The main result of such a computer simulation is a "snapshot" of the system as it might actually evolve in real time.

As an example, a version of an inventory stocking model was simulated. In this model a company keeps track of a particular type of item in stock. At the beginning of each week it uses the following type of reordering policy: If the current inventory is sufficiently low, it orders enough to bring the inventory up to a prescribed level; otherwise, it orders no items that week. During the week customers arrive at random times and request random numbers of items. If there are enough items in stock, the customers' requests are satisfied immediately; otherwise, they are put on a waiting list until a new order arrives. There are three types of costs the company wants to investigate: (1) ordering costs of new items, (2) inventory costs of having excess stock on the shelves, and (3) shortage costs of having customers wait for out-of-stock items. The company would like to know the average cost per week for each of these over a 36-week period, given values of the system parameters. (These system parameters include things such as the unit ordering cost, the fixed cost per order, the average time between customer requests, and so on. It is assumed that these are known, so that they can be fed into the computer simulation program.)

When this model is simulated over a 36-week period, it is not difficult to keep track of any desired costs. However, because of the random numbers used in the simulation, it is important to realize that a simulated cost from any single simulation run is a random variable drawn from the population distribution of all such costs. Therefore, if we want to estimate the mean of this distribution, we must simulate the entire 36-week period several times and use the concepts from the past few chapters to form point estimates and confidence intervals. Also, it is more likely that we will have small sample sizes. This is because a given simulation run is usually time-consuming and expensive; hence we may not be able to afford many runs.

To illustrate the analysis, we simulated the 36-week period of the inventory system 15 times (using different random numbers each time). The system parameters were set at fixed levels. For each run we kept track of the average ordering costs per week (X), the average cost per week of holding inventory (Y), the average cost per week of making customers wait (Z), and the average total cost per week ($T = X + Y + Z$). The results are shown in Table 8.11. From these results we can estimate the true mean of any of these cost types. For example, a point estimate of μ_X, the mean ordering cost per week, is the average over the 15 runs, $\overline{X}$ = \$97.59. Similarly, a 95% confidence interval for μ_X is

$$\overline{X} \pm t_{.025,14} \, \text{StdErr}(\overline{X}) = 97.59 \pm 2.145\left(\frac{5.54}{\sqrt{15}}\right) = 97.59 \pm 3.07$$

or from \$94.52 to \$100.66. Similarly, point estimates and 95% confidence intervals for the other three types of costs are shown in the table. The only way to improve on these estimates, that is, to obtain shorter confidence intervals, is to run the simulation more than 15 times.

Table 8.11

Run Number	X	Y	Z	T
1	88.53	29.02	.28	117.83
2	102.56	23.86	3.84	130.26
3	97.08	27.30	4.05	128.43
4	95.25	25.26	1.68	122.18
5	98.75	25.62	1.82	126.19
6	101.94	23.19	1.97	127.11
7	101.11	25.64	.39	127.14
8	97.00	26.62	.84	124.45
9	100.22	25.52	1.64	127.37
10	94.47	25.12	1.64	121.24
11	104.72	23.28	5.85	133.85
12	94.69	26.30	.52	121.52
13	107.36	23.08	2.95	133.39
14	90.06	26.82	1.80	118.67
15	90.06	25.34	1.76	117.15
Mean	97.59	25.46	2.07	125.12
Std. dev.	5.54	1.65	1.53	5.29
95% C.I.	94.52–100.66	24.55–26.37	1.22–2.92	122.19–128.05

Glossary of Terms

t distribution a symmetric, bell-shaped distribution with slightly more variance than a $N(0, 1)$ distribution; sometimes called the Student t distribution

Degrees of freedom the parameter (or parameters) of the distributions in this chapter; in general, it is the sample size minus the number of nuisance parameters that have to be estimated

Notation $t_{\alpha,\nu}$ the number with area α to its right under a t density with ν degrees of freedom

Chi-square and F distributions two distributions of positive random variables useful for studying variances

Notation $\chi^2_{\alpha,\nu}$ the number with area α to its right under a chi-square density with ν degrees of freedom

Notation F_{α,ν_1,ν_2} the number with area α to its right under an F density with ν_1 degrees of freedom in the numerator and ν_2 degrees of freedom in the denominator

Important Formulas

1. Formula for t when estimating a mean

$$t = \frac{\overline{X} - \mu}{s/\sqrt{n}}$$

2. Formula for t when estimating the difference between two means and the variances are equal

$$t = \frac{(\overline{X}_1 - \overline{X}_2) - (\mu_1 - \mu_2)}{s_p \sqrt{1/n_1 + 1/n_2}}$$

where

$$s_p^2 = \frac{(n_1 - 1)s_1^2 + (n_2 - 1)s_2^2}{n_1 + n_2 - 2}$$

3. Formula for t when estimating the difference between two means and the variances are not necessarily equal

$$t = \frac{(\overline{X}_1 - \overline{X}_2) - (\mu_1 - \mu_2)}{\sqrt{s_1^2/n_1 + s_2^2/n_2}}$$

4. Formula for the approximate degrees of freedom when estimating the difference between two means and the variances are not necessarily equal

$$\overline{n} \approx \frac{(s_1^2/n_1 + s_2^2/n_2)^2}{(s_1^2/n_1)^2/(n_1 - 1) + (s_2^2/n_2)^2/(n_2 - 1)}$$

5. Formula for χ^2 when estimating a variance

$$\chi^2 = \frac{(n - 1)s^2}{\sigma^2}$$

6. Formula for F when comparing two variances

$$F = \frac{s_1^2/\sigma_1^2}{s_2^2/\sigma_2^2}$$

7. Confidence interval formulas in this chapter—see Table 8.9

End-of-Chapter Problems

42. The following data represent a sample of telephone bills for 15 randomly selected families: 27.40, 22.10, 28.41, 35.12, 26.50, 28.14, 29.31, 37.20, 20.10, 25.14, 26.33, 35.90, 30.21, 23.60, and 24.95.
   a. Find the sample variance s^2 of these data from the definition of s^2, that is, $s^2 = \Sigma (X_i - \overline{X})^2/(n - 1)$.
   b. Find the sample variance s^2 from the computing formula for s^2. Check that it is the same answer as you obtained in part (a).
   c. If the distribution of all phone bills is normal, find a 95% confidence interval for the mean of this distribution. Then find a 95% confidence interval for the standard deviation of this distribution.

43. For a random sample of books offered by two competing book clubs, the following prices have been observed.

Book Club 1	Book Club 2
$14.95	$13.50
13.95	11.99
15.95	12.99
11.95	10.99
10.95	11.50
13.95	10.99
11.50	11.50
14.95	9.99
18.50	8.50
10.95	13.99
	10.50
	16.99
	6.99
	12.50
	9.99

   a. Find the two sample variances of prices, s_1^2 and s_2^2. Then, assuming that the two population variances are equal, find the pooled estimate s_p^2 of this common variance.
   b. Find the t value for the difference between the two sample means, $\overline{X}_1 - \overline{X}_2$, assuming the two population means are equal and the two population variances are equal.
   c. Find the probability of obtaining a t value at least as large in absolute value as the one in part (b) for typical random samples of these sizes. Again assume equal population means and equal population variances.

44. Using the same data as in Problem 43, but not assuming equal population variances, do the following.
   a. Find the t value for $\overline{X}_1 - \overline{X}_2$ if the two population means are equal.
   b. Find the associated degrees of freedom parameter $\overline{n}$ for this t value.
   c. Find the probability of obtaining a t value at least as large in absolute value as the one in part (b) for typical random samples with these sample sizes.

45. Again referring to the data in Problem 43, find two 95% confidence intervals for the difference between the mean prices for the two book clubs, one where the population variances are assumed equal and the other where they are not assumed equal.

46. As of 1985 it has been reported that experienced sales professionals earn quite a lot more than they did in 1983.
   a. Assume that the population distributions of salaries in 1983 and 1985 are normal. If two samples of 10 experienced sales professionals, sample 1 taken in 1985 and sample 2 taken in 1983, yield sample means of $31,300 and $26,400, and sample standard deviations of $2320 and $2140, find a 90% confidence interval for the difference between the

mean salary in 1985 and the mean salary in 1983. Assume equal population variances.

b. If the difference between population mean salaries in 1985 and 1983 is really $3460, find the t value for the difference between means, using the sample data in part (a). Is this t value unusual? Answer with an appropriate probability calculation.

*47. One industry has reported that the average training cost of a salesperson is $12,630. (This average is taken over all companies in the industry.) Suppose that a random sample of 15 companies in this industry are chosen. They report a sample mean training cost of $13,420 and a sample standard deviation of $2130.

a. Find the probability of observing as large a t value for the mean as the observed t value if the $12,630 figure is correct. Assume that the population distribution of training costs is normal.

b. If it is *known* that the population standard deviation is $\sigma = \$2700$ (and the population mean is still $12,630), find the probability of observing as large a sample mean as $13,420 from a sample of size $n = 15$.

c. How are parts (a) and (b) related? Do they contradict one another? Explain.

48. It is well known that the average man is older when he marries for the first time than the average woman on her first marriage. Consider the two (independent) samples below, one of men and one of women. Each number represents the age when first married.

Men	Women
25	20
31	18
19	21
23	32
30	22
26	29
27	25
29	22
24	18
25	19
27	26
29	25
31	23

a. Find the pooled estimate of the variance of ages from the combined samples, assuming that the variance of men's

ages and the variance of women's ages at first marriage are equal.

b. Assuming that the male and female populations of ages are normal, calculate the t value for the difference between the sample means of men and women when the population mean difference is 2.5.

c. Find the probability of observing a t value for the mean difference as large as the one in part (b).

49. Repeat parts (b) and (c) of Problem 48, but do not assume that the population variances for men and women are equal.

50. Referring to Problems 48 and 49, calculate 95% confidence intervals for the difference between the mean female and male ages when first married. For the first confidence interval assume equal population variances; for the second do not assume equal population variances.

51. It has been reported that Americans eat less beef today than they used to. Consider two samples of 15 people each, one taken in 1981 and one in 1985, with sample means of 78.3 and 75.2 pounds of beef per person, and sample standard deviations of 10.6 and 11.2 pounds per person. Assume that the distribution of beef consumption each year is normal.

a. Find a 90% confidence interval for the difference between the mean amounts of beef consumed in 1981 and 1985. Assume equal variances for the two years.

b. Find a 90% confidence interval for σ_1^2/σ_2^2, where σ_1^2 is the variance of beef consumption in 1981 and σ_2^2 is the similar variance in 1985. Does this confidence interval tend to support the assumption in part (a) that σ_1^2 and σ_2^2 are equal? Explain.

52. A random sample of 12 retailers who specialize in toy sales are asked to estimate the percentage of their annual toy sales that occur during the last three weeks of the year. Their responses are as follows: 55, 61, 47, 56, 62, 57, 51, 68, 54, 45, 69, and 60. Would you consider the resulting t value for the mean of these percentages to be abnormally low if the average percentage, taken over all retailers, is 60% and the population distribution of percentages is normal? (This 60% figure is, in fact, the national average.) Back up your answer with an appropriate probability calculation.

*53. Consider two samples with equal sample sizes ($n_1 = n_2$).

a. Show algebraically that the standard error of $\bar{X}_1 - \bar{X}_2$, and hence the t value for this difference, is the same whether or not we assume equal population variances. (To simplify the algebra, let n denote the common sample size.)

b. If, in addition, the two sample variances are equal ($s_1^2 = s_2^2$), show algebraically that the degrees of freedom $\bar{n}$ from

Section 8.3 reduces to $n_1 + n_2 - 2$. (In this part let n denote the common sample size and let s^2 denote the common sample variance.)

54. We often hear that people in the United States watch too much television. To examine this, we ask a random sample of 20 teenagers to keep track of their TV viewing times per week, and we ask a random sample of 20 people in their 30s to do the same. The teenage sample has mean 45 hours, 20 minutes and standard deviation 5 hours, 25 minutes. The people in their 30s have sample mean 35 hours, 37 minutes and sample standard deviation 7 hours, 25 minutes. Assume that the distribution of television viewing time across the teenage population is normal with mean and standard deviation μ_1 and σ_1. The distribution for people in their 30s is also normal, with mean and standard deviation μ_2 and σ_2.
   a. Find a 95% confidence interval for μ_1. Do the same for σ_1.
   b. Find a 95% confidence interval for μ_2. Do the same for σ_2.
   c. Find a 95% confidence interval for $\mu_1 - \mu_2$, assuming that $\sigma_1^2 = \sigma_2^2$.
   d. Find a 95% confidence interval for σ_1^2/σ_2^2. Does it appear from this confidence interval that the assumption in part (c) is reasonable?

55. A recent study looked at a large sample (over 400) of "dog" companies. (Reference: B. D. Gelb, "Strategic Planning for the Under-Dog," *Business Horizons*, Vol. 25, 1982, pp. 8–18.) These companies were identified as those inferior in certain financial aspects. The average return on investment (ROI) for these companies is 18.5% (before interest and taxes) and the standard deviation is 4.7%. The distribution of these ROIs is approximately normal.
   a. If a random 12 of these companies are selected, what is the probability that these 12 have an average ROI of at least 15%? (Consider the 400-plus companies described above as the population.)
   b. What is the probability that the ROIs of the 12 companies in part (a) have a sample standard deviation of at least 2.4%?

*56. Consider the income levels of recent applicants for welfare. The population is known to be normally distributed. For a random sample of 25 applicants, we find that $\Sigma X_i = 92,451$ and $\Sigma (X_i - \overline{X})^2 = 24,016,254$.
   a. Find point estimates of μ and σ based on this information.
   b. What is the probability of observing as low a t value as the one from this sample if the population mean is 4345?

c. What is the probability of observing as low a sample standard deviation as the one observed if the population standard deviation is 1321?

*57. Certain tubes produced by a company have a mean lifetime of 900 hours and a standard deviation of 80 hours. The distribution of these lifetimes is approximately normal. The company sends out 1000 lots of 20 tubes each.
   a. In how many of the lots can we expect the sample mean lifetime to exceed 910 hours?
   b. In how many of the lots can we expect the sample standard deviation of the lifetimes to exceed 100 hours?

*58. Assume that ball bearings have a mean diameter of .5 inch. The standard deviation of diameters of all such ball bearings is .01 inch. Also, the distribution of the diameters is normal.
   a. How likely is it that a sample of 25 ball bearings will have a sample mean between .497 and .503 inch?
   b. How likely is it that the sample standard deviation of the diameters of these 25 ball bearings will be between .008 and .012 inch?
   c. How likely is it that neither of the events in parts (a) and (b) will occur? (For this part, use the fact that the sample mean and the sample standard deviation from a normal population are *independent* random variables, and think of intersections.)

*59. For the telephone bill data in Problem 42, let s^2 be the sample variance, let σ^2 be the population variance, and let $\chi^2 = (n - 1)s^2/\sigma^2$. If α is the probability of observing a χ^2 value at least as large as the one observed, find the value of σ^2 that makes α equal to .05; that makes α equal to .01. Then interpret your findings in words.

60. The public television stations in many cities hold annual fund-raising drives in order to make enough money to continue high-quality programming. For one station a random sample of 12 individual contributors shows the following contributions (in dollars): 65, 125, 35, 70, 60, 45, 20, 135, 70, 95, 100, and 25.
   a. Assuming that the population of contributions is normally distributed, find a 95% confidence interval for the mean amount per contribution.
   b. Find a 95% confidence interval for the standard deviation of amount per contribution.

*61. We are often interested in a sum of squared deviations from a mean. Show algebraically that the following two equations are true.
   a. $\sum (X_i - \mu)^2 = \sum X_i^2 - 2n\mu\overline{X} + n\mu^2$
   b. $\sum (X_i - \overline{X})^2 = \sum X_i^2 - n\overline{X}^2$

*62. Consider the pooled variance s_p^2 from Section 8.3:

$$s_p^2 = \frac{(n_1 - 1)s_1^2 + (n_2 - 1)s_2^2}{n_1 + n_2 - 2}$$

Show algebraically that this is equivalent to

$$s_p^2 = \frac{\Sigma X_i^2 - n_1\overline{X}_1^2 - n_2\overline{X}_2^2}{n_1 + n_2 - 2}$$

where the sum of squares is taken over all $n_1 + n_2$ observations in the two samples. Then calculate s_p^2 for the following data by both formulas and check that they agree.

Sample 1	Sample 2
25	29
43	24
27	25
15	17
18	32
16	51
25	27
	33
	51

*63. A random sample of n natural gas bills in a given community has a sample standard deviation of \$35.20. Assume that the population standard deviation is \$29.30. If it is claimed that a sample standard deviation this much greater than the population standard deviation is only about .10, find (approximately) what the sample size n must have been. (Use trial and error on n, together with the chi-square table.)

*64. If you believe that the variances from two normal populations are equal, would you be surprised if two independent random samples, of size approximately 100 each, had sample standard deviations of $s_1 = 10$ and $s_2 = 15$? Why or why not? Answer by calculating an appropriate probability based on the F distribution.

65. A newspaper article in 1983 listed the 1982–1983 tuitions for 10 well-known private universities. These data are as follows: \$8820, \$8000, \$8085, \$8700, \$8427, \$8380, \$8190, \$8290, \$8220, and \$8370. Assuming that this sample is representative of all private universities and that the distribution of tuitions for these universities is normal, find a 95% confidence interval for the mean of this distribution. Do the same for the standard deviation of this distribution.

*66. Continuing Problem 19 (p. 367), assume that students and faculty have the same population mean usage (as well as the same population variance). That is, the faculty and students can be considered as one large population. Find a 95% confidence interval for the mean usage of this population. Do the same for the standard deviation of this population. (Pool the two samples into one large sample, and use the appropriate formulas from Chapter 2 for merging means and variances from separate samples.)

*67. In Section 8.4 we used computer simulation to generate 10,000 sample variances (s^2's) for samples of size 30 from a $N(100, 10^2)$ population. The first 100 s^2 values are shown in Table 8.5. For now, consider these 100 values as a random sample of size 100 from the sampling distribution of the sample variance. Also assume that this distribution is approximately normal. (According to Figure 8.5, this is not an unreasonable assumption.)

a. Use the fact that the sample mean and sample standard deviation of these 100 numbers are 101.28 and 26.88 to obtain a 95% confidence interval for the mean of the sampling distribution of s^2. Then find a 95% confidence interval for the standard deviation of the sampling distribution of s^2.

b. Do the confidence intervals in part (a) include the true mean and true standard deviation of the sampling distribution of s^2? [Recall from Section 8.4 that $E(s^2) = \sigma^2$ and $\text{Var}(s^2) = 2\sigma^4/(n - 1)$.]

68. Consider a normal population with μ and σ^2 unknown. If we take two separate, independent samples of sizes $n_1 = 15$ and $n_2 = 20$ and use these to obtain two 95% confidence intervals for μ, can we be absolutely sure that the confidence interval based on the larger sample ($n_2 = 20$) will be the shorter of the two? Why or why not?

69. Referring to the quality control data used in Application 5.1 and again in Application 6.2, find a 95% confidence interval for the population mean and a 95% confidence interval for the population standard deviation, assuming that the population is normal. Which of these would be most disturbing to the quality control engineers? Discuss.

*70. In 1981, Jung performed an experiment to see how much variation exists in new car dealers' prices of popular automobiles. (Reference: Allen F. Jung, "Finding a Better Deal on a New Car," *Business Horizons*, Vol. 26, 1983, pp. 34–36.) Posing as a potential customer, he visited a number of new car dealers in Toronto. At each dealership he got a quote for a 1982 Chevrolet Caprice Classic and a 1982 Ford LTD, each with standard equipment. (Each quote was obtained after the usual bargaining process.) Although the factory-suggested list prices for these cars were approximately $11,530 and $11,532, the mean quotes he obtained were $10,601 for the Chevy and $10,528 for the Ford. The standard deviations of these quotes were $228 for the Chevy and $239 for the Ford. Jung did not report the sample size (number of dealers visited), but we will assume that it was 20.

a. Find a 95% confidence interval for the mean quoted price of a 1982 Chevrolet Caprice Classic, taken over all deal- erships in the relevant population. Do the same for the 1982 Ford LTD.

b. Find a 95% confidence interval for the population standard deviation of quoted prices of the Chevy. Do the same for the Ford.

c. If we used the data above and the method from this chapter to find a 95% confidence interval for the difference be- tween the mean quoted prices of the Chevy and the Ford, why might we make an error? (Think of correlation.)

Computer Problems

(These problems are to be used in conjunction with the computer software package.)

1. Referring to the grade point averages and test scores in Table II of Appendix D, consider only the scores on the first 20 students. Use the SAMPMEAN program to find (i) a 95% confidence interval for the mean undergraduate GPA; (ii) a 90% confidence interval for the standard deviation of all under- graduate GPA's. Then repeat, finding these confidence inter- vals for graduate GPA's.

2. Continuing Problem 1 (and again using only the data from the first 20 students), use the SAMPMEAN program to find a 95% confidence interval for the difference between the mean verbal percentile and the mean quantitative percentile.

3. Now continue Problem 2, but use the data on the first 40

students to find a 95% confidence interval for the proportion of students who achieved a higher percentile on the verbal part than on the quantitative part. Use the PROPORTN program. Then repeat, this time basing the confidence interval on the last 40 students.

4. As you are watching television, keep track of the number of times each commercial states the brand name of the product being advertised. Gather this data on 20 separate commercials, but do not use commercials for any given brand more than once. Then use the SAMPMEAN program to find a 90% con- fidence interval for the mean number of times the brand name is stated. Also, use this program to find a 90% confidence interval for the standard deviation of this number. Then as time permits, repeat this experiment several times to see how your confidence intervals vary from sample to sample.

APPENDIX 8A

Robustness to the Normal Assumption

The main feature that distinguishes this chapter from Chapter 7 is that we now allow the sample sizes to be small. To compensate for this, we are forced to assume normal population distributions. Since this is a rather strong assumption (many populations are *not* normally distributed), we need to see whether the methods in this chapter are valid when the normal assumption is violated. If they are valid, at least for moderate departures from normality, we say the methods are *robust*. As we will see, the methods that use the t distribution for studying means are fairly robust, whereas the methods that use the chi-square or F distributions for studying variances are not very robust.

To test for robustness, we again resorted to computer simulation. First, we chose several nonnormal populations that differed in their departure from normality. The population densities chosen are shown in Figure 8.16. Notice

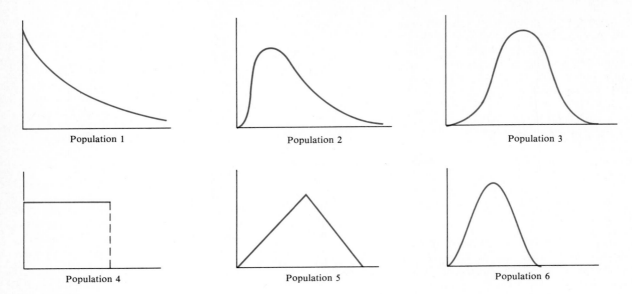

Figure 8.16
Population Densities for Simulation Experiment

that populations 1, 2, and 3 are all skewed to the right, although population 1 is much more skewed than population 3. Populations 4, 5, and 6, on the other hand, are symmetric, but only population 6 is really bell-shaped. From each of these populations, we simulated 5000 samples of size 11, 5000 samples of size 21, and 5000 samples of size 31. For each sample we calculated the sample mean $\overline{X}$ and the sample variance s^2.

If these populations were normal, we would expect 5% of the samples of size n to have a t value greater than $t_{.05,n-1}$. Here the t value is $(\overline{X} - \mu)/(s/\sqrt{n})$. Similarly, 10% of the samples should have a t value greater than $t_{.10,n-1}$. For example, 5% of the samples of size 11 should have a t value greater than $t_{.05,10} = 1.812$ and 10% should have a t value greater than $t_{.10,10} = 1.372$. The actual percentages of samples with t values greater than the tabulated t values are shown in Table 8.12.

Table 8.12   Fraction of Simulated t Values Greater Than $t_{\alpha,n-1}$

	$\alpha = .05$			$\alpha = .10$		
Population	$n = 11$	$n = 21$	$n = 31$	$n = 11$	$n = 21$	$n = 31$
1	.0149	.0200	.0221	.0512	.0627	.0650
2	.0332	.0357	.0393	.0794	.0811	.0873
3	.0395	.0425	.0460	.0864	.0901	.0897
4	.0495	.0473	.0457	.0941	.0947	.0960
5	.0506	.0509	.0471	.0949	.1007	.0965
6	.0539	.0475	.0458	.1016	.0915	.0986

Notice that for populations 1, 2, and 3, the percentage of t values in the 5% and 10% tails are less than expected. This is particularly true for population 1, which is extremely nonnormal. However, for populations 4, 5, and 6, the percentages are fairly close to what we would expect if these populations were normal. The difference is basically that populations 1, 2, and 3 are skewed, whereas populations 4, 5, and 6 are symmetric. So calculations based on the t distribution appear to be fairly robust to the normal assumption if the population is symmetric.

Using the same method, we tested robustness for the chi-square and F distributions. Again, if the populations were normal, we would expect 5% of the simulated chi-square statistics $(n - 1)s^2/\sigma^2$ to be larger than $\chi^2_{.05,n-1}$ and 10% to be larger than $\chi^2_{.10,n-1}$. Similarly, by treating the 5000 samples for a given sample size as 2500 pairs of samples, we would expect 5% of the resulting ratios s_1^2/s_2^2 to be greater than $F_{.05,n-1,n-1}$ and 10% to be greater than $F_{.10,n-1,n-1}$. The actual percentages are shown in Tables 8.13 and 8.14.

The percentages in these tables show that if the populations are nonnormal, chi-square and F calculations based on normality can be very misleading. For example, for the very nonnormal population 1, many more chi-square and F values are in the right-hand tail than we expect. In contrast, for population 4 there are many fewer values in the right-hand tail than we expect.

Table 8.13   Fraction of Simulated χ^2 Values Greater Than $\chi^2_{\alpha,n-1}$

	$\alpha = .05$			$\alpha = .10$		
Population	$n = 11$	$n = 21$	$n = 31$	$n = 11$	$n = 21$	$n = 31$
1	.1209	.1500	.1526	.1628	.1933	.1987
2	.0769	.0815	.0864	.1266	.1301	.1362
3	.0645	.0650	.0689	.1138	.1143	.1180
4	.0039	.0042	.0037	.0310	.0258	.0231
5	.0263	.0245	.0251	.0645	.0621	.0624
6	.0448	.0468	.0447	.0973	.0950	.0967

Table 8.14   Fraction of Simulated F Values Greater Than $F_{\alpha,n-1,n-1}$

	$\alpha = .05$			$\alpha = .10$		
Population	$n = 11$	$n = 21$	$n = 31$	$n = 11$	$n = 21$	$n = 31$
1	.2308	.2714	.2758	.3210	.3532	.3658
2	.0836	.0932	.0942	.1548	.1610	.1632
3	.0670	.0702	.0672	.1214	.1234	.1254
4	.0086	.0040	.0036	.0224	.0156	.0162
5	.0241	.0223	.0218	.0681	.0652	.0648
6	.0432	.0426	.0440	.0914	.0972	.0976

Only for populations 3 and 6, which are reasonably normally shaped, are the percentages close to 5% and 10%.

The implication of this simulation experiment is that if the populations are nonnormal, the inferences we have discussed in this chapter may not be correct. This is especially true for inferences on variances. For example, a confidence interval for σ^2 with "nominal" confidence level 95% may really have confidence level 75% or even 98%, depending on the shape of the population distribution. Of course, this means that we should not trust these inferences, particularly for small sample sizes, unless we can check that the population distribution is at least approximately normally shaped.

APPENDIX 8B

Relationships Among Distributions in This Chapter

This appendix is intended only for those readers who wish to probe a little further into the mathematics of sampling distributions. It examines the relationships between the t, chi-square, and F distributions, and how each of these is intimately related to the normal distribution. This section is entirely optional. However, students who read it will better understand why these distributions continue to appear in future chapters in various contexts. There really is a pattern to it all.

Throughout this section we assume that $X_1, X_2, \ldots, X_n$ represent a random sample of size n from a $N(\mu, \sigma^2)$ population. This normal assumption is absolutely necessary. Without it, the results in this section are at best approximately true. By standardizing each X_i, we obtain a random sample $Z_1, Z_2, \ldots, Z_n$ from a $N(0, 1)$ population. As usual, the transformation is $Z_i = (X_i - \mu)/\sigma$ for each i.

The first result is that the sum of the squares of the Z's is a chi-square random variable with n degrees of freedom.

$$\frac{\Sigma (X_i - \mu)^2}{\sigma^2} = \sum Z_i^2$$

is a chi-square random variable with n degrees of freedom

This is the context in which the chi-square distribution arises: as a sum of squares of standardized normal random variables.

If we cannot compute a given Z_i because μ is unknown, we replace μ by its estimate $\overline{X}$ to obtain $\hat{Z}_i = (X_i - \overline{X})/\sigma$. Now the result is that the sum of the squares of the $\hat{Z}$'s is a chi-square random variable with $n - 1$ degrees of freedom. We lose a degree of freedom because μ must be estimated. But we have

$$\sum \hat{Z}_i^2 = \sum \frac{(X_i - \overline{X})^2}{\sigma^2} = (n - 1)\left[\frac{\sum (X_i - \overline{X})^2/(n - 1)}{\sigma^2}\right] = \frac{(n - 1)s^2}{\sigma^2}$$

Therefore, we have rediscovered the main result from Section 8.4.

$$\frac{(n - 1)s^2}{\sigma^2}$$

has a chi-square distribution with $n - 1$ degrees of freedom

A t random variable with ν degrees of freedom is defined as the ratio of two independent random variables; the numerator is a $N(0, 1)$ random variable and the denominator is the square root of a chi-square random variable divided by its degrees of freedom.

A t random variable with ν degrees of freedom has the form

$$\frac{Z}{\sqrt{\chi^2/\nu}}$$

where Z is $N(0, 1)$, χ^2 is chi-square with ν degrees of freedom, and Z and χ^2 are independent.

In this chapter, we let the $N(0, 1)$ random variable Z be $(\overline{X} - \mu)/(\sigma/\sqrt{n})$, the standardized $\overline{X}$. For the χ^2 random variable, we use $(n - 1)s^2/\sigma^2$, which has $\nu = n - 1$ degrees of freedom. We also use the possibly surprising fact that the sample mean $\overline{X}$ and the sample variance s^2 drawn from a normal population are *independent* random variables, even though they come from the same sample. This implies that $Z = (\overline{X} - \mu)/(\sigma/\sqrt{n})$ and $\chi^2 = (n - 1)s^2/\sigma^2$ are independent random variables. Therefore, $Z/\sqrt{\chi^2/(n - 1)}$ is a t random variable with $n - 1$ degrees of freedom. But we may rewrite this ratio as

$$\frac{Z}{\sqrt{\chi^2/(n - 1)}} = \frac{(\overline{X} - \mu)/(\sigma/\sqrt{n})}{\sqrt{s^2/\sigma^2}} = \frac{\overline{X} - \mu}{s/\sqrt{n}}$$

This gives us the main result of Section 8.2, which is summarized in the next box.

$$\frac{\overline{X} - \mu}{s/\sqrt{n}}$$

has a t distribution with $n - 1$ degrees of freedom

Finally, an F random variable with ν_1 degrees of freedom in the numerator and ν_2 degrees of freedom in the denominator is defined as the ratio of two independent chi-square random variables χ_1^2 and χ_2^2, each divided by its degrees of freedom. That is,

An F random variable has the form

$$F = \frac{\chi_1^2/\nu_1}{\chi_2^2/\nu_2}$$

where χ_1^2 and χ_2^2 are independent chi-square random variables with ν_1 and ν_2 degrees of freedom, respectively.

To apply this result, let s_1^2 and s_2^2 be the sample variances, based on sample sizes n_1 and n_2, from two independent normal populations with variances σ_1^2 and σ_2^2. Then $(n_1 - 1)s_1^2/\sigma_1^2$ and $(n_2 - 1)s_2^2/\sigma_2^2$ are independent chi-square random variables with $n_1 - 1$ and $n_2 - 1$ degrees of freedom, respectively. If we divide each of these by its degrees of freedom and then form a ratio of the resulting quantities, we obtain $(s_1^2/\sigma_1^2)/(s_2^2/\sigma_2^2)$. This yields the main result from Section 8.5.

$$\frac{s_1^2/\sigma_1^2}{s_2^2/\sigma_2^2}$$

has an F distribution with $n_1 - 1$ and $n_2 - 1$ degrees of freedom

One final relationship between these distributions is the following. Suppose that we square a t random variable of the form $Z/\sqrt{\chi^2/\nu}$. The result is $Z^2/(\chi^2/\nu)$. But the numerator, Z^2, is a chi-square random variable with 1 degree of freedom (by the definition of chi-square random variables given earlier in this appendix). Therefore, the ratio $Z^2/(\chi^2/\nu)$ is a ratio of two independent chi-square random variables, each divided by its degrees of freedom. This means that it has an F distribution.

> The square of a t random variable with ν degrees of freedom is an F random variable with 1 and ν degrees of freedom.

We will see an illustration of this relationship when we study regression.

References

BREIMAN, L. *Statistics: With a View Toward Applications.* Boston: Houghton Mifflin, 1973.

CANAVOS, G. C. *Applied Probability and Statistical Methods.* Boston: Little, Brown, 1984.

HOGG, R. V. and CRAIG, A. T. *Introduction to Mathematical Statistics,* 4th ed. New York: Macmillan, 1978.

MOOD, A. M., GRAYBILL, F. A., and BOES, D. C. *Introduction to the Theory of Statistics,* 3rd ed. New York: McGraw-Hill, 1974.

NETER, J., WASSERMAN, W., and WHITMORE, G. A. *Applied Statistics,* 2nd ed. Boston: Allyn & Bacon, 1982.

CHAPTER 9

Hypothesis Testing

Objectives

1. To learn the difference between null and alternative hypotheses.
2. To learn the meaning of type I errors, type II errors, and *p*-values.
3. To understand what it means for a sample result to be statistically significant.
4. To learn when to use a one-tailed test and when to use a two-tailed test.
5. To learn how to perform hypothesis tests for proportions, means, and variances.
6. To understand how two-tailed hypothesis tests are related to confidence intervals.
7. To learn how to calculate the probabilities of type II errors and how these are related to sample size.

Contents

When a package of a consumer item states that it contains a certain quantity, we as consumers can be confident that the package really does contain this much. For example, we can be confident that 12-ounce beer cans actually contain 12 ounces of beer. Or can we? Skeptics, one of whom we will discuss later in this chapter, may try to prove the hypothesis that some products contain less, on the average, than their packages advertise. To test their hypothesis, they conduct an experiment. They examine a random sample of "12-ounce" beer cans and see whether the average amount per can is really less than 12 ounces.

This is a typical hypothesis-testing problem. The skeptics try to prove their hypothesis by discrediting the claim of the product. However, we will see in this chapter that the burden of proof is on the skeptics. They have to amass a good deal of conclusive evidence before they can legitimately claim that consumers are being cheated. In the beer can example, we discover just how much evidence is necessary when we pursue this example later in this chapter.

9.1

Introduction

The subject of this chapter is hypothesis testing, a topic very closely connected to estimation and confidence intervals. In many applications the investigator already has some preconceived theory, called a hypothesis, that the data will either tend to support or refute. In this case the results of the study are usually stated as a confirmation or a denial of the specific hypothesis rather than as a confidence interval for some population parameter.

A typical example of hypothesis testing is the following. Suppose that a laundry detergent company believes it can capture more of the market if it uses a new packaging design. At least this is what management is told by the people in the product design division of the company. Management, however, being somewhat reluctant to deviate from proven packaging designs, refuses to believe the design people's claim until this claim has been confirmed in a test market.

To test which side is correct, an experiment is conducted. In this experiment a randomly chosen test group of supermarkets stock the product packaged in the new design. After a certain length of time, sales figures are examined to see whether the new design has resulted in increased sales. Let $\overline{X}$ be the mean sales level for the test group, and let μ_0 be the mean sales level for the stores that use the traditional design. (We assume that μ_0 is well known from historical data.) Once $\overline{X}$ is observed, the design people's claim can certainly be rejected if $\overline{X}$ is less than μ_0, because the new design has actually produced *lower* sales than the traditional design. If $\overline{X}$ is greater than μ_0 but not much greater, management may decide to attribute the increase in sales to a lucky sample, not to a more effective design. Only if $\overline{X}$ is much larger than μ_0 will management be convinced that the new design is more effective, for this is the only case where a lucky sample can be ruled out as the cause of the difference between $\overline{X}$ and μ_0.

The discussion above suggests that management will choose some "threshold" level such that if $\overline{X}$ is less than μ_0 or exceeds μ_0 by less than the threshold level, they will reject the design people's claim, whereas if $\overline{X}$ exceeds μ_0 by more than the threshold level, they will accept the claim. Of course, each of these possibilities leads to concrete actions. If the claim is rejected, management may decide to scrap the new design forever, or they may attempt to improve the design. If the designers' claim is accepted, management will probably discontinue use of the traditional design and switch to the new design.

This example is typical of all hypothesis-testing problems in the following respects. First, there is a set of competing hypotheses (whether or not the new design is better than the traditional design), and the problem is to discover which of the hypotheses is true. Second, an experiment is performed (use the new design in several randomly selected stores) to gather data that can be used to test the hypotheses. Third, a decision rule is used to see which hypothesis should be accepted as true (accept the new designers' claim only if $\overline{X}$ minus μ_0 exceeds some threshold). Finally, based on the outcome of the experiment, a concrete action is taken (scrap the new design or replace the traditional design with it).

9.2

General Concepts in Hypothesis Testing

In this section we discuss several concepts common to all hypothesis-testing problems. Then in later sections we apply these concepts to tests of particular population parameters.

Null and Alternative Hypotheses

In any hypothesis-testing problem we are concerned with some aspect of one or more populations. This may be the value of a numerical parameter, such as the mean or the difference between two means, or it may be more general, such as the entire shape of a population density function. In either case, there is a true, but unknown, "state" of the population. For example, we may hypothesize that the mean income in a city is at least $17,000 or that the shape of the income distribution is normal. However, we do not know for certain whether these statements are true, so all we can do is infer the truth from sample data.

We divide the set of all possibilities into two mutually exclusive subsets. These two subsets are treated as two competing hypotheses, and the goal is to infer which of them includes the true state of the population. For example, let μ be the mean annual amount manufacturing companies spend on pollution control. Then the two competing hypotheses might be (1) $\mu \leq \$50{,}000$, and (2) $\mu > \$50{,}000$. The first hypothesis is that the average manufacturing company spends no more than $\$50{,}000$ on pollution control, whereas the second is that the average is more than $\$50{,}000$. One and only of these hypotheses is true, and we must infer the truth from available sample data.

In hypothesis testing the two competing hypotheses are not treated in a symmetric manner. We always denote one of the hypotheses as H_0; this is called the *null hypothesis*. The other hypothesis is denoted as H_a and is called the *alternative hypothesis*. Since they are not treated equally, it makes a difference which we call H_0 and which we call H_a. The key to deciding which is which is the following: the burden of proof is *always* on the alternative hypothesis H_a. This means that H_0 cannot be rejected unless there is overwhelming evidence in favor of H_a. If there is a relatively small amount of evidence in favor of H_a, we still might not reject H_0. This is reflected in Figure 9.1.

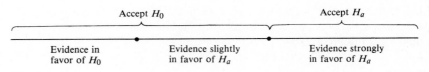

Figure 9.1

> The two competing hypotheses are called the null hypothesis (H_0) and the alternative hypothesis (H_a). The burden of proof is always on the alternative hypothesis.

The null hypothesis can often be equated with the "status quo" or the "current thinking." The alternative hypothesis is then the "new theory" that is trying to displace current thinking. It is often called the "research hypothesis." Usually, this is the hypothesis that an investigator is attempting to prove. The following examples exhibit some typical possibilities.

EXAMPLE 9.1

The classic example concerns a person who is being tried for a crime. The two hypotheses are that he is innocent and that he is guilty. We usually do not know which is true, so we rely on evidence to help make the decision. In the United States at least, a person is considered innocent until proven guilty. Therefore, the null hypothesis is that the person is innocent. A small amount of circumstantial evidence indicating guilt is usually not enough to send the suspect to jail. A great deal of conclusive evidence must be presented before the alternative hypothesis of guilt is accepted and the person is sent to jail.

EXAMPLE 9.2

Suppose that medical scientists claim they have developed a safe new drug that cures arthritis better than any drug on the market. Now the two competing claims are that the new drug is better than any other existing arthritis drugs, and that the new drug is no better than what is already available. Before this new drug can be marketed, the Food and Drug Administration (FDA) requires that an extensive set of tests be done to prove that the claimed effect really exists. Since the burden of proof is clearly on the new drug, the null hypothesis is that the new drug is no better than what already exists. Unless scientific tests are very favorable to the new drug, the null hypothesis will not be rejected, which means that the drug will not be marketed.

EXAMPLE 9.3

Consider the new product design already discussed in this chapter. Here the two hypotheses are that the new design will increase sales and that the new design will at best leave sales as they are. In this case management plays the role of the devil's advocate. Management is unwilling to introduce the new design unless it can be proven more effective. Since the burden of proof is on the new design, the null hypothesis is that the new design is not more effective.

Let the mean sales level with the traditional design be μ_0, and let μ be the mean sales level that would result if all companies used the new design. Then the null and alternative hypotheses are $H_0: \mu = \mu_0$ and $H_a: \mu > \mu_0$. (The null hypothesis is written as an equality to reflect management's belief that even though the new design might not increase sales, at least it will not decrease them.)

We have stated that hypothesis-testing problems are really decision problems with two possible decisions: accept H_0 or accept H_a. In practice, the situation is not always this symmetric. If there is indeed enough evidence to reject H_0 and accept H_a, we are usually confident that H_a is true. This is because so much evidence in favor of H_a is required before H_a can be accepted. But if there is not enough evidence to reject H_0, we cannot necessarily state that H_0 is true. Referring to the guilty–innocent example, we are confident that most people sent to jail are really guilty. This is because a conviction requires so much evidence. But most of us believe that many people set free are not innocent; there is simply not enough evidence to convict them. In general, whenever we ''accept'' H_0, it is probably more accurate to say that we cannot reject H_0. In these cases the truth of H_0 is often still in doubt, and more information is needed to decide the issue one way or the other.

> ''Accepting'' H_0 usually means that there is not enough evidence to reject it. In this case it is more accurate to say that H_0 cannot be rejected.

Rejection Region

In order to make a decision between rejecting and not rejecting H_0, we usually collect sample data. We then devise a decision rule that is based on these sample data. If the sample evidence strongly favors H_a, we reject H_0; otherwise, we do not reject it. In all hypothesis tests in this book, the decision rule is very simple to describe. First, we use the sample data to compute a *test statistic*. This test statistic is usually related to one of the sampling distributions discussed in earlier chapters, such as the normal or chi-square distributions. Then if the test statistic is far enough out on the appropriate tail (or tails) of this sampling distribution, we reject H_0; otherwise, we do not reject it. The set of values of the test statistic that lead to rejection of H_0 is called the *rejection region*.

> The rejection region is the set of values of the test statistic that lead to rejection of H_0.

To illustrate this idea, consider the laundry detergent company from Example 9.3. They are testing H_0: $\mu = \mu_0$ versus H_a: $\mu > \mu_0$, where μ is the mean sales if all stores switched to the new packaging design. As we indicated earlier, H_0 will be rejected if the mean sales $\overline{X}$ from a sample of stores packaging the new design is considerably larger than μ_0. Since the standard error of $\overline{X}$ is $\sigma/\sqrt{n}$, we know that the z statistic $(\overline{X} - \mu_0)/(\sigma/\sqrt{n})$ has a standard normal distribution when H_0 is true. Therefore, if this z statistic is far enough out on the right-hand tail of the standard normal density, we reject H_0. The corresponding rejection region is shown in Figure 9.2. The borderline value that defines the rejection region, labeled z^* in the figure, is chosen so that a small area falls to the right of it. More precisely, this value is determined by the type I error probability, to be discussed next.

Given H_0 and H_a, there are only two possible decisions. Either we reject H_0 or we do not. But for each of these decisions, there is a possibility of making an error, as shown in Table 9.1.

Type I and Type II Errors

Table 9.1

		True State	
		H_0 True	H_a True
Decision	Accept H_0 (Reject H_a)	Correct decision	Type II error
	Reject H_0 (Accept H_a)	Type I error	Correct decision

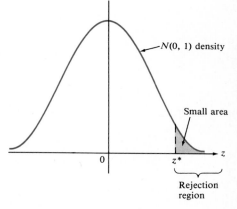

Figure 9.2

The two possible errors in Table 9.1 have different names. The error of rejecting H_0 when H_0 is true is called a *type I error*. The opposite error of not rejecting H_0 when H_a is true is called a *type II error*. These two types of errors are labeled differently to indicate that they are not considered equally important.

> Type I error: rejecting H_0 when H_0 is true
> Type II error: not rejecting H_0 when H_a is true

Recall that the burden of proof is on H_a. This means we want to be very sure that H_a is correct before we reject H_0. The reason is that we consider a type I error to be the more costly error. For example, we want to be very sure that we do not send an innocent person to jail, even if this means letting a few (or maybe even many) guilty persons go free. Therefore, we wish to keep the probability of a type I error very small, even if it makes the probability of a type II error relatively large.

Unfortunately, we cannot generally keep the probability of a type I error and the probability of a type II error *simultaneously* small. In fact, by requiring the probability of a type I error to be small, we are usually forced to accept whatever probability of type II error results; we no longer have any control over it (except by gathering more evidence, as we discuss later).

The usual procedure is as follows. Let α and β denote the probability of a type I error and a type II error, respectively. First, we choose a small value of α, usually .10, .05, or .01, and we choose a decision rule so that the probability of a type I error is at most α. Next, we can do one of two things. If a sample size has already been chosen, we can compute the probability of a type II error, β. Whatever this value of β is, we must live with it. Alternatively, we can choose a sample size large enough to produce an acceptably low value of β. However, the sample size does not affect the probability of a type I error; its maximum value is still α.

> The maximum probability of a type I error is α; it is chosen first and remains fixed. Then we have no control over the probability of a type II error, β, except by increasing the sample size.

Let's return to the laundry detergent example. Suppose that management wants to be 95% certain that the new packaging design is superior before it will reject the traditional design. This implies an α value of .05. In other words, if the new design is not superior (H_0 is true), there will be only a .05 probability of going with the new design. Now recall that in this example, the rejection region is where the test statistic z is greater than some critical value z^* (see Figure 9.2). The probability of this occurring when $\mu = \mu_0$ is the area to the right of z^*. Since we want this area to be .05, we set $z^* = z_{.05} = 1.645$. Thus the rejection region is $z > 1.645$, as shown in Figure 9.3a.

Figure 9.3a is relevant for showing the probability of a type I error because it shows the distribution of z when H_0 is true, that is, when $\mu = \mu_0$. However, when H_a is true, this figure is not relevant for showing the probability of a type II error. This is because $z = (\overline{X} - \mu_0)/(\sigma/\sqrt{n})$ has a mean greater than 0 when $\mu > \mu_0$, so that the distribution of z is shifted to the right. Two possibilities, for two possible values of μ greater than μ_0, are shown in Figures 9.3b and c. In each graph the type II error probability β is the area to the left of 1.645, for this is where we will (incorrectly) fail to reject H_0. But this area is clearly larger in Figure 9.3b than in Figure 9.3c. The intuitive reason is that the true mean in Figure 9.3c is larger than the mean in Figure 9.3b (although both are larger than μ_0). Therefore, it is easier to distinguish between μ and μ_0 in Figure 9.3c, and the probability of a type II error is correspondingly smaller.

There is one final point to make in this example. When the null hypothesis is stated as H_0: $\mu = \mu_0$, it reflects management's implicit belief that even if the new design is no better, at least it is no worse. However, if management admits the possibility of a decrease in sales with the new design, the null hypothesis should be stated as H_0: $\mu \leq \mu_0$. In this case the rejection region remains exactly as before, but the type I error probability depends on the

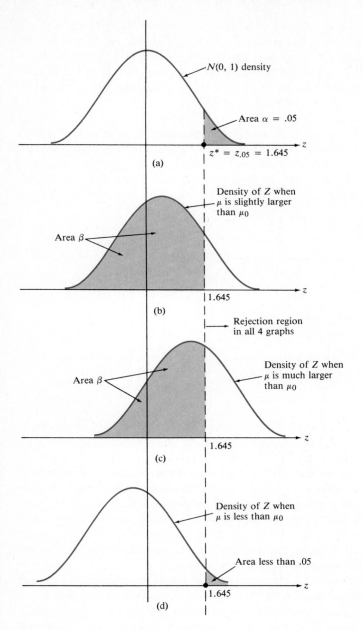

Figure 9.3

value of μ. Consider a value of μ less than μ_0. Then the distribution of $z = (\bar{X} - \mu_0)/(\sigma/\sqrt{n})$ is shifted to the left, as in Figure 9.3d, so that the type I error probability, that is, the area to the right of 1.645, is *less* than $\alpha = .05$. This is why we stated earlier that α is the *maximum* type I error probability. It always occurs when the true value of the parameter, in this case μ, is on the borderline between H_0 and H_a.

Power of a Test

Since β is the probability of not rejecting H_0 when H_a is true, $1 - \beta$ is the probability of correctly rejecting H_0 when H_a is true. Furthermore, we have already seen that α is the maximum probability of rejecting H_0 when H_0 is true. These statements are shown graphically in Figure 9.4 for the laundry detergent example.

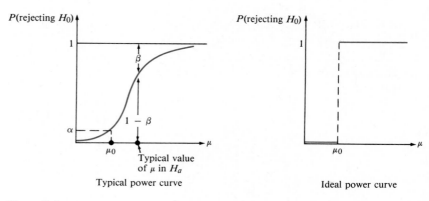

Figure 9.4

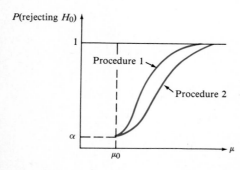

Figure 9.5

The graphs in this figure, often called *power curves,* show the probability of rejecting H_0 for all values of μ. This curve illustrates how the probability of a type II error is fairly large unless the true value of μ is a good bit larger than the borderline value between H_0 and H_a. In contrast, the curve on the right is called the "ideal" power curve because it shows that H_0 is rejected if and only if H_0 is false. Unfortunately, we cannot achieve an ideal power curve unless we sample the entire population.

If there are two or more decision rules available for testing a certain pair of hypotheses, and they are all to be used on the same data, we say that one decision rule is more *powerful* than the others if it produces uniformly lower type II error probabilities than the others (given the same α value for each rule). Intuitively, a more powerful decision rule is better able, in the sense of using the data more efficiently, to discriminate between H_0 and H_a. In Figure 9.5, the power curve for decision rule 1 is above the power curve for rule 2 for all values in H_a. Therefore, each β value is smaller for rule 1 than for rule 2, and we conclude that rule 1 is more powerful (hence better) than rule 2.

> One decision rule is more powerful than another if it produces lower type II error probabilities (for a given value of α and sample size n).

As we have indicated, type II errors are considered less important than type I errors. In fact, β is not even calculated in many applications. There are several reasons for this. One reason is that it is time-consuming. In the laundry detergent example the probability of a type II error is not too difficult to compute for any specific value of μ, but the entire power curve necessitates a good many of these calculations. In other hypothesis-testing examples such as we will see in later chapters, the type II error probabilities may be practically impossible to calculate. The difficulty is that unless H_0 is true, we often do not know the sampling distribution required to calculate β.

Although β is not (or cannot be) calculated, we should not forget that it exists and is often sizable. If we reject H_0, we can be fairly confident that no mistake has been made. In this case the probability of an error is no greater than α. But if there is not enough evidence to reject H_0, we cannot be so confident. This is the reason for the earlier caution about "accepting" H_0. If H_0 cannot be rejected, it is better to state that "we cannot reject H_0"; the truth of H_0 may still be very much in doubt.

In the context of hypothesis testing, we often state that a sample result is "statistically significant." This does not necessarily mean that the result is "important"; this may or may not be the case. Instead, it means that the sample result actually observed would be quite *unexpected* if the null hypothesis were true. Since this provides grounds for rejecting the null hypothesis, we may state the following general definition.

Significance of a Hypothesis Test

> Statistically significant sample results are those that lead to the rejection of H_0.

Refer again to the laundry detergent example. If management chooses an α value of .05, the sample results will be statistically significant only if the test statistic z is greater than $z_{.05} = 1.645$. Notice that the values of z that are statistically significant depend on the significance level α. For example, the test statistic $z = 1.75$ is statistically significant when $\alpha = .05$ (since $z_{.05} = 1.645$), but it is not significant when $\alpha = .025$ (since $z_{.025} = 1.96$). So when we say that a result is statistically significant, we must also qualify this by reporting the value of α being used. This value is called the *significance level* of the test. The usual terminology is to say that a result is significant at, say, the 5% level (or the .05 level). This corresponds to α = .05.

> A sample result is statistically significant at the 5% level if and only if it leads to rejection of H_0 when the type I error probability α is .05. Similar statements hold for the 10%, 1%, or any other significance levels.

In general, the lower the value of α, the more unusual the sample has to be, assuming that H_0 is true, before we can reject H_0. So a sample result that is significant at, say, the 5% level is automatically significant at the 10% level. However, it might not be significant at the 1% level.

Reporting p-Values

The discussion above implies that statistically significant results, and hence accept–reject decisions, depend critically on the value of α. But which value of α should be used? Unfortunately, for many decision makers this is a fairly arbitrary choice. An alternative to making this choice is simply to report *how* unusual the observed sample is, assuming that H_0 is correct. This is done by reporting the "*p*-value" (*p* for probability) of the sample. The definition of a *p*-value is given below.

> The *p*-value of a sample is the probability of observing a sample at least as unlikely as the one observed if H_0 is true.

For example, in the laundry detergent example we saw that a *z* value of 1.75 is significant at the 5% level but not at the 2.5% level. But *p*-values allow us to be more specific than this. Since $1.75 = z_{.04}$ (area .04 lies to the right of 1.75), the *p*-value of this sample is .04. This means that we would reject the null hypothesis at the 4% level or at any higher level.

We highly recommend reporting the *p*-value in any hypothesis testing situation. Admittedly, reporting the *p*-value does not solve the decision problem of choosing between H_0 and H_a and then acting on this decision. Ultimately, the person responsible for making the decision must "stick his neck out" and accept or reject H_0. But a reported *p*-value can only help the decision maker make this final decision.

One-Tailed Versus Two-Tailed Tests

In many hypothesis-testing situations, including all of those we discuss in this chapter, the hypotheses involve the value of a numerical population parameter such as p, μ, or σ^2. The resulting hypothesis tests are then either "one-tailed" or "two-tailed." The laundry detergent example and a variation of it illustrate these two types.

If management assumes that there is virtually no chance that the new design will reduce sales, but it is skeptical that the new design will do much to improve sales, the only kind of sample information that will eliminate this skepticism is a large value of $\overline{X}$. Thus the null hypothesis is $H_0: \mu = \mu_0$ (or $H_0: \mu \le \mu_0$) and the alternative is $H_a: \mu > \mu_0$. Since only values of $\overline{X}$ significantly larger than μ_0 lead to rejection of H_0, we call this a one-tailed test.

In contrast, assume that management has no idea which of two new product designs, labeled 1 and 2, will produce more sales. Prior to testing, there is no reason to believe that either design is significantly better than the other. Assume that the first of these designs has been thoroughly tested and is known to produce a mean sales level of μ_0. The mean sales level of the second, μ, is unknown and is estimated by the mean sales level $\overline{X}$ from a random sample of stores stocking this design. Now the null hypothesis is $H_0: \mu = \mu_0$ and the alternative is $H_a: \mu \ne \mu_0$. This is called a two-tailed test because values of $\overline{X}$ significantly larger than μ_0 and values of $\overline{X}$ significantly smaller than μ_0 *both* lead to rejection of H_0.

How do we know whether to use a one-tailed or a two-tailed test? There is no *mathematical* way to answer this question. It depends entirely on the context of the problem and the biases of the decision maker. In general, if we are virtually sure that the unknown parameter cannot be on one side of the value specified in H_0, we use a one-tailed test. Otherwise, we use a two-tailed test.

Problems for Section 9.2

1. Is is true that if α is the probability of a type I error and β is the probability of a type II error, α and β must add to 1? Why or why not?

2. If we are able to reject H_0 in favor of H_a at the $\alpha = .05$ level, is it true that we can also reject H_0 at the $\alpha = .01$ level? Why or why not?

3. If we are able to reject $H_0: \mu = 10$ in favor of $H_a: \mu > 10$ at the $\alpha = .05$ level, is it true that we can also reject this H_0 in favor of $H_a: \mu \ne 10$ at the $\alpha = .15$ level? Why or why not?

4. If we wish to test $H_0: \mu = 20$ versus $H_a: \mu > 20$, is it true that the probability of a type II error is greater when the true μ is 22 than when it is 23? Why or why not?

5. Many separate, independent, identically run experiments are performed to test $H_0: \mu = 10$ versus $H_a: \mu > 10$, each at the 5% level. If the true mean is $\mu = 11$ in every case, is it true that in approximately 5% of these experiments, a type I error will be made? Why or why not?

6. If we reject H_0 in favor of H_a at the 5% level for some particular sample, is it true that the *p*-value of this sample must be less than or equal to .05? Why or why not?

7. Suppose it is estimated that 2% of all people who are innocent go to jail and 20% of all guilty people go free. We wish to decide whether to convict a certain person, recognizing that in our legal system a person is presumed innocent until "proven" guilty. When will type I and type II errors occur, and what are their probabilities?

* 8. Referring to Problem 7, suppose that a jury believes, after hearing all the evidence, that the probability is .7 that a particular person is guilty. However, the jury also believes that the "cost" of sending an innocent person to jail is twice as

large as the "cost" of letting a guilty person go free. What decision should the jury make to minimize the expected cost? How can you reconcile the reasoning in this problem with the reasoning we have been using in this chapter? (Remember that the expected cost is the sum of possible costs times their probabilities.)

9.3

Hypothesis Tests for a Population Mean

In this section we use the ideas from Section 9.2 to develop large-sample hypothesis tests for a population mean. These include one-tailed and two-tailed tests. We will also discuss p-values for the tests and type II error probabilities. Throughout this section we will assume that the sample size n is large enough ($n \geq 30$) to ensure that the sampling distribution of the sample mean is approximately normal.

One-Tailed Test

Given any population characteristic with an unknown mean μ, the tests in this section are all of the form H_0: $\mu \leq \mu_0$ versus H_a: $\mu > \mu_0$, or H_0: $\mu \geq \mu_0$ versus H_a: $\mu < \mu_0$, where μ_0 is a given hypothesized value. In either case the subscript on μ_0 is standard; it indicates that μ_0 is the value of μ at the borderline between H_0 and H_a, and that it belongs to H_0. (Notice that the equality part of the inequality sign always goes with H_0.) If H_a is $\mu > \mu_0$, we call the test a *right-tailed* test; if H_a is $\mu < \mu_0$, we call it a *left-tailed* test. For both of these one-tailed tests, the rejection region is based on the test statistic $z = (\overline{X} - \mu_0)/(\sigma/\sqrt{n})$. In a right-tailed test the rejection region is $z > z_\alpha$, where α is the significance level. Similarly, in a left-tailed test the rejection region is $z < -z_\alpha$.

When performing any one-tailed test on μ, it is best to go through the following steps in a systematic manner. (These steps are basic to all the hypothesis tests in this book. Only the details differ from one test to another.)

Procedure for a One-Tailed Test of the Population Mean

1. From the context of the problem, formulate the hypotheses. That is, decide whether the test should be right-tailed or left-tailed, and decide on the value of μ_0.
2. Choose a significance level α. (Usually, this is .10, .05, or .01, but any value is permissible. Remember, the smaller the value of α, the more difficult it will be to reject H_0.)
3. Collect n observations and calculate the test statistic $z = (\overline{X} - \mu_0)/(\sigma/\sqrt{n})$. If σ is unknown, substitute the sample standard deviation s.

4. Look up the tabulated value z_α in Appendix B.
5. For a right-tailed test, reject H_0 if $z > z_\alpha$; for a left-tailed test, reject H_0 if $z < -z_\alpha$ (see Figure 9.6).
6. State the final decision in the context of the particular problem.

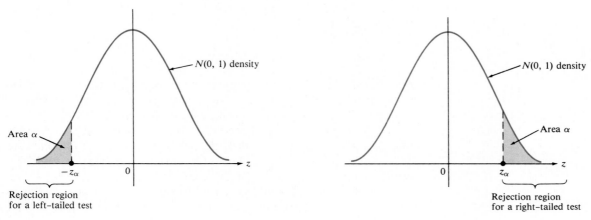

Figure 9.6

Although this procedure is based on the test statistic z, it is implicitly based on $\overline{X}$ also. For example, for the right-tailed test, the rejection region $z > z_\alpha$ is equivalent to

$$\overline{X} > \mu_0 + z_\alpha\left(\frac{\sigma}{\sqrt{n}}\right)$$

In words, H_0 is rejected only if $\overline{X}$ is at least z_α standard errors (of $\overline{X}$) to the right of the hypothesized value μ_0. Perhaps this is a more intuitive way of viewing the test because it is expressed in terms of the original units of measurement. However, the procedure based upon z is probably the most popular method of performing the test. [In fact, every decision rule in this chapter can be stated in terms of tabulated quantities (z, t, χ^2, and F values), or equivalently in terms of the point estimates themselves ($\overline{X}$, $\hat{p}$, and s^2). However, we have omitted the latter versions of the tests simply to avoid any possible confusion.]

EXAMPLE 9.4

A group of consumer advocates wishes to test whether a particular brand of tire is living up to the company's claim of "at least 30,000 miles of safe use.'' The consumer group doubts this claim. Eventually, it would like to publish that this claim is false, but it wants to be 95% sure that if it does publish this result, it is correct. Fifty of these tires (each on a different car) are observed in actual driving conditions. Each tire is run until it is judged unusable for safe driving. The 50 observed mileages have mean 29,275 miles. Should the consumer group publish that these tires are not living up to the company's claim? Assume that the standard deviation of mileages for all tires of this brand is $\sigma = 3465$ miles.

SOLUTION

We solve this example by going through the six steps listed above. (1) (State the hypotheses.) This example concerns a mean μ, the mean mileage attained by all tires of this brand. The hypothesized value μ_0 is 30,000 miles, as claimed by the tire company. Since the research hypothesis of the consumer group is that μ is less than 30,000, the null and alternative hypotheses are H_0: $\mu \geq 30,000$ and H_a: $\mu < 30,000$. (2) (Decide on a value of α.) In this example a type I error occurs if the company's claim is correct and the consumer group publishes the opposite. Since the consumer group wants to be 95% certain of not making this error, $\alpha = .05$. (3) (Compute the test statistic.) The test statistic z is given by

$$z = \frac{\overline{X} - \mu}{\sigma/\sqrt{n}} = \frac{29,275 - 30,000}{3465/\sqrt{50}} = -1.48$$

(4) (Find the relevant tabulated value.) Since $\alpha = .05$ and the test is a left-tailed test, the relevant z value is $-z_{.05} = -1.645$. (5) (Make the decision.) The computed z value -1.48 is not less than -1.645, so H_0 cannot be rejected at the 5% significance level. (6) (State the decision in terms of the particular problem.) The consumer group should not publish negative findings about this company's tires. It would take an unacceptably high risk if it did so.

---

p-Value for the One-Tailed Test

We can also compute the *p*-value of a given sample. This *p*-value indicates how far out on the appropriate tail of the $N(0, 1)$ density the test statistic z is. For example, if H_0 is $\mu \leq \mu_0$, and there is, say, .07 area to the right of z, the *p*-value is .07. This means that we can reject H_0 at the 7% significance level or at any higher level. If H_0 is $\mu \geq \mu_0$, we instead see how far out on the left-hand tail z is. If .07 area lies to the left of z, this again means that we can reject H_0 at the 7% level or any higher level. Notice that this is exactly the case in Example 9.4. Since approximately .07 area lies to the left of -1.48 under the standard normal curve, the *p*-value of this sample is .07.

This provides another explanation of why H_0 could not be rejected at the .05 level.

We now consider probabilities of type II errors for H_0: $\mu \geq \mu_0$ versus H_a: $\mu < \mu_0$. (The H_0: $\mu \leq \mu_0$ case is entirely analogous.) In Example 9.4 we saw that a sample mean of $\overline{X} = 29,275$, based on $n = 50$ tires (and a population standard deviation $\sigma = 3465$), does not lead to rejection of H_0 at the 5% level. Since H_0 is not rejected, no type I error is possible. But a type II error is possible. In fact, the probability of committing a type II error is the probability of observing a z value greater than $-z_\alpha$ (and thus not rejecting H_0) when the true μ is less than 30,000. Since this is equivalent to $\overline{X}$ being greater than $\mu_0 - z_\alpha(\sigma/\sqrt{n})$, the probability of a type II error is

$$P\left[\overline{X} \geq \mu_0 - z_\alpha\left(\frac{\sigma}{\sqrt{n}}\right)\right] = P\left[\overline{X} \geq 30,000 - 1.645\left(\frac{3465}{\sqrt{50}}\right)\right] = P(\overline{X} \geq 29,194)$$

To evaluate this, recall that when μ is less than μ_0, $\overline{X}$ is normally distributed with mean μ (not μ_0) and standard deviation $\sigma/\sqrt{n}$. For example, assume that μ is 29,500, a value in H_a. Then the probability of a type II error is as follows (see Figure 9.7):

$$P(\overline{X} \geq 29,194) = P\left(Z \geq \frac{29,194 - 29,500}{3465/\sqrt{50}}\right) = P(Z \geq -.624) = .733$$

It is important to realize that the Z in this calculation is a typical standard normal random variable; it is not the z test statistic found earlier. This is because we are now subtracting the given mean 29,500, not $\mu_0 = 30,000$, from $\overline{X}$.

It is not atypical to obtain this large a type II error probability. As stated earlier in this chapter, we are often forced to accept a type II error probability, however large it may be, because α and n are often prescribed ahead of time. But suppose that we are able to choose the sample size n in order to reduce this probability to an acceptably low level. How do we do this? It can be shown that if we want the type II error probability to be a specified value β when the true value of μ is μ_a (a for alternative), the required sample size is given by the following formula.

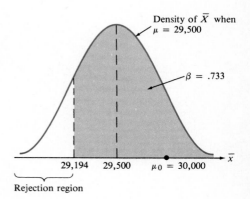

Type II Error for a One-Tailed Test

Density of $\overline{X}$ when $\mu = 29,500$

$\beta = .733$

29,194   29,500 $\mu_0 = 30,000$ $\overline{x}$

Rejection region

Figure 9.7
Illustration of Type II Error Probability

Sample Size Required for an Acceptable Value of β

$$n = \frac{(z_\alpha + z_\beta)^2\sigma^2}{(\mu_0 - \mu_a)^2}$$

Continuing Example 9.4, let's find the number of tires that must be sampled if we want the probability of a type II error to be .20 when the population mean μ is 29,500 miles. Then $\beta = .20$, $\mu_a = 29,500$, and $z_\beta = z_{.20} = .842$ (from Table Ib in Appendix B), so we have

$$n = \frac{(z_\alpha + z_\beta)^2 \sigma^2}{(\mu_0 - \mu_a)^2} = \frac{(1.645 + .842)^2 (3465)^2}{(30,000 - 29,500)^2} \approx 297$$

The implication is that if the consumer group wants to be 80% certain of rejecting the tire company's claim when the true mean mileage is only 29,500 miles, it must test 297 tires. Again, this is typical. Unless the sample size is increased considerably, the probability of a type II error is usually quite large.

Two-Tailed Test for the Mean

In many situations the investigator believes that if the true value of μ is not μ_0, it must be on a particular side of μ_0. This is when a one-tailed test is appropriate. But if the investigator has no idea which side of μ_0 the true μ is on, a two-tailed test is appropriate. This has the form H_0: $\mu = \mu_0$ versus H_a: $\mu \neq \mu_0$ for a specified μ_0.

The test procedure is very similar to the one-tailed test procedure. The two basic differences are that (1) the rejection region contains large positive *and* large negative z values, and (2) probability $\alpha/2$ must be put into each tail in order to obtain an α significance level. The procedure is listed below.

Procedure for a Two-Tailed Test of the Population Mean

1. From the context of the problem, formulate the hypotheses. That is, decide on the value of μ_0.
2. Choose a significance level α.
3. Calculate the test statistic $z = (\overline{X} - \mu_0)/(\sigma/\sqrt{n})$. If σ is unknown, substitute the sample standard deviation s.
4. Look up the tabulated value $z_{\alpha/2}$ in Appendix B.
5. Reject H_0 if $z < -z_{\alpha/2}$ or $z > z_{\alpha/2}$ (see Figure 9.8).
6. State the decision in the context of the particular problem.

One fairly subtle point should be made about the difference between one-tailed and two-tailed tests (for μ or any other parameter). We should choose between a one-tailed and a two-tailed test *before* the sample results are observed. We should not wait for the sample data to suggest which type of test to use, because the sample data *always* suggest that μ is on one side of μ_0. After all, any numerical value of $\overline{X}$ has to be to the right of μ_0 or the left of μ_0 (except in the very unusual case where $\overline{X}$ equals μ_0). But just because $\overline{X}$ is to the right of μ_0, say, we should not run a one-tailed test. If we thought

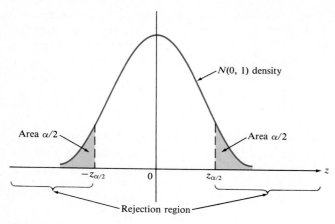

Figure 9.8

that a two-tailed test was appropriate *before* the sample was observed, we should not switch to a one-tailed test *after* the sample is observed.

EXAMPLE 9.5

A study is performed in a large midwestern city to determine whether the average monthly grocery bill per four-person family in that city is significantly different from the national average. A random sample of 40 four-person families in this city shows a mean grocery bill for a given month of $365. Assume a standard deviation in this city of $35 across families. Also assume that the national average is $353. Is the evidence significant at the .05 level that the mean for this city is different from the national mean?

SOLUTION

The six steps of the solution are as follows. (1) We want to test H_0: $\mu = \mu_0$ versus H_a: $\mu \neq \mu_0$, where μ is the mean in this city and $\mu_0 = 353$ is the national average. (2) It is given that $\alpha = .05$. (3) The test statistic z is

$$z = \frac{\overline{X} - \mu_0}{\sigma/\sqrt{n}} = \frac{365 - 353}{35/\sqrt{40}} = 2.17$$

(4) The tabulated z value is $z_{\alpha/2} = z_{.025} = 1.96$. (5) Since $2.17 > 1.96$, there is enough evidence to reject H_0. (6) We can conclude that four-person families in this city spend a significantly different amount on groceries than the national average.

For the sake of comparison, suppose that the data in this example are used to perform the *one-tailed* test of H_0: $\mu = 353$ versus H_a: $\mu > 353$ at the 5% level. Now we reject H_0 only if z is greater than $z_{.05} = 1.645$, and we use the *same z* value as above. Because 2.17 is greater than 1.645, we are again able to reject H_0. But suppose that we chose $\alpha = .02$ for both tests. Then for the two-tailed test, $z_{\alpha/2} = z_{.01} = 2.327$, which means that H_0 could not be rejected, but for the one-tailed test, $z_\alpha = z_{.02} = 2.054$, which means that H_0 could be rejected.

As this comparison shows, it is easier to obtain significant results, that is, results that lead to rejection of H_0, for a one-tailed test than for a two-tailed test, given the same α value. Another way of stating this is that any significant sample results for a two-tailed test are also significant for the appropriate one-tailed test, given the same significance level for both tests.

p-Value for a Two-Tailed Test

The *p*-value for a two-tailed test is somewhat less intuitive than it is for a one-tailed test. Recall that the *p*-value says how unusual a given sample result is; it is the probability of a sample result at least as unusual as the one observed, assuming that H_0 is true. In the present context, "unusual" means an abnormally large positive or negative value of z. So to find the *p*-value for a given test statistic z, we calculate the probability of a z value this far out on *either* tail of the $N(0,1)$ density.

For example, if the computed z value is $z = 2.17$, as in Example 9.5, the *p*-value is shown in Figure 9.9 to be $2(.015) = .030$. This is because the area to the right of 2.17 and the area to the left of -2.17 are both .015. Thus we would reject H_0 at any significance level 3% or above. (Notice that the *p*-value for $z = -2.17$ would also be .030, by the same reasoning.)

Two-Tailed Tests and Confidence Intervals

For a two-tailed test there is an extra bit of insight we can gain by relating the nonrejection region to a confidence interval for μ. We just saw that H_0: $\mu = \mu_0$ cannot be rejected if z is between $-z_{\alpha/2}$ and $z_{\alpha/2}$. In terms of $\overline{X}$, this is equivalent to

$$\mu_0 - z_{\alpha/2}\left(\frac{\sigma}{\sqrt{n}}\right) \le \overline{X} \le \mu_0 + z_{\alpha/2}\left(\frac{\sigma}{\sqrt{n}}\right)$$

But we can manipulate this inequality (multiply through by -1 and then add $\overline{X} + \mu_0$ to each side) to obtain

$$\overline{X} - z_{\alpha/2}\left(\frac{\sigma}{\sqrt{n}}\right) \le \mu_0 \le \overline{X} + z_{\alpha/2}\left(\frac{\sigma}{\sqrt{n}}\right)$$

Now recall that a confidence interval for μ is also of this form:

$$\overline{X} \pm z_{\alpha/2}\left(\frac{\sigma}{\sqrt{n}}\right)$$

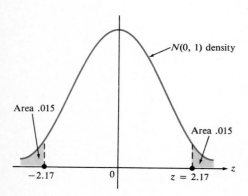

Area .015

Area .015

$N(0, 1)$ density

-2.17 0 $z = 2.17$ z

Figure 9.9

Therefore, we can perform the hypothesis test as follows: Reject H_0 if and only if μ_0 falls outside the corresponding confidence interval for μ.

> *Equivalent Test for H_0: $\mu = \mu_0$ Versus H_a: $\mu \neq \mu_0$*
>
> Form a confidence interval (with confidence level $1 - \alpha$) for μ, and reject H_0 if and only if μ_0 is outside this confidence interval.

Returning to Example 9.5 where we tested H_0: $\mu = 353$ versus H_a: $\mu \neq 353$ with $\overline{X} = 365$, $\sigma = 35$, $\alpha = .05$, and $n = 40$, a 95% confidence interval for μ is

$$\overline{X} \pm z_{\alpha/2}\left(\frac{\sigma}{\sqrt{n}}\right) = 365 \pm 1.96\left(\frac{35}{\sqrt{40}}\right) = 365 \pm 10.85$$

or from 354.15 to 375.85. Since $\mu_0 = 353$ is not within this interval, we have a second, equivalent reason for rejecting H_0 at the 5% significance level. Furthermore, we would reject H_0: $\mu = \mu_0$ at the 5% level for any national average μ_0 less than \$354.15 or greater than \$375.85.

The procedure above is valid for a two-tailed test of *any* population parameter, not just μ. To test H_0: $\theta = \theta_0$ versus H_a: $\theta \neq \theta_0$, where θ is any population parameter and θ_0 is the hypothesized value of θ, first find a confidence interval for θ with confidence level $1 - \alpha$. Then reject H_0 at the α level only if θ_0 falls outside this confidence interval. (This works only for two-tailed tests. There is a relationship between one-tailed tests and a type of confidence interval called a one-sided confidence interval, but we will not discuss one-sided confidence intervals in this book.)

Type II Error Probabilities for a Two-Tailed Test

The test for H_0: $\mu = \mu_0$ versus H_a: $\mu \neq \mu_0$ says H_0 cannot be rejected if z is between $-z_{\alpha/2}$ and $z_{\alpha/2}$. If z is within these limits and the true μ does not equal μ_0, we make a type II error. In this section we show how to calculate a type II error probability for any value of μ not equal to μ_0.

Again we consider the test of H_0: $\mu = \mu_0$ versus H_a: $\mu \neq \mu_0$, with $\mu_0 = 353$. Assuming that $\alpha = .05$ and $\sigma = 35$, the non-rejection region $-1.96 \leq z \leq 1.96$ can be written equivalently in terms of $\overline{X}$ as

$$353 - 1.96\left(\frac{35}{\sqrt{n}}\right) \leq \overline{X} \leq 353 + 1.96\left(\frac{35}{\sqrt{n}}\right)$$

When $\mu \neq \mu_0$, the probability of this occurring is the probability of a type II error. To calculate this probability for any μ not equal to μ_0, we use the fact that $\overline{X}$ is approximately normal with mean μ (not μ_0) and standard

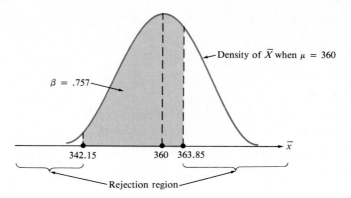

Figure 9.10
Illustration of Type II Error Probability

deviation $35/\sqrt{n}$. For example, when $n = 40$ and $\mu = 360$, the type II error probability β is as follows (see Figure 9.10).

$$\beta = P\left[353 - 1.96\left(\frac{35}{\sqrt{40}}\right) \le \overline{X} \le 353 + 1.96\left(\frac{35}{\sqrt{40}}\right)\right]$$

$$= P(342.15 \le \overline{X} \le 363.85)$$

$$= P\left(\frac{342.15 - 360}{35/\sqrt{40}} \le Z \le \frac{363.85 - 360}{35/\sqrt{40}}\right)$$

$$= P(-3.23 \le Z \le .70) = .757$$

As in the one-tailed case, the Z value in this calculation is not the test statistic z; it is a typical standard normal random variable found by subtracting the true mean, $\mu = 360$, from $\overline{X}$ and then dividing by the standard deviation $\sigma/\sqrt{n}$.

   This calculation shows that even when the true mean is \$7 above the hypothesized value, there is a .757 probability that H_0 will not be rejected, based on a sample size of 40. The only way to reduce this type II error probability is to increase the sample size. As with one-tailed tests, there is a formula for the sample size required to obtain a value β when μ equals a specific value μ_a in H_a. It is as follows.

Sample Size Required for an Acceptable Value of β

$$n = \frac{(z_{\alpha/2} + z_{\beta})^2\sigma^2}{(\mu_0 - \mu_a)^2}$$

Notice that this formula is exactly the same as the one-tailed formula, except that z_α has been replaced by $z_{\alpha/2}$.

To see how this formula can be used, suppose that we wish to reduce the value of β in the example above from .757 to .10 when $\mu = 360$. Then $\alpha = .05$, $\beta = .10$, $\mu_0 = 353$, $\mu_a = 360$, and $z_\beta = z_{.10} = 1.282$, so that the required sample size is

$$n = \frac{(1.96 + 1.282)^2(35)^2}{(353 - 360)^2} \approx 263$$

This again illustrates how difficult it is to reduce type II error probabilities to an acceptable level.

Problems for Section 9.3

9. Suppose that we wish to test H_0: $\mu = 10$ versus H_a: $\mu > 10$ at the 5% level. Also, suppose that we observe values of $\overline{X}$ and s when $n = 40$ that do not lead to rejection of H_0. Is it true that we might reject H_0 if we observed the *same* values of $\overline{X}$ and s from a sample with a sample size larger than 40? Why or why not?

10. Suppose that we observe a sample of size n from a normal population. The sample mean and sample standard deviation are $\overline{X}$ and s. If we are able to reject H_0: $\mu = \mu_0$ in favor of a two-tailed alternative at the 10% level, is it true that we can definitely reject H_0 in favor of the appropriate one-tailed alternative at the 8% level? Why or why not?

11. Consider a test of H_0: $\mu = 100$ versus H_a: $\mu > 100$ for a normal population with a known value of $\sigma = 10$. We choose $\alpha = .05$.
   a. Which values of $\overline{X}$ lead to rejection of H_0 when $n = 35$?
   b. What is the probability of a type II error when $\mu = 105$ and $n = 35$?
   c. Answer parts (a) and (b) when $n = 100$; when $n = 250$.

12. In 1983 statistics showed that steel workers were the highest paid blue-collar workers, with an average wage of $14.39 per hour. Automobile workers, on the other hand, averaged only $13.07 per hour. (Reference: *Time*, Mar. 14, 1983, p. 64.) Suppose that a random sample of 30 steel workers taken today shows a sample mean wage of $15.03 per hour with a sample standard deviation of $1.29 per hour. A similar sample of 35 automobile workers shows a sample mean of $13.50 and a sample standard deviation of $1.14.
   a. Is the steel worker sample enough evidence to reject the null hypothesis that steel workers today average no more than 20 cents above the 1983 mean? Use $\alpha = .05$.
   b. Answer the same question as in part (a) for the automobile workers.

13. A company can tolerate .05 milligram per liter (mg/liter) of impurities in a raw material needed for manufacturing its product. Because the laboratory test for the impurities is subject to experimental error, the company tests each batch 30 times. Assume that the experimental error has mean 0, so that each reading is an unbiased estimate of the true amount of impurities in the batch. For a particular batch of the raw material, the mean of the 30 test readings is .058 mg/liter and the standard deviation is .009 mg/liter.
   a. Find a 95% confidence interval for the true amount of impurities in this batch.
   b. Do the data provide sufficient evidence to indicate that the amount of impurities in this batch exceeds .054 mg/liter? Test when $\alpha = .025$.

14. A machine produces handballs with a mean bounce height that is supposed to be 46 inches when dropped from a given height. In an experiment 35 balls are dropped. The mean bounce height is 44.8 inches, and the standard deviation of these heights is 2.1 inches. If the distribution of all bounce heights is normal with mean μ, for which values of μ_0 would you reject H_0: $\mu = \mu_0$ in favor of H_a: $\mu < \mu_0$ at the 5% level?

15. An efficiency expert claims that by introducing a new type of machinery into a production process, he can substantially decrease the time required for production. Because of the

expense involved in purchasing and maintaining the new machinery, management figures that unless the production time can be decreased by at least 8 minutes per unit produced, it should not buy this machinery. The mean time to produce one unit with the current machinery is 76 minutes. Suppose that management observes an experiment with the new machinery where 45 units are produced with a mean time of 66.9 minutes and a standard deviation of 2.3 minutes. Should it be sufficiently convinced at the 5% level that the new machinery is worth the price?

*16. The current mean age of all Americans is approximately 30, and one prediction is that it could increase to 35 in the next decade because of the relatively low birth rate. (Reference: G. J. Stolnitz, "Our Main Population Patterns: Radical Shifts, Cloudy Prospects," *Business Horizons,* Vol. 25, 1982, pp. 91–99.) Suppose that a random sample of n people taken 10 years from now shows a sample mean age of 31.1 and a sample standard deviation of 5.5. If we can reject the null hypothesis at the 5% level that the average age in the whole population has not increased from the current level of 30, what is the smallest value that n could be?

17. A random sample of $n = 200$ savings accounts in a local community shows a mean percentage increase in savings account values of 7.2% over the past 12 months and a standard deviation of 5.6%. Assume that the mean of all percentage increases (or percentage decreases, if negative) is μ.
   a. Find a 95% confidence interval for μ.
   b. How would you use part (a) to test H_0: $\mu = \mu_0$ versus H_a: $\mu \neq \mu_0$ at the 5% level for any specific μ_0? Which μ_0's would lead to rejection of H_0?

18. On an examination given to students at a large number of different schools, the mean grade is 78.3 and the standard deviation of grades is 7.4. These figures are taken to be population figures. At one particular school where 30 students are sampled, the sample mean grade is 75.9. Does this sample indicate at the 5% level that the (population) mean score for this school is significantly different from the population mean for all schools? First test with a one-tailed alternative; then test with a two-tailed alternative.

19. A consumer agency claims that a jelly company does not put the required amount of jelly in its 10-ounce jars. A sample of 40 jars are selected and weighed. From past experience it is known that the standard deviation of weights of jelly in all jars is .25 ounce. The agency wants to be 95% sure that the company is indeed not putting an average of at least 10 ounces in its jars before it (the agency) makes any public accusation. How small must the sample mean for the 40 jars be before the agency will make an accusation against the jelly company? Answer the same question if the sample size is 80 instead of 40.

*20. Referring to Problem 19, suppose that the mean weight of all the company's jelly jars is 9.90 ounces. What is the probability that the agency makes a type II error when the sample size is 40; when the sample size is 80? In words, what is a type II error for this problem?

*21. Assume that under present working conditions in a certain plant, the distribution of the number of parts produced in one hour has mean 146 and standard deviation 20. A change is proposed that may change the mean but will leave the standard deviation as it is. Let μ be the new mean. We wish to test H_0: $\mu = 146$ versus H_a: $\mu \neq 146$, by examining parts from a sample of $n = 30$ hours under the new conditions.
   a. For a 5% significance level, find the relevant rejection region in terms of the sample mean. That is, find a region such that we reject H_0 only if $\overline{X}$ falls in this region.
   b. Using the rejection region from part (a), what is the probability of making a type II error if the new mean is really $\mu = 149$; if $\mu = 152$?

22. A group of scientists are experimenting with a possible new "quick" cure for a common disease. Using the current methods for curing the disease, the time until a patient recovers completely is known to be normally distributed with mean 13.5 days. Using the new method on 30 patients, the scientists observe that the mean time to recovery is 11.8 days and the standard deviation is 3.8 days. They will publish their results in the form "Our method reduces the mean time to recovery" only if they are 95% confident that this statement is correct.
   a. Set up their problem of whether to publish as a hypothesis-testing problem.
   b. State in words what type I and type II errors are in the particular context of this problem.
   c. Given that you are the resident statistician, would you recommend publishing or not publishing? Why?

Hypothesis Tests for Other Population Parameters

In Section 9.3 we discussed hypothesis tests for a population mean μ in depth. We could repeat this discussion for each of the other parameters of interest, such as p and σ^2, but it is not necessary to do so, at least not in the same depth as above, because hypothesis tests for these parameters are very similar to those for μ. Therefore, in this section we merely state the forms of the hypothesis tests and conclude with examples that implement these tests.

The notation is exactly the same as in the past few chapters. This is because the same sampling distributions play the key role in establishing the forms of these hypothesis tests. For each test, α is the maximum allowed type I error probability. Also, each parameter subscripted with a 0 denotes the hypothesized value of the parameter being tested. (In the case of differences, such as $\mu_1 - \mu_2$, we write D_0 to indicate that the value of the *difference*, not the individual values μ_1 and μ_2, is being hypothesized.) Of course, these hypothesized values must be deduced from the context of any specific problem.

The tests for the various parameters are summarized in Table 9.2. This table not only makes implementation of the tests straightforward, but it also highlights the similarities between the tests.

It is important to realize that each of these tests is based on several crucial assumptions. The first is that the samples are *random* samples from the population. This means that the individual observations are independent of

Forms of the Tests

Table 9.2

Test group 1   Parameter of interest: p
   Assumptions: Sample size is large ($np(1 - p) \geq 5$).
   Computed quantities:
      Sample proportion, $\hat{p}$
      Standard error of $\hat{p}$: $\text{StdErr}(\hat{p}) = \sqrt{p_0(1 - p_0)/n}$
      Test statistic: $z = (\hat{p} - p_0)/\text{StdErr}(\hat{p})$
   A. $H_0: p \leq p_0$ versus $H_a: p > p_0$
      Rejection region: $z > z_\alpha$
   B. $H_0: p \geq p_0$ versus $H_a: p < p_0$
      Rejection region: $z < -z_\alpha$

(continued)

Table 9.2   *(continued)*

  C. H_0: $p = p_0$ versus H_a: $p \neq p_0$
      Rejection region: $z > z_{\alpha/2}$ or $z < -z_{\alpha/2}$

Test group 2   Parameter of interest: $p_1 - p_2$
    Assumptions: Sample sizes are large ($n_1 p_1 (1 - p_1) \geq 5$, $n_2 p_2 (1 - p_2) \geq 5$).
    Computed quantities:
      Difference between sample proportions, $\hat{p}_1 - \hat{p}_2$
      Pooled sample proportion: $\hat{p} = (n_1 \hat{p}_1 + n_2 \hat{p}_2)/(n_1 + n_2)$
      Standard error of $\hat{p}_1 - \hat{p}_2$: $\text{StdErr}(\hat{p}_1 - \hat{p}_2) = \sqrt{\hat{p}(1 - \hat{p})(1/n_1 + 1/n_2)}$
      Test statistic: $z = (\hat{p}_1 - \hat{p}_2)/\text{StdErr}(\hat{p}_1 - \hat{p}_2)$
  A. H_0: $p_1 - p_2 \leq 0$ versus H_a: $p_1 - p_2 > 0$
      Rejection region: $z > z_\alpha$
  B. H_0: $p_1 - p_2 \geq 0$ versus H_a: $p_1 - p_2 < 0$
      Rejection region: $z < -z_\alpha$
  C. H_0: $p_1 - p_2 = 0$ versus H_a: $p_1 - p_2 \neq 0$
      Rejection region: $z > z_{\alpha/2}$ or $z < -z_{\alpha/2}$

Test group 3   Parameter of interest: μ
    Assumptions: Sample size is large ($n \geq 30$).
    Computed quantities:
      Sample mean: $\overline{X}$
      Sample variance: s^2
      Standard error of $\overline{X}$: $\text{StdErr}(\overline{X}) = \sigma/\sqrt{n}$ (Use s in place of σ if σ is
       unknown)
      Test statistic: $z = (\overline{X} - \mu_0)/\text{StdErr}(\overline{X})$
  A. H_0: $\mu \leq \mu_0$ versus H_a: $\mu > \mu_0$
      Rejection region: $z > z_\alpha$
  B. H_0: $\mu \geq \mu_0$ versus H_a: $\mu < \mu_0$
      Rejection region: $z < -z_\alpha$
  C. H_0: $\mu = \mu_0$ versus H_a: $\mu \neq \mu_0$
      Rejection region: $z > z_{\alpha/2}$ or $z < -z_{\alpha/2}$

Test group 4   Parameter of interest: μ
    Assumptions: Population is normal; sample size is small ($n < 30$).
    Computed quantities:
      Sample mean: $\overline{X}$
      Sample variance: s^2
      Standard error of $\overline{X}$: $\text{StdErr}(\overline{X}) = s/\sqrt{n}$
      Test statistic: $t = (\overline{X} - \mu_0)/\text{StdErr}(\overline{X})$
      Degrees of freedom: $n - 1$
  A. H_0: $\mu \leq \mu_0$ versus H_a: $\mu > \mu_0$
      Rejection region: $t > t_{\alpha, n-1}$
  B. H_0: $\mu \geq \mu_0$ versus H_a: $\mu < \mu_0$
      Rejection region: $t < -t_{\alpha, n-1}$
  C. H_0: $\mu = \mu_0$ versus H_a: $\mu \neq \mu_0$
      Rejection region: $t > t_{\alpha/2, n-1}$ or $t < -t_{\alpha/2, n-1}$

Table 9.2 *(continued)*

Test group 5 Parameter of interest: $\mu_1 - \mu_2$

Assumptions: Sample sizes are large ($n_1 \geq 30$, $n_2 \geq 30$); observations from two samples are independent.

Computed quantities:

Difference between sample means: $\overline{X}_1 - \overline{X}_2$

Sample variances: s_1^2, s_2^2

Standard error of $\overline{X}_1 - \overline{X}_2$: $\text{StdErr}(\overline{X}_1 - \overline{X}_2) = \sqrt{\sigma_1^2/n_1 + \sigma_2^2/n_2}$ (Use s_1^2, s_2^2 in place of σ_1^2, σ_2^2 if σ's are unknown)

Test statistic: $z = [(\overline{X}_1 - \overline{X}_2) - D_0]/\text{StdErr}(\overline{X}_1 - \overline{X}_2)$

A. $H_0: \mu_1 - \mu_2 \leq D_0$ versus $H_a: \mu_1 - \mu_2 > D_0$

Rejection region: $z > z_\alpha$

B. $H_0: \mu_1 - \mu_2 \geq D_0$ versus $H_a: \mu_1 - \mu_2 < D_0$

Rejection region: $z < -z_\alpha$

C. $H_0: \mu_1 - \mu_2 = D_0$ versus $H_a: \mu_1 - \mu_2 \neq D_0$

Rejection region: $z > z_{\alpha/2}$ or $z < -z_{\alpha/2}$

Test group 6 Parameter of interest: $\mu_1 - \mu_2$

Assumptions: Populations are normal; sample sizes are small ($n_1 < 30$, $n_2 < 30$); population variances are equal; observations from two populations are independent.

Computed quantities:

Difference between sample means: $\overline{X}_1 - \overline{X}_2$

Sample variances: s_1^2, s_2^2

Pooled sample variance: $s_p^2 = [(n_1 - 1)s_1^2 + (n_2 - 1)s_2^2]/(n_1 + n_2 - 2)$

Standard error of $\overline{X}_1 - \overline{X}_2$: $\text{StdErr}(\overline{X}_1 - \overline{X}_2) = s_p\sqrt{1/n_1 + 1/n_2}$

Test statistic: $t = [(\overline{X}_1 - \overline{X}_2) - D_0]/\text{StdErr}(\overline{X}_1 - \overline{X}_2)$

Degrees of freedom: $n_1 + n_2 - 2$

A. $H_0: \mu_1 - \mu_2 \leq D_0$ versus $H_a: \mu_1 - \mu_2 > D_0$

Rejection region: $t > t_{\alpha, n_1 + n_2 - 2}$

B. $H_0: \mu_1 - \mu_2 \geq D_0$ versus $H_a: \mu_1 - \mu_2 < D_0$

Rejection region: $t < -t_{\alpha, n_1 + n_2 - 2}$

C. $H_0: \mu_1 - \mu_2 = D_0$ versus $H_a: \mu_1 - \mu_2 \neq D_0$

Rejection region: $t > t_{\alpha/2, n_1 + n_2 - 2}$ or $t < -t_{\alpha/2, n_1 + n_2 - 2}$

Test group 7 Parameter of interest: $\mu_1 - \mu_2$

Assumptions: Populations are normal; samples sizes are small ($n_1 < 30$, $n_2 < 30$); population variances are not equal; observations from two samples are independent.

Computed quantities:

Difference between sample means: $\overline{X}_1 - \overline{X}_2$

Sample variances: s_1^2, s_2^2

Standard error of $\overline{X}_1 - \overline{X}_2$: $\text{StdErr}(\overline{X}_1 - \overline{X}_2) = \sqrt{s_1^2/n_1 + s_2^2/n_2}$

Test statistic: $t = [(\overline{X}_1 - \overline{X}_2) - D_0]/\text{StdErr}(\overline{X}_1 - \overline{X}_2)$

Degrees of freedom: $\overline{n}$, where

$$\overline{n} \approx \frac{(s_1^2/n_1 + s_2^2/n_2)^2}{(s_1^2/n_1)^2/(n_1 - 1) + (s_2^2/n_2)^2/(n_2 - 1)}$$

(continued)

Table 9.2   (*continued*)

A. H_0: $\mu_1 - \mu_2 \leq D_0$ versus H_a: $\mu_1 - \mu_2 > D_0$
   Rejection region: $t > t_{\alpha,\bar{n}}$

B. H_0: $\mu_1 - \mu_2 \geq D_0$ versus H_a: $\mu_1 - \mu_2 < D_0$
   Rejection region: $t < -t_{\alpha,\bar{n}}$

C. H_0: $\mu_1 - \mu_2 = D_0$ versus H_a: $\mu_1 - \mu_2 \neq D_0$
   Rejection region: $t > t_{\alpha/2,\bar{n}}$ or $t < -t_{\alpha/2,\bar{n}}$

Test group 8   Parameter of interest: σ^2 (or σ)
   Assumptions: Population is normal.
   Computed quantities:
      Sample variance: s^2
      Test statistic: $\chi^2 = (n-1)s^2/\sigma_0^2$
      Degrees of freedom: $n - 1$

A. H_0: $\sigma^2 \leq \sigma_0^2$ versus H_a: $\sigma^2 > \sigma_0^2$
   Rejection region: $\chi^2 > \chi_{\alpha,n-1}^2$

B. H_0: $\sigma^2 \geq \sigma_0^2$ versus H_a: $\sigma^2 < \sigma_0^2$
   Rejection region: $\chi^2 < \chi_{1-\alpha,n-1}^2$

C. H_0: $\sigma^2 = \sigma_0^2$ versus H_a: $\sigma^2 \neq \sigma_0^2$
   Rejection region: $\chi^2 > \chi_{\alpha/2,n-1}^2$ or $\chi^2 < \chi_{1-\alpha/2,n-1}^2$

Test group 9   Parameter of interest: σ_1^2/σ_2^2
   Assumptions: Populations are normal; two samples are independent.
   Computed quantities:
      Sample variances: s_1^2, s_2^2
      Test statistic: $F = s_1^2/s_2^2$
      Degrees of freedom: $n_1 - 1$ (numerator) and $n_2 - 1$ (denominator)

A. H_0: $\sigma_1^2/\sigma_2^2 \leq 1$ versus H_a: $\sigma_1^2/\sigma_2^2 > 1$
   Rejection region: $F > F_{\alpha,n_1-1,n_2-1}$

B. H_0: $\sigma_1^2/\sigma_2^2 = 1$ versus H_a: $\sigma_1^2/\sigma_2^2 \neq 1$
   Rejection region: $F > F_{\alpha/2,n_1-1,n_2-1}$ or $1/F > F_{\alpha/2,n_2-1,n_1-1}$

Test group 10 (Matched-pairs test)   Parameter of interest: μ_D, the mean of the differences
   Assumptions: Population of differences is normal; each observation from
      population 1 is paired with an observation from population 2.
   Computed quantities:
      Sample mean of the differences: $\overline{X}_D$
      Sample variance of the differences: s_D^2
      Standard error of $\overline{X}_D$: StdErr$(\overline{X}_D) = s_D/\sqrt{n}$
      Test statistic: $t = (\overline{X}_D - D_0)/\text{StdErr}(\overline{X}_D)$
      Degrees of freedom: $n - 1$

A. H_0: $\mu_D \leq D_0$ versus H_a: $\mu_D > D_0$
   Rejection region: $t > t_{\alpha,n-1}$

B. H_0: $\mu_D \geq D_0$ versus H_a: $\mu_D < D_0$
   Rejection region: $t < -t_{\alpha,n-1}$

C. H_0: $\mu_D = D_0$ versus H_a: $\mu_D \neq D_0$
   Rejection region: $t > t_{\alpha/2,n-1}$ or $t < -t_{\alpha/2,n-1}$

one another and that for any given sample size, all possible samples are equally likely. Second, an assumption of normality is always lurking in the background. Essentially, this means that the sample sizes must be large enough for the Central Limit Theorem to apply or the populations must be normal. Finally, when two populations are involved, such as in the tests of $\mu_1 - \mu_2$, the two samples are assumed to be independent of one another. (The only exception is test group 10, which we discuss in Section 9.5.)

The consequence of violating these assumptions and performing the tests as if the assumptions were true is that the actual type I error probability may not be the specified value α. For example, we may run the test at the $\alpha = .05$ level, but because of a lack of independence, say, the actual type I error probability may be .25. A thorough discussion of the seriousness of failing to satisfy the various assumptions is beyond the level of this book. Basically, lack of independence tends to be more serious than lack of normality. But in applied problems, we should always try to determine whether the data fit the assumptions before proceeding blindly with the following tests. In many cases a trained statistician can suggest a different test that is more appropriate. In Chapter 13 we discuss alternatives to several of the tests given here.

Numerical Examples of Hypothesis Tests

As the material in Table 9.2 indicates, it is relatively straightforward to perform the appropriate hypothesis test once the hypotheses are given. Much of the difficulty in real problems involves the formulation of the hypotheses in the first place. We must choose the parameter to be tested and then develop H_0 and H_a. After this, the rest is arithmetic. The following examples illustrate both the formulation and computational aspects of these tests. For the reader's convenience, we continue to solve these examples by going through the six basic steps: (1) state the hypotheses, (2) determine α, (3) calculate a test statistic, (4) look up the relevant tabulated value, (5) make the decision, and (6) state the decision in the context of the particular problem.

EXAMPLE 9.6

An encyclopedia company sells a large percentage of its encyclopedias by employing door-to-door salespeople. Over the past decade, monthly sales per employee stayed fairly steady at an average rate of 10 sets sold per month. Recently, however, the company has been putting its door-to-door salespeople through a new and hopefully more effective training course. Subsequent to this new training program, sales of 25 randomly selected employees were recorded for a particular month. The average was 13.2 sales and the standard deviation was 5.3. The company believes the added expense of the new training program is justified only if an employee sells, on the average, at least 1.5 more sets per month with the new training program than without it. Is there significant evidence, at the 5% level, to indicate that sales have increased this much? What about at the 10% level? Assume that the distribution of the number of sets sold per month is normal.

SOLUTION

(1) Let μ be the mean monthly sales per employee who has had the new training program. Since the previous mean sales level was 10, the new training program is justified only if $\mu > 10 + 1.5$, that is, only if $\mu > 11.5$. Since the company is evidently skeptical of the new program unless sample evidence proves its superiority, the hypotheses are H_0: $\mu \leq 11.5$ versus H_a: $\mu > 11.5$. (2) We will use $\alpha = .05$ first and then see what happens when $\alpha = .10$. (3) Because this is a test of a mean and the sample size is relatively small, we use Test 4A from Table 9.2, with $n = 25$, $\mu_0 = 11.5$, $\overline{X} = 13.2$, and $s = 5.3$. The test statistic is a t value:

$$t = \frac{\overline{X} - \mu_0}{\text{StdErr}(\overline{X})} = \frac{13.2 - 11.5}{5.3/5} = 1.60$$

(4) The tabulated t value is $t_{.05,24} = 1.71$. (5) Since the calculated t value is *not* greater than 1.71, we cannot reject H_0 at the 5% significance level. (6) We must conclude that the training program is not worth the money.

But for a 10% significance level, $t_{.10,24} = 1.32$. Because this is less than the calculated t value, we *could* reject H_0 at the 10% level. In other words, the p-value for this sample is somewhere between .05 and .10 (see Figure 9.11).

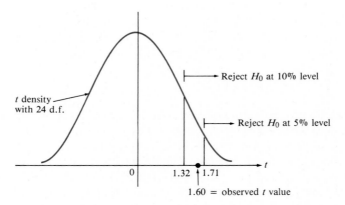

Figure 9.11

EXAMPLE 9.7

Two teams of workers assemble automobile engines at a manufacturing plant. Another group inspects a random sample of the teams' assemblies and judges each assembly to be acceptable or unacceptable. A random sample of 127 assemblies from team 1 shows 12 unacceptable assemblies. A similar random sample of 98 assemblies from team 2 shows five unacceptable assemblies. Is this enough evidence to conclude, at the 10% level, that the two teams differ with respect to their proportions of unacceptable assemblies?

SOLUTION

(1) Let p_1 and p_2 be the proportions of *all* assemblies produced by teams 1 and 2 that are unacceptable. Evidently, management will assume that p_1 equals p_2 unless there is significant evidence to the contrary. This means the two hypotheses are H_0: $p_1 - p_2 = 0$ (or $p_1 = p_2$) versus H_a: $p_1 - p_2 \neq 0$ (or $p_1 \neq p_2$). (2) The α value is given as .10. (3) Because this a test of the difference between two proportions, we use Test 2C from Table 9.2 with $\hat{p}_1 = {}^{12}\!/_{127} = .094$, $\hat{p}_2 = {}^5\!/_{98} = .051$, $n_1 = 127$, and $n_2 = 98$. To obtain the standard error of $\hat{p}_1 - \hat{p}_2$ when H_0 is true, we first compute the "pooled" $\hat{p}$. (Notice that the numerator of $\hat{p}$ listed in the table, $n_1\hat{p}_1 + n_2\hat{p}_2$, is simply the total number of unacceptable items in the two samples.)

$$\hat{p} = \frac{n_1\hat{p}_1 + n_2\hat{p}_2}{n_1 + n_2} = \frac{12 + 5}{127 + 98} = .076$$

Then the standard error of $\hat{p}_1 - \hat{p}_2$ when H_0 is true is

$$\text{StdErr}(\hat{p}_1 - \hat{p}_2) = \sqrt{\hat{p}(1 - \hat{p})\left(\frac{1}{n_1} + \frac{1}{n_2}\right)} = .0356$$

The resulting test statistic is

$$z = \frac{\hat{p}_1 - \hat{p}_2}{\text{StdErr}(\hat{p}_1 - \hat{p}_2)} = 1.21$$

(4) The relevant tabulated value is $z_{\alpha/2} = z_{.05} = 1.645$. (5) Since 1.21 is not greater in magnitude than 1.645, we cannot reject H_0. (6) We cannot conclude at the 10% significance level that the two teams are different. In fact, since $1.21 = z_{.113} = z_{.226/2}$, we could only reject H_0 at the 22.6% level (or any higher level). This is illustrated in Figure 9.12 (p. 436).

Because this is a two-tailed test, an alternative way to perform the test is to calculate a 90% confidence interval for $p_1 - p_2$ and see whether the H_0

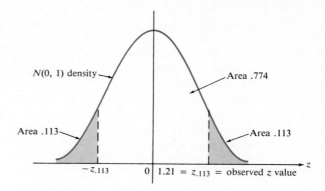

Figure 9.12

value of $p_1 - p_2$, namely 0, falls within this confidence interval. From Chapter 7 the appropriate confidence interval is

$$\hat{p}_1 - \hat{p}_2 \pm z_{\alpha/2} \sqrt{\frac{\hat{p}_1(1 - \hat{p}_1)}{n_1} + \frac{\hat{p}_2(1 - \hat{p}_2)}{n_2}}$$

$$= (.094 - .051) \pm 1.645 \sqrt{\frac{.094(.906)}{127} + \frac{.051(.949)}{98}}$$

$$= .043 \pm .056$$

This interval extends from a negative number, $-.013$, to a positive number, $.099$, so that it does include the value 0. This provides a second, equivalent reason for not rejecting H_0 at the 10% level.

The following example concerns a test for the difference between two means when the sample sizes are small and the population variances are unknown. From Table 9.2 we see that there are two tests available, the distinction being whether we assume equal population variances. Therefore, it is a good idea to use Test 9B first to see whether the equal population variance assumption is a reasonable one. (Many books include only Test 6, not Test 7. However, Test 7 is preferred when the sample variances are widely different, especially when the sample sizes are also widely different.)

EXAMPLE 9.8

A large department store would like to know whether delinquent credit card purchasers (those who do not pay within six months, say) make larger purchases on the average than those who pay promptly. They randomly select

15 credit card purchases made more than six months ago that have not yet been paid. The mean of these is $96.51, and the standard deviation is $58.20. They also select a group of 20 purchases that were paid promptly. The mean of these is $78.71, and the standard deviation $40.23. Can the store conclude, at the 5% significance level, that delinquent payments are generally for larger amounts than prompt payments? Assume that the distributions of payments for both groups of customers are normal.

SOLUTION

Let μ_1 be the mean of all delinquent bills, and let μ_2 be the mean of all bills paid promptly. The store wants to know if there is enough evidence to conclude that μ_1 is greater than μ_2. Therefore, the test involves a comparison between two means. Since the sample sizes are relatively small, we must choose between test groups 6 and 7. The difference between these two test groups is whether we can assume equal variances of delinquent payments and prompt payments. So as a first step, we test this assumption.

The six steps for this preliminary test are as follows. (1) Let σ_1^2 and σ_2^2 be the variances of all delinquent bills and promptly paid bills, respectively. Since we want to test whether these are equal, the relevant hypotheses are $H_0: \sigma_1^2/\sigma_2^2 = 1$ versus $H_a: \sigma_1^2/\sigma_2^2 \neq 1$. (2) No α value is given for this test, so we arbitrarily choose $\alpha = .05$. (3) For a test of equality between two variances, we use Test 9B. The test statistic is an F value,

$$F = \frac{s_1^2}{s_2^2} = \frac{58.20^2}{40.23^2} = 2.09$$

(4) The relevant tabulated F value is $F_{\alpha/2, n_1-1, n_2-1} = F_{.025, 14, 19}$. From Table V, this is approximately 2.64. (5) Since 2.09 is not greater than 2.64, we cannot reject H_0. (6) We cannot conclude that the variances of delinquent bills and promptly paid bills are significantly different.

Now that this preliminary test has been performed, we return to the original problem and present the six steps for its solution. (1) The store wants to know if there is enough evidence to conclude that $\mu_1 > \mu_2$. In this case the burden of proof is on showing that delinquent payments are larger, so the hypotheses are $H_0: \mu_1 - \mu_2 \leq 0$ versus $H_a: \mu_1 - \mu_2 > 0$. (2) The α value is given as .05. (3) Because of the results of the preliminary test on variances, we use Test 6A with $D_0 = 0$. The pooled variance is

$$s_p^2 = \frac{(n_1 - 1)s_1^2 + (n_2 - 1)s_2^2}{n_1 + n_2 - 2}$$

$$= \frac{14(58.20)^2 + 19(40.23)^2}{15 + 20 - 2} = 48.67^2$$

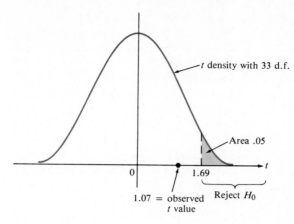

Figure 9.13

This leads to the standard error of $\overline{X}_1 - \overline{X}_2$, namely

$$\text{StdErr}(\overline{X}_1 - \overline{X}_2) = 48.67 \sqrt{\frac{1}{15} + \frac{1}{20}} = 16.62$$

Then the test statistic t is

$$t = \frac{(\overline{X}_1 - \overline{X}_2) - D_0}{\text{StdErr}(\overline{X}_1 - \overline{X}_2)} = \frac{(96.51 - 78.71) - 0}{16.62} = 1.07$$

(4) The degrees of freedom parameter for the relevant t distribution is $n_1 + n_2 - 2 = 33$. Therefore, the tabulated t value is $t_{.05,33}$, which is approximately 1.69. (5) As Figure 9.13 shows, the calculated t statistic is well below 1.69, so we cannot reject H_0. (6) The store cannot conclude at the 5% significance level that delinquent bills are larger on the average than promptly paid bills.

EXAMPLE 9.9

A television network decides to cancel one of its shows if it is convinced that less than 14% of the viewing public are watching this show. First, if a random sample of 1500 households is selected, what sample proportions will lead to the show's cancellation? Assume a 5% significance level. Second, what is the probability that the show will not be canceled if 13.4% of the entire viewing population are watching it?

SOLUTION

(1) In this example we interpret the phrase "if it (the network) is convinced" to imply that the network will keep the show unless strong evidence indicates it should be canceled. So if p is the proportion of the viewing public who watch the show, the hypotheses are H_0: $p \geq .14$ (keep the show) versus H_a: $p < .14$ (cancel it). (2) The value of α is given as .05. (3) To answer the first question, we use Test 1B with $p_0 = .14$. According to Table 9.2, the rejection region is $z < -z_\alpha$, where z is given by

$$z = \frac{\hat{p} - p_0}{\sqrt{p_0(1 - p_0)/n}} = \frac{\hat{p} - .14}{\sqrt{.14(.86)/1500}} = \frac{\hat{p} - .14}{.00896}$$

But from the way the question is phrased, we want the rejection region stated in terms of the sample proportion, $\hat{p}$. From the formula for z, it is clear that $z < -z_\alpha$ if and only if $\hat{p} < .14 - z_\alpha(.00896)$. (4) The tabulated value is $z_{.05} = 1.645$. (5) We reject H_0 only if $\hat{p} < .125$ [since $.14 - 1.645(.00896) = .125$]. (6) The network should cancel the show only if less than $\frac{1}{8}$ of the sampled viewers are watching it.

Referring to the second question, when only 13.4% of the entire population are watching the show, it should be canceled. However, this will be done only if $\hat{p} < .125$. The probability of not doing so is a type II error probability. To calculate it, we must use $p = .134$ and $\sqrt{.134(.866)/1500} = .00880$ as the mean and standard deviation when standardizing $\hat{p}$:

$$P(\text{not canceling when } p = .134) = P(\hat{p} \geq .125) = P\left(Z \geq \frac{.125 - .134}{.00880}\right)$$

$$= P(Z \geq -1.02) = .846$$

This means there is about an 85% chance of taking the *wrong* action (continuing the show) when 13.4% of the public are watching it. The reason for this large error probability is that .134 is so close to the H_0 value of .14. To distinguish between these values, a sample size even larger than 1500 is required.

EXAMPLE 9.10

A natural gas company in Ohio knows that during the years of "cheap energy," the monthly gas bills during the winter for single-family houses had a standard deviation that stayed relatively constant at $15. With more expensive energy, however, the company hypothesizes that gas bills are varying more widely than they used to. To test this theory, the company examines the monthly gas bills of 20 randomly selected single-family houses during the month of January. These show a mean of $96.42 and a standard deviation of $26.23. Is the company's theory about increased variability supported at the 1% level? Assume that gas bills are currently varying according to a normal distribution.

SOLUTION

(1) Let σ be the standard deviation of current monthly gas bills for the relevant population of houses, and let $\sigma_0 = 15$ be the standard deviation of gas bills for this population during the years of cheap energy. Then the hypotheses are H_0: $\sigma \leq 15$ versus H_a: $\sigma > 15$. Equivalently, these can be stated as H_0: $\sigma^2 \leq 225$ versus H_a: $\sigma^2 > 225$. (2) The value of α is given as .01. (3) Since this is a test of a single population variance, we use Test 8A from Table 9.2, with $s = 26.23$. The test statistic is a chi-square value:

$$\chi^2 = \frac{(n-1)s^2}{\sigma_0^2} = \frac{19(26.23)^2}{15^2} = 58.10$$

(4) There are $n - 1 = 19$ degrees of freedom, so the relevant tabulated value is $\chi^2_{\alpha,n-1} = \chi^2_{.01,19} = 36.19$. (5) Since the calculated χ^2 value is well above 36.19, we can reject H_0. (6) The company has good reason to claim that gas bills *do* vary more now than they used to.

EXAMPLE 9.11

Consider an undergraduate business major who is trying to decide whether she should go on to earn her MBA degree. She decides to do so only if she can be convinced that graduates with MBA degrees earn at least $5000 per year more, on the average, than those with bachelor's degrees, after each has been working for five years. To test this hypothesis, she does some investigating and finds salaries for a random group of 30 business people who earned their MBAs five years ago and 35 who earned their bachelor's degrees five years ago. If the standard deviations of salaries of *all* such business people are known to be $6500 (for MBAs) and $5600 (for bachelors), how large a difference in mean salaries must she observe before she will be convinced, at the 10% level, to earn her MBA degree? Then if the actual mean difference between people with MBAs and bachelor's degrees (over the whole population) is really $6000, what is the probability that she will not go on to earn her MBA degree?

SOLUTION

(1) Let the subscripts 1 and 2 denote MBA and bachelor's degrees, respectively. Then she will go on to earn her MBA degree only if she is convinced that $\mu_1 - \mu_2 > 5000$. So she should test H_0: $\mu_1 - \mu_2 \leq 5000$ versus H_a: $\mu_1 - \mu_2 > 5000$. (2) The value of α is given as .10. (3) Since the sample

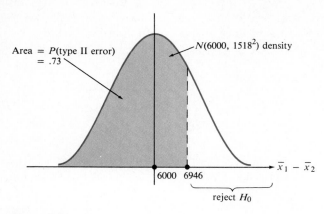

Figure 9.14

sizes are relatively large, we can use Test 5A from Table 9.2 with $n_1 = 30$, $n_2 = 35$, and $D_0 = 5000$. This test says to reject H_0 when z is greater than z_α, or equivalently, when $\overline{X}_1 - \overline{X}_2$ is greater than the critical value

$$D_0 + z_\alpha \text{StdErr}(\overline{X}_1 - \overline{X}_2) = 5000 + z_\alpha(1518)$$

Here we found $\text{StdErr}(\overline{X}_1 - \overline{X}_2)$ from the calculation

$$\text{StdErr}(\overline{X}_1 - \overline{X}_2) = \sqrt{\frac{\sigma_1^2}{n_1} + \frac{\sigma_2^2}{n_2}} = \sqrt{\frac{6500^2}{30} + \frac{5600^2}{35}} = 1518$$

(4) The tabulated z value is $z_{.10} = 1.282$. (5) Therefore, H_0 should be rejected when $z > 1.282$, that is, when $\overline{X}_1 - \overline{X}_2$ is greater than \$6946 [since 5000 + 1.282(1518) = 6946]. (6) The answer to the first question is that she should go on to obtain her MBA degree (reject H_0) only if she observes at least a \$6946 mean difference between the two groups of salaries.

For the second question, if the true mean difference is $\mu_1 - \mu_2 = 6000$, the probability that she will (mistakenly) not go on to earn an MBA degree is the probability that she observes a value of $\overline{X}_1 - \overline{X}_2$ less than \$6946 (see Figure 9.14). Since the standard error of $\overline{X}_1 - \overline{X}_2$ is still 1518, this probability is

$$P(\overline{X}_1 - \overline{X}_2 \leq 6946 \text{ when } \mu_1 - \mu_2 = 6000) = P\left(Z \leq \frac{6946 - 6000}{1518}\right)$$
$$= P(Z \leq .623) = .73$$

This is a type II error probability. It says that even when $\mu_1 - \mu_2$ is really \$6000, the probability is .73 that she will not be sufficiently convinced that confidence intervals $r = \sqrt{\dfrac{\hat{p}(1-\hat{p})}{n}}$

test of null $r = \sqrt{\dfrac{p_0(1-p_0)}{n}}$

the salary difference is at least $5000. This is one more example where relatively small sample sizes produce a large type II error probability.

Problems for Section 9.4
Proportions

23. By the end of 1981, it was reported that approximately 27% of all families had cable television. (Reference: J. T. Rothe, M. G. Harvey, and G. C. Michael, "Perspectives on the New Television," *Business Horizons,* Vol. 25, 1982, pp. 55–62.) A random sample of 75 families is chosen in 1986 and 29 of them have cable television. Is this enough evidence to conclude at the 5% significance level that the population percentage of families with cable television is up at least eight percentage points from 1981?

24. We wish to test the claim made in a recent business journal that at least 5% of the work force suffers from alcoholism. (Reference: R. J. Tersine and J. Hazeldine, "Alcoholism: A Productivity Hangover," *Business Horizons,* Vol. 25, 1982, pp. 68–72.) A sample of n workers is chosen, and it is observed that 6% of them suffer from alcoholism.
    a. Is the claim of the journal supported at the 10% level by this evidence if $n = 150$? What is the associated p-value?
    b. How large would n have to be to make this sample evidence significant at the 1% level?

25. An article in a news magazine claimed that 75% of all instamatic cameras are bought by women. Suppose that the owner of a camera store records over a period of several months that 78 out of 129 instamatic camera purchasers are women.
    a. Based on these data, find a 95% confidence interval for the proportion of all instamatic cameras bought by women.
    b. Given the answer to part (a), can you reject the claim of the magazine at the 5% significance level? Use a two-tailed test.
    c. If the true proportion of all instamatic cameras bought by women is .69, could you be making a type II error in part (b)? Explain.

*26. We would like to know whether we can reject the null hypothesis, at the 10% level, that no more than 20% of the households in Indiana make more than $30,000 per year.
    a. If 200 households are chosen at random, how many of them would have to be earning more than $30,000 per year in order for us to reject H_0?
    b. Assume that the true proportion of all Indiana households

with yearly incomes of at least $30,000 is .217. Find the probability of making a type II error with a sample of size $n = 200$. [Use the answer to part (a).]

27. When the television show "M*A*S*H" had its last episode in 1983, it attracted the largest viewing audience in the history of television. (Reference: *Time,* Mar. 14, 1983, p. 79.) Assume that in a random sample of 150 viewers, 113 watched this episode of "M*A*S*H." Let p be the proportion of *all* viewers who watched the show.
    a. Find a 95% confidence interval for p based on the sample above.
    b. Is the sample above enough evidence to reject the null hypothesis that no more than 72% of the public watched the show? Use $\alpha = .05$. What is the p-value for this sample?

28. An article in a business magazine claims that 7.3% of the industrial salesforce are women. If you took a random sample of 140 salespeople and found that 13 of them were women, would you be able to reject the null hypothesis that 7.3% of the salesforce are women? Use $\alpha = .05$ and answer the question for a one-tailed alternative; for a two-tailed alternative.

29. In one 1971 study, 143 out of a randomly selected 1700 employees were found to have a drinking problem. (Reference: R. J. Tersine and J. Hazeldine, "Alcoholism: A Productivity Hangover," *Business Horizons,* Vol. 25, 1982, pp. 68–72.)
    a. Find a 95% confidence interval for the proportion of all employees with a drinking problem in 1971.
    b. If p is the proportion of all employees with a drinking problem in 1986, and we wish to test H_0: $p = p_0$ versus a two-tailed alternative at the 5% significance level, for which values of p_0 would the same sample evidence as above (143 out of 1700) lead to rejection of H_0?

30. One study of 387 television commercials showed that only 185 of them had any "informational content." (Reference: A. Resnik and B. L. Stern, "An Analysis of Information Content in Television Advertising," *Journal of Marketing,*

Vol. 41, 1977, pp. 50–53.) Is this strong enough evidence to support the claim (the alternative hypothesis) that less than half of all television commercials have no informational content? Use $\alpha = .05$. What is the p-value for this sample?

31. Security experts have claimed that if a full-scale investigation were made, it would reveal that at least 50% of all company employees are involved in company-related theft. (Reference: R. J. Tersine and R. S. Russell, "Internal Theft: The Multi-Billion-Dollar Disappearing Act," *Business Horizons,* Vol. 24, 1981, pp. 11–20.)

    a. Would a sample of 450 employees, 237 of whom were shown to be involved in company-related theft, be enough evidence to support the experts' claim at the 5% level?

    b. For a sample of 450 employees, how many of them would have to be involved in company-related theft to support the experts' claim at the 5% level?

*32. Continuing Problem 31, assume that the actual proportion involved in company-related theft is .53. If we decide to accept the experts' claim only if at least 243 out of 450 are involved in company-related theft, what is the probability of a type II error?

33. A survey of 200 randomly selected women in the age bracket 18 to 45 shows that 57 have never had children. Would you reject the claim of the 1979 census survey that one-third of all women in this age bracket have never had children? (Reference: G. J. Stolnitz, "Our Main Population Patterns: Radical Shifts, Cloudy Prospects," *Business Horizons,* Vol. 25, 1982, pp. 91–99.) Use $\alpha = .10$ and a two-tailed test. What is the p-value for this sample?

34. In a 1982 poll 56% of 1250 Americans sampled favored a "sink or swim" attitude toward large companies in financial trouble. That is, these 56% were against the federal government bailing large companies out of their financial troubles.

    a. Find a 99% confidence interval for the population proportion of Americans who favored the sink-or-swim attitude.

    b. Based on your answer to part (a), would you reject the claim that the proportion who favored the sink-or-swim attitude is equal to .59? Use a two-tailed test with $\alpha = .01$.

35. In a recent study of 641 employees, 47.9% of them reported they did nothing regular in terms of exercise. (Reference: R. Kreitner, "Personal Wellness: It's Just Good Business," *Business Horizons,* Vol. 25, 1982, pp. 28–35.) Would you reject the null hypothesis that at least half of all workers do not exercise regularly, using $\alpha = .025$? What is the p-value for this sample?

36. A firm buys parts from a distributor. In the past, 15% of the parts were unusable. The distributor claims that the quality has recently improved so that no more than 10% of the parts are now unusable. Suppose that the firm places an order for 10,000 parts. A sample of 400 are randomly selected from the 10,000 parts, and 47 of these are unusable.

    a. Is this enough evidence to reject the distributor's claim at the 5% level? What is the p-value for this sample?

    b. Is this enough sample evidence to reject the null hypothesis that the distributor's quality control is no better than it used to be? Again, test at the 5% level.

37. We wish to test H_0: $p = .5$ versus H_a: $p > .5$, where p is the proportion of all customers who buy brand A in a two-brand market. In one city we observe 400 people, 216 of whom buy brand A. In another city, we observe 1000 people, 540 of whom buy brand A. Are the sample results from either city significant at the 5% level? Consider the two cities separately. (Remember that a "significant" sample result is one that leads to rejection of H_0.) How can you generalize from the results of this problem?

38. An insurance company groups a large number of people together as being similar drivers in the sense that each experiences the same probability p of having an accident every time he or she goes on a trip of at least 50 miles. Before the 55-mph speed limit was in effect, extremely large amounts of data showed this probability to be .007. Since the introduction of the 55-mph speed limit, a sample of 5000 such 50-mile-or-over trips produces 27 accidents. On this basis the insurance company reports in its newsletter that accidents among this group of drivers have gone down significantly.

    a. What is the company's probability of type I error when making this statement? That is, what is the p-value for the sample?

    b. How would your answer to part (a) change if the sample results are instead 54 accidents out of 10,000 trips?

Means, Differences Between Means

39. Some resort locations charge exorbitant prices for even modest accommodations. For example, one magazine article reported that a family would have to pay at least $200 per night for minimal accommodations in Aspen, Colorado, during the peak season. (Reference: *Time,* Feb. 14, 1983, p. 19.) Suppose that a random sample of 20 families staying in Aspen

is taken, and the prices they pay per night are as follows: 215, 185, 230, 245, 195, 225, 200, 215, 180, 175, 195, 255, 220, 210, 215, 195, 180, 175, 235, and 240. Do these prices support the (alternative) hypothesis that the average price per night for all families staying in Aspen is at least $200 at the 5% significance level? (Assume that the distribution of all prices is normal.)

40. It has been hypothesized that families with cable television watch more television than families without the cable. (Reference: J. T. Rothe, M. G. Harvey, and G. C. Michael, "Perspectives on the New Television," *Business Horizons*, Vol. 25, 1982, pp. 55–62.) To test this claim, two random samples are chosen. Fifteen families with cable report an average viewing time of 40.7 hours per week and a standard deviation of 7.3 hours per week, while 20 families without cable report an average viewing time of 38.2 hours per week and a standard deviation of 6.8 hours per week. Assuming that the populations of viewing times are normal with the same variance, does this sample information support the stated hypothesis at the 10% significance level? What is the (approximate) p-value for this sample data?

41. Referring to the data in Problem 12 (p. 427), do the two samples represent enough evidence to accept the alternative hypothesis that today's steel workers earn at least $1.25 per hour more than today's auto workers? Again use $\alpha = .05$, and assume equal population variances.

42. Consider the following sample data for the weights (in pounds) of athletic and nonathletic men, all approximately 5 feet 10 inches tall and of medium build.

Athletic Men	Nonathletic Men
151	152
148	153
156	149
155	162
157	165
161	168
158	157
168	178
149	161
174	186

a. Calculate the sample means and standard deviations of the weights of the two groups.
b. Treating the weights as independent random samples, can the null hypothesis that the population mean weight of athletic men is at least as large as that of nonathletic men be rejected at the 10% level? Assume equal population variances.

43. In a fixed period of time, 10 discount stores from different parts of the country are sampled, and their gross sales figures for this period are tabulated. In units of $100,000, these 10 sales figures are 3.8, 2.7, 4.1, 5.2, 2.5, 3.4, 3.9, 2.2, 5.6, and 4.4. Assume that the gross sales figures for all such discount stores for this period are normally distributed with mean μ.
a. Find a 95% confidence interval for μ.
b. Find the approximate p-value for a test of H_0: $\mu = 3$ versus H_a: $\mu > 3$. For which values of α would you reject H_0 in favor of H_a?

44. Using a relatively expensive brand of gasoline, the mean number of miles per gallon traveled by 15 similar automobiles under similar conditions is 22.6, and the standard deviation is 3.8 mpg. Using a cheaper brand of gasoline on a different sample of 15 automobiles, the mean mpg is 21.4 and the standard deviation is 4.4 mpg. Is this enough evidence to conclude that the mean mpg for the more expensive gasoline is higher? Test at the 5% level. (Assume that the two population variances are equal.)

45. To test the effects of a new fertilizer on wheat production, a tract of land is divided into 60 sections of equal area. All sections have nearly identical qualities as to soil, exposure to sunlight, and so on. The new fertilizer is applied to 30 of the sections, and the old fertilizer is applied to the other 30 sections. The mean number of bushels of wheat harvested per section using the new fertilizer is 19.5 bushels, and the standard deviation is .73 bushel. The corresponding mean and standard deviation for the sections using the old fertilizer are 17.9 bushels and .53 bushel, respectively. Is there enough sample evidence to claim that the new fertilizer produces a higher mean yield than the old fertilizer? Test at the 1% level. Do not assume equal population variances.

Differences Between Proportions

46. A manufacturer of ¼-inch bolts produces these bolts on two different machines. Random samples of 200 bolts manufactured by machine 1 and 100 bolts manufactured by machine 2 are examined. These samples show 19 and 5 defective bolts, respectively.
a. Is there enough evidence to accept the hypothesis that the

two machines are producing different proportions of defective bolts? Use $\alpha = .05$.

  b. Is there enough evidence to accept the hypothesis that the first machine is producing a higher proportion of defective bolts than the second machine? Again use $\alpha = .05$.

47. In a study to assess various effects of using a female model in television advertising, each of 150 male subjects is shown photographs of two televisions matched for price, color, and size, but of different makes. One television is shown with a female model and one without a model to 75 of the subjects (sample 1), and both televisions are shown without a female model to the other 75 subjects (sample 2). In sample 1 the television shown with the model is judged to be more expensive by 51 subjects, while in sample 2 the same television is judged to be more expensive by 39 subjects. Do these results indicate that using a female model influences the perceived expensiveness of a television? Use $\alpha = .05$ and a one-tailed test. What is the associated p-value?

48. In the past few years the percentage of married couples in which both partners have full-time jobs has definitely been increasing. Consider random samples of 100 married couples in 1985 and another 125 married couples in 1986. The data show that 41 of the 1985 couples are two-job families, whereas 55 of the 1986 couples are two-job families. Is this significant evidence at the 10% level that the proportion of couples with two jobs has increased from 1985 to 1986? What is the p-value for these sample results?

49. Consider two slot machines at a Las Vegas casino. They appear to be identical, but a player suspects that one of them will produce a higher proportion of wins than the other. He plays one of the machines 150 times and wins 12 times. He plays the other one 175 times and wins 17 times. At what significance level can the player reject the null hypothesis that the two machines are identical in terms of their proportions of wins?

50. A company that is marketing a new set of children's books mails a brochure about the books, together with a reply form, to a large number of families on a mailing list. In addition, it phones a randomly selected subset of these families and describes the books with a short 1-minute message. In one typical community, 97 of the 756 families not contacted by phone reply that they are willing to try the books for the stated trial period. In the same community 182 other families are contacted by phone (as well as by mail) and 33 reply that they are willing to try the books. Can you accept the alternative hypothesis that phone contact affects the proportion of those who are willing to try the books? Use a two-tailed test at the 5% level.

*51. For testing the difference between two proportions, we use $\hat{p}(1 - \hat{p})(1/n_1 + 1/n_2)$ as the (approximate) variance of $\hat{p}_1 - \hat{p}_2$, where $\hat{p}$ is the pooled sample proportion. Explain why this is reasonable when the H_0 value of $p_1 - p_2$ is 0. Why would this not be a good approximation when the H_0 value of $p_1 - p_2$ is a nonzero number. What would you recommend using for the variance of $\hat{p}_1 - \hat{p}_2$ in that case?

Variances

52. Given the sample of families in Problem 39, can you reject the null hypothesis at the 5% level that the standard deviation of prices paid per night by all families staying in Aspen is no greater than $18?

53. Referring to Problem 12 (p. 427), let σ_1^2 be today's variance of all steel workers' wages. Define σ_2^2 similarly for automobile workers. Assume that the population distributions of wages are normal for both groups of workers.

  a. Given the sample data in Problem 12, for which values of σ_0^2 could you reject $H_0: \sigma_1^2 \geq \sigma_0^2$ in favor of $H_a: \sigma_1^2 < \sigma_0^2$ at the 10% level?

  b. Answer part (a) with σ_1^2 replaced by σ_2^2. [That is, do part (a) for the automobile workers.]

54. Continuing Problem 53, can you reject $H_0: \sigma_1^2/\sigma_2^2 = 1$ in favor of $H_a: \sigma_1^2/\sigma_2^2 \neq 1$ at the 10% level? Can you reject $H_0: \sigma_2^2/\sigma_1^2 \leq 1$ in favor of $H_a: \sigma_2^2/\sigma_1^2 > 1$ at the 10% level?

55. Referring to the data in Problem 42, can you reject the null hypothesis at the 5% level that the variance in weight among all athletic men is different than the variance in weight among all nonathletic men?

*56. Suppose that you sample two normal populations independently. The variances of these populations are σ_1^2 and σ_2^2. You take random samples of sizes n_1 and n_2 and observe sample variances of s_1^2 and s_2^2.

  a. If $n_1 = n_2 = 21$, how large must the fraction s_1/s_2 be before you can reject the null hypothesis that σ_1^2 is no greater than σ_2^2 at the 5% significance level?

  b. Answer part (a) when $n_1 = n_2 = 41$.

c. If s_1 is 25% larger than s_2, approximately how large must n_1 and n_2 be if you are able to reject the null hypothesis in part (a) at the 5% level? (Again assume that n_1 and n_2 are equal, and refer to the F tables.)

57. The standard deviation of the breaking strengths of certain cables has been 350 pounds. After a change was introduced in the manufacturing process, however, the breaking strengths of a sample of 15 cables had a standard deviation of 410 pounds. Is this apparent increase in variability significant at the 5% level? Given the limits of the chi-square table, what can you conclude about the p-value for this sample? (Assume a normal distribution of breaking strengths.)

58. A production process produces parts where the weight is crit-ical. A sample of size $n = 25$ yields the statistics for weight as follows: $\overline{X} = 1.243$ ounces and $s = .027$ ounce.
   a. Find a 95% confidence interval for the standard deviation σ of the weights of all parts produced, assuming that the distribution of these weights is normal.
   b. Use part (a) to test the hypothesis $H_0: \sigma^2 = \sigma_0^2$ versus H_a: $\sigma^2 \neq \sigma_0^2$. For which values of σ_0^2 can you reject H_0 at the 5% level?

59. Referring to Problem 58, suppose that a second sample of size $n = 21$ is taken a few days later. It shows $\overline{X} = 1.237$ and $s = .034$. Is there enough sample evidence to conclude at the 10% level that the variance in weight has increased from the previous day? Why is an F test, not a chi-square test, appropriate?

9.5

The Matched-Pairs t Test

We mentioned that all the tests in Section 9.4 are valid only if certain in-dependence assumptions are met. When these independence assumptions are clearly violated, the application of any of the tests above can produce a much different type I error probability than expected. In this section we look at one type of problem where an independence assumption is clearly violated, and we develop a new test to deal with it.

To motivate this new test, consider the following example. A speed-read-ing program claims that it can increase people's reading speeds by at least 100 words per minute on the average. To test this claim, the company teaches the course to 15 randomly selected people. Their reading speeds, in words per minute, are measured before the course and after the course, with the results shown in Table 9.3. (The subscripts 1, 2, and D denote before, after, and difference.)

To test the claim of the program, we test $H_0: \mu_2 - \mu_1 \leq 100$ versus H_a: $\mu_2 - \mu_1 > 100$. Since the sample standard deviations s_1 and s_2 are nearly equal, we can assume that $\sigma_1 = \sigma_2$ and use Test 6A from Table 9.2. Then the pooled variance s_p^2 is

$$s_p^2 = \frac{(n_1 - 1)s_1^2 + (n_2 - 1)s_2^2}{n_1 + n_2 - 2}$$

$$= \frac{14(168.8)^2 + 14(172.1)^2}{28} = 170.5^2$$

Table 9.3

Person	Reading Speed Before	Reading Speed After	Difference (Increase)
1	375	480	105
2	250	520	270
3	325	610	285
4	540	620	80
5	180	290	110
6	240	380	140
7	650	710	60
8	420	580	160
9	120	195	75
10	520	680	160
11	250	370	120
12	190	350	160
13	425	575	150
14	615	820	205
15	200	420	220
	$\overline{X}_1 = 353.4$	$\overline{X}_2 = 506.7$	$\overline{X}_D = 153.3$
	$s_1 = 168.8$	$s_2 = 172.1$	$s_D = 67.6$

and the resulting t statistic is

$$t = \frac{(\overline{X}_2 - \overline{X}_1) - D_0}{s_p\sqrt{1/n_1 + 1/n_2}} = \frac{153.3 - 100}{170.5\sqrt{1/15 + 1/15}} = .86$$

This t value is not even significant at the 10% level because $t_{.10,28} = 1.31$. So by using this test, we cannot accept the company's claim at the 10% level (or at any lower level).

But the tests for differences between means discussed so far (test groups 5, 6, and 7 from Table 9.2) assume that the two samples are independent of one another. This assumption is clearly not valid in this example. Since every person is paired with himself or herself in the sense that every person takes both the before-test and the after-test, high before-test scores tend to be paired with high after-test scores, and low before-test scores tend to be paired with low after-test scores. If all of the people had approximately equal reading abilities, this lack of independence would not cause a problem. But they obviously do not. Some people read much faster than others, both before the course and after it. This creates an extra source of variance, namely, the variance in people's reading abilities. If we use Test 6A as above, this extra source of variance tends to obscure the effectiveness of the course.

We can get around this problem by using only the *last* column of numbers in Table 9.3, the differences, to test H_0: $\mu_D \leq 100$ versus H_a: $\mu_D > 100$. Here μ_D equals $\mu_2 - \mu_1$, the mean *difference* between after-test and before-test scores. Now we perform the test by treating the 15 differences in Table 9.3 as a random sample from the *single* population of differences. We assume that this population of differences is normally distributed. The sample mean and standard error of the sample differences are labeled $\overline{X}_D$ and s_D and are shown in the table. Since we now have a single population, we proceed as in Test 4A, the small-sample test for a single mean. The required t statistic is

$$t = \frac{\overline{X}_D - D_0}{\text{StdErr}(\overline{X}_D)} = \frac{153.3 - 100}{67.6/\sqrt{15}} = 3.05$$

and the relevant degrees of freedom parameter is $n - 1 = 14$. This t value is significant even at the 1% level ($\alpha = .01$) because $t_{.01,14} = 2.624$. So we can safely reject H_0 and accept the claim of the company. This is a very different result, and a more valid one, than that obtained using Test 6A.

The test above is called a *matched-pairs t test*. It is appropriate whenever there is a natural correspondence between the members of the two samples. In essence, each member of the sample is paired with itself. Although the members may differ significantly from one another, we care only about the differences between the two samples. In this case it is best not to use one of the tests in groups 5, 6, or 7, which test for differences between two population means. Instead, we should use Test 4 on the *single* population of differences. This special use of Test 4 has been listed separately as Test 10 in Table 9.2.

The following example illustrates another application where a matched-pairs t test is appropriate.

EXAMPLE 9.12

A manufacturing plant that employs a large number of blue-collar workers pays these workers every other Friday. The personnel department believes that there is a tendency for the absentee rate to be higher on the Monday following a payday than on the payday itself, and it wishes to test this hypothesis statistically. Looking over its records, it finds the information on absenteeism listed in Table 9.4. Is this information sufficient to conclude, at the 5% level, that there is more absenteeism on Mondays following paydays than on paydays?

SOLUTION

Here we have two samples of absentee figures, one for paydays and one for the Mondays following these paydays. It is probably reasonable to assume that the observations in either of these samples are independent of one another because they are separated by at least two-week periods. However, the ob-

Table 9.4

Pay Period	Absent on Friday	Absent on Following Monday	Difference (Monday − Friday)
1	25	34	9
2	15	21	6
3	42	47	5
4	29	28	−1
5	37	48	11
6	19	27	8
7	14	16	2
8	28	23	−5
9	31	40	9
10	21	26	5
11	32	32	0
12	20	31	11
13	29	35	6
	$\overline{X}_2 = 26.31$	$\overline{X}_1 = 31.38$	$\overline{X}_D = 5.08$
	$s_2 = 8.34$	$s_1 = 9.53$	$s_D = 4.87$

servation on a payday is *not* independent of the observation on the following Monday. If a large number of workers are absent on a payday, for example, there is a good chance that there will be a larger-than-average number of workers absent the following Monday. This is due to illnesses (or self-imposed vacations) that last more than three days. Therefore, the usual t test for a difference between two means is not appropriate, and we should use a matched-pairs t test instead.

To emphasize that this test is very similar to the other tests in this chapter, we again list the six basic steps. (1) We need to test H_0: $\mu_D \leq 0$ versus H_a: $\mu_D > 0$, where μ_D is the mean difference between the number absent on a Monday and the number absent on the previous payday. (2) The relevant value of α is .05. (3) For the 13 pay periods observed, the required t statistic is

$$t = \frac{\overline{X}_D - D_0}{\text{StdErr}(\overline{X}_D)} = \frac{5.08 - 0}{4.87/\sqrt{13}} = 3.76$$

(4) Since there are 13 pay periods, there are $13 - 1 = 12$ degrees of freedom, so the tabulated t value is $t_{.05,12} = 1.78$. (5) We can safely reject H_0 because 3.76 is much greater than 1.78. (6) Based on these data, there definitely appears to be more absenteeism on Mondays following paydays than on the paydays themselves.

Problems for Section 9.5

60. A study is performed to investigate whether husbands rate a new television show any differently than their wives. Fifteen couples watch the show and are then asked to rate its quality on a 0–100 scale. Each person rates the show without consulting his or her spouse. The ratings are shown below.

Husband	Wife
55	70
35	45
50	45
75	65
85	70
65	65
40	35
60	70
55	50
75	55
45	50
80	65
55	60
60	70
40	35

   a. If we want to test whether the mean rating for husbands is any different from the mean rating for their wives, why is a matched-pairs test appropriate? What distribution should be normal for the matched-pairs t test to be valid? Be specific.
   b. Use a matched-pairs t test to test the equal means hypothesis versus a two-tailed alternative at the 10% level.

61. A person in charge of a company's motor pool is trying to determine statistically whether there is any difference in mileage between two brands of gasoline (a cheap one and an expensive one). He chooses eight cars from the pool and runs each of them for several tankfuls with each brand of gasoline. He computes the mpg for the expensive brand minus the mpg for the cheap brand for each car. The mean of these differences is 1.47 mpg and the standard deviation of the differences is 1.50 mpg. He will use the more expensive gasoline only if he is persuaded at the 5% level that the mean difference in mpg over all cars is positive.
   a. Set this up as a hypothesis-testing situation and determine what decision the person should make.

   b. Why should this problem be solved with a matched-pairs test? What is the disadvantage (for this particular problem) of not using a matched-pairs test?

62. Ten golfers are asked to hit two brands of golf balls to test for differences in distance. The results are shown below. Each observation is the average distance of several drives by each golfer with each brand of ball. The question is whether we can conclude at the 10% level that the two brands produce different mean distances.

Golfer	Type 1	Type 2
1	270	265
2	235	245
3	225	205
4	285	260
5	220	225
6	245	235
7	265	260
8	275	250
9	245	250
10	280	275

   a. Why is a matched-pairs test appropriate for this problem?
   b. Can we reject the equal-mean-distance hypothesis in favor of a two-tailed alternative at the 10% level?
   c. Construct a 90% confidence level for the mean difference between the distances for the two brands of balls. How does this support your answer to part (b)?

*63. In 1982 married people got some relief from the "marriage penalty" on their income taxes. Suppose that we wish to test $H_0: \mu_{1982} - \mu_{1981} = \mu_0$ versus $H_a: \mu_{1982} - \mu_{1981} > \mu_0$, where μ_{1982} and μ_{1981} are the mean refunds (or payments, for negative values) for married couples in 1982 and 1981. We randomly sample 10 married couples and observe their refunds (or payments, if negative) for 1981 and 1982. These are shown below.

Couple	1981	1982
1	$ 125	$ 573
2	297	673
3	− 347	132
4	1036	984
5	− 563	430 (*continued*)

Couple	1981	1982
6	469	430
7	−704	−250
8	219	346
9	1250	1589
10	−321	−500

a. Why is a matched-pairs design appropriate here?

b. Assuming that $\mu_0 = 150$, use Test 6A from Table 9.2, with $\alpha = .05$, to test H_0. Then use a matched-pairs t test to test H_0, also with $\alpha = .05$. Compare the results.

c. Using a matched-pairs t test, for which values of μ_0 are the sample data above significant at the 5% level?

Summary

The topic of this chapter, hypothesis testing, is certainly one of the most important areas in statistics. The purpose of hypothesis testing is to choose between two hypotheses, the null hypothesis, which the investigator is usually trying to disprove, and the alternative hypothesis, which the investigator is usually trying to establish. A decision rule is designed so that the type I error probability of rejecting a true null hypothesis is small, usually .10, .05, or .01. The probability of a type II error, not rejecting the null hypothesis when it is false, is often sizable and can be controlled only by increasing the sample size (or by finding a more powerful test). The statistical significance of the test is the maximum acceptable probability of a type I error, and significant sample evidence is sample evidence that leads to the rejection of the null hypothesis. A very useful piece of information is the p-value of a sample. This is the probability of observing at least as unusual a sample as the one observed, given that the null hypothesis is true. If the p-value is sufficiently small, the null hypothesis can be rejected.

The actual mechanics of performing the tests in this chapter are very straightforward. In every case the test can be performed by computing a test statistic, looking up a tabulated value from Appendix B, and rejecting or not rejecting the null hypothesis based on a comparison of these two numbers. The similarities among the tests for the various parameters are highlighted in Table 9.2. Furthermore, this table shows how the same sampling distributions we learned in the previous three chapters are again used in hypothesis testing.

Applications

Application 9.1 It is well known that many companies are investing in gymnasiums and other exercise facilities so that their employees can get in better physical shape. However, it has not been proved that the cost of these facilities is worthwhile in terms of higher employee productivity. Do physically fit employees perform better? This question was the subject of a research study by Edwards and Gettman in 1980. (Reference: Sandra

E. Edwards and Larry R. Gettman, "The Effect of Employee Physical Fitness on Job Performance," *Personnel Administrator,* Vol. 25, 1980, pp. 41–44.) They selected 22 commercial real estate investment brokers who were not currently exercising regularly but expressed an interest in doing so. These people were put through a standard 12-week fitness program. By the end of this program, tests showed that they were in significantly better physical shape than when they started. But did they perform their work better?

To answer this question, Edwards and Gettman selected a "control" group of 22 employees who did *not* go through the training program. For the control group and the test group, monetary commissions were measured during a 24-week period before the training program and during a second 24-week period after the training program. If the training program had the desired effect, any increase in commissions for the training group should be higher than for the control group. This appeared to be the case. The mean commissions for the training group were $68,216 (before) and $85,950 (after), for a mean increase of $17,734. The standard deviation of these increases was very large, $45,936. For the control group, the similar figures were $41,983 (before) and $41,210 (after) for a mean increase of −$773 (a decrease). Here the standard deviation was also large, $41,432. Let μ_1 and μ_2 be the mean increase in commissions for all people with and without the benefit of the training program, respectively. Then we should test H_0: $\mu_1 - \mu_2 \leq 0$ versus H_a: $\mu_1 - \mu_2 > 0$. The test statistic is the usual t statistic for differences:

$$t = \frac{17,734 - (-773)}{\sqrt{45,936^2/22 + 41,432^2/22}} = 1.403$$

(The simplified formula for the variance term, as compared to the formula shown in test group 6, can be used because of equal sample sizes.) With over 40 degrees of freedom, this t value is not significant at the 5% level, although it is significant at the 10% level. So in spite of the large mean increase for the training group and the mean *decrease* for the control group, we cannot say conclusively that the training program makes a difference. As Edwards and Gettman correctly point out, the problem here is high variance. Because the members of each group varied so much from one another, the difference between group means is difficult to detect. We discuss this problem of "within-group variation" more extensively in Chapter 10 when we study analysis of variance.

Application 9.2   If you wonder whether 12-ounce soft drink cans really contain 12 ounces of soft drink or your gallon container of milk really contains a gallon of milk, you are not alone. According to a 1984 *Wall*

Street Journal article, the state of West Virginia, led by inspector Kenneth Butcher, is continually on the watch for product packages that contain less than they claim. (Reference: *Wall Street Journal,* Nov. 26, 1984.) Butcher, head of the consumer protection division of the state's labor department, makes periodic visits to supermarkets throughout the state. If he and his staff find a product that fails to measure up to the correct weight or volume advertised, they stamp it ILLEGAL FOR SALE, which prohibits its sale until the shortfall is rectified. According to the article, Mr. Butcher's crew of 26 inspectors have, in the past year, stamped ILLEGAL FOR SALE on $3 million of chemicals, 180,000 gallons of milk, oceans of orange juice, warehouses full of beer, and a long list of other items, including hams, charcoal briquettes, plastic bags, salt, and bottled water.

For example, at one point several prominent brewing companies received this stamp on their 12-ounce beer cans because they were on the average up to one-tenth of an ounce short per can. Of course, the inspectors realize that some shortfalls may be the result of sampling error. That is, the population of beer cans may contain at least 12 ounces per can, although the particular sample observed comes up short. Therefore, the inspectors may want to guard against the type I error of stamping such a sample ILLEGAL FOR SALE. Is an average shortfall of $\frac{1}{10}$ ounce per can enough to justify the illegal stamp given that a maximum type I probability of .05 is tolerated? The answer depends on the sample size and the standard deviation within the sample. Formally, we are testing H_0: $\mu \geq 12$ versus H_a: $\mu < 12$, where μ is the population mean of all beer cans. The test is run so that H_0 is rejected, and the cans are stamped illegal, only if

$$\frac{\overline{X} - 12}{\sigma/\sqrt{n}} < -z_{.05}$$

that is, only if $(12 - \overline{X}) > 1.645\sigma/\sqrt{n}$. If the critical shortfall to be detected is .1 ounce, the rejection region is where $.1 > 1.645\sigma/\sqrt{n}$. Rearranging, the sample is rejected only if $n > 1.645^2\sigma^2/.1^2 = 270.6\sigma^2$. For example, if $\sigma = .2$ (measured in ounces per can), n must be at least 11 cans. In this case, if the average of 11 (or more) cans is short by at least .1 ounce on the average, the inspectors can stamp the cans illegal and be at least 95% certain that no type I error has been committed.

Application 9.3   The purpose of a management information system (MIS) is to give managers timely data so that they can make intelligent decisions for their companies. However, it is not always clear what type of information is most useful for making these decisions. In a controlled experiment, Chervany and Dickson tested for differences in performance between subjects who were shown raw data about company operations and those who were shown the same data except in statistically summarized form. (Reference: Norman L. Chervany and Gary W. Dickson, "An Experimental Evaluation of Information Overload in a Production Environment," *Management Science,* Vol. 20, No. 10, 1974, pp. 1135–1344.) The data related to a production company's inventory levels, stockouts, and demands. The subjects seeing the raw data (RD) were shown daily levels of each of these quantities for each type of item produced. The subjects seeing the statistically summarized data (SSD) were shown averages and standard deviations of these daily quantities, as well as several other summary measures. Then each subject was asked to make decisions on future production levels. These decisions were fed into a computer, and on the basis of randomly generated future demands, the performance of each subject, in terms of average weekly cost, was measured. There were also two other performance measures for each subject: (1) decision time, the average amount of time elapsed between the time a subject received his information and submitted his next decision; and (2) decision confidence, the subject's level of confidence that he had made a good decision, measured on a seven-point scale.

The researchers reported the results of tests for the mean differences between the two groups on each of the performance measures. These tests were run as matched-pairs t tests, based on 11 subjects in each group who were paired according to scores from a previously taken standardized test. The researchers also reported results of F tests for differences between variances of performance measures for the two groups. A summary of the results is shown in Table 9.5. Each mean difference is the mean for the RD group minus the mean for the SSD group. For the total cost measure the ratio of variances is the variance of the RD group divided by the variance of the SSD group. For the decision time and decision confidence measures, the variances are reversed in this ratio; that is, the variance of the SSD group is in the numerator.

As these results show, the SSD group performed considerably better in

Table 9.5

	Total Cost	Decision Time	Decision Confidence
Mean difference	$1483	−4.7 min	.636
Level of significance	.18	.05	.12
Ratio of variances	1.984	1.057	5.307
Level of significance	.15	*	.02

*Reported only as "not significant."

terms of cost, although the difference is statistically significant only at the 18% level. Also, the SSD group had considerably less variation in their costs, but again the difference is significant only at the 15% level. With respect to decision time, the SSD group took a significantly longer time to make decisions, but perhaps surprisingly, they had somewhat less confidence than the RD group that they had made good decisions. As Chervany and Dickson surmise, the SSD group apparently saw problems with company operations, particularly with stockouts, that the RD group missed. By trying to come to grips with these problems, they managed to reduce costs, but it took them slightly longer, and they worried more that they might not have solved the problems successfully.

Glossary of Terms

Null and alternative hypotheses   the two conflicting hypotheses in any hypothesis-testing problem; the burden of proof is always on the alternative hypothesis

Type I error   the error committed when H_0 is true but is rejected; its probability is labeled α

Type II error   the error committed when H_a is true but H_0 is not rejected; its probability is labeled β

Power curve   the graph of the probability of rejecting H_0 for all possible values of the population parameter

Power of a test   the probability $1 - \beta$ of rejecting H_0 when H_a is true

Statistically significant results   sample results that lead to the rejection of H_0

Significance level of a test   the maximum acceptable probability of a type I error

p-value of a sample   the probability of observing a sample result at least as unlikely as the one observed, assuming that H_0 is true

Rejection region for a test   the values of a sample statistic that lead to rejection of H_0

One-tailed test   a test where rejection of H_0 occurs only for sample statistics in one tail of the appropriate distribution

Two-tailed test   a test where rejection of H_0 occurs for sample statistics in either tail of the appropriate distribution

Matched-pairs t test   a test for the difference between two means when the observations come in matched pairs

Important Formulas

1. Formulas for the tests in this chapter—see Table 9.2

End-of-Chapter Problems

64. If we wish to test H_0: $p = .5$ versus H_a: $p \neq .5$ at the 5% level, is it possible to assure that the probability of a type II error will be less than .05 when the true p is .52? If so, how? If not, why not? (Just give an intuitive argument; no calculations are necessary.)

65. In 1983 there was a very large increase in natural gas prices, followed by much complaining from consumers. Consider the samples of residential monthly gas bills (during January) at the top of the next page.

1982	1983
$ 85.20	$ 93.25
69.75	115.27
120.30	155.30
76.15	122.25
83.25	96.43
65.73	115.48
101.24	130.26
	115.73
	105.47

a. Assuming that the standard deviation of gas prices for all homes stayed the same during the two years, test the claim that the mean gas price per month rose by at least $25 from 1982 to 1983. Use a 5% significance level.

b. How do you know that a matched-pairs test should not be used for these data?

66. In a test for a proportion, is it possible that H_0 will be rejected at the 5% level in favor of a one-tailed alternative, but will not be rejected at the 5% level in favor of a two-tailed alternative? Provide a numerical example to back up your answer.

67. The Democratic candidate in an upcoming election has decided that if a random sample of voters taken six weeks before the election convinces him that he will lose, he will undertake an expensive "crash" campaign. He must be convinced at the 5% level.

a. Set up his problem as a hypothesis-testing problem; that is, supply the null and alternative hypotheses. (Assume that he will lose unless he gets at least 50% of the votes.)

b. If 250 people are sampled, what type of sample information will convince him to undertake the crash campaign? Be specific.

c. Describe in words a type II error for this particular problem.

68. A psychologist wishes to give her standard screening examination to recent job applicants to decide whether today's job seekers achieve higher scores than applicants from 10 years ago. If they do, she will use a new examination in the future. The test is to be administered to a random sample of $n = 25$ persons. In analyzing the results, the psychologist wishes to allow only a 5% chance of incorrectly changing procedures when the actual mean screening examination score (for today's population) is less than or equal to 86, the historical mean figure from 10 years ago. If the sample group achieves a mean score of 88 points and a standard deviation of 10 points, should the present screening examination be retained or changed? (List your hypotheses first.)

*69. Suppose that we send a questionnaire to a random sample of recent MBA graduates from a particular university. The 14 women in this sample respond that their starting salary was $25,630, whereas the 18 men in the sample respond that their average starting salary was $27,860. Assume that the variance of all MBA starting salaries is the same for men and women. If we wish to test whether the mean starting salary is larger for men than for women, what value of the pooled sample standard deviation s_p makes us indifferent between accepting and rejecting this (alternative) hypothesis at the 5% level? If the observed value of s_p is larger than this, should we reject or not reject the null hypothesis at the 5% level?

*70. A report in the 1940s stated that 30% of all employees claimed that they would not tolerate employee theft in their companies. (Reference: R. J. Tersine and R. S. Russell, "Internal Theft: The Multi-Billion-Dollar Disappearing Act," *Business Horizons*, Vol. 24, 1981, pp. 11–20.) Suppose that a current study asks the same questions and finds that 25% of the employees questioned would not tolerate employee theft. Let p be the current proportion of all employees who would not tolerate employee theft, and left H_0 be that p is no less than the 1940s proportion, .30. If we are able to reject H_0 on the basis of the current sample data at the 5% level, what is the smallest the current sample size could have been?

71. A manufacturer is interested in the difference in mean monthly complaints about two of his products. Over a period of 12 months ($n = 12$), he observes the following sample means and standard deviations for complaints per month for the two products: $\overline{X}_1 = 17.2$, $s_1 = 4.6$, $\overline{X}_2 = 25.1$, and $s_2 = 5.3$.

a. Test the hypothesis at the 10% level that the two population variances are equal. Assume that the distribution of the number of complaints per month is normal for each product.

b. Assuming that the two population variances *are* equal, test the claim (H_a) that product 2 receives at least four more complaints per month than product 1. Again, use a 10% level of significance.

*72. A pair of dice are tossed 100 times, and it is observed that a sum of seven appears 23 times. Test the hypothesis that the dice are not "loaded" (where loaded means not well balanced), using $\alpha = .05$ and a two-tailed test. (What proportion of sevens would you expect from a balanced pair of dice?)

*73. A company claims that at least 95% of the parts it supplies to its customers conform to specifications.

a. If an examination of 200 randomly selected parts reveals that 17 are faulty, at what significance level can the company's claim be rejected?

b. Assume that the company's claim is really wrong, and in fact, only 93% of all its parts meet specifications. If a sample of size $n = 200$ is selected to test the company's claim at the 5% level, what is the probability of making a type II error? What type of sample results lead to a type II error? Be specific.

74. A sample of 24 electric light bulbs produced by manufacturer 1 have a mean lifetime of 1193 hours and a standard deviation of 91 hours. A sample of 12 similar light bulbs produced by manufacturer 2 have a mean lifetime of 1237 hours and a standard deviation of 129 hours.
   a. Assuming that the two populations of lifetimes are normally distributed with equal variances, can you reject the null hypothesis that the mean lifetimes of the two manufacturers' light bulbs are the same at the 10% level?
   b. Answer the question in part (a) if you do not make the equal-variance assumption.
   c. Using an F test, can you reject the null hypothesis that the two populations have equal variances at the 10% level?

*75. Assume it is known that in 1980, 55.4% of the families in a large city favored school bussing. Today we wish to use sample evidence to test the null hypothesis that the proportion favoring school bussing in this city has not changed since 1980. The significance level is set at $\alpha = .05$. If we want the probability of making a type II error to be .20 if today's percentage favoring bussing is actually 49.6%, is $n = 500$ a large enough sample size?

*76. How does the answer to Problem 75 change when the null hypothesis is that today's percentage favoring bussing is at least 55.4% (a one-sided test)?

*77. Suppose that we wish to test whether athletes perform better or worse under stress. We perform the following experiment. Each of n athletes is told in a practice session to perform a certain athletic maneuver. The proportion who do so successfully is $\hat{p}_1$. Then in real competition these same athletes are required to perform the same maneuver. Now the proportion who are successful is $\hat{p}_2$. If we are interested in whether the population $p_1 - p_2$ is 0, explain why the test shown for $p_1 - p_2$ in Table 9.2 is not appropriate here. (Here p_1 is the proportion of all athletes who would be successful in practice, and p_2 is the similar proportion in stress situations.) Reason as in Section 9.5.

*78. Referring to Problem 77, let X_{1i} equal 1 or 0 depending on whether athlete i is successful or unsuccessful in the practice session. Define X_{2i} similarly for the competition session.
   a. In terms of the population proportions p_1 and p_2, find the expected value of the difference $X_{1i} - X_{2i}$. (Use the defi-

nition of expected value and the rules for expected values in Chapter 4.)
   b. Why is the variance of $X_{1i} - X_{2i}$ probably not equal to the sum $p_1(1 - p_1) + p_2(1 - p_2)$, even though the variance of X_{1i} is $p_1(1 - p_1)$ and the variance of X_{2i} is $p_2(1 - p_2)$? (What about independence?)
   c. Let σ_D^2 equal the variance of $X_{1i} - X_{2i}$, and assume that σ_D^2 is known. Explain why the following test can be used to test $H_0: p_1 - p_2 = 0$ versus $H_a: p_1 - p_2 \neq 0$ at the α level (provided that n is large).

$$\text{Reject } H_0 \text{ only if } \left| \frac{\Sigma X_{1i}/n - \Sigma X_{2i}/n}{\sigma_D/\sqrt{n}} \right| > z_{\alpha/2}$$

(*Hint:* Explain what $\Sigma X_{1i}/n$ and $\Sigma X_{2i}/n$ represent, and then describe the sampling distribution of $\hat{p}_1 - \hat{p}_2$.)

79. A production supervisor for a "widget" company has been keeping careful records for several years on the diameter of the widgets being produced. When the equipment is in good condition, he knows that the mean diameter is 3.002 inches and the standard deviation is .026 inch. He is worried now, however, because a random sample of 25 of today's widgets shows a mean diameter of 3.004 inches and a standard deviation of .034 inch.
   a. Find a 95% confidence interval for the standard deviation of the diameters of all of today's widgets.
   b. Is today's sample enough evidence to reject the null hypothesis that today's standard deviation is no greater than usual, using a 5% significance level? Why is the result from part (a) not applicable here?

*80. In an executive program, 20 executives take a minicourse on decision making under uncertainty. Each of the executives receives a score from a test given on the first day of class (to test their previous knowledge of the subject material). These scores are $X_1, X_2, \ldots, X_{20}$. After the course, they all take a similar test and receive scores $Y_1, Y_2, \ldots, Y_{20}$. The results are summarized as $\overline{X} = 52.3$, $\overline{Y} = 75.6$, and $\Sigma (Y_i - X_i)^2 = 12835$, where this sum is over all 20 executives. Use a matched-pairs test to test the (alternative) hypothesis at the 5% level that the average increase from the first test to the second test would be at least 15 points if the tests (and the course) were given to a large population of similar executives. (The hard part here is to find the sample standard deviation of the differences.)

*81. Consider two samples, each of size 25, taken from two normal populations. We wish to use a two-tailed test to test whether the population variances are the same. The significance level is set at 5%. Suppose the sample results show that the two sample standard deviations satisfy $s_1 = ks_2$, where k is some number (not necessarily an integer) greater than 1. How large would k have to be before we could reject the equal-variance hypothesis?

*82. A statistician develops a method for finding a 90% confidence interval for some population parameter θ. He then simulates 500 samples on a computer and uses his method to compute a 90% confidence interval for θ from each sample. Since this is a controlled experiment, he actually knows the true value of θ, and therefore he is able to see how many of the 500 confidence intervals include this true value of θ. If it turns out that 407 of these intervals include θ, can you reject the null hypothesis at the 5% level that his method produces confidence intervals with confidence level at least 90%? (The idea here is that because $^{407}\!/_{500}$ is less than .90, we have evidence that the actual confidence level from his method may be less than 90%.) Use a one-tailed test.

83. A 1982 article in the *Wall Street Journal* reports that the steady erosion in consumers' loyalty toward well-known brands may have halted in the past year, that is, in 1981. (Reference: *Wall Street Journal*, Jan. 7, 1982.) Until that time, shoppers had gradually been lured away from national brands toward private-label and generic brands of such items as soap, margarine, and waxed paper. The article quotes the results of an annual survey of 2000 male and 2000 female household heads. Each was asked if he or she agrees with the statement "I try to stick to well-known brand names." The proportions agreeing are shown below.

	1975	1976	1977	1978	1979	1980	1981
Women	.74	.74	.72	.72	.66	.56	.58
Men	.80	.82	.77	.75	.74	.64	.65

a. Let $p_{M,t}$ be the population proportion of all males agreeing with this statement in year t, and let $p_{F,t}$ be the similar proportion of females. Can you reject the null hypothesis that $p_{M,t} \le p_{F,t}$ in favor of $p_{M,t} > p_{F,t}$ for $t = 1975$; for $t = 1981$? Use a 5% significance level.
b. Can you reject the null hypothesis that $p_{M,1978} \le p_{M,1979}$ in favor of $p_{M,1978} > p_{M,1979}$ at the 5% level? What about the similar hypotheses for women?
c. Can you reject H_0: $p_{M,1980} - p_{M,1981} = 0$ in favor of a two-tailed alternative at the 5% level? What about the similar hypotheses for women?

84. Many of today's managers reach a position where they believe, often correctly, that they will never be promoted any further up the organizational ladder. As Near explains, this probably has more to do with organizational constraints than with managerial abilities; there may simply be too few jobs at the top and too many entrenched people occupying them. (Reference: Janet P. Near, "Reactions to the Career Plateau," *Business Horizons*, Vol. 27, 1984, pp. 75–79.) Near refers to managers who expect no further promotions as "plateaued" managers (P's). The others are called nonplateaued (NP's). In a study of 200 managers from various firms, she found that 98 were P's and 102 were NP's. The main objective of the study was to locate differences between the P's and the NP's. Several of her findings are shown below.

	Among P's	Among NP's
Proportion under 40 years old	.35	.68
Proportion who have not attended college	.53	.36
Proportion who rate their supervisors favorably	.43	.73
Proportion who are highly satisfied with their jobs	.28	.33
Proportion who work less than 50 hours per week on average	.63	.67

a. Let p be the proportion of all U.S. managers who are P's. For which values of p_0 would you reject H_0: $p = p_0$ in favor of H_a: $p \ne p_0$ at the .05 significance level?
b. For each of the five categories listed in the table, test whether the proportion of P's is significantly different from the proportion of NP's. That is, perform five separate tests. Run each as a two-tailed test at the .10 significance level.

*85. It is quite possible with present technology to "time compress" television commercials. This means a commercial that in normal time runs, say, for 30 seconds can be speeded up so that it runs for 24 or fewer seconds with no voice tone or other obvious distortions. Schlinger et al. performed an experiment to see how people react to time-compressed commercials. (Reference: Mary Jane Rawlins Schlinger, Linda F. Alwitt, Kathleen E. McCarthy, and Leila Green, "Effects of Time Compression on Attitudes and Information Processing," *Journal of Marketing*, Vol. 47, 1983, pp. 70–85.) Two commercials, labeled A and B, were used. The normal time for each commercial was 30 seconds, whereas the time-compressed versions were 24 seconds. The experiment employed 240 subjects, split into four groups of 60 each. One group watched the regular version of commercial *A,* another watched the time-compressed version of *A,* and the other two groups were assigned similarly to commercial *B.* The results showed that there were several statistically significant differences between the regular and time-compressed groups with respect to the number of ideas remembered from the commercials and attitudes toward the commercials. However, perhaps the most important finding concerned buying intentions. After viewing a commercial, each subject was asked to measure "purchase interest" on a 1 ("definitely would not buy") to 5 ("definitely would buy") scale. According to the researchers, there were no significant differences between the regular and time-compressed groups for commercial *A* or for commercial *B.* Average interest in purchasing the *A* brand was 3.28 for regular-time viewers and 3.05 for time-compressed viewers. The similar averages for commercial *B* viewers were 4.29 and 4.31. Assuming equal sample standard deviations for the regular and time-compressed groups, how small must this common standard deviation have been so that these means were not significantly different at the 5% level? Assume a two-tailed test. Answer the question separately for commercials *A* and *B.*

86. The concept of quality circles for enhancing productivity is one that started in Japan but has spread to the United States in recent years. O'Donnell and O'Donnell conducted a 1982 study to determine the number of U.S. companies with quality circles. (Reference: Merle O'Donnell and Robert J. O'Donnell, "Quality Circles—A Fad or a Real Winner?" *Business Horizons,* Vol. 27, 1984, pp. 48–52.) They report that 205 of 417 companies sampled are either using or are about to begin using quality circles. Let *p* be the proportion of all U.S. companies using or about to use quality circles. For what values of p_0 would you reject H_0: $p \leq p_0$ versus H_a: $p > p_0$ at the 5% significance level? Answer the same question for the 10% significance level.

*87. Many manufacturing companies are now using computerized materials requirements planning (MRP) systems to expedite orders and control in-process inventories. These systems provide relatively sophisticated methods for incorporating manufacturing lead times, timing of customer orders, and other variables into an overall production plan. In a survey of 433 companies with MRP systems, Anderson and Schroeder found that the average lead time in delivery decreased from 71.4 days before the installation of an MRP system to 58.9 days after its installation. (Reference: John C. Anderson and Roger G. Schroeder, "Getting Results from Your MRP System," *Business Horizons,* Vol. 27, 1984, pp. 57–64.) Let μ_D be

the mean decrease in delivery lead time across all companies that have installed MRP systems. Suppose that we wish to test H_0: $\mu_D \leq 10$ versus H_a: $\mu_D > 10$.

a. Why is a matched-pairs test necessary?

b. The observed standard deviation of the *differences* was not reported in the study above. What values of this standard deviation would lead to rejection of H_0 at the 5% level; at the 10% level?

88. There is a great deal of skepticism by the U.S. population toward business practices. Some analysts who would like to remove this skepticism believe the cause is the population's lack of knowledge of business and economics. Their claim is that if people knew more about business and economics, they would be more favorably disposed toward business practices. Fox and Calder, however, question this claim. (Reference: Karen F. A. Fox and Bobby Calder, "The Right Kind of Business Advocacy," *Business Horizons,* Vol. 28, 1985, pp. 7–11.) They write: "If people knew more about business and economics, wouldn't they like business better? The answer to that question is no. As long as economic conditions are bad, business should accept that public attitudes will be negative. Or, better, business should accept that these attitudes cannot be changed by educational campaigns supplying information about the economic system." Several educational campaigns have attempted to resolve this issue. Suppose we wish to test the claim that the increased education from these campaigns creates a more favorable attitude toward business practices. Before the campaign we ask 150 randomly selected people whether they believe U.S. businesses, on the average, are run in an efficient and responsible manner; 89 of the sampled people respond affirmatively. One year later, after the educational campaign, 100 randomly chosen people who have been exposed to the campaign are asked the same question; now 68 respond affirmatively. Can you reject the claim at the 10% level that the educational campaign has not created a more favorable attitude toward business? What is the *p*-value of the sample results?

89. There has recently been considerable concern as to whether MBA students are acquiring the knowledge and skills necessary for the business world. In an extensive study, Jenkins, Reizenstein, and Rodgers questioned two groups of people to discover their opinions of MBA education. (Reference: Roger L. Jenkins, Richard C. Reizenstein, and F. G. Rodgers, "Report Cards on the MBA," *Harvard Business Review,* Sept.–Oct. 1984, pp. 20–30.) One group, the "corporate community," was composed of Fortune 500 presidents and personnel directors, as well as a group of 1978 MBA grad-

uates. There were 684 people in this group. The other group, the "business school community," was composed of 395 deans and faculty members from the better known business schools. A small part of the results of this study is shown below. For each statement, the proportion of people from each group who agree with the statement is shown. Considering each statement separately, which have significantly different proportions between the two groups at the .05 level? (Use two-tailed tests.)

Statement	Corporate Community	Business School Community
MBA program should deemphasize short-term decision making in favor of long-term planning.	.377	.346
The ideal MBA graduate is a generalist, not a specialist.	.628	.632
The ideal MBA program should focus strongly on quantitative analysis.	.593	.577
MBA graduates should have a functional area specialty in addition to a general business core.	.685	.546
MBA programs should focus on application of theories.	.744	.781

*90. Television advertisers are increasingly aware of a problem called zapping. (Compare with Application 3.2.) This is the viewer practice of eliminating advertisements. For example, one form of zapping occurs when viewers switch channels when an ad comes on. This practice is becoming more and more prevalent as more channels, especially continuous programming channels, are available. It is also simplified by the presence of remote control devices. Kaplan reported the results of a 1983 Nielsen study on channel switching during prime time viewing. (Reference: Barry M. Kaplan, "Zapping—The Real Issue Is Communication," *Journal of Advertising Research,* Vol. 25, 1985, pp. 9–12.) The accompanying proportions of viewers who switched channels were observed. These proportions indicate that households with remote-control devices switch more often, during both commercial and noncommercial minutes, than viewers without these devices. But are the differences statistically significant? This depends on the sample sizes, which were not reported.

	Proportion Who Switched	
	During Commercial Minutes	During Noncommercial Minutes
Households with remote devices	.071	.046
Households without remote devices	.045	.028

a. Assume that the number of sampled households with remote control devices was only one-third as large as the number sampled without remote-control devices. Considering the commercial minutes only, how large must the sample sizes have been to make the differences above significant at the .01 level? Assume that a one-tailed test was run. (Be careful when finding the pooled sample proportion $\hat{p}$.)

b. Answer part (a) for the noncommercial minutes.

*91. According to a 1982 *Wall Street Journal* article, people are holding on to their automobiles longer than in the past. (Reference: *Wall Street Journal,* Jan. 7, 1982.) For example, the average age of the cars on the road went from 5.5 years in 1970 to 6.6 years in 1980. Although the article suggests that this may be a temporary effect of higher interest rates and other factors, it also suggests that it may be evidence of a long-term trend. If this is true and we project this trend linearly through 1990, we can expect an average age of approximately 7.7 years by 1990. Suppose that we take a random sample of 100 cars on the road in 1990 and observe an average age of $\overline{X}$ years and a standard deviation of 2.7 years.

a. How large would $\overline{X}$ have to be before we could reject the null hypothesis H_0: $\mu \leq 7.7$ in favor of H_a: $\mu > 7.7$ at the 5% significance level? (Here μ represents the average age of all cars on the road in 1990.)

b. If we are told that the true σ for 1990 is 2.3, how does the answer to part (a) change? In this case, if the true mean μ is 8.0, what is the resulting type II error probability?

*92. In an article on quality of life, Kahn reports that a sizable proportion of adults believe their work intrudes on other parts of their lives. (Reference: Robert L. Kahn, "Productive Behavior Through the Life Course: An Essay on the Quality of Life," *Human Resource Management,* Vol. 23, 1984, pp. 5–22.) He summarizes the findings of a 1977 study that questioned a sample of employed men and women in the United States about their feelings toward work and leisure. In particular, this study asked people to respond to two questions: (1) Would you like to spend less time working so that you could spend more time with your (husband/wife) and children, even if it meant having less money? and (2) Would you like to spend more time working in order to have more money, even if it meant spending less time with your (husband/wife) and children? The results are shown here. The numbers are the observed proportions. The p's are the unknown population proportions.

Men

Preference	Both Wife and Children in Household ($n = 652$)	Wife but No Children in Household ($n = 358$)
Less time working, more time with family	.419 $p_{1,1}$	.391 $p_{2,1}$
More time working, less time with family	.124 $p_{1,2}$	.123 $p_{2,2}$
Neither more nor less time with family	.457 $p_{1,3}$	.486 $p_{2,3}$

Women

Preference	Both Husband and Children in Household ($n = 319$)	Husband but No Children in Household ($n = 185$)	Children but No Husband in Household ($n = 89$)
Less time working, more time with family	.511 $p_{3,1}$	.395 $p_{4,1}$	.348 $p_{5,1}$
More time working, less time with family	.047 $p_{3,2}$	.065 $p_{4,2}$	.090 $p_{5,2}$
Neither more nor less time with family	.442 $p_{3,3}$	.541 $p_{4,3}$	.562 $p_{5,3}$

Find the p-values for each of the following null hypotheses, each assuming a one-tailed alternative: (a) H_0: $p_{1,1} \leq p_{2,1}$; (b) H_0: $p_{5,2} \leq p_{4,2}$; (c) H_0: $p_{5,2} + p_{5,3} \leq p_{4,2} + p_{4,3}$. For which of these would you reject H_0 at the 10% level?

Computer Problems

(These problems are to be used in conjunction with the computer software package.)

1. Referring to the housing data in Table III of Appendix D, use the SAMPMEAN program to test whether the mean appraised value and the mean selling price are equal. Use a 5% significance level, and base your test on the last 30 observations only. Then, using these same observations, find a 95% confidence interval for the difference between the mean appraised value and the mean selling price.

2. Use the DIFFRNCE program and the cost of living data in Table VII of Appendix D to test whether there is a significant difference between the mean housing cost in selected western states (California, Oregon, Washington, Nevada, and Arizona) and selected eastern states (New York, Pennsylvania, Maryland, and New Jersey). Use a 5% significance level. Also, find a 95% confidence interval for this mean difference. Then repeat for mean differences between grocery items, utilities, and miscellaneous goods and services. (Test each of these separately.)

3. Go home and look at the mint dates on all the pennies you can find. Can you reject the null hypothesis that the mean age of all pennies in circulation is at least 4 years? Can you reject the null hypothesis that at least 50% of all pennies in circulation are at least 4 years old? Use the SAMPMEAN program to answer the first question, and use the PROPORTN program to answer the second question. Use a 5% significance level for each question. (Round off the ages you observe to the nearest year. For example, a 1985 penny in 1987 is assumed to be 2 years old.)

4. Continuing Problem 3, look at all the silver-colored coins you can find (nickels, dimes, quarters, and half-dollars). Can you reject the null hypothesis that the average age of all pennies in circulation is at least as great as the average age of all silver-colored coins in circulation? Use the DIFFRNCE program with a 10% significance level.

References

BREIMAN, L. *Statistics: With a View Toward Applications.* Boston: Houghton Mifflin, 1973.

CANAVOS, G. C. *Applied Probability and Statistical Methods.* Boston: Little, Brown, 1984.

HOGG, R. V. and CRAIG, A. T. *Introduction to Mathematical Statistics,* 4th ed. New York: Macmillan, 1978.

MOOD, A. M., GRAYBILL, F. A., and BOES, D. C. *Introduction to the Theory of Statistics,* 3rd ed. New York: McGraw-Hill, 1974.

NETER, J., WASSERMAN, W., and WHITMORE, G. A. *Applied Statistics,* 2nd ed. Boston: Allyn & Bacon, 1982.

CHAPTER 10

Analysis of Variance

1. To learn that analysis of variance is a technique for testing for differences among several population means.
2. To learn some of the terminology associated with experimental design, including factors, treatment levels, blocking, main effects, and interactions.
3. To understand how analysis of variance is based on breaking up the total variation into several sources of variation and then comparing the individual sources by means of F tests.
4. To learn how to analyze three particular analysis of variance designs: one-way ANOVA, a randomized block design, and two-way ANOVA.

Contents

Researchers in marketing and other areas of business often perform a controlled experiment to discover how consumers behave. Usually, the experiment consists of using a separate "treatment" on each of several consumer groups, measuring a response from each consumer, and then trying to infer whether different treatments make the groups behave differently from one another on the average. For example, one experiment we will examine consisted of showing different groups of consumers pieces of carpeting differentiated by quality and price tag. Each consumer was then asked to rate the quality of the carpet sample he or she observed. It is natural to hypothesize that consumers would give the highest ratings to the carpet samples that indeed had the highest quality. However, it is also conceivable that consumers could be misled by price and therefore give a high rating to a low-quality, high-priced carpet and a low rating to a high-quality, low-priced carpet.

The purpose of such an experiment is to see whether these types of behavior really exist. The problem, however, is that consumers *within* a given group (who all see the same carpet sample) may differ significantly from one another in their ratings. This variation makes it difficult for the researcher to infer whether there are real differences, on average, *between* the groups. In this chapter we learn a powerful method called analysis of variance that is appropriate for analyzing this type of experiment. Essentially, this method tells us when we can infer from perceived sample differences that true population differences exist.

10.1

Introduction

In this chapter we study a method called analysis of variance, abbreviated ANOVA. This method generalizes a hypothesis test that we learned in Chapter 9. There we learned how to test the hypothesis that the means of two populations are equal. Analysis of variance generalizes this by testing whether the means of *more* than two populations are equal. Usually, the "populations" are subsets of one population that have been treated in different ways. As an example, suppose that a population of college students is randomly divided into several groups, and each group is then taught by a different teaching method. Then the purpose of ANOVA is to test whether the different groups learn significantly different amounts, as measured by some type of standardized test.

In this example the variable used to test the hypothesis of equal means is the test score on a standardized test. In ANOVA terminology this is called the *dependent variable*. In contrast, the variable we are manipulating, "teaching method," is called a *factor*. The "values" of a factor, here the types of teaching methods used, are called the *treatment levels* of the factor. In other words, a factor is a categorical variable, with the categories being the treatment levels.

> A factor is a categorical variable that is manipulated within an ANOVA study. Its values are called treatment levels. We are interested in the effect of the levels of a factor on a quantitative dependent variable.

Sometimes an ANOVA study has more than one factor. For instance, a second factor in the teaching example might be the sex of the teacher. Then we would be interested in whether male teachers are any more or less effective than female teachers. Of course, the two levels of this factor are "male" and "female." An analysis of variance is usually classified according to the number of factors present. We refer to an analysis of variance with N factors as an *N-way ANOVA*. Therefore, one-way ANOVA means that there is only one factor used at a number of levels, two-way ANOVA means that there are two factors each used at a number of levels, and so on. In this chapter we discuss only one-way and two-way ANOVA, the two most common types.

> An *N*-way ANOVA is a study with N factors.

The overall analysis of variance study is usually called an *experiment*. Sometimes the "experiment" is what we usually think of as an experiment, namely, a laboratory experiment run under closely controlled conditions. In agriculture, for example, where ANOVA is used extensively, it is usually possible to run a controlled experiment. In business and economics, however, it is often much more difficult, if not impossible, to control the conditions as we would like to do. There we must often accept the data in whatever form they come to us.

The individual observations are associated with the *experimental units* of the experiment. In the school example, each student is an experimental unit. If the experimental units are assigned to the treatment levels according to a specific experimental design, we obtain *experimental data*. Otherwise, we obtain *observational data*. The data in the school example would be termed experimental data if we purposely assigned students to different teaching methods to balance out varying student abilities, class sizes, and other pertinent factors across the different teaching methods. However, if an investigator had to gather data from classes that were already formed and underway, the resulting data would be termed observational data.

Usually, we prefer to obtain data from a carefully designed experiment. Then we can use the data more efficiently, and extraneous factors do not obscure the main results we are seeking. This can often be done, even in business and economics. (Of course, this requires the investigator to know a good deal about the proper design of experiments, a topic we just barely touch on in this chapter.) However, there are many situations in business and economics where we must be content with observational data; they are the only data available.

10.2
One-Way ANOVA

In this section we learn how to test the hypothesis of equal treatment level means when there is a single factor. Before proceeding with the details, however, we take a look at the subject from an intuitive point of view. In particular, we learn why the subject is called analysis of *variance* even though we are primarily interested in *means*.

Suppose that there is one factor at three different levels, labeled 1, 2, and 3. For example, these might correspond to three different teaching methods. We denote the dependent variable by Y (with appropriate subscripts as we need them). Since we are interested in the differences, if any, between the *population* means of the Y's for the three treatment levels, we examine the three *sample* means, labeled $\overline{Y}_1$, $\overline{Y}_2$, and $\overline{Y}_3$. In the school example, these sample means correspond to the average test scores for the three groups of students in the study. We need to know how different these three sample means have to be before we can reject the null hypothesis of equal population means. This is where variances enter the analysis.

Consider the two diagrams in Figure 10.1. In each of these diagrams, the three $\overline{Y}$'s are shown by horizontal bars. As we see, these sample means are not equal; they satisfy $\overline{Y}_1 < \overline{Y}_2 < \overline{Y}_3$. Notice that the individual observations, shown by dots, vary more around their means in Figure 10.1b than in Figure 10.1a. This increased variance within each treatment level in Figure 10.1b tends to obscure the differences between the three $\overline{Y}$'s. That is, we are not sure whether the differences between the $\overline{Y}$'s are due to differences between the (unobserved) population means or to sampling variation. This is because the large variances make us very unsure of the exact locations of the population means. In Figure 10.1a, however, there is very little variation within each treatment level, so it appears that the observed differences between the $\overline{Y}$'s are due to *real* differences between the population means. Given the data

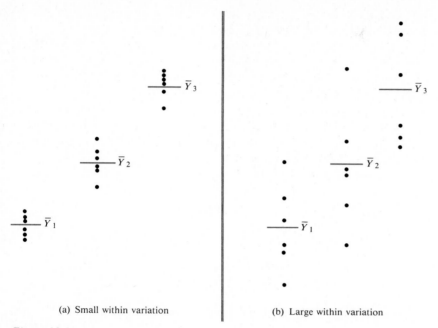

(a) Small within variation (b) Large within variation

Figure 10.1

in Figure 10.1a, we would probably reject the null hypothesis of equal population means; given the data in Figure 10.1b, we would probably not be able to reject this null hypothesis.

This is the basic idea in all ANOVA studies. We look at several types of variation to see whether an equal-means hypothesis can be rejected. In one-way ANOVA, there are two such types of variation. One of them occurs because the $\bar{Y}$'s vary from one treatment level to another. This is called the *between* variation. The other occurs because of the random variation within each treatment level. This is called the *within* variation. If the between variation is large compared to the within variation, we tend to reject the equal-means hypothesis (Figure 10.1a). Otherwise, we may not be able to reject it (Figure 10.1b).

We now state the statistical model for one-way ANOVA, and we list the assumptions for this model. All the statistical analysis is based on these assumptions, so if they are not valid, neither are the statistical results.

Since this discussion concerns one-way ANOVA, there is only one factor. We assume that there are J treatment levels for this factor, and that n_j experimental units are assigned to level j. Then the total number of observations, denoted by n, is the sum of the n_j's.

The One-Way ANOVA Model

> ### Total Number of Observations
>
> $$n = n_1 + n_2 + \cdots + n_J$$

Let Y_{ij} be the value of the dependent variable for the ith experimental unit assigned to level j, and let $\overline{Y}_j$ be the mean of the n_j observations from level j. A typical setup when $J = 3$, $n_1 = 5$, $n_2 = 7$, and $n_3 = 4$ is shown in Table 10.1. Each of the 16 Y_{ij}'s in this table corresponds to the observed value from a single experimental unit.

The statistical model is that

$$Y_{ij} = \mu_j + \epsilon_{ij}$$

where

$$\mu_j = \text{population mean for level } j$$
$$\epsilon_{ij} = \text{a random error term for observation } Y_{ij}$$

We assume that the errors are independent random variables from a normal population with mean 0 and variance σ^2. In symbols, ϵ_{ij} is $N(0, \sigma^2)$, and the ϵ's are independent of one another. These assumptions imply that Y_{ij} has a $N(\mu_j, \sigma^2)$ distribution and that the Y_{ij}'s are independent random variables (see Figure 10.2). (All ANOVA models, including those in later sections of this chapter, make assumptions similar to these. Each observation is written as the sum of several quantities, one of which is a random error term. Then the errors are assumed to be independent and normally distributed. We will not continue to list the assumptions for each model in this chapter, but the reader should be aware that they are always present.)

When we write that the variance of the error terms is σ^2, without any subscripts, we are implying that the Y_{ij}'s for one treatment level do not vary

Table 10.1 A Typical One-Way ANOVA Design with $J = 3$, $n_1 = 5$, $n_2 = 7$, $n_3 = 4$

Treatment Level		
1	2	3
Y_{11}	Y_{12}	Y_{13}
Y_{21}	Y_{22}	Y_{23}
Y_{31}	Y_{32}	Y_{33}
Y_{41}	Y_{42}	Y_{43}
Y_{51}	Y_{52}	
	Y_{62}	
	Y_{72}	

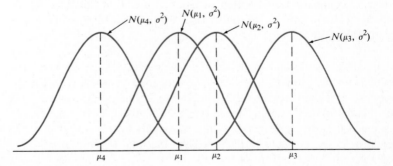

Figure 10.2

any more than for any other treatment level. [This is the same assumption that we made in Chapter 9, test group 6, when we tested for differences between *two* population means (see Table 9.2).] This equal-variance assumption is sometimes quite clearly violated. However, the only time that we really need to be concerned is when the sample sizes, n_1 through n_J, also vary widely. If the variances differ from one treatment level to the next but the sample sizes are roughly equal, no serious mistakes will occur.

The critical assumption is the independence assumption. If the experimental units are assigned completely randomly to the different treatment levels, the error terms are usually independent. However, we sometimes deliberately match subjects across treatment levels according to an extraneous factor, exactly as we did in the matched-pairs test in Chapter 9. This is called *blocking* and will be discussed separately in Section 10.3.

The Method

In this section we present an *F* test for the hypothesis

$$H_0: \mu_1 = \mu_2 = \cdots = \mu_J$$

versus the alternative that not all the means are equal. The idea is to separate the total variation of the Y's from their overall mean into a between variation (variation between the treatment means) and a within variation (variation of the observations within each treatment level). Then these two are compared as we discussed above.

Specifically, let $\overline{\overline{Y}}$ be the mean of all n observations. This is given by

$$\overline{\overline{Y}} = \frac{\Sigma \Sigma Y_{ij}}{n}$$

The double summation simply means that we sum over all treatment groups (j) and over all observations within each treatment level (i). In short, we sum over all n observations. Then the total variation, denoted SST for sum of squares total, is the sum of squared deviations about the overall mean $\overline{\overline{Y}}$.

$$\text{SST} = \sum \sum (Y_{ij} - \overline{\overline{Y}})^2$$

We now separate SST into two sums of squares, labeled SSTr (for sum of squares for treatments) and SSE (for sum of squared errors). The "between" sum of squares, SSTr, is due to differences between the treatment levels. It measures the variation of the separate $\overline{Y}_j$'s from the overall mean $\overline{\overline{Y}}$. The appropriate formula is

$$\text{SSTr} = \sum n_j (\overline{Y}_j - \overline{\overline{Y}})^2$$

where this sum is over the J treatment levels. Notice that the presence of the n_j's gives more weight to the treatment levels with the most observations.

The "within" sum of squares, SSE, is due to random variation within the treatment levels. It measures the variation of the Y_{ij}'s in a given level from the mean $\overline{Y}_j$ of this level. The formula for SSE is

$$SSE = \sum \left[\sum (Y_{ij} - \overline{Y}_j)^2 \right]$$

Here the inner summation is over all observations i within treatment level j, while the outer summation is over all treatment levels j. This formula says that we first find the variation within a given treatment level j (the sum enclosed in brackets), and then we sum over all treatment levels.

Although it is by no means obvious, it can be shown by algebra that the sums of squares are related by

$$SST = SSTr + SSE$$

Before we give numerical examples of these sums of squares, we first present computational formulas for them. The formulas above, while more meaningful as definitions, are difficult to use because they require squared deviations from means. Fortunately, they are equivalent to the following computational formulas. (These are similar to the computational formula for the sample variance that we used in previous chapters.)

Computational Formulas for SST, SSTr, and SSE

$$SST = \sum \sum Y_{ij}^2 - \frac{(\sum \sum Y_{ij})^2}{n}$$

$$SSTr = \sum \frac{(\sum Y_{ij})^2}{n_j} - \frac{(\sum \sum Y_{ij})^2}{n}$$

$$SSE = SST - SSTr$$

These formulas require sums of raw data and sums of squares of raw data only; no deviations from means are required. As we will see, SST is not needed for the ANOVA F test. Its main use is to find SSE from the formula $SSE = SST - SSTr$.

Each of the SS's above has an associated degrees of freedom. For SST, the degrees of freedom is $n - 1$; for SSTr, it is $J - 1$; for SSE, it is $n - J$. Notice that these degrees of freedom also add up:

$$n - 1 = (J - 1) + (n - J)$$

or

$$\text{df for SST} = (\text{df for SSTr}) + (\text{df for SSE})$$

As with SST, the degrees of freedom for SST will not be used in the ANOVA test. It is used only as an arithmetic check for the other degrees of freedom.

When we divide the SS's by their degrees of freedom, we obtain "mean squares." The two mean squares required for ANOVA are the mean square for treatments, MSTr, given by

$$\text{MSTr} = \frac{\text{SSTr}}{J - 1}$$

and the mean squared error, MSE, given by

$$\text{MSE} = \frac{\text{SSE}}{n - J}$$

From these we form an F ratio used to test the equal-means hypothesis:

$$F = \frac{\text{MSTr}}{\text{MSE}}$$

When the null hypothesis of equal means is true, this F ratio has an F distribution with $(J - 1)$ and $(n - J)$ degrees of freedom.

The reason we form this ratio of MS's is that when the population means are equal, MSTr and MSE are both unbiased estimates of σ^2. In fact, their general expected values (whether or not H_0 is true) are given by

$$E(\text{MSTr}) = \sigma^2 + \frac{\Sigma n_j(\mu_j - \mu)^2}{J - 1}$$

and

$$E(\text{MSE}) = \sigma^2$$

where μ is a weighted sum of the μ_j's, namely $\Sigma\, n_j\mu_j/n$. If all the μ_j's are equal, they all equal μ, and $E(\text{MSTr}) = E(\text{MSE}) = \sigma^2$. But if H_0 is not true, $E(\text{MSTr})$ is greater than σ^2, so that $E(\text{MSTr})$ is greater than $E(\text{MSE})$. This means the F ratio should be close to 1 when H_0 is true, and it should be larger than 1 when H_0 is false. This leads to the following one-way ANOVA test.

> *One-Way ANOVA Test for Equality of Means*
>
> Reject H_0 (equal means) at the α level if $F > F_{\alpha, J-1, n-J}$.

EXAMPLE 10.1

Consider a large chain of supermarkets that sell their own brand of potato chips in addition to many other name brands. Management would like to know whether the type of display used for the store brand has any effect on sales. Since there are four types of displays being considered, management decides to choose 24 similar stores to serve as the experimental units. A random six of these are instructed to use display type 1, another random six are instructed to use display type 2, a third random six are instructed to use display type 3, and the final six stores are instructed to use display type 4. For a period of one month, each store keeps track of the fraction of total potato chips sales that are of the store brand. (This *fraction,* rather than total store brand sales, is used as the dependent variable because different stores tend to sell different total amounts of potato chips.) The data for the 24 stores are shown in Table 10.2. Notice that one of the stores using display type 3 is marked with a "*". This store did not follow instructions properly, so its observation is disregarded. Do the data in Table 10.2 suggest different mean proportions of store brand sales? Use an F test with a 10% significance level.

Table 10.2

	Display Types			
	1	2	3	4
	.26	.28	.35	.15
	.21	.35	.37	.19
	.32	.19	.26	.21
	.14	.27	*	.23
	.20	.21	.23	.31
	.25	.29	.32	.16
ΣY_{ij}:	1.38	1.59	1.53	1.25
ΣY_{ij}^2:	.3362	.4381	.4823	.2773

Grand totals: $\Sigma (\Sigma Y_{ij}) = 5.75$, $\Sigma (\Sigma Y_{ij}^2) = 1.5339$

SOLUTION

The relevant sample sizes are $n_1 = 6$, $n_2 = 6$, $n_3 = 5$, and $n_4 = 6$, so that $n = n_1 + n_2 + n_3 + n_4 = 23$. The "preliminary" sums we need are:

> ### Sum of All Squares
>
> $$\sum \sum Y_{ij}^2 = .26^2 + .21^2 + \cdots + .31^2 + .16^2 = 1.5339$$
>
> ### Sum of Observations from Each Display Type
>
> $$\sum Y_{i1} = .26 + .21 + .32 + .14 + .20 + .25 = 1.38$$
> $$\sum Y_{i2} = .28 + .35 + .19 + .27 + .21 + .29 = 1.59$$
> $$\sum Y_{i3} = .35 + .37 + .26 + .23 + .32 = 1.53$$
> $$\sum Y_{i4} = .15 + .19 + .21 + .23 + .31 + .16 = 1.25$$
>
> ### Sum of All Observations
>
> $$\sum \sum Y_{ij} = 1.38 + 1.59 + 1.53 + 1.25 = 5.75$$

(These sums are also shown in Table 10.2.) From these sums, we immediately find the sample means:

$$\bar{Y}_1 = \frac{1.38}{6} = .23 \quad \bar{Y}_2 = \frac{1.59}{6} = .265$$

$$\bar{Y}_3 = \frac{1.53}{5} = .306 \quad \bar{Y}_4 = \frac{1.25}{6} = .2083$$

These sample means indicate that the different display types have different effectiveness levels, display type 3 being the most effective and display type 4 being the least effective. The purpose of the F test, however, is to show whether these observed differences can be attributed to chance alone or are generalizable to the population of all stores.

The computational formulas for the SS's use the sums calculated above:

$$SST = 1.5339 - \frac{5.75^2}{23} = .0964$$

$$SSTr = \left(\frac{1.38^2}{6} + \frac{1.59^2}{6} + \frac{1.53^2}{5} + \frac{1.25^2}{6} \right) - \frac{5.75^2}{23} = .0298$$

$$SSE = .0964 - .0298 = .0666$$

Since the degrees of freedom of SST, SSTr, and SSE are $23 - 1 = 22$, $4 - 1 = 3$, and $23 - 4 = 19$, the mean squares we need are

$$MSTr = \frac{.0298}{3} = .00993$$

and

$$MSE = \frac{.0666}{19} = .00351$$

Therefore, the F ratio is

$$F = \frac{.00993}{.00351} = 2.83$$

The degrees of freedom for this F ratio are 3 and 19. Because $F_{.10,3,19} = 2.40$, which is less than 2.83, we can reject the equal-means hypothesis at the 10% significance level. There do seem to be differences in mean sales effectiveness between the four display types.

The results of an ANOVA study are usually summarized in an *ANOVA table*. In an ANOVA table we always show the sources of variation, the degrees of freedom, the sums of squares, the mean squares, and any relevant F ratios. The ANOVA table for this example is shown in Table 10.3. The "significance" value in the right-hand column is the p-value corresponding to the calculated F ratio. In this example it is between .05 and .10 because 2.83 is between 3.13 ($= F_{.05,3,19}$) and 2.40 ($= F_{.10,3,19}$). This p-value implies that we cannot reject H_0 at the 5% level but we can reject it at the 10% level.

Table 10.3   ANOVA Table for Example 10.1

Source	SS	df	MS	F	Significance
Treatment	.0298	3	.00993	2.83	Between .05
Error	.0666	19	.00351		and .10
Total*	.0964	22			

*This row is used for an arithmetic check only and is often omitted.

Confidence Intervals for Differences Between Means

Suppose that the F test leads to the rejection of H_0. Then we accept that there are real differences between the treatment level means. In this case it is natural to ask which treatment levels are significantly different from which others. We provide an answer to this question in this section.

Consider any two treatment levels, j and k. The corresponding population means are μ_j and μ_k. If we want to test whether μ_j and μ_k are equal, we can proceed as in Chapter 9, where we tested the difference between two population means. In particular, we can calculate a 95% confidence interval for $\mu_j - \mu_k$ and then reject the null hypothesis H_0: $\mu_j - \mu_k = 0$ at the 5% level if this confidence interval does not include the value 0.

The approach above is fine if we are interested in testing only one pair of means. However, there is a problem with this approach if we want to test all possible pairs. If $J = 4$, for example, we could test any of the six differences $(\mu_1 - \mu_2)$, $(\mu_1 - \mu_3)$, $(\mu_1 - \mu_4)$, $(\mu_2 - \mu_3)$, $(\mu_2 - \mu_4)$, or $(\mu_3 - \mu_4)$. [In general, there are $\binom{J}{2} = J(J - 1)/2$ possible differences, because this is the number of *pairs* of levels that can be chosen from a total of J levels.] If we make a 95% confidence interval statement about each of these differences, each statement has a .05 probability of being incorrect. But this implies that the probability of *at least one* incorrect statement is considerably greater than .05, possibly as much as 6 times .05. (Compare this with Example 3.10.)

The approach we now discuss makes a *simultaneous* statement about all possible differences, so that the entire statement has only .05 probability (or whatever α level we choose) of being incorrect. The procedure is to compute a confidence interval for each difference and then to accept as significantly nonzero only those differences whose confidence intervals do not include the value 0. The formula for the confidence intervals is as follows.

> *Simultaneous Confidence Intervals for Each* $\mu_j - \mu_k$ *with Overall Confidence Level* $1 - \alpha$
>
> $$(\overline{Y}_j - \overline{Y}_k) \pm \sqrt{(J - 1)F_{\alpha, J-1, n-J}\mathrm{MSE}\left(\frac{1}{n_j} + \frac{1}{n_k}\right)}$$

The interpretation is that if we compute the confidence interval above for each pair of treatment levels, we have confidence level $1 - \alpha$ that *each* $\mu_j - \mu_k$ will be captured within its confidence interval. (This approach is due to Scheffé. Another method due to Tukey is available for equal sample sizes, but we will not discuss it here.)

EXAMPLE 10.1 (continued)

For the display data in Table 10.2, find a set of simultaneous 90% confidence intervals for all possible differences of means. Which of these differences are significantly nonzero?

SOLUTION

We use the confidence interval formula above to find the confidence intervals for each of the six possible differences. For example, the confidence interval for $\mu_1 - \mu_2$ is

$$(\overline{Y}_1 - \overline{Y}_2) \pm \sqrt{(J - 1)F_{.10, 3, 19}\mathrm{MSE}\left(\frac{1}{n_1} + \frac{1}{n_2}\right)}$$

or

$$(.23 - .265) \pm \sqrt{3(2.40)(.00351)\left(\frac{1}{6} + \frac{1}{6}\right)} = -.035 \pm .092$$

Table 10.4   Simultaneous 90% Confidence Intervals

Difference	Confidence Interval
$\mu_1 - \mu_2$	$-.127$ to $.057$
$\mu_1 - \mu_3$	$-.172$ to $.020$
$\mu_1 - \mu_4$	$-.070$ to $.114$
$\mu_2 - \mu_3$	$-.137$ to $.055$
$\mu_2 - \mu_4$	$-.035$ to $.149$
$\mu_3 - \mu_4$	$.002$ to $.194$

This extends from $-.127$ to $.057$. (We do not need to look at the confidence interval for $\mu_2 - \mu_1$ separately because it is the negative of the one we just found; it extends from $-.057$ to $.127$.) The other confidence intervals are computed similarly and are shown in Table 10.4. As we see, there is only one significantly nonzero difference, $\mu_3 - \mu_4$. Therefore, we can only conclude that μ_3 and μ_4 are significantly different. Of course, this is what we would expect since $\overline{Y}_3$ and $\overline{Y}_4$ differ by a larger amount than any other pair of $\overline{Y}$'s. The other confidence intervals all include the value 0, so we are not convinced that the corresponding population means differ.

For the ANOVA designs in the following sections of this chapter, it is possible to compute confidence intervals for differences between pairs of means as we have done here. However, we will describe only the relevant F tests. Readers who wish to learn more about simultaneous confidence intervals for other ANOVA designs are advised to consult a more advanced statistics text or a book devoted entirely to analysis of variance.

Problems for Section 10.2

1. In one-way ANOVA, why are MSE and MSTr random variables? Explain how (in an intuitive sense) their expected values are consistent with the one-way ANOVA F test.

2. For each of the following sets of parameters and summary statistics, how large must MSTr be before the null hypothesis in a one-way ANOVA will be rejected at the 5% level; at the 10% level?
   a. $J = 4$, $n_1 = n_2 = n_3 = n_4 = 20$, MSE $= 250$
   b. $J = 4$, $n_1 = n_2 = n_3 = n_4 = 30$, MSE $= 250$
   c. $J = 4$, $n_1 = n_2 = n_3 = n_4 = 30$, MSE $= 500$
   d. $J = 8$, $n_1 = n_2 = n_3 = n_4 = n_5 = n_6 = n_7 = n_8 = 20$, MSE $= 250$

3. In a one-way ANOVA, suppose that the sample data provide us with enough evidence to reject H_0. Explain exactly what we are then accepting. For example, is it possible we are accepting that $\mu_1 = \mu_2 = \cdots = \mu_{J-1}$ but that $\mu_{J-1} \neq \mu_J$?

4. In Example 10.1, draw a diagram of the potato chip data similar to Figure 10.1. Does your diagram indicate any differences in the mean fractions of sales of the store brand? Considering the within variance for any given display, do the differences between the display means appear to be real, that is, not simply the result of random (within) variation?

5. It is hypothesized that the average price of a box of a well-known brand of cereal differs among various-sized cities. A study is undertaken where five cities from each of three size categories are chosen randomly, and then the average cereal price for all supermarkets in each city is observed. The data are shown below.

| | Size of City | |
Small	Medium	Large
1.78	1.65	1.64
1.72	1.70	1.60
1.70	1.63	1.62
1.74	1.71	1.65
1.69	1.73	1.68

   a. Let μ_i be the mean of these average prices over all cities in size category i. Can you reject the null hypothesis that $\mu_1 = \mu_2 = \mu_3$ at the 10% level? Answer by running the appropriate F test. In words, what do you conclude from this test?
   b. Find simultaneous 90% confidence intervals for $\mu_1 - \mu_2$, $\mu_1 - \mu_3$, and $\mu_2 - \mu_3$. In terms of the test in part (a), what do these confidence intervals tell you?

6. Although four similar small-car models exhibit similar mpg sticker ratings, there is some skepticism as to whether their mean mpg values are really equal. To test this equal-mean hypothesis, five cars of each model are driven for 10,000 miles under nearly identical driving conditions. The observed mpg values are shown below.

Model 1	Model 2	Model 3	Model 4
32.5	34.6	29.7	30.4
33.6	35.7	28.5	29.1
30.1	36.8	29.1	27.1
35.1	35.0	30.2	27.1
34.2	36.1	31.2	28.5

a. Draw a figure similar to Figure 10.1 to detect any evidence of unequal means. Does your figure support the null hypothesis of equal means?
b. Calculate the appropriate ANOVA table and use it to test for equal mean mpg values across car models at the 10% level.
c. Which models, if any, have significantly higher mean mpg values than which others? Answer by calculating simultaneous 90% confidence intervals.

7. Analysis of variance has been used in many agricultural experiments. As an example, suppose that a farmer with many acres of corn experiments with three different types of fertilizer. He selects 24 acres of land and randomly assigns each fertilizer to 8 acres. The yields (in bushels per acre) are shown below.

Fertilizer Type

1	2	3
96	107	113
105	98	108
100	112	116
103	101	110
99	105	112
106	99	105
108	102	114
101	110	112

a. Find the sample mean and sample standard deviation of corn yield for each fertilizer. Considering the magnitudes of the differences between sample means and the magnitudes of the standard errors of the sample means, do you believe that there are any real differences between the fertilizers with respect to yield? Explain.

b. Calculate the ANOVA table and then use it to test for differences between fertilizer types. Use a 1% significance level.

8. Three different types of tread design are tested on several similar cars to see whether any of these is better than any others in terms of tire lifetime. Eight cars use tread design 1, five use design 2, and five use design 3. Each car is run over similar roads until the tires on the car are no longer safe. The total mileage for each car is then recorded. Letting $\bar{Y}_1$, $\bar{Y}_2$, and $\bar{Y}_3$ be the sample mean mileages from the three designs, it is found that $\bar{Y}_1 = 42.1$, $\bar{Y}_2 = 36.2$, and $\bar{Y}_3 = 41.4$ (in thousands of miles). Within each group, the sum of squares is also calculated. These sums are

$$\sum Y_{i1}^2 = 14308$$
$$\sum Y_{i2}^2 = 6589$$
$$\sum Y_{i3}^2 = 8705$$

where Y_{ij} is the mileage (in thousands of miles) for car i using tread design j.
a. Fill in the appropriate ANOVA table and test the F value at the 5% level. In words, what do you conclude?
b. Find a confidence interval for each $\mu_k - \mu_j$ so that you are 95% sure each of these differences is within its appropriate interval.
c. On the basis of part (b), which tread designs are significantly better (at the 5% significance level) than which others?

9. A hotel manager would like to know whether people who pay by different methods have different-sized bills. He divides all customers into four categories: those who pay by check or cash, those who pay with VISA or MasterCard, those who pay with an American Express card, and those who use some other type of charge card. He then collects the following data on daily bills. (These bills contain the room charge, plus any other charges to the customer's account.)

Check/Cash	VISA/MC	American Express	Other
67.50	74.55	85.75	65.40
71.55	79.35	77.25	70.40
64.55	70.25	91.25	77.40
68.95	75.15	80.45	69.50
74.55	81.55	84.50	65.75
	83.50	90.15	

a. Calculate the sample means and standard deviations for each of the categories of customers. Does it appear that the equal variance assumption of one-way ANOVA is satisfied?

b. Test whether the different categories of customers have different-sized bills. Use a 10% significance level.

c. Find simultaneous 90% confidence intervals for all pairs of differences between means. Which of these differences, if any, are significantly nonzero at the 10% level?

10. A study of women with undergraduate business degrees shows the following starting salaries as a function of their major within business.

a. Is there any reason to doubt the equal-variance assumption made in the one-way ANOVA model? Answer by calculating the individual sample variances.

Major			
Accounting	Marketing	Finance	Management
21,450	18,350	19,325	17,320
25,650	17,845	19,550	16,450
22,630	18,430	21,640	20,135
27,110	17,645	22,760	17,340
19,440	18,635	20,550	18,635
27,330		19,875	
20,835		18,890	
		21,650	

b. Assuming equal variances, can you reject the null hypothesis at the 10% level that the mean starting salary is the same for each of the majors within business?

10.3

A Randomized Block Design

In some ANOVA studies there are one or more factors that affect the dependent variable *besides* those factors being considered explicitly. If these other factors are not controlled properly, they can mask the differences in treatment levels that we are hoping to detect. In this section we discuss the simplest ANOVA design for handling these extraneous factors.

To motivate the material in this section, we look at a typical example. Suppose that a Miami based air-conditioning company wishes to test four prototype air-conditioners. The dependent variable is the number of days an air-conditioner will work before its motor needs major repair. In this example the company is interested in only one factor, type of air-conditioner, at four different levels. However, the company suspects that the type of use might affect the time until repair. In particular, these air-conditioners are used in three environments: (1) in computer facilities, where they are on continuously throughout the day; (2) in factories, where they are on much of the time but are occasionally turned off; and (3) in residential homes, where they are off a significant portion of the time. The company suspects that the different environments may tend to obscure real differences among the four types of air-conditioners.

In this example there are really two factors, type of air-conditioner and type of environment, but the company is interested primarily in the first of these. To control for the environment, however, they assign each type of air-conditioner to each of the three environments in a random manner. Then if environment has any effect on time until repair, it will be felt equally over the four types of air-conditioners. (The idea is very similar to the matched-pairs test in Chapter 9.)

In ANOVA terminology the extraneous variable, environment, is called a *blocking variable*. This terminology is used because we separate the data into "blocks," one block for each level of the blocking variable. When we design an experiment to deal with a blocking variable explicitly, we say that the experiment has a *randomized block design*.

In general, suppose that there is one factor of interest with J possible levels, and there is one blocking variable with K possible levels. Then it is customary to run the experiment with JK experimental units, that is, JK observations. For example, if there are four factor levels and three levels of the blocking variable as in the air-conditioning example, we need observations on 12 air-conditioners. In this case we would randomly assign one experimental unit (an air-conditioner) to each of the 12 possible factor-block combinations.

A possible design is shown in Table 10.5. Here it is assumed that experimental units 1 through 3 are type 1 air-conditioners, units 4 through 6 are type 2's, units 7 through 9 are type 3's, and units 10 through 12 are type 4's. The numbers in the body of the table show which experimental units are assigned to the various blocks.

Table 10.5 A Randomized Block Design

		Treatment Level (Air-Conditioner Type)			
		1	2	3	4
Block (Environment)	1	2	5	8	12
	2	3	4	9	10
	3	1	6	7	11

The method for testing the equal-means hypothesis in a randomized block design is very similar to the one-way ANOVA method we studied earlier. We first state the hypothesis that we wish to test. Let $\mu_1, \mu_2, \ldots, \mu_J$ be the population means for treatment levels 1 through J. It is understood that any one of these, μ_j say, is an average over all levels of the blocking variable when treatment level j is used exclusively. Then the null hypothesis is

$$H_0: \mu_1 = \mu_2 = \cdots = \mu_J$$

The alternative is that the means are not all equal.

To test this hypothesis, we again break the sum of squares total, SST, into several sums of squares. Now there are *three* sources of variation, not just two. There is the variation between treatment levels, the variation due to random error, and the variation between blocks. The associated sums of squares are labeled SSTr, SSE, and SSB. The formula relating these is

$$SST = SSTr + SSB + SSE$$

In essence, we isolate the extraneous influence of the blocking variable by separating SSB from the other sums of squares. Then we can concentrate on the effect of the treatment levels by comparing SSTr to SSE as we did in Section 10.2.

The notation used for the computational formulas is somewhat different than before. This notation is listed below. (Notice that we have put a single subscript on the Y's. Although this is slightly inconsistent with the double-subscripting from the preceding section, it is done to make the notation less complex and will be continued throughout this chapter.)

$$n = JK = \text{total number of observations}$$
$$Y_i = \text{observation } i \ (i = 1 \text{ through } n)$$
$$\sum Y_i = \text{sum of all } n \text{ observations}$$
$$\sum Y_i^2 = \text{sum of the squares of all } n \text{ observations}$$
$$T_j = \text{sum of the } K \text{ observations in treatment level } j \ (j = 1 \text{ through } J)$$
$$B_k = \text{sum of the } J \text{ observations in block } k \ (k = 1 \text{ through } K)$$

Then the computational formulas for the SS's are as follows:

Computational Formulas for Sums of Squares

$$SST = \sum Y_i^2 - \frac{(\sum Y_i)^2}{n}$$

$$SSTr = \frac{(\sum T_j^2)}{K} - \frac{(\sum Y_i)^2}{n}$$

$$SSB = \frac{(\sum B_k^2)}{J} - \frac{(\sum Y_i)^2}{n}$$

$$SSE = SST - SSTr - SSB$$

The degrees of freedom for the SS's are given below. Notice that they again add up to the degrees of freedom for SST.

Degrees of Freedom

$$\underset{\text{total}}{n - 1} = \underset{\text{treatment}}{(J - 1)} + \underset{\text{block}}{(K - 1)} + \underset{\text{error}}{(n - J - K + 1)}$$

From here on, the procedure is exactly as in one-way ANOVA. We divide SSTr and SSE by their degrees of freedom to obtain MSTr and MSE:

$$\text{MSTr} = \frac{\text{SSTr}}{J - 1} \qquad \text{MSE} = \frac{\text{SSE}}{n - J - K + 1}$$

Then we form the F ratio:

$$F = \frac{\text{MSTr}}{\text{MSE}}$$

The resulting test for equal means is:

> *Test for Equality of Treatment Means*
>
> Reject H_0 (equal treatment means) at the α level if $F > F_{\alpha, J-1, n-J-K+1}$.

It is also possible to test the equality of the *block* means by a similar F test. We let $\text{MSB} = \text{SSB}/(K - 1)$ and $F = \text{MSB}/\text{MSE}$. If F exceeds $F_{\alpha, K-1, n-J-K+1}$, we conclude that the means for the blocks, averaged across treatment levels, are not equal. Although this is not our primary concern, a rejection of the equal-block mean hypothesis does confirm that we were wise to separate the data into blocks in the first place. Most computer outputs for ANOVA report both F ratios, the one for treatments and the one for blocks. We will follow this convention as well.

EXAMPLE 10.2

Suppose that the air-conditioning company discussed earlier tests the four types of air-conditioners by assigning one of each type to each of the three

Table 10.6 Data for Air-Conditioner Example

		Treatment Levels (Air-Conditioner Types)				
		1	2	3	4	B_k
	1	151.3	163.7	175.4	189.2	679.6
Blocks (Environments)	2	137.2	170.7	164.2	146.3	618.4
	3	115.1	125.4	150.3	155.2	546.0
	T_j	403.6	459.8	489.9	490.7	

$$\Sigma Y_i = 1844.0 \qquad \Sigma Y_i^2 = 288{,}229.14$$

environments. The 12 air-conditioners are observed until they require repair, and the number of days each lasts (while on) is recorded. The data are shown in Table 10.6 (p. 481). Is there significant evidence at the 5% level to conclude that the mean times until repair for the four types of air-conditioners are different?

SOLUTION

The values of n, J, and K are $n = 12$, $J = 4$, and $K = 3$. We first calculate the preliminary sums of observations and squared observations.

Sums for Treatments

$$T_1 = 151.3 + 137.2 + 115.1 = 403.6$$
$$T_2 = 163.7 + 170.7 + 125.4 = 459.8$$
$$T_3 = 175.4 + 164.2 + 150.3 = 489.9$$
$$T_4 = 189.2 + 146.3 + 155.2 = 490.7$$

Sums for Blocks

$$B_1 = 151.3 + 163.7 + 175.4 + 189.2 = 679.6$$
$$B_2 = 137.2 + 170.7 + 164.2 + 146.3 = 618.4$$
$$B_3 = 115.1 + 125.4 + 150.3 + 155.2 = 546.0$$

Sum of All Observations

$$\sum Y_i = \sum T_j = 403.6 + 459.8 + 489.9 + 490.7 = 1844.0$$
$$(\text{or} = \sum B_k = 679.6 + 618.4 + 546.0 = 1844.0)$$

Sum of Squares of All Observations

$$\sum Y_i^2 = 151.3^2 + 137.2^2 + \cdots + 146.3^2 + 155.2^2 = 288{,}229.14$$

(These sums are also shown in Table 10.6.) From these preliminary sums we obtain the SS's.

$$\text{SST} = 288{,}229.14 - \frac{1844.0^2}{12} = 4867.8$$

$$\text{SSTr} = \frac{403.6^2 + 459.8^2 + 489.9^2 + 490.7^2}{3} - \frac{1844.0^2}{12} = 1671.2$$

$$\text{SSB} = \frac{679.6^2 + 618.4^2 + 546.0^2}{4} - \frac{1844.0^2}{12} = 2236.3$$

$$\text{SSE} = 4867.8 - 1671.2 - 2236.3 = 960.3$$

Next, we find MSTr and MSE as

$$\text{MSTr} = \frac{1671.2}{4 - 1} = 557.1$$

$$\text{MSE} = \frac{960.3}{12 - 4 - 3 + 1} = 160.1$$

Finally, the F ratio, with 3 and 6 degrees of freedom, is

$$F = \frac{557.1}{160.1} = 3.48$$

Since $F_{.05,3,6} = 4.76$, the calculated F ratio is not quite large enough to be significant at the 5% level. That is, in spite of the apparent differences between types of air-conditioners, we cannot say with 95% confidence that the population means are different. (This F ratio would be significant at the 10% level, however, since $F_{.10,3,6} = 3.29$.) The results from this example are summarized in the ANOVA table in Table 10.7. Notice that the F ratio for differences between *block* means is also listed. It *is* significant at the 5% level.

Table 10.7 ANOVA Table for Example 10.2

Source	SS	df	MS	F	Significance
Treatment	1671.2	3	557.1	3.48	Between .05 and .10
Block	2236.3	2	1118.15	6.99	Between .025 and .05
Error	960.1	6	160.0		
Total	4867.8	11			

Although the F ratio for treatment means is not significant at the 5% level, the randomized block design does help us to see differences between the types of air-conditioners. The reason is that the different environments do seem to affect the types of air-conditioners in similar ways. Namely, environment 1 tends to produce longer times until repair than environment 3, with environment 2 usually being in the middle. If we had ignored the environment and had used the one-way ANOVA method from Section 10.3 (with three observations per treatment level), the resulting F ratio would have been much smaller. That is, the differences between air-conditioners would have been even less significant.

Problems for Section 10.3

11. A certain type of women's cologne is sold in either "splash-on" or spray bottles. The price of an 8-ounce bottle is the same for splash-on and spray, so the only difference in sales is attributed to women's preferences. The numbers of bottles sold for a sample of 10 department stores over a one-week period are shown below.

Store	Splash-on	Spray
1	18	15
2	35	25
3	12	16
4	45	40
5	31	33
6	28	26
7	15	13
8	51	42
9	17	19
10	28	24

a. If we want to test for equal sales of splash-on and spray bottles, why is a randomized block design preferable to a one-way ANOVA design? What is the blocking variable?
b. Use the block design to test for equal means at the 10% level.
c. Now test for equal means by using the matched-pairs t test from Chapter 9. (This is possible because there are only two treatment levels.) Check that the square of the t statistic is equal to the F statistic from part (b). (In this sense, the two tests are equivalent.)

12. A factory has four assembly lines producing the same product. The production supervisor suspects that because of different machines or perhaps different worker abilities, the lines are producing at different rates. The data shown below represent the numbers of pieces completed during each of several hours for the various lines.

Hour	Line 1	Line 2	Line 3	Line 4
9–10 A.M.	134	126	154	129
10–11 A.M.	125	115	146	125
1–2 P.M.	115	120	139	120
3–4 P.M.	120	125	145	131
4–5 P.M.	112	118	132	130

a. Use a one-way ANOVA to test for different means among the four lines. Use a 5% significance level.
b. Is there any reason to believe that the hour of the day should be used as a blocking variable? Use it as a blocking variable and rerun the test from part (a) in the appropriate manner. Do you obtain the same conclusion?

13. Golf ball manufacturers frequently make claims that they make the "longest ball," that is, the ball that goes the farthest. To see which ball really goes the farthest, a sample of golfers, ranging from very long hitters to relatively short hitters, are asked to hit several drives with each of four brands of golf balls. The data below represent the average-length drive (in yards) for each golfer and each brand of golf ball.

Golfer	Brand 1	Brand 2	Brand 3	Brand 4
1	231	242	225	218
2	185	195	201	178
3	201	220	215	219
4	265	272	254	271
5	163	179	156	160
6	230	251	245	235
7	213	230	225	217

a. Why is a randomized block design appropriate here? What would we lose by using a one-way ANOVA design as in Section 10.2 instead of a randomized block design?
b. Using a block design, test for significant differences in length between the four brands of golf balls. Use a 5% significance level.
c. From your calculations in part (b), what (if anything) confirms that it was a good idea to use a randomized block design?

*14. One small town has five real estate appraisers. It is hypothesized that some of them give consistently lower appraisals than others. Discuss in some detail how you would test this hypothesis. In particular, why would a randomized block design probably be a good idea? What would the factor be; what would the blocking variable be? What advantage would this randomized block design have over a one-way ANOVA design?

15. To test the relative effectiveness of five competing brands of sleeping pills, 10 people who have trouble getting to sleep

are used in an experiment. Each person is monitored for five consecutive nights. On each night the person takes a different brand of sleeping pill, and then the time until the person goes to sleep is recorded. That is, each person uses all five brands exactly once, although the order in which they are used is varied randomly from one person to another. The accompanying times (in minutes) are observed.

a. Assuming that the sequence in which a person takes the various brands is not important, discuss why a randomized block design is appropriate here. What is the blocking variable?

b. Calculate the appropriate ANOVA table and use it to test for any significant differences between the five brands. Use a 1% significance level.

Person	Brand 1	Brand 2	Brand 3	Brand 4	Brand 5
1	15	17	22	10	16
2	26	21	23	17	30
3	17	19	21	12	25
4	10	16	18	11	23
5	19	26	25	21	32
6	45	61	53	32	49
7	31	21	45	21	35
8	43	33	36	28	28
9	13	18	15	14	19
10	17	25	31	24	28

10.4
Two-Way ANOVA

The last design we consider in this chapter is two-way ANOVA. This means that there are two separate factors, each used at several treatment levels. Our objective is to see how the dependent variable is affected by various levels of each factor separately, and how it is affected by various *combinations* of factor levels. The design in this section is similar to the randomized block design in that there are again two factors. However, the blocking variable in a randomized block design is introduced only because we need to control for it; our primary interest is in the other factor. In two-way ANOVA, both factors are considered to be equally important.

We pursue the following example of two-way ANOVA in this section. Suppose a company that sells vacuum cleaners door to door wants to judge the sales effectiveness of two characteristics: (1) factor A, the type of sales presentation used by its salespeople; and (2) factor B, the type of previous experience or training its salespeople have had in door-to-door sales.

There are two types of presentations the company wishes to test. These two levels of factor A are the "hard-sell" approach, level 1, and the more relaxed "soft-sell" approach, level 2. The company differentiates between four levels of past experience/training. These levels of factor B are labeled 1 through 4 and are defined as

1. no past experience as a salesperson, no formal training in how to be a salesperson.

2. no past experience, some formal training.
3. some past experience, no formal training.
4. some past experience, some formal training.

To see how presentation and experience/training affect sales, the company runs an experiment with 24 of its recent hirees, six of whom fall into each of the four experience/training levels described above. Each of the 24 employees is assigned randomly to a given sales region, where the 24 sales regions are chosen to be as similar as possible. Within each group of six salespeople at a given experience/training level, three are told to use a hard-sell approach and the other three are told to use a soft-sell approach. Of course, the hard-sellers and the soft-sellers are instructed very specifically in the types of presentation they are supposed to use.

During a six-month period, the number of sales for each of the 24 salespeople is recorded. These data are shown in Table 10.8. The company wishes to infer from these data whether the different presentations and experience/training backgrounds cause significant differences in sales.

Table 10.8   Data for Vacuum Cleaner Example

| | | Factor B Experience Level | | | |
		1	2	3	4
	Hard Sell	61	63	81	96
		65	74	69	89
Factor A		51	70	72	97
Presentation	Soft Sell	58	49	81	99
		70	60	90	76
		67	62	75	89

Before we learn the formal ANOVA method for solving the company's problem, it is useful to look at the data in Table 10.8 from an intuitive point of view. For each of the 12 cells (combinations of factor levels), we can compute the sample mean sales. These sample means are shown in Table 10.9. This table also shows the sample means as one factor is held constant and the other is allowed to vary. These sample means are shown in the margins. For example, the average sales for the 12 salespeople using the hard-sell approach is 74; the average sales for the 6 salespeople with no sales experience and no formal training is 62.

The sample means in the margins of Table 10.9 indicate what we call the *main effects* from the data. That is, they show how the levels of a given

Table 10.9   Sample Means for Vacuum Cleaner Example

		Factor B Experience Level				
		1	2	3	4	
Factor A	Hard Sell	59	69	74	94	74
Presentation	Soft Sell	65	57	82	88	73
		62	63	78	91	

factor affect sales when we average over the levels of the other factor. The main effect of presentation appears to be minimal, since the average for hard sales is just barely above the average for soft sales. On the other hand, the main effect of experience/training appears to be significant, since the means for categories 3 and 4 are a good deal larger than the means for categories 1 and 2. Judging by the main effects, the method of presentation does not seem to matter, but experience as a salesperson definitely appears to make a difference.

If we look at the individual cell means, however, we see a somewhat different pattern. For the salespeople with no formal training, levels 1 and 3, the soft-sell approach seems to produce higher sales; for the salespeople with formal training, the opposite is true. This is called an *interaction effect*. An interaction effect occurs whenever the pattern of cell means over the levels of one factor changes as we vary the level of the other factor. In other words, certain combinations of factor levels produce patterns of means that could not be predicted from main effects alone. (Although we did not mention it at the time, one assumption of the randomized block design is that there is *no* interaction between the blocking variable and factor being manipulated.) The main effect of presentation in this example is almost zero, but for any level of the experience/training factor, the type of presentation appears to make a difference. In cases like this, where interaction effects are present, the main effects are often considered less important.

For this example we can also see the interaction effect by graphing the four mean sales levels under the soft-sell approach and again under the hard-sell approach. As Figure 10.3 (p. 488) illustrates, these two graphs exhibit the different patterns described above.

We now present the formal statistical analysis. We denote the two factors by A and B. Factor A is assumed to have J levels, while factor B has K levels. This produces JK cells, one for each combination of factor levels. We randomly assign m experimental units to each of these cells, so that the total number of observations, n, is equal to mJK. (This is called a *balanced design* because the same number of experimental units, m, are assigned to

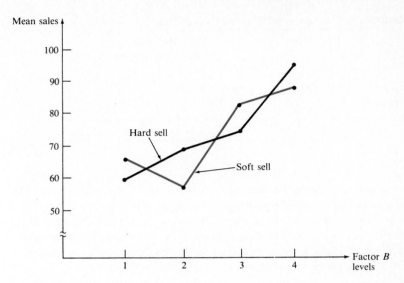

Figure 10.3

each of the JK joint factor levels.) Then we find the following sums:

$\sum Y_i$ = sum of all n observations
$\sum Y_i^2$ = sum of the squares of all n observations
AB_{jk} = sum of the m observations using levels j and k
      of factors A and B (= cell j, k sum)
A_j = sum of the mK observations using level j of factor A (= row j sum)
B_k = sum of the mJ observations using level k of factor B (= column k sum)

Using the sums above, we again form sums of squares. Now the total sum of squares, SST, is broken into four sums of squares, one due to factor A alone (SSA), one due to factor B alone (SSB), one due to the interaction between factors A and B (SSAB), and finally, one due to the random variation within the individual cells (SSE). (Note that SSB now stands for sum of squares for factor B, not sum of squares for the blocking variable, as in Section 10.3.) The formula that relates these is

$$SST = SSA + SSB + SSAB + SSE$$

Their degrees of freedom are given by

$$n - 1 = (J - 1) + (K - 1) + (J - 1)(K - 1) + (m - 1)JK$$
$$\text{total} \qquad A \qquad\qquad B \qquad\quad \text{interaction} \qquad\qquad \text{error}$$

Computationally, we find the SS's by the following formulas.

$$SST = \sum Y_i^2 - \frac{(\sum Y_i)^2}{n}$$

$$SSA = \frac{\sum A_j^2}{mK} - \frac{(\sum Y_i)^2}{n}$$

$$SSB = \frac{\sum B_k^2}{mJ} - \frac{(\sum Y_i)^2}{n}$$

$$SSAB = \frac{\sum \sum AB_{jk}^2}{m} - SSA - SSB - \frac{(\sum Y_i)^2}{n}$$

$$SSE = SST - SSA - SSB - SSAB$$

(The double summation for SSAB indicates that we should sum over all JK cells.)

In two-way ANOVA we form three F ratios, two for the main effects of A and B, and one for the interaction effect. These F ratios are

$$F_A = \frac{MSA}{MSE}, \qquad F_B = \frac{MSB}{MSE}, \qquad F_{AB} = \frac{MSAB}{MSE}$$

where

$$MSA = \frac{SSA}{J-1} \qquad MSB = \frac{SSB}{K-1}$$

$$MSAB = \frac{SSAB}{(J-1)(K-1)} \qquad MSE = \frac{SSE}{(m-1)JK}$$

If F_A exceeds $F_{\alpha, J-1, (m-1)JK}$, we reject the null hypothesis that factor A has no main effect. This implies that the means for the different levels of factor A (after averaging over the levels of factor B) are not all equal. A similar statement holds for factor B if F_B exceeds $F_{\alpha, K-1, (m-1)JK}$. Finally, if F_{AB} exceeds $F_{\alpha, (J-1)(K-1), (m-1)JK}$, we reject the null hypothesis of no interaction effect. In this case there is a significant pattern of cell means that cannot be seen by looking at the main effects alone.

Usually, we look for interactions first. If the corresponding F ratio is significant, we may not be too concerned with the significance of the main effects. In this case we are more interested in the pattern of cell means than in their row or column averages. But if the F ratio for interactions is not significant, the main effects take on more importance.

EXAMPLE 10.3

Use two-way ANOVA to uncover any significant main effects and/or interactions for the vacuum cleaner sales data in Table 10.8.

SOLUTION

We first summarize the preliminary sums in Table 10.10. Then the SS's are

$$SST = 134,326 - \frac{1764^2}{24} = 4672$$

$$SSA = \frac{888^2 + 876^2}{12} - \frac{1764^2}{24} = 6$$

$$SSB = \frac{372^2 + 378^2 + 468^2 + 546^2}{6} - \frac{1764^2}{24} = 3414$$

$$SSAB = \frac{177^2 + 207^2 + 222^2 + 282^2 + 195^2 + 171^2 + 246^2 + 264^2}{3}$$

$$- 6 - 3414 - \frac{1764^2}{24} = 414$$

$$SSE = 4672 - 6 - 3414 - 414 = 838$$

The rest of the calculations are summarized in the ANOVA table in Table 10.11.

Table 10.10 Preliminary Sums for Example 10.3

		Factor B				
		1	2	3	4	
Factor A	1	$AB_{11} = 177$	$AB_{12} = 207$	$AB_{13} = 222$	$AB_{14} = 282$	$A_1 = 888$
	2	$AB_{21} = 195$	$AB_{22} = 171$	$AB_{23} = 246$	$AB_{24} = 264$	$A_2 = 876$
		$B_1 = 372$	$B_2 = 378$	$B_3 = 468$	$B_4 = 546$	

$$\Sigma Y_i = 1764 \qquad \Sigma Y_i^2 = 134,326$$

Table 10.11 ANOVA Table for Example 10.3

Source	SS	df	MS	F	Significance
Main effect A	6	1	6	$F_A = .115$	Greater than .10
Main effect B	3414	3	1138	$F_B = 21.73$	Less than .01
AB interaction	414	3	138	$F_{AB} = 2.63$	Between .05 and .10
Error	838	16	52.375		
Total	4672	23			

As we suspected from our earlier discussion, the interaction effect is fairly significant. Since $F_{.10,3,16} = 2.46$ and $F_{.05,3,16} = 3.24$, the interaction is significant somewhere between the 5% and 10% levels. The main effect of presentation is not close to being significant, whereas the main effect of experience/training is very significant, well beyond the 1% level.

What does the vacuum cleaner company learn from this analysis? Probably it is interested primarily in the data in Table 10.9. This table indicates that sales experience and formal training do enable a salesperson to make more sales. Beyond this, however, it appears that there is an interaction between the type of presentation and the amount of experience/training. Salespeople with no formal training tend to be more successful with the soft-sell approach; salespeople with formal training can afford to use the hard-sell approach.

Problems for Section 10.4

16. Referring to Problem 7 (p. 477), suppose that a second factor to be tested, in addition to fertilizer, is the type of corn planted, of which there are four varieties. Now the farmer selects 36 acres for his experiment. Each of the 12 combinations of fertilizer type and corn variety is randomly assigned to three of the 36 acres. The resulting yields are shown below.

		Fertilizer Type		
		1	2	3
	1	105	101	110
		100	96	112
		104	100	115
	2	100	108	116
		9	105	110
		103	110	115
Corn Variety	3	110	114	109
		105	110	112
		104	116	106
	4	105	101	112
		109	99	115
		100	104	110

a. Calculate the mean yields for each combination of fertilizer and corn variety. Also calculate the mean yield for each fertilizer (an average over 12 acres) and for each corn variety (an average over 9 acres).

b. Repeat part (a) with "standard deviation" replacing "mean."

c. Given the numbers from part (a), do you believe that there are any main effects or interactions? Intuitively, how might the numbers from part (b) affect your answer to this question?

17. Calculate the appropriate ANOVA table for the data in Problem 16. Use it to test for any significant main effects or interactions at the 5% level. Then explain your results in words. If you were the farmer, how might the results of this experiment affect your future decisions?

18. The people performing the golf ball experiment in Problem 13 (p. 484) believe there may be some interaction between

Temperature (°F)	Brand 1	Brand 2	Brand 3	Brand 4
40	220	235	231	215
	225	241	225	210
	227	243	221	219
	218	237	227	223
65	230	253	231	247
	228	261	240	251
	235	250	235	255
	225	248	236	258
90	250	261	255	270
	246	255	260	275
	245	263	265	278
	251	265	258	271

golf ball brand and temperature. To test for this, a ball machine (a type of robot that hits golf balls) is used instead of
real golfers. It hits each brand of ball four times at each of
three air temperatures: 40°F, 65°F, and 90°F. The results are
shown in the preceding table.

a. Calculate the appropriate ANOVA table. Are there any
   significant main effects at the 5% level? What are they?
b. Are there any significant interactions (again at the 5%
   level)? Explain.
c. If you were a serious golfer, what would you regard as
   the most important findings of this experiment?

19. A study is done on a sample of residential homes to discover
whether the size of the monthly heating bill depends on the
type of heat or the type of home. Specifically, two types of
heat are examined: gas and heating oil. Also, all homes are
classified into two types: those with at least two stories and
those on a single level. In a single community, five houses
of each type, using each type of heat, are located, and their
heating bills for January of the current year are observed.
(The homes in the study are roughly equivalent in terms of
overall square footage and level of insulation.) The results
are shown below.

	Gas	Oil
Single level	125.65	147.82
	145.62	133.29
	175.19	155.63
	105.78	176.34
	128.10	153.26
Two or more	164.53	178.43
levels	153.25	167.41
	195.26	174.28
	168.99	182.53
	146.25	171.29

a. Fill in a table of means (as in Table 10.9) and draw a
   graph of these means (as in Figure 10.3). Are there any
   apparent main effects or interactions? Explain.
b. Calculate the appropriate ANOVA table and use it to test
   for significant main effects and interactions at the 5% level.
   Discuss your findings in words.

20. A used-car dealer would like to know whether the amount of
money spent on a car depends on (1) the age of the buyer,

and (2) whether the buyer is accompanied by a spouse. The
following data on 24 recent car purchases show the purchase
prices. Test for any significant main effects and interactions
at the 10% level, and discuss your findings in words.

Age	With Spouse	Not with Spouse
20–35	7,870	10,250
	8,350	9,735
	11,450	14,530
	10,255	11,640
36–50	8,955	12,460
	7,555	15,605
	10,340	13,420
	7,450	10,540
51–65	12,540	8,320
	14,550	10,460
	16,365	12,540
	15,210	13,125

21. A two-way ANOVA is used to test for differences in inventory turnover. One factor is type of store (grocery, department, and variety); the other factor is season (winter, spring,
summer, and fall). Three stores are sampled from each combination of factor levels, so that there are 36 observations
total. The mean inventory turnover levels (defined as percentages of total stock turned over in a fixed period of time)
are shown below.

	Type of Store		
	Grocery	Department	Variety
Winter	7.43	6.70	5.05
	7.98	5.76	5.63
	6.89	6.02	6.09
Spring	8.35	7.15	6.54
	8.21	7.35	6.99
	7.15	6.35	6.45
Summer	9.25	8.22	7.17
	8.65	8.36	7.95
	8.45	8.20	8.15
Fall	8.15	7.74	6.32
	8.47	8.96	6.21
	8.35	8.73	5.58

Imagine that I am your boss and know nothing about ANOVA. Calculate the table of means and the ANOVA table, and explain their contents to me. (Do not worry about every detail; just cover the high points in a way that a nonstatistical person can comprehend.)

10.5
ANOVA and Computer Packages

It is possible to avoid the tedious arithmetic in ANOVA studies by using a computer package. All of the multipurpose statistical packages we discuss in the regression chapters also do various forms of ANOVA. For the most part, it is straightforward to command the computer to do the appropriate analysis. Basically, all the user has to do is input the data in the appropriate format and then command the computer to use the appropriate ANOVA program. However, there are a good many ANOVA designs that we have not mentioned in this chapter. Since the ANOVA computer programs are usually equipped to deal with most of these designs, it is helpful to know more about potential experimental designs—at least the jargon—before attempting to use these programs. Fortunately, most of the manuals that accompany the computer packages include a write-up of each topic before the corresponding program is described. In the case of ANOVA, this write-up is probably sufficient to enable users to run the designs described in this chapter. (We have also included BASIC programs in the disk accompanying this text that perform ANOVA tests.)

Summary

Analysis of variance, or ANOVA, is a set of procedures for testing the difference between means of several populations. Usually, the populations differ in that they are given different treatment levels of one or more factors. There are many ways of doing this, and in fact there is a whole body of statistical literature devoted to the topic of experimental design. We have examined only three of the simplest experimental designs: one-way ANOVA, a randomized block design, and two-way ANOVA. In each case the primary objective is to see whether different treatments lead to significantly different mean values of a specified dependent variable.

Although analysis of variance tests for differences between means, variances play an extremely important role. Basically, we need to see whether the variances of observations within the individual treatment levels are small compared to the variance of the treatment level means. The question is resolved by calculating one or more ratios of mean-squared errors, called

F ratios, and displaying this information in an ANOVA table. If an F ratio is sufficiently large, the appropriate equal-means hypothesis can be rejected. In this case there are methods for calculating confidence intervals for each pair of means, so that we can see which means are significantly different from which others.

Applications

Application 10.1   Does background music have any effect on shoppers? Evidently, most store managers believe that it does because of its frequent use. But Milliman, in a *Journal of Marketing* article, questioned whether this belief is supported by hard evidence. (Reference: Ronald E. Milliman, "Using Background Music to Affect the Behavior of Supermarket Shoppers," *Journal of Marketing,* Vol. 46, 1982, pp. 86–91.) He conducted an experiment in a southwestern supermarket to test whether music, as well as the speed of the music, has an effect on shoppers. He used two dependent variables: the pace of the shoppers through the store (operationalized as the length of time it took them to pass through two specified points in the store) and the level of sales. The independent variable, or factor, was music, set at three levels: no music, slow music, and fast music. ("Fast" and "slow" music were given specific operational definitions.) For a total of nine weeks, the music setting was alternated daily: no music on Sunday, fast music on Monday, slow music on Tuesday, no music on Wednesday, and so on.

Milliman then used one-way ANOVA to analyze the results. Using pace as the dependent variable, the resulting F value of 4.85 was significant at the .01 level. The mean values of this variable were 108.93 seconds for fast music, 119.86 seconds for no music, and 127.53 seconds for slow music, indicating that customers moved fastest through the store when fast music was playing and slowest when slow music was playing. In fact, individual tests of the pairwise differences indicated that the difference in pace between the slow and fast settings was significant at the .01 level, but neither of the other two pairwise differences were significant at the .05 level.

Similarly, using total sales as the dependent variable, the F value of 3.21 was significant at the .05 level. Here again, the test for individual pairwise differences showed only one significant difference, namely that sales were significantly higher with slow music than with fast music.

Milliman interpreted these findings as saying that the speed of the music does make a difference. When the music is slow, people tend to move more slowly and buy more. When the music is fast, exactly the opposite effects occur.

Application 10.2   With the widespread use of computers in today's businesses, there are a significant number of employees whose primary responsibility is data entry from a keyboard. In a study of these key-entry operators, Ives and Chervany note that these jobs can be very repetitious and dull, resulting in poor attitudes and high absenteeism. (Reference: Blake Ives and Normal L. Chervany, "Alternative Data Entry Technologies and Settings: Impact on Worker Attitudes and Behavior," *Information and Management,* Vol. 6, 1983, pp. 37–47.) However, they also discuss two changes in these jobs that might make them more stimulating. The first is the move toward decentralization. Instead of having all key-entry operators sitting in one central location within the data processing department, many companies are moving these people into user groups, where the data are generated and used. The second change is improvement in key-entry technology. Many of today's systems have a programmable microprocessor, often permitting sophisticated reformatting of data, complex error checking procedures, and the collection of operator productivity statistics.

Ives and Chervany ran an experiment designed to check whether the move toward decentralization and/or technology improvement has a significant effect on worker attitudes or job performance. To do this, they sampled 326 key-entry operators from the Minneapolis–St. Paul area. Each of these was classified as working in a centralized (C) or decentralized (DC) job, with one of three levels of technology, low (L), medium (M), or high (H). Although this gives 6 (= 3 × 2) combinations, two of the combinations, C/H and DC/L, were not used due to very small numbers of workers in these groups. The remaining four combinations, C/L, C/M, DC/M, and DC/H, were used as the treatment levels in a one-way ANOVA design. There were several dependent variables, each tested separately. These included employee attitudes toward several aspects of their jobs (task identity, skill variety, task significance, feedback from the job, and autonomy on the job), supervisors' ratings of worker productivity, and absenteeism. All of these variables were measured on a seven-point scale (1 = worst, 7 = best), except for absenteeism, which was the number of days absent in the past six months. The sample means and F statistics for each dependent variable are shown in Table 10.12 (p. 496). The F values denoted by * are significant at the .05 level; those denoted by ** are significant at the .01 level.

For those dependent variables with significant F values, the significant pairwise differences (at the .05 level) are shown in Table 10.13 with $+$'s and $-$'s. For example, the "$-$" under "C/M minus DC/M" for the task significance variable means that workers in a centralized, medium-technology environment regard their jobs as less significant (in the sense of important) than those in a decentralized, medium-technology environ-

Table 10.12

Dependent Variable	C/L ($n = 80$)	C/M ($n = 107$)	DC/M ($n = 56$)	DC/H ($n = 83$)	F ratio
Task identity	4.51	4.49	4.64	4.32	.38
Skill variety	3.31	3.34	3.37	3.53	.59
Task significance	5.20	5.48	5.73	5.67	2.72*
Feedback from job	4.00	4.64	4.75	4.78	15.20**
Autonomy	3.75	3.26	4.00	4.69	4.75*
Internal work motivation	5.31	5.47	5.26	5.36	2.56
General job satisfaction	4.21	4.48	4.20	4.67	.81
Supervisor productivity rating	5.42	5.67	5.58	5.61	.96
Single-day absences	2.19	3.21	3.22	2.00	1.14
Total-day absences	3.74	4.84	4.40	3.08	3.10*

Table 10.13

	C/L minus C/M	DC/M minus DC/H	C/M minus DC/M
Task significance	−		−
Autonomy	+	−	−
Feedback from job	+		
Total-day absences	−	+	

ment. As another example, the "+" under the "DC/M minus DC/H" for the absenteeism variable means that the workers in a decentralized, medium-technology environment are absent more often than those in a decentralized, high-technology environment. The differences in these two examples are in the direction expected by the researchers, but the results are not all as expected. For example, the "+" under "C/L minus C/M" for the autonomy variable means that for workers in a centralized environment, those with a low technology feel that they have more autonomy in their jobs than those with a medium technology. Although Ives and Chervany present a rather complex reason for this contrary-to-expected result, it is the type of result that probably raises more questions than it answers.

Application 10.3   Consumers use cues such as product characteristics, store image, brand name, and price to differentiate among products and to form impressions of their quality. To the extent that these cues affect the consumer decision process, they are obviously important to the retailer, who must deal with the task of merchandise planning. Wheatley, Chiu, and Goldman performed an experiment to see how consumers' perceived quality of a product is affected by two types of cues: extrinsic cues, such as price, that can be manipulated by the retailer, and intrinsic cues, such as density of a garment's fiber, that are intrinsic to the product itself. (Reference: John J. Wheatley, John S. Y. Chiu, and Arieh Goldman, "Physical Quality, Price, and Perceptions of Product Quality: Implications for Retailers," *Journal of Retailing,* Vol. 57, 1981, pp. 100–115.) The experimental design was a two-way ANOVA design, where the dependent variable was the perceived quality of a carpet sample, and the two factors were an intrinsic cue (actual quality, as measured by carpet backing and density and length of fibers), and an extrinsic cue (price). Each factor was used at three levels.

More specifically, the experiment used nine squares of carpet, all of the same color. Three of these were "low" quality, usually retailing for $9 per square yard, three were of "medium" quality, usually retailing for $11 per square yard, and three were of "high" quality, usually retailing for $13 per square yard. However, in the experiment one of the low-quality squares was marked $9, another was marked $11, and the third was marked $13. The same pricing procedure was used for the medium- and high-quality squares. In other words, only three of the squares were priced correctly. The experiment used 171 subjects who had purchased carpeting at least once. They were randomly split into nine groups of 19 subjects each. After being allowed to inspect all nine squares, each subject was asked to rate the quality of a particular square on a 1-to-5 scale, where 1 indicates very low quality and 5 indicates very high quality. For example, the 19 subjects assigned to the medium-quality square with a $9 price tag were asked to rate that square's quality.

The mean quality perceptions for each of the nine quality–price combinations, as well as row and column averages, are shown in Table 10.14. These indicate that the subjects were able to distinguish increases in actual

Table 10.14

		Quality Low	Quality Medium	Quality High	Mean
	Low	2.3158	2.8947	2.8421	2.6842
Price	Medium	2.6316	3.4737	3.1579	3.0877
	High	2.6842	3.6316	4.1053	3.4737
	Mean	2.5439	3.3333	3.3684	

Table 10.15   ANOVA Table

Source of Variation	SS	df	MS	F
Physical cue	24.784	2	12.392	14.50
Price	17.766	2	8.883	10.40
Interaction	5.883	4	1.471	1.72
Error	138.421	162	.854	

quality (the column averages), and that they perceived higher-priced samples as being of higher quality (the row averages). These indications are verified statistically by the ANOVA table shown in Table 10.15. The F values for the main effects of actual quality and price are highly significant, with p-values less than .001, but the interaction effect is not significant even at the .10 level.

Glossary of Terms

Dependent variable   the quantitative variable that is measured in an analysis of variance

Factors   the categorical variables that are manipulated in an analysis of variance

Treatment levels   the categorical values of the factors

N-way ANOVA   an analysis of variance with N factors

Between variation   the variation between the different treatment means

Within variation   the variation of the observations within a given treatment level

Blocking variable   an extraneous variable that is controlled in an ANOVA experimental design

Randomized block design   an experimental design that explicitly controls for different levels of a blocking variable

Main effect in a two-way ANOVA   the effect of varying the levels of one factor, averaged over the levels of the other factor

Interactions in a two-way ANOVA   any effects from varying the levels of both factors that cannot be predicted from the main effects alone

Important Formulas

1. One-way ANOVA computational formulas

$$\text{SST} = \sum \sum Y_{ij}^2 - \frac{(\sum \sum Y_{ij})^2}{n}$$

$$\text{SSTr} = \sum \frac{(\sum Y_{ij})^2}{n_j} - \frac{(\sum \sum Y_{ij})^2}{n}$$

$$\text{SSE} = \text{SST} - \text{SSTr}$$

2. Test statistic for one-way ANOVA

$$F = \frac{\text{MSTr}}{\text{MSE}} = \frac{\text{SSTr}/(J - 1)}{\text{SSE}/(n - J)}$$

3. Simultaneous confidence intervals for each $\mu_j - \mu_k$ in one-way ANOVA

$$(\bar{Y}_j - \bar{Y}_k) \pm \sqrt{(J - 1)F_{\alpha, J-1, n-J}\text{MSE}\left(\frac{1}{n_j} + \frac{1}{n_k}\right)}$$

4. Randomized block design computational formulas

$$\text{SST} = \sum Y_i^2 - \frac{(\Sigma \, Y_i)^2}{n}$$

$$\text{SSTr} = \frac{\Sigma \, T_j^2}{K} - \frac{(\Sigma \, Y_i)^2}{n}$$

$$\text{SSB} = \frac{\Sigma \, B_k^2}{J} - \frac{(\Sigma \, Y_i)^2}{n}$$

$$\text{SSE} = \text{SST} - \text{SSTr} - \text{SSB}$$

where

$$T_j = \text{sum of observations in treatment level } j$$
$$B_k = \text{sum of observations in block } k$$

5. Test statistic for randomized block design

$$F = \frac{\text{MSTr}}{\text{MSE}} = \frac{\text{SSTr}/(J - 1)}{\text{SSE}/(n - J - K + 1)}$$

6. Two-way ANOVA computational formulas

$$\text{SST} = \sum Y_i^2 - \frac{(\Sigma \, Y_i)^2}{n}$$

$$\text{SSA} = \frac{\Sigma \, A_j^2}{mK} - \frac{(\Sigma \, Y_i)^2}{n}$$

$$\text{SSB} = \frac{\Sigma \, B_k^2}{mJ} - \frac{(\Sigma \, Y_i)^2}{n}$$

$$\text{SSAB} = \frac{\Sigma \Sigma \, AB_{jk}^2}{m} - \text{SSA} - \text{SSB} - \frac{(\Sigma \, Y_i)^2}{n}$$

$$\text{SSE} = \text{SST} - \text{SSA} - \text{SSB} - \text{SSAB}$$

where

$$A_j = \text{sum of observations for factor } A, \text{ treatment level } j$$
$$B_k = \text{sum of observations for factor } B, \text{ treatment level } k$$
$$AB_{jk} = \text{sum of observations in cell } j, k$$

7. Test statistics for two-way ANOVA

$$F_A = \frac{\text{MSA}}{\text{MSE}} \qquad F_B = \frac{\text{MSB}}{\text{MSE}} \qquad F_{AB} = \frac{\text{MSAB}}{\text{MSE}}$$

where

$$\text{MSA} = \frac{\text{SSA}}{J - 1} \qquad \text{MSB} = \frac{\text{SSB}}{K - 1}$$

$$\text{MSAB} = \frac{\text{SSAB}}{(J - 1)(K - 1)} \qquad \text{MSE} = \frac{\text{SSE}}{(m - 1)JK}$$

End-of-Chapter Problems

22. The following table shows median salary (in $1000s) for computer majors from a well-known university. These are classified by terminal degree and years of work experience. Each cell contains one graduate only.

Experience (Years)	Undergraduate	Graduate
1–3	24.8	31.5
4–6	30.2	33.8
7–9	34.1	37.3
10–12	36.1	41.2
13–15	42.1	40.3
16–20	37.6	42.7

a. In this part of the problem, ignore the degrees and use one-way ANOVA to test whether years of experience makes a significant difference in mean salary levels. Use a 5% significance level.

b. Now analyze the data as in part (a) but use "degree" as a blocking variable. How do your conclusions change, if at all?

23. Assume that the data in the 12 cells in Problem 22 are really means, based on 10 graduates per cell. Now we would like

to run a two-way ANOVA using both terminal degree and years of work experience as factors.

a. Why is it impossible to carry out a two-way ANOVA with the data that are given? What is missing?

b. In spite of part (a), do the given cell means indicate any probable main effects or interactions? If so, what are they?

24. In two-way ANOVA we are often not as interested in main effects once we discover significant interactions. Explain intuitively why this is the case.

*25. Four professors at a well-known university have taught an undergraduate statistics course for a number of years. Each student in each class receives an overall score for the class between 0 and 100. The sample means $\bar{Y}_j$, the sample standard deviations s_j, and the sample sizes n_j for a random sample of students from each professor's classes are shown below.

Class j	n_j	$\bar{Y}_j$	s_j
1	52	78	5.3
2	43	73	8.2
3	75	81	4.1
4	62	71	6.3

Do the calculations necessary to test for significant differences between the mean scores for the four professors. Test at the 5% level. (Recall the computing formula for sample variance to obtain the necessary sums of squares.)

26. In a one-way ANOVA, we could find the usual confidence interval for the difference between any pair of μ's, even if there are more than two μ's in the study. We proceed basically as in Chapter 8, except that we use MSE in the formula for the standard error of $\bar{Y}_i - \bar{Y}_j$. Specifically, a confidence interval for $\mu_i - \mu_j$ with confidence level $1 - \alpha$ is given by

$$\bar{Y}_i - \bar{Y}_j \pm t_{\alpha/2, n-J}\, s \sqrt{\frac{1}{n_i} + \frac{1}{n_j}}$$

where s is the square root of MSE. Using the data from Example 10.1, find a 90% confidence interval for $\mu_1 - \mu_2$. Then repeat for each of the other five pairs of μ's. Why are these confidence intervals different from those in Table 10.4? Would you expect them to be shorter or longer? Why?

27. Explain why it is inappropriate to use individual confidence intervals for differences between means (specifically those in Problem 26) when we want to make a statement about many such differences with overall confidence level $1 - \alpha$.

28. A second way to get around the simultaneous confidence interval problem is as follows. If we wish to make confidence interval statements about r differences simultaneously with overall confidence level $1 - \alpha$, each confidence interval can be of the form presented in Problem 26, but with $t_{\alpha/2, n-J}$ replaced by $t_{\alpha/2r, n-J}$. For example, if $\alpha = .10$ and $r = 6$, each individual confidence interval is formed from $t_{.10./12, n-J}$, or $t_{.0083, n-J}$, and has confidence level $1 - .0083 = .9917$. In this case it can be shown that the *overall* confidence level, that is, the probability that each of the r confidence interval statements is correct, is at least the required .90. Use this procedure to develop a set of simultaneous confidence intervals with overall confidence level at least .90 for the potato chip data in Example 10.1. (Use the fact that $t_{.0083, 19}$ equals 2.629.) Compare these confidence intervals with those in Table 10.4. Which set has the shortest lengths?

29. A number of coffee drinkers are chosen to take part in a taste comparison test. Each person is asked to taste each of five brands of coffee and rate them on a 1-to-10 scale. (Each person tastes the brands in a random order.) The object of the test is to discover whether the mean ratings for the five brands are equal. Which experimental design is appropriate? Explain.

30. For Problem 29, suppose that the observed ratings are shown below. Can you conclude that there are significant differences between the five brands at the 5% level? Answer by calculating the appropriate ANOVA table and testing the appropriate F value.

Brand 1	Brand 2	Brand 3	Brand 4	Brand 5
5	7	8	3	5
7	9	7	4	7
8	6	9	7	3
6	8	6	5	4
9	6	7	7	5
7	6	8	4	6
8	6	7	5	6

31. In one large city there is fierce competition among three of the best-known national fast-food chains. Each of these claims to have the most sales. To test their claims, sales are monitored on five randomly selected weeks. The resulting sales (in dollars) are shown below.

Week	Chain 1	Chain 2	Chain 3
1	2769	2954	3121
2	2614	2852	2954
3	3420	3615	3537
4	3821	4013	4154
5	2853	3045	3265

a. Use a one-way ANOVA design to test for significant mean differences between the three food chains in this city. Use a 10% significance level.

b. Why might a randomized block design be appropriate here? What is the blocking variable?

c. Test the same hypothesis as in part (a), but now use a randomized block design. Again use a 10% level. Do you reach the same conclusion? Is there numerical evidence in your ANOVA table to suggest that you were wise to use a randomized block design? What is it?

*32. A telephone company would like to know how many operators to have on duty during various four-hour shifts. This of course depends on the mean number of incoming calls during these periods of the day. The shifts in question are from 8 A.M. to noon, from noon to 4 P.M., from 4 P.M. to 8 P.M., and from 8 P.M. to midnight. The company collects data on the number of calls received per hour for each of these shifts. Each observation is an average over the four hours in a shift, and the data are collected over a 10-day period. Discuss how you could help the company analyze its problem by means of the techniques in this chapter. In particular, how might simultaneous confidence intervals be useful?

*33. In a one-way ANOVA with three treatment levels, labeled 1, 2, and 3, suppose that we test H_0: $\mu_1 = \mu_2 = \mu_3$ as follows. For each of the three differences, $\mu_1 - \mu_2$, $\mu_1 - \mu_3$, and $\mu_2 - \mu_3$, we use the test in Chapter 9 for the difference between two means. For example, we test H_0: $\mu_1 - \mu_2 = 0$ versus H_a: $\mu_1 - \mu_2 \neq 0$, and similarly for $\mu_1 - \mu_3$ and $\mu_2 - \mu_3$. Then if we can reject H_0 for any of these three tests, we reject H_0: $\mu_1 = \mu_2 = \mu_3$. What is the problem with this procedure? In particular, what can you say about its significance level, that is, its probability of a type I error?

*34. In a one-way ANOVA, let s_j^2 be the sample variance of the observations in level j. How is MSE related to the s_j^2's? (Look at the original formula in this chapter for SSE.) Is it correct to say that MSE is a weighted average of the s_j^2's? (A weighted average of the s_j^2's is of the form $\Sigma\, w_j s_j^2$, where the "weights," the w_j's, are nonnegative numbers that sum to 1.) Why or why not?

35. In a test to see which types of alkaline batteries last longer than others, three of the most popular brands are put in children's toys and then run continuously until the toys stop functioning. Each toy requires one battery, and 10 batteries of each brand are tested. The following times (in hours) are observed.

Brand 1	Brand 2	Brand 3
8.4	6.5	7.4
7.9	7.1	8.0
7.4	7.4	6.9
8.1	6.7	7.1
8.9	9.1	5.8
9.3	6.4	7.1
7.9	6.8	8.0
8.4	7.1	7.7
7.5	6.1	8.3
9.4	7.0	8.3

a. Calculate the sample means and the sample standard deviations for each brand. Do the sample means appear to be very different? Considering the magnitudes of these differences and the magnitudes of the standard errors of the sample means, do you believe the differences between means can be attributed solely to random (within) variation? (Don't run any formal tests; just answer intuitively.)

b. Now run a formal ANOVA test to see whether the null hypothesis of equal means can be rejected at the 10% level.

36. In Problem 35, calculate simultaneous 90% confidence intervals for all differences between pairs of means. (How many pairs are there?) Which brands, if any, have significantly longer lifetimes than which others?

37. In Problem 35, suppose that some of the toys require a single AA battery, while others require a single C battery. Now we would like to see how battery lifetimes depend on battery size (AA or C) as well as on brand. To do this, a new experiment is run with 36 batteries total. There are 12 of each brand, and for each brand there are six AA's and six C's. The data on lifetimes are given below.

	Brand 1	Brand 2	Brand 3
AA	7.4	8.2	9.2
	8.2	6.7	7.1
	9.2	7.1	8.5
	7.9	6.6	7.1
	8.6	8.1	8.8
	6.9	8.5	9.4
C	8.9	9.2	10.5
	9.2	7.9	9.4
	7.8	9.5	11.6
	9.1	7.9	9.7
	8.9	8.3	10.6
	9.1	7.2	11.1

a. Calculate the sample means and arrange them in a table such as Table 10.9. Do there appear to be any main effects? Explain.

b. Graph the cell means (as in Figure 10.3) to see whether any interaction effects are apparent. Do there appear to be any interactions? Explain.

c. Calculate the ANOVA table corresponding to these data and discuss any significant F values (at the 5% level) and their implications.

*38. It is certainly reasonable to hypothesize that the job satisfaction level of people in managerial positions is related to the amount of travel required of them, as well as their marital status. Discuss in some detail how you would test this hypothesis. In particular, why would a two-factor design be appropriate? What are the factors, and how would you define their levels? What is the dependent variable, and how would you obtain data on it? What results might you expect concerning main effects and interactions? Are there any particular interactions you might expect to observe?

39. It has been hypothesized that different segments of the female population have different attitudes toward the current issues concerning women, such as women's right to equal pay, women's access to jobs traditionally held by men, women's place in the home, and so on. Suppose that women are divided into the following categories: (1) married "housewives", (2) married women with relatively low-paying jobs, (3) married women with relatively high-paying jobs, (4) unmarried women with no jobs or relatively low-paying jobs, and (5) unmarried women with relatively high-paying jobs. A randomly selected group of 10 women in each category are given a 100-item test. The scores on this test range from 0 to 100, with a low score reflecting disagreement with most of the "women's movement," and a high score reflecting agreement with most of the women's movement. The scores are shown below.

		Category		
1	2	3	4	5
54	67	86	68	77
67	84	61	58	72
57	81	63	69	58
42	62	94	58	82
71	83	71	72	83
48	62	82	91	58
51	77	92	72	66
61	89	78	71	57
57	64	68	79	92
73	58	92	71	87

a. Do these data support the hypothesis that not all groups of women have the same attitudes about the role of women? Test at the 5% significance level.
b. Find simultaneous 90% confidence intervals for each $\mu_i - \mu_j$, where μ_i is the mean score on the test for all women in group i. Which mean differences are significantly nonzero?
c. Given the results in parts (a) and (b), if you were writing a report of this experiment in a women's magazine, what would you report as the most important findings?

*40. Consider the randomized block design in Section 10.3. There we have J levels of a factor, K values of the blocking variable, and a single observation for each level–block combination. Now suppose that we ignore the blocking variable and proceed as in Section 10.2 with a one-way ANOVA design with K observations per level. Show algebraically that SST and SSTr are unaffected, that is, they are the same for the block design and the one-way design, but that SSE for the one-way design equals SSB + SSE for the block design.

41. The manager of a certain business is trying to decide which of three personal computer brands to buy for his company. He is particularly interested in which of these three brands is easiest to learn. To test this, he acquires one computer of each brand and selects a popular software program compatible with each computer. He then selects 18 employees, randomly assigns six of these employees to each computer, and measures the time required to "master" the program. (The employees work independently of one another, so that they do not have the chance to learn from one another.) The learning times (in minutes) are shown below.

Computer 1	Computer 2	Computer 3
53	69	32
87	34	46
61	57	28
42	29	33
57	59	47
39	72	55

a. Which of the three computers would you suggest that the manager buy, given that all other factors, such as price, are equal? Why?
b. To test whether there are any significant differences between the mean learning times on the three brands, which design is appropriate, a one-way ANOVA or a randomized block design? Explain your reasoning.
c. Using your answer from part (b), run the appropriate test at the 5% significance level. What is your conclusion? Does this affect your answer to part (a)? Explain.

*42. Sometimes the one-way ANOVA model is written as

$$Y_{ij} = \mu + \tau_j + \epsilon_{ij}$$

where Y_{ij} and ϵ_{ij} are defined as in Section 10.2. Now μ is the overall mean for all treatment levels, and τ_j is referred to as the "mean treatment effect" for level j.
a. If the null hypothesis of equal means is true, what does this imply about the τ_j's?
b. If there are four treatment levels, and we observe the sample means $\bar{Y}_1 = 23$, $\bar{Y}_2 = 25$, $\bar{Y}_3 = 30$, and $\bar{Y}_4 = 26$, each based on the same number of observations, how would you estimate τ_1, τ_2, τ_3, and τ_4?

43. With regard to Application 10.3, Wheatley, Chiu, and Goldman found no statistically significant interaction between actual quality and price in their carpet experiment. This may be because there really is no interaction or because the sample

sizes were not large enough to prove the existence of an interaction. Does the table of means indicate any possible interaction that might be worth pursuing in a larger experiment? Discuss.

Computer Problems

(These problems are to be used in conjunction with the computer software package.)

1. Referring to the data on grade point averages and test scores in Table II of Appendix D, suppose the first 25 scores are for undergraduate business majors, the next 25 scores are for undergraduate humanities majors, the next 25 scores are for undergraduate physical sciences majors, and the last 25 scores are for undergraduate social sciences majors. For this problem, consider only the first 10 students in each of these four categories.
   a. Use the ANOVA program to test at the 5% level whether there are any significant differences among the four groups with respect to mean graduate GPA's.
   b. Repeat part (a) when the dependent variable is the verbal test percentile.
   c. Repeat part (a) when the dependent variable is the quantitative test percentile.

2. For this problem refer to the housing data in Table III of Appendix D. We would like to see whether the mean selling price is significantly affected by the number of bedrooms. Consider the first 50 houses as three groups: those with two bedrooms,

those with three bedrooms, and those with four or more bedrooms.
   a. Use the ANOVA program to test whether there are any significant differences in mean selling price among these three groups. Use a 10% significance level.
   b. Find simultaneous 90% confidence intervals for the differences between mean selling prices for the three groups.

3. Repeat Problem 2, now using appraised value instead of selling price as the dependent variable.

4. Referring to the cost of living data in Table VII of Appendix D, use the ANOVA program to test whether there are any differences among California, Florida, New York, and Texas cities with respect to the mean index of (i) grocery items; (ii) housing; (iii) transportation; (iv) miscellaneous goods and services. (You will have to run ANOVA four times, once for each of these measures.) Use a 5% significance level.

5. Use the ANOVA program and the TWOWAY program to solve Problem 12 of this chapter (p. 484).

6. Use the TWOWAY program to solve Problem 18 of this chapter (p. 491).

References

GUENTHER, W. C. *Analysis of Variance*. Englewood Cliffs, N.J.: Prentice-Hall, 1964.

KLEINBAUM, D. G. and KUPPER, L. L. *Applied Regression Analysis and Other Multivariable Methods*. North Scituate, Mass., 1978 (available from PWS Publishers, Boston).

MENDENHALL, W. and SINCICH, T. *A Second Course in Business Statistics: Regression Analysis*, 2nd ed. San Francisco: Dellen (a division of Macmillan), 1986.

NIE, N., HULL, C. H., JENKINS, J. G., STEINBRENNER, K., and BENT, D. H. *Statistical Package for the Social Sciences*, 2nd ed. New York: McGraw-Hill, 1975.

CHAPTER 11

Simple Linear Regression and Correlation

Objectives

1. To learn how a regression equation relates an independent variable to a dependent variable.
2. To see how a scattergram indicates the presence or absence of a linear relationship between two variables.
3. To examine the statistical assumptions of the linear regression model.
4. To learn how to calculate the least squares estimates of the regression coefficients.
5. To learn how to find the standard error of estimate for a regression equation.
6. To see how correlation is related to linear regression.
7. To learn a measure of the strength of a linear fit, r^2.
8. To learn how to use an ANOVA table to test the significance of a linear fit.
9. To develop confidence intervals and hypothesis tests for the regression coefficients.
10. To see how to use regression for prediction.

Contents

*F*inancial analysts are continually trying to understand what causes stock prices to change so that they can predict future price changes. A standard approach is to examine price changes of a particular stock in relationship to price changes of a "market index," composed of a wide variety of stocks. From such an examination of, say, weekly price changes over a period of several years, the analysts might be able to conclude, for example, that a 1% increase (or decrease) in the market index is typically accompanied by a 1.5% increase (or decrease) of the price of the particular stock. Although this does not necessarily imply that a change in the market index *causes* a change in the price of the stock, it does imply that information about the market index will be helpful in predicting future price changes of the stock.

Probably the most popular method for conducting this analysis is to build a "linear regression equation" that relates the two variables, stock price change and market index change. This is an equation that has the variable of interest, stock price change, on one side and a linear function of the other variable, market index change, on the other side. This linear function is then used to explain or predict the variable of interest. As we will see, the job of the statistician is to estimate the parameters (slope and intercept) of the regression equation on the basis of sample data, and then to test the explanatory or predictive power of the estimated equation. As we will also see, the subject of regression is closely tied to correlation. If stock price changes and market index changes are highly correlated (as discussed in Chapter 2), the estimated regression equation will be capable of fairly accurate predictions; if these variables are practically uncorrelated, the regression equation will be of little use.

11.1

Introduction

Until now we have been concerned primarily with the properties of a *single* variable from a population. For example, the techniques in previous chapters enable us to study household income in a given population, so that we can estimate the mean income, the variance of incomes, and so on. In this chapter and Chapter 12, we learn a very useful method for relating two or more variables from a population. We will no longer be as interested in the properties of a single variable as we are in the way two or more variables are related. The technique that quantifies the relationship between several variables is called *regression analysis*. We will learn only a special case of general regression analysis, called *linear* regression.

To gain some insight into regression, it is useful to proceed directly to an example. Consider a cross section of houses in a given city. Suppose that we choose one of these houses at random and attempt to predict its cost, labeled Y. Assuming that we know nothing about this particular house, the best we can do is guess that it is an "average" house and that its cost is therefore equal to the *mean* cost of all houses in the population. Obviously, our guess can differ widely from the actual cost of the house. The house could be in the poorer section of the city, so that our guess would probably be on the high side, or it could be in the wealthy section of the city, so that our guess would probably be on the low side.

The problem here is that we do not know enough about the house to predict its cost accurately. But there are obviously variables related to the cost of the house. For example, it would be helpful to know the square footage of the house, the number of bedrooms, the type of construction, and probably others. If we knew the values of these variables, we could undoubtedly make a more accurate prediction. In particular, if μ is the mean cost of all houses, and we observe a house with, say, an unusually large square footage, our estimate of the cost of this house will be larger than μ. If we learn, on the other hand, that the house has only one bedroom, our estimate of the cost of the house will be lower than μ.

Regression is a method that quantifies these ideas. In any regression analysis there is a variable $Y,$ such as the cost of a house, that we wish to predict. As in Chapter 10, this variable is called the *dependent variable*. There are also one or more other variables, labeled X_1, X_2, and so on, such as square footage and the number of bedrooms, that are related to the dependent variable. These variables are called the *independent variables*. If there is a single independent variable $X,$ the method is called *simple regression*. If there are two or more independent variables, the method is called *multiple regression*. (In either case there is only *one* dependent variable.) In this chapter we study simple regression. We examine multiple regression in Chapter 12.

> The dependent variable, labeled Y, is the variable we wish to predict. The independent variable or variables, labeled by X's, are the variables we use to predict Y.

Regression analysis is typically used in two types of situations. The situation described above, where we try to predict the cost of a house from the characteristics of the house, deals with *cross-sectional data*. Here we are interested in the characteristics of a population at a given point in time, so we sample a cross section of the population. Regression analysis is also used for analyzing *time series data*. In this case the dependent variable and the independent variables are each measured periodically (monthly, say) throughout time. For example, government economists use regression analysis to predict GNP in terms of other variables, such as interest rates, unemployment, the money supply, and government spending. For time series data, the problem is to predict future values of the dependent variable given observed (or predicted) values of the independent variables.

Although regression is applicable to both cross-sectional and time series data, we will concentrate more heavily on cross-sectional data in these two regression chapters. There are two reasons for this. First, regression analysis of time series data presents several difficulties that we will not cover in an introductory text. Second, we devote an entire chapter, Chapter 14, to time series analysis. Included in that chapter will be a discussion of the special role of regression in time series contexts.

There are two primary objectives in regression analysis. One of these is prediction. In particular, we wish to predict values of the dependent variable from given values of the independent variables. The other objective of regression analysis is to understand the relationship between two or more variables so that we can better understand the way the world operates. For example, we may be more interested in quantifying the relationship between housing costs and square footage than predicting the cost of any particular house.

The first step in any regression analysis is to estimate an equation that relates the dependent variable to the independent variables. This *regression equation* tells us "how the world operates" since it quantifies the relationship between the variables. Then if we wish, we may use this equation for prediction purposes. Therefore, the two goals of regression analysis, understanding the way the world operates and predicting, are both achieved by examining the regression equation.

11.2

The Linear Regression Model

In this section we investigate the reasoning behind the linear regression model. The basic ideas are quite simple and can be understood by examining scattergrams of the sample data. Scattergrams suggest the type of relationship, if any, that exists between two variables, and they lead us to a quantitative form of this relationship. However, we must look beyond scattergrams if we wish to use regression for statistical inference. In that case we must introduce a *statistical model* that is supported by the sample data.

Scattergrams: Evidence of a Regression Line

In Chapter 2 we briefly discussed relationships between two variables and showed how they can be illustrated graphically with scattergrams. We now examine these topics in further detail. Suppose that we are interested in the

relationship between housing costs (Y) and square footages (X) for a particular population of houses. If we collect data for n houses in this population,
we will have n pairs of numbers of the form (X_i, Y_i). The cost of the ith
house is Y_i and its square footage is X_i. For $n = 15$, Table 11.1 lists a
possible set of data.

By examining the data in Table 11.1, we gain some appreciation of the
relationship between housing costs and square footages. In particular, it appears that houses with more square footage cost more and that houses with
less square footage cost less. This is certainly expected. However, suppose
that we want to predict the cost of a house (not included in the sample) with
1560 square feet. Or suppose that we want to predict how much more a house
would cost if it had 1800 instead of 1600 square feet. The tabular form of
the data is not really sufficient to answer these questions because it does not
suggest a precise *form* of the relationship between cost and square footage.

A scattergram makes the relationship between the variables much more
obvious. For each pair (X_i, Y_i), we plot a point on a two-dimensional graph.
As usual, the X axis is the horizontal axis and the Y axis is the vertical axis.
The scattergram is the resulting cluster of points. The scattergram of the data
in Table 11.1 is shown in Figure 11.1a (p. 510). Notice that the points tend
to rise as we look from left to right. This means there is a *positive* relationship
between housing cost and square footage, so that the cost increases as the
square footage increases.

One important aspect of Figure 11.1a is that the points tend to cluster
around a straight line. Admittedly, no single straight line goes through each
point exactly, but the line shown in Figure 11.1b provides a fairly good fit
to the 15 points.

Now recall that the equation of any line, in slope–intercept form, is

$$Y = a + bX$$

(The reader might wish to consult Appendix A for a brief discussion of linear
equations.) Here a is the Y intercept (the Y value when $X = 0$) and b is the
slope (the change in Y for a unit change in X). This means that a is measured
in the same units as Y (thousands of dollars) and b is measured in Y units
divided by X units (thousands of dollars per hundred square feet). From the
graph it appears that a is approximately -60 and b is approximately 8.
(Although it cannot be seen in Figure 11.1b, the -60 was found graphically
by extending the line below the X axis until it hit the Y axis.)

If the line in Figure 11.1b fits the population of *all* houses in the population
reasonably well, the questions we asked earlier can be answered fairly easily.
Specifically, if a house has 1560 square feet, its predicted cost is

$$Y = a + b(15.60) = -60 + 8(15.60) = 64.8 \quad \text{(or \$64,800)}$$

(Notice that the cost variable Y is measured in thousands of dollars and the
square footage variable X is measured in hundreds of square feet.) Next,

Table 11.1

Housing Cost Y ($1000s)	Square Footage X (100s of Square Feet)
75.90	17.5
61.00	15.9
110.00	21.0
83.50	18.0
94.60	18.9
54.50	13.6
96.00	20.5
70.70	17.6
50.75	15.0
69.40	16.5
87.50	17.0
105.00	19.2
76.50	18.0
103.20	21.5
59.00	16.0

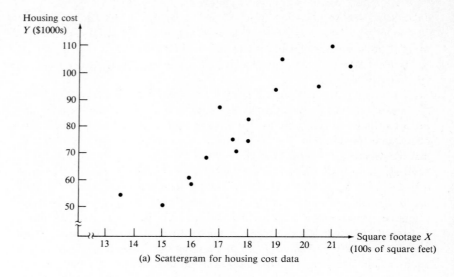

(a) Scattergram for housing cost data

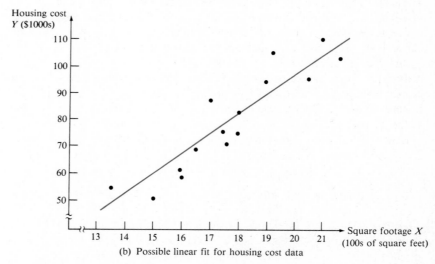

(b) Possible linear fit for housing cost data

Figure 11.1

suppose that the square footage of a house changes from 1600 to 1800 square feet. Then the change in X, labeled ΔX, is 2. Therefore, the predicted change in Y, labeled ΔY, is

$$\Delta Y = b(\Delta X) = 8(2) = 16 \quad \text{(or \$16,000)}$$

This discussion suggests that if we can find the equation of a straight line that fits the points in the scattergram reasonably well, this equation is very

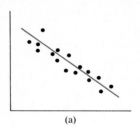
(a)

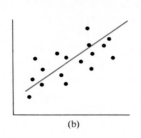
(b)

(c)

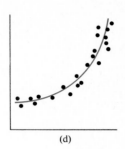
(d)

Figure 11.2
Scattergrams Showing Various Relationships

useful for understanding the relationship between the variables and for prediction. Actually, we will not use the scattergram directly to estimate the
parameters of the straight line. For that purpose we will go back to the
numerical data in Table 11.1 and use regression *formulas* to find more precise
estimates of *a* and *b*. The real purpose of a scattergram is to let us see quickly
whether there is any relationship between *X* and *Y* worth pursuing. In particular, we wish to know whether a straight-line fit is plausible.

The scattergrams in Figure 11.2 show some of the possibilities. In Figure
11.2a there is a good linear fit of a "negative" relationship (where the line
slopes downward from left to right). The graph in Figure 11.2b suggests a
positive linear relationship, but the points are obviously not as tightly clus-
tered around *any* straight line as they are in Figure 11.2a. The graph in Figure
11.2c shows a swarm of points that do not appear to fit any pattern, linear
or otherwise. When we observe a scattergram such as this, there is little point
in trying to use regression formulas to relate *Y* and *X*. The graph clearly
shows that no relationship exists, and no mathematical formulas will be able
to find one.

The final graph in Figure 11.2d shows a relationship between *X* and *Y,* but
not a linear one. If our objective is to predict *Y* values from *X* values, and
if we know the equation of the curve that fits the data (as shown in the graph),
the prediction will be just as successful as if we have a linear fit. However,
it is not quite as simple to *estimate* a nonlinear fit as a linear one. We postpone
further discussion of nonlinear relationships until Chapter 12.

The Statistical Model

Suppose that a scattergram indicates a linear relationship between two variables, such as housing cost and square footage. What does this really mean?
That is, if we believe on the basis of sample data that the *X*'s and *Y*'s are
"linearly related," what do we believe is true of the entire population of *X*'s
and *Y*'s? In this section we formulate a statistical model that provides an
answer to this question.

Consider a fixed value of *X,* such as $X = 1.5$ (1500 square feet). If we
look at *all* houses in the population with this value of *X,* that is, all 1500-

square-foot houses, we know that their costs vary. The mean cost of all these 1500-square-foot houses is labeled $\mu_{Y|X=1.5}$ (read "the mean of Y given that $X = 1.5$"), and the variance of these costs is labeled $\sigma^2_{Y|X=1.5}$ (read "the variance of Y given that $X = 1.5$"). This variance measures how the costs of 1500-square-foot houses vary throughout the population.

In general, if we choose any value of X and measure all members of the population with this value of X, the mean and variance of the associated values of Y are labeled $\mu_{Y|X}$ and $\sigma^2_{Y|X}$.

$$\mu_{Y|X} = \text{mean of all } Y \text{ values for a fixed } X \text{ value}$$
$$\sigma^2_{Y|X} = \text{variance of all } Y \text{ values for a fixed } X \text{ value}$$

We realize that not all of the (X, Y) points are likely to lie on a single straight line. However, the regression model assumes that the *means*, $\mu_{Y|X}$, do lie on a single straight line. This straight line is called the *population regression line*. In other words, the population regression line is the line consisting of all points of the form $(X, \mu_{Y|X})$. Its equation is given below.

> *Population Regression Line*
>
> $$\mu_{Y|X} = \beta_0 + \beta_1 X$$

Here we have relabeled the Y-intercept as β_0 and the slope as β_1. The reason for this notation, instead of a and b, is that it extends more naturally to multiple regression equations, the topic of Chapter 12.

The population regression line for the housing cost example is illustrated in Figure 11.3. For several X values we plot a few of the many (X, Y) points. As the graph shows, the Y values for a given X do not all lie on the straight line; some are above the line and others are below it. But the assumption is that the mean of these values does lie on the line for each value of X.

Usually, we are not as interested in the mean of all Y's as we are in a *single* value of Y. For example, we may not be as interested in the mean cost of all 1500-square-foot houses as we are in the cost of a particular 1500-square-foot house. To express a single Y value in terms of the regression equation, we write any Y value as the sum of its mean, $\mu_{Y|X}$, and an "error" term, labeled ϵ (the Greek lowercase letter "epsilon"). Since the mean is $\beta_0 + \beta_1 X$, this leads to the following equation.

> *Regression Equation for a Single Observation*
>
> $$Y = \beta_0 + \beta_1 X + \epsilon$$

The error term ϵ measures the difference between a single Y and the mean of all Y's for a fixed X. If $\epsilon = 0$, the point (X, Y) lies on the population

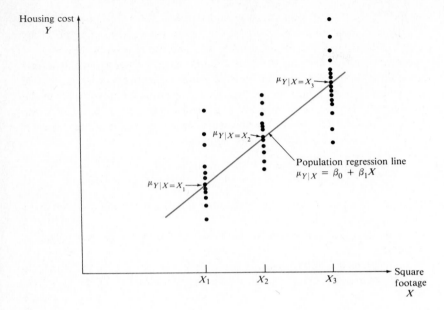

Figure 11.3
Population Regression Line for Housing Cost Example with Some Representative
(*X, Y*) Points

regression line. If $\epsilon \neq 0$, the point is either above the line ($\epsilon > 0$) or below
it ($\epsilon < 0$). The assumption that the mean $\mu_{Y|X}$ is on the regression line is
equivalent to the assumption that the mean of the ϵ's (for a given X) is 0.
That is, the positive errors cancel the negative errors.

The graph in Figure 11.4 shows a population regression line and several

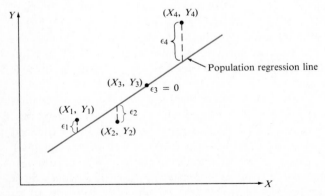

Figure 11.4
Error Terms for a Regression Line

selected (X, Y) points. Notice that ϵ_1 and ϵ_4 are positive, ϵ_2 is negative, and ϵ_3 is 0. Also, notice how we can "see" the error terms in the graph. They are the *vertical* distances between the points and the regression line.

To use regression analysis for statistical inference, we need to make several assumptions about the way in which the *population* scattergram varies around the regression line. Equivalently, we need to make assumptions about the error terms. The usual assumptions are listed below. These are called the *OLS assumptions*. (OLS stands for ordinary least squares. In the next section we see the reason for the term "least squares.")

OLS Assumptions for the Model $Y = \beta_0 + \beta_1 X + \epsilon$

1. There is a population regression line such that the mean of all error terms around this line equals 0.
2. The errors have a common variance σ_e^2, the same for each value of X.
3. The errors are normally distributed.
4. The errors are probabilistically independent of one another.

More compactly, the OLS assumptions state that the error terms are independent $N(0, \sigma_e^2)$ random variables.

Discussion of the Assumptions

Assumption 1: Earlier we assumed that the mean of all Y's with a given X lies on the regression line. This is equivalent to saying that the errors have mean 0. Some error terms are positive and some are negative, but their average is assumed to be 0.

Assumption 2: Suppose that we fix X and consider all observations with this value of X. Then the variance of the corresponding Y values is $\sigma_{Y|X}^2$. Assumption 2 implies that this variance is the same constant, labeled σ_e^2, for each X. For example, if Y is the cost of a house and X is its square footage, assumption 2 implies that the costs of 1300-square-foot houses vary just as much as the costs of 2000-square-foot houses. (More advanced discussions of regression refer to this constant-error-variance assumption as *homoscedasticity*. Its opposite, an error variance that depends on the value of X, is called *heteroscedasticity*.)

Assumption 3: This assumption implies that the distribution of all Y values for a given X is normally shaped. Together with the first two assumptions, it implies that the Y values must also be normal, with mean $\beta_0 + \beta_1 X$ and variance σ_e^2. Figure 11.5 illustrates this assumption as well as assumptions 1 and 2. For several values of X, we see normal curves centered on the regression line. Each curve is the population density function of Y values for a given X. Notice that each curve has the same spread, as measured by σ_e^2.

Assumption 4: The independence assumption means that we cannot predict

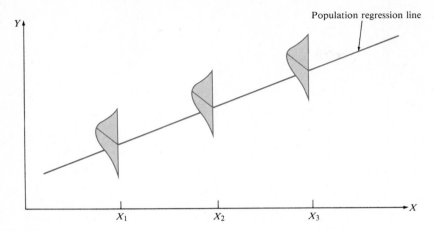

Figure 11.5
Distribution of Y-Values for fixed X: Illustrations of Assumptions 1–3

one error term from any of the others. For cross-sectional data this assumption is usually justified. However, it often fails to hold in time series contexts.

To illustrate the meaning of assumption 4, suppose that the dependent variable (now labeled Y_t, t for time) is the number of calculators sold in time period t, and the independent variable (now labeled X_t) is the price of an average calculator in period t. Then a scattergram of (X_t, Y_t) points might appear as in Figure 11.6 (p. 516). Because the price of calculators has been decreasing continually over time, the sequence of points, in the order they were observed, proceeds from lower right to upper left.

Notice that the error terms in Figure 11.6 follow a definite pattern. For a while they are positive, then they are negative, then positive, and so on. So if we are told that ϵ_6 is positive, we will tend to predict that ϵ_7 is also positive; if we are told that ϵ_{13} is negative, we will tend to predict that ϵ_{14} is also negative. This means that the successive error terms are *not* independent, as assumed, but are instead said to be *autocorrelated*. Autocorrelation is practically always present in time series data, which means that assumption 4 is practically always violated. This is the primary reason we must be very careful when we apply regression analysis to time series data.

The OLS assumptions listed above are ideal assumptions. It is unlikely that these assumptions are ever entirely valid, and it is also unlikely that we can ever fully check their validity. However, all the statistical results in this chapter and Chapter 12 depend on the validity of these OLS assumptions. If the assumptions are valid or at least approximately valid, the conclusions from the regression analysis are also valid. But if the assumptions are grossly violated, the regression analysis will probably yield invalid conclusions. Fortunately, all good computer packages that perform regression analysis supply

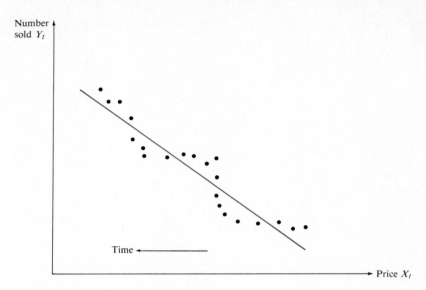

Figure 11.6
Autocorrelated Error Terms

diagnostics for testing the validity of the OLS assumptions. We discuss some of these diagnostics in Chapter 12.

The following example illustrates the type of data we would expect from a population that satisfies the OLS assumptions.

EXAMPLE 11.1

The data in Table 11.2 represent a sample of housing costs and square footages for 75 houses. Here we have selected three specific values of square footage and 25 houses with each of these square footages. For each square footage we calculate estimates of the mean and variance of costs. (These are only estimates because we do not have data on *all* houses with these square footages.)

Looking at the mean housing costs for the three square footages, we see that they lie near the line

$$Y = -70 + 9X$$

as shown in Figure 11.7 (p. 518). (Again, the graph must be expanded to see that the line crosses the Y axis at approximately -70.) The error terms are the vertical distances between the actual points and this regression line. Since the 25 points for any given square footage are approximately sym-

Table 11.2 Housing Costs (in $1000s) for Three Selected Square Footages

Costs for $X = 1400$ Square Feet	Costs for $X = 1700$ Square Feet	Costs for $X = 2000$ Square Feet
52.9	72.9	112.9
60.5	80.3	121.9
64.6	92.5	123.2
66.8	87.6	120.4
60.0	86.7	108.0
51.8	77.1	103.7
58.3	95.1	118.9
55.2	86.3	104.7
72.4	75.1	114.9
55.5	75.4	105.0
66.4	81.9	92.3
71.9	98.4	99.7
47.2	79.3	110.7
60.5	85.4	98.5
53.8	62.7	101.6
46.0	72.7	91.9
32.7	80.7	120.0
57.3	88.1	119.9
55.9	70.7	100.6
40.8	85.7	114.6
43.0	77.8	115.1
55.2	88.2	99.9
74.8	107.8	114.9
54.1	77.9	109.9
46.8	77.1	123.2
Mean: 56.2	82.5	109.9
Std. dev.: 10.2	9.7	9.6

metrically placed on either side of the line, the errors cancel. Thus assumption 1 appears to be satisfied. Assumption 2 also appears to be satisfied because the three variances (shown in the table) are nearly equal. This can also be seen from the scattergram, where the three spreads around the regression line are approximately the same.

Assumption 3 is more difficult to check with only 25 points for each square footage, but the histogram of the 25 costs for any given square footage is probably not nonnormal enough to invalidate the normality assumption. (In a formal test of normality, as we will present in Chapter 13, we would pool all 75 error terms and look at the resulting histogram to test for normality.)

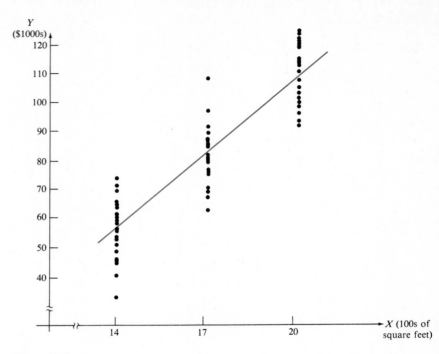

Figure 11.7
Scattergram for Data in Table 11.2

Finally, since these data are cross-sectional data, we have no reason to doubt the validity of assumption 4.

Interpretation of the Regression Coefficients

So far, we have looked at the regression line from a geometric point of view. That is, we have seen how β_0 is the Y intercept and β_1 is the slope. We now consider the economic (or physical) interpretation of these parameters.

The Y intercept β_0 is the mean of all Y values with an X value equal to 0. Therefore, β_0 is what we expect Y to be when X is 0. In some cases this interpretation is meaningful. For example, financial analysts use regression to predict the change in a particular stock's price, Y, from the change in the price, X, of a "market" portfolio of stocks. Since X and Y are both *changes* in price, they may be positive, negative, or zero. Then β_0 is the predicted change in the stock's price if the market's price does not change.

In many other situations, however, this interpretation of β_0 is not meaningful. This occurs when it is physically impossible for X to equal 0. It also occurs when one relationship between X and Y holds for "typical" values of X, but a different relationship holds for X close to 0. In the housing cost versus square footage example, β_0 literally represents the cost of a house with zero square feet. But this is obviously meaningless. First, a house with zero square feet does not exist. Second, we probably built our regression equation from a sample of houses with "typical" square footages, say, from 800 to 2500 square feet. Therefore, it is not valid to assume that the *same* linear relationship holds for square footages outside this range.

The slope parameter β_1 is usually the more important of the two parameters. Although β_0 often has no meaningful interpretation, β_1 always does. Since β_1 is a slope, it measures a rate of change, namely the expected change in Y when X increases by 1 unit. For example, suppose that the true β_1 for the housing cost example is 8. Then if one house is 100 square feet (1 unit of X) larger than another, we expect that the first house will cost \$8000 (8 units of Y) more than the second.

There are two important things to notice about β_1. First, its units are Y units divided by X units. In the example above, Y was measured in \$1000s and X was measured in units of 100 square feet, so β_1 is measured in \$1000s per 100 square feet. If we decided to measure Y in dollars and X in square feet, β_1 would be measured in dollars per square foot. Its value in the example would change from 8 to .8.

Second, the value of β_1 is valid only for the range of X's that we observe in the sample. If the estimate of β_1 is 8 (in \$1000s per 100 square feet), and this estimate is based on a sample of houses with less than 2500 square feet, we cannot say what will happen outside this range. For example, we do not necessarily expect the difference in cost between a 3500-square-foot house and a 3600-square-foot house to be \$8000. These square footages are outside the range of the sample, so the estimated value of β_1 might not be valid for these square footages.

Problems for Section 11.2

1. If X and Y have a positive relationship, what do you expect a scattergram of (X, Y) points to look like? What do you expect it to look like if X and Y have a negative relationship?

2. If the line $Y = 10 - 25X$ appears to fit a scattergram of (X, Y) points, how would you expect Y to change if X increased by 12 units; if X decreased by 6 units? What can you say about the expected value of Y if X is between 30 and 35 units?

3. For the scattergrams on p. 520, how successful are we likely to be in finding a linear relationship between X and Y? Explain.

4. The mean of all Y values in a population, given $X = 30$, is 350. Similarly, the mean of all Y values, given $X = 45$, is 630.

   a. Assuming that a linear regression line fits this population, find the population regression line, that is, find β_0 and β_1.
   b. Use part (a) to find $\mu_{Y|X = 38}$.

5. Suppose that we wish to estimate a regression equation of managers' salaries (Y) versus years of work experience (X). Why might you expect assumption 2 (the constant variance assumption) to be violated?

6. The scattergram on p. 520 shows number of sales of a recently developed product (Y) versus months since the product has been on the market (X). How does this graph indicate that assumption 4 is violated?

7. A regression equation of average miles per gallon (Y) versus engine size (X), measured in cubic inches, turns out to be $Y = 40 - .1X$.

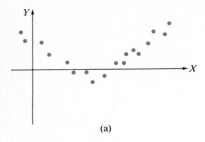

(a)

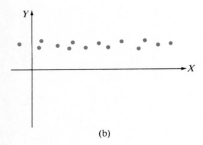

(b)

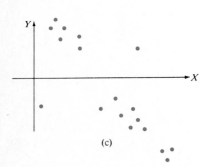

(c)

Scattergrams for Problem 3

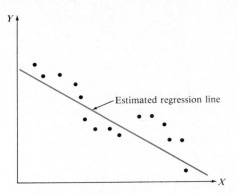

Scattergram for Problem 6

the price of a particular stock reacts to changes in the market index.

a. If the true relationship can be written as $Y_t = \beta_0 + \beta_1 X_t + \epsilon$, how can you interpret the parameters β_0 and β_1? Make sure that your explanations pertain to this particular problem.

b. The true relationship for one stock has $\beta_1 = 1.5$, while for another stock, $\beta_1 = .5$. Discuss the qualitative difference between these two stocks. Which would you classify as the riskier of the two? Why?

9. Suppose that a sample of 150 income tax returns are analyzed by means of regression. The dependent variable Y is the amount of taxes actually paid, and the independent variable X is the gross annual income.

a. Give any reasons you can think of why a linear fit for these data might not be a very good one.

b. If a linear fit were reasonably good, what would be the economic interpretation of the slope β_1 be? Give a range of values where you might expect to find β_1. (Assume that all Y's and X's are measured in dollars.)

c. Why might you expect assumption 2 (the constant variance assumption) to be violated?

10. Consider a population of homes in a given city. Let Y_i be the assessed valuation of home i, and let X_i be the size of the lot it is on.

a. If you saw a scattergram of (X, Y) points, what shape would you expect? Why?

b. Suppose that the relationship between Y and X for the entire population of homes satisfies the four OLS assumptions. If we took a census of all homes in this population, explain what we would find. That is, explain exactly what it means (in this particular context) when we say the OLS assumptions hold.

a. If one car's engine size is 20 cubic inches larger than another's, what relationship do you expect between the average miles per gallon for the two cars?

b. What practical significance do you attach to the Y-intercept value ($\beta_0 = 40$)?

8. Let Y_t be the change in price of a particular company's stock from time period $t - 1$ to time period t, and let X_t be the change in value of a composite market index from time period $t - 1$ to time period t. Financial analysts often attempt to regress Y_t on X_t, that is, estimate a regression equation with Y_t as the dependent variable. This allows them to see how

In this section we examine a method for estimating the regression parameters β_0 and β_1. We assume that a population regression line exists when a sample of (X, Y) points swarm around a straight line. However, there may be quite a few lines that appear to fit the scattergram equally well. Which do we choose?

This is an estimation problem quite different from any we have seen so far. In earlier chapters we learned how to estimate μ, p, and other population parameters. In each case there were "natural" estimates, such as the sample mean and the sample proportion. Now there are no natural estimates of β_0 and β_1, so we will develop a method for finding them. This method is called the *method of least squares*.

Recall that the regression equation for the *i*th observation is

$$Y_i = \beta_0 + \beta_1 X_i + \epsilon_i$$

Here the error term ϵ_i is the vertical distance from the observed Y_i value to the population regression line (see Figure 11.8). Since we do not know the true values of β_0 and β_1, we cannot calculate the value of ϵ_i. However, we can estimate it as follows.

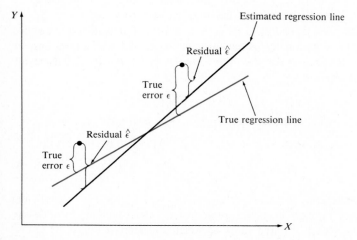

Figure 11.8
Difference Between True Errors and Residuals

Suppose that we choose $\hat{\beta}_0$ and $\hat{\beta}_1$ as estimates of β_0 and β_1. Then the *estimated* regression equation is given below.

Estimated Regression Equation

$$\hat{Y}_i = \hat{\beta}_0 + \hat{\beta}_1 X_i$$

Here $\hat{Y}_i$ is the estimated value of Y_i, based on the estimated regression equation.

In general, $\hat{Y}_i$ does not equal Y_i. There are two reasons for this. First, we calculate $\hat{Y}_i$ from the estimated, not the true, regression equation. Second, even if we knew β_0 and β_1, we could still not predict Y_i with certainty because of the unknown error term. The difference between the observed value Y_i and its estimate $\hat{Y}_i$ is called the *residual* and is labeled $\hat{\epsilon}_i$.

Equation for the Residual

$$\hat{\epsilon}_i = Y_i - \hat{Y}_i$$

Geometrically, the residuals are the vertical distances between the observed points and the *estimated* regression line, as shown in Figure 11.8. Notice from the figure how the "true" error term ϵ_i differs from the residual $\hat{\epsilon}_i$. The true error term is the distance between the point and the population regression line, which is unobservable. The residual, on the other hand, is the distance between the point and the estimated regression line.

It is intuitively clear that a line provides a good fit to the sample data if it results in small residuals. This is the idea we use to find $\hat{\beta}_0$ and $\hat{\beta}_1$. In particular, we choose $\hat{\beta}_0$ and $\hat{\beta}_1$ to minimize the sum of the squared residuals, $\Sigma \hat{\epsilon}_i^2$. For readers with a calculus background, Appendix 11A shows how to perform the minimization and how the formulas below for $\hat{\beta}_0$ and $\hat{\beta}_1$ result from this minimization.

Criterion for Choosing the OLS Estimates

$\hat{\beta}_0$ and $\hat{\beta}_1$ are chosen to minimize $\Sigma \hat{\epsilon}_i^2$, the sum of the squared residuals.

Before presenting the formulas for $\hat{\beta}_0$ and $\hat{\beta}_1$, we develop a bit of notation that will be used throughout this chapter. In fact, almost all the formulas in this chapter are based on three sums of squares and cross products. These are:

$SS_{XX} = \sum (X_i - \overline{X})^2$ = sum of squared deviations of X's from their mean
$SS_{YY} = \sum (Y_i - \overline{Y})^2$ = sum of squared deviations of Y's from their mean
$SS_{XY} = \sum (X_i - \overline{X})(Y_i - \overline{Y})$ = sum of cross-products of deviations from means

The simplest way to find SS_{XX}, SS_{YY}, and SS_{XY}, given the sample data (X_1, Y_1), (X_2, Y_2), . . . , (X_n, Y_n), is as follows. First we find five "preliminary" sums from the raw data:

$$\begin{array}{ccc} \sum X_i, \ \sum Y_i & \sum X_i^2, \ \sum Y_i^2 & \sum X_iY_i \\ \text{sums of data} & \text{sums of squares} & \text{sum of cross-products} \end{array}$$

Then the computational formulas for SS_{XX}, SS_{YY}, and SS_{XY} are

$$SS_{XX} = \sum X_i^2 - \frac{(\sum X_i)^2}{n}$$

$$SS_{YY} = \sum Y_i^2 - \frac{(\sum Y_i)^2}{n}$$

$$SS_{XY} = \sum X_iY_i - \frac{(\sum X_i)(\sum Y_i)}{n}$$

The sum of squared deviations SS_{XX} measures the amount of variation of the X's in the sample. In fact, there is a very simple relationship between the sample variance of the X's, s_X^2, and SS_{XX}:

$$s_X^2 = \frac{SS_{XX}}{n - 1}$$

Similarly, SS_{YY} measures the amount of variation of the Y's in the sample. It is related to the sample variance of the Y's by

$$s_Y^2 = \frac{SS_{YY}}{n - 1}$$

Finally, the sum of cross-products SS_{XY} measures the amount of "covariation" between the X's and Y's in the sample. It is related to the sample covariance, s_{XY}, by

$$s_{XY} = \frac{SS_{XY}}{n - 1}$$

If the magnitude of SS_{XY} is large (relative to SS_{XX} and SS_{YY}), X and Y tend to have a strong linear relationship. If the magnitude of SS_{XY} is relatively small, X and Y tend to have no linear relationship, and it is doubtful that regression analysis will be very useful.

The formulas for the OLS estimates $\hat{\beta}_0$ and $\hat{\beta}_1$ can now be given very compactly. (SS_{YY} is not needed in these particular formulas, but it will be used later.)

Formulas for Estimated Regression Coefficients

$$\hat{\beta}_1 = \frac{SS_{XY}}{SS_{XX}}$$

$$\hat{\beta}_0 = \overline{Y} - \hat{\beta}_1\overline{X}$$

We first find $\hat{\beta}_1$ as the ratio of SS_{XY} to SS_{XX}. Then we find $\hat{\beta}_0$ by using $\hat{\beta}_1$ and the sample means of the X's and Y's.

From the equation for $\hat{\beta}_0$, notice that

$$\overline{Y} = \hat{\beta}_0 + \hat{\beta}_1\overline{X}$$

This says that the regression line passes through the point $(\overline{X}, \overline{Y})$ whose coordinates are the sample means.

EXAMPLE 11.2

For the housing cost data listed in Table 11.1, find the sums of squares and cross-products SS_{XX}, SS_{YY}, and SS_{XY}. Then find the OLS estimates $\hat{\beta}_0$ and $\hat{\beta}_1$.

SOLUTION

We first find the five preliminary sums from the raw data. These are shown in Table 11.3.

From the sums in Table 11.3, we obtain

$$SS_{YY} = \sum Y_i^2 - \frac{(\sum Y_i)^2}{n} = 100{,}744.62 - \frac{1197.55^2}{15} = 5136.22$$

$$SS_{XX} = \sum X_i^2 - \frac{(\sum X_i)^2}{n} = 4793.4 - \frac{266.2^2}{15} = 69.24$$

$$SS_{XY} = \sum X_iY_i - \frac{(\sum X_i)(\sum Y_i)}{n} = 21{,}802.3 - \frac{266.2(1197.55)}{15} = 549.78$$

Finally, we have

$$\hat{\beta}_1 = \frac{SS_{XY}}{SS_{XX}} = \frac{549.78}{69.24} = 7.940$$

Table 11.3 Worksheet for Housing Cost Example

Y	X	X^2	Y^2	XY
75.90	17.5	306.25	5,760.81	1,328.25
61.00	15.9	252.81	3,721.00	969.90
110.00	21.0	441.00	12,100.00	2,310.00
83.50	18.0	324.00	6,972.25	1,503.00
94.60	18.9	357.21	8,949.16	1,787.94
54.50	13.6	184.96	2,970.25	741.20
96.00	20.5	420.25	9,216.00	1,968.00
70.70	17.6	309.76	4,998.49	1,244.32
50.75	15.0	225.00	2,575.56	761.25
69.40	16.5	272.25	4,816.36	1,145.10
87.50	17.0	289.00	7,656.25	1,487.50
105.00	19.2	368.64	11,025.00	2,016.00
76.50	18.0	324.00	5,852.25	1,377.00
103.20	21.5	462.25	10,650.24	2,218.80
59.00	16.0	256.00	3,481.00	944.00
Sum: 1,197.55	266.2	4,793.38	100,744.62	21,802.26

and

$$\hat{\beta}_0 = \bar{Y} - \hat{\beta}_1\bar{X} = \frac{1197.55}{15} - 7.940\left(\frac{266.2}{15}\right) = -61.072$$

Therefore, the estimated regression line is

$$\hat{Y} = -61.072 + 7.940X$$

The positive value of $\hat{\beta}_1$ confirms that as square footage increases, so does the cost of a house. In fact, we estimate that the cost increase for a house with 100 extra square feet is $\hat{\beta}_1 = 7.940$, or \$7940. (The negative value of $\hat{\beta}_0$ has no real significance because an X value equal to 0 is physically impossible.)

EXAMPLE 11.3

A study of middle- to upper-level managers is undertaken to investigate the relationship between salary level and years of work experience. A random sample of 20 managers is chosen, with the results given in Table 11.4 (p. 526). Do these data indicate that salary is linearly related to years of work experience? If so, find the estimated regression equation.

Table 11.4 Worksheet for Salary Example

Salary Y ($1000s)	Years of Experience X	X^2	Y^2	XY
29.5	7	49	870.25	206.5
33.7	10	100	1,135.69	337.0
25.2	5	25	635.04	126.0
41.6	12	144	1,730.56	499.2
52.8	15	225	2,787.84	792.0
43.0	9	81	1,849.00	387.0
37.2	12	144	1,383.84	446.4
26.1	8	64	681.21	208.8
41.3	9	81	1,705.69	371.7
29.5	10	100	870.25	295.0
22.4	5	25	501.76	112.0
55.7	25	625	3,102.49	1,392.5
61.2	18	324	3,745.44	1,101.6
41.3	15	225	1,705.69	619.5
28.5	12	144	812.25	342.0
35.4	10	100	1,253.16	354.0
27.3	6	36	745.29	163.8
50.5	19	361	2,550.25	959.5
43.1	15	225	1,857.61	646.5
38.5	13	169	1,482.25	500.5
Sum: 763.8	235	3,247	31,405.56	9,861.5

SOLUTION

The scattergram shown in Figure 11.9 shows that salaries tend to increase as years of work experience increase, and that a linear relationship between these variables is certainly plausible. We notice that the managers in the sample are somewhat limited in that their years of experience vary between 5 and 25 years. Therefore, any linear relationship we find is valid only for this range.

For the data in Table 11.4, we calculate the five preliminary sums to be $\Sigma X_i = 235$, $\Sigma Y_i = 763.8$, $\Sigma X_i^2 = 3247$, $\Sigma Y_i^2 = 31,405.56$, and $\Sigma X_i Y_i = 9861.5$. (These calculations are shown in Table 11.4.) From these sums, we find

$$SS_{XX} = 485.75 \qquad SS_{YY} = 2236.1 \qquad SS_{XY} = 886.85$$

Finally, the estimates of the slope and Y intercept are

$$\hat{\beta}_1 = \frac{886.85}{485.75} = 1.826$$

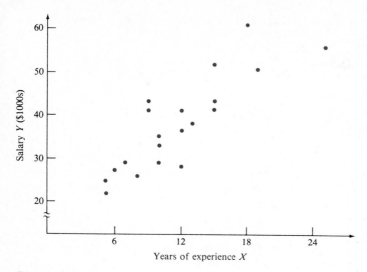

Figure 11.9
Scattergram for Salary Data

and

$$\hat{\beta}_0 = \frac{763.8}{20} - 1.826\left(\frac{235}{20}\right) = 16.735$$

Therefore, the estimated regression equation is

$$\hat{Y} = 16.735 + 1.826X$$

Again, the $\hat{\beta}_0$ value is probably not meaningful. We might expect it to indicate the salary of a typical manager with zero work experience. But no managers in the sample have zero work experience, so we would be going beyond the range of the sample if we interpreted $\hat{\beta}_0$ in this way. On the other hand, $\hat{\beta}_1$ has a very meaningful interpretation. For every extra year of experience, a manager can expect to earn an extra $\hat{\beta}_1$, or \$1826, of salary. Alternatively, if manager *A* has one more year of work experience than manager *B*, we expect manager *A* to earn \$1826 more than manager *B*.

In this section we have not really done any statistical *inference*. We have merely fitted a line to a scattergram of points by an optimization method called least squares. However, the fitted line is not likely to be the true line. After all, the true line is based on an entire population, and we see only a sample of this population. In the following sections we see how to estimate the size of the errors we make when we use the fitted line to make statistical inferences.

11.4

Estimation of the Error Variance

The key to statistical inference in regression analysis is the error variance σ_e^2. Recall that this variance measures the variability of the errors around their mean of 0. Alternatively, σ_e^2 measures the variability of the Y's around the population regression line.

As usual, it is somewhat easier to interpret the standard deviation σ_e because it is measured in the same units as the dependent variable Y. The intuitive meaning of σ_e is as follows. Suppose that we know the true values of β_0 and β_1. Then the expected value of Y is $\beta_0 + \beta_1 X$. But an individual observation differs from this expected value by a random amount ϵ that has standard deviation σ_e. From the usual normal approximation (see Rule 4.2), the probability is approximately .68 that this random error will have magnitude less than σ_e, and the probability is approximately .95 that its magnitude will be less than $2\sigma_e$. In other words, we expect about 68% of the observed Y's to be within one σ_e of the regression line, and we expect about 95% of them to be within two σ_e's of the regression line. This is illustrated in Figure 11.10.

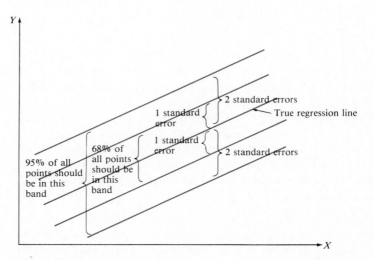

Figure 11.10
Geometric Meaning of the Standard Error of Estimate

Unfortunately, σ_e is an unknown population parameter. Like β_0 and β_1, its value must be estimated from the sample data. Since σ_e^2 is the variance of the errors, we estimate it from the observed residuals. The appropriate formula for this estimate, labeled s_e^2, is shown below.

Estimate of σ_e^2

$$s_e^2 = \frac{\Sigma \text{ squared residuals}}{n-2} = \frac{\Sigma \hat{\epsilon}_i^2}{n-2} = \frac{\Sigma (Y_i - \hat{Y}_i)^2}{n-2}$$

This estimate is not quite an *average* of the squared residuals because we divide by $n - 2$, not n. The reason for the $n - 2$ is that we lose 2 degrees of freedom when we estimate β_0 and β_1. Also, this denominator makes s_e^2 an unbiased estimate of σ_e^2.

The square root of s_e^2 is called the *standard error of estimate*. If s_e is small, then $\hat{Y}_i$ (the estimated value) is likely to be close to Y_i (the observed value). If s_e is large, $\hat{Y}_i$ is likely to be quite far from Y_i. As a rule of thumb, we expect about 95% of the $\hat{Y}$'s to be within 2 standard errors of the corresponding Y's.

The formula for s_e^2 above is not very convenient for hand calculation. A much easier way is as follows. Let SSE stand for sum of squared errors:

$$SSE = \sum (Y_i - \hat{Y}_i)^2$$

It has the following computational formula.

Computational Formula for SSE

$$SSE = SS_{YY} - \hat{\beta}_1 SS_{XY}$$

Then the standard error of estimate s_e follows directly from SSE.

Standard Error of Estimate

$$s_e = \sqrt{\frac{SSE}{n-2}}$$

EXAMPLE 11.2 (continued)

For the housing cost data in Table 11.1, find the standard error of estimate. Then determine how many of the $\hat{Y}$'s are within 1 or 2 standard errors of the corresponding Y's.

Table 11.5

Y	Estimated Y	Residual
75.90	77.88	−1.98
61.00	65.17	−4.17
110.00	105.67	4.33
83.50	81.85	1.65
94.60	88.99	5.61
54.50	46.91	7.59
96.00	101.70	−5.70
70.70	78.67	−7.97*
50.75	58.03	−7.28
69.40	69.94	−0.54
87.50	73.91	13.59*
105.00	91.38	13.62*
76.50	81.85	−5.35
103.20	109.64	−6.44
59.00	65.97	−6.97

*Between 1 and 2 standard errors (s_e = 7.70) in magnitude.

SOLUTION

For these data we found that $\hat{\beta}_1 = 7.940$, $SS_{XY} = 549.78$, and $SS_{YY} = 5136.22$. Using the computational formula for SSE, we have

$$SSE = SS_{YY} - \hat{\beta}_1 SS_{XY} = 5136.22 - 7.940(549.78) = 770.97$$

This leads directly to the standard error s_e:

$$s_e = \sqrt{\frac{SSE}{(n-2)}} = \sqrt{\frac{770.97}{13}} = 7.700$$

Since housing costs are measured in $1000s, the value of s_e should be interpreted as $7700. The interpretation of this value is that it measures the magnitude of the expected differences between the $\hat{Y}$'s and the Y's. In particular, about 68% of the $\hat{Y}$'s should be within $7700 of the corresponding Y's, and about 95% of the $\hat{Y}$'s should be within $15,400 of the corresponding Y's.

We illustrate this in Table 11.5 and Figure 11.11. In Table 11.5 we list the estimated housing costs (the $\hat{Y}$'s) next to the observed costs. Each $\hat{Y}$ is

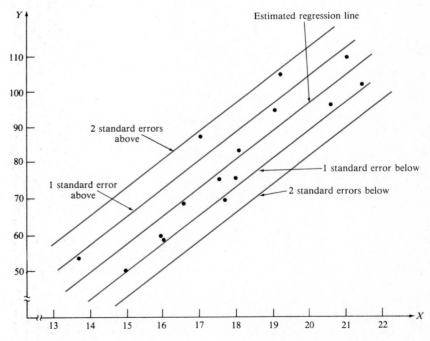

Figure 11.11

found by plugging the appropriate square footage X into the estimated regression equation. For each observation we list the residual, $\hat{\epsilon} = Y - \hat{Y}$. Notice that only 3 of the 15 residuals are larger in absolute value than 1 standard error, and none are larger than 2 standard errors. This is not quite what we expected from the rule of thumb, but it is fairly close, especially for such a small sample size. Figure 11.11 shows these results graphically. Here we see that 12 of 15 points lie within a band that extends 1 standard error on either side of the regression line. The other three points lie in the next band, which extends 2 standard errors beyond the regression line. No points lie beyond this second band.

11.5

Measures of the Goodness of a Linear Fit

In this section we present two related measures of the strength of the linear relationship between the independent and dependent variables. The formulas for $\hat{\beta}_0$ and $\hat{\beta}_1$ allow us to fit a linear equation through *any* set of points. However, the "fit" may be a very poor one if the variables are not linearly related. The measures in this section show us numerically what a scattergram shows us geometrically. Intuitively, these measures indicate whether any linear equation can be successful in predicting the dependent variable Y from the independent variable X.

The Correlation Coefficient

We first discuss the role of correlation in regression analysis. As we have seen in Chapters 2 and 4, a correlation is a number between -1 and $+1$ that measures the relationship between two variables X and Y. Specifically, in regression analysis it measures the presence or absence of a *linear* relationship between the independent and dependent variables. The correlation measures how tightly the points in a scattergram cluster around a straight line. If they do cluster tightly around some line, the magnitude (absolute value) of the correlation is close to 1. If they do not, the correlation is close to 0.

When we talk about a "high" correlation, we mean that the correlation is close to -1 or to $+1$. If it is close to -1, the variables vary negatively, that is, in opposite directions; if it is close to $+1$, the variables vary positively. For example, we would expect a large *negative* correlation between demand and price, since demand tends to decrease as price increases, and vice versa. However, we would expect a large *positive* correlation between the demand for peanut butter and the demand for jelly, because many people tend to buy both or neither.

If the correlation between two variables is near 0, all we can conclude is that these variables are not *linearly* related. In most cases this means that there is no relationship between the variables, so that the scattergram is a shapeless swarm of points, as in Figure 11.12a. However, it is possible that two variables with a near-zero correlation are related nonlinearly, as in Figure 11.12b. Although this is somewhat unusual, it can happen. Therefore, we should always examine a scattergram before concluding that there is no relationship between variables with a low correlation; they could be related nonlinearly.

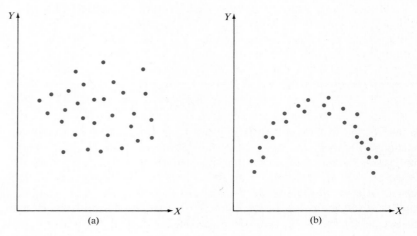

Figure 11.12
Two Types of Scattergrams That Exhibit Zero Correlation

The population correlation between two variables X and Y is usually labeled ρ (the Greek letter "rho"). Like the mean μ and the variance σ^2, ρ is a parameter that cannot be calculated unless the entire population is sampled. Therefore, we calculate an estimate of ρ, labeled r, from the available sample data. (If there are more than two variables under discussion, we often subscript ρ or r by a particular pair of variables. For example, r_{XY} is the correlation between X and Y, r_{XZ} is the correlation between X and Z, and so on. We omit these subscripts when there is no chance for confusion.)

The formula for r is given below. (This formula is equivalent to the formula given in Chapter 2.)

Formula for Correlation

$$r = \frac{SS_{XY}}{\sqrt{SS_{XX}SS_{YY}}}$$

As an example, the correlation between housing costs and square footages in Example 11.2 is

$$r = \frac{SS_{XY}}{\sqrt{SS_{XX}SS_{YY}}} = \frac{549.78}{\sqrt{69.24(5136.22)}} = .922$$

This high number indicates a fairly strong linear relationship between the housing costs and square footages in this sample.

The only time that r can equal -1 or $+1$ is when there is an *exact* linear relationship between X and Y. In this case all the (X, Y) points in the scattergram lie on a single straight line. For example, if X is temperature in Celsius degrees and Y is temperature in Fahrenheit degrees, then the relationship between Y and X is $Y = (\%_5)X + 32$, and the correlation between X and Y is 1. But for variables where there is no exact relationship, the best we can obtain is an r close to -1 or $+1$. How close is "close"? Is $r = .75$ a "high" correlation? What about $-.65$? Usually, it is up to the investigator to decide which correlations are sufficiently large. However, in the next subsection we give an intuitive meaning to the *square* of r which does shed some light on this issue.

One important property of the correlation is that it is unaffected by rescaling the data or adding a constant to each observation. To illustrate this property, recall from the housing cost example that Y is measured in \$1000s and X is measured in units of 100s of square feet. Now suppose that we multiply each Y by 1000 and each X by 100. Then the costs are measured in dollars, and the square footages are measured in square feet. However, the correlation between the variables does not change; it is still .922.

We saw above that the correlation measures the strength of the linear relationship between two variables. In this section we look at another measure that indicates the strength of the linear relationship between two variables. This measure is called the *coefficient of determination*. Although the coefficient of determination turns out to be nothing more than the square of the correlation (for *simple* linear regression), its derivation lends some valuable insight into the subject. Furthermore, the coefficient of determination carries over to *multiple* regression somewhat more naturally than correlation.

The Coefficient of Determination: r^2

Let's return to the data on housing costs once again. These costs vary around the sample mean housing cost, $\overline{Y}$. How can we explain this variation? Is it purely random variation, or is there a natural way of explaining it? A look at the graph in Figure 11.13 (p. 534) gives us a clue. For any particular observation, the difference between Y_i and the mean $\overline{Y}$ is $Y_i - \overline{Y}$. Part of this difference is expected once we look at the square footage of the house. If the house has a large square footage, we do not expect Y_i to equal $\overline{Y}$; we expect it to be considerably larger than $\overline{Y}$. On the other side, if the house has a small square footage, we expect Y_i to be smaller than $\overline{Y}$. Only for houses with average square footages do we expect Y_i to be close to $\overline{Y}$.

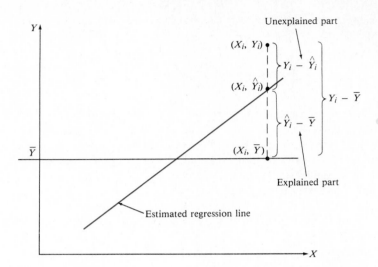

Figure 11.13

The estimated regression line clarifies this idea. If we are given the square footage X_i, we do not expect Y_i to equal $\overline{Y}$; we expect it to equal $\hat{Y}_i$, the estimated cost. Thus part of the difference $Y_i - \overline{Y}$ is explained by the fact that different houses have different square footages. The explained part of this difference, as shown in the figure, is $\hat{Y}_i - \overline{Y}$. The part left unexplained is the difference $Y_i - \hat{Y}_i$. This is the random residual that square footage alone cannot account for.

Now it is obvious, either from algebra or from the graph in Figure 11.13, that for each observation, we have

$$Y_i - \overline{Y} = (Y_i - \hat{Y}_i) + (\hat{Y}_i - \overline{Y})$$

By summing over all observations, we obtain

$$\sum (Y_i - \overline{Y}) = \sum (Y_i - \hat{Y}_i) + \sum (\hat{Y}_i - \overline{Y})$$

This equation is almost what we want, but not quite. Although it is not immediately obvious, it can be shown that

$$\sum (Y_i - \overline{Y})^2 = \sum (Y_i - \hat{Y}_i)^2 + \sum (\hat{Y}_i - \overline{Y})^2$$

From left to right, these three summations are called the *total variation,* the *unexplained variation,* and the *explained variation.* Therefore, this formula separates the total variation into two parts, an explained part and an unexplained part.

We have seen two of these sums of squares before. The total variation, $\Sigma \, (Y_i - \overline{Y})^2$, is simply SS_{YY}. We will also denote this sum by SST, for sum of squares total.

$$SST = \text{total variation} = \sum (Y_i - \overline{Y})^2 = SS_{YY}$$

The unexplained variation, $\Sigma \, (Y_i - \hat{Y}_i)^2$, is the sum of squared errors, SSE. This is the sum we minimized to find the OLS estimators $\hat{\beta}_0$ and $\hat{\beta}_1$. (We also saw this sum when we estimated σ_e^2.)

$$SSE = \text{unexplained variation} = \sum (Y_i - \hat{Y}_i)^2$$

Finally, the explained variation, $\Sigma \, (\hat{Y}_i - \overline{Y})^2$, is a new quantity. We denote this sum by SSR, for sum of squares due to regression.

$$SSR = \text{explained variation} = \sum (\hat{Y}_i - \overline{Y})^2$$

Using the SS notation, the equation relating SST, SSE, and SSR is simply

$$SST = SSE + SSR$$

If X and Y are linearly related, the regression line should explain a large percentage of the total variation of the Y's. If X and Y are not linearly related, the fitted regression line will probably explain very little of the total variation. So to measure the relationship between X and Y, we calculate the *fraction* of total variation explained by the regression. This fraction is labeled r^2 and is called the coefficient of determination.

Formula for Coefficient of Determination (r^2)

$$r^2 = \frac{SSR}{SST}$$

Alternatively, $r^2 = 1 - \dfrac{SSE}{SST}$

To find r^2 numerically, we need SST and SSR (or SSE). A convenient computational procedure is as follows. First, find SST by the computing formula for SS_{YY}. Next, find SSR from the fact that $SSR = \hat{\beta}_1 SS_{XY}$. (This fact requires proof, but we omit it here.) Since $\hat{\beta}_1 = SS_{XY}/SS_{XX}$, we may also write $SSR = (SS_{XY})^2/SS_{XX}$. Finally, calculate SSE by subtraction: $SSE = SST - SSR$.

> *Computational Procedure for SST, SSR, and SSE*
>
> $$SST = SS_{YY}$$
>
> $$SSR = \frac{(SS_{XY})^2}{SS_{XX}}$$
>
> $$SSE = SST - SSR$$

There is a good reason for denoting the coefficient of determination by r^2. It turns out that r^2 is the square of the correlation between X and Y. Since $SSR = (SS_{XY})^2/SS_{XX}$ and $SST = SS_{YY}$, we have

$$r^2 = \frac{SSR}{SST} = \frac{(SS_{XY})^2/SS_{XX}}{SS_{YY}} = \frac{SS_{XY}^2}{SS_{XX}SS_{YY}}$$

and the latter expression is the square of the formula for r. Thus we have an arithmetic check for r^2. We can either calculate r^2 as SSR/SST, or we can find r from the formula for correlation and then square it. Aside from rounding error, the two answers should be the same.

EXAMPLE 11.3 (continued)

For the salary data in Table 11.4, find the percentage of total variation of salaries that can be explained by years of experience.

SOLUTION

From previous calculations we have $SS_{XX} = 485.75$, $SS_{YY} = 2236.1$, and $SS_{XY} = 886.85$. Therefore,

$$SST = SS_{YY} = 2236.1$$

$$SSR = \frac{(SS_{XY})^2}{SS_{XX}} = \frac{886.85^2}{485.75} = 1619.2$$

and

$$r^2 = \frac{SSR}{SST} = \frac{1619.2}{2236.1} = .724$$

This says that 72.4% of the total variation of salaries is explained by years of experience. Alternatively, a fraction SSE/SST = .276, or 27.6%, of the variation is left unexplained. Notice that the correlation between salaries and years of experience is the square root of .724, or .851.

Because r^2 is the square of a correlation, the magnitude of r^2 is *less* than the magnitude of r. For example, if $r = \pm.8$, then $r^2 = .64$; if $r = \pm.3$, then $r^2 = .09$. So to obtain a high r^2 value, we must obtain an even higher correlation. To explain 64% of the total variation, for instance, the correlation must be $\pm.8$; to explain 90% of the total variation, the correlation must be $\pm\sqrt{.9} = \pm.949$. So unless the independent and dependent variables are highly correlated, we cannot expect the regression line to explain a large percentage of the total variation.

Again we may ask how large is "large." Is the regression line doing a good job if it explains 85% of the total variation? What about 65%? As with correlations, no exact guidelines can be given. Most investigators hope to get an r^2 value of .8 or above, but they are often forced to settle for an r^2 value of .5 or below. Even in the latter case, however, they are not entirely unsuccessful. Although an r^2 of .5 means that 50% of the variation has been left unexplained, it also means that the regression line has been able to explain the other 50%.

A Test for Goodness of Fit:
The ANOVA Table

In regression analysis we are attempting to see whether one or more independent variables can explain at least a fraction of the total variation of the dependent variable. If this fraction is greater than zero, we know that the independent variable or variables have *some* explanatory power. Of course, all we see is a sample of the population. So it is possible that this sample will indicate a linear relationship even when there is no such relationship in the total population. In terms of r^2, we may observe a moderately large r^2 value when in fact the population version of r^2, namely ρ^2, is close to 0. In this section we present a method for testing whether there is any *statistically significant* linear relationship exhibited by the sample data.

The hypotheses for this test may be stated in terms of β_1. The null hypothesis is essentially that the independent variable has no explanatory power whatsoever. This is equivalent to stating that β_1 is 0. The reason is that if β_1 is 0, the regression line is horizontal, and we will predict the *same* value of Y regardless of the value of X. The alternative hypothesis is that β_1 does not equal 0.

Hypotheses for the Presence of a Linear Relationship

$$H_0: \beta_1 = 0 \quad \text{versus} \quad H_a: \beta_1 \neq 0$$

We use an F test to test these hypotheses. Basically, we want to see whether the explained part of the total variation, SSR, is large in comparison to the unexplained part, SSE. When it is, we will tend to reject H_0 and conclude that there is at least some linear relationship between X and Y. Each of the sums of squares has an associated degrees of freedom parameter. For SSR, the degrees of freedom is 1, and for SSE, the degrees of freedom is

$n - 2$. To calculate the F statistic used in the test, we form a ratio of these sums of squares, each divided by its degrees of freedom.

As in Chapter 10, when we divide a sum of squares by its degrees of freedom, we call the ratio a *mean square*. Therefore, $SSE/(n - 2)$ is called the mean-squared error and is labeled MSE, while $SSR/1$ is called the mean square for the regression and is labeled MSR. The F ratio formed by dividing these mean squares is

$$F = \frac{SSR/1}{SSE/(n - 2)}$$

When the null hypothesis is true, this ratio has an F distribution with 1 and $n - 2$ degrees of freedom. In this case each mean square, MSE and MSR, is an unbiased estimate of the error variance σ_e^2, so that we expect F to be fairly close to 1. But when the alternative hypothesis is true, MSR will generally be larger than MSE, and we will tend to see an F ratio well out in the right-hand tail of this F distribution. Therefore, the test is performed as follows (see Figure 11.14).

Test for Significance of a Linear Relationship

Reject H_0 at the α level if $F > F_{\alpha, 1, n-2}$.

Usually, the ingredients for this test are summarized in an *analysis of variance* (ANOVA) table. Exactly as in Chapter 10, this table lists the sums

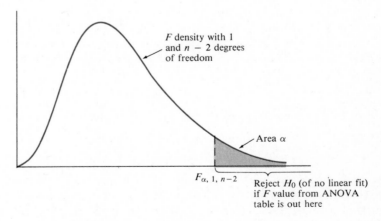

Figure 11.14
F Test for a Significant Linear Fit

of squares, the degrees of freedom, the mean squares, and finally the F ratio. The typical form of an ANOVA table is shown in Table 11.6.

Table 11.6 Typical ANOVA Table for Simple Regression*

Source	SS	df	MS	F
Regression	SSR	1	$MSR = SSR/1$	MSR/MSE
Error	SSE	$n - 2$	$MSE = SSE/(n - 2)$	

*The ''total'' row shown in Chapter 10 is usually omitted in an ANOVA table for regression.

EXAMPLE 11.3 (continued)

For the salary data in Table 11.4, test the significance of the linear relationship between salaries and years of experience by using an F test. Use a 5% significance level.

SOLUTION

From previous calculations we have SSR $= 1619.2$ and SSE $= 616.9$. Then the ANOVA table follows easily and is shown in Table 11.7.

Table 11.7 ANOVA Table for Salary Example

Source	SS	df	MS	F
Regression	1619.2	1	$1619.2/1 = 1619.2$	$1619.2/34.27 = 47.2$
Error	616.9	18	$616.9/18 = 34.27$	

Strictly speaking, we should compare 47.2 with the tabulated F value with 1 and 18 degrees of freedom. This is $F_{.05,1,18} = 4.41$. A quick glance at the F table, however, shows that most of the F values are between 1 and 5. Therefore, an observed F ratio of 47.2 is extremely far out in the tail, and H_0 can be rejected at *any* reasonable significance level. We point this out because F ratios in regression are often extremely large, so that no table lookup is required. In this example there is no doubt that years of experience does have some explanatory power for predicting salaries.

Problems for Sections 11.3, 11.4, 11.5

11. The following seven pairs of X's and Y's are observed.

X	Y
125	160
85	130
105	165
90	115
75	95
145	175
120	145

a. Draw a scattergram of these data. Does a linear fit appear plausible? What do you believe the sign of β_1 will be, negative or positive?

b. Find the sums SS_{XX}, SS_{YY}, and SS_{XY} for these data, and use them to estimate the regression equation relating Y to X.

c. Does the estimated regression line appear to fit the points in the scattergram adequately? Answer by superimposing it on the scattergram from part (a).

12. From the answer to Problem 11, part (b), calculate $\hat{Y}_i$ and $\hat{\epsilon}_i$ for each of the seven observations. Then find the sum of the squared residuals. Could this sum be made any smaller by choosing different values of $\hat{\beta}_0$ and/or $\hat{\beta}_1$? Explain.

13. Find SSE, s_e^2, and s_e for the data in Problem 11 from the formulas in the text. Then use the answer from Problem 12 to check your results.

14. A regression analysis is run on a sample of 25 X's and Y's and it is found that 20 of the 25 resulting residuals are less than 15 units in magnitude. What does this tell you about the approximate magnitude of the standard error s_e? Why?

15. The following data represent the numbers of sales (Y) of various brands of men's shirts versus the prices (X) of these for a given week at a local department store.

Price	Number Sold
$17.50	332
17.25	405
16.50	330
20.00	312
14.75	434
17.00	310 (*continued*)

Price	Number Sold
18.75	331
16.50	404
18.25	324
19.00	341
17.75	379
16.75	356
14.50	383
20.50	284

a. Draw a scattergram of these data.

b. Find the correlation between number of shirts sold and their price. Does the value of this correlation appear to correspond to the scattergram? Explain.

16. Consider the following set of X's and Y's.

X	Y
24	37
33	41
54	76
12	25
43	51
37	47
57	71
14	30

a. Find the correlation between the X's and the Y's.

b. Transform each X value to a W by the formula $W = -3 + 2X$. Transform each Y value to a Z by the formula $Z = 6 + 3Y$. Then find the correlation between the W's and the Z's directly from the formula for correlation. Compare this correlation with the one found in part (a). They should be equal. Why?

17. For the data in Problem 15, find the estimated regression equation and use it to calculate each $\hat{Y}_i$. Next, calculate the sums $\Sigma (Y_i - \bar{Y})^2$, $\Sigma (Y_i - \hat{Y}_i)^2$, and $\Sigma (\hat{Y}_i - \bar{Y})^2$ directly (not from the formulas given in the text). Verify that SST = SSR + SSE. Finally, check that the computational formulas for SST, SSR, and SSE given in the text give you the same results.

18. Again using the data in Problem 15, what percentage of the total variation in men's shirts sales can be explained by price?

Is the percentage you found a sample statistic or a population parameter? Explain.

19. Suppose that a regression equation of Y versus X is able to explain 76.8% of the total variation of the Y's in the sample from their mean $\overline{Y}$. What is the magnitude of the correlation between the X's and the Y's? Can you tell whether this correlation is positive or negative? Why or why not?

20. Explain why $\rho = 0$ is equivalent to $\beta_1 = 0$. That is, if the population correlation ρ between the Y's and the X's is 0, why is the slope of the regression line equal to 0, and vice versa? If we know that both of these are 0, why will a knowledge of X be worthless in terms of predicting Y?

21. Which entry in the ANOVA table is the square of the standard error of estimate, s_e? Which population parameter is this entry an estimate of?

22. Fill in the ANOVA table for the data given in Problem 15. Test the significance of a linear relationship between shirt sales and price at the 10% level. In words, what is your conclusion?

23. A sample of 15 houses produces the following data on price and square footage.

Square Feet (100s)	Price ($1000s)
15.79	61.800
15.73	75.940
15.08	53.800
18.04	78.550
13.72	74.670
15.66	53.350
16.87	72.700
15.15	79.300
16.60	67.560
17.16	79.100
16.20	81.460
15.42	66.000
13.62	56.810
18.35	82.500
14.52	59.110

a. Fit a least squares regression line to these data.
b. Pool these data with the data in Table 11.1 of the text to obtain one large data set. Fit a least squares regression line to this combined data set. (Make use of earlier calculations as much as possible.)

24. For each part of Problem 23, compute the standard error of estimate s_e, the r^2 value, and the ANOVA table. Which data set, the one given in Problem 23 or the combined set, has the most significant F value? (Why can't you answer this question just by comparing the magnitudes of the F's?)

25. Why would you expect s_e, the standard error of estimate, to be less than s_Y, the standard error (or sample standard deviation) of the Y's? How could you use the information in the ANOVA table to obtain the ratio of s_e to s_Y?

26. A marketing manager is interested in the ability of consumers to judge the price of an item from a simple inspection of the item. To investigate this he randomly selects 12 pieces of material worth $2 per yard, 12 pieces worth $3 per yard, 12 pieces worth $4 per yard, and 12 pieces worth $5 per yard. Each person in a panel of consumers guesses the price of each piece of material, and the guesses are then averaged. The data below show the resulting 48 averages (one for each piece of material).

	Actual Price			
	2	3	4	5
	2.37	4.46	3.51	4.09
	2.98	2.80	3.53	3.87
	2.33	2.12	3.60	4.25
	3.33	2.13	3.63	4.77
	2.10	3.25	4.25	4.51
Average	2.68	3.78	2.77	3.69
"Guess" Price	3.35	3.59	3.49	3.40
	2.27	2.64	3.69	5.10
	2.29	2.56	3.40	4.40
	2.91	2.66	3.10	4.59
	2.73	4.09	4.40	5.09
	2.12	3.87	4.59	4.87

a. Find the estimated regression equation that relates the average "guess" price (Y) to the actual price (X). (Notice there are 48 observations, but these include only four distinct X values.)
b. What is the correlation between the X's and Y's?
c. What percentage of the total variation of the dependent variable is left unexplained by the regression equation?
d. Fill in the ANOVA table and use it to test whether the regression is significant at the 5% and/or 1% levels.
e. Find an estimate of σ^2, the variance of the error terms in the regression model.

27. In trying to explain the number of common colds reported during the winter, it is believed that the average weekly temperature might be a significant factor. The following data have been reported, where each data point refers to a given week in a particular town. (Assume that all towns referred to in this problem have roughly equal populations.)

Number of Colds Reported	Average Temperature (°F)
57	22
37	38
43	19
52	21
21	38
85	5
42	28
25	32
97	12
65	16

a. Find the correlation between the number of colds and the average temperature from the data given.
b. Calculate the coefficients of the estimated regression equation (where the number of colds is the dependent variable).
c. Fill in an ANOVA table to test for the significance of the regression as a whole (at the 5% level).
d. Find the value of r^2, the proportion of variance explained.

28. Referring to Problem 27, find the 10 $\hat{Y}_i$ values corresponding to the 10 given X_i values. What is the correlation between the calculated $\hat{Y}_i$'s and the original Y_i's? Then find the percentage of Y_i's falling within 1 standard error of estimate of the corresponding $\hat{Y}_i$'s. What would you expect this percentage to be (approximately)?

29. In developing guidelines for the type of energy-saving investments likely to be economically justified for homeowners, a utility company needed to estimate 1981 utility costs for houses of various ages. A sample of 18 homes was selected, with the following observations.

Age of House	1981 Utility Costs
6	$711
7	728
8	736
9	761
9	744
10	769 (*continued*)

Age of House	1981 Utility Costs
10	790
11	737
11	753
12	775
12	785
13	792
14	810
15	867
16	872
17	880
18	929
19	964

a. Estimate the regression equation relating 1981 utility costs (Y) to the ages of the houses (X).
b. Fill in the ANOVA table for this regression. Is the F ratio significant at the 5% level?
c. Compute the percentage of variation of the Y's explained by the regression. What is the correlation between the Y's and the X's? How are these two answers related?

30. A car rental company with branches in many cities found the following data for the number of cars rented (Y) versus the number of competing car rental agencies (X) within a 10-mile radius. (Each of these observations comes from a midsized city, and none of the agencies are located at airports.)

Number of Competing Agencies	Number of Cars Rented
4	88
4	119
3	89
6	73
2	136
4	79
5	84
3	120
4	82
5	88
3	106
4	98

a. Draw a scattergram of these data. Does it seem to imply a linear relationship?

b. Estimate the linear regression equation for explaining car rentals in terms of the number of competing agencies.

c. Find the correlation between the dependent and independent variables. What percentage of the total variation in total car rentals is explained by the number of competitors?

d. Fill in an ANOVA table and use the F value in this table to test the relevant hypothesis at the 1% level. What is this hypothesis in words, and how should the conclusion of the test be interpreted?

31. The following data represent a sample of several baseball players' batting averages in successive years. We are interested in whether there is a linear relationship between the averages in one year and the averages in the following year.

Average in One Year	Average in Next Year
.261	.246
.260	.299
.247	.225
.306	.294
.219	.264
.258	.227
.283	.275
.248	.281
.277	.263
.288	.291
.268	.293
.254	.263
.218	.227
.312	.282
.236	.252

a. Find the correlation between these two sets of batting averages.

b. Estimate the regression equation where X is the batting average in one year and Y is the batting average in the following year.

c. Find the standard error of estimate for the equation in part (b). What does it tell us in words (for this particular example)?

*32. Referring to Problem 31, let $Z = Y - X$ be the change in batting average from one year to the next.

a. Can you deduce the estimated regression equation of Z on X directly from the results of Problem 31? What is it? What about the correlation between Z and X?

b. Go through the formal steps of regressing Z on X and finding the correlation between Z and X. Do they agree with your "guesses" from part (a)?

33. The following data indicate the relationship between the amount of money put into savings (Y) in a given year and the after-tax income (X) in that year for a sample of families.

After-Tax Income ($1000s)	Savings ($1000s)
24.250	1.920
24.050	3.475
21.790	1.245
17.030	2.285
23.820	1.340
28.060	2.875
22.030	2.910
27.110	2.480
29.060	3.350
25.570	3.280
16.700	1.100
33.250	3.180

a. Draw a scattergram of Y versus X.

b. Let Z be the fraction of after-tax income put into savings. Draw a scattergram of Z versus X.

c. Estimate the regression equation with X as the independent variable and Y as the dependent variable. Then repeat with Z as the dependent variable. Discuss any differences or similarities between these two equations.

34. Find the r^2 values for each regression equation estimated in part (c) of Problem 33. Can you think of a possible problem of interpretation when trying to compare two r^2 values from equations with the same independent variable but different *dependent* variables? (Remember that r^2 is the percentage of the variation of the dependent variable explained by the regression.)

35. In the fruit-packing business, where workers are paid "by the piece," that is, per box packed, the relationship between the number of boxes packed per hour (Y) and the months of experience (X) is being investigated. The following data are collected for a randomly selected set of workers.

Months of Experience	Boxes per Hour
17	22
17	30
13	18
28	31
7	23
16	19
22	27
14	27
21	25
23	30
19	29
15	23
6	17
30	29

a. Draw a scattergram of these data. Does it appear to support a linear fit?

b. Estimate the regression equation of Y versus X.

c. Test the significance of the equation from part (b) by means of an ANOVA table. Use a 5% significance level. What is the value of s_e, the standard error of estimate?

36. The television networks wish to find the relationship between the ratings for their new fall shows and the number of advertisements for these new shows seen by the average viewer. Over a several-year span the following data have been collected. Here Y is the average rating of a new show for its first five weeks and X is the average number of advertisements for the show seen by potential viewers.

Number of Ads	Rating
7	.092
6	.181
6	.072
10	.144
4	.153
6	.060
8	.129
6	.161
8	.115
9	.156
7	.167
3	.092
11	.168
5	.121
4	.094

a. Draw a scattergram of these data. Can you think of plausible reasons why it has the shape it has?

b. Estimate the regression equation of Y versus X.

c. Calculate the percentage of variation of the dependent variable explained by the independent variable.

11.6

Confidence Intervals and Hypothesis Tests for the β's

In this section we investigate the errors made in estimating β_0 and β_1 by $\hat{\beta}_0$ and $\hat{\beta}_1$. The estimates $\hat{\beta}_0$ and $\hat{\beta}_1$ obviously depend on the particular X's and Y's in the sample. If we saw many different samples, all from the same population, we would calculate many different values of $\hat{\beta}_0$ and $\hat{\beta}_1$. Therefore, $\hat{\beta}_0$ and $\hat{\beta}_1$ are random variables with sampling distributions. In the usual way, knowledge of these sampling distributions allows us to find confidence intervals for β_0 and β_1 and to perform hypothesis tests on them. For most of this section, we concentrate on the slope parameter β_1 because it is usually more important in applied studies. However, we also list the corresponding results for the intercept term β_0.

We first consider the mean and variance of the sampling distribution of $\hat{\beta}_1$. It can be shown that the mean of $\hat{\beta}_1$ is exactly what we want it to be, namely β_1. In words, $\hat{\beta}_1$ is an unbiased estimate of β_1, so that there is no tendency for it to underestimate or overestimate β_1. The variance of $\hat{\beta}_1$ is σ_e^2/SS_{XX}, where σ_e^2 is the variance of the error terms.

$$
\textit{Mean and Variance of } \hat{\beta}_1
$$
$$
E(\hat{\beta}_1) = \beta_1 \qquad \mathrm{Var}(\hat{\beta}_1) = \frac{\sigma_e^2}{SS_{XX}}
$$

As usual, the square root of the variance of $\hat{\beta}_1$ measures the magnitude of the error made in estimating β_1 by $\hat{\beta}_1$. If this variance is large, there is a high probability that $\hat{\beta}_1$ is far from β_1. Therefore, in applied studies we always want the variance of $\hat{\beta}_1$ to be as small as possible.

Since we do not know the error variance σ_e^2, we cannot calculate the true variance of $\hat{\beta}_1$. However, an unbiased estimate of this variance is found by substituting the previously discussed estimate s_e^2 for σ_e^2. The resulting estimate of $\mathrm{Var}(\hat{\beta}_1)$ is s_e^2/SS_{XX}. The square root of this quantity is called the *standard error of* $\hat{\beta}_1$ and is labeled $\mathrm{StdErr}(\hat{\beta}_1)$.

$$
\textit{Standard Error of } \hat{\beta}_1
$$
$$
\mathrm{StdErr}(\hat{\beta}_1) = \frac{s_e}{\sqrt{SS_{XX}}}
$$

To make inferences about β_1, we use the fact that the standardized random variable $(\hat{\beta}_1 - \beta_1)/\mathrm{StdErr}(\hat{\beta}_1)$ has a t distribution with $n - 2$ degrees of freedom. This leads to the following confidence interval for β_1.

$$
\textit{Confidence Interval for } \beta_1 \textit{ with Confidence Level } 1 - \alpha
$$
$$
\hat{\beta}_1 \pm t_{\alpha/2, n-2} \mathrm{StdErr}(\hat{\beta}_1)
$$

Notice that this confidence interval is centered at $\hat{\beta}_1$ and extends a multiple of $\mathrm{StdErr}(\hat{\beta}_1)$ on either side. The multiplying factor is a t value found from Appendix B.

If we wish to test a hypothesis about β_1, we again use the t distribution. Suppose that we want to test $H_0: \beta_1 = (\beta_1)_0$ versus a one-tailed or two-tailed alternative. Here $(\beta_1)_0$ is any specified value of β_1. Then we calculate a t statistic that measures the number of standard errors $\hat{\beta}_1$ is from $(\beta_1)_0$. The formula for the test statistic t is as shown in the next box.

> *Computed t Statistic for Testing* H_0: $\beta_1 = (\beta_1)_0$
>
> $$t = \frac{\hat{\beta}_1 - (\beta_1)_0}{\text{StdErr}(\hat{\beta}_1)}$$

We reject H_0 only if this t value is far enough out in the appropriate tail (or tails) of the relevant t distribution.

> *Hypothesis Tests for* H_0: $\beta_1 = (\beta_1)_0$
>
> One-tailed alternatives
>
> $$H_a: \beta_1 > (\beta_1)_0$$
>
> Reject H_0 at the α level when $t > t_{\alpha, n-2}$.
>
> $$H_a: \beta_1 < (\beta_1)_0$$
>
> Reject H_0 at the α level when $t < -t_{\alpha, n-2}$.
>
> Two-tailed alternative H_a: $\beta_1 \neq (\beta_1)_0$
>
> Reject H_0 at the α level when $|t| > t_{\alpha/2, n-2}$.

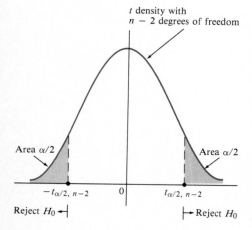

t density with *n* − 2 degrees of freedom

Area $\alpha/2$ Area $\alpha/2$

$-t_{\alpha/2,\, n-2}$ 0 $t_{\alpha/2,\, n-2}$

Reject H_0 ⊣   ⊢ Reject H_0

Figure 11.15
Rejection Region for Test of H_0: $\beta_1 = 0$
Versus H_a: $\beta_1 \neq 0$

There is one particular test on β_1 that is almost always run. This is the two-tailed test of H_0: $\beta_1 = 0$ versus H_a: $\beta_1 \neq 0$. From the instructions above, we see that H_0 should be rejected if $|t| > t_{\alpha/2, n-2}$, where the formula for t [with $(\beta_1)_0 = 0$] reduces to $t = \hat{\beta}_1/\text{StdErr}(\hat{\beta}_1)$ (see Figure 11.15). The reason this particular test is run is that it is a test of the predictive ability of the independent variable, as we discussed in Section 11.5. (Mathematically, the F test in Section 11.5 is equivalent to this t test, because the square of this t statistic is equal to the F statistic in the ANOVA table.) If X is completely unrelated to Y in a linear way, we may as well predict the same value of Y regardless of the value of X. This is consistent with a horizontal regression line ($\beta_1 = 0$). But if there is significant evidence that the independent variable does have predictive ability, we will tend to see a large t statistic and reject the null hypothesis that $\beta_1 = 0$.

The analysis above may also be done for the intercept parameter β_0. We list the results below. (For the hypothesis tests, $(\beta_0)_0$ is the null hypothesis value of β_0, and $t = [\hat{\beta}_0 - (\beta_0)_0]/\text{StdErr}(\hat{\beta}_0)$ is the test statistic.)

Properties of the Sampling Distribution of $\hat{\beta}_0$

$$E(\hat{\beta}_0) = \beta_0 \qquad \text{Var}(\hat{\beta}_0) = \sigma_e^2\left(\frac{1}{n} + \frac{\overline{X}^2}{\text{SS}_{XX}}\right)$$

$$\text{StdErr}(\hat{\beta}_0) = s_e\sqrt{\frac{1}{n} + \frac{\overline{X}^2}{\text{SS}_{XX}}}$$

$(\hat{\beta}_0 - \beta_0)/\text{StdErr}(\hat{\beta}_0)$ has a t distribution with $n - 2$ degrees of freedom

Confidence Interval for β_0 *with Confidence Level* $1 - \alpha$

$$\hat{\beta}_0 \pm t_{\alpha/2, n-2}\, \text{StdErr}(\hat{\beta}_0)$$

Hypothesis Tests for H_0: $\beta_0 = (\beta_0)_0$

One-tailed alternatives

$$H_a: \beta_0 > (\beta_0)_0$$

Reject H_0 at the α level when $t > t_{\alpha, n-2}$.

$$H_a: \beta_0 < (\beta_0)_0$$

Reject H_0 at the α level when $t < -t_{\alpha, n-2}$.

Two-tailed alternative H_a: $\beta_0 \neq (\beta_0)_0$

Reject H_0 at the α level when $|t| > t_{\alpha/2, n-2}$.

EXAMPLE 11.2 (continued)

For the housing cost data in Table 11.1, find 95% confidence intervals for the slope and intercept of the true regression line.

SOLUTION

From previous calculations we know that the estimated regression equation is $\hat{Y} = -61.072 + 7.940X$. This says that $\hat{\beta}_0 = -61.072$ and $\hat{\beta}_1 = 7.940$ are unbiased estimates of β_0 and β_1. To find 95% confidence intervals for these parameters, we first need the standard errors of $\hat{\beta}_0$ and $\hat{\beta}_1$. These are

$$\text{StdErr}(\hat{\beta}_0) = s_e \sqrt{\frac{1}{n} + \frac{\overline{X}^2}{SS_{XX}}}$$

$$= 7.700 \sqrt{\frac{1}{15} + \frac{17.75^2}{69.24}} = 16.55$$

(since 17.75 is the mean of the X's), and

$$\text{StdErr}(\hat{\beta}_1) = \frac{s_e}{\sqrt{SS_{XX}}} = \frac{7.700}{\sqrt{69.24}} = .925$$

For a 95% confidence interval, we set $\alpha = .05$, so that $t_{\alpha/2, n-2} = t_{.025, 13} = 2.160$. Then the required confidence intervals are

$$\hat{\beta}_0 \pm t_{.025, 13} \, \text{StdErr}(\hat{\beta}_0) = -61.072 \pm 2.160(16.55)$$
$$\text{(from } -96.82 \text{ to } -25.32)$$

and

$$\hat{\beta}_1 \pm t_{.025, 13} \, \text{StdErr}(\hat{\beta}_1) = 7.940 \pm 2.160(.925)$$
$$\text{(from } 5.942 \text{ to } 9.938)$$

This final interval says we are 95% confident that the expected increase in cost for a house with an extra 100 square feet is between \$5942 and \$9938.

In applied studies, regression equations are usually reported by listing the estimated equation with the standard errors of the $\hat{\beta}$'s below the corresponding coefficients. The standard error of estimate, s_e, and the r^2 value are usually listed next to the equation also. For the housing cost example we can summarize the findings as

$$\hat{Y} = -61.072 + 7.940\,X \qquad s_e = 7.700$$
$$\phantom{\hat{Y} =} (16.55) \quad (.925) \qquad r^2 = .850$$

EXAMPLE 11.3 (continued)

For managers of the type investigated in the salary example, it is hypothesized that the average salary increase per extra year of experience is greater than \$1500. Does the regression analysis support this hypothesis at the 5% level?

SOLUTION

Since the regression equation for this example relates salary linearly to years of experience, the slope term β_1 is the average salary increase per extra year of experience. Therefore, we need to test H_0: $\beta_1 = 1.5$ (because salaries are in \$1000s) versus H_a: $\beta_1 > 1.5$. From previous calculations we know that $\hat{\beta}_1 = 1.826$, and we can compute $\text{StdErr}(\hat{\beta}_1)$ as

$$\text{StdErr}(\hat{\beta}_1) = \frac{s_e}{\sqrt{\text{SS}_{XX}}}$$

For this example, $\text{SS}_{XX} = 485.75$, and s_e^2 is given by

$$s_e^2 = \frac{\text{SSE}}{n-2} = \frac{616.9}{18} = 34.27$$

Therefore,

$$\text{StdErr}(\hat{\beta}_1) = \frac{\sqrt{34.27}}{\sqrt{485.75}} = .266$$

Then the calculated t statistic is

$$t = \frac{\hat{\beta}_1 - (\beta_1)_0}{\text{StdErr}(\hat{\beta}_1)} = \frac{1.826 - 1.5}{.266} = 1.23$$

Since $t_{\alpha, n-2} = t_{.05, 18} = 1.734$, the calculated t value is *not* far enough out in the tail. Therefore, there is not enough evidence to support the claim that salaries increase by more than \$1500 per extra year of work experience.

11.7
Prediction

We now discuss prediction, the focal point of many applied studies. Up to now we have discussed two distinct values of the dependent variable, the Y's and the $\hat{Y}$'s. The Y's are the observed values, whereas the $\hat{Y}$'s are the estimated values and are found by plugging the observed X's into the estimated regression equation. However, these $\hat{Y}$'s are calculated mainly to test the fit of the proposed regression equation. Obviously, there is no real need to predict the values of the sample Y's because these Y's are already known. What we will learn in this section is how to predict the Y's for members of the population *not* in the original sample.

A typical situation where prediction is important is as follows. Suppose that a chain of discount stores such as K-mart is planning to open a new store at one of several locations. Their executives would like to locate the new store in the location that generates the highest sales, but they are uncertain which location this is. Therefore, they gather data on sales and possible explanatory variables (such as demographic data) from a sample of existing locations. They use these data to build a regression equation for sales as a function of the explanatory variables. If the regression equation provides a good fit to the stores in the sample, the company feels confident that it can use this equation to predict sales in the proposed locations given the values of the explanatory variables for these locations. Presumably, the company will then build the new store in the location with the highest predicted sales figure.

As we all know, prediction can be a very risky business. Different people's predictions not only vary widely from one another, but they often tend to be far from accurate. We see this phenomenon even with "experts," such as government economists, whose predictions often do not come true. Before we discuss the particular details of prediction in regression analysis, it is worth discussing some of the reasons for our inability to make accurate predictions in general.

1. Probably the most important reason for large prediction errors is that the model on which we base our predictions is not sufficiently realistic to incorporate all the critical factors. Sometimes these factors are intangibles that simply cannot be incorporated into any mathematical model but are nevertheless important. In the housing cost example, there are undoubtedly intangible qualities of houses that cannot be captured by the square footage, the number of bedrooms, or other easily quantified explanatory variables.

2. A second problem occurs when we try to predict values outside the range of values used to build the model. We mentioned this problem earlier in the context of housing costs. If an equation relates housing costs to square footages for houses with 800 to 2500 square feet, we are certainly taking a risk when we use this equation to predict the cost of a house with, say, 4000 square feet. This is called *extrapolation* and is always a dangerous practice in prediction problems.

3. The model we use for prediction is based on a particular sample from the population, and we use all the peculiarities of this sample to estimate the population parameters. Therefore, the model usually fits the data in the sample much better than it fits the rest of the population. When we attempt to predict values for the other members of the population, we may not do nearly as well as we do when we "predict" values for the members of the sample. (Sometimes investigators randomly split a large data set into two halves. One half is used to estimate the parameters of the model. This estimated model is then used to "predict" the other half of the data and to see how well the predicted values match the actual values. Often the estimated model does not fit the second half of the data nearly as well as it fits the first half.)

4. Even if we overcome the foregoing problems, we still have to contend with the inherent randomness that occurs in almost all prediction problems.

Unfortunately, this is one aspect of the problem that we can never eliminate completely.

In regression analysis there are two prediction problems that we will discuss. The first occurs when we choose a particular value of the independent variable, labeled X_0, and try to predict the *mean* of all Y's corresponding to $X = X_0$. For example, we might wish to predict the mean cost of all houses with 1600 square feet. The second prediction problem is when we try to predict the value of Y for a *single* observation. In the housing cost example, we might wish to predict the cost of a particular house with 1600 square feet.

Intuitively, there is a big difference between predicting the mean of many Y's (all with the same X) and predicting a single Y with this X. In the former case, we do not need to worry about high Y's and low Y's because they will tend to cancel each other in the calculation of the mean. But when we are predicting an individual Y, we must be aware of the possibility of observing one of the relatively high or low Y's associated with this X. The difference between these two prediction problems is reflected in their standard errors. The standard error of the mean of all Y's is considerably smaller than the standard error of an individual Y.

Geometrically, we can also see the difference between the two problems. Suppose that X_0 is given and we want to predict the mean of all Y's with this X. Using our earlier notation, this is $\mu_{Y|X_0}$. Let $\hat{\mu}_{Y|X_0}$ be the predicted value of $\mu_{Y|X_0}$. Then as we see in Figure 11.16, the only reason $\hat{\mu}_{Y|X_0}$ is not equal

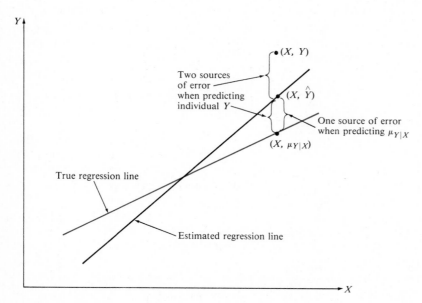

Figure 11.16
Comparison of Errors for the Two Prediction Problems

to the correct value $\mu_{Y|X_0}$ is that we have not estimated the population regression line correctly. That is, $\hat{\beta}_0$ and $\hat{\beta}_1$ are not in general equal to β_0 and β_1. However, when we try to predict an individual Y, we do not expect it to lie exactly on the population regression line. This is because of the random error term associated with this particular observation. Therefore, there are two sources of prediction error in this case: (1) we do not have the true population regression line, and (2) there is a random error term associated with this observation that is impossible to predict. These two sources of prediction error are also illustrated in Figure 11.16.

The analysis of the two problems is very similar. For both problems we make exactly the same "point prediction," or best guess. This is found by substituting X_0 into the estimated regression equation. Letting $\hat{Y}_0$ be the point prediction for the individual prediction problem and $\hat{\mu}_{Y|X_0}$ be the point prediction for the mean prediction problem, we have

> *Point Prediction for the Two Prediction Problems*
>
> $$\hat{\mu}_{Y|X_0} = \hat{Y}_0 = \hat{\beta}_0 + \hat{\beta}_1 X_0$$

In words, no matter whether we are predicting the mean of all Y's or an individual Y, we predict the value to be the height of the estimated regression line above X_0 (see Figure 11.17).

We now examine the standard errors for the two problems. The formulas for these standard errors are given below. We let StdErr(mean) denote the standard error of the mean of the Y's, and we let StdErr($\hat{Y}_0$) denote the standard error of an individual Y.

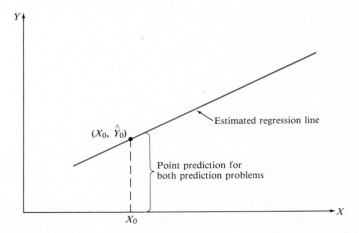

Figure 11.17

$$Standard\ Error\ of\ \hat{\mu}_{Y|X_0}$$

$$\text{StdErr(mean)} = s_e \sqrt{\frac{1}{n} + \frac{(X_0 - \overline{X})^2}{SS_{XX}}}$$

$$Standard\ Error\ of\ \hat{Y}_0$$

$$\text{StdErr}(\hat{Y}_0) = s_e \sqrt{1 + \frac{1}{n} + \frac{(X_0 - \overline{X})^2}{SS_{XX}}}$$

There are several things to notice about these formulas. First, notice that the formulas both depend on the value of X_0. In particular, they depend on the distance between X_0 and the mean $\overline{X}$ of the X's in the sample. The standard errors are both minimized when X_0 equals $\overline{X}$, and they grow steadily as X_0 gets farther away from $\overline{X}$ on either side. This is intuitive. It means that we are able to predict more accurately for values of X_0 close to the mean of the X's in the sample. When we try to predict for X_0 values farther away from the typical X's in the sample, the standard errors of prediction naturally increase, so that our predictions become less accurate. In fact, when X_0 is outside the range of the X's in the sample, prediction amounts to extrapolation, and this is always risky.

However, if the X's in the sample vary widely and X_0 is not too far from the sample mean $\overline{X}$, then $(X_0 - \overline{X})^2$ is often much smaller than SS_{XX}. In this case we can approximate StdErr(mean) and StdErr($\hat{Y}_0$) very well by ignoring the $(X_0 - \overline{X})^2/SS_{XX}$ term. In fact, if n is fairly large, we can also ignore the $1/n$ term in the formula for StdErr($\hat{Y}_0$). Then we have the approximate formulas:

Approximate Standard Errors of Prediction

$$\text{StdErr(mean)} \approx \frac{s_e}{\sqrt{n}}$$

$$\text{StdErr}(\hat{Y}_0) \approx s_e$$

In most cases these approximations are acceptable, although the exact formulas are, of course, preferred.

We may use these standard errors of prediction to compute confidence intervals. We first examine the mean $\mu_{Y|X_0}$. In this case the quantity we are trying to predict is a population parameter, a mean. Therefore, we proceed exactly as in earlier chapters. The details are shown below. A graph of 95% confidence intervals for $\mu_{Y|X_0}$ for all possible values of X_0, referred to as a *confidence interval band,* is shown in Figure 11.18 (p. 554).

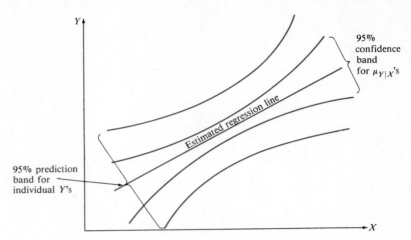

Figure 11.18
95% Confidence and Prediction Bands

Confidence Interval for $\mu_{Y|X_0}$ *with Confidence Level* $1 - \alpha$

$$\hat{\beta}_0 + \hat{\beta}_1 X_0 \pm t_{\alpha/2, n-2} \text{ StdErr(mean)}$$

When we are predicting an individual Y, the interpretation is somewhat different. An individual Y is *not* a population parameter like a mean. Instead, it is a random observation, which we estimate by $\hat{Y}_0$. The mean of this estimate is approximated by $\hat{\beta}_0 + \hat{\beta}_1 X_0$, and its standard error is $\text{StdErr}(\hat{Y}_0)$. The resulting confidence interval for Y is usually called a *prediction interval*. It is given as follows.

Prediction Interval for an Individual Y

$$\hat{\beta}_0 + \hat{\beta}_1 X_0 \pm t_{\alpha/2, n-2} \text{ StdErr}(\hat{Y}_0)$$

This prediction interval has the following interpretation. If we observe many members of the population, each with its own X_0 value, and we calculate the prediction interval above for each observation, the fraction of these intervals that contain the observed Y values will be approximately $1 - \alpha$.

Since an individual Y is a random variable, we can also calculate probabilities associated with it. For example, suppose that the predicted value of an individual Y is $\hat{\beta}_0 + \hat{\beta}_1 X_0 = 15.3$, and the associated standard error is $\text{StdErr}(\hat{Y}_0) = 2.3$. Then we may find the probability that the actual value of Y is greater than 18.7, say. Strictly speaking, this should be done by using the t distribution, but if the sample size is reasonably large, we may use the normal distribution as an approximation. (This approximation is used primarily because of the limitations of the t table.) The normal calculation is

$$P(Y > 18.7) = P\left(Z > \frac{18.7 - 15.3}{2.3}\right) = P(Z > 1.48) = .07$$

EXAMPLE 11.2 (continued)

Suppose that the data in Table 11.1 have been used to build a regression equation for housing cost as a function of square footage. For a randomly selected house with 1750 square feet, calculate the probability that the predicted cost differs from the actual cost by more than $5000.

SOLUTION

From previous calculations we have $\overline{X} = 17.75$ (1775 square feet), $SS_{XX} = 69.24$, $s_e = 7.700$, $\hat{\beta}_0 = -61.072$, and $\hat{\beta}_1 = 7.940$. For a 1750-square-foot house, $X_0 = 17.50$, so the predicted Y value is

$$\hat{Y}_0 = \hat{\beta}_0 + \hat{\beta}_1 X_0 = -61.072 + 7.940(17.50) = 77.878 \quad \text{(or \$77,878)}$$

and the standard error is

$$\text{StdErr}(\hat{Y}_0) = 7.700 \sqrt{1 + \frac{1}{15} + \frac{(17.5 - 17.75)^2}{69.24}} = 7.956 \quad \text{(or \$7956)}$$

The probability that the actual cost and the predicted cost differ by more than $5000 is the probability that the actual Y is outside the interval from $77,878 - \$5000$ to $77,878 + \$5000$. This probability is given by

$$P(Y < 72.878 \text{ or } Y > 82.878) = 2P(Y > 82.878) \quad \text{(by symmetry)}$$
$$= 2P\left(Z > \frac{82.878 - 77.878}{7.956}\right)$$
$$= 2P(Z > .628) = .53$$

As we see, the probability is slightly greater than .5 that the predicted value will be off by more than $5000.

EXAMPLE 11.3 (continued)

Referring again to the data in Table 11.4, consider the subset of managers in the population who have exactly 12 years of experience. Find an estimate and a 95% confidence interval for the mean salary of these managers.

SOLUTION

From previous calculations we know that $\overline{X} = 11.75$, $SS_{XX} = 485.75$, $s_e = 5.854$, $\hat{\beta}_0 = 16.735$, and $\hat{\beta}_1 = 1.826$. The X_0 requested for this example is 12, so the point prediction of the mean is

$$\hat{\mu}_{Y|X_0} = \hat{\beta}_0 + \hat{\beta}_1 X_0 = 16.735 + 1.826(12) = 38.647 \quad (\text{or } \$38,647)$$

and the standard error is

$$\text{StdErr(mean)} = 5.854 \sqrt{\frac{1}{20} + \frac{(12 - 11.75)^2}{485.75}} = 1.311 \quad (\text{or } \$1311)$$

This gives a 95% confidence interval for $\mu_{Y|X_0}$ of

$$38.647 \pm t_{.025,18}(1.311) = 38.647 \pm 2.101(1.311)$$

or from \$35,893 to \$41,401. In words, we are 95% confident that the mean salary of all managers in the population with 12 years of experience is between \$35,893 and \$41,401.

Problems for Sections 11.6, 11.7

37. a. Referring to the data in Problem 15 (p. 540), find a 95% confidence interval for the expected increase in the number of shirts sold when the price of a shirt decreases by \$1.
   b. Can you conclude at the 10% level that the expected decrease in shirt sales when price increases by \$1 is more than 15? That is, can you reject the null hypothesis that it is no more than 15?

38. The following data relate the number of days absent from work per year (Y) to yearly income (X) for a sample of employees in a large company.

Income ($1000s)	Days Absent
19.350	7
19.190	17
17.250	7
26.120	8
13.170	18
18.990	5
22.625	8
17.450	16
21.810	7
23.480	10 (*continued*)

Income ($1000s)	Days Absent
20.490	14
18.285	10
12.880	12
27.075	4
15.585	13
14.420	11

a. Estimate the regression line that relates Y to X.
b. Predict the mean number of days absent per year for all employees who earn \$16,500 per year. Find a 95% confidence interval for this mean.
c. Find a 95% prediction interval for the number of days a particular employee with income \$16,500 will be absent during the next year. Why is this interval wider than the confidence interval found in part (b)?
d. For the employee in part (c), find the probability that he will be absent at least eight days in the coming year.

39. The following data relate the number of persons entering a discount store (X) (in hundreds) to the total sales volume (Y) (in \$1000s) on seven randomly selected Saturdays.

X	3	5	8	5	2	1	6
Y	6.7	7.2	10.3	8.2	6.9	3.7	8.3

a. What is your best estimate of mean total sales volume averaged over *all* Saturdays if you ignore all information about the number of persons entering the store?

b. Find a 95% confidence interval for the quantity estimated in part (a). (This can be done entirely from the material learned in Chapter 8.)

c. What is your best estimate of total sales volume on a particular Saturday when 400 persons entered the store? [Unlike parts (a) and (b), you should not ignore the information on the number of people entering the store.]

d. Find a 95% prediction interval for the quantity estimated in part (c).

40. The marketing manager in Problem 26 (p. 541) wants to test the hypothesis that if the actual price changes by a certain amount, the average "guess" price will change by the *same* amount. Set this up as an appropriate hypothesis-testing problem, and perform the test at the 5% significance level. (Use a two-tailed test.)

41. The following data were collected during the 10-year period from 1969 to 1978. Let Y_t be the number of building permits in year t, and let X_t be the interest rate (as a percentage) in year t.

Year	Interest Rate (Percent)	Building Permits
1969	6.5	2165
1970	6.0	2984
1971	6.5	2780
1972	7.5	1940
1973	8.5	1750
1974	9.5	1535
1975	10.0	962
1976	9.0	1310
1977	11.0	856
1978	12.0	776

a. Estimate the regression equation $Y_t = \beta_0 + \beta_1 X_t + e_t$, that is, find $\hat{\beta}_0$ and $\hat{\beta}_1$.

b. Calculate (by any method) the correlation between interest rate and number of building permits.

c. Fill in the ANOVA table and test the resulting F value for significance at the 5% level; at the 1% level.

d. Find a 95% confidence interval for β_1.

e. Find a 95% prediction interval for Y in 1979 if the interest rate in 1979 was 11.5%.

42. a. Referring to the data in Problem 27 (p. 542), consider a large number of towns, each with an average temperature of 20°F. Find a point estimate and a 95% confidence interval for the predicted *average* number of colds per week in these towns.

b. If a similar-sized town in Florida averages 70°F during the winter, how many colds would you predict they have per week? How can you "interpret" this answer?

43. a. Referring to the data in Problem 29 (p. 542), compute a 95% confidence interval for β_1; for β_0.

b. How probable is it that a 12-year-old house had a 1981 utility bill below $750? (Find the estimated utility cost and its standard error, and do a normal probability calculation.)

44. The following data are for workloads at 10 distribution centers maintained in overseas locations by a multinational firm. The X's are thousands of "work units" performed during the reporting period, and the Y's are thousands of manhours required.

Thousands of Work Units	Thousands of Manhours
5.0	27.5
3.5	20.1
10.0	50.5
5.0	26.3
6.5	33.5
6.0	32.4
7.1	36.8
2.5	15.5
3.0	18.3
4.2	22.0

a. Find the correlation between the X's and Y's. What percentage of the total variation of Y does X explain?

b. Find the estimated regression equation for Y in terms of X.

c. Find a 95% prediction interval for the number of manhours required at another location that performed 8100 work units.

45. A fast-foods restaurant wishes to see how its sales in a given week are related to the number of ads it runs in local newspapers during the week. Data from eight randomly selected weeks are shown on p. 558.

Number of Ads	Sales ($1000s)
7	13.980
6	16.850
5	12.930
10	16.360
4	12.045
6	15.180
8	15.470
6	16.010

a. Estimate the linear regression equation of sales versus number of ads.

b. Find a 90% confidence interval for the increase in sales the restaurant can expect when its ads increase by four from one week to the next.

46. a. Referring to Problem 45, find a 90% prediction interval for the level of sales for a week in which 9 ads are run. What is the probability that the sales in this week will be at least $18,200?

b. Find a 90% confidence interval for the mean level of sales in all weeks in which the restaurant runs 9 ads. How do you explain the difference between this interval and the one you calculated in part (a)?

47. a. Referring to the data in Problem 31 (p. 543), test the hypothesis that $\beta_1 = 1$ versus a two-tailed alternative at the 10% level. State in words why this might be a reasonable hypothesis to test (for this particular example).

b. Consider a player who batted .278 in 1985. Predict his batting average in 1986. What is the probability that his average in 1986 is over .300?

48. One of the major automobile makers wishes to estimate the relationship between the number of cars sold per month and the number of salespeople at a given dealership. The following data are collected from a representative sample of 15 dealerships.

Number of Salespeople	Number of Cars Sold
10	36
9	48
8	30
13	48
7	38
9	31
11	43
9	43 *(continued)*

Number of Salespeople	Number of Cars Sold
11	40
12	47
9	37
6	29
13	45
8	36
7	31

a. Estimate the linear regression equation that relates sales to the number of salespeople.

b. Does it appear that the addition of one salesperson will increase sales by more than two cars per month? (Treat this as the alternative hypothesis and test at the 10% level.)

c. For a dealership not included in the sample, find a 95% prediction interval for the number cars sold per month, given that it employs 12 salespeople.

49. A study was performed to estimate the relationship between average driving speed on interstate highways and the annual number of accidents on these highways. A sample of 25 stretches of interstate highways throughout the country were selected. These were chosen to be as similar as possible with respect to weather, terrain, level of traffic, and so on, except that some were patrolled more heavily than others. (The effect of patrolling was to reduce the average driving speed.) The following regression equation was estimated, where Y is the number of accidents observed in a year and X is the average driving speed:

$$\hat{Y} = -209.6 + 4.3X$$

with $s_{\beta_0} = 15.7$, $s_{\beta_1} = 1.4$, $s_e = 4.1$, and $r^2 = .62$. The average driving speeds (the X's) were all between 50 and 65 miles per hour.

a. Explain the meaning of the information given by this equation and the summary statistics.

b. Are you able to conclude with 99% confidence that stretches of interstate highway (similar to these) have fewer accidents when their driving speeds are lower? (Formulate appropriate null and alternative hypotheses and perform the appropriate test on them.)

50. a. Referring to Problem 49, find an *approximate* 95% confidence interval for the mean number of accidents per year on all similar stretches of interstate highways with an average mph of 58. (Use the approximate standard error of prediction discussed in the text.)

b. Find an *approximate* 95% prediction interval for the number of accidents in one year for a single stretch of interstate highway with an average mph of 58.

c. Explain the difference between parts (a) and (b).

d. Why are the answers in parts (a) and (b) only approximate, and why is it impossible to find the exact answers from the data that are given?

51. a. Referring to the data in Problem 36 (p. 544), test the

hypothesis that $\beta_1 = 0$ (versus a two-tailed alternative) at the 10% level, and form a 90% confidence interval for β_1.

b. Calculate the correlation between the Y's and the X's.

c. How do the answers to parts (a) and (b) go along with the appearance of the scattergram in part (a) of Problem 36?

11.8

Simple Regression and Computer Packages

Throughout this chapter we have emphasized formulas for calculating the important quantities in simple linear regression. With some practice these formulas can be used quickly and easily to solve regression problems. However, there are faster methods available. First, many hand calculators are programmed to do simple linear regression. In particular, they are capable of showing sums of squares and cross-products, correlations, and the regression coefficients, $\hat{\beta}_0$ and $\hat{\beta}_1$. (Most calculators label these coefficients a and b.)

Second, there are a number of computer packages that perform many forms of regression analysis, including simple linear regression. We will say much more about these in Chapter 12, when we study multiple regression. But an example of the computer output that can be obtained is shown below in Exhibit 11.1. This output is from the computer package SPSS (Statistical Package for the Social Sciences). To obtain it we read the data on housing costs and square feet from Table 11.1 into the computer and instructed the package to perform a simple regression analysis with cost as the dependent variable. Among the important features in this output are (1) the r^2 value (R SQUARE), .85, (2) the s_e value (STANDARD ERROR), 7.69, (3) the F value from the ANOVA table, 73.74, (4) the regression coefficients (in

Exhibit 11.1 SPSS Printout for Simple Regression Analysis

MULTIPLE R		.92202	ANALYSIS OF VARIANCE				
R SQUARE		.85013		DF	SUM OF SQUARES	MEAN SQUARE	
ADJUSTED R SQUARE		.83860	REGRESSION	1	4363.96989	4363.96989	
STANDARD ERROR		7.69288	RESIDUAL	13	769.34611	59.18047	

$$F = 73.74003 \quad \text{SIGNIF } F = .0000$$

VARIABLES IN THE EQUATION

VARIABLE	B	SE B	95 CONFDNCE INTRVL B		BETA	T	SIG T
SQFT	7.94024	.92466	5.94263	9.93784	.92202	8.587	.0000
(CONSTANT)	-61.07273	16.52940	-96.78233	-25.36314		-3.695	.0027

the "B" column), 7.940 and -61.072, and (5) the standard errors, 95% confidence intervals, and t values for these coefficients (in the "SE B," "95 CONFDNCE INTRVL B," and "T" columns, respectively). Aside from slight round-off, these are the same quantities as those found in Example 11.2.

Summary

This chapter has begun the discussion of one of the most important modeling devices in statistics, linear regression. The simple linear regression model states that the mean values of a dependent variable, for each value of an independent variable, lie along a straight line. We can observe the presence or absence of a regression line geometrically by looking at a scattergram of the observations. The least squares formulas then allow us to calculate numerically what the scattergram shows us geometrically. These formulas are based on minimizing the sum of the squared errors (or vertical distances) between the observations and the estimated regression line.

The least squares line can be fitted to any set of observations. However, the statistical analysis in regression shows whether the regression line represents an improvement, in terms of being able to predict the dependent variable, over no regression at all. Two particular measures of importance are the standard error of estimate, s_e, and the coefficient of determination, r^2. The standard error of estimate measures the standard deviation of the error term in the population regression equation. A good fit will have a small value of s_e because approximately 95% of the observed values of the dependent variable are within 2 s_e's of the values predicted by the regression line. The coefficient of determination is the proportion of the variation of the dependent variable explained by the regression equation. Most researchers believe that if r^2 is not fairly large, the regression analysis has not been a success. For r^2 to be large, its square root, the magnitude of the correlation between the dependent and independent variable, also has to be large. In this sense, the correlation measures the strength of a linear fit between a pair of variables.

One of the principal uses of regression is to predict the value of the dependent variable from the value of the independent variable for a member of the population not in the original sample. The point estimate is always the value given by the estimated regression equation. However, the standard error of this point estimate is proportional to s_e, so that predictions can have very large standard errors unless the estimated regression line provides a good fit to the original observations.

Applications

Application 11.1   All managers tend to come in contact with stressful situations that cause them physical and psychological strain, but the article by Weiss suggests that information systems (IS) managers are particularly subject to stress. (Reference: Madeline Weiss, "Effects of Work Stress and Social Support on Information Systems Managers," *MIS Quarterly,* Vol. 7, 1983, pp. 29–41.) In a large study of 241 IS managers, she questioned the managers about the stress factors of their jobs and the resulting personal feelings of strain. The stress factors included job overload (too much work or work beyond one's capacity), lack of feedback (lack of information about one's job performance), being in an innovative role (having to bring about change in the organization), and eight others. Weiss hypothesized that the combined effect of these stress factors is positively related to the amount of strain felt by the IS managers. To test this hypothesis, she asked several questions relating to the stress factors and several relating to the feeling of strain. After combining (averaging) the stress-related responses into a composite stress index and combining the strain-related responses into a composite strain index, she ran a simple regression of the strain index (the dependent variable) on the stress index (the independent variable). The estimated coefficient of stress was indeed positive and highly significant ($t = 8.06$, significant at the .0005 level), indicating that as the stress factors increase, so do the feelings of strain. The r^2 value for this equation was .21.

Weiss also hypothesized that feelings of strain decrease when the manager receives more social support during the job. Social support is defined by Weiss as the "flow of emotional concern, instrumental aid, information, and/or appraisal (information relevant to self-evaluation) between people." To test her hypothesis, she again used the strain index as the dependent variable in a simple regression analysis, but this time she used a social support index as the independent variable. As expected, the coefficient of social support was negative and significant ($t = -3.86$, significant at the .0005 level), indicating that strain tends to decrease as social support increases. The r^2 value for this equation was only .06.

The results above are fairly typical of studies with large samples. If the sample size is sufficiently large, and if there is any relationship at all between two variables, this relationship will be found beyond the shadow of a doubt. In this study stress factors definitely have some positive effect on strain, and social support definitely has some negative effect on strain. We know this from the large magnitudes of the t values quoted above.

But the relatively low r^2 values indicate that a large proportion of the variation of the dependent variable remains unexplained by stress and/or social support. In other words, there are undoubtedly other variables that affect the amount of job-related strain felt by IS managers. So although the results of Weiss's study are those she desired, they probably do not tell the whole story.

Application 11.2   In assessing the riskiness of a particular company's stock, financial analysts often regress the return for the stock against a market index, where this market index represents the return from a portfolio of many diverse stocks. By examining the coefficient of the market index (often called the "BETA" for this stock), we can see how sensitive this stock is to changes in the overall market. In particular, if the coefficient is less than 1, a given percentage change in the market index will produce a smaller percentage change in that particular stock. Exactly the opposite is true when the coefficient is greater than 1. For this reason stocks with a BETA less than 1 are often considered less risky than those with a BETA greater than 1.

To illustrate these ideas, we ran a regression of Revlon's stock versus a market index of 500 stocks. The dependent variable Y_t is the percentage change in Revlon's stock price from one week to the next, that is, from week $t - 1$ to week t. The independent variable X_t is the percentage change in the market index for the same period. We estimated the equation

$$Y_t = \beta_0 + \beta_1 X_t + \epsilon_t$$

by using weekly data from the beginning of 1978 to the end of 1981. In all, there were 208 observations of Y_t and X_t. The estimated equation is

$$\hat{Y}_t = -.230 + .996X_t$$

The standard errors of the coefficients are $\text{StdErr}(\hat{\beta}_0) = .240$ and $\text{StdErr}(\hat{\beta}_1) = .116$. The standard error of estimate is $s_e = 3.45$, and the r^2 value is .262.

Clearly, this estimated equation does not explain everything about changes in Revlon's stock price. The r^2 value implies that only 26.2% of the total variation in the dependent variable has been accounted for, and the s_e value implies that a predicted percentage change, $\hat{Y}_t$, could easily be off by 6% or more from the actual change, Y_t. However, the estimated coefficient of the market index X_t is very close to 1. To financial analysts, this means that Revlon stock is neither very risky nor completely riskless. Instead, it tends to move with the market as a whole.

Glossary of Terms

Dependent variable the variable that a regression analysis is trying to explain or predict

Independent variables the variables used to explain or predict the dependent variable

Simple linear regression a regression analysis that uses a single independent variable in a linear equation

Residual the difference between the observed and estimated values of the dependent variable

Standard error of estimate the estimated standard deviation of the error term

Coefficient of determination the proportion of variance of the dependent variable explained by the regression

Important Formulas

1. Population regression equation

$$\mu_{Y|X} = \beta_0 + \beta_1 X$$

where $\mu_{Y|X}$ is the mean of all Y's with a fixed X

2. Regression equation for a single observation

$$Y = \beta_0 + \beta_1 X + \epsilon$$

3. Estimated regression equation

$$\hat{Y} = \hat{\beta}_0 + \hat{\beta}_1 X$$

4. Formula for a residual

$$\hat{\epsilon}_i = Y_i - \hat{Y}_i$$

5. Sums of squares useful in this chapter

$$SS_{XX} = \sum X_i^2 - \frac{(\sum X_i)^2}{n}$$

$$SS_{YY} = \sum Y_i^2 - \frac{(\sum Y_i)^2}{n}$$

$$SS_{XY} = \sum X_i Y_i - \frac{(\sum X_i)(\sum Y_i)}{n}$$

6. Least squares estimates of β_0 and β_1

$$\hat{\beta}_1 = \frac{SS_{XY}}{SS_{XX}}$$

$$\hat{\beta}_0 = \bar{Y} - \hat{\beta}_1 \bar{X}$$

7. Standard error of estimate

$$s_e = \sqrt{\frac{\text{SSE}}{n-2}}$$

where

$$\text{SSE} = \sum (Y_i - \hat{Y}_i)^2 = \text{SS}_{YY} - \hat{\beta}_1 \text{SS}_{XY}$$

8. Formula for r^2

$$r^2 = \frac{\text{SSR}}{\text{SST}}$$

where

$$\text{SSR} = \frac{(\text{SS}_{XY})^2}{\text{SS}_{XX}} \qquad \text{SST} = \text{SS}_{YY}$$

9. Formula for F in the ANOVA table

$$F = \frac{\text{MSR}}{\text{MSE}} = \frac{\text{SSR}}{\text{SSE}/(n-2)}$$

10. Standard error of $\hat{\beta}_1$

$$\text{StdErr}(\hat{\beta}_1) = \frac{s_e}{\sqrt{\text{SS}_{XX}}}$$

11. Confidence interval for β_1

$$\hat{\beta}_1 \pm t_{\alpha/2, n-2} \, \text{StdErr}(\hat{\beta}_1)$$

12. Test statistic for testing H_0: $\beta_1 = (\beta_1)_0$

$$t = \frac{\hat{\beta}_1 - (\beta_1)_0}{\text{StdErr}(\hat{\beta}_1)}$$

13. Standard error for predicting an individual Y value when $X = X_0$

$$\text{StdErr}(\hat{Y}_0) = s_e \sqrt{1 + \frac{1}{n} + \frac{(X_0 - \bar{X})^2}{\text{SS}_{XX}}}$$

14. Prediction interval for an individual Y when $X = X_0$

$$\hat{\beta}_0 + \hat{\beta}_1 X_0 \pm t_{\alpha/2, n-2} \, \text{StdErr}(\hat{Y}_0)$$

15. Standard error for predicting the mean of all Y values when $X = X_0$

$$\text{StdErr(mean)} = s_e \sqrt{\frac{1}{n} + \frac{(X_0 - \bar{X})^2}{SS_{XX}}}$$

16. Confidence interval for the mean of all Y values when $X = X_0$

$$\hat{\beta}_0 + \hat{\beta}_1 X_0 \pm t_{\alpha/2, n-2} \, \text{StdErr(mean)}$$

End-of-Chapter Problems

52. Consider a population regression equation of Y versus X.
   a. Why is an error term necessary?
   b. What is the difference between the error term ϵ_i and the residual $\hat{\epsilon}_i = Y_i - \hat{Y}_i$ for a particular observation i? Which of these is observable?

53. If a 95% confidence interval for the slope coefficient β_1 extends from .53 to .94, is it necessarily true that the F ratio from the ANOVA table will be significant at the 5% level? Why or why not?

54. An insurance company wishes to investigate the relationship between a person's annual income and the amount of whole-life insurance the person has. Fourteen people are chosen at random. If Y_i and X_i are, respectively, the yearly income and whole-life insurance coverage for the ith person (both measured in \$1000s), the following sums are found: $\Sigma X_i = 275$, $\Sigma X_i^2 = 7493$, $\Sigma Y_i = 463.6$, $\Sigma Y_i^2 = 17,564.42$, and $\Sigma X_i Y_i = 11,101.2$.
   a. Calculate SS_{XX}, SS_{YY}, SS_{XY}, and the correlation r.
   b. Estimate the regression equation for Y as a function of X.
   c. What is the residual for a person whose income is \$40,000 and who has \$35,000 of whole-life insurance?
   d. Find a 90% confidence interval for β_1. What is the interpretation of β_1 in this problem?
   e. Find the predicted income, along with a 90% prediction interval for this income, for a person who owns \$20,000 of whole-life insurance.

*55. For the data in Problem 54, suppose that we want, instead, to use X (insurance owned) as the dependent variable and Y (income) as the independent variable in order to estimate the equation $X = \alpha_0 + \alpha_1 Y + \epsilon$. (Here we use α's to distinguish them from the β's used in the equation with Y as the dependent variable.) Check numerically that the OLS estimates $\hat{\alpha}_0$ and $\hat{\alpha}_1$ found by switching the roles of X and Y in the usual regression formulas are *not* the same as those that would be found by solving for X in terms of Y in the answer to Problem 54, part (b). That is, show numerically that $\hat{\alpha}_0$ and $\hat{\alpha}_1$ are not equal to $-\hat{\beta}_0/\hat{\beta}_1$ and $1/\hat{\beta}_1$, respectively. Can you explain this difference? (Think geometrically about what is being minimized with OLS estimates.)

*56. The time required for machine operators to set up a complicated piece of machinery typically depends on the number of weeks of training they have had. The following data reflect this, where two machinists were observed in various phases of their training periods. (A *different* pair of machinists were observed each week.)

Week of Training	Setup Time (Minutes)	
	Machinist 1	Machinist 2
1	9.5	10.2
2	9.0	6.4
3	5.5	7.1
4	5.8	6.8
5	6.6	5.3
6	5.5	7.3
7	5.2	5.4
8	4.9	7.6
9	5.9	4.2
10	4.5	6.3

a. Letting X be the number of weeks of training and Y be the number of minutes of setup time, estimate the associated regression equation $\hat{Y} = \hat{\beta}_0 + \hat{\beta}_1 X$.

b. Suppose that management believes Y might be better explained by the equation $Y = \alpha_0 + \alpha_1 Z$, where $Z = 1/X$. Find $\hat{\alpha}_0$ and $\hat{\alpha}_1$, the estimates of α_0 and α_1. (First transform each X to a Z, and then use the usual regression formulas on the Y's and Z's.)

c. Which of the equations above seems to give the better fit? Illustrate graphically and numerically.

d. If another machinist has been in training six weeks, give a point prediction and a 95% prediction interval for his amount of setup time using (1) the equation in part (a), and (2) the equation in part (b).

*57. Sometimes the original data, the X's and Y's, are standardized before a regression is run. That is, we let $U_i = (X_i - \overline{X})/s_X$ and $V_i = (Y_i - \overline{Y})/s_Y$ for each observation i. (Here s_X and s_Y are the respective sample standard deviations of the original X's and Y's.) Then we regress the V_i's on the U_i's by the usual formulas. Do this for the data in Problem 39 (page 556). Check that the estimated slope of this equation is the *correlation* between the X's and the Y's.

*58. Referring to the method in Problem 57, show in general that when the standardized Y's (the V's) are regressed on the standardized X's (the U's) the estimated intercept term is 0, and the estimated slope coefficient is r, the correlation between the X's and Y's.

59. The following data on 10 randomly selected cities were obtained from U.S. census data. (Reference: *Places Rated Almanac*, 1982.) The variable AVEX is the average expenditure per student in grades K–12, and the variable AVSAL is the average salary per teacher in these grades.

City	AVEX ($1000s)	AVSAL ($1000s)
Asheville, NC	1.585	13.176
Baltimore, MD	1.781	17.712
Buffalo, NY	2.098	19.824
Columbia, SC	1.241	11.400
Denver, CO	1.944	15.336
Gainesville, FL	1.642	14.148
Lubbock, TX	1.173	11.292
Nashville, TN	1.324	13.680
Pittsburgh, PA	1.523	15.228
Terre Haute, IN	1.256	13.464

a. If you had to estimate AVEX for a city outside this sample without knowing its AVSAL, what would your estimate be, and what would the standard error of this estimate be?

b. Answer the questions in part (a) for a city outside the sample with an observed value of AVSAL equal to 15.8. In doing so, develop the regression equation for AVEX in terms of AVSAL.

60. A cereal company would like to know how the number of "new triers" (customers who buy a given brand for the first time) is related to a brand's market share. The following data show the results of a survey of several cereal brands. The dependent variable Y is the *fraction* of all sales to people who never bought the brand before.

Market Share (Percent)	Fraction of New Triers
5.8	.090
6.7	.183
5.1	.065
8.0	.138
3.7	.154
5.7	.059
6.9	.124
5.2	.162
6.6	.106
7.2	.146

a. Estimate the linear regression equation that relates Y to X.

b. Use an ANOVA table to test whether there is a significant linear relationship between the fraction of new triers and a brand's market share at the 5% significance level.

c. Run a t test on β_1 that is equivalent to the test in part (b). Why are the two tests equivalent?

*61. For the data in Problem 48 (p. 558), let $Z_i = \ln(X_i)$, the natural logarithm of the number of salespeople in dealership i. The values of the Z's are shown below.

X	$Z = \ln(X)$
10	2.303
9	2.197
8	2.079
13	2.565
7	1.946
9	2.197
11	2.398
9	2.197 *(continued)*

X	$Z = \ln(X)$
11	2.398
12	2.485
9	2.197
6	1.792
13	2.565
8	2.079
7	1.946

a. Why is it plausible that the Z's might be better predictors of sales than the X's? (Refer to Appendix A for information on the logarithm function.)

b. Estimate the linear regression equation with sales as the dependent variable and the logarithm of salespeople as the independent variable.

c. If the number of salespeople increases from eight to nine, what does the equation in part (b) predict will happen to sales? Answer the same question if the number of salespeople increases from four to five. Why are the two answers different?

d. Calculate the r^2 value for the equation estimated in part (b) and compare it to the r^2 value found in Problem 48. Do the same for the standard error of estimate. What conclusion can you draw?

*62. Suppose that we calculate the correlation between the X's and Y's for any set of data. We then estimate the equation $\hat{Y} = \hat{\beta}_0 + \hat{\beta}_1 X$ and calculate the correlation between the $\hat{Y}$'s and the Y's. From your knowledge of correlation, why should the two correlations above be equal? Check that they are the same by finding both correlations for the housing cost data in Table 11.1.

63. For the data in Problem 35 (p. 543), let $Z = 1/X$, the reciprocal of the number of months of experience, for each worker.

a. Calculate Z_i for each worker, and draw a scattergram of the Y's versus the Z's. Does it appear to be more nearly linear than the scattergram of Y's versus X's from Problem 35?

b. Estimate the regression equation with Y as the dependent variable and Z as the independent variable.

c. Test the significance of the regression equation from part (b) by means of an ANOVA table at the 10% significance level. How does the F ratio compare to the F ratio in Problem 35? How does the standard error of estimate s_e compare to the s_e value from Problem 35? What do you conclude from these comparisons?

*64. It can be argued (and tested) that families with higher incomes pay more per year in medical costs (including those costs reimbursed by medical insurance). Suppose that a regression equation with medical costs as the dependent variable and family income as the independent variable is estimated from a large sample of families with a wide range of incomes. If the slope parameter of this equation (β_1) is shown to be significantly greater than 0, does this support the argument above? Why or why not? Does this evidence imply that families with higher incomes get sick more often? Why or why not?

*65. Some new restaurants start out with huge crowds that either continue or decline as time passes, whereas others are slower starters. Consider the following data on 15 similar-sized, similar-style restaurants from a large city. The dependent variable Y is the average number of customers per day during the 13th month of operation for each restaurant, and the independent variable X is the similar number for the first month of operation.

1st Month	13th Month
113	114
121	128
197	116
103	110
139	124
153	144
173	143
162	128
133	140
167	135
143	110
90	142
190	144
132	109
145	149

a. Draw a scattergram of these data. What can you conclude from it about the appropriateness of a linear fit?

b. Estimate the regression equation of Y versus X, and calculate the resulting correlation r.

c. Eliminate the two restaurants from the sample that appear (from the scattergram) to be outliers, and estimate the regression equation for the remaining observations. Calculate its r^2 value.

d. What conclusions can you draw from a comparison of the results from parts (b) and (c)? Which part do you believe has the more "valid" equation? Explain. (The answer to this question may not be as straightforward as it seems.)

*66. How would you react to the statement that if we take *any* two variables X and Y and we gather large enough sample sizes, the F test for the significance of a linear relationship will probably be significant, regardless of the presence of any *real* linear relationship between the two variables?

Computer Problems

(These problems are to be used in conjunction with the computer software package.)

1. Referring to the housing data in Table III of Appendix D, use the SREGRESS program to estimate a regression equation using actual selling price as the dependent variable and appraised value as the independent variable. Use only the data on the first 35 houses. Can you reject the null hypothesis at the 5% level that the coefficient of the independent variable equals 1? Can you reject the null hypothesis, again at the 5% level, that the constant term equals 0?

2. Use the SREGRESS program on the stock price data in Table VIII of Appendix D to see whether Revlon's stock price in one week is related to the stock price in the previous week. Specifically, let the dependent variable be Revlon's stock price in week t, and let the independent variable be the stock price in week $t - 1$. As an example, the last observation will have $Y = 30.5$ and $X = 29.75$, the next-to-last observation will have $Y = 29.75$ and $X = 29.75$, and so on. Use only the last 40 weeks of data in this problem. Discuss your findings. What are the prediction and the standard error of prediction for Revlon's stock price in week 210? Do the residuals appear to be autocorrelated? (You may answer this question intuitively, by "eyeballing" the residuals, or by entering the residuals into the AUTOCORR program.)

APPENDIX 11A

Derivation of the Least Squares Estimates

In Section 11.3 we presented formulas for the least squares estimates $\hat{\beta}_0$ and $\hat{\beta}_1$. These estimates result from minimizing the sum of the squared residuals. To perform this minimization and derive the least squares estimates, we need to use differential calculus. Therefore, this appendix is intended only for those who have studied optimization in a calculus context.

Our notation is the same as before. We let Y_i be the ith observed value, and we let $\hat{Y}_i = \hat{\beta}_0 + \hat{\beta}_1 X_i$ be the estimated value of Y_i when $\hat{\beta}_0$ and $\hat{\beta}_1$ are used to estimate β_0 and β_1. Then the objective is to find the values of $\hat{\beta}_0$ and $\hat{\beta}_1$ that minimize the function

$$g(\hat{\beta}_0, \hat{\beta}_1) = \sum (Y_i - \hat{Y}_i)^2 = \sum (Y_i - \hat{\beta}_0 - \hat{\beta}_1 X_i)^2$$

Writing this function as $g(\hat{\beta}_0, \hat{\beta}_1)$ emphasizes the fact that $\hat{\beta}_0$ and $\hat{\beta}_1$ are the variables we wish to choose.

To minimize $g(\hat{\beta}_0, \hat{\beta}_1)$, we set its two partial derivatives equal to 0 and solve the resulting two equations for $\hat{\beta}_0$ and $\hat{\beta}_1$. We have

$$\frac{\partial g}{\partial \hat{\beta}_0} = -2 \sum (Y_i - \hat{\beta}_0 - \hat{\beta}_1 X_i) = 0$$

and

$$\frac{\partial g}{\partial \hat{\beta}_1} = -2 \sum (Y_i - \hat{\beta}_0 - \hat{\beta}_1 X_i)X_i = 0$$

The first equation can be simplified to yield

$$\sum Y_i = n\hat{\beta}_0 + \hat{\beta}_1 \sum X_i$$

Dividing by n, this is equivalent to

$$\hat{\beta}_0 = \overline{Y} - \hat{\beta}_1 \overline{X}$$

This equation shows how we obtain $\hat{\beta}_0$ from $\hat{\beta}_1$; it is the same equation for $\hat{\beta}_0$ as in Section 11.3.

To obtain $\hat{\beta}_1$, we use the equation $\partial g/\partial \hat{\beta}_1 = 0$. This equation may be rewritten as

$$\sum X_i Y_i = \hat{\beta}_0 \sum X_i + \hat{\beta}_1 \sum X_i^2$$

or, using the equation $\hat{\beta}_0 = \overline{Y} - \hat{\beta}_1 \overline{X}$, as

$$\sum X_i Y_i = \frac{(\sum X_i)(\sum Y_i)}{n} - \frac{\hat{\beta}_1(\sum X_i)^2}{n} + \hat{\beta}_1(\sum X_i^2)$$

Solving for $\hat{\beta}_1$, we obtain

$$\hat{\beta}_1 = \frac{\sum X_i Y_i - (\sum X_i)(\sum Y_i)/n}{\sum X_i^2 - (\sum X_i)^2/n} = \frac{SS_{XY}}{SS_{XX}}$$

This is the same formula for $\hat{\beta}_1$ as in Section 11.3.

References

DRAPER, N. and SMITH, H. *Applied Regression Analysis,* 2nd ed. New York: Wiley, 1981.

KLEINBAUM, D. G. and KUPPER, L. L. *Applied Regression Analysis and Other Multivariable Methods.* North Scituate, Mass., 1978 (available from PWS Publishers, Boston).

LING, R. F. and ROBERTS, H. V. *IDA: A User's Guide to the IDA Interactive Data Analysis and Forecasting System.* New York: McGraw-Hill, 1982.

MENDENHALL, W. and SINCICH, T. *A Second Course in Business Statistics: Regression Analysis,* 2nd ed. San Francisco: Dellen (a division of Macmillan), 1986.

NETER, J., WASSERMAN, W., and KUTNER, M. H. *Applied Linear Regression Models.* Homewood, Ill.: Richard D. Irwin, 1983.

NIE, N., HULL, C. H., JENKINS, J. G., STEINBRENNER, K., and BENT, D. H. *Statistical Package for the Social Sciences,* 2nd ed. New York: McGraw-Hill, 1975.

NORUSIS, M. J. *SPSS Introductory Guide: Basic Statistics and Operations.* New York: McGraw-Hill, 1982.

WONNACOTT, R. J. and WONNACOTT, T. H. *Econometrics.* New York: Wiley, 1970.

CHAPTER 12

Multiple Regression Analysis

Objectives

1. To understand the purposes of multiple regression.
2. To learn how to interpret the coefficients of a multiple regression equation.
3. To generalize the statistical concepts learned in Chapter 11.
4. To learn how to interpret multiple regression output from computer packages.
5. To learn the meaning and advantages of stepwise regression.
6. To learn when to use dummy variables, nonlinear terms, and interaction terms.
7. To learn how to interpret diagnostic messages generated by computer packages.

Contents

Since many more wives are working now than in previous years, a natural concern of retailers is whether families with working wives spend more for consumer goods than families without working wives. This question was examined in a study that we will pursue later in this chapter. The study selected random samples of families with and without working wives. Then for each of several durable goods, such as refrigerators, a regression equation was estimated for each set of families. Each equation used only those families who had bought the item in the past year, and for these families the dependent variable was the price paid for the item. The principal result of the study was that families with working wives did not differ significantly from those without working wives with respect to this dependent variable.

However, there are several differences between this regression analysis and the regression analysis from Chapter 11. The main difference is there are now several independent variables, all of which help to explain the dependent variable. In the above study these independent variables included family income, the family's net assets, and others. A second difference is in interpretation. In particular, since family income is included as an independent variable, the foregoing conclusion does not mean exactly what it appears to mean. As we will see, it implies that families with and without working wives do not differ significantly with respect to the purchase price of durable goods, provided that they have the *same* income. Put in this light, the conclusion now seems much more reasonable.

12.1

Introduction

In this chapter we continue our study of linear regression, but we generalize the regression model in one important direction. We now allow any number of independent variables to be included in the equation for the dependent variable. Recall that the purpose of regression is to explain the observed variation in the dependent variable so that (1) we can better understand "how the world works," and (2) we can predict values of the dependent variable outside of the sample. In Chapter 11 we saw that one independent variable often explains a significant percentage of the variation of the dependent variable. Therefore, it stands to reason that the *combined* effect of several independent variables might be even more useful in explaining the variation of the dependent variable.

There are several important differences and also many similarities between simple regression and multiple regression. We will certainly point out the similarities when they occur. For example, statistical concepts such as the standard error of estimate, the coefficient of determination, the ANOVA table, and others are practically identical to those in simple regression. However, we need to be aware of the important differences between multiple regression and simple regression. Probably the most obvious of these differences is that multiple regression requires a computer for its many tedious calculations. Therefore, part of this chapter is devoted to explaining computer packages that perform multiple regression analysis. Besides this obvious difference, there are several other more subtle differences. For example, it is not always clear which independent variables should be used in the regression equation; in fact, there is often an overabundance of possible independent variables from which to choose. Furthermore, the coefficient of a given independent variable can depend on which *other* independent variables are included in the equation. This means that we must be very careful when we interpret these coefficients.

This chapter may appear quite different from Chapter 11, in spite of the fact that they both deal with regression. In Chapter 11 we not only explained the regression model, its assumptions, and its statistical properties, but also presented a good many formulas suitable for hand calculations. So in Chapter 11 it is possible to become overly concerned with formulas and lose sight of the overall purpose of regression. This should not be a problem in this chapter. Since we let a computer do most of the "number-crunching," we are able to devote our energies to building good regression equations and interpreting the numerical results. (It is certainly possible to perform simple regression by means of a computer package. However, the calculations are so simple to do by hand that the computer approach may be more trouble than it is worth.)

Before proceeding, we emphasize that multiple regression analysis is undoubtedly one of the most frequently used statistical methods in business and economics. Certainly, one of the reasons for this is that multiple regression computer packages are widely available and are fairly simple to use. But there is more to it than ease of use. Business people and economists are constantly trying to understand relationships between business and economic variables. Although multiple regression is not the only statistical method used in problems of this type, it is the best known and probably the most general of all such methods.

Because multiple regression is fairly simple to use and is applicable to so many real-world problems, there is a great danger of using the method incorrectly or in situations where it does not apply. For this reason, potential users of multiple regression should have a thorough understanding of the method. They should understand the model itself, the assumptions behind the model, the type of computer output produced (including diagnostic messages that point to violations of the assumptions), and possible ways of generating better regression equations. Although we discuss each of these topics, we cannot hope to make the reader an expert in multiple regression in such a short space. An entire course (or more) and a great deal of practical experience are required before a person can possibly master this complex subject.

12.2
The Multiple Regression Model

In this section we discuss the multiple regression model and the statistical assumptions behind it. Most of the material in this section is reminiscent of Chapter 11, but there are several important differences. For example, the role of scattergrams is somewhat more limited than it was before. Also, we must be more careful how we interpret the regression coefficients.

The Regression Equation

As in Chapter 11, all multiple regression analyses attempt to explain or predict the value of a single dependent variable Y. However, there are now several independent variables possibly related to Y. If there are k of these independent variables, we label them $X_1, X_2, \ldots, X_k$. Our basic assumption in multiple regression is that the dependent variable Y is related to the independent variables $X_1, X_2, \ldots, X_k$ by the linear equation below.

Regression Equation for a Single Y

$$Y = \beta_0 + \beta_1 X_1 + \beta_2 X_2 + \cdots + \beta_k X_k + \epsilon$$

The β's are again the regression coefficients, and ϵ is the random error term. Furthermore, we assume that the population mean of all Y's for fixed values of the X's, written $\mu_{Y|X_1,X_2,\ldots,X_k}$, lies on a population regression line. The equation for this population regression line is given below.

Population Regression Line

$$\mu_{Y|X_1,X_2,\ldots,X_k} = \beta_0 + \beta_1 X_1 + \beta_2 X_2 + \cdots + \beta_k X_k$$

By writing the regression line in this form, there are several assumptions we are making. First, we are assuming linearity. This means that the expression on the right-hand side of the equation is a constant (β_0) plus the sum of constants (β_1 through β_k) times variables. This linearity assumption is not quite as restrictive as it appears, because we are allowed to use *any* form of variables for X_1 through X_k, including nonlinear expressions. We will see examples of this in Section 12.7.

A second assumption is that the variables in the equation, X_1, X_2, . . . , X_k, are precisely those variables that *belong* in the equation. This was not an issue in simple regression, where we restricted ourselves to a single independent variable. But when we allow any number of independent variables in the equation, how do we know which ones belong?

This question can lead to a rather philosophical discussion of whether there is a single "true" population equation. This is an interesting issue (about which much has been written), but unfortunately, it is one that can never be resolved in practical applications. That is, we can never be absolutely sure whether the independent variables we have included are those, and only those, that belong. All we can do is attempt to include the variables that produce the best fit. As a practical consideration, most people desire *parsimony*, which in this context means adequately explaining the dependent variable with the *fewest* possible number of independent variables. So if the usefulness of a potential independent variable is questionable, it is often omitted from the equation.

The error term ϵ plays an important role in this discussion. Probably no applied study ever includes *all* of the independent variables related to the dependent variable. Perhaps some are omitted because of a desire for parsimony, some are omitted because the data are not available, and some are omitted because the investigator fails to see their importance. In these cases one component of the error term is the effect of the omitted variables. When we study residuals, the estimates of the error terms, we will see how these residuals change as we build equations with different sets of independent variables. Again, this is because the residuals act in part as "proxies" for the omitted variables. When variables are added to or deleted from the equation, the residuals usually reflect the changes.

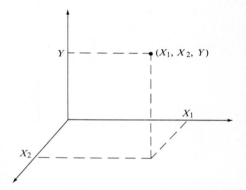

Figure 12.1

Scattergrams

We saw in Chapter 11 that scattergrams are very useful for deciding whether a linear relationship exists between a dependent variable and a single independent variable. In multiple regression, however, scattergrams are sometimes less useful because of our inability to draw graphs in more than two dimensions. Since we live in three-dimensional space, we can *imagine* a scattergram of points when there are only three variables: a Y and two X's. In fact, we can even attempt to draw such a scattergram on a piece of paper. Each observation in the sample is a triple of the form (X_1, X_2, Y). This can be located in a three-dimensional graph as shown in Figure 12.1. Here the two horizontal axes are the X_1 and X_2 axes and the vertical axis is the Y axis. If we have a sample of n points, then by locating each of them on the graph, we can produce a three-dimensional scattergram. The linear regression as-

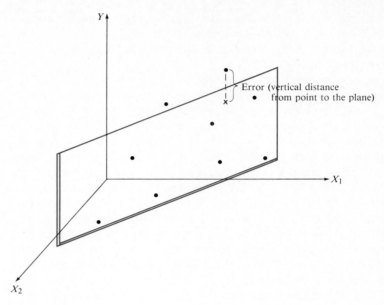

Error (vertical distance from point to the plane)

Figure 12.2
Scattergram in Three Dimensions

sumption is that a *plane* (the three-dimensional analogue of a line) will fit these points fairly closely. This is illustrated in Figure 12.2.

Unfortunately, it is virtually impossible to see the "shape" of the three-dimensional scattergram when it is drawn on a two-dimensional piece of paper. Therefore, we cannot tell whether a linear fit is reasonable. All we can do is imagine what a linear fit would look like. Furthermore, the situation only gets worse when we have more than two independent variables, because we cannot even attempt to draw graphs in more than three dimensions. So when we talk about regression lines (or more precisely, regression planes) in multiple regression, we are appealing mainly to the reader's imagination; we very rarely attempt to draw the graphs.

Nevertheless, scattergrams can still be helpful. Suppose that we are attempting to discover whether a linear fit with several independent variables is reasonable. Then we can draw a sequence of scattergrams, each of which shows the dependent variable versus a *single* independent variable. For example, if X_1, X_2, and X_3 are the independent variables, we can draw three scattergrams, one of Y versus X_1, one of Y versus X_2, and one of Y versus X_3. Presumably, if each of these produces a good linear fit, the combination of all three should also produce a good linear fit. This is not a foolproof method, however, as the following example shows.

Table 12.1

Y	X_1	X_2
9	3	1
16	4	7
25	5	15
36	6	25
49	7	37
64	8	51
81	9	67
100	10	85

EXAMPLE 12.1

Consider the data in Table 12.1. There are two independent variables, X_1 and X_2, and 8 observations. Clearly, Y is the *square* of X_1 for each observation. This implies that the scattergram of Y versus X_1, shown in Figure 12.3a, is far from linear. The scattergram of Y versus X_2 in Figure 12.3b, on the other hand, is very nearly linear. On the basis of these scattergrams, we would probably conclude that no linear equation that includes X_1 could possibly provide a good fit to the data. However, notice that for each of the eight observations, the equation

$$Y = 5 + X_1 + X_2$$

holds *exactly*. Therefore, by using X_1 and X_2 in the equation for Y, we obtain a perfect linear fit!

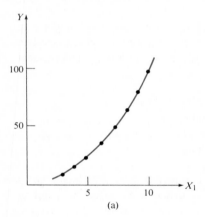
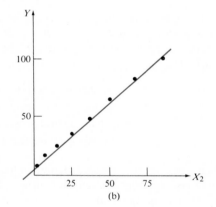

Figure 12.3

This example indicates that when a single independent variable does not appear to be linearly related to Y, as indicated by a scattergram of Y versus it only, this variable may still be a candidate for a *multiple* regression equation. So our advice is to use scattergrams for indications of linear fits but to proceed cautiously. When we look at the effect of a single independent variable on Y, we are ignoring the simultaneous effects of *other* independent variables on Y. These other effects can be estimated only by considering the multiple regression equation as a whole.

The parameters of a multiple regression equation are the coefficients β_0, β_1, . . . , β_k. In later sections we will see how to estimate these coefficients, but

Interpretation of the
Regression Coefficients

> *Assumptions of the Multiple Regression Model*
>
> 1. The error terms have mean 0.
> 2. The variance of the error terms, for any fixed set of X's, is a constant σ_e^2, that does not depend on the values of the X's.
> 3. The error terms are normally distributed.
> 4. The error terms are independent of one another, that is, there is no autocorrelation.

If we can imagine the population scattergram of points and the population regression "plane" passing through these points, an error term is the vertical distance from a point to this plane (see Figure 12.2). Assumption 1 says that the positive errors cancel the negative errors. Assumption 2 says that the variation of errors for any fixed values of the independent variables is independent of these values. In particular, the errors do not tend to vary any more or less for large X's than for small X's. Assumption 3 says that the distribution of the error terms is *normal* with mean 0 and variance σ_e^2. Finally, as we discussed in Chapter 11, assumption 4 is made primarily for time series data. In this case we do not want any noticeable time pattern of error terms to exist.

There is one other assumption that we make in multiple regression. Although it is not really a "statistical" assumption, it is very important for the numerical analysis. We assume that there are no exact linear relationships between the *independent* variables. If the independent variables are X_1, X_2, . . . , X_k, we say there is an exact linear relationship between them if any one of them, say X_k, can be written as a linear combination of the others, that is, if there are constants c_0 through c_{k-1} with

$$X_k = c_0 + c_1 X_1 + \cdots + c_{k-1} X_{k-1}$$

for *each* member of the population. If there is such a relationship, we say that there is *exact multicollinearity*.

> Exact multicollinearity exists when one independent variable can be written as a linear combination of the others.

To illustrate, suppose that X_1, X_2, and X_3 are defined as in the cola example: X_1 is the amount spent on television ads, X_2 is the amount spent on radio ads, and X_3 is the amount spent on all other ads. Then we should not include the independent variable X, defined as the sum $X_1 + X_2 + X_3$. This variable, which represents total advertising, is a linear combination of the other independent variables X_1, X_2, and X_3 since it is their sum. It should be clear that there is no real need to include X in the equation for sales, given that the other advertising variables are in the equation.

It is usually simple to avoid exact multicollinearity. For example, we make sure that no independent variable is a sum of several others, and that we have not included the *same* variable as two separate independent variables, one measured in feet, say, and one measured in meters. Such cases are easy to avoid because they are easy to recognize. But in many applications it is difficult to avoid *approximate* multicollinearity, where some of the independent variables are *nearly* linear combinations of the others. We discuss this phenomenon and the problems it creates in Section 12.8.

The statistical assumptions presented here are even more difficult to check than the corresponding assumptions in simple linear regression. We do not expect all of them to hold exactly, but we do want to detect gross violations. Fortunately, the standard multiple regression computer packages provide a series of *diagnostic* messages that indicate possible violations of the assumptions. Because it is important to know whether the assumptions are violated, it is important to know which diagnostic messages are available and how to interpret them. We will discuss briefly in Section 12.9 the diagnostics that are available.

Problems for Section 12.2

1. The following data represent the average monthly utility bills (electricity and heating) during winter months for a sample of 15 households in Pennsylvania. Also shown are the average thermostat settings, square footages of the houses, and income levels for these households. Using average monthly utility bill as the dependent variable, draw three separate scattergrams, one for each independent variable versus the dependent variable. Does a multiple linear regression equation appear plausible? Are any nonlinearities suggested by the scattergrams? Explain.

Utility Bill	Thermostat Setting (°F)	Square Footage	Income ($1000s)
$150.90	71	1609	19.170
170.70	71	1945	22.935
128.45	69	1665	19.345
151.65	71	1465	19.665
114.60	67	1495	18.555
119.15	67	1395	19.450
154.65	71	1585	22.250
161.60	70	1935	24.825
158.60	70	1550	24.385

(*continued*)

Utility Bill	Thermostat Setting (°F)	Square Footage	Income ($1000s)
$111.30	67	1265	18.950
146.60	70	1505	20.040
141.05	69	1575	23.315
131.65	67	1485	25.350
132.30	68	1350	15.045
142.85	72	1675	20.170

2. For the car data in Table 12.2, draw a scattergram of MPG versus each of the four independent variables. Do these individual scattergrams indicate that a multiple linear regression equation will probably be successful in explaining MPG? Why or why not? Are there any indications of nonlinearity?

3. What principle is illustrated by the data in Table 12.1? Is there any foolproof way to know from two-dimensional scattergrams whether we will be successful in using a *multiple regression* equation to predict a dependent variable? Explain.

4. In what sense is the error term ϵ a "proxy" for omitted variables in a multiple regression equation? How do we know

in any practical problem whether one or more variables have been omitted?

5. Why do some (usually more advanced) textbooks on multiple regression use notation such as $\beta_{3.1245}$ for the regression coefficients? How is this coefficient different from $\beta_{3.12}$? Why will the estimates of these two coefficients probably not be the same?

6. Suppose that we regress a dependent variable Y on the independent variables X_1, X_2, X_3, X_4, and assume that for each member of the population, the X's are related by

$$X_1 + 2X_2 - 3X_3 + 4X_4 = 0$$

Why does this imply that exact multicollinearity is present? (Verify that it is present by using the definition of a linear combination given in Section 12.2.) Would you need all four independent variables to predict Y? Why or why not?

7. The population of households in Problem 1 have average monthly utility bills that are related to the other three variables by the following population regression equation:

$$BILL = \beta_0 + \beta_1 THERM + \beta_2 SQFT + \beta_3 INCOME + \epsilon$$

a. Explain exactly how each of the three coefficients (β_1, β_2, β_3) in this equation should be interpreted.
b. What do you expect would happen to a family's monthly utility bill if they raised their thermostat setting by 2°F to celebrate the father's $300 per month raise in salary?
c. Answer the question in part (b) if the family there also moved to a house with 2000 extra square feet (in addition to the higher thermostat setting and the higher income).

8. Suppose that we use time series data to regress monthly sales against number of employees for a store that has been experiencing increasing sales and increasing employee levels over the past few years. If monthly sales vary more now than they did previously, is this a probable cause of autocorrelation of the error terms? If so, why? If not, which other OLS assumption is likely to be violated?

12.3

The Least Squares Solution

In this section we learn how to use the sample data to estimate the regression coefficients β_0, β_1, . . . , β_k. The notation is the same as in Section 12.2. The dependent variable is Y, and the independent variables are X_1, X_2, . . . , X_k. The equation relating these is

$$Y = \beta_0 + \beta_1 X_1 + \beta_2 X_2 + \cdots + \beta_k X_k + \epsilon$$

where the ϵ's are normally distributed with mean 0 and variance σ_e^2. We will concentrate only on estimating this particular equation. That is, we will not compare this equation with other possible equations formed by omitting or adding independent variables. (Comparison of alternative equations will be studied briefly in Section 12.10.)

The Least Squares Method

The method used to estimate the coefficients of the regression equation is in theory exactly the same as the method used in Chapter 11; it differs only in numerical complexity. The method is again called ordinary least squares, or OLS. Consider a random sample of size n chosen from the population. The measurements on the ith member of the sample are denoted by Y_i, X_{1i}, X_{2i},

. . . , X_{ki}. If we estimate Y_i by a linear combination of X_{1i} through X_{ki}, using $\hat{\beta}_0, \hat{\beta}_1, \ldots, \hat{\beta}_k$ as estimates of the true regression parameters, the estimate of Y_i is denoted by $\hat{Y}_i$ and can be written as

$$\hat{Y}_i = \hat{\beta}_0 + \hat{\beta}_1 X_{1i} + \hat{\beta}_2 X_{2i} + \cdots + \hat{\beta}_k X_{ki}$$

This equation is called the *estimated regression equation*.

Estimated Regression Equation

$$\hat{Y} = \hat{\beta}_0 + \hat{\beta}_1 X_1 + \hat{\beta}_2 X_2 + \cdots + \hat{\beta}_k X_k$$

(Here we have omitted the subscript i for clarity.) As before, Y is the *observed* value of the dependent variable, $\hat{Y}$ is the *estimated* value of Y, and $\hat{\beta}_0$ through $\hat{\beta}_k$ are estimates of the true β's.

The difference between Y_i and $\hat{Y}_i$ is called the ith residual and is labeled $\hat{\epsilon}_i$. Again the "^" is put over $\hat{\epsilon}_i$ because this residual is only an estimate of the true but unobservable error term ϵ_i.

Residual for the ith *Member of the Sample*

$$\hat{\epsilon}_i = Y_i - \hat{Y}_i = Y_i - \hat{\beta}_0 - \hat{\beta}_1 X_{1i} - \cdots - \hat{\beta}_k X_{ki}$$

Since a good fit means having small residuals, we choose the $\hat{\beta}$'s in order to minimize the sum of the squared residuals. The resulting estimates are called the OLS estimates.

The OLS estimates $\hat{\beta}_0$ through $\hat{\beta}_k$ are chosen so as to minimize the sum of the squared residuals.

So far, the analogy between least squares estimation in multiple regression and simple regression is exact. However, it is no longer possible to give simple formulas for the $\hat{\beta}$'s as we did in Chapter 11. (The relevant formulas are most easily expressed in *matrix* notation, but we have not included them here.)

Although we cannot give simple formulas for the $\hat{\beta}$'s, we can explain how they are found. To minimize the sum of the squared residuals, we use differential calculus to obtain conditions the $\hat{\beta}$'s must satisfy. These conditions are $k + 1$ linear equations in $k + 1$ unknowns, $\hat{\beta}_0, \hat{\beta}_1, \ldots, \hat{\beta}_k$. These equations are called the *normal equations*. They can be written as shown in the next box. (Here each sum is from $i = 1$ to $i = n$.)

> *Normal Equations for OLS Estimates*
>
> $$\hat{\beta}_0 + \hat{\beta}_1\bar{X}_1 + \hat{\beta}_2\bar{X}_2 + \cdots + \hat{\beta}_k\bar{X}_k = \bar{Y}$$
>
> $$\hat{\beta}_0 \sum X_{1i} + \hat{\beta}_1 \sum X_{1i}^2 + \hat{\beta}_2 \sum X_{1i}X_{2i} + \cdots + \hat{\beta}_k \sum X_{1i}X_{ki} = \sum X_{1i}Y_i$$
>
> $$\hat{\beta}_0 \sum X_{2i} + \hat{\beta}_1 \sum X_{1i}X_{2i} + \hat{\beta}_2 \sum X_{2i}^2 + \cdots + \hat{\beta}_k \sum X_{2i}X_{ki} = \sum X_{2i}Y_i$$
>
> $$\cdots\cdots\cdots$$
>
> $$\hat{\beta}_0 \sum X_{ki} + \hat{\beta}_1 \sum X_{1i}X_{ki} + \hat{\beta}_2 \sum X_{2i}X_{ki} + \cdots + \hat{\beta}_k \sum X_{ki}^2 = \sum X_{ki}Y_i$$

For example, if $k = 2$, the three normal equations are

$$\hat{\beta}_0 + \hat{\beta}_1\bar{X}_1 + \hat{\beta}_2\bar{X}_2 = \bar{Y}$$

$$\hat{\beta}_0 \sum X_{1i} + \hat{\beta}_1 \sum X_{1i}^2 + \hat{\beta}_2 \sum X_{1i}X_{2i} = \sum X_{1i}Y_i$$

$$\hat{\beta}_0 \sum X_{2i} + \hat{\beta}_1 \sum X_{1i}X_{2i} + \hat{\beta}_2 \sum X_{2i}^2 = \sum X_{2i}Y_i$$

In general, the first equation is formed by substituting sample means for variables in the regression equation itself (and dropping the error term). Each other equation is formed by (1) multiplying the regression equation through by a particular independent variable, and then (2) summing over the n observations in the sample.

Once the sums in the normal equation are calculated from the raw data, we obtain $k + 1$ linear equations in $k + 1$ unknowns. Unfortunately, the whole process is fairly tedious to perform by hand, particularly when k is greater than 2 or 3. It can be done, but there is an easier way: we let a computer do the work for us.

Computer Output

As we discussed briefly in Chapter 11, there are many computer packages available to solve the normal equations and to do many other regression calculations. Most of these are multipurpose packages that perform other statistical analyses besides regression. For example, most of them also do analysis of variance. Some of the better known packages are SPSS, BIOMED, SAS, MINITAB, and IDA. These "names" are abbreviations or acronyms for the actual names of the packages. For example, SPSS, perhaps the best known of the available packages, stands for Statistical Package for the Social Sciences. Each of these packages is a large computer program written as a sequence of subprograms. Each subprogram is designed to perform a particular statistical method that is too tedious to do by hand.

In general, the packages are similar in that they perform essentially the same set of statistical analyses. However, the commands required to implement the programs vary greatly from package to package. One basic difference is that some packages, such as SPSS and SAS, are written for "batch mode," whereas others, notably IDA, are written for "interactive mode." (By the time this book appears, SPSS and probably others will be available in an interactive version.) In batch mode we give the computer a set of instructions all at once, and then the computer provides the output all at once. In interactive mode, however, we sit at a terminal and "talk" to the computer. That is, we give it a command, it gives us an answer, we give it another command, it gives us a second answer, and so on. At the present time, it is probably fair to say that most statistical analyses (including regression) are done in batch mode. However, interactive packages are clearly the trend for the future.

We do *not* have to be computer programmers to use these packages. For any package we need to know (1) what each subprogram is designed to do (regression, analysis of variance, or whatever), (2) how to input the data into the computer and how to command the computer to perform the required statistical method, and (3) how to read and interpret the output. A user of any of these packages needs to obtain the appropriate manual, such as an SPSS manual, in order to learn aspects (1) and (2) above. Each package contains different subprograms, and more important, each package has its own idiosyncrasies in terms of data input and procedural commands. We will not attempt to teach these aspects here because there are so many options available. Instead, we advise users to find what they need from the appropriate manuals at their school or company.

What we will learn is the type of output provided by two widely used packages, SPSS and IDA. Although the commands for obtaining output from these two packages are quite different, their outputs are very similar. In fact, the output from practically any regression package is similar to the outputs from SPSS and IDA. Therefore, a person who knows how to interpret these outputs should have no trouble reading outputs from other packages.

An Example

The best way to proceed is to illustrate output from a particular example. The data in Table 12.2 (p. 586) show several characteristics for each of 33 automobile models. These data were collected from 1982 issues of *Consumer Reports*. We let the dependent variable be MPG, the miles per gallon experienced over a 15,000-mile test. (In this example and many others with real data, it is customary to let the variable names be meaningful abbreviations, such as MPG, rather than abstract symbols such as Y, X_1, X_2, etc.) The independent variables are (1) WT, the weight of the car (in pounds); (2) PRICE, the lowest base sticker price of this model (in dollars); (3) ENG, the engine size of the car (in cubic inches); and (4) REV, the number of engine revolutions per mile. Then the regression equation we wish to estimate is

$$\text{MPG} = \beta_0 + \beta_1 \text{ENG} + \beta_2 \text{WT} + \beta_3 \text{PRICE} + \beta_4 \text{REV} + \epsilon$$

Based on our knowledge of cars, we probably expect MPG to decrease as WT and ENG increase. Therefore, we expect β_1 and β_2 to be negative. The relationships between MPG and PRICE and between MPG and REV are probably less clear.

Table 12.2

MPG	PRICE	ENG	REV	WT	Model
28.6	6,278	112	2,570	2,450	Chevrolet Cavalier
34.5	4,997	98	3,335	2,135	Chevrolet Chevette
29.7	7,739	133	2,410	2,620	Datsun 200SX
30.3	5,139	91	2,775	2,020	Datsun 210
32.2	4,799	91	2,515	1,965	Honda Civic
30.3	7,995	107	2,625	2,140	Honda Prelude
25.9	7,545	120	2,785	2,635	Mazda 626
30.9	5,295	91	3,230	2,025	Mazda GLC
30.3	5,502	98	2,595	2,090	Mercury Lynx
33.0	5,543	86	2,715	1,950	Plymouth Champ
34.1	5,799	105	2,340	2,200	Plymouth Horizon
32.6	4,995	85	3,395	1,865	Renault Le Car
27.8	7,398	100	3,255	2,320	Renault 181
28.0	6,169	109	2,435	2,065	Subaru
31.9	4,998	89	2,765	2,050	Toyota Corolla Tercel
34.9	5,578	79	2,550	1,755	Toyota Starlet
28.3	8,375	105	2,510	2,190	Volkswagen Jetta
30.3	5,990	105	2,505	1,980	Volkswagen Rabbit
19.7	5,954	151	2,510	2,960	AMC Concord
14.6	8,719	258	1,855	3,480	AMC Eagle
19.6	8,712	231	1,965	3,320	Buick Regal
31.3	13,665	121	2,730	2,950	Audi 5000
21.0	11,049	146	2,980	2,930	Datsun 810 Maxima
26.8	5,990	135	2,415	2,465	Dodge Aries
14.9	7,750	225	2,320	3,425	Dodge Diplomat
20.1	5,985	140	2,635	2,905	Ford Fairmont Futura
18.4	7,126	232	2,110	3,010	Ford Granada
26.3	20,989	146	3,100	3,250	Mercedes-Benz 240D
26.1	10,990	141	3,110	3,130	Peugot 505
23.3	6,964	151	2,020	2,685	Pontiac Phoenix
23.3	12,249	168	2,150	2,900	Toyota Cressida
27.5	10,045	145	2,375	3,160	Volvo
18.0	8,221	229	2,090	3,630	Chevrolet Impala

The results of a regression analysis are shown in Exhibit 12.1. This is output from the SPSS package. Again, we will not explain how we commanded the computer to give us this output, except to say that we read the data in Table 12.2 into the computer and instructed it to perform a regression analysis with MPG as the dependent variable. To obtain the estimates of the β's, the computer solved the five normal equations in five unknowns, $\hat{\beta}_0$ through $\hat{\beta}_4$. The results are shown under the column marked "B". The variable listed as "(CONSTANT)" corresponds to the intercept term, so that $\hat{\beta}_0 = 48.236$. (The "E" in these numbers instructs us to move the decimal

Exhibit 12.1 SPSS Regression Analysis for Data of Table 12.2

			VARIABLES IN THE EQUATION				
VARIABLE	B	SE B	95% CONFDNCE INTRVL B		BETA	T	SIG T
WT	-0.00430	0.00227	-0.00896	0.35603E-03	-0.41033	-1.892	0.0689
REV	-0.00108	0.00152	-0.00419	0.00203	-0.07534	-0.713	0.4817
PRICE	0.34135E-03	0.1872E-03	-0.42063E-04	0.72475E-03	0.19412	1.824	0.0789
ENG	-0.07626	0.02502	-0.12750	-0.02501	-0.65486	-3.048	0.0050
(CONSTANT)	48.23554	4.94829	38.09942	58.37165		9.748	0.0000

point a certain number of places to the left or right. For example, .2E02 means .2 times 10^2, or 20.0, and .2E$-$02 means .2 times 10^{-2}, or .002.) The estimated equation is therefore

$$\widehat{MPG} = 48.236 - .0763ENG - .00430WT + .000341PRICE - .00108REV$$

This equation indicates that MPG is positively related to PRICE and negatively related to WT, ENG, and REV. For example, if the weight of a car increases by 100 pounds and its PRICE, ENG, and REV remain the same, we expect the MPG to decrease by $100\hat{\beta}_2$, or .430 mile per gallon. On the other hand, if two cars are alike in terms of WT, ENG, and REV, but one costs $100 more than the other, we expect the MPG to be $100\hat{\beta}_3$, or .0341 mile per gallon, higher for the more expensive car.

The positive coefficient of PRICE may be surprising. We tend to think of more expensive cars as larger cars that require more gas. But remember that the coefficient of PRICE is the effect on MPG of an increase in PRICE, given that the other independent variables remain constant. Therefore, the sign of the PRICE coefficient may indicate that if we can build a more expensive car and keep its WT, ENG, and REV the same, the extra expense results in extra MPG.

We have labeled the regression coefficients as β's, so why do we look at the "B" column, not the "BETA" column, to find the estimates $\hat{\beta}_0$ through $\hat{\beta}_4$? This is because the numbers in the "BETA" column in SPSS output are also estimated regression coefficients, but for an equation using *standardized* variables. (Some computer packages do not provide these BETAs.) That is, if we had first standardized all the variables (by subtracting from each observation the appropriate mean and then dividing each by the appropriate standard deviation), the numbers in the "BETA" column would be the $\hat{\beta}$'s for the regression equation with the standardized variables. In this equation all variables would be "unitless," so that the relative magnitudes of their $\hat{\beta}$'s would more accurately reflect their relative importance in explaining the dependent variable. Since ENG and WT have the BETAs with the largest magnitudes, it appears they are the two most important variables in terms of explaining MPG.

12.4

Other Statistical Quantities in Multiple Regression Output

Exactly as in simple regression analysis, there are several other important statistical quantities. These include the standard error of estimate, the coefficient of determination, the standard errors of the $\hat{\beta}$'s, the ANOVA table, and a number of correlations. Since these have interpretations very similar to their interpretations in Chapter 11, we will not explain them in much detail. Also, we will say very little about calculating these quantities because the computer packages do the calculations for us.

The Standard Error of Estimate

We again need to estimate the variance of the error terms, σ_e^2. The estimate we use is the sum of the squared residuals (the same sum that we minimize to obtain the OLS estimates of the β's), divided by the appropriate degrees of freedom. We again denote the sum of squared residuals by SSE. The degrees of freedom is no longer $n - 2$ but $n - k - 1$, where k is the number of independent variables. (Notice that we subtract the number of estimated coefficients, $k + 1$, from the sample size to obtain the degrees of freedom.) Letting s_e^2 denote the estimate of σ_e^2, we have

---

Estimate of the Error Variance σ_e^2

$$s_e^2 = \frac{SSE}{n - k - 1}$$

The square root of this estimate, s_e, is again called the *standard error of estimate*. Its value indicates how large the differences between the observed Y's and the estimated $\hat{Y}$'s tend to be. We expect about 68% of these differences to be less than 1 standard error and about 95% of them to be less than 2 standard errors.

Standard Error of Estimate

$$s_e = \sqrt{\frac{SSE}{n - k - 1}}$$

The standard error of estimate is found as "STANDARD ERROR" in the SPSS output (see Exhibit 12.2). For the car example, it is $s_e = 2.40$. This value is in the same units as the dependent variable, that is, miles per gallon. It indicates that for about 68% of the cars in the sample (or in the population as a whole), the difference between the actual MPG and the $\widehat{\text{MPG}}$ from the regression equation should be less than 2.40 miles per gallon.

Exhibit 12.2 SPSS Output Showing Standard Error of Estimate

```
MULTIPLE R              0.92054
R SQUARE                0.84739
ADJUSTED R SQUARE       0.82559
STANDARD ERROR          2.39638
```

The Coefficient of Determination, R^2

As in simple regression, we hope that a significant percentage of the total variation of the dependent variable can be explained by the combined effect of the independent variables. If SST is the total variation of the dependent variable, SSR is the part explained by the regression equation, and SSE is the part left unexplained (the same SSE as above), then

$$SST = SSR + SSE$$

The proportion of variation explained is again called the *coefficient of determination,* or the "multiple R^2." (Because most computer packages label this quantity R^2, we will switch to the capital R notation in this chapter.)

Coefficient of Determination

$$R^2 = \text{fraction of variation explained} = \frac{SSR}{SST} = 1 - \frac{SSE}{SST}$$

Many users of regression analysis consider R^2 to be the most important indicator of the "success" of their analysis. If R^2 is high, above .7 say, they believe their regression equation does a good job in explaining the dependent variable; if R^2 is low, below .5 say, they believe their equation is not worth much. This probably overstates the importance of R^2, for there are many other important aspects of a regression output to consider as well. But there is no doubt that R^2 is one of the key indicators of the explanatory power of a regression equation.

One important mathematical property of R^2 is that if we add an extra independent variable to a regression equation and reestimate the equation, R^2 *cannot decrease.* In fact, it almost always increases. (The only time R^2 does not increase is when the extra variable is completely uncorrelated with the residuals from the equation estimated so far.) Therefore, we can sometimes obtain an artificially high R^2 by adding many independent variables to the equation and finding that some of them, purely by chance, help to explain the dependent variable.

In an intuitive sense, this is not a very scientific way of obtaining a good regression equation. We should add variables to the equation because they are related to the dependent variable, not just because they happen to increase R^2. For this reason, most computer outputs report an "adjusted R^2." This R^2 value does *not* always increase when a new independent variable is added to the equation. Essentially, if the new variable does not explain enough to justify its presence in the equation, the adjusted R^2 can *decrease*. If this occurs, the new variable should probably be omitted from the equation.

For the car example, the R^2 value is .847 (see Exhibit 12.3). This says that 84.7% of the total variation of the MPGs in the sample is explained by the variables WT, PRICE, ENG, and REV. Because this is a reasonably large percentage, the proposed regression equation is fairly successful in explaining MPG.

Exhibit 12.3   SPSS Output Showing Value
                   of R^2

MULTIPLE R	0.92054
R SQUARE	0.84739
ADJUSTED R SQUARE	0.82559
STANDARD ERROR	2.39638

The ANOVA Table

The test of the explanatory power of the regression equation as a whole is again contained in an ANOVA table. This test attempts to discover whether the independent variables, *as a whole,* have any significant explanatory power. If they had absolutely no explanatory power, the population equivalent of R^2 would equal 0, and the coefficients of the independent variables, β_1 through β_k, would equal 0. So we may phrase the hypotheses for this test as follows.

Hypotheses for Testing the Overall Fit

H_0: $\beta_1 = \beta_2 = \cdots = \beta_k = 0$ versus H_a: at least one β_i is not 0

The ANOVA table presents the ingredients for an F test of these hypotheses. If the F value in the table is sufficiently large, we reject H_0 and conclude that at least one of β_1 through β_k is nonzero. That is, we conclude that the combined effect of the independent variables *is* useful in explaining the dependent variable.

The form of the ANOVA table is identical to those in Chapter 11 except that the degrees of freedom are different. In Table 12.3 we show the general form. (Notice that the mean squared error, MSE, is the estimate of σ_e^2 we saw earlier in this chapter. That is, MSE $= s_e^2$.)

Table 12.3   Typical Form of ANOVA Table

Source	SS	df	MS	F	Significance
Regression	SSR	k	SSR/k	MSR/MSE	p-value of F
Residual	SSE	$n - k - 1$	SSE/$(n - k - 1)$		

The F value is the ratio of two sums of squares, each divided by its degrees of freedom. Many computer outputs also show the p-value of this F ratio. This tells us how far out in the right-hand tail the F ratio is (and it saves us a table lookup). So if the p-value is very low, we reject H_0 and accept the significance of the linear fit.

In most multiple regression analyses with a reasonable amount of data, the F ratio in the ANOVA table has a very low p-value, so that the results are easily *statistically* significant. However, this only means that the independent variables (as a whole) have some explanatory power. In many cases the investigator must use his or her best judgment as to whether this explanatory power has any *practical* significance. After all, there are a large number of variables in the real world that are slightly related. What we are really searching for, however, are those variables that are related in a meaningful way.

The F ratio in the car example is 38.87. With 4 and 28 degrees of freedom, the associated p-value, listed as "SIGNIF F," is .000 rounded to three decimal places (see Exhibit 12.4). So there is little doubt that at least one of β_1 through β_4 is not equal to 0. Therefore, the combination of these independent variables certainly appears to be useful in explaining MPG.

Exhibit 12.4   SPSS Output Showing F Ratio and Associated p-Value

```
ANALYSIS OF VARIANCE
                  DF        SUM OF SQUARES       MEAN SQUARE
REGRESSION         4           892.81512         223.20378
RESIDUAL          28           160.79450           5.74266
F =      38.86766    SIGNIF F = 0.0000
```

The overall test of significance in the ANOVA table tells us whether the *combined* effect of the independent variables is significant. Now we look at their *individual* effects. There are several relevant pieces of output.

Statistics on the Individual β Coefficients

First, the standard errors of the $\hat{\beta}$'s indicate how far the estimated $\hat{\beta}$'s are likely to be from the true β's. These are shown in the "SE B" column to the right of the "B" column (see Exhibit 12.5). Generally, when an estimated regression equation is reported in a study, the standard errors of the $\hat{\beta}$'s are shown below the $\hat{\beta}$'s. So we would report the equation in the car example as follows:

$$\widehat{MPG} = 48.236 - .0763ENG - .00430WT + .000341PRICE - .00108REV$$
$$(4.948) \quad (.0250) \quad\quad (.00227) \quad\quad (.000187) \quad\quad (.00152)$$

Given these standard errors, the computer can easily find confidence intervals for the β's. (Most computer packages report 95% confidence intervals.) The limits of these confidence intervals are found by going approximately 2 standard errors on either side of the estimated $\hat{\beta}$'s. For instance, the standard error of $\hat{\beta}_2$, the estimate of the WT coefficient, is .00227. This leads to a 95% confidence interval for the true β_2 that extends from $-.00896$ to .00036. This interval and the confidence intervals for the other β's in the car example also appear in Exhibit 12.5.

Exhibit 12.5   SPSS Output Showing Standard Errors of $\hat{\beta}$'s

```
------------------------------ VARIABLES IN THE EQUATION ------------------------------

VARIABLE            B           SE B        95% CONFDNCE INTRVL B       BETA        T       SIG T
WT              -0.00430      0.00227     -0.00896   0.35603E-03     -0.41033   -1.892    0.0689
REV             -0.00108      0.00152     -0.00419   0.00203         -0.07534   -0.713    0.4817
PRICE        0.34135E-03   0.1872E-03   -0.42063E-04   0.72475E-03    0.19412    1.824    0.0789
ENG             -0.07626      0.02502     -0.12750   -0.02501        -0.65486   -3.048    0.0050
(CONSTANT)      48.23554      4.94829      38.09942   58.37165                    9.748    0.0000
```

The computer output also allows us to test hypotheses on the individual β's. The tests that are performed most often are for the hypotheses

$$H_0: \beta_i = 0 \quad \text{versus} \quad H_a: \beta_i \neq 0$$

If H_0 is true, the coefficient of X_i is 0, which implies that X_i is not needed in the equation. However, we must be very careful when interpreting these hypotheses. If we accept that β_1 is 0, for example, we are saying that X_1 does not help to explain the dependent variable *given* that the other independent variables are already in the equation. This is *not* the same as saying that X_1 is unrelated to Y. It simply says that the other independent variables have already explained a portion of Y, and X_1 cannot explain anything *more* about Y. It is very possible that X_1 is related to Y but is not needed once the other independent variables are in the equation.

This phenomenon often occurs when the independent variables are related to each other in a linear way. As an example, suppose that we are trying to explain salaries in a given industry by age, years of experience in the industry, and seniority with the present company. Since each of these variables is probably related to salary, the overall F test will probably be significant when all three variables are included in the equation. However, it is possible that we could not reject *any* of the individual hypotheses H_0: $\beta_1 = 0$, H_0: $\beta_2 = 0$, or H_0: $\beta_3 = 0$. The reason is that age, years of experience, and seniority are obviously related to one another. Therefore, when any two of these are already in the equation for salary, the third is probably not needed. (We will reexamine this example in Section 12.8 when we discuss multicollinearity.)

The SPSS output provides a t test for the hypothesis that an individual β equals 0. For each independent variable, a t value is shown in the "T" column (see Exhibit 12.5). This t value can actually be calculated very easily by the formula

$$t = \frac{\hat{\beta}_i}{\text{StdErr}(\hat{\beta}_i)}$$

If the absolute value of this t value is sufficiently large, we reject H_0. But if the t value is small, so that the standard error of $\hat{\beta}_i$ is large relative to $\hat{\beta}_i$, we cannot reject the hypothesis that the true β_i is 0.

Again, many computer packages essentially run this test for us since they give us the p-value corresponding to each t statistic. [In some computer packages, including earlier versions of SPSS, this p-value is shown under an F statistic instead of a t statistic. The reason is that the individual t test is equivalent to an individual F test (for a two-tailed test). Either test can be used.] In SPSS output the p-values are listed in the "SIG T" column (see Exhibit 12.6). If any particular p-value is small, we can reject the hypothesis that the corresponding β is 0. However, if a p-value is fairly large, larger than .10 say, then the usefulness of this variable, given that the other variables are included, is doubtful.

For the car example there is only one variable with a p-value less than .05, namely ENG. The p-values for PRICE and WT, .079 and .069, are also

Exhibit 12.6 SPSS Output Showing p-Values for t Tests

VARIABLE	B	SE B	95% CONFDNCE INTRVL B		BETA	T	SIG T
WT	-0.00430	0.00227	-0.00896	0.35603E-03	-0.41033	-1.892	0.0689
REV	-0.00108	0.00152	-0.00419	0.00203	-0.07534	-0.713	0.4817
PRICE	0.34135E-03	0.1872E-03	-0.42063E-04	0.72475E-03	0.19412	1.824	0.0789
ENG	-0.07626	0.02502	-0.12750	-0.02501	-0.65486	-3.048	0.0050
(CONSTANT)	48.23554	4.94829	38.09942	58.37165		9.748	0.0000

fairly small. (The "CONSTANT" term also has a low p-value, but we are usually not concerned with its significance.) Therefore, the coefficient of ENG is significantly nonzero at the 5% level, given that WT, PRICE, and REV are already in the equation. Because of their low t values, a similar statement cannot be made for the other three variables. However, this does not *necessarily* mean we should drop these variables from the equation. Possibly REV should be dropped, but a substantial decrease in R^2 might occur if PRICE, WT, and REV are all dropped. As a rule of thumb, it is best to drop only those variables that (1) have high p-values, and (2) have no strong economic or physical support for being in the equation in the first place.

Correlations

There are several relevant correlations in a multiple regression output. Recall that a correlation measures the strength of a linear relationship between *any* pair of variables. Since there are several variables in a multiple regression analysis, we have many possible correlations.

The square root of the multiple R^2 is again a correlation. However, it does not have the same interpretation as in Chapter 11. That is, it is no longer the correlation between the independent variable and the dependent variable. This interpretation would not even make sense here because there are *several* independent variables, not just one. Instead, this number R is the correlation between the actual Y's and estimated $\hat{Y}$'s. (It is labeled "MULTIPLE R" in most computer outputs.) If the Y's and the $\hat{Y}$'s are close to one another, then R is large, and we have an indication of a good fit. In this case, of course, R^2 is also large, and the F value in the ANOVA table is probably very significant. The multiple R for the car example is .921, a very large correlation. (It can be seen in Exhibit 12.3.)

The computer also supplies correlations between all pairs of original variables. These include correlations between independent variables and the dependent variable, as well as correlations between pairs of independent variables. In fact, if there are k independent variables, there are k correlations between the dependent variable and independent variables, and $k(k - 1)/2$ correlations between pairs of independent variables. All of these correlations, called *simple* correlations, are shown in a *correlation matrix*.

The correlation matrix for the car data appears in Exhibit 12.7. By looking at the MPG column, we see how each independent variable is correlated with the dependent variable. One way to interpret these simple correlations between Y and the X's is as follows. If a given independent variable were used *by itself* in a regression equation for MPG, the square of the associated simple correlation is the fraction of the total variation in MPG that would be explained by this independent variable alone. For example, WT would explain a fraction $(-.84)^2$, or 71%, of the total variation of MPG if it were the only independent variable in the equation. In contrast, PRICE by itself would explain only $(-.26)^2$, or 7%, of the total variation of MPG.

Exhibit 12.7 Correlation Matrix

```
CORRELATION
              MPG       PRICE        ENG        REV         WT
MPG         1.000      -0.258     -0.905      0.529     -0.840
PRICE      -0.258       1.000      0.319      0.035      0.587
ENG        -0.905       0.319      1.000     -0.646      0.879
REV         0.529       0.035     -0.646      1.000     -0.425
WT         -0.840       0.587      0.879     -0.425      1.000
```

If we look at simple correlations between pairs of independent variables, it is sometimes easy to be misled. For example, the correlation between WT and ENG, .88, is fairly high. This suggests that WT and ENG *may* be saying the same thing about MPG, so that only one of them is really needed in the equation for MPG. In fact, this may account for the relatively low *t* value for WT that we saw earlier.

However, high simple correlations between independent variables do not necessarily imply that one or more of these variables should be omitted from the equation. The same is true for independent variables having a low correlation with the dependent variable. The simple correlation matrix alone does not always indicate the results of a *multiple* regression analysis. The best advice is to look at the simple correlation matrix for possible important or unimportant independent variables, but to reserve judgment until the rest of the multiple regression output is examined.

12.5

Stepwise Regression

The computer output we discussed above is relevant when the regression equation is estimated "all at once." In this section we discuss a slightly different equation-building option that most computer packages possess. This is called *stepwise regression*.

In stepwise regression the computer does not build one big equation with all the independent variables included. It builds a *sequence* of equations, the first equation including only one independent variable, and each succeeding equation including one extra independent variable. We say that the independent variables are entered one at a time in a stepwise manner. Furthermore, they are entered in a definite order.

The first equation includes the independent variable most highly correlated with the dependent variable. Then the second independent variable entered is the one that explains the most of what remains unexplained after the first variable. Similarly, the third independent variable entered is the one that explains the most of what remains unexplained after the first two independent variables. After each variable is entered, the computer also checks whether any of the previously entered variables can be discarded from the equation. This occurs when the effect of such a variable can be explained by a combination of other variables that have entered the equation by that time. (Not all regression packages make this check.) This process of entering variables and possibly discarding variables continues until (1) all the independent variables have entered, or (2) the independent variables not in the equation explain an insignificant amount of the variation left unexplained. If the latter case occurs, the final equation does not include all the potential independent variables.

The reason stepwise regression is popular is that we are able to see the steps involved in building the final equation. We are able to see which variables enter in which order, and we can see how each explains a certain portion of the dependent variable's total variation. Of course, the output for stepwise regression is generally much more lengthy than the output for the "all at once" approach. This is because we get all of the output described in the previous sections for *each* equation built. If there are 10 potential independent variables, for example, we obtain complete output for as many as 10 successively larger equations. Much of this output is usually disregarded. Usually, we are concerned primarily with (1) the order in which the independent variables enter, and (2) the output for the *last* equation.

However, there is one interesting aspect of the successive outputs worth mentioning. The estimated coefficient of an independent variable included early in the stepwise procedure generally *changes* as other independent variables enter the equation. This reinforces what we said earlier in this chapter, namely, that the value of any $\hat{\beta}_i$ depends on the *other* independent variables included in the equation.

A portion of the stepwise regression output for the car example is summarized below. Here we report only the successive equations that were estimated, together with the standard errors of the $\hat{\beta}$'s, the standard errors of estimate, and the R^2 values.

Equation 1

$$\widehat{MPG} = 40.927 - \underset{(.0089)}{.1054 ENG}$$

$$s_e = 2.48 \qquad R^2 = .819$$

Equation 2

$$\widehat{MPG} = 43.512 - \underset{(.019)}{.085 ENG} - \underset{(.00167)}{.00205 WT}$$

$$s_e = 2.46 \qquad R^2 = .828$$

Equation 3

$$\widehat{MPG} = 45.220 - \underset{(.0208)}{.0665ENG} - \underset{(.00219)}{.00469WT} + \underset{(.00185)}{.000328PRICE}$$

$$s_e = 2.38 \qquad R^2 = .845$$

Equation 4

$$\widehat{MPG} = 48.236 - \underset{(.0250)}{.0763ENG} - \underset{(.00227)}{.00430WT} + \underset{(.000187)}{.000341PRICE}$$

$$- \underset{(.00152)}{.00108REV}$$

$$s_e = 2.40 \qquad R^2 = .847$$

Clearly, ENG is the most important independent variable for explaining MPG. Once ENG is in the equation, the other independent variables cause R^2 to change only slightly. However, the effect of ENG on MPG, as measured by its $\hat{\beta}_1$ value, does change as more variables are added to the equation. It goes from an original value of $-.1054$ to a final value of $-.0763$. Also, the standard error of $\hat{\beta}_1$ increases from an original value of .0089 to a final value of .0250. The reason for this increase in the standard error is probably that ENG is related to the other independent variables. When several variables, such as WT and ENG, say similar things about the dependent variable, we cannot tell how to distribute their *individual* effects, as measured by their $\hat{\beta}$'s. Therefore, the standard errors of these $\hat{\beta}$'s may increase when each is included in the equation. We will have more to say about this when we discuss multicollinearity in Section 12.8.

Most people would agree that equation 3 is "better" than equation 4 because it has a lower standard error s_e. The equations above were obtained from SPSS by forcing the computer to estimate all four equations. But the user of SPSS has control of several parameters that tell the computer when to quit. For reasonable settings of these parameters, the computer would probably quit after equation 3 and never even estimate equation 4.

It is important to realize that the final equation from the stepwise output (if it includes all the independent variables) is the *same* as the equation from the "all at once" approach. The two methods use exactly the same least squares procedure to estimate a given equation. Consequently, their end products are the same. The only difference is that we are able to see the intermediate equations when we use the stepwise option.

12.6

Prediction

The prediction problem in multiple regression is the same as in simple regression. After estimating a regression equation from sample data, we may want to predict the value of the dependent variable for other members of the population. As in Chapter 11, we may be interested in the value of an individual Y for a fixed set of X's or the mean of all Y's with these X's. In either problem we want to obtain a point prediction and the standard error of this point prediction.

Suppose that there are k independent variables, and we fix their values at $X_1, X_2, \ldots, X_k$. Then to predict an individual Y with these X's or the mean of all Y's with these X's, we simply substitute the X's into the estimated regression equation.

> ### Predicted Value of an Individual Y or the Mean of all Y's
>
> $$\hat{Y} = \hat{\mu}_{Y|X_1, \ldots, X_k} = \hat{\beta}_0 + \hat{\beta}_1 X_1 + \hat{\beta}_2 X_2 + \cdots + \hat{\beta}_k X_k$$

The standard errors for the two prediction problems are given by complicated formulas. Some computer packages supply these standard errors and some do not. (SPSS does not, for example.) However, we may approximate these standard errors very easily and fairly accurately. Of course, these approximations should be used only when the available computer package does not supply the exact standard errors.

> ### Approximate Standard Errors of Prediction
>
> $$\text{StdErr}(\hat{Y}) \approx s_e$$
>
> $$\text{StdErr}(\text{mean}) \approx \frac{s_e}{\sqrt{n}}$$

As an example, suppose that we want to predict the MPG for a car with WT = 2665, ENG = 140, PRICE = 6345, and REV = 2335. (These are the specifications for a 1982 Ford Mustang.) The point prediction of MPG is found by substituting these values into the estimated regression equation. This gives

$$\widehat{\text{MPG}} = 48.236 - .0763(140) - .00430(2665) + .000341(6345) - .00108(2335)$$
$$= 25.74$$

The standard error of this prediction, StdErr($\widehat{MPG}$), is approximately $s_e =$ 2.40 miles per gallon. The exact value of StdErr($\widehat{MPG}$) is not reported in SPSS, but from the interactive package IDA, we find that StdErr($\widehat{MPG}$) for this car is 2.48. Therefore, we may conclude, with approximately 95% confidence, that the actual MPG for a particular 1982 Ford Mustang is no more than 2 standard errors on either side of the predicted value, that is, from $25.74 - 4.96 = 20.78$ to $25.74 + 4.96 = 30.70$.

Problems for Sections 12.3, 12.4, 12.5, 12.6

9. Discuss the differences and similarities between parameter estimation for simple versus multiple regression. Are the principles involved any different? What about the computational aspects?

10. Suppose that we regress Y against two independent variables, X_1 and X_2. What property does the OLS regression "plane" have with respect to a geometrical swarm of points (as in Figure 12.2)? That is, what does it minimize from a geometric point of view?

11. Calculate the necessary sums in order to write down the normal equations for the data in Problem 1 (p. 581), using only thermostat setting and square footage as independent variables. (The only unknowns in your answer should be $\hat{\beta}_0$, $\hat{\beta}_1$, and $\hat{\beta}_2$.)

*12. a. Show that if there is only *one* independent variable, the solution of the two normal equations (for $\hat{\beta}_0$ and $\hat{\beta}_1$) gives the same values of $\hat{\beta}_0$ and $\hat{\beta}_1$ as we saw in Chapter 11. Do this by writing down the two normal equations and then solving them for the two unknowns $\hat{\beta}_0$ and $\hat{\beta}_1$. (*Hint:* Solve the first normal equation for $\hat{\beta}_0$ in terms of $\hat{\beta}_1$. Then substitute this expression for $\hat{\beta}_0$ into the second equation and solve for $\hat{\beta}_1$.)
   b. Illustrate the result in part (a) numerically by using the data from Problem 1 (p. 581) with square footage as the only independent variable.

13. The IDA output for the data in Problem 1 (p. 581) includes the following information.

a. What is the estimated regression equation?
b. Explain what the numbers in the "B (STD.V)" column mean. Be specific. Based on the relative magnitudes of the numbers in this column, which variables seem to be most important in terms of their influence on the dependent variable? Why?
c. Why are magnitudes of the numbers in the "B" column possibly misleading in terms of judging the relative importance of the independent variables?

14. Several of the $\hat{Y}$'s from the equation in Problem 13 are shown below.

Actual Bill	Estimated Bill
150.90	149.73
170.70	162.23
128.45	137.64
151.65	148.24
114.60	120.02
119.15	119.99
154.65	154.98
161.60	158.87
158.60	151.65
111.30	116.91
146.60	
141.05	
131.65	
132.30	
142.85	

IDA Output for Problem 13

VARIABLE	B(STD.V)	B	STD.ERROR(B)	T
THERM	0.6601	6.6706E+00	1.6257E+00	4.103
SQFT	0.1763	1.6650E-02	1.7604E-02	0.946
INCOME	0.2935	1.8364E+00	9.5538E-01	1.922
CONSTANT	0	-3.8858E+02	1.0204E+02	-3.781

a. Calculate the rest of the $\hat{Y}$'s, and then calculate the 15 residuals. These should average to 0 (except for possible round-off). Check that this is the case.

b. How many of the residuals in part (a) are within 1 standard error of 0? Is this approximately what you would expect? Explain.

15. The SPSS output for the data in Problem 1 (p. 581) is shown below.

a. What is the value of the standard error of estimate? Explain its meaning intuitively for this example.

b. What is the value of R^2? What does this tell us?

c. How significant is the F value in the ANOVA table? Explain what it means for F to be significant.

d. List the standard errors and 95% confidence intervals for the coefficients of the three independent variables. Explain what the numbers in the "SIG T" column mean.

e. Are there any important correlations between pairs of independent variables? If so, could these cause any problems? Explain intuitively.

SPSS Output for Problem 15

```
MULTIPLE R          .90670    ANALYSIS OF VARIANCE
R SQUARE            .82210                 DF      SUM OF SQUARES    MEAN SQUARE
ADJUSTED R SQUARE   .77359    REGRESSION    3        3638.43685      1212.81228
STANDARD ERROR     8.46021    RESIDUAL     11         787.32715        71.57520

                    F =    16.94459    SIGNIF F =   .0002

                  ---- VARIABLES IN THE EQUATION ----

VARIABLE          B         SE B     95 CONFDNCE INTRVL B      BETA        T      SIG T

INCOME        1.83637     .95538    -.26640      3.93913     .29349      1.922    .0809
THERM         6.67059    1.62572    3.09240     10.24879     .66006      4.103    .0018
SQFT           .01665     .01760    -.02210       .05540     .17627       .946    .3646
(CONSTANT)  -385.88184  102.04466  -610.48059  -161.28309               -3.781    .0030

             CORRELATION

                      BILL      THERM      SQFT     INCOME

        BILL        1.000       .822       .725      .516
        THERM        .822      1.000       .595      .195
        SQFT         .725       .595      1.000      .532
        INCOME       .516       .195       .532     1.000
```

16. The SPSS output for a stepwise regression of the data in Problem 1 (p. 581) is summarized on p. 601.

a. Given the correlation matrix displayed in Problem 15, do the independent variables enter in the order you would have expected? Why or why not?

b. Write the three regression equations that were estimated.

c. Does each successive equation appear to be significantly "better" than the one before it? Back up your answer with appropriate numbers.

17. The simple correlations between a dependent variable Y and three independent variables X_1, X_2, and X_3 are as follows:

$r_{YX_1} = .7$, $r_{YX_2} = .65$, $r_{YX_3} = .5$, $r_{X_1X_2} = .9$, $r_{X_1X_3} = -.1$, and $r_{X_2X_3} = .1$.

a. If you ran a stepwise regression on the data, in which order would the independent variables probably enter? Why?

b. Would your answer to part (a) change if r_{YX_2} and $r_{X_1X_2}$ were instead $-.65$ and $-.9$, respectively? Explain.

18. a. Use the data in Problem 1 (p. 581) and the output from Problems 13 and 15 to predict the average monthly utility bill for a household with a thermostat setting of 68.4°F, a house with 1600 square feet, and an income of $23,000.

b. What is the approximate standard error of prediction for this household? Why is this answer only approximate, and why can't you be more exact, given the output shown?

SPSS Stepwise Regression Output for Problem 16

```
VARIABLE(S) ENTERED ON STEP NUMBER 1..      THERM

MULTIPLE R               .82228      ANALYSIS OF VARIANCE
R SQUARE                 .67614                 DF      SUM OF SQUARES     MEAN SQUARE
ADJUSTED R SQUARE        .65123      REGRESSION    1         2992.43100     2992.43100
STANDARD ERROR         10.50030      RESIDUAL     13         1433.33300      110.25638

                         F =     27.14066    SIGNIF F =  .0002
───────────────────────── VARIABLES IN THE EQUATION ─────────────────────────

VARIABLE            B          SE B      95 CONFDNCE INTRVL B        BETA        T      SIG T

THERM            8.31000      1.59511       4.86397     11.75603    .82228     5.210    .0002
(CONSTANT)    -435.09000    110.62757    -674.08632   -196.09368            -3.933    .0017

VARIABLE(S) ENTERED ON STEP NUMBER 2..      INCOME

MULTIPLE R               .89869      ANALYSIS OF VARIANCE
R SQUARE                 .80764                 DF      SUM OF SQUARES     MEAN SQUARE
ADJUSTED R SQUARE        .77558      REGRESSION    2         3574.41156     1787.20578
STANDARD ERROR          8.42295      RESIDUAL     12          851.35244       70.94604

                         F =     25.19106    SIGNIF F =  .0001
───────────────────────── VARIABLES IN THE EQUATION ─────────────────────────

VARIABLE            B          SE B      95 CONFDNCE INTRVL B        BETA        T      SIG T

THERM            7.58063      1.30463       4.73808     10.42318    .75010     5.811    .0001
INCOME           2.31349       .80775        .55355      4.07343    .36974     2.864    .0142
(CONSTANT)    -432.86442     88.74466    -626.22240   -239.50644            -4.878    .0004

VARIABLE(S) ENTERED ON STEP NUMBER  3..      SQFT

MULTIPLE R               .90670      ANALYSIS OF VARIANCE
R SQUARE                 .82210                 DF      SUM OF SQUARES     MEAN SQUARE
ADJUSTED R SQUARE        .77359      REGRESSION    3         3638.43685     1212.81228
STANDARD ERROR          8.46021      RESIDUAL     11          787.32715       71.57520

                         F =     16.94459    SIGNIF F =  .0002
───────────────────────── VARIABLES IN THE EQUATION ─────────────────────────

VARIABLE            B          SE B      95 CONFDNCE INTRVL B        BETA        T      SIG T

THERM            6.67059      1.62572       3.09240     10.24879    .66006     4.103    .0018
INCOME           1.83637       .95538       -.26640      3.93913    .29349     1.922    .0809
SQFT              .01665       .01760       -.02210       .05540    .17627      .946    .3646
(CONSTANT)    -385.88184    102.04466    -610.48059   -161.28309            -3.781    .0030
```

19. In a multiple regression output, suppose that the coefficient of some independent variable has a t value that is not significant. Explain why this does not necessarily mean that this variable is unrelated to the dependent variable. Could the simple correlation between this variable and the dependent variable be large? Explain.

20. The following regression equation has been estimated on the basis of a sample of size 25.

$$\hat{Y} = 4.76 + 2.32X_1 - .76X_2 + 8.4X_3$$

The standard errors of $\hat{\beta}_1$, $\hat{\beta}_2$, and $\hat{\beta}_3$ are .75, .62, and 2.4, respectively. It is also known that SSR = 2901 and SST = 4753.

a. Find the standard error of estimate and the multiple R^2 for this equation.

b. The square root of R^2 may be interpreted as a correlation between two variables. Which two variables? Be specific.

   c. Which of the three coefficients, $\hat{\beta}_1$, $\hat{\beta}_2$, and $\hat{\beta}_3$, are significantly nonzero at the 5% level?

   d. Determine whether the regression as a whole is significant at the 5% level by completing the ANOVA table. What does it mean to say that the regression as a whole is significant at the 5% level?

21. How could the value of s_e^2 *increase* if we added a variable to a multiple regression equation that had very little relationship to the dependent variable? (What will happen to the numerator and denominator in the formula for s_e^2?)

22. A chain of discount stores used regression to estimate the yearly profit per store on the basis of several independent variables. Among these variables were X_1, the average daily number of customers per store for the 6 peak months; X_2, the average daily number of customers for the other 6 months; and X_3, the average daily number of customers for the entire year. Explain what is wrong with this approach. What estimation problems will it cause?

23. The F value in the ANOVA table allows us to test the significance of the regression equation as a whole. In what sense is there a possible difference between the *statistical* significance of an estimated regression equation and its *practical* significance? Which does the F test measure? Give an example where a regression equation might be statistically significant but not practically significant.

24. Suppose that you are given a multiple regression output from a new computer package. The only information you receive about the regression coefficients are the $\hat{\beta}$'s and their standard errors, the s_β's. How could you use these to obtain 95% confidence intervals for the β's? Be specific.

12.7

Modeling Possibilities

In this section we examine several ways of improving the fit of a regression equation. We do this by introducing new types of independent variables. These include nonlinear variables, interactive variables, and "dummy" variables. The techniques in this section provide us with many alternative approaches to modeling the relationship between a dependent variable and potential independent variables. In many applications these techniques produce significantly better fits than we could obtain without them.

As the title of this section suggests, these techniques are modeling *possibilities*. They provide a wide variety of independent variables from which to choose. However, this does not mean that it is wise to include all or even many of these new independent variables in any one regression equation. The chances are that only a few, if any, will significantly improve the linear fit. Knowing which independent variables to include requires a great deal of practical experience with regression, as well as a thorough understanding of the particular problem to be solved.

Dummy Variables

Some potential independent variables cannot be measured on a quantitative scale because they are qualitative, or categorical, variables. Nevertheless, they may be related to the dependent variable. In this case we can include them in the regression equation as "dummy" variables. Dummy variables are variables that indicate the category a given observation is in. They are usually "coded" to have values 0 or 1. If a dummy variable for a given category equals 1, the observation is in that category; if it equals 0, the observation is not in that category.

> Dummy variables are variables used to indicate the value of categorical variables. Their values are usually coded as 0 or 1.

Take the car data, for example. One categorical variable possibly related to MPG is the nationality of the car. Suppose that we separate all cars into two categories: U.S. cars and foreign cars. Then we may define a dummy variable FOR as

$$FOR = \begin{cases} 1 & \text{if the car is foreign made} \\ 0 & \text{if the car is made in the United States} \end{cases}$$

Now consider the following regression equation for MPG:

$$MPG = \beta_0 + \beta_1 ENG + \beta_2 WT + \beta_3 PRICE + \beta_4 REV + \beta_5 FOR + \epsilon$$

For any U.S. car, FOR equals 0, and this equation becomes

$$MPG = \beta_0 + \beta_1 ENG + \beta_2 WT + \beta_3 PRICE + \beta_4 REV + \epsilon$$

But for any foreign car, FOR equals 1, and the equation becomes

$$MPG = (\beta_0 + \beta_5) + \beta_1 ENG + \beta_2 WT + \beta_3 PRICE + \beta_4 REV + \epsilon$$

Geometrically, we can imagine two separate regression planes for MPG, one for U.S. cars and one for foreign cars. Because β_5 appears only in the intercept term, these two planes are parallel, but they cross the Y axis at different levels.

Using any computer package, we can estimate β_5, along with the other β's, by inputting a 1 or a 0 for each car in the sample. The relevant output from IDA is shown in Exhibit 12.8. As we see, the estimated equation is as

Exhibit 12.8 IDA Regression Analysis Output

```
VARIABLE   B(STD.V)        B           STD.ERROR(B)       T

PRICE       0.2299      4.0419E-04      2.1665E-04       1.866
ENG        -0.6679     -7.7771E-02      2.5438E-02      -3.057
REV        -0.0691     -9.9303E-04      1.5432E-03      -0.643
WT         -0.4363     -4.5736E-03      2.3451E-03      -1.950
FOR        -0.0601     -6.8732E-01      1.1512E+00      -0.597
CONSTANT    0           4.8816E+01      5.0996E+00       9.572

                 MULTIPLE R      R-SQUARE
UNADJUSTED         0.9216         0.8494
  ADJUSTED         0.9064         0.8215

STD. DEV. OF RESIDUALS = 2.4244E+00
N =   33
```

follows (notice that in IDA output, the $\hat{\beta}$'s are found in the "B" column; the "B (STD.V)" column is the same as the "BETA" column in SPSS output):

$$\widehat{\text{MPG}} = 48.816 - .0778\text{ENG} - .00457\text{WT} + .000404\text{PRICE} \\ - .000993\text{REV} - .687\text{FOR}$$

The estimated value of β_5 is $\hat{\beta}_5 = -.687$. The interpretation is that the average MPG for a foreign car is .687 mile per gallon lower than the average MPG for a U.S. car given that the other independent variables are comparable for the two groups. However, the t value for $\hat{\beta}_5$ is quite low ($-.597$). This means that we cannot reject the null hypothesis that β_5 equals 0. In other words, there is not enough evidence to conclude that U.S. and foreign cars really differ with respect to MPG.

To generalize the example above, consider a categorical variable with more than two possible categories. Then several dummy variables are necessary. In general, we need one less dummy variable than the number of categories. One category (any one of them) is called the *base* category. Then there is one dummy variable for every category other than the base category.

> There is always one less dummy variable than the number of possible categories. These dummy variables are all relative to a base category.

For example, suppose that we separate cars into three groups: U.S., European, and Japanese. We arbitrarily choose U.S. cars to be the base category and then define the dummy variables EUR and JAP as follows:

$$\text{EUR} = \begin{cases} 1 & \text{if the car is made in Europe} \\ 0 & \text{otherwise} \end{cases}$$

and

$$\text{JAP} = \begin{cases} 1 & \text{if the car is made in Japan} \\ 0 & \text{otherwise} \end{cases}$$

Notice that U.S. cars have $\text{EUR} = 0$ and $\text{JAP} = 0$, European cars have $\text{EUR} = 1$ and $\text{JAP} = 0$, and Japanese cars have $\text{EUR} = 0$ and $\text{JAP} = 1$.

Now consider the regression equation for MPG with the two dummy variables included:

$$\text{MPG} = \beta_0 + \beta_1\text{ENG} + \beta_2\text{WT} + \beta_3\text{PRICE} \\ + \beta_4\text{REV} + \beta_5\text{EUR} + \beta_6\text{JAP} + \epsilon$$

For U.S. cars, this becomes

$$MPG = \beta_0 + \beta_1 ENG + \beta_2 WT + \beta_3 PRICE + \beta_4 REV + \epsilon$$

For European cars, EUR $= 1$, so the equation becomes

$$MPG = (\beta_0 + \beta_5) + \beta_1 ENG + \beta_2 WT + \beta_3 PRICE + \beta_4 REV + \epsilon$$

Finally, for Japanese cars, JAP $= 1$, so the equation becomes

$$MPG = (\beta_0 + \beta_6) + \beta_1 ENG + \beta_2 WT + \beta_3 PRICE + \beta_4 REV + \epsilon$$

The only difference between these three equations is that they have different constant terms, that is, different Y intercepts.

The IDA output for this equation is shown in Exhibit 12.9. Now the estimated equation for MPG, using these two dummy variables, is

$$\widehat{MPG} = 49.951 - .0762 ENG - .00474 WT + .000361 PRICE - .00126 REV + .105 EUR - .937 JAP$$

Since the intercept terms for the three groups are 49.951 (U.S.), 49.951 + .105 = 50.056 (European), and 49.951 − .937 = 49.014 (Japanese), we expect the average Japanese MPGs to be slightly less than the U.S. MPGs and the average U.S. MPGs to be slightly less than the European MPGs. However, the t values for $\hat{\beta}_5$ and $\hat{\beta}_6$ are both quite low (.069 and − .782). Therefore, we can probably attribute the apparent difference between the three groups' MPGs to chance alone.

We did not find any of the dummy variables in the car example to be significantly different from 0, so we can conclude that these variables are not

Exhibit 12.9 IDA Output for Regression with Two Dummy Variables

VARIABLE	B(STD.V)	B	STD.ERROR(B)	T
PRICE	0.2055	3.6128E-04	2.2441E-04	1.610
ENG	-0.6541	-7.6173E-02	2.5679E-02	-2.966
REV	-0.0878	-1.2616E-03	1.5883E-03	-0.794
WT	-0.4523	-4.7412E-03	2.3693E-03	-2.001
EUR	0.0080	1.0511E-01	1.5176E+00	0.069
JAP	-0.0782	-9.3744E-01	1.1993E+00	-0.782
CONSTANT	0	4.9951E+01	5.3212E+00	9.387

	MULTIPLE R	R-SQUARE
UNADJUSTED	0.9236	0.8531
ADJUSTED	0.9051	0.8192

STD. DEV. OF RESIDUALS = 2.4401E+00
N = 33

very helpful in explaining MPG. In particular, the variable FOR caused the multiple R^2 to increase only slightly, from .847 to .849. Similarly, the variables EUR and JAP increased R^2 only slightly, from .847 to .853. Neither of these R^2 increases is significant. However, we should not conclude that dummy variables never improve a fit; they often do. Indeed, the addition of dummy variables has been an extremely important modeling device in many applied regression analyses. (In Appendix 12A we illustrate how one-way ANOVA can be carried out entirely by means of regression analysis with the use of dummy variables.)

Nonlinear Terms

The term multiple *linear* regression implies to many people that no nonlinear variables can enter the equation. This is not the case. What we mean by linear regression is that the regression equation is linear in the *coefficients,* the β's. There can be no terms such as $\beta_1^3 X_1$, $X_1^{\beta_1}$, $\beta_1\beta_2 X_1$, and so on, that are nonlinear in the β's. However, we are allowed to include terms such as $\beta_1 X_1^2$, $\beta_1 \log(X_1)$, and $\beta_1 X_1 X_2$, which are nonlinear in the X's but are linear in β_1. We simply treat nonlinear expressions such as X_1^2, $\log(X_1)$, and $X_1 X_2$ as new independent variables. This opens many possibilities for obtaining significantly better fits than we could obtain otherwise.

The simplest case is where there are only two variables, a dependent variable Y and an independent variable X. Consider the scattergrams in Figure 12.4. If we tried to fit the equation $Y = \beta_0 + \beta_1 X$ to these data, we would not be very successful because the variables are not linearly related.

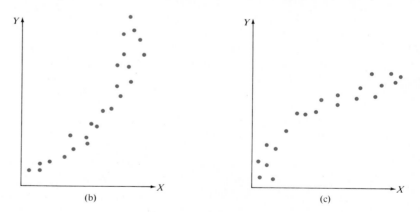

Figure 12.4
Nonlinear Scattergrams

The relationship in Figure 12.4a is one where Y first increases (at a decreasing rate), then decreases (at an increasing rate), as X increases. One situation where this might occur is when X is the amount of service (number of checkout people, for example) provided at a department store and Y is the store's profit. For low service levels, customers tire of waiting and take their business elsewhere; for high service levels, there are too many people on the payroll. There is a point somewhere in the middle where profits reach their maximum.

The scattergram for this type of situation suggests a *quadratic* curve. This curve has the form

$$Y = \beta_0 + \beta_1 X + \beta_2 X^2 + \epsilon$$

(The error term is again added because the points in the scattergram do not all lie on any single quadratic curve.) This equation becomes a linear regression equation by defining $X_1 = X$ and $X_2 = X^2$. This yields

$$Y = \beta_0 + \beta_1 X_1 + \beta_2 X_2 + \epsilon$$

which we can estimate in the usual way. (Many computer packages are capable of calculating the nonlinear terms for us. For instance, in the equation above we would input the X's and then command the computer to generate the squared values.)

For the scattergram in Figure 12.4b, Y increases at an increasing rate as X increases. This behavior might not continue if we keep increasing X forever, but it does occur for the range of X's considered in the sample. A typical application is when sales of a product are growing over time. For example, let Y be the number of companies that own microcomputers and let X be the number of years since microcomputers were introduced. Then the X axis is the time axis, and the scattergram shows how the use of microcomputers has been growing over time. One way to model this type of "growth curve" is to introduce the variable e^X, where e is the special constant 2.718. . . . Then we estimate the equation

$$Y = \beta_0 + \beta_1 e^X + \epsilon$$

By letting $X_1 = e^X$, we obtain

$$Y = \beta_0 + \beta_1 X_1 + \epsilon$$

which is the type of equation we know how to handle. We will use regression to estimate this growth curve in Chapter 14.

Finally, for the scattergram in Figure 12.4c, Y increases at a decreasing rate as X increases. An important application of this behavior is when Y is a company's total operating cost and X is its level of output. Then Y increases at a decreasing rate, due to economies of scale for higher output levels. To model this, we introduce variables that increase at a decreasing rate, the two most common being $\sqrt{X}$ and $\log(X)$. For example, we might try estimating the equation

$$Y = \beta_0 + \beta_1 \log(X) + \epsilon$$

As before, we make this linear by defining $X_1 = \log(X)$ and then proceeding as usual.

If we begin with more than one independent variable, nonlinearities are more difficult to detect and model appropriately. If we draw a series of scattergrams, each showing the relationship between the dependent variable and one of the independent variables, apparent nonlinearities may not require nonlinear terms in a *multiple* regression equation. We saw an example of this in Example 12.1. However, this example is probably the exception rather than the rule. If the individual scattergrams exhibit nonlinear shapes, it is a good idea to try the appropriate nonlinear terms in a multiple regression equation.

For example, suppose that there are two potential independent variables, X_1 and X_2, and their individual scattergrams against Y appear as in Figure 12.5. Then it is likely that the equation

$$Y = \beta_0 + \beta_1 X_1 + \beta_2 X_2 + \beta_3 X_2^2 + \epsilon$$

will provide a good fit to the data. To estimate this equation, we define a new variable, $X_3 = X_2^2$, and proceed as usual with the equation

$$Y = \beta_0 + \beta_1 X_1 + \beta_2 X_2 + \beta_3 X_3 + \epsilon$$

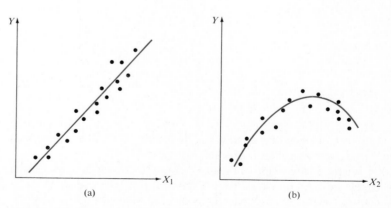

Figure 12.5
Evidence of a Nonlinear Relationship in Multiple Regression

EXAMPLE 12.2

Consider a company that experiences varying production levels and operating costs over time. The data in Table 12.4 show operating costs (COST), numbers of items produced (UNITS), and total overtime hours (OVERTM) for a random sample of 20 weeks. Find a relationship between the dependent variable COST and the independent variables UNITS and OVERTM.

Table 12.4

COST	OVERTM	UNITS	COST	OVERTM	UNITS
35.5	8	7	199.2	17	44
50.3	12	8	201.3	11	51
73.2	10	12	202.1	12	53
97.2	16	14	205.1	18	74
145.5	25	21	225.1	20	59
136.2	13	23	244.2	28	62
150.3	19	25	227.1	14	67
124.5	8	12	226.0	12	70
175.5	21	15	237.1	15	72
200.3	19	65	230.5	12	75

SOLUTION

If we use IDA to estimate an equation with UNITS and OVERTM entered linearly, we obtain the output shown in Exhibit 12.10. The resulting equation is

$$\widehat{COST} = 37.15 + 2.83\ OVERTM + 2.13 UNITS$$

Exhibit 12.10 IDA Regression Analysis for Data of Table 12.4

```
VARIABLE      B(STD.V)        B           STD.ERROR(B)      T

OVERTM        0.2362      2.8358E+00      1.1262E+00      2.518
UNITS         0.8479      2.1305E+00      2.3570E-01      9.039
CONSTANT      0           3.7150E+01      1.9069E+01      1.948

                 MULTIPLE R       R-SQUARE
UNADJUSTED        0.9256          0.8567
 ADJUSTED         0.9164          0.8398

STD. DEV. OF RESIDUALS = 2.5875E+01
N =    20
```

Exhibit 12.11 Scattergram of COST Versus UNITS

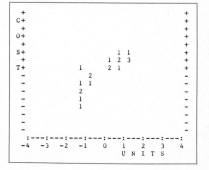

Although this equation provides a fairly good fit, the scattergram of COST versus UNITS shown in Exhibit 12.11 suggests a nonlinear relationship, where COST increases at a decreasing rate. (Each number in this scattergram indicates the number of data points at a given spot on the graph.) Therefore, two other regression equations were estimated with UNITS replaced by the (natural) logarithm of UNITS (labeled LOG) and the square root of UNITS (labeled SQRT), respectively. The results are

$$\widehat{COST} = -102.27 + \underset{(.895)}{1.653} \text{ OVERTM} + \underset{(5.86)}{71.15 \text{LOG}}$$

$$s_e = 20.03 \qquad R^2 = .91$$

and

$$\widehat{COST} = -22.45 + \underset{(.996)}{2.296} \text{ OVERTM} + \underset{(2.43)}{25.75 \text{SQRT}}$$

$$s_e = 22.64 \qquad R^2 = .89$$

Based on the s_e and R^2 values, the company would probably accept the logarithmic fit as the best of the three.

Interaction Terms

In this section we study a specific type of nonlinear term called an interaction term. This term is the product of two (or possibly more) independent variables. As its name suggests, it is useful when the interaction of the independent variables has an effect on Y that cannot be accounted for by their separate contributions.

Suppose that we believe Y is related to X_1 and X_2 by the equation

$$Y = 5 + 3X_1 + 2X_2 + \epsilon$$

One implication of this equation is that if we hold one of the variables constant, then Y is linearly related to the other variable. For example, if $X_2 = 6$, the equation becomes

$$Y = 17 + 3X_1 + \epsilon$$

If $X_2 = -2$, the equation becomes

$$Y = 1 + 3X_1 + \epsilon$$

The only difference between these two equations is their Y intercepts; their slopes are both 3. In other words, the marginal effect of X_1 on Y is the *same* regardless of the value of X_2. If X_2 is held constant at any value, and X_1 increases by 1 unit, we expect Y to increase by 3 units.

Now suppose that we do not believe the population behaves this way. In particular, suppose that Y is linearly related to X_1 when X_2 is held constant, but the slope (as well as the Y intercept) of this linear relationship depends on the value of X_2. We can model this by introducing the interaction variable $X_1 X_2$ (the product of X_1 and X_2) and estimating the equation

$$Y = \beta_0 + \beta_1 X_1 + \beta_2 X_2 + \beta_3 X_1 X_2 + \epsilon$$

(As in the preceding section, we would define a new variable $X_3 = X_1 X_2$ and perform the estimation in the usual way.)

To see the implication of this new equation, suppose that the β's turn out to be $\beta_0 = 4$, $\beta_1 = 2$, $\beta_2 = 5$, and $\beta_3 = 1$, so that the true equation is

$$Y = 4 + 2X_1 + 5X_2 + X_1 X_2 + \epsilon$$

Rewriting this, we have

$$Y = (4 + 5X_2) + (2 + X_2)X_1 + \epsilon$$

Therefore, if X_2 is held constant, Y is linearly related to X_1 with Y intercept $4 + 5X_2$ and slope $2 + X_2$, both of which depend on the value of X_2. For example, if $X_2 = 1$, this equation becomes

$$Y = 9 + 3X_1 + \epsilon$$

but if $X_2 = -1$, it becomes

$$Y = -1 + X_1 + \epsilon$$

These lines are contrasted in Figure 12.6.

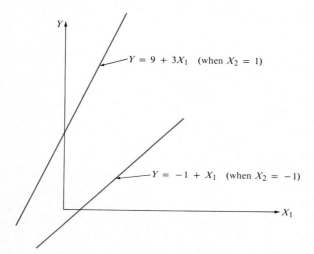

Figure 12.6
The Interaction Effect Between X_1 and X_2

It is very difficult to tell by means of scattergrams whether an interaction term belongs in an equation. The problem is that if we draw the scattergram of Y versus X_1, we are *not* able to keep X_2 constant. So even if this scattergram is really a mixture of several lines with different slopes (one for each X_2 value), this is practically impossible to detect. The best advice is to introduce interaction terms only if there is prior evidence that the marginal effect of one variable depends on the values of the other variables.

EXAMPLE 12.3

For MBA graduates, starting salaries depend, among other things, on their prior work experience and class standing in their MBA class. The data in Table 12.5 show the number of years of prior work experience (YEARS), class standing (CLASS), and starting salary (SAL) for a random sample of MBA's. (Class standing is expressed as a percentile; salary is expressed in $1000s.) Does there appear to be any interaction between years of work experience and class standing in terms of explaining starting salary?

SOLUTION

To answer this question, we use IDA to estimate two regression equations with SAL as the dependent variable. The first equation includes YEARS and CLASS only; the second equation includes these two variables plus the interaction variable YEARS*CLASS (where "*" means "times"). The results are shown below.

Equation without interaction term

$$\widehat{SAL} = 20.223 + 1.298\text{YEARS} + .0421\text{CLASS}$$
$$\qquad\qquad (.204) \qquad\qquad (.0154)$$

$$s_e = 1.71 \qquad R^2 = .814$$

Equation with interaction term

$$\widehat{SAL} = 17.409 + 2.214\text{YEARS} + .0917\text{CLASS} - .0156\text{YEARS}*\text{CLASS}$$
$$\qquad\qquad (.388) \qquad\qquad (.0228) \qquad\qquad (.0060)$$

$$s_e = 1.40 \qquad R^2 = .885$$

It certainly appears that the interaction term improves the fit. We see that (1) the coefficient of YEARS*CLASS is large (in comparison to its standard error), (2) the standard error s_e decreases from 1.71 to 1.40, and (3) the R^2 value increases from .814 to .885. From the second equation it appears that salary increases with years of experience (since 2.214 is positive) but that the rate of increase is *less* for people with a higher class standing (since $-.0156$ is negative). This is the interaction effect.

Table 12.5

SAL	YEARS	CLASS
19.20	0	25
26.36	0	89
23.26	1	33
24.72	1	76
24.18	2	47
22.70	2	21
23.36	3	12
27.42	3	94
26.92	4	57
31.86	5	69
30.62	6	41
29.10	4	10
29.78	5	82
28.96	6	28
31.10	7	90

25. Suppose that we try to explain a person's reading speed (in words per minute) in terms of his or her IQ and whether he or she has ever taken a speed-reading course. The following equation is estimated from a group of 50 people.

$$\widehat{\text{SPEED}} = -1151.6 + 105.3\text{RC} + 13.56 \text{ IQ}$$

Here RC (for reading course) is a dummy variable that equals 1 for people who have taken such a course, and equals 0 otherwise.
   a. Interpret the coefficient of RC; of IQ.
   b. For a person who has had a speed-reading course and has an IQ of 105, predict his or her reading speed. Answer this same question if the person has not had such a course but has the same IQ of 105.
   c. How can you explain the large negative constant term, -1151.6, in light of the fact that most people have reading speeds from 200 to 800 words per minute?

26. Consider a regression analysis where one of the predictors of the dependent variable is the major an MBA graduate had in school. The possible categories are finance, marketing, accounting, and "other." If we wish to use dummy variables to incorporate this information, how many dummy variables are necessary, and how would you code them for any particular MBA graduate? Be specific.

27. A record club wishes to explain the number of records its members have purchased in the past year by the number of months they have been in the club and the record category they are in. There are three categories: classical, country-western, and rock. Based on a sample of 100 members, the following equation is estimated:

$$\widehat{\text{PURCH}} = 12.26 - 1.41\text{CLASS} \\ + 7.73\text{ROCK} + .115\text{MONTHS}$$

Here CLASS equals 1 if a member is in the classical category, and equals 0 otherwise. Similarly, ROCK equals 1 if a member is in the rock category, and equals 0 otherwise.
   a. Interpret exactly what the equation above is saying. Does the average rate at which members buy records (that is, records purchased per year) depend on the category they are in? Explain.
   b. How many records would you predict a country-western fan has bought if he or she has been in the club for two

years? What about a rock fan who has been in the club for five years?

28. A department store ran an experiment to estimate the effect of the number of salespeople on the average profit (sales revenue minus wages and other expenses) per day. Why do you think the relationship between these variables might be nonlinear? Why in particular might the relationship be approximately quadratic? Draw a graph of the relationship you might expect. In this case what equation would you estimate, that is, which independent variables would you include?

29. For Example 12.2, use the three equations estimated to obtain three separate predictions of operating cost when 24 units are produced and 37 hours of overtime are used. Given the information you have, what are the approximate standard errors of these three predictions? Which prediction do you believe is the most accurate?

30. Referring to Example 12.3, consider an MBA graduate with two years of work experience who is in the 85th percentile of her class and another MBA graduate with one year of work experience who is in the 65th percentile of his class. How much more would you expect the first MBA graduate to obtain in starting salary than the second? Give two answers, one using the equation without the interaction term and one using the equation with the interaction term.

31. Suppose that we include an interaction term in the speed-reading equation of Problem 25, and the new equation is estimated as follows.

$$\widehat{\text{SPEED}} = -1132.9 + 107.4\text{RC} + 12.32 \text{ IQ} + 1.7\text{RC}*\text{IQ}$$

   a. What is the estimated equation for a person who has never had a speed-reading course; for a person who has had such a course?
   b. Predict a person's reading speed if he or she has an IQ of 105 and has never had a speed-reading course. Do the same for a person with an IQ of 105 who has had a speed-reading course.
   c. Interpret the coefficient 1.7 of the interaction term RC*IQ. Be specific.

32. As a variation of the car example from the text, the following three equations were estimated:

$$\text{MPG} = \beta_0 + \beta_1\text{WT} + \beta_2\text{HP} + \epsilon$$
$$\text{MPG} = \beta_0 + \beta_1\text{WT} + \beta_2\text{HP} + \beta_3\text{WT}*\text{HP} + \epsilon$$

Outputs for Problem 32

```
MULTIPLE R                    .818
R SQUARE                      .668
ADJUSTED R SQUARE             .659
STANDARD ERROR               3.407

ANALYSIS OF VARIANCE

                DF        SS        MS         F       SIG F

REGRESSION       2     1731.47    865.74     74.57     .000
RESIDUAL        74      859.21     11.61

VARIABLES IN THE EQUATION

                 B        SE B      BETA       T       SIG T

HP            -.042       .011     -.379    -3.818     .000
WT            -.0044     .885E-03  -.496    -4.999     .000
(CONST)      37.319     1.725               21.637     .000
```

```
MULTIPLE R                    .834
R SQUARE                      .695
ADJUSTED R SQUARE             .683
STANDARD ERROR               3.288

ANALYSIS OF VARIANCE

                DF        SS        MS         F       SIG F

REGRESSION       3     1801.53    600.51     55.55     .000
RESIDUAL        73      789.15     10.81

VARIABLES IN THE EQUATION

                 B        SE B      BETA       T       SIG T
WT*HP         .275E-04   .108E-04   1.061     2.546     .013
WT           -.0082      .0017      -.920    -4.792     .000
HP           -.119       .032      -1.075    -3.711     .000
(CONST)      47.163     4.210               11.203     .000
```

```
MULTIPLE R                    .849
R SQUARE                      .721
ADJUSTED R SQUARE             .693
STANDARD ERROR               3.236

ANALYSIS OF VARIANCE

                DF        SS        MS         F       SIG F

REGRESSION       7     1868.35    266.91     25.50     .000
RESIDUAL        69      722.33     10.47

VARIABLES IN THE EQUATION

                 B        SE B      BETA       T       SIG T

WT*HP         .513E-04   .317E-04   1.981     1.619     .110
WT           -.0126      .0030     -1.410    -4.182     .000
HP           -.164       .099      -1.482    -1.660     .101
D           -23.91      13.82      -1.983    -1.730     .088
D*WT*HP      -.527E-04   .375E-04  -2.707    -1.407     .164
D*WT          .0101      .0048      2.781     2.126     .037
D*HP          .121       .118       1.805     1.027     .308
(CONST)      56.113     7.808                 7.186     .000
```

and

$$\text{MPG} = \beta_0 + \beta_1\text{WT} + \beta_2\text{HP} + \beta_3\text{WT}*\text{HP} + \beta_4\text{D}$$

$$+ \beta_5\text{D}*\text{WT} + \beta_6\text{D}*\text{HP} + \beta_7\text{D}*\text{WT}*\text{HP} + \epsilon$$

The variables MPG and WT are as before, HP means horsepower, D is a dummy variable for price (D = 1 for cars with price greater than $10,000, D = 0 for cars with price less than $10,000), and "∗" indicates multiplication. The outputs for the three equations are shown on p. 614. Consider a car that weighs 2450 pounds, has 88 horsepower, and costs $6290. Use each of the three estimated equations to predict this car's MPG. Repeat the calculations for a car that weighs 2930 pounds, has 103 horsepower, and costs $11,050.

33. A researcher estimated the equation

$$Y = \beta_0 + \beta_1 X_1 + \beta_2 X_2 + \beta_3 X_3 + \epsilon$$

for 25 randomly selected senior citizens. The variables are as follows. The dependent variable Y is the number of hours per day the person watches TV, X_1 indicates the marital status of the person ($X_1 = 1$ if married, $X_1 = 0$ otherwise), X_2 is the person's age in years, and X_3 is the person's amount of education in years. The multiple regression output is shown below.

a. For a randomly selected 75-year-old married person who had 12 years of education, predict the number of hours per day this person watches TV. Is this prediction likely to be off by more than an hour? Why or why not?

b. Test the significance of the overall regression equation at the 5% level; at the 1% level.

c. Find a 95% confidence interval for β_2. Also, test the null hypothesis that $\beta_2 = 0$ versus a two-tailed alternative at the 5% level. How are the answers to these two questions about β_2 related?

d. Interpret the estimate of β_1 in words. That is, how does it relate marital status to the dependent variable? Be specific.

Output for Problem 33

MULTIPLE R	.7918
R SQUARE	.6269
STD. ERROR OF EST.	.7524

ANALYSIS OF VARIANCE

	DF	SS	MS	F
REGRESSION	3	19.972	6.657	11.760
RESIDUAL	21	11.888	.566	

INDIVIDUAL ANALYSIS OF VARIABLES

VARIABLE	COEFFICIENT	STD. ERROR	T VALUE
(CONSTANT)	1.414		
MARITAL STATUS	-1.174	.315	-3.727
AGE	.040	.032	1.250
YEARS EDUCATION	-.151	.050	-3.020

34. In what sense is the following regression equation linear and in what sense is it nonlinear? Would you be able to estimate its coefficients by OLS, given data on Y, X_1, and X_2? If not, why? If so, how?

$$Y = \beta_0 + \beta_1 X_1 + \beta_2 X_1 X_2^3 + \beta_3 \log(X_1 X_2) + \epsilon$$

35. Answer the same questions as in Problem 34 for the following regression equation.

$$Y = \beta_0 + \beta_1 X_1^2 + \beta_2 X_2^2 + \beta_1\beta_2 X_1 X_2 + \epsilon$$

*36. Suppose that we wish to regress starting salaries of MBA graduates on their class standing (percentile of their graduating class) and their sex. The three independent variables are

CLASS (class standing), SEX (1 for men, 0 for women), and CLASS*SEX (the product of CLASS and SEX).

a. How do you interpret the coefficient of SEX? How do you interpret the coefficient of CLASS*SEX? In particular, if both of these coefficients are negative, what does this say about starting salaries?

b. If the coefficient of CLASS is positive and the coefficients of SEX and CLASS*SEX are negative, graph two straight lines (on the same graph), one showing the relationship between starting salary and class standing for men, and the other showing this relationship for women.

12.8

Multicollinearity

In Section 12.2 we said that we do not want any exact linear relationships to exist between the independent variables. For example, we do not want one of them to be the sum of several of the others, and we do not want any of them to be proportional to any of the others. This is called exact multicollinearity and is usually easy to avoid by being careful. However, we often have *near* multicollinearity, where several of the independent variables are nearly linearly related to one another. In this case these independent variables often explain the same things about the dependent variable. In this section we will see how multicollinearity can cause estimation problems.

To understand why multicollinearity is undesirable, let's reexamine the cola example from the beginning of this chapter. We again let the dependent variable Y be cola sales for a given month, and we let the independent variables X_1, X_2, and X_3 be advertising variables for various types of advertising. Now if we let X_4 be the total amount of advertising, then $X_4 = X_1 + X_2 + X_3$. (We ignore the temperature variable that was used earlier.) Then the regression equation is

$$Y = \beta_0 + \beta_1 X_1 + \beta_2 X_2 + \beta_3 X_3 + \beta_4 X_4 + \epsilon$$

By substituting $X_1 + X_2 + X_3$ for X_4, this equation becomes

$$Y = \beta_0 + (\beta_1 + \beta_4)X_1 + (\beta_2 + \beta_4)X_2 + (\beta_3 + \beta_4)X_3 + \epsilon$$

If we try to estimate the original regression equation (with X_4 as a separate variable), it will be impossible to estimate β_1 through β_4 uniquely. The problem is that we can only estimate the *sums* $\beta_1 + \beta_4$, $\beta_2 + \beta_4$, and $\beta_3 + \beta_4$, not the individual β's. To see why this is true, suppose it turns out that the true values of these sums are $\beta_1 + \beta_4 = 5$, $\beta_2 + \beta_4 = 4$, and $\beta_3 + \beta_4 = 3$. Then there are infinitely many individual β's that produce these sums. For example, we could have $\beta_1 = 3$, $\beta_2 = 2$, $\beta_3 = 1$, and $\beta_4 = 2$, or $\beta_1 = 2.5$, $\beta_2 = 1.5$, $\beta_3 = .5$, and $\beta_4 = 2.5$. When we include the same explanatory variable more than once (television advertising, for instance, is included in X_1 and X_4), we cannot distinguish the *separate* influences on the dependent variable. This is why we can determine only the sums of the β's, not the individual β's.

This is why we try to avoid multicollinearity. In the example above, it is easy to avoid. We simply omit X_4. In other situations multicollinearity is not this easy to avoid. Consider an example mentioned earlier, where we would like to explain salaries in a given industry by age, years of experience in the industry, and seniority in the present company. These independent variables are definitely related, and we would expect to see fairly high simple correlations between pairs of them. However, the three variables are not exactly the same, so we may decide to include all three in the equation for salary. What problems will this cause?

The main problem is that we will not be able to distinguish their separate influences on the dependent variable. This means that we will probably not obtain very accurate estimates of their β's. In particular, the standard errors of the individual β's will probably be quite large, so that their individual t statistics will be fairly small. This does *not* mean that the overall regression will be a failure. It is quite possible that the combination of these three variables will explain a high percentage of the variation of salaries, and that it will be very useful for prediction. We simply will not be able to estimate the *individual* effects of the three independent variables.

When multicollinearity is present, there are two options available. First, we can omit one or more of the variables causing the multicollinearity. In the example above we could omit one or two of the independent variables, say age and/or seniority, and hopefully, obtain nearly as high an R^2 value without them. The other option is to leave all the independent variables in the equation even though they are related. If we do this, we must recognize that the estimates of the individual β's may not be very accurate, even though the overall F ratio (in the ANOVA table) may be very significant.

12.9

Diagnostics

Multiple regression analysis is frequently as much an art as a science. When we have real data with many potential independent variables, there are usually many possibilities. Given an easy-to-use computer package such as SPSS or IDA, it is relatively simple to try many of these possibilities. However, we must always be aware of the basic assumptions underlying the regression model. If these assumptions are grossly violated, the *statistical* analysis we perform may be incorrect.

Fortunately, all regression packages provide us with diagnostics that indicate whether any of the basic assumptions have been violated. If we do detect violations of the assumptions, corrective measures should be taken. We will not discuss these corrective measures in much detail, for they belong in a more advanced statistics book. In this section we simply discuss some of the diagnostics available.

Nonlinear Pattern of Residuals

When a computer package estimates a regression equation, it calculates the residuals (the $\hat{e}$'s) and can then plot these on a scattergram versus any of the other variables in the study. These scattergrams often indicate undesirable behavior. One particularly interesting scattergram is of residuals versus the estimated values of the dependent variable (the $\hat{Y}$'s). If the estimated linear fit is a good one, the residuals should not only have a mean of 0 but should also vary *randomly* around 0. That is, there should be no detectable patterns.

The graphs in Figure 12.7 show two possible scattergrams of residuals versus $\hat{Y}$'s. The graph in Figure 12.7a is what we want to see. The residuals vary randomly around the horizontal axis. However, the residuals in Figure 12.7b exhibit a definite nonlinear pattern. For small and large $\hat{Y}$'s they are positive, but for $\hat{Y}$'s in the middle range, they are negative. This type of behavior suggests that we should use one or more nonlinear variables in the equation, as in Section 12.7.

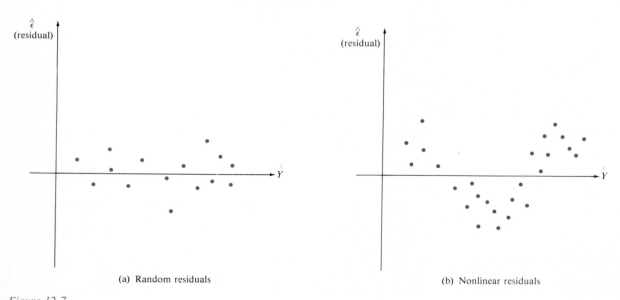

(a) Random residuals   (b) Nonlinear residuals

Figure 12.7

Nonconstant Error Variance

Another purpose of the residual scattergrams is to detect a nonconstant error variance. From the basic assumptions we know that the error variance should remain constant at different levels of the independent variables. This implies the residuals should not vary any more or less for large $\hat{Y}$'s than for small $\hat{Y}$'s. For example, if Y is household income, the variation of incomes should not be any greater for the high-income groups than for the low-income groups.

The scattergram in Figure 12.8 illustrates a nonconstant error variance. For small $\hat{Y}$'s the residuals are tightly bunched around the horizontal axis, but for large $\hat{Y}$'s they are more spread out. If this pattern exists and we do nothing to remedy it, the standard error of estimate, s_e, will be misleading. It will be too large for small Y's and too small for large Y's.

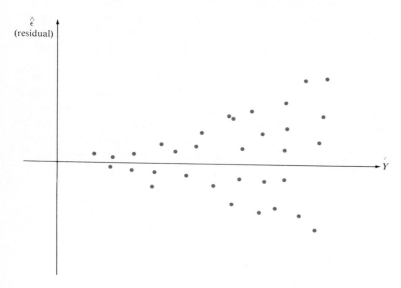

Figure 12.8
Nonconstant Error Variance

One common remedy for the type of nonconstant error variance shown in Figure 12.8 is to use $\log(Y)$, rather than Y, as the dependent variable. The logarithm function essentially spreads out the small Y's and compresses the large Y's. This often results in a more nearly constant error variance.

Nonnormality of the Errors

The assumption of normally distributed error terms implies that the histogram of the residuals should be approximately symmetric and bell-shaped. Most regression packages allow us to check this by providing the residual histogram and other graphical evidence. For relatively small samples, however, it is very difficult to distinguish between normality and nonnormality. There are simply too few residuals to show us the true shape of the residual distribution. Therefore, we can only look for obvious departures from normality, such as obvious skewness to the left or the right.

Nonnormality of the residuals and nonconstant error variance commonly go together. Referring again to the population of incomes, there is likely to be a greater residual variance for the high-income group than for the low-income group. The distribution of residuals is also likely to be skewed to the right. Therefore, the logarithmic transformation of Y mentioned above can often remove the skewness and the nonconstant error variance simultaneously.

Autocorrelation

When we have time series data (as opposed to cross-sectional data), the errors in nearby time periods are often correlated with one another. We call this autocorrelation. If autocorrelation is present, the errors are *not* independent as we have assumed, and the standard regression analysis may contain serious mistakes.

It is difficult to deal with autocorrelation, but it is fairly simple to detect it. Durbin and Watson, two well-known statisticians, have devised a statistic for detecting autocorrelation. This *Durbin–Watson statistic* has a value between 0 and 4. If it is close enough to 2 (as determined by special tables), there is no significant evidence of autocorrelation. But if its value is close to 0 or to 4, there is probably an autocorrelation problem (see Figure 12.9).

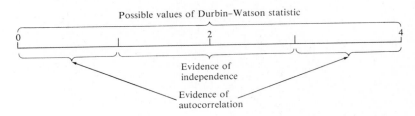

Figure 12.9
Durbin–Watson Statistic

Fortunately, this Durbin–Watson statistic is a part of most computer regression outputs. We will have more to say about autocorrelation in time series data in Chapter 14.

> The Durbin–Watson statistic is used to indicate autocorrelation. A value close to 2 indicates that successive residuals are independent; a value close to 0 or 4 indicates autocorrelation.

Outliers

Outliers are members of the sample that are quite different from the "typical" members. They may have unusual Y values, X values, residual values, or any combination of these. The problem created by outliers is that they can exert an undue influence on the regression equation as a whole. For example, one outlier can completely "tilt" a regression line and can seriously deflate an R^2 value. The scattergram in Figure 12.10 indicates how this can occur.

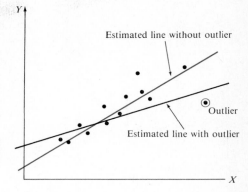

Figure 12.10
An "Influential" Outlier

As with autocorrelation, outliers are difficult to deal with (we should *not* simply throw them away!), but they are relatively easy to locate. The NEW REGRESSION subprogram of SPSS, for example, lists the worst outliers with respect to several criteria. These include (1) the observations with the largest residuals; (2) the observations with X values farthest from the typical values in the sample; and (3) the most "influential" observations, that is, those such as the point in Figure 12.10 that tilt the whole regression line. Once we know which observations are outliers, we can attempt to deal with them on an individual basis.

12.10

A Test for Comparing Two Regression Equations

When there are many potential independent variables in a regression study, it is difficult to select the ones to include in the regression equation. If we add variables that do not belong, they may have undesirable effects on the equation as a whole. For example, the standard errors of the $\hat{\beta}$'s may increase because of multicollinearity. In this section we present a useful procedure for testing the effectiveness of adding variables to an existing equation. In effect, we test whether a large equation is significantly better than a small equation.

To be specific, let the "small" equation be

$$Y = \beta_0 + \beta_1 X_1 + \cdots + \beta_k X_k + \epsilon$$

and let the "large" equation be

$$Y = \beta_0 + \beta_1 X_1 + \cdots + \beta_k X_k + \beta_{k+1} X_{k+1} + \cdots + \beta_{k+j} X_{k+j} + \epsilon$$

The small equation is called the *reduced model* and the large equation is called the *complete model*. Notice that the complete model has all the independent variables from the reduced model, plus j others, X_{k+1} through X_{k+j}.

If the complete model is no better than the reduced model, the coefficients of the extra variables must be 0. Therefore, the null hypothesis we test is

$$H_0: \beta_{k+1} = \beta_{k+2} = \cdots = \beta_{k+j} = 0$$

The alternative is that at least one of these β's is not zero. If we reject H_0, we are saying that the complete model is significantly better than the reduced model. But if we cannot reject H_0, it is probably safe to omit the extra variables from the equation.

The test of H_0 is an F test. We estimate both equations (by IDA, say) and locate their SSE's in the respective ANOVA tables. Let SSE_R and SSE_C be the SSE's for the reduced model and the complete model. Then the test is as follows.

Test for the Superiority of the Complete Model

Compute the following F ratio:

$$F = \frac{(SSE_R - SSE_C)/j}{SSE_C/(n - k - j - 1)}$$

Reject H_0 at the α level if $F > F_{\alpha, j, n-k-j-1}$

As an example, consider once again the car data in Table 12.2. We saw that ENG is the only independent variable with a significantly nonzero $\hat{\beta}$ at the 5% level. This suggests testing whether the complete model,

$$MPG = \beta_0 + \beta_1 ENG + \beta_2 WT + \beta_3 PRICE + \beta_4 REV + \epsilon$$

is significantly better than the reduced model,

$$MPG = \beta_0 + \beta_1 ENG + \epsilon$$

Here the reduced model has only one independent variable and the complete model has three extra independent variables, so $k = 1$ and $j = 3$.

Exhibit 12.12 ANOVA Tables for Complete and Reduced Models

```
 ANOVA TABLE FOR COMPLETE MODEL

   SOURCE        SS         DF        MS          F
 REGRESSION   8.92815E+02    4     2.23204E+02   38.87
 RESIDUALS    1.60795E+02   28     5.74266E+00
   TOTAL      1.05361E+03   32     3.29253E+01

 ANOVA TABLE FOR REDUCED MODEL

   SOURCE        SS         DF        MS          F
 REGRESSION   8.62860E+02    1     8.62860E+02   140.23
 RESIDUALS    1.90750E+02   31     6.15323E+00
   TOTAL      1.05361E+03   32     3.29253E+01
```

The ANOVA tables for these two equations are shown in Exhibit 12.12. We see that $SSE_C = 160.80$ and $SSE_R = 190.75$. The F ratio is therefore

$$F = \frac{(190.75 - 160.80)/3}{160.80/(33 - 1 - 3 - 1)} = 1.74$$

With $k = 3$ and $n - k - j - 1 = 28$ degrees of freedom, this F value is not significant at the 5% level (since $F_{.05,3,28} = 2.95$). Therefore, we cannot reject the null hypothesis that $\beta_2 = \beta_3 = \beta_4 = 0$. In other words, once ENG is in the equation for MPG, the other variables WT, PRICE, and REV do not add significantly to the fit. For reasons of parsimony, we may decide to omit these variables from the equation.

Problems for Sections 12.8, 12.9, 12.10

37. Suppose that we wish to predict a person's height by means of the length of his feet. We let HT be the person's height, RT be the length of his right foot, and LT be the length of his left foot. If we use multiple regression to express HT in terms of RT and LT, why will we get a rather extreme case of multicollinearity? Does this mean the standard errors of the coefficients of RT and LT will be large? Does it mean the standard error of estimate will necessarily be large? Does it mean our prediction of HT based on values of RT and LT will necessarily be inaccurate? Explain.

38. Consider a multiple regression analysis with three independent variables. If the F value in the ANOVA table is significantly large but the t values for $\hat{\beta}_1$, $\hat{\beta}_2$, and $\hat{\beta}_3$ are each insignificant, explain why multicollinearity is probably present and why it is producing this effect of a large F and small t's. Is this equation likely to be any good for predicting values of the dependent variable? Why or why not?

39. If multicollinearity exists between several of the independent variables, explain why the standard errors of their corresponding $\hat{\beta}$'s are likely to be large.

40. Suppose that a graph of the residuals versus the estimated Y's shows that the variance of the residuals increases as the Y's increase and the distribution of the residuals is skewed to the right. Which logarithm transformation might you try, and why might it remedy both violations of the OLS assumptions?

41. For each of the graphs on p. 624, discuss any obvious vio-

lations of the OLS assumptions. What might you do in each case to remedy the situation?

42. Suppose that one time series Y_t is regressed on one or more other time series. Which of the time series of residuals on p. 624 exhibits obvious autocorrelation? Explain.

43. What type of data is the Durbin–Watson statistic useful for, and what is it used to indicate? Which values of this statistic indicate potential problems with an OLS approach?

44. A study of taxpayers is undertaken to see how the amount of taxes (TAX) paid in a given year depends on several variables. These variables are household income (INC), number of children in the family (CHILD), number of people in the family with full-time or part-time jobs (JOBS), and amount of contributions donated to various organizations (CONTRIB). The outputs shown on p. 625 are obtained from IDA. These show what happens when INC is the only variable included and when all four variables are included. Can you conclude at the 10% level that the inclusion of CHILD, JOBS, and CONTRIB significantly improves the equation for TAX? That is, is the equation with all four variables significantly better than the equation with only INC?

45. Consider the equations estimated in Problem 32 (p. 613). Is the second equation a significant improvement over the first? Is the third equation a significant improvement over the second? Use the method from Section 12.10 to answer these questions, with a 10% significance level for each question.

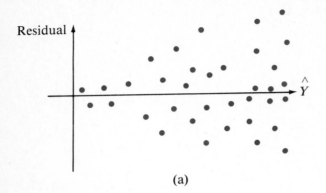

(a)

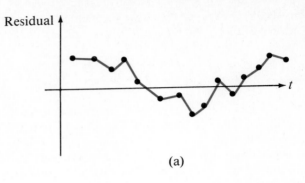

(a)

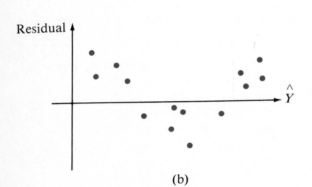

(b)

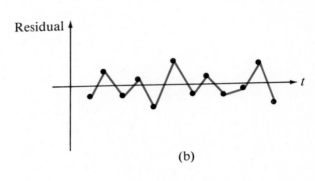

(b)

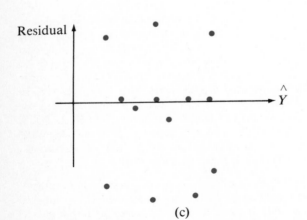

(c)

Graphs for Problem 41

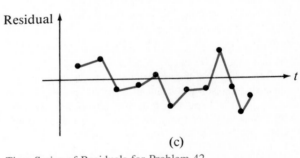

(c)

Time Series of Residuals for Problem 42

IDA Output for Problem 44

```
VARIABLE     B(STD.V)          B          STD.ERROR(B)        T

INC           0.8485      1.3878E-01       2.0402E-02       6.802
CONSTANT      0           1.3168E+03       5.6796E+02       2.319

                      MULTIPLE R        R-SQUARE
UNADJUSTED            0.8485            0.7199
 ADJUSTED            0.8393            0.7044

STD. DEV. OF RESIDUALS = 7.6484E+02
N =   20

   ANOVA

   SOURCE           SS          DF          MS           F
REGRESSION     2.70666E+07       1      2.70666E+07     46.27
RESIDUALS      1.05296E+07      18      5.84978E+05
   TOTAL       3.75962E+07      19      1.97875E+06

VARIABLE     B(STD.V)          B          STD.ERROR(B)        T

INC           0.9379      1.5340E-01       2.1984E-02       6.978
CHILD         0.1096      1.6516E+02       1.6926E+02       0.976
JOBS          0.2324      4.0230E+02       2.2932E+02       1.754
CONTRI       -0.4769     -8.2873E+00       2.3196E+00      -3.573
CONSTANT      0           1.2169E+03       4.5292E+02       2.687

                      MULTIPLE R        R-SQUARE
UNADJUSTED            0.9337            0.8718
 ADJUSTED            0.9152            0.8376

STD. DEV. OF RESIDUALS = 5.6691E+02
N =   20

   ANOVA

   SOURCE           SS          DF          MS           F
REGRESSION     3.27754E+07       4      8.19384E+06     25.50
RESIDUALS      4.82082E+06      15      3.21388E+05
   TOTAL       3.75962E+07      19      1.97875E+06
```

*46. Again referring to Problem 32 (p. 613), suppose that you want to test the hypothesis H_0: $\beta_5 = \beta_6 = \beta_7 = 0$ versus the alternative that at least one of these β's is nonzero. Why is the output in Problem 32 insufficient for testing this hypothesis? Explain what further output you would need, and how you would use it.

12.11

An Example

We conclude our study of multiple regression by examining a typical example with real data. The data come from *Places Rated Almanac*, a book with a wealth of information on a large group of U.S. metropolitan areas. (The data in this almanac are U.S. Census Bureau data.) We have selected data from a random sample of 30 of the cities listed. These data are shown in Table

Table 12.6

	CHEMP	INC	TAX	UNEMP	POP80	POP70	W1	W2	HOUSE	UTIL	HS39	CRIME	FWAY	EDUC
Altoona, PA	12.91	20,104	1355	10.3	136,621	135,356	0	1	39,725	971	67.7	217.4	5	1149
Asheville, NC	19.39	20,966	1903	5.9	177,761	161,059	1	0	48,184	938	38.5	278.3	26	1585
Birmingham, AL	22.47	23,231	1544	9.8	847,360	767,230	1	0	51,013	886	29.2	623.2	152	1207
Boston, MA	11.52	26,090	4691	4.0	2,763,357	2,899,101	1	0	65,805	729	56.2	648.2	176	2107
Charleston, WV	33.40	26,738	1649	7.4	269,595	257,140	1	0	51,796	888	40.1	271.4	52	1354
Columbia, SC	27.14	23,725	1907	4.6	408,176	322,880	0	0	54,502	901	15.1	916.2	16	1241
Decatur, IL	15.35	26,749	1576	11.0	131,375	125,010	0	1	44,114	1030	43.6	320.4	2	1267
Erie, PA	17.88	24,125	1767	9.3	279,780	263,654	1	0	46,492	874	52.1	298.9	6	1607
Fresno, CA	26.95	26,668	3679	9.4	515,013	413,329	0	0	71,605	599	20.2	845.9	17	1700
Grand Rapids, MI	27.76	25,466	2116	9.0	601,680	539,225	0	1	44,074	794	39.6	377.6	54	1748
Hartford, CT	16.80	27,702	2310	5.1	726,114	720,581	0	0	59,251	892	37.2	503.8	110	1784
Knoxville, TN	31.45	22,521	863	5.4	476,517	409,409	1	0	47,600	1036	27.2	374.5	44	1275
Lancaster, PA	19.14	25,067	1950	5.4	362,346	320,079	1	0	57,160	1088	49.2	112.1	14	1541
Lansing, MI	22.75	25,942	2344	10.7	468,482	424,271	0	0	45,465	864	40.0	292.1	33	1567
Lincoln, NE	18.07	26,992	1875	3.5	192,884	167,972	0	0	53,260	848	34.4	264.3	17	1495
Los Angeles, CA	18.02	29,792	5132	8.1	7,477,657	7,041,980	1	0	113,985	558	23.5	1205.1	562	1749
Lubbock, TX	34.11	24,219	1046	4.3	211,651	179,295	0	0	46,452	866	10.4	591.8	41	1173
Miami, FL	23.14	28,042	1521	5.2	1,625,979	1,267,792	1	0	74,239	814	12.9	1372.6	92	1812
Newark, NJ	11.60	29,435	4852	7.0	1,965,304	2,057,468	1	0	85,089	758	48.2	856.5	88	1984
New Haven, CT	13.10	25,344	1849	6.6	417,592	411,287	1	0	49,464	809	44.1	399.0	61	1719
Orlando, FL	41.02	25,237	926	5.5	700,699	453,270	0	0	51,552	796	11.8	908.5	66	1480
Philadelphia, PA	10.27	25,585	2419	6.5	4,716,818	4,824,110	1	0	64,975	845	48.4	528.9	285	1726
Pueblo, CO	30.29	24,316	2294	6.4	125,972	118,238	0	0	45,041	586	39.6	840.5	28	1621
St. Cloud, MN	31.12	19,861	2899	5.8	163,256	134,585	0	0	49,680	978	39.6	62.8	5	1821
San José, CA	36.61	32,411	5516	4.8	1,295,071	1,065,313	1	0	119,860	537	9.6	416.1	89	1813
Shreveport, LA	24.80	22,891	948	6.5	376,646	336,000	0	0	45,732	658	23.3	599.9	41	1289
Steubenville, OH	18.21	25,480	1533	8.8	163,099	166,385	0	1	51,748	829	49.2	202.4	32	1327
Trenton, NJ	18.10	27,189	4192	5.0	307,863	304,116	1	0	73,515	933	46.2	547.9	50	1912
Tulsa, OK	29.77	27,248	1572	5.2	689,628	549,154	0	0	44,713	863	26.2	468.0	78	1278
Youngstown, OH	14.49	24,697	1321	12.0	531,350	537,124	0	1	55,750	873	42.2	356.4	85	1519

CHEMP = predicted percentage increase in employment from 1980 to 1990
INC = average household income
TAX = average sum of state, sales, and property taxes
UNEMP = unemployment percentage
POP80 = population in 1980
POP70 = population in 1970

$$W1 = \begin{cases} 1 & \text{if city's weather is rated in top third of all large cities} \\ 0 & \text{otherwise} \end{cases}$$

$$W2 = \begin{cases} 1 & \text{if city's weather is rated in middle third of all large cities} \\ 0 & \text{otherwise} \end{cases}$$

HOUSE = average market value of all homes
UTIL = average yearly utility bill
HS39 = percentage of city's houses built before 1939
CRIME = number of violent crimes per 100,000 people
FWAY = number of freeway miles
EDUC = average amount spent per student in grades K–12

12.6. The dependent variable we have chosen is CHEMP, the percentage change in employment from 1980 to 1990, as predicted in 1980 by a complicated Census Bureau prediction scheme. The potential independent variables capture many aspects of the cities included. These range from population levels in 1970 and 1980 (POP70 and POP80) to the number of violent crimes per 100,000 people (CRIME) to dummy variables on weather quality (W1 and W2). The definitions of the independent variables are given in Table 12.6.

This regression problem is a difficult one. Which variables in Table 12.6 should be included in the regression equation? Are there any variables that are significantly related to CHEMP but are not included in Table 12.6? Are there other dummy variables, nonlinear terms, or interaction terms that should be used? Would the fit be improved by using a nonlinear transformation of CHEMP, such as its logarithm, as the dependent variable? An applied regression analysis must attempt to answer these questions.

We used IDA to estimate several possible equations for these data. These include the equation with all 13 independent variables entering (linearly), as well as several with only a subset of the 13 independent variables and/or nonlinear transformations of these. The equation shown below is one of the best equations we found. It balances the desire for a high R^2 value against the desire for parsimony. (Readers with access to a computer package may wish to search for an even better equation; there may be one.)

$$\widehat{CHEMP} = 51.56 - \underset{(.103)}{.481HS39} - \underset{(.00428)}{.00792CRIME} - \underset{(.000134)}{.000268HOUSE}$$

$$+ \underset{(.0000127)}{.0000216POP80} - \underset{(.0000128)}{.0000226POP70} + \underset{(.000164)}{.000322TAX}$$

$$s_e = 4.99 \qquad R^2 = .710$$

There are several interesting points to notice about this equation. First, the R^2 value is not as high as we are used to seeing in the typical "textbook" examples. But for real data, $R^2 = .710$ is not bad at all. Second, the most significant variable by far is HS39, the percentage of a city's houses built before 1939. (This was evidently not due to chance. HS39 was the most significant variable in another run we tried, this one using a *different* sample of 30 cities.) Since the coefficient of HS39 is negative, cities with a large percentage of old houses are less likely to have a large percentage increase in employment by 1990. From the signs of the other regression coefficients, we see that the change in employment is positively related to the population in 1980 and taxes, whereas it is negatively related to crime, housing values, and the population in 1970.

With regard to the population variables, we note that the coefficients of POP70 and POP80 are practically the same, but with opposite signs. This suggests that the relevant population variable might be POP80 − POP70, that is, the increase (or decrease) in population from 1970 to 1980. Since the coefficient of this difference is positive (approximately .000022, the common magnitude of the coefficients of POP70 and POP80), cities with large increases in population during the 1970s are the most likely to experience large percentage increases in employment during the 1980s. To test this observation, we tried one other run, with the variable DPOP = POP80 − POP70 as a substitute for POP80 and POP70. The resulting equation is shown below.

Exhibit 12.13   Scattergram of Residuals Versus Estimated Dependent Variable

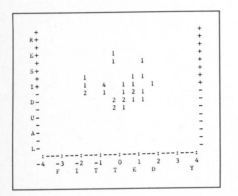

$$\widehat{CHEMP} = 55.91 - \underset{(.0931)}{.526 HS39} - \underset{(.00387)}{.00978 CRIME} - \underset{(.000124)}{.000318 HOUSE}$$

$$+ \underset{(.0000127)}{.0000209 DPOP} + \underset{(.000163)}{.000340 TAX}$$

$$s_e = 5.00 \qquad R^2 = .697$$

Obviously, this equation is very similar to the equation above. Because it has one less variable, however, it is probably preferred. (The slight decrease in R^2 is negligible.)

The scattergram of residuals versus the estimated dependent variable for this final equation is shown in Exhibit 12.13. There do not appear to be any pronounced patterns, such as nonlinearity or nonconstant residual variance. Therefore, we may conclude that the assumptions of the least squares model are approximately valid and that a reasonably good fit has been obtained.

Summary

In this chapter we have continued the discussion of linear regression in an important direction. We now allow more than one independent variable in the equation for the dependent variable. As in simple regression, we estimate the multiple regression equation by a least squares approach. We also interpret statistical quantities such as the standard error of estimate, the R^2 value, confidence intervals for the regression coefficients, and so on, very much as we did in simple regression. The main difference from a computational point of view is that almost all multiple regression analyses are performed by a computer; the computations are simply too tedious to perform by hand. However, most computerized regression packages, such as SPSS and IDA, are relatively easy to use, and their outputs are very similar to one another.

When we are allowed to have more than one independent variable in the regression equation, it is usually difficult to know which variables to include. We saw that a variable can be related to the dependent variable, but nevertheless be omitted from the regression equation because other variables explain the same things about the dependent variable. We also looked at several possible types of independent variables that might not be immediately obvious. These include dummy variables (for modeling categorical variables), nonlinear variables, and interaction variables. It is usually not necessary or wise to include many of these possibilities in any single regression equation, but a small number of them can sometimes improve the fit significantly.

With a computerized regression package in hand, it is relatively simple to keep trying potential regression equations until a good fit (large R^2, say) is found. However, we should always be aware of the danger of violating the regression assumptions. Most computer packages allow us to check whether these assumptions are met, at least approximately, by including helpful diagnostics. We did not analyze these diagnostics in much depth because of the elementary nature of this text, but they are an important part of any applied regression analysis and should not be ignored.

Applications

Application 12.1 In a 1977 paper Strober and Weinberg presented results of a study of purchases of durable goods and other expensive items for families with nonworking wives (NWW) versus those with working wives (WW). (Reference: Myra H. Strober and Charles B. Weinberg, "Working Wives and Major Family Expenditures," *Journal of Consumer Research,* Vol. 4, 1977, pp. 141–146.) Their hypothesis was that after controlling for several variables, particularly income, the NWW and WW families would not differ with respect to the amount spent on durable goods, expensive hobby and recreation items, and vacations. In other words, they expected that a WW family and a NWW family with the same income who purchased these items would spend approximately the same amount on them.

To test this hypothesis, they selected samples of families who had purchased the various items in the past year, and used data from these families to estimate several regression equations. Each regression equation had as its dependent variable the amount spent in the previous year for a given item. For example, the dependent variable for one equation was the amount spent on a color television set in the past year. (This equation included data only from those families who had bought a color television set in the past year.) The independent variables in each equation were as follows:

$$
\begin{aligned}
\text{INC} &= \text{family income} \\
\text{NASTS} &= \text{family's net assets} \\
\text{YOUNG} &= \text{dummy variable for age} \\
&\quad \text{(1 if husband is 35 or younger, 0 otherwise)} \\
\text{MOVREC} &= \text{dummy variable for moving recently} \\
&\quad \text{(1 if family moved within past two years, 0 otherwise)} \\
\text{WWD1} &= \text{dummy variable for working wives} \\
&\quad \text{(1 if wife worked during past year, 0 otherwise)} \\
\text{WWD2} &= \text{dummy variable for recent working wives} \\
&\quad \text{(1 if wife worked during past year but } not \text{ during previous} \\
&\quad \text{2 years, 0 otherwise)}
\end{aligned}
$$

The results from the regression analysis are shown in Table 12.7.

Table 12.7

Independent Variable	Dependent Variable (Dollar Expenditures)				
	Refrigerator	B&W TV	Color TV	Furniture	Dryer
(Constant)	198.33	98.89	505.80	196.94	68.03
INC	.0051*	.0099	−.0021	.0076	.0119*
NASTS	−.0001	−.0015	.0007*	.0037*	−.0003
YOUNG	−2.34	16.71	−36.52	−20.54	−2.64
MOVREC	34.62	−34.71	88.46	429.61*	−40.14
WWD1	38.49	108.10*	27.52	9.55	−62.94
WWD2	72.06	−172.66	−81.55	292.45*	6.19
R^2	.080	.059	.035	.193	.283

*Indicates significantly nonzero at the 5% level.

There are several things to notice about these results. First, by including variables such as income (INC) in the equations explicitly, we control for these variables. Therefore, the coefficients of WWD1 and WWD2 indicate the effect on expenditures of having a working wife, *given* that income and the other independent variables are held constant. Second, most of the variables in these equations are statistically insignificant. These include the WWD1 and WWD2 variables, except in two instances. This tends to confirm the authors' suspicions that the working status of the wife is not relevant. (If the working status were really not relevant, we would expect WWD1 and WWD2 to be 0.) Finally, a marketing manager might want to investigate the entire issue more thoroughly before basing any decisions on these regression results. The low R^2 values suggest that better regression equations, perhaps with different or more independent variables, could explain more of the variation in the dependent variables.

Application 12.2   In a study performed several years ago, Platt and McCarthy employed multiple regression analysis to explain variations in compensation among the chief executive officers (CEOs) of large companies. (Reference: Harlan D. Platt and Daniel J. McCarthy, "Executive Compensation: Performance and Patience," *Business Horizons*, Vol. 28, 1985, pp. 48–53.) Their primary objective was to discover whether levels of compensation are affected more by short-run considerations ("I'll earn more now if my company does well in the short run") or long-run considerations ("my best method for obtaining high compensation is to stay with my company for a long time"). The study used as its dependent variable the total compensation for each of the 100 highest paid CEOs in 1981. This variable was defined as the sum of salary, bonuses, and other benefits (measured in $1000s).

The following potential independent variables were considered. To capture short-run effects, the average of the company's previous five years' percentage changes in earnings per share (EPS), and the projected percentage change in next year's EPS were used. To capture the long-run effect, age and years as CEO, two admittedly correlated variables, were used. Dummy variables for the CEO's background (founder, administration, finance, legal, marketing, operations, or technical area) were also considered. Finally, the researchers considered several nonlinear and interaction terms based on the variables above.

The best fit is shown in Table 12.8. It implies that compensation increases as the square of years as CEO, it increases linearly with age, and there is a negative interaction effect between years as CEO and age. Also, the positive coefficient of the finance background dummy variable indicates that, all else equal, finance people earn approximately $867,000 per year more than average. (To appreciate this huge difference, it should be pointed out that the CEOs in the sample were among the highest paid executives in the country. Many of their total compensation packages were above $10,000,000!)

Table 12.8 Regression Results (Dependent Variable: CEO Compensation)

Independent Variable	Estimated Coefficient
(Constant)	−3493.00
Years CEO	898.70
(Years CEO) squared	9.28
(Years CEO) × Age	−17.19
Age	88.27
Finance background	867.44

$R^2 = .1944$

Platt and McCarthy draw several conclusions from this analysis. First, it appears that CEOs should indeed concentrate on long-run considerations, namely, those that keep them on their jobs the longest. Second, the absence of the short-run company-related variables from the equation (their coefficients were statistically insignificant) helps to confirm the conjecture that CEOs who concentrate on earning the quick dollar for their companies may not be acting in their best self-interest. Finally, the positive coefficient of the financial background variable may imply that financial people possess skills that are vitally important, and firms therefore outbid one another for the best financial talent.

Application 12.3   A common term in marketing is user share. This is defined in an article by Raj as the proportion of all buyers of a product who purchase a particular company's brand. (Reference: S. P. Raj, "Striking a Balance Between Brand 'Popularity' and Brand Loyalty," *Journal of Marketing,* Vol. 49, 1985, pp. 53–59.) As Raj points out, however, the customers who purchase a particular brand may do so exclusively, or they may switch brands from time to time. So besides a measure of user share, the company may also want a measure of brand loyalty, defined by Raj as the proportion of all buyers of a particular brand who buy this brand exclusively. For example, if 150 out of 1000 consumers purchase brand *A* at least once during a certain period, brand *A*'s user share is .15. But if only 30 of these 150 buyers buy brand *A* and no other brands during this period, brand *A*'s loyalty index is .20.

Raj conducted a study of many different products and product brands to see how brand loyalty is related to user share. To do so, he used a regression model. The data set was gathered from consumer purchase patterns for approximately 20,000 households during 1976. For each product brand included in the study, an "observation" consisted of the user share (the dependent variable) and the brand loyalty (the independent variable) for that brand. The products were divided into five categories, as shown in Table 12.9. A separate regression equation was estimated for each of these product categories. A combined regression equation for all 1091 brands was also estimated.

It became clear that the relationship between user share (US) and brand loyalty (BL) was not linear, but was instead quadratic. Therefore, the

Table 12.9

Product Code	Product Type	Number of Products in Product Type	Number of Brands in Product Type
P1	Food	31	315
P2	Pet food	7	61
P3	Personal care	28	460
P4	Household goods	15	138
P5	Tobacco	5	117
All		86	1091

Table 12.10

Product Code	$\hat{\beta}_0$	$\hat{\beta}_1$	R^2
P1	2.66	.006	.50
P2	1.29	.006	.34
P3	1.27	.003	.28
P4	.60	.008	.60
P5	1.27	.002	.13
All	1.93	.004	.29

following equation was estimated for each product category as well as for the combined group of all products:

$$US = \beta_0 + \beta_1 BL^2 + \epsilon$$

The results are shown in tabular (Table 12.10) and graphical form (Figure 12.11). As these results for each product category show, user share not only increases as brand loyalty increases, but it increases at an increasing rate. The possible implication for marketing managers is that it is wise to build a loyal group of followers because this is likely to have a beneficial effect on the brand's total share of the market.

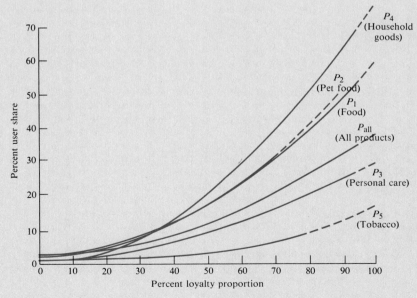

Figure 12.11

Glossary of Terms

Multiple regression   a regression analysis with more than one independent variable

Interpretation of β_i   the expected change in Y when X_i increases by 1 unit and the other independent variables are held constant

Normal equations   the equations that must be solved to find the least squares estimates $\hat{\beta}_0$ through $\hat{\beta}_k$

SPSS, SAS, BIOMED, MINITAB, and IDA   some of the computer packages that perform multiple regression analysis

Standard error of estimate, coefficient of determination (R^2), and ANOVA table   statistical quantities with the same interpretations as in Chapter 11

Overall F test for a regression equation   a test to determine whether the independent variables (as a whole) explain a significant amount of the total variation of the dependent variable

Individual t test for a single β_i   a test to determine whether a single variable X_i is useful in explaining the dependent variable, given that the other independent variables are already in the equation

Stepwise regression   a method for building a regression equation where the independent variables enter one at a time in order of decreasing importance

Dummy variables   independent variables used to indicate which of several categories an observation is in

Nonlinear terms   nonlinear functions of one or more independent variables; often useful when a scattergram does not appear to be linear

Interaction terms   products of independent variables that allow the effect of one independent variable to depend on the values of other independent variables

Multicollinearity   a situation where several independent variables are exactly or nearly linearly related

Durbin–Watson statistic   a statistic for testing the presence of autocorrelated error terms, especially for time series data; if the statistic is close to 2 (as determined by special tables), autocorrelation is no problem

Important Formulas

1. Regression equation for a single Y

$$Y = \beta_0 + \beta_1 X_1 + \beta_2 X_2 + \cdots + \beta_k X_k + \epsilon$$

2. Estimated regression equation

$$\hat{Y} = \hat{\beta}_0 + \hat{\beta}_1 X_1 + \hat{\beta}_2 X_2 + \cdots + \hat{\beta}_k X_k$$

3. Approximate standard errors of prediction

$$\text{StdErr}(\hat{Y}) \approx s_e$$

$$\text{StdErr(mean)} \approx \frac{s_e}{\sqrt{n}}$$

4. Test statistic for the superiority of a complete model (with $k + j$ independent variables) over a reduced model (with only k of these variables)

$$F = \frac{(\text{SSE}_R - \text{SSE}_C)/j}{\text{SSE}_C/(n - k - j - 1)}$$

End-of-Chapter Problems

47. Financial analysts often attempt to explain the percentage change in a given stock's price by means of a multiple regression equation. Consider a company in the cosmetics industry. Let Y_t be the percentage change in the stock's price from week $t - 1$ to week t. That is, $Y_t = (P_t - P_{t-1})/P_{t-1}$, where P_{t-1} and P_t are the prices in week $t - 1$ and week t, respectively. Also, let X_{1t} be the percentage change in a typical market portfolio's price from week $t - 1$ to week t, and let X_{2t} be the similar percentage change for a portfolio of stocks in the cosmetics industry. We gather stock prices for a number of consecutive weeks and estimate the following equation:

$$Y_t = \beta_0 + \beta_1 X_{1t} + \beta_2 X_{2t} + \epsilon_t$$

a. If the estimates of β_1 and β_2 are approximately .5 and .7, what can we say about the reaction of this stock's price to changes in the market in general and to changes in the cosmetics industry? Be specific.

b. Would you expect X_{1t} to stay constant if X_{2t} changes? Would you expect X_{2t} to stay constant if X_{1t} changes? Explain.

c. For this equation, does β_0 have any economic interpretation? If so, what is it? What value would you expect β_0 to be near? Explain.

48. Consider the following correlation matrix between a dependent variable Y and three potential independent variables, X_1, X_2, and X_3. In a stepwise regression, which variable would enter the regression equation first, and why? What percentage of the total variation of Y would this variable explain by itself? Which variable would probably enter the equation second, and why? Does it appear that multicollinearity is a problem with the data? Why or why not?

	Y	X_1	X_2	X_3
Y	1.00			
X_1	.35	1.00		
X_2	.76	.09	1.00	
X_3	−.89	−.25	−.30	1.00

49. A factory supervisor needs to find some way of predicting the effectiveness of each of his employees on a machine that is critical to the operation of the factory. The supervisor lists five factors he believes are related to effectiveness on the critical machine: (1) years of machinist experience (YRS), (2) seniority with the company (SEN), (3) effectiveness rating on the machinist's current job (JOBEFF), (4) age (AGE), and (5) score on an emotional stability test (EMOT). Twenty em-

Output for Problem 49

```
VARIABLE        COEFFICIENT     STANDARD ERROR OF COEFFICIENT

YRS               .653                    .178
SEN               .011                    .220
JOBEFF            .040                    .131
AGE              -.161                    .171
EMOT              .094                    .016
(CONSTANT)        .414                    .083

MULTIPLE CORRELATION COEFFICIENT (R) = .908
STANDARD ERROR OF ESTIMATE = 5.901

ANOVA TABLE:

SOURCE          SS          DF      MS      F       SIGNIFICANCE

   SSR        1704.1
   SSE
   SST        2066.9
```

ployees are randomly selected and given the emotional test. Each is assigned to the critical machine and is measured for effectiveness (EFF). (EFF and JOBEFF are measured as percentages between 0 and 100. EMOT is measured on a scale from 200 to 700.) A regression package gives the output shown on p. 635.

a. Fill in the rest of the ANOVA table. What does it tell us?
b. What percentage of total variation (of EFF) has been explained?
c. Does the small regression coefficient of SEN, compared to its large standard error, necessarily mean that SEN is not linearly related to EFF? Why or why not?
d. If another of the employees has YRS = 20, SEN = 12, JOBEFF = 80, AGE = 55, and EMOT = 550, what is the prediction of his EFF? What is the (approximate) probability that his EFF will be below 50?
e. Might multicollinearity be a problem with these data? Why? What difficulty does it cause in terms of estimating the regression coefficients?

50. Referring to Problem 49, suppose that we replace the AGE variable by a dummy variable DAGE. This variable equals 1 if AGE is at least 50, and it equals 0 if AGE is less than 50. If the estimated coefficient of DAGE is −3.7, how do you interpret this? Be specific.

*51. Referring to Problems 49 and 50, suppose that the regression equation for EFF is run again with only three independent variables: YRS, DAGE (as in Problem 50), and YRS*DAGE (the product of DAGE and YRS). The estimated equation is as follows:

$$\widehat{EFF} = 25.01 + 1.23YRS - 2.72DAGE + .37YRS*DAGE,$$

$$s_e = 5.79 \qquad R^2 = .856$$

How would you interpret these findings to a boss who knows very little about multiple regression?

52. A marketing study is performed on 110 households to see how the purchase rate of a commonly purchased good is related to the income level, educational level, and family size of the household. Each household is monitored for 36 consecutive months. The dependent variable PUR is the average number of purchases made per month over the 36-month interval. The independent variables are as follows. INC is the household's average income over the period (in $1000s). The education level of the head of the household is categorized into three levels: 13 or more years, 9 to 12 years, and 0 to 8 years. There are dummy variables E1 and E2 for the first two

categories (for example, E1 = 1 for a head of household in the 13-or-over category, E1 = 0 otherwise), and the 0-to-8 category is considered the base category. Similarly, household size is categorized into four levels: three members, four or five members, six or more members, and one or two members. There are dummy variables H1, H2, and H3 for the first three of these categories (for example, H1 = 1 for a household with three members, H1 = 0 otherwise), and the one- or two-member category is considered the base category. The results from a multiple regression package are shown below.

Output for Problem 52

VARIABLE	COEFF	STDERR	T
MULTIPLE R	.379		
R SQUARE	.143		
ADJUSTED R SQUARE	.142		
STANDARD ERROR	3.180		
INC	−.082	.013	−6.31
E1	.880	.141	6.24
E2	.565	.160	3.53
H1	.817	.156	5.24
H2	.931	.149	6.25
H3	5.364	.229	23.42
(CONST)	2.116	.105	20.15

a. Based on the estimated regression equation, what does the income variable say about the dependent variable PUR?
b. Interpret the effect of the level of education (of the head of the household) on the dependent variable. Be specific.
c. Interpret the effect of household size on the dependent variable. Be specific.
d. How many purchases per month would you predict for a household with annual income $15,000 if there are three people in the household and the head of the household got through high school but never went to college?

53. Consider a company that gives each of its prospective managers four separate tests for judging their potential. For a sample of 30 managers, the test scores and the subsequent job effectiveness ratings (JOBEFF) given one year later are shown here.

JOBEFF	TEST1	TEST2	TEST3	TEST4
30	51	62	62	57
53	77	63	55	56
43	72	57	50	45
40	51	54	49	57

(continued)

JOBEFF	TEST1	TEST2	TEST3	TEST4
59	85	72	51	50
78	82	62	68	79
67	81	75	65	70
49	46	55	64	75
38	64	68	62	49
57	95	74	71	55
59	78	66	72	64
22	49	42	35	43
80	73	85	72	68
56	76	62	66	59
59	76	79	62	62
70	78	66	82	80
66	74	68	46	56
82	77	89	70	70
67	93	84	90	74
69	68	71	85	77
44	58	71	58	57
48	54	62	45	61
57	80	71	66	64
65	89	68	87	74
56	66	79	60	56
61	81	61	62	58
41	54	73	63	62
79	86	75	81	72
56	86	80	74	62
58	62	65	49	54

a. The matrix of simple correlations for these data is as follows. Does it appear that a multiple regression equation for JOBEFF, with the test scores as independent variables, will be successful? Can you foresee any problems in obtaining accurate estimates of the regression coefficients? Explain.

	JOBEFF	TEST1	TEST2	TEST3	TEST4
JOBEFF	1.00				
TEST1	.68	1.00			
TEST2	.63	.53	1.00		
TEST3	.61	.58	.55	1.00	
TEST4	.69	.30	.36	.78	1.00

b. The IDA regression output is shown below. Write out the estimated regression equation and provide 95% confidence intervals for the coefficients of the test scores. How do you explain the negative coefficient of TEST3, given the positive correlation between JOBEFF and TEST3?

c. Can you reject the null hypothesis that the four test scores as a whole have no predictive ability for job effectiveness at the 1% level? Why or why not?

d. If a new prospective manager has test scores of 83, 74, 65, and 77, what do you predict his job effectiveness rating will be in one year? What is the approximate standard error of this prediction?

IDA Output for Problem 53

```
VARIABLE    B(STD.V)        B          STD.ERROR(B)      T
TEST 1       0.5738     6.0966E-01     1.1227E-01     5.430
TEST 2       0.3414     4.9238E-01     1.4436E-01     3.411
TEST 3      -0.5573    -6.1300E-01     1.7505E-01    -3.502
TEST 4       0.8319     1.2223E+00     1.9264E-01     6.345
CONSTANT     0         -5.7450E+01     1.0276E+01    -5.591

                    MULTIPLE R      R-SQUARE
UNADJUSTED           0.9185         0.8437
 ADJUSTED            0.9048         0.8187

STD. DEV. OF RESIDUALS = 6.2040E+00
N =   30

    SOURCE           SS         DF        MS          F
REGRESSION     5.19274E+03      4    1.29818E+03    33.73
RESIDUALS      9.62230E+02     25    3.84892E+01
   TOTAL       6.15497E+03     29    2.12240E+02
```

54. The estimated job effectiveness ratings for the 30 managers in Problem 53 are shown below. Calculate the corresponding residuals and then graph the residuals versus the estimated job effectiveness ratings in a scattergram. Do any of the usual regression assumptions appear to be violated? Explain.

Actual JOBEFF	Estimated JOBEFF	Actual JOBEFF	Estimated JOBEFF
30	35.8	70	70.1
53	55.3	66	61.4
43	38.9	82	76.0
40	39.9	67	75.9
59	59.7	69	61.0
78	78.0	44	47.0
67	74.6	48	53.0
49	50.1	57	64.1
38	36.9	65	67.4
57	60.6	56	53.4

Actual JOBEFF	Estimated JOBEFF	Actual JOBEFF	Estimated JOBEFF
59	56.7	61	54.9
22	24.2	41	48.6
80	67.9	79	70.3
56	51.1	56	64.8
59	65.6	58	48.3

55. The data in Problem 53 were also analyzed by means of stepwise regression with the IDA program. The output is shown below. Suppose that your task is to explain the most important aspects of this output to a boss who knows practically nothing about multiple regression. What would you tell him? In particular, does it appear that each equation is significantly "better" than the one before it? (You do not need to answer the latter question with formal tests.)

IDA Output for Problem 55

```
MULT. R = 0.6923   S.E. RES. = 1.06993E+01   F = 25.77

VARIABLE    B(STD.V)        B         STD.ERROR(B)        T

TEST4        0.6923      1.0172E+00    2.0039E-01       5.076
CONSTANT     0          -6.2358E+00    1.2616E+01      -0.494


MULT. R = 0.8522   S.E. RES. = 7.90022E+00   F = 35.81

VARIABLE    B(STD.V)        B         STD.ERROR(B)        T

TEST4        0.5379      7.9033E-01    1.5494E-01       5.101
TEST1        0.5204      5.5294E-01    1.1204E-01       4.935
CONSTANT     0          -3.1974E+01    1.0676E+01      -2.995


MULT. R = 0.8780   S.E. RES. = 7.36406E+00   F = 29.17

VARIABLE    B(STD.V)        B         STD.ERROR(B)        T

TEST4        0.8091      1.1888E+00    2.2836E-01       5.206
TEST1        0.6764      7.1867E-01    1.2775E-01       5.626
TEST3       -0.4095     -4.5039E-01    1.9993E-01      -2.253
CONSTANT     0          -3.9848E+01    1.0548E+01      -3.778


MULT. R = 0.9185   S.E. RES. = 6.20397E+00   F = 33.73

VARIABLE    B(STD.V)        B         STD.ERROR(B)        T

TEST4        0.8319      1.2223E+00    1.9264E-01       6.345
TEST1        0.5738      6.0966E-01    1.1227E-01       5.430
TEST3       -0.5573     -6.1300E-01    1.7505E-01      -3.502
TEST2        0.3414      4.9238E-01    1.4436E-01       3.411
CONSTANT     0          -5.7450E+01    1.0276E+01      -5.591
```

56. A study of 14 midwestern counties shows the following data that relate per capita annual income (in $1000s) to the percentage of the work force engaged in agriculture and the average number of years of schooling for people over 25 years old. The three variables are labeled INC, AGRPCT, and EDUC. Draw a scattergram of INC versus AGRPCT; of INC versus EDUC. Do the relationships between these variables appear to be positive or negative (or neither)? Is a linear fit of INC versus AGRPCT and EDUC plausible? Explain.

INC	AGRPCT	EDUC
9.786	8.2	8.92
9.731	11.4	11.94
8.002	8.4	9.61
9.900	8.8	8.18
10.875	8.3	10.96
9.152	11.3	10.77
9.142	9.6	10.62
10.647	8.1	10.14
7.629	10.1	7.26
12.367	6.5	10.04
10.667	10.7	10.42
9.576	10.8	10.44
13.197	7.7	11.42
9.647	9.9	8.66

57. The IDA output for the data in Problem 56 is shown below.
   a. Write out the estimated regression equation.

b. Find 95% confidence intervals for the coefficients of AGRPCT and EDUC. Based on these, can you reject the (separate) null hypotheses that these coefficients are zero, assuming a two-tailed alternative and a 5% significance level for each test?
c. Use the information in the ANOVA table to test the significance of the overall regression equation at the 1% level. Interpret your conclusion in words.

58. a. Using the estimated regression equation from Problem 57, predict the per capita annual income and find the approximate standard error of this prediction for a county with 6.6% of the work force engaged in agriculture and an average education level of 11.35 years.
   b. Output from the IDA program (not shown) tells us that the standard error of prediction for the county in part (a) is really 1.24 (in $1000s). Explain why there is a difference between this answer and your answer in part (a).

59. The data on p. 640 show how demand for a particular product varies with the price of the product, the price of a competing product, and the income of the population for 20 small communities. The variables are defined more precisely as follows:

DEMAND = average quantity demanded per day
PRICE = average price per unit (averaged over all stores in the community that sell the product)
COMPET = average price per unit of a competing product
INCOME = average monthly income per household in the community

IDA Output for Problem 57

```
VARIABLE    B(STD.V)        B           STD.ERROR(B)      T

AGRPCT      -0.6065    -6.0796E-01      1.9395E-01      -3.135
EDUC         0.5525     6.3404E-01      2.2206E-01       2.855
CONSTANT     0          9.3470E+00      2.6942E+00       3.469

                    MULTIPLE R       R-SQUARE
UNADJUSTED            0.7707          0.5939
ADJUSTED             0.7212          0.5201

STD. DEV. OF RESIDUALS = 1.0337E+00
N =    14

  ANOVA

  SOURCE          SS          DF         MS            F
REGRESSION    1.71924E+01      2     8.59619E+00      8.04
RESIDUALS     1.17545E+01     11     1.06859E+00
  TOTAL       2.89468E+01     13     2.22668E+00
```

IDA Output for Problem 59

```
VARIABLE    B(STD.V)        B         STD.ERROR(B)      T

PRICE       -0.8271    -7.1701E+00     7.6313E-01     -9.396
INCOME       0.2578     1.0941E-02     4.1428E-03      2.641
COMPET       0.4804     5.3945E+00     1.1510E+00      4.687
CONSTANT     0          4.9707E+01     1.4275E+01      3.482

                MULTIPLE R        R-SQUARE
UNADJUSTED        0.9514           0.9052
 ADJUSTED         0.9420           0.8874

STD. DEV. OF RESIDUALS = 2.6917E+00
N =   20

 ANOVA

  SOURCE          SS         DF        MS            F
REGRESSION    1.10703E+03     3     3.69009E+02     50.93
RESIDUALS     1.15922E+02    16     7.24512E+00
 TOTAL        1.22295E+03    19     6.43658E+01
```

DEMAND	PRICE	COMPET	INCOME
39	14.65	13.98	1380
45	15.35	16.15	1480
41	14.30	14.80	1670
35	13.90	13.45	1250
53	13.10	14.98	1525
47	14.98	15.70	1700
56	13.65	14.90	1925
37	15.60	15.75	1725
47	14.85	15.70	1540
31	15.55	14.45	1467
33	15.05	13.80	1305
49	14.40	15.70	1600
52	13.65	15.00	1859
50	13.67	14.85	1460
29	15.70	14.80	1236
45	14.80	15.37	1547
43	14.50	15.25	1520
38	14.20	14.78	1340
30	16.70	15.40	1505
39	16.15	15.81	1725

	DEMAND	PRICE	COMPET	INCOME
DEMAND	1.00			
PRICE	-.70	1.00		
COMPET	.62	-.13	1.00	
INCOME	.34	.33	.52	1.00

b. The regression output from IDA, with demand as the dependent variable, is shown at the top of the page. What do you expect to happen to demand if the price of the product and the price of the competing product both increase by $1?

c. Test (separately) whether the three coefficients of the independent variables are significantly nonzero. Use two-tailed tests at the 5% level.

60. Referring to the data from Problem 59, the outputs from two other regression equations (with INCOME omitted and with COMPET omitted, respectively) are shown on p. 641. Test (separately) whether the "complete" model from Problem 59 is significantly better than these "reduced" models. Test each at the 5% level.

a. The matrix of simple correlations for these four variables is shown above. Are all the signs (positive or negative) what you would expect? Explain.

61. For the equation in Problem 59, the 20 estimated demands are shown in the accompanying table. Calculate the corresponding residuals, and plot them in a scattergram. Based on

Output for Problem 60

```
VARIABLE     B(STD.V)          B        STD.ERROR(B)        T

PRICE        -0.9148      -7.9307E+00     8.2156E-01      -9.653
COMPET        0.6445       7.2374E+00     1.0642E+00       6.801
CONSTANT      0            5.0043E+01     1.6595E+01       3.016

                    MULTIPLE R         R-SQUARE
UNADJUSTED           0.9295             0.8639
 ADJUSTED            0.9208             0.8479

STD. DEV. OF RESIDUALS = 3.1291E+00
N =   20

  ANOVA

  SOURCE            SS          DF           MS            F
REGRESSION    1.05649E+03       2       5.28247E+02     53.95
RESIDUALS     1.66455E+02      17       9.79148E+00
  TOTAL       1.22295E+03      19       6.43658E+01

VARIABLE     B(STD.V)          B        STD.ERROR(B)        T

PRICE        -0.6326      -5.4844E+00     1.0058E+00      -5.453
INCOME        0.5352       2.2712E-02     4.9237E-03       4.613
CONSTANT      0            8.7847E+01     1.7527E+01       5.012

                    MULTIPLE R         R-SQUARE
UNADJUSTED           0.8804             0.7751
 ADJUSTED            0.8652             0.7486

STD. DEV. OF RESIDUALS = 4.0225E+00
N =   20

  ANOVA

  SOURCE            SS          DF           MS            F
REGRESSION    9.47887E+02       2       4.73944E+02     29.29
RESIDUALS     2.75063E+02      17       1.61802E+01
  TOTAL       1.22295E+03      19       6.43658E+01
```

this graph, do there appear to be any violations of the usual regression assumptions? Explain.

Actual Demand	Estimated Demand	Actual Demand	Estimated Demand
39	35.2	33	30.5
45	43.0	49	48.7
41	45.3	52	53.1
35	36.3	50	47.8
53	53.3	29	30.5
47	45.6	45	43.4
56	53.3	43	44.6
37	41.7	38	42.3
47	44.8	30	29.5
31	32.2	39	38.1

62. A chain of discount stores has collected the following data from 16 branch locations. The variables are defined as follows:

SALES = average weekly gross sales (in $100s)
POP = target population within a 5-mile radius (in 1000s)
INCPC = annual per capita income for the target population
COMPET = number of competitors within a 5-mile radius

SALES	POP	INCPC	COMPET
196	5.18	5567	4
194	7.59	6809	7
166	6.47	5882	7
195	4.34	5608	4
209	5.76	6217	5
217	6.91	5954	5

(*continued*)

SALES	POP	INCPC	COMPET
164	4.68	4863	5
235	6.22	5658	3
240	6.48	8024	5
229	7.06	6224	5
176	4.42	5380	4
169	4.82	6246	6
225	7.48	5696	5
190	6.28	7303	7
254	7.41	8095	4
224	7.62	6652	6

The estimated regression equation for these data, using SALES as the dependent variable, is

$$\widehat{SALES} = 119.2 + 16.12POP + .0119\ INCPC - 17.17COMPET$$

$$R^2 = .942 \qquad s_e = 7.613$$

a. Can we say that POP and COMPET are more important than INCPC for predicting SALES just because the magnitudes of their coefficients are larger? Explain.
b. Are the signs of the regression coefficients (negative or positive) what you would expect? Explain.
c. The regression output shows that the standard errors of the coefficients for POP, INCPC, and COMPET are 2.05, .0026, and 1.74, respectively. Which of the three independent variables have significantly nonzero coefficients? Use two-tailed tests at the 5% level.

63. The discount chain in Problem 62 is planning to open a new branch at one of three possible locations. The values of POP, INCPC, and COMPET at these three locations are shown below.

Location	POP	INCPC	COMPET
1	6.32	4895	4
2	4.57	7345	5
3	5.96	4567	7

a. Based on predictions from the estimated regression equation, which location appears to be the most attractive? Support your answer with appropriate calculations.
b. Considering the magnitudes of the differences between the three predictions you made in part (a) and the (approximate) standard errors of these predictions, how confident are you that the location you found to be best in part (a) will actually have the highest sales level? Explain. (No *exact* calculations are intended here.)

64. In an agriculture experiment, the number of pounds of fertilizer and the number of pounds of insecticide were varied over 15 equal-sized plots of land in order to judge their effects on corn yield (in bushels per plot). The following data were obtained.

Corn Yield	Fertilizer	Insecticide
68.9	16.9	14.2
68.7	19.9	16.2
60.0	15.0	14.8
69.5	17.7	13.4
74.4	18.5	16.1
65.7	17.5	15.4
73.2	18.0	15.3
58.1	16.0	12.2
81.8	18.6	15.7
73.3	20.4	15.0
67.9	19.1	14.9
86.0	20.8	16.7
68.2	18.3	13.6
62.8	16.5	12.8
65.7	17.5	15.4

a. Draw a scattergram of corn yield versus amount of fertilizer; of corn yield versus amount of insecticide. Do these graphs appear to be linear?
b. The matrix of simple correlations between the three variables is shown below. Which variable explains the most about corn yield for these data? What is a lower bound for the R^2 value when both independent variables enter the equation for corn yield linearly?

Matrix of simple correlations

	Corn Yield	Fertilizer	Insecticide
Corn Yield	1.00		
Fertilizer	.76	1.00	
Insecticide	.67	.62	1.00

c. Might multicollinearity be present in these data? Why or why not?

65. Referring to Problem 64, the estimated equation for corn yield is

$$\widehat{CORN} = -4.52 + 2.60FERT + 1.85\ INSECT$$

The standard errors of the coefficients of FERT and INSECT are 1.02 and 1.26, respectively. The standard error of estimate is 4.81, and the R^2 value is .64.

a. Test (separately) whether the coefficients of fertilizer and insecticide are significantly positive. Use one-tailed tests at the 5% level.

b. What is the correlation between the observed corn yields and the corn yields estimated from the regression equation?

c. Is there any practical significance to the negative constant term (-4.52) in the equation above?

d. Output (not shown) from the IDA program shows that if FERT and INSECT are set equal to 18.2 and 15.7, respectively, the predicted corn yield is 71.80. Furthermore, it shows that the standard error for an individual observation is 5.08, while the standard error for the average of all such observations is 1.64. Use the equations from the text to verify that these answers are (at least approximately) correct. Interpret the standard errors in words.

66. For the equation from Problem 65, the scattergram of residuals versus estimated corn yields is shown below. (This is taken from the IDA output, where each number in the graph tells how many observations are at any particular point on the graph.) Which of the regression assumptions appears to be violated? Explain.

Scattergram for Problem 66

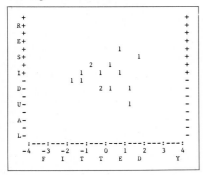

67. In a study of earnings of 1393 business economists, the following equation was estimated. (Reference: N. L. Preston and E. R. Fiedler, "Overworked and Underpaid?" *Business Economics*, Vol. 15, 1980, pp. 9–15.)

$$\hat{Y} = 9.393 + .224X_1 + .019X_2 + .049X_3$$
$$+ .190X_4 + .245X_5 - .180X_6 - .281X_7$$
$$- .266X_8 + .067X_9 + .078X_{10} + .122X_{11}$$

The variables are

Y = natural logarithm of total compensation
X_1 = natural logarithm of number of years of professional experience
X_2 = number of persons supervised
X_3 = number of years of college education
X_4 = dummy variable (1 for men, 0 for women)
X_5 = dummy variable (1 if employed in securities and investment industry, 0 otherwise)
X_6 = dummy variable (1 if employed in nonprofit research organization, 0 otherwise)
X_7 = dummy variable (1 if employed in government, 0 otherwise)
X_8 = dummy variable (1 if employed in an academic institution, 0 otherwise)
X_9 = dummy variable (1 if employed in New York City, 0 otherwise)
X_{10} = dummy variable (1 if employed as an "economic advisor," 0 otherwise)
X_{11} = dummy variable (1 if employed as a "general administration economist," 0 otherwise)

a. Interpret the coefficients of X_5 and X_6.

b. Do all the coefficients have the signs (positive or negative) that you would expect? Discuss.

c. Assume that the standard errors of the coefficients of X_1 through X_{11} are .0010, .0012, .0041, .029, .037, .049, .036, .034, .022, .028, and .027. Calculate a 95% confidence interval for each of these coefficients. Which of these confidence intervals include 0? How does this relate to your answer in part (b)?

68. Referring to Problem 67, predict the total compensation of a business economist who has 10 years of professional experience, supervises three other employees, has earned a master's degree (in six years), is male, and is employed in an investment company in New York City. (Assume that he is not considered an "economic advisor" or a "general administration economist.") Note that you will have to convert from natural logarithm of dollars to dollars.

69. With regard to the regression equation developed by Platt and McCarthy (see Application 12.2), consider a CEO who has been in his position for 10 years and has a financial background. Find a point prediction of his total yearly compensation if he is 50 years old; if he is 55 years old. Explain why the difference between these two predictions is not $5 \times 88{,}270$, where 88,270 is the coefficient of the age variable.

70. A cross-sectional study of women past childbearing age intends to discover how the number of children a woman has

depends on her education level, her job status, and the number of children she thought she would have when she first got married. The following data are obtained from a sample of 30 women. The variables are:

CHILD = number of children the woman has had
INTEND = number of children the woman says she intended to have when she got married
JOB = dummy variable (1 if the woman had a full-time or part-time job during her childbearing years, 0 otherwise)
EDUC = dummy variable (1 if the woman went to college, 0 otherwise)

CHILD	INTEND	JOB	EDUC
3	3	0	1
2	3	1	0
1	2	1	0
2	1	0	1
0	2	1	1
2	2	0	0
1	1	1	1
3	2	1	0
4	2	1	0
2	3	0	1

(*continued*)

CHILD	INTEND	JOB	EDUC
1	3	0	0
3	2	0	0
1	4	1	1
0	0	1	1
2	1	1	1
4	3	0	1
5	6	0	0
2	4	0	1
1	0	1	0
0	1	1	1
3	1	1	1
2	1	0	0
2	2	0	1
4	2	1	0
2	3	0	0
1	1	1	1
0	0	1	1
3	3	0	0
2	1	1	1
2	2	0	0

The IDA output for these data is shown below.

IDA Output for Problem 70

```
VARIABLE    B(STD.V)          B          STD.ERROR(B)       T

INTEND      0.4082        3.9614E-01     1.7786E-01       2.227
JOB        -0.1209       -3.0663E-01     4.6094E-01      -0.665
EDUC       -0.2511       -6.3675E-01     4.1347E-01      -1.540
CONSTANT     0           1.6976E+00      6.1414E-01       2.764

                     MULTIPLE R         R-SQUARE
UNADJUSTED            0.5934            0.3522
 ADJUSTED             0.5267            0.2774

STD. DEV. OF RESIDUALS = 1.0936E+00
N =    30

 ANOVA

 SOURCE           SS          DF          MS              F
REGRESSION    1.69034E+01      3      5.63448E+00       4.71
RESIDUALS     3.10966E+01     26      1.19602E+00
 TOTAL        4.80000E+01     29      1.65517E+00
```

a. What is the estimated regression equation? How do you interpret the coefficients of JOB and EDUC? Be specific.
b. Are these three independent variables as a whole useful in predicting the number of children a woman has had? Use a 5% significance level.
c. Which of the three independent variables, taken separately, is useful for predicting the dependent variable, given that the other two independent variables are already in the equation? Base your answer on a 5% significance level.
d. How accurately is this equation likely to predict the number of children a woman will have?

*71. It can be shown that the variance of $\hat{\beta}_j$ (for any $j \geq 1$) is given by

$$s_{\hat{\beta}_j}^2 = \frac{s_e^2}{SS_{jj}(1 - R_j^2)}$$

Here SS_{jj} is the sum of squared deviations of the X_j values about their mean, and R_j^2 is the R^2 value that would result if X_j were regressed on all the other independent variables, that is, if X_j were treated as the dependent variable.

a. Why might R_j^2 be large when multicollinearity involving X_j is present?

b. Explain the effect that multicollinearity can have on the standard errors of the $\hat{\beta}$'s by referring to the formula for $s_{\hat{\beta}_j}^2$ above.

c. Give an intuitive reason for the effect described in part (b).

72. In a study of 208 California residents who had obtained car repairs during the previous year, Biehal estimated a regression equation using level of dissatisfaction as the dependent variable. (Reference: Gabriel J. Biehal, "Consumers' Prior Experiences and Perceptions in Auto Repair Choice," *Journal of Marketing*, Vol. 47, 1983, pp. 82–91.) This variable was measured on a scale where higher values represent more customer dissatisfaction with the repair shop. The independent variables were (1) the repair cost (REPAIR), (2) the number of previous times this repair shop has been used by the customer, (3) whether the problem was corrected on the first visit, and (4) the level of information search used by the customer prior to having the car repaired. More explicit definitions of variables (2), (3), and (4) are as follows. The number of previous times the repair shop had been used was divided into four categories: never before, 1 or 2 times, 3 to 5 times, and more than 5 times. Dummy variables D1, D2, and D3 were used for the last three categories, and the first category was used as the base category. Variable (3), whether the problem was corrected on the first visit, was also modeled as a dummy variable, D4. It was coded as 0 if the problem was corrected on the first visit, 1 otherwise. Finally, variable (4), level of information search, INFO, was a combination of the number of phone calls made to repair companies (PHONE), the number of visits to repair shops (VISIT), and the number of friends contacted about repair information (FRIEND). For technical reasons, the INFO variable was defined as

$$INFO = .82PHONE + .68VISIT + .64FRIEND$$

Given these definitions, the following multiple regression coefficients were estimated.

Variable	Coefficient
(Constant)	2.14
REPAIR	.03
D1	−.34
D2	−.26
D3	−.72*
D4	2.54**
INFO	−.15*

A * means significant at the 5% level; a ** means significant at the 1% level.

a. Are any of these findings, either significance or lack of it, or the signs of the coefficients, contrary to intuition? Answer by discussing what each of the coefficients implies.

b. Consider two customers, A and B. Customer A used a repair shop he had never used before, his repair cost was $175, the problem was corrected the first time, and his information search consisted of contacting two friends. Customer B, on the other hand, used a repair shop she had used twice before, her repair cost was $250, the problem was not corrected the first time, and her information search consisted of visiting three repair shops and making four phone calls. According to the regression equation, which of these two customers would you expect to be more dissatisfied with the service?

73. Referring to the Futrell, Parasuraman study of job satisfaction and salesforce turnover (see Chapter 7, Problem 66), the authors hypothesized that not only was job satisfaction related to turnover, but that the form and strength of this relationship was related to job performance. To test this, they estimated two multiple regression equations, one for the 130 "low performers" in the sample and the other for the 133 "high performers." For each equation the dependent variable was the salesperson's stated "propensity to leave," and the independent variables were the five measured components of job satisfaction: pay, promotion, co-workers, work, and supervision. The estimated regression equations are shown on p. 646. Discuss in intuitive terms whether the authors' hypotheses appear to hold. In particular, what role does job performance appear to play? How certain can we be that the true signs of the coefficients (in either equation) are the same as the signs of the estimated coefficients?

	Regression Coefficient	Standard Error of Coefficient			Regression Coefficient	Standard Error of Coefficient
High-performer equation				Low-performer equation		
Satisfaction with:				Satisfaction with:		
Pay	.003	.007		Pay	−.006	.007
Promotion	−.012	.006		Promotion	−.009	.006
Co-workers	−.009	.011		Co-workers	.016	.010
Work	−.017	.010		Work	−.050	.011
Supervision	−.013	.009		Supervision	−.027	.010

Computer Problems

(These problems are to be used in conjunction with the computer software package.)

1. Consider the data on grade point averages and test scores in Table II of Appendix D. In this problem we would like to develop a regression equation for GGPA, the graduate grade point average.

   a. Using the MREGRESS program, enter the data on all four variables for the first 30 students. Use GGPA as the dependent variable. Then estimate the equation that includes (i) undergraduate GPA only; (ii) the verbal and quantitative percentiles only; (iii) all three independent variables. Comment on whether the last equation appears to be much better than the first two.

   b. Test formally whether test percentiles improve the fit significantly, given that undergraduate GPA is already in the equation. Use a 5% level. Then turn this around. That is, test whether undergraduate GPA improves the fit, given that test percentiles are already in the equation. Again use a 5% level.

   c. Using the estimated equation that includes all three independent variables, find a point prediction and the standard error of this prediction for the GGPA of a student with a 3.42 undergraduate GPA and verbal and quantitative test percentiles of 67 and 91. Repeat for a student with a 3.17 undergraduate GPA and verbal and quantitative percentiles of 82 and 64.

2. The data in Table VIII of Appendix D show weekly percentage changes in stock prices as well as the stock prices themselves.

   Use the MREGRESS program to see how well percentage changes in the price of Revlon stock can be explained by the percentage changes in stocks in the drug industry, stocks in the cosmetics industry, and stocks comprising the market index. Use the last 30 weekly percentage changes only. Is this equation (with three independent variables) significantly better than the equation that has the percentage change in the market index as the only independent variable? Use a 5% significance level.

3. The data set in Table IX of Appendix D is similar to the data in Section 12.11, except that a different sample of 30 cities is used. Use the MREGRESS program to run the same multiple regression equations as were listed in Section 12.11. Do the results from this sample appear to be similar to the results from the previous sample? Discuss.

4. Use the MREGRESS program on the data in Problem 53 (p. 636), with JOBEFF again as the dependent variable. Use the output to answer the questions in Problem 53.

5. Use the MREGRESS program on the data Problem 56 (p. 639), with INC as the dependent variable. Then answer the questions in Problems 56, 57, and 58. In particular, verify the standard error of prediction claimed in Problem 58, part (b).

6. Use the MREGRESS program on the data in Problem 59 (p. 639), with DEMAND as the dependent variable. Then use the output to answer the questions in Problems 59, 60, and 61.

Using Regression Analysis to Perform One-Way ANOVA

In this appendix we show how one-way ANOVA is a special case of multiple regression, where all the independent variables are dummy variables. This means that we can analyze a one-way ANOVA problem on the computer by using any of the available *regression* packages. Although this appendix deals only with one-way ANOVA, there is a similar connection between other ANOVA designs and multiple regression.

Suppose that the single factor has J possible treatment levels, labeled 1 through J. Then we choose any one of these to be the "base" level, and we define a dummy variable for each of the other levels. Suppose that level J is chosen as the base level. Then for any level j between 1 and $J - 1$, we let X_j be the corresponding dummy variable. Its value is 1 if the observation comes from treatment level j, and its value is 0 otherwise. (These 0's and 1's are read into a computer exactly like the values of any other independent variable.) The regression equation we estimate is

$$Y = \beta_0 + \beta_1 X_1 + \beta_2 X_2 + \cdots + \beta_{J-1} X_{J-1} + \epsilon$$

It can be shown that the least squares estimates of the β's are

$$\hat{\beta}_0 = \overline{Y}_J, \quad \hat{\beta}_1 = \overline{Y}_1 - \overline{Y}_J, \quad \hat{\beta}_2 = \overline{Y}_2 - \overline{Y}_J, \quad \ldots, \quad \hat{\beta}_{J-1} = \overline{Y}_{J-1} - \overline{Y}_J$$

where the $\overline{Y}$'s are the sample means for the various treatment levels. Therefore, tests for differences between treatment means are equivalent to tests on the β's. Furthermore, it can be shown that the ANOVA F test from Chapter 10 is the *same* as the overall F test from this chapter. In particular, rejection of the equal treatment means hypothesis is equivalent to rejection of the regression hypothesis that β_1 through β_{J-1} equal 0.

To illustrate this procedure, reconsider Example 10.1. There the problem was to see whether any of four types of displays made a significant difference in the fraction of store-brand potato chips sold. Earlier we ran the usual ANOVA F test and rejected the equal means hypothesis at the 10% level. An alternative method is to use dummy variables in the multiple regression procedure suggested here. We first select one of the treatment levels (display types), say level 4, as the base level, and then encode dummy variables X_1, X_2, and X_3 for the other three display types. For example, the observation for the third store using display type 2 (see Table 10.2) has $Y = .19$, $X_1 = 0$, $X_2 = 1$, $X_3 = 0$, whereas the fifth store using display type 4 has

$Y = .31$, $X_1 = 0$, $X_2 = 0$, $X_3 = 0$. If we input these values, plus similar values for the other 21 observations, into a multiple regression package, we obtain $\hat{\beta}_0 = \overline{Y}_4 = .2083$, $\hat{\beta}_1 = \overline{Y}_1 - \overline{Y}_4 = .0217$, $\hat{\beta}_2 = \overline{Y}_2 - \overline{Y}_4 = .0567$, and $\hat{\beta}_3 = \overline{Y}_3 - \overline{Y}_4 = .0977$. More important, the F value from the ANOVA table (from the multiple regression output) is still 2.83. With the same degrees of freedom as before, this again leads to rejection of the equal-means hypothesis at the 10% level.

References

DRAPER, N. and SMITH, H. *Applied Regression Analysis,* 2nd ed. New York: Wiley, 1981.

KLEINBAUM, D. G. and KUPPER, L. L. *Applied Regression Analysis and Other Multivariable Methods.* North Scituate, Mass., 1978 (available from PWS Publishers, Boston).

LING, R. F. and ROBERTS, H. V. *IDA: A User's Guide to the IDA Interactive Data Analysis and Forecasting System.* New York: McGraw-Hill, 1982.

MENDENHALL, W. and SINCICH, T. *A Second Course in Business Statistics: Regression Analysis,* 2nd ed. San Francisco: Dellen (a division of Macmillan), 1986.

NETER, J., WASSERMAN, W., and KUTNER, M. H. *Applied Linear Regression Models.* Homewood, Ill.: Richard D. Irwin, 1983.

NIE, N., HULL, C. H., JENKINS, J. G., STEINBRENNER, K., and BENT, D. H. *Statistical Package for the Social Sciences,* 2nd ed. New York: McGraw-Hill, 1975.

NORUSIS, M. J. *SPSS Introductory Guide: Basic Statistics and Operations.* New York: McGraw-Hill, 1982.

WONNACOTT, R. J. and WONNACOTT, T. H. *Econometrics.* New York: Wiley, 1970.

CHAPTER 13

Goodness-of-Fit Tests and Nonparametric Statistics

Objectives

1. To learn statistical procedures that are valid under less restrictive conditions than the parametric tests in previous chapters.
2. To learn the advantages and disadvantages of nonparametric tests in comparison to previous tests.
3. To learn a chi-square goodness-of-fit test that is applicable to categorical data.
4. To learn a chi-square test for independence between two attributes.
5. To learn several nonparametric tests for the difference between two means.
6. To learn a nonparametric analogue of the one-way ANOVA F test.
7. To learn two nonparametric measures that indicate the strength of a relationship between two variables.
8. To learn a "runs" test for randomness.

Contents

With the introduction of computers into virtually all types of businesses, there has been a sharp increase in the development and use of management information systems. These are computerized systems that allow management to keep track of practically any information (accounting data, marketing forecasts, inventory, etc.) that might be of use in making decisions. However, because these systems consume large amounts of time and money in the development stages, it is important that they be developed correctly on the first attempt. To date, there have been two basic approaches to developing these systems. One approach is to develop the system according to preset "stages," with little input from the potential users, whereas the other approach is to develop a crude system quickly and then let potential users modify this system gradually as they see fit.

One study attempted to discover which of these two approaches is favored by users. Teams of potential users were paired according to several criteria and were instructed to develop information systems. For each pair of teams, one team was instructed to use the first approach, while the other team was told to use the second approach. After the development of the systems, the teams were questioned about their reactions to the development approach they used, and the results were analyzed statistically to see if there were differences between the two groups of teams. Although this sounds like a perfect setting for the matched-pairs t test from Chapter 9, the assumptions behind that test were questionable. Therefore, a "nonparametric" test for paired differences was used instead. As we will see, the advantage of this type of test is that it requires weaker assumptions. Its potential disadvantage is that it is not as powerful as tests that we have studied in previous chapters.

13.1

Introduction

In this chapter we continue our study of statistical inference, but we will now learn procedures that require less restrictive assumptions than those in earlier chapters. These procedures are called *nonparametric,* or sometimes *distribution-free,* procedures. The terms "nonparametric" and "distribution-free" indicate how the procedures in this chapter differ from those in earlier chapters. The earlier procedures are all similar in that (1) they deal with specific parameters, such as p, μ, and σ^2; and (2) they assume normal or approximately normal population distributions. In this chapter we relax both of these assumptions. Many of the hypothesis tests in this chapter cannot be stated in terms of a single parameter, and most of them require no specific population distribution. Thus, they are applicable in many situations where the earlier tests do not apply.

If the assumptions of the previous chapters do apply, then the methods in this chapter are not as powerful as the previous methods. Essentially, they do not use the sample data as efficiently as the methods based on normality. But when the assumptions of previous chapters do not apply, the methods discussed here should be used instead. Not only do they yield more valid inferences, but research has shown that they are surprisingly powerful.

13.2
The Chi-Square Goodness-of-Fit Test

Perhaps the most widely known and used test in this chapter is the chi-square goodness-of-fit test. (The chi-square tests in Sections 13.2, 13.3, and 13.4 have no analogues in previous chapters.) This test applies to *categorical* data. Suppose that there are several well-defined categories and that each observation falls into exactly one of these categories. First we hypothesize the proportions of the total population in the various categories. These imply a population histogram, such as in Figure 13.1a. Then we gather a random sample from the population and count the number of observations in each category; this gives a sample proportion for each category. These sample proportions can be shown in a histogram as in Figure 13.1b. If the hypoth-

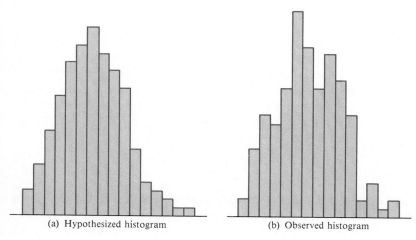

(a) Hypothesized histogram   (b) Observed histogram

Figure 13.1

esized proportions are the true ones, the population and sample histograms should be similar. That is, there should be a good fit between them, hence the name "goodness-of-fit test."

The reason we need a formal test for deciding whether the hypothesized proportions are true is that looks can be deceiving. How can we tell, for instance, whether the fit between Figures 13.1a and 13.1b is good enough? Certainly, we do not expect a perfect fit because of sampling variation. But it is hard to tell by looking at the two histograms whether the differences between them are due to sampling variation or an incorrect hypothesis. The chi-square test resolves this question; it tells us whether the perceived differences are statistically significant.

The Test for Multinomial Data

The first version of the chi-square test we present is when the data are already in categorical form. We assume that there are M distinct categories, labeled $1, 2, \ldots, M$, and that each observation is in exactly one of these categories. This means that the data need not be quantitative. For example, the categories could be different brands of soap detergent. Then the observations might tell us which brand each person in the sample favors. Or the categories could be different amounts of education. Then the observations might tell us how far each person in the sample progressed in school.

It is also possible for the data to be quantitative data that have been categorized. As an example, suppose that the variable of interest is the daily change in the price of a stock. Rather than analyzing the actual numerical changes in stock prices, we could divide all stock price changes into three categories: (1) changes that are decreases of at least one point, (2) changes that are increases of at least one point, and (3) changes of magnitude less than one point. The stock price data can then be treated as categorical data.

We often refer to the types of data listed above as *multinomial* data. The word "multinomial" is a generalization of the word "binomial." Recall that the term "binomial" refers to data categorized into two types. Similarly, multinomial data are the frequency counts for data categorized into more than two types. With binomial data, we usually let p denote the proportion of the population of one type, so that a proportion $1 - p$ are of the other type. Similarly, with multinomial data we let $p_1, p_2, \ldots, p_M$ denote the proportions of the population in the respective categories. Since every member of the population must be in exactly one category, we have

$$p_1 + p_2 + \cdots + p_M = 1$$

Now suppose that we select a random sample of size n from the population. Before we observe the sample, the number of sampled members from category i is a random variable; we let E_i be the expected value of this random variable. Then it is easy to show that E_i is related to the proportion p_i by the following formula.

> *Expected Number in Category i*
>
> $$E_i = np_i$$

This expression is intuitive. For example, if 25% of the population are in category 5, and we choose a random sample of 200 members, we expect $200(.25) = 50$ of these, plus or minus sampling variation, to be in category 5.

For any *particular* sample of size n, let O_i (O for observed) be the actual number of observations in category i. There is no formula for the O_i's; we simply count the number of observations in each category.

If the p_i's used to calculate the E_i's (from $E_i = np_i$) are the *true* population proportions, the E_i's and O_i's ought to be close to each other. Again, we say that there should be a good fit. If the hypothesized p_i's are not the true ones, however, the E_i's and O_i's will probably differ substantially. The test statistic used to measure the "distance" between the E_i's and O_i's is labeled χ^2 and is given as follows.

> *Chi-Square Test Statistic*
>
> $$\chi^2 = \sum \frac{(O_i - E_i)^2}{E_i}$$

When the p_i's are the true population proportions, it can be shown that under most conditions, this test statistic is approximately chi-square distributed with $M - 1$ degrees of freedom. (The necessary conditions are that n is reasonably large and none of the E_i's is too small.)

We now convert these facts into a formal hypothesis test. The null hypothesis is

> H_0: $p_1, p_2, \ldots, p_M$ are the true population proportions

and the alternative is that these p_i's are not the true proportions. (Notice that in any particular problem, the p_i's in H_0 are M specified numbers that sum to 1.) Since the numerators of the test statistic, the $(O_i - E_i)^2$'s, will tend to be small when H_0 is true and large when H_0 is false, we reject H_0 only when the chi-square test statistic is sufficiently large.

> *Chi-Square Goodness-of-Fit Test*
>
> Reject H_0 (the proposed fit) at the α level if $\chi^2 > \chi^2_{\alpha, M-1}$.

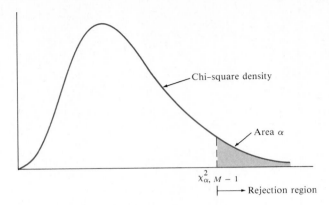

Figure 13.2

Figure 13.2 illustrates the rejection region as the right-hand tail of the appropriate chi-square density.

EXAMPLE 13.1

Consider a large company that hires mostly college students for entry-level positions. The company categorizes its hirees as follows:

  1: white male with a business degree
  2: white male with a nonbusiness degree
  3: white female with a business degree
  4: white female with a nonbusiness degree
  5: minority with a business degree
  6: minority with a nonbusiness degree

The company senses that because of its conscious or unconscious hiring policies and because of changing mixes of college students, today's mix of hirees is somewhat different than it was 10 years ago. From extensive company records, the proportions in the six categories 10 years ago are found to be

$$p_1 = .54, \quad p_2 = .21, \quad p_3 = .11, \quad p_4 = .05, \quad p_5 = .03, \quad p_6 = .06$$

A random sample of 200 recent hirees results in the observed values

$$O_1 = 95, \quad O_2 = 38, \quad O_3 = 35, \quad O_4 = 12, \quad O_5 = 12, \quad O_6 = 8$$

Is there enough evidence in this sample to conclude at the 5% level that the company's mix of hirees is different now than it was 10 years ago?

SOLUTION

The null hypothesis is that today's proportions in the six categories are the same as the proportions 10 years ago. We test this by calculating the chi-square test statistic, which has a chi-square distribution with $6 - 1 = 5$ degrees of freedom if H_0 is true. The necessary calculations are shown in Table 13.1.

Table 13.1

Category	O_i	p_i	E_i	$(O_i - E_i)^2/E_i$
1	95	.54	108	1.565
2	38	.21	42	.381
3	35	.11	22	7.682
4	12	.05	10	.400
5	12	.03	6	6.000
6	8	.06	12	1.333
Total	200	1.00	200	17.361

From the right-hand column, we see that the test statistic is 17.361. This must be compared with the tabulated chi-square value with 5 degrees of freedom that cuts off area .05 in the right-hand tail, namely $\chi^2_{.05,5} = 11.070$. Since 17.361 is greater than 11.070, we reject H_0 at the 5% level. In other words, there is significant evidence that the current mix of hirees is different than it was 10 years ago.

There are several aspects of the chi-square test that we wish to point out.

1. As Table 13.1 illustrates, the O_i's and E_i's must each sum to n, the sample size. This serves as an arithmetic check. Also, even though the O_i's are always integers (since they arise from counts), the E_i's should generally *not* be rounded to integer values. This can seriously distort the χ^2 value.
2. The E_i in the denominator of $(O_i - E_i)^2/E_i$ has an important effect. In particular, the categories with small E_i's contribute relatively more to the test statistic. For instance, compare categories 1 and 5 in Table 13.1. Category 5 contributes about four times as much to the test statistic as category 1, even though its $O_i - E_i$ is only about half as large. This means that rejection of H_0 is often due to the categories with the *smallest* proportions.
3. If we reject H_0, as in the example above, we are only accepting that the p_i's specified by H_0 are not the true ones. We are not accepting

that any *specific* alternative set of p_i's are true. In Example 13.1, we are not saying how the mix of hirees has changed over the past 10 years when we reject H_0. However, it appears from the data that the change is due primarily to increased numbers of women and minorities from business schools.

One special case of this chi-square test is when the p_i's are hypothesized to be equal. Then the null hypothesis is

$$H_0: p_1 = p_2 = \cdots = p_M = \frac{1}{M}$$

In this case each E_i is equal to n/M because we expect an equal number of observations in each of the categories. Because of equal E_i's, the chi-square test statistic can be simplified (with the help of some algebra):

> ### *Test Statistic for Equally Probable Categories*
>
> $$\chi^2 = \frac{M}{n} \sum O_i^2 - n$$

Other than this simplification, the test is run exactly as before, as shown in the following example.

EXAMPLE 13.2

It is hypothesized that the same number of police calls arise in 10 sections of a city. During a one-week period, the frequencies of police calls shown in Table 13.2 are observed. Can we reject the equal proportion hypothesis at the 5% level on the basis of these data?

SOLUTION

From the table we see that the total number of police calls for the week is $n = 589$. The chi-square test statistic is therefore

$$\chi^2 = \frac{M}{n} \sum O_i^2 - n = \frac{10}{589} (35,543) - 589 = 14.45$$

With $M - 1 = 9$ degrees of freedom, the relevant chi-square value from the chi-square table is $\chi^2_{.05,9} = 16.92$. Since 14.45 is less than 16.92, we cannot reject the equal proportion hypothesis at the 5% level. This is despite the seemingly large variation among the O's.

Table 13.2

Section	O_i	O_i^2
1	53	2,809
2	71	5,041
3	47	2,209
4	62	3,844
5	75	5,625
6	44	1,936
7	58	3,364
8	61	3,721
9	63	3,969
10	55	3,025
Total	589	35,543

In many statistical applications it is convenient to assume that a population distribution has some particular form. Presumably we make this assumption so that we can apply a particular statistical procedure. We now see how to test such an assumption by means of the chi-square goodness-of-fit test.

The specific population distribution we will test in this section is the normal distribution. We do this because we must frequently assume that a given population is normally distributed. However, the goodness-of-fit test we describe in this section can be performed for *any* hypothesized population distribution. We choose the normal distribution simply because it is so important and because we are so familiar with it.

The idea behind the test is illustrated in Figure 13.3. The curve shown is a specified normal density. The null hypothesis is that this normal density represents the population distribution. Because the chi-square test works with categorical data, we must first divide the possible observations into M interval categories, specified by $M - 1$ "break points." For example, a category might be defined as all values greater than 20 and less than or equal to 30. The break points, together with Table Ia in Appendix B, then allow us to find the probabilities of the various categories. These are the areas under the curve between the break points. We label these probabilities p_1 through p_M:

$$p_i = \text{probability of an observation being in category } i$$

Alternatively, we may choose the categories implicitly by choosing their probabilities, the p_i's. Then we can find the break points that produce these p_i's by using Table Ib. An example will illustrate this procedure.

Once we have the break points and the p_i's, we proceed basically as before. For a sample of size n, we let $E_i = np_i$ be the expected number of observations in category i, and we let O_i be the observed number of observations in category i. If the null hypothesis is true, the test statistic

$$\chi^2 = \sum \frac{(O_i - E_i)^2}{E_i}$$

again has a chi-square distribution. If the p_i's are all equal to $1/M$, we may use the simplified chi-square formula discussed above, namely

$$\chi^2 = \frac{M}{n} \sum O_i^2 - n$$

There is one difficulty, however. The null hypothesis, which can be written as

H_0: the population is normally distributed

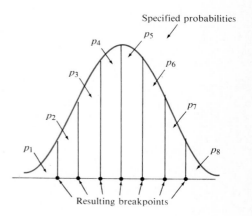

Figure 13.3

does not specify *which* normal distribution is the true one. That is, we do not know which mean μ and variance σ^2 to use. So we first use the data to estimate μ and σ^2 by their usual estimates, $\overline{X}$ and s^2. Then we see whether the data fit this particular normal distribution. For example, if we calculate that $\overline{X} = 37$ and $s^2 = 16$, we test whether the data fit a $N(37, 16)$ distribution. (The idea is that if the data do not fit this particular normal distribution, they will certainly not fit any other normal distribution.) But by estimating μ and σ^2, we lose 2 degrees of freedom. Therefore, the resulting test statistic has a chi-square distribution with $(M - 1) - 2 = M - 3$ degrees of freedom. (Although it is less common, it is possible to test whether a population is normal with *given* values of μ and σ^2. In this case we do not need to estimate μ and σ^2, and the resulting degrees of freedom parameter for the chi-square test is $M - 1$.)

The usual procedure is to choose somewhere between 5 and 10 *equally probable* categories. This means that we make p_1 through p_M equal to $1/M$. Then all the E_i's equal n/M. The work goes into locating the break points so that we can find the O_i's.

The procedure is illustrated in Figure 13.4. Suppose that we want to find $M - 1$ break points that divide a $N(\mu, \sigma^2)$ density into M equal areas. To be specific, we will solve this problem when $M = 8$. We first use Table 1b to locate the break points that divide a $N(0, 1)$ density into $M = 8$ equal parts, each with area $1/8$. The rightmost break point must be $z_{1/8} = z_{.125} = 1.15$ because we require it to have area $1/8$ to its right. The next break point must be $z_{2/8} = z_{.25} = .67$ because it must have a *total* area $2/8$ to its right. The procedure continues until we find all seven break points. (Notice from the figure how symmetry around 0 simplifies the procedure.) Then we use these $N(0, 1)$ break points to find the $N(\mu, \sigma^2)$ break points we really need.

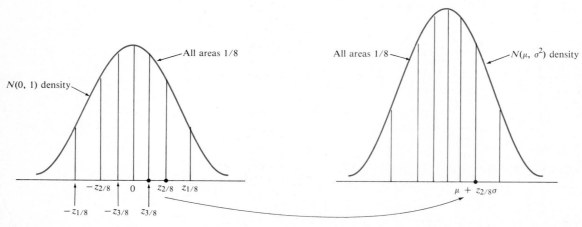

Figure 13.4

Each z value is multiplied by σ and then added to μ. (Notice that this procedure is the opposite of standardizing. That is, if $Z = (X - \mu)/\sigma$, then $X = \sigma Z + \mu$.) The resulting break points define the categories and allow us to find the O_i's.

EXAMPLE 13.3

Consider a hardware retailer who is having difficulty determining the correct stocking policy for a frequently demanded item. A consultant assures him that there is a mathematical model that will determine the best stocking policy, but this model is based on the assumption of normally distributed daily demands. The retailer consults his records and finds the number of items demanded on 75 selected days. These data are shown in Table 13.3. Is there enough evidence from these data to reject the null hypothesis of normally distributed daily demands? Use eight equally probable categories in a chi-square goodness-of-fit test at the 10% level.

Table 13.3

16	52	27	39	21	46	32	12	59	26	39	15
21	30	46	41	32	8	17	23	41	27	16	28
37	42	51	7	28	35	25	17	19	26	29	35
59	62	31	26	30	26	45	18	23	29	35	42
18	5	61	27	30	31	29	18	12	52	69	71
15	20	38	41	23	26	43	27	34	42	39	62
12	20	10									

Sum of observations = 2366
Sum of squares = 91,324

SOLUTION

We first estimate μ and σ^2. From the sums shown in the table, we calculate $\overline{X}$ and s^2 in the usual way:

$$\overline{X} = \sum \frac{X_i}{n} = 31.55$$

and

$$s^2 = \frac{\sum X_i^2 - n\overline{X}^2}{n - 1} = 225.47 = 15.02^2$$

Now we use the method in Figure 13.4 to find the seven break points that define the eight categories of demands. These are shown in Figure 13.5. For

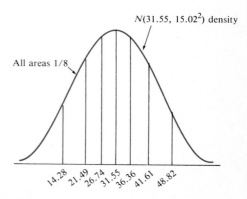

Figure 13.5

Table 13.4

Category	O_i	p_i	E_i	$(O_i - E_i)^2/E_i$
Less than 14.28	7	⅛	⁷⁵⁄₈	.602
14.28–21.49	14	⅛	⁷⁵⁄₈	2.282
21.49–26.74	9	⅛	⁷⁵⁄₈	.015
26.74–31.55	14	⅛	⁷⁵⁄₈	2.282
31.55–36.36	6	⅛	⁷⁵⁄₈	1.215
36.36–41.61	8	⅛	⁷⁵⁄₈	.202
41.61–48.82	7	⅛	⁷⁵⁄₈	.602
Greater than 48.82	10	⅛	⁷⁵⁄₈	.042
Total	75	1	75	7.242

example, the rightmost break point is

$$\overline{X} + z_{.125}s = 31.55 + 1.15(15.02) = 48.82$$

So any observation above 48.82 is in the rightmost category; there are 10 such observations. The tabulation of the other O_i's and the calculation of the chi-square test statistic are straightforward and are shown in Table 13.4. Alternatively, the test statistic can be found (more easily) from

$$\chi^2 = \frac{M}{n} \sum O_i^2 - n = \frac{8}{75} (771) - 75 = 7.24$$

This follows because the categories are equally likely under H_0. With eight categories there are $8 - 3 = 5$ degrees of freedom, so the tabulated chi-square value we require is $\chi^2_{.10,5} = 9.236$. The calculated test statistic is only 7.242, which means we *cannot* reject a normal fit at the 10% level. In other words, if the population distribution is really normal, the distribution of data we have obtained is not terribly unusual. We would expect to obtain this "poor" a fit in over 10% of all such samples. The conclusion is that the retailer can feel fairly confident about using the consultant's model.

The principal drawback of the chi-square goodness-of-fit test for normality is its lack of power. This means that if the population is not normal, there may still be a high probability of not rejecting the null hypothesis of normality and thus committing a type II error. This is especially likely when the true population distribution is not *too* nonnormal, say, approximately bell-shaped and approximately symmetric. For example, it is quite possible that the true population distribution in Example 13.3 is nonnormal, but that our test failed to detect this. There are other goodness-of-fit tests, most notably the Kolmogorov–Smirnov (K-S) test and the Lilliefors test, that are somewhat more difficult to use but tend to produce fewer type II errors. We refer the reader to more advanced statistics books for a discussion of these other tests.

13.3
A Chi-Square Test for Independence

In this section we extend the chi-square test to a somewhat different situation. Suppose that a population can be categorized in two different ways. We will examine whether there is any relationship between the two types of categories.

As an example, suppose that we categorize a group of people according to their smoking habits and their drinking habits. The question we want to explore is whether there is any relationship between a person's drinking and smoking habits. If there is no such relationship, we say that the two qualities are *independent*. Otherwise, we say that there is some form of *dependence*. In this section we learn a chi-square test for independence that is very similar to the test in the preceding section.

In the smoking–drinking example, suppose that each person is in one of three possible smoking categories: heavy smoker (HS), light smoker (LS), or nonsmoker (NS). Similarly, each person is classified as a heavy drinker (HD), a light drinker (LD), or a nondrinker (ND). Then each person is in one of nine joint smoking–drinking categories. If we select a random sample of n people from this population, the results can be listed in a two-way *contingency table*, as discussed in Chapter 2. For $n = 200$, Table 13.5 lists the results of a possible sample.

Table 13.5

		Drinking			
		ND	LD	HD	
	NS	41	42	10	93
Smoking	LS	15	38	8	61
	HS	6	29	11	46
		62	109	29	

The numbers in the nine cells are joint frequencies. For example, 41 people are neither smokers nor drinkers. The numbers in the margins are marginal frequencies. These are row sums and column sums of the joint frequencies. For example, 93 people are nonsmokers, and 62 people are nondrinkers.

Notice that the marginal frequencies for smoking sum to $n = 200$, as do the marginal frequencies for drinking.

The intuitive notion behind independence is the following. Suppose that we choose a person at random. Before observing his or her smoking habits, we would predict that this person's chances of being a heavy drinker, say, are 29 out of 200, because 29 out of the 200 people in the sample are heavy drinkers. But if smoking and drinking are independent, we should make this same prediction, 29 out of 200, *regardless* of the smoking category this person is in. In other words, independence implies that all types of smokers have the *same* likelihood of being heavy drinkers. If smoking and drinking are not independent, however, we might find, for example, that nonsmokers are less likely than heavy smokers to be heavy drinkers. This is one form (of many possible forms) of dependence.

The data in Table 13.5 indicate some dependence. The proportion of the entire sample who drink heavily, for example, is .145 ($= {}^{29}\!/_{200}$). But for the nonsmokers, the proportion of heavy drinkers is .108 ($= {}^{10}\!/_{93}$), for the light smokers, it is .131 ($= {}^{8}\!/_{61}$), and for the heavy smokers, it is .239 ($= {}^{11}\!/_{46}$). Similarly, a proportion .31 ($= {}^{62}\!/_{200}$) of the sample do not drink, but for the nonsmokers, this proportion is .441 ($= {}^{41}\!/_{93}$), for the light smokers, it is .246 ($= {}^{15}\!/_{61}$), and for the heavy smokers, it is .130 ($= {}^{6}\!/_{46}$).

These figures indicate that drinking and smoking tend to go together. As usual, however, we must ask whether this conclusion is generalizable to the whole population or is due to sampling variation. We use a chi-square test to answer this question.

In general, denote the row categories by $A_1, A_2, \ldots, A_r$, with r being the number of rows. Similarly, denote the c column categories by $B_1, B_2, \ldots, B_c$. In the example above, the A's are NS, LS, and HS, the B's are ND, LD, and HD, and $r = c = 3$. Then let AB_{ij} be the joint category A_i and B_j (the intersection of A_i and B_j). We observe the number in category AB_{ij}, for each i, j pair. This observed number is labeled O_{ij}. If independence exists, the number we expect to see in category AB_{ij} is labeled E_{ij} and is given as follows.

Expected Number in Joint Category AB_{ij}, Given Independence

$$E_{ij} = \frac{R_i C_j}{n}$$

where R_i = marginal sum of O_{ij}'s in row i

C_j = marginal sum of O_{ij}'s in column j

n = sample size

(We provide a rationale for this formula below.)

As in Section 13.2, we test independence by seeing how far the O_{ij}'s are from the E_{ij}'s. The test statistic is almost the same as before.

> ### Chi-Square Statistic for Test of Independence
> $$\chi^2 = \sum \sum \frac{(O_{ij} - E_{ij})^2}{E_{ij}}$$

The double summation means that we sum over all possible i and j, that is, over all joint categories.

The null hypothesis we are testing is

> H_0: the row and column attributes are independent

versus the alternative that some form of dependence exists. It has been shown that if H_0 is true (and if each E_{ij} is no less than 1), the test statistic has a chi-square distribution with $(r-1)(c-1)$ degrees of freedom. Therefore, the test is as follows.

> ### Chi-Square Test for Independence
> Reject H_0 (independence) at the α level if $\chi^2 > \chi^2_{\alpha,(r-1)(c-1)}$.

The reason we set E_{ij} equal to $R_i C_j / n$ can be explained by a probability argument. Let $P(AB_{ij})$ be the probability that a randomly selected person falls into the joint category AB_{ij}. Then if we assume independence, the multiplication rule for intersections of independent events yields

$$P(AB_{ij}) = P(A_i \text{ and } B_j) = P(A_i)P(B_j)$$

Since we do not know $P(A_i)$ or $P(B_j)$, we approximate them by the relative frequencies R_i/n and C_j/n, so that

$$P(AB_{ij}) \approx \frac{R_i C_j}{n^2}$$

Finally, the expected number in joint category AB_{ij} is the sample size n times the probability $P(AB_{ij})$ that any given sampled member is in this category. This gives

$$E_{ij} = nP(AB_{ij}) \approx n\left(\frac{R_i C_j}{n^2}\right) = \frac{R_i C_j}{n}$$

EXAMPLE 13.4

At what level of significance can we reject the null hypothesis of independence between smoking and drinking, based on the data in Table 13.5?

SOLUTION

We first calculate the E_{ij}'s and the $(O_{ij} - E_{ij})^2/E_{ij}$'s. These, together with the given O_{ij}'s, are shown in Table 13.6. In each cell, O_{ij} is shown in the upper left triangle, E_{ij} is shown in the lower right triangle, and $(O_{ij} - E_{ij})^2/E_{ij}$ is shown between them. The test statistic is

$$\chi^2 = 5.14 + 1.49 + \cdots + 2.81 = 17.31$$

With $(3 - 1)(3 - 1) = 4$ degrees of freedom, this has a p-value less than .01 because $\chi^2_{.01,4} = 13.277$. Therefore, we are reasonably sure that drinking and smoking habits *are* related. That is, we can be reasonably confident that the independence assumption is false.

A glance at the individual $(O_{ij} - E_{ij})^2/E_{ij}$'s indicates the categories that contribute most highly to dependence. The three largest $(O_{ij} - E_{ij})^2/E_{ij}$'s occur in the NS/ND, HS/ND, and HS/HD categories. There are more people who neither smoke nor drink than we would expect $(O_{ij} > E_{ij})$. Similarly, there are more people who drink heavily and smoke heavily than we would expect $(O_{ij} > E_{ij})$, and there are fewer nondrinkers who smoke heavily than

Table 13.6

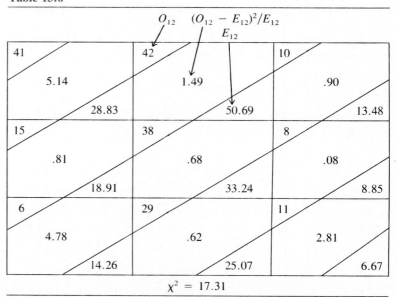

$$\chi^2 = 17.31$$

we would expect $(O_{ij} < E_{ij})$. Again, this evidence points to the fact that smoking and drinking habits are positively related.

13.4
A Chi-Square Test for Differences Between Several Proportions

In this section we present one further chi-square test that is mathematically identical to the test for independence in Section 13.3. The only difference is the context. Now we suppose that there are r populations for which a single categorical variable is measured. The objective is to test whether there are significant differences between these populations with respect to the *proportions* falling in the various categories.

As an example, suppose that there are four candidates running in a state election. Before the election, a poll is taken to discover voter preferences in three important congressional districts. The results are shown in Table 13.7. The numbers in the 12 cells represent the numbers of sampled voters in each district who intend to vote for the respective candidates. The marginal totals at the right are the sample sizes for the three districts, and the bottom marginal totals are the total numbers supporting the four candidates. In each cell we show in parentheses the proportions of the sampled voters in that district who intend to vote for the various candidates.

The proportions in Table 13.7 are certainly not the same from district to district, but are they significantly different? Mathematically, this is the same as asking whether there is significant dependence between the row attribute (district) and the column attribute (candidate). Therefore, the same test applies as in the preceding section. We compare observed frequencies with expected frequencies and see if the resulting chi-square test statistic is significantly large.

Table 13.7

		Candidate				
		1	2	3	4	
	1	52 (.26)	34 (.17)	80 (.40)	34 (.17)	200
District	2	33 (.22)	15 (.10)	78 (.52)	24 (.16)	150
	3	66 (.22)	54 (.18)	141 (.47)	39 (.13)	300
		151	103	299	97	

In general, we label the populations 1 through r. (These are the row categories.) We label the categories of data 1 through c. (These are the column categories.) Then O_{ij} is the observed number from population i in category j. As before, the expected number from population i in category j is given by

$$E_{ij} = \frac{R_i C_j}{n}$$

where

R_i = sample size from population i (row total i)
C_j = total number in category j (column total j)
n = total sample size

The null hypothesis is that the population proportions in the various categories are the same for each population. To test this, we form the same test statistic as in the preceding section:

$$\chi^2 = \sum \sum \frac{(O_{ij} - E_{ij})^2}{E_{ij}}$$

When the null hypothesis is true, this statistic has a chi-square distribution with $(r - 1)(c - 1)$ degrees of freedom. Therefore, the test is as before.

Test for Equal Proportions Across Populations

Reject H_0 (equal proportions) at the α level if $\chi^2 > \chi^2_{\alpha,(r-1)(c-1)}$.

EXAMPLE 13.5

Given the data in Table 13.7, do the proportions voting for the four candidates differ significantly from district to district?

SOLUTION

We again form a table of O_{ij}'s, E_{ij}'s, and $(O_{ij} - E_{ij})^2/E_{ij}$'s. Using the same format as in Table 13.6, we show these numbers in Table 13.8. The test statistic is

$$\chi^2 = .66 + .17 + \cdots + .74 = 9.50$$

and there are $(3 - 1)(4 - 1) = 6$ degrees of freedom. Since $\chi^2_{.10,6} = 10.645$, the test statistic is not significant even at the 10% level. We probably do not wish to conclude that the districts have *exactly* the same proportions, but we cannot reject the equal-proportions hypothesis at the 10% level.

Table 13.8

52 .66 46.46	34 .17 31.69	80 1.57 92.00	34 .58 29.85
33 .10 34.85	15 3.24 23.77	78 1.17 69.00	24 .12 22.38
66 .20 69.69	54 .88 47.54	141 .07 138.00	39 .74 44.77

$$\chi^2 = 9.50$$

In this example we cannot reject H_0. However, if H_0 were rejected, we could pinpoint the places where differences exist by locating the cells with the highest $(O_{ij} - E_{ij})^2/E_{ij}$'s. These cells, of course, are the ones that contribute most heavily to the chi-square test statistic. In this example the cell with the largest $(O_{ij} - E_{ij})^2/E_{ij}$ is the cell from district 2 supporting candidate 2. If district 2 had the same proportions as the other two districts, we would expect more of its voters to support candidate 2 (and less to support candidate 3).

Problems for Sections 13.2, 13.3, 13.4

1. In one city a department store branch has extensive records that show the proportions of customers who favor the five brands of men's dress shirts carried by the store. These are given by $p_1 = .26$, $p_2 = .12$, $p_3 = .22$, $p_4 = .29$, and $p_5 = .11$. In a different city a new branch of this department store is about to open. A survey of 200 prospective shoppers at this store reveals the following numbers who name brands 1 through 5 as their favorites: 47, 32, 37, 64, and 20. Do these numbers suggest that the proportions favoring the five brands in the new city differ from those in the first city? Test at the 10% level.

2. Solve Example 13.3 by using 10, rather than 8, equally probable categories. First locate the nine z values from Table Ib that divide a $N(0, 1)$ density into 10 equally probable categories. Then use these z values to locate the break points for the particular normal density in this example. Finally, find the O_i's and run the chi-square test at the 10% level with the appropriate degrees of freedom.

3. The following table presents data on the numbers of moving traffic offenses during the past five years for various age groups.

		Number of Traffic Offenses			
		0	1–2	3–4	5 or more
Age	16–25	6	24	20	10
	26–50	12	18	6	4
	51–75	4	16	8	3

a. Calculate the E_{ij}'s, given an independence assumption.

b. Before running a chi-square test, are there any indications of a lack of independence? What are they?

c. Test for independence of age and frequency of traffic violations at the 10% level.

4. For the data in Problem 3, give estimates of the probabilities of a randomly selected person falling into the various joint categories (1) without making any independence assumption, and (2) with an independence assumption.

5. Random samples of people within four socioeconomic groups in a Major League baseball city were asked how often they went to a baseball game in the past year. The frequencies are shown below. Use a chi-square test to test whether the proportions falling into the various attendance categories differ significantly among the four groups at the 10% level.

Number of Games Attended

		0	1–2	3–5	6 or more
	1	26	49	12	13
Socioeconomic	2	43	26	18	13
Group	3	54	43	17	6
	4	24	29	18	9

6. A study in 1958 showed that when married couples buy cars, the wife makes the decision 4% of the time, the husband and wife share the decision 31% of the time, the husband makes the decision 56% of the time, and a third party makes the decision 9% of the time. Suppose that a study of 200 of today's car-buying couples shows that 18 wives made the decision, 75 couples shared in the decision, 92 husbands made the decision, and in the remainder of the cases, a third party made the decision. Use a chi-square goodness-of-fit test, with $\alpha = .05$, to test whether today's couples are significantly different from those in 1958 with respect to their car-buying decision process.

7. U.S. Department of Labor statistics from 1954 show the following breakdown of employees into job classifications. Next to these are similar numbers for 1974. (Reference: Bureau of Labor Statistics, U.S. Department of Labor.) The 1954 values are based on the entire population. Assume the 1974 values are based on a sample of 1000 laborers. Do these figures represent a significant shift during the 20-year interval? Test at the 1% level. Explain exactly what you are accepting or rejecting with this test.

Job Category	1954 (Percent)	1974 (Percent)
Professional, technical	8.9	14.0
Managers, officials	9.8	10.1
Clerical	13.1	17.4
Sales	6.4	6.3
Craftsmen, foremen	13.6	13.3
Industrial workers	20.7	16.7
Nonfarm laborers	6.3	5.4
Household help	2.9	1.4
Service workers	8.2	12.0
Farm laborers	10.1	3.4

8. A city government conducted a survey to determine whether the occurrence of various crimes varies from one part of the city to another. The city was divided into three regions, and the following data were collected.

Region	Number of Homicides	Number of Car Thefts	Number of Cases of Grand Larceny
1	15	251	208
2	19	172	293
3	8	105	125

Using a chi-square test, determine whether there is significant dependence between the regions and the types of crime. Use $\alpha = .05$.

9. The numbers of books borrowed from a public library during the five days of a particular week are given below. Test the hypothesis that the number of books borrowed does not depend on the day of the week, using a significance level of 10%. Repeat at the 5% level.

Day	Number Borrowed
Monday	135
Tuesday	108
Wednesday	120
Thursday	114
Friday	146

10. The following data represent the results of an experiment that investigated the effect of vaccinating laboratory animals to protect against a particular disease. Test the hypothesis that there is no difference between the vaccinated and unvaccinated groups at the 5% level.

	Got Disease	Did Not Get Disease
Vaccinated	9	42
Not vaccinated	17	28

11. An experiment was performed on a group of patients who complained that they had trouble sleeping. Some were given sleeping pills, while others were given sugar pills (although they all thought they were getting sleeping pills). Both groups were asked later whether the pills helped them. Their responses are shown below.

	Slept Well	Slept Poorly
Took sleeping pills	44	10
Did not take sleeping pills	81	35

a. Assuming that all patients told the truth, test the hypothesis that there is no difference between the perceived effectiveness of the sleeping pills and the sugar pills at a significance level of 5%. Use a chi-square test.

b. Use the (two-tailed) test for the difference between two population proportions from Chapter 9 to test the equal-proportion hypothesis in part (a). Do you obtain the same conclusion? Why might a one-tailed test be more appropriate for these data? Do you reach the same conclusion when you use a one-tailed test from Chapter 9?

12. On a particular proposal of national importance, Democrats, Republicans, and Independents cast votes as indicated in the table below. Is there enough evidence to indicate that there are differences between the parties with respect to this proposal? Use $\alpha = .10$.

	In Favor	Opposed	Undecided
Democrats	185	154	65
Republicans	153	159	37
Independents	27	21	13

13. The results of a survey taken to determine whether the age of a driver 21 years of age and older has any effect on the number of automobile accidents in which he or she is involved are shown in the next column. Does it appear that the number of accidents is independent of the age of the driver? Test at the 10% level. If there are any indications of a lack of independence, what are they?

		Age of Driver				
		21–30	31–40	41–50	51–60	61–70
Number of Accidents	0	748	821	786	720	672
	1	74	60	51	66	50
	2	31	25	22	16	15
	3 or more	9	10	6	5	7

*14. This problem is concerned with the effect of sample size on the chi-square goodness-of-fit test from Section 13.2. Suppose researcher 1 hypothesizes population proportions $p_1, p_2, \ldots, p_M$ and observes frequencies $O_1, O_2, \ldots, O_M$, based on a sample of size n. Researcher 2 hypothesizes exactly the same population proportions, but his sample size is $2n$, and his O's are exactly twice as large as the O's for researcher 1. How are their E's related? How are their computed χ^2 values related? Given that they both use the same α value, will they both use the same tabulated χ^2 value? Which researcher is more likely to be able to reject H_0? Explain.

15. The percentages of all students majoring in various fields of study at a group of major universities in 1978 are shown below. Beside these percentages are similar percentages for a sample of 1000 students at these universities in 1985. Using a chi-square goodness-of-fit test at the 5% level, test whether there has been a significant shift from 1978 to 1985.

Major	1978 (Percent)	1985 (Percent)
Arts, humanities	9.7	7.9
Biology	10.7	10.6
Business	6.9	13.1
Education	3.1	2.0
Engineering	14.7	17.9
Physical sciences	8.3	6.9
Professional fields	17.0	16.2
Premed	15.1	14.1
Social sciences	14.5	11.3

16. In a large study of all U.S. universities, students were classified into one of five political categories. The percentages in these categories are shown below. A much smaller study of 250 students from two prominent California universities produced the frequencies also shown on the next page. Does the political mix from these California schools differ significantly from the mix found in all U.S. universities? Use $\alpha = .10$.

Category	All U.S. Universities (Percent)	Students in Sample (Percent)
Far left	1.8	1.6
Liberal	18.9	25.2
Middle of road	59.9	48.8
Conservative	18.4	23.2
Far right	1.0	1.2

17. A 1985 *Wall Street Journal* article reported results of a survey indicating that MBA graduates are shifting from jobs in management consulting to those in investment banking. (Reference: *Wall Street Journal*, July 31, 1985.) This is evidently the result of exciting new aspects of investment-banking jobs, as well as higher starting salaries in these jobs. The survey reported on 1980, 1982, and 1984 graduates from a number of U.S. business schools. Selected results are shown below. Do these results present significant evidence at the .05 level to reject the null hypothesis that the proportions of MBA graduates going into the various job categories stayed constant over the three years? Answer by assuming that the survey was based on 200 MBA graduates each year. Then repeat, assuming that it was based on 600 MBA graduates each year. Do the statistical tests tend to confirm the conclusion of the article as stated above? Discuss.

	Average Percent of Graduating Class		
	1980	1982	1984
Management consulting	12.0	10.5	12.5
Investment banking	6.5	12.0	10.0
Financial services	15.0	17.5	14.0
Manufacturing	29.0	24.5	23.0
Other	37.5	35.5	40.5

*18. The following data represent weekly sales of a given product at each of 80 branch locations of a discount store. The mean and standard deviation of sales, taken over all 80 locations, are $356 and $68, respectively. The numbers of locations falling into various categories are shown below. Use a chi-square goodness-of-fit test to test whether these data are consistent with a normal distribution. Test at the 10% level. (Here you need to calculate the E_i's by finding the probabil-

ities of a $N(356, 68^2)$ random variable falling into the various categories.)

Sales Category	Number of Observations
Less than $250.00	5
$250.00–$319.99	14
$320.00–$354.99	23
$355.00–$389.99	17
$390.00–$459.99	16
$460.00 or more	5

19. In a required sophomore computer class at a large undergraduate business school, the grade distribution has traditionally been as shown below. During the current semester, 5 randomly selected sections of the course with a total 200 students produced the distribution also shown below. Is there significant evidence that the grading pattern is different now than it has been traditionally? Use $\alpha = .10$.

Grade	Traditional (Percent)	Current (Percent)
A	15	18
B	25	29
C	30	26
D	20	16
F	10	11

20. A poll is taken to see whether the news program a person regularly watches depends on his or her political preference. The answers from 500 respondents are shown below. Use a chi-square test to test whether there is any significant dependence between a person's favorite news station and his or her political preference. Use a 10% significance level.

	Favorite News Station			
	CBS	NBC	ABC	Other
Democrat	75	57	69	19
Republican	63	78	59	35
Other	12	9	13	11

21. A survey of sixth graders is taken to determine whether their reading levels depend on the level of wealth in their families.

The following data are found.

		Low	Reading Level Medium Low	Medium High	High
Family Income ($1000s)	10–20	15	12	8	5
	20–40	10	27	13	10
	40 or more	7	12	6	5

a. Transform these frequencies into proportions for each level of wealth. That is, the proportions in each wealth group should sum to 1.

b. Use a chi-square test to test whether the proportions from part (a) differ significantly from one wealth group to another. Use $\alpha = .05$.

22. People from a large eastern city, a large western city, and a medium-sized midwest city were asked whether they subscribe to a particular news magazine and/or a particular sports magazine. The observed frequencies are as follows.

	Eastern	Western	Midwestern
Both news and sports	7	9	9
News only	12	18	5
Sports only	9	8	3
Neither	12	15	13

a. Can you conclude at the 10% level that the proportions in the various subscription categories differ among the three cities? Use a chi-square test.

b. Which categories contribute most heavily to the chi-square test statistic? What does this lead you to believe?

13.5

Nonparametric Tests for Differences Between Two Populations

In this section we present three tests for deciding whether two populations are different with respect to a given variable. These tests are analogues of the tests for differences between two means from Chapter 9. Now, however, the tests require fewer assumptions than those in Chapter 9.

Specifically, in Chapter 9 we required that (1) the data be measured numerically on at least an interval scale, usually a ratio scale, and (2) the populations be at least approximately normally distributed unless the sample sizes are large. (Although the first of these assumptions was never mentioned explicitly, it was implicit in all the examples we considered.) If these assumptions hold, the "parametric" tests for differences between means given in Chapter 9 are preferred to the tests given here. However, there are situations where these assumptions are at best questionable, and the tests we present here can be used instead. Two particular situations that require the methods of this section are the following.

1. The variable of interest cannot be measured on an interval or a ratio scale, but can only be measured on an ordinal scale. For example, in a taste test of two brands of chocolate, a person may not feel qualified to rate the two brands numerically, but may only be able to rate one

brand as *better* than another. The tests in Chapter 9 cannot handle ordinal data such as these.
2. The variable may be measurable on an interval or ratio scale, but may not even be approximately normally distributed. Then the tests in this section, being distribution-free, are preferred to those requiring normality. This is particularly true when the sample sizes are small.

The greatest advantage, then, of the tests in this section is that they make fewer assumptions about the data. Their main disadvantage is that they are not as powerful as the tests based on normality. This means that they are not as good at discriminating between two populations that are in fact not equal. In terms of hypothesis testing terminology, if a nonparametric test and a normal test are used on the same data, at the same level of significance, the nonparametric test is more likely to commit a type II error. The reason is that the nonparametric tests ignore some aspects of the data that the normal tests put to good use. This is why we prefer the normal tests of Chapter 9 to the nonparametric tests *if* the relevant assumptions hold. (We should not be overly critical of the lack of power of nonparametric tests. Researchers have shown that the best nonparametric tests are nearly as powerful as the normal tests, even when the normal assumptions hold.)

The Wilcoxon (Mann–Whitney) Rank Sum Test

The first test we discuss is analogous to the test for the difference between two population means, given independent samples. (See test groups 5, 6, and 7 from Table 9.2.) This test is called the Wilcoxon rank sum test, after the statistician Wilcoxon. It is also referred to as the Mann–Whitney test, for the two statisticians who developed an equivalent form of the test. The only assumptions we make are the following.

1. The samples taken from the two populations are independent of one another.
2. The two population distributions are shaped exactly alike, so that they have the same variance. However, one is shifted an amount δ (the Greek lowercase letter delta) to the right of the other, as shown in Figure 13.6.

Then the hypotheses are

$$H_0: \delta = 0 \quad \text{versus} \quad H_a: \delta \neq 0$$

(Throughout this section we discuss two-tailed tests only. By making the obvious modifications, we can convert these to one-tailed tests.) Since the whole population 1 distribution is simply a shifted version of the population 2 distribution, the difference between their means is also δ. Therefore, the

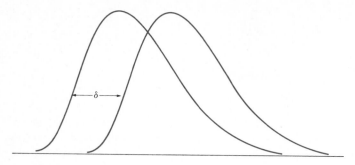

Figure 13.6
Two Densities Shaped Alike with One Shifted by an Amount δ

hypotheses above are equivalent to

$$H_0: \mu_1 = \mu_2 \quad \text{versus} \quad H_a: \mu_1 \neq \mu_2$$

To test H_0, we obtain random samples of sizes n_1 and n_2 from the two populations. Next, instead of using the observed data directly, we pool the two samples and rank the $n_1 + n_2$ observations from smallest to largest. The smallest observation receives rank 1 and the largest receives rank $n_1 + n_2$. If there are ties, each observation in the tie receives the *average* of the ranks these observations would receive if they were not tied. For example, if two observations have value 18, and if there are exactly five observations with values less than 18, the two tied observations both receive rank $(6 + 7)/2$, or 6.5. If three observations were tied with value 18, they would all receive rank $(6 + 7 + 8)/3$, or 7.

The statistic used to test H_0 is labeled W. It is found by summing the *ranks* of the n_1 observations from population 1.

Test Statistic for the Rank Sum Test

W = sum of the ranks of the n_1 population 1 observations

(An equivalent test for H_0 is based on the sum of the ranks of the n_2 population 2 observations.)

To gain an intuitive understanding of the rank sum test, we examine the values W can have. Suppose that the population 1 density is far to the left of the population 2 density ($\mu_1 < \mu_2$). Then most of the small ranks are given to the n_1 population 1 observations, and W is small. In fact, the smallest it can be is when the population 1 observations receive ranks 1 through n_1. It can be shown that the sum of these ranks is $n_1(n_1 + 1)/2$.

Minimum Value of W

$$1 + 2 + \cdots + n_1 = \frac{n_1(n_1 + 1)}{2}$$

On the other hand, if $\mu_1 > \mu_2$, the large ranks go to the population 1 observations, and W is large. The largest it can be is when the population 1 observations receive ranks $n_2 + 1$ through $n_1 + n_2$. In this case the sum is shown below.

Maximum Value of W

$$(n_2 + 1) + (n_2 + 2) + \cdots + (n_1 + n_2) = n_1 n_2 + \frac{n_1(n_1 + 1)}{2}$$

For example, if $n_1 = 10$ and $n_2 = 15$, the smallest possible value of W is

$$\frac{10(11)}{2} = 55$$

and its largest possible value is

$$10(15) + \frac{10(11)}{2} = 205$$

Intuitively, if H_0 is false, most of the population 1 observations will be to one side of most of the population 2 observations. In this case W will be close to one of the extremes above. But if H_0 is true, the population 1 and population 2 observations will be mixed together and W will have a value near the middle of the two extremes. These ideas form the basis of the rank sum test.

The exact sampling distribution of W when H_0 is true is complicated. It has been tabulated, but we do not need these special tables unless n_1 and n_2 are quite small. If n_1 and n_2 are both 10 or more, it has been shown that the sampling distribution of W is approximately normal. (Even though W is approximately normal, this is still a nonparametric test. This is because the population distributions are *not* necessarily normal.) The mean and standard error of W depend only on the sample sizes n_1 and n_2, as shown below.

$$E(W) = \frac{n_1(n_1 + n_2 + 1)}{2} \qquad \text{StdErr}(W) = \sqrt{\frac{n_1 n_2(n_1 + n_2 + 1)}{12}}$$

The test of equal populations uses these values exactly as we have done before.

Test of H_0: $\delta = 0$ ($\mu_1 = \mu_2$) Versus H_a: $\delta \neq 0$ ($\mu_1 \neq \mu_2$)

$$\text{Define } z = \frac{W - E(W)}{\text{StdErr}(W)}.$$

Reject H_0 at the α level if $|z| > z_{\alpha/2}$.

If the test statistic z is less than $-z_{\alpha/2}$, we conclude that population 1 observations tend to be less than population 2 observations. If z is greater than $z_{\alpha/2}$, we make the opposite conclusion.

EXAMPLE 13.6

An automobile dealer sells two types of new cars, a U.S. model and a Japanese model. He would like to know whether these two models differ with respect to the time until the first major engine repair is needed. His records show the following data for a sample of 20 U.S. cars (sample 1) and 15 Japanese cars (sample 2). The data are listed in Table 13.9. Does the Wilcoxon rank sum test indicate that the U.S. and Japanese population distributions (for these models) differ at the $\alpha = .10$ level?

SOLUTION

In Table 13.10 (p. 676) we have arranged the cars within each sample in increasing order and have then merged the two samples. The ranks are shown next to the cars, along with a designation of their nationalities. The test statistic W is the total of the U.S. ranks. Its value is

$$W = 1 + 2 + 3 + 4.5 + \cdots + 35 = 313$$

Since the minimum and maximum values of W are

$$\frac{n_1(n_1 + 1)}{2} = \frac{20(21)}{2} = 210$$

and

$$n_1 n_2 + \frac{n_1(n_1 + 1)}{2} = 20(15) + \frac{20(21)}{2} = 510$$

the observed value of W seems fairly low. (These minimum and maximum values are not really needed for the test, but they help us to see whether the observed value of W is unusually low or high.) To test for significance, we

Table 13.9

Time Until First Engine Problem (Months)

U.S.		Japan	
21	25	25	36
19	31	53	41
31	51	29	18
22	23	38	27
27	30	26	38
37	26	43	45
39	15	55	20
42	35	28	
16	18		
12	61		

Table 13.10

Observation	Combined Rank	Nationality	Observation	Combined Rank	Nationality
12	1	U.S.	30	19	U.S.
15	2	U.S.	31	20.5	U.S.
16	3	U.S.	31	20.5	U.S.
18	4.5	U.S.	35	22	U.S.
18	4.5	Japan	36	23	Japan
19	6	U.S.	37	24	U.S.
20	7	Japan	38	25.5	Japan
21	8	U.S.	38	25.5	Japan
22	9	U.S.	39	27	U.S.
23	10	U.S.	41	28	Japan
25	11.5	U.S.	42	29	U.S.
25	11.5	Japan	43	30	Japan
26	13.5	U.S.	45	31	Japan
26	13.5	Japan	51	32	U.S.
27	15.5	U.S.	53	33	Japan
27	15.5	Japan	55	34	Japan
28	17	Japan	61	35	U.S.
29	18	Japan			

standardize W by subtracting its mean,

$$E(W) = \frac{n_1(n_1 + n_2 + 1)}{2} = \frac{20(36)}{2} = 360$$

and dividing by its standard error,

$$\text{StdErr}(W) = \sqrt{\frac{n_1 n_2 (n_1 + n_2 + 1)}{12}} = \sqrt{\frac{20(15)(36)}{12}} = 30$$

The resulting z value is

$$z = \frac{W - E(W)}{\text{StdErr}(W)} = \frac{313 - 360}{30} = -1.57$$

With $\alpha = .10$, $z_{\alpha/2} = z_{.05} = 1.645$. Therefore, the calculated z value is not quite large enough in magnitude to reject the equal-population-distributions hypothesis. The data provide an indication that U.S. cars need repair sooner than Japanese cars, but the difference is not quite statistically significant.

For the sake of comparison, suppose that the standard t test is used to test H_0: $\mu_1 = \mu_2$ versus H_a: $\mu_1 \neq \mu_2$. (There is nothing about this particular data set that makes the t test invalid.) Then the relevant test is test 6C from Table

9.2. The individual means and standard deviations are calculated from the original data (not the ranks) to be

$$\overline{X}_1 = 29.05 \qquad \overline{X}_2 = 34.80 \qquad s_1 = 12.44 \qquad s_2 = 11.30$$

and the pooled variance is

$$s_p^2 = \frac{19(12.44)^2 + 14(11.30)^2}{33} = 11.97^2$$

Therefore, the resulting t statistic is

$$t = \frac{29.05 - 34.80}{11.97\sqrt{1/20 + 1/15}} = -1.41$$

This t test (with 33 degrees of freedom) is very close to the z value (-1.57) from the rank sum test. So each test leads to the same conclusion that H_0 cannot be rejected at the 10% level.

As we indicated earlier, the rank sum test and the t test do not always give the same answer, even when they both apply. The t test is more powerful (when the populations are normal) because it uses the actual numerical values of the observations, not just their ranks. When we use only the ranks, we are essentially throwing away information that the t test can use to good advantage. Therefore, we again stress that the rank sum test is preferred to the t test only when the assumptions of the t test do not appear to be valid.

In this section and the next, we present two tests for the equality of two population distributions when observations are obtained in *matched pairs*. These tests are therefore analogues of the matched-pairs t test presented in Chapter 9. (See test group 10 in Table 9.2.) The fact that observations come in pairs, each pair being an observation from population 1 and one from population 2, means that the two samples are usually not independent. Therefore, the rank sum test just presented is not valid because it assumes independence of the samples.

The first matched-pairs test we examine is called a *sign* test. This term is used because we base the test on the sign, plus or minus, of the difference between the observations within each pair. The sign test is not a very powerful test because it throws away so much of the sample information. In fact, it is probably the least powerful test in this chapter. But it is still used because it is so simple to implement and because its assumptions are so weak. The only assumptions made are the following.

1. The sample observations must be paired in a natural way, with one observation in each pair from each population. The observations within

A Sign Test for Matched-Pairs Data

a pair need not be independent, but any pair of observations must be independent of any other pair.

2. The two population distributions do not need to have the same shape (as in Figure 13.6). All we require is that when H_0 is true, the observations in any matched pair are equally likely to be in either order. That is, we must have $P(X_1 > X_2) = P(X_2 > X_1) = .5$, where X_1 is an observation from population 1 and X_2 is its matched observation from population 2.

This second assumption is very weak. It means that the two population distributions do not need to have the same variance. Furthermore, the observations do not even have to be numerical. All we require is the ability to rank the two observations within a given pair as a "larger" and a "smaller." Then the null hypothesis states that the two possible rankings in any pair are equally likely. Therefore, this test is particularly well suited to ordinal data, where we only rank the observations in relation to one another.

The test itself is based on the binomial distribution. For any pair of observations, we define the probability p as

$$p = P(X_1 > X_2)$$

where X_1 and X_2 are defined as above. We will ignore the possibility of a tie within a given pair. (If some ties are present, the usual procedure is to discard these tied pairs and work only with the pairs that are not tied.) The hypotheses are then

$$H_0: p = .5 \quad \text{versus} \quad H_a: p \neq .5$$

We conduct the test for H_0 exactly as we conducted the test for a population proportion p in Chapter 9. First, we label any pair where the population 1 observation is larger than the population 2 observation as a " $+$ ". The other pairs are labeled with a " $-$ ". If there are n pairs in all, we count the number of these that are $+$'s and denote this number by S. Then S is a binomial random variable with mean and standard error as given below.

$$E(S) = np \quad \text{StdErr}(S) = \sqrt{np(1-p)}$$

In particular, if H_0 is true, $p = .5$, so that

$$E(S) = \frac{n}{2} \quad \text{StdErr}(S) = \frac{\sqrt{n}}{2}$$

For reasonably large sample sizes ($n > 15$, say), S is approximately normally distributed. Therefore, the test statistic is a z value:

$$z = \frac{S - E(S)}{\text{StdErr}(S)}$$

When H_0 is true, a slight amount of simplification gives the following.

Test Statistic for Sign Test

$$z = \frac{2S - n}{\sqrt{n}}$$

The test for H_0 is the usual two-tailed z test.

Sign Test

Reject H_0 at the α level if $|z| > z_{\alpha/2}$.

This test is extremely simple to perform. We only need to count the number of $+$'s, calculate the z value, and compare it to a tabulated z value. The following example illustrates the simplicity of the test.

EXAMPLE 13.7

A panel of 20 consumers are asked to rate two brands of chocolate. Each consumer is instructed to write a "$+$" if he or she prefers brand 1 (the one with the red label) and to write a "$-$" if he or she prefers brand 2 (the one with the blue label). In case the consumers cannot distinguish between the two brands, they are allowed to write a "0". The results of this experiment are shown in Table 13.11. Use the sign test to determine whether one brand is preferred significantly more often than the other. Use $\alpha = .05$.

Table 13.11

Consumer	Preference	Consumer	Preference
1	−	11	−
2	−	12	0
3	+	13	−
4	0	14	−
5	−	15	−
6	−	16	+
7	−	17	0
8	+	18	+
9	−	19	−
10	+	20	−

SOLUTION

First, we disregard the observations for consumers 4, 12, and 17, as they are unable to rank the two brands. This leaves 17 observations, and we see that

$S = 5$. The z value is

$$z = \frac{2S - n}{\sqrt{n}} = \frac{10 - 17}{\sqrt{17}} = -1.70$$

At the $\alpha = .05$ level, we compare this z value to $z_{\alpha/2} = z_{.025} = 1.96$. Since the magnitude of -1.70 is not greater than 1.96, we cannot reject H_0. There is close to enough, but not quite enough, evidence to conclude that the second brand is preferred more often than the first.

To show how the sign test can also be used on numerical data, we consider one further example. This example will be used later to compare the sign test with other matched-pairs tests.

EXAMPLE 13.8

A tire manufacturer wishes to compare two tread designs, A and B. He selects a random sample of 20 cars and places one A type and one B type on each car. These are placed randomly on the four possible tire positions of any given car. (The remaining two positions are filled by another type of tire.) These 20 cars are run for 15,000 miles over a number of types of driving conditions. At the end of the experiment, the depth of tread is measured at the baldest part of each A and B tire. The results are shown in Table 13.12. Do the two types of tires differ significantly? Use the sign test with $\alpha = .10$.

Table 13.12   Tread Depths (Millimeters)

Car	A	B	Sign	Car	A	B	Sign
1	5.75	5.90	−	11	4.50	4.80	−
2	6.35	6.85	−	12	3.95	4.50	−
3	4.20	5.15	−	13	6.30	5.90	+
4	6.15	5.90	+	14	6.25	7.10	−
5	5.30	5.40	−	15	5.05	4.95	+
6	6.35	6.00	+	16	4.15	5.10	−
7	4.15	4.50	−	17	3.70	4.50	−
8	7.25	7.45	−	18	6.20	6.95	−
9	5.10	4.95	+	19	4.75	4.80	−
10	6.35	6.40	−	20	6.05	6.80	−

SOLUTION

There are $n = 20$ pairs of observations and $S = 5$ of these are $+$'s. The z statistic is

$$z = \frac{10 - 20}{\sqrt{20}} = -2.24$$

Since $z_{\alpha/2} = z_{.05} = 1.645$ and the magnitude of -2.24 is greater than 1.645, we can conclude that there are significant differences between the two types of tires.

Notice that the example above *does* require a matched-pairs test. This is because the driving conditions, the drivers, and the types of cars themselves are likely to vary from one observation (car) to another. As we discussed in Chapter 9, this is the type of extraneous variation that a matched-pairs test controls for.

We now discuss a generalization of the sign test. The weakness of the sign test is that it assigns only a "$+$" or a "$-$" to each difference. It ignores the *magnitudes* of the differences. For example, a small positive difference essentially cancels a large negative difference. The test in this section uses not only the signs of the differences but also the *ranks* of their magnitudes. As such, it is somewhat similar to the rank sum test discussed earlier. (Both are due to Wilcoxon.) However, the rank sum test deals with *independent* samples; the present test deals with *matched-pairs* samples.

Basically, the signed rank test falls between the matched-pairs t test of Chapter 9 and the sign test above in terms of its power and its assumptions. The signed rank test is more powerful than the sign test but is less powerful than the t test. This is because it ignores some aspects of the data (it uses only ranks of the differences), but it ignores less than the sign test does. However, the signed rank test makes more assumptions than the sign test and fewer assumptions than the t test. In particular, it requires the following.

1. The sample observations must come in pairs, with independence between the various pairs.
2. The distribution of the paired differences must be symmetric, but not necessarily normal. That is, if X_1 is a population 1 observation and X_2 is its matched observation from population 2, then the distribution of $X_1 - X_2$ must be symmetric.

If the distribution of the differences is not only symmetric but also normal, the t test should be used instead. At the other extreme, if the distribution of the differences is not even symmetric, the sign test should be used instead.

The test itself is straightforward. We first calculate the differences for the n pairs of observations. Pairs with 0 differences (ties) are discarded. Then we rank the pairs from 1 to n according to the *magnitudes* of their differences. The same convention for ranking ties that was used in the rank sum test is used here also. That is, we assign an *average* ranking to differences with tied ranks. For each positive difference we attach a plus sign to its rank; for each negative difference we attach a minus sign to its rank. The test statistic, denoted by V, is the sum of the ranks with *plus* signs.

A Signed Rank Test for Matched Pairs

> ### *Signed Rank Test Statistic*
>
> V = sum of the ranks with plus signs

The hypotheses are

$$H_0: \mu_D = 0 \quad \text{versus} \quad H_a: \mu_D \neq 0$$

where μ_D is the mean of the differences, averaged over the population of matched pairs. If H_0 is true, we not only expect approximately as many positive differences as negative differences, but we also expect the sum of the ranks with plus signs to be approximately half of the sum of all n ranks. Since it can be shown that the sum of all n ranks is $n(n + 1)/2$, we expect the test statistic V to be close to $n(n + 1)/4$.

More specifically, it has been shown that for most sample sizes we encounter, the sampling distribution of V is approximately normal with mean and standard error as given below.

$$E(V) = \frac{n(n + 1)}{4} \qquad \text{StdErr}(V) = \sqrt{\frac{n(n + 1)(2n + 1)}{24}}$$

Therefore, we base the test on the z value

$$z = \frac{V - E(V)}{\text{StdErr}(V)}$$

The test for H_0 is the usual z test.

> ### *Signed Rank Test*
>
> Reject H_0 at the α level if $|z| > z_{\alpha/2}$.

EXAMPLE 13.8 (continued)

For the data in Table 13.12, use the signed rank test to see whether there are significant differences between the two types of tires. Again use $\alpha = .10$. Then use the matched-pairs t test from Chapter 9 to test the same hypothesis.

SOLUTION

For the signed rank test we first rank the magnitudes of the differences. These differences, together with their signed ranks, are shown in Table 13.13. The

Table 13.13

Car	Difference	Signed Rank	Car	Difference	Signed Rank
1	−.15	−5.5	11	−.30	−9
2	−.50	−13	12	−.55	−14
3	−.95	−19.5	13	.40	+12
4	.25	+8	14	−.85	−18
5	−.10	−3.5	15	.10	+3.5
6	.35	+10.5	16	−.95	−19.5
7	−.35	−10.5	17	−.80	−17
8	−.20	−7	18	−.75	−15.5
9	.15	+5.5	19	−.05	−1.5
10	−.05	−1.5	20	−.75	−15.5

sum of the ranks with plus signs is

$$V = 8 + 10.5 + 5.5 + 12 + 3.5 = 39.5$$

If H_0 is true, then

$$E(V) = \frac{20(21)}{4} = 105 \qquad \text{StdErr}(V) = \sqrt{\frac{20(21)(41)}{24}} = 26.79$$

This gives a z value of

$$z = \frac{39.5 - 105}{26.79} = -2.44$$

Since $z_{\alpha/2} = z_{.05} = 1.645$, the calculated z value is definitely significant at the 10% level. Therefore, we can reject the null hypothesis. This is the same conclusion that we obtained from the sign test.

For the matched-pairs t test from Chapter 9, we need the sample mean and sample standard deviation of the 20 differences (not their ranks). These are calculated to be

$$\overline{X}_D = -.303 \qquad s_D = .440$$

The t statistic when H_0 is true ($\mu_D = 0$) is

$$t = \frac{\overline{X}_D - 0}{\text{StdErr}(\overline{X}_D)} = \frac{-.303}{.440/\sqrt{20}} = -3.08$$

[Recall that $\text{StdErr}(\overline{X}_D) = s_D/\sqrt{n}$.] This t value must be compared with the tabulated t value at the $\alpha/2 = .05$ level with $n - 1 = 19$ degrees of freedom, namely $t_{.05,19} = 1.729$. Again, the calculated t value is easily large enough in magnitude to be significant at the 10% level. Therefore, all three matched-pairs tests lead to rejection of H_0 for this example.

One drawback of the signed rank test as we have presented it is that it does not work well when there are many ties in the ranking procedure. If there are a large number of ties, the sampling distribution of the test statistic V is not as we have claimed, and the test must be modified slightly. Although we do not present the modification here, we do point out the problem. To eliminate ties, we may have to discriminate more in the *measurement* of the data than is really possible. For example, the tire data in Table 13.12 suggest that tread depths can be measured only to the nearest five-hundredths of a millimeter. This is what leads to so many tied ranks in Table 13.13.

13.6

The Kruskal–Wallis Test for Comparing More Than Two Populations

We now extend the Wilcoxon rank sum test from Section 13.5 to a test for differences between *more* than two independent populations. The test presented here, called the Kruskal–Wallis test, is a direct analogue of the one-way ANOVA test from Chapter 10. The difference between the test given here and the ANOVA test in Chapter 10 is that the present test is a nonparametric test. In particular, it does not require the populations to be normally distributed. Therefore, the previous comments in this chapter apply here as well. The Kruskal–Wallis test is not as powerful as the test based on normality (when normality is present), but it is valid in situations where the usual ANOVA assumptions do not hold.

This test is a direct extension of the Wilcoxon rank sum test. Both its assumptions and its procedure are very similar. The assumptions are as follows.

1. Independent samples are taken from K populations, where $K \geq 3$. The sample size for the population k sample is n_k.
2. Each population distribution has the same shape (including the same variance), but this shape need not be normal. (See Figure 13.7 for an example.)
3. The sample sizes, the n_k's, should each be at least 5.

The null hypothesis is that the K population distributions are identical. In particular, this implies that their means are the same. The alternative is that

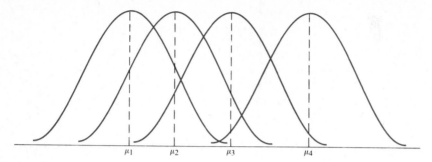

Figure 13.7
Four Populations with the Same Shape, Different Means

at least one distribution is different from at least one other. To test H_0, we again rank the entire set of data from 1 to $n_1 + n_2 + \cdots + n_K$. That is, we pool the K samples into one large sample and then rank the observations from smallest (rank 1) to largest (rank $n_1 + n_2 + \cdots + n_K$). If there is a tie, we assign each member of the tie an average ranking as we have done previously.

After the data have been ranked, we let $T_1, T_2, \ldots, T_K$ be the sums of the rankings in samples 1 through K, respectively. Intuitively, if the *averages* of the rankings for the K samples, T_1/n_1 through T_K/n_K, are roughly the same, this evidence supports H_0. To build a statistical test for H_0, we form the test statistic H, defined as follows.

> *Kruskal–Wallis Test Statistic*
>
> $$H = \frac{12}{n(n+1)} \sum \frac{T_k^2}{n_k} - 3(n+1)$$

Here n is the total number of observations. It has been shown that when H_0 is true, the H statistic has a chi-square distribution with $K - 1$ degrees of freedom. When H_0 is not true, the H statistic will tend to fall in the right-hand tail of this chi-square density. So the test has the following form.

> *Kruskal–Wallis Test*
>
> Reject H_0 (equal population distributions) at the α level if $H > \chi^2_{\alpha, K-1}$.

Table 13.14

	Company		
1	2	3	4
64	81	53	59
73	73	49	62
55	67	55	68
76	85	61	48
43	69	71	51
78	72	66	60
71	84		

EXAMPLE 13.9

The data in Table 13.14 represent the results of a study of work-time for new managers at four companies. Each manager in the study was asked to estimate the average number of hours per week spent on work-related projects. Is there evidence of significant differences between the four companies with respect to the amount of work-time per week? Test this at the 10% level.

SOLUTION

For this example, $K = 4$, $n_1 = n_2 = 7$, $n_3 = n_4 = 6$, and $n = 26$. In Table 13.15 we show the ranks of the 26 observations (in parentheses) along with the original data. We also show the sum of the ranks for each company. A quick look at the data (either the original data or the rankings) indicates that company 2 managers spend more time working than managers from companies 1, 3, or 4. The Kruskal–Wallis test simply tells us whether this apparent difference is real or is due to chance. The test statistic is

$$H = \frac{12}{26 \times 27} \left(\frac{102.5^2}{7} + \frac{144.5^2}{7} + \frac{55^2}{6} + \frac{49^2}{6} \right) - 3 \times 27 = 11.10$$

We compare this value of H with the chi-square value $\chi^2_{.10,3} = 6.25$. Since the test statistic is greater than this tabulated value, we can conclude with 90% confidence that there really are differences between the four companies.

Table 13.15

	Company		
	1	2	3	4
---	---	---	---	---
	64 (12)	81 (24)	53 (5)	59 (8)
	73 (20.5)	73 (20.5)	49 (3)	62 (11)
	55 (6.5)	67 (14)	55 (6.5)	68 (15)
	76 (22)	85 (26)	61 (10)	48 (2)
	43 (1)	69 (16)	71 (17.5)	51 (4)
	78 (23)	72 (19)	66 (13)	60 (9)
	71 (17.5)	84 (25)		
T_k:	102.5	144.5	55	49
n_k:	7	7	6	6

As with the Wilcoxon rank sum test, there is a problem when there are many ties in the ranking procedure. Furthermore, it is very possible that there will be frequent ties. In the example above it is likely that many managers in an actual study would round their work times to the nearest multiple of 5, such as 70, 65, 85, and so on. This obviously increases the chances of ties. When there are many ties, a modification of the Kruskal–Wallis test may be necessary to ensure the validity of the test. Such a modification is available, but we do not present it here.

Problems for Sections 13.5, 13.6

23. The approximate histograms of data collected from two populations appear as follows. If we wish to test for equality of the two population means, why might the rank sum test be preferred to the *t* test from Chapter 9? What disadvantage is there to the rank sum test; to the *t* test?

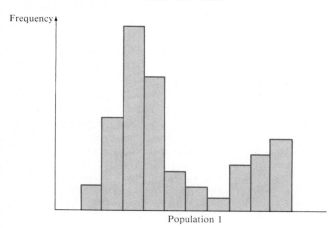

Population 1

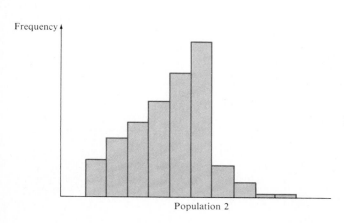

Population 2

24. A sample of credit card purchase amounts is gathered from each of two competing department stores. The data are shown below.

Purchase Amounts for Store 1	Purchase Amounts for Store 2
$17.95	$26.63
16.53	35.32
54.76	16.53
19.86	25.43
20.54	67.32
25.65	24.33
24.21	76.32
13.27	32.15
78.32	23.15
25.47	

a. Rank these data from largest to smallest, and calculate the Wilcoxon rank sum W.

b. Use the rank sum test to test whether either store's credit card purchase amounts are larger on the average than the other store's amounts. Use $\alpha = .10$. What is the p-value for this test?

c. Run a *t* test on these data. Do you get the same conclusion as in part (b)?

d. For these particular data, why might the *t* test be inappropriate?

25. A panel of 25 husband and wife pairs are asked to rate the president's handling of the economy on a 1-to-10 scale. The ratings are shown at the top of p. 688.

a. Use the sign test to test whether husbands tend to rate the president significantly higher or lower than wives. Use $\alpha = .05$.

b. In what sense does the sign test ignore some aspects of

Husband's Rating	Wife's Rating	Husband's Rating	Wife's Rating
9	7	6	3
7	3	5	4
8	9	6	5
9	8	8	6
3	3	3	3
5	6	6	7
7	5	9	10
4	5	5	2
8	9	7	8
2	2	8	5
6	7	7	4
6	7	9	7
8	5		

the data? Is anything that appears to be useful being ignored when we use the sign test on these particular data? Why or why not?

26. Tennis players often complain about having to play "under the lights," that is, at night on a lighted court. To test whether it really makes a difference, 20 players of varying abilities are given 100 balls to hit during the day and another 100 to hit under the lights. (To keep as much control over the experiment as possible, the balls are fed to each player by a ball machine.) For each session, the number of shots each player gets back into a target area is recorded. These results are shown below.

Player	Shots in Target During the Day	Shots in Target at Night
1	32	25
2	15	17
3	22	20
4	43	36
5	18	17
6	13	18
7	31	22
8	21	23
9	16	9
10	35	29
11	16	20
12	31	34
13	21	20
14	16	13

(continued)

Player	Shots in Target During the Day	Shots in Target at Night
15	25	20
16	20	17
17	15	11
18	9	14
19	15	9
20	32	33

a. Use the signed rank test to test whether players tend to perform differently during the day than during the night. Use $\alpha = .05$.
b. Why is a matched-pairs test necessary for this problem?
c. Why is a one-tailed test probably preferred to the two-tailed test you performed in part (a)? Modify the test in the obvious way to make it a one-tailed test, and then perform it on these data at the 5% level.

27. A group of 12 executives are asked to rate their perceived effectiveness of a widely used quantitative technique, linear programming, as it relates to their particular companies. The executives are then given a crash course in linear programming, after which they are again asked to rate their perceived effectiveness of the technique. The results are shown below. Each rating is on a 0-to-100 scale. Use the signed rank test to test whether there is a significant difference between the ratings before and after the course. Test at the 10% level.

Executive	Before Rating	After Rating
1	55	60
2	45	40
3	65	85
4	70	55
5	75	80
6	25	35
7	40	75
8	80	60
9	50	35
10	65	70
11	35	50
12	45	65

28. To see how a description of a product affects customers' reactions to the product, the manufacturer of a new product asks 30 subjects to rate the product from 0 to 100. Before the experiment is performed, half of the subjects are shown

a fairly technical, facts-oriented description of the product, while the other half are shown a less technical, more emotionally oriented description. The following ratings are obtained. Use Wilcoxon's rank sum test to test whether a significant difference between the mean ratings exists at the 10% level.

Facts-Oriented Group Ratings	Emotionally Oriented Group Ratings
76	57
56	49
87	70
37	66
48	71
56	51
68	49
72	55
85	59
61	50
75	60
54	48
69	87
55	45
85	55

*29. a. What are the minimum and maximum values of the Wilcoxon rank sum statistic W when the sample sizes are $n_1 = 50$ and $n_2 = 100$; when $n_1 = 75$ and $n_2 = 75$?

b. What values of W are significant (that is, lead to rejection of H_0) at the 10% level when $n_1 = 50$ and $n_2 = 100$; when $n_1 = 75$ and $n_2 = 75$?

30. A long-distance runner recorded 10 of his times for the 2-mile run in 1982 and 15 of his times for the same distance in 1984. When these 25 times are merged, the rankings of the 10 1982 times are (in increasing order) 1, 2, 3, 5, 7, 10, 13, 16, 17, and 18. Is there significant evidence that his mean time in 1982 is different from his mean time in 1984? Use the Wilcoxon rank sum test with $\alpha = .05$.

31. Two groups of women are asked to rate a type of laundry detergent on a scale from 1 to 10. One group consists of 10 housewives who have no outside job, and the other group consists of 12 wives who have a full-time job. The conjecture is that the housewives may have a superior knowledge of brands of laundry detergent, so that they may rate this particular brand more consistently good or bad than do the working wives. The ratings are shown in the next column.

Housewives' Ratings	Working Wives' Ratings
7	6
8	4
6	10
8	7
6	4
7	9
5	5
7	8
8	3
9	5
	10
	6

a. Rank the combined group of ratings. Why are tied ranks likely to be so common?

b. Does the rank sum test indicate that the housewives and working wives differ significantly with respect to their ratings of this brand of detergent? Use $\alpha = .05$.

32. An advertiser ran a test on 50 subjects to see whether the type of ad has an effect on how well people remember the ad. Each subject was shown two types of ads for similar products and was then asked several questions about each ad. Based on the answers to these questions, each subject received a pair of scores, one for each type of ad. The results of the test showed that 17 of the subjects scored higher on the first type of ad, 30 scored higher on the second type of ad, and 3 scored equally well on both ads. Test the null hypothesis at the 10% level that on the average, the two types of ads produce equal scores on this memory test. Use the sign test. Repeat at the 5% level. With the data given, could you use any other test? Explain.

33. Run the sign test on the data from Example 9.12. For the sake of comparison, reinterpret the t test done there as a two-tailed test. Compare the p-values of the sign test and the t test. Which test do you believe should be preferred? Why?

34. In an experiment using student subjects, a researcher is attempting to gauge the effectiveness of various types of incentives on task performance. Each student is confronted with a sequence of fairly complicated tasks. During half of the experiment, he or she is rewarded monetarily each time a task is completed successfully. During the other half of the experiment, the rewards are given less frequently and more irregularly. Each student receives a total score for each half of the experiment. The results for 15 students are shown

below. The researcher wishes to test whether the type of reward schedule affects the scores.

Student	First-Half Score	Second-Half Score
1	35	27
2	45	42
3	53	45
4	29	26
5	31	36
6	41	42
7	47	43
8	27	30
9	16	19
10	41	36
11	36	32
12	27	25
13	39	41
14	24	19
15	42	37

a. Use the matched-pairs t test (two-tailed) from Chapter 9 with $\alpha = .05$. What is the associated p-value?
b. Use the sign test, again with $\alpha = .05$. Also find the p-value for this test.
c. Use the signed rank test, again with $\alpha = .05$. What is its p-value?
d. Which of the three tests above do you believe should be preferred for this example? Why?

35. To discover whether husbands or wives tend to keep up more on current events, 15 husband-and-wife pairs are given a 50-question test on current news items. Their scores are shown below.

Husbands' Scores	Wives' Scores	Husbands' Scores	Wives' Scores
35	32	35	37
24	19	22	21
25	22	33	26
43	45	42	36
32	36	33	21
19	17	40	32
27	18	25	17
23	27		

a. Use the sign test to test whether husbands differ significantly from their wives on their knowledge of current events (at least for the items asked on this test). Use $\alpha = .05$. What is the p-value for this test?
b. Repeat part (a), but now use the signed rank test.

36. A company with a large chain of discount stores has decided to launch an advertising campaign to attract customers to its film-developing services. Three types of advertising, labeled A, B, and C, are being considered. The company randomly chooses 18 of its discount stores and divides these into three groups of six stores each. These three groups are told to use the three advertising methods. After one month the percentage increases in film-developing sales are measured. These are shown below. Use a nonparametric test to test whether the three types of advertising methods produce significantly different increases in film-developing sales. Use a 10% significance level.

	Percent Increase	
Advertising Type A	Advertising Type B	Advertising Type C
8.2	6.1	10.2
7.2	4.7	5.1
9.3	5.8	7.7
4.6	4.9	7.1
10.3	6.9	5.5
9.8	3.5	8.8

37. Two fast-foods restaurants located across the street from one another are continually claiming superiority in terms of numbers of customers served. To settle this issue, the numbers of customers served at each restaurant over a 15-day interval are observed. The data are shown below.

Day	Restaurant 1	Restaurant 2
1	225	237
2	186	199
3	265	280
4	206	196
5	255	276
6	342	330
7	205	256
8	266	257
9	176	182
10	345	376
11	195	208	(continued)

Day	Restaurant 1	Restaurant 2
12	277	291
13	164	171
14	205	189
15	168	179

a. Why is a matched-pairs test appropriate here?
b. Test for any significant differences between the two restaurants in terms of the average number of customers per day. Use the signed rank test at the 10% level.

38. There are three English teachers at the senior level in a particular high school. Students are assigned randomly to these three teachers. At the beginning of the senior year a test of reading, writing, and vocabulary skills is given to each student. They take a similar test at the end of the year. The percentage increases (or decreases, if negative) in test scores for a random sample of students from the three classes are shown below. Can you conclude at the 5% significance level that there are any differences in teaching effectiveness among the three teachers? Use a nonparametric test.

	Percent Change	
Teacher 1	Teacher 2	Teacher 3
15	10	22
8	11	12
9	2	11
−2	7	8
10	−1	12
16	6	4
5	−5	10
8	0	2
11	13	7
12	7	
9		

39. Consider three publishing companies that compete vigorously in the business textbook market at the university level. The following data show the number of adoptions a randomly selected set of textbooks achieved in their first two years on the market. (An adoption occurs when a university's business school decides to use the book.) Is there enough evidence to conclude at the 10% level that the publishing companies have different degrees of success in terms of the number of adoptions?

Company 1	Company 2	Company 3
12,275	5,760	15,450
8,330	10,410	18,365
6,235	12,555	14,650
10,670	9,875	11,540
5,760	12,560	9,510
12,100	7,250	13,790
		8,320

a. Test this by using the Kruskal–Wallis test.
b. Test this by using the one-way ANOVA test from Chapter 10.
c. Which of the two tests above do you believe should be preferred for this example? Why?

40. A test is performed to see whether different brands of men's cotton tennis shirts differ from one another with respect to durability. Several shirts of each of four brands are put through simulated wearing conditions. This test includes stretching, stains and spills, and many washings. At the end of the test each shirt is rated on a 25-point scale for overall appearance. The results are shown below. Do there appear to be significant differences among the four brands? Use the Kruskal–Wallis test at the 5% significance level.

Brand 1	Brand 2	Brand 3	Brand 4
21	18	16	20
23	15	19	16
20	17	14	15
19	15	18	20
24	13	18	22
18	19	17	21

41. Three different models of cars are tested for their ability to withstand the impact of a collision. Several cars of each model are crashed into a wall at a speed of 35 mph, and the resulting damage is rated on a 0-to-100 scale (100 being the worst damage). The results are shown below. Is there enough evidence to conclude that these three models differ on the average with respect to their ability to withstand the impact of a collision? Use a Kruskal–Wallis test with $\alpha = .05$.

Model 1	Model 2	Model 3
46	57	32
39	61	41
54	41	37
62	55	44
71	48	27

13.7

Two Nonparametric Measures of Association Between Two Variables

In several previous chapters we have investigated the relationship between two sets of observations, labeled X's and Y's, and we have measured the strength of this relationship by the correlation between the X's and Y's. The correlation we have discussed is sometimes called the *Pearson* correlation coefficient, after the statistician Pearson. It is the relevant measure when the X's and Y's are quantitative variables. In this section we introduce two other measures of association between two variables, the *Spearman rank correlation coefficient* and *Kendall's tau*. Both of these are numbers between -1 and $+1$ and can be interpreted in much the same way as the Pearson correlation. Namely, if their values are close to -1 or $+1$, the X's and Y's have a strong relationship, whereas if their values are close to 0, the X's and Y's are probably not related. The reason for introducing these measures is that they are valid even when the X's and Y's are ordinal (ranked) data.

The Spearman rank correlation coefficient, labeled r_S, is used in the following situation. Suppose that we gather random samples of size n from each of two populations in such a way that the observations (the X's and Y's) come in matched pairs. The data within each sample are at least ordinal, which means that the n X's and the n Y's can be ranked from smallest (rank 1) to largest (rank n). Then the correlation r_S measures whether the ranks in the two samples tend to go in the same direction, go in the opposite direction, or are not related at all. For any pair X_i and Y_i, let d_i be the difference between their ranks. For example, if X_1 is the fifth smallest X and Y_1 is the eight smallest Y, then $d_1 = 5 - 8 = -3$. Then r_S is defined as follows.

Spearman Rank Correlation Coefficient

$$r_S = 1 - \frac{6(\Sigma\, d_i^2)}{n(n^2 - 1)}$$

It can be shown that r_S is the usual (Pearson) correlation between the *rankings*. Therefore, it must be between -1 and $+1$.

Consider the rankings, corresponding to three possible pairs of samples, shown in Table 13.16. For the samples on the left, the ranks of the members of any pair are the same. Therefore, each $d_i = 0$, and $r_S = 1$. We say that these two samples are perfectly correlated, large being matched with large

Table 13.16

1	1		1	5		1	4
2	2		2	4		2	5
3	3		3	3		3	2
4	4		4	2		4	1
5	5		5	1		5	3
Perfect positive correlation			Perfect negative correlation			Moderate negative correlation	

and small being matched with small. In a case like this, where the rankings are identical for the two samples, r_S is always equal to 1.

For the samples in the middle, the two sets of rankings are exactly opposite. Now large observations are matched with small observations, and vice versa. The value of r_S is

$$r_S = 1 - \frac{6[(-4)^2 + (-2)^2 + 0^2 + 2^2 + 4^2]}{5(24)} = -1$$

In fact, it can be shown that when the ranks go in exactly the opposite order, r_S is always equal to -1. This is called perfect negative correlation.

Finally, the samples on the right show less extreme behavior. Now r_S is

$$r_S = 1 - \frac{6[(-3)^2 + (-3)^2 + 1^2 + 3^2 + 2^2]}{5(24)} = -.6$$

The negative value of r_S indicates that large population 1 ranks *tend* to go with small population 2 ranks and vice versa, but there is not perfect negative correlation.

In general, if r_S is positive, the large population 1 observations tend to be matched with the large population 2 observations, and the small population 1 observations tend to be matched with the small population 2 observations. The closer r_S is to $+1$, the greater this tendency is. The exact opposite statements are true when r_S is negative. If r_S is close to 0 (negative or positive), all we can say is that the ranks for population 1 do not appear to be related to the ranks for population 2 in any meaningful way.

The second measure of association is called Kendall's tau. (The Greek lowercase letter tau, τ, corresponds to our t.) Again, we assume that the observations (the X's and Y's) from the two populations are at least ordinal and come in matched pairs. Consider any pair of paired observations, (X_i, Y_i) and (X_j, Y_j). We say these two pairs are *concordant* if $X_i > X_j$ and $Y_i > Y_j$ or if $X_i < X_j$ and $Y_i < Y_j$. Otherwise, they are *discordant*. In an intuitive sense, when two pairs are concordant, we have evidence of positive correlation between the X's and Y's. The opposite is true when two pairs are discordant. In general, there are $n(n - 1)/2$ ways we can choose two pairs from a total of n pairs. Therefore, we can have as many as $n(n - 1)/2$ concordant pairs and as few as 0. Let K be the number of concordant pairs minus the number of discordant pairs. Then K is between $-n(n - 1)/2$ (when all pairs are discordant) and $n(n - 1)/2$ (when all pairs are concordant). Kendall's tau scales K so that it is between -1 and $+1$.

Kendall's Tau

$$\tau = \frac{2K}{n(n - 1)}$$

where K = (number of concordant pairs) $-$ (number of discordant pairs)

Again, the intuition is that if (X_i, Y_i) and (X_j, Y_j) are concordant, the X's and Y's go in the same direction. If they are discordant, the X's and Y's go in opposite directions. Therefore, a large number of concordant pairs (that is, a large K or a large τ) implies that the X's and Y's are *positively* related. Similarly, a large number of discordant pairs implies that the X's and Y's are negatively related. Only if K (or τ) is close to 0 can we conclude that the X's and Y's are unrelated.

A primary advantage of using Kendall's tau instead of the Pearson correlation (for quantitative data) is that Kendall's tau tends to be more resistant to outliers in the sample. (This is similar to the way in which the median is less sensitive to extreme observations than the mean.) One disadvantage of Kendall's tau is that it is tedious to calculate. To calculate K, we need to check $n(n - 1)/2$ pairs for concordance. For example, if $n = 10$, we need to check $10(9)/2 = 45$ pairs: (X_1, Y_1) versus (X_2, Y_2), (X_1, Y_1) versus (X_3, Y_3), and so on.

EXAMPLE 13.10

The data in Table 13.17 represent the number of murders (per 100,000 population) and the number of motor vehicle thefts (also per 100,000 population) in eight large U.S. cities in 1980. Calculate the Spearman rank correlation coefficient between the number of murders (X) and the number of vehicle thefts (Y). Then calculate Kendall's tau for these data.

SOLUTION

The last three columns of the table show how the cities are ranked with respect to murders and vehicle thefts, as well as the squared differences

Table 13.17

City	Murders X_i	Vehicle Theft Y_i	X_i Ranking	Y_i Ranking	d_i^2
Dallas	35.4	869	7	2	25
San Francisco	16.3	1208	2	5	9
New York	25.8	1428	3	6	9
Los Angeles	34.2	1452	6	7	1
Houston	39.1	1737	8	8	0
Chicago	28.9	1031	5	3	4
Philadelphia	25.9	1070	4	4	0
Indianapolis	15.3	542	1	1	0

between these rankings. The Spearman correlation is

$$r_S = 1 - \frac{6(\Sigma \, d_i^2)}{n(n^2 - 1)} = 1 - \frac{6(48)}{8(63)} = .429$$

This indicates a positive relationship between the two types of crime.

To obtain Kendall's tau, we have to check concordance for all pairs of cities. With eight cities, there are $8(7)/2 = 28$ pairs. For example, San Francisco and Los Angeles are concordant because $16.3 < 34.2$ and $1208 < 1452$ (both types of crime are worse in Los Angeles). However, Dallas and San Francisco are discordant because $35.4 > 16.3$ but $869 < 1208$ (murder is worse in Dallas, but vehicle theft is worse in San Francisco). The reader can check that exactly 18 of the 28 pairs of cities are concordant; the other 10 are discordant. Therefore, $K = 18 - 10 = 8$ and Kendall's tau is

$$\tau = \frac{2K}{n(n - 1)} = \frac{2(8)}{8(7)} = .286$$

This also indicates a positive relationship between the two types of crime, although its magnitude is less than r_S. [For the sake of comparison, the usual (Pearson) correlation from previous chapters is .567.]

13.8

A Runs Test for Randomness

The final test in this chapter deals with a problem quite different from any that we have discussed so far. This is a test for randomness. It applies to the following types of situations.

1. Consider a baseball player who comes to bat many times during a season. His successive at-bats are either successes (he gets on base) or failures (he makes an out). The question is whether his sequence of successes and failures are randomly mixed or they tend to come in streaks. Most baseball players believe the latter because they constantly talk about "hot streaks" and "slumps."

2. Consider a door-to-door salesman who is successful (makes a sale) on about 35% of his calls. Again, we might ask whether his 35% successful calls are randomly mixed with the 65% unsuccessful calls. If they are not, it is probably evidence that some of his days (or some of the neighborhoods) are good ones, while others are not so good.

3. Consider the sequence of daily closing prices of a given stock. On some days the price increases from the previous day, and on other days the price decreases. Is there any pattern to the sequence of increases and decreases, or are they randomly mixed? Investors are certainly interested in this question, for if the answer is that increases and decreases are randomly mixed, it becomes very difficult to play the stock market successfully.

The common element in these examples is a sequence of observations, where each observation is one of two types. This recalls our discussion of the binomial distribution, where we labeled the two types A's and B's. One of the critical assumptions of the binomial distribution is that the successive trials are probabilistically independent. This means that if p is the overall proportion of trials resulting in A's, then the probability of an A on the current trial is p, *regardless* of the outcome of the previous trial. This independence assumption is exactly what we want to test in this section. If it holds, we say that the results of the successive trials are *randomly mixed*.

There are essentially two possible types of nonrandom sequences. These are shown in Figure 13.8. In the sequence on the left, the A's and B's alternate too often. Even though we expect half A's and half B's, for example, we do not necessarily expect them to alternate as A, then B, then A, then B, and so on. The opposite of this pattern is shown in the sequence on the right. Here the A's and B's do not alternate often enough, and we obtain streaks. A random sequence should fall somewhere between the two sequences shown in the figure.

$A \ B \ A \ B \ A \ B \ A \ B \ A \ B \ A \ B \ A \ B$ ——→ Time $A \ A \ A \ A \ B \ B \ B \ A \ A \ A \ A \ B \ B \ B$ ——→ Time

Figure 13.8
Two Types of Nonrandom Sequences

One way to measure the randomness of a sequence is to count the number of streaks of consecutive A's or consecutive B's. Each such streak is called a *run*.

A run of length n is a sequence of n consecutive observations of one type, either A's or B's.

In the sequence on the left in Figure 13.8, there are 14 runs, each of length 1. In the sequence on the right, there are four runs, of lengths 4, 3, 4, and 3.

There are tests of randomness that use both the number of runs and the lengths of the runs. The test we present here, however, uses only the *number* of runs in the sequence. As such, it is simpler but not as powerful as tests that use both the number of runs and their lengths.

The runs test is very simple to apply. First we define:

$$n = \text{total number of observations in the sample}$$
$$n_A = \text{number of } A\text{'s in the sample}$$
$$n_B = \text{number of } B\text{'s in the sample}$$
$$R = \text{number of runs in the sample}$$

For relatively small values of n ($n \le 20$), the sampling distribution of R is given by special tables. But when n is reasonably large ($n > 20$), this distribution is approximately normal. When the null hypothesis of randomness is true, the mean and standard error of R are as given below.

$$E(R) = \frac{n + 2n_A n_B}{n}$$

$$\text{StdErr}(R) = \sqrt{\frac{2n_A n_B (2n_A n_B - n)}{n^2(n - 1)}}$$

Since there is evidence of nonrandomness when R is too small *or* when R is too large, the test is a two-tailed test.

Runs Test for Randomness (for $n > 20$)

$$\text{Compute } z = \frac{R - E(R)}{\text{StdErr}(R)}$$

Reject H_0 (randomness) at the α level if $|z| > z_{\alpha/2}$.

This test is very simple to perform. To calculate the z statistic, all we need are (1) the sample size n; (2) the numbers of A's and B's in the sample, n_A and n_B; and (3) the number of runs, R.

EXAMPLE 13.11

An investor has kept track of the stock price of a particular stock for the past 50 trading days. Each day he records a "$+$" if the price increases from the previous day's price, and he records a "$-$" if it decreases or remains constant. (We use the symbols $+$ and $-$, rather than A and B, for this example because they are more suggestive of increases and decreases.) The sequence of $+$'s and $-$'s is shown in Figure 13.9. Is there significant evidence of nonrandomness in this sequence? Use $\alpha = .10$ for the two-tailed test.

$+ + + + - + + - - - + - - + + - + + + + - - + - - - - + - - - - - + + + - + - - + + + + - - + + +$

Time (days)

Figure 13.9

SOLUTION

For this sequence there are 50 observations, 27 of which are $+$'s and 23 of which are $-$'s. There are also 21 runs. Therefore, $n = 50$, $n_A = 27$, $n_B = 23$, and $R = 21$. The expected value and standard error of R are

$$E(R) = \frac{50 + 2(27)(23)}{50} = 25.84$$

and

$$\text{StdErr}(R) = \sqrt{\frac{2(27)(23)[2(27)(23) - 50]}{50^2(49)}} = 3.48$$

Since the observed value of R is below the expected value of R, there is some evidence of nonrandomness. Specifically, the $+$'s and $-$'s seem to be coming in streaks. To test whether this apparent nonrandomness is the result of chance alone, we form the test statistic,

$$z = \frac{R - E(R)}{\text{StdErr}(R)} = \frac{21 - 25.84}{3.48} = -1.39$$

For a two-tailed test with $\alpha = .10$, the tabulated z value we require is $z_{.05} = 1.645$. Since -1.39 is *not* larger in absolute value than 1.645, we cannot reject the hypothesis of randomness at the 10% level. Evidently, the sequence is not as nonrandom as it looks.

Notice that this test for randomness has nothing to do with whether the proportion of A's is close to $\frac{1}{2}$. Randomness (or the lack of it) can exist if the proportion of A's is close to 0, close to 1, or anywhere in between. The randomness test only examines whether the A's in the sample, however many there are, alternate with the B's in a random manner.

Problems for Sections 13.7, 13.8

42. The following data are collected from 15 men. They show the annual salary and the value of the automobile owned for each man.

Salary	Automobile Value	Salary	Automobile Value
$25,400	$ 7,350	$29,350	$15,600
36,700	10,400	52,400	6,700
19,450	5,400	46,130	16,430
28,250	9,750	27,500	7,100
65,790	17,820	21,650	4,610
43,100	11,500	57,320	11,440
18,320	6,780	42,890	17,650
35,800	10,300		

   a. Rank the 15 salaries and the 15 automobile values, and then calculate the Spearman rank correlation coefficient. Interpret its value.
   b. For each of the possible pairs of men, check whether they are concordant or discordant. Then calculate K, the difference between the number of concordant pairs and discordant pairs, and use it to find Kendall's tau.
   c. Compute the usual (Pearson) correlation for these data. Compare the three measures of association between salaries and automobile values. Do they all say basically the same thing?

43. A group of 12 husbands and wives are asked to rate a new restaurant on a 1-to-20 scale. The ratings are shown below.

Husbands' Ratings	Wives' Ratings
16	14
17	13
10	8
9	15
12	9
15	16
19	17
7	10

(*continued*)

Husbands' Ratings	Wives' Ratings
11	12
13	11
18	19
8	7

   a. Calculate the Spearman rank correlation coefficient from these ratings. Intuitively, what does it tell us?
   b. For the sake of comparison, calculate the Pearson correlation for the data above. (Do *not* convert the ratings to ranks; work with the ratings themselves.) Do the two correlations seem to be saying the same thing?

44. A test is given to each new employee at a particular company. This test is divided into two parts. One part concerns the employee's technical knowledge of the business this company is involved in. The second part tests whether the employees have leadership qualities that will eventually lead them into management positions. The results of the test for 10 new employees are shown below.

Technical Knowledge	Leadership Ability
33	41
42	39
26	35
29	26
30	37
45	38
22	31
36	43
46	42
27	30

   a. Find the Spearman rank correlation coefficient for these data, and interpret it.

b. Verify that the Pearson correlation between the *ranks* from part (a) is the same as the Spearman correlation found in part (a).

c. Find Kendall's tau for these data. Does it seem to be saying the same thing as the Spearman correlation? Explain.

45. Consider a door-to-door salesman who makes 50 calls over a period of several days. He is successful on calls numbered 2, 4, 8, 10, 14, 15, 16, 21, 22, 27, 35, 36, 37, 48, and 49.

a. Count the number of runs in his sequence of 50 successes and failures. To the naked eye, does there appear to be any evidence of nonrandomness? If so, what type?

b. Use the runs test to test whether there is a significant degree of nonrandomness at the 10% level.

*46. A baseball player comes to bat 60 successive times over a 15-game stretch, and he is able to get on base 19 of these times. How many or how few runs would his sequence of 60 at-bats have to contain before you could infer a lack of randomness at the 10% level; at the 5% level?

47. During the months of September and October, the following sequence of days on which it rained (R) or did not rain (NR) was observed. Does this sequence indicate a pattern of nonrandomness that is significant at the 10% level? Are there more or less than the expected number of runs?

Date	Weather	Date	Weather	Date	Weather
9/1	R	9/7	R	9/13	R
9/2	R	9/8	R	9/14	R
9/3	R	9/9	NR	9/15	R
9/4	NR	9/10	NR	9/16	NR
9/5	NR	9/11	NR	9/17	NR
9/6	NR	9/12	NR	9/18	NR

Date	Weather	Date	Weather	Date	Weather
9/19	R	10/3	R	10/17	NR
9/20	NR	10/4	R	10/18	NR
9/21	NR	10/5	NR	10/19	NR
9/22	NR	10/6	R	10/20	NR
9/23	NR	10/7	R	10/21	R
9/24	NR	10/8	R	10/22	NR
9/25	R	10/9	NR	10/23	NR
9/26	NR	10/10	NR	10/24	NR
9/27	R	10/11	NR	10/25	NR
9/28	NR	10/12	R	10/26	R
9/29	R	10/13	NR	10/27	NR
9/30	R	10/14	NR	10/28	NR
10/1	R	10/15	NR	10/29	NR
10/2	NR	10/16	NR	10/30	NR
				10/31	NR

48. Before observing a sequence of A's and B's, if we have reason to believe that any lack of randomness will have a *particular* form (either too many runs or too few runs), we can use a one-tailed test that is the obvious modification of the two-tailed test presented in the text. That is, we reject the hypothesis of randomness only if the same z test statistic is far enough in the appropriate tail of the standard normal distribution.

a. Carry out this one-tailed test at the 10% level for the data presented in Problem 47 when the alternative hypothesis is that the rainy days and nonrainy days tend to come in streaks.

b. In general, which test is more likely to lead to the rejection of H_0 (for a given significance level), the one-tailed or the two-tailed test? Why?

Summary

The purpose of this chapter has been to present a variety of statistical methods that fall outside the category of "parametric" methods discussed in Chapters 6 through 10. Some of these, including the chi-square tests for goodness of fit and independence, and the runs test for randomness, do not have any counterparts in previous chapters. Others, such as the Wilcoxon rank sum test, the sign test, and the Kruskal–Wallis test, are analogous to tests presented in Chapters 9 and 10. However, the procedures given here do not require the assumptions of normality on which the previous tests were based. For this reason the procedures in this chapter apply to more situations than those based on normality. On the other hand, nonparametric procedures are typically less powerful than procedures based on normality. This is because nonparametric procedures typically ignore aspects of the data that parametric procedures put to good use.

Although the tests in this chapter are based on different assumptions than those we learned earlier, they are still performed in basically the same manner. Each test is performed by comparing a test statistic with a tabulated value and then making the appropriate reject or do not reject decision. When the sample sizes are small, the tabulated values that are needed for the comparison appear in special tables not given in this book. However, when the sample sizes are reasonably large, the test statistics have approximately the same sampling distributions that we already know (normal and chi-square). This makes the tests in this chapter very easy to implement.

Applications

Application 13.1 The development of management information systems (MISs), both as an academic subject and as a management tool, has seen a tremendous increase in the past 10 to 15 years. In practice, a design group, a team of people trained in business and computer science, develops an MIS for a user group. The completed system provides the user group with timely information necessary for making important decisions. For example, an MIS for an oil and gas company may enable the company to perform costing and reporting of its chemical products, track its manpower utilization, and track its transportation of crude oil.

There are two basic methods for developing an MIS. The more traditional method is called the life-cycle approach. In this method the designers go through a prescribed sequence of steps, the end product of which is a completed MIS. A somewhat more recent method is the prototype approach. In this method the designers patch together a skeletal MIS, the prototype. Then by a series of interactions with the users, this prototype is developed into a finished product. The basic difference between the two approaches is that with the life-cycle approach, there is no system at all until the completed system, whereas with the prototype approach, there is a prototype, however crude, from the very beginning of the project.

Alavi performed an experiment with groups of MBA students to test for differences between users' and designers' reactions to a life-cycle approach versus a prototype approach. (Reference: Maryam Alavi, "An Assessment of the Prototyping Approach to Information Systems Development," *Communications of the ACM*, Vol. 27, 1984, pp. 556–563.) Nine groups of users (typical MBA students) were paired with nine groups of designers (MIS majors) to construct an MIS for the support of a new plant investment decision in the chemical industry. These nine pairs were then divided randomly into life-cycle teams and prototype teams, and each was instructed very carefully on how it was to proceed with the designs of the MIS.

After several weeks of development, the teams were asked to complete questionnaires, the results of which were used to test for differences between the life-cycle and prototype teams. The responses to the questionnaires were on a 1-to-5 scale. For example, one of the items on the questionnaire was, "I used the information system reports in analyzing the case and arriving at my decisions." For this statement the users could respond from 1 (completely false) to 5 (completely true). Because of the nature of the data (a five-point scale) and also because of the small sample sizes involved, Alavi decided to use the Wilcoxon test, rather than a *t* test, to test for differences. Selected results are shown in Table 13.18. In each case the numbers next to each group are means from the 1-to-5 scale, where 1 is always interpreted as "low," 5 as "high." The *p*-values listed are all *p*-values for a two-tailed test of a given difference. Therefore, any *p*-value below .05, say, implies that we would reject the null hypothesis of no difference between groups for that particular variable at the 5% level.

Table 13.18

Dependent Variable	Prototype Group	Life-Cycle Group	*p*-Value
Overall favorable evaluation of the information system	4.53	3.42	.007
Overall satisfaction with the information system	4.40	3.21	.011
Timeliness of output reports	4.53	4.53	.523
Accuracy of output reports	4.06	2.64	.002
Ease of use of the information system	3.46	3.07	.345
Helpfulness of output reports	4.21	3.14	.007

These results indicate that users are generally more satisfied with a prototype approach. This is probably because they have more interaction with the system as it is being developed. However, a potential drawback to the prototype approach is reflected by the "ease of management and control of design process" question. As Alavi points out, this may be because the "lack of explicit planning and control guidelines [in the prototype approach] may bring about a reduction in the discipline needed for proper management.''

Application 13.2   Although the number of executive positions in business that are filled by women is still relatively small, it is growing. With the relatively large number of women acquiring MBA degrees, this trend is likely to continue. Forbes and Piercy conducted a study to learn about today's women executives. (Reference: J. Benjamin Forbes and James E. Piercy, ''Rising to the Top: Executive Women in 1983 and Beyond,'' *Business Horizons,* Vol. 26, 1983, pp. 38–47.) Using *Standard and Poor's Register of Corporations, Directors, and Executives,* they found 1262 women listed as company executives as of 1981. Included in this listing were a number of characteristics of these female executives. For example, they found the distribution of education and region of employment shown in Table 13.19.

Table 13.19

| | Region of Employment | | | |
Education	Northeast (Percent)	Central (Percent)	South (Percent)	West (Percent)
Less than degree	41.6	53.0	53.3	53.3
Undergraduate degree only	35.3	28.9	34.1	33.3
Graduate degree	23.1	18.1	12.6	13.4
Total	100.0	100.0	100.0	100.0

Now that we have studied the chi-square test for equality of proportions across different subpopulations, it is natural to want to test for differences in education levels across the four geographical regions. However, there are two reasons that we will not do this. First, it is not appropriate. The data in Table 13.19 describe the *entire* population of female executives, so there is nothing left to infer. We perform a statistical test only when we have a *sample* from a population, but in this case we have the whole population. Perhaps one could argue that the 1262 women are a sample from all present and future female executives, and that we can make inferences about future executives from this sample. However, it is risky to make such inferences because the relationship between education and region of employment could easily change in the future.

The second reason for not performing a chi-square test is the large sample size. Even if this sample were a random sample from a larger population and a chi-square test were appropriate, the large sample size practically guarantees significant differences between the regions. The reasoning is that in the population there are bound to be some differences, however small, between the regions. If the sample size is small, there is a good chance of not detecting these if they are fairly small. But with a large sample size such as 1262, these population differences will almost certainly be visible. The reader can check that the chi-square statistic we would obtain is approximately 24.4. With $(3 - 1)(4 - 1) = 6$ degrees of freedom, this is significant at the .001 level. In other words, the test indicates beyond all doubt that there are statistical differences in education level between the regions. We are not saying that a formal statistical test should never be run when the sample size is extremely large; we are simply predicting that the results in this case will almost always be statistically significant.

Glossary of Terms

Goodness-of-fit tests   tests that determine whether an observed distribution provides a good fit to a hypothesized population distribution

Multinomial data   data that represent the frequencies of observations in each of several categories

Chi-square test for independence   a test that determines whether two attributes are related in the population

Chi-square test for differences between proportions in r populations   a test that determines whether the proportions falling into various categories differ among r specified populations

Wilcoxon (or Mann–Whitney) rank sum test   a test for the difference between means from two independent populations; uses only ranks of the observations

Sign test for matched pairs   a test for the difference between two populations when the observations come in matched pairs that can be ranked "smaller" and "larger"

Signed rank test for matched pairs   a test for the difference between two populations when the observations come in matched pairs; uses only signed ranks of the observations

Kruskal–Wallis test   a test for differences between K independent populations; uses only ranks of the observations

Spearman rank correlation coefficient   a number between -1 and $+1$ that measures whether two matched sets of rankings are related

Kendall's tau   a number between -1 and $+1$ that measures whether two variables are related

Runs test for randomness   a test to determine whether the observations in a sequence of A's and B's are randomly mixed

Important Formulas

1. Chi-square test statistic for all chi-square tests in this chapter (except the Kruskal–Wallis test)

$$\chi^2 = \sum \frac{(O - E)^2}{E}$$

where the sum is over all categories, E stands for expected frequency, and O stands for observed frequency

2. Formula for E_{ij} in the chi-square test for independence

$$E_{ij} = \frac{R_i C_j}{n}$$

where R_i = row i total, C_j = column j total, and n = sample size

3. Test statistic for Wilcoxon rank sum test

$$z = \frac{W - E(W)}{\text{StdErr}(W)}$$

where W = sum of n_1 population 1 ranks, and

$$E(W) = \frac{n_1(n_1 + n_2 + 1)}{2} \qquad \text{StdErr}(W) = \sqrt{\frac{n_1 n_2(n_1 + n_2 + 1)}{12}}$$

4. Test statistic for sign test

$$z = \frac{2S - n}{\sqrt{n}}$$

where S = number of paired observations where the population 1 observation is larger

5. Test statistic for signed rank test

$$z = \frac{V - E(V)}{\text{StdErr}(V)}$$

where V = sum of ranks of the positive differences, and

$$E(V) = \frac{n(n + 1)}{4} \qquad \text{StdErr}(V) = \sqrt{\frac{n(n + 1)(2n + 1)}{24}}$$

6. Test statistic for Kruskal–Wallis test (a chi-square statistic)

$$H = \frac{12}{n(n + 1)} \sum \frac{T_k^2}{n_k} - 3(n + 1)$$

where T_k = sum of ranks for population k

7. Formula for Spearman rank correlation

$$r_S = 1 - \frac{6(\Sigma \, d_i^2)}{n(n^2 - 1)}$$

where d_i^2 is the squared difference between the rankings in the ith matched pair

8. Formula for Kendall's tau

$$\tau = \frac{2K}{n(n-1)}$$

where K is the number of concordant pairs minus the number of discordant pairs

9. Test statistic for runs test

$$z = \frac{R - E(R)}{\text{StdErr}(R)}$$

where R = number of runs, and

$$E(R) = \frac{n + 2n_A n_B}{n} \qquad \text{StdErr}(R) = \sqrt{\frac{2n_A n_B (2n_A n_B - n)}{n^2(n-1)}}$$

End-of-Chapter Problems

*49. In a chi-square goodness-of-fit test, suppose that the hypothesized proportions in M categories are $p_1, p_2, \ldots, p_M$. (These are specific *known* numbers that sum to 1.) It turns out that the probability of a type II error, when the true proportions are really different from $p_1, p_2, \ldots, p_M$, is very difficult to calculate. Explain in as much detail as possible why this is the case. (Keep in mind how the test is run and think in terms of sampling distributions.)

*50. Three coins are tossed a total of 240 times each, and each time the number of heads is observed. The results are shown below.

	0 heads	1 head	2 heads	3 heads
Observed frequency	24	108	85	23

a. If the coins are well balanced, use the binomial distribution to calculate the proportions of the 240 tosses you would expect to observe in the four categories above.
b. Using part (a), use a chi-square goodness-of-fit test, with $\alpha = .05$, to test whether we can reject the hypothesis that the coins are well balanced.

*51. In 100 different batches of 50 parts each, the numbers of defectives are counted. The data are shown below. (No batch has more than three defectives.)

k	0	1	2	3
Number of batches with k defectives	27	54	12	7

a. Find $\hat{p}$, the sample proportion of all items inspected that are defective.
b. Using the value of $\hat{p}$ from part (a) (as an estimate of the population proportion p) and the binomial distribution (with $n = 50$), find the probability of a batch having 0 defectives; 1 defective; 2 defectives; 3 or more defectives.
c. Using the proportions from part (b), find the expected frequencies (the E_i's) in each of the four categories above. Then use a chi-square goodness-of-fit test, with $\alpha = .05$ (and 2 degrees of freedom), to test whether these E_i's are significantly different from the observed frequencies. Why are there only 2, not 3, degrees of freedom?

*52. If the test in Problem 51, part (c), shows that the E_i's and O_i's are significantly different, the null hypothesis you reject is that a binomial model is appropriate. What possible reasons are there that a binomial model would *not* be appropriate? Be specific. (Recall the assumptions behind a binomial model from Chapter 5.)

*53. Many queueing (waiting-line) models in operations research assume that the number of "events" in a given period of time follows a Poisson distribution. Check whether this is reasonable for the following data, when the Poisson parameter is assumed to be $\lambda = 1.4$. Use a chi-square goodness-of-fit test at the 5% level. (*Hint:* Cumulative Poisson probabilities are tabulated in Appendix B.)

i = number of calls per hour	0	1	2	3	4 or more
O_i = number of one hour periods with i calls per hour	10	15	8	3	4

*54. A gambler in Las Vegas is playing a game where the outcome depends on the sum of the faces showing when two dice are thrown. After a streak of "bad luck," the gambler accuses the house of playing with unfair dice. To demonstrate that there is no cheating going on, a member of the house throws the two dice repeatedly to "prove" that the dice are fair. How would you use the results of 500 tosses of the two dice, plus statistical theory, to settle the argument? Be as specific as possible about your method. In particular, discuss what you expect to see from the 500 tosses if the dice are fair.

55. At several major airports around the country, data were collected on the number of cars rented from the four existing car rental companies. (Assume in this problem that there are only four car rental companies.) These data are shown below. Is there enough evidence in these data to conclude at the 10% level that the market shares of these rental companies differ significantly among these airports? What is the relevant population in this problem, and in what sense do we have only a sample from this population?

	Rental Company			
	1	2	3	4
Airport 1	68	73	45	29
Airport 2	54	67	51	33
Airport 3	69	85	44	41
Airport 4	51	72	38	25

56. The number of telephone calls made to a company's main office during any 5-minute interval is hypothesized to follow a Poisson distribution with mean $\lambda = 4$. From the Poisson tables this implies the following probabilities, where X is the random number of calls in any 5-minute interval.

k	$P(k$ Calls in 5 Minutes$)$
0	.0183
1	.0733
2	.1465
3	.1954
4	.1953
5	.1563
6	.1042
7	.0596
8 or more	.0511

The actual distribution of calls received in 100 consecutive 5-minute intervals is shown in the following frequency table. Are these data consistent with the Poisson probabilities? Use a chi-square goodness-of-fit test with $\alpha = .05$.

k	Number of 5-Minute Intervals with k Calls
0	3
1	9
2	18
3	14
4	21
5	10
6	6
7	9
8 or more	10

*57. Consider a normal population with mean 100 and standard deviation 15.
   a. Find seven break points that divide this distribution into eight equally probable categories.
   b. Find seven break points that divide this distribution into eight categories which, from left to right, have probabilities .05, .10, .15, .20, .20, .15, .10, and .05.
   c. Discuss how both of the sets of break points above could be used in a chi-square goodness-of-fit test for normality for a set of data with mean 100 and standard deviation 15. Which would probably be preferred? Why?

*58. a. Show algebraically that the chi-square test statistic for independence can be written as

$$\chi^2 = \sum \sum \frac{n(p_{ij} - \hat{p}_{ij})^2}{p_{ij}}$$

where p_{ij} is the expected proportion in category i, j given independence; that is, $p_{ij} = R_i C_j / n^2$, and $\hat{p}_{ij}$ is the proportion observed to be in category i, j. (This is the formula for χ^2 presented in many statistics books.)

b. Calculate the p_{ij}'s and $\hat{p}_{ij}$'s from the data in Problem 20 (p. 670) and then calculate the χ^2 test statistic from the formula in part (a). Check that it equals the value found in Problem 20.

*59. In Chapter 9 we presented a normal test for the equality of two proportions. In Section 13.4 we presented a test for the equality of several proportions among several populations.

a. In the test from this chapter, assume there are two categories and two populations; that is, the resulting contingency table is 2×2. Explain how this test and the test from Chapter 9 are testing the same thing (assuming the test from Chapter 9 is conducted as a two-tailed test).

b. It can be shown that a chi-square random variable with 1 degree of freedom is equal to the square of a standard normal (Z) random variable. Therefore, the chi-square test from this chapter and the normal test from Chapter 9 are actually equivalent in the 2×2 case. Perform the normal test on the data from Problem 10 (p. 668), and verify that the square of the z test statistic equals the χ^2 test statistic (aside from round-off error). Also, verify that the square of the relevant tabulated z value (for a two-tailed test) is equal to the relevant tabulated χ^2 value.

60. A study of 35 graduating MBAs is conducted to see whether MBAs who go into "people-oriented" jobs earn the same starting salary as those who go into more technical jobs. The study shows that 19 of the MBA's are going into people-oriented jobs and that the rankings of their starting salaries, with respect to all 35 salaries, are 1, 3, 4, 5, 7, 10, 12, 14, 16, 17, 18, 20, 22.5, 24, 25, 26, 27.5, 30, and 31. Is there significant evidence that MBAs with people-oriented jobs tend to earn any more or less on the average than MBAs with more technical jobs? Answer by performing a rank sum test at the 10% level.

*61. Numerical data from two populations are gathered. The sample sizes are $n_1 = n_2 = 80$. The histograms of the two samples are both approximately symmetric and bell-shaped. The objective is to compare the means of the two populations.

a. Why is a test from Chapter 9 preferred to the rank sum test from this chapter?

b. The sample means are $\bar{X}_1 = 65$ and $\bar{X}_2 = 60$, and the pooled sample variance is $s_p^2 = 389$. What is the p-value for these data if a two-tailed test from Chapter 9 is used?

c. How far above its mean would the rank sum statistic W have to be to have the same p-value as the test statistic in part (b)?

*62. A group of 100 people are asked to rate their impressions of the "social responsibility" of a well-known company. These 100 people are then provided with some in-depth information about the company, and they listen to several addresses given by important people within the company. Finally, they are asked to reassess their original ratings. Let X be the number who revise their ratings upward, and let Y be the number who revise their ratings downward. (Assume that $X + Y = 100$.) We wish to use the sign test on these data to test whether the in-depth information has had any effect.

a. What values do you expect X and Y to have if the null hypothesis is true?

b. How much must X and Y differ before the (two-tailed) alternative hypothesis will be accepted at the 10% level?

c. Why might a one-tailed test be preferred over a two-tailed test? What would the null and alternative hypotheses be for the one-tailed test?

*63. Suppose that we wish to use the signed rank test on a sample of 60 matched pairs, with a significance level of 10%.

a. How large could the test statistic V possibly be; how small could it possibly be? When would these two extremes occur?

b. How large or small would V have to be before we could reject the null hypothesis? (The answer should be specific numerical values.)

64. A group of 30 overweight women is split into two groups of 15 each. Each woman in group 1 is matched as closely as possible with a woman in group 2 with respect to weight, body frame, and other relevant physical characteristics. The two groups then go on two types of diets for a one-month period. The weight losses are shown below. Does the signed rank test indicate that the two diets produce significantly different results at the 10% level?

Group 1	Group 2	Group 1	Group 2
13	9	9	6
5	7	11	16
10	11	8	12
6	8	15	19

(continued)

Group 1	Group 2	Group 1	Group 2
12	10	13	12
4	7	7	8
11	17	5	11
7	10		

65. The signed rank test presented is really valid only for relatively large sample sizes. The version that is valid for small sample sizes is as follows. First, rank the differences in the same way as before, with ranks for positive differences receiving plus signs and ranks for negative differences receiving minus signs. Let V^+ and V^- be the sum of the magnitudes of the ranks with plus signs and minus signs, respectively, and let V be the smaller of V^+ and V^-. Then reject the null hypothesis of equal population means if V is *smaller* than V_0, where V_0 depends on α and n and is tabulated in several statistics books. For example, when there are $n = 15$ matched pairs, the critical values V_0 are $V_0 = 30$ (when $\alpha = .10$) and $V_0 = 25$ (when $\alpha = .05$). Rework Problem 37 by using this more precise form of the signed rank test. Do you still reach the same conclusion in terms of accepting or rejecting H_0?

66. After the winter thaw, 23 homeowners who had lost most of their lawns to the drought the preceding summer reseeded their lawns with four different types of grass seed mixtures. Each person watered and fertilized his lawn according to directions for 6 weeks. At that time each of the 23 lawns was rated by a lawn care specialist on a 1-to-20 scale for overall quality. The results are given below. Can you conclude at the 10% level that there are any significant differences among the four grass seed mixtures?

Mixture 1	Mixture 2	Mixture 3	Mixture 4
12	15	10	11
13	16	9	8
14	14	13	10
8	12	7	12
10	17	15	14
12	15	8	

67. An allergy test is performed on 10 patients. Two critical parts of the test are the patients' reactions to pollen and their reactions to molds. When a patient is allergic to either of these, a red mark appears on the skin where the substance has been injected. The larger the red mark, the more allergic the patient is. The sizes of the red marks (diameters in millimeters) are shown in the next column.

Patient	Reaction to Pollen	Reaction to Molds
1	19	12
2	24	18
3	10	7
4	13	16
5	18	15
6	14	11
7	6	9
8	11	14
9	8	5
10	12	17

a. Find the Spearman rank correlation coefficient for these data and interpret it.
b. Interpret a concordance and a discordance between a given pair of patients. How many of each are there in the given data. What is Kendall's tau for these data?

*68. When we discussed the binomial distribution in earlier chapters, we made two assumptions about a sequence of trials resulting in A's and B's: (1) the results of the successive trials are probabilistically independent, and (2) the probability of an A on any trial remains constant at some value p. Now suppose that we observe a gambler who plays a game that is part skill and part luck. On a sequence of 35 consecutive gambles, he loses almost all of the first half of the gambles, and he wins almost all of the last half of the gambles. How does this type of sequence of outcomes imply that *either* of the two binomial assumptions listed above might be violated? That is, why might you suspect that the independence assumption is violated; why might you suspect that the assumption of a constant probability p is violated? How would you test whether a binomial model is valid?

*69. Consider a sequence of 5 A's and B's that results in 2 A's and 3 B's. If all orderings of the A's and B's are equally likely, find the exact probability distribution of the number of runs by listing all possible sequences of 2 A's and 3 B's. Repeat when the sequence contains 1 A and 4 B's.

*70. Watson and Driver conducted an experiment to determine whether the form of data presentation in an information system has an effect on the users' recall of the information. (Reference: Collin J. Watson and Russel W. Driver, "The Influence of Computer Graphics on the Recall of Information," *MIS Quarterly*, Vol. 7, 1983, pp. 45–53.) Specifically, they hypothesized that users who see a three-dimensional graphical display of data (on a computer screen) will recall the data differently than will those who see a tabular display of the same data. The experiment used 29 student subjects. One group saw a tabular distribution of the number of medical graduates from a particular medical school who settled in the various states of the United States. The other group saw a three-dimensional map of the United States with "bumps" on each state proportional in height to the number of medical graduates who settled there. After being allowed to study these data for a minute, the subjects in each group were given a list, not necessarily in rank order, of the six states with the largest number of medical graduates. They were then asked to put this list in rank order. A Spearman correlation between the true rank order and the subject's rank order was computed for each subject. These 29 correlations are shown below. Watson and Driver used the usual t test for differences to conclude that the correlations for the tabular group were not significantly different from those for the graphical group. (Here the "observations" for the t test were the correlations.) Run a Wilcoxon test on this sample of correlations to see if you reach the same conclusion. Use a two-tailed test at the 5% significance level.

Graphics		Tabular	
.980	.900	.786	.557
.786	.757	.980	.900
.557	.357	.929	.700
.700	.786	.786	.470
.470	.929	.929	.414
.786	.986	.470	.814
.814	.929	.986	.786
.786			

*71. In 1971 the Federal Trade Commission (FTC) adopted a program to regulate advertising claims. The program required advertisers of selected products to submit on demand all possible evidence substantiating claims of product safety, performance, effectiveness, quality, or comparative price. Many people feared that advertisers, in their desire to avoid FTC investigations, would shy away from claims that could be challenged ("this antiperspirant keeps you 20% drier than other leading brands"), and would instead tend toward claims that were either inherently verifiable ("this antiperspirant comes in a roll-on container") or impossible to verify ("this antiperspirant will make you feel fresher than you've ever felt before"). Healey and Kassarjian performed a before-after study to see if this was the case. (Reference: John S. Healey and Harold H. Kassarjian, "Advertising Substantiation and Ad-

vertiser Response: A Content Analysis of Magazine Advertisements," *Journal of Marketing*, Vol. 47, 1983, pp. 107–117.) They selected four products, two of which required substantiation by the FTC ruling (antiperspirants and pet foods) and two of which did not (skin lotions and prepared foods). For each of these products, they performed a comparative analysis of many magazine ads before the FTC ruling (1970) and after the ruling (1976). Their hypothesis was that the affected products would experience a trend toward fewer claims that could be challenged and more claims that were inherently verifiable or impossible to verify. They also hypothesized that no such trend would be apparent for the products not affected by the FTC ruling. The results of the study are shown below. (The number of claims for each product is the total number of claims for safety, performance, etc., found in all magazine ads sampled.) Treating each product separately, perform the relevant chi-square test at the 5% level to see whether there is a significant difference between 1970 and 1976. Discuss whether the differences go in the direction hypothesized by Healey and Kassarjian.

	Affected Industries			
	Antiperspirants		Pet Foods	
	1970	1976	1970	1976
Number of claims	157	284	193	276
Number inherently verifiable	44	153	73	160
Number that could be challenged	105	34	98	39
Number with gross exaggeration	8	97	22	77

	Unaffected Industries			
	Skin Lotions		Prepared Foods	
	1970	1976	1970	1976
Number of claims	282	282	238	249
Number inherently verifiable	68	112	143	162
Number that could be challenged	118	102	62	42
Number with gross exaggeration	96	68	33	45

*72. In Application 5.2 we saw data on the number of alignment errors found in airplane inspections, and we examined whether these data could come from a Poisson population distribution. At that time we were not equipped to test a Poisson fit statistically, but now we are. Using the data and calculations from Application 5.2, test the goodness of the Poisson fit at the 10% level. Use the categories 0–4, 5–6, 7–8, 9–11,

12–14, and 15 or more (measured in errors per plane). Why are there 4, not 5, degrees of freedom?

*73. Survey samplers desire as large a response rate to their questionnaires as possible. Nonresponses imply lost mailing and processing costs, plus possible nonresponse bias as described in Application 1.1. Jobber and Sanderson conducted an experiment to test the effectiveness of two factors on survey response rates. (Reference: David Jobber and Stuart Sanderson, "The Effects of a Prior Letter and Coloured Questionnaire Paper on Mail Survey Response Rates," *Journal of the Market Research Society,* Vol. 25, 1983, pp. 339–348.) These were (1) the presence or absence of a prior letter to the potential respondents, briefly previewing the purpose of the study; and (2) the color of the questionnaire, either blue or white. The color factor was examined because it was believed that a nonwhite color might be more noticeable on a respondent's desk, and hence the response rate might increase. The experiment consisted of sending a marketing survey to 800 randomly selected textile companies. These were split evenly among the four factor combinations: no prior letter/white, prior letter/white, no prior letter/blue, and prior letter/blue. The results are shown below.

Factor Combination	Number of Responses
Prior letter/white	108
Prior letter/blue	107
No prior letter/white	114
No prior letter/blue	128

a. Use a chi-square test at the .05 level to see whether any of these four questionnaire methods produces a significantly different response rate than any others. (Refer to Section 13.4.)

b. (Requires knowledge of Section 10.4.) Jobber and Sanderson analyzed the data above by using two-way ANOVA. The dependent variable indicated whether a company responded. It was coded as 1 for each respondent and 0 for each nonrespondent. The authors state that even though this is not a continuous variable, let alone a normally distributed variable, two-way ANOVA is still applicable because of the large sample sizes. Perform a two-way ANOVA on these data. What results do you obtain, and how do they compare to the results from part (a)?

74. In a 1977 article Resnick and Stern presented their results from a study on information content in TV commercials. (Reference: Alan Resnik and Bruce L. Stern, "An Analysis of Information Content in Television Advertising," *Journal of Marketing,* Vol. 41, 1977, pp. 50–53.) The purpose of this study was to see how many commercials contain information about the product that can really help a customer to make an intelligent choice. They selected 14 criteria for judging whether a commercial has information content: whether it says anything about price, quality, performance, availability, safety, and nine other criteria. They then played 378 videotaped commercials to a panel of trained experts who judged which, if any, of the 14 criteria were present. The following table shows how many of the 14 criteria were present in each of several commercial classifications.

Commercial Type	Number of 14 Criteria Present		
	0	1	2 or More
Food	82	44	18
Institutional	6	11	7
Personal care products	54	25	14
Laundry, household products	27	19	6
Hobbies, toys, transportation	8	15	6
Other	13	13	10

a. Using the entire set of 378 commercials as one large sample, calculate a 95% confidence interval for the proportion of all commercials that possess none of the 14 criteria. (Resnick and Stern referred to these as commercials with no information content.)

b. Use a chi-square test at the .05 level to test whether the number of information criteria present depends on the commercial classification.

75. In 1976, Charles Lehman, a marketing researcher, performed a telephone survey to discover whether men's attitudes toward future availability of oil had any bearing on the types of cars they intended to buy. (Reference: Charles C. Lehman, "The Ambiguities of 'Actionable' Research," *Journal of Marketing,* Vol. 41, 1977, pp. 21–23.) Out of 980 respondents, 379 were labeled optimists, while 112 were labeled pessimists. The optimists were those who said there was almost no chance or a slight chance that oil shipments would be limited or cut off, and also that there was a fairly good chance or it was almost certain that the United States would find more oil or develop new energy sources. The pessimists were those who responded in exactly the opposite manner. Then these 491 optimists and pessimists were asked what size car they thought their next car would be. The results are shown on p. 712. Is

it possible to reject the null hypothesis that there is no difference between the optimists and pessimists with respect to the size of the next car they intend to buy? Use a .05 significance level.

Type of Car	Optimists	Pessimists
Subcompact	34	26
Compact	84	28
Intermediate	140	39
Full size	121	19

76. One function of the Federal Trade Commission is to check that TV commercials use terms that are understood by the viewing public. To see whether this function is being performed effectively, Cunningham and Cunningham administered a 12-question true–false test to a random sample of 2200 Texas residents. (Reference: Isabella C. M. Cunningham and William H. Cunningham, "Standards for Advertising Regulation," *Journal of Marketing,* Vol. 41, 1977, pp. 92–97.) Each question required the respondent to know the meaning of a certain term used frequently in commercials. For example, two of the questions, with the terms italicized and the correct answers in parentheses, were:

A *100% solid-state TV* has only one conventional tube, which is the picture tube. (True); and *Disk brakes* are a type of air brake. (False)

The respondents were instructed not to guess; if they did not know the answer, they were instructed to reply "don't know." The results for the two questions above, categorized by the education level of the respondents, are shown below. (Note that only 598 of the 2200 people sampled responded.)

100% Solid-State Question

Category	Sample Size	True	False	Don't Know
Did not complete high school	41	20	7	14
High school graduate	120	65	21	34
Attended college	204	99	36	69
College graduate	145	79	16	50
Attended post college	88	50	10	28

Disk-Brake Question

Category	Sample Size	True	False	Don't Know
Did not complete high school	41	6	22	13
High school graduate	120	18	75	27
Attended college	204	27	120	57
College graduate	145	10	87	48
Attended post college	88	8	61	19

a. Based on the subjects' responses to the solid-state question, can you conclude at the 5% significance level that differences exist across the five education groups? Answer this for the disk-brake question.
b. Find a 95% confidence interval for the proportion of the entire population who could not answer the solid-state question correctly. Do the same for the disk-brake question.

Computer Problems

(These problems are to be used in conjunction with the computer software package.)

1. Referring to the data on school teachers in Table I of Appendix D, calculate the Spearman correlation coefficient between the number of teachers (at all levels) and the average salary per teacher. To do this, first use the SUMMARY program to rank each variable from smallest to largest, and then calculate the Spearman correlation by hand. Alternatively, this correlation can be found by entering the *ranks* (1 to 50) into the SUM-MARY program and having the program calculate the usual (Pearson) correlation for the ranks.

2. Referring to the data on grade point averages and test scores in Table II of Appendix D, use the NORMFIT program to test whether the undergraduate GPAs for these 100 students come from a normal population. Use a 1% significance level.

3. Assume that the data on grade point averages and test scores in Table II of Appendix D are for the current MBA class at a

given university. This university believes that the proportions of all its MBA students (past, present, and future) with verbal and quantitative test scores in various categories are as shown below. Can you reject these null hypotheses at the 5% level on the basis of the data in Table II? Use the CHISQR program to test the hypothesis on verbal scores and the hypothesis on quantitative scores separately.

Verbal		Quantitative	
Category	Percentage	Category	Percentage
Less than 50	2	Less than 50	5
50 to 59	8	50 to 59	10
60 to 69	25	60 to 69	20
70 to 79	25	70 to 79	30
80 to 89	20	80 to 89	20
90 to 99	20	90 to 99	15

4. Using the cost of living data in Table VII of Appendix D, we would like to test whether the cost of living depends on the region of the country. One way to do this is to use a chi-square test for equality of proportions. We divide the United States into regions, and we break the index scale into several categories. Then we test whether the proportions in the various categories differ among regions. Use the CHISQR program to perform this test at the 5% level when the following regions and categories are specified. The five regions are: (1) California, Hawaii, Alaska, Washington, Oregon, Arizona, New Mexico, and Texas; (2) Montana, Idaho, Wyoming, Utah, Nevada, Colorado, and Oklahoma; (3) North Dakota, South Dakota, Nebraska, Kansas, Iowa, Minnesota, Wisconsin, Missouri, Illinois, and Indiana; (4) Louisiana, Arkansas, Mississippi, Alabama, Florida, Georgia, Tennessee, North Carolina, South Carolina, Virginia, and Kentucky; and (5) Ohio, Michigan, West Virginia, Maryland, Delaware, New Jersey, New York, Pennsylvania, Massachusetts, Connecticut, Rhode Island, Vermont, New Hampshire, and Maine. The four categories for the all-items cost of living index are: (1) below 95; (2) at least 95 and below 100; (3) at least 100 and below 105; and (4) at least 105.

References

BREIMAN, L. *Statistics: With a View Toward Applications.* Boston: Houghton Mifflin, 1973.

CONOVER, W. J. *Practical Nonparametric Statistics,* 2nd ed. New York: Wiley, 1980.

GIBBONS, J. D. *Nonparametric Statistical Inference.* New York: McGraw-Hill, 1971.

NETER, J., WASSERMAN, W., and WHITMORE, G. A. *Applied Statistics,* 2nd ed. Boston: Allyn & Bacon, 1982.

CHAPTER 14

Time Series Analysis, Forecasting, and Index Numbers

Objectives

1. To learn the four components of a time series: trend, seasonal, cyclic, and irregular.
2. To learn how to use regression to measure a linear or an exponential trend.
3. To learn how to extract the cyclic component from a time series of yearly observations.
4. To see how moving averages smooth a time series, and to learn how they are used in the ratio to moving average method to identify the seasonal component of a time series.
5. To learn how exponential smoothing methods can be used to track and forecast a time series.
6. To look more deeply into the role of regression in time series analysis.
7. To learn how to compute index numbers, and to learn how these index numbers (particularly the Consumer Price Index) are interpreted.

Contents

An important concept in economics is a product's price elasticity. This is defined as the percentage change in the product's sales for a given percentage change in the product's price. Price elasticity is often difficult to estimate because it is not always possible to vary price systematically and observe the resulting changes in sales. However, one study we examine in this chapter found a perfect setting for estimating price elasticity. This study observed sales and price of presweetened and other types of cereals at a period during the 1970s when sugar prices, and hence presweetened cereal prices, rose significantly. By observing changes in price and changes in sales over time, the study was able to estimate the price elasticity of cereal products as a whole and presweetened cereals in particular.

The method used in this study was to observe cereal sales, cereal prices, and related variables (such as advertising levels) over time, and then relate the resulting time series. Actually, the statistical method used was multiple regression, a method we have already studied. However, regression analysis in a time series context poses several problems that we have not covered in earlier chapters. In particular, we must deal explicitly with autocorrelated time series, that is, time series where observations separated by a given number of time periods are correlated with one another. Autocorrelation is only one of several statistical concepts peculiar to time series data that we examine in this chapter.

14.1

Introduction

Business and economic data generally fall into two categories, cross-sectional data and time series data. Cross-sectional data occur when we measure a subset of a population at approximately the same point in time. Time series data occur when we measure a single characteristic of a population, such as unemployment or a company's sales, at successive points in time. Most of the analysis we have done in previous chapters is suited more naturally to cross-sectional data. We now learn how to deal with some of the special problems presented by time series data. For example, we mentioned in the regression chapters that although regression can be adapted to time series data, the ordinary least squares assumptions are usually violated. Therefore, if we do wish to use regression, we have to check the assumptions thoroughly and possibly vary the technique. Although the analysis can become quite complicated, we discuss some of the basic ideas in this chapter.

Probably the most important use of time series analysis is forecasting. Here we observe past measurements of a variable, such as a company's sales, and then try to forecast future values. We cannot overemphasize the importance of good forecasting methods in business and economics. Government economists need to forecast economic variables such as GNP, unemployment, inflation, productivity, and so on, so that the president and Congress can set policies wisely. Business executives need to forecast demands for their products so that they can set production levels sensibly. Security analysts need to forecast movements in the stock market so that they can buy and sell at the correct times. Farmers need to forecast weather accurately to avoid disastrous losses.

Unfortunately, forecasting is a very difficult task, especially when we are attempting to make long-range forecasts. Typically, we base forecasts on observations made in the past. We then *extrapolate* from the past to the future. There are two problems with this approach. The first is a technical problem. It is not always easy to recognize patterns in past data that can then be extrapolated into the future. Often there is a lot of irregularity, or "noise," in the past data. So in much of this chapter, we examine basic techniques for separating the significant patterns from the noise. We point out that entire books and scores of scholarly papers have been devoted to this type of analysis, so we will only scratch the surface of a difficult topic.

The other problem is that there are no guarantees that past patterns will continue in the future. The OPEC countries could raise their oil prices again, a company's competitor could introduce a brand-new product into the market, the bottom could fall out of the stock market, and so on. Each of these "shocks" to the system being studied could drastically alter the future in a highly unpredictable way. Of course, if these shocks themselves can be predicted, we can take them into account, along with our analysis of past behavior, to forecast the future. But it is more likely that these shocks are totally unexpected or at least do not occur in a predictable manner or at a predictable time. This does not mean that a forecaster should admit defeat, however. It simply explains why forecasts are often way off the mark.

This chapter is different from most of the other chapters in this book in one important respect. Most of the time series analysis and forecasting methods we study here are "ad hoc" methods. That is, they are not based on statistical assumptions that allow us to perform statistical inference. For example, we will not be able to quote confidence intervals for our forecasts because we will not make enough assumptions to infer sampling distributions of these forecasts. There are forecasting models that make statistical assumptions and then proceed to perform statistical inference on the results. However, these models are generally difficult mathematically, so we do not cover them in this book. Instead, we discuss methods that are intuitive, are used frequently in the business world, and have performed well in terms of providing useful forecasts.

14.2

Components of Time Series Data

In Chapter 2 we discussed a useful graphical means of depicting time series data, namely, time series graphs. We now use these time series graphs to help explain and identify four important components of a time series. These components are called the trend component, the seasonal component, the cyclic component, and the irregular (or noise) component.

Let's start by looking at a very simple time series. This is a time series where every observation is the same. Such a series is shown in Figure 14.1. The graph in this figure shows time (t) on the horizontal axis and the observation values (Y) on the vertical axis. It is assumed that Y is measured at regularly spaced intervals, usually days, weeks, months, quarters, or years, with Y_t being the value of the observation at time period t. As indicated in Figure 14.1, the individual observation points are usually joined by straight lines to make any patterns in the time series more apparent. Since all observations in this time series are equal, the resulting time series graph is a horizontal line. We refer to this time series as the *base* series. Below we show more interesting time series built from this base series.

If the observations increase or decrease regularly through time, we say that the time series has a *trend* (sometimes called a secular trend). The graphs in Figure 14.2 illustrate several possible trends. The *linear* trend in Figure 14.2a occurs if a company's sales, for example, increase by the same amount from

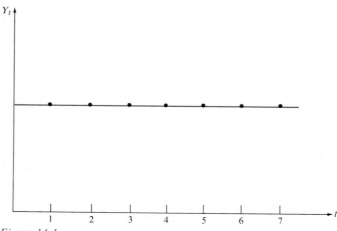

Figure 14.1
The Base Series

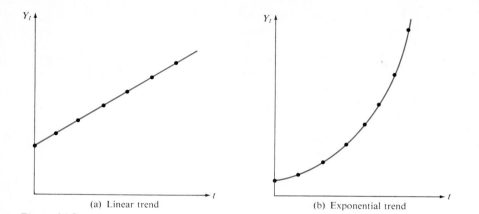

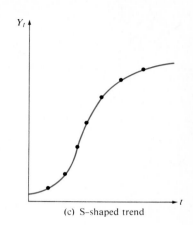

(a) Linear trend

(b) Exponential trend

(c) S–shaped trend

Figure 14.2

period to period. This constant per period change is then the slope of the linear trend line. The curve in Figure 14.2b is an *exponential* trend curve. It occurs in a business such as the personal computer business, where sales are increasing at a tremendous rate. For this type of curve, the *percentage* increase in Y_t from period to period remains constant. The curve in Figure 14.2c is an *S-shaped* trend curve. For example, this type of trend curve is appropriate for a new product that takes a while to catch on, then exhibits a rapid increase in market share as the public becomes aware of it, and finally tapers off to a fairly constant level. The curves in Figure 14.2 all represent *upward* trends. Of course, we could just as well have *downward* trends of the same types.

Many time series have a seasonal component. For example, a company's sales of swimming pool equipment increase every spring, then stay relatively high during the summer, and then drop off until next spring, at which time the yearly pattern repeats itself. An important aspect of the seasonal component is that it tends to be predictable from one year to the next. That is, the *same* seasonal pattern tends to repeat itself every year.

In Figure 14.3 (p. 720) we show two possible seasonal patterns. In Figure 14.3a there is nothing but the seasonal component. That is, if there were no seasonal variation, we would have the base series from Figure 14.1. In Figure 14.3b we show a seasonal pattern superimposed on a linear trend line.

The third component of a time series is the cyclic component. By studying past movements of many business and economic variables, it becomes apparent that there are business cycles that affect many variables in similar ways. For example, during a recession housing starts generally go down, unemployment goes up, stock prices go down, and so on. But when the recession is over, all these variables tend to move in the opposite direction.

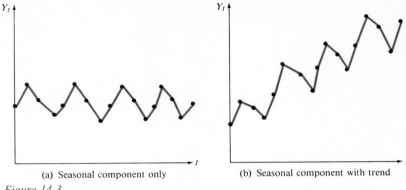

(a) Seasonal component only   (b) Seasonal component with trend

Figure 14.3

We know that the cyclic component exists for many time series because we are able to see it as periodic swings in the levels of the time series graphs. However, the cyclic component is harder to predict than the seasonal component. The reason is that seasonal variation is much more regular. For example, swimming pool supplies sales *always* start to increase during the spring. Cyclic variation, on the other hand, is more irregular for the simple reason that the "business cycle" does not always have the same length. A further distinction is that the length of a seasonal cycle is generally one year; the length of a business cycle is generally much longer than one year.

The graphs in Figure 14.4 illustrate the cyclic component of a time series. In Figure 14.4a cyclic variation is superimposed on the base series from Figure 14.1. In Figure 14.4b this same cyclic variation is superimposed on the series from Figure 14.3b. The resulting graph has trend, seasonal variation, and cyclic variation.

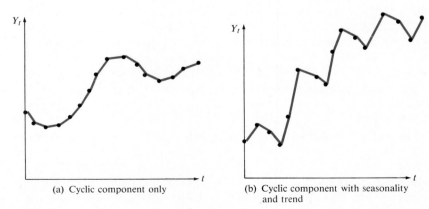

(a) Cyclic component only   (b) Cyclic component with seasonality
                                       and trend

Figure 14.4

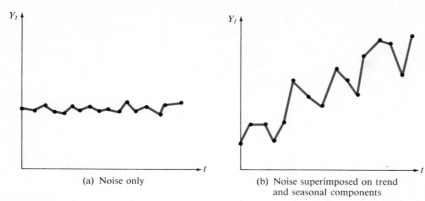

(a) Noise only   (b) Noise superimposed on trend and seasonal components

Figure 14.5

The final component in a time series is called the irregular component, or simply *noise*. This unpredictable component gives most time series graphs their irregular, jagged-edge appearances. Usually, a time series can be determined only to a certain extent by its trend, seasonal, and cyclic components. Then other factors determine the rest. These other factors may be inherent randomness, unpredictable "shocks" to the system, the unpredictable behavior of human beings who interact with the system, and probably others. Whatever these factors are, however, there is no doubt that they exist and that they combine to create a certain amount of unpredictability in almost all time series.

In Figures 14.5 and 14.6 we show the effect that noise can have on a time series graph. The graph on the left of each figure shows the irregular component only, superimposed on the base series. Then on the right of each figure, the irregular component is superimposed on the trend-with-seasonal-

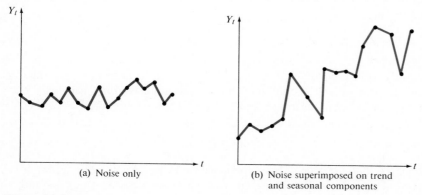

(a) Noise only   (b) Noise superimposed on trend and seasonal components

Figure 14.6

component graph from Figure 14.3b. The difference between Figures 14.5 and 14.6 is the relative magnitude of the noise. When it is small, as in Figure 14.5, the other components emerge fairly clearly; they are not disguised by the noise. But if the noise is large in magnitude, as in Figure 14.6, the noise makes it very difficult to distinguish the other components.

14.3

Measuring the Trend Component

In this section we use least squares analysis to quantify the trend component of a time series. This is particularly important in the case where the trend component is the dominant component. In fact, we make the implicit assumption in this section that the other three components can be combined into a single "noise" component, and that this noise component is relatively small compared to the trend. Then our problem is much as it was in regression: to fit a regression (trend) line or (trend) curve to the time series graph. The dependent variable is Y_t (or a transformation of Y_t) and the independent variable is time t.

Linear Trend Line

If the graph of Y_t is approximately linear, we can estimate the linear relationship:

$$Y_t = \beta_0 + \beta_1 t + \epsilon_t$$

The parameter β_0 represents the value of Y_t at time 0 (if this is meaningful). More important, β_1 represents the expected change in Y_t from one time period to the next. The term ϵ_t is the noise component. We estimate the regression equation,

$$\hat{Y}_t = \hat{\beta}_0 + \hat{\beta}_1 t$$

exactly as in Chapter 11. We simply substitute the subscript t for i and the independent variable t for X_i in the regression formulas from Chapter 11. The following example illustrates the mechanics of this procedure.

EXAMPLE 14.1

Suppose that a company has experienced a fairly constant rise in the sales level of one of its (nonseasonal) products over the past few years, as shown by the quarterly sales data (measured in $1000s) in Table 14.1. The time

Table 14.1 Worksheet for Sales Example

Year	t	Y_t	t^2	tY_t
1982	1	51.3	1	51.3
	2	54.6	4	109.2
	3	55.9	9	167.7
	4	57.3	16	229.2
1983	5	60.6	25	303.0
	6	61.4	36	368.4
	7	65.0	49	455.0
	8	67.1	64	536.8
1984	9	67.7	81	609.3
	10	70.2	100	702.0
	11	71.1	121	782.1
	12	73.1	144	877.2
1985	13	77.3	169	1004.9
	14	77.8	196	1089.2
	15	78.1	225	1171.5
	16	82.0	256	1312.0
Sum:	136	1070.5	1496	9768.8

series graph of these data in Figure 14.7 appears to be linear except for some irregular variation. Fit a linear equation to these data by using the least squares regression approach. Then use the estimated equation to forecast the sales for the next four quarters.

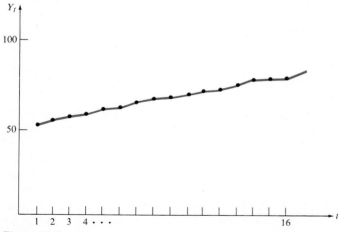

Figure 14.7

SOLUTION

Using the same notation as in Chapter 11 and recalling that time t is now the independent variable, we have

$$SS_{XX} = \sum t^2 - \frac{(\sum t)^2}{n} = 1496 - \frac{136^2}{16} = 340$$

$$SS_{XY} = \sum tY_t - \frac{(\sum t)(\sum Y_t)}{n} = 9768.8 - \frac{136(1070.5)}{16} = 669.55$$

(The required sums are shown in Table 14.1.) Then we have

$$\hat{\beta}_1 = \frac{SS_{XY}}{SS_{XX}} = \frac{669.55}{340} = 1.97$$

and $\hat{\beta}_0$ is found from

$$\hat{\beta}_0 = \frac{\sum Y_t - \hat{\beta}_1 \sum t}{n} = \frac{1070.5 - 1.97(136)}{16} = 50.16$$

So the estimated equation is

$$\hat{Y}_t = 50.16 + 1.97t$$

This equation estimates that sales are increasing by approximately $1970 per quarter.

The forecasts for the next four quarters (of 1986) are found by substituting $t = 17, 18, 19, 20$ into the estimated regression equation. These forecasts are:

$$\hat{Y}_{17} = 50.16 + 1.97(17) = 83.65 \text{ (or } \$83,650)$$
$$\hat{Y}_{18} = 50.16 + 1.97(18) = 85.62 \text{ (or } \$85,620)$$
$$\hat{Y}_{19} = 50.16 + 1.97(19) = 87.59 \text{ (or } \$87,590)$$
$$\hat{Y}_{20} = 50.16 + 1.97(20) = 89.56 \text{ (or } \$89,560)$$

Equivalently, we may take the estimate for the fourth quarter of 1985 (when $t = 16$) and keep adding $1970 to obtain the forecast for each succeeding quarter.

Exponential Trend Curve

In some cases we do not observe a constant change in Y_t each period, but instead observe a constant *percentage* change in Y_t each period. A simple example of this behavior occurs when we put an amount Y_1 into a savings account and let it and its subsequent interest grow at an interest rate of r per period. For instance, if $Y_1 = \$1000$ and the monthly interest rate is 1% ($r = .01$), then $Y_2 = 1.01Y_1 = \$1010$, $Y_3 = 1.01Y_2 = \$1020.10$, $Y_4 = 1.01Y_3 = \$1030.30$, and so on. Each Y is 1% larger than the previous value Y.

A *linear* trend line is not appropriate for this type of time series. Instead, we need to fit the following *exponential* curve:

$$Y_t = \beta_0 e^{\beta_1 t}$$

where β_0 and β_1 are unknown parameters and e is the special number 2.718 . . . . Notice that β_0 is the expected value of Y at time 0, because $e^0 = 1$. To interpret β_1, we look at the ratio of two successive Y's and use the rules of exponents:

$$\frac{Y_{t+1}}{Y_t} = \frac{\beta_0 e^{\beta_1(t+1)}}{\beta_0 e^{\beta_1 t}} = e^{\beta_1}$$

If β_1 is positive, e^{β_1} is greater than 1, and we expect Y_{t+1} to be greater than Y_t. That is, we expect the level of the time series to increase through time. The opposite is true if β_1 is negative, for then e^{β_1} is less than 1. Notice also that the percentage change from period t to period $t + 1$ is

$$\frac{Y_{t+1} - Y_t}{Y_t} \times 100 = \left(\frac{Y_{t+1}}{Y_t} - 1\right) \times 100 = (e^{\beta_1} - 1) \times 100$$

As we promised, this percentage change is indeed a constant, independent of time t.

To estimate β_0 and β_1, there are two possible approaches. The most popular approach is to assume a *multiplicative* error term ϵ_t, so that the equation for Y_t becomes $Y_t = \beta_0 e^{\beta_1 t}\epsilon_t$. Then we take natural logarithms of both sides and use the rules of logarithms to obtain

$$\ln(Y_t) = \beta_0 + \beta_1 t + \epsilon_t$$

(The reader may wish to consult Appendix A for a brief discussion of exponential and logarithmic functions.) This is exactly the same as the equation for a linear trend line except that the dependent variable is now $\ln(Y_t)$, not Y_t. Therefore, we can find a least squares fit to this line by using the same procedure as in Example 14.1, but we must first replace each Y_t by its logarithm, $\ln(Y_t)$. An example will be shown below.

The second approach is to assume an *additive* error term ϵ_t, so that the equation for Y_t becomes $Y_t = \beta_0 e^{\beta_1 t} + \epsilon_t$. Instead of transforming this equation logarithmically, we directly find a least squares fit to the exponential curve. This means that we find values $\hat{\beta}_0$ and $\hat{\beta}_1$ that minimize the sum of squared residuals

$$\sum (Y_t - \hat{\beta}_0 e^{\hat{\beta}_1 t})^2$$

Unfortunately, this is a difficult minimization problem for which no nice formulas (for $\hat{\beta}_0$ and $\hat{\beta}_1$) exist. To solve this problem, we need to resort to a computerized nonlinear optimization technique.

Several researchers have pointed out that (1) these two approaches can give quite different estimates of β_0 and β_1, and (2) the second approach may be a more valid approach. Nevertheless, we will illustrate only the first approach numerically because it is by far the easier of the two.

We note that it may be difficult to tell whether an exponential trend curve is appropriate simply by looking at the time series graph on *regular* graph paper. However, if we plot Y_t against t on *semilog* graph paper, an exponential trend corresponds to a *straight* line. (Semilog graph paper is special graph paper where the scale on the vertical axis is purposely distorted in a particular way.) Algebraically, we can tell whether an exponential fit is likely to be better than a linear fit by comparing the ratios Y_t/Y_{t-1} with the differences $Y_t - Y_{t-1}$. If the differences remain fairly constant for all values of t, a linear trend line is appropriate. But if the ratios Y_t/Y_{t-1} remain fairly constant, an exponential trend curve is probably more appropriate.

For a linear trend, the differences $Y_t - Y_{t-1}$ should remain fairly constant. For an exponential trend, the ratios Y_t/Y_{t-1} should remain fairly constant.

EXAMPLE 14.2

Suppose that a company sells several products, one of which is being phased out. Because the company is not promoting this product vigorously, most of its sales are in response to past advertising. As a result, the sales (measured in $1000s) are beginning to decline, as shown in Table 14.2. Fit an exponential trend curve to these data and explain why the fit is likely to be good. Then use the estimated equation to forecast sales for the next three months.

SOLUTION

The third column of Table 14.2 shows the ratio of Y_t to the previous month's sales, Y_{t-1}, for each $t \geq 2$. Because these ratios stay reasonably constant between .92 and .98, we have reason to believe that the percentage decrease in sales each month is practically constant and that an exponentially declining trend curve will provide a good fit. To estimate this fit, we use the least squares regression formulas from Chapter 11 with $\ln(Y_t)$ as the dependent

Table 14.2 Worksheet for Example 14.2

Month t	Y_t	Y_t/Y_{t-1}	$\ln(Y_t)$	t^2	$t \ln(Y_t)$
1	24.5	—	3.20	1	3.20
2	23.4	.955	3.15	4	6.30
3	22.6	.966	3.12	9	9.36
4	21.0	.929	3.04	16	12.18
5	20.3	.967	3.01	25	15.05
6	19.1	.941	2.95	36	17.70
7	18.4	.963	2.91	49	20.39
8	17.1	.929	2.84	64	22.71
9	16.4	.959	2.80	81	25.18
10	15.6	.951	2.75	100	27.47
11	15.3	.981	2.73	121	30.01
12	14.2	.928	2.65	144	31.84
13	13.7	.965	2.62	169	34.03
14	13.3	.971	2.59	196	36.23
15	12.7	.955	2.54	225	38.12
Sum: 120			42.90	1240	329.76

variable and t as the independent variable. From the calculations shown in Table 14.2, we see that the required sums of squares and cross products for the least squares solution are

$$SS_{XY} = \sum (t)(\ln Y_t) - \frac{(\sum t)(\sum \ln Y_t)}{n} = 329.76 - \frac{120(42.90)}{15} = -13.44$$

and

$$SS_{XX} = \sum t^2 - \frac{(\sum t)^2}{n} = 1240 - \frac{(120)^2}{15} = 280$$

These imply that

$$\hat{\beta}_1 = \frac{SS_{XY}}{SS_{XX}} = \frac{-13.44}{280} = -.048$$

and

$$\hat{\beta}_0 = \frac{(\sum \ln Y_t - \hat{\beta}_1 \sum t)}{n} = \frac{42.90 - (-.048)(120)}{15} = 3.244$$

Thus the estimated regression equation is

$$\ln(Y_t) = 3.244 - .048t$$

Alternatively, if we raise each side to the power e and recall that $e^{\ln x} = x$ for any x, we obtain

$$\hat{Y}_t = e^{3.244}e^{-.048t} = 25.636(.953)^t$$

Here we see that the factor $e^{-.048} = .953$ leads to the approximate 5% decrease in sales per month. We use this final formula for $\hat{Y}_t$ to forecast future sales. For the next three months, we have

$$\hat{Y}_{16} = 25.636(.953)^{16} = 11.867 \quad \text{(or \$11,867)}$$
$$\hat{Y}_{17} = 25.636(.953)^{17} = 11.309 \quad \text{(or \$11,309)}$$
$$\hat{Y}_{18} = 25.636(.953)^{18} = 10.778 \quad \text{(or \$10,778)}$$

Notice that these forecasts could also be obtained by estimating Y_{15} from the regression equation and then successively multiplying by .953 to obtain each succeeding month's forecast.

Problems for Sections 14.2, 14.3

1. What is the difference between the seasonal component and the cyclic component of a time series? Why is one more difficult to forecast than the other?

2. If you observe yearly data (one observation per year) for a given variable, which of the four components of time series are you able to see? Explain.

3. For each of the following time series, explain the extent to which you believe a trend component, a seasonal component, and a cyclic component are present. Assume that each series consists of monthly data.
   a. Sales of new model cars.
   b. Construction starts of new homes.
   c. Amount of rainfall in Chicago.
   d. Wage rates for hourly workers in the steel industry.

4. Why is it more difficult to identify the trend, cyclic, and/or seasonal components of the time series in the figure on the bottom than the one on the top?

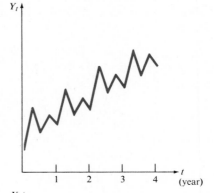

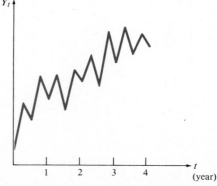

5. Consider the following data on average yearly electricity bills for a sample of households in a given location.

Year	Average Electricity Bill	Year	Average Electricity Bill
1969	$345	1977	$567
1970	368	1978	589
1971	387	1979	642
1972	417	1980	671
1973	441	1981	703
1974	459	1982	745
1975	498	1983	783
1976	532		

a. Let $t = 1$ correspond to 1969 and graph the resulting time series. Does a linear trend appear to be plausible?

b. Estimate the regression equation $Y_t = \beta_0 + \beta_1 t + \epsilon$.

c. Forecast the average yearly electricity bills for 1984, 1985, and 1986.

6. Fit an exponential trend curve to the electricity bill data in Problem 5. The natural logarithms of these data are given below. Then use the estimated equation to forecast the average electricity bills for 1984, 1985, and 1986.

Year	Logarithm of Average Electricity Bill	Year	Logarithm of Average Electricity Bill
1969	5.844	1977	6.340
1970	5.908	1978	6.378
1971	5.958	1979	6.465
1072	6.033	1980	6.509
1973	6.089	1981	6.555
1974	6.129	1982	6.613
1975	6.211	1983	6.663
1976	6.277		

7. a. For the data given in Problem 5, calculate the differences $Y_t - Y_{t-1}$ and the ratios Y_t/Y_{t-1} for all t. Based on these, which do you believe provides a better fit, a linear trend or an exponential trend? Explain your reasoning.

b. For the years 1969–1983, compare the residuals $Y_t - \hat{Y}_t$ from the estimated equations in Problems 5 and 6. Based on these, which equation appears to give the better fit? Answer by calculating the sum of the squared residuals for each.

8. The dollar amounts of direct U.S. investments abroad from 1965 to 1980 are shown in the next column. (Reference: "More Foreigners Bet Their Money on America," *U.S. News & World Report*, Dec. 15, 1980, p. 37.)

Year	Direct U.S. Investment Abroad (Billions of Dollars)
1965	50
1966	53
1967	59
1968	65
1969	71
1970	79
1971	86
1972	94
1973	104
1974	113
1975	128
1976	140
1977	148
1978	172
1979	193
1980	213

a. Graph this time series. Does it appear to be growing linearly or exponentially over time?

b. Fit an exponential trend curve to these data. (Here $t = 1$ corresponds to 1965.) Then use the resulting equation to estimate total U.S. investments abroad for 1981, 1982, and 1983.

9. The numbers of vehicles on the road (in millions) from 1970 to 1980 are shown below. (Reference: National Safety Council, *Accident Facts*, 1981, p. 59.)

Year	Number of Vehicles (Millions)
1970	111.2
1971	116.3
1972	122.3
1973	129.8
1974	134.9
1975	137.9
1976	143.5
1977	148.8
1978	153.6
1979	159.6
1980	164.9

a. Graph this time series. Does a linear trend appear to fit the data well?

b. Estimate the equation that expresses the number of vehicles on the road (Y_t) as a linear function of time t. Let $t = 1$ correspond to 1970.

c. Use the answer in part (b) to forecast Y_t for 1981, 1982, and 1983.

10. The following data represent average interest rates (Y_t) on new homes from 1968 to 1981. (Reference: Federal Home Loan Bank Board.) (These are on conventional first mortgages.)

Year	Average Interest Rates (Percent)
1968	6.83
1969	7.66
1970	8.27
1971	7.59
1972	7.45
1973	7.78
1974	8.71
1975	8.75
1976	8.76
1977	8.80
1978	9.30
1979	10.48
1980	12.25
1981	14.16

a. Graph this time series.
b. Calculate the differences $Y_t - Y_{t-1}$ and the ratios Y_t/Y_{t-1} for each year t, starting with 1969.
c. Based on parts (a) and (b), which do you believe would provide a better fit, a linear trend line or an exponential trend curve?

11. For the data in Problem 10, estimate an exponential trend curve. The appropriate natural logarithms are given below. Why might it be hazardous to forecast interest rates on first mortgages for years after 1981 from the estimated equation?

Year	Logarithm of Average Interest Rate	Year	Logarithm of Average Interest Rate
1968	1.921	1975	2.169
1969	2.036	1976	2.170
1970	2.113	1977	2.175
1971	2.027	1978	2.230
1972	2.008	1979	2.349
1973	2.052	1980	2.506
1974	2.164	1981	2.650

14.4

Measuring the Cyclic and Seasonal Components

In Section 14.3 we showed how to measure the trend component of a time series, assuming that the seasonal, cyclic, and irregular components can be combined into a relatively minor "noise" component. Clearly, there are time series for which this assumption cannot be made. These are cases where the seasonal and/or cyclic components are important in their own right and should be measured separately from the trend component.

One popular model that helps us to do this is the following *multiplicative* model. (There is also an *additive* model that is sometimes used, but we will not consider it here.) Let Y_t be the measurement variable, and let T_t, S_t, C_t, and I_t be, respectively, the trend, seasonal, cyclic, and irregular components of Y_t. Then we postulate that Y_t satisfies the following equation.

Multiplicative Model

$$Y_t = T_t \times S_t \times C_t \times I_t$$

Often we omit the subscript t and simply write $Y = T \times S \times C \times I$.

Our job is to measure the individual components of this multiplicative formula. We will look at two special cases. The first case is when the data are *yearly* data and our objective is to isolate the trend and cyclical components. The second case is when the data are *monthly* or *quarterly* data and our objective is to discover any seasonal patterns that exist.

Consider yearly data on a given variable Y_t. Then by definition there can be no seasonal component in these data because we have combined all the seasons into a *single* yearly observation. This means that the multiplicative equation becomes

$$Y_t = T_t \times C_t \times I_t$$

Dividing by the trend T_t, we obtain

$$\frac{Y_t}{T_t} = C_t \times I_t$$

This equation provides the clue for measuring the cyclic component C_t. We first measure the trend line (or trend curve) by an appropriate method. For example, we could use one of the regression techniques discussed in the preceding section. The resulting estimated value of Y_t, labeled $\hat{Y}_t$ above, becomes the estimate of the trend T_t, that is, $T_t = \hat{Y}_t$. We then divide each Y_t by its trend estimate T_t in order to *detrend* the data. What remains is a "noisy" estimate of C_t, namely $C_t \times I_t$. Because we have no reason to believe that any particular I_t is abnormally large or small, we treat the noise component as if it were not present and use Y_t/T_t as the estimate of C_t:

Obtaining T and C from Yearly Data

> *Estimate of C_t*
>
> $$C_t \approx \frac{Y_t}{T_t}$$

The simplest way to interpret this cyclic component numerically is to multiply it by 100%. Then it shows what percentage of the trend that particular year's observation is. The following example illustrates the procedure.

EXAMPLE 14.3

The data in Table 14.3 (p. 732) represent the total income (in $1,000,000s) of all life insurance companies from the years 1971 through 1981. Investigate the trend and cyclic components of these data.

SOLUTION

The last two columns in Table 14.3 show the successive changes in the Y_t's $(Y_t - Y_{t-1})$ and the fractional changes (Y_t/Y_{t-1}). Since the quotients

Table 14.3

Year	t	Y_t	$Y_t - Y_{t-1}$	Y_t/Y_{t-1}
1971	1	54,202	—	—
1972	2	58,848	4,646	1.09
1973	3	64,753	5,905	1.10
1974	4	70,010	5,257	1.08
1975	5	78,022	8,012	1.11
1976	6	88,558	10,536	1.14
1977	7	97,985	9,427	1.11
1978	8	108,206	10,221	1.10
1979	9	119,139	10,933	1.10
1980	10	132,489	13,350	1.11
1981	11	151,865	19,376	1.15

Y_t/Y_{t-1} are more nearly constant than the differences $Y_t - Y_{t-1}$, we have reason to believe that an exponential trend will provide a better fit to these data than a linear trend. Therefore, we first estimate the equation

$$\ln(Y_t) = \beta_0 + \beta_1 t + \epsilon_t$$

Proceeding exactly as in Example 14.2, we obtain the estimated regression equation

$$\ln(\hat{Y}_t) = 10.771 + .103t$$

Solving for $\hat{Y}_t$ (by raising each side to the power e), we obtain

$$\hat{Y}_t = e^{10.771}e^{.103t} = 47620(1.108)^t$$

This is the (estimated) trend component, T_t. Now we divide each observation Y_t by its trend estimate $\hat{Y}_t$ (or T_t) to estimate the cyclic component for that year. The results are shown in Table 14.4.

Table 14.4

Year	t	Y_t	$\hat{Y}_t = T_t$	$C_t = Y_t/T_t$
1971	1	54,202	52,763	1.027
1972	2	58,848	58,461	1.007
1973	3	64,753	64,775	1.000
1974	4	70,010	71,771	.975
1975	5	78,022	79,522	.981
1976	6	88,558	88,111	1.005
1977	7	97,985	97,626	1.004
1978	8	108,206	108,170	1.000
1979	9	119,139	119,853	.994
1980	10	132,489	132,797	.998
1981	11	151,865	147,139	1.032

As the numbers in Table 14.4 indicate, there is very little cyclic variation for insurance company incomes during these years. The C_t for 1981 shows that Y_t is 3.2% above the trend curve, and the C_t for 1974 shows that Y_t is 2.5% below the trend curve. These are the two largest percentage departures from the trend curve. Actually, since the ratio Y_t/T_t includes the noise component I_t as well as the cyclic component C_t, the small departures from the trend curve can probably be attributed as much to noise as to any definite cyclic variation. This example supports the contention of insurance people that their income is *not* affected by the ups and downs of business cycles.

EXAMPLE 14.4

The data in Table 14.5 represent the annual sales (in \$1,000,000s) of all U.S. automobile dealers from 1968 to 1980. Perform the same analysis as in Example 14.3 on these data.

Table 14.5

Year	t	Y_t	$Y_t - Y_{t-1}$	Y_t/Y_{t-1}	$\hat{Y}_t = T_t$	$C_t = Y_t/T_t$
1968	1	57,289	—	—	53,977	1.061
1969	2	60,337	3,048	1.053	59,375	1.016
1970	3	57,545	−2,792	.954	65,312	.881
1971	4	70,874	13,329	1.232	71,843	.987
1972	5	81,094	10,220	1.144	79,028	1.026
1973	6	94,787	13,693	1.169	86,930	1.090
1974	7	87,476	−7,311	.923	95,624	.915
1975	8	96,762	9,286	1.106	105,186	.920
1976	9	118,860	22,098	1.228	115,704	1.027
1977	10	137,091	18,231	1.153	127,275	1.077
1978	11	153,277	16,186	1.118	140,002	1.095
1979	12	161,110	7,833	1.051	154,003	1.046
1980	13	148,799	−12,311	.924	169,403	.878

SOLUTION

In contrast to Example 14.3, it is clear from the $Y_t - Y_{t-1}$ and the Y_t/Y_{t-1} columns that neither a linear trend line nor an exponential trend curve will fit these data perfectly. In other words, there does seem to be some cyclic variation. We again choose to fit the trend by an exponential curve because the ratios Y_t/Y_{t-1} are somewhat more constant than the differences $Y_t - Y_{t-1}$. The regression analysis gives the following estimated regression equation:

$$\ln(\hat{Y}_t) = 10.801 + .095t$$

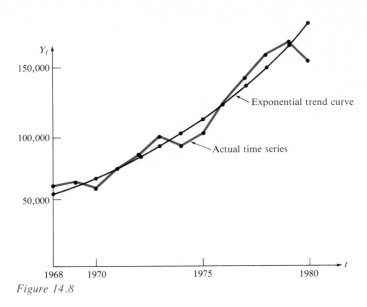

Figure 14.8

This can be transformed to the trend curve

$$T_t = \hat{Y}_t = 49{,}070(1.100)^t$$

Finally, the estimated cyclic factors are Y_t/T_t. All the trend and cyclic values are shown in Table 14.5.

In fact, we see quite a lot of cyclic variation in automobile sales. This is illustrated graphically in Figure 14.8. For example, the best years for automobile dealers were 1973 and 1978, when their sales were 9.0% and 9.5% above the trend curve. In contrast, 1970 and 1980 were poor years. In these years sales were down 11.9% and 12.2% below the trend curve. This example makes it apparent that automobile sales *are* affected by business cycles, particularly when things are going badly!

We point out that the technique in this section should be used primarily for identifying the cyclic component of historical data. Unfortunately, it is not likely to be very accurate for predicting cyclic variation of future data. For example, even if we are successful in determining the cyclical pattern of a company's sales, we may not be able to predict *future* cyclical patterns. There are more sophisticated methods for identifying "turning points" in a time series pattern, such as the point where sales have bottomed out and will then proceed to recover, but we will not discuss these methods in this book.

In this section we learn one of several existing methods for identifying the seasonal component of a time series. This component is usually much more predictable than the cyclic component. The difficulty with predicting cyclic patterns is that they do not repeat themselves in a regular manner. Seasonal patterns, on the other hand, are more likely to repeat themselves in the future. Therefore, a method for identifying a seasonal pattern is especially useful because it can be used to forecast the future behavior of the time series, particularly the short-term future.

To measure the seasonal factor for each period, we again use the multiplicative equation $Y = T \times C \times S \times I$. Dividing by $T \times C$, we obtain

$$\frac{Y}{T \times C} = S \times I$$

This equation implies that if we can "divide out" the trend and cyclic components from the observations, all that remains is a noisy estimate, $S \times I$, of the seasonal component. As in the preceding section, we will use this noisy estimate as an estimate of S itself. The problem, then, is to estimate $T \times C$, that is, to see what the time series would look like if there were no seasonal variation. We do this by "smoothing" the data to eliminate much of the seasonal variation. The smoothing method we will use is called the method of *centered moving averages*.

In general, a *moving average* is an average of the observations from several consecutive time periods. Suppose that there are M observations per year. Normally, we have $M = 4$ (for quarterly data) or $M = 12$ (for monthly data). Then to compute a moving average sequence, we compute successive averages of M consecutive observations. For example, with quarterly data, the first moving average is the average of the observations from quarters 1 through 4, the second moving average is the average for quarters 2 through 5, the third moving average is the average for quarters 3 through 6, and so on. This is illustrated in Table 14.6 (p. 736) with quarterly data ($M = 4$). The data in this table represent new privately owned housing starts in the period 1977 to 1981.

The only problem with this moving average procedure is that M is an *even* number. This means that the middle of each moving average, timewise, falls *between* two quarters. We would instead like to have each moving average correspond to a particular quarter. The remedy is to compute *centered* moving averages. Each centered moving average is the average of two consecutive moving averages.

As an example, the average of the four quarters in 1977 corresponds to the end of quarter 2, 1977, or to the beginning of quarter 3, 1977. Similarly, the next average, of quarter 2, 1977 through quarter 1, 1978, corresponds to the end of quarter 3, 1977, or to the beginning of quarter 4, 1977. If we average these two averages, we obtain a centered moving average that cor-

Table 14.6

Year	Quarter	Y_t	Moving Average	CMA_t	$S_t = Y_t/CMA_t$
1977	1	367.4			
	2	581.1			
	3	561.5	496.8	488.7	1.15
	4	477.1	480.5	471.8	1.01
1978	1	302.2	463.0	450.3	.67
	2	511.3	437.6	430.4	1.19
	3	459.8	423.1	424.3	1.08
	4	419.1	425.4	422.2	.99
1979	1	311.3	419.0	415.9	.75
	2	485.9	412.7	404.2	1.20
	3	434.6	395.7	384.2	1.13
	4	351.1	372.6	345.6	1.02
1980	1	218.7	318.5	306.9	.71
	2	269.7	295.2	296.5	.91*
	3	341.4	297.8	301.1	1.13
	4	361.3	304.4	308.3	1.17*
1981	1	245.3	312.1	298.6	.82
	2	300.4	285.1	262.9	1.14
	3	233.5	240.7		
	4	183.6			

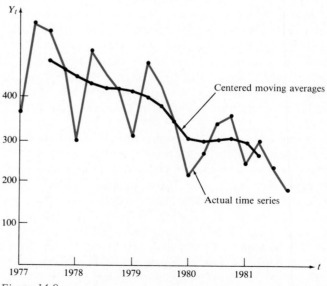

Figure 14.9

responds to the middle of quarter 3, 1977. For this reason we identify 488.7, the average of the two moving averages 496.8 and 480.5, with quarter 3, 1977.

All the centered moving averages for this example are shown in Table 14.6 and are graphed, together with the original time series, in Figure 14.9. Clearly, the centered moving average graph is much smoother than the graph of the original time series.

The real purpose of moving averages or centered moving averages is to smooth out seasonal variations in the data. Therefore, these centered moving averages are estimates of $T \times C$, the product of the trend and cyclic components. Symbolically, if we let CMA_t be the centered moving average corresponding to period t, we have

> ### Estimate of Trend and Cyclic Components
>
> $$T_t \times C_t \approx CMA_t$$

Notice that some of the time periods have no associated centered moving averages. In general, there will be a half year's worth missing at the beginning and at the end of the time series. These missing averages generally create no problems, however, if the time series is sufficiently long.

Once we have found the centered moving averages, we can compute estimates of the seasonal component. For period t we have

> ### Estimate of Seasonal Component
>
> $$S_t \approx \frac{Y_t}{CMA_t}$$

Since these estimates of the seasonal factors are ratios formed by centered moving averages, this method for estimating the seasonal component is called the *ratio-to-moving average method*.

> The ratio-to-moving average method uses the ratios of observations to centered moving averages to estimate the seasonal component of a time series.

The estimated S_t values are shown in the right-hand column of Table 14.6. Perhaps the best way to interpret S_t is to multiply the equation above by 100%. This tells us by what percentage a given period's observation differs from the corresponding centered moving average. For example, the value of

S_9 (the first quarter of 1979) is .75. This shows that housing starts were 75% as large as the smoothed average for this quarter. In contrast, $S_{10} = 1.20$ shows that housing starts were 20% above the smoothed average for the second quarter of 1979.

If we wish to use the seasonal factors for forecasting, we can average all the first quarter S_t's to provide an overall first quarter seasonal factor. This estimate of an "average" quarter 1 seasonal component is labeled $\overline{S}_1$. In this example it is

$$\overline{S}_1 = \frac{.67 + .75 + .71 + .82}{4} = .74$$

In the absence of other relevant information about housing starts in the future, we forecast that housing starts for the first quarters of future years will be approximately 26% below the extrapolated trend-cyclic smoothed averages for these quarters. Similarly, the averages of the seasonal factors for the other quarters are

$$\overline{S}_2 = \frac{1.19 + 1.20 + .91 + 1.14}{4} = 1.11 \text{ (or 11\% above normal)}$$

$$\overline{S}_3 = \frac{1.15 + 1.08 + 1.13 + 1.13}{4} = 1.12 \text{ (or 12\% above normal)}$$

$$\overline{S}_4 = \frac{1.01 + .99 + 1.02 + 1.17}{4} = 1.05 \text{ (or 5\% above normal)}$$

Notice that the seasonal patterns are fairly stable from year to year. The only seasonal factors that appear to break the pattern are S_{14} (second quarter, 1980) and S_{16} (fourth quarter, 1980), which we have starred in Table 14.6. Because the rest of the S_t's for any given quarter stay fairly constant from year to year, we have reason to believe that these values will remain stable in the future. Hence, we may be fairly confident that the *seasonal* component of our forecasts will be reasonably accurate.

Problems for Section 14.4

12. Estimate the cyclic component for the time series in Problem 5 (p. 729) in two ways: (1) use the estimated linear trend from Problem 5 to detrend the data, and (2) use the estimated exponential trend from Problem 6 (p. 729) to detrend the data. Do the two resulting cyclic patterns appear to be similar?

13. The following data represent annual sales total (in $1,000,000s) for lumber and building materials for the years 1968–1980. (Reference: U.S. Department of Commerce.)

Year	Annual Sales ($1,000,000s)	Year	Annual Sales ($1,000,000s)
1968	10,295	1975	17,938
1969	10,918	1976	22,480
1970	11,248	1977	27,127
1971	12,930	1978	31,490
1972	14,956	1979	35,255
1973	17,242	1980	33,682
1974	17,830		

a. Estimate an exponential trend for these data.

b. Detrend these data by using the result from part (a) and then estimate the cyclic component.

c. Graph the time series C_t found in part (b). Discuss any obvious qualities of the cyclic component that you can see in this graph.

14. Explain why we use centered moving averages rather than moving averages in the ratio-to-moving average method. Be explicit.

15. The following data represent quarterly expenditures (in billions of dollars) for plants and equipment in the manufacturing industry for the years 1973–1979. (Reference: U.S. Department of Commerce.)

Year	Quarter	Expenditures (Billions of Dollars)
1973	1	7.80
	2	9.16
	3	9.62
	4	11.43
1974	1	9.49
	2	11.27
	3	11.62
	4	13.63
1975	1	10.84
	2	12.15
	3	11.67
	4	13.30
1976	1	10.96
	2	12.66
	3	13.48
	4	15.38
1977	1	12.52
	2	14.84
	3	15.60
	4	17.19
1978	1	13.67
	2	16.76
	3	16.89
	4	20.30
1979	1	15.88
	2	19.08
	3	24.93
	4	30.42

a. Estimate the seasonal component of these data by using the ratio-to-moving average method.

b. If you used the trend and cyclic components to arrive at a forecast of expenditures for the first quarter 1980, by what seasonal factor would you adjust this forecast?

16. The following data represent per capita consumption of soft drinks in the United States from 1970 to 1979. (Each observation is the average number of 12-ounce containers consumed per person.)

Year	Per Capita Consumption
1970	241.9
1971	258.7
1972	270.9
1973	286.4
1974	286.3
1975	292.7
1976	328.7
1977	359.0
1978	382.7
1979	399.6

a. Fit a linear trend line to the yearly totals.

b. Using the equation from part (a), estimate the cyclic component C_t. Can you see any obvious patterns?

17. The following data represent quarterly returns per share of Coca-Cola stock from 1960 to 1969. Graph these data on a time series graph. Does there appear to be a trend? What about seasonal variation? How would you account for this particular type of seasonal variation; that is, can you think of any reasons for its presence?

Year	Quarter 1	2	3	4
1960	.13	.21	.26	.12
1961	.15	.21	.27	.14
1962	.16	.24	.30	.16
1963	.18	.26	.33	.18
1964	.22	.31	.39	.22
1965	.26	.36	.45	.26
1966	.31	.42	.52	.31
1967	.35	.47	.59	.35
1968	.38	.51	.66	.38
1969	.42	.57	.74	.42

18. For the data in Problem 17, use the ratio-to-moving average method to estimate the seasonal component. Does it appear to be relatively constant for these years? Explain.

19. Consider the quarterly data on a company's sales on p. 740. Suppose you are told that the relevant seasonal factors for deseasonalizing this data set are .9, 1.4, .8, and .9. (For

example, first quarter sales average about 90% of all quarterly sales.) Use these factors to deseasonalize the data. Then graph both the original series and the deseasonalized series. Do the given seasonal factors appear to be satisfactory? Explain.

Year	Quarter	Sales ($1000s)
1984	1	121.8
	2	186.7
	3	110.5
	4	113.6

(continued)

Year	Quarter	Sales ($1000s)
1985	1	131.3
	2	174.6
	3	117.5
	4	107.6
1986	1	115.1
	2	169.4
	3	125.4
	4	109.4

14.5

Exponential Smoothing

We have already seen one method for smoothing an irregular time series: moving averages. We now examine a second smoothing method called *exponential smoothing*. Although this method may not be as intuitive as the moving average method, it is very convenient to implement, either by hand or on a computer. Its data requirements are minimal, and its flexibility usually allows us to make reasonably accurate forecasts from the smoothed series.

Simple Exponential Smoothing

We begin by discussing the most basic version of exponential smoothing, called *simple* exponential smoothing. This version is primarily useful when we expect no pronounced trends, seasonal variation, or cyclic variation in the data. This means that we believe the time series is essentially "flat" except for the unpredictable noise. In this case the purpose of the method is to smooth out the irregularities in the data and then extrapolate the smoothed series into the future.

As usual, we denote the observation at time t by Y_t. Since we believe the time series would remain at a fairly constant level if it were not for the noise, we let L_t (L for level) be the estimate of that level at time t. We also let F_{t+1} be the forecast of Y_{t+1}, made at time t. Then the formulas for simple exponential smoothing are as follows.

Simple Exponential Smoothing Formulas

Smoothed level at time t

$$L_t = \alpha Y_t + (1 - \alpha)L_{t-1}$$

Forecast of Y_{t+1} made at time t

$$F_{t+1} = L_t$$

The formula for F_{t+1} is intuitive. Once we have estimated the level of the time series in period t, L_t, we forecast that the next observation, Y_{t+1}, will equal this smoothed level L_t.

The formula for L_t is the crux of exponential smoothing. Here α is a *smoothing constant* (not to be confused with our earlier uses of the symbol α) that must be between 0 and 1. The formula says to calculate L_t as a weighted average of the current observation Y_t and the smoothed level from the preceding period, L_{t-1}. The weight α is attached to Y_t, and the weight $(1 - \alpha)$ is attached to L_{t-1}. If the observations begin with time period $t = 1$, we first find L_1, then we find L_2 from L_1, then we find L_3 from L_2, and so on. To get started, we must estimate L_0, the level of the series one period before we start collecting data. This is because L_1 satisfies

$$L_1 = \alpha Y_1 + (1 - \alpha)L_0$$

Once we estimate L_0, the rest of the L_t's can be computed in "stepladder" fashion. A numerical example will be given below.

The role of the smoothing constant α can be understood better if we rewrite the formula for L_t as

$$L_t = \alpha(Y_t - L_{t-1}) + L_{t-1}$$

Since the forecast of Y_t made at time $t - 1$ is $F_t = L_{t-1}$, the equation above becomes

$$L_t = \alpha(Y_t - F_t) + L_{t-1}$$

This means that the smoothed level at time t, L_t, is the smoothed level at time $t - 1$, L_{t-1}, plus α times the forecast error in forecasting Y_t, namely $Y_t - F_t$. (By time t, this forecasting error will be known.) Since α is positive, this implies that we will revise our estimate of the level upward ($L_t > L_{t-1}$) if the previous forecast was too low ($Y_t > F_t$), and we will revise it downward ($L_t < L_{t-1}$) if the previous forecast was too high ($Y_t < F_t$). This certainly makes sense from an intuitive standpoint.

The amount of revision is determined by the magnitude of α. If α is close to 0, $\alpha(Y_t - F_t)$ is small and L_t is practically equal to L_{t-1}. But if α is close to 1, we react quickly to the previous forecast error, and L_t can be quite different from L_{t-1}. Therefore, a low value of α smooths the data more than a high value of α. If we want the smoothed levels, and hence the forecasts, to react quickly to sudden changes in the observations, we should choose a relatively large value of α. But if we want the smoothed time series, and hence the forecasts, to be resistant to noise, a small α value is recommended.

The choice is still a difficult one, however, because it is difficult a priori to say which shifts in the Y_t's are significant and which are only noise. In actual practice, α is usually chosen to be somewhere in the interval from .1

to .5. The following example illustrates the effect different α values can have on forecasts.

EXAMPLE 14.5

The data in Table 14.7 represent the number of deaths from automobile accidents per 100,000 people in the United States from 1965 to 1980. Use simple exponential smoothing with $\alpha = .3$ to smooth these data. Repeat the calculations with $\alpha = .8$. What are the forecasts for 1981 with these two α values? Use $L_0 = 25$ (the actual 1964 figure).

Table 14.7

Year	t	Y_t Number of Deaths per 100,000 People
1965	1	25.4
1966	2	27.1
1967	3	26.8
1968	4	27.5
1969	5	27.7
1970	6	26.8
1971	7	26.4
1972	8	27.0
1973	9	26.5
1974	10	22.0
1975	11	21.5
1976	12	21.9
1977	13	22.9
1978	14	24.0
1979	15	24.0
1980	16	23.2

SOLUTION

The solution is summarized in Table 14.8. For each $t \geq 1$, we find L_t from the defining formula $L_t = \alpha Y_t + (1 - \alpha)L_{t-1}$, starting with $L_0 = 25$. For example, the first two calculations with $\alpha = .3$ are

$$L_1 = \alpha Y_1 + (1 - \alpha)L_0 = .3(25.4) + .7(25.0) = 25.12$$
$$L_2 = \alpha Y_2 + (1 - \alpha)L_1 = .3(27.1) + .7(25.12) = 25.71$$

Notice that we needed the value of L_1 from the first calculation to calculate L_2. Similarly, we will need this value of L_2 to calculate L_3. This is what we mean by saying that the calculations proceed in "stepladder" fashion.

The forecast of Y_2 made in period 1 is labeled F_2 and is given by $L_1 =$

Table 14.8

Year	t	Y_t	$\alpha = .3$			$\alpha = .8$		
			L_t	F_t	E_t	L_t	F_t	E_t
1964	0	—	25.0	—	—	25.0	—	—
1965	1	25.4	25.12	25.0	.40	25.32	25.0	.40
1966	2	27.1	25.71	25.12	1.98	26.74	25.32	1.78
1967	3	26.8	26.04	25.71	1.09	26.79	26.74	.06
1968	4	27.5	26.48	26.04	1.46	27.36	26.79	.71
1969	5	27.7	26.85	26.48	1.22	27.63	27.36	.34
1970	6	26.8	26.84	26.85	−.05	26.97	27.63	−.83
1971	7	26.4	26.71	26.84	−.44	26.51	26.97	−.57
1972	8	27.0	26.80	26.71	.29	26.90	26.51	.49
1973	9	26.5	26.71	26.80	−.30	26.58	26.90	−.40
1974	10	22.0	25.30	26.71	−4.71	22.92	26.58	−4.58
1975	11	21.5	24.16	25.30	−3.80	21.78	22.92	−1.42
1976	12	21.9	23.48	24.16	−2.26	21.88	21.78	.12
1977	13	22.9	23.31	23.48	−.58	22.70	21.88	1.02
1978	14	24.0	23.52	23.31	.69	23.74	22.70	1.30
1979	15	24.0	23.66	23.52	.48	23.95	23.74	.26
1980	16	23.2	23.52	23.66	−.46	23.35	23.95	−.75
1981	17			23.52			23.35	
				MAD = 1.26			MAD = .94	

25.12. Since the actual Y_2 is 27.1, the forecast error in period 2, labeled E_2, is given by

$$E_2 = Y_2 - F_2 = 27.1 - 25.12 = 1.98$$

Since this error is positive (we underestimated Y_2), the smoothed level L_2 is larger than L_1. Similarly, the forecast of Y_3 made in period 2 is $F_3 = L_2 = 25.71$. The forecast error in period 3 is

$$E_3 = Y_3 - F_3 = 26.8 - 25.71 = 1.09$$

Since this is also positive, we know that L_3 will be larger than L_2. Jumping ahead, we see from the table that the final forecast is for 1981, made in 1980. Its value is $F_{17} = 23.52$ (with $\alpha = .3$) and $F_{17} = 23.35$ (with $\alpha = .8$).

The original observations and the smoothed values are graphed in Figure 14.10 (p. 744). As we promised, the smoothed series with $\alpha = .8$ reacts quickly to changes in the original series, whereas the series with $\alpha = .3$ is smoother. In particular, when the series decreases abruptly in 1974, the smoothed series with $\alpha = .8$ picks up this change much more quickly than

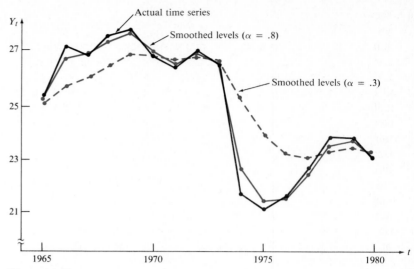

Figure 14.10

the one with $\alpha = .3$. Is this good or bad? For these particular data, the observations after 1973 remain at a lower level than they were before 1973, so the smoothed series, which picks up this change quickly, is probably preferred.

One way of measuring whether one smoothing constant is better than another is to find the average of the absolute values of the forecast errors, the E_t's. This average is called the *mean absolute deviation*, or MAD. (This is a special case of the MAD measure we discussed in Chapter 2.) Algebraically, MAD is defined as:

> *Mean Absolute Deviation*
>
> $$\text{MAD} = \sum \frac{|E_t|}{N} = \sum \frac{|Y_t - F_t|}{N} \qquad \text{where } N = \text{number of periods}$$

For the accident data, we see from Table 14.8 that MAD $= 1.26$ for $\alpha = .3$ and MAD $= .94$ for $\alpha = .8$. Therefore, exponential smoothing does a better job of "forecasting" the known data when $\alpha = .8$ than when $\alpha = .3$. This does not guarantee, however, that *future* forecasts based on $\alpha = .8$ will be more accurate than those based on $\alpha = .3$. We simply have no way of knowing.

Winters' Exponential Smoothing Method

Simple exponential smoothing usually works fairly well with time series with no pronounced trend and no obvious seasonal variation. But if a time series has either of these characteristics, the simple exponential smoothing model does not do a very good job of "tracking" the series. The forecasts tend to lag behind the trend, and the seasonal variation is nearly ignored altogether. In this section we present a generalization of simple exponential smoothing due to Winters that takes trend and seasonality into account. Although this method is considerably more tedious to compute by hand than simple exponential smoothing, it is very well suited to computer programming. (The computer package that accompanies this text includes a BASIC program for performing Winters' method.) Winters' method is also a fairly powerful method that managers can understand intuitively, regardless of whether they can work through the equations.

We again find a smoothed level L_t for the series at any time t. Now we can think of L_t as the approximate level the series would equal throughout the future if the trend were discontinued and there were no seasonality. Because there may be a trend, however, we introduce an estimate of the trend at time t, labeled T_t. This trend estimate is the amount we expect the series to increase (or decrease, if negative) in one time period, again if seasonality were not present.

Finally, to account for the seasonality in period t, we introduce the seasonal factor S_t. The interpretation of this factor is identical to that in Section 14.2. For example, if $S_t = .90$, we expect Y_t for this period to be 90% as large as the average for an entire year. In the other direction, if $S_t = 1.10$, we expect Y_t for this period to be 10% higher than the average for an entire year. Furthermore, if there are M periods in a year, we expect two S's separated by M periods, S_t and S_{t+M} say, to be nearly equal. For example, the seasonal factor for January 1982 ought to be close to the seasonal factor for January 1981. However, the method does not force these two factors to be identical.

The equations for Winters' method rely on three smoothing constants, α, β, and γ. The only comments we make about the choice of these constants are that (1) they should each be between 0 and 1; (2) the larger these constants are, the quicker the forecasts react to sudden changes in the overall level (α), the trend (β), and the seasonality factors (γ); and (3) these three constants are usually chosen to be in the interval from .1 to .5. In general, a practitioner must use trial and error to choose good values of these smoothing constants in any particular application.

The equations for Winters' method are given below.

Formulas for Winters' Method

Revised level

$$L_t = \frac{\alpha Y_t}{S_{t-M}} + (1 - \alpha)(L_{t-1} + T_{t-1})$$

Revised trend

$$T_t = \beta(L_t - L_{t-1}) + (1 - \beta)T_{t-1}$$

Revised seasonality factor

$$S_t = \frac{\gamma Y_t}{L_t} + (1 - \gamma)S_{t-M}$$

Forecast of Y_{t+1} (made in period t)

$$F_{t+1} = (L_t + T_t)S_{t-M+1}$$

These equations are easier to understand if we make the following observations:

1. Y_t/S_{t-M} is the *deseasonalized* value of Y_t, based on the seasonal factor from exactly one year ago. For example, if t corresponds to January 1981, then $t - M$ corresponds to January 1980.
2. $L_{t-1} + T_{t-1}$ is the expected deseasonalized level of the series in period t. That is, this is what we would forecast Y_t to be if there were no seasonality.
3. $L_t - L_{t-1}$ is the estimate of the trend in period t.
4. Y_t/L_t is an estimate of the seasonal factor in period t, as is the seasonal factor from a year ago, S_{t-M}.
5. S_{t-M+1} is the seasonal factor from a year ago next period. For example, if we are standing in January 1982, this is the seasonal factor from February 1981. This factor is used to seasonalize the level $L_t + T_t$ and thereby produce the forecast F_{t+1} of Y_{t+1}.

To operationalize these formulas, starting from period $t = 1$, we first need an initial estimate of the level, L_0, an initial estimate of the trend, T_0, and estimates of the whole past year's seasonal factors, labeled S_{-M+1} through S_0. For quarterly data, these would be S_{-3} through S_0; for monthly data, they would be S_{-11} through S_0. We then set $t = 1$ and successively calculate L_1, then T_1, then S_1, and then F_2. Next we set $t = 2$ and repeat, calculating L_2, then T_2, then S_2, and then F_3. We continue until we have calculated all these quantities for each value of t.

This computational procedure is not meant for hand calculation. In spite of its basic simplicity, there are too many arithmetic operations required to make it feasible. As with multiple regression, we definitely recommend using a computer to perform the calculations.

EXAMPLE 14.6

The data in Table 14.9 represent U.S. beer production (in millions of barrels) for the 60 months from January 1977 to December 1981. As we would expect, these data are clearly seasonal, rising in the summer months and falling in the winter months. There is also a slight upward trend, as indicated by the successive yearly totals. Therefore, a simple exponential smoothing model would not track these data very well. Instead, we use Winters' model, starting with $L_0 = 13.6$, $T_0 = .4$, and the following seasonal adjustment factors (corresponding to January through December): $S_{-11} = .9$, $S_{-10} = .9$, $S_{-9} = .9$, $S_{-8} = 1.0$, $S_{-7} = 1.1$, $S_{-6} = 1.2$, $S_{-5} = 1.2$, $S_{-4} = 1.2$, $S_{-3} = 1.0$, $S_{-2} = 1.0$, $S_{-1} = .8$, and $S_0 = .8$. These starting values were chosen from several considerations:

1. The average of the twelve 1976 observations (not shown) was 13.6; this is the estimate of L_0.
2. The average per month increase from the beginning of 1974 to the end of 1976 was approximately .4; this is the estimate of T_0.
3. The seasonal pattern for 1976 was roughly that of S_{-11} to S_0.

The α, β, and γ values chosen are .2, .1, and .5, respectively. These relatively small values imply that the values of the L_t's, T_t's, and S_t's will remain fairly stable over the entire time period unless dramatic changes occur in the series itself. (We tried larger values of α, β, and γ, but they all resulted in larger values of MAD.)

Table 14.9 U.S. Beer Production (Millions of Barrels)

	1977	1978	1979	1980	1981
January	11.98	12.87	13.83	14.64	13.31
February	11.48	12.71	13.57	14.72	14.58
March	16.20	15.86	16.89	16.56	16.72
April	16.03	15.62	16.34	16.36	17.68
May	16.79	16.57	16.97	17.97	18.87
June	16.90	16.88	16.77	17.93	18.63
July	15.92	16.74	16.94	18.72	18.80
August	15.31	17.61	16.76	17.02	17.72
September	13.26	14.63	14.70	16.29	15.72
October	12.61	14.01	14.43	14.95	14.61
November	12.02	12.71	13.14	13.02	13.12
December	12.01	12.87	12.18	13.32	13.14
Total	170.51	179.08	182.52	191.50	192.90

We used the computer program EXSMOOTH in the package accompanying this text to evaluate the L_t's, T_t's, S_t's, and F_t's. The resulting output is shown in Table 14.10. This program also calculates the forecast errors $E_t = Y_t - F_t$, and MAD, the mean absolute deviation of these errors. The following observations can be made about these data.

Table 14.10

Year	January	February	March	April	May	June	July	August	September	October	November	December
1977	12.60	12.82	12.88	15.48	17.63	19.56	19.49	19.16	15.58	15.33	11.95	12.09
1978	13.46	13.15	15.12	15.82	16.94	17.86	17.43	17.26	14.90	14.76	12.71	12.72
1979	13.94	13.73	16.33	16.57	17.61	18.20	17.71	17.88	14.87	14.47	12.79	12.88
1980	13.74	13.66	16.81	16.52	17.36	17.85	17.93	18.31	15.55	15.41	13.74	13.18
1981	14.97	14.41	16.83	16.56	17.97	18.30	18.71	18.07	16.26	15.34	13.48	13.31

Forecasts (F_t)

Year	January	February	March	April	May	June	July	August	September	October	November	December
1977	−.62	−1.34	3.32	.55	−.84	−2.66	−3.57	−3.85	−2.32	−2.72	.07	−.08
1978	−.59	−.44	.74	−.20	−.37	−.98	−.69	.35	−.27	−.75	.00	.15
1979	−.11	−.16	.56	−.23	−.64	−1.43	−.77	−1.12	−.17	−.04	.35	−.70
1980	.90	1.06	−.25	−.16	.61	.08	.79	−1.29	.74	−.46	−.72	.14
1981	−1.66	.17	−.11	1.12	.90	.33	.09	−.35	−.54	−.73	−.36	−.17

Errors (E_t)

Year	January	February	March	April	May	June	July	August	September	October	November	December
1977	13.86	13.95	15.04	15.59	15.87	15.86	15.64	15.33	15.12	14.79	14.96	15.10
1978	15.12	15.16	15.45	15.56	15.63	15.60	15.59	15.76	15.82	15.77	15.86	15.99
1979	16.06	16.11	16.32	16.37	16.35	16.17	16.09	15.93	15.92	15.93	16.04	15.89
1980	16.11	16.40	16.41	16.43	16.59	16.67	16.87	16.71	16.92	16.89	16.77	16.85
1981	16.52	16.57	16.56	16.79	16.99	17.10	17.17	17.16	17.09	16.97	16.90	16.87

Smoothed levels (L_t)

Year	January	February	March	April	May	June	July	August	September	October	November	December
1977	.39	.36	.43	.44	.43	.38	.32	.26	.21	.16	.16	.16
1978	.14	.13	.15	.14	.14	.12	.11	.11	.11	.09	.09	.10
1979	.09	.09	.10	.10	.08	.06	.04	.02	.02	.02	.03	.01
1980	.03	.06	.05	.05	.06	.06	.08	.05	.07	.06	.04	.04
1981	.01	.01	.01	.03	.05	.05	.06	.05	.04	.02	.01	.01

Trends (T_t)

Year	January	February	March	April	May	June	July	August	September	October	November	December
1977	.88	.86	.99	1.01	1.08	1.13	1.11	1.10	.94	.93	.80	.80
1978	.87	.85	1.01	1.01	1.07	1.11	1.09	1.11	.93	.91	.80	.80
1979	.86	.85	1.02	1.00	1.05	1.07	1.07	1.08	.93	.91	.81	.78
1980	.89	.87	1.02	1.00	1.07	1.07	1.09	1.05	.94	.90	.79	.79
1981	.85	.88	1.01	1.03	1.09	1.08	1.09	1.04	.93	.88	.78	.78

Seasonality Factors (S_t)

1. The smoothed averages (the L_t's) remain fairly constant over time, certainly more so than the time series itself. However, these smoothed averages do exhibit some trend and a small amount of seasonality. This is not uncommon.

2. The trends are all positive, but they quickly decrease to a level well below our original "guess," $T_0 = .4$. This is in spite of the fact that the smoothing constant for trend, $\beta = .1$, is very low.

3. The seasonality factors remain fairly close to our original estimates of them. This means that the same seasonal pattern appears to continue from year to year.

4. The errors are relatively small, and perhaps even more important, they alternate between positive and negative in a fairly random way. If there were a definite pattern to the positives and negatives, we would suspect that the forecast errors were more than just noise. In this case we would attempt to remove the nonnoise component from the errors by using different smoothing constants or a different forecasting method altogether.

In the example above we have used the word "forecast," but we have not attempted to forecast any values we did not already know. Given values of beer production through 1981, a forecaster should attempt to forecast values *after* 1981. This can be done by using the following equation. Here t represents the last time period for which we have an observation, and k represents the number of periods we are forecasting ahead.

Forecast of Y_{t+k} (Made at Time t)

$$= (L_t + kT_t)S_{t-M+k}$$

In this formula, L_t is the current smoothed level, kT_t is the amount of trend that should be added for k periods in the future, and S_{t-M+k} is the appropriate seasonality factor for k periods in the future.

We used this formula to forecast beer production in 1982. These forecasts are shown in Table 14.11 (p. 750). Again, these values were found from the EXSMOOTH computer program. However, hand calculations are certainly possible. For example, the forecast for June 1982, made at the end of 1981, is

$$F_{60+6} = (L_{60} + 6T_{60})S_{60-12+6} = [16.87 + 6(.01)]1.08 = 18.28$$

Notice that the seasonal factor, S_{54}, is from June 1981, exactly one year prior to the month for which the forecast is being made.

Table 14.11   Forecasts of 1982 Made
in December 1981

Month	Forecast
January	14.35
February	14.86
March	17.07
April	17.42
May	18.44
June	18.28
July	18.46
August	17.63
September	15.77
October	14.93
November	13.24
December	13.25

14.6

Forecasting with Regression

In this section we look at ways of using regression for time series analysis and forecasting. This may appear to be a very natural approach to time series analysis, given what we know about regression. First, the computer packages available for doing regression are simple to use and are easily accessible. Second, many time series are related in obvious ways to other time series. For example, monthly sales levels are related to monthly advertising levels, so it seems natural to regress sales on advertising. Then we would forecast future sales by substituting planned advertising levels into the estimated regression equation.

Regression is indeed used in time series analysis, as we discussed in Chapters 11 and 12. However, we encounter difficulties when we attempt to use ordinary least squares regression for time series data. The most serious of these difficulties is autocorrelated errors, that is, errors that are correlated with one another. Basically, these occur when the errors in successive time periods exhibit some type of nonrandom pattern. They might remain positive for several consecutive months, then become negative for several consecutive months, then become positive again, and so on. Or they might exhibit a seasonal pattern. Whenever autocorrelation occurs, there is a good chance that the results of an ordinary least squares analysis are not entirely valid.

A related difficulty is how to deal with *lagged* variables. These are values of the variables that were observed in previous time periods. The need for these is often clear. For example, if we wish to explain sales by advertising, the following regression equation might be estimated:

$$\text{SALES}_t = \beta_0 + \beta_1 \text{AD}_t + \beta_2 \text{AD}_{t-1} + \beta_3 \text{AD}_{t-2} + \epsilon_t$$

Here AD_t, AD_{t-1}, and AD_{t-2} are the advertising levels in months t, $t-1$, and $t-2$, respectively. The variables AD_{t-1} and AD_{t-2} are the lagged variables; they represent past time periods. We say that AD_{t-1} is lagged one period and that AD_{t-2} is lagged two periods. The equation above is a natural one to test, for it is quite plausible that current sales depend not only on this month's advertising level, but also on advertising levels from the past two months.

There is no particular difficulty in *estimating* the equation above. We simply treat AD_{t-2}, AD_{t-1}, and AD_t as three separate independent variables and proceed as usual. The difficulties are (1) knowing *which* lagged variables to include in the equation, and (2) knowing whether the presence of lagged variables will create violations of the ordinary least squares assumptions, particularly autocorrelation. We will not discuss these two issues in much detail because they are quite difficult to resolve. In fact, they are the subject of a whole area of statistics called *econometrics*. We will only discuss some of the most important points.

If the only lagged variables to be introduced are lagged *independent* variables, all we need to do is determine how many periods in the past have a significant influence on the present. Should advertising levels from more than two months be used in the equation, or are their effects no longer important given the advertising levels from more recent months? Questions such as these can usually be answered by fitting several regression equations and noticing at which lags the β values start to drop off. For example, if the AD_{t-2} term has a relatively small estimated β coefficient, we might decide to ignore lags of two months or more. Consider the following example.

EXAMPLE 14.7

The data in Table 14.12 (pp. 752–753) represent monthly sales (in hundreds of units) and monthly advertising levels (as a percentage of total expenses) for a particular company. These data are from January 1976 through January 1980. Examine the relationship between sales and advertising, using lagged values of advertising if necessary. (The data in this example have been chosen so that trend and seasonality are not an issue.) Then use the final regression equation to forecast sales for February and March of 1980 if advertising levels in these two months are 5.372% and 7.920%.

Table 14.12

Month	SALES	AD	AD (lag 1)	AD (lag 2)
1/76	91.821	3.922	8.779	2.595
2/76	55.675	4.284	3.922	8.779
3/76	77.561	7.664	4.284	3.922
4/76	87.197	7.469	7.664	4.284
5/76	97.415	7.847	7.469	7.664
6/76	116.103	9.486	7.847	7.469
7/76	69.545	1.732	9.486	7.847
8/76	50.198	4.631	1.732	9.486
9/76	47.994	4.518	4.631	1.732
10/76	67.203	8.803	4.518	4.631
11/76	90.945	5.542	8.803	4.518
12/76	87.389	5.455	5.542	8.803
1/77	76.727	5.985	5.455	5.542
2/77	94.960	7.047	5.985	5.455
3/77	97.576	6.075	7.047	5.985
4/77	86.183	8.001	6.075	7.047
5/77	104.139	7.790	8.001	6.075
6/77	120.274	9.151	7.790	8.001
7/77	106.735	5.058	9.151	7.790
8/77	73.033	5.696	5.058	9.151
9/77	80.359	7.465	5.696	5.058
10/77	90.218	4.660	7.465	5.696
11/77	79.446	6.457	4.660	7.465
12/77	56.687	3.834	6.457	4.660
1/78	65.372	7.038	3.834	6.457

SOLUTION

The last two columns of Table 14.12 show the lagged advertising levels, for lags of 1 and 2 months, respectively. Notice that the lag 1 levels are shifted by one month from the original advertising column and that they begin one month earlier (with December 1975). Similarly, the lag 2 levels are shifted by two months from the original advertising levels, and they begin with the

Exhibit 14.1   Correlations Among Independent Variables in Example 14.7

	SALES	AD	AD-1	AD-2
SALES	1.00			
AD	0.61	1.00		
AD-1	0.67	0.06	1.00	
AD-2	0.04	-0.11	0.01	1.00

Table 14.12 Continued

Month	SALES	AD	AD (lag 1)	AD (lag 2)
2/78	73.277	4.239	7.038	3.834
3/78	31.716	3.982	4.239	7.038
4/78	68.436	6.074	3.982	4.239
5/78	85.267	7.527	6.074	3.982
6/78	89.608	6.171	7.527	6.074
7/78	82.782	5.585	6.171	7.527
8/78	57.363	2.946	5.585	6.171
9/78	65.492	5.441	2.946	5.585
10/78	98.284	4.854	5.441	2.946
11/78	75.362	5.959	4.854	5.441
12/78	82.595	6.343	5.959	4.854
1/79	57.097	3.283	6.343	5.959
2/79	25.548	1.305	3.283	6.343
3/79	24.903	4.042	1.305	3.283
4/79	92.552	10.029	4.042	1.305
5/79	92.990	4.049	10.029	4.042
6/79	79.059	5.657	4.049	10.029
7/79	72.833	6.511	5.657	4.049
8/79	86.196	6.133	6.511	5.657
9/79	51.182	3.725	6.133	6.511
10/79	48.145	3.660	3.725	6.133
11/79	72.812	6.286	3.660	3.725
12/79	78.282	5.651	6.286	3.660
1/80	82.041	3.790	5.651	6.286

November 1975 level. The dependent variable is $SALES_t$, while the possible independent variables are AD_t, AD_{t-1}, and AD_{t-2}. (These variables are labeled AD, AD-1, and AD-2 in the following exhibits, all of which come from the IDA computer package.) The correlations between these variables are shown in Exhibit 14.1. Here we see that AD_t and AD_{t-1} are highly correlated with $SALES_t$ and that AD_{t-2} is only slightly correlated with $SALES_t$. This suggests that AD_t and AD_{t-1} should be in the equation for $SALES_t$, but that AD_{t-2} may not be needed. The correlation matrix also shows that the independent variables are practically uncorrelated with one another. This means that multicollinearity is not a problem in this example.

The scattergrams (again from IDA) shown in Exhibit 14.2 (p. 754) confirm the relationships between the independent and dependent variables. (Each number in these scattergrams tells how many points lie in a given position on the graph.) We see a definite indication of an upward-sloping straight line in the graphs of $SALES_t$ versus AD_t and $SALES_t$ versus AD_{t-1}, but we see no such indication in the graph of $SALES_t$ versus AD_{t-2}.

Exhibit 14.2   Scattergrams of Dependent Versus Independent
Variables

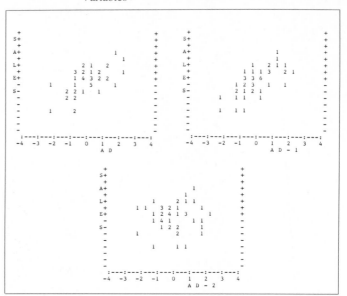

We estimated three regression equations, one with AD_t only, one with AD_t and AD_{t-1} only, and one with all three independent variables. Exhibit 14.3 shows the coefficients of these three equations as well as their summary statistics. It is clear that the second equation is a definite improvement over the first (since R^2 increases from .374 to .781), but that the third equation is only a minor improvement over the second (since R^2 increases only from .781 to .790). Nevertheless, the t value for the coefficient of AD_{t-2} in the third equation is 1.45, which is significantly nonzero at the 20% level (for a two-tailed test). Therefore, we may wish to keep AD_{t-2} in the equation. The ANOVA table for this final equation is shown in Exhibit 14.4. It leaves no doubt that advertising values are useful in explaining sales.

Because the data in this example are time series data, autocorrelation is a potential problem. Therefore, we show a plot of the residuals (versus time) in Exhibit 14.5. Since the errors vary fairly randomly (there are no obvious patterns), we conclude that autocorrelated errors are not a serious problem in this example. This conclusion is supported by the Durbin–Watson statistic (not shown) of 1.63, which is reasonably close to 2.

If we wish to forecast sales in February and March 1980, we use the equation (from Exhibit 14.3)

$$\widehat{SALES}_t = -6.2 + 6.448AD_t + 6.936AD_{t-1} + 1.055AD_{t-2}$$

Exhibit 14.3 Outputs for Three Regression Equations for Example 14.7

```
VARIABLE      B(STD.V)          B          STD.ERROR(B)      T

AD             0.6119      6.7682E+00      1.2762E+00      5.303
CONSTANT       0           3.8041E+01      7.6226E+00      4.991

                    MULTIPLE R          R-SQUARE
UNADJUSTED           0.6119              0.3744
 ADJUSTED            0.6009              0.3611

STD. DEV. OF RESIDUALS = 1.6763E+01
N =   49

VARIABLE      B(STD.V)          B          STD.ERROR(B)      T

AD             0.5716      6.3230E+00      7.6563E-01      8.259
AD-1           0.6385      6.9510E+00      7.5346E-01      9.225
CONSTANT       0           4.4273E-01      6.1188E+00      0.072

                    MULTIPLE R          R-SQUARE
UNADJUSTED           0.8835              0.7805
 ADJUSTED            0.8780              0.7710

STD. DEV. OF RESIDUALS = 1.0036E+01
N =   49

VARIABLE      B(STD.V)          B          STD.ERROR(B)      T

AD             0.5829      6.4475E+00      7.6149E-01      8.467
AD-1           0.6371      6.9358E+00      7.4468E-01      9.314
AD-2           0.0996      1.0552E+00      7.2798E-01      1.450
CONSTANT       0          -6.2009E+00      7.5876E+00     -0.817

                    MULTIPLE R          R-SQUARE
UNADJUSTED           0.8890              0.7903
 ADJUSTED            0.8811              0.7763

STD. DEV. OF RESIDUALS = 9.9185E+00
N =   49
```

In February 1980, the relevant advertising levels are $AD_t = 5.372$ (February 1980), $AD_{t-1} = 3.790$ (January 1980), and $AD_{t-2} = 5.651$ (December 1979). The resulting forecast of sales is

$$\widehat{SALES} = -6.2 + 6.448(5.372) + 6.936(3.790) + 1.055(5.651)$$
$$= 60.688 \quad \text{(or 6069 units)}$$

Exhibit 14.4 ANOVA For Final Regression Equation in Example 14.7

```
ANOVA

 SOURCE           SS         DF          MS            F
REGRESSION    1.66826E+04     3      5.56088E+03    56.53
RESIDUALS     4.42692E+03    45      9.83761E+01
 TOTAL        2.11096E+04    48      4.39782E+02
```

Exhibit 14.5   Plot of Residuals Versus Time

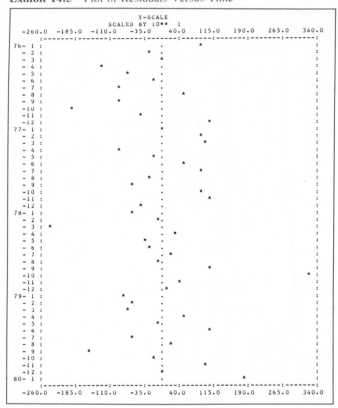

For March 1980, the relevant advertising levels are $AD_t = 7.920$ (March 1980), $AD_{t-1} = 5.372$ (February 1980), and $AD_{t-2} = 3.790$ (January 1980). The resulting forecast of sales is

$$\widehat{SALES} = -6.2 + 6.448(7.920) + 6.936(5.372) + 1.055(3.790)$$
$$= 86.127 \quad \text{(or 8613 units)}$$

There are other lagged terms that we can include in a regression equation besides lagged independent variables. We are allowed, and it is perfectly sensible, to include lagged *dependent* variables on the right-hand side of the equation. One possibility is as follows:

$$SALES_t = \beta_0 + \beta_1 SALES_{t-1} + \beta_2 AD_t + \beta_3 AD_{t-1} + \epsilon_t$$

Now the sales level in month t is being explained by sales in the previous month and advertising levels in the current month and the previous month. One other possibility is to include lagged values of the error terms, with coefficients that must be estimated. One possibility is

$$\text{SALES}_t = \beta_0 + \beta_1 \text{SALES}_{t-1} + \beta_2 \text{AD}_t + \beta_3 \text{AD}_{t-1} + \beta_4 \epsilon_{t-1} + \epsilon_t$$

When we use lagged terms in regression equations, particularly lagged dependent variables and lagged error terms, we are practically assured of significant autocorrelation. This autocorrelation is not necessarily bad; it simply has to be dealt with explicitly, and the ordinary least squares analysis from Chapters 11 and 12 does not do this. One of the best known and systematic methods for dealing with these types of equations and the associated autocorrelation is the *Box–Jenkins method* (named for its two originators). In Box–Jenkins time series analysis, the *only* variables on the right-hand side of the regression equation are lagged dependent variables and the current and lagged error terms. So for these models, the time series is explaining itself entirely by its *own* past movements. The Box–Jenkins approach has become very popular recently, partly because of its great flexibility and partly because it has been computerized. (It is in the most recent version of SPSS and in IDA, for example.) From a mathematical standpoint, however, the Box–Jenkins approach is quite difficult, and we will not discuss it any further in this book.

Measuring Autocorrelation

We have talked about a sequence of errors being autocorrelated. We now see how to measure autocorrelation. There are really no new concepts involved. All we need to do is specialize the correlation formula from Chapter 2 (or Chapter 11) to a somewhat new situation.

Consider two sequences of observations, $X_1, X_2, \ldots, X_n$ and $Y_1, Y_2, \ldots, Y_n$. We assume that these sequences come in pairs, so that X_1 is paired with Y_1, X_2 is paired with Y_2, and so on. Then from Chapter 2, the correlation between these two sequences is

$$r = \frac{\sum X_i Y_i - (\sum X_i)(\sum Y_i)/n}{\sqrt{\sum X_i^2 - (\sum X_i)^2/n}\ \sqrt{\sum Y_i^2 - (\sum Y_i)^2/n}}$$

This formula holds for *any* two sequences that can be paired.

Now consider a time series $Y_1, Y_2, \ldots, Y_T$, and let k be any positive integer. (The value of k will typically be much less than the number of observations T.) Suppose that we pair the original Y's with Y's that are lagged k periods, as indicated below:

$$
\begin{array}{cccc|cccccc}
Y_1 & Y_2 & \cdots & Y_k & Y_{k+1} & Y_{k+2} & \cdots & Y_{T-1} & & Y_T \\
 & & & & Y_1 & Y_2 & \cdots & Y_{T-k-1} & & Y_{T-k}
\end{array}
$$

The sequence on the bottom is k periods off, observation by observation, from the sequence on the top. Because there are no observations before period 1, the first k observations on the top cannot be paired with any observations below. Therefore, we have only $T - k$ *pairs* of observations. We define the *autocorrelation of lag k* of the series to be the (usual) correlation between these two paired sequences of $T - k$ observations each. Letting r_k be the symbol for this autocorrelation, the formula for r_k is given below.

$$\textit{Autocorrelation of Lag k}$$

$$r_k = \frac{\Sigma\, Y_t Y_{t-k} - (\Sigma\, Y_t)(\Sigma\, Y_{t-k})/(T - k)}{\sqrt{\Sigma\, Y_t^2 - (\Sigma\, Y_t)^2/(T - k)}\ \sqrt{\Sigma\, Y_{t-k}^2 - (\Sigma\, Y_{t-k})^2/(T - k)}}$$

Since r_k is a correlation, its value is always between -1 and $+1$. Its magnitude tells us how strong the relationship is between an observation at one point in time and the corresponding observation k periods ago. The usual value of k we examine is $k = 1$. This is because r_1 indicates the correlation between *adjacent* observations. If the data are seasonal, we might also be interested in r_4 (for quarterly data) or r_{12} (for monthly data). As an example, if a product is seasonal, monthly sales in June might be correlated with sales in the previous May (measured by r_1) and with sales in the previous June (measured by r_{12}).

Many computer packages relieve us of the arithmetic calculations required

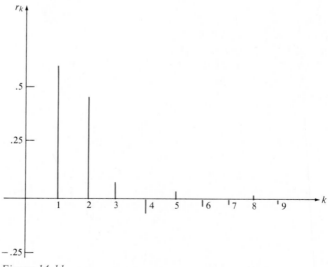

Figure 14.11
Correlogram

to compute the r_k's. For example, these can be found from IDA by using the command "AUTO." A graph of these r_k values versus k, called a *correlogram*, is also provided by most packages. The correlogram shown in Figure 14.11, for example, indicates fairly high positive autocorrelations at lags 1 and 2 and rather negligible autocorrelations at higher lags. A correlogram is indispensable for more sophisticated approaches to time series analysis, such as the Box–Jenkins method.

EXAMPLE 14.7 (continued)

Examine the autocorrelations between the residuals for the sales versus advertising regression equation that uses AD_t, AD_{t-1}, and AD_{t-2} as the independent variables. Do this for all lags k from 1 to 12.

SOLUTION

The values of r_k for k from 1 to 12 would be extremely tedious to calculate by hand. However, we obtain them easily from IDA by using the command "AUTO" and then specifying the variable desired (RESIDUAL) and the maximum number of lags (12). The information in Exhibit 14.6 is received.

Exhibit 14.6 Examination of Autocorrelations for Example 14.7

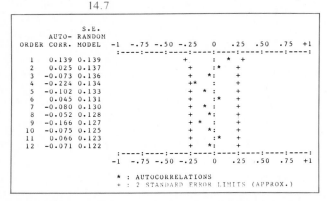

(Here "ORDER" refers to lags.) The values under "AUTOCORR." are the r_k's. For example, $r_2 = .025$, a very small correlation. The "S.E. RANDOM MODEL" column shows the standard error of each r_k if there were really no autocorrelation in the population. (The mean of each r_k would then be 0.) Therefore, if each r_k in the diagram (shown by a *) is within the 2 standard error limits (shown by +'s), we can be reasonably confident that autocorrelated errors are not a problem. Obviously, each r_k is within these limits in the diagram. So we have another confirmation (in addition to those discussed earlier) that there is no serious autocorrelation in this example.

Problems for Sections 14.5, 14.6

20. Explain the effect of using a small value of the smoothing constant α in simple exponential smoothing. How is this different from using a large value of α? Why is it difficult to predict which will be better for forecasting the future?

21. a. Exponentially smooth the accident data in Table 14.7, but now use the smoothing constant $\alpha = .1$. (Use $L_0 = 25$.)
    b. Graph the levels from part (a) as a time series, and verify that you obtain a "smoother" graph than either graph in Figure 14.10. Why would you expect it to be smoother?

22. How is Winters' method better than simple exponential smoothing? Are there any reasons you can think of why a manager would prefer to use simple exponential smoothing rather than Winters' method?

23. The equations for L_t, T_t, and S_t in Winters' method are each weighted averages of two separate estimates of these quantities. For example, L_t is a weighted average of Y_t/S_{t-M} and $L_{t-1} + T_{t-1}$. Explain intuitively why each of these equations (the one for L_t, the one for T_t, and the one for S_t) makes sense.

24. Is the quantity $S_t L_t$ a seasonalized or deseasonalized estimate of Y_t? What should you do to deseasonalize the value Y_t, divide by the appropriate S or multiply by it? Explain and illustrate with a numerical example.

25. Suppose that we have quarterly data for 1976 through 1980 (20 observations). After using a computer program to implement Winters' method, we obtain $L_{20} = 760$, $T_{20} = 10$, $S_{17} = .9$, $S_{18} = 1.2$, $S_{19} = 1.2$, and $S_{20} = .7$.
    a. Describe any trend and seasonal patterns that appear to be present.
    b. Forecast the values of Y for the four quarters of 1981.

26. For the beer data in Table 14.9, use simple exponential smoothing with $L_0 = 13.6$ and $\alpha = .3$ to obtain forecasts for 1977 and 1978. (That is, work through only two years of data.) Compare these with the forecasts in Table 14.10. Does it appear that the forecasts in Table 14.10 are better? Illustrate graphically. (Plot the sequence of actual observations together with both sequences of forecasts.) Calculate MAD.

27. Suppose that we estimate a regression equation for Y_t and find the following estimated $\hat{Y}_t$'s. Graph the residuals, the $\hat{\epsilon}_t$'s. Would you say that autocorrelated errors present a serious problem? Explain. Calculate r_1, the one-period autocorrelation for the $\hat{\epsilon}$'s.

t	Y Observed	Y Estimated
1	13.718	13.877
2	13.771	13.879
3	13.912	13.858
4	13.949	13.866
5	13.924	13.883
6	13.944	13.950
7	14.119	14.022
8	14.184	14.143
9	14.218	14.207
10	14.262	14.222
11	14.306	14.283
12	14.222	14.278
13	14.276	14.291
14	14.285	14.328
15	14.359	14.362

28. Consider the following two possible graphs of residuals from a regression analysis. What would you expect of r_1, the autocorrelation of lag 1, for each of these graphs? Would you expect r_1 to be large or small in magnitude? What about its sign, positive or negative? Explain your reasoning.

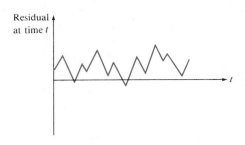

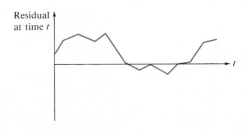

29. Use simple exponential smoothing with $\alpha = .3$ and $L_0 = .13$ to smooth the data in Problem 17 (p. 739). Then calculate the forecast errors $E_t = Y_t - F_t$ and graph them on a time series graph. Explain the presence of any obvious patterns, if any, in this graph.

30. The data shown below exhibit a perfect linear trend, that is, each observation is 3 units higher than the previous observation.

t	Observation
1	10
2	13
3	16
4	19
5	22
6	25
7	28
8	31
9	34
10	37

a. Starting with $L_0 = 7$, use simple exponential smoothing with $\alpha = .5$ to find the forecasts (the F_t's) of these data.
b. Graph the Y_t's and the F_t's on the same graph.
c. What appears to happen when you use simple exponential smoothing to forecast a time series with a linear trend?

31. The total sales Y_t (in millions of dollars) of all eating and drinking establishments in the United States was regressed against total sales X_t (also in millions of dollars) of all grocery stores in the United States and time t from 1969 to 1980. (Reference: U.S. Department of Commerce.) That is, Y_t was explained by the two independent variables X_t and t. The following data were used to produce the estimated regression equation shown below.

$$\hat{Y}_t = -8376 - 83.375t + .481X_t$$

Year	t	X_t	Y_t
1969	1	74,460	28,084
1970	2	82,474	31,463
1971	3	85,330	32,868

(continued)

Year	t	X_t	Y_t
1972	4	91,685	36,180
1973	5	103,508	40,402
1974	6	117,199	44,673
1975	7	129,182	51,067
1976	8	138,172	57,211
1977	9	147,759	63,276
1978	10	162,705	70,679
1979	11	182,365	79,576
1980	12	202,065	86,612

a. Calculate the residuals, $Y_t - \hat{Y}_t$, and graph these residuals on a time series graph. Does there appear to be any autocorrelation of the residuals?
b. Calculate r_1, the autocorrelation of the residuals corresponding to a one-year lag. Does its value go along with your answer to problem (a)? Explain.

32. The following correlogram of the residuals from a time series regression analysis is obtained. Each period corresponds to a quarter (three months). Explain what this graph tells us about the autocorrelation pattern of the residuals.

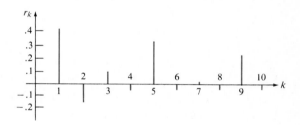

33. Consider a time series of gas bills for a homeowner in Michigan who heats his house with natural gas. Each month for a period of several years we observe the quantity of gas used, Y_t, measured in hundreds of cubic feet. Assuming that the homeowner has not made any radical changes in his heating system during these years, what would we expect r_1, r_6, and r_{12} to be (approximately)? Explain. (Here r_k is the autocorrelation between Y's taken k months apart.)

14.7

Index Numbers

Economic variables, particularly prices, are constantly changing through time. It is convenient and often necessary to compare these variables at two or more points in time. Index numbers provide a meaningful way of doing this. The Consumer Price Index (CPI) is one of the most popular indexes. If its value is 227 in a given year, for example, we know that current prices are approximately 127% above the prices in a "base" period (1967), when the index was equal to 100. Since there are so many references to index numbers in magazines, in newspapers, and on television, it is important for people in business and economics to have an understanding of these indexes. In this section we see how index numbers are computed, and we see their implications as well as their shortcomings.

Price Relatives and Aggregate Price Indexes

Suppose that we wish to compare the price of a given product at two different points in time. The simplest way to do this is to call one of the time periods the *base* period and to compare the price in the other time period with the price in the base period. We do this by means of a *price relative*. Letting the subscript 0 denote the base period, the subscript t denote the other time period, and letting P_t and P_0 denote the prices for these periods, we have

$$\text{\textit{Price Relative at Time t}}$$

$$\frac{P_t}{P_0} \times 100$$

As usual, the factor 100 converts the ratio P_t/P_0 into a percentage. Therefore, the price relative tells us what percentage of the base price the price in period t is. For example, suppose that a gallon of regular gasoline cost \$1.00 in the base period, and four years later it cost \$1.30. Then the price relative for this later time period is

$$\frac{P_t}{P_0} \times 100 = \frac{1.30}{1.00} \times 100 = 130$$

We interpret this by saying that the price at the later time period is 30% larger than in the base period.

A price relative can be computed for each product separately, but we often want an *aggregate* index of price changes for all products. Clearly, some prices go up and some go down, but what we want is the overall effect. One way to measure the overall price change is given by the following *unweighted aggregate price index*, labeled UWI_t.

$$\text{\textit{Unweighted Aggregate Price Index}}$$

$$\text{UWI}_t = \frac{\sum P_{it}}{\sum P_{i0}} \times 100$$

Here P_{it} and P_{i0} are the prices of product i in time period t and the base period, respectively, and the sums are taken over all products.

To illustrate this aggregate index and its shortcomings, suppose that we are considering four products: a shirt, a gallon of milk, a lawn mower, and a sofa. The prices of these in the base period and the current period are shown in Table 14.13. The price relatives for these products are also shown.

Table 14.13

Product	i	P_{i0}	P_{it}	$P_{it}/P_{i0} \times 100$
Shirt	1	$ 12	$ 18	150
Gallon of milk	2	1.60	2	125
Lawn mower	3	150	250	167
Sofa	4	400	800	200

The unweighted aggregate price index is given by

$$\text{UWI}_t = \frac{\Sigma P_{it}}{\Sigma P_{i0}} \times 100$$

$$= \frac{18 + 2 + 250 + 800}{12 + 1.60 + 150 + 400} \times 100 = 190$$

Apparently prices rose by 90%. But notice that this index is primarily a result of the price increases in the two expensive products, sofas and lawn mowers. To make this more apparent, assume instead that the price of a gallon of milk increases from $1.60 to $4.80, for a price relative of 300. This huge increase in the price of milk hardly changes the unweighted index. Its new value (rounded to the nearest integer) is

$$\text{UWI}_t = \frac{18 + 4.80 + 250 + 800}{12 + 1.60 + 150 + 400} \times 100 = 190$$

But if the price of a sofa increases from $400 to $1000 (instead of $800), for a price relative of 250, the unweighted index changes dramatically. Now its value is

$$\text{UWI}_t = \frac{18 + 2 + 250 + 1000}{12 + 1.60 + 150 + 400} \times 100 = 225$$

As consumers, we do not want an aggregate price index to be so heavily influenced by expensive products we buy infrequently. In the example above, our cost of living will probably not change much if lawn mowers or sofas increase in price because we buy these items so infrequently. But for a typical family (with a lot of hungry, growing children!), price increases in food items such as milk can make a relatively large difference in the family's yearly expenses. In order to reflect each product's *usage* as well as its per unit price, we use a *weighted aggregate price index*, labeled WI_t.

Weighted Aggregate Price Index

$$\text{WI}_t = \frac{\sum P_{it}Q_i}{\sum P_{i0}Q_i} \times 100$$

Here Q_i is the average quantity of product i purchased per year, so that $P_{it}Q_i$ is the total amount spent on product i in period t.

To see how this index compares with the unweighted index, again consider the four products and their prices listed in Table 14.13. Suppose that the average family buys 25 shirts per year, 75 gallons of milk per year, a new lawn mower every four years, and a new sofa every five years. These translate into the average yearly quantities $Q_1 = 25$, $Q_2 = 75$, $Q_3 = \frac{1}{4} = .25$, and $Q_4 = \frac{1}{5} = .2$. Then the weighted aggregate index is

$$\text{WI}_t = \frac{18 \times 25 + 2 \times 75 + 250 \times .25 + 800 \times .2}{12 \times 25 + 1.60 \times 75 + 150 \times .25 + 400 \times .2} \times 100 = 153$$

This is much less than $\text{UWI}_t = 190$, for the simple reason that the typical family's most used items (shirts and milk) have not gone up in price as much as the items they purchase infrequently.

The weighted index can be expressed in an alternative way, as a weighted average of the price relatives for the various products. (In general, a *weighted average* of any n numbers $x_1, x_2, \ldots, x_n$, with nonnegative weights $w_1, w_2, \ldots, w_n$, is the ratio $\sum x_i w_i / \sum w_i$. This average is always between the largest and the smallest of the x's.) We write

$$\text{WI}_t = \frac{\sum P_{it}Q_i}{\sum P_{i0}Q_i} \times 100$$

$$= \frac{\sum (P_{it}/P_{i0} \times 100)P_{i0}Q_i}{\sum P_{i0}Q_i}$$

$$= \frac{\sum (P_{it}/P_{i0} \times 100)w_i}{\sum w_i}$$

$$= \frac{\sum (\text{price relative of product } i)w_i}{\sum w_i}$$

where the weight w_i is the total amount paid for product i with base period prices, $P_{i0}Q_i$. This formula gives us another (equivalent) way of computing

WI$_t$. It also explains why the weighted aggregate price index is always between the smallest and the largest of the price relatives. In the above example $w_1 = 12(25) = 300$, $w_2 = 1.60(75) = 120$, $w_3 = 150(.25) = 37.50$, and $w_4 = 400(.2) = 80$. So we can also compute WI$_t$ from

$$\text{WI}_t = \frac{\Sigma\ (P_{it}/P_{i0} \times 100)w_i}{\Sigma\ w_i}$$

$$= \frac{150(300)\ +\ 125(120)\ +\ 167(37.5)\ +\ 200(80)}{300\ +\ 120\ +\ 37.5\ +\ 80}$$

$$= 153$$

Notice that the price relative for shirts receives the largest weight, while the price relative for lawn mowers receives the smallest weight.

An unweighted aggregate price index is clearly inferior to one that is weighted, so we will not consider unweighted indexes any more in this chapter. But even with weighted indexes, we have a practical problem. How do we choose the quantities, the Q's, to be used in the weighting scheme? The problem is that buying patterns change through the years. For example, people are spending large amounts of money on personal computer equipment and exercise equipment, items they hardly ever purchased in earlier years. If the Q's for these products are measured by the base period quantities, or even by the average yearly quantities for all years since the base period, they will underestimate the importance of these products for today's consumers. In a case like this, it is difficult to decide which Q's we should use in the weighting formula. Should we use the earlier ones, the later ones, or some type of average? We will look at three possibilities below.

It seems natural that if we use a base year for comparing current prices, we should also use the quantities purchased in the base year for the weighted index. If we do so, the resulting index is called a *Laspeyres index*. It is given by

Laspeyres Index

Laspeyres Price Index

$$\frac{\Sigma\ P_{it}Q_{i0}}{\Sigma\ P_{i0}Q_{i0}} \times 100$$

Here Q_{i0} is the quantity of product i purchased in the base year.

There are distinct advantages and disadvantages to this index. The main advantages are that (1) the quantities, the Q's, need to be estimated for only one year, the base year; and (2) the indexes for all years that use the same base are directly comparable, each being based on the same "shopping cart" of goods. The main disadvantage of the Laspeyres index is what we discussed above. Consumer buying habits may have changed significantly from the base year. If the base year Q's no longer represent what today's consumers buy, the Laspeyres index can be very misleading.

Paasche Index

Since the base year Q's may no longer be current, perhaps we should base the index on the current Q's. If we do so, we obtain the *Paasche index*, given by

> ### Paasche Price Index
>
> $$\frac{\Sigma P_{it} Q_{it}}{\Sigma P_{i0} Q_{it}} \times 100$$

Here Q_{it} is the quantity of product i purchased in period t, so that $P_{it} Q_{it}$ is the total amount spent for product i in period t.

The advantage of the Paasche index is an obvious one, namely, that we are comparing the total price of today's goods with the total price this *same* amount of goods would have cost (if it had been purchased) in the base period. There are, unfortunately, two disadvantages to using this index. The first is that the Q's must be updated every year, which can be a very costly, time-consuming job. The second disadvantage is that indexes for different years (with the same base year) are not directly comparable because they are based on different quantities. This tends to defeat the original purpose of the price index, namely, to make meaningful comparisons of price levels in different time periods. For these reasons, a Paasche index is seldom used.

Fixed Weights Index

A compromise between the two methods discussed above is to choose a representative year (other than the base year) and then use the quantities from this year for the indexes of all future years. (As a practical matter, if consumer behavior changes significantly from what it was in the representative year, the Q's may be updated from time to time. This is done, for example, with the CPI.) The resulting index is called a *fixed weights index* and is given by

> ### Fixed Weights Price Index
>
> $$\frac{\Sigma P_{it} Q_i}{\Sigma P_{i0} Q_i} \times 100$$

Here Q_i is the quantity of product i purchased in a representative year, so that $P_{it} Q_i$ is the amount that would be spent on product i in period t if this same quantity were purchased in period t.

There are none of the obvious disadvantages of the fixed weights index that we discussed with the Laspeyres and Paasche indexes. If the representative year is chosen carefully (and the Q's are updated as necessary, as mentioned in the preceding paragraph), the fixed weights index allows us to make a meaningful comparison between today's prices and those of recent years. The weights do not become outdated as quickly as they do for a Laspeyres index, and we avoid the expense of estimating new Q's *every* year as with the Paasche index.

To illustrate these weighted indexes, consider the hypothetical data for four products listed in Table 14.14. The prices and quantities of these products for the years 1979 through 1985 are shown. We let 1979 be the base year. The prices are in dollars and are the top figure in each cell. The quantities are in millions and are the bottom figure in each cell.

Table 14.14

	Year						
Product	1979	1980	1981	1982	1983	1984	1985
1	22	22	23	23	26	27	30
	18	16	15	15	14	15	16
2	1.50	1.60	1.50	1.70	2.00	2.10	2.30
	215	200	220	230	210	200	190
3	10	15	17	18	20	21	22
	35	35	30	30	28	30	33
4	100	105	110	110	105	105	110
	8	10	12	12	15	18	15

The Laspeyres index uses the quantities (and prices) in the base year (1979) column for computing *each* year's index. For example, the 1983 index is

$$\frac{26(18) + 2(215) + 20(35) + 105(8)}{20(18) + 1.5(215) + 10(35) + 100(8)} \times 100 = 133$$

The Paasche index uses the quantities for each separate year to calculate that year's index. For example, the 1983 Paasche index is

$$\frac{26(14) + 2(210) + 20(28) + 105(15)}{20(14) + 1.5(210) + 10(28) + 100(15)} \times 100 = 123$$

The fixed weights index uses the quantities from a representative year to compute each year's index. For illustrative purposes we use 1981 as the

Table 14.15

	Year						
Index	1979	1980	1981	1982	1983	1984	1985
Laspeyres	100	115	121	125	133	137	146
Paasche	100	114	118	121	123	124	135
Fixed weights	100	112	118	121	126	129	138

representative year. Then again using 1983 as an example, its fixed weights index is

$$\frac{26(15) + 2(220) + 20(30) + 105(12)}{20(15) + 1.5(220) + 10(30) + 100(12)} \times 100 = 126$$

All the price indexes for these seven years are shown in Table 14.15. The differences between the three types of indexes become even more apparent when we graph them as a time series, as in Figure 14.12.

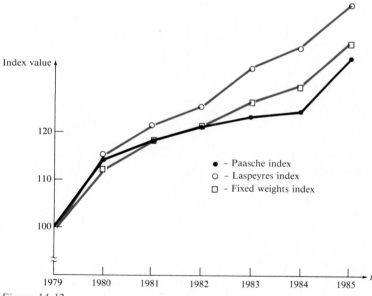

Figure 14.12

The Consumer Price Index

The Consumer Price Index (CPI) is undoubtedly the best known of all the many indexes that are computed regularly. It is also one of the most important indexes in terms of its real effects on economic decisions. Therefore, we will close this section by discussing the meaning of the CPI, some of its effects on other economic variables, and some of its deficiencies.

The CPI is a measure of the cost of living for the typical family in the United States. It is based on a "shopping cart" of approximately 400 items that Americans buy regularly, such as food items, medical supplies, housing, transportation, and clothing. The 400 items included in the list comprise a representative sample of all items Americans purchase, and the list is updated periodically to reflect changes in buying habits. From these 400 items a type of fixed weights index is computed, with 1967 as the base year. (This base year is due to change in the future.) The quantities, the Q's, that make up the weights are not really "fixed" but are updated whenever necessary. It should be noted that the gathering of data for estimating and updating the Q's is very complicated, time-consuming, and expensive.

It is sometimes tempting to regard the CPI as a curiosity item and to underestimate its importance. For example, a family that owns a house, has a low mortgage rate, and does very little driving may not be too concerned if rises in mortgage rates, housing costs, and gasoline prices cause the CPI to increase dramatically. This family might argue that regardless of the CPI, its own cost of living depends on price changes in the specific items it typically purchases. This argument, however, neglects the fact that many economic variables are tied directly to changes in the CPI. For example, many unions have agreements whereby their wages automatically increase by a certain percentage of the increase in the CPI. Similarly, Social Security payments increase automatically when the CPI increases. Therefore, we are all directly or indirectly affected by changes in the CPI, regardless of whether we are heavy users of the items measured by the CPI. Bunke underscores the importance of the CPI in the following quote. (Reference: Harvey C. Bunke, "Indexing—It Grows on You," *Business Horizons*, Vol. 25, 1982, pp. 3–8.)

And so, in practice, indexing takes on a great importance because it is a determinant of how much of the economic pie each of us gets. Rather than some mysterious abstraction, it is an everyday pocketbook factor which affects the real income of everyone from the production worker in Peoria, Illinois, to the retiree living in Ft. Myers, Florida's Leisure Village, to the totally disabled Vietnam veteran in Seattle, Washington. Those who enjoy the benefits of indexing fight to retain it; those who don't have it, want it—all of which has made for steadily increasing use of indexing in recent years. Indeed, so great is the tendency to add the CPI escalator to everything from child support to collective bargaining contracts that the Bureau of Labor Statistics is unable to maintain an up-to-date list of the CPI index. Indexing, rather than being the property of a few statistical purists enchanted with the prospect of constructing the perfect model, is increasingly a matter of popular and political interest. About the twenty-fifth of each month millions of Americans watch the six o'clock news, intent on learning how much the CPI went up during the previous month.

The CPI is by no means a perfect indicator of the cost of living. There are bound to be several difficulties with any such index, no matter how it is computed. We list several of these.

1. Not all people buy the same items in the same quantities. Therefore, any index is an "average" that underestimates real price changes for some families and overestimates them for others.
2. It is virtually impossible to figure *quality* changes into any price index. If an item increases in price by 30% but its quality increases by at least this amount, is it fair to say that the item is really more expensive? What if the price remains the same but the quality deteriorates? Such quality changes obviously occur, but it is very difficult for any price index to capture them.
3. It is difficult to choose the "correct" base year. If prices in the base year are abnormally low, for example, the CPI in future years will be inflated. Also, it is difficult to know when to change the base year. If this is not done often enough, people are not able to make meaningful comparisons because they cannot remember what life was like that many years ago. But if the base year is changed too often, there are obvious costs involved.

The CPI suffers from the problems noted above and undoubtedly, others as well. But in spite of the fact that economists are continually trying to improve on the CPI, no general price index for consumers is ever likely to measure everyone's real cost of living accurately.

Problems for Section 14.7

34. Consider the following five products, with given prices (P_{i0}) in a base period, given prices (P_{it}) in a later period t, and average quantities purchased per year.

Product	Price in Base Year	Price in Year t	Average Quantity Purchased
1	$ 4.50	$ 5.65	55
2	20.70	29.45	10
3	150.89	141.59	1
4	35.79	48.89	5
5	680.00	850.00	.25

a. Calculate the price relatives for each of the five products.
b. Calculate the unweighted aggregate price index for these

five products in period t. Does this index underestimate or overestimate the real effect of price increases for an average consumer? Explain.
c. Calculate the weighted aggregate price index for these products in period t by two equivalent formulas, one using price relatives explicitly and one not using price relatives explicitly. Why is the answer between the smallest and largest of the five price relatives?

35. Other than the expense of updating the Q's each year, what is the major disadvantage of using a Paasche index? Why is this particularly serious when buying habits change significantly over time?

36. Given the following data on four representative products, calculate the Laspeyres index, the Paasche index, and the fixed weights index for all years after the base year, 1979.

Use 1981 as the representative year for the fixed weights index. (In each cell the top number is the per unit price, and the bottom number is the quantity consumed per person.)

| | | \multicolumn{5}{c}{Year} | | | | |
		1979	1980	1981	1982	1983
	1	$6.50	$7.00	$7.50	$8.00	$8.50
		25	30	35	30	35
	2	$25.00	$27.50	$30.00	$35.00	$40.00
		12	14	15	17	18
Product	3	$85.00	$90.00	$90.00	$95.00	$95.00
		2	2	2	2	2
	4	$15.00	$20.00	$28.00	$35.00	$40.00
		20	18	15	12	12

37. Consider a small company that has been monitoring its expenses over the past several years. The most important of these expenses are shown below. Using 1981 as the base year, calculate an unweighted aggregate price index for this company for the years 1982, 1983, and 1984. Is this unweighted index a useful measure of the company's increased costs during this period? Why or why not?

	1981	1982	1983	1984
Energy costs	$ 1,985	$ 2,140	$ 2,456	$ 2,754
Wages	15,450	17,590	19,740	23,450
Raw material	12,660	16,540	19,780	21,350
Equipment	7,650	7,420	7,790	8,320

38. Why is an unweighted aggregate price index usually inferior to a weighted index? Which types of products will the unweighted index tend to overemphasize, and which will it tend to underemphasize?

39. The following data represent prices and quantity of sales for the four leading brands of men's sport shirts at a particular department store. Calculate the Laspeyres price index for these shirts for each year, using 1978 as the base year. Compare this with a fixed weights price index that uses 1980 as the representative year.

| | | \multicolumn{5}{c}{Year} | | | | |
		1978	1979	1980	1981	1982
	1	$13.50	$13.75	$13.75	$14.00	$14.50
		525	570	660	690	770
	2	$18.00	$18.25	$18.75	$19.00	$20.00
Brand		380	450	360	320	350
of	3	$28.00	$29.00	$31.00	$33.00	$35.00
Shirt		460	520	540	580	620
	4	$35.50	$37.50	$38.00	$38.00	$38.50
		270	290	260	280	250

40. a. For the data in Problem 39, calculate the price relatives for each type of shirt in 1982, using 1978 as the base year. Then recalculate the Laspeyres index for 1982 as a weighted average of price relatives. What are the weights?

   b. For these same data, calculate the price relatives for the five brands of shirts in 1982, using 1980 as the base year. Then recalculate the fixed weights index for 1982 (again with 1980 as the representative year) as a weighted average of these price relatives. Now what are the weights?

Summary

One of the most important applications of statistics is analysis of time series data and forecasting. This chapter has presented a brief introduction to some of the methods most commonly used. Some of these methods, such as the ratio-to-moving average method, are "ad hoc" methods. That is, they are not based on statistical assumptions about a population from which a random sample is taken. This means that we cannot perform hypothesis tests or calculate confidence intervals as we did in earlier chapters. We simply do the numerical calculations and report the results. However, these ad hoc methods have been studied and applied for years with good results; they sometimes even outperform methods that are considerably more sophisticated and are based strictly on statistical theory.

Not all of the methods in this chapter have this ad hoc quality, however. There is a whole area of regression-type models, called Box–Jenkins models, that can be used to analyze time series data and make forecasts. (Even some exponential smoothing models are special cases of Box–Jenkins models.) This general category of models differs from the regression models we studied in Chapters 11 and 12 in two regards: (1) we now allow lagged variables, including lagged dependent variables and lagged error terms, on the right-hand side of the equation; and (2) we have to be very explicit about dealing with autocorrelation. The required analysis is well beyond the level of this book, but it is important to realize that Box–Jenkins models are being used increasingly often in applied time series studies.

Applications

Application 14.1   As we have seen, quantitative forecasting methods can be fairly complicated and usually require computer implementation. This statement pertains to methods we have discussed plus a number we have not discussed. Carbone and Gorr ran an experiment to see if forecasts using quantitative methods are really superior to those made by simply "eyeballing" the series and making an informed guess. (Reference: Robert Carbone and Wilpen L. Gorr, "Accuracy of Judgmental Forecasting of Time Series," *Decision Sciences,* Vol. 16, 1985, pp. 153–160.) They presented 10 time series (graphs plus data listings) to seven teams of students in a forecasting course. The most recent 6, 8, or 18 observations (depending on yearly, quarterly, or monthly data) were omitted from each series; the students were asked to forecast these observations. First, the students were asked to make eyeball judgment forecasts. Then they were instructed to use three objective, computerized methods to make forecasts. These methods had all been covered recently in the forecasting class. Finally, in light of the objective forecasts they had just made, the students were given an opportunity to revise their original eyeball judgment forecasts.

The variable used to judge the accuracy of any team's forecasts was the average of the absolute percentage forecast errors (APFEs). Carbone and Gorr found that the differences between the APFEs from each quantitative method and those from the original eyeball judgments were easily significant at the .01 level. In each case the objective forecasts were significantly better than the eyeball forecasts. On the other hand, the revised eyeball forecasts were superior to the objective forecasts for two of the three objective methods. These results lead us to believe that forecasting with the naked eye alone is not very reliable. When we look at a time series graph, we may not see subtle patterns or trends. However, a totally objective, computerized method may also not be optimal. It appears that a combination of eyeball judgment and a quantitative method may be the best strategy in many situations.

Application 14.2   An important concept in economics is a product's price elasticity, defined as the ratio of the product's percentage change in demand to a given percentage change in its price. If a product has a large elasticity (greater in magnitude than 1, say), its sales will be strongly affected by a price change. If the product's elasticity is small, however, price changes will have only a small effect on sales. Neslin and Shoemaker did a recent study on the elasticity of presweetened cereals. (Reference: Scott A. Neslin and Robert W. Shoemaker, ''Using a Natural Experiment to Estimate Price Elasticity: The 1974 Sugar Shortage and the Ready-to-Eat Cereal Market,'' *Journal of Marketing,* Vol. 47, 1983, pp. 44–57.) They used time series data from the three-year period 1973–1975 because there was a large increase in the price of sugar during this period. This led to a simultaneous increase in the price of presweetened cereals, so that a study of demand changes as a function of price changes could be performed naturally.

As Neslin and Shoemaker realized, however, other variables were changing during this period that could have a confounding effect on the demand-price relationship. These included (1) advertising; (2) new products on the market, particularly granola brands; (3) competition, in terms of price changes and advertising levels of other cereals; and (4) growth trends in the cereal industry. Therefore, the researchers used a rather involved method for estimating the desired elasticity.

First, they defined the following variables.

i labels the three major cereal subcategories: $i = 1$ for presweetened cereals, $i = 2$ for low-sugar cereals, $i = 3$ for granolas

t $= 1, \ldots , 36$ labels the 36 months beginning January 1973 and ending December 1975

V_{it} = sales in ounces of subcategory i in period t

V_t = total cereal sales in ounces in period t

A_{it} = advertising expenditures (\$) of subcategory i in period t

A_t = total cereal advertising expenditures in period t

P_{it} = average price per ounce of subcategory i in period t

D_t = number of granola brands available during period t

To obtain an aggregate price index for all cereals in period t, they defined

$$P_t = W_1 P_{1t} + W_2 P_{2t} + W_3 P_{3t}$$

where W_i is the long-term average market share of subcategory i in the overall cereal market.

Next, they used regression analysis to estimate three relationships:

1. The relationship between overall cereal sales, price, advertising, and time:

$$\ln(V_t) = \alpha_1 + \beta_1 \ln(P_t) + \beta_2 \ln(A_t) + \beta_3 t$$

2. The relationship between relative sales, relative prices, and relative advertising levels for presweetened and low-sugar cereals:

$$\ln\left(\frac{V_{1t}}{V_{2t}}\right) = \alpha_2 + \beta_4 \ln\left(\frac{P_{1t}}{P_{2t}}\right) + \beta_5 \ln\left(\frac{A_{1t}}{A_{2t}}\right)$$

3. The relationship between relative sales, relative prices, relative advertising levels for presweetened and granola cereals, and the number of granola brands on the market:

$$\ln\left(\frac{V_{1t}}{V_{3t}}\right) = \alpha_3 + \beta_6 \ln\left(\frac{P_{1t}}{P_{3t}}\right) + \beta_7 \ln\left(\frac{A_{1t}}{A_{3t}}\right) + \beta_8 \ln(D_t)$$

(Natural logarithms of variables, rather than the variables themselves, were used as dependent and independent variables for economic reasons; this is a common practice in studies of this type. Also, the number of granola brands on the market, D_t, was used in the third equation because the number of granola brands available grew quickly during the 1973–1975 period.) The purchase behaviors of over 3000 families were used to estimate the equations above. The estimated coefficients are shown below.

First equation: $\hat{\alpha}_1 = 10.69, \hat{\beta}_1 = -.312,$
$\hat{\beta}_2 = .050, \hat{\beta}_3 = .005, R^2 = .65$

Second equation: $\hat{\alpha}_2 = -.092, \hat{\beta}_4 = -2.574,$
$\hat{\beta}_5 = -.069, R^2 = .60$

Third equation: $\hat{\alpha}_3 = 3.120, \hat{\beta}_6 = -2.257,$
$\hat{\beta}_7 = .340, \hat{\beta}_8 = -.953, R^2 = .79$

There are two elasticities that result from this analysis. One is the elasticity of the cereal industry as a whole, β_1. It measures how the demand for cereal will change when the price index (P_t) of all cereals changes. The estimated value, $\hat{\beta}_1 = -.312$, a relatively low value, indicates that cereal sales as a whole are relatively insensitive to price. On the other hand, it can be shown algebraically that the elasticity of presweetened cereals is given by the expression

$$\text{elasticity} = \frac{W_1 P_{1t}}{\sum W_i P_{it}} \beta_1 + \frac{V_{2t}}{\sum V_{it}} \beta_4 + \frac{V_{3t}}{\sum V_{it}} \beta_6$$

(Each summation is over i, the subcategories of cereals.) This shows that the elasticity of presweetened cereal is composed of three factors. The first, the β_1 term, reflects the change in total cereal sales caused by a change in the price of presweetened cereals. The second and third factors, the β_4 and β_6 terms, reflect the substitution of one cereal for another (low sugar or granola for presweetened) that results from a price increase in presweetened cereals. By using the estimated β's and averaging the expression above over all time periods, Neslin and Shoemaker found an elasticity for presweetened cereals of -1.967. This suggests that if the price of presweetened cereal increases (and all else remains constant), sales in this category will fall substantially. Some people will switch from cereals to a different type of breakfast, while others will switch to other types of cereal. The latter substitution effect partially explains why the elasticity of presweetened cereals, -1.967, is so much larger in magnitude than the elasticity of cereals as a whole, $-.312$.

Glossary of Terms

Components of time series data trend, seasonal, cyclic, and irregular (noise)

Linear trend line a trend line that is appropriate when the differences between consecutive observations remain fairly constant from period to period

Exponential trend curve a trend curve that is appropriate when the percentage changes between consecutive observations remain fairly constant over time

Moving average sequence a sequence of averages of a fixed number of consecutive observations

Centered moving averages averages of two consecutive moving averages; used when the moving averages are calculated from an even number of observations

Exponential smoothing models methods for smoothing a time series and forecasting where observations in the past receive less weight than more recent observations (see Problem 49)

Winters' exponential smoothing model a more complicated exponential smoothing model that incorporates trend and seasonality

Lagged variables variables from previous time periods; in regression they may be independent variables, dependent variables, or error terms

Autocorrelation of lag k the correlation between two versions of the same time series, where one version is shifted k periods from the other

Weighted price indexes indexes that show how the current average price level compares to the average price level in a base period

Possible weighted price indexes Laspeyres index (uses quantities from the base period), Paasche index (uses quantities from the current period), and fixed weights index (uses quantities from a representative period)

Consumer price index (CPI) the best known weighted price index; measures the current cost of living

Important Formulas

1. Formula for the multiplicative model

$$Y_t = T_t \times S_t \times C_t \times I_t$$

where T_t is the trend component, S_t is the seasonal component, C_t is the cyclic component, and I_t is the irregular (noise) component

2. Formula for the cyclic component estimated from yearly data

$$C_t \approx \frac{Y_t}{T_t}$$

where T_t is an estimate of the trend

3. Ratio-to-moving average estimate of the seasonal component

$$S_t \approx \frac{Y_t}{\text{CMA}_t}$$

where CMA_t is the centered moving average for period t

4. Simple exponential smoothing formulas

$$L_t = \alpha Y_t + (1 - \alpha)L_{t-1} \qquad F_{t+1} = L_t$$

where L_t is the smoothed level in period t, and F_{t+1} is the forecast of Y_{t+1} made in period t

5. Formula for a weighted aggregate price index

$$\text{WI}_t = \frac{\Sigma P_{it}Q_i}{\Sigma P_{i0}Q_i} \times 100$$

End-of-Chapter Problems

41. The data below represent personal savings (in billions of dollars) for all people in the United States from 1958 to 1977. (Reference: U.S. Department of Commerce.) Draw a time series graph of these data. From this graph, does it appear that a linear trend line will fit the data well? What about an exponential trend curve?

Year	Personal Savings (Billions of Dollars)	Year	Personal Savings (Billions of Dollars)
1958	21.7	1968	38.1
1959	18.8	1969	35.1
1960	17.1	1970	50.6
1961	20.2	1971	57.3
1962	20.4	1972	49.4
1963	18.8	1973	70.3
1964	26.1	1974	71.7
1965	30.3	1975	83.6
1966	33.0	1976	68.0
1967	40.9	1977	66.9

*42. Suppose that we estimate an exponential trend curve to be

$$\ln(\hat{Y}_t) = 3.42 - 4.12t$$

a. Show explicitly how this equation implies that the estimated percentage change in Y from period $t - 1$ to period t, namely $(\hat{Y}_t - \hat{Y}_{t-1})/\hat{Y}_{t-1}$, remains constant for all values of t. What is the value of this constant? (*Hint:* Solve for $\hat{Y}_t$ and then calculate the ratio $\hat{Y}_t/\hat{Y}_{t-1}$.)

b. Calculate the estimated percentage change in Y from each period to the next by using the estimated regression equation.

*43. Although we discussed only two types of trend curves (linear and exponential), many others are possible. For example, consider a variable that first increases at a high rate but then increases at a lower rate in later periods. A time series of such a variable might appear as in the following graph.

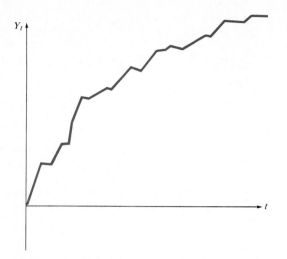

a. List one or more business or economic variables that behave in this way.

b. We might expect that the relationship between such a variable Y_t and time t to be of the form

$$Y_t = \beta_0 + \beta_1 \ln(t) + \epsilon_t$$

where $\ln(t)$ is the natural logarithm of time t. Estimate β_0 and β_1 for this equation by least squares regression for the following data. [First transform t to $\ln(t)$ to obtain the values of the independent variable.]

Year	t	Y_t
1975	1	152
1976	2	165
1977	3	180
1978	4	182
1979	5	191
1980	6	197
1981	7	196
1982	8	203
1983	9	206
1984	10	205
1985	11	211
1986	12	214

44. The following data represent total retail sales in the United States (in billions of dollars) from 1970 to 1980. (Reference: U.S. Department of Commerce.) For this problem consider only the yearly totals.

	1971	1972	1973	1974	1975	1976	1977	1978	1979	1980
January	28.64	30.73	36.43	38.23	41.66	47.46	49.88	53.34	62.55	70.56
February	27.71	31.05	35.58	36.85	40.15	45.77	49.88	53.80	61.33	70.62
March	31.74	36.08	41.86	42.82	45.17	52.02	58.40	65.12	73.04	75.99
I	88.09	97.86	113.87	117.90	126.98	145.25	158.16	172.26	196.92	217.17
April	33.36	35.27	41.24	44.28	45.88	54.49	60.18	64.23	71.28	75.15
May	33.79	38.02	43.58	47.12	51.19	54.71	60.57	68.41	75.55	79.20
June	34.70	38.75	44.11	46.00	49.50	55.92	61.63	69.59	75.61	77.36
II	101.85	112.04	128.93	137.40	146.57	165.12	182.38	202.23	222.44	231.71
July	34.46	37.17	42.19	46.40	50.39	56.52	61.12	67.10	72.92	79.86
August	33.79	38.24	43.79	48.95	51.20	55.01	62.07	69.72	78.76	81.74
September	33.92	37.65	41.36	44.14	48.47	53.55	59.68	66.82	73.46	77.58
III	102.17	113.06	127.34	139.49	150.06	165.08	182.87	203.64	225.14	239.18
October	35.40	38.92	44.01	46.58	51.97	56.15	62.25	69.29	77.37	84.00
November	35.89	39.94	44.94	46.67	50.96	56.62	63.48	72.01	79.89	83.81
December	42.82	47.24	50.43	52.92	61.59	69.13	76.05	85.23	92.55	100.80
IV	114.11	126.10	139.38	146.17	164.52	181.90	201.78	226.53	249.81	268.61
Year	406.22	449.06	509.52	540.96	588.13	657.35	725.19	804.66	894.31	956.67

a. Fit a linear trend line to the yearly totals.

b. Using the answer to part (a), estimate the cyclic component. Does this component suggest that yearly retail sales were affected by whatever business cycles existed? Explain.

45. The table in Problem 44 also shows quarterly totals. Using these totals for 1977 to 1980 only, calculate the moving averages and centered moving averages for these quarterly data. Then calculate the approximate seasonal component from the centered moving averages.

46. Do the same as in Problem 45, except with the given monthly data, not the aggregated quarterly data. Are the seasonal values for the monthly data consistent with the seasonal values for the quarterly data (from Problem 45)? Explain.

*47. Suppose that you are calculating 12-month moving averages and you have just calculated the average, call it MA, for the months September 1982 through August 1983. Now you want the next average, from October 1982 through September 1983. Show that this average can be calculated by adding $(Y_{S,83} - Y_{S,82})/12$ to the previous moving average, MA. (Here $Y_{S,82}$ and $Y_{S,83}$ are the September 1982 and 1983 observations, respectively.) Why would this principle save a lot of time when calculating moving averages for a long series of monthly data? Illustrate the principle for the first four 12-month averages calculated in Problem 46.

48. The same source that listed the data on retail sales in Problem 44 also gave the following "seasonally adjusted" data on retail sales for 1979 and 1980. (Reference: U.S. Department of Commerce.) Graph the two series (for 1979 and 1980 only) on the same graph. Does the seasonally adjusted graph appear to have less seasonal variation?

	1979	1980
January	71.40	79.56
February	71.70	78.90
March	72.59	77.60
April	72.61	76.40
May	73.19	75.98
June	73.49	77.84
July	74.21	79.49
August	75.62	79.83
September	76.82	80.62
October	76.42	81.55
November	76.94	82.76
December	77.48	83.44

*49. In simple exponential smoothing the formula $L_t = \alpha Y_t + (1 - \alpha)L_{t-1}$ holds for each $t \geq 1$. Therefore, replacing t by $t - 1$, we have $L_{t-1} = \alpha Y_{t-1} + (1 - \alpha)L_{t-2}$. Plugging this value for L_{t-1} back into the equation for L_t, we obtain

$$L_t = \alpha Y_t + (1 - \alpha)[\alpha Y_{t-1} + (1 - \alpha)L_{t-2}]$$
$$= \alpha Y_t + \alpha(1 - \alpha)Y_{t-1} + (1 - \alpha)^2 L_{t-2}$$

But we could continue this substitution by plugging in the expression $\alpha Y_{t-2} + (1 - \alpha)L_{t-3}$ for L_{t-2}, then plugging in a similar expression for L_{t-3}, and so on.

a. Show that if we continue this procedure, L_t will eventually be a sum of terms involving Y_t, Y_{t-1}, Y_{t-2}, and so on, down to Y_1 and L_0, and that the coefficient of Y_{t-k} is $\alpha(1 - \alpha)^k$, for $k \geq 1$.

b. Calculate the coefficients $\alpha(1 - \alpha)^k$ for $k = 1$; for $k = 2$; for $k = 3$; for $k = 4$; for $k = 5$. Do this when $\alpha = .1$; when $\alpha = .5$; when $\alpha = .8$.

c. Comment on the following statement, given the results from parts (a) and (b). Simple exponential smoothing expresses the current level of the series as a weighted average of the current observation and all previous observations, with the more recent observations receiving more weight, especially when α is close to 1.

*50. Given that the simple exponential smoothing equation can be written as $L_t = \alpha E_t + L_{t-1}$, where E_t is the forecast error $Y_t - F_t$, why do we want α to be between 0 and 1? (Try several trial values for L_{t-1}, F_t, and Y_t to see what happens if α is negative or α is greater than 1.)

*51. A version of Winters' exponential smoothing model that might be especially useful for yearly data considers only the level L_t and the trend T_t; it ignores the seasonal factors (the S_t's). It is given by the equations:

$$L_t = \alpha Y_t + (1 - \alpha)(L_{t-1} + T_{t-1})$$
$$T_t = \beta(L_t - L_{t-1}) + (1 - \beta)T_{t-1}$$
$$F_{t+1} = L_t + T_t = \text{forecast of } Y_{t+1} \text{ made at time } t$$

Only L_0, T_0, α, and β need to be specified in advance. Then the following are calculated (in this order): L_1, T_1, F_2, L_2, T_2, F_3, and so on.

a. Illustrate the required calculations for the following data on total mortgage debt outstanding (in billions of dollars) in the United States from 1969 to 1977. (Reference: Federal Housing Administration.) Use $L_0 = 400$, $T_0 = 25$, $\alpha = .2$, and $\beta = .3$.

Year	Mortgage Debt Outstanding (Billions of Dollars)
1969	425.3
1970	451.7
1971	499.8
1972	603.4
1973	682.3
1974	742.5
1975	801.6
1976	889.3
1977	1019.7

b. Graph the actual data on a time series graph. Then graph the forecasts (the F_t's) on the same graph. Explain why the method does such a poor job of forecasting these data.

52. Continuing Problem 51, if year t is the last observation, what value would $L_t + kT_t$ be a reasonable forecast of? Use your calculations from Problem 51 to forecast total mortgage debt outstanding for 1978, 1979, and 1980. What do you suspect about the accuracy of these particular forecasts? Explain.

53. The following data represent the results of a regression equation used to estimate Y_t, personal consumption expenditures, from 1956 to 1970. The estimates, the $\hat{Y}_t$'s, are shown for each year. Calculate the one-period lag autocorrelation r_1 of the residuals, where the residual in period t is $\hat{\epsilon}_t = Y_t - \hat{Y}_t$. Does your calculation suggest that autocorrelation might cause a problem in this regression analysis? Explain.

Year	t	Observed Personal Consumption (Billions of 1958 Dollars)	Estimated Personal Consumption (Billions of 1958 Dollars)
1956	1	281.4	261.421
1957	2	288.1	276.603
1958	3	290.0	291.784
1959	4	307.3	306.966
1960	5	316.1	322.148
1961	6	322.5	337.330
1962	7	338.4	352.512
1963	8	353.3	367.693
1964	9	373.7	382.875
1965	10	397.7	398.057
1966	11	418.1	413.239
1967	12	430.1	428.421
1968	13	452.7	443.602
1969	14	469.1	458.784
1970	15	476.9	473.966

54. The following data represent ticket prices and the number of passengers flown for several of an airline's most popular routes.

		Year			
		1980	1981	1982	1983
Route	1	$379 10,252	$395 12,342	$420 13,567	$450 13,732
	2	$545 4,763	$568 4,429	$574 3,985	$580 3,876
	3	$168 20,685	$176 24,784	$165 26,432	$158 28,421
	4	$265 6,450	$279 6,725	$294 6,650	$320 6,984

a. Calculate the Paasche price index for each of these years, using 1980 as the base year.

b. Why is it difficult to compare the different years' Paasche indexes, especially with data such as these?

55. Calculate the Laspeyres index for each year from the data given in Problem 54. Why is it meaningful to compare the different years' Laspeyres indexes? What is the potential disadvantage to using the Laspeyres index, particularly for these data? For these particular data, does it really make any difference?

56. The following graph shows how production of Porsches has varied over a 20-year span. (Reference: Porsche advertising brochure, 1983.) Clearly there has been an overall upward trend, but this upward movement has not been very smooth. Read each year's production figure from the graph to the nearest 500 units and use these figures to calculate r_1, the one-period lag autocorrelation. Interpret its value in light of what you see in this particular graph.

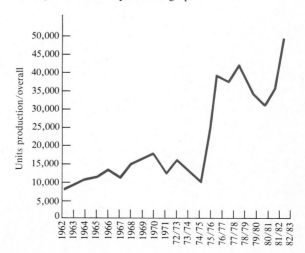

57. Since 1945 the total amount of transfer payments to individuals in the United States has grown tremendously. These are payments, such as Social Security and Medicare, that people receive directly from Washington and state and local governments. The following table shows how these payments have grown from 1945 to 1980. (Reference: *U.S. News & World Report*, Mar. 2, 1981.) Fit an exponential curve of the form $Y_t = \beta_0 e^{\beta_1 t}$ to the data, where Y_t is the total of transfer payments in year t (measured in billions of dollars), and t is measured in years, starting with $t = 1$ in 1945. Then use the estimated equation to predict Y_t for 1987.

Year	Total Transfer Payments (Billions of Dollars)
1945	5.6
1950	14.4
1955	16.2
1960	27.0
1965	37.6
1970	76.1
1975	170.9
1980	283.9

Computer Problems

(These problems are to be used in conjunction with the computer software package.)

1. Referring to the life insurance data in Table IV of Appendix D, use the SREGRESS program to fit a linear trend line for the amount of insurance owned. Start this with 1955. Then use the transformation ability of SREGRESS to fit an exponential trend line to the same time series. Use each equation to predict the amount of life insurance owned in 1982, 1983, and 1984.

2. a. Referring to the data on durable goods in Table VI of Appendix D, use the SREGRESS program to fit a linear trend to the yearly totals from 1963 to 1980. Then use the AUTOCORR program to calculate the autocorrelations of the residuals for lags of 1, 2, and 3 years. How can you interpret these autocorrelations? Does it appear that the OLS assumption of no autocorrelation is seriously violated?

   b. Repeat part (a), but now use an exponential trend instead of a linear trend. Does it appear that you get better results?

3. Again referring to the data on durable goods in Table VI of Appendix D, use the MOVAVE program to find seasonal factors for the 4 quarters. Use all of the data from 1963 to 1980. Does it appear that these seasonal factors have remained constant during this time period?

4. Now use the EXSMOOTH program on the durable goods quarterly data in Table VI of Appendix D. Use an initial level $L_0 = 1.4$, an initial trend $T_0 = .6$, and initial seasonal factors .8, 1, 1, and 1.2. Also, use smoothing constants $\alpha = .3$, $\beta = .4$, and $\gamma = .2$. Run the program only with the data from 1963 to 1979. Then forecast the quarterly data for 1980 and compare your forecasts to the actual data. Finally, try different values of α, β, and/or γ to see if you can reduce the value of MAD or improve the 1980 forecasts.

5. If you worked Problem 29 (p. 761; based on the data on Coca-Cola returns shown in Problem 17), you found that simple exponential smoothing does a very poor job of forecasting data that has obvious seasonality. Now use the EXSMOOTH program to perform Winters' method on these data. Use an initial level $L_0 = .13$ and smoothing constant $\alpha = .3$, as in Problem 29. Also, use an initial trend $T_0 = .05$, initial seasonal factors of .8, 1.15, 1.25, and .8, and smoothing constants $\beta = .3$ and $\gamma = .4$. Then use the AUTOCORR program to find the autocorrelations of lags 1, 2, 3, and 4 quarters for the forecast errors. (Write down the forecast errors from EXSMOOTH and use these as inputs to AUTOCORR.)

6. Use the MREGRESS program on the sales and advertising data in Table 14.12 (pp. 752–753). As in Example 14.7, let SALES, be the dependent variable, and let AD_t, AD_{t-1}, and AD_{t-2} be the independent variables. Verify that the equation given in Example 14.7 is correct. Then use the residuals from the MREGRESS output as input to the AUTOCORR program to find the autocorrelations for lags of 1, 2, 3, and 4 months.

References

DANNENBRING, D. G. and STARR, M. K. *Management Science, An Introduction*. New York: McGraw-Hill, 1981.

GUJARATI, D. *Basic Econometrics*. New York: McGraw-Hill, 1978.

LING, R. F. and ROBERTS, H. V. *IDA: A User's Guide to the IDA Interactive Data Analysis and Forecasting System*. New York: McGraw-Hill, 1982.

NELSON, C. R. *Applied Time Series Analysis for Managerial Forecasting*. San Francisco: Holden-Day, 1973.

U.S. Department of Labor, *The Consumer Price Index: Concepts and Content over the Years*. Bureau of Labor Statistics, Bulletin 2134-2, Apr. 1984.

WONNACOTT, R. J. and WONNACOTT, T. H. *Econometrics*. New York: Wiley, 1970.

CHAPTER 15

Decision Making Under Uncertainty

Objectives

1. To learn several criteria for making good decisions under uncertainty, particularly the expected monetary value (EMV) criterion.
2. To learn how to build and solve decision trees.
3. To understand the meaning of certainty equivalents.
4. To learn how Bayes' rule can be used to revise probabilities as new information becomes available.
5. To learn how to find the value of sample information and perfect information.
6. To learn the meaning of risk and the role of utility functions.

Contents

*I*n the context of quality control, when a company receives a batch of manufactured items, it often must decide on an "acceptance plan." The idea is that there are probably some items in the batch, labeled defectives, that need rework before they can meet product specifications, and it is usually less costly to rework these defectives at an early stage than at a later stage. Therefore, the company must decide on a plan whereby it balances the cost of inspecting items immediately, so that defectives can be reworked early, with the cost of not inspecting and then having to rework defective items at a later stage. For example, the plan might be to inspect 15% of the items in the batch, and then inspect the rest of the batch only if more than 10% of the items inspected originally are found to be defective.

Any such plan has uncertainties and costs associated with it. The uncertainties arise because the company does not know how many defectives are in the batch or how many defectives an inspection will turn up. The costs include the cost of inspection plus the cost of reworking defective items either at an early stage or a later stage. The company's objective is to find a plan that will, in some sense, minimize the anticipated costs. In this chapter we see exactly what cost criteria we should minimize in a problem characterized by uncertainty, and then we see how to carry out the minimization.

15.1

Introduction

Business firms vary in many respects, but two interests they have in common are that (1) they are uncertain about the future, and (2) they must make decisions today with outcomes that depend on the future. Even we as individuals are faced with many such decisions on a day-to-day basis. Some of these are fairly minor, such as whether to carry an umbrella to work when the sky is cloudy, or whether to place a small bet with a friend on the result of an upcoming football game. Other decisions are much more important. Should we put our house up for sale now and attempt to buy a new house, or should we wait for the interest rates to come down? Should we put our savings into long-term fixed-rate bonds, or should we invest in short-term assets, with the expectation that interest rates will increase and we will be able to reinvest at the higher rates?

These kinds of decisions concern all of us because they affect *our* money, however large the amounts might be. Therefore, we want to make good decisions. However, most of us do not try to solve these problems in a systematic, mathematical way. We usually get some advice from experts, talk it over at home, and finally make a decision.

Business firms, on the other hand, differ from individuals in two important respects. First, the decisions they must make typically involve large sums of money. A few terrible (or unlucky) decisions could bankrupt a firm. Second, these important decisions must be made continually. Therefore, companies want to know how to make good decisions on a routine basis. They will be out of business if they fail to do so.

There is no doubt that the ability to make good business decisions depends largely on business experience and good judgment. An intelligent business executive with years of experience is probably able to make many successful day-to-day decisions without the aid of formal decision-making procedures. In fact, some executives distrust formal procedures because they believe these procedures attempt to replace human judgment and experience. However, many of today's business problems are too complex to solve successfully without the aid of a formal procedure. These problems often involve a large number of possible decisions, a large number of potential outcomes, the assessment of likelihoods, risk trade-offs, and tricky timing. Even the most intelligent and experienced executives can benefit from formal decision-making procedures when they are faced with this degree of complexity. This is why many companies are now using formal decision-making procedures, or they are hiring trained consultants to perform the analysis for them.

We stress that the analysis in this chapter should be used primarily as an *aid* in the overall decision-making process. The procedures in this chapter use only mathematical models of reality. As such, they do not incorporate many of the intangible elements that are important in any decision-making problem. Only judgment and experience can deal with these intangible elements successfully, but judgment and experience *can* be aided by formal procedures. In short, people ultimately make the decisions, but in complex situations they should welcome the input from formal decision-making procedures.

There is one idea in this chapter that we must always keep in mind. We will *not* be able to give a prescription for making perfect decisions. For all the applications we will discuss, a decision must be made *now,* even though some of the relevant information will not be known until later. So we are forced to make probability assessments about future outcomes and then make the best possible decision. We have control of the current decision, but that is all. We cannot control the future, at least not completely, so it may not turn out the way we hoped or predicted. This means that after the future reveals itself, it may be tempting to look back and criticize the decision that was made, especially if it had unfortunate consequences. That is, it may be tempting to ''second-guess'' the decision.

But second-guessing a decision is not really fair. We assume that the decision-maker acts rationally at the time the decision has to be made. He obtains all relevant information, he makes probability assessments about future outcomes consistent with his beliefs and the available information, he takes into account his company's feelings toward risk, and he integrates these in a sensible way to find the best decision. Without perfect foresight, this is the best anyone can do. If the future turns out differently than expected and the decision proves to be an unfortunate one, the decision maker should not be blamed. He was simply unlucky. Presumably, his rational, systematic approach will be rewarded in the majority of applications.

In this chapter we systematically discuss many of the intuitive notions mentioned in the paragraphs above. These include the assessment of probabilities of future outcomes, the revision of probabilities as new information becomes available, the method for choosing the "best" decision, the value of information for improving decision making, and the way in which attitudes toward risk influence decision making.

15.2

Possible Approaches Toward Decision Making Under Uncertainty

In this section we begin our study of decision making under uncertainty by examining a very simple example. Despite the simplicity of the example, the solution is by no means obvious. The main difficulty is that there is no obvious criterion for judging the various decisions and choosing the "best" decision. We need to define what is meant by "best." Although there are several acceptable ways of doing this, we will settle on one of these definitions and continue to use it throughout the majority of this chapter.

Sets of Decisions, States of Nature, and Payoff and Cost Tables

In all decision problems involving uncertainty, there are three elements that must be defined. The first is the set of possible decisions. Before a company can possibly choose the best decision, it must list the set of all possible decisions. As a rule, this list should be as complete as possible. Unless a particular decision is clearly not as good as some other decision, it should not be omitted from the list.

The second element is a list of possible outcomes of the uncertain aspects of the problem. The possible outcomes are usually called the *states of nature*. Then a given state of nature is any of the possible outcomes that might occur. The outcome that actually occurs is called the *true* state of nature.

> The states of nature are the possible future outcomes. The true state of nature is the outcome that actually occurs.

The third element is called the *payoff table*. For each possible decision d and each possible state of nature s, the decision maker receives a monetary payoff. This payoff is labeled $r(d, s)$ to emphasize its dependence on the decision d and outcome s. If $r(d, s)$ is positive, it represents a profit for the decision maker. But if $r(d, s)$ is negative, it represents a cost. Since there is a payoff $r(d, s)$ for each d and s, we can summarize the payoffs in a payoff table, as shown in Table 15.1. (In this table there are N possible decisions and M possible states of nature.)

Table 15.1 Typical Payoff Table

		Possible States of Nature			
		s_1	s_2	. . .	s_M
	d_1	$r(d_1, s_1)$	$r(d_1, s_2)$		$r(d_1, s_M)$
	d_2	$r(d_2, s_1)$	$r(d_2, s_2)$		$r(d_2, s_M)$
Possible Decisions	$\cdot$ $\cdot$ $\cdot$				
	d_N	$r(d_N, s_1)$	$r(d_N, s_2)$		$r(d_N, s_M)$

> The payoff table lists the monetary outcomes for the various decisions and states of nature.

Some authors prefer to talk of *costs,* labeled $c(d, s)$, and *cost tables* of these. Then $c(d, s)$ is the negative of $r(d, s)$, so that a positive $c(d, s)$ represents a cost and a negative $c(d, s)$ represents a profit. Since there are no essential differences between payoff and cost tables, we will feel free to alternate between them, depending on which is more natural for a given problem.

A cost table as defined here should not be confused with a *loss* (or *opportunity loss*) table. For each state of nature, the opportunity loss resulting from any particular decision shows how much worse off we are by not choosing the best decision. For example, the loss table corresponding to the payoff table in Table 15.2a (p. 788) is shown in Table 15.2b. Since the payoffs in Table 15.2a are all positive, there is no possibility of incurring any losses in terms of out-of-pocket costs. However, the losses shown in Table 15.2b show how much profit is forgone by not choosing the best decision in any given column. Notice that the opportunity loss from choosing the best decision in any given column is 0; the corresponding cells are marked with asterisks.

From here on, we will work only with payoff and cost tables, not opportunity loss tables. However, it is worth mentioning that the principal criterion

Table 15.2

	s_1	s_2	s_3			s_1	s_2	s_3
d_1	100	150	75		d_1	100	0*	85
d_2	90	50	160		d_2	110	100	0*
d_3	200	130	70		d_3	0*	20	90
	(a) Payoff table					(b) Opportunity loss table		

for choosing the best decision, the EMV criterion (to be discussed shortly), leads to the same decisions regardless of whether a payoff table, a cost table, or an opportunity loss table is used. This is the primary reason we do not need to consider loss tables in the rest of this chapter.

Given the set of decisions, the states of nature, and the payoff or cost table, many decision-making situations evolve as follows. (In a later section we will refer to these types of problems as *single-stage* decision problems.) First, the decision maker chooses one of the decisions from his list. Next, one of the possible states of nature occurs. Again, we call this outcome the *true* state of nature. Finally, the decision and the true state of nature combine to yield a payoff or cost. This three-step sequence is illustrated in Figure 15.1.

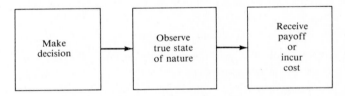

Figure 15.1
Evolution of a Single-Stage Decision Problem

Let's look at the middle step of this three-step sequence. How is the true state of nature chosen? In this chapter we assume that this outcome is chosen by an indifferent "force" called nature. (Alternative terms for nature in this context are "fate" and "chance.") By indifferent, we mean that nature's choice of outcome is essentially independent of our decision. In particular, it is not specifically chosen to help or hurt us. In other words, we have no reason to be pessimistic and believe that nature is "out to get us," or to be optimistic and believe that nature is going out of her way to help us.

To explore this idea one step further, the typical situation in this chapter can be described as a decision maker playing a "game" against an indifferent opponent called nature. This is quite different from situations where the outcomes of a company's decisions are affected by the decisions of consciously "hostile" opponents. For example, suppose that company A is deciding whether to undertake a costly advertising campaign. If undertaken, the success or failure of this campaign depends largely on company B's advertising plans. In this situation company B is definitely not an indifferent opponent; any market share company A gains will probably be at company B's expense, and company B knows this. This type of problem, where two or more competitors make decisions that will affect one another, is a much more difficult problem than we can tackle in this book. (It falls under the category of *game theory,* a topic we will not discuss.) So from here on, we will assume that the decision-maker's "opponent," nature, selects outcomes independently of the decisions chosen.

We now illustrate several possible approaches to decision making under uncertainty for the following simplified example. Consider a candy company that knows it will need 10 tons of sugar six months from now. The company has two basic options. It can buy the sugar at the going price when it needs it, six months from now, or it can buy a futures contract today. This contract guarantees delivery of the sugar in six months but at today's prices. In other words, the contract is a type of insurance against sugar prices increasing significantly. To keep the problem small, we assume that the possible futures contracts available are for 5 tons or 10 tons only. Also, we will rule out buying or selling futures contracts in the intervening months. Then the company's three possible decisions are:

Possible Decision-Making Criteria for a Simple Example

d_1: buy a futures contract for 10 tons
d_2: buy a futures contract for 5 tons and buy the other 5 tons in six months
d_3: buy all 10 tons in six months

The monetary information is as follows. The price of sugar bought now for delivery in six months is 8.51 cents per pound. The transactions cost for a 5-ton futures contract is $65; for a 10-ton contract, it is $110. (This explains why the company does not need to consider buying two 5-ton futures contracts; the transactions cost would be too high compared to one 10-ton contract.) Finally, the company assumes that the possible prices of sugar six months from now (in cents per pound) are 7.8, 8.3, 8.7, 9.1, and 9.6. The company wants to make the decision that results in the least-cost way of meeting its sugar requirement.

In this example the only uncertainty involves the price of sugar in six months. So we let the states of nature be the possible prices in six months. Then we obtain the cost table shown in Table 15.3 (p. 790). (We use a cost table instead of a payoff table because all monetary consequences are costs, not profits.) Each entry in this table is the cost of obtaining the sugar, given the decision and the price of sugar in six months. For example,

$$c(d_2, s_3) = .0851(10{,}000) + .087(10{,}000) + 65 = \$1786$$

Table 15.3   Cost Table for Sugar Example (Dollars)

		Possible Sugar Prices in Six Months (Cents per Pound)				
		7.8	8.3	8.7	9.1	9.6
Possible Decisions	d_1	1812	1812	1812	1812	1812
	d_2	1696	1746	1786	1826	1876
	d_3	1560	1660	1740	1820	1920

Notice that the top row of this table is constant. This is because the price of sugar six months from now is irrelevant if the company contracts for all 10 tons of sugar today.

Unfortunately, there is still no obvious *best* decision. The decision that turns out to be best depends on the true state of nature. For example, if s_4 is true, the best decision is d_1. But if s_1 is true, d_3 is best. What we need is a criterion for selecting the "best" decision before the true state of nature is observed.

Before doing this, we point out one possibly surprising aspect of this example. By examining the columns of Table 15.3, we see that there is no state of nature for which the decision d_2 is best; it is *always* second or third best. But this does not necessarily mean that we will never choose d_2. The only time we can eliminate a decision from consideration is when it is *dominated* by another decision. This happens when its costs are higher (or its payoffs are lower) than those of some other decision for *every* state of nature.

Decision $\overline{d}$ dominates d if

$$r(d, s) \leq r(\overline{d}, s) \text{ for each } s$$

$$[\text{or } c(d, s) \geq c(\overline{d}, s) \text{ for each } s]$$

If decision $\overline{d}$ dominates decision d, decision d can be eliminated from consideration.

For example, in Table 15.4 we show a payoff table where decision d is dominated by decision $\overline{d}$. This follows because $r(d, s) \leq r(\overline{d}, s)$ for *each s*. In the sugar example, no decision, not even d_2, is dominated by another decision. Therefore, we cannot automatically eliminate any of them from consideration.

Minimax Criterion

The first criterion we discuss is the pessimist's criterion. The pessimist assumes that nature is an enemy who will do her best to hurt him, no matter what he does. Therefore, his plan is to minimize his cost, assuming that the

Table 15.4 Payoff Table Where d Is Dominated by $\bar{d}$

		Possible States of Nature			
		s_1	s_2	s_3	s_4
	.				
	.				
	.				
Possible	d	57	49	105	220
Decisions	$\bar{d}$	68	50	170	220
	.				
	.				
	.				

worst will occur. In particular, he makes the decision that minimizes his maximum cost. This decision is called the *minimax* decision.

> The minimax decision is the decision that minimizes the maximum cost. It is a very conservative decision.

(A *maximin* decision is the mirror image of a minimax decision but is used for payoff, not cost, tables. It is the decision that maximizes the minimum payoff.)

   The minimax decision is simple to find. For each decision (each row) in the cost table, we find the maximum cost in that row and write it in the margin. Then we locate the row that minimizes these maximums. As Table 15.5 indicates, the minimax decision for the sugar example is d_1. If the pessimist makes this decision, he is assured of a cost no greater than $1812. (In fact, for this problem his cost will be $1812 for sure.)

Table 15.5 Minimax and Minimin Decisions for the Sugar Example

		Possible Sugar Prices in Six Months					Max.	Min.
		7.8	8.3	8.7	9.1	9.6		
	d_1	1812	1812	1812	1812	1812	⟨1812⟩	1812
Possible	d_2	1696	1746	1786	1826	1876	1876	1696
Decisions	d_3	1560	1660	1740	1820	1920	1920	⟨1560⟩

↑	↑
Choose d_1	Choose d_3
for	for
minimax	minimin

Minimin Criterion

The opposite of a minimax decision is a *minimin* decision. This is the decision an extreme optimist chooses. He believes that no matter what he does, nature will do her best to help him. Therefore, he finds the decision that minimizes the minimum cost. That is, in each row he finds the best (lowest) cost and chooses the decision that corresponds to the best of these.

> The minimin decision is the decision that corresponds to the smallest cost in the entire cost table. It is often a very risky decision.

(The mirror image of a minimin decision when using a payoff table is called a *maximax* decision. It is the decision that corresponds to the highest possible payoff.)

The minimin decision rule is very easy to find. We simply find the minimum cost in the entire cost table and use the corresponding decision. The minimin decision for the sugar example is also illustrated in Table 15.5. As the table shows, d_3 is the optimist's decision.

Criticisms of Minimax and Minimin Criteria

We have presented minimax and minimin decision rules because they are used in some real-world applications. But for many problems, both of these rules have some obvious drawbacks and can lead to poor decisions. The problem is that they fail to take into account (1) the sizes of the numerical differences between the various costs, and (2) the probabilities of the various states of nature.

For example, consider the cost table in Table 15.6. The minimax decision is d_1 because $101 is less than $102. But the small difference between these costs is much less than the potential savings possible if we choose d_2 and s_1 occurs. Furthermore, if all available information indicates that s_1 is much more *probable* than s_2, then d_2 becomes even more attractive. The minimax decision maker is so conservative that he ignores these attractive aspects of decision d_2.

Table 15.6

	s_1	s_2	Max.
d_1	100	101	101 ← Minimax decision
d_2	0	102	102

A minimin decision maker may be even worse. For example, given the cost table in Table 15.7, he will choose d_1. However, he is risking a cost of $1000 in order to save $10. This risk is especially serious if the $1000 cost could put his company in serious financial difficulty and/or outcome s_2 is

Table 15.7

	s_1	s_2	Min.
d_1	0	1000	0 ← Minimin decision
d_2	10	10	10

much more probable than s_1. The minimin decision maker is sometimes too optimistic; he ignores the possible disastrous consequences of his decisions.

Obviously, these small examples have been contrived to show the worst aspects of minimax and minimin decision rules. But even in less extreme situations, we can usually make better, more rational, decisions by taking probabilities of future outcomes into consideration. A procedure for doing this will be discussed next.

Problems for Section 15.2

1. Explain how possible decisions and possible outcomes are used to build a payoff table. How can these be converted to a cost table? How can they be converted to a opportunity loss table? Illustrate on the following payoff table.

		States of Nature			
		1	2	3	4
	1	45	−35	0	120
Decisions	2	20	−20	10	80
	3	75	−85	40	30

2. The following cost table shows the monetary outcomes when four decisions are available and three states of nature are possible. Convert this to a payoff table for the same decisions and states of nature. Then convert it to an opportunity loss table. What is the minimax decision? (Which table should you use to find this?)

		States of Nature		
		1	2	3
	1	55	−10	75
	2	20	0	40
Decisions	3	25	25	25
	4	15	−10	80

3. For the cost table in Problem 2, are there any dominated decisions? Is it obvious which of the undominated decisions should be chosen? Explain.

4. Why are the maximin decision from a payoff table and the minimax decision from the corresponding cost table necessarily the same? Illustrate with the following payoff table.

		States of Nature			
		1	2	3	4
	1	50	−30	20	0
	2	30	−10	10	10
Decisions	3	80	−40	30	−10
	4	20	20	20	20

5. Consider a cost table with no dominated decisions. Show by means of a two-decision, three-state problem that it is possible for the minimin decision to be the same as the minimax decision.

6. Consider an investor with $5000 to invest. He has the following options: (1) he can invest in a risk-free savings account with a guaranteed 8% annual return; (2) he can invest in a fairly safe stock, where the possible return rates are 7% or 11%; or (3) he can invest in a fairly risky stock where the possible return rates are 1% or 17%. Furthermore, he can put all his money into any one of the options above, or he can

split his $5000 into two $2500 investments in any two of the options above.

a. Construct the investor's payoff table. Why is a payoff table more natural than a cost table for this problem?

b. Construct the investor's opportunity loss table for this problem. In what sense are the values in this table "losses"?

c. Are there any dominated decisions? If so, which ones? If not, why not?

d. What is the maximin strategy? What is the maximax strategy?

e. How might you criticize the maximin and the maximax criteria for this problem?

15.3

Expected Monetary Value (EMV) Criterion

In this section we present a criterion that explicitly trades off differences between the various payoffs (or costs) and the probabilities of the states of nature. As we have seen, the minimax and minimin decisions fail to take into account the probabilities of the states of nature. However, any decision maker has some idea, no matter how imprecise, of these probabilities. These probabilities are usually partly objective and partly subjective assessments (as discussed in Chapter 3). That is, they are based partly on historical data and partly on the decision maker's subjective beliefs about the future. Because of the subjective component, these probability assessments will probably differ from one person to the next. But some person must ultimately make a decision. Therefore, he may as well spend some time assessing the required probabilities and then incorporate his assessments into the decision-making process.

Suppose that the states of nature are labeled $s_1, s_2, \ldots, s_M$, and their probabilities are assessed to be $P(s_1), P(s_2), \ldots, P(s_M)$. Because one and only one of the states of nature can be the true state, these probabilities must sum to 1:

$$\sum P(s) = 1$$

Once we assess these probabilities, we use them and the payoff (or cost) table to find the best decision. For a single decision d, we weight the payoffs $r(d, s)$ by their probabilities $P(s)$ and sum over all states of nature to obtain an *expected* payoff, labeled $R(d)$.

> *Expected Payoff from Using Decision d*
> $$R(d) = \sum r(d, s)P(s)$$

If we are working with costs instead of payoffs, the expected cost, labeled $C(d)$, is found by replacing $r(d, s)$ by $c(d, s)$.

> ### Expected Cost from Using Decision d
>
> $$C(d) = \sum c(d, s)P(s)$$

The reader should recall from Chapter 4 that the above expressions for expected payoff and expected cost are actually "expected values." That is, they are sums of possible values (of payoffs or costs) times probabilities.

How do we interpret an expected payoff? It is not necessarily the most likely payoff or the payoff that we expect to receive. For example, if $r(d, s_1) = \$100$, $r(d, s_2) = \$0$, and $P(s_1) = P(s_2) = .5$, then

$$R(d) = 100(.5) + 0(.5) = \$50$$

But $50 is not a possible payoff; the only possible payoffs are $0 and $100. One way that we can interpret this expected value of $50 is that if we could repeat the "experiment" many times, we would receive $100 about half the time and $0 about half the time. Therefore, the *average* payoff in the long run would be near $50. Unfortunately, this interpretation is of little use if the decision problem occurs only once.

On the other hand, researchers who have studied the theoretical, even philosophical, aspects of decision making under uncertainty have shown that expected payoffs (or costs) play a very prominent role. Specifically, they have shown that in many situations, a rational person should choose the decision that maximizes the expected payoff or minimizes the expected cost. Since payoffs and costs are usually in monetary amounts, this criterion is called the *expected monetary value* criterion, or simply the EMV criterion.

> Using the EMV criterion, we choose the decision that maximizes the expected payoff $R(d)$ or minimizes the expected cost $C(d)$.

We now return to the sugar example. If we wish to use the EMV criterion, we must first assess probabilities of the possible sugar prices in six months. There is no simple way to do this, nor is there a "right answer." We can examine past sugar prices, we can read relevant newspapers and periodicals, and we can consult with experts in the sugar industry. But eventually, we must decide on five probabilities that sum to 1 and reflect our beliefs about future sugar prices.

Suppose that we have made the probability assessments shown below the cost table in Table 15.8 (p. 796). Then the rest is straightforward. For each decision we weight the costs in that row by the probabilities, and then we sum these products to obtain the expected cost $C(d)$. Finally, we choose the

Table 15.8

| | | Possible Sugar Prices in Six Months | | | | | EMV | |
		7.8	8.3	8.7	9.1	9.6		
	d_1	1812	1812	1812	1812	1812	1812	
Possible Decisions	d_2	1696	1746	1786	1826	1876	1793	
	d_3	1560	1660	1740	1820	1920	1754	← Best
		.05	.25	.35	.20	.15	← Probabilities	

decision that has the smallest $C(d)$. The calculations are shown below.

$$C(d_1) = 1812(.05) + 1812(.25) + 1812(.35) + 1812(.20) + 1812(.15)$$
$$= \$1812$$
$$C(d_2) = 1696(.05) + 1746(.25) + 1786(.35) + 1826(.20) + 1876(.15)$$
$$= \$1793$$
$$C(d_3) = 1560(.05) + 1660(.25) + 1740(.35) + 1820(.20) + 1920(.15)$$
$$= \$1754$$

Because $C(d_3)$ is the smallest, it is the best decision according to the EMV criterion. Evidently, the company should take the risk of waiting for six months before buying any sugar.

Since the assessed probabilities in Table 15.8 are at best "educated guesses," it is useful to see how sensitive the optimal decision is to these probabilities. That is, if these probabilities change slightly, will d_3 remain the optimal decision? First, notice that $C(d_1)$ does not depend on the probabilities at all; its value is always \$1812 because $c(d_1, s)$ equals \$1812 for each state of nature. In words, the uncertainty about sugar prices in six months is irrelevant if we buy a futures contract today. But $C(d_2)$ and $C(d_3)$ will change if the probabilities change.

For example, consider the two new sets of probabilities shown in Tables 15.9a and b. In Table 15.9a we have

$$C(d_1) = \$1812$$
$$C(d_2) = 1696(.04) + 1746(.28) + 1786(.38) + 1826(.18) + 1876(.12)$$
$$= \$1789.20$$
$$C(d_3) = 1560(.04) + 1660(.28) + 1740(.38) + 1820(.18) + 1920(.12)$$
$$= \$1746.40$$

In this case d_3 is still the best decision, with an expected cost of \$1746.40. However, in Table 15.9b the expected costs are

$C(d_1) = \$1812$

$C(d_2) = 1696(.01) + 1746(.14) + 1786(.20) + 1826(.30) + 1876(.35)$
$= \$1823$

$C(d_3) = 1560(.01) + 1660(.14) + 1740(.20) + 1820(.30) + 1920(.35)$
$= \$1814$

Now d_1 is the best decision, with an expected cost of $1812. Intuitively, the reason for the change is that high prices in the future are now more probable, so we should contract for the lower price now.

Table 15.9

	7.8	8.3	8.7	9.1	9.6	EMV	
d_1	1812	1812	1812	1812	1812	1812	
d_2	1696	1746	1786	1826	1876	1789.2	
d_3	1560	1660	1740	1820	1920	1746.4	← Best
	.04	.28	.38	.18	.12	← Probabilities	

(a)

	7.8	8.3	8.7	9.1	9.6	EMV	
d_1	1812	1812	1812	1812	1812	1812	← Best
d_2	1696	1746	1786	1826	1876	1823	
d_3	1560	1660	1740	1820	1920	1814	
	.01	.14	.20	.30	.35	← Probabilities	

(b)

The type of analysis described above is called *sensitivity analysis*. We see how sensitive the optimal decision is to changes in the problem parameters, here the probabilities. A sensitivity analysis is always a useful part of the decision process, especially in applications where some of the problem parameters, such as the probabilities, are not known exactly. Obviously, if a decision remains optimal for moderate changes in the input parameters, we have more confidence that it is really the correct decision.

With the EMV criterion, we act as if there is a single number characterizing that decision's monetary consequences. This single number is its EMV. This means that any "gamble" with a given EMV is treated the same as a "sure thing" with the same dollar value. For example, using the data in Table 15.8, we saw that $C(d_2) = \$1793$. We know that this value is an *expected* value, that is, a weighted average of the possible costs when d_2 is used. But when

Certainty Equivalents

we use the EMV criterion, we act as if the cost from d_2 is \$1793 *for sure*. In other words, we act as if we are indifferent between taking the gamble that d_2 represents and paying out a certain \$1793.

Since the EMV of a decision is treated the same as a certain dollar payoff (or cost) of this amount, we refer to the EMV as a *certainty equivalent*. A more formal definition of a certainty equivalent is given below.

> A certainty equivalent for a given gamble is an amount such that we are indifferent between taking the gamble and receiving (or paying) this amount for sure.

When EMV is the decision criterion, the certainty equivalent of a gamble is simply its EMV. The concept of certainty equivalents is extremely important in decision making under uncertainty and will be discussed more fully throughout this chapter.

15.4
Decision Trees for Single-Stage Decision Problems

In Section 15.3 we saw how to use the EMV criterion to find the optimal decision for "single-stage" decision problems. These single-stage decision problems evolve through time as shown in Figure 15.1 (p. 788). First, the decision maker chooses a decision from his list, then nature reveals the true state of nature, and finally the decision maker receives a payoff or incurs a cost. (Notice that the sugar example has this basic structure.)

For any problem of this form, we can represent its decisions, states of nature, payoffs or costs, probabilities, and solution very conveniently in a *decision tree*. A decision tree is much easier to "see" than to explain in words, so we present the decision tree for the sugar example, with data from Table 15.8, in Figure 15.2 (p. 800).

There are several conventions we follow when we build decision trees. These are listed below.

> *Decision Tree Conventions*
>
> 1. Decision trees are composed of *nodes* (circles and squares) and *branches* (straight lines).

2. The nodes represent points in time. A *decision node* (a square) is a time when the decision maker makes a decision. A *probability node* (a circle) is a time when an uncertain outcome is revealed.

3. Time proceeds from left to right. This means that any sequence of branches leading into a node (from the left) have already been observed. Any branches to the right of a given node have not yet occurred.

4. Branches leading out of (to the right of) a decision node represent the possible decisions; the decision maker may choose which of these branches he prefers. Branches leading out of probability nodes represent the possible outcomes of uncertain events; the decision maker has no control over which of these will occur.

5. Probabilities are listed on probability branches. (We put them in parentheses for the sake of clarity.) These probabilities are *conditional* on the events that have already been observed. Also, the probabilities on branches leading out of a given node must sum to 1.

6. Payoffs or costs are shown at the tips of the rightmost branches. These monetary values depend on the decisions and outcomes to the left of them.

For the typical single-stage decision problem pictured in Figure 15.1, these conventions are easy to follow. Figure 15.2 illustrates this. Going from left to right, there is a decision node, followed by a sequence of decision branches. Each of these leads to a probability node, followed by probability branches for the various states of nature. Finally, the numbers from the payoff or cost table are shown at the tips of the probability branches.

Sometimes parts of the payoffs or costs do not depend on the uncertain outcomes. In these cases it is permissible, even preferable, to put these payoffs or costs where they occur in time. In case the *entire* monetary outcome of a given decision is independent of the uncertain outcomes, we may eliminate the corresponding probability node and probability branches altogether. These ideas are illustrated in Figure 15.3 (p. 801) for the sugar example. In this decision tree we have put the transactions costs from d_1 and d_2 on the decision branches where they occur, and we have put the certain $1702 purchase price for d_1 at the tip of its decision branch. This decision tree is entirely equivalent to the decision tree in Figure 15.2. (The only caution is to avoid double-counting. If a payoff or a cost is put on the branch where it occurs, it should not also be included at the tips of the rightmost branches.)

Now that we have built and labeled this decision tree, we need to "solve" it. This procedure is called *folding back* on the tree. Actually, folding back is a very simple procedure because there are only two operations to remem-

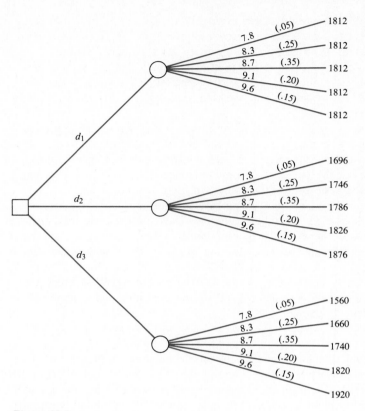

Figure 15.2
Decision Tree for the Sugar Example

ber. Starting from the *right* of the tree and proceeding to the left, we

1. Take expected values (sums of monetary values times probabilities) at probability nodes.
2. Take maximums (for payoffs) or minimums (for costs) at decision nodes.

These operations are illustrated for the sugar example in Figure 15.4 (p. 802). Our first step is to take expected values for the two probability nodes. These expected values, listed in triangles above the probability nodes, are the expected costs, not counting transactions costs, of decisions d_2 and d_3. Then we fold back to the decision node by taking the minimum of $1702 + 110$, $1728 + 65$, and 1754. Since this minimum is 1754, we put 1754 in a triangle above the decision node. We also put a mark (/ /) on the decision d_3 branch to indicate that d_3 is the best decision.

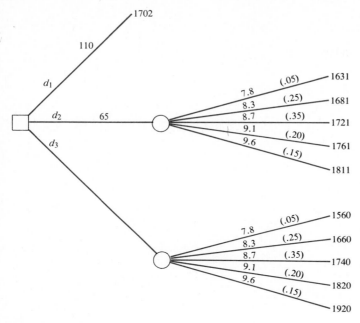

Figure 15.3
Alternate Decision Tree for the Sugar Example

The key to this folding-back procedure, especially for more complex decision trees, is to understand what the numbers in the triangles represent. There will be a number inside a triangle above every node that has uncertain outcomes to the right of it. Each of these numbers is a certainty equivalent. It tells us how much we are willing to trade the future for if we ever get to the point in time represented by that node. For example, the 1728 above the top probability node in Figure 15.4 means that *if* we have already made decision d_2 and have paid the $65 transactions cost, we are indifferent between paying $1728 for the sugar now and gambling on its price in six months. In the same way, the 1754 above the decision node means that we are indifferent between paying $1754 for the sugar now and gambling on its price in six months.

The fact that the numbers in triangles are certainty equivalents has an important implication. It means that once we have found the first few of these certainty equivalents and have written them above the appropriate nodes, everything to the *right* of these nodes is irrelevant for the remainder of the folding-back procedure. For example, once we find the certainty equivalents 1728 and 1754 for the probability nodes in Figure 15.4, the *remaining* decision problem is equivalent to the simplified decision tree in Figure 15.5.

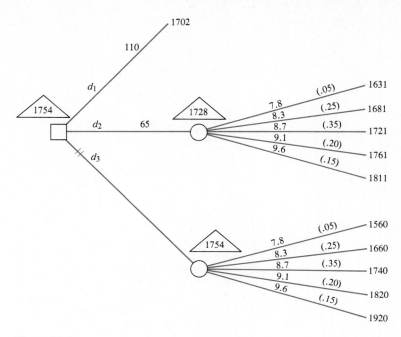

Figure 15.4
Decision Tree Solution for the Sugar Example

In essence, the certainty equivalents summarize all the necessary monetary information to the right of them.

We now present several examples of the one-stage decision problems described in Figure 15.1.

Figure 15.5

An Equivalent Decision Tree for the Sugar Example

EXAMPLE 15.1

A chain of supermarkets requires 24,000 fluorescent light bulbs for its stores. There are two suppliers of these bulbs. Supplier A offers them at $2.00 per bulb and will replace any defectives with guaranteed good ones for $2.00 each. Supplier B offers them at $2.05 per bulb and guarantees to replace defectives for $1.00 each. From past experience, the distribution of the proportion of defective bulbs (from either supplier) is given below.

Proportion Defective	Probability
.03	.1
.04	.2
.05	.4
.06	.3

For example, the probability is .4 that 5%, or 1200, of the 24,000 bulbs will be defective. The supermarket plans to sell them for $2.25 apiece and charge nothing for replacement of defectives. From which supplier should it buy the bulbs, and what is its optimal expected profit?

SOLUTION

The possible states of nature are the possible proportions defective, and the possible decisions are to buy from A or B. The payoffs are receipts from customers minus payments to the supplier. For example, the payoff from going with supplier B and seeing 4% defectives is

$$24,000(2.25) - 24,000(2.05) - 24,000(.04)(1.00) = \$3840$$

The complete payoff table is shown in Table 15.10.

Table 15.10   Payoff Table for Example 15.1

		Proportion Defective			
		.03	.04	.05	.06
Supplier	A	4560	4080	3600	3120
	B	4080	3840	3600	3360

This payoff table leads directly to the decision tree shown in Figure 15.6. By folding back, we see that supplier A offers a slightly better deal. The supermarket's expected profit from supplier A's bulbs is $3648.

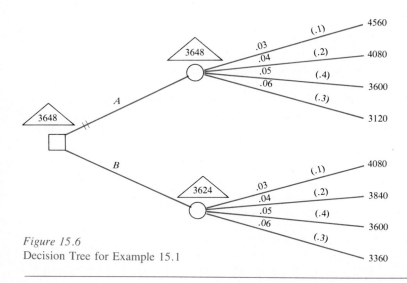

Figure 15.6
Decision Tree for Example 15.1

EXAMPLE 15.2

In trying to decide how to design a space vehicle, NASA needs to know whether to provide zero, one, or two "backup" systems for an important part of the vehicle. The first backup system (if provided) comes into use only if the original system fails. The second backup (if provided) comes into use only if the original system and the first backup both fail. The engineers claim that each system, independently of the others, has a .01 probability of failing if called into use. Each backup system costs $70,000 to produce and install. Once in flight, the mission will fail only if the original system and all backups fail. The cost of a mission failure (in addition to production costs) is assessed at $8,000,000. How many backups should be provided to minimize total expected costs?

SOLUTION

The possible decisions are to provide zero, one, or two backup systems. The states of nature are that the mission succeeds, s_1, or that it fails, s_2. The probabilities of these depend on the decision taken. In particular, if i backup systems are provided, the mission fails only if $i + 1$ systems (the original and the i backups) all fail. Using the multiplication rule for independent events, we have

$$P(s_2 \text{ with } i \text{ backups}) = (.01)^{i+1}$$
$$P(s_1) = 1 - P(s_2) = 1 - (.01)^{i+1}$$

For example, if two backups are provided, $P(s_2) = (.01)^3 = .000001$ and $P(s_1) = .999999$.

The relevant decision tree is shown in Figure 15.7. Notice that we have put the costs of the backups on the decision branches where they occur. We see that the optimal decision is to include one backup system. This decision results in an expected cost of $70,800; $70,000 of this is the certain cost of the backup system, and $800 is the expected cost from a possible mission failure.

EXAMPLE 15.3

Mr. Foyt has just bought a new $15,000 car. Being an average driver, he believes that his chances of having an accident in the next year are 1 out of 20. If he does have an accident, the types of accidents, their conditional

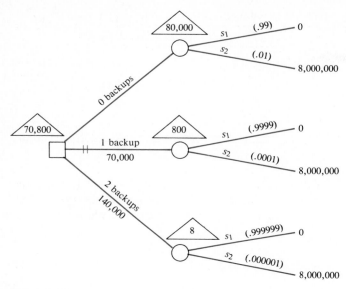

Figure 15.7
Decision Tree for Example 15.2

probabilities (conditional on having an accident), and damage amounts are shown below.

Type	1	2	3	4
Probability	.6	.2	.1	.1
Damage	$100	$500	$2000	$15,000

How much should Mr. Foyt be willing to pay for $150-deductible collision insurance? (With this type of insurance, he pays the first $150 if he causes an accident, and the insurance company pays the rest.)

SOLUTION

Let C be the yearly premium for the $150-deductible insurance. We will find the price C such that Mr. Foyt is indifferent between buying and not buying the insurance. His cost table is shown in Table 15.11 (p. 806). The important thing to notice is that the damage amount, if over $150, is irrelevant to Mr. Foyt if he buys the insurance.

To fill in a decision tree, we need the (unconditional) probabilities of the various outcomes. Let A be the event that Mr. Foyt has an accident and let A_i be the event that he has an accident of type i, $i = 1, 2, 3, 4$. We are given that $P(A) = \frac{1}{20} = .05$. We are also given the conditional probabilities

Table 15.11   Cost Table for Example 15.3

	No Accident	Types of Accidents			
		A_1	A_2	A_3	A_4
With Insurance	C	$C + 100$	$C + 150$	$C + 150$	$C + 150$
Without Insurance	0	100	500	2000	15,000

$P(A_1|A) = .6$, $P(A_2|A) = .2$, $P(A_3|A) = .1$, and $P(A_4|A) = .1$. Using the multiplication rule for conditional probabilities and the fact that $P(A_i \text{ and } A)$ equals $P(A_i)$ (because A occurs for certain if A_i occurs), we have

$$P(A_i) = P(A_i|A)P(A) = \begin{cases} .03 & i = 1 \\ .01 & i = 2 \\ .005 & i = 3 \\ .005 & i = 4 \end{cases}$$

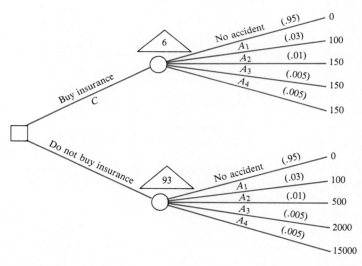

Figure 15.8
Decision Tree for Example 15.3

We use these probabilities in the decision tree in Figure 15.8. This figure shows that the expected collision claim without insurance is \$93, and the expected collision claim with insurance is \$6. Thus, if $C = \$93 - \$6 =$

$87, Mr. Foyt is indifferent between insurance and no insurance. In fact, $87 is the *most* he should be willing to pay for this insurance.

EXAMPLE 15.4

Precision Incorporated, a company that specializes in scientific instruments, has been invited to make a bid on a large government contract. The contract calls for a specific number of these instruments to be delivered during the coming year. The bids must be sealed (so that no company knows what the others are bidding), and the low bid wins the contract. Precision estimates that it will cost $5000 to prepare a bid and $95,000 to supply the instruments if it wins the contract. The options it decides to consider are (1) to make no bid, (2) to bid $115,000, (3) to bid $120,000, and (4) to bid $125,000. On the basis of past contracts of this type, Precision believes that the low bid from the competition, if there is any competition, has the following probability distribution.

Low Bid	Probability
Less than $115,000	.2
Between $115,000 and $120,000	.4
Between $120,000 and $125,000	.3
Greater than $125,000	.1

However, there is a 30% chance that there will be no competing bids. Precision wants a decision that maximizes the expected value of its net profit.

SOLUTION

We first label the states of nature as

s_1: no competition
s_2: lowest competing bid is less than $115,000
s_3: lowest competing bid is between $115,000 and $120,000
s_4: lowest competing bid is between $120,000 and $125,000
s_5: lowest competing bid is greater than $125,000

We are given that $P(s_1) = .3$. The probabilities of the other states of nature are their conditional probabilities, given competition, times the probability of competition, .7. For example, $P(s_2) = .4(.7) = .28$. The payoff is 0 if Precision does not bid. Otherwise, it equals $-$$5000 if the bid is not won, and it equals the bid amount minus $95,000 minus $5000 if the bid is won.

We use these facts to fill in the payoff table shown in Table 15.12 (p. 808) and the decision tree shown in Figure 15.9. Notice that we do not need five

Table 15.12 Payoff Table for Example 15.4

		Competition's Low Bid ($1000s)				
		No Bid	< 115	> 115 < 120	> 120 < 125	> 125
	No Bid	0	0	0	0	0
Company A's	115	15	−5	15	15	15
Bid	120	20	−5	−5	20	20
($1000s)	125	25	−5	−5	−5	25
		.3	.14	.28	.21	.07 ← Probabilities

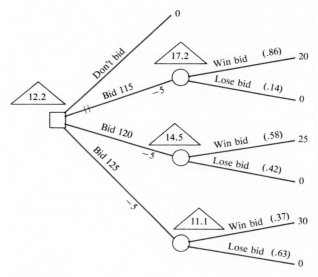

Figure 15.9
Decision Tree for Example 15.4 (in $1000s)

probability branches for each probability node; all we need are two branches that tell whether Precision wins or loses the bid. The largest expected profit is 12.2, or $12,200, from bidding $115,000.

Problems for Sections 15.3, 15.4

7. For the cost table in Problem 2 (p. 793), assume that the first two states of nature (s_1 and s_2) are equally likely, and the probability of the third, s_3, is p. Find the decision that minimizes the EMV when $p = .1$; when $p = .3$; when $p = .5$; when $p = .7$; when $p = .9$. How sensitive to the value of p is the optimal decision?

8. A gambler makes a bet where he loses $100 with probability .2, he loses $50 with probability .4, he wins $50 with probability .3, and he wins $300 with probability .1. If EMV is his decision criterion, calculate the certainty equivalent of this bet, and explain exactly what it means. Should he make the bet? Why or why not?

9. Draw a decision tree for Problem 7 when $p = .5$, and then solve it. Compare the "ingredients" of this solution with your calculations in Problem 7.

10. Suppose that the decision tree for Example 15.2 is changed so that the costs of producing the backups are included in the costs at the rightmost tips of the decision tree (rather than under the decision branches where they occur, as in Figure 15.7). Rework the problem this way and confirm that the answer is the same.

11. A company is considering the introduction of two new products to the market. Research and development costs for product 1 are $90,000; for product 2, the figure is $75,000. The success of these products depends on the general economy and on the consumers' reaction to these products. These can be summarized by three states of nature: s_1 (good), s_2 (fair), and s_3 (poor). The company's revenues (not counting research and development costs) for introducing product 1 only, product 2 only, or both products, are shown below (in $1000s). The probabilities of the states nature are also shown below. The company has four options: introduce neither product, introduce product 1 only, introduce product 2 only, or introduce both products. The first option entails no costs since research and development have not yet begun.

		States of Nature		
		s_1	s_2	s_3
Decisions on Which Products to Introduce	Neither	0	0	0
	1 only	250	130	60
	2 only	210	115	55
	Both	410	195	100
	Probabilities	.3	.5	.2

a. Construct a payoff table for this problem.
b. Solve the company's problem of maximizing EMV by means of a decision tree. What is the best decision? What is the associated EMV, and how can it be interpreted as a certainty equivalent?

12. Consider a company that is trying to decide whether to ship some equipment now or wait until the threat of a dock strike is over. The costs, including shipping costs and delay costs, are shown in the following table. The probabilities of a dock strike or no dock strike are p and $1 - p$, as shown below the table. For which values of p does shipping now minimize the company's expected cost?

	Strike	No Strike
Ship Now	$6000	$400
Wait	$1000	$1000
Probabilities	p	$1 - p$

13. In Example 15.2 of Section 15.4, we could also define the states of nature as the possible numbers of system failures. For example, if two backups are included, there are three states of nature: no failures, one failure, and two failures. Draw the appropriate decision tree with this definition of states of nature, label it, and solve it. (You should obtain the same optimal decision and corresponding EMV as in the example.)

14. In Example 15.3 of Section 15.4, assume that $250-deductible collision insurance is also available. How much less would Mr. Foyt be willing to pay for this than for $150-deductible insurance? Intuitively, why is $150-deductible insurance not worth $100 more than $250-deductible insurance?

15. A drugstore that provides film-developing services is trying to decide on its pricing policy for 24-print rolls of color film. It will choose one of the following options (and then use it for all customers): (1) charge a flat $5.25 per roll, or (2) charge 24 cents for each print the customer decides to accept. From past data, the probability distribution of the number of prints a typical customer refuses is given below. Use a decision tree to find the pricing policy that maximizes the store's EMV. If the store's cost of developing a 24-print roll is C dollars, is the answer to the problem dependent on the value of C? Explain.

k	0	1	2	3	4	5
P(refusing k prints)	.55	.15	.10	.08	.07	.05

*16. Consider the case of Souvenirs, Inc., which is in charge of manufacturing and distributing various types of souvenirs for the upcoming Olympics games. The company is undecided about the quantity of each item that should be produced. On the one hand, a profit can be made for each souvenir made and sold. On the other hand, Olympics souvenirs that are not sold prior to the Olympics are practically worthless afterward.

For one particular souvenir, the total cost per unit of producing and marketing is $2. Each unit is then sold for $3.50. The uncertainty arises because the demand for this souvenir is unknown. It is treated as a random variable with the following distribution. Assuming that the company must produce this souvenir in batches of 1000 units, how many batches should be produced to maximize the expected profit? (Calculate the expected profit from producing k batches, for $k = 5, 6, 7, 8, 9, 10$.)

Demand (1000s)	Probability
5	.1
6	.2
7	.2
8	.3
9	.1
10	.1

15.5

Using Information to Revise Probabilities: Bayes' Rule

Before we can use the EMV criterion, we must assess probabilities of the various states of nature. To assess these probabilities, we often proceed rather informally. We look at relevant historical data, we read current information in newspapers or periodicals, we consult with experts, and we use our own subjective beliefs about the uncertain outcomes. The only mathematical rule is that the probabilities must be nonnegative and sum to 1. The probabilities that we assess are often called *prior* probabilities, because they are assessed prior to any further information gathering.

In many situations, however, we have the opportunity to learn more about the states of nature *before* we make a final decision. At some cost we may be able to learn information that is related to the true state of nature. After receiving this information, we need to make a formal revision of the prior probabilities. The revised probabilities are called *posterior* probabilities, because they are obtained after, or posterior to, receiving the information. In this section we discuss the mechanism for revising probabilities.

A typical example will clarify the ideas. Suppose that a company is trying to decide whether to hire a particular person, Mr. Wright, for a very demanding job. If he is hired for the job, there are only two possible outcomes:

s_1: he is a success at the job
s_2: he is a failure at the job

The people in personnel examine Mr. Wright's past academic and professional record, they interview him, and they see how many similar people were successful at similar jobs. As a result of this effort, they assess the prior probabilities $P(s_1) = .6$ and $P(s_2) = .4$ for the two possible outcomes.

There is one other relevant piece of information the company plans to obtain. This is the result of a specially designed aptitude and stress test that

Mr. Wright must take. There are three possible outcomes of this test, labeled x_1, x_2, and x_3. These are defined as

x_1: his score is in the lower third of all test scores
x_2: his score is in the middle third of all test scores
x_3: his score is in the top third of all test scores

After we observe his test scores, we need to revise the prior probabilities. For example, if x_1 occurs, we expect the posterior probability of s_1 given x_1, written $P(s_1|x_1)$, to be lower than the prior probability $P(s_1)$. This is because a low test score (x_1) is not likely to accompany a successful employee (s_1). The question is how to obtain a numerical value for $P(s_1|x_1)$ and similar posterior probabilities.

The first step is to notice that the outcome of the test is random. This means that we need to attach probabilities to x_1, x_2, and x_3. One way to assess these probabilities is as follows. Suppose that this test has been given to many other applicants, and their subsequent successes or failures on similar jobs have been recorded. The historical data might appear as in Table 15.13a. The numbers inside the cells show the number of people with a given test score who went on to become successes or failures. For example, 27 of the people who scored in the middle third went on to become successes. These frequencies can easily be translated into conditional probabilities of the form $P(x|s)$. For example, of the 87 people who were eventual successes, 27 scored x_2 on the test. Therefore,

$$P(x_2|s_1) = \frac{27}{87} = .310$$

This probability and similar conditional probabilities are shown in Table 15.13b. Notice that the column sums are 1. This is because *some* x has to occur for any given s.

Of course, the probabilities listed in Table 15.13b are only relative frequencies from historical data. They may or may not be relevant for Mr.

Table 15.13

	s_1	s_2			s_1	s_2	
x_1	20	20		x_1	$^{20}/_{87}$ = .230	$^{20}/_{34}$ = .588	
x_2	27	9		x_2	$^{27}/_{87}$ = .310	$^{9}/_{34}$ = .265	
x_3	40	5		x_3	$^{40}/_{87}$ = .460	$^{5}/_{34}$ = .147	
	87	34	← Sums		1	1	← Sums

(a) Frequency table of historical data

(b) Likelihoods from historical data

Wright's situation. However, for lack of any better evidence, we will assume that these same probabilities do apply to Mr. Wright.

In decision making terminology, the probabilities in Table 15.13b are called *likelihoods*. More precisely, likelihoods are the probabilities of the possible information outcomes, given the various states of nature. A likelihood such as $P(x_2|s_1) = .310$ says that 31% of all people who went on to become successes scored x_2 on the test. Now we need to combine the likelihoods with the prior probabilities to obtain posterior probabilities. This is done by means of a very important result called *Bayes' rule*.

The general form of Bayes' rule is as follows.

Bayes' Rule for Revising Probabilities

$$P(s_i|x_j) = \frac{P(x_j|s_i)P(s_i)}{\sum\limits_{k} P(x_j|s_k)P(s_k)}$$

The key to remembering this rule is that it expresses a posterior probability as a ratio of two expressions. The numerator is always a likelihood times a prior, and the denominator is always the sum of likelihoods times priors. In the formula, s_i is any particular state of nature, x_j is any particular information outcome, and the sum (on k) in the denominator is over all possible states of nature.

The denominator in Bayes' rule is important in its own right. It is the marginal (or unconditional) probability of the information outcome x_j.

Marginal Probability of x_j

$$P(x_j) = \sum\limits_{k} P(x_j|s_k)P(s_k)$$

Bayes' rule is illustrated for Mr. Wright's data in Table 15.14. At the top we list the prior probabilities of s_1 and s_2. Then for each test result x, there are three rows. The first row lists the likelihoods for each state of nature. The second row lists the products of likelihoods times priors, and its shows the sum of these products in the right-hand margin. The third row lists the ratios of likelihoods times priors to the marginal probability of the corresponding x. These ratios are the desired posterior probabilities of s_1 and s_2. Notice that $P(s_1|x)$ and $P(s_2|x)$ sum to 1 for each x. This follows because exactly one of s_1 or s_2 must occur, regardless of the x that occurs. Also notice that the marginal probabilities of the three x's sum to 1, because exactly one of these x's must occur.

Table 15.14 Bayes' Rule Calculations

	s_1	s_2	
Prior ———→	.6	.4	
Likelihood ———			
Likelihood times prior ———	→ .230	.588	
x_1	→.6(.230) = .138	.4(.588) = .235	.373
Posterior —→	.138/.373 = .370	.235/.373 = .630	
x_2	.310 .6(.310) = .186 .186/.292 = .637	.265 .4(.265) = .106 .106/.292 = .363	.292
x_3	.460 .6(.460) = .276 .276/.335 = .824	.147 .4(.147) = .059 .059/.335 = .176	.335 ↑ Marginals for x

If we compare $P(s_1|x_1)$, $P(s_1|x_2)$, and $P(s_1|x_3)$, we see that these go basically in the direction we would expect. If Mr. Wright scores in the lower third (x_1), his revised probability of being successful is only .370; if he scores in the middle third (x_2), his probability of being successful increases slightly to .637; if he scores in the upper third (x_3), his probability of being successful increases to .824.

We now look at two typical applications of Bayes' rule.

EXAMPLE 15.5

Consider a population of men and women, each of whom expresses a preference for brand A or brand B of a given product. The data in Table 15.15 show that 50% of the women prefer brand A, whereas only 30% of the men prefer brand A. Assume that 45% of the population are women. If a randomly selected person prefers brand A, what is the probability that this person is a woman? If another randomly selected person prefers brand B, what is the probability that this person is a man?

Table 15.15

Women		Men	
Prefer A	Prefer B	Prefer A	Prefer B
50%	50%	30%	70%

SOLUTION

Define the following events:

s_1: a woman is selected
s_2: a man is selected
x_1: the person selected prefers brand A
x_2: the person selected prefers brand B

We are given $P(x_1|s_1) = .5$, $P(x_1|s_2) = .3$, and $P(s_1) = .45$. The first question asks for $P(s_1|x_1)$, the probability that a person who prefers brand A is a woman. By Bayes' rule, we have

$$P(s_1|x_1) = \frac{P(x_1|s_1)P(s_1)}{P(x_1|s_1)P(s_1) + P(x_1|s_2)P(s_2)} = \frac{.5(.45)}{.5(.45) + .3(.55)} = .577$$

The second question asks for $P(s_2|x_2)$, the probability that a person who prefers brand B is a man. Notice that we are now dealing with the subset of the population who prefer brand B. This is a totally different subset than the subset from the first question, that is, the subset who prefer brand A. Therefore, $P(s_2|x_2)$ is *not* 1 minus the answer to the first question, a mistake that is commonly made. From Bayes' rule, we have

$$P(s_2|x_2) = \frac{P(x_2|s_2)P(s_2)}{P(x_2|s_1)P(s_1) + P(x_2|s_2)P(s_2)} = \frac{.7(.55)}{.5(.45) + .7(.55)} = .631$$

The answer to the first question implies that 57.7% of all people who prefer brand A are women; the other 42.3% are men. The answer to the second question implies that 63.1% of all people who prefer brand B are men; the other 36.9% are women.

EXAMPLE 15.6

A marketing research group wants to find the population proportion p of people who believe a new brand of window cleaner is better than any similar product on the market. The research group believes there are only three possible values of p: .2, .25, and .3. For lack of any better information, it believes these values are equally likely to be the true p. (In a real application, we would assume many more possible values of p, probably a whole continuum of values.) To learn more about p, the group sends a questionnaire to 100 randomly chosen members of the population. The results of this questionnaire show that 29 out of the 100 people believe the new product is the best on the market. Find the revised probabilities for the true value of p.

SOLUTION

In this problem there are three states of nature, s_1, s_2, and s_3, corresponding to .2, .25, and .3, the possible values of p. Prior to the questionnaire, these are assumed equally likely, so the prior probabilities are $P(s_1) = P(s_2) = P(s_3) = \frac{1}{3}$. The information from the questionnaire is the number of responses favoring the new product. But if p is the proportion of the entire population who favor the new product, the number of sampled members who favor the new product is binomially distributed with parameters $n = 100$ and p. Specifically, the likelihood of 29 favorable responses out of 100 is

$$P(29 \text{ out of } 100 | \text{true } p) = \binom{100}{29} p^{29}(1 - p)^{71}$$

Letting x denote the outcome "29 out of 100 are favorable responses," we can evaluate $P(x|s_i)$ for any s_i. For example,

$$P(x|s_2) = P(29 \text{ out of } 100 | \text{true } p = .25) = \binom{100}{29}(.25)^{29}(.75)^{71}$$

Now we use Bayes' rule to find the posterior probabilities of the form $P(s_i|x)$. The calculations are shown below.

$$P(s_1|x) = P(\text{true } p = .2 \mid 29 \text{ out of } 100)$$

$$= \frac{\binom{100}{29}(.2)^{29}(.8)^{71}(\frac{1}{3})}{\binom{100}{29}(.2)^{29}(.8)^{71}(\frac{1}{3}) + \binom{100}{29}(.25)^{29}(.75)^{71}(\frac{1}{3}) + \binom{100}{29}(.3)^{29}(.7)^{71}(\frac{1}{3})}$$

$$= \frac{(.2)^{29}(.8)^{71}}{(.2)^{29}(.8)^{71} + (.25)^{29}(.75)^{71} + (.3)^{29}(.7)^{71}} = .058$$

Similarly,

$$P(s_2|x) = P(\text{true } p = .25 | 29 \text{ out of } 100)$$

$$= \frac{(.25)^{29}(.75)^{71}}{(.2)^{29}(.8)^{71} + (.25)^{29}(.75)^{71} + (.3)^{29}(.7)^{71}} = .381$$

and

$$P(s_3|x) = P(\text{true } p = .3 \mid 29 \text{ out of } 100)$$

$$= \frac{(.3)^{29}(.7)^{71}}{(.2)^{29}(.8)^{71} + (.25)^{29}(.75)^{71} + (.3)^{29}(.7)^{71}} = .561$$

Notice that the factor $\binom{100}{29}$, common to each likelihood, can be canceled from the numerator and denominator in each probability calculation. It is also possible to cancel the prior probabilities (the $\frac{1}{3}$'s), but this is possible only because of the equally likely assumption.

The posterior probabilities on p are quite different from the prior probabilities. The marketing research group initially has no idea which of the three possible values of p is the true one, so it assigns equal prior probabilities. But the information from the questionnaire is fairly strong evidence in favor of $p = .3$ and is strong evidence against $p = .2$. This is shown by the small posterior probability of $p = .2$, namely $P(s_1|x) = .058$, and the large posterior probability of $p = .3$, namely $P(s_3|x) = .561$. The probability of $p = .25$ increases only slightly, from $\frac{1}{3}$ to .381.

Before leaving this section, we emphasize that not all decision problems with sample information require Bayes' rule. This depends entirely on the probabilities we are given in the statement of a problem and those we need in the decision tree. An example where Bayes' rule is not needed is the following.

EXAMPLE 15.7

Suppose that the Toys for Tots company is contemplating a new advertising campaign to increase its share of the market. The marketing people in the company assume that the increase in market share can be 0%, 5%, or 10%. These are the three states of nature. However, before the final stages of the new campaign are undertaken (that is, before it is too late to back out), Toys for Tots will be able to observe whether its main competitor is about to undertake a similar campaign. If the competitor does undertake its campaign, Toys for Tots assesses the probabilities of its three possible increases to be .5, .3, and .2. If the competitor does not undertake its campaign, Toys for Tots believes that the probabilities of these three possible increases are .1, .4, and .5.

In this example a likelihood would be of the form

$$P(\text{competitor's plan} \mid \text{increase in Toys for Tots's market share})$$

and Bayes' rule would be used to convert this to a posterior probability of the form

$$P(\text{increase in Toys for Tots's market share} \mid \text{competitor's plan})$$

However, the likelihoods are not given in the problem statement. Instead, the posterior probabilities are given directly. Therefore, when Toys for Tots is making its final stage decision, after observing its competitor's plan, it does *not* need to use Bayes' rule; the probabilities it needs are exactly those that are given.

17. A person enters the hospital, and there is some initial suspicion that he has a specific disease. In fact, as a result of a preliminary examination, the doctors believe the probability is .1 that he has this disease. To gain more information, an expensive test is administered to the patient. This test is not perfectly accurate. It gives a positive response (that is, indicates the disease is present) in 5% of all patients who do not have the disease, and it gives a negative response (that is, indicates the disease is not present) in 7% of all patients who do have the disease.
    a. What are the states of nature and the prior probabilities for this problem?
    b. What are the possible results of the test?
    c. What are the likelihoods?
    d. What is the probability of a positive test result for this particular patient?
    e. If this person's test results are positive, use Bayes' rule to find the posterior probability that he has the disease.
    f. If this person's test results are negative, use Bayes' rule to find the posterior probability that he does not have the disease.

18. Consider a population of 1000 people, 400 of whom are college graduates. It is known that 150 of the college graduates earn at least $30,000 per year, and 100 of the noncollege graduates make at least $30,000 per year.
    a. What is the probability that a randomly chosen person makes at least $30,000 per year?
    b. If a randomly chosen person makes at least $30,000 per year, what is the probability that this person is a college graduate?
    c. If a randomly chosen person makes less than $30,000 per year, what is the probability that this person is a college graduate?

19. An oil company is planning to drill for oil on a particular site. On similar sites in the past, drilling has yielded "successful" amounts of oil 30% of the time. The company first decides to obtain seismic readings. In the past, similar seismic readings have been optimistic on 60% of the successful sites, and they have been pessimistic on 70% of the unsuccessful sites.
    a. Given that the present reading turns out to be optimistic, calculate the probability that the current site will be successful. Find the probability of this same event if the current reading is pessimistic.
    b. If drilling costs $10,000 and the oil from a successful and an unsuccessful site yield revenues (not counting drilling costs) of $25,000 and $5000, respectively, find the expected profit, given a pessimistic reading. Based on your answer, what would you suggest to the company if this reading is obtained?

20. A company is thinking of changing the packaging design of a certain product. The marketing people believe the probability is .7 that this change will increase profits. The change is tried in a limited test market, and it results in reduced profits. The probability is .2 that this test market result would occur even though the new design would increase profits nationally. However, if the new design would not increase profits nationally, the probability of the observed test market result is .9. Given the test market result, what is the revised probability that the new design will increase profits nationally?

21. Most baseball teams win much more regularly when they play at their home field. One particular team wins 58% of its home games and only 45% of its away games. Half of its games are at home and half are away. If we hear that this team has just won a game but we are not told where the game was played, what is the probability that it was played at the team's home field?

*22. If we hear that the baseball team in Problem 21 just won both games of a doubleheader (two games played on the same day on the same field), what is the probability that these games were played at the team's home field?

23. In a state with mandatory yearly automobile inspections, it is estimated that 15% of all cars have problems that need to be corrected. Unfortunately, the inspections fail to catch these problems, whenever they are present, 10% of the time. Consider a car that is inspected and nothing is found to be wrong. What is the probability that there is indeed something wrong that the inspection has failed to catch? (Assume that if there is really nothing wrong, the inspection will not find anything wrong.)

24. A financial analyst has just received information that could affect the price of a particular stock in the next few days. He is 75% certain that the information is correct. If it is correct,

he assesses that the price of the stock will fall in the next few days with probability .8, and that it will rise or remain unchanged with probability .2. If the information is incorrect, he believes that the two possibilities above are equally likely.

a. If the price of the stock falls in the next few days, what is the probability that the information was correct?

b. If the price of the stock does not fall, what is the probability that the information was correct?

15.6

More Complicated Decision Trees

Many realistic decision problems are more complicated than the single-stage problems we have examined so far. The decision maker often has to make decisions in stages, and decisions in the early stages usually have a direct bearing on the decisions he will want (or be able) to make in the later stages. It is impossible to categorize all possible types of decision problems because there is virtually no limit to the variety of possible situations. However, most problems have decision trees where decision nodes and probability nodes alternate. First, a decision is made, next an outcome is observed, next another decision is made, next another outcome is observed, and so on. At the end a payoff is received or a cost is incurred. Often the outcomes of the early probability branches influence the probabilities of the later probability branches. In these cases Bayes' rule is usually necessary.

One particular type of problem is shown in Figure 15.10. We call this a *two-stage* decision problem. In this problem there is one final decision that must eventually be made. After this decision is made, the true state of nature will be revealed, and a payoff or cost will result. But before this final decision is made, the decision maker has a chance to do one or more "sampling experiments." This sampling, which generally costs money, is done to learn more about the true state of nature. The hope is that the information will enable the decision maker to make a better decision.

If we do decide to perform a sampling experiment, the results of the sample will not be known until after the experiment. (If we knew the sample results

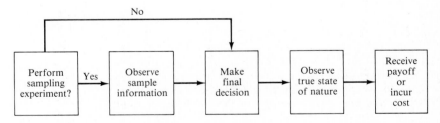

Figure 15.10
Two-Stage Decision Problem

ahead of time, there would be no point in wasting money on the experiment.)
After the sample results are known, we can then decide which final decision
to make. Clearly, this final decision may depend on the particular sample
information received. If we receive one piece of information, we may make
decision d_1, if we receive another piece of information, we may instead make
decision d_2, and so on. So the solution to this type of problem is not a single
decision but rather a complete contingency plan that specifies the correct
decision for every possible piece of sample information. The following example illustrates these ideas.

EXAMPLE 15.8

Mr. Stevens wishes to buy a tractor-lawn mower from the Rider company.
The company buys these mowers for $5000 and is currently selling them for
$5200. Because $5200 is more cash than Mr. Stevens has, he asks if he can
pay on an installment plan. Under this plan he pays a $200 down payment
and the other $5000 over the next 15 months. The company needs to decide
whether to let him do this, because it has recently been having problems with
people defaulting on installment loans. The company's experience shows that
10% of its customers default, and on these it can expect to recover only 20%
of the loan value.

   Before making a decision on Mr. Stevens's request, the company can buy
credit-rating information on him. This information will show that he is in the
high risk (HR), medium risk (MR), or low risk (LR) category. Also the
credit-rating service claims the following conditional probabilities (obtained
from historical frequencies). Here D stands for default, and ND stands for
no default.

$$P(HR|D) = .65 \quad P(MR|D) = .30 \quad P(LR|D) = .05$$
$$P(HR|ND) = .20 \quad P(MR|ND) = .25 \quad P(LR|ND) = .55$$

For example, $P(HR|D) = .65$ means that 65% of people who eventually
default were rated in the high-risk category. The rating service charges $30
for its information. What should Rider do?

SOLUTION

The first decision is whether to buy the credit-rating information. If Rider
does buy it, the decision on Mr. Stevens's request can be delayed until the
rating is received. Otherwise, the decision on Mr. Stevens's request can be
made right away. If Rider buys the credit-rating information, it will need to
base its final decision on the probability of default, given the credit rating.
The prior probability of default is $P(D) = .10$, and the likelihoods of the
ratings, given default or no default, are given above. We need to use Bayes'
rule to find the posterior probability of default for each possible rating. For

example,

$$P(\text{D}|\text{HR}) = \frac{P(\text{HR}|\text{D})P(\text{D})}{P(\text{HR}|\text{D})P(\text{D}) + P(\text{HR}|\text{ND})P(\text{ND})} = \frac{.65(.1)}{.65(.1) + .20(.9)} = .2653$$

Similarly,

$$P(\text{D}|\text{MR}) = \frac{P(\text{MR}|\text{D})P(\text{D})}{P(\text{MR}|\text{D})P(\text{D}) + P(\text{MR}|\text{ND})P(\text{ND})} = \frac{.30(.1)}{.30(.1) + .25(.9)} = .1176$$

and

$$P(\text{D}|\text{LR}) = \frac{P(\text{LR}|\text{D})P(\text{D})}{P(\text{LR}|\text{D})P(\text{D}) + P(\text{LR}|\text{ND})P(\text{ND})} = \frac{.05(.1)}{.05(.1) + .55(.9)} = .01$$

Because D or ND must occur for any credit rating, we have

$$P(\text{ND}|\text{HR}) = 1 - P(\text{D}|\text{HR}) = 1 - .2653 = .7347$$
$$P(\text{ND}|\text{MR}) = 1 - P(\text{D}|\text{MR}) = 1 - .1176 = .8824$$
$$P(\text{ND}|\text{LR}) = 1 - P(\text{D}|\text{LR}) = 1 - .01 = .99$$

The only other probabilities needed for the decision tree are $P(\text{HR})$, $P(\text{MR})$, and $P(\text{LR})$, the probabilities of the various credit ratings. These are not the likelihoods given earlier because the default status of Mr. Stevens is not known until *after* the rating is received. However, we have these probabilities in the calculations above. They are the denominators in the Bayes' rule formulas. For example,

$$P(\text{HR}) = P(\text{HR}|\text{D})P(\text{D}) + P(\text{HR}|\text{ND})P(\text{ND}) = .65(.1) + .20(.9) = .245$$

The others are $P(\text{MR}) = .255$ and $P(\text{LR}) = .5$. (Check that these three probabilities sum to 1, as they should.)

The decision tree for this example is shown in Figure 15.11. The numbers to the right represent Rider's profit or loss on this tractor-lawn mower, not counting the payment to the credit-rating service. In particular, the -3800 represents the \$200 down payment, plus the 20% recovered from the default, minus the \$5000 the company paid for the mower. (We assume that if the installment loan is not granted, Mr. Stevens will not buy the mower.) The top part of the tree shows that if no credit rating is available, the company should not issue the loan. However, if the credit rating is purchased, there is a 50–50 chance that the LR rating will result, in which case the loan is profitable. In fact, the expected profit of \$80 from having the rating and then proceeding optimally is more than enough to cover the cost of the rating. To summarize Figure 15.11, the company should purchase the rating and then

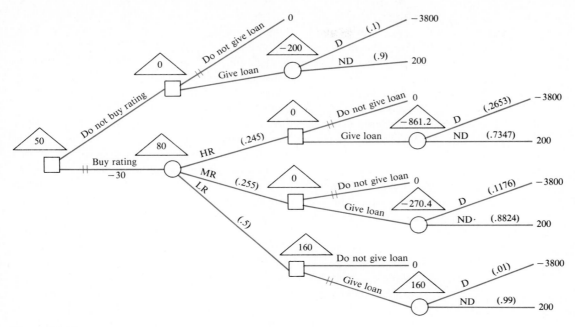

Figure 15.11
Decision Tree for Example 15.8

grant the loan only if a LR rating is received. The expected net profit is $50 from using this strategy.

The important thing to notice about the decision tree in Example 15.8 is that it follows all the conventions for decision trees listed earlier. We especially emphasize the timing convention. Because time moves from left to right, all nodes and branches toward the right of the tree are conditional on the events (decisions and outcomes) to the left of them. This has two important implications. First, when we are building the "skeleton" of the tree, we need to put the nodes and branches in the proper order, namely, as they evolve through time. This may sound obvious, but it is probably the cause of more errors in decision problems than anything else. Second, the probabilities on the probability branches are conditional on those events, and only those events, that have occurred to the left of them. The required probabilities may or may not be those given in the data. In case they are not, Bayes' rule is probably necessary.

There are really no new ideas or formulas involved when we go from single-stage problems to more complicated problems. We still build decision trees according to the conventions listed earlier and then fold back on them (from right to left) to obtain the solution. Also, the key to the folding-back process is still the set of numbers in the triangles, the certainty equivalents. These have the same interpretation as before, that is, they summarize all decisions and outcomes to the right of them. The principal difficulties in these more complex problems are (1) understanding the problem thoroughly, particularly the possible options and their timing; (2) drawing the appropriate decision tree; and (3) labeling it with the appropriate probabilities and monetary values. After the decision tree has been drawn and labeled appropriately, the solution procedure is straightforward.

We now present several examples to illustrate the many kinds of problems that are possible. These examples are purposely not the same as the "typical" two-stage problem in Example 15.8. Instead, we present a variety of problem types in order to stress the flexibility required in dealing with different decision problems.

EXAMPLE 15.9

A paper company in the state of Washington currently has an option to buy a piece of land with good timber forest on it. The current selling price is $1,200,000. The company does not actually need the timber from this land for another two months, but its management people fear that another company might buy the land in the next two months. They assess there is 1 chance out of 20 that another company will buy the land in the coming month. If this does not occur, there is 1 chance out of 10 that another company will buy the land in the following month. If the company does not take advantage of its current option, it can attempt to buy the land in one month or in two months if it is still available.

The company's incentive for delaying the purchase is that their financial experts believe that the price of the land may fall significantly in one or both of the next two months. The possible price decreases and their probabilities are shown in Table 15.16. The top table shows the (marginal) probabilities of the possible price decreases in the first month. The bottom table shows the conditional probabilities of the possible price decreases in month 2, *given* the price decrease in month 1.

If the company purchases the land, it believes that it can gross $1,800,000. (This does not count the cost of purchasing the land.) But if it does not purchase the land, it believes that it can make $350,000 from alternative investments. What should the company do?

SOLUTION

The company definitely wants to buy this land because its net profit of at least $600,000 is much better than the net profit of $350,000 it could make on alternative investments. But the problem is whether to wait for a lower selling price and risk losing the option to buy the land, or buy the land while

Table 15.16 Probabilities for Example 15.9

		Price Decrease in Month 1		
		0	30,000	60,000
		.5	.3	.2

		Price Decrease in Month 2		
		0	30,000	60,000
Given Price	0	.2	.5	.3
Decrease	30,000	.5	.4	.1
in Month 1	60,000	.7	.25	.05

it is available. The relevant decision tree is shown in Figure 15.12 (p. 824). All monetary values are in $1000s. The numbers on the various ''buy'' branches are the purchase prices at the time the land is purchased. The probability branches are combinations of the events CB and CNB (competitor buys or does not buy the land) and the possible price decreases. The probabilities of these branches are fairly simple to obtain because Bayes' rule is not needed. For example, suppose that the price decrease in month 1 is $60,000. Then the probability that a competitor does not buy the land in month 2 and the price decrease in month 2 is $30,000 is the product of the two individual probabilities, namely .9(.25) = .225. (We are implicitly assuming that the competitors' choice to buy or not buy is independent of the amount of the price decrease. A more realistic assumption could be made without complicating the problem substantially.)

The optimal decision is as follows. The company should risk losing the land by delaying its purchase until a month from now, and at that time it should buy the land only if the price is less than $1,200,000. If the month 1 price is still $1,200,000, the company should wait another month and then buy the land if it is still available. The expected net profit from this policy is $609,682.50, which is only $9682.50 more than would be obtained by buying the land right away.

EXAMPLE 15.10

The physical plant at an eastern university uses coal for heating university buildings in the winter. Even though it is currently only June, the people in charge of energy planning have to start making plans for obtaining adequate winter coal supplies. (They especially realize the importance of this because they were caught short the previous winter and had to pay exorbitant prices

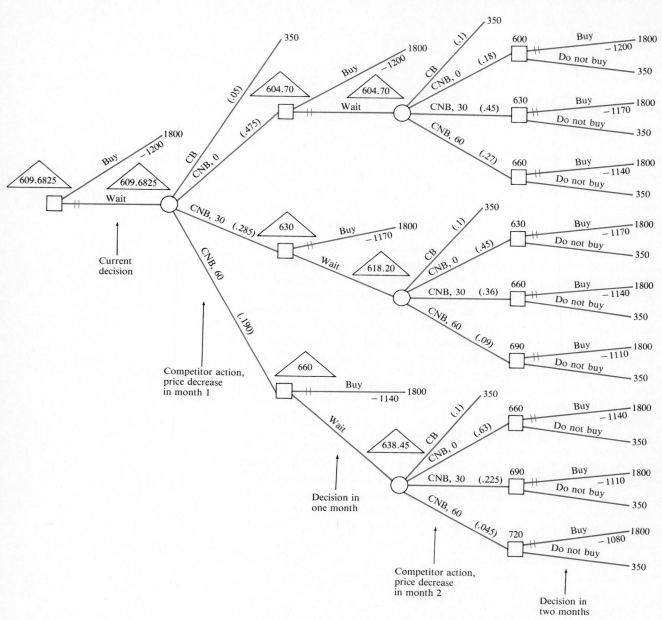

Figure 15.12

for coal.) The normal coal requirement for the winter months is 130,000 tons. For a mild winter, the requirement is only 125,000 tons, but for a severe winter, the requirement is 140,000 tons. They presently have an option to buy a contract for any amount of coal at $9.85 per ton. They may delay the purchase until early November, at which time the contract price will be $10.05 per ton. If the winter months arrive and there is not enough coal on hand, they estimate that the spot price of coal will be $10.65 per ton. If there is more than enough coal on hand, it will be valued at $9.50 per ton. This value reflects the fact that the coal can be used for the *next* winter, but that the university's money has been tied up for a whole year.

By early November, the planners will have observed the type of fall weather and will be better able to predict the winter weather. Their current probabilities for fall weather (mild fall, normal fall, or severe fall) are

$$P(MF) = .2 \qquad P(NF) = .4 \qquad P(SF) = .4$$

Once the fall weather is observed, they will use the probabilities in Table 15.17 to find the probabilities of winter weather. The probabilities in this table, obtained from historical weather data, show the probabilities of winter weather, given fall weather. For example, the table indicates that for years with a mild fall, a mild winter occurred 60% of the time.

The university's energy planners want to find a strategy that minimizes the expected cost of supplying the necessary coal. They decide to consider only contracts for multiples of 5000 tons.

Table 15.17 Probabilities of Winter Weather, Given Fall Weather, in Example 15.10

	MW	NW	SW
MF	.6	.3	.1
NF	.2	.6	.2
SF	.1	.3	.6

SOLUTION

The timing of events is: (1) the planners decide how much to buy in June, (2) fall weather is observed, (3) the planners decide how much to buy in November, (4) winter weather is observed, and (5) extra coal is purchased if necessary. The possible options are to buy from 125,000 to 140,000 tons in June and to supplement this in November. The total amount bought in June and November should not be greater than 140,000 tons.

The fact that we learn about winter weather when we observe fall weather suggests that Bayes' rule is necessary. However, we are given exactly those probabilities that are required in the decision tree, namely, marginal (or unconditional) probabilities of fall weather, and conditional probabilities of winter weather, given fall weather. Therefore, no probability revision is necessary for this problem.

The decision tree for this example is shown in Figure 15.13 (pp. 826–827). The monetary values are costs (in $1000s), not profits. This means that if coal is left over, its value at $9.50 per ton is shown as a negative number. The costs of the purchases in June and November are shown on the branches where they occur. Since the number of nodes and branches quickly multiplies as we go from left to right, we have summarized the final probability nodes

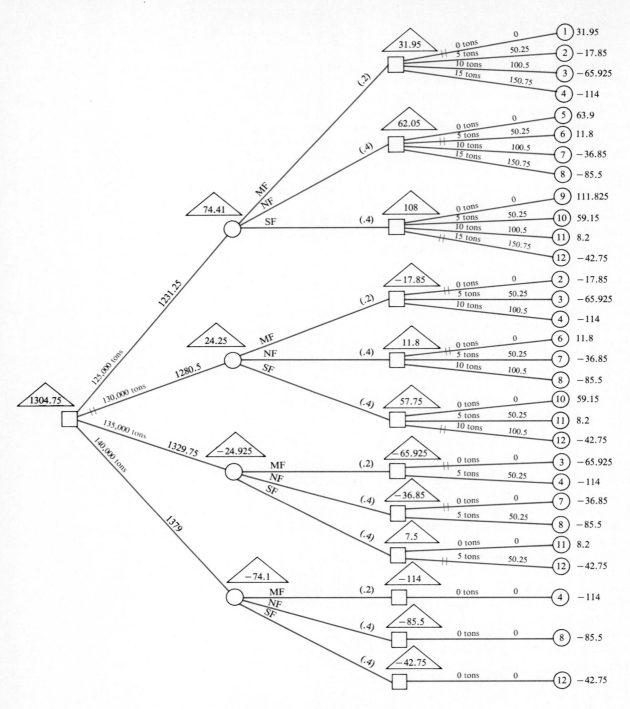

(a) Decision tree for Example 15.10

Figure 15.13

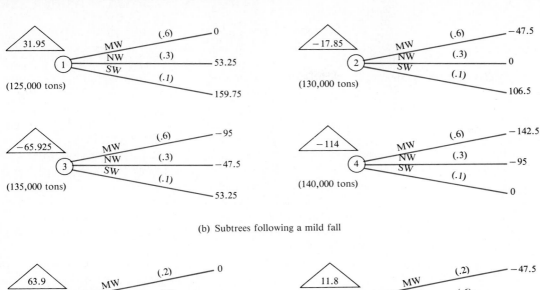

(b) Subtrees following a mild fall

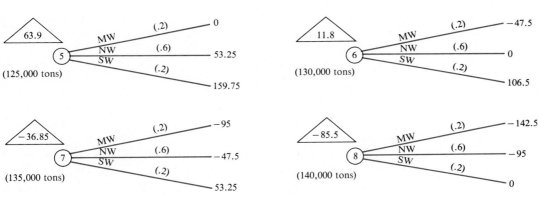

(c) Subtrees following a normal fall

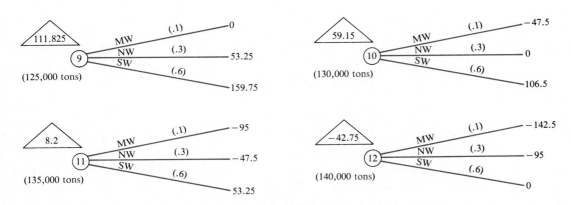

(d) Subtrees following a severe fall

and branches in Figure 15.13b–d. In these figures we show 12 "subtrees," one for each combination of fall weather and coal inventory (shown below the nodes) after the November purchase. (The numbers inside the 12 circle nodes are for identification purposes only.) The information from these "subtrees" is used in the main decision tree in Figure 15.13a.

In spite of the many calculations, the optimal policy is fairly simple to state. The university should buy 130,000 tons in June, it should buy nothing in November if fall weather is mild or normal, and it should buy 10,000 tons in November if fall weather is severe. The total expected cost from this strategy is $1,304,750. However, the optimality of this policy is probably quite sensitive to changes in the parameters of the problem. This is because several other policies have expected costs just slightly above the optimal expected cost. In fact, as far as the energy planners are concerned, one of the most important pieces of information from this decision analysis is that several different policies give very similar expected costs.

EXAMPLE 15.11

Western Fruit Company is a large fruit distributor based in California. Western Fruit owns its own orchards, picks the fruit, packs it, and sells it to eastern supermarket chains. The sales manager, Mr. Davis, currently has a request for an order of 4000 boxes of peaches at $5.70 per box from one of Western's most important customers, Wissingers Food Stores. The order is for a fairly uncommon variety of peaches, and Wissingers stipulates that it will accept delivery no later than June 26. It is currently June 5, and Mr. Davis is worried about taking the order. On the one hand, he does not want to refuse large orders from Wissingers because Wissingers might take its business elsewhere. In fact, Mr. Davis estimates that if Wissingers does not receive the order from Western on time and in good shape, Western has a 30% chance of losing $5000 profit and a 10% chance of losing $10,000 profit from potential Wissingers orders in future months.

On the other hand, the growers advise him that 4000 boxes of peaches of this particular type will not be ready for shipment until June 19 or June 22. (June 20 and June 21 are weekend days, when almost no packing takes place.) If the shipment leaves on June 19, it will arrive in the east on time, but if it does not leave until June 22, there is a 40% chance that it will not arrive on time. The growers currently find it difficult to assess the probability of having the peaches ready by June 19. However, they believe they will have a more precise estimate of this probability by June 12. At this time they will either have an "early" or "late" indication, and these are believed to be equally likely. Given an early indication, the probability of having the peaches ready by June 19 is .9; given a late indication, this probability is only .3. Mr. Davis replies that June 12 may be too late; he believes there is a 20% chance that Wissingers will have bought the peaches from a competitor if Western delays this long. There is one other problem, especially with this variety of peaches. Because of possible refrigeration problems, the peaches might decay by the time they reach their destination. The probability of this event is only .05, but if it occurs, Western Fruit, not Wissingers, is stuck with the peaches.

The cost information is as follows. The cost of getting the peaches into packaged form (picking, packing, and materials) is $3.50 per box. The transportation cost is $.65 per box. If the peaches are shipped and they decay, they can be salvaged for only $1.00 per box (whether or not they arrive late). If they arrive in good shape but are late, they can be sold on consignment (to another customer) for $4.00 per box. Finally, if Mr. Davis refuses the order, he figures that he can make a net profit of $.30 per box on these peaches by selling them to other (less interested) customers.

Mr. Davis has the options of accepting or refusing the order now or delaying until June 12. If he delays until June 12 and Wissingers has not bought from a competitor by then, he can still accept or refuse the order at that time. What should he do to maximize his total expected profit?

SOLUTION

The main difficulty in this example is sorting out the given data and getting everything in the correct chronological order. The only necessary probability not given explicitly is the current probability of having the shipment ready by June 19. Since Mr. Davis will receive an early indication (EI) or a late indication (LI) on June 12, his current probability that the peaches will be ready by June 19 is

$$P(\text{June 19}) = P(\text{June 19 and EI}) + P(\text{June 19 and LI})$$
$$= P(\text{June 19|EI})P(\text{EI}) + P(\text{June 19|LI})P(\text{LI})$$
$$= (.9)(.5) + (.3)(.5) = .6$$

From this point, all the necessary data are summarized in Figure 15.14 (pp. 830–831). As in Example 15.10, we separate the decision tree into several parts. (This is done simply to save space.) The main decision tree is shown in Figure 15.14a. Identical parts of the decision tree appear in several places, so we summarize these "subtrees" in Figure 15.14b. These subtrees begin with probability nodes labeled 1, 2, and 3. Node 1 occurs when the order is accepted and is shipped on June 22. Node 2 occurs when the order is accepted and is shipped on June 19, or when it is shipped on June 22 and arrives on time. Node 3 occurs when Mr. Davis refuses the order, or when he delays and Wissingers buys the peaches elsewhere.

The optimal policy is to accept the order on June 5, with an expected profit of $3721.40. It appears that the possibility of losing Wissingers' business and the possibility of a good profit on this order are the overriding concerns. Because of these, Mr. Davis's decision is not affected by the possibility of

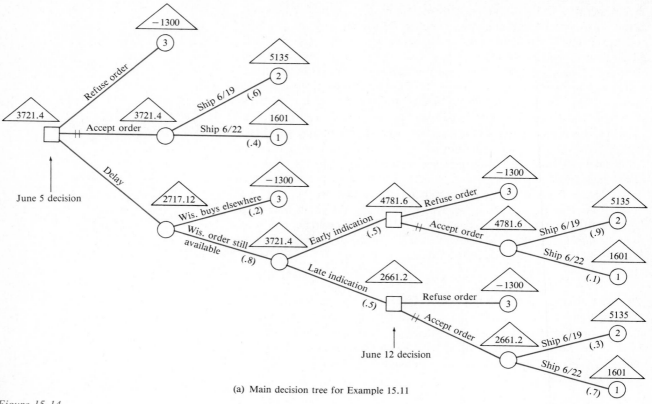

Figure 15.14

(a) Main decision tree for Example 15.11

late shipment and/or decay. Notice that if he *did* decide to delay his decision until June 12, he would then accept the order, whether he received an early or late indication. This is the main reason he does not delay his decision. In the terminology of Section 15.7, the information he receives on June 12 is of no value to him because he would make the same decision—accept the order—with or without this information.

The examples above show some of the many possible types of multistage decision problems. Each decision tree reflects the context of the particular problem. Different decision problems require different-looking decision trees, and there is no sense in getting locked into any particular pattern. However, all the decision trees follow the conventions listed earlier in this chapter, and the folding-back process is always done in the same way. The following tips are useful for solving any complicated decision problem.

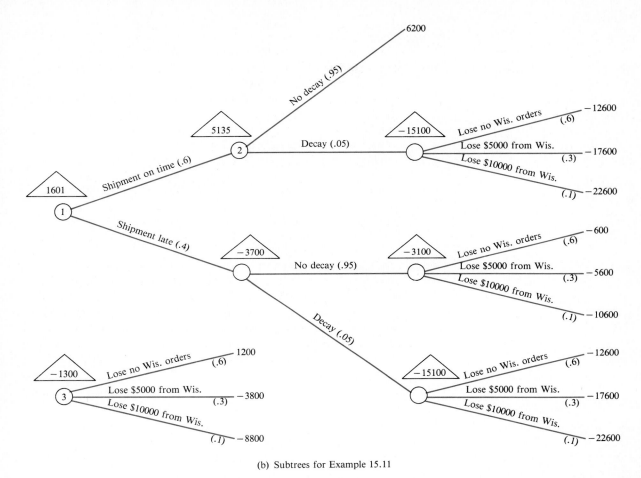

(b) Subtrees for Example 15.11

> ## Tips for Solving Complicated Decision Problems
>
> 1. Understand the problem thoroughly. What are the possible decisions, what are the possible outcomes, what are the monetary consequences, and what is the timing, that is, which events occur in which order? By drawing "trial" decision trees as you are acquainting yourself with the problem, you will gain a better understanding of the problem, especially its timing.
> 2. As you are drawing the decision tree, break it into several pieces, as we did in Examples 15.10 and 15.11. This is especially conven-

ient when the same sequence of nodes, branches, and dollars amounts occurs several times in the tree. It may even give you some insight into which problem parameters are exerting the greatest influence on the solution of the problem.

3. Translate the probabilities given in the problem into the probabilities required on the decision tree. Sometimes this requires Bayes' rule, buy not always. Sometimes the given probabilities are exactly those needed, but again, not always. The key is to imagine that you are standing at a given probability node and are about to observe an outcome stemming from this node. Then the probabilities on the branches leading from this node are conditional on everything you have observed so far.

4. When you put a cost or payoff on the decision branch where it occurs, do *not* include this cost or payoff at the far right of the decision tree. This would be double-counting.

5. Fold back from right to left, and do not forget to include any of the costs or payoffs that are located on the decision branches where they occur.

6. Look at the decision you have chosen as optimal and at its EMV. Do they make sense or are they drastically different from what you expected? If the latter is true, go back through the decision tree and see whether you violated any of the principles we have discussed.

15.7

The Value of Information

In many applications a decision maker would like to delay the final decision until more information is available. By having more information, the decision maker can learn more about the uncertain events and thereby make better decisions. However, this information is usually not free. The question is whether it is worth its price. In this section we see how to value information in a decision-making context.

We first look at *sample* information, the type of information we usually receive when we conduct an experiment, take a poll, or delay a decision until some related event can be observed. Sample information is also called *imperfect* information, because it does not remove all of the uncertainty about the future. In contrast, the best we could obtain is *perfect* information. This is information that removes all uncertainty; it specifies with certainty which outcome will occur. Although it is almost never practical or physically possible to obtain perfect information, we will see how the value of perfect information is useful even when we are ultimately interested in the value of sample information.

The value of information is always related to uncertainty about the future. We currently have some possibly vague ideas about the probabilities of future outcomes, given by the prior probabilities, and we believe that we could do better by obtaining relevant information and then revising these probabilities. Therefore, the concept of information value relates to any of the decision problems we have discussed so far. However, to keep the exposition fairly simple, we will relate information value to the two-stage decision problem shown in Figure 15.10 (p. 818). This figure indicates that we have the option of performing one or more "sampling experiments," each with its associated cost. After the results of these experiments are known, we make the final decision, the true state of nature is revealed, and a payoff or cost results. The initial decision problem can then be phrased in one of two ways: (1) given the costs of the available experiments, which one, if any, should we perform; or (2) what is the most we would be willing to pay for any of the available experiments?

To answer these questions for a specific example, let's return to Example 15.8. In this example, the Rider company needs to make a credit-granting decision on a loan requested by Mr. Stevens. Prior to this decision, the company can obtain information about Mr. Stevens from a credit-rating service. Intuitively, this information is worthwhile to the company for the following reason. If the information shows that Mr. Stevens is a high-risk customer, Rider knows not to take a chance on him; if the information shows that he is a low-risk customer, Rider can feel confident in granting him the loan. (If the information shows that he is a medium-risk customer, Rider is not much better off than before it received the information. Notice the similarity between the prior probability of default, .1, and the posterior probability of default given the medium risk information, .1176.) In no case is the credit-rating information perfect, for it does not specify with certainty whether Mr. Stevens will default, but it does appear to be worth having.

To see how to value the credit-rating information numerically, we examine the partial decision tree in Figure 15.15 (p. 834). This is part of the decision tree from Figure 15.11 with the cost of the credit-rating service, $30, replaced by a variable C. The optimal decision for each of the rightmost decision nodes is also shown.

This figure shows us all the important aspects of the information:

1. The information must be worth something because it changes the credit-granting decision in one instance. Without information, the best decision is not to grant the loan. But if the information is available and it shows that Mr. Stevens is in the low-risk category, the best decision is to grant him the loan.

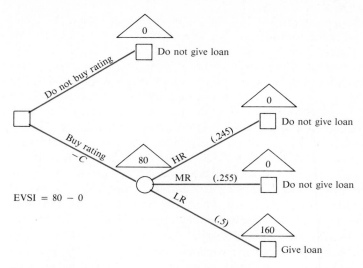

Figure 15.15
Value of Sample Information in Example 15.8

2. The *actual* value of the information is not known until it is received. In two cases, the high- and medium-risk cases, the information is worthless, because Rider does not change its final decision after receiving this information. Only in the low-risk case is the information worth something. So when we are deciding whether to buy the information, we cannot judge it by its actual value, which is unknown at the time. Instead, we must judge it by its *expected* value.

3. If Rider does purchase the information, its expected profit is $80 minus the information cost C. This makes it clear that the company should buy the information if and only if it costs less than $80. In particular, we saw in Example 15.8 that the information should be purchased when it costs only $30.

The example above is typical. It leads us to the following definition of the *expected value of sample information,* abbreviated EVSI.

> The expected value of sample information, EVSI, equals the difference between the EMV with sample information and the EMV without sample information. It is the most we are willing to pay for the sample information.

In the Rider example, the expected value of the credit-rating information is

$$\text{EVSI} = \$80 - \$0 = \$80$$

The EVSI for *any* information is always nonnegative; we cannot do worse with information than without it. (After all, we always have the option of ignoring the information.) However, it is possible to have EVSI = 0. This happens whenever the final decision without information is the same as the decision with information *regardless* of the sample information received. In this case it does not make sense to pay for information that will in no way influence the final decision.

As we have seen, sample information is imperfect because it does not remove all uncertainty about the future. Now imagine that we could buy information that would remove all future uncertainty. How much would we be willing to pay for this perfect information?

Again, we answer this question in the context of the credit-granting example. Now we ignore the credit-rating service, and we imagine that there is a sealed envelope whose contents say whether Mr. Stevens will default or will not default. (We admit that no such envelope exists, but the usefulness of this assumption will soon be seen.) How much would Rider pay for the envelope? To answer this question, we solve the decision tree in Figure 15.16. This tree indicates that we *first* discover the contents of the envelope (where the probabilities of default and no default are the prior probabilities), and then we make the correct decision. Of course, the correct decision is obvious once we know the contents of the envelope. If Mr. Stevens will default, he should not be given the loan; if he will not default, he should be given the loan.

Now we compare the EMV for this decision tree, $180, with the EMV for the tree with no information, namely $0. The difference, $180, is what we would be willing to pay for the perfect information in the envelope. This difference is called the *expected value of perfect information*, or EVPI.

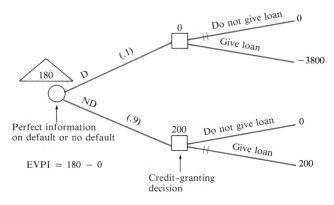

Figure 15.16
Value of Perfect Information for Example 15.8

> The expected value of perfect information, EVPI, equals the difference between the EMV with perfect information and the EMV without information. It is the most we would be willing to pay for information that removes all uncertainty.

Why do we consider perfect information when it is almost never for sale at any price? There are two reasons. First, EVPI is usually simple to calculate, much more so than EVSI. Second, EVSI is *never* greater than EVPI, because imperfect information is never better than perfect information. Therefore, if the price of sample information is greater than EVPI, we should not buy it, whether or not we are able to calculate its EVSI. The following example illustrates how convenient this fact can be.

EXAMPLE 15.12

Mattari, a company that manufactures video games for kids (and adults), is currently trying to decide which of two new video games to market in the upcoming months. One of these, Gallactic Missiles, is modeled after a popular competitor's game, and Mattari is fairly certain that it would be a success. The other game, Monopolize, is more risky because it has no direct counterpart among the competitors' games. However, if it caught on, Mattari could realize a substantial profit. The marketing people at Mattari estimate the payoff table and prior probabilities shown in Table 15.18. The payoffs (in $100s) are shown in the margins and indicate how much each game would be worth if it were the one marketed. The probabilities are joint probabilities for both games' success levels. For example, the marketing people believe the probability is .2 that both games would have a high level of success if they were both marketed.

Table 15.18 Joint Probabilities for Success Levels and Possible Profits ($100s) for Example 15.12

		Success Levels for Monopolize			Profits from Gallactic Missiles
		High	Medium	Low	
Success Levels for Gallactic Missiles	High	.2	.35	.05	1000
	Low	.1	.15	.15	750
Profits from Monopolize		2000	800	100	

Because large amounts of money are at stake in this decision problem, Mattari would like to obtain more information about success probabilities before making the final decision. Again the marketing people are called in. They list many possibilities for gathering such information. These range from sending out questionnaires or running controlled experiments with paid subjects to elaborate test markets in various regions of the country. Two things they agree on are that (1) it would be very difficult to estimate the probabilities of the sample results (that would be needed on a decision tree), and (2) the better information-gathering schemes would be quite expensive.

Find a reasonable way for Mattari to proceed.

SOLUTION

The decision tree in Figure 15.17 is relevant if Mattari pays for no extra information and uses only the data in Table 15.18. (The probabilities in this tree are marginal probabilities, that is, row sums and column sums from the table.) The best decision is to market Monopolize, with an EMV of $102,000.

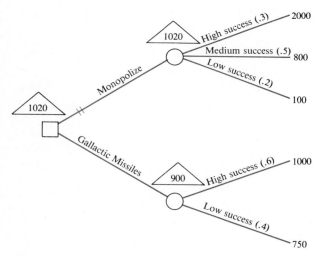

Figure 15.17
Decision Tree with No Extra Information for Example 15.12

If Mattari does try to evaluate all possible ways of gathering sample information on success probabilities, the resulting decision tree could become very complicated. There are many options, some of which could be used simultaneously or could even be contingent on the results of others. For example, a test market might be used only if the results of a questionnaire are inconclusive. Besides these complexities, the problem of assessing the

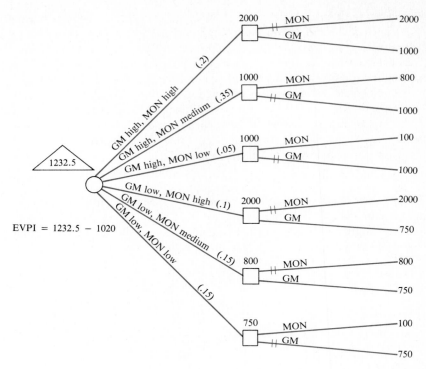

Figure 15.18
Value of Perfect Information for Example 15.12

required probabilities for the sample information branches would be difficult, to say the least.

Therefore, a reasonable alternative is to find the EVPI. From Figure 15.18, the EMV Mattari could obtain with perfect information is $123,250. This implies that

$$\text{EVPI} = \$123{,}250 - \$102{,}000 = \$21{,}250$$

Since EVSI is no greater than EVPI (and for most sample information, it is much less), Mattari knows that *no* sample information can be worth more than $21,250. Therefore, the company may decide to forget about gathering sample information (and ignore the complicated decision trees) unless good sample information can be obtained for considerably less than $21,250.

Problems for Sections 15.6, 15.7

25. A publishing company is trying to decide whether to publish a new biology textbook. Based on a thorough reading of the manuscript, the editor in charge assesses the following states of nature and their probabilities. The payoffs (or costs, if negative) for each state of nature are also shown. Before making a decision, the company can collect information about the chances of the book's success by doing an in-depth survey of university biology teachers. The results of similar surveys (for science books) taken in the past are also shown below. For example, similar surveys have indicated moderate success for 13 of the 29 books that turned out to be very successful.

Current Assessments

State	Probability	Payoff (If Published)
Very successful	.2	$100,000
Moderate success	.3	20,000
Very little success	.5	−50,000

Historical Frequencies

		Actual		
		Very Successful	Moderate Success	Very Little Success
Survey Indication	Very successful	15	14	3
	Moderate success	13	18	10
	Very little success	1	6	12

a. Draw and label a decision tree that can be used to solve the company's problem. (Use the EMV criterion.)
b. If the survey costs money, what is the most the company would be willing to pay for it?
c. If the actual cost of the survey is less than the amount found in part (b), what should the company do?

26. Suppose that the company in Problem 12 (p. 809) can purchase imperfect information at a cost of $100. This information will either say, "yes, there will be a strike" or "no, there will not be a strike." The probability of a "yes," given there will actually be a strike, is .7; the probability of a "no," given there will not be a strike, is .8.

a. Build a decision tree for analyzing the company's problem when $p = .15$. What strategy minimizes its total expected cost, and what is this expected cost?
b. Find EVSI for this problem. Also find EVPI. Again use $p = .15$.

*27. A firm is considering marketing a new product. For simplicity, assume that the events of interest are $s_1 =$ "new product is a success" and $s_2 =$ "new product is a failure." The prior probabilities are $P(s_1) = p$ and $P(s_2) = 1 - p$. If the product is marketed and it is a failure, the firm will suffer a loss of $300,000. If the product is marketed and it is a success, the firm will obtain a profit of $500,000. There is no cost (or profit) from not marketing the product. The firm is also considering taking a survey, the results of which can be classified as favorable, neutral, or unfavorable. The conditional probabilities for the results of the survey are

$$P(\text{favorable}|s_1) = .6 \qquad P(\text{favorable}|s_2) = .1$$
$$P(\text{neutral}|s_1) = .3 \qquad P(\text{neutral}|s_2) = .2$$
$$P(\text{unfavorable}|s_1) = .1 \qquad P(\text{unfavorable}|s_2) = .7$$

The survey costs C dollars.
a. What is the *largest* amount the firm should pay for perfect information if $p = .4$; if $p = .5$?
b. If $p = .4$, find the expected value of sample information. What is the expected net gain from the survey (over no survey) if $C = \$10,000$ and $p = .4$?

28. A product manager wishes to determine whether her company should market a new toothpaste. The present value of all future profits from a successful toothpaste is $1,200,000, whereas failure of the brand would result in a loss of $500,000. Not marketing the product would not affect profits from the company's other products. The manager has judged that the probability of success is .5. Before making her decision, however, the manager can spend $50,000 for a consumer testing program. Consumer testing will either be favorable (with probability .4) or unfavorable (with probability .6). Given a favorable test, the probability of eventual product success is judged to be .8. Given an unfavorable test, the probability of eventual success is judged to be only .3.
a. Given that EMV is the decision criterion, what strategy should the manager use, and what is the optimal EMV? Use a decision tree.
b. What are EVSI and EVPI?

29. A homeowner is trying to decide whether to install a heat pump in his house. There is a fairly large initial expense in doing so, and this expense will be recovered only if the winter weather for the next few years is sufficiently bad. After looking at historical records and consulting with experts on heating, he assesses the following heating costs for the next five years, with and without the heat pump, as a function of the weather. The probabilities of the different types of weather are also shown. The homeowner is basing his decision on expected total costs for the next five years.

Weather

	Mild	Normal	Colder than Normal	Severe
Without pump	$1700	$1900	$2300	$2600
With pump	$1450	$1550	$1800	$2000
Probabilities	$.2(1 - p)$	$.5(1 - p)$	$.3(1 - p)$	p

a. If $p = .1$, what is the most that he will be willing to pay for the heat pump?

b. If the heat pump costs $400, how large must p be before the heat pump is worth the cost?

30. In Problem 29, what is the EVPI (about weather) to the homeowner if the heat pump costs $400? That is, what is the most he would be willing to pay now for perfect information about the weather for the next five years? Solve when $p = .05$; when $p = .15$.

31. Consider Example 15.12, where the company is trying to decide between Gallactic Missiles and Monopolize. Suppose that sample information can be obtained. There are two possibilities for this sample information. The first of these has probability $\frac{1}{3}$; given that it occurs, the probabilities in Table 15.18 are revised to those shown below on the left. The second possibility has probability $\frac{2}{3}$; given that it occurs, the probabilities in Table 15.18 are revised to those below on the right.

	Revised probabilities for first possible sample information				Revised probabilities for second possible sample information		
	High	Medium	Low		High	Medium	Low
High	.10	.15	.09	High	.25	.45	.03
Low	.16	.25	.25	Low	.07	.10	.10

a. If the company decides to obtain the sample information, what is its optimal strategy and the corresponding EMV (not counting the cost of the information)?

b. What is EVSI? How can you explain its value intuitively for this problem?

15.8

Utility Functions and Attitudes Toward Risk

In the preceding sections we have assumed that the decision-maker is indifferent between a sure dollar amount and a gamble with the same expected value. This means that the EMV of a gamble acts as a certainty equivalent. But most decision makers would prefer a sure $500,000 to a gamble that pays $0 or $1,000,000 with probability .5 each, even though the EMV of this gamble is $500,000. In this case most people believe that increasing their wealth from $0 to $500,000 is much more important than increasing it from $500,000 to $1,000,000.

An even more striking example is a gamble where $1,000,000 could be won or lost, with probability .5 each. The EMV of this gamble, $0, is the same as the payoff from not gambling at all, but most people would prefer not to risk the gamble. The possibility of a disastrous loss outweighs the attractiveness of a large gain. In fact, most people would pay for insurance to avoid this kind of gamble. For these people a sure loss (the insurance premium) is preferable to a risky gamble with an EMV of $0.

The simple truth is that when relatively small amounts of money are at stake, people are willing to base their decisions on the EMV criterion. But when the possible payoffs or losses are large, most people try to avoid risks. This means that they are willing to sacrifice some EMV to avoid risky gambles. Given that this type of behavior is common, we need to modify the EMV criterion to be consistent with observed behavior. To do so, we introduce *utility functions*. These functions measure companies' or individuals' preferences for different amounts of money. (Strictly speaking, a utility function can also measure preferences for nonmonetary consequences, but we will not discuss this possibility here.) Then our new criterion becomes: choose the decision with the highest expected utility. We refer to this criterion as the *EU criterion*.

EU Criterion

Choose the decision with the highest expected utility.

From a practical point of view, the greatest difficulty in using the EU criterion is assessing a company's or individual's utility function. This function measures preferences for different amounts of money, and in doing so, it automatically incorporates attitudes toward risk. But since these attitudes differ from company to company and from person to person, there is no universal utility function that can be used for everyone. In this section we sketch a procedure for assessing a particular individual's utility function.

Mathematically, a utility function is a function that assigns a number, $U(x)$, to any dollar payoff x. (If $x < 0$, x represents a cost.) The value $U(x)$ is called the utility of x and is measured in nonmonetary units sometimes called *utiles*. It is often convenient to set $U(0) = 0$, which says that the utility of receiving $0 is 0, but this is not required. In fact, if a person's utility function is $U(x)$, this person will make exactly the same decisions as a person whose utility function is $\overline{U}(x)$, where $\overline{U}(x) = aU(x) + b$ for any constants a and b (with $a > 0$). The fact that two constants (a and b) can be chosen arbitrarily means that when we are assessing a person's utility function, we may assign *any* two utility values, such as $U(0)$ and $U(100)$, arbitrarily.

Assessing Utility Functions

When assessing a utility function any two utility values can be chosen arbitrarily.

But how do we then find $U(x)$ for other x's? The trick is to ask the person when he is indifferent between various sure dollar amounts and various simple gambles. By asking enough questions, we can discover what his utility function looks like. In general, we give him the choice of the following two options:

I. A payoff of x for sure.
II. A payoff of x_1 with probability $1 - p$, or a payoff of x_2 with probability p.

Three of the four numbers, x, x_1, x_2, and p, are fixed, and the other is adjusted until the person is indifferent between options I and II. When this occurs, the utility of the sure payoff, $U(x)$, must equal the *expected* utility of the gamble, $(1 - p)U(x_1) + pU(x_2)$. So we set

$$U(x) = (1 - p)U(x_1) + pU(x_2)$$

This generally leads to a new utility function value. The procedure is illustrated in the following example.

EXAMPLE 15.13

Ms. Harris, a decision analysis expert, has been called in as a consultant for some important decisions the Into the Woods furniture company must soon make. Ms. Harris discusses the problem with Mr. Shields, the president of the company, and discovers that large possible profits and losses are at stake. Therefore, both people believe that the company's attitude toward risk requires the use of the EU criterion instead of the EMV criterion.

To find Mr. Shields's utility function, Ms. Harris first asks him the largest possible loss and the largest possible profit he can imagine occurring. These are $200,000 and $300,000, respectively. Ms. Harris explains that any two utility values can be assigned arbitrarily, so she sets $U(-200,000) = 0$ and $U(300,000) = 1$. [*Any* values besides 0 and 1 could be used as long as $U(-200,000)$ is less than $U(300,000)$, but 0 and 1 make the arithmetic simple.] She then explains that she wants Mr. Shields to say when he is indifferent between the following two options:

I. A payoff of x for sure.
II. A loss of $200,000 with probability $1 - p$, or a payoff of $300,000 with probability p.

In particular, Ms. Harris will specify the value of p and Mr. Shields must supply the "indifference value," x. Mr. Shields's responses for various values of p are shown in Table 15.19. The EMV of each gamble in option II is

Table 15.19 Indifference Values in Example 15.13

p	Mr. Shields's x	EMV for Option II
.1	−160	−150
.2	−120	−100
.3	−85	−50
.4	−40	0
.5	0	50
.6	50	100
.7	100	150
.8	160	200
.9	230	250

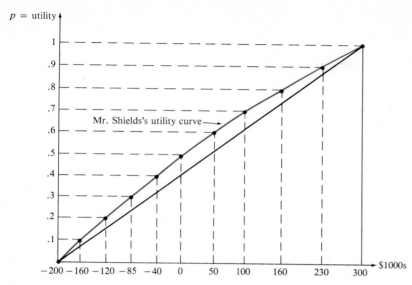

Figure 15.19
Utility Curve in Example 15.13

also shown for comparison. Notice that for every p, Mr. Shields is willing to sacrifice some EMV to avoid gamble II.

When Mr. Shields is indifferent between I and II, we know that

$$U(x) = (1 - p)U(-200,000) + pU(300,000) = (1 - p)(0) + p(1) = p$$

Therefore, Table 15.19 directly translates into nine points on the *utility curve* shown in Figure 15.19. We have drawn a smooth curve through these points to estimate Mr. Shields's utility function for all possible dollar values. The straight line below the utility curve is the utility "curve" that would result if Mr. Shields were indifferent between a sure thing and a gamble with the *same* EMV, that is, if the middle and right-hand columns of Table 15.19 were equal. The fact that his actual utility curve is above this straight line implies that he prefers to avoid risks.

The example above shows only one way of assessing a person's utility function. As an alternative, Ms. Harris could supply the value x in option I and then ask for the indifference value of p. The difficulty with any such method is that unless the respondent thoroughly understands the procedure, he is likely to contradict himself as the questioning proceeds. The idea behind assessing utility functions is straightforward, but doing it *accurately* is not an easy task. (To appreciate the difficulty, try assessing your own utility function.) Therefore, specially trained consultants are often called in to help obtain a company's utility function.

Shapes of Utility Functions

We know that different companies or individuals have different utility functions because of their different attitudes toward risk. However, the general shapes of their utility functions are usually fairly similar. They are usually shaped like Mr. Shields's utility curve in Figure 15.19. This is called an increasing, concave utility curve. The "increasing" part means that the curve rises from left to right. This simply means that he prefers more money to less money; *all* utility curves have this property. The "concave" part means that the curve rises less steeply as we look from left to right. (For those who have studied calculus, the curve is concave if its second derivative is less than or equal to 0.) Behaviorally, a utility curve is concave if the person is *risk averse,* that is, if he is willing to sacrifice some EMV to avoid a gamble. Since Mr. Shields is in this category, we know that his utility curve must be concave.

> Concave utility curves are appropriate for risk-averse people. These people prefer a sure thing to a gamble with the same EMV.

The graphs in Figure 15.20 show some possible shapes for utility curves. The utility curve in Figure 15.20a is concave, as we discussed above. It is appropriate for a risk-averse person. The *linear* utility curve in Figure 15.20b is appropriate for a person who is *risk neutral*. This means that he is indifferent between a sure thing and a gamble with the same EMV. This is the type of person who should use EMV as his decision-making criterion. Therefore, all of the examples we solved earlier in this chapter are appropriate for people with a linear utility function.

> The EMV criterion is appropriate for a person with a linear utility function and who is therefore risk neutral.

The opposite of a risk-averse person is a *risk taker*. This person would rather take a gamble with a given EMV than a sure thing with the same monetary value. (Before concluding that there are no such people in the world, go to the Las Vegas casinos!) A risk taker's utility curve is shown in Figure 15.20c. We say that this curve is *convex,* the opposite of concave. Realistically, many people are willing to gamble for small amounts of money, even if the odds are against them, but they become risk averse for large amounts. These people have utility functions as in Figure 15.20d. This curve is concave for extreme losses or gains but is convex for moderate dollar amounts.

Figure 15.20
Shapes of Utility Curves

Finally, the curve in Figure 15.20e helps to justify our use of the EMV criterion throughout most of this chapter. It is appropriate for the many companies that are risk averse when extreme amounts of money are at stake, but are practically risk neutral when more moderate dollar amounts are involved. Of course, an extreme amount for one company is a moderate amount for another. But in each of the EMV examples we have solved, we have made the implicit assumption that the dollar amounts involved are in the middle portion of that particular company's utility graph. This means that they may base their decisions on the EMV criterion.

We now learn how to solve decision problems when the EU criterion is used instead of the EMV criterion. The modifications from our earlier procedure are relatively minor once the utility function has been specified. We still build decision trees as before, and we still fold back on them in the same way. There are only two changes we need to make.

Solving Decision Problems with the Expected Utility Criterion

1. *All* costs and payoffs must be put at the right of the decision tree. This means that we should no longer put monetary values on the decision branches where they occur in time. (The reason for this change is that otherwise we will find the sum of the utilities of the separate monetary values. This is generally not equal to the utility of the total monetary value, which is the required utility.)
2. All monetary values at the right of the decision tree should be replaced by their utility values before folding back. Then the folding-back process consists of taking expected *utilities* at probability nodes and maximums of expected utilities at decision nodes.

The concept of certainty equivalents takes on a slightly different meaning. For example, suppose that we solve a decision tree and the optimal decision has an expected utility of .7. Also, suppose that the utility of $965 is .7, that is, $U(965) = .7$. Then the decision maker is indifferent between a sure payoff of \$965 and the gamble the decision tree represents. The reason this is different from before is that the EMV of the gamble is *greater* than \$965 (if the person is risk averse). Again, this means that a risk-averse person is willing to sacrifice some EMV to avoid a risky gamble.

We illustrate these ideas in the following example, a continuation of Example 15.13.

EXAMPLE 15.13 (continued)

Ms. Harris, the consultant for the Into the Woods furniture company, has already estimated Mr. Shields's utility function. This is shown in Figure 15.19. Now he asks her to help solve the following decision problem. The company, which makes hand-crafted wood furniture, has traditionally specialized in dining room sets and various types of "reading" chairs. Mr. Shields is now planning to expand into cushioned sofas (the chairs are currently all wood) and/or bookshelves. These types of items were made previously but only for custom orders. Mr. Shields's current idea is to produce them in mass quantities for cost savings. However, he is not sure that the public is willing to buy the rather expensive, high-quality items he has in mind. He and his accountant estimate the probabilities of success for the two items (shown in parentheses) and the possible payoffs in Table 15.20a. These figures assume that only one of the items is produced and that all extra capacity is used for this item. If both items are produced, each will use half of the extra capacity. Then the joint probabilities of success and the payoffs are shown in Table 15.20b. Which items should the company produce to maximize its expected utility?

Table 15.20   Payoff Tables (\$1000s) and Probabilities for Example 15.13

| | Success Level | | | | Success Level for Sofas | |
	High	Low			High	Low
Sofas	300 (.6)	−200 (.4)	Success Levels for Bookshelves	High	210 (.45)	−35 (.25)
Bookshelves	150 (.7)	−80 (.3)		Low	95 (.15)	−150 (.15)
	(a) Only one item produced				(b) Both items produced	

SOLUTION

The decision tree for this problem is straightforward, as shown in Figure 15.21. If the problem were to maximize EMV, the solution would be to

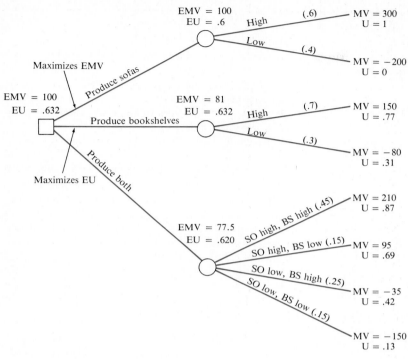

Figure 15.21
Decision Tree for Example 15.13 (SO for Sofas, BS for Bookshelves)

produce sofas only, with an EMV of $100,000. However, the company is risk averse and sofas are the riskier of the two items. Therefore, we suspect that maximizing EU might lead to a different decision. This is what happens. Below each monetary value (MV) on the right, we show its utility (*U*). These are found from Figure 15.19 by reading up from the dollar amount to the utility curve and then to the left to find the utility value. The highest EU is .632, from producing bookshelves only. The company's utility function discourages risk so much that the decision to produce sofas only is now the worst decision!

We can interpret the maximum expected utility of .632 as a certainty equivalent. From Figure 15.19, we see that a utility value of .632 corresponds to a dollar amount of approximately $65,000. This means that the company is indifferent between a sure $65,000 and the gamble that results from making bookshelves only. Since the company could make an EMV of $100,000 from producing sofas only, it is willing to sacrifice $35,000 of EMV to avoid a considerable amount of risk.

Problems for Section 15.8

32. An investor is considering an investment with the following potential payoffs.

Payoff	Probability
− $1000	.2
0	.1
1000	.3
2000	.2
3000	.1
4000	.1

He assesses his utility for various amounts of money x as follows:

x	$U(x)$
− $1000	0
− 500	.16
0	.30
500	.43
1000	.55
1500	.66
2000	.77
3000	.94
4000	1.08

a. Graph his utility function and interpret the shape of the curve.

b. The investor has three options. He can make the investment, he can take a half-share in the investment (where he gains or loses only half of the amounts shown, with the same probabilities), or he can forget the whole thing. What should he do to maximize his expected utility?

33. Suppose that the utility function for the manager in Problem 28 is $U(x)$, where x is expressed in $1000s. Given that the following utilities are supplied, what should the manager do to maximize his expected utility?

$$U(-550) = -.733 \quad U(-500) = -.649 \quad U(-50) = -.051$$
$$U(0) = 0 \qquad U(1150) = .683 \quad U(1200) = .698$$

34. Suppose that the probabilities for Example 15.13 in Table

15.20a are changed from .6, .4, .7, and .3 to .61, .39, .65, and .35.

a. Is the EMV maximizing decision still the same? What is the new maximum EMV?

b. Is the EU maximizing decision still the same? What is the new maximum EU?

c. Referring to Figure 15.19, what dollar amount is equivalent to the maximum EU from part (b)? By using the decision from part (b), how much EMV is being sacrificed? Explain.

*35. An author of a new textbook is trying to decide which of two publishing companies, A or B, to sign with. Company A will sell the book for $25, and it will pay the author a flat 15% on each book sold. Shown below is its estimate of the distribution of copies that it will be able to sell over the book's useful lifetime. Company B, on the other hand, will sell the book for $24. It will pay the author 14% on each of the first 20,000 copies sold and 18% on each further copy sold. Its estimate of the distribution of sales is also shown below.

Copies Sold	Probability (Assessed by A)	Probability (Assessed by B)
10,000	.35	.40
20,000	.25	.25
30,000	.20	.15
40,000	.15	.10
50,000	.05	.10

a. If the author wishes to maximize his expected profit, which publishing company should he choose?

b. Now assume that the author is quite risk averse and has the following utility function:

$$U(x) = -(x - b)^2$$

where x is measured in $1000s and b is a given constant. What is the author's best decision when $b = 210$?

36. In Problem 35, part (b), $U(x)$ is negative for all values of x and all values of b. Does this matter? Explain.

*37. The accompanying table shows the monetary payoffs for each decision and each state of nature. Below each payoff is the utility of the payoff, found from the decision maker's utility function. Probabilities are shown at the bottom of the table.

		States of Nature		
		1	2	3
	1	$1,000 110	−$1,000 92	$0 100
Decisions	2	$10,000 190	−$10,000 0	$500 106
	3	$6,000 156	−$5,000 55	$1,000 110
Probabilities		.2	.18	.62

a. Find the decision that maximizes the expected utility.

b. Let $U(x)$ be the utility function for this decision maker. Suppose that another decision maker also has this decision problem. The utility function for this second decision maker, $\hat{U}(x)$, satisfies $\hat{U}(x) = a + bU(x)$, where a and b are given constants, with b positive. Show algebraically that the second decision maker's best decision is the same as the first decision maker's, regardless of the values of a and b.

Summary

This chapter has been our first exposure to optimization. We first learned several sensible methods for maximizing profits or minimizing costs when there are uncertain outcomes that affect the decision process. The most popular approach uses the EMV criterion: Maximize the expected profit or minimize the expected cost. A convenient way of doing this is to form a decision tree, labeled with the information from the payoff or cost table and the probabilities of uncertain outcomes. We then fold back on this decision tree to find the best decision strategy and its associated EMV. When information can be obtained prior to making the final decision, Bayes' rule can be used to update probabilities of outcomes, and the expected value of sample information, the most a rational person should pay for the sample information, can be calculated. Furthermore, the expected value of perfect information provides an upper bound on the most a rational person should pay for *any* information.

In the last section of this chapter we explained how the EMV criterion should be modified when the decision maker is risk averse, especially when large profits and/or losses are at stake. In this case we need to assess the decision maker's utility function, which encodes his feelings toward risk, and then use the expected utility criterion to find the best decision strategy. We saw that a risk-averse person is often willing to give up some EMV in order to avoid risk.

Applications

Application 15.1 Members of a bargaining team hired by management to negotiate an upcoming union contract can often find themselves in a seemingly no-win situation. Either they give away more than is necessary or they risk causing a costly strike that the company cannot afford. Winter developed a decision-tree model that can help a bargaining team plan its strategy with management. (Reference: Frederick W. Winter, "An Application of Computerized Decision Tree Models in Management-Union Bargaining," *Interfaces,* Vol. 15, 1985, pp. 74–80.) This model was developed for a client company that manufactures heavy industrial goods. Each year the company must negotiate approximately six contracts with 15 different unions. Since these unions are highly organized and aggressive, negotiating teams must continually deal with the real possibility of a strike.

The decision process is basically that management decides on a final package it is prepared to offer, and then the union decides to accept this package or take some action, usually a strike. The complicating aspect is that this process is repeated over several weeks or months because each side believes that a strike can dislodge the opponent from an unfavorable position. Thus, management's strategy necessarily becomes a contingency plan, such as: offer package 1 before a strike, offer it again during the first week of a strike, offer package 2 during the second week of a strike, offer package 3 during the third week of a strike, and so on. The type of decision tree that leads to such a plan may look as shown in Figure 15.22.

Quoting Winter, the objective of his decision-tree model was "to develop a tool that would permit the negotiator to realize a more favorable bargaining outcome through improved decision making." His model did indeed achieve this goal. That is, there is every indication that the model did save the company money. However, he also points out various unexpected by-products of the approach itself that may be important in many other real-world applications of decision models.

First, the model required management to perform a careful calculation of the costs of each package offered to the union. In fact, this step was so crucial that the company created a microcomputer program to figure in cost-of-living allowances, wage compression, and other complicated factors automatically. This program alone gave the company a better understanding of labor costs than it had ever had before. Second, the model forced management to assess explicit strike probabilities during each week of the negotiating process. This probability assessment had never been done formally before. Third, the results from the decision tree not only provided a best strategy and an expected cost from this strategy; it also provided a breakdown of the possible costs and their probabilities for *any* strategy management might want to consider. Finally, the negotiating team felt that by developing this decision model in cooperation with management, they obtained much more insight into the thoughts and feelings of management. In short, the use of the model helped the team to understand alternative packages from management's perspective.

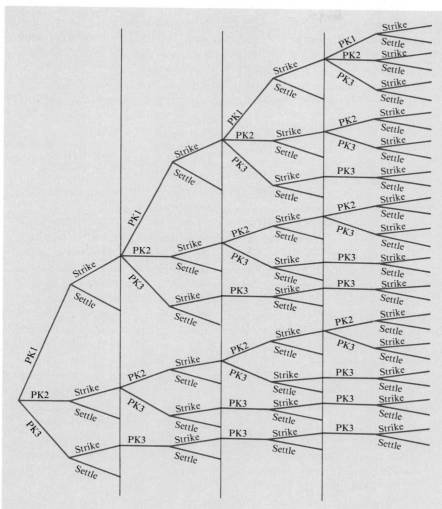

Figure 15.22
Decision Tree for a Three-Strike Period, Three-Bargaining-Package Situation

Application 15.2   A good example of decision making under uncertainty is the problem of finding an optimal acceptance plan in quality control. Manufacturing companies routinely receive shipments of items to be used in assembly of final products. Since some of these items are defective and need rework, the goal is to find these defectives ahead of time, when it is cheaper to rework them. A typical decision rule is as follows. Upon receipt of a lot of N items, the company samples n of these at a cost of c_s each, and reworks all defectives found at a cost of c_r per defective. If k or fewer defectives are found, this lot is "accepted." This means that the lot is used for further production, and any further defective items (from the $N - n$ not inspected) are reworked as they are found at cost c_d per defective. Here $c_d > c_r$; this reflects the fact that it is cheaper to rework items at an earlier stage in the process. On the other hand, if more than k defectives are found in the sample, the lot is "rejected." This means that the remaining $N - n$ items are inspected right away, and all defectives are reworked at the "cheaper" cost c_r. The decision variables in this plan are n, the sample size, and k, the cutoff value for accepting or rejecting.

For typical lot sizes on the order of 1000 items, this can lead to a huge decision tree. There is a decision branch for each possible n ($= 0, 1, 2, \ldots, N$), and for each n there is a decision branch for each possible k ($= 0, 1, 2, \ldots, n$). Then for each combination of n and k, there are probability branches for the possible numbers of defectives found in the sample. Adding to the complexity of the problem is the fact that Bayes' rule is generally needed to update hundreds of probabilities. This is a problem where a computer is clearly necessary. However, we will now show how a fairly easy set of calculations, together with the concept of EVPI, can provide useful information, such as an upper limit on the sample size n we need to consider.

The following numerical example is taken from an article by Moskowitz. (Reference: Herbert Moskowitz, "Selecting Bayesian Acceptance Plans for Quality Control by Pattern Search," *AIIE Transactions*, Vol. 9, 1977, pp. 396–408.) Its input parameters are $N = 1000$, $c_s = \$.28$, $c_r = \$1.60$, and $c_d = \$3.00$. We assume that the company believes a proportion f of these 1000 items are defective, where f is modeled as a discrete random variable with the distribution shown in Table 15.21. For example, the company believes the probability is .1875 that 15% (or 150) of the 1000 items are defective.

Without performing any sampling at all, the company could accept or reject the lot. The expected cost of the accept decision is

$$E(\text{accept}) = Nc_d \sum f\, p(f)$$
$$= 1000(3.00)[.05(.0625) + \cdots + .35(.0625)] = \$600$$

This is the lot size times the later "expensive" cost of reworking a defective times the expected fraction of defectives. The expected cost of the reject decision is

$$E(\text{reject}) = Nc_s + Nc_r \sum f\, p(f)$$
$$= 1000(.28) + 1000(1.60)][.05(.0625) + \cdots + .35(.0625)] = \$600$$

Table 15.21

Proportion Defective f	Prior Probability
.05	.0625
.10	.1250
.15	.1875
.20	.2500
.25	.1875
.30	.1250
.35	.0625

This is the cost of inspecting the entire lot plus the expected cost of reworking all defectives at the "cheap" cost. The fact that the expected costs from accepting and rejecting are both $600 is purely coincidental, but it does imply that with no sampling, we are indifferent between accepting and rejecting the lot; the expected cost is $600 either way.

To obtain EVPI, suppose that the company knows the value of *f before* it has to make a reject-accept decision. Then the cost of accepting is $Nc_d f = 3000f$, and the cost of rejecting is $Nc_s + Nc_r f = 280 + 1600f$. The correct decision depends on *f*. In fact, it is easy to verify that $3000f \le 280 + 1600f$ (accept is better) only if $f \le .20$. So the company should accept the lot if it is told that $f \le .20$, and it should reject the lot otherwise. This leads to the tree for finding the expected cost under perfect information on *f* shown in Figure 15.23.

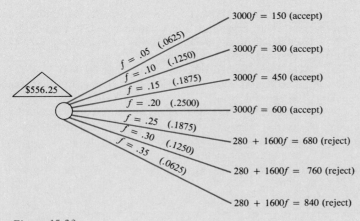

Figure 15.23

Now we know that the expected cost with perfect information is $556.25, and the expected cost with no sample information is $600. Therefore, EVPI is the difference:

$$EVPI = 600 - 556.25 = \$43.75$$

This means that the most *any* information can be worth is $43.75. Since the cost of sampling is $.28 per item, the maximum number of items the company should consider sampling is 43.75/.28, or 156 items. Sampling more than 156 items is guaranteed to be less than optimal. Unfortunately, as Moskowitz illustrates, there is still a lot of work to do to find the optimal sampling plan parameters, *n* and *k*. But the results above limit this work to some extent. Moreover, we know that any values of n and k that yield an expected cost close to \$556.25 must be very close to optimal. (For the sake of curiosity, Moskowitz reports that the optimal n and k are 90 and 17, respectively; these yield an expected cost of \$562.11. This strategy entails sampling 90 items and accepting the lot only if 17 or fewer defectives are found.)

Glossary of Terms

States of nature   the uncertain outcomes over which the decision maker has no control

Payoff (or cost) tables   tables that show the monetary payoffs (or costs) for all possible decisions and all possible states of nature

Minimax decision   the decision that minimizes the maximum possible cost

Minimin decision   the decision that minimizes the minimum possible cost

EMV criterion   choose the decision that minimizes the expected monetary value (EMV) of the possible costs or maximizes the EMV of the possible payoffs

Certainty equivalent   the dollar amount such that a decision maker is indifferent between obtaining this amount for sure and participating in a specified gamble

Decision tree   a graphical device for summarizing and solving decision problems with uncertain outcomes

Folding back in a decision tree   numerically solving a decision tree, following the conventions: (1) take expected values at probability nodes, and (2) maximize expected payoffs (or minimize expected costs) at decision nodes

Bayes' rule   a formula for converting prior probabilities into posterior probabilities as new information is received

Likelihoods (in the context of Bayes' rule)   the probabilities of sample information given the states of nature

EVSI (the expected value of sample information)   the most a decision maker is willing to pay for a particular type of sample information

EVPI (the expected value of perfect information)   the most a decision maker is willing to pay for perfect information

Utility function   a function that encodes a person's or company's preferences for money and attitudes toward risk

EU criterion   choose the decision with the highest expected utility

Important Formulas

1. Formula for EMV

$$\text{EMV}(d) = C(d) = \sum c(d, s)P(s) \qquad \text{for costs}$$

$$\text{EMV}(d) = R(d) = \sum r(d, s)P(s) \qquad \text{for payoffs}$$

2. Bayes' rule

$$P(s_i|x_j) = \frac{P(x_j|s_i)P(s_i)}{\sum\limits_{k} P(x_j|s_k)P(s_k)}$$

where s_i is a particular state of nature and x_j is a particular piece of sample information

3. Formula for EVSI

$$\text{EVSI} = (\text{EMV with sample information}) - (\text{EMV without it})$$

4. Formula for EVPI

$$\text{EVPI} = (\text{EMV with perfect information}) - (\text{EMV without any information})$$

End-of-Chapter Problems

*38. Suppose that we are given a payoff table for any single-stage decision problem, and we find the decision according to the EMV criterion. If we had used the EMV criterion on the table of opportunity losses instead, show in general why the *same* optimal decision would result. (*Hint:* Show that the expected opportunity loss from any decision d equals a constant K minus the expected payoff from d, when K is the same for all decisions d.)

39. Illustrate the result from Problem 38 by working Example 15.1 in terms of opportunity losses. Explain in words the meaning of the optimal EMV for this version of the problem. That is, how can you interpret the expected opportunity loss?

*40. Referring to Problem 6 (p. 793), suppose that the investor uses the EMV criterion. Let r_1 and r_2 be, respectively, the returns from the safe stock and the risky stock, and assume $P(r_1 = 7\%, r_2 = 1\%) = p_1$, $P(r_1 = 11\%, r_2 = 1\%) = p_2$, $P(r_1 = 7\%, r_2 = 17\%) = p_3$, and $P(r_1 = 11\%, r_2 = 17\%) = p_4$.

a. If $p_1 = .15$, $p_2 = .3$, $p_3 = .35$, and $p_4 = .2$, find the investor's best decision and the corresponding EMV.

b. Let $p_5 = p_1 + p_3$ and $p_6 = p_1 + p_2$. For what values of p_5 is investing all $5000 in the safe stock better than investing all $5000 in the savings account? For what values of p_6 is investing all $5000 in the risky stock better than investing all $5000 in the savings account?

c. Continuing part (b), suppose that p_5 is fixed at some value between 0 and 1. Given this value of p_5, for what values of p_6 is investing all $5000 in the risky stock better than investing all $5000 in the safe stock?

*41. Continuing Problem 40, show that for any values of p_1, p_2, p_3, and p_4, diversifying among the stocks (that is, investing $2500 in the safe stock and $2500 in the risky stock) is never better in terms of EMV than putting all $5000 into the better of the two stocks. (*Hint:* If X is the random return from the safe stock when all $5000 is invested in it, and Y is the

random return from the risky return when all $5000 is invested in it, express the return from diversifying in terms of X and Y. Then use the rules of expected values from Chapter 4.)

*42. Continuing Problems 40 and 41, consider a risk-averse investor who is an expected utility maximizer. His utility function $U(x)$ is tabulated below. Here x is the total amount of money he will have in one year, principal plus interest.

x	$U(x)$	x	$U(x)$
$5050	15.9	$5475	38.1
5200	24.8	5550	41.1
5225	26.2	5600	43.0
5300	30.1	5625	43.9
5350	32.5	5700	46.5
5375	33.7	5850	51.2
5400	34.8		

a. Why is it conceivable that he might now want to diversify (as described in Problem 41), whereas this was never a good idea with the EMV criterion? Give an intuitive answer.

b. Using the same probabilities as in Problem 40, part (a), find the investor's best strategy.

c. What dollar value is equivalent to the optimal expected utility from part (b)? Compare this dollar value with the optimal EMV from Problem 40, part (a). How can you interpret the difference between these two values?

43. A farmer is trying to decide whether to purchase an irrigation system for his 25 acres of cropland this year or next year. Because of other investments he could make with his money this year, he figures that the real cost of purchasing an irrigation system this year, as opposed to next year, is $600. An irrigation system is of value to the farmer this year only if there is a fairly dry or very dry season. If the season is fairly

dry, he expects irrigation to result in an increased yield of 1 ton per acre, as compared to the output without the system. If there is a very dry season, irrigation will result in an increase of 3 tons per acre. The farmer nets $24 per ton. If he believes that the probability of a fairly dry season this year is .40 and the probability of a very dry season is .25, should he irrigate this year or wait until next year? (Assume that he will certainly install the system next year if he does not do it this year.)

*44. Reconsider Mr. Foyt's situation in Example 15.3 of Section 15.4. There we assumed that he used EMV as his decision criterion. Now suppose that he is risk averse, with the utility function $U(x) = 1 - e^{-.0001x}$. (Here x is any possible monetary gain or loss, and e is the special number 2.718. . . .) With the same data as in the example, see whether he would be willing to buy the $150-deductible car insurance if it costs $100. (Remember to put the cost of the insurance at the right-hand tips of the decision tree.)

*45. Continuing Problem 44, how much would Mr. Foyt be willing to pay for $150-deductible car insurance? (*Hint:* In the expression for the expected utility from buying the insurance at any given cost, use the fact that $e^{a+b} = e^a e^b$ for any numbers a and b. Then set the expected utility from buying insurance equal to the expected utility from not buying insurance, and solve for the cost of insurance.)

*46. Imagine that I can play either of two slot machines, marked A and B. I am told that one of these is the "good" one, meaning that any time I play it, I win with probability .4. The other is the "bad" one; each time I play it, I win with probability .2.
   a. If my current probability that machine A is the good one is p, and if I play machine A next, what is the probability that I will win? (The answer should be an expression involving p.)
   b. Suppose that my current probability that machine A is the good one is .6. If I play machine A three times in a row and win all three times, what is the posterior probability that machine A is the good one?
   c. Suppose that my current probability that A is the good one is .6. If I play A once and lose and then play B once and win, what is the posterior probability that A is the good one?

47. Suppose that you are trying to sell your house. Each time you get an offer, you must decide whether to accept it, knowing that if you reject the offer, you cannot change your mind later on; that is, a rejected offer is gone forever. At the present time, you have an offer for $65,000, and you must make up

your mind whether to accept it. You believe you will receive only one more offer, for an amount X, at time T months from now, where X and T are random variables with joint distribution given by the following table. Determine your best decision by means of a decision tree, given that each month you wait costs you $700 in upkeep, rent, and so on. Also, determine your optimal expected net profit. (Assume that you will certainly accept the current offer or the next one.)

		\$62,000	X \$66,000	\$70,000
T	1	.1	.2	.3
	2	.1	.1	.2

48. Reconsider the houseselling dilemma in Problem 47. Everything is the same as before, except that you now believe you will receive exactly two more offers, one a month from now and the other two months from now. (So unlike Problem 47, there is no uncertainty in the *timing* of future offers.) The values of these offers are random variables X_1 and X_2 with joint distribution given by the following table. Draw the relevant decision tree, assuming that you incur a $700 cost per month for each month your house remains unsold. Solve for your best strategy, and your optimal expected net profit. (Assume that you will accept the current offer or one of the next two offers for sure.)

		X_2 \$63,000	\$67,000
X_1	\$64,000	.3	.2
	\$66,000	.2	.3

49. An educator is trying to teach a technique to a group of students. After a particular lecture, the instructor believes that 60% of the students have mastered the technique. A test is then given. The instructor believes that 15% of the students who have not mastered the technique will get lucky and pass the test. On the other hand, he believes that 10% of the students who have mastered the technique will get careless and fail the test.
   a. If a given student passes the test, what is the probability that this student has mastered the technique?
   b. If a given student fails the test, what is the probability that this student has not mastered the technique?
   c. What percentage of the students do you expect to pass the test?

50. Let A be any event, and let $B_1, B_2, \ldots, B_n$ be any n mutually exclusive events such that one of the B's must occur.
   a. Show that $P(A) = \Sigma\, P(A|B_i)P(B_i)$.
   b. How is the result in part (a) related to Bayes' rule? Be specific.

51. A small steel company has been offered a deal where it can make a potential $8,000 profit by delivering an order of steel by the first of next month. There is a .6 probability that on account of other orders, this order could not be completed in time. In this case the company could either buy steel from a competitor, with a net loss of $5000, or it could simply say "sorry" to its customer and let the customer find the steel elsewhere. However, if the latter option is used, the company assesses the following losses of future revenue from this customer (and their probabilities), due to a loss of goodwill. The other option the company has is to refuse to accept the order right away; this entails no loss of goodwill. The company wishes to make the decision that maximizes its profit. What should it do? Solve by means of a decision tree.

Loss ($1000s)	Probability
0	.4
5	.4
10	.1
15	.1

*52. In Problem 51 assume that the company receives the order on May 1, and the due date is June 1. The options in Problem 51 are all available, but now the company can also delay its decision on whether to accept the order until May 10, when it will be more certain of its ability to get the order finished on time. The only "cost" of this delay is that there is a .4 probability that the customer will take its business elsewhere. If the company does delay the decision until May 10, there are two possibilities. With probability .2, the company will know by that time that the order can certainly be finished on time; with probability .8, it will know that there is a 75% chance that the order will not be finished on time.
   a. Draw the "skeleton" of the required decision tree.
   b. Label the tree with the required probabilities and monetary values.
   c. Find the decision strategy that maximizes the expected profit.

*53. Mr. Jones is attempting to sell his farm. He currently has an offer from Mr. Smith for $175,000, but Mr. Smith wants a yes or no answer on his offer right away. If Mr. Jones delays, there is a .6 probability that Mr. Smith will withdraw his offer. With probability .4, Mr. Smith's offer will remain in force for at least one month. Mr. Jones knows of one other person, Mr. Brown, who is also planning to make an offer, but he will not be able to do so until one month from now. He assumes that the possible offers from Mr. Brown and their probabilities are as shown below. Until he sells the farm, he incurs expenses of $1350 per month. If he is an EMV maximizer, what should he do: accept Mr. Brown's offer now or wait for Mr. Smith's offer? Assume that he will accept one of these two offers for sure. (Note that if he delays, there is some possibility that Mr. Smith's offer will still be available and that it will exceed Mr. Brown's offer.)

Brown's Offer ($1000s)	Probability
170	.5
175	.2
180	.2
185	.1

54. In Problem 53, how much would it be worth to Mr. Jones to know the exact value of Mr. Brown's offer right now?

*55. A salvage crew is trying to locate a plane that wrecked in the Pacific Ocean. The relevant section of the ocean (where the wreck is known to have occurred) is divided into four subsections. Based on available information, the crew believes the probabilities that the wreck is in the various subsections are .3, .2, .4, and .1, respectively. However, a search of any subsection has probability .2 of failing to discover the wreck even if it is there. If a search of subsection 3 fails to find the wreck, find the revised probabilities of the wreck being in the various subsections. Answer the same question if the unsuccessful search is made in subsection 1; in subsection 2; in subsection 4.

*56. Answer Problem 55 if a search of subsection 3 and a subsequent search of subsection 1 both fail to find the wreck. (*Hint:* Apply Bayes' rule to find the posterior probabilities after the unsuccessful search of subsection 3. Then use these posterior probabilities as new "prior" probabilities and apply Bayes' rule again to find the new posterior probabilities after the unsuccessful search of subsection 1.)

*57. Assume that the crew in Problems 55 and 56 always chooses the next subsection to search as the one with the highest current probability of containing the wreck. (Of course, this applies only when all the previous searches have been unsuccessful.) Where should the first three searches take place if all three are necessary? Back up your answer with relevant probabilities. (Use the answers from Problems 55 and 56.)

*58. Referring to Problem 35 (p. 848), suppose that the author believes the distribution of sales will be the same, regardless of the publishing company he chooses. He believes there is a 35% chance that this distribution is the one predicted by company A, and there is a 65% chance that it is the one predicted by company B. (In other words, he believes that one, but not both, of the publishing companies has provided the correct distribution.) Now what should the author's decision be, assuming that he is an EMV maximizer?

*59. In order to discover an executive's utility function, a consultant uses the following procedure. She explains to the executive that he (the executive) can choose between the following two options:

   I. Receive $100 for certain.
   II. Gamble on winning Y dollars or 0 dollars.

The gamble in II is very simple. There is a jar with 100 marbles, R of which are red and 100 − R of which are blue. The executive must close his eyes and select one of the marbles at random. If he selects a red one, he wins Y dollars; otherwise, he wins 0 dollars. Now the consultant explains that she will specify the number R, and then the executive must supply the value Y such that he is indifferent between I and II. This procedure is repeated with several values of R, and the following responses are given.

Consultant's R	Executive's Y
20	$580
40	280
60	180
80	135

a. If the executive's utility function is $U(x)$, and we specify that $U(0) = 0$ and $U(100) = 1$, evaluate the utility of four other dollar values.
b. Do the executive's responses indicate that he is risk averse? Why or why not?
c. If the executive is risk averse, what must be true of his response Y when $R = 75$? Be specific.

*60. You have been given the opportunity to become a full or limited partner in a company. A full partnership costs $100,000. You believe that the present value of income you could make from this partnership is a random variable X with a given distribution. If you do not become a partner, you believe the present value of income you could make by investing the $100,000 in other ways is a known constant A. If you become a limited partner, you pay the corresponding portion of the entering fee and you receive the corresponding portions of X and A. For example, if you purchase a 75% partnership, it costs you $75,000, and the present value of your income is $.75X + .25A$. Show that if you are an EMV maximizer, you should either become a full partner or no partner at all, depending on the values of A and $E(X)$, the expected value of X. That is, you should never become a limited partner. Why might this not be the case if you are a risk-averse expected utility maximizer?

Computer Problems

(These problems are to be used in conjunction with the computer software package.)

1. For the following payoff table, two sets of probabilities are shown. Use the PROBDIST program with the first set of probabilities to find the decision that maximizes the EMV. Then use this program again with the second set of probabilities to find the maximum EMV. Is the same decision optimal for both sets of probabilities? Is the extra information provided by the PROBDIST (on variance and standard deviation) of any use in this problem?

		States of Nature					
		1	2	3	4	5	6
	1	700	400	100	0	−600	−1000
Decisions	2	500	300	50	−20	−400	−700
	3	200	100	0	−40	−100	−400
Probability Set 1		.2	.2	.1	.1	.1	.3
Probability Set 2		.4	.3	.1	.1	.05	.05

2. An investor is thinking of investing $10,000 in two possible investments. The profits from the two investments (per dollar

invested) are random variables labeled X_1 and X_2. The joint distribution of X_1 and X_2 is given below. If the investor puts a_1 dollars into investment 1 and a_2 dollars into investment 2, where $a_1 + a_2 = 10,000$, then the profit from the investment is $a_1X_1 + a_2X_2$. The investor has a utility function that is "quadratic," which means that if X is a random profit, then $EU(X) = -b_1E(X^2) + b_2E(X)$ for some positive constants b_1 and b_2. Since $\text{Var}(X) = E(X^2) - [E(X)]^2$ for any random variable X, the expected utility can also be expressed as $EU(X) = -b_1\text{Var}(X) - b_1[E(X)]^2 + b_2E(X)$.

| | | Return from Investment 1 | |
	.05	.10	.15
Return from Investment 2 .05	.06	.15	.10
.10	.12	.25	.06
.15	.12	.10	.04

a. For the present case the random profit is $a_1X_1 + a_2X_2$. This has expected value $a_1E(X_1) + a_2E(X_2)$ and variance $a_1^2\text{Var}(X_1) + a_2^2\text{Var}(X_2) + 2a_1a_2\text{Cov}(X_1, X_2)$. Use the **PROBDIST** program to find this expected value and this variance when $a_1 = 4,000$ and $a_2 = 6,000$; when $a_1 = 8,000$ and $a_2 = 2,000$.

b. Assume $b_1 = 1$ and $b_2 = 10,000$. Use the results from part (a) to find the investor's expected utility when $a_1 = 4,000$ and $a_2 = 6,000$; when $a_1 = 8,000$ and $a_2 = 2,000$. Which of these two investments is better from an expected utility point of view? Which is better from an EMV point of view?

References

Bunn, D. W. *Applied Decision Analysis*. New York: McGraw-Hill, 1984.

Lindley, D. V. *Making Decisions*. London: Wiley, 1971.

Winkler, R. L. *Introduction to Bayesian Inference and Decision*. New York: Holt, Rinehart and Winston, 1972.

Methods of Survey Sampling

When the members of Congress propose tax changes, they obviously need to know how these changes will affect taxpayers. One method for finding this information is to select a representative sample of recent tax returns and see how these returns would be affected by the proposed tax changes. As we will see later in this chapter, this is the method actually used. In fact, the effects of various changes on a representative sample of tax returns are investigated on a daily basis. Therefore, if the method is to be feasible, the sample must be as small as possible in addition to being representative. The question is how this representative sample should be selected.

The only sampling method we have discussed so far is called "simple" random sampling. Here every member of the population has an equal chance of being selected. However, there are other types of random samples that are better than simple random samples in certain situations. The method actually used for selecting tax returns is called stratified sampling. Here the population of tax returns is separated into groups, called strata, such that the returns in any group are similar to one another in some predefined sense. (For example, they might have approximately the same adjusted gross income.) Then a simple random sample is selected from each group, and these simple random samples are combined to make up the overall sample. As we will see, the benefit of a stratified sample is that a given level of accuracy can sometimes be achieved by means of a smaller sample size.

16.1

Introduction

Throughout most of this book, we have learned how to infer characteristics of a population from the characteristics of a random sample. In this chapter we give an overview of the methods survey samplers use to select the samples in the first place. We discussed this topic in general terms in Chapter 1. There we saw that two of the primary objectives in sample selection are (1) to minimize sampling costs, and (2) to minimize sampling error.

The first of these objectives explains why we do not take a census of the entire population. It costs too much. So we sample no more of the population than necessary to obtain the desired accuracy. With regard to the second objective, minimizing sample error, we saw in Chapter 1 that certain types of errors can be avoided by not "building in" any biases in the sample. For example, if we survey a population to learn about TV viewing preferences, we should not sample exclusively from the teenage population or from the college graduate population. Either of these could lead to obvious biases. However, when we sample *randomly* from a given population, there is no way to avoid being unlucky and obtaining an unrepresentative sample. Since we cannot avoid sampling errors, we do the next best thing. We learn how to measure sampling error by using probability theory.

The basic ideas in this chapter are not new. When we want to infer the value of a population parameter from a randomly selected sample, we first need to estimate this parameter by means of a sample estimate. Since this sample estimate is not likely to equal the population parameter, we need to measure the standard error of the estimate and build a confidence interval for the parameter. To accomplish this, we require properties of the sampling distribution of the sample estimate. For *simple* random sampling, the type of random sampling discussed in earlier chapters, we already know the relevant statistical quantities. For the new sampling schemes in this chapter, we learn how to calculate the appropriate sample estimates and their associated standard errors. As a by-product we also learn sample size formulas that guarantee sufficiently small sampling errors with high probability.

16.2
Some Sampling Terminology

Before we learn about specific sampling methods, it is useful to become acquainted with some of the terminology used in sampling discussions. We begin by defining the relevant population.

> The population is the set of all members about which a study intends to make inferences.

It is important to realize that a population is defined in relationship to any particular study. Any person planning a survey should first decide which population the conclusions of the study will concern, so that the sample can be chosen from *this* population. For example, if a marketing research group plans to use a questionnaire to infer consumers' reactions to a new product, it must first decide which population of consumers it is interested in: all consumers, consumers over 21 years old, consumers who do most of their shopping in shopping malls, or others. Once the relevant consumer population has been chosen, a sample from this population can then be surveyed. Of course, it follows that any inferences made from the study pertain only to this population.

Before we can choose a sample from a given population, we need to have a list of all the members of the population. This list is called a *frame,* and the potential sample members are called *sampling units.* Depending on the application, the sampling units could be individual people, households, companies, cities, or others.

> A sampling unit is one of the possible members of the population that could be chosen in a sample.

> A frame is a list of the sampling units in the population.

In this chapter we assume the population is finite and consists of N sampling units. We also assume that a frame of these N sampling units is available. Obviously, there are situations where a complete frame is practically impossible to obtain. For example, if we want to take a survey of the attitudes of all unemployed teenagers in Chicago, it would be very difficult, if not impossible, to obtain a complete frame of them. In this situation all we can hope to do is obtain as complete a listing as possible and then choose a random sample from this partial frame. If the partial frame omits any significant segments of the population (which a complete frame would include), the resulting sample could be biased. For instance, if we use the Yellow Pages of a Los Angeles telephone book to choose a sample of restaurants, we automatically omit all restaurants that do not advertise in the Yellow Pages. Depending on the purposes of the study, this may or may not be a serious omission.

For completeness, we introduce two other terms. These are the two broad categories of samples that are possible: *probability samples* and *judgmental samples.*

> A probability sample is a sample in which the sampling units are chosen from the population by means of a random mechanism (such as a random number table).

> A judgmental sample is a sample where the sampling units are not chosen randomly, but are chosen according to the sampler's judgment.

We will not discuss judgmental samples in this book. The reason is very simple. There is no way to measure the amount of sampling error committed when we use a judgmental sample because the rules of probability do not apply. Furthermore, it is very difficult to choose a representative sample from a population *without* using some random mechanism. Since our judgments are not as good as we think, judgmental samples are likely to contain our own built-in biases. Therefore, we will concentrate only on probability samples in the rest of this chapter.

16.3

Simple Random Sampling

In this section we discuss simple random samples, their properties, and methods for obtaining them. Much of this section is review from Chapters 6 and 7, because we were really talking about simple random samples when we used the term "random sample" in those chapters. In this section, however, we will be more explicit about the role of the population size N than we were in earlier chapters. Our emphasis in this section (and in other sections of this chapter) is on estimating the population mean μ or a population proportion p.

Suppose that a population has N sampling units and we wish to sample n of these. Then a simple random sample, taken without replacement, is defined as follows.

> A simple random sample of size n, taken without replacement, is chosen in such a way that every possible sample of size n has the same probability of being chosen.

A similar definition could be given for a simple random sample taken *with* replacement. However, we do not do so because almost all random samples in the real world are taken without replacement, where no sampling unit can be chosen more than once.

Our first objective is to learn how to select the members of the sample. We need a random mechanism for choosing the sample so that every possible sample of size n has the same chance of being chosen. As an example, consider the frame of 40 families with annual incomes shown in Table 16.1 (p. 866). Suppose that we wish to choose a simple random sample of size 10. Below we describe two possible methods for doing this.

In the first method we use a table of random digits. This is a table, such as the one shown in Table 16.2, where the successive numbers (here five-digit numbers) have been selected from all possible five-digit numbers to have certain properties of "randomness." In particular, there is no pattern

Selecting a Simple Random Sample

Table 16.1   A Frame of 40 Household Incomes

Family	Income	Family	Income
1	$24,550	21	$37,690
2	23,240	22	15,330
3	17,650	23	21,150
4	23,670	24	13,450
5	32,640	25	45,250
6	27,500	26	33,210
7	37,900	27	17,890
8	54,370	28	41,200
9	14,690	29	18,330
10	23,900	30	25,490
11	26,220	31	37,350
12	47,630	32	23,140
13	56,730	33	32,700
14	26,510	34	42,100
15	14,320	35	17,640
16	19,670	36	43,990
17	23,180	37	16,540
18	26,770	38	15,420
19	34,600	39	27,550
20	17,830	40	46,870

Table 16.2   A Table of Five-Digit Random Numbers

88860	16874	47839	22258	82971
04202	67156	99000	42938	36662
32094	18661	11139	26130	25585
96053	93209	77020	49728	82775
39890	96003	58847	30230	74758
77889	82612	51429	70018	05479
86942	05365	21819	24309	64893
02378	04760	28244	24714	03950
60294	66842	17259	65377	48691
60436	19937	44747	69278	83873
69401	76665	28618	54830	10147
84160	11331	37672	01224	77215
83234	48764	98233	61352	31502
24191	02808	54719	21514	85819
46767	87107	25102	16624	53116
29336	49862	31251	91096	76455
74230	02709	17462	83181	68011
81169	71175	25032	53041	15782
63712	33568	33673	65464	82151
29202	01775	59585	97254	50002

to these numbers, which means that we cannot predict any number from the numbers before it or after it. Also, the numbers in the table have the property that *any* five-digit number is as likely to appear as any other. Given this table of random numbers, we can choose the sample of size 10 from the frame in Table 16.1 as follows.

First, we start at any number in the random number table, say the number 88860 in the top left-hand corner. Since the population size is 40, a number with only two digits, we ignore the last three digits of the random number. This leaves the number 88. Then the method is to select the sampling unit labeled by this number if the number is less than or equal to 40 (which it is not). Otherwise, we go to the next random number in Table 16.2 and look at the number formed by its first two digits. In general, if the first two digits of the next random number is less than or equal to 40, *and* if we have not yet selected the sampling unit labeled by this number, this sampling unit is added to the sample. Otherwise, we go to the next random number. The procedure continues until 10 sampling units have been selected.

Table 16.3 (p. 868) illustrates this method for the random numbers in Table 16.2 when we start with the random number in the upper left-hand corner and work down and then to the right. (We could have started at any other point in the table and the same procedure would still be valid.)

A second method that is perhaps more difficult to do by hand but is well suited to computer programming works as follows. Again we use a table of random digits (or a similar computer-generated set of random numbers) to draw a random subset of size 10 from a population of size 40. First, we divide the interval from 0 to 1 into 40 equal-length intervals. These all have length $1/40$. The first extends from 0 to $1/40$, the second from $1/40$ to $2/40$, and so on. Now we select the first random number from the random number table, put a decimal point in front of it (to place it between 0 and 1), and see which of the 40 intervals it is in. Again starting in the upper left-hand corner of Table 16.2, the random number is .88860. Since this is between $35/40$ and $36/40$, the 36th out of 40 intervals, we choose the 36th sampling unit from Table 16.1 as the first member of the sample, and we eliminate this sampling unit from the frame (see Figure 16.1).

Figure 16.1

Table 16.3   Sample Chosen by Method 1

Random Number (First Two Digits)	Choice	Salary
88	Ignore	—
04	Family 4	$23,670
32	Family 32	23,140
96	Ignore	—
39	Family 39	27,550
77	Ignore	—
86	Ignore	—
02	Family 2	23,240
60	Ignore	—
60	Ignore	—
69	Ignore	—
84	Ignore	—
83	Ignore	—
24	Family 24	13,450
46	Ignore	—
29	Family 29	18,330
74	Ignore	—
81	Ignore	—
63	Ignore	—
29	Family 29 already chosen	—
16	Family 16	19,670
67	Ignore	—
18	Family 18	26,770
93	Ignore	—
96	Ignore	—
82	Ignore	—
05	Family 5	32,640
04	Family 4 already chosen	—
66	Ignore	—
19	Family 19	34,600

Next we divide the interval from 0 to 1 into 39 intervals of length $\frac{1}{39}$ each, select the second random number (04202) from Table 16.2 and put a decimal in front of it, and see which of the 39 intervals it is in. Since .04202 is between $\frac{1}{39}$ and $\frac{2}{39}$, the second of the 39 intervals, the second sampling unit of the remaining 39 in the frame is selected as the next member of the sample, and it is eliminated from the frame.

The next step is to divide the interval from 0 to 1 into 38 intervals of length $\frac{1}{38}$ each, and to see which of these intervals the next random number is in. This determines the third member of the sample. This procedure continues in the same manner until 10 members have been selected for the sample. The 10 members chosen in this way are shown in Table 16.4.

Table 16.4 Sample Chosen by Method 2

Random Number (As a Decimal)	Relevant Interval	Choice	Salary
.88860	$^{35}/_{40}$–$^{36}/_{40}$	Family 36	43,990
.04202	$^{1}/_{39}$–$^{2}/_{39}$	Family 2	23,240
.32094	$^{12}/_{38}$–$^{13}/_{38}$	Family 14 (13th remaining family)	26,510
.96053	$^{35}/_{37}$–$^{36}/_{37}$	Family 39 (36th remaining family)	27,550
.39890	$^{14}/_{36}$–$^{15}/_{36}$	Family 17 (15th remaining family)	23,180
.77889	$^{27}/_{35}$–$^{28}/_{35}$	Family 31 (28th remaining family)	37,350
.86942	$^{29}/_{34}$–$^{30}/_{34}$	Family 34 (30th remaining family)	42,100
.02378	$^{0}/_{33}$–$^{1}/_{33}$	Family 1	24,550
.60294	$^{19}/_{32}$–$^{20}/_{32}$	Family 24 (20th remaining family)	13,450
.60436	$^{18}/_{31}$–$^{19}/_{31}$	Family 23 (19th remaining family)	21,150

One advantage of this second method is that it requires only n random numbers to obtain a sample of size n. None of the random numbers are "wasted" as they are with the first method. An apparent disadvantage of the second method is the difficulty in determining which interval a given random number is in. However, there is a simple way to determine this. For example, consider the third step of the method (with the same data as above). We can tell that .32094 (the third random number in Table 16.2) is in the 13th of 38 equal-length intervals as follows. We multiply 38 by .32094 to obtain 12.19572, and then we round *up* to the next integer, 13. This tells us to add the 13th of the remaining sampling units to the sample. The general procedure is shown below.

> If m sampling units are left in the frame and r (between 0 and 1) is the next random number in the random number table, let k be the integer obtained by rounding the product mr up to the next integer. Then the kth sampling unit of those remaining in the frame is added to the sample.

Clearly, it makes a difference which of the two methods we use and where we start in the random number table. This is because different methods and/or different starting points result in different samples. However, the choice is irrelevant in the sense that each method is *valid*. That is, each method has the required property that the sample it selects qualifies as a simple random sample. Therefore, the choice of method is largely a matter of convenience.

Confidence Intervals for a Simple Random Sample

Once we have chosen the n sampling units in the sample, we want to use the information from them to estimate the population mean or a population proportion. As in previous chapters, we use the sample mean $\overline{X}$ and the sample proportion $\hat{p}$ as point estimates of the population mean μ and a population proportion p.

To measure the accuracy of these estimates, we need their standard errors. These standard errors are:

$$\textit{Standard Error of } \overline{X}$$

$$\text{StdErr}(\overline{X}) = \sqrt{\frac{N - n}{N - 1}} \frac{\sigma}{\sqrt{n}}$$

$$\textit{Standard Error of } \hat{p}$$

$$\text{StdErr}(\hat{p}) = \sqrt{\frac{N - n}{N - 1}} \sqrt{\frac{p(1 - p)}{n}}$$

Notice that these standard errors are not quite the same as those we saw in Chapters 6 and 7. The standard errors from Chapters 6 and 7 require that the observations be independent. When sampling is done *without* replacement from a finite population, this independence assumption does not hold, and we must modify the standard errors by the *finite population correction factor*, $\sqrt{(N - n)/(N - 1)}$. When the sample size n is a small fraction of the population size N, the finite population correction factor is close to 1 and can safely be ignored. As a rule of thumb, it is usually ignored when n/N is less than .05, that is, when less than 5% of the population is sampled.

If σ and p are unknown, the standard errors above cannot be evaluated. In this case we estimate them by substituting $\hat{p}$ for p and s for σ, where s is the sample standard deviation:

$$s = \sqrt{\frac{\sum X_i^2 - n\overline{X}^2}{n - 1}}$$

Then the estimated standard errors are:

$$\textit{Estimated Standard Error of } \overline{X}$$

$$\text{StdErr}(\overline{X}) = \sqrt{\frac{N - n}{N - 1}} \frac{s}{\sqrt{n}}$$

> ### *Estimated Standard Error of $\hat{p}$*
>
> $$\text{StdErr}(\hat{p}) = \sqrt{\frac{N - n}{N - 1}} \sqrt{\frac{\hat{p}(1 - \hat{p})}{n}}$$

We could now proceed to obtain confidence intervals for μ and p in the usual way. In survey sampling, however, it is customary to quote upper and lower bounds for these population parameters. The usual way to do this is to go out plus or minus 2 standard errors from the point estimate. There is actually nothing new about this approach. Since the sampling distributions of $\overline{X}$ and $\hat{p}$ are approximately normal with approximately .95 area within 2 standard deviations of their means, we are really just quoting approximate 95% confidence intervals for μ and p with this "new" approach. (By using appropriate multiples other than 2, we can of course obtain 90% confidence intervals, 99% confidence intervals, or any other confidence intervals we desire.)

> ### *Approximate 95% Confidence Interval for μ*
>
> $$\overline{X} \pm 2 \text{ StdErr}(\overline{X})$$
>
> ### *Approximate 95% Confidence Interval for p*
>
> $$\hat{p} \pm 2 \text{ StdErr}(\hat{p})$$

In each case the term we are adding and subtracting is called a *bound on the error*. The reason is that when we estimate μ by $\overline{X}$, for example, we are approximately 95% sure that the resulting error $|\overline{X} - \mu|$ will be no greater than 2 standard errors of $\overline{X}$ in magnitude (see Figure 16.2).

Maximum probable error when we estimate μ by $\overline{X}$

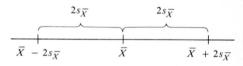

Figure 16.2

EXAMPLE 16.1

Find a point estimate and an approximate 95% confidence interval for (1) the mean income, and (2) the proportion of incomes over $25,000 for the population shown in Table 16.1. Do this from the samples found from method 1 (Table 16.3) and from method 2 (Table 16.4).

SOLUTION

The sample incomes from method 1 are: 23,240, 23,670, 32,640, 19,670, 26,770, 34,600, 13,450, 18,330, 23,140, and 27,550. These give

$$\overline{X} = \frac{23,240 + \cdots + 27,550}{10} = 24,306$$

$$s = \sqrt{\frac{(23,240^2 + \cdots + 27,550^2) - 10(24,306)^2}{9}} = 6412$$

and

$$\hat{p} = \frac{4}{10} = .4$$

Therefore, the estimated standard errors of $\overline{X}$ and $\hat{p}$ are

$$\text{StdErr}(\overline{X}) = \sqrt{\frac{40 - 10}{40 - 1}} \frac{6412}{\sqrt{10}} = 1778$$

and

$$\text{StdErr}(\hat{p}) = \sqrt{\frac{40 - 10}{40 - 1}} \sqrt{\frac{.4(.6)}{10}} = .136$$

(Notice that we include the finite population correction factor because $n/N = .25$ is much larger than the .05 guideline.) The resulting confidence interval for μ is $24,306 \pm 2(1778)$, or from \$20,750 to \$27,862. For p, it is $.4 \pm 2(.136)$, or from .128 to .672.

If we use the sample selected by method 2, the sample incomes are: 24,550, 37,350, 23,240, 26,510, 23,180, 21,150, 13,450, 42,100, 43,990, and 27,550. Now we have $\overline{X} = 28,307$, $s = 9774$, and $\hat{p} = .5$. The resulting standard errors are $\text{StdErr}(\overline{X}) = 2711$ and $\text{StdErr}(\hat{p}) = .139$, and the confidence intervals for μ and p are from \$22,885 to \$33,729 and from .222 to .778, respectively.

Since we have the entire population listed in Table 16.1, we can find the true values of μ and p; these are \$28,646.50 and $21/40 = .525$. (Also, the true value of σ is \$11,567.29.) Therefore, we see that the confidence interval from the method 1 sample does *not* include μ. Part of the reason is that its $\overline{X}$ is too low, but notice that its estimate of σ is also too low. This produces a confidence interval that is not only centered at the wrong place but is also too short. The confidence interval for μ based on the method 2 sample is much more on the mark. Of course, this does not imply that method 1 is any worse than method 2; it was just the unluckier of the two in this example.

Sample Size Selection for Simple Random Sampling

Once we have chosen a sample size and a sample of this size, we can proceed as above to obtain point estimates and confidence intervals for the population parameters we require. The first stage of the whole procedure, however, is to select the sample size n. We want n to be reasonably small so that sampling costs are minimized, but we also want it to be large enough so that sampling errors are not too large. For example, if we estimate μ by $\overline{X}$, the error is $|\overline{X} - \mu|$, and this error has approximately a 95% chance of being less than

2 standard errors of $\overline{X}$. Therefore, we will choose n so that two times the standard error of $\overline{X}$ is no larger than a preassigned error bound B (exactly as in Chapter 7).

To find the required value of n for estimating the mean μ, we set two times the standard error of $\overline{X}$ equal to B and solve for n. This leads to the following formula.

Required Sample Size for Estimating μ

$$n = \frac{N\sigma^2}{\sigma^2 + (N - 1)B^2/4}$$

In a similar way, we can find the required sample size for estimating a proportion p.

Required Sample Size for Estimating p

$$n = \frac{Np(1 - p)}{p(1 - p) + (N - 1)B^2/4}$$

The problem with both of these formulas is that they contain population parameters, σ^2 and p, that are unknown when the sample size is being selected. The question is what we can use in place of these unknown values. As in Chapter 7, we provide several suggestions.

One suggestion is to approximate σ and/or p by appropriate values and then use these approximations in the formulas for n. A convenient approximation for σ is

$$\sigma \approx \frac{\text{range in population}}{4}$$

where "range in population" is the largest value in the population minus the smallest value. For a proportion p, we can either guess a value of p or simply substitute .5 for p in the formula for n. If we guess a value of p, we should err toward .5 rather than toward 0 or 1, so that the resulting sample size n will be large enough to accomplish its purpose. If we do substitute .5 for p, the resulting n will definitely be large enough.

Another suggestion is as follows. First estimate σ^2 and/or p with a small "preliminary" sample of size n_0. The resulting estimates are labeled s_0^2 and $\hat{p}_0$. Next, substitute these values for σ^2 or p in the sample size formulas above to find the required total sample size n. Finally, collect a *remaining* sample of size $n - n_0$ and merge these sampling units with the original n_0 sampling units to produce the total sample. (This method was also discussed in Chapter 7.)

As an example, suppose that we want to estimate μ from a population of size $N = 10,000$, and we want the bound on the error to be approximately equal to 50. If we believe that most of the population have values between 2300 and 3800, an approximate value of σ is $(3800 - 2300)/4 = 375$. This leads to the following value of n:

$$n = \frac{N\sigma^2}{\sigma^2 + (N - 1)B^2/4}$$

$$= \frac{10,000(375)^2}{375^2 + 9999(50)^2/4} = 220$$

Alternatively, suppose that we take a preliminary sample of size $n_0 = 30$, and the resulting sample standard deviation is $s_0 = 325$. Then the approximate total sample size required is

$$n = \frac{Ns_0^2}{s_0^2 + (N - 1)B^2/4}$$

$$= \frac{10,000(325)^2}{325^2 + 9999(50)^2/4} = 166$$

In this case an extra $166 - 30 = 136$ sampling units must be sampled to obtain the entire sample. As this example illustrates, the final value of n depends critically on the value of σ^2 used.

EXAMPLE 16.2

Suppose that we wish to find the proportion of the 57,358 families in a given city who got refunds from their federal tax returns. We want the error bound for this proportion to be no more than .02. Find the required sample size n under three assumptions: (1) we substitute .5 for p in the formula for n; (2) we guess that p will be at least .6; and (3) a preliminary sample of 100 families shows that 71 received refunds.

SOLUTION

The only difference between the three answers is the value of p we use in the formula

$$n = \frac{57,358p(1 - p)}{p(1 - p) + 57,357(.02)^2/4}$$

If we use $p = .5$, we obtain an upper bound for the required n; it is 2396. If we know that p is at least .6, we also obtain an upper bound for the required n; it is 2304. (These sample sizes are upper bounds on the required n in the sense that they are more than adequate to produce the desired error bound.) Finally, if a preliminary sample of size $n_0 = 100$ shows that $\hat{p}_0 = .71$, the approximate required value of n is 1988. In this case we would need to sample 1888 *more* families. Notice that as p gets farther away from .5 (on either side), the required value of n decreases.

From an intuitive point of view, it seems reasonable that the larger the population size, the larger the sample size must be to achieve a prescribed level of accuracy. For example, it seems reasonable that to estimate the mean age of a population with 1,000,000 people, we have to sample more people than if the population had only 1000 people. However, this reasoning is *not* correct. The following two observations are in direct conflict with common intuition.

1. When the population size N is reasonably large, the required sample size is practically independent of N. For example, suppose that we are estimating μ, the error bound B is 10, and the standard deviation σ is 30. Then for population sizes $N = 1000$, $N = 100,000$, and $N = 1,000,000$, the required sample sizes are $n = 35$, $n = 36$, and $n = 36$. Similar results hold for estimating a proportion.

2. The proportion of the population that must be sampled to achieve a given level of accuracy *decreases* as the population size N increases. For example, again suppose that we are estimating μ, the error bound B is 10, and the standard deviation σ is 30. Then the required sample sizes for populations of size $N = 50$, $N = 100$, and $N = 500$ are $n = 21$, $n = 27$, and $n = 34$. This means that the proportions of these three populations that must be sampled are $21/50 = .42$, $27/100 = .27$, and $34/500 = .068$. The conclusion is that a large percentage of a small population must be sampled, whereas only a small percentage of a large population must be sampled.

Problems for Sections 16.2, 16.3

1. The city government of Jefferson City wishes to gather information about the assessed valuation of all single-family dwellings within the city limits. What is the relevant population? What must a frame for this problem include? What are the sampling units?

2. Answer the same questions as in Problem 1 in the context where K mart is interested in total weekly sales of garden equipment for all its member stores in the United States.

3. Consider a population of five members labeled A, B, C, D, and E. Display all possible samples of size 3. What property does a simple random sample of size 3, drawn without replacement, from this population have? List all such samples.

4. Use the first method in Section 16.3 to choose a simple random sample of size 10 from the population in Table 16.1. Now, however, start at the bottom right of the random number table (Table 16.2) and work up and to the left.

5. Use the second method in Section 16.3 to choose a simple random sample of size 10 from the population in Table 16.1. Now start at the top of the left-hand column in Table 16.2 but work across and then down (not down and then across as in the example in the text).

6. For a population of size 10,000, calculate the finite population correction factor for the standard errors of $\overline{X}$ and $\hat{p}$ when $n = 100$; when $n = 500$; when $n = 1000$. Use trial and error (or any other method) to see how small n must be before this correction factor is less than or equal to .90.

7. When we are interested in the mean and we say that $2s_{\overline{x}}$ is a bound on the error, exactly what error are we talking about? In what sense is $2s_{\overline{x}}$ a bound on this error? (Are we sure that the error will be less than this bound?) How is the magnitude of this bound related to the length of a confidence interval for μ?

8. Rework Example 16.1 by using the sample you found in Problem 4.

9. Rework Example 16.1 by using the sample you found in Problem 5.

10. After a severe winter the maintenance department of an eastern city wishes to estimate the mean cost per city block that is required to repair weather-worn streets. The department decides to base its total estimate on a simple random sample of n of the city's 10,000 city blocks of streets, and it wants the estimate to be off by no more than $5.
   a. Approximately how large should n be if the city is convinced that the amount of damage on almost all blocks is between $50 and $200?
   b. Approximately how large should n be if a preliminary sample of 15 blocks shows a mean damage amount per block of $76 and a standard deviation of $32?

11. A company that is marketing a new brand of dessert wishes to know the proportion of the 30,000 wives in a given city who are aware of the product through television or magazine advertising. It knows that it cannot obtain this fraction exactly without a census, so it is content to obtain a 95% confidence interval for the proportion.
   a. What sample size will guarantee a 95% confidence interval of length no greater than .05?
   b. If a preliminary sample of 50 wives shows that 17 are aware of the product, how many more wives must be sampled to obtain a 95% confidence interval of approximate length .05?

12. Consider a population with 50 members, 5 of whom are women. How many simple random samples of size 15 can be chosen from this population? How many of these samples have no women? What is the probability of choosing a simple random sample with no women?

13. Consider working Example 16.1 for *every* possible sample of size 10. What fraction of the 95% confidence intervals for μ will include the true mean μ? Explain.

14. A study is being done in a large city to see how automobile repair costs vary from one repair shop to another. The people doing the study plan to take a car requiring body repair to a sample of repair shops for estimates of repair costs. They know there are 56 shops in this city that can do the required repair work, and they estimate that the range in costs is approximately from $150 to $300.
   a. What is a reasonable estimate of the population standard deviation of repair costs in this city?
   b. Using the estimate in part (a), how many shops should they obtain estimates from if they want an error bound on their estimate of the overall mean repair cost in this city to be no greater than $5?
   c. How much will the answer to part (b) change if they discover that the estimate of σ used in part (b) is 50% larger than the true σ?

16.4

Stratified Sampling

In this section we present an alternative to simple random sampling that is used in many real applications. Suppose that we can identify various subpopulations within the total population. These subpopulations are called *strata*. Instead of taking a simple random sample from the entire population, it may make more sense to select a simple random sample from each stratum separately. This sampling method is called *stratified sampling*. It is a particularly useful approach when there is considerable variation between the various strata but relatively little variation within a given stratum.

> In stratified sampling, we divide the population into relatively homogeneous strata and take a simple random sample from each stratum.

There are several advantages to stratified sampling. One obvious advantage is that we obtain separate estimates within each stratum, which we would not obtain if we took a simple random sample from the entire population. Even if we eventually plan to pool the samples from the individual strata, it cannot hurt to have the total sample broken down into separate samples at first.

The second advantage of stratified sampling is that the sampling error of the resulting population estimate can be reduced by sampling appropriately from the strata. The idea here is that there is usually much less variance *within* the individual strata than in the population as a whole. So by choosing the sample sizes for the individual strata appropriately, we can generally obtain a smaller standard error for a given sampling cost than we could obtain from a simple random sample at the same cost. Alternatively, we can achieve the same level of accuracy at a lower sampling cost.

Probably the greatest difficulty in using stratified sampling is that we must identify the strata. As an example, suppose a company that advertises its product on television wishes to estimate the reaction of viewers to the advertising. Here the population consists of all viewers who have seen the advertising. But what are the appropriate strata? The answer depends on the company's objectives and its product. The company could stratify the population by sex, by income, by amount of television watched, by the amount of the product class consumed, and probably others. Then after the company has defined the strata in an unambiguous way, it must compile a frame for each stratum. Clearly, this is no easy task. However, it must be done if the company is to select a simple random sample from each stratum.

Choosing the Individual Sample Sizes

Suppose that we have identified J nonoverlapping strata in a given population, and we wish to perform stratified sampling. The first thing we must do is choose the sampling units that comprise the sample. Let N be the total population size and let N_j be the population size of stratum j. Similarly, let n be the total sample size and let n_j be the sample size selected from stratum j. Then we have

$$N_1 + N_2 + \cdots + N_J = N$$

and

$$n_1 + n_2 + \cdots + n_J = n$$

Once we have selected the sample sizes $n_1, n_2, \ldots, n_J$, we proceed as in Section 16.3 to select a *simple* random sample of the appropriate size from each stratum. That is, we use the frame for each stratum and a table of random numbers to choose the sampling units for that stratum. Since this method is identical to the one described in the preceding section, we will not give an illustration of it here.

What we do need to discuss is the choice of the individual sample sizes n_1 through n_J, given that the total sample size n has been chosen. (Selection of n will be discussed later.) There are many ways that we could choose numbers n_1 through n_J that sum to n, but we will discuss only the two most popular methods, *proportional* sample sizes and *optimal* sample sizes.

Proportional sample sizes are certainly the simplest to understand and implement. The idea is that if a given stratum contains a certain percentage of the population, its sample size should be the *same* proportion of the total sample size n. For example, if 25% of the population are in stratum 1, then 25% of the sample should come from stratum 1. Formally, let F_j be the proportion of the population in stratum j, that is, $F_j = N_j/N$. Then n_j is determined by the following formula.

> ### Proportional Sample Sizes in Stratified Sampling
>
> $$n_j = F_j n \qquad j = 1, 2, \ldots, J$$

The advantage of proportional sample sizes is that they are very easy to determine. The disadvantage is that they ignore differences in variances among the strata. To illustrate, suppose that we are attempting to estimate the population mean μ of employee salaries in a large company. There are three strata, of sizes $N_1 = 1400$, $N_2 = 500$, and $N_3 = 100$, so that $F_1 = 1400/2000 = .7$, $F_2 = 500/2000 = .25$, and $F_3 = 100/2000 = .05$. Stratum 1 includes all blue-collar workers, stratum 2 includes foremen and middle level managers, and stratum 3 includes high-level managers and executives. Suppose that the individual standard deviations of the salaries in these three strata are $\sigma_1 = \$2000$, $\sigma_2 = \$5000$, and $\sigma_3 = \$10,000$. This implies that the salaries are progressively more variable as we move from stratum 1 to stratum 3.

If we use proportional sample sizes, 70% of the sample will come from stratum 1, 25% will come from stratum 2, and 5% will come from stratum 3. But in spite of its small population size, stratum 3 is likely to have a large effect on the sampling error of the estimate of the population mean. This is because of its large standard deviation. On the other hand, we probably do not need to sample so heavily from stratum 1 because it has a small standard deviation; a relatively few members from this stratum should give us a good idea of its mean.

In this example it is better to choose the individual sample sizes by taking the standard deviations of the strata into effect. The optimal way to do this is shown below.

Optimal Sample Sizes for Stratified Sampling

$$n_j = \frac{N_j \sigma_j}{N_1 \sigma_1 + N_2 \sigma_2 + \cdots + N_J \sigma_J} n \qquad j = 1, 2, \ldots, J$$

For the example above, the optimal sample sizes are

$$n_1 = \frac{1400(2000)}{6,300,000} n = .444n$$

$$n_2 = \frac{500(5000)}{6,300,000} n = .397n$$

$$n_3 = \frac{100(10,000)}{6,300,000} n = .159n$$

where the denominator in each expression above was found from

$$N_1 \sigma_1 + N_2 \sigma_2 + N_3 \sigma_3 = 1400(2000) + 500(5000) + 100(10,000) = 6,300,000$$

Now only 44.4% of the sample comes from stratum 1, whereas almost 16% of the sample comes from stratum 3. Obviously, this is a much different allocation than with proportional sample sizes. The difference is that strata with higher standard deviations now have proportionally larger sample sizes.

The difficulty in obtaining optimal sample sizes is that we generally do not know the σ_j's for the individual strata. In this case we may substitute an approximation for each σ_j in the formula above. The resulting n_j's will be approximately optimal. (This discussion of optimal sample sizes is relevant only if we are estimating the population mean. If we are estimating a population proportion, similar formulas exist, but we do not present them here.)

Once we have chosen the sample sizes n_1 through n_J and have collected simple random samples of these sizes from the individual strata, we can combine these samples to estimate the population mean or a population proportion. We present the formulas for doing so in this section.

Since each stratum can be considered a separate population, everything we said about simple random sampling in Section 16.3 applies here if we concentrate on only one stratum at a time. In particular, we use $\overline{X}_j$, the sample mean of the stratum j observations, as a point estimate of μ_j, the stratum j

Point Estimates and Confidence Intervals with Stratified Sampling population mean. The standard error of $\overline{X}_j$ is approximated by

$$\text{StdErr}(\overline{X}_j) = \sqrt{\frac{N_j - n_j}{N_j - 1}} \frac{s_j}{\sqrt{n_j}}$$

where s_j is the sample standard deviation of the stratum j observations. Then $\overline{X}_j \pm 2\,\text{StdErr}(\overline{X}_j)$ is an approximate 95% confidence interval for μ_j. Similar statements hold for estimating proportions.

Now to combine these sample statistics into estimates of the *total* population parameters, we use the following formulas. (Any parameter without a subscript refers to the entire population; subscripted parameters refer to particular strata. Also, F_j still denotes the fraction of the population in stratum j.)

Formula for the Population Mean μ

$$\mu = F_1\mu_1 + F_2\mu_2 + \cdots + F_J\mu_J$$

Formula for a Population Proportion p

$$p = F_1p_1 + F_2p_2 + \cdots + F_Jp_J$$

If we wish to estimate the population mean μ, the formulas above (plus a variance formula not shown here) lead to the following point estimate of μ and standard error of this point estimate:

Point Estimate of μ

$$\overline{X} = F_1\overline{X}_1 + \cdots + F_J\overline{X}_J$$

Estimated Standard Error of $\overline{X}$

$$\text{StdErr}(\overline{X}) = \sqrt{F_1^2 s_{\overline{X}_1}^2 + \cdots + F_J^2 s_{\overline{X}_J}^2}$$

$$\text{where } s_{\overline{X}_j}^2 = \frac{(N_j - n_j)}{(N_j - 1)} \frac{s_j^2}{n_j}$$

Approximate 95% Confidence Interval for μ

$$\overline{X} \pm 2\,\text{StdErr}(\overline{X})$$

The similar formulas for estimating a population proportion p are:

Point Estimate of p

$$\hat{p} = F_1\hat{p}_1 + \cdots + F_J\hat{p}_J$$

> *Estimated Standard Error of $\hat{p}$*
>
> $$\text{StdErr}(\hat{p}) = \sqrt{F_1^2 s_{\hat{p}_1}^2 + \cdots + F_J^2 s_{\hat{p}_J}^2}$$
>
> where $s_{\hat{p}_j}^2 = \dfrac{N_j - n_j}{N_j - 1} \dfrac{\hat{p}_j(1 - \hat{p}_j)}{n_j}$
>
> *Approximate 95% Confidence Interval for p*
>
> $$\hat{p} \pm 2\,\text{StdErr}(\hat{p})$$

According to the usual convention, we have used the notation $\overline{X}$ and $\hat{p}$ for the point estimates of μ and p. However, it is important to realize that $\overline{X}$ is not the usual sample mean, that is, it is not the average of all n observations. Instead, it is a weighted average of the sample means from the individual strata. Similarly, $\hat{p}$ is not the proportion of all members in the sample with the specified property; it is a weighted average of the individual sample proportions. We also point out that the finite population correction factors for the standard errors of $\overline{X}_j$ and $\hat{p}_j$, namely $\sqrt{(N_j - n_j)/(N_j - 1)}$, can be ignored when n_j/N_j is less than or equal to .05.

The following example illustrates the effect stratified sampling can have on the standard error of $\overline{X}$. In this example we assume that the population standard deviation σ and the strata standard deviations σ_1 through σ_J are known so that they (instead of their sample estimates) can be used in the formulas for the standard error of $\overline{X}$.

EXAMPLE 16.3

Consider a population of size $N = 10{,}000$. We wish to use a sample of size $n = 500$ to estimate the mean μ. This population can be divided into three strata with sizes $N_1 = 5000$, $N_2 = 3000$, and $N_3 = 2000$, so that $F_1 = .5$, $F_2 = .3$, and $F_3 = .2$. The means and standard deviations of these strata are $\mu_1 = 500$, $\mu_2 = 800$, $\mu_3 = 1200$, $\sigma_1 = 100$, $\sigma_2 = 300$, and $\sigma_3 = 500$. Find the standard error of $\overline{X}$ when (1) a simple random sample is taken from the entire population, (2) stratified sampling is used with proportional sample sizes, and (3) stratified sampling is used with optimal sample sizes. Use the fact that the variance σ^2 of the entire population is given by

$$\sigma^2 = \sum F_j \sigma_j^2 + \sum F_j \mu_j^2 - \left(\sum F_j \mu_j \right)^2$$

SOLUTION

(1) For simple random sampling, the standard error of $\overline{X}$ is $\sigma/\sqrt{n}$, where from the preceding formula,

$$\sigma^2 = (.5\sigma_1^2 + .3\sigma_2^2 + .2\sigma_3^2) + (.5\mu_1^2 + .3\mu_2^2 + .2\mu_3^2)$$
$$- (.5\mu_1 + .3\mu_2 + .2\mu_3)^2 = 392.56^2$$

So the standard error of $\overline{X}$ is

$$\text{StdErr}(\overline{X}) = \frac{\sigma}{\sqrt{n}} = \frac{392.56}{\sqrt{500}} = 17.56$$

(We omit the finite population correction factors in all parts of this example because the sample sizes are small relative to the population sizes.)

(2) For stratified sampling with proportional sample sizes, the sample sizes are $n_1 = .5n = 250$, $n_2 = .3n = 150$, and $n_3 = .2n = 100$. The standard error of the sample mean $\overline{X}_j$ from stratum j is

$$\text{StdErr}(\overline{X}_j) = \frac{\sigma_j}{\sqrt{n_j}}$$

This leads to $\text{StdErr}(\overline{X}_1) = 100/\sqrt{250} = 6.325$ for stratum 1, and similarly, $\text{StdErr}(\overline{X}_2) = 24.495$ and $\text{StdErr}(\overline{X}_3) = 50.000$ for strata 2 and 3. The resulting standard error of the overall sample mean $\overline{X}$ is

$$\text{StdErr}(\overline{X}) = \sqrt{.5^2(6.325)^2 + .3^2(24.495)^2 + .2^2(50.000)^2} = 12.81$$

Notice that each term in the square root above is the square of an F_j times the square of the corresponding $\text{StdErr}(\overline{X}_j)$.

(3) For stratified sampling with optimal sample sizes, the sample size for stratum 1 is

$$n_1 = \frac{N_1\sigma_1}{N_1\sigma_1 + N_2\sigma_2 + N_3\sigma_3}\, n = 104$$

Similarly, $n_2 = 188$ and $n_3 = 208$. Using the same formulas as in part (2) (but with different n_j values), we obtain $\text{StdErr}(\overline{X}_1) = 9.806$, $\text{StdErr}(\overline{X}_2) = 21.880$, $\text{StdErr}(\overline{X}_3) = 34.669$, and finally, $\text{StdErr}(\overline{X}) = 10.73$.

Comparing the standard errors of $\overline{X}$ from parts (1), (2), and (3), we see that stratified sampling indeed leads to a lower standard error than simple random sampling (17.56 versus 12.81 and 10.73). Also, the standard error with optimal sample sizes is about 16% lower than the standard error with proportional sample sizes. However, part of this reduction results from knowing the individual σ_j's. If these are unknown and must be estimated, the optimal sample size method may not do as well as the proportional sample size method. Therefore, the main lesson to be learned from this example is that stratified sampling with proportional or optimal sample sizes can produce a significantly lower standard error of $\overline{X}$ than simple random sampling.

We now present an example that illustrates the stratified sampling formulas when we start with the raw sample data.

EXAMPLE 16.4

Suppose that a textbook company wants to investigate the net amount university students pay for books in a given year. (The *net* amount is studied because many students, particularly undergraduates, sell their books after the course is over.) The company performs its study at a large university with 31,320 students. The total student population at this university is divided into three strata: undergraduates, master's students, and doctoral students. The sizes of these three strata are $N_1 = 20,315$, $N_2 = 9130$, and $N_3 = 1875$, so that $F_1 = .649$, $F_2 = .291$, and $F_3 = .060$. Since the company does not have nearly enough time to interview all the students, it decides to use stratified sampling with proportional sample sizes and a total sample of 50 students. This results in individual sample sizes of $n_1 = 32$, $n_2 = 15$, and $n_3 = 3$. Because the doctoral students are practically neglected by this allocation, however, the company decides to alter these slightly to $n_1 = 29$, $n_2 = 14$, and $n_3 = 7$. (It argues that these may be closer to the *optimal* sample sizes anyway.) Simple random samples of these sizes are selected from the three strata, and the resulting observations are shown in Table 16.5. Use these data to find (1) a point estimate and a 95% confidence interval for the mean net amount spent over the entire student population, and (2) a point

Table 16.5

	Undergraduate		Masters	Doctoral
	128	131	156	167
	57	109	195	185
	115	185	128	215
	93	66	105	169
	175	97	170	306
	67	135	210	207
	45	77	166	251
	92	121	96	
	129	119	145	
	143	85	132	
	105	145	87	
	91	120	123	
	87	165	186	
	164	112	146	
	152			
Mean:	114.14		146.07	214.29
Std. dev.:	35.70		37.09	49.93

estimate and a 95% confidence interval for the proportion of all students who spend more than \$130 per year.

(1) As the table shows, the sample means are $\overline{X}_1 = 114.14$, $\overline{X}_2 = 146.07$, and $\overline{X}_3 = 214.29$. The resulting point estimate of the population mean is

$$\overline{X} = \sum F_j \overline{X}_j = .649(114.14) + .291(146.07) + .060(214.29) = \$129.44$$

The sample standard deviations, also shown in the table, are $s_1 = 35.70$, $s_2 = 37.09$, and $s_3 = 49.93$. We use these to calculate an estimated standard error of $\overline{X}$. (The finite population correction factors are dropped because each n_j is so small relative to N_j.)

$$\text{StdErr}(\overline{X}) = \sqrt{\sum F_j^2 s_{\overline{X}_j}^2} = \sqrt{\sum \frac{F_j^2 s_j^2}{n_j}}$$

$$= \sqrt{\frac{.649^2(35.70)^2}{29} + \frac{.291^2(37.09)^2}{14} + \frac{.060^2(49.93)^2}{7}} = \$5.30$$

The resulting confidence interval for the population mean μ is $\overline{X} \pm 2\,\text{StdErr}(\overline{X})$, or from \$118.84 to \$140.04. Notice that this interval is closest to the undergraduate and masters' sample means. This is because there are more of these students in the population.

(2) From the table, the three sample proportions of expenditures over \$130 are $\hat{p}_1 = 9/29$, $\hat{p}_2 = 9/14$, and $\hat{p}_3 = 7/7 = 1$. This gives an estimate of the overall proportion:

$$\hat{p} = \sum F_j \hat{p}_j = .649\left(\frac{9}{29}\right) + .291\left(\frac{9}{14}\right) + .060(1) = .448$$

The estimated standard error of $\hat{p}$ (again ignoring the finite population correction factors) is

$$\text{StdErr}(\hat{p}) = \sqrt{\sum F_j^2 s_{\hat{p}_j}^2} = \sqrt{\sum \frac{F_j^2 \hat{p}_j(1 - \hat{p}_j)}{n_j}}$$

$$= \sqrt{\frac{.649^2(\frac{9}{29})(\frac{20}{29})}{29} + \frac{.291^2(\frac{9}{14})(\frac{5}{14})}{14} + \frac{.060^2(1)(0)}{7}} = .067$$

A 95% confidence interval for the population proportion p is $\hat{p} \pm 2\,\text{StdErr}(\hat{p})$, or from .314 to .582. Again, this interval is affected more by the undergraduate and masters' sample proportions, because there are more of these students.

If we want the maximum difference between the population parameter (μ or p) and its estimate ($\overline{X}$ or $\hat{p}$) to be less than some prescribed value B with 95% confidence, we must select the appropriate total sample size n. With stratified sampling, however, we cannot choose n intelligently until we know how we are going to divide n into the individual sample sizes n_1 through n_J. In this section, therefore, we assume that *proportional* sample sizes are being used, and we then present formulas for the total sample size required.

First we discuss the mean. If B is the prescribed error bound on $\overline{X}$, so that the desired confidence interval has length $2B$, the formula for n is as given below.

> *Sample Size for Estimating μ with Stratified Sampling*
>
> $$n = \frac{\Sigma\, N_j \sigma_j^2}{\Sigma\, F_j \sigma_j^2 + NB^2/4}$$

As usual, this formula requires standard deviations, the σ_j's, which are probably not known. Therefore, we again recommend using the range approximation,

$$\sigma_j \approx \frac{\text{range in stratum } j}{4}$$

as an estimate of σ_j if no other estimates are available.

If we are interested in a proportion p and we want the error bound on the difference between p and $\hat{p}$ to be no greater than B, a conservative sample size is as follows.

> *Sample Size for Estimating p with Stratified Sampling*
>
> $$n = \frac{N}{1 + NB^2}$$

This value is conservative in the sense that it will certainly do the job required, but it may be larger than is really needed. This latter statement is especially true when p is close to 0 or 1.

EXAMPLE 16.5

Given the population sizes in Example 16.4, find the required sample sizes n, n_1, n_2, and n_3 when we want an error bound on $\overline{X}$ to be $B = \$3.00$. Assume that we have estimates of σ_1, σ_2, and σ_3 equal to $\$33$, $\$38$, and $\$50$, respectively. Then find the required sample sizes n, n_1, n_2, and n_3 when we want the error bound on the population proportion of expenditures greater than \$130 to be $B = .05$.

For estimating the mean, we have

$$n = \frac{\Sigma N_j \sigma_j^2}{\Sigma F_j \sigma_j^2 + NB^2/4} = 557$$

Since we plan to use proportional sample sizes, the individual sample sizes are $n_1 = F_1(557) = 361$, $n_2 = F_2(557) = 162$, and $n_3 = n - n_1 - n_2 = 34$.

For estimating the proportion, the required sample size is

$$n = \frac{N}{1 + NB^2} = 395$$

Now the individual sample sizes are $n_1 = F_1(395) = 256$, $n_2 = F_2(395) = 115$, and $n_3 = n - n_1 - n_2 = 24$.

Problems for Section 16.4

15. A study is attempting to estimate the average mortgage rate paid by all homeowners in a given city. Why might a stratified sample, where the strata are determined by the number of years since the home was purchased, be preferable to a simple random sample?

16. In Problem 15 suppose that there are 25,000 mortgages. These are stratified as follows: 7000 of the homes were purchased at least 15 years ago, 8000 were purchased between 8 and 15 years ago, 7500 were purchased between 3 and 8 years ago, and the other 2500 were purchased in the past 3 years. A stratified sampling scheme has been chosen with a total sample size of $n = 200$.
    a. If proportional sample sizes are used, what should they be?
    b. Assume that the relevant standard deviations for the four strata are known to be approximately $\sigma_1 = 1.2$, $\sigma_2 = 1.4$, $\sigma_3 = 2.1$, and $\sigma_4 = 1.7$. If optimal sample sizes are used, what should they be?

17. Discuss in some detail how you would choose the members to be sampled in Problem 16, part (a). That is, what frames would be necessary, and how would random number tables be used?

18. Rework Example 16.4, part (1), assuming the same sample means $\bar{X}_1$, $\bar{X}_2$, and $\bar{X}_3$, and the same sample standard deviations s_1, s_2, and s_3. Now, however, assume that these are based on sample sizes of $n_1 = 406$, $n_2 = 183$, and $n_3 = 35$. (Is it safe to ignore the finite population correction factors?)

19. Rework Example 16.4, part (2), with the same sample sizes as in Problem 18. Assume that the numbers in the three strata observed to have net expenditures over \$130 are 134, 127, and 31, respectively.

20. We wish to estimate the mean salary of all 1000 employees in a city government. These employees are stratified by job classification into four strata. The numbers of employees in these strata are 360, 280, 240, and 120. The ranges of salaries in the strata are known to be from \$12,000 to \$15,000, from \$10,000 to \$16,000, from \$14,000 to \$20,000, and from \$15,000 to \$30,000. If proportional sample sizes are to be

used, find the required sample sizes needed to obtain a 95% confidence interval for μ with an error bound of approximately $200.

21. For the data given in Problem 20, how large should the sample sizes be to ensure that the error bound for the estimation of p, the proportion of all employees earning at least $14,000, is no greater than .05? What can you say about the length of the resulting 95% confidence interval for p if the true p is considerably less than .5?

22. Consider a population that has been divided into three strata. The relevant population sizes are $N_1 = 2000$, $N_2 = 5000$, and $N_3 = 13,000$, and the relevant variances are $\sigma_1^2 = 100$, $\sigma_2^2 = 10$, and $\sigma_3^2 = 1$. We wish to estimate the mean μ of the population by using stratified sampling with a total sample size of $n = 500$.
   a. What sample sizes should we use under the proportional sample size scheme?
   b. What sample sizes should we use under the optimal sample size scheme?
   c. Explain why the sample sizes in part (b) lead to a smaller standard error of $\overline{X}$ than those in part (a). Give an intuitive argument, using the particular data given in this problem.

23. Suppose that a population of size 15,000 can be divided into four strata of sizes 3000, 5000, 6000, and 1000. The means and standard deviations of the variable in question for these strata are $\mu_1 = 100$, $\mu_2 = 80$, $\mu_3 = 130$, $\mu_4 = 60$, $\sigma_1 = 20$, $\sigma_2 = 10$, $\sigma_3 = 30$, and $\sigma_4 = 10$. We plan to estimate the mean μ of this population by means of a random sample of size 900. Proceed as in Example 16.3 to compare the standard errors of $\overline{X}$ for simple random sampling and stratified sampling with proportional sample sizes.

24. We wish to estimate the interest rate paid on bonds issued during a given period of time. The population of all bonds is stratified by their ratings: Aaa, Aa, A, Bb, and B. (The higher the rating, the less risky the bond.) Based on sample sizes of 8, 11, 14, 15, and 17, the sample mean rates are 8.2, 9.1, 10.1, 12.7, and 14.2. The sample standard deviations are .9, 1.1, 1.2, 1.4, and 1.6.
   a. If these sample sizes are proportional sample sizes and there are 520 bonds total, what are the population sizes for the five different ratings?
   b. Find an approximate 95% confidence interval for the mean rate of all Aaa bonds; of all B bonds.
   c. Find an approximate 95% confidence interval for the mean rate of all 520 bonds.

25. In Problem 22 assume that the sample means from the three strata are 25.7, 32.5, and 40.3, and the sample standard deviations are 11.1, 3.7, and 1.4. Assume that the population variances are not known and that the proportional sample sizes found in Problem 22, part (a), are used. Find a point estimate and a 95% confidence interval for the mean of each stratum separately. Then find a point estimate and a 95% confidence interval for the population mean.

26. A study is done to estimate the average number of cigarette ads in 25 of the most popular magazines, where the average is over all issues of these magazines for a period of one year. These magazines are stratified into news magazines, sports magazines, women's magazines, and all others. There are 450 issues total during the year, and the numbers in the four categories are 120, 135, 85, and 110. The following sample data are found from a stratified sample of the 450 issues.

Stratum	Sample Size	Number of Cigarette Ads in Issues Sampled
News	10	3, 1, 3, 2, 4, 2, 2, 3, 1, 2
Sports	12	4, 5, 3, 6, 2, 5, 4, 6, 5, 3, 4, 3
Women's	8	4, 2, 3, 5, 1, 3, 4, 2
Others	10	4, 2, 5, 4, 1, 6, 4, 5, 2, 3

   a. Find a point estimate of the mean number of cigarette ads per issue. What is a bound on the error of this estimate? (Use finite population correction factors.)
   b. If you wanted to reduce the bound on the error in part (a) to .2 and you were going to use proportional sample sizes, how many issues from each strata should be examined? Approximate the required standard deviations by the sample standard deviations from the data in part (a).

27. Based on the data in Problem 26, find a point estimate of the proportion of all issues during the year with more than three cigarette ads. What is a bound on the error of this estimate?

28. Assume that the data in Problem 26 represent a *simple* random sample from the population of all 450 issues. Now answer the questions in Problem 26, part (a). Compare your answers with those in Problem 26, part (a).

29. A population with 1000 members can be stratified into four groups of sizes 100, 280, 420, and 200. We wish to estimate the proportion p of this population with a certain property.
   a. A stratified sample gives the results on p. 888. Estimate the proportion p and give a 95% confidence interval for it.

Stratum	Sample Size	Number in Sample with the Specified Property
1	10	6
2	28	15
3	42	26
4	20	9

b. Suppose that the data in part (a) represent a *simple* random sample of size 100 from this population. (That is, we ignore the strata.) Now answer the questions in part (a). Compare your answers with those in part (a).

16.5

Cluster Sampling

Stratified sampling is useful when there are segments of the population with different characteristics. The strategy is to obtain a cross section of *each* segment and then pool them to learn about the population as a whole. In other applications the population may be grouped into "clusters," geographically or otherwise, such that each cluster is a small version of the entire population. Then we can obtain representative information about the population by randomly choosing several of the clusters and studying the chosen clusters in detail. This method of sampling is called *cluster sampling*.

> In cluster sampling, we take a simple random sample of the clusters and then take a census of the selected clusters.

Cluster sampling is not necessarily more efficient than simple random sampling in terms of producing a smaller standard error. However, there are usually practical reasons for preferring cluster sampling to simple random sampling. For example, suppose that a political pollster wants to investigate the attitudes of Americans with regard to the candidates in the upcoming election. It would certainly require a great deal of work to obtain a frame of the entire U.S. voting population and then survey a simple random sample from this frame. Instead, the pollster could choose several representative cities (or sections of cities) and survey these in detail. If the people in each cluster are geographically close to one another, as they would be in this example, the survey is probably simpler and less costly from a purely physical standpoint.

The assumption made in cluster sampling is that each cluster is a small microcosm of the entire population. This is why we believe an in-depth study of a few clusters will tell us what we need to know about the entire population. However, some clusters are obviously different than others. Therefore, if we sample a relatively small number of clusters, there is some chance that we will obtain an unrepresentative sample of clusters. The only way to avoid this is to choose a larger sample size (of clusters) in the first place. We discuss sample size selection briefly later in this section.

Once we choose the clusters in the sample, we do not always need to take an entire *census* of each cluster chosen. This may not be worth the time or money. In some sample designs, we survey only a subset of the sampling units within each selected cluster. If this subset is selected randomly, the resulting sampling scheme is called *two-stage cluster sampling*. We will not discuss this method of sampling any further in this book, however.

In this section we provide formulas for the point estimates and confidence intervals for the population mean μ and a population proportion p when cluster sampling is performed. These formulas require some new notation, which is summarized below.

Estimates and Confidence Intervals for Cluster Sampling

M = number of clusters in the population
m = number of clusters sampled
n_i = sample size (and population size) of cluster i
$\bar{n}$ = average sample size per cluster sampled = $(\Sigma\, n_i)/m$
t_i = sum of the observations in cluster i
p_i = proportion of the observations in cluster i with a specified property

The formulas below show how to estimate the population mean μ. Note that the estimate of μ is simply the average of all the observations, that is, the sum of the observations divided by the total sample size.

Point Estimate of μ with Cluster Sampling

$$\bar{X} = \frac{\Sigma\, t_i}{\Sigma\, n_i}$$

Standard Error of $\bar{X}$

$$\text{StdErr}(\bar{X}) = \sqrt{\left(\frac{M - m}{Mm\bar{n}^2}\right)\frac{\Sigma\,(t_i - n_i\bar{X})^2}{(m - 1)}}$$

Approximate 95% Confidence Interval for μ

$$\bar{X} \pm 2\,\text{StdErr}(\bar{X})$$

If we are interested in the population proportion p that have a specified property, the formulas in the box on p. 890 apply. Again, notice that the point estimate of p is simply the proportion of all sampled members with the specified property.

> *Point Estimate of p with Cluster Sampling*
>
> $$\hat{p} = \frac{\sum n_i p_i}{\sum n_i}$$
>
> *Standard Error of $\hat{p}$*
>
> $$\text{StdErr } (\hat{p}) = \sqrt{\left(\frac{M - m}{Mm\bar{n}^2}\right) \frac{\sum n_i^2 (p_i - \hat{p})^2}{m - 1}}$$
>
> *Approximate 95% Confidence Interval for p*
>
> $$\hat{p} \pm 2 \text{ StdErr}(\hat{p})$$

EXAMPLE 16.6

A consumer group lobbying for ceilings on natural gas prices takes a survey to discover monthly gas bills paid by households in a large midwestern city. Rather than taking a simple random sample from the entire city, the agency divides the city into 125 districts and then samples all households in 10 randomly selected districts. Each household is asked for its average gas bill over the past 24 months. The sample results are shown in Table 16.6. Use this information to obtain a point estimate and a 95% confidence interval for (1) the mean average monthly gas bill per household, μ, and (2) the proportion p of all households with an average monthly gas bill of at least $70.

Table 16.6

District	Sample Size (Households)	Average Monthly Bill (Dollars)	Number with an Average Monthly Bill over $70
1	230	76.20	101
2	115	59.14	43
3	128	65.71	62
4	205	74.20	114
5	102	77.50	59
6	186	56.19	82
7	153	66.93	75
8	221	61.47	103
9	167	73.26	95
10	118	58.33	61

SOLUTION

Using the notation above, we have $M = 125$, $m = 10$, and

$$\bar{n} = \frac{\Sigma n_i}{m} = \frac{230 + 115 + \cdots + 118}{10} = 162.5$$

For estimating the mean, the required sum t_i for district i is found by multiplying the average by the sample size in district i. For example, $t_1 = 230(76.20) = 17{,}526$. Therefore, the point estimate of μ is

$$\bar{X} = \frac{230(76.20) + \cdots + 118(58.33)}{230 + \cdots + 118} = \$67.23$$

and the standard error of $\bar{X}$ is

$$\sqrt{\frac{125 - 10}{125(10)(162.5)^2} \cdot \frac{[17{,}526 - 230(67.23)]^2 + \cdots + [6882.94 - 118(67.23)]^2}{9}}$$
$$= 2.51$$

This leads to a 95% confidence interval for μ of $67.23 \pm 2(2.51)$, or from \$62.21 to \$72.25.

For estimating the proportion of average gas bills over \$70, notice that $n_i p_i$ (in the formula for $\hat{p}$) is the number in district i with average gas bills over \$70. This means that the products $n_i p_i$ are given directly in the last column of Table 16.6. Therefore, the point estimate of the population proportion p is

$$\hat{p} = \frac{101 + 43 + \cdots + 61}{230 + 115 + \cdots + 118} = \frac{795}{1625} = .489$$

The standard error of $\hat{p}$ is then

$$\sqrt{\frac{125 - 10}{125(10)(162.5)^2} \cdot \frac{230^2(.439 - .489)^2 + \cdots + 118^2(.517 - .489)^2}{9}} = .018$$

This gives a 95% confidence interval for p of $.489 \pm 2(.018)$, or from .453 to .525.

When we perform cluster sampling, there is only one sample size to choose, namely, the number of clusters to be selected, m. As stated earlier, we want to make m large enough to avoid excessively large standard errors of $\bar{X}$ and/or $\hat{p}$. Since the formulas for these standard errors are fairly complicated functions of m, there are no simple prescriptions for selecting m. Therefore, we

Sample Size Selection with Cluster Sampling

merely state that, in general, it is a good idea to sample as many *small* clusters as possible. This implies that we should define the clusters so that they are relatively small sections of the population. For more details on sample size selection for cluster sampling, we refer the reader to more advanced texts on survey sampling.

16.6

Systematic Sampling

One final sampling scheme that is very easy to implement is called *systematic sampling*. This scheme has practically the same probabilistic properties as simple random sampling, which means that once we have selected the sampling units, we can use the same formulas for estimates and confidence intervals presented in Section 16.3. Therefore, in this section we only describe how systematic sampling is performed.

Consider a population frame that consists of N members, listed 1 through N. We wish to select a sample of size n from this frame. We will assume that N is an exact multiple of n, and we will set N/n equal to the integer k. For example, if $N = 1000$ and $n = 50$, then $k = 20$. In systematic sampling we begin by randomly choosing any number between 1 and k. Suppose that this choice is the number j (so that $1 \leq j \leq k$). Then we choose sampling units j, $j + k$, $j + 2k$, and so on, up to $j + (n - 1)k$, from the population frame. In other words, we randomly select one of the first k from the list, and then we select every kth sampling unit after the first one. As an example, suppose that $N = 1000$ and $n = 50$, so that $k = 20$. If the random integer selected between 1 and 20 is $j = 13$, then we choose sampling units 13, 33, 53, and so on, up to 993.

It should be clear why this is a convenient way to select a sample. For example, if we want to choose a sample of size 100 from a phone book with 3200 entries, all we have to do is select one of the first 32 names and then select every 32nd name after this one. In a situation such as this, there is no reason why the resulting systematic sample is any more or less representative than a simple random sample, provided that the alphabetical order of the names has nothing to do with the characteristic of interest. In general, unless there is some inherent periodic property in the population frame (such as, every tenth name represents a millionaire), a systematic sample is just as "random" as a simple random sample. Hence, it is chosen in many applications because of its convenience.

Problems for Sections 16.5, 16.6

30. Consider a study whose purpose is to investigate the effects on blue-collar workers of recent high unemployment in small towns in the industrial section of the East. Why might a cluster sampling scheme be preferable to simple random sampling? How would it work? Why would some type of two-stage cluster sampling almost surely be used if interviewing is expensive in terms of time and money?

31. A national labor union with 325 local chapters wants to estimate the fraction p of its members who support a new policy. Rather than take a census of all members, the union takes a census of 12 randomly chosen local chapters. The numbers belonging to these chapters and the numbers supporting the new policy are shown below. Find a point estimate and a 95% confidence interval for p.

Chapter	Number in Chapter	Number Who Support the New Policy
1	45	36
2	75	57
3	64	47
4	95	72
5	69	51
6	47	29
7	88	63
8	71	51
9	105	74
10	58	33
11	70	45
12	113	91

32. As long as the labor union in Problem 31 is polling its members, it decides to ask what percentage increase in wages members believe the union should request in upcoming contract talks. (The members are reminded that large increases in wages are likely to mean smaller increases in various fringe benefits.) The same local chapters polled in Problem 31 recommend the following average percentage increases in wages.
   a. Find a point estimate of the average percentage increase that would be recommended by all union members (if they were all polled). Calculate the standard error of this estimate.

Chapter	Average Percent Increase Recommended
1	5.23
2	6.31
3	5.78
4	5.91
5	5.28
6	6.03
7	6.22
8	5.74
9	6.73
10	5.44
11	5.87
12	6.34

   b. Is it likely that the average percentage increase that would be requested by all union members is at least 6.5? Be explicit in your answer.

33. Educators in a certain county in New York would like to measure the proportion p of all elementary school students who were absent at least 5% of the past school year. They randomly select seven of the 48 elementary schools in the county and collect the following data on the children in these schools. Find an estimate of p and a 95% confidence interval for p.

School	Enrollment	Number Absent at Least 5% of the Time
1	293	37
2	573	87
3	312	42
4	501	76
5	164	31
6	321	55
7	212	27

34. The same educators in Problem 33 would also like to measure μ, the average number of days each elementary school student was absent. Records from the seven schools sampled

yield the following data. Find an estimate of μ and a bound on the error of this estimate.

School	Average Number of Days Absent
1	4.73
2	6.35
3	3.81
4	2.98
5	6.02
6	5.28
7	4.91

35. In the cluster sampling formula for the standard error of the sample mean $\overline{X}$, there are no sample variance terms for the individual clusters sampled. Terms such as these are usually needed to indicate the accuracy of the sample means (here the sample means of the individual clusters). Why are these terms not needed here?

*36. The AMA (American Medical Association) wishes to publish data on the average amount charged by doctors for a routine office visit. In one particular state there are 59 counties. The AMA randomly chooses eight of these and asks the doctors in these counties how much they charge. The following data

are obtained. Find an interval such that the AMA can be 95% confident of being correct if it publishes that the average price of an office visit for this state is within the interval.

County	Number of Doctors	Average Charge
1	73	$15.47
2	28	13.45
3	55	16.74
4	48	15.32
5	39	14.67
6	87	17.42
7	60	16.33
8	51	18.21

37. What might be the advantages of selecting the data in Problem 36 as described there, rather than choosing a simple random sample of all doctors in the state? Do you believe that cluster sampling in this example is a good idea? Explain.

38. Suppose that a systematic sample of size 150 is to be chosen from a frame of 5250 people.
   a. What is the role (if any) of a random number table in choosing this sample? How would it be used?
   b. How many systematic samples of size 150 could be chosen from this population?

Summary

The purpose of this chapter has been to expand the coverage of statistical inference to more general sampling schemes. Most discussions of sampling deal with simple random samples taken from a very large population, where every sample of a given sample size has the same probability of being chosen. We have seen how a random number generator can be used to select a simple random sample from a given population frame. We have also seen how the formulas from Chapter 7 are modified when the sample size is a reasonably large percentage of the population size.

The latter part of the chapter emphasized that actual surveys often use random samples other than simple random samples. A stratified sampling scheme is appropriate when the population can be divided into natural groupings, called strata. If the members of a given stratum are fairly similar but the strata are quite different, stratified sampling can be effective in lowering the overall standard error of the sample mean or a sample proportion. In contrast, cluster sampling is useful when the population is composed of many relatively small "clusters," each a microcosm of the entire population. Then we randomly choose a set of clusters, and do an in-depth survey of the clusters chosen. If the members of a given cluster are close to each other geographically, cluster sampling is especially attractive from a cost point of view. Finally, systematic sampling is similar to simple random sampling in terms of its statistical properties. However, it is often much easier to administer. Here we sample every kth person from the population frame. If the ordering of sampling units in the frame has no obvious periodic properties, systematic sampling should provide just as representative a sample as any other sampling scheme.

Applications

Application 16.1   As we have seen throughout this book, one of the primary uses of statistics is to use sample data to infer population characteristics. According to what we have learned so far, the main reason we cannot make perfect inferences is that there is sampling error, the result of unrepresentative samples. To minimize sampling error, we use probability samples to avoid systematic biases and we use large sample sizes to gain precision. However, Assael and Keon suggest that we should perhaps be more concerned with *nonsampling error* than with sampling error. (Reference: Henry Assael and John Keon, "Nonsampling vs. Sampling Errors in Survey Research," *Journal of Marketing,* Vol. 46, 1982, pp. 114–123.) They define nonsampling error to be composed of two components, nonresponse error and response error. Nonresponse error occurs when the members of the sample who decide not to respond differ in an important way from the respondents. Response error occurs when the respondents do not respond accurately to the survey's questions. They may purposely misreport information, they may have faulty recall, they may be tired, or they may be affected by a variety of other factors.

As an example (the one used by Assael and Keon), suppose that the purpose of a survey is to find the mean phone bill for a population of small businesses. A questionnaire is sent to a large sample of these businesses, and 60% of the sampled businesses respond. The average phone bill of the respondents is $135 per month. Although the true mean of *all* the sampled businesses might be very close to the population mean (small sampling error), it may be that the true sample mean is not $135, the observed sample mean. For example, Assael and Keon found that (1) respondents had significantly higher phone bills than nonrespondents, and (2) respondents reported phone bills that were 14% higher than actual. Both of these factors imply that the true mean of the entire sample, and hence the population mean, is considerably less than $135. Unfortunately, the probabilistic analysis we have been discussing would not catch this large upward bias because it deals only with sampling error, not with nonsampling error.

Assael and Keon conclude that the traditional emphasis on large sample sizes, used to decrease sampling error, may be misplaced. Essentially, they argue that sampling error is already under control, and that by increasing sample size, the possibility of larger nonsampling error results. They suggest instead that more care be taken to reduce the nonsampling error. Possibly this can be achieved by using an appropriate survey method. For example, they suggest that mail and drop-off delivery methods are more effective than telephone or personal interview methods when surveying small businesses. In general, the key is to use a survey method that (1) ensures accurate responses from the respondents, and (2) does not tend to generate a set of nonrespondents who are significantly different than the respondents.

Application 16.2   When congressional committees and other federal agencies in Washington contemplate changes in tax laws, they frequently ask the Office of Tax Analysis (OTA) to provide information on how the tax changes will affect the various groups of taxpayers. The OTA finds this information by "simulating" the changes on a randomly selected representative sample of taxpayers. That is, it discovers how the tax returns for these sampled taxpayers would be affected by the proposed changes. This is a time-consuming process, and the OTA's job is made even more difficult because (1) the information is sought quickly, often within a day; and (2) the OTA has to run literally thousands of these simulations per year. Therefore it is essential that the sample of taxpayers be as small as possible, in addition to being representative.

Mulvey reports a methodology for choosing this sample. (Reference: John M. Mulvey, "Reducing the U.S. Treasury's Taxpayer Data Base by Optimization," *Interfaces,* Vol. 10, 1980, pp. 101–111.) Actually, he explains that the OTA already had a representative subset of approximately 155,000 taxpayers. For each of these, there was information on 192 attributes, such as adjusted gross income, taxes paid, salary and wages, total tax credits, pensions, and so on. This represents an enormous amount of data, so the OTA wanted to reduce the sample size to about 75,000 without losing any of the representativeness of the original large sample. One idea was to stratify the 155,000 sample in some way and then choose representative members from each stratum to be in the smaller sample. The question, though, was how to define the strata. For example, if the strata were based only on a single attribute, such as adjusted gross income, the small sample might resemble the large sample very closely with respect to adjusted gross income, but the resemblance might not be very good with respect to other important attributes.

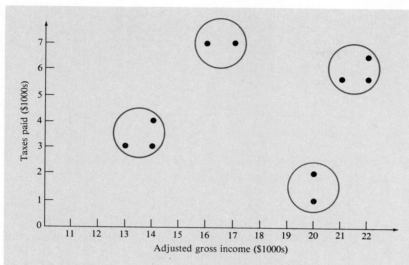

Figure 16.3

Therefore, Mulvey decided to define strata in a more sophisticated manner. He used an intricate computer program to separate the 155,000 taxpayers into strata such that the taxpayers within each stratum were similar with respect to two attributes, adjusted gross income and taxes paid. His idea can be depicted graphically as in Figure 16.3, where each point represents a single taxpayer. From the 10 points shown, the four strata, or groupings, are shown by circles. Mulvey then chose representative taxpayers from each grouping so that the total sample size was approximately 75,000. As he reports, the resemblance between the original large sample and the newly created small sample was very good. In particular, the percentage differences between means and standard deviations for the two samples were less than 2% for most of the important attributes. This was good enough for the OTA, which has been using the reduced sample (or updated versions of it) since 1980.

Glossary of Terms

Sampling unit   any potential member of a sample
Frame   a list of the sampling units in the population
Probability sample   a sample chosen by a random mechanism
Judgmental sample   a sample chosen by the sampler's judgment
Simple random sample of size *n*   a random sample where each possible sample of size *n* has the same chance of being chosen

Stratified sampling   a sampling scheme where a simple random sample is chosen from each stratum in the population; works well when the sampling units are homogeneous within each stratum but the strata differ from one another
Cluster sampling   a sampling scheme where a simple random sample of clusters is chosen from all clusters. and a census is

taken of the selected clusters; works well when each cluster is a small microcosm of the entire population

Two-stage cluster sampling same as cluster sampling except that only a random sample of each selected cluster is chosen

Systematic sampling a sampling scheme where one of the first k sampling units is chosen randomly and then every kth sampling unit after this one is added to the sample

---

Important Formulas

1. Approximate 95% confidence interval for the population mean μ for all sampling schemes in this chapter

$$\overline{X} \pm 2\ \text{StdErr}(\overline{X})$$

where $\overline{X}$ is the point estimate of μ and $\text{StdErr}(\overline{X})$ is the estimated standard error of $\overline{X}$

2. Approximate 95% confidence interval for a population proportion p for all sampling schemes in this chapter

$$\hat{p} \pm 2\ \text{StdErr}(\hat{p})$$

where $\hat{p}$ is a point estimate of p and $\text{StdErr}(\hat{p})$ is the estimated standard error of $\hat{p}$

3. Estimated standard errors of $\overline{X}$ and $\hat{p}$ with simple random sampling

$$\text{StdErr}(\overline{X}) = \sqrt{\frac{N-n}{N-1}}\ \frac{s}{\sqrt{n}}$$

$$\text{StdErr}(\hat{p}) = \sqrt{\frac{N-n}{N-1}}\ \sqrt{\frac{\hat{p}(1-\hat{p})}{n}}$$

4. Finite population correction factor for standard errors in this chapter (which can be ignored when n/N is less than .05)

$$\sqrt{\frac{N-n}{N-1}}$$

5. Sample size required to make the difference between $\overline{X}$ and μ less than B with simple random sampling

$$n = \frac{N\sigma^2}{\sigma^2 + (N-1)B^2/4}$$

6. Sample size required to make the difference between $\hat{p}$ and p less than B with simple random sampling

$$n = \frac{Np(1 - p)}{p(1 - p) + (N - 1)B^2/4}$$

7. Proportional sample sizes with stratified sampling

$$n_j = F_j n \qquad j = 1, 2, \ldots, J$$

where F_j is the fraction of the population in stratum j

8. Optimal sample sizes with stratified sampling

$$n_j = \frac{N_j \sigma_j}{N_1 \sigma_1 + N_2 \sigma_2 + \cdots + N_J \sigma_J} n \qquad j = 1, 2, \ldots, J$$

9. Estimates of μ and p with stratified sampling

$$\overline{X} = \sum F_j \overline{X}_j$$
$$\hat{p} = \sum F_j \hat{p}_j$$

10. Standard errors of $\overline{X}$ and $\hat{p}$ with stratified sampling

$$\text{StdErr}(\overline{X}) = \sqrt{F_1^2 s_{\overline{X}_1}^2 + \cdots + F_J^2 s_{\overline{X}_J}^2}$$

where

$$s_{\overline{X}_j}^2 = \frac{N_j - n_j}{N_j - 1} \frac{s_j^2}{n_j}$$

$$\text{StdErr}(\hat{p}) = \sqrt{F_1^2 s_{\hat{p}_1}^2 + \cdots + F_J^2 s_{\hat{p}_J}^2}$$

where

$$s_{\hat{p}_j}^2 = \frac{N_j - n_j}{N_j - 1} \frac{\hat{p}_j(1 - \hat{p}_j)}{n_j}$$

11. Sample size required to make the difference between $\overline{X}$ and μ less than B with stratified sampling (proportional sample sizes)

$$n = \frac{\sum N_j \sigma_j^2}{\sum F_j \sigma_j^2 + NB^2/4}$$

12. Sample size required to make the difference between $\hat{p}$ and p less than B with stratified sampling (proportional sample sizes)

$$n = \frac{N}{1 + NB^2}$$

13. Estimates of μ and p with cluster sampling

$$\overline{X} = \frac{\text{sum of all observations}}{\text{total sample size}}$$

$$\hat{p} = \frac{\text{number of observations with a specified property}}{\text{total sample size}}$$

14. Standard errors of $\overline{X}$ and $\hat{p}$ with cluster sampling (see Section 16.5 for notation)

$$\text{StdErr}(\overline{X}) = \sqrt{\left(\frac{M - m}{Mm\overline{n}^2}\right) \frac{\Sigma (t_i - n_i\overline{X})^2}{m - 1}}$$

$$\text{StdErr}(\hat{p}) = \sqrt{\left(\frac{M - m}{Mm\overline{n}^2}\right) \frac{\Sigma n_i^2(p_i - \hat{p})^2}{m - 1}}$$

End-of-Chapter Problems

39. Consider a population with 10 members. We wish to choose a simple random sample with n members. Calculate the number of such samples for $n = 3$. Then repeat the calculation for each n between 1 and 10. Graph this number versus n by erecting a "spike" of the appropriate height above each integer n.

*40. We would like to estimate the mean of a population of size N by a simple random sample. The population variance is known to be equal to 1, and we want the size of the error bound for μ to be B. What is the approximate effect on the required sample size n of halving the size of the required error bound, that is, reducing it from B to $B/2$? Refer to the relevant formula for n.

41. Although we have used the notation $\overline{X}$ for the estimate of the population mean μ in Section 16.4, this estimate is in general not really a sample mean; that is, it is not the sum of all observations divided by the sample size n. Why not? (Illustrate with a small numerical example.) Is there a case where $\overline{X}$ is really a sample mean in the usual sense? When is this? Why do we not use the average of all the observations to estimate μ in stratified sampling?

42. A consumer group in a large city wishes to find the average price charged for a particular brand of cold medicine, where the average is taken over all stores that sell the brand.

a. A simple random sample of 15 stores shows the following prices. Estimate the mean over all stores and find a 95% confidence interval for this mean, assuming that there are 150 stores that sell the product. How does the answer change if 300 stores sell the product? (Use the finite population correction factor.)

Store	Price	Store	Price
1	$3.75	9	$2.79
2	2.89	10	3.15
3	3.35	11	3.10
4	3.64	12	4.05
5	2.98	13	3.77
6	3.05	14	3.49
7	3.87	15	2.80
8	3.65		

b. If you were designing the survey and you wanted the resulting 95% confidence interval for the mean to be no longer than 10 cents, how large would your sample need to be if there are 150 stores total; if there are 300 stores total? Use the sample standard deviation from part (a) to estimate σ.

43. a. Using the same data as in Problem 42, part (a), find a point estimate and a 95% confidence interval for the proportion of all stores that charge at least $3.20 for the product. Again solve the problem for the case when there are 150 stores and for the case when there are 300 stores.

   b. How many stores must be sampled to reduce the length of the confidence interval for the proportion in part (a) to .10? Use the value of $\hat{p}$ from part (a) in the formula for the required sample size. Answer the question when there are 150 stores total and when there are 300 stores total.

44. Suppose that the consumer group in Problem 42 first decides to stratify the population of all stores selling the cold medicine into four groups: drugstores, supermarkets, convenience stores (such as 7-11's), and others (such as discount stores). The number of stores in the 4 strata are 29, 35, 42, and 38. The consumer group is interested in the mean price charged for the cold medicine.

   a. If proportional sample sizes are used, what should these sample sizes be if a total sample of 25 stores is to be used? (Round your answers to integers.)

   b. If the consumer group wants a bound on the difference between its estimate and the true mean to be no greater than 5 cents, and proportional sample sizes are to be used, what should these sample sizes be? Assume that the standard deviations in the four strata are all equal to 25 cents.

45. With the data in Problem 44 and the proportional sample sizes found in part (a) of that problem, find a point estimate and a 95% confidence interval for the mean price if the sample means are $3.74, $3.59, $4.21, and $3.21. Assume that the sample standard deviations for the four strata are $.28, $.21, $.15, and $.32.

46. Again using the data from Problem 44, suppose that the consumer group wishes to estimate the proportion of all stores that charge at least $3.50 for the medicine. What sample sizes are needed if proportional sample sizes are to be used and the bound on the error is required to be no greater than .15? (Round your answers to integers.)

47. Suppose that the sample sizes prescribed in Problem 46 are used in that problem, and the numbers of stores in the four strata charging more than $3.50 are 3, 4, 6, and 4. Find a point estimate and a 95% confidence interval for the proportion of all stores that charge at least $3.50. Is the length of this confidence interval close to what was prescribed in Problem 46?

48. We wish to estimate a population proportion p. Compare the total sample size required in simple random sampling and stratified sampling when the population size is 500 and the error bound is required to be less than .10. (Assume that p is approximately .5 in the simple random sample formula.)

49. If stratified sampling is to be used in a population of 500 members to estimate a proportion p having a certain property, find the error bound for $\hat{p}$ when proportional sample sizes are used, there are three strata, the total sample size found in Problem 48 is used, and the numbers in the samples having this property are 7, 20, and 14, respectively. Assume that there are 100 members in stratum 1, 250 members in stratum 2, and 150 members in stratum 3. Then find a point estimate and a 95% confidence interval for p. Is the length of the confidence interval as short as it was supposed to be, as prescribed in Problem 48?

50. The following data have been collected from a population with 10,000 members. The population has been divided into three strata of sizes 2000, 3000, and 5000, respectively. The members of a stratified sample have been asked how much they spend per year on records and cassette tapes and whether they purchase more records than cassette tapes.

Stratum	Sample Size	Average Amount Spent	Standard Deviation of Amounts Spent	Number Who Purchase More Records
1	100	$75.60	$49.50	57
2	150	54.80	65.20	69
3	250	62.70	45.45	127

   a. Find the standard error of each stratum's sample mean expenditures for records and tapes. Then calculate a point estimate of the mean expenditure for the entire population, and calculate the standard error of this estimate.

   b. Find the standard error of each stratum's sample proportion of members who purchase more records than cassettes. Then calculate a point estimate of the proportion of the entire population who purchase more records than cassettes, and calculate the standard error of this estimate.

51. A discount chain of stores with 450 member stores wishes to know how satisfied its employees are with their working conditions. Management randomly selects 10 of the member stores

and gives a questionnaire to each employee at these stores. The questionnaire contains 15 questions on aspects of their jobs. For each of these, the employees must mark that they are (1) very satisfied, (2) mildly satisfied, (3) mildly dissatisfied, or (4) very dissatisfied. The company is interested in μ, the average number of "very satisfied" responses per employee, averaged over all employees, and p, the proportion of all employees who mark "very dissatisfied" on at least two of the 15 questions. The following data are observed.

Store	Number of Employees	Average Number of "Very Satisfied" Responses	Number Who Mark "Very Dissatisfied" at Least Twice
1	75	6.72	65
2	58	4.85	31
3	88	3.71	32
4	61	4.66	43
5	78	7.51	67
6	85	2.54	29
7	46	4.48	37
8	68	6.11	53
9	75	3.87	52
10	53	4.01	42

a. Find a point estimate of μ and the standard error of this estimate.

b. Find a point estimate of p and the standard error of this estimate.

52. Time-share condominiums are a relatively new idea where people can buy a condominium for a specified week of each year, usually for vacation purposes. A company that offers time-share owners the opportunity to "trade" their week for a week at another time-sharing resort wishes to know p, the proportion of all time-share owners who have used this trading service in the 350 resorts offering time sharing. The company randomly chooses 15 of these resorts and questions each of the owners at these resorts. The following data are found. Find a point estimate and a 95% confidence interval for the desired proportion p.

Resort	Number of Owners	Number Who Have Used the Trading Service
1	65	21
2	124	42
3	42	10
4	157	85

(continued)

Resort	Number of Owners	Number Who Have Used the Trading Service
5	135	72
6	78	34
7	69	21
8	105	33
9	176	101
10	98	38
11	57	18
12	138	77
13	68	35
14	165	86
15	140	56

53. The company offering the trading service in Problem 52 would also like to know the average income of all time-share owners in the 350 resorts. The following income data are obtained from the 15 resorts sampled. Find a point estimate and a 95% confidence interval for the average income of all time-share owners in these 350 resorts.

Resort	Average Income of Owners ($1000s)	Resort	Average Income of Owners ($1000s)
1	46.7	9	51.3
2	53.2	10	44.2
3	39.8	11	41.8
4	62.5	12	53.8
5	48.7	13	36.2
6	35.7	14	65.4
7	57.1	15	49.9
8	72.5		

54. A candidate for mayor of a fairly large city hires a pollster to gauge voters' opinions and voting intentions. One particular issue the pollster is asked to examine is voters' knowledge of this candidate's position on waste disposal. The pollster randomly selects 10 of the 125 voting districts in the city and asks each registered voter within these 10 districts whether he or she is aware of the candidate's position on waste disposal. The accompanying data are found. Can the candidate be fairly certain that at least 25% of the registered voters are aware of his position on waste disposal? Answer by first calculating an appropriate confidence interval.

District	Number of Voters Registered	Number Aware of Candidates's Position
1	445	112
2	237	63
3	327	98
4	198	61
5	376	98
6	265	76
7	534	149
8	351	87
9	276	78
10	512	148

55. State explicitly how the cluster sample in Problem 52 could be chosen. What is the role of a random number table, and how would it be used?

56. During the 1970s the Federal Trade Commission (FTC) proposed several rules to regulate advertising practices in such industries as food, drugs, and appliances. Recently, the Reagan administration has favored the substitution of government regulatory programs with industry self-regulation. In 1983, LaBarbera surveyed 446 trade associations to see how many had adopted an advertising self-regulation program among the member firms. (Reference: Priscilla A. LaBarbera, "The Diffusion of Trade Association Advertising Self-Regulation," *Journal of Marketing,* Vol. 47, 1983, pp. 58–67.) Of these 446 trade associations, 110 responded that they had adopted self-regulation programs. Given that there are between 1000 and 2000 trade associations whose members engage in advertising, find a 95% confidence interval for the proportion of these that have adopted self-regulation programs. Do this assuming there are exactly 1000 trade associations. Then repeat the calculation, assuming that there are exactly 2000 trade associations. Why must you use the finite population correction factor in each case? How is your answer affected by the population size?

Computer Problems

(These problems are to be used in conjunction with the computer software package.)

1. Use the RNSAMPLE program to choose a sample of 15 houses from the data on 150 houses in Table III of Appendix D. Then use the SAMPMEAN program on this sample to find a 90% confidence interval for the mean difference between appraised value and selling price. Note that SAMPMEAN does not incorporate finite population correction factors. What would the 90% confidence interval be if this correction factor were used? (For this last question, use the results from SAMPMEAN and then work the rest by hand.)

2. Consider a population with 100 members. By the definition of a simple random sample, every member of the population has an equal chance of being selected, so if we sample, say, 10 members, any given member should have 1 chance out of 10 of being selected. This implies that if we repeatedly selected random samples of size 10 from this population, then any particular member ought to be chosen about 10% of the time. Use the RNSAMPLE program and the PROPORTN programs to test this. Run the RNSAMPLE program 40 times, each time choosing a sample of size 10 from a population of size 100. For each sample, keep track of whether member number 37 is selected. (If you have some other favorite number between 1 and 100, use it instead.) Then use the PROPORTN program to find a 90% confidence interval for the proportion of times member number 37 would be selected in the long run, and test whether you can reject the null hypothesis that this proportion equals .10. Use a 10% significance level for this test.

3. Suppose we would like to select a stratified sample from the cities listed in Table VII of Appendix D, where the strata correspond to regions of the country. In particular, there are five regions, defined as in Computer Problem 4 of Chapter 13 (p. 713). Explain how you would use the RNSAMPLE program to select the sample, given prescribed sample sizes for each stratum. Then carry out your procedure when the sample sizes for the five regions are 8, 7, 10, 6, and 13. Your answer should include the list of the cities selected in each region.

References

COCHRAN, W. G. *Sampling Techniques,* 3rd ed. New York: Wiley, 1977.

SCHEAFFER, R. L., MENDENHALL, W., and OTT, L. *Elementary Survey Sampling,* 2nd ed. North Scituate, Mass.: Duxbury, 1979 (available from PWS Publishers, Boston).

Mathematical Background

Contents

Symbols and Conventions

When we write mathematical formulas, we need to use various symbols to "stand for" the numbers we will "plug in" later. As in high school algebra, where the symbols *a, b, c, x, y, z,* and others are used frequently, we are allowed to use a wide variety of symbols to express statistical variables. There are no rules that say an *x* must be used in one situation, an *a* must be used in another situation, and so on. We are allowed to use practically any symbols we like as long as we are consistent.

Although there are no rules to tell us which symbols to use, there are a number of conventions that we follow. Essentially, we try to use symbols that (1) suggest the corresponding statistical ideas, and (2) are the same as those used by the majority of other statistics books. For example, the Greek letters μ (mu) and σ (sigma) are consistently used in statistics books to denote the mean and standard deviation of a population.

Once we have defined the symbols in any given problem, it is important to be consistent throughout the problem. For example, if p stands for the proportion of a population who have gone to college, and $\hat{p}$ stands for an estimate of p, then p and $\hat{p}$ mean different things and should not be confused. One could ask why p is used for the population proportion and $\hat{p}$ is used for the estimate of p. The answer to this question has more to do with historical tradition than anything else, but the important point is that if we agree to follow this tradition, we must do so *consistently*.

We now discuss several symbols that may be new to the reader. These are particularly important in statistics.

Subscripts

In high school algebra there is rarely a need to work with more than two or three variables at a time. Therefore, the variables are usually distinct letters of the alphabet, the most frequent being *x, y,* and *z.* In statistics, however, there are often a large number of variables, typically one for each member of a sample. Therefore, it is convenient to use numerical subscripts on a single letter of the alphabet, such as *x,* to label the variables.

For example, if we measure the heights of 100 people, we might denote their heights by the variables $x_1, x_2, \ldots, x_{100}$, where the " . . ." means "and so on, up to." Then x_1 is the height of the first person, x_2 is the height of the second person, and so on. If we wish to denote the height of a "typical" person, we use notation such as x_i, which literally means the height of the *i*th member in the sample. The subscripts *i, j,* and *k* are generally used as "typical" subscripts.

Sometimes it is convenient to use two subscripts (separated by commas, if necessary to avoid ambiguity) to denote variables. Suppose that we measure the heights of 10 people in each of 15 cities. Then we might label the 150 heights with *single* subscripts as $x_1, x_2, \ldots, x_{150}$, or we could use *double* subscripts on the x's:

$$x_{1,1}, \ldots, x_{1,10}; x_{2,1}, \ldots, x_{2,10}; \ldots; x_{15,1}, \ldots, x_{15,10}$$

Now we have divided the 150 heights into 15 natural groups of 10 each. The first subscript tells which city the person comes from, and the second subscript tells which number the person is within that city. The variable $x_{7,3}$, for example, is the height of the third person from the seventh city. In general, $x_{i,j}$ is the jth person from the ith city. There is no rule that tells us when to use single subscripts and when to use double subscripts; it is purely a matter of convenience. Double subscripting in the example above allows us to identify which height goes with which person much more easily.

One advantage of subscripted variables is that we can then use summation notation. We will have more to say about summation notation later in this appendix.

So, statistics is all Greek to you? Perhaps the reason is that there are quite a few Greek symbols used, even in beginning statistics texts. Again, the reason that many of these are used has more to do with historical tradition than anything else, but there are two practical reasons for using Greek symbols. First, by taking advantage of the Greek alphabet, we have more symbols than we would have otherwise. The second reason is that a Greek letter is often used to denote a population parameter, whereas the corresponding Ro-

Greek Letters

Greek Letter	Use(s) in This Book	Chapter(s) Used
α (alpha)	Error probability	Many
	Smoothing constant	14
β (beta)	Type II error probability	9
	Regression coefficient	11, 12, 14
	Smoothing constant	14
γ (gamma)	Smoothing constant	14
δ (delta)	A difference between means	13
Δ (capital delta)	Signifies a differencing operation	11
μ (mu)	Population mean	Many
σ (sigma)	Population standard deviation	Many
Σ (capital sigma)	Summation sign	Many
ν (nu)	Degrees of freedom parameter	8
π (pi)	The special number 3.14159 . . .	5
χ (chi)	Used for chi-square distributions	8, 9, 13
λ (lambda)	Parameter of a Poisson distribution	5
ϵ (epsilon)	Error term	10, 11, 12, 14
ρ (rho)	Population correlation coefficient	4, 11
τ (tau)	Kendall's tau	13

man letter is used to denote the sample estimate of this parameter. For example, the Greek letter ρ (rho) corresponds to the Roman letter r, so it is customary to let ρ be the population correlation coefficient and to let r be the sample estimate of ρ.

The particular Greek letters used in this text are summarized in the preceding table. Beside each letter we list its main use or uses in statistics.

A.2

Functions and Functional Notation

Functions and functional notation are common to every branch of mathematics, and statistics is no exception. As we have indicated by the title of this section, there are really two aspects of this topic: the concept of functions and the notation used to describe them.

The idea behind functions is quite simple. Conceptually, there is an "input-output machine," called a function. When we put numerical inputs into the machine, they are transformed by the function into other numerical outputs. The only rule is that the same input always produces the same output. This is described in Figure A.1.

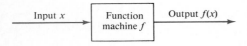

Figure A.1
A "Function Machine"

If the input x is a single number, we say that f is a function of one variable. If x is a list of n numbers, written $x = (x_1, x_2, \ldots, x_n)$, f is a function of n variables. In either case the *output* of a function is a single number. We write the output as $y = f(x)$ [or $y = f(x_1, x_2, \ldots, x_n)$] to emphasize its dependence on the input and the function f.

Given the input, how do we know the value of the output? The usual way is that f is defined by means of a formula. For instance, we might have $f(x) = x^2 + 1$. This formula says that f takes the input, squares it, and adds 1 to produce the output. Alternatively, we sometimes define a function by a table of numbers, as in Table A.1. For each value of x, this table shows the value of $f(x)$. The main drawback to a tabular representation is that if we need $f(x)$ for some x not tabulated, we are stuck. Therefore, most functions are defined by a formula.

Suppose that $f(x)$ is given by the formula $f(x) = x^2 + 1$. In this formula the variable x is merely a "placeholder." That is, x is simply a convenient label for a typical input. It is sometimes called the *argument* of the function.

Table A.1 Function Defined in Tabular Form	
x	$f(x)$
1	15
2	18
3	27
4	38
5	46
6	59
7	79
8	86
9	105
10	154

> The argument of a function f is the input variable (or expression) inside the parentheses next to f.

It is irrelevant how we label the argument of a function. We could label it t, p, σ or anything else. The important part is what the formula $f(x) =$

$x^2 + 1$ says. It says to take the argument, square it, and add 1. Several examples are given below to illustrate the possibilities.

EXAMPLE A.1

Let $f(x) = x^2 + 1$. Alternative ways of defining f are $f(t) = t^2 + 1$, $f(\sigma) = \sigma^2 + 1$, or many others. Numerical examples are

$$f(2) = 2^2 + 1 = 5 \qquad f(-3) = (-3)^2 + 1 = 10$$
$$f(1.1) = 1.1^2 + 1 = 2.21$$

We also have

$$f(3p) = (3p)^2 + 1 = 9p^2 + 1 \qquad f(2t^4) = (2t^4)^2 + 1 = 4t^8 + 1$$

We can even evaluate a function at another function value. For example,

$$f[f(2)] = [f(2)]^2 + 1 = (2^2 + 1)^2 + 1 = 5^2 + 1 = 26$$

EXAMPLE A.2

Define the functions f and g by $f(x) = 3x + 4$ and $g(x) = (x + 1)^2$. Then we may evaluate f at the value $g(x)$ as follows. [Here $g(x)$ is the argument of the function f.]

$$f[g(x)] = f[(x + 1)^2] = 3(x + 1)^2 + 4$$
$$= (3x^2 + 6x + 3) + 4 = 3x^2 + 6x + 7$$

Similarly, we can evaluate g at the value $f(x)$. [Now $f(x)$ is the argument of the function g.]

$$g[f(x)] = g(3x + 4) = [(3x + 4) + 1]^2 = 9x^2 + 30x + 25$$

Numerically, when $x = 2$, we have $f[g(2)] = 3(2)^2 + 6(2) + 7 = 31$ and $g[f(2)] = 9(2)^2 + 30(2) + 25 = 121$. As this example shows, we have to be careful about the order of the operations. In general, $f[g(x)]$ is *not* equal to $g[f(x)]$.

EXAMPLE A.3

Let $f(x, y) = x + y^2$. The new aspect of this example is that f is now a function of two variables. (Notice that the symbol y is being used as an *input* for this example.) Nevertheless, the comments made earlier still apply. That is, regardless of how the two arguments (inputs) are labeled, the formula says to add the argument on the left to the square of the argument on the right to produce the function value. For example,

$$f(2, 4) = 2 + 4^2 = 18 \qquad f(4, 2) = 4 + 2^2 = 8 \qquad f(y, x) = y + x^2$$

Linear Functions

One particularly important function in statistics is a linear function. The reason for the term ''linear'' is that the graphs of linear functions (of a single variable) are straight lines. A linear function of one variable can be written as follows.

> ### Linear Function of a Single Variable
> $$f(x) = a + bx$$

Here a and b are given constants. A linear function of the n variables x_1, x_2, . . . , x_n can be written similarly.

> ### Linear Function of n Variables
> $$f(x_1, x_2, \ldots, x_n) = a + b_1 x_1 + b_2 x_2 + \cdots + b_n x_n$$

Again, a, b_1, b_2, . . . , b_n are given constants.

The important practical implication of a linear function is that if a particular input, say x, is changed by an amount Δx, the value of the function changes by an amount $b(\Delta x)$, where b is the coefficient of x. In the single-variable case, this follows because

$$f(x + \Delta x) - f(x) = [a + b(x + \Delta x)] - (a + bx) = b(\Delta x)$$

In the multiple-variable case, suppose that we change the value of variable x_1 and keep the other variables constant. Then

$$f(x_1 + \Delta x_1, x_2, \ldots, x_n) - f(x_1, x_2, \ldots, x_n)$$
$$= [a + b_1(x_1 + \Delta x_1) + b_2 x_2 + \cdots + b_n x_n]$$
$$- (a + b_1 x_1 + b_2 x_2 + \cdots + b_n x_n)$$
$$= b_1(\Delta x_1)$$

A similar result holds if we change any variable other than x_1 and keep the rest constant. Notice that the change in the function value depends only on the change in the x being varied and not on the levels of any of the x's. This is one of the distinctive properties of linear functions.

We now study linear functions of a single variable in some detail. Let $y = a + bx$. As we saw above, if x changes by an amount Δx, then y changes by an amount $\Delta y = b(\Delta x)$. In particular, if $\Delta x = 1$, then $\Delta y = b$. For example, if $b = 2$, then y increases by 2 units for every unit increase in x. If $b = -2$, then y *decreases* 2 units for every unit increase in x. The constant b is called the *slope* of the linear function. The role of the other constant, a, is simple. It is the *y intercept,* because $y = a + b(0) = a$ when $x = 0$. Therefore, when a straight line is written in the form $y = a + bx$, we say that it is written in *slope-intercept* form.

There are several ways to graph a straight line. We show two methods, both of which are simple and lead to the same graph.

Method 1: Put the equation in slope-intercept form: $y = a + bx$. Then draw a line with slope b crossing the y axis at height a. (Notice that the higher the absolute value of the slope b, the steeper the line becomes. If $b > 0$, the line slopes upward to the right; if $b < 0$, the line slopes downward to the right; if $b = 0$, the line is horizontal.)

Method 2: No matter what form the equation of the line has, find the x intercept by setting $y = 0$, and find the y intercept by setting $x = 0$. Then draw a straight line through these two intercepts.

These two methods are equivalent in the sense that they both produce the same line. However, the second method is usually quicker and easier.

EXAMPLE A.4

Graph the line $3x + 4y = 12$.

SOLUTION

For method 1 we must first solve for y. We subtract $3x$ from both sides and divide both sides by 4 to obtain $y = 3 - (\frac{3}{4})x$. This means that the slope is $-\frac{3}{4}$, so that the line goes down 3 units for every 4 units to the right. The y intercept is 3, which means that the graph goes through the point $(0, 3)$. For method 2 we set $x = 0$ to obtain $y = 3$ (the y intercept) and set $y = 0$ to obtain $x = 4$ (the x intercept). Then we draw a straight line through the points $(0, 3)$ and $(4, 0)$. The graph of this line is shown in Figure A.2.

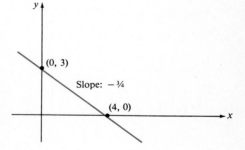

Figure A.2
Graph of $3x + 4y = 12$

EXAMPLE A.5

Find the equation of the line that passes through the points $(2, 1)$ and $(-1, 3)$.

SOLUTION

Suppose that the line is written in the form $y = a + bx$. First we find the slope b. In going from $(2, 1)$ to $(-1, 3)$, the change in x is $\Delta x =$

$2 - (-1) = 3$, and the change in y is $\Delta y = 1 - 3 = -2$. Therefore, $b = \Delta y/\Delta x = -\frac{2}{3}$. To solve for the y intercept, we substitute the coordinates of *either* point into the equation $y = a - (\frac{2}{3})x$. For example, using the point (2, 1), we have $1 = a - (\frac{2}{3})(2)$, or $a = \frac{7}{3}$. So the equation of the line is $y = \frac{7}{3} - (\frac{2}{3})x$. We graph this line by drawing a straight line through the two original points (2, 1) and (-1, 3). The resulting line is shown in Figure A.3.

Exponential Functions

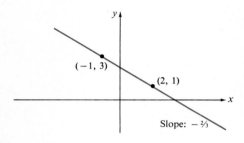

Figure A.3
Graph of $y = \frac{7}{3} - \frac{2}{3}x$

For any number $a > 0$, the function a^x is called an *exponential* function. The number a is called the *base*, and x is called the *exponent*. The most common base is the special number $e = 2.718\ldots$, which has a number of attractive properties. For example, it can be shown that if one dollar is put into a savings institution that compounds interest *continuously* at an annual rate of, say, 6%, this dollar grows to $e^{.06x}$ dollars in x years. In a year it grows to $e^{.06} = 1.0618$ dollars, in two years it grows to $e^{.12} = 1.1275$ dollars, and so on. To compute these numbers, we can refer to published tables of the exponential function, or we can use the "e^x" button that appears on many calculators. (There is often a "y^x" button as well for bases other than e.)

The main property of exponential functions is as follows.

Rule for Multiplying Exponentials with the Same Base

$$a^x a^y = a^{x+y} \qquad \text{for any } a > 0$$

As a special case,

$$e^x e^y = e^{x+y}$$

In words, if we multiply two numbers with the same base, we simply add their exponents.

In Figure A.4 we show the graphs of several exponential functions. The key property of these graphs is the extremely rapid increase of a^x (when $a > 1$) for large positive values of x, and of a^x (when $a < 1$) for large negative values of x.

Logarithmic Functions

A generation ago logarithms were used for multiplying or dividing large numbers. This tedious process involved looking up logarithms and antilogarithms in tables and performing the arithmetic on the logarithms instead of the original numbers. Because of the availability of today's calculators, not only has the need for tables of logarithms been eliminated, but logarithms themselves are no longer needed for ordinary multiplication and division. Nevertheless, logarithms are still encountered in many branches of mathe-

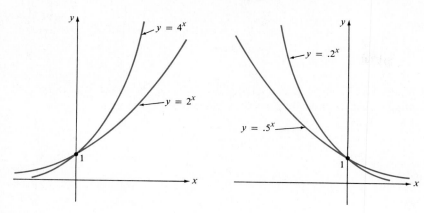

Figure A.4
Exponential Functions

matics, including statistics. Below we look at several properties of logarithms that make them useful.

The definition of $\log_a x$, read "the logarithm of x to the base a," is that it is the number y such that $a^y = x$.

> ## Meaning of a Logarithm
>
> $y = \log_a x$ means that $a^y = x$

The number a ($a > 0$) is called the base of the logarithm, and the logarithm itself, y, is the exponent. Since $a^y > 0$ for any y, $x = a^y$ must be positive, which means that $\log_a x$ is defined only when $x > 0$.

> $\log_a x$ is not defined for $x \leq 0$

The base we encounter most often is e, the special number from the preceding section. Then it is customary to write $\ln(x)$ instead of $\log_e x$ and to refer to this logarithm as the *natural* logarithm. Furthermore, when the base is not important in a particular discussion, we sometimes use the simplified notation $\log(x)$.

By the definition of logarithms, it follows that the logarithm function and the exponential function (with the same base) are "inverse functions" of one another. That is, they "undo" one another in the sense that

$$\log_a(a^x) = x$$

and

$$a^{\log_a x} = x$$

For this reason the exponential function $y = a^x$ is sometimes called the *antilogarithm* function. In particular, when $a = e$, we have

$$\ln(e^x) = x$$

and

$$e^{\ln(x)} = x$$

(In fact, to obtain e^x on some calculators, it is necessary to hit the inverse button "INV" and then the "ln(x)" button.) Letting $x = 0$ and noticing that $a^0 = 1$ for any a, we obtain

$$\log_a 1 = 0 \qquad \text{for any } a > 0$$

The basic rules of logarithms are given below. Here a is any positive number.

Rules of Logarithms

$$\log_a(xy) = \log_a x + \log_a y$$

$$\log_a\left(\frac{x}{y}\right) = \log_a x - \log_a y$$

$$\log_a\left(\frac{1}{x}\right) = -\log_a x$$

$$\log_a(x^b) = b \log_a x$$

Probably the most important of these is the first, which states that "the log of a product is the sum of the logs." Often we need to deal with a product. If we would rather deal with a sum (for mathematical simplicity), we may take the logarithm of the product, which converts the product into a sum. This transformation is used frequently in statistics.

The graph of the function $y = \log_a x$ is shown in Figure A.5. Notice that it decreases rapidly as x approaches 0, it increases fairly slowly as x increases, and its x intercept is the point (1, 0).

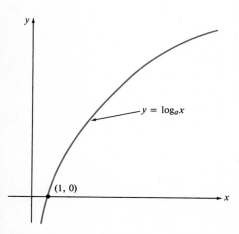

Figure A.5
Logarithmic Function

In statistics we are frequently required to sum a number of variables. An important benefit of using subscripted variables is that we can use *summation notation* to denote these sums. For example, suppose that we want to sum the variables x_1, x_2, x_3, and x_4. This sum can be written as $x_1 + x_2 + x_3 + x_4$, but we often prefer to write it more compactly, using summation notation, as

$$x_1 + x_2 + x_3 + x_4 = \sum_{i=1}^{4} x_i$$

This summation notation consists of several parts. The "Σ" (the capital Greek letter sigma) denotes "summation." The notation below and above Σ (namely, "$i = 1$" and "4") means that we sum over every integer subscript i from 1 to 4. The subscripted variable x_i indicates which variables to sum. The subscript i could be replaced by any other subscript everywhere it appears, and the meaning of the summation would not be changed. For example,

$$\sum_{i=1}^{4} x_i = \sum_{j=1}^{4} x_j = \sum_{k=1}^{4} x_k$$

These all mean the same thing: $x_1 + x_2 + x_3 + x_4$. The letters i, j, k, l, m, and n are the subscripts used most often in summation notation. Often we see the even more abbreviated notation $\Sigma\, x_i$. This means that we should sum x_i over all subscripts i for which x_i is defined. The relevant range is usually clear from the context of the problem.

Sometimes we wish to sum double-subscripted variables. Then we need two Σ's, that is, *double summation notation*. The limits above and below each Σ indicate which indices to sum over for each subscript. For example,

$$\sum_{i=1}^{8} \sum_{j=1}^{5} x_{i,j} = (x_{1,1} + \cdots + x_{1,5}) + (x_{2,1} + \cdots + x_{2,5})$$
$$+ \cdots + (x_{8,1} + \cdots + x_{8,5})$$

Notice there are 40 numbers in this sum. The most convenient way to think of double summation is as two repeated single summations. That is, we can write

$$\sum_{i=1}^{8} \sum_{j=1}^{5} x_{i,j} = \sum_{i=1}^{8} \left(\sum_{j=1}^{5} x_{i,j} \right)$$

$$= \sum_{j=1}^{5} x_{1,j} + \sum_{j=1}^{5} x_{2,j} + \cdots + \sum_{j=1}^{5} x_{8,j}$$

In each of the summations on the right, the subscript on the left is constant, and we sum over the subscript on the right. If we write the summation above as $\sum \sum x_{i,j}$, it is understood that i and j vary over all values for which $x_{i,j}$ is defined. Again, this is usually clear from the context.

The following examples illustrate some of the uses of summation notation.

EXAMPLE A.6

Suppose that $x_i = i^2$ for each i between 1 and 6. Then

$$\sum_{i=1}^{6} x_i = \sum_{i=1}^{6} i^2 = 1^2 + 2^2 + 3^2 + 4^2 + 5^2 + 6^2 = 91$$

EXAMPLE A.7

Suppose that $p_1 = .3$, $p_2 = .5$, $p_3 = .2$, $x_1 = 20$, $x_2 = 35$, and $x_3 = -5$. Then

$$\sum_{i=1}^{3} p_i x_i = p_1 x_1 + p_2 x_2 + p_3 x_3 = .3(20) + .5(35) + .2(-5) = 22.5$$

EXAMPLE A.8

Suppose that $x_{i,j} = i + j^2$ for each i between 1 and 3, and each j between 1 and 2. Then

$$\sum_{i=1}^{3} \sum_{j=1}^{2} x_{i,j} = \sum_{i=1}^{3} \left[\sum_{j=1}^{2} (i + j^2) \right]$$

$$= \sum_{j=1}^{2} (1 + j^2) + \sum_{j=1}^{2} (2 + j^2) + \sum_{j=1}^{2} (3 + j^2)$$

$$= [(1 + 1^2) + (1 + 2^2)] + [(2 + 1^2) + (2 + 2^2)]$$

$$+ [(3 + 1^2) + (3 + 2^2)]$$

$$= 27$$

Summation notation is simply a shorthand notation for a familiar arithmetic operation, addition. Therefore, the rules for manipulating summation notation are the familiar rules of addition. The most important of these rules are listed below.

Important Rules for Summation Notation

$$\sum_{i=1}^{n} c = nc \qquad \text{where } c \text{ is any constant}$$

$$\sum_{i=1}^{n} ax_i = a\left(\sum_{i=1}^{n} x_i\right) \qquad \text{where } a \text{ is any constant}$$

$$\sum_{i=1}^{n} (x_i + y_i) = \sum_{i=1}^{n} x_i + \sum_{i=1}^{n} y_i$$

EXAMPLE A.9

The temperature at the Indianapolis airport was measured at hourly intervals from 10 A.M. until 4 P.M. Let x_i be the value of the ith measurement, measured in Fahrenheit degrees. These measurements are shown in Table A.2. Use summation notation and the rules above to find the average of the seven temperatures, expressed in Fahrenheit degrees and then in Celsius degrees. Use the fact that Celsius is related to Fahrenheit by $C = (\frac{5}{9})(F - 32)$.

Table A.2

Time	i	Temperature (x_i)
10 A.M.	1	68
11 A.M.	2	72
12 P.M.	3	74
1 P.M.	4	75
2 P.M.	5	75
3 P.M.	6	74
4 P.M.	7	73

SOLUTION

The average of the seven temperatures is the sum of them divided by 7. In Fahrenheit degrees, this average is

$$\frac{\sum_{i=1}^{7} x_i}{7} = \frac{68 + 72 + 74 + 75 + 75 + 74 + 73}{7} = \frac{511}{7} = 73$$

Next let y_i be the value of the ith measurement, measured in Celsius degrees. Since $y_i = (\frac{5}{9})(x_i - 32) = (\frac{5}{9})x_i - (\frac{160}{9})$, we may use the rules for summation notation to obtain

$$
\begin{aligned}
\sum_{i=1}^{7} y_i &= \sum_{i=1}^{7} \left(\frac{5}{9} x_i - \frac{160}{9} \right) \\
&= \sum_{i=1}^{7} \frac{5}{9} x_i - \sum_{i=1}^{7} \frac{160}{9} \\
&= \frac{5}{9} \left(\sum_{i=1}^{7} x_i \right) - 7 \left(\frac{160}{9} \right) \\
&= \frac{5}{9} (511) - 7 \left(\frac{160}{9} \right) = 159.44
\end{aligned}
$$

Therefore, the average of the Celsius measurements is 159.44/7, or 22.78.

EXAMPLE A.10

Simplify the summation

$$
\sum_{i=1}^{n} (x_i - c)^2
$$

where c is any constant and n is any integer. Then evaluate this sum when $n = 4$, $c = 11.79$, $x_1 = 8$, $x_2 = 9$, $x_3 = 14$, and $x_4 = 15$.

SOLUTION

We first write out the square $(x_i - c)^2$ as

$$
(x_i - c)^2 = x_i^2 - 2cx_i + c^2
$$

Then by the summation rules, we have

$$
\begin{aligned}
\sum_{i=1}^{n} (x_i - c)^2 &= \sum_{i=1}^{n} (x_i^2 - 2cx_i + c^2) \\
&= \left(\sum_{i=1}^{n} x_i^2 \right) - 2c \left(\sum_{i=1}^{n} x_i \right) + nc^2
\end{aligned}
$$

To evaluate this expression, we need the sums $\sum x_i^2$ and $\sum x_i$. For the numerical example, these are

$$
\sum_{i=1}^{4} x_i = 8 + 9 + 14 + 15 = 46
$$

and

$$\sum_{i=1}^{4} x_i^2 = 8^2 + 9^2 + 14^2 + 15^2 = 566$$

Plugging in these values, we obtain

$$\sum_{i=1}^{4} (x_i - 11.79)^2 = 566 - 2(11.79)(46) + 4(11.79)^2 = 37.3364$$

Statistical Tables

Contents

Table Ia   Cumulative Probabilities for the Standard Normal Distribution
This table gives probabilities p to the left of given z values for the
standard normal distribution.

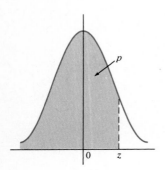

z	.00	.01	.02	.03	.04	.05	.06	.07	.08	.09
0	.5000	.5040	.5080	.5120	.5160	.5199	.5239	.5279	.5319	.5359
.1	.5398	.5438	.5478	.5517	.5557	.5596	.5636	.5675	.5714	.5753
.2	.5793	.5832	.5871	.5910	.5948	.5987	.6026	.6064	.6103	.6141
.3	.6179	.6217	.6255	.6293	.6331	.6368	.6406	.6443	.6480	.6517
.4	.6554	.6591	.6628	.6664	.6700	.6736	.6772	.6808	.6844	.6879
.5	.6915	.6950	.6985	.7019	.7054	.7088	.7123	.7157	.7190	.7224
.6	.7257	.7291	.7324	.7357	.7389	.7422	.7454	.7486	.7517	.7549
.7	.7580	.7611	.7642	.7673	.7704	.7734	.7764	.7794	.7823	.7852
.8	.7881	.7910	.7939	.7967	.7995	.8023	.8051	.8078	.8106	.8133
.9	.8159	.8186	.8212	.8238	.8264	.8289	.8315	.8340	.8365	.8389
1.0	.8413	.8438	.8461	.8485	.8508	.8531	.8554	.8577	.8599	.8621
1.1	.8643	.8665	.8686	.8708	.8729	.8749	.8770	.8790	.8810	.8830
1.2	.8849	.8869	.8888	.8907	.8925	.8944	.8962	.8980	.8997	.9015
1.3	.9032	.9049	.9066	.9082	.9099	.9115	.9131	.9147	.9162	.9177
1.4	.9192	.9207	.9222	.9236	.9251	.9265	.9279	.9292	.9306	.9319
1.5	.9332	.9345	.9357	.9370	.9382	.9394	.9406	.9418	.9429	.9441
1.6	.9452	.9463	.9474	.9484	.9495	.9505	.9515	.9525	.9535	.9545
1.7	.9554	.9564	.9573	.9582	.9591	.9599	.9608	.9616	.9625	.9633
1.8	.9641	.9649	.9656	.9664	.9671	.9678	.9686	.9693	.9699	.9706
1.9	.9713	.9719	.9726	.9732	.9738	.9744	.9750	.9756	.9761	.9767
2.0	.9772	.9778	.9783	.9788	.9793	.9798	.9803	.9808	.9812	.9817
2.1	.9821	.9826	.9830	.9834	.9838	.9842	.9846	.9850	.9854	.9857
2.2	.9861	.9864	.9868	.9871	.9875	.9878	.9881	.9884	.9887	.9890
2.3	.9893	.9896	.9898	.9901	.9904	.9906	.9909	.9911	.9913	.9916
2.4	.9918	.9920	.9922	.9925	.9927	.9929	.9931	.9932	.9934	.9936
2.5	.9938	.9940	.9941	.9943	.9945	.9946	.9948	.9949	.9951	.9952
2.6	.9953	.9955	.9956	.9957	.9959	.9960	.9961	.9962	.9963	.9964
2.7	.9965	.9966	.9967	.9968	.9969	.9970	.9971	.9972	.9973	.9974
2.8	.9974	.9975	.9976	.9977	.9977	.9978	.9979	.9979	.9980	.9981
2.9	.9981	.9982	.9982	.9983	.9984	.9984	.9985	.9985	.9986	.9986
3.0	.9987	.9987	.9987	.9988	.9988	.9989	.9989	.9989	.9990	.9990
3.1	.9990	.9991	.9991	.9991	.9992	.9992	.9992	.9992	.9993	.9993
3.2	.9993	.9993	.9994	.9994	.9994	.9994	.9994	.9995	.9995	.9995
3.3	.9995	.9995	.9995	.9996	.9996	.9996	.9996	.9996	.9996	.9997
3.4	.9997	.9997	.9997	.9997	.9997	.9997	.9997	.9997	.9997	.9998

Example: The probability that a standard normal (Z) random variable is less than 1.53 is found
at the intersection of the 1.5 row and the .03 column. This gives $P(Z < 1.53) = .9370$. By
symmetry, $P(Z > -1.53) = .9370$, so that $P(Z < -1.53) = 1 - .9370 = .0630$.

Table Ib   Percentiles of the Standard Normal Distribution
This table gives values that have specified probabilities p to the left of them for the standard normal distribution.

p	.000	.005	.010	.015	.020	.025	.030	.035	.040	.045
.500	.000	.013	.025	.038	.050	.063	.075	.088	.100	.113
.550	.126	.138	.151	.164	.176	.189	.202	.215	.228	.240
.600	.253	.266	.279	.292	.306	.319	.332	.345	.359	.372
.650	.385	.399	.413	.426	.440	.454	.468	.482	.496	.510
.700	.524	.539	.553	.568	.583	.598	.613	.628	.643	.659
.750	.675	.690	.706	.723	.739	.755	.772	.789	.806	.824
.800	.842	.860	.878	.897	.915	.935	.954	.974	.995	1.015
.850	1.036	1.058	1.080	1.103	1.126	1.150	1.175	1.200	1.227	1.254
.900	1.282	1.311	1.341	1.372	1.405	1.440	1.476	1.514	1.555	1.598
.950	1.645	1.695	1.751	1.812	1.881	1.960	2.054	2.171	2.326	2.576

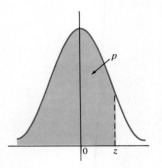

Example: To find the number with area .735 to the left of it under the standard normal curve, locate the tabled entry at the intersection of the .700 row and the .035 column. This gives $P(Z < .628) = .735$. To find the number with area .265 to the left of it under the standard normal curve, use symmetry and the fact that $.265 = 1 - .735$ to obtain $P(Z < -.628) = .265$.

Table II   Cumulative Probabilities for the Binomial Distribution
This table gives probabilities of being less than or equal to specified
values of k for binomial distributions with given values of n and p.

n	k	.05	.10	.20	.30	.40	.50
1	0	.9500	.9000	.8000	.7000	.6000	.5000
	1	1.0000	1.0000	1.0000	1.0000	1.0000	1.000
2	0	.9025	.8100	.6400	.4900	.3600	.2500
	1	.9975	.9900	.9600	.9100	.8400	.7500
	2	1.0000	1.0000	1.0000	1.0000	1.0000	1.0000
3	0	.8574	.7290	.5120	.3430	.2160	.1250
	1	.9927	.9720	.8960	.7840	.6480	.5000
	2	.9999	.9990	.9920	.9730	.9360	.8750
	3	1.0000	1.0000	1.0000	1.0000	1.0000	1.0000
4	0	.8145	.6561	.4096	.2401	.1296	.0625
	1	.9860	.9477	.8192	.6517	.4752	.3125
	2	.9995	.9963	.9728	.9163	.8208	.6875
	3	1.0000	.9999	.9984	.9919	.9744	.9375
	4		1.0000	1.0000	1.0000	1.0000	1.0000
5	0	.7738	.5905	.3277	.1681	.0778	.0313
	1	.9774	.9185	.7373	.5282	.3370	.1875
	2	.9988	.9914	.9421	.8369	.6826	.5000
	3	1.0000	.9995	.9933	.9692	.9130	.8125
	4		1.0000	.9997	.9976	.9898	.9688
	5			1.0000	1.0000	1.0000	1.0000

Example: The probability of 4 or fewer A's when there are 7 trials and each has probability
.20 of producing an A is .9953. For a value of p above .50, switch the roles of the A's and B's.
For instance, to find the probability of 4 or fewer A's when there are 7 trials and the probability
of an A is .70, notice that this is the same as the probability of 3 or more B's in 7 trials when
the probability of a B is .30. But this is 1 minus the probability of 2 or fewer B's, and this latter
probability, from the table with $k = 2$, $n = 7$, and $p = .30$, is .6471. So the original probability
is $1 - .6471 = .3529$.

Table II Continued

n	k	.05	.10	.20	.30	.40	.50
					p		
6	0	.7351	.5314	.2621	.1176	.0467	.0156
	1	.9672	.8857	.6554	.4202	.2333	.1094
	2	.9978	.9841	.9011	.7443	.5443	.3438
	3	.9999	.9987	.9830	.9295	.8208	.6563
	4	1.0000	.9999	.9984	.9891	.9590	.8906
	5		1.0000	.9999	.9993	.9959	.9844
	6			1.0000	1.0000	1.0000	1.0000
7	0	.6983	.4783	.2097	.0824	.0280	.0078
	1	.9556	.8503	.5767	.3294	.1586	.0625
	2	.9962	.9743	.8520	.6471	.4199	.2266
	3	.9998	.9973	.9667	.8740	.7102	.5000
	4	1.0000	.9998	.9953	.9712	.9037	.7734
	5		1.0000	.9996	.9962	.9812	.9375
	6			1.0000	.9998	.9984	.9922
	7				1.0000	1.0000	1.0000
8	0	.6634	.4305	.1678	.0576	.0168	.0039
	1	.9428	.8131	.5033	.2553	.1064	.0352
	2	.9942	.9619	.7969	.5518	.3154	.1445
	3	.9996	.9950	.9437	.8059	.5941	.3633
	4	1.0000	.9996	.9896	.9420	.8263	.6367
	5		1.0000	.9988	.9887	.9502	.8555
	6			.9999	.9987	.9915	.9648
	7			1.0000	.9999	.9993	.9961
	8				1.0000	1.0000	1.0000
9	0	.6302	.3874	.1342	.0404	.0101	.0020
	1	.9288	.7748	.4362	.1960	.0705	.0195
	2	.9916	.9470	.7382	.4628	.2318	.0898
	3	.9994	.9917	.9144	.7297	.4826	.2539
	4	1.0000	.9991	.9804	.9012	.7334	.5000
	5		.9999	.9969	.9747	.9006	.7461
	6		1.0000	.9997	.9957	.9750	.9102
	7			1.0000	.9996	.9962	.9805
	8				1.0000	.9997	.9980
	9					1.0000	1.0000
10	0	.5987	.3487	.1074	.0282	.0060	.0010
	1	.9139	.7361	.3758	.1493	.0464	.0107
	2	.9885	.9298	.6778	.3828	.1673	.0547
	3	.9990	.9872	.8791	.6496	.3823	.1719
	4	.9999	.9984	.9672	.8497	.6331	.3770
	5	1.0000	.9999	.9936	.9526	.8338	.6230
	6		1.0000	.9991	.9894	.9452	.8281
	7			.9999	.9999	.9877	.9453
	8			1.0000	1.0000	.9983	.9893
	9					.9999	.9990
	10					1.0000	1.0000

Table II Continued

n	k	.05	.10	.20	.30	.40	.50
11	0	.5688	.3138	.0859	.0198	.0036	.0005
	1	.8981	.6974	.3221	.1130	.0302	.0059
	2	.9848	.9104	.6174	.3127	.1189	.0327
	3	.9984	.9815	.8369	.5696	.2963	.1133
	4	.9999	.9972	.9496	.7897	.5328	.2744
	5	1.0000	.9997	.9883	.9218	.7535	.5000
	6		1.0000	.9980	.9784	.9006	.7256
	7			.9998	.9957	.9707	.8867
	8			1.0000	.9994	.9941	.9673
	9				1.0000	.9993	.9941
	10					1.0000	.9995
	11						1.0000
12	0	.5404	.2824	.0687	.0138	.0022	.0002
	1	.8816	.6590	.2749	.0850	.0196	.0032
	2	.9804	.8891	.5583	.2528	.0834	.0193
	3	.9978	.9744	.7946	.4925	.2253	.0730
	4	.9998	.9957	.9274	.7237	.4382	.1938
	5	1.0000	.9995	.9806	.8821	.6652	.3872
	6		.9999	.9961	.9614	.8418	.6128
	7		1.0000	.9994	.9905	.9427	.8062
	8			.9999	.9983	.9847	.9270
	9			1.0000	.9998	.9972	.9807
	10				1.0000	.9997	.9968
	11					1.0000	.9998
	12						1.0000
13	0	.5133	.2542	.0550	.0097	.0013	.0001
	1	.8646	.6213	.2336	.0637	.0126	.0017
	2	.9755	.8661	.5017	.2025	.0579	.0112
	3	.9969	.9658	.7473	.4206	.1686	.0461
	4	.9997	.9935	.9009	.6543	.3530	.1334
	5	1.0000	.9991	.9700	.8346	.5744	.2905
	6		.9999	.9930	.9376	.7712	.5000
	7		1.0000	.9988	.9818	.9023	.7095
	8			.9998	.9960	.9679	.8666
	9			1.0000	.9993	.9922	.9539
	10				.9999	.9987	.9888
	11				1.0000	.9999	.9983
	12					1.0000	.9999
	13						1.0000

Table II Continued

n	k	.05	.10	.20	.30	.40	.50
14	0	.4877	.2288	.0440	.0068	.0008	.0001
	1	.8470	.5846	.1979	.0475	.0081	.0009
	2	.9699	.8416	.4481	.1608	.0398	.0065
	3	.9958	.9559	.6982	.3552	.1243	.0287
	4	.9996	.9908	.8702	.5842	.2793	.0898
	5	1.0000	.9985	.9561	.7805	.4859	.2120
	6		.9998	.9884	.9067	.6925	.3953
	7		1.0000	.9976	.9685	.8499	.6047
	8			.9996	.9917	.9417	.7880
	9			1.0000	.9983	.9825	.9102
	10				.9998	.9961	.9713
	11				1.0000	.9994	.9935
	12					.9999	.9991
	13					1.0000	.9999
	14						1.0000
15	0	.4633	.2059	.0352	.0047	.0005	.0000
	1	.8290	.5490	.1671	.0353	.0052	.0005
	2	.9638	.8159	.3980	.1268	.0271	.0037
	3	.9945	.9444	.6482	.2969	.0905	.0176
	4	.9994	.9873	.8358	.5155	.2173	.0592
	5	.9999	.9978	.9389	.7216	.4032	.1509
	6	1.0000	.9997	.9819	.8689	.6098	.3036
	7		1.0000	.9958	.9500	.7869	.5000
	8			.9992	.9848	.9050	.6964
	9			.9999	.9963	.9662	.8491
	10			1.0000	.9993	.9907	.9408
	11				.9999	.9981	.9824
	12				1.0000	.9997	.9963
	13					1.0000	.9995
	14						1.0000
16	0	.4401	.1853	.0281	.0033	.0003	.0000
	1	.8108	.5147	.1407	.0261	.0033	.0003
	2	.9571	.7892	.3518	.0994	.0183	.0021
	3	.9930	.9316	.5981	.2459	.0651	.0106
	4	.9991	.9830	.7982	.4499	.1666	.0384
	5	.9999	.9967	.9183	.6598	.3288	.1051
	6	1.0000	.9995	.9733	.8247	.5272	.2272
	7		.9999	.9930	.9256	.7161	.4018
	8		1.0000	.9985	.9743	.8577	.5982
	9			.9998	.9929	.9417	.7728
	10			1.0000	.9984	.9809	.8949
	11				.9997	.9951	.9616
	12				1.0000	.9991	.9894
	13					.9999	.9979
	14					1.0000	.9997
	15						1.0000

Table II　Continued

n	k	.05	.10	.20	.30	.40	.50
17	0	.4181	.1668	.0225	.0023	.0002	.0000
	1	.7922	.4818	.1182	.0193	.0021	.0001
	2	.9497	.7618	.3096	.0774	.0123	.0012
	3	.9912	.9174	.5489	.2019	.0464	.0064
	4	.9988	.9779	.7582	.3887	.1260	.0245
	5	.9999	.9953	.8943	.5968	.2639	.0717
	6	1.0000	.9992	.9623	.7752	.4478	.1662
	7		.9999	.9891	.8954	.6405	.3145
	8		1.0000	.9974	.9597	.8011	.5000
	9			.9995	.9873	.9081	.6855
	10			.9999	.9968	.9652	.8338
	11			1.0000	.9993	.9894	.9283
	12				.9999	.9975	.9755
	13				1.0000	.9995	.9936
	14					.9999	.9988
	15					1.0000	.9999
	16						1.0000
18	0	.3972	.1501	.0180	.0016	.0001	.0000
	1	.7735	.4503	.0991	.0142	.0013	.0001
	2	.9419	.7338	.2713	.0600	.0082	.0007
	3	.9891	.9018	.5010	.1646	.0328	.0038
	4	.9985	.9718	.7164	.3327	.0942	.0154
	5	.9998	.9936	.8671	.5344	.2088	.0481
	6	1.0000	.9988	.9487	.7217	.3743	.1189
	7		.9998	.9837	.8593	.5634	.2403
	8		1.0000	.9957	.9404	.7368	.4073
	9			.9991	.9790	.8653	.5927
	10			.9998	.9939	.9424	.7597
	11			1.000	.9986	.9797	.8811
	12				.9997	.9942	.9519
	13				1.0000	.9987	.9846
	14					.9998	.9962
	15					1.0000	.9993
	16						.9999
	17						1.0000

Table II   Continued

n	k	.05	.10	.20	.30	.40	.50
					p		
19	0	.3774	.1351	.0144	.0011	.0001	.0000
	1	.7547	.4203	.0829	.0104	.0008	.0000
	2	.9335	.7054	.2369	.0462	.0055	.0004
	3	.9868	.8850	.4551	.1332	.0230	.0022
	4	.9980	.9648	.6733	.2822	.0696	.0096
	5	.9998	.9914	.8369	.4739	.1629	.0318
	6	1.0000	.9983	.9324	.6655	.3081	.0835
	7		.9997	.9767	.8180	.4878	.1796
	8		1.0000	.9933	.9161	.6675	.3238
	9			.9984	.9674	.8139	.5000
	10			.9997	.9895	.9115	.6762
	11			.9999	.9972	.9648	.8204
	12			1.0000	.9994	.9884	.9165
	13				.9999	.9969	.9682
	14				1.0000	.9994	.9904
	15					.9999	.9978
	16					1.0000	.9996
	17						1.0000
20	0	.3585	.1216	.0115	.0008	.0000	.0000
	1	.7358	.3917	.0692	.0076	.0005	.0000
	2	.9245	.6769	.2061	.0355	.0036	.0002
	3	.9841	.8670	.4114	.1071	.0160	.0013
	4	.9974	.9568	.6296	.2375	.0510	.0059
	5	.9997	.9887	.8042	.4164	.1256	.0207
	6	1.0000	.9976	.9133	.6080	.2500	.0577
	7		.9996	.9679	.7723	.4159	.1316
	8		.9999	.9900	.8867	.5956	.2517
	9		1.0000	.9974	.9520	.7553	.4119
	10			.9994	.9829	.8725	.5881
	11			.9999	.9949	.9435	.7483
	12			1.0000	.9987	.9790	.8684
	13				.9997	.9935	.9423
	14				1.0000	.9984	.9793
	15					.9997	.9941
	16					1.0000	.9987
	17						.9998
	18						1.0000

Table II   Continued

n	k	.05	.10	.20	.30	.40	.50
50	0	.0769	.0052	.0000	.0000	.0000	.0000
	1	.2794	.0338	.0002	.0000	.0000	.0000
	2	.5405	.1117	.0013	.0000	.0000	.0000
	3	.7604	.2503	.0057	.0000	.0000	.0000
	4	.8964	.4312	.0185	.0002	.0000	.0000
	5	.9622	.6161	.0480	.0007	.0000	.0000
	6	.9882	.7702	.1034	.0025	.0000	.0000
	7	.9968	.8779	.1904	.0073	.0001	.0000
	8	.9992	.9421	.3073	.0183	.0002	.0000
	9	.9998	.9755	.4437	.0402	.0008	.0000
	10	1.0000	.9906	.5836	.0789	.0022	.0000
	11		.9968	.7107	.1390	.0057	.0000
	12		.9990	.8139	.2229	.0133	.0002
	13		.9997	.8894	.3279	.0280	.0005
	14		.9999	.9393	.4468	.0540	.0013
	15		1.0000	.9692	.5692	.0955	.0033
	16			.9856	.6839	.1561	.0077
	17			.9937	.7822	.2369	.0164
	18			.9975	.8594	.3356	.0325
	19			.9991	.9152	.4465	.0595
	20			.9997	.9522	.5610	.1013
	21			.9999	.9749	.6701	.1611
	22			1.0000	.9877	.7660	.2399
	23				.9944	.8438	.3359
	24				.9976	.9022	.4439
	25				.9991	.9427	.5561
	26				.9997	.9686	.6641
	27				.9999	.9840	.7601
	28				1.0000	.9924	.8389
	29					.9966	.8987
	30					.9986	.9405
	31					.9995	.9675
	32					.9998	.9836
	33					.9999	.9923
	34					1.0000	.9967
	35						.9987
	36						.9995
	37						.9998
	38						1.0000

Table II Continued

n	k	.05	.10	.20	.30	.40	.50	n	k	.20	.30	.40	.50
100	0	.0059	.0000	.0000	.0000	.0000	.0000	100	36	.9999	.9201	.2386	.0033
	1	.0371	.0003	.0000	.0000	.0000	.0000		37	1.0000	.9470	.3068	.0060
	2	.1183	.0019	.0000	.0000	.0000	.0000		38		.9660	.3822	.0105
	3	.2578	.0078	.0000	.0000	.0000	.0000		39		.9790	.4621	.0176
	4	.4360	.0237	.0000	.0000	.0000	.0000		40		.9875	.5433	.0284
	5	.6160	.0576	.0000	.0000	.0000	.0000						
	6	.7660	.1172	.0001	.0000	.0000	.0000		41		.9928	.6225	.0443
	7	.8720	.2061	.0003	.0000	.0000	.0000		42		.9960	.6967	.0666
	8	.9369	.3209	.0009	.0000	.0000	.0000		43		.9979	.7635	.0967
	9	.9718	.4513	.0023	.0000	.0000	.0000		44		.9989	.8211	.1356
	10	.9885	.5832	.0057	.0000	.0000	.0000		45		.9995	.8689	.1841
	11	.9957	.7030	.0126	.0000	.0000	.0000		46		.9997	.9070	.2421
	12	.9985	.8018	.0253	.0000	.0000	.0000		47		.9999	.9362	.3086
	13	.9995	.8761	.0469	.0001	.0000	.0000		48		.9999	.9577	.3822
	14	.9999	.9274	.0804	.0002	.0000	.0000		49		1.0000	.9729	.4602
	15	1.0000	.9601	.1285	.0004	.0000	.0000		50			.9832	.5398
	16		.9794	.1923	.0010	.0000	.0000		51			.9900	.6178
	17		.9900	.2712	.0022	.0000	.0000		52			.9942	.6914
	18		.9954	.3621	.0045	.0000	.0000		53			.9968	.7579
	19		.9980	.4602	.0089	.0000	.0000		54			.9983	.8159
	20		.9992	.5595	.0165	.0000	.0000		55			.9991	.8644
	21		.9997	.6540	.0288	.0000	.0000		56			.9996	.9033
	22		.9999	.7389	.0479	.0001	.0000		57			.9998	.9334
	23		1.0000	.8109	.0755	.0003	.0000		58			.9999	.9557
	24			.8686	.1136	.0006	.0000		59			1.0000	.9716
	25			.9125	.1631	.0012	.0000		60				.9824
	26			.9442	.2244	.0024	.0000		61				.9895
	27			.9658	.2964	.0046	.0000		62				.9940
	28			.9800	.3768	.0084	.0000		63				.9967
	29			.9888	.4623	.0148	.0000		64				.9982
	30			.9939	.5491	.0248	.0000		65				.9991
	31			.9969	.6331	.0398	.0001		66				.9996
	32			.9984	.7107	.0615	.0002		67				.9998
	33			.9993	.7793	.0913	.0004		68				.9999
	34			.9997	.8371	.1303	.0009		69				1.0000
	35			.9999	.8839	.1795	.0018						

Table III Percentiles of the t Distribution

This table gives values with specified probabilities to the right of them for the specified t distributions.

Degrees of freedom ν	Right-hand tail probability α			
	.10	.05	.025	.01
1	3.078	6.314	12.706	31.821
2	1.886	2.920	4.303	6.965
3	1.638	2.353	3.182	4.541
4	1.533	2.132	2.776	3.747
5	1.476	2.015	2.571	3.365
6	1.440	1.943	2.447	3.143
7	1.415	1.895	2.365	2.998
8	1.397	1.860	2.306	2.896
9	1.383	1.833	2.262	2.821
10	1.372	1.812	2.228	2.764
11	1.363	1.796	2.201	2.718
12	1.356	1.782	2.179	2.681
13	1.350	1.771	2.160	2.650
14	1.345	1.761	2.145	2.624
15	1.341	1.753	2.131	2.602
16	1.337	1.746	2.120	2.583
17	1.333	1.740	2.110	2.567
18	1.330	1.734	2.101	2.552
19	1.328	1.729	2.093	2.539
20	1.325	1.725	2.086	2.528
21	1.323	1.721	2.080	2.518
22	1.321	1.717	2.074	2.508
23	1.319	1.714	2.069	2.500
24	1.318	1.711	2.064	2.492
25	1.316	1.708	2.060	2.485
26	1.315	1.706	2.056	2.479
27	1.314	1.703	2.052	2.473
28	1.313	1.701	2.048	2.467
29	1.311	1.699	2.045	2.462
30	1.310	1.697	2.042	2.457
40	1.303	1.684	2.021	2.423
60	1.296	1.671	2.000	2.390
120	1.289	1.658	1.980	2.358
z_α	1.282	1.645	1.960	2.326

Example: For a t distribution with 20 degrees of freedom, the probability of being greater than 1.725 is .05. By symmetry, the probability of being to the left of -1.725 is also .05.

Source: E. S. Pearson and H. O. Hartley, *Biometrika Tables for Statisticians*, Vol. I. London: Cambridge University Press, 1966.

Table IV Percentiles of the Chi-Square Distribution
This table gives values with specified probabilities to the right of them for the specified chi-square distributions.

Degrees of freedom ν	Right-hand tail probability α							
	.99	.975	.95	.90	.10	.05	.025	.01
1	.0002	.0010	.0039	.0158	2.706	3.841	5.024	6.635
2	.020	.051	.103	.211	4.605	5.991	7.378	9.210
3	.115	.216	.352	.584	6.251	7.815	9.348	11.345
4	.297	.484	.711	1.064	7.779	9.488	11.143	13.277
5	.554	.831	1.145	1.610	9.236	11.071	12.833	15.086
6	.872	1.237	1.635	2.204	10.645	12.592	14.449	16.812
7	1.239	1.690	2.167	2.833	12.017	14.067	16.013	18.475
8	1.646	2.180	2.733	3.490	13.362	15.507	17.535	20.090
9	2.088	2.700	3.325	4.168	14.684	16.919	19.023	21.666
10	2.558	3.247	3.940	4.865	15.987	18.307	20.483	23.209
11	3.053	3.816	4.575	5.578	17.275	19.675	21.920	24.725
12	3.571	4.404	5.226	6.304	18.549	21.026	23.337	26.217
13	4.107	5.009	5.892	7.042	19.812	22.362	24.736	27.688
14	4.660	5.629	6.571	7.790	21.064	23.685	26.119	29.141
15	5.229	6.262	7.261	8.547	22.307	24.996	27.488	30.578
16	5.812	6.908	7.962	9.312	23.542	26.296	28.845	32.000
17	6.408	7.564	8.672	10.085	24.769	27.587	30.191	33.409
18	7.015	8.231	9.390	10.865	25.989	28.869	31.526	34.805
19	7.633	8.907	10.117	11.651	27.204	30.144	32.852	36.191
20	8.620	9.591	10.851	12.443	28.412	31.410	34.170	37.566
21	8.897	10.283	11.591	13.240	29.615	32.671	35.479	38.932
22	9.542	10.982	12.338	14.042	30.813	33.924	36.781	40.289
23	10.196	11.689	13.091	14.848	32.007	35.173	38.076	41.638
24	10.856	12.401	13.848	15.659	33.196	36.415	39.364	42.980
25	11.524	13.120	14.611	16.473	34.382	37.653	40.647	44.314
26	12.198	13.844	15.379	17.292	35.563	38.885	41.923	45.642
27	12.879	14.573	16.151	18.114	36.741	40.113	43.194	46.963
28	13.565	15.308	16.928	18.939	37.916	41.337	44.461	48.278
29	14.257	16.047	17.708	19.768	39.088	42.557	45.722	49.588
30	14.954	16.791	18.493	20.599	40.256	43.773	46.979	50.892
40	22.164	24.433	26.509	29.051	51.805	55.759	59.342	63.691
50	29.707	32.357	34.764	37.689	63.167	67.505	71.420	76.154
60	37.485	40.481	43.188	46.459	74.397	79.082	83.298	88.379
70	45.442	48.758	51.739	55.329	85.527	90.531	95.023	100.425
80	53.540	57.153	60.392	64.278	96.578	101.879	106.629	112.329
90	61.754	65.647	69.126	73.291	107.565	113.145	118.136	124.116
100	70.065	74.222	77.930	82.358	118.498	124.342	129.561	135.807
z_α	−2.326	−1.960	−1.645	−1.282	1.282	1.645	1.960	2.326

Example: For a chi-square distribution with 13 degrees of freedom, the probability of being greater than 4.107 is .99; the probability of being greater than 27.688 is .01.

Source: From Table IV of Fisher and Yates, *Statistical Tables for Biological, Agricultural and Medical Research,* published by Longman Group Ltd., London (previously published by Oliver & Boyd, Edinburgh, 1963).

Table V   Percentiles of the *F* Distribution

This table gives values with specified probabilities to the right of them for the specified *F* distributions. Actually, this is a series of 4 separate tables, one each for the right-hand tail probabilities .10, .05, .025, and .01.

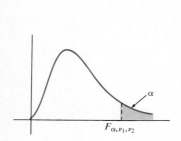

F_{α, ν_1, ν_2}

$$\alpha = .10$$

ν_1 ν_2	NUMERATOR DEGREES OF FREEDOM								
	1	2	3	4	5	6	7	8	9
1	39.86	49.50	53.59	55.83	57.24	58.20	58.91	59.44	59.86
2	8.53	9.00	9.16	9.24	9.29	9.33	9.35	9.37	9.38
3	5.54	5.46	5.39	5.34	5.31	5.28	5.27	5.25	5.24
4	4.54	4.32	4.19	4.11	4.05	4.01	3.98	3.95	3.94
5	4.06	3.78	3.62	3.52	3.45	3.40	3.37	3.34	3.32
6	3.78	3.46	3.29	3.18	3.11	3.05	3.01	2.98	2.96
7	3.59	3.26	3.07	2.96	2.88	2.83	2.78	2.75	2.72
8	3.46	3.11	2.92	2.81	2.73	2.67	2.62	2.59	2.56
9	3.36	3.01	2.81	2.69	2.61	2.55	2.51	2.47	2.44
10	3.29	2.92	2.73	2.61	2.52	2.46	2.41	2.38	2.35
11	3.23	2.86	2.66	2.54	2.45	2.39	2.34	2.30	2.27
12	3.18	2.81	2.61	2.48	2.39	2.33	2.28	2.24	2.21
13	3.14	2.76	2.56	2.43	2.35	2.28	2.23	2.20	2.16
14	3.10	2.73	2.52	2.39	2.31	2.24	2.19	2.15	2.12
15	3.07	2.70	2.49	2.36	2.27	2.21	2.16	2.12	2.09
16	3.05	2.67	2.46	2.33	2.24	2.18	2.13	2.09	2.06
17	3.03	2.64	2.44	2.31	2.22	2.15	2.10	2.06	2.03
18	3.01	2.62	2.42	2.29	2.20	2.13	2.08	2.04	2.00
19	2.99	2.61	2.40	2.27	2.18	2.11	2.06	2.02	1.98
20	2.97	2.59	2.38	2.25	2.16	2.09	2.04	2.00	1.96
21	2.96	2.57	2.36	2.23	2.14	2.08	2.02	1.98	1.95
22	2.95	2.56	2.35	2.22	2.13	2.06	2.01	1.97	1.93
23	2.94	2.55	2.34	2.21	2.11	2.05	1.99	1.95	1.92
24	2.93	2.54	2.33	2.19	2.10	2.04	1.98	1.94	1.91
25	2.92	2.53	2.32	2.18	2.09	2.02	1.97	1.93	1.89
26	2.91	2.52	2.31	2.17	2.08	2.01	1.96	1.92	1.88
27	2.90	2.51	2.30	2.17	2.07	2.00	1.95	1.91	1.87
28	2.89	2.50	2.29	2.16	2.06	2.00	1.94	1.90	1.87
29	2.89	2.50	2.28	2.15	2.06	1.99	1.93	1.89	1.86
30	2.88	2.49	2.28	2.14	2.05	1.98	1.93	1.88	1.85
40	2.84	2.44	2.23	2.09	2.00	1.93	1.87	1.83	1.79
60	2.79	2.39	2.18	2.04	1.95	1.87	1.82	1.77	1.74
120	2.75	2.35	2.13	1.99	1.90	1.82	1.77	1.72	1.68
∞	2.71	2.30	2.08	1.94	1.85	1.77	1.72	1.67	1.63

DENOMINATOR DEGREES OF FREEDOM

Example: For an *F* distribution with 4 and 20 degrees of freedom, the probability of being greater than 2.25 is .10. Since an *F* random variable is a ratio, we can take reciprocals and state that for an *F* distribution with 20 and 4 degrees of freedom, the probability of being *less* than 1/2.25 is .10.

$\alpha = .10$

ν_2	NUMERATOR DEGREES OF FREEDOM ν_1									
	10	12	15	20	24	30	40	60	120	∞
1	60.19	60.71	61.22	61.74	62.00	62.26	62.53	62.79	63.06	63.33
2	9.39	9.41	9.42	9.44	9.45	9.46	9.47	9.47	9.48	9.49
3	5.23	5.22	5.20	5.18	5.18	5.17	5.16	5.15	5.14	5.13
4	3.92	3.90	3.87	3.84	3.83	3.82	3.80	3.79	3.78	3.76
5	3.30	3.27	3.24	3.21	3.19	3.17	3.16	3.14	3.12	3.10
6	2.94	2.90	2.87	2.84	2.82	2.80	2.78	2.76	2.74	2.72
7	2.70	2.67	2.63	2.59	2.58	2.56	2.54	2.51	2.49	2.47
8	2.54	2.50	2.46	2.42	2.40	2.38	2.36	2.34	2.32	2.29
9	2.42	2.38	2.34	2.30	2.28	2.25	2.23	2.21	2.18	2.16
10	2.32	2.28	2.24	2.20	2.18	2.16	2.13	2.11	2.08	2.06
11	2.25	2.21	2.17	2.12	2.10	2.08	2.05	2.03	2.00	1.97
12	2.19	2.15	2.10	2.06	2.04	2.01	1.99	1.96	1.93	1.90
13	2.14	2.10	2.05	2.01	1.98	1.96	1.93	1.90	1.88	1.85
14	2.10	2.05	2.01	1.96	1.94	1.91	1.89	1.86	1.83	1.80
15	2.06	2.02	1.97	1.92	1.90	1.87	1.85	1.82	1.79	1.76
16	2.03	1.99	1.94	1.89	1.87	1.84	1.81	1.78	1.75	1.72
17	2.00	1.96	1.91	1.86	1.84	1.81	1.78	1.75	1.72	1.69
18	1.98	1.93	1.89	1.84	1.81	1.78	1.75	1.72	1.69	1.66
19	1.96	1.91	1.86	1.81	1.79	1.76	1.73	1.70	1.67	1.63
20	1.94	1.89	1.84	1.79	1.77	1.74	1.71	1.68	1.64	1.61
21	1.92	1.87	1.83	1.78	1.75	1.72	1.69	1.66	1.62	1.59
22	1.90	1.86	1.81	1.76	1.73	1.70	1.67	1.64	1.60	1.57
23	1.89	1.84	1.80	1.74	1.72	1.69	1.66	1.62	1.59	1.55
24	1.88	1.83	1.78	1.73	1.70	1.67	1.64	1.61	1.57	1.53
25	1.87	1.82	1.77	1.72	1.69	1.66	1.63	1.59	1.56	1.52
26	1.86	1.81	1.76	1.71	1.68	1.65	1.61	1.58	1.54	1.50
27	1.85	1.80	1.75	1.70	1.67	1.64	1.60	1.57	1.53	1.49
28	1.84	1.79	1.74	1.69	1.66	1.63	1.59	1.56	1.52	1.48
29	1.83	1.78	1.73	1.68	1.65	1.62	1.58	1.55	1.51	1.47
30	1.82	1.77	1.72	1.67	1.64	1.61	1.57	1.54	1.50	1.46
40	1.76	1.71	1.66	1.61	1.57	1.54	1.51	1.47	1.42	1.38
60	1.71	1.66	1.60	1.54	1.51	1.48	1.44	1.40	1.35	1.29
120	1.65	1.60	1.55	1.48	1.45	1.41	1.37	1.32	1.26	1.19
∞	1.60	1.55	1.49	1.42	1.38	1.34	1.30	1.24	1.17	1.00

DENOMINATOR DEGREES OF FREEDOM

Table V Continued

$$\alpha = .05$$

v_1 / v_2	NUMERATOR DEGREES OF FREEDOM								
	1	2	3	4	5	6	7	8	9
1	161.4	199.5	215.7	224.6	230.2	234.0	236.8	238.9	240.5
2	18.51	19.00	19.16	19.25	19.30	19.33	19.35	19.37	19.38
3	10.13	9.55	9.28	9.12	9.01	8.94	8.89	8.85	8.81
4	7.71	6.94	6.59	6.39	6.26	6.16	6.09	6.04	6.00
5	6.61	5.79	5.41	5.19	5.05	4.95	4.88	4.82	4.77
6	5.99	5.14	4.76	4.53	4.39	4.28	4.21	4.15	4.10
7	5.59	4.74	4.35	4.12	3.97	3.87	3.79	3.73	3.68
8	5.32	4.46	4.07	3.84	3.69	3.58	3.50	3.44	3.39
9	5.12	4.26	3.86	3.63	3.48	3.37	3.29	3.23	3.18
10	4.96	4.10	3.71	3.48	3.33	3.22	3.14	3.07	3.02
11	4.84	3.98	3.59	3.36	3.20	3.09	3.01	2.95	2.90
12	4.75	3.89	3.49	3.26	3.11	3.00	2.91	2.85	2.80
13	4.67	3.81	3.41	3.18	3.03	2.92	2.83	2.77	2.71
14	4.60	3.74	3.34	3.11	2.96	2.85	2.76	2.70	2.65
15	4.54	3.68	3.29	3.06	2.90	2.79	2.71	2.64	2.59
16	4.49	3.63	3.24	3.01	2.85	2.74	2.66	2.59	2.54
17	4.45	3.59	3.20	2.96	2.81	2.70	2.61	2.55	2.49
18	4.41	3.55	3.16	2.93	2.77	2.66	2.58	2.51	2.46
19	4.38	3.52	3.13	2.90	2.74	2.63	2.54	2.48	2.42
20	4.35	3.49	3.10	2.87	2.71	2.60	2.51	2.45	2.39
21	4.32	3.47	3.07	2.84	2.68	2.57	2.49	2.42	2.37
22	4.30	3.44	3.05	2.82	2.66	2.55	2.46	2.40	2.34
23	4.28	3.42	3.03	2.80	2.64	2.53	2.44	2.37	2.32
24	4.26	3.40	3.01	2.78	2.62	2.51	2.42	2.36	2.30
25	4.24	3.39	2.99	2.76	2.60	2.49	2.40	2.34	2.28
26	4.23	3.37	2.98	2.74	2.59	2.47	2.39	2.32	2.27
27	4.21	3.35	2.96	2.73	2.57	2.46	2.37	2.31	2.25
28	4.20	3.34	2.95	2.71	2.56	2.45	2.36	2.29	2.24
29	4.18	3.33	2.93	2.70	2.55	2.43	2.35	2.28	2.22
30	4.17	3.32	2.92	2.69	2.53	2.42	2.33	2.27	2.21
40	4.08	3.23	2.84	2.61	2.45	2.34	2.25	2.18	2.12
60	4.00	3.15	2.76	2.53	2.37	2.25	2.17	2.10	2.04
120	3.92	3.07	2.68	2.45	2.29	2.17	2.09	2.02	1.96
∞	3.84	3.00	2.60	2.37	2.21	2.10	2.01	1.94	1.88

DENOMINATOR DEGREES OF FREEDOM

$$\alpha = .05$$

ν_2 \ ν_1	10	12	15	20	24	30	40	60	120	∞
				NUMERATOR DEGREES OF FREEDOM						
1	241.9	243.9	245.9	248.0	249.1	250.1	251.1	252.2	253.3	254.3
2	19.40	19.41	19.43	19.45	19.45	19.46	19.47	19.48	19.49	19.50
3	8.79	8.74	8.70	8.66	8.64	8.62	8.59	8.57	8.55	8.53
4	5.96	5.91	5.86	5.80	5.77	5.75	5.72	5.69	5.66	5.63
5	4.74	4.68	4.62	4.56	4.53	4.50	4.46	4.43	4.40	4.36
6	4.06	4.00	3.94	3.87	3.84	3.81	3.77	3.74	3.70	3.67
7	3.64	3.57	3.51	3.44	3.41	3.38	3.34	3.30	3.27	3.23
8	3.35	3.28	3.22	3.15	3.12	3.08	3.04	3.01	2.97	2.93
9	3.14	3.07	3.01	2.94	2.90	2.86	2.83	2.79	2.75	2.71
10	2.98	2.91	2.85	2.77	2.74	2.70	2.66	2.62	2.58	2.54
11	2.85	2.79	2.72	2.65	2.61	2.57	2.53	2.49	2.45	2.40
12	2.75	2.69	2.62	2.54	2.51	2.47	2.43	2.38	2.34	2.30
13	2.67	2.60	2.53	2.46	2.42	2.38	2.34	2.30	2.25	2.21
14	2.60	2.53	2.46	2.39	2.35	2.31	2.27	2.22	2.18	2.13
15	2.54	2.48	2.40	2.33	2.29	2.25	2.20	2.16	2.11	2.07
16	2.49	2.42	2.35	2.28	2.24	2.19	2.15	2.11	2.06	2.01
17	2.45	2.38	2.31	2.23	2.19	2.15	2.10	2.06	2.01	1.96
18	2.41	2.34	2.27	2.19	2.15	2.11	2.06	2.02	1.97	1.92
19	2.38	2.31	2.23	2.16	2.11	2.07	2.03	1.98	1.93	1.88
20	2.35	2.28	2.20	2.12	2.08	2.04	1.99	1.95	1.90	1.84
21	2.32	2.25	2.18	2.10	2.05	2.01	1.96	1.92	1.87	1.81
22	2.30	2.23	2.15	2.07	2.03	1.98	1.94	1.89	1.84	1.78
23	2.27	2.20	2.13	2.05	2.01	1.96	1.91	1.86	1.81	1.76
24	2.25	2.18	2.11	2.03	1.98	1.94	1.89	1.84	1.79	1.73
25	2.24	2.16	2.09	2.01	1.96	1.92	1.87	1.82	1.77	1.71
26	2.22	2.15	2.07	1.99	1.95	1.90	1.85	1.80	1.75	1.69
27	2.20	2.13	2.06	1.97	1.93	1.88	1.84	1.79	1.73	1.67
28	2.19	2.12	2.04	1.96	1.91	1.87	1.82	1.77	1.71	1.65
29	2.18	2.10	2.03	1.94	1.90	1.85	1.81	1.75	1.70	1.64
30	2.16	2.09	2.01	1.93	1.89	1.84	1.79	1.74	1.68	1.62
40	2.08	2.00	1.92	1.84	1.79	1.74	1.69	1.64	1.58	1.51
60	1.99	1.92	1.84	1.75	1.70	1.65	1.59	1.53	1.47	1.39
120	1.91	1.83	1.75	1.66	1.61	1.55	1.50	1.43	1.35	1.25
∞	1.83	1.75	1.67	1.57	1.52	1.46	1.39	1.32	1.22	1.00

DENOMINATOR DEGREES OF FREEDOM

Table V   Continued

$$\alpha = .025$$

ν_2 \ ν_1	NUMERATOR DEGREES OF FREEDOM								
	1	2	3	4	5	6	7	8	9
1	647.8	799.5	864.2	899.6	921.8	937.1	948.2	956.7	963.3
2	38.51	39.00	39.17	39.25	39.30	39.33	39.36	39.37	39.39
3	17.44	16.04	15.44	15.10	14.88	14.73	14.62	14.54	14.47
4	12.22	10.65	9.98	9.60	9.36	9.20	9.07	8.98	8.90
5	10.01	8.43	7.76	7.39	7.15	6.98	6.85	6.76	6.68
6	8.81	7.26	6.60	6.23	5.99	5.82	5.70	5.60	5.52
7	8.07	6.54	5.89	5.52	5.29	5.12	4.99	4.90	4.82
8	7.57	6.06	5.42	5.05	4.82	4.65	4.53	4.43	4.36
9	7.21	5.71	5.08	4.72	4.48	4.32	4.20	4.10	4.03
10	6.94	5.46	4.83	4.47	4.24	4.07	3.95	3.85	3.78
11	6.72	5.26	4.63	4.28	4.04	3.88	3.76	3.66	3.59
12	6.55	5.10	4.47	4.12	3.89	3.73	3.61	3.51	3.44
13	6.41	4.97	4.35	4.00	3.77	3.60	3.48	3.39	3.31
14	6.30	4.86	4.24	3.89	3.66	3.50	3.38	3.29	3.21
15	6.20	4.77	4.15	3.80	3.58	3.41	3.29	3.20	3.12
16	6.12	4.69	4.08	3.73	3.50	3.34	3.22	3.12	3.05
17	6.04	4.62	4.01	3.66	3.44	3.28	3.16	3.06	2.98
18	5.98	4.56	3.95	3.61	3.38	3.22	3.10	3.01	2.93
19	5.92	4.51	3.90	3.56	3.33	3.17	3.05	2.96	2.88
20	5.87	4.46	3.86	3.51	3.29	3.13	3.01	2.91	2.84
21	5.83	4.42	3.82	3.48	3.25	3.09	2.97	2.87	2.80
22	5.79	4.38	3.78	3.44	3.22	3.05	2.93	2.84	2.76
23	5.75	4.35	3.75	3.41	3.18	3.02	2.90	2.81	2.73
24	5.72	4.32	3.72	3.38	3.15	2.99	2.87	2.78	2.70
25	5.69	4.29	3.69	3.35	3.13	2.97	2.85	2.75	2.68
26	5.66	4.27	3.67	3.33	3.10	2.94	2.82	2.73	2.65
27	5.63	4.24	3.65	3.31	3.08	2.92	2.80	2.71	2.63
28	5.61	4.22	3.63	3.29	3.06	2.90	2.78	2.69	2.61
29	5.59	4.20	3.61	3.27	3.04	2.88	2.76	2.67	2.59
30	5.57	4.18	3.59	3.25	3.03	2.87	2.75	2.65	2.57
40	5.42	4.05	3.46	3.13	2.90	2.74	2.62	2.53	2.45
60	5.29	3.93	3.34	3.01	2.79	2.63	2.51	2.41	2.33
120	5.15	3.80	3.23	2.89	2.67	2.52	2.39	2.30	2.22
∞	5.02	3.69	3.12	2.79	2.57	2.41	2.29	2.19	2.11

DENOMINATOR DEGREES OF FREEDOM

$$\alpha = .025$$

ν_1 ν_2	NUMERATOR DEGREES OF FREEDOM									
	10	12	15	20	24	30	40	60	120	∞
1	968.6	976.7	984.9	993.1	997.2	1001	1006	1010	1014	1018
2	39.40	39.41	39.43	39.45	39.46	39.46	39.47	39.48	39.49	39.50
3	14.42	14.34	14.25	14.17	14.12	14.08	14.04	13.99	13.95	13.90
4	8.84	8.75	8.66	8.56	8.51	8.46	8.41	8.36	8.31	8.26
5	6.62	6.52	6.43	6.33	6.28	6.23	6.18	6.12	6.07	6.02
6	5.46	5.37	5.27	5.17	5.12	5.07	5.01	4.96	4.90	4.85
7	4.76	4.67	4.57	4.47	4.42	4.36	4.31	4.25	4.20	4.14
8	4.30	4.20	4.10	4.00	3.95	3.89	3.84	3.78	3.73	3.67
9	3.96	3.87	3.77	3.67	3.61	3.56	3.51	3.45	3.39	3.33
10	3.72	3.62	3.52	3.42	3.37	3.31	3.26	3.20	3.14	3.08
11	3.53	3.43	3.33	3.23	3.17	3.12	3.06	3.00	2.94	2.88
12	3.37	3.28	3.18	3.07	3.02	2.96	2.91	2.85	2.79	2.72
13	3.25	3.15	3.05	2.95	2.89	2.84	2.78	2.72	2.66	2.60
14	3.15	3.05	2.95	2.84	2.79	2.73	2.67	2.61	2.55	2.49
15	3.06	2.96	2.86	2.76	2.70	2.64	2.59	2.52	2.46	2.40
16	2.99	2.89	2.79	2.68	2.63	2.57	2.51	2.45	2.38	2.32
17	2.92	2.82	2.72	2.62	2.56	2.50	2.44	2.38	2.32	2.25
18	2.87	2.77	2.67	2.56	2.50	2.44	2.38	2.32	2.26	2.19
19	2.82	2.72	2.62	2.51	2.45	2.39	2.33	2.27	2.20	2.13
20	2.77	2.68	2.57	2.46	2.41	2.35	2.29	2.22	2.16	2.09
21	2.73	2.64	2.53	2.42	2.37	2.31	2.25	2.18	2.11	2.04
22	2.70	2.60	2.50	2.39	2.33	2.27	2.21	2.14	2.08	2.00
23	2.67	2.57	2.47	2.36	2.30	2.24	2.18	2.11	2.04	1.97
24	2.64	2.54	2.44	2.33	2.27	2.21	2.15	2.08	2.01	1.94
25	2.61	2.51	2.41	2.30	2.24	2.18	2.12	2.05	1.98	1.91
26	2.59	2.49	2.39	2.28	2.22	2.16	2.09	2.03	1.95	1.88
27	2.57	2.47	2.36	2.25	2.19	2.13	2.07	2.00	1.93	1.85
28	2.55	2.45	2.34	2.23	2.17	2.11	2.05	1.98	1.91	1.83
29	2.53	2.43	2.32	2.21	2.15	2.09	2.03	1.96	1.89	1.81
30	2.51	2.41	2.31	2.20	2.14	2.07	2.01	1.94	1.87	1.79
40	2.39	2.29	2.18	2.07	2.01	1.94	1.88	1.80	1.72	1.64
60	2.27	2.17	2.06	1.94	1.88	1.82	1.74	1.67	1.58	1.48
120	2.16	2.05	1.94	1.82	1.76	1.69	1.61	1.53	1.43	1.31
∞	2.05	1.94	1.83	1.71	1.64	1.57	1.48	1.39	1.27	1.00

DENOMINATOR DEGREES OF FREEDOM

Table V   Continued

$$\alpha = .01$$

ν_1 ν_2	NUMERATOR DEGREES OF FREEDOM								
	1	2	3	4	5	6	7	8	9
1	4,052	4,999.5	5,403	5,625	5,764	5,859	5,928	5,982	6,022
2	98.50	99.00	99.17	99.25	99.30	99.33	99.36	99.37	99.39
3	34.12	30.82	29.46	28.71	28.24	27.91	27.67	27.49	27.35
4	21.20	18.00	16.69	15.98	15.52	15.21	14.98	14.80	14.66
5	16.26	13.27	12.06	11.39	10.97	10.67	10.46	10.29	10.16
6	13.75	10.92	9.78	9.15	8.75	8.47	8.26	8.10	7.98
7	12.25	9.55	8.45	7.85	7.46	7.19	6.99	6.84	6.72
8	11.26	8.65	7.59	7.01	6.63	6.37	6.18	6.03	5.91
9	10.56	8.02	6.99	6.42	6.06	5.80	5.61	5.47	5.35
10	10.04	7.56	6.55	5.99	5.64	5.39	5.20	5.06	4.94
11	9.65	7.21	6.22	5.67	5.32	5.07	4.89	4.74	4.63
12	9.33	6.93	5.95	5.41	5.06	4.82	4.64	4.50	4.39
13	9.07	6.70	5.74	5.21	4.86	4.62	4.44	4.30	4.19
14	8.86	6.51	5.56	5.04	4.69	4.46	4.28	4.14	4.03
15	8.68	6.36	5.42	4.89	4.56	4.32	4.14	4.00	3.89
16	8.53	6.23	5.29	4.77	4.44	4.20	4.03	3.89	3.78
17	8.40	6.11	5.18	4.67	4.34	4.10	3.93	3.79	3.68
18	8.29	6.01	5.09	4.58	4.25	4.01	3.84	3.71	3.60
19	8.18	5.93	5.01	4.50	4.17	3.94	3.77	3.63	3.52
20	8.10	5.85	4.94	4.43	4.10	3.87	3.70	3.56	3.46
21	8.02	5.78	4.87	4.37	4.04	3.81	3.64	3.51	3.40
22	7.95	5.72	4.82	4.31	3.99	3.76	3.59	3.45	3.35
23	7.88	5.66	4.76	4.26	3.94	3.71	3.54	3.41	3.30
24	7.82	5.61	4.72	4.22	3.90	3.67	3.50	3.36	3.26
25	7.77	5.57	4.68	4.18	3.85	3.63	3.46	3.32	3.22
26	7.72	5.53	4.64	4.14	3.82	3.59	3.42	3.29	3.18
27	7.68	5.49	4.60	4.11	3.78	3.56	3.39	3.26	3.15
28	7.64	5.45	4.57	4.07	3.75	3.53	3.36	3.23	3.12
29	7.60	5.42	4.54	4.04	3.73	3.50	3.33	3.20	3.09
30	7.56	5.39	4.51	4.02	3.70	3.47	3.30	3.17	3.07
40	7.31	5.18	4.31	3.83	3.51	3.29	3.12	2.99	2.89
60	7.08	4.98	4.13	3.65	3.34	3.12	2.95	2.82	2.72
120	6.85	4.79	3.95	3.48	3.17	2.96	2.79	2.66	2.56
∞	6.63	4.61	3.78	3.32	3.02	2.80	2.64	2.51	2.41

DENOMINATOR DEGREES OF FREEDOM

$$\alpha = .01$$

ν_2	NUMERATOR DEGREES OF FREEDOM									
ν_1	10	12	15	20	24	30	40	60	120	∞
1	6,056	6,106	6,157	6,209	6,235	6,261	6,287	6,313	6,339	6,366
2	99.40	99.42	99.43	99.45	99.46	99.47	99.47	99.48	99.49	99.50
3	27.23	27.05	26.87	26.69	26.60	26.50	26.41	26.32	26.22	26.13
4	14.55	14.37	14.20	14.02	13.93	13.84	13.75	13.65	13.56	13.46
5	10.05	9.89	9.72	9.55	9.47	9.38	9.29	9.20	9.11	9.02
6	7.87	7.72	7.56	7.40	7.31	7.23	7.14	7.06	6.97	6.88
7	6.62	6.47	6.31	6.16	6.07	5.99	5.91	5.82	5.74	5.65
8	5.81	5.67	5.52	5.36	5.28	5.20	5.12	5.03	4.95	4.86
9	5.26	5.11	4.96	4.81	4.73	4.65	4.57	4.48	4.40	4.31
10	4.85	4.71	4.56	4.41	4.33	4.25	4.17	4.08	4.00	3.91
11	4.54	4.40	4.25	4.10	4.02	3.94	3.86	3.78	3.69	3.60
12	4.30	4.16	4.01	3.86	3.78	3.70	3.62	3.54	3.45	3.36
13	4.10	3.96	3.82	3.66	3.59	3.51	3.43	3.34	3.25	3.17
14	3.94	3.80	3.66	3.51	3.43	3.35	3.27	3.18	3.09	3.00
15	3.80	3.67	3.52	3.37	3.29	3.21	3.13	3.05	2.96	2.87
16	3.69	3.55	3.41	3.26	3.18	3.10	3.02	2.93	2.84	2.75
17	3.59	3.46	3.31	3.16	3.08	3.00	2.92	2.83	2.75	2.65
18	3.51	3.37	3.23	3.08	3.00	2.92	2.84	2.75	2.66	2.57
19	3.43	3.30	3.15	3.00	2.92	2.84	2.76	2.67	2.58	2.49
20	3.37	3.23	3.09	2.94	2.86	2.78	2.69	2.61	2.52	2.42
21	3.31	3.17	3.03	2.88	2.80	2.72	2.64	2.55	2.46	2.36
22	3.26	3.12	2.98	2.83	2.75	2.67	2.58	2.50	2.40	2.31
23	3.21	3.07	2.93	2.78	2.70	2.62	2.54	2.45	2.35	2.26
24	3.17	3.03	2.89	2.74	2.66	2.58	2.49	2.40	2.31	2.21
25	3.13	2.99	2.85	2.70	2.62	2.54	2.45	2.36	2.27	2.17
26	3.09	2.96	2.81	2.66	2.58	2.50	2.42	2.33	2.23	2.13
27	3.06	2.93	2.78	2.63	2.55	2.47	2.38	2.29	2.20	2.10
28	3.03	2.90	2.75	2.60	2.52	2.44	2.35	2.26	2.17	2.06
29	3.00	2.87	2.73	2.57	2.49	2.41	2.33	2.23	2.14	2.03
30	2.98	2.84	2.70	2.55	2.47	2.39	2.30	2.21	2.11	2.01
40	2.80	2.66	2.52	2.37	2.29	2.20	2.11	2.02	1.92	1.80
60	2.63	2.50	2.35	2.20	2.12	2.03	1.94	1.84	1.73	1.60
120	2.47	2.34	2.19	2.03	1.95	1.86	1.76	1.66	1.53	1.38
∞	2.32	2.18	2.04	1.88	1.79	1.70	1.59	1.47	1.32	1.00

DENOMINATOR DEGREES OF FREEDOM

Table VI Cumulative Probabilities for the Poisson Distribution
This table gives probabilities of being less than or equal to specified values of k for Poisson distributions with given values of λ.

					λ					
k	.1	.2	.3	.4	.5	.6	.7	.8	.9	1.0
0	.9048	.8187	.7408	.6703	.6065	.5488	.4966	.4493	.4066	.3679
1	.9953	.9825	.9631	.9384	.9098	.8781	.8442	.8088	.7725	.7358
2	.9998	.9989	.9964	.9921	.9856	.9769	.9659	.9526	.9371	.9197
3	1.0000	.9999	.9997	.9992	.9982	.9966	.9942	.9909	.9865	.9810
4	1.0000	1.0000	1.0000	.9999	.9998	.9996	.9992	.9986	.9977	.9963
5	1.0000	1.0000	1.0000	1.0000	1.0000	1.0000	.9999	.9998	.9997	.9994
6	1.0000	1.0000	1.0000	1.0000	1.0000	1.0000	1.0000	1.0000	1.0000	.9999
7	1.0000	1.0000	1.0000	1.0000	1.0000	1.0000	1.0000	1.0000	1.0000	1.0000

					λ					
k	1.1	1.2	1.3	1.4	1.5	1.6	1.7	1.8	1.9	2.0
0	.3329	.3012	.2725	.2466	.2231	.2019	.1827	.1653	.1496	.1353
1	.6990	.6626	.6268	.5918	.5578	.5249	.4932	.4628	.4338	.4060
2	.9004	.8795	.8571	.8335	.8088	.7834	.7572	.7306	.7037	.6767
3	.9743	.9662	.9569	.9463	.9344	.9212	.9068	.8913	.8747	.8571
4	.9946	.9923	.9893	.9857	.9814	.9763	.9704	.9636	.9559	.9473
5	.9990	.9985	.9978	.9968	.9955	.9940	.9920	.9896	.9868	.9834
6	.9999	.9997	.9996	.9994	.9991	.9987	.9981	.9974	.9966	.9955
7	1.0000	1.0000	.9999	.9999	.9998	.9997	.9996	.9994	.9992	.9989
8	1.0000	1.0000	1.0000	1.0000	1.0000	1.0000	.9999	.9999	.9998	.9998
9	1.0000	1.0000	1.0000	1.0000	1.0000	1.0000	1.0000	1.0000	1.0000	1.0000

					λ					
k	2.1	2.2	2.3	2.4	2.5	2.6	2.7	2.8	2.9	3.0
0	.1225	.1108	.1003	.0907	.0821	.0743	.0672	.0608	.0550	.0498
1	.3796	.3546	.3309	.3084	.2873	.2674	.2487	.2311	.2146	.1991
2	.6496	.6227	.5960	.5697	.5438	.5184	.4936	.4695	.4460	.4232
3	.8386	.8194	.7993	.7787	.7576	.7360	.7141	.6919	.6696	.6472
4	.9379	.9275	.9162	.9041	.8912	.8774	.8629	.8477	.8318	.8153
5	.9796	.9751	.9700	.9643	.9580	.9510	.9433	.9349	.9258	.9161
6	.9941	.9925	.9906	.9884	.9858	.9828	.9794	.9756	.9713	.9665
7	.9985	.9980	.9974	.9967	.9958	.9947	.9934	.9919	.9901	.9881
8	.9997	.9995	.9994	.9991	.9989	.9985	.9981	.9976	.9969	.9962
9	.9999	.9999	.9999	.9998	.9997	.9996	.9995	.9993	.9991	.9989
10	1.0000	1.0000	1.0000	1.0000	.9999	.9999	.9999	.9998	.9998	.9997
11	1.0000	1.0000	1.0000	1.0000	1.0000	1.0000	1.0000	1.0000	.9999	.9999
12	1.0000	1.0000	1.0000	1.0000	1.0000	1.0000	1.0000	1.0000	1.0000	1.0000

Example: The probability of a Poisson random variable with mean 3.4 being less than or equal to 2 is .3397.

k	λ									
	3.1	3.2	3.3	3.4	3.5	3.6	3.7	3.8	3.9	4.0
0	.0450	.0408	.0369	.0334	.0302	.0273	.0247	.0224	.0202	.0183
1	.1847	.1712	.1586	.1468	.1359	.1257	.1162	.1074	.0992	.0916
2	.4012	.3799	.3594	.3397	.3208	.3027	.2854	.2689	.2531	.2381
3	.6248	.6025	.5803	.5584	.5366	.5152	.4942	.4735	.4533	.4335
4	.7982	.7806	.7626	.7442	.7254	.7064	.6872	.6678	.6484	.6288
5	.9057	.8946	.8829	.8705	.8576	.8441	.8301	.8156	.8006	.7851
6	.9612	.9554	.9490	.9421	.9347	.9267	.9182	.9091	.8995	.8893
7	.9858	.9832	.9802	.9769	.9733	.9692	.9648	.9599	.9546	.9489
8	.9953	.9943	.9931	.9917	.9901	.9883	.9863	.9840	.9815	.9786
9	.9986	.9982	.9978	.9973	.9967	.9960	.9952	.9942	.9931	.9919
10	.9996	.9995	.9994	.9992	.9990	.9987	.9984	.9981	.9977	.9972
11	.9999	.9999	.9998	.9998	.9997	.9996	.9995	.9994	.9993	.9991
12	1.0000	1.0000	1.0000	.9999	.9999	.9999	.9999	.9998	.9998	.9997
13	1.0000	1.0000	1.0000	1.0000	1.0000	1.0000	1.0000	1.0000	.9999	.9999
14	1.0000	1.0000	1.0000	1.0000	1.0000	1.0000	1.0000	1.0000	1.0000	1.0000

k	λ									
	4.1	4.2	4.3	4.4	4.5	4.6	4.7	4.8	4.9	5.0
0	.0166	.0150	.0136	.0123	.0111	.0101	.0091	.0082	.0074	.0067
1	.0845	.0780	.0719	.0663	.0611	.0563	.0518	.0477	.0439	.0404
2	.2238	.2102	.1974	.1851	.1736	.1626	.1523	.1425	.1333	.1247
3	.4142	.3954	.3772	.3595	.3423	.3257	.3097	.2942	.2793	.2650
4	.6093	.5898	.5704	.5512	.5321	.5132	.4946	.4763	.4582	.4405
5	.7693	.7531	.7367	.7199	.7029	.6858	.6684	.6510	.6335	.6160
6	.8786	.8675	.8558	.8436	.8311	.8180	.8046	.7908	.7767	.7622
7	.9427	.9361	.9290	.9214	.9134	.9049	.8960	.8867	.8769	.8666
8	.9755	.9721	.9683	.9642	.9597	.9549	.9497	.9442	.9382	.9319
9	.9905	.9889	.9871	.9851	.9829	.9805	.9778	.9749	.9717	.9682
10	.9966	.9959	.9952	.9943	.9933	.9922	.9910	.9896	.9880	.9863
11	.9989	.9986	.9983	.9980	.9976	.9971	.9966	.9960	.9953	.9945
12	.9997	.9996	.9995	.9993	.9992	.9990	.9988	.9986	.9983	.9980
13	.9999	.9999	.9998	.9998	.9997	.9997	.9996	.9995	.9994	.9993
14	1.0000	1.0000	1.0000	.9999	.9999	.9999	.9999	.9999	.9998	.9998
15	1.0000	1.0000	1.0000	1.0000	1.0000	1.0000	1.0000	1.0000	.9999	.9999
16	1.0000	1.0000	1.0000	1.0000	1.0000	1.0000	1.0000	1.0000	1.0000	1.0000

Table VI Continued

					λ					
k	5.1	5.2	5.3	5.4	5.5	5.6	5.7	5.8	5.9	6.0
0	.0061	.0055	.0050	.0045	.0041	.0037	.0033	.0030	.0027	.0025
1	.0372	.0342	.0314	.0289	.0266	.0244	.0224	.0206	.0189	.0174
2	.1165	.1088	.1016	.0948	.0884	.0824	.0768	.0715	.0666	.0620
3	.2513	.2381	.2254	.2133	.2017	.1906	.1801	.1700	.1604	.1512
4	.4231	.4061	.3895	.3733	.3575	.3422	.3272	.3127	.2987	.2851
5	.5984	.5809	.5635	.5461	.5289	.5119	.4950	.4783	.4619	.4457
6	.7474	.7324	.7171	.7017	.6860	.6703	.6544	.6384	.6224	.6063
7	.8560	.8449	.8335	.8217	.8095	.7970	.7842	.7710	.7576	.7440
8	.9252	.9181	.9106	.9026	.8944	.8857	.8766	.8672	.8574	.8472
9	.9644	.9603	.9559	.9512	.9462	.9409	.9352	.9292	.9228	.9161
10	.9844	.9823	.9800	.9775	.9747	.9718	.9686	.9651	.9614	.9574
11	.9937	.9927	.9916	.9904	.9890	.9875	.9859	.9840	.9821	.9799
12	.9976	.9972	.9967	.9962	.9955	.9949	.9941	.9932	.9922	.9912
13	.9992	.9990	.9988	.9986	.9983	.9980	.9977	.9973	.9969	.9964
14	.9997	.9997	.9996	.9995	.9994	.9993	.9991	.9990	.9988	.9986
15	.9999	.9999	.9999	.9998	.9998	.9998	.9997	.9996	.9996	.9995
16	1.0000	1.0000	1.0000	.9999	.9999	.9999	.9999	.9999	.9999	.9998
17	1.0000	1.0000	1.0000	1.0000	1.0000	1.0000	1.0000	1.0000	1.0000	.9999
18	1.0000	1.0000	1.0000	1.0000	1.0000	1.0000	1.0000	1.0000	1.0000	1.0000

					λ					
k	6.1	6.2	6.3	6.4	6.5	6.6	6.7	6.8	6.9	7.0
0	.0022	.0020	.0018	.0017	.0015	.0014	.0012	.0011	.0010	.0009
1	.0159	.0146	.0134	.0123	.0113	.0103	.0095	.0087	.0080	.0073
2	.0577	.0536	.0498	.0463	.0430	.0400	.0371	.0344	.0320	.0296
3	.1425	.1342	.1264	.1189	.1119	.1052	.0988	.0928	.0871	.0818
4	.2719	.2592	.2469	.2351	.2237	.2127	.2022	.1920	.1823	.1730
5	.4298	.4141	.3988	.3837	.3690	.3547	.3407	.3270	.3137	.3007
6	.5902	.5742	.5582	.5423	.5265	.5108	.4953	.4799	.4647	.4497
7	.7301	.7160	.7018	.6873	.6728	.6581	.6433	.6285	.6136	.5987
8	.8367	.8259	.8148	.8033	.7916	.7796	.7673	.7548	.7420	.7291
9	.9090	.9016	.8939	.8858	.8774	.8686	.8596	.8502	.8405	.8305
10	.9531	.9486	.9437	.9386	.9332	.9274	.9214	.9151	.9084	.9015
11	.9776	.9750	.9723	.9693	.9661	.9627	.9591	.9552	.9510	.9466
12	.9900	.9887	.9873	.9857	.9840	.9821	.9801	.9779	.9755	.9730
13	.9958	.9952	.9945	.9937	.9929	.9920	.9909	.9898	.9885	.9872
14	.9984	.9981	.9978	.9974	.9970	.9966	.9961	.9956	.9950	.9943
15	.9994	.9993	.9992	.9990	.9988	.9986	.9984	.9982	.9979	.9976
16	.9998	.9997	.9997	.9996	.9996	.9995	.9994	.9993	.9992	.9990
17	.9999	.9999	.9999	.9999	.9998	.9998	.9998	.9997	.9997	.9996
18	1.0000	1.0000	1.0000	1.0000	.9999	.9999	.9999	.9999	.9999	.9999
19	1.0000	1.0000	1.0000	1.0000	1.0000	1.0000	1.0000	1.0000	1.0000	.9999
20	1.0000	1.0000	1.0000	1.0000	1.0000	1.0000	1.0000	1.0000	1.0000	1.0000

k	\u03bb									
	7.1	7.2	7.3	7.4	7.5	7.6	7.7	7.8	7.9	8.0
0	.0008	.0007	.0007	.0006	.0006	.0005	.0005	.0004	.0004	.0003
1	.0067	.0061	.0056	.0051	.0047	.0043	.0039	.0036	.0033	.0030
2	.0275	.0255	.0236	.0219	.0203	.0188	.0174	.0161	.0149	.0138
3	.0767	.0719	.0674	.0632	.0591	.0554	.0518	.0485	.0453	.0424
4	.1641	.1555	.1473	.1395	.1321	.1249	.1181	.1117	.1055	.0996
5	.2881	.2759	.2640	.2526	.2414	.2307	.2203	.2103	.2006	.1912
6	.4349	.4204	.4060	.3920	.3782	.3646	.3514	.3384	.3257	.3134
7	.5838	.5689	.5541	.5393	.5246	.5100	.4956	.4812	.4670	.4530
8	.7160	.7027	.6892	.6757	.6620	.6482	.6343	.6204	.6065	.5926
9	.8202	.8096	.7988	.7877	.7764	.7649	.7531	.7411	.7290	.7166
10	.8942	.8867	.8788	.8707	.8622	.8535	.8445	.8352	.8257	.8159
11	.9420	.9371	.9319	.9265	.9208	.9148	.9085	.9020	.8952	.8881
12	.9703	.9673	.9642	.9609	.9573	.9536	.9496	.9453	.9409	.9362
13	.9857	.9841	.9824	.9805	.9784	.9762	.9739	.9714	.9687	.9658
14	.9935	.9927	.9918	.9908	.9897	.9886	.9873	.9859	.9844	.9827
15	.9972	.9968	.9964	.9959	.9954	.9948	.9941	.9934	.9926	.9918
16	.9989	.9987	.9985	.9983	.9980	.9978	.9974	.9971	.9967	.9963
17	.9996	.9995	.9994	.9993	.9992	.9991	.9989	.9988	.9986	.9984
18	.9998	.9998	.9998	.9997	.9997	.9996	.9996	.9995	.9994	.9993
19	.9999	.9999	.9999	.9999	.9999	.9999	.9998	.9998	.9998	.9997
20	1.0000	1.0000	1.0000	1.0000	1.0000	.9999	.9999	.9999	.9999	.9999
21	1.0000	1.0000	1.0000	1.0000	1.0000	1.0000	1.0000	1.0000	1.0000	1.0000

Table VI   Continued

					λ					
k	8.1	8.2	8.3	8.4	8.5	8.6	8.7	8.8	8.9	9.0
0	.0003	.0003	.0002	.0002	.0002	.0002	.0002	.0002	.0001	.0001
1	.0028	.0025	.0023	.0021	.0019	.0018	.0016	.0015	.0014	.0012
2	.0127	.0118	.0109	.0100	.0093	.0086	.0079	.0073	.0068	.0062
3	.0396	.0370	.0346	.0323	.0301	.0281	.0262	.0244	.0228	.0212
4	.0941	.0887	.0837	.0789	.0744	.0701	.0660	.0621	.0584	.0550
5	.1822	.1736	.1653	.1573	.1496	.1422	.1352	.1284	.1219	.1157
6	.3013	.2896	.2781	.2670	.2562	.2457	.2355	.2256	.2160	.2068
7	.4391	.4254	.4119	.3987	.3856	.3728	.3602	.3478	.3357	.3239
8	.5786	.5647	.5508	.5369	.5231	.5094	.4958	.4823	.4689	.4557
9	.7041	.6915	.6788	.6659	.6530	.6400	.6269	.6137	.6006	.5874
10	.8058	.7955	.7850	.7743	.7634	.7522	.7409	.7294	.7178	.7060
11	.8807	.8731	.8652	.8571	.8487	.8400	.8311	.8220	.8126	.8030
12	.9313	.9261	.9207	.9150	.9091	.9029	.8965	.8898	.8829	.8758
13	.9628	.9595	.9561	.9524	.9486	.9445	.9403	.9358	.9311	.9262
14	.9810	.9791	.9771	.9749	.9726	.9701	.9675	.9647	.9617	.9585
15	.9908	.9898	.9887	.9875	.9862	.9847	.9832	.9816	.9798	.9780
16	.9958	.9953	.9947	.9941	.9934	.9926	.9918	.9909	.9899	.9889
17	.9982	.9979	.9976	.9973	.9970	.9966	.9962	.9957	.9952	.9947
18	.9992	.9991	.9990	.9989	.9987	.9985	.9983	.9981	.9978	.9976
19	.9997	.9996	.9996	.9995	.9995	.9994	.9993	.9992	.9991	.9989
20	.9999	.9999	.9998	.9998	.9998	.9997	.9997	.9997	.9996	.9996
21	1.0000	.9999	.9999	.9999	.9999	.9999	.9999	.9999	.9998	.9998
22	1.0000	1.0000	1.0000	1.0000	1.0000	1.0000	1.0000	.9999	.9999	.9999
23	1.0000	1.0000	1.0000	1.0000	1.0000	1.0000	1.0000	1.0000	1.0000	1.0000

k	9.1	9.2	9.3	9.4	9.5	9.6	9.7	9.8	9.9	10.0
0	.0001	.0001	.0001	.0001	.0001	.0001	.0001	.0001	.0001	.0000
1	.0011	.0010	.0009	.0009	.0008	.0007	.0007	.0006	.0005	.0005
2	.0058	.0053	.0049	.0045	.0042	.0038	.0035	.0033	.0030	.0028
3	.0198	.0184	.0172	.0160	.0149	.0138	.0129	.0120	.0111	.0103
4	.0517	.0486	.0456	.0429	.0403	.0378	.0355	.0333	.0312	.0293
5	.1098	.1041	.0987	.0935	.0885	.0838	.0793	.0750	.0710	.0671
6	.1978	.1892	.1808	.1727	.1650	.1575	.1502	.1433	.1366	.1301
7	.3123	.3010	.2900	.2792	.2687	.2584	.2485	.2388	.2294	.2202
8	.4426	.4296	.4168	.4042	.3918	.3796	.3676	.3558	.3442	.3328
9	.5742	.5611	.5479	.5349	.5218	.5089	.4960	.4832	.4705	.4579
10	.6941	.6820	.6699	.6576	.6453	.6330	.6205	.6080	.5955	.5830
11	.7932	.7832	.7730	.7626	.7520	.7412	.7303	.7193	.7081	.6968
12	.8684	.8607	.8529	.8448	.8364	.8279	.8191	.8101	.8009	.7916
13	.9210	.9156	.9100	.9042	.8981	.8919	.8853	.8786	.8716	.8645
14	.9552	.9517	.9480	.9441	.9400	.9357	.9312	.9265	.9216	.9165
15	.9760	.9738	.9715	.9691	.9665	.9638	.9609	.9579	.9546	.9513
16	.9878	.9865	.9852	.9838	.9823	.9806	.9789	.9770	.9751	.9730
17	.9941	.9934	.9927	.9919	.9911	.9902	.9892	.9881	.9869	.9857
18	.9973	.9969	.9966	.9962	.9957	.9952	.9947	.9941	.9935	.9928
19	.9988	.9986	.9985	.9983	.9980	.9978	.9975	.9972	.9969	.9965
20	.9995	.9994	.9993	.9992	.9991	.9990	.9989	.9987	.9986	.9984
21	.9998	.9998	.9997	.9997	.9996	.9996	.9995	.9995	.9994	.9993
22	.9999	.9999	.9999	.9999	.9998	.9998	.9998	.9998	.9997	.9997
23	1.0000	1.0000	1.0000	.9999	.9999	.9999	.9999	.9999	.9999	.9999
24	1.0000	1.0000	1.0000	1.0000	1.0000	1.0000	1.0000	1.0000	.9999	.9999
25	1.0000	1.0000	1.0000	1.0000	1.0000	1.0000	1.0000	1.0000	1.0000	1.0000

(Column header group: λ)

Table VI Continued

k	λ									
	11.0	12.0	13.0	14.0	15.0	16.0	17.0	18.0	19.0	20.0
0	.0000	.0000	.0000	.0000	.0000	.0000	.0000	.0000	.0000	.0000
1	.0002	.0001	.0000	.0000	.0000	.0000	.0000	.0000	.0000	.0000
2	.0012	.0005	.0002	.0001	.0000	.0000	.0000	.0000	.0000	.0000
3	.0049	.0023	.0011	.0005	.0002	.0001	.0000	.0000	.0000	.0000
4	.0151	.0076	.0037	.0018	.0009	.0004	.0002	.0001	.0000	.0000
5	.0375	.0203	.0107	.0055	.0028	.0014	.0007	.0003	.0002	.0001
6	.0786	.0458	.0259	.0142	.0076	.0040	.0021	.0010	.0005	.0003
7	.1432	.0895	.0540	.0316	.0180	.0100	.0054	.0029	.0015	.0008
8	.2320	.1550	.0998	.0621	.0374	.0220	.0126	.0071	.0039	.0021
9	.3405	.2424	.1658	.1094	.0699	.0433	.0261	.0154	.0089	.0050
10	.4599	.3472	.2517	.1757	.1185	.0774	.0491	.0304	.0183	.0108
11	.5793	.4616	.3532	.2600	.1847	.1270	.0847	.0549	.0347	.0214
12	.6887	.5760	.4631	.3585	.2676	.1931	.1350	.0917	.0606	.0390
13	.7813	.6815	.5730	.4644	.3632	.2745	.2009	.1426	.0984	.0661
14	.8540	.7720	.6751	.5704	.4656	.3675	.2808	.2081	.1497	.1049
15	.9074	.8444	.7636	.6694	.5681	.4667	.3714	.2866	.2148	.1565
16	.9441	.8987	.8355	.7559	.6641	.5660	.4677	.3750	.2920	.2211
17	.9678	.9370	.8905	.8272	.7489	.6593	.5640	.4686	.3784	.2970
18	.9823	.9626	.9302	.8826	.8195	.7423	.6549	.5622	.4695	.3814
19	.9907	.9787	.9573	.9235	.8752	.8122	.7363	.6509	.5606	.4703
20	.9953	.9884	.9750	.9521	.9170	.8682	.8055	.7307	.6472	.5591
21	.9977	.9939	.9859	.9711	.9469	.9108	.8615	.7991	.7255	.6437
22	.9989	.9969	.9924	.9833	.9672	.9418	.9047	.8551	.7931	.7206
23	.9995	.9985	.9960	.9907	.9805	.9633	.9367	.8989	.8490	.7875
24	.9998	.9993	.9980	.9950	.9888	.9777	.9593	.9317	.8933	.8432
25	.9999	.9997	.9990	.9974	.9938	.9869	.9747	.9554	.9269	.8878
26	1.0000	.9999	.9995	.9987	.9967	.9925	.9848	.9718	.9514	.9221
27	1.0000	.9999	.9998	.9994	.9983	.9959	.9912	.9827	.9687	.9475
28	1.0000	1.0000	.9999	.9997	.9991	.9978	.9950	.9897	.9805	.9657
29	1.0000	1.0000	1.0000	.9999	.9996	.9989	.9973	.9940	.9881	.9782
30	1.0000	1.0000	1.0000	.9999	.9998	.9994	.9985	.9967	.9930	.9865
31	1.0000	1.0000	1.0000	1.0000	.9999	.9997	.9992	.9982	.9960	.9919
32	1.0000	1.0000	1.0000	1.0000	.9999	.9999	.9996	.9990	.9978	.9953
33	1.0000	1.0000	1.0000	1.0000	1.0000	.9999	.9998	.9995	.9988	.9973
34	1.0000	1.0000	1.0000	1.0000	1.0000	1.0000	.9999	.9997	.9994	.9985
35	1.0000	1.0000	1.0000	1.0000	1.0000	1.0000	.9999	.9999	.9997	.9992
36	1.0000	1.0000	1.0000	1.0000	1.0000	1.0000	1.0000	.9999	.9998	.9996
37	1.0000	1.0000	1.0000	1.0000	1.0000	1.0000	1.0000	1.0000	.9999	.9998
38	1.0000	1.0000	1.0000	1.0000	1.0000	1.0000	1.0000	1.0000	1.0000	.9999
39	1.0000	1.0000	1.0000	1.0000	1.0000	1.0000	1.0000	1.0000	1.0000	.9999
40	1.0000	1.0000	1.0000	1.0000	1.0000	1.0000	1.0000	1.0000	1.0000	1.0000

Manual for Statistics Software Package

Contents

Sample Problems

C.1

Introduction

In statistics there are concepts and there are calculations. The main purpose of this text is to explain the concepts and to illustrate the calculations by means of numerical examples, usually examples with small data sets. But as we have indicated throughout the text, most statistics users take advantage of computers to perform many of the necessary calculations, particularly in the typical business situations where large data sets are involved. Most frequently, powerful all-purpose statistical packages such as SPSS, SAS, IDA, BMD, and MINITAB are used on large mainframe computers or on somewhat smaller minicomputers. The advantages of these packages are that (1) they are extremely versatile—that is, they can perform a wide variety of statistical techniques; (2) they use the ability of large computers to perform numerous calculations very quickly; (3) they have the ability to retrieve data sets entered previously and save output for later use; and (4) they are widely accepted by a large audience.

However, there are drawbacks to these large statistical packages. Perhaps the two greatest drawbacks are that (1) they require access to a mainframe computer or minicomputer (although some are making inroads into the microcomputer area); (2) more importantly, they take time to learn. Typically the user must acquire a rather thick manual and wade through relevant parts of it before any statistical analysis is possible. To avoid both of these drawbacks, we have included a statistical computer package with this text that is suitable for IBM microcomputers or any of the many IBM-compatible microcomputers. (This appendix is geared to IBMs and IBM-compatibles. However, for users with Apple systems, a mini-manual and an accompanying diskette are also available from Macmillan Publishing Company.) The statistical programs in this package are not as powerful—they do not do as many things—as the packages mentioned above, but they are extremely easy to use, and they are very convenient for anyone with access to the appropriate microcomputers. In addition, they are capable of performing the majority of the statistical techniques discussed in this introductory text, which means they should be perfectly adequate for introductory statistics students.

The purpose of this appendix is to provide a brief explanation of the package. Included in this explanation are: (1) a description of the computer hardware and software needed; (2) a summary of the programs included in the package; (3) a short "how-do-do-it" manual; and (4) a few miscellaneous tips on using the computer. Beyond this, however, you will see that once you learn how to get the programs started, almost everything you need to know is explained on the screen as you work at the computer.

C.2

Hardware and Software Requirements

As stated above, this statistical package is written for IBM or IBM-compatible microcomputers. Therefore, users must have access to an IBM or an IBM-compatible system, including a keyboard, a screen, at least one disk drive, and (only if you desire written output) an accompanying printer. A variety of microcomputers (including Zeniths, Compaqs, and others) are, to various extents, compatible with the IBM microcomputer. If you are unsure whether your school's microcomputers are IBM-compatible, ask your computer consultant. Or better yet, try this package on them. The worst that can happen is that they won't work!

The above requirements are hardware requirements. There is also one software requirement. To get started, you will need the "Disk Operating System," or DOS, diskette that came with your computer. This DOS diskette has two purposes. First, it gets the computer started, somewhat like an ignition system starts a car. We say it "boots" the system. If you turned on your computer without first inserting the DOS diskette, nothing useful would happen. The second use of the DOS diskette is that it contains BASIC, the language in which these statistical programs are written. There are various versions of BASIC, all very similar, and the chances are that the version on your DOS diskette will work with this package. Again, if you have any questions about the version of BASIC on your DOS diskette, ask your computer consultant.

C.3

Summary of Programs

This package is a set of programs, written in the BASIC language, that allow you to perform the most important techniques discussed in the text. There is also a MENU program. The MENU program explains (on the screen) how to use the package, and it provides a "menu," or list, of the programs available. This makes it easy for you to choose which program you want to run. Although the MENU program provides a brief explanation of each program, we will also do this here for reference purposes. The 21 programs, in the order in which they are listed in the MENU program, are as follows. (*Note:* All of the remaining information in this section is summarized on the screen when the package is run, so if you would like to jump ahead to the how-to-do-it explanation in Section C.4, feel free to do so.)

SUMMARY   This program provides summary data, as in Chapter 2, for a single set of observations or a set of paired observations (X's and Y's). The outputs include means, variances, standard deviations, medians, mean absolute deviations, and observations shown in increasing order of magnitude. In case paired observations are entered, the covariance, correlation, and a scattergram are also provided. The only user inputs are the sample size and the observations.

WOREPLCE (short for "without replacement")   This program calculates probabilities for the experiment of sampling without replacement from a finite population of A's and B's. It uses the formula from Chapter 3 (or the hypergeometric formula in Chapter 5). It also has the option of approximating exact probabilities by means of computer simulation. Specifically, the user enters the population size, the number of A's in the population, the sample size, and any desired integer k. Then the program calculates the probability of k or fewer A's in the sample.

PROBDIST (short for "probability distribution")   This program calculates summary statistics for the probability distribution of a single discrete random variable or the joint (bivariate) distribution of two discrete random variables. The outputs include means, variances, and standard deviations. In the bivariate case, the marginal distributions and the covariance and correlation are also provided. The only user inputs are the probability descriptions—that is, the possible values and their probabilities.

BINOMIAL   This program calculates binomial probabilities. It is capable of reproducing any of the information in the binomial tables, plus it can "fill in the gaps"—that is, it can perform calculations for values of n and/or p that are not in the binomial tables. The user must supply the values of n and p. Then the program can calculate any binomial probability, or it can find the integer with a specified probability to the left of it.

POISSON   This program is similar to the BINOMIAL program, except that it works with Poisson probabilities. The only user input is the mean of the Poisson distribution.

NORMAL   This program is also similar to the BINOMIAL program, except that it works with normal probabilities. It is capable of performing any of the normal probability calculations that appear in the text. The only user inputs are the mean and standard deviation of the normal distribution. Then the program can calculate any normal probability for this mean and standard deviation, or it can find the value that has a specified probability to the left of it.

SIMULATE   This program simulates 1000 random samples from any inputted parent distribution, and it shows the resulting distribution of the 1000 sample means. This is similar to the demonstration of the "empirical" sampling distribution of the sample mean in Section 6.6. The only user input is the description of the parent distribution—that is, its possible values and their probabilities. Then the program lists the mean and standard deviation of the 1000 simulated sample means. It also lists how many of these fall into various categories, and it compares these frequencies with the theoretical frequencies that would result if the population were normal.

SAMPMEAN (short for "sample mean")   This program calculates a confidence interval for the population mean or the t-value for a hypothesis test on the population mean. This mean can be the mean of a single distribution if a single set of observations is entered, or it can be the mean of differences if a set of matched pairs is entered. The program can also calculate a confidence interval for the population variance or a chi-square value for a hypothesis test on the population variance. In the single-distribution case, the user can enter the set of observations or simply the observed sample mean and standard deviation of the set. Similarly, for the matched-pairs case, the user can enter the set of matched pairs or simply the observed sample mean and standard deviation of the set of differences.

DIFFRNCE (short for "difference")   This program calculates a confidence interval for the difference between two population means or the t-value for a hypothesis test on this difference. The outputs are given with and without the assumption of equal population variances. The program can also calculate a confidence interval for the ratio of the two population variances or the F-value for a hypothesis test on this ratio. For either sample, the user can enter the set of observations or simply the observed sample mean and standard deviation of the set.

PROPORTN (short for "proportion")   This program calculates a confidence interval for a population proportion or the difference between two population proportions. It can also calculate the z-value for a hypothesis test on a population proportion or the difference between two population proportions. The only user inputs are the sample size(s) and sample proportion(s).

ANOVA (short for "analysis of variance")   This program runs a test for equality of population means when there are two or more populations (i.e., treatment levels), as in Chapter 10. The outputs include the standard ANOVA table and simultaneous confidence intervals for all pairs of population mean differences. The only user inputs are the number of treatment levels, sample sizes, and observations.

TWOWAY   This program performs a one-way ANOVA with a blocking variable or a two-way ANOVA, as discussed in the latter sections of Chapter 10. For either design, the outputs include the ANOVA table for a test of equal means and, in the two-way case, a test of an interaction effect. The only user inputs are the numbers of treatment (or block) levels, sample sizes, and observations.

SREGRESS (short for "simple regression")   This program performs a regression analysis when there is a single independent variable. It provides all of the statistical outputs described in Chapter 11; in addition, it provides a couple useful scattergrams. The user must specify which of the two variables is the dependent variable and then enter the sample size and the observations on each variable. Besides being able to run the usual regression analysis, the user may also transform either of the variables (by a square, reciprocal, or logarithm transformation) and then run the regression analysis on the transformed observations.

MREGRESS (short for "multiple regression")   This program performs a multiple regression analysis where there are up to thirteen independent variables. It provides practically all of the statistical outputs described in Chapter 12, and also several useful scattergrams. The user must enter the sample size and the observations for the dependent variable and all potential independent variables. Then the program can be run several times, so that the user can choose which independent variables to include in the regression equation on each run.

CHISQR (short for "chi-square")   This program performs a chi-square goodness-of-fit test as in Section 13.2, or it performs a chi-square test for independence or a chi-square test for equality of proportions as in Sections 13.3 and 13.4. For the goodness-of-fit test, the user must enter the number of categories, the observed frequency in each category, and the expected proportion in each category (as specified by the null hypothesis). For the independence test or the test for equal proportions, the only user inputs are the number of row and column categories and the observed frequency in each cell.

NORMFIT (short for "normal fit")   This program uses the chi-square goodness-of-fit test in Chapter 13 to test whether a set of observations comes from a normal population. The program automatically forms a set of equal-probability categories, based on the sample mean and sample standard deviation, and then it calculates the chi-square test statistic from these categories. The only user inputs are the sample size and the observations.

MOVAVE (short for "moving averages")   This program calculates the centered moving averages for a time series of observations and uses the ratio-to-moving-average method in Chapter 14 to estimate the seasonal factors for this time series. The output includes a time series graph of the observations, with a superimposed graph of the centered moving averages. The only user inputs are the sample size, whether the data are monthly or quarterly, and the time series of observations.

EXSMOOTH (short for "exponential smoothing")   This program performs exponential smoothing on a time series of observations, and it provides forecasts of future observations, based on the smoothed series. The program can do simple exponential smoothing, or it can perform Winters' method if trend and/or seasonality in the time series are suspected. The output includes the smoothed series, the forecasts, and a time series graph of the observations, with a superimposed graph of the smoothed series. The user inputs include the sample size, the time series of observations, the smoothing constants, and "starting" values for the exponential smoothing procedure. The program can be run several times, each time using different smoothing constants or different starting values.

AUTOCORR (short for "autocorrelation")   This program calculates autocorrelations for a time series of observations, as described in Section 14.6. The user may specify the number of lags desired. The only user inputs are the sample size, the time series of observations, and the number of lags desired.

RNSAMPLE (short for "random sample")   This program selects a random sample from a finite population, as described in Section 16.3. The output consists of the "identification numbers" of the members sampled. The only user inputs are the population size and the sample size.

BLCKJACK (short for "blackjack")   This program is a bonus. It allows the user to play a realistic version of the popular game blackjack. Not even statistics should be all work and no play! Rules of the game are supplied on the screen when this program is run.

C.4

A Short How-to-do-it Manual

The principal strength of this package is its ease of use. Only a few instructions are necessary. After these are learned, even a person with no computer experience should be able to run the package with no difficulties. So put any of your fears about computers behind you, and read on. (*Note:* The following instructions are written specifically for the IBM microcomputer. It is possible that slight alterations may be necessary for IBM-compatibles. Ask your computer consultant if you have any problems.)

The first thing you have to do is "boot" the system and get the computer ready to read BASIC. Here are the necessary steps.

1. Put the DOS diskette into disk drive A. This is the disk drive on the left if your computer has two disk drives. (When inserting this and other diskettes, make sure that the label side of the diskette is facing up and that the label is the last part of the diskette to enter the disk drive.)

2. Turn the computer on and turn the screen on. You will hear some "whirring" for about 30 seconds before you finally see writing on the screen. This is normal.

3. Hit the "Caps Lock" key. (The reason is that many questions in this package require a yes/no answer. The programs are written so that "Y" and "N" are understood, but "y" and "n" are not. So make sure you are typing in CAPITAL letters.)

4. In response to current time and current date, type in the current time and date, or simply press the "RETURN" key (the key with the crooked arrow; it is just to the left of the "Home" key).

5. Now you should see A> on the screen. This is the operating system's prompt for an instruction. Type BASICA (yes, there should be an "A" at the end of "BASIC") and press the "RETURN" key. This gets the computer ready to read BASIC programs. Again you will hear a little whirring, but in a couple seconds you should see the BASIC prompt, namely "Ok".

6. Take the DOS diskette out of the disk drive and replace it in drive A with the diskette that accompanies this text. (See step 1 for instructions on how to insert a diskette.)

Now you are all ready to run the statistical package. Since you are now in "BASIC mode," you will see a listing of things you can do at the bottom of the screen. Only two of these are relevant for this package, numbers 2 and 3. Number 3 allows you to "load" a program, such as "BINOMIAL," into the computer's memory. Number 2 then enables you to "run" the program that is in the computer's memory. These instructions are carried out by pressing the "F3" key (to load) or the "F2" key (to run). Notice that these "F" keys are located on the far left side of the keyboard.

Any time you see the "Ok" prompt, you can do one of several things:

1. You can load and run the MENU program. (This is the recommended option the first few times you run the package.) To do this:
a. Press the "F3" key, type MENU, and press the "RETURN" key.

b. Press the "F2" key.

c. Follow the instructions on the screen.

2. You can load and run any of the 21 programs listed in Section C.3. This allows experienced users to bypass the MENU program. To run "BINOMIAL," for example:

a. Press the "F3" key, type BINOMIAL, and press the "RETURN" key.

b. Press the "F2" key.

c. Follow the instructions on the screen.

3. If there is already a program in the computer's memory (which might be the case, for example, if you aborted a previous program you were running), you do not need to load it again. If you want to run this program:

a. Press the "F2" key.

b. Follow the instructions on the screen.

4. You may quit. Simply take the diskette out of the disk drive and turn the system off.

Terminating a Program

The programs in this package have been written to minimize the chance of user errors. For example, every time the user enters a list of observations, there is an option to correct keypunch errors after the data have been entered. Or as another example, if a program asks the user for a probability and the response is something inappropriate such as $-.3$ or 2.7, the program replies that probabilities must be between 0 and 1, and the user is given another chance.

However, there are times when you will want to get out of a program before it is finished. This might be because of an incorrect data entry that was caught too late, it might be because you have seen all you need to see, or it might be because a program (such as SIMULATE, for example) is taking more time than you have to spend. There is a very easy way to terminate any program. Simply hit the "Ctrl" key and the "Break" key simultaneously. (The "Break" key on the IBM keyboard is the upper right-most key. On other keyboards it might be located elsewhere.) So always remember:

> To terminate a program, press the "Ctrl" and "Break" keys *simultaneously*.

When you terminate a program in this manner, you will be returned to the "Ok" prompt. At this point the program you just terminated is still in the computer's memory, and you may proceed with any of the four options discussed earlier in this section.

C.5

Other Information

1. In all of the programs in this package, you will be asked to supply numerical values. Here are two things to remember.

a. Never put a comma within a numerical value. For example, the number "one million" should be entered as 1000000, not as 1,000,000. If you enter 1,000,000 (with the commas), the computer will think you have entered three separate numbers: 1, 000, and 000. Obviously, this is not what you want. The same problem occurs when the computer asks you for a single number and you mistakenly enter two or more numbers, separated by commas. In this case the computer will give you a "redo" message, prompting you to enter a single number, not several numbers.

b. If the program asks for more than one number, all on one line and separated by commas (such as it might for a matched pair of observations), you will get a message to "redo" if you hit the "RETURN" key between numbers. For example, if you are supposed to enter the pair 14,57—all on one line—and you type 14 and then RETURN before the 57, the message will prompt you for the pair. This gives you a chance to correct your error (of not entering both numbers on the same line), and then you can proceed normally.

2. You may sometimes see very large or very small numbers written on the screen in "scientific notation." For example, you may see $4.567E+05$ or $3.221E-04$. These numbers mean 4.567 times 10 to the 5th power, and 3.221 times 10 to the -4th power, respectively. That is, $4.567E+05$ equals 456700 (move the decimal 5 places to the right), and $3.221E-04$ equals .0003221 (move the decimal 4 places to the left). The computer writes numbers in scientific notation simply to save space.

3. Sometimes you will make keypunch errors as you are entering data or answering the program's questions. There are two possible remedies, depending on when you spot the error.

a. If you have not yet pressed the "RETURN" key (to enter your response), then you can press the left arrow key (above the "RETURN" key at the top of the keyboard) one or more times. The effect of this is to backspace and erase. (Pressing the "Ctrl" and the "H" keys simultaneously has the same effect and is more convenient for some typists.)

b. If you have already pressed the "RETURN" key, then you may get a chance later in the program to correct your error. For example, when a list of observations is required, all the programs give you a chance to look at your data and make any necessary changes. But there are times when you will not have a chance to correct your error. In this case your best bet is probably to terminate the program (as discussed above) and then rerun it with the correct responses.

4. All of the programs in this package end with a question such as "Would you like to rerun the program with new data?" If you answer "N" to this question, then you are automatically returned to the "MENU" program, from which you can make your next selection, if any. If you get tired of always being returned to the "MENU" program, then you may want to terminate the current program (press "Ctrl" and "Break" simultaneously) instead of answering "N" to the question. As usual, this returns you to the "Ok" prompt, from which you can immediately load and run any program you want.

5. Several of the programs (SUMMARY, SREGRESS, MREGRESS, MOVAVE, and EXSMOOTH) are written to provide scattergrams and time series graphs. Most computers should provide these graphs with no difficulties. However, some computers are not equipped with adaptors that enable them to do graphics. Furthermore, some versions of BASIC do not understand all of the program's graphics instructions. Therefore, when you get to the graphics parts of these programs, a couple things could occur. The first is that you simply will not see any graphics. In this case you will be able to continue with the rest of the program. The second is that you will get an error message, followed by the "Ok" prompt. This means you are out of the current program and will have to run this program or load and run another program if you want to continue. But even in this case, the only thing you lost was that you were not able to see the graphics.

6. Computers sometimes do strange things with numbers. One example you will probably see is when a decimal number, such as .09, is recorded and printed as .0899999 or .0900001. There is nothing you can do about this, but fortunately, it has no practical effect on the final answer.

7. If you are hooked up to a printer, it is sometimes nice to get a paper copy of the results you see on the screen. This is easy to accomplish. First load your printer with paper and turn it on. Then just press the "Ctrl" and "PrtSc" keys simultaneously, and everything you see on the screen will also be printed. To stop printing, press these same keys again. To start printing again, press them again, and so on. (Notice on the IBM PC keyboard that the "PrtSc" key is just below the "RETURN" key.)

SAMPLE PROBLEM 1

Consider a hotel manager who wants to find a reasonable overbooking policy for a given night. The hotel has 100 empty rooms, and it has many more than 100 demands for reservations. Each person who makes a reservation shows up with probability .8. The hotel manager wants to know how many reservations he can make so that the probability of no more than 100 people showing up is no greater than .95. That is, he wants to be 95% sure that he does not run out of rooms. Also, he wants to know the probability that there will be at least 10 vacant rooms if he uses this overbooking policy.

SOLUTION

The computer output from BINOMIAL shows how this problem was solved. First, some trial and error was used to find the correct value of *n,* the number of reservations made. If $n = 117$, the probability of not running out of rooms is too small, .949, whereas if $n = 116$, it is large enough, .968. Therefore, the manager should make 116 reservations. Then if he does make 116 reservations, the probability of at least 10 vacant rooms is the probability that no more than 90 people will show up, .291. In other words, if 116 reservations are made, the probability is greater than .95 that everyone will have a room, and the probability is approximately .70 that at least 90% of the rooms will be occupied.

```
LOAD"BINOMIAL
Ok
RUN
BINOMIAL PROGRAM - REVISED 7/86

DO YOU WANT AN EXPLANATION OF THIS PROGRAM (Y OR N) ? Y

THIS PROGRAM PERFORMS CALCULATIONS FOR THE BINOMIAL DISTRIBUTION. IT CAN
CALCULATE THE PROBABILITY OF BEING BETWEEN TWO INPUTTED VALUES, OR IT CAN FIND
THE SMALLEST INTEGER WITH A SPECIFIED PROBABILITY TO ITS LEFT.

THE MAXIMUM NUMBER OF TRIALS IS 1500.

PRESS THE RETURN KEY TO RUN THE PROGRAM.?
HOW MANY TRIALS ARE THERE ? 116

WHAT IS THE PROBABILITY OF AN 'A' ON EACH TRIAL ? .8

THE PROBABILITY OF AN 'A' ON EACH OF  116  TRIALS IS  .8

ENTER 1 IF YOU WANT TO CALCULATE A PROBABILITY; ENTER 2 IF YOU WANT TO FIND AN
INTEGER WITH A SPECIFIED PROBABILITY TO ITS LEFT.

1 OR 2 ? 1
THIS PROGRAM FINDS THE PROBABILITY OF BEING BETWEEN 2 INTEGERS (INCLUSIVE).

WHAT ARE THESE 2 INTEGERS? ENTER THE SMALLER INTEGER FIRST AND SEPARATE BY A
COMMA.

(NOTE: IF YOU ENTER THE SAME INTEGER TWICE, THE PROGRAM CALCULATES THE
PROBABILITY OF THIS VALUE.)

? 0,100

THE PROBABILITY OF BEING BETWEEN  0  AND  100  (INCLUSIVE) IS 0.96783

DO YOU WANT TO DO ANOTHER CALCULATION WITH THE SAME PARAMETERS (Y OR N) ? N

DO YOU WANT TO DO ANOTHER CALCULATION WITH ANOTHER SET OF PARAMETERS
(Y OR N) ? Y
HOW MANY TRIALS ARE THERE ? 117

WHAT IS THE PROBABILITY OF AN 'A' ON EACH TRIAL ? .8

THE PROBABILITY OF AN 'A' ON EACH OF  117  TRIALS IS  .8
```

```
ENTER 1 IF YOU WANT TO CALCULATE A PROBABILITY; ENTER 2 IF YOU WANT TO FIND AN
INTEGER WITH A SPECIFIED PROBABILITY TO ITS LEFT.

1 OR 2 ? 1
THIS PROGRAM FINDS THE PROBABILITY OF BEING BETWEEN 2 INTEGERS (INCLUSIVE).

WHAT ARE THESE 2 INTEGERS? ENTER THE SMALLER INTEGER FIRST AND SEPARATE BY A
COMMA.

(NOTE: IF YOU ENTER THE SAME INTEGER TWICE, THE PROGRAM CALCULATES THE
PROBABILITY OF THIS VALUE.)

? 0,100

THE PROBABILITY OF BEING BETWEEN  0  AND  100  (INCLUSIVE) IS 0.94928

DO YOU WANT TO DO ANOTHER CALCULATION WITH THE SAME PARAMETERS (Y OR N) ? N

DO YOU WANT TO DO ANOTHER CALCULATION WITH ANOTHER SET OF PARAMETERS
(Y OR N) ? Y
HOW MANY TRIALS ARE THERE ? 116

WHAT IS THE PROBABILITY OF AN 'A' ON EACH TRIAL ? .8

THE PROBABILITY OF AN 'A' ON EACH OF  116  TRIALS IS  .8

ENTER 1 IF YOU WANT TO CALCULATE A PROBABILITY; ENTER 2 IF YOU WANT TO FIND AN
INTEGER WITH A SPECIFIED PROBABILITY TO ITS LEFT.

1 OR 2 ? 1
THIS PROGRAM FINDS THE PROBABILITY OF BEING BETWEEN 2 INTEGERS (INCLUSIVE).

WHAT ARE THESE 2 INTEGERS? ENTER THE SMALLER INTEGER FIRST AND SEPARATE BY A
COMMA.

(NOTE: IF YOU ENTER THE SAME INTEGER TWICE, THE PROGRAM CALCULATES THE
PROBABILITY OF THIS VALUE.)

? 0,90

THE PROBABILITY OF BEING BETWEEN  0  AND  90  (INCLUSIVE) IS 0.29107

DO YOU WANT TO DO ANOTHER CALCULATION WITH THE SAME PARAMETERS (Y OR N) ? N

DO YOU WANT TO DO ANOTHER CALCULATION WITH ANOTHER SET OF PARAMETERS
(Y OR N) ? N
MENU PROGRAM - REVISED 7/86

ENTER 1 IF YOU WANT AN EXPLANATION; ENTER 2 IF YOU WANT TO GO TO THE MENU;
ENTER 3 IF YOU WANT TO QUIT.

1, 2, OR 3 ? 3
TAKE THE DISK OUT OF THE DISK DRIVE AND TURN OFF THE COMPUTER.
Ok
```

SAMPLE PROBLEM 2

Suppose we obtain a random sample of 20 car repair bills from a local repair shop. The dollar amounts are: 225, 167, 79, 154, 264, 133, 126, 85, 167, 205, 98, 145, 152, 64, 173, 134, 105, 62, 168, and 105. Use the computer package to: (1) test the null hypothesis that the mean repair bill for all repairs at this shop is at least $150, with a 5% significance level; (2) find a 95% confidence interval for the mean repair bill; (3) test the null hypothesis that the standard deviation of all repair bills is no greater than $45, with a 90% significance level; and (4) find a 90% confidence interval for the standard deviation of all repair bills.

SOLUTION

The SAMPMEAN program was constructed to solve exactly these problems. For (1), the t statistic is $-.796$, whereas the tabulated value for a one-tailed test, with 19 degrees of freedom, is -1.729. (This value had to be found from the t table; the computer does not supply it.) Therefore, the null hypothesis cannot be rejected. For (2), the confidence interval for the mean extends from \$115.69 to \$165.41. For (3), the chi-square test statistic is 26.478, whereas the tabulated value for a one-tailed test, with 19 degrees of freedom, is 27.204. Again, the null hypothesis cannot be rejected, although it is fairly close. Finally, for (4), the confidence interval for the standard deviation extends from \$42.17 to \$72.80.

```
LOAD"SAMPMEAN
Ok
RUN
SAMPLE MEAN PROGRAM - REVISED 9/86

DO YOU WANT AN EXPLANATION OF THIS PROGRAM (Y OR N) ? Y

THIS PROGRAM CALCULATES THE SAMPLE MEAN AND SAMPLE STANDARD DEVIATION FOR A
SINGLE SAMPLE OF OBSERVATIONS. THE INPUTS INCLUDE THE SAMPLE SIZE AND THE OB-
SERVATIONS. IT IS ALSO POSSIBLE FOR THE SAMPLE TO BE A SAMPLE OF DIFFERENCES
FROM MATCHED PAIRS DATA. IN THIS CASE THE INPUT INCLUDES THE SAMPLE SIZE AND
THE MATCHED PAIRS. IN EITHER CASE THE OUTPUT INCLUDES THE STANDARD ERROR OF THE
SAMPLE MEAN AND THE T STATISTIC FOR A TEST OF THE POPULATION MEAN, AS WELL AS
A CONFIDENCE INTERVAL FOR THE POPULATION MEAN. IT IS ALSO POSSIBLE TO RUN
A TEST OR FORM A CONFIDENCE INTERVAL FOR THE POPULATION VARIANCE OR THE
POPULATION STANDARD DEVIATION.

THE PROGRAM ALLOWS YOU TO TYPE IN DATA FROM THE TERMINAL OR ACCESS DATA FROM A
DATA DISK. IN THE FORMER CASE YOU HAVE THE OPTION OF TYPING IN INDIVIDUAL
OBSERVATIONS OR SIMPLY SUMMARY MEASURES (MEANS AND STANDARD DEVIATIONS).

THERE MAY BE AS MANY AS 250 OBSERVATIONS (OR MATCHED PAIRS OF OBSERVATIONS).

PRESS THE RETURN KEY TO RUN THE PROGRAM.?
ENTER 1 IF YOU WANT TO TYPE IN DATA FROM THE TERMINAL; ENTER 2 IF YOU WANT TO
ACCESS A DATA SET STORED ON A DATA DISK.

1 OR 2 ? 1

ENTER THE SAMPLE SIZE. ? 20

ENTER 1 IF YOU WANT TO WORK WITH A SAMPLE OF INDIVIDUAL OBSERVATIONS; ENTER 2
IF YOU WANT TO WORK WITH A SAMPLE OF MATCHED PAIRS OF OBSERVATIONS.

1 OR 2 ? 1
ENTER 1 IF YOU WANT TO ENTER THE INDIVIDUAL OBSERVATIONS; ENTER 2 IF YOU WANT
TO ENTER ONLY SUMMARY DATA (SAMPLE MEAN AND STANDARD DEVIATION).

1 OR 2 ? 1
ENTER THE  20  OBSERVATIONS (ONE PER LINE).

BY THE WAY, DON'T WORRY IF YOU MAKE AN ERROR ENTERING THE DATA. YOU'LL HAVE A
CHANCE TO CORRECT ANY ERRORS AFTER THE DATA HAVE ALL BEEN ENTERED.

? 225
? 167
? 79
? 154
? 264
? 133
? 126
? 85
? 167
? 205
? 98
? 145
? 152
? 64
? 173
```

```
? 134
? 105
? 62
? 168
? 105
IT'S ALWAYS A GOOD IDEA TO PROOFREAD THE INPUT DATA.

HERE ARE THE OBSERVATION NUMBERS (I) AND THE OBSERVATIONS (X):

  I    X        I    X        I    X        I    X        I    X

  1   225       2   167       3    79       4   154       5   264
  6   133       7   126       8    85       9   167      10   205
 11    98      12   145      13   152      14    64      15   173
 16   134      17   105      18    62      19   168      20   105


DO YOU WANT TO MAKE ANY CHANGES (Y OR N) ? N
THE MEAN AND STANDARD DEVIATION OF THE OBSERVATIONS ARE  140.55  AND
 53.12198

THE STANDARD ERROR OF THE MEAN IS  11.87843

PRESS THE RETURN KEY TO SEE MORE.?
DO YOU WANT TO DO A HYPOTHESIS TEST FOR THE POPULATION
MEAN (Y OR N)? Y

WHAT IS THE HYPOTHESIZED MEAN ? 150

THE T STATISTIC FOR THIS TEST IS -.7955592 . IT HAS  19  DEGREES OF FREEDOM.

TO PERFORM THE TEST, COMPARE THIS T STATISTIC WITH THE APPROPRIATE VALUE FROM
THE T TABLE WITH  19  DEGREES OF FREEDOM.

PRESS THE RETURN KEY TO SEE MORE.?
DO YOU WANT TO FIND A CONFIDENCE INTERVAL FOR THE POPULATION MEAN
(Y OR N)? Y

ENTER THE CONFIDENCE LEVEL (SUCH AS 95 FOR A 95% CONFIDENCE INTERVAL). ? 95

ENTER THE APPROPRIATE T VALUE FROM THE T TABLE. (YOU MAY ENTER A Z VALUE FROM
THE NORMAL TABLE IF THE SAMPLE SIZE IS SUFFICIENTLY LARGE.)
? 2.093

A  95 % CONFIDENCE INTERVAL FOR THE POPULATION MEAN EXTENDS FROM
 115.6885  TO  165.4116

PRESS THE RETURN KEY TO SEE MORE.?
DO YOU WANT TO PERFORM A HYPOTHESIS TEST ON THE POPULATION VARIANCE OR THE
POPULATION STANDARD DEVIATION (Y OR N) ? Y

ENTER THE HYPOTHESIZED POPULATION STANDARD DEVIATION. ? 45

THE CHI-SQUARE VALUE FOR THIS TEST IS  26.4775 . TO RUN THE TEST, COMPARE
THIS WITH THE APPROPRIATE CHI-SQUARE VALUE FROM THE TABLE WITH  19
DEGREES OF FREEDOM.

PRESS THE RETURN KEY TO SEE MORE.?
DO YOU WANT TO FORM A CONFIDENCE INTERVAL FOR THE POPULATION VARIANCE OR THE
POPULATION STANDARD DEVIATION (Y OR N) ? Y

ENTER THE CONFIDENCE LEVEL (SUCH AS 95 FOR A 95% CONFIDENCE INTERVAL). ? 90

ENTER THE TWO APPROPRIATE CHI-SQUARE VALUES FROM THE TABLE (ONE FOR EACH TAIL).
ENTER THE SMALLER OF THESE FIRST AND SEPARATE THEM WITH A COMMA.
? 10.117,30.144

THE  90 % CONFIDENCE INTERVAL FOR THE POPULATION VARIANCE EXTENDS FROM
 1778.694  TO  5299.688

THE  90 % CONFIDENCE INTERVAL FOR THE POPULATION STANDARD DEVIATIONS EXTENDS
FROM  42.17457  TO  72.79896

PRESS THE RETURN KEY TO SEE MORE.?
DO YOU WANT TO REPEAT THE PROGRAM WITH NEW DATA (Y OR N) ? N
MENU PROGRAM - REVISED 7/86

ENTER 1 IF YOU WANT AN EXPLANATION; ENTER 2 IF YOU WANT TO GO TO THE MENU;
ENTER 3 IF YOU WANT TO QUIT.

1, 2, OR 3 ? 3
TAKE THE DISK OUT OF THE DISK DRIVE AND TURN OFF THE COMPUTER.
Ok
```

SAMPLE PROBLEM 3

Use the computer package to perform the regression analysis for the salary data in Table 11.4. Since the scattergram of these data (in Figure 11.9) suggests a slight nonlinearity, run the regression again, this time using the logarithm of salary as the dependent variable. Then use each estimated equation to estimate the mean salary for all managers who have 12 years of work experience.

SOLUTION

Since there is only one independent variable, we use the SREGRESS program to perform the analysis. The estimated regression for a straight line relationship is $Y = 16.738 + 1.826X$. The corresponding standard error of estimate is 5.85, and the r-square value is .724. The estimated regression equation using $\log(Y)$ as the dependent variable is $\log(Y) = 3.051 + .0471X$. The standard error of estimate is now .157, and the r-square value is .707. (These are difficult to compare to the previous values, because the standard error is now in log units, and the r-square is the proportion of the variation of the log units explained. However, it appears that the two fits are equally good.) The predicted mean salary for all managers with 12 years of experience is $38,646 from the first equation. From the second equation we get an estimated log of average salary from the prediction. This is 3.616. The approximate estimate of average salary is then the antilog of this value, or $37,202. (On a computer screen, several scattergrams would appear in the midst of this output. However, these do not appear on a printed copy of the output.)

```
LOAD"SREGRESS
Ok
RUN
SIMPLE REGRESSION PROGRAM - REVISED 9/86

DO YOU WANT AN EXPLANATION OF THIS PROGRAM (Y OR N) ? Y

THIS PROGRAM PERFORMS A REGRESSION ANALYSIS WITH A SINGLE INDEPENDENT VARIABLE.
THE INPUTS ARE THE NUMBER OF OBSERVATIONS (NO MORE THAN 250), AND THE OBSER-
VATIONS. ALL OF THE STATISTICAL QUANTITIES DISCUSSED IN CHAPTER 11 ARE GIVEN.
THE PROGRAM ALSO PROVIDES TWO USEFUL SCATTERGRAMS, AND IT ALLOWS YOU TO USE
SEVERAL NONLINEAR TRANSFORMATIONS OF THE DEPENDENT OR INDEPENDENT VARIABLES.

THE PROGRAM ALLOWS YOU TO TYPE IN DATA FROM THE TERMINAL OR ACCESS DATA FROM A
DATA DISK. IT ALSO ALLOWS YOU TO SAVE THE Y'S, THE ESTIMATED Y'S (THE Y-HAT'S),
AND THE RESIDUALS ON A DATA DISK FOR POSSIBLE FURTHER USE WITH THIS PROGRAM OR
ONE OF THE OTHER PROGRAMS IN THIS PACKAGE.

PRESS THE RETURN KEY TO RUN THE PROGRAM ?
ENTER 1 IF YOU WANT TO TYPE IN DATA FROM THE TERMINAL; ENTER 2 IF YOU WANT TO
ACCESS A DATA SET FROM A DATA DISK.

1 OR 2 ? 1
HOW MANY OBSERVATIONS ARE THERE ? 20

ENTER THE DATA IN PAIRS, FIRST AN X (INDEPENDENT VARIABLE), THEN A Y (DEPENDENT
VARIABLE), SEPARATED BY A COMMA.

BY THE WAY, DON'T WORRY IF YOU MAKE AN ERROR ENTERING THE DATA. YOU'LL HAVE A
CHANCE TO CORRECT ANY ERRORS AFTER THE DATA HAVE ALL BEEN ENTERED.
```

```
OBSERVATION NUMBER  1
? 7,29.5

OBSERVATION NUMBER  2
? 10,33.7

OBSERVATION NUMBER  3
? 5,25.2

OBSERVATION NUMBER  4
? 12,41.6

OBSERVATION NUMBER  5
? 15,52.8

OBSERVATION NUMBER  6
? 9,43.0

OBSERVATION NUMBER  7
? 12,37.2

OBSERVATION NUMBER  8
? 8,26.1

OBSERVATION NUMBER  9
? 9,41.3

OBSERVATION NUMBER  10

? 10,29.5

OBSERVATION NUMBER  11
? 5,22.4

OBSERVATION NUMBER  12
? 25,55.7

OBSERVATION NUMBER  13
? 18,61.2

OBSERVATION NUMBER  14
? 15,41.3

OBSERVATION NUMBER  15
? 12,28.5

OBSERVATION NUMBER  16
? 10,35.4

OBSERVATION NUMBER  17
? 6,27.3

OBSERVATION NUMBER  18
? 19,50.5

OBSERVATION NUMBER  19
? 15,43.1

OBSERVATION NUMBER  20
? 13,38.5
IT'S ALWAYS A GOOD IDEA TO PROOFREAD THE DATA.

HERE ARE THE OBSERVATION NUMBERS (J) AND THE OBSERVATIONS (X) FOR THE INDEPEN-
DENT VARIABLE:

J    X        J    X        J    X        J    X        J    X

1    7        2    10       3    5        4    12       5    15
6    9        7    12       8    8        9    9        10   10
11   5        12   25       13   18       14   15       15   12
16   10       17   6        18   19       19   15       20   13


DO YOU WANT TO MAKE ANY CHANGES (Y OR N) ? N
HERE ARE THE OBSERVATION NUMBERS (J) AND THE OBSERVATIONS (Y) FOR THE DEPENDENT
VARIABLE:

J    Y        J    Y        J    Y        J    Y        J    Y

1    29.5     2    33.7     3    25.2     4    41.6     5    52.8
6    43       7    37.2     8    26.1     9    41.3     10   29.5
11   22.4     12   55.7     13   61.2     14   41.3     15   28.5
16   35.4     17   27.3     18   50.5     19   43.1     20   38.5
```

```
DO YOU WANT TO MAKE ANY CHANGES (Y OR N) ? N
THIS PROGRAM ALLOWS YOU TO WORK WITH NONLINEAR FUNCTIONS OF THE X'S AND/OR Y'S
INSTEAD OF THE X'S AND Y'S THEMSELVES. IN PARTICULAR, YOU MAY SQUARE A VARIABLE
OR TAKE ITS RECIPROCAL OR TAKE ITS NATURAL LOGARITHM.

DO YOU WANT TO TRANSFORM THE INDEPENDENT VARIABLE (Y OR N) ? N


DO YOU WANT TO TRANSFORM THE DEPENDENT VARIABLE (Y OR N) ? N


PRESS THE RETURN KEY TO SEE MORE ?
THE MEAN OF THE  X'S IS  11.75

THE MEAN OF THE  Y'S IS  38.19

THE STAND. DEV. OF THE  X'S IS  5.056263

THE STAND. DEV. OF THE  Y'S IS  10.84833

THE CORRELATION BETWEEN THE  X'S AND THE  Y'S IS +0.8510

THE ESTIMATED REGRESSION EQUATION IS:

Y =  16.73764  +  ( 1.825733 ) X

PRESS THE RETURN KEY TO SEE MORE ?
THE  Y'S, THEIR ESTIMATES, AND THE RESIDUALS ARE AS FOLLOWS.


Y              EST. Y              RESIDUAL

29.5           29.51777           -1.776886E-02
33.7           34.99497           -1.294964
25.2           25.8663            -.6663018
41.6           38.64643           2.953568
52.8           44.12363           8.676372
43             33.16924           9.830765
37.2           38.64643           -1.44643
26.1           31.3435            -5.243502
41.3           33.16924           8.130764
29.5           34.99497           -5.494965
22.4           25.8663            -3.466303
55.7           62.38096           -6.680954
61.2           49.60083           11.59918
41.3           44.12363           -2.823628
28.5           38.64643           -10.14643

PRESS THE RETURN KEY TO SEE MORE ?
Y              EST. Y              RESIDUAL

35.4           34.99497           .4050369
27.3           27.69204           -.3920365
50.5           51.42656           -.9265594
43.1           44.12363           -1.023628
38.5           40.47217           -1.972164

PRESS THE RETURN KEY TO SEE MORE ?
WOULD YOU LIKE TO SAVE THE Y'S, Y-HAT'S AND RESIDUALS THAT YOU JUST SAW ON A
DATA DISK (Y OR N) ? Y

PUT YOUR DATA DISK IN DRIVE B.

YOU MUST NAME THE FILE WHERE YOU ARE GOING TO STORE THIS DATA SET. THE NAME
MUST BE OF THE FORM B:FILENAME.TXT, WHERE 'FILENAME' IS THE PARTICULAR NAME OF
THIS DATA FILE. MAKE SURE THIS IS NOT THE SAME NAME AS THAT OF ANY OTHER FILE
ON YOUR DATA DISK, AND MAKE SURE YOU WRITE DOWN THE FILE NAME AND ITS CONTENTS
SO THAT YOU CAN REMEMBER THIS FOR FUTURE USE.

ENTER THE NAME OF YOUR DATA FILE ? B:EXAMPLE3.TXT

FOR FUTURE REFERENCE THIS DATA FILE NOW HAS THE Y'S STORED AS VARIABLE 1, THE
Y-HAT'S STORED AS VARIABLE 2, AND THE RESIDUALS STORED AS VARIABLE 3.

PRESS THE RETURN KEY TO SEE MORE. ?
THE STANDARD ERROR OF ESTIMATE IS  5.854177

THE R-SQUARE VALUE IS  .7241166
THEREFORE,  72.41166 % OF THE TOTAL VARIATION IS EXPLAINED.

THE STANDARD ERROR AND T VALUE FOR BETA1 ARE  .2656192  AND  6.873498
```

THE STANDARD ERROR AND T VALUE FOR BETA0 ARE 3.38443 AND 4.945483

THE ANOVA TABLE FOR A TEST OF THE OVERALL FIT IS SHOWN BELOW:

SOURCE	SS	DF	MS	F
REGR	1619.15	1	1619.15	47.24497
ERROR	616.8849	18	34.27138	
TOTAL	2236.035	19		

PRESS THE RETURN KEY TO SEE MORE ?
DO YOU WANT TO DO ANY PREDICTION (Y OR N) ? Y

ENTER AN (UNTRANSFORMED) X VALUE FOR THE PREDICTION ? 12

THE PREDICTED Y VALUE IS 38.64643

THE STAND. ERR. FOR AN INDIVIDUAL Y IS 5.999114

THE STAND. ERR. FOR THE MEAN OF ALL Y'S WITH THIS X IS 1.310717

DO YOU WANT TO DO ANY MORE PREDICTION (Y OR N) ? N

PRESS THE RETURN KEY TO SEE A SCATTERGRAM OF THE X'S
(HORIZONTAL AXIS) VERSUS THE Y'S, AND A GRAPH OF THE
ESTIMATED REGRESSION LINE. (THE HORIZONTAL LINE IN THIS GRAPH CORRESPONDS
TO THE MEAN OF THE Y'S; THE VERTICAL LINE CORRESPONDS TO
THE MEAN OF THE X'S.)

NOTE: SOME IBM PERSONAL COMPUTERS ARE NOT EQUIPPED WITH AN ADAPTER THAT ALLOWS
YOU TO DO GRAPHICS. IF YOU ARE USING ONE OF THESE, THEN YOU WON'T BE ABLE TO
SEE ANY SCATTERGRAMS. BUT THAT'S THE ONLY PART OF THIS PROGRAM YOU WON'T SEE.

NOW PRESS THE RETURN KEY ?
PRESS THE RETURN KEY TO CLEAR THE SCREEN ?
PRESS THE RETURN KEY TO SEE A SCATTERGRAM OF THE X'S
(HORIZONTAL AXIS) VERSUS THE RESIDUALS. (THE VERTICAL LINE IN THIS GRAPH
CORRESPONDS TO THE MEAN OF THE X'S; THE HORIZONTAL LINE
CORRESPONDS TO 'RESIDUALS=0'.)

NOW PRESS THE RETURN KEY ?
PRESS THE RETURN KEY TO CLEAR THE SCREEN ?
DO YOU WANT TO REPEAT THE PROGRAM WITH THE SAME OBSERVATIONS BY USING NEW
TRANSFORMATIONS OF THE X'S AND/OR THE Y'S (Y OR N) ? Y

THIS PROGRAM ALLOWS YOU TO WORK WITH NONLINEAR FUNCTIONS OF THE X'S AND/OR Y'S
INSTEAD OF THE X'S AND Y'S THEMSELVES. IN PARTICULAR, YOU MAY SQUARE A VARIABLE
OR TAKE ITS RECIPROCAL OR TAKE ITS NATURAL LOGARITHM.

DO YOU WANT TO TRANSFORM THE INDEPENDENT VARIABLE (Y OR N) ? N

DO YOU WANT TO TRANSFORM THE DEPENDENT VARIABLE (Y OR N) ? Y

ENTER 1 IF YOU WANT TO SQUARE THE Y'S; ENTER 2 IF YOU WANT TO TAKE RECIPROCALS
OF THE Y'S; ENTER 3 IF YOU WANT TO TAKE LOGARITHMS OF THE Y'S.

1, 2, OR 3 ? 3

FROM HERE ON THE ANALYSIS IS DONE IN TERMS OF TRANSFORMED VARIABLES.

PRESS THE RETURN KEY TO SEE MORE ?
THE MEAN OF THE X'S IS 11.75

THE MEAN OF THE TRANSFORMED Y'S IS 3.604588

THE STAND. DEV. OF THE X'S IS 5.056263

THE STAND. DEV. OF THE TRANSFORMED Y'S IS .283151

THE CORRELATION BETWEEN THE X'S AND THE TRANSFORMED Y'S IS +0.8411

THE ESTIMATED REGRESSION EQUATION IS:

$LOG(Y) = 3.051163 + (4.710004E-02) X$

```
PRESS THE RETURN KEY TO SEE MORE ?
THE TRANSFORMED Y'S, THEIR ESTIMATES, AND THE RESIDUALS ARE AS FOLLOWS.

   LOG(Y)          EST. LOG(Y)        RESIDUAL

   3.38439         3.380863           3.527403E-03
   3.517498        3.522163          -4.665137E-03
   3.226844        3.286663          -5.981875E-02
   3.7281          3.616363           .111737
   3.966511        3.757663           .2088482
   3.7612          3.475063           .2861374
   3.616309        3.616363          -5.435944E-05
   3.261935        3.427963          -.1660276
   3.720863        3.475063           .2457996
   3.38439         3.522163          -.1377728
   3.109061        3.286663          -.1776016
   4.01998         4.228664          -.2086835
   4.114147        3.898963           .215184
   3.720863        3.757663          -3.680062E-02
   3.349904        3.616363          -.266459


PRESS THE RETURN KEY TO SEE MORE ?
   LOG(Y)          EST. LOG(Y)        RESIDUAL

   3.566712        3.522163           4.454899E-02
   3.306887        3.333763          -2.687597E-02
   3.921974        3.946063          -2.408981E-02
   3.763523        3.757663           5.860091E-03
   3.650658        3.663463          -1.280499E-02


PRESS THE RETURN KEY TO SEE MORE ?
WOULD YOU LIKE TO SAVE THE Y'S, Y-HAT'S AND RESIDUALS THAT YOU JUST SAW ON A
DATA DISK (Y OR N) ? N

PRESS THE RETURN KEY TO SEE MORE. ?
THE STANDARD ERROR OF ESTIMATE IS   .1573657

THE R-SQUARE VALUE IS   .7073866
THEREFORE,  70.73866 % OF THE TOTAL VARIATION IS EXPLAINED.

THE STANDARD ERROR AND T VALUE FOR BETA1 ARE  7.14009E-03  AND  6.596562

THE STANDARD ERROR AND T VALUE FOR BETA0 ARE  9.097662E-02  AND  33.53787

THE ANOVA TABLE FOR A TEST OF THE OVERALL FIT IS SHOWN BELOW:

SOURCE     SS          DF        MS              F
REGR     1.077595       1      1.077595        43.51462
ERROR     .4457515     18      2.476397E-02
TOTAL    1.523346      19

PRESS THE RETURN KEY TO SEE MORE ?
DO YOU WANT TO DO ANY PREDICTION (Y OR N) ? Y

ENTER AN (UNTRANSFORMED) X VALUE FOR THE PREDICTION ? 12

THE PREDICTED TRANSFORMED Y VALUE IS  3.616363

THE STAND. ERR. FOR AN INDIVIDUAL TRANSFORMED Y IS   .1612618

THE STAND. ERR. FOR THE MEAN OF ALL TRANSFORMED Y'S WITH THIS X IS
   3.523329E-02

DO YOU WANT TO DO ANY MORE PREDICTION (Y OR N) ? N

PRESS THE RETURN KEY TO SEE A SCATTERGRAM OF THE  X'S
(HORIZONTAL AXIS) VERSUS THE TRANSFORMED Y'S, AND A GRAPH OF THE
ESTIMATED REGRESSION LINE. (THE HORIZONTAL LINE IN THIS GRAPH CORRESPONDS
TO THE MEAN OF THE TRANSFORMED Y'S; THE VERTICAL LINE CORRESPONDS TO
THE MEAN OF THE  X'S.)

NOTE: SOME IBM PERSONAL COMPUTERS ARE NOT EQUIPPED WITH AN ADAPTER THAT ALLOWS
YOU TO DO GRAPHICS. IF YOU ARE USING ONE OF THESE, THEN YOU WON'T BE ABLE TO
SEE ANY SCATTERGRAMS. BUT THAT'S THE ONLY PART OF THIS PROGRAM YOU WON'T SEE.

NOW PRESS THE RETURN KEY ?
```

```
PRESS THE RETURN KEY TO CLEAR THE SCREEN ?
PRESS THE RETURN KEY TO SEE A SCATTERGRAM OF THE  X'S
(HORIZONTAL AXIS) VERSUS THE RESIDUALS. (THE VERTICAL LINE IN THIS GRAPH
CORRESPONDS TO THE MEAN OF THE  X'S; THE HORIZONTAL LINE
CORRESPONDS TO 'RESIDUALS=0'.)

NOW PRESS THE RETURN KEY ?
PRESS THE RETURN KEY TO CLEAR THE SCREEN ?
DO YOU WANT TO REPEAT THE PROGRAM WITH THE SAME OBSERVATIONS BY USING NEW
TRANSFORMATIONS OF THE X'S AND/OR THE Y'S (Y OR N) ? N

DO YOU WANT TO REPEAT THE PROGRAM WITH NEW DATA (Y OR N) ? N
MENU PROGRAM - REVISED 9/86

ENTER 1 IF YOU WANT AN EXPLANATION; ENTER 2 IF YOU WANT TO GO TO THE MENU;
ENTER 3 IF YOU WANT TO QUIT.

1, 2, OR 3 ? 3
TAKE THE DISK OUT OF THE DISK DRIVE AND TURN OFF THE COMPUTER.
Ok
```

SAMPLE PROBLEM 4

In Chapter 2 we presented a contingency table for studying the relationship between coffee consumption and age. See Table 2.5. Now use a chi-square test on these data to see whether coffee consumption is independent of age. Use a 1% significance level.

SOLUTION

This type of analysis can be performed by the CHISQR program. The chi-square statistic is 108.38, whereas the tabulated value, with 6 degrees of freedom, is 15.086. (Again, this tabulated value must be looked up; it is not provided by the computer.) Therefore, the independence hypothesis can definitely be rejected. By looking at the ''(O-E)-square over E'' column, we can see where the largest departures from independence occur. In particular, there are many more older people in the light consumption category than expected, there are many fewer older people in the medium heavy and heavy categories than expected, and there are many more middle-aged people in the medium heavy category than expected.

```
LOAD"CHISQR
Ok
RUN
CHI-SQUARE PROGRAM - REVISED 7/86

DO YOU WANT AN EXPLANATION OF THIS PROGRAM (Y OR N) ? Y

THIS PROGRAM CALCULATES THE EXPECTED FREQUENCIES AND THE CHI-SQUARE STATISTIC
USED TO TEST FOR GOODNESS-OF-FIT (SECTION 13.2), INDEPENDENCE (SECTION 13.3),
OR EQUAL PROPORTIONS (SECTION 13.4). THE ONLY INPUTS ARE THE OBSERVED FRE-
QUENCIES IN THE VARIOUS CATEGORIES AND (FOR THE GOODNESS-OF-FIT TEST ONLY) THE
EXPECTED PROPORTIONS IN THE CATEGORIES.

THERE MAY BE AS MANY AS 10 ROW CATEGORIES AND AS MANY AS 10 COLUMN CATEGORIES.
IF THE NUMBER OF COLUMN CATEGORIES IS 1, THEN THE CHI-SQUARE VALUE IS FOR THE
GOODNESS-OF-FIT TEST IN SECTION 13.2. OTHERWISE, IT IS FOR THE INDEPENDENCE
TEST IN SECTION 13.3 OR THE EQUAL PROPORTIONS TEST IN SECTION 13.4.

PRESS THE RETURN KEY TO RUN THE PROGRAM.?
ENTER 1 IF YOU WANT TO RUN A CHI-SQUARE GOODNESS-OF-FIT TEST (SECTION 13.2);
ENTER 2 IF YOU WANT TO RUN A TEST FOR INDEPENDENCE OR A TEST FOR EQUALITY OF
PROPORTIONS (SECTIONS 13.3, 13.4).
```

```
1 OR 2 ? 2
HOW MANY ROW CATEGORIES ARE THERE ? 4

HOW MANY COLUMN CATEGORIES ARE THERE ? 3

NOW INPUT THE OBSERVED FREQUENCIES IN EACH CELL, ONE ROW AT A TIME. (ENTER ONE
FREQUENCY PER LINE.)

INPUT THE OBSERVED FREQUENCIES FOR ROW  1
? 85
? 45
? 95

INPUT THE OBSERVED FREQUENCIES FOR ROW  2
? 90
? 55
? 50

INPUT THE OBSERVED FREQUENCIES FOR ROW  3
? 90
? 115
? 30

INPUT THE OBSERVED FREQUENCIES FOR ROW  4
? 135
? 85
? 25


HERE ARE THE OBSERVED FREQUENCIES, THE EXPECTED FREQUENCIES, AND THE
((O-E) SQUARED OVER E)'S USED TO FIND THE CHI-SQUARE STATISTIC.

DATA FOR ROW  1

O            E                    (O-E) SQUARED OVER E

85           100                  2.25
45           75                   12
95           50                   40.5

PRESS THE RETURN KEY TO SEE MORE.?
DATA FOR ROW  2

O            E                    (O-E) SQUARED OVER E

90           86.66666             .1282053
55           65                   1.538462
50           43.33333             1.025641

PRESS THE RETURN KEY TO SEE MORE.?
DATA FOR ROW  3

O            E                    (O-E) SQUARED OVER E

90           104.4444             1.997636
115          78.33334             17.16312
30           52.22222             9.456264

PRESS THE RETURN KEY TO SEE MORE.?
DATA FOR ROW  4

O            E                    (O-E) SQUARED OVER E

135          108.8889             6.26134
85           81.66666             .1360546
25           54.44445             15.92404

PRESS THE RETURN KEY TO SEE MORE.?
THE CHI-SQUARE STATISTIC IS  108.3808 . IT HAS  6  DEGREES OF FREEDOM.

TO PERFORM THE RELEVANT HYPOTHESIS TEST, COMPARE THE ABOVE CHI-SQUARE VALUE
WITH THE APPROPRIATE VALUE FROM THE CHI-SQUARE TABLE.

DO YOU WISH TO REPEAT THE PROGRAM WITH NEW DATA (Y OR N) ? N
MENU PROGRAM - REVISED 7/86

ENTER 1 IF YOU WANT AN EXPLANATION; ENTER 2 IF YOU WANT TO GO TO THE MENU;
ENTER 3 IF YOU WANT TO QUIT.

1, 2, OR 3 ? 3
TAKE THE DISK OUT OF THE DISK DRIVE AND TURN OFF THE COMPUTER.
Ok
```

Data Sets

Contents

Table I   Number and Average Salary of Classroom Teachers, 1983

State	Total	Teachers (1000) Elementary	Secondary	Total	Average Salary ($1,000) Elementary	Secondary
Alabama	39.4	20.0	19.4	17.9	17.4	18.0
Alaska	5.6	3.1	2.5	34.0	33.8	34.2
Arizona	28.9	19.9	8.9	18.8	18.6	19.3
Arkansas	23.5	11.5	12.0	15.2	14.8	15.5
California	170.4	104.6	65.8	23.6	23.2	24.5
Colorado	29.0	15.0	14.0	21.5	21.1	22.3
Connecticut	31.6	18.9	12.8	20.8	20.5	21.4
Delaware	5.3	2.5	2.9	20.7	20.1	21.2
District of Columbia	4.9	2.9	2.0	26.0	26.1	26.0
Florida	82.0	46.5	35.5	18.5	18.7	18.1
Georgia	57.0	34.7	22.3	17.4	17.1	17.8
Hawaii	8.1	5.0	3.1	24.8	25.3	24.0
Idaho	10.1	5.4	4.8	17.5	16.9	18.3
Illinois	104.2	67.8	36.4	22.6	21.7	24.2
Indiana	50.7	25.5	25.2	20.1	19.7	20.5
Iowa	31.0	14.6	16.4	18.7	18.0	19.4
Kansas	26.3	14.5	11.8	18.3	18.2	18.4
Kentucky	32.2	21.0	11.2	18.4	17.9	19.2
Louisiana	42.5	23.8	18.7	19.3	18.8	19.7
Maine	12.3	7.8	4.5	15.3	16.6	15.8
Maryland	37.7	18.1	19.7	22.8	21.8	23.1
Massachusetts	52.0	22.0	30.0	19.0	18.8	19.2
Michigan	77.2	40.1	37.1	24.0	23.7	24.2
Minnesota	40.6	19.4	21.2	22.3	21.5	23.1
Mississippi	24.8	13.7	11.2	14.3	14.0	14.6
Missouri	48.3	24.0	24.3	17.7	17.3	18.2
Montana	8.9	5.0	3.9	19.5	18.8	20.3
Nebraska	16.2	8.1	8.1	17.4	16.7	18.2
Nevada	7.4	3.9	3.5	20.9	20.6	21.3
New Hampshire	10.1	5.3	4.8	15.4	15.3	15.5
New Jersey	73.3	41.8	31.5	21.6	21.2	22.2
New Mexico	14.3	6.9	7.3	20.6	20.3	21.0
New York	163.1	73.8	89.3	25.1	24.3	25.7
North Carolina	56.5	34.2	22.3	17.8	17.8	17.8
North Dakota	7.5	4.7	2.8	18.4	17.7	19.1
Ohio	95.0	53.4	41.6	20.4	19.9	21.0

Source: National Education Association, Washington, D.C., *Estimates of School Statistics,* 1982–1983.

Table I   Continued

State	Total	Teachers (1000) Elementary	Secondary	Total	Average Salary ($1,000) Elementary	Secondary
Oklahoma	33.9	17.9	16.0	18.1	17.7	18.6
Oregon	24.5	15.0	9.5	22.3	21.9	23.1
Pennsylvania	102.7	47.2	55.5	21.0	20.5	21.3
Rhode Island	8.8	4.7	4.1	23.2	24.1	22.2
South Carolina	32.1	20.1	12.0	16.4	15.9	17.0
South Dakota	8.0	5.3	2.7	15.6	15.4	16.0
Tennessee	39.2	24.5	14.8	17.4	17.4	17.5
Texas	166.8	92.8	74.0	19.5	19.0	20.1
Utah	14.9	9.1	5.8	19.7	19.1	20.6
Vermont	6.6	3.0	3.6	15.3	14.9	15.8
Virginia	56.9	33.7	23.2	18.7	18.0	19.7
Washington	34.5	18.4	16.1	23.4	23.0	23.9
West Virginia	22.0	12.7	9.3	17.4	17.3	17.5
Wisconsin	52.2	28.8	23.4	20.9	20.5	21.5
Wyoming	7.3	4.0	3.3	24.0	22.7	24.3

Table II   Hypothetical Data on Student Grade-Point Averages and Standardized Test Scores

Student	UGPA	GGPA	VERB	QUAN	Student	UGPA	GGPA	VERB	QUAN
1	3.07	3.37	62	57	11	2.86	3.23	60	58
2	3.06	3.73	89	80	12	2.79	3.28	75	73
3	2.76	3.52	77	74	13	3.35	3.75	68	72
4	3.05	3.25	60	80	14	3.00	3.53	92	93
5	3.19	3.48	72	83	15	3.64	3.78	97	77
6	3.27	3.66	71	73	16	3.34	3.77	82	79
7	2.74	3.26	56	70	17	3.52	3.51	67	79
8	3.45	3.58	61	68	18	2.94	3.05	56	64
9	3.50	3.63	95	86	19	3.15	3.37	86	87
10	3.40	3.70	73	81	20	3.26	3.77	64	77

Legend: UGPA: Undergraduate grade-point average.
GGPA: Graduate grade-point average.
VERB: Percentile ranking on verbal section of standardized test.
QUAN: Percentile ranking on quantitative section of standardized test.

Table II   Continued

Student	UGPA	GGPA	VERB	QUAN	Student	UGPA	GGPA	VERB	QUAN
21	3.01	3.58	62	76	61	3.40	3.83	83	65
22	3.50	3.59	87	71	62	2.66	3.18	60	39
23	2.85	2.91	60	43	63	3.21	3.56	82	88
24	2.77	3.30	75	66	64	2.98	3.16	62	68
25	3.09	3.39	66	97	65	3.14	3.65	62	70
26	3.29	3.55	53	75	66	2.48	3.23	69	80
27	3.18	3.48	60	60	67	3.20	3.42	61	57
28	3.27	3.69	58	76	68	3.35	3.85	74	54
29	2.67	3.06	83	87	69	2.83	3.27	59	85
30	3.26	3.64	65	84	70	3.07	3.35	71	80
31	3.46	3.74	56	68	71	2.38	3.16	44	56
32	3.09	3.72	76	54	72	2.99	3.54	84	76
33	3.53	3.50	65	59	73	2.92	3.29	80	69
34	2.88	3.17	77	60	74	3.28	3.73	89	67
35	3.20	3.55	66	83	75	3.11	3.57	66	47
36	2.95	3.17	38	59	76	2.81	3.17	83	58
37	2.88	3.26	63	85	77	3.53	3.82	80	95
38	3.17	3.79	75	59	78	3.75	3.86	86	98
39	3.05	3.27	65	66	79	2.75	3.35	81	74
40	3.48	3.69	96	75	80	3.30	3.58	67	63
41	2.79	3.31	99	70	81	2.79	3.41	95	76
42	2.76	3.20	64	66	82	3.33	3.59	68	65
43	3.11	3.69	82	97	83	3.20	3.42	82	57
44	2.96	3.28	93	90	84	3.00	3.42	65	77
45	3.64	3.71	74	64	85	2.81	3.40	44	84
46	3.72	3.83	80	91	86	2.94	3.80	78	89
47	3.31	3.54	83	85	87	2.93	3.55	76	73
48	3.04	3.41	65	66	88	3.10	3.58	86	73
49	3.34	3.55	95	97	89	3.05	3.83	82	51
50	2.80	3.16	40	55	90	3.30	3.19	59	66
51	3.22	3.32	64	87	91	3.42	3.93	94	85
52	2.76	3.57	77	74	92	2.84	3.17	57	69
53	3.38	3.90	94	80	93	2.77	3.14	62	58
54	3.38	3.56	98	99	94	3.34	3.41	73	60
55	3.22	3.62	91	99	95	3.31	3.81	89	78
56	2.72	3.11	55	62	96	3.13	3.45	64	68
57	3.49	3.76	68	49	97	2.95	3.68	85	84
58	2.72	3.13	63	51	98	3.59	3.57	90	77
59	3.31	3.79	66	77	99	2.78	3.07	58	65
60	3.32	3.49	84	70	100	3.19	3.53	43	63

Table III Hypothetical Data on Recently Sold Houses

House	VALUE	PRICE	SQFT	BEDRM
1	71.330	68.490	15.90	2
2	70.980	87.530	19.80	4
3	58.130	72.980	17.00	3
4	70.440	61.540	15.30	2
5	76.570	75.350	17.60	3
6	80.130	86.070	18.10	3
7	57.530	58.520	13.80	2
8	87.700	83.880	19.30	3
9	89.730	86.860	21.70	4
10	85.270	89.510	18.50	4
11	62.570	58.640	14.70	2
12	59.650	60.530	16.50	3
13	83.360	91.990	18.20	3
14	68.500	75.570	19.65	4
15	95.550	97.790	22.70	5
16	82.870	92.900	19.90	4
17	90.500	81.050	18.60	4
18	61.990	53.610	14.10	2
19	74.610	69.340	19.10	4
20	68.910	79.010	16.10	2
21	89.820	85.140	20.70	4
22	62.140	51.230	14.20	2
23	58.300	61.140	16.40	3
24	72.420	69.890	16.50	4
25	80.930	80.240	15.70	3
26	76.010	75.120	16.10	2
27	80.040	87.470	16.50	3
28	54.340	47.060	16.70	3
29	79.530	84.800	17.20	3
30	88.210	92.260	17.00	3
31	72.050	87.250	18.30	2
32	90.830	80.590	17.80	3
33	63.490	55.730	16.70	3
34	77.080	79.490	17.10	3
35	66.300	56.200	12.10	2
36	63.480	60.290	15.20	4
37	75.700	84.350	18.60	3
38	70.390	62.780	15.90	3
39	88.930	90.250	22.00	4
40	59.370	61.870	20.50	4

Legend: VALUE: Appraised value of house ($1000s).
PRICE: Recent selling price of house ($1000s).
SQFT: Square footage of house (100s sq. ft.).
BEDRM: Number of bedrooms in house.

Table III   Continued

House	VALUE	PRICE	SQFT	BEDRM
41	58.090	55.470	14.90	2
42	73.220	85.880	19.20	4
43	66.720	62.270	19.20	4
44	96.130	92.840	19.60	3
45	99.190	100.030	20.80	5
46	81.780	79.350	19.50	4
47	69.910	70.080	16.10	2
48	83.120	81.110	21.00	5
49	59.700	53.770	13.80	2
50	77.660	67.300	16.40	3
51	58.170	75.440	17.10	2
52	89.660	95.460	21.70	4
53	84.700	82.130	21.60	5
54	77.740	83.460	20.40	4
55	56.440	51.950	14.40	2
56	81.810	93.330	17.80	3
57	89.200	93.690	18.50	3
58	56.340	50.610	13.40	2
59	81.900	77.350	19.50	3
60	85.460	96.520	20.30	3
61	54.090	53.550	14.10	2
62	77.440	80.200	19.20	4
63	67.590	58.200	15.20	2
64	74.330	83.760	16.50	2
65	77.540	81.320	18.10	3
66	46.110	54.330	14.70	2
67	76.890	72.540	16.10	2
68	83.550	91.960	19.10	3
69	61.270	60.450	14.60	2
70	71.470	67.290	17.00	3
71	41.930	49.410	13.30	2
72	67.970	76.510	18.70	4
73	64.560	62.080	17.50	3
74	80.160	89.920	20.50	4
75	73.170	79.540	16.80	2
76	60.150	54.550	17.30	2
77	91.100	97.390	20.40	4
78	100.580	102.030	21.00	5
79	57.870	63.550	17.30	3
80	81.100	81.930	17.40	3

House	VALUE	PRICE	SQFT	BEDRM
81	59.310	67.040	19.20	3
82	82.430	82.890	17.80	3
83	76.890	72.680	18.80	3
84	68.290	70.090	16.00	2
85	60.220	66.740	14.80	2
86	65.740	76.450	18.20	3
87	65.570	69.430	19.30	4
88	72.650	78.820	19.30	3
89	70.730	75.620	18.40	3
90	81.250	65.890	15.80	3
91	86.400	93.240	21.90	4
92	61.590	54.230	14.10	2
93	58.530	52.600	14.60	2
94	82.960	75.260	18.10	3
95	81.560	90.380	20.70	3
96	74.020	73.270	16.40	2
97	66.310	73.270	18.90	4
98	93.700	84.680	21.30	4
99	58.040	49.460	13.90	2
100	76.530	78.380	14.30	2
101	81.130	85.710	18.50	3
102	73.940	77.270	18.80	4
103	44.010	52.040	17.00	3
104	67.350	58.790	15.78	3
105	49.250	44.830	14.00	2
106	74.210	81.230	17.20	3
107	45.060	53.780	15.40	2
108	69.230	80.300	16.60	3
109	70.310	76.870	20.50	4
110	69.150	60.440	14.80	3
111	90.410	85.140	19.50	3
112	51.560	51.700	15.40	2
113	67.200	63.450	15.30	3
114	45.070	47.900	14.60	2
115	67.150	64.050	17.50	3
116	85.820	78.530	18.20	3
117	72.240	71.290	16.20	3
118	74.100	84.920	18.90	4
119	78.560	76.160	16.50	3
120	81.630	75.720	16.00	2

Table III   Continued

House	VALUE	PRICE	SQFT	BEDRM
121	60.370	71.450	18.30	4
122	58.830	54.570	14.70	2
123	64.490	69.560	16.90	3
124	80.570	89.550	19.30	4
125	73.620	80.820	19.70	2
126	45.050	51.550	15.30	2
127	87.090	82.760	20.30	5
128	55.430	64.250	18.30	3
129	65.370	72.320	20.70	3
130	55.970	61.450	16.30	2
131	65.210	72.450	15.80	3
132	70.370	75.830	17.60	3
133	59.750	65.760	18.10	4
134	60.930	65.840	17.10	3
135	66.800	75.320	18.90	3
136	58.820	60.140	16.40	2
137	84.080	87.530	20.10	4
138	82.490	84.940	17.30	3
139	80.550	76.010	17.70	4
140	70.360	59.330	17.50	4
141	64.270	71.150	16.60	3
142	107.730	112.360	25.10	5
143	69.190	77.170	17.00	2
144	65.180	64.710	16.60	3
145	97.510	88.650	21.10	4
146	66.670	68.520	14.30	2
147	77.570	72.020	17.10	4
148	73.460	68.030	15.80	2
149	103.570	108.060	23.50	5
150	58.460	54.920	14.20	2

Table IV Ordinary Life Insurance in Force in the United States

Year	Number Policies (1,000,000s)	Amount ($1,000,000s)	Year	Number Policies (1,000,000s)	Amount ($1,000,000s)
1900	3	6,124	1955	80	216,812
1905	5	9,585	1956	83	238.348
1910	6	11,783	1957	87	264,949
1915	9	16,650	1958	89	288,607
1920	16	32,018	1959	93	317,158
1925	23	52,892	1960	95	341,881
1930	32	78,576	1961	97	366,141
1935	33	70,684	1962	99	391,048
1936	33	72,361	1963	102	420,808
1937	34	74,836	1964	104	457,868
1938	35	75,772	1965	107	499,638
1939	36	77,121	1966	109	541,022
1940	37	79,346	1967	113	584,570
1941	39	82,525	1968	116	633,392
1942	41	85,139	1969	118	682,453
1943	43	89,596	1970	120	734,730
1944	46	95,085	1971	123	792,318
1945	48	101,550	1972	126	853,911
1946	53	112,818	1973	128	928,192
1947	56	122,393	1974	131	1,009,038
1948	58	131,158	1975	134	1,083,421
1949	61	138,862	1976	137	1,177,672
1950	64	149,116	1977	139	1,289,321
1951	67	159,109	1978	142	1,425,095
1952	70	170,875	1979	146	1,585,878
1953	73	185,007	1980	148	1,760,474
1954	76	198,599	1981	149	1,987,080

Sources: *Spectator Year Book* and American Council of Life Insurance.

Table V   Per Capita Personal Income, Actual and Projected (in 1978 Dollars)

State	1978	2000	Increase	State	1978	2000	Increase
Alabama	6326	12216	93%	Montana	6915	12662	83%
Alaska	10850	17006	57	Nebraska	7544	13101	74
Arizona	7385	13032	76	Nevada	9378	14432	54
Arkansas	6122	11415	86	New Hampshire	7379	12569	70
California	8916	14381	61	New Jersey	8775	14465	65
Colorado	8117	13857	71	New Mexico	6599	11970	81
Connecticut	8915	15235	60	New York	8229	13784	68
Delaware	8531	14553	60	North Carolina	6639	12176	83
District of Columbia	9599	16317	70	North Dakota	7433	13184	77
Florida	7578	13206	74	Ohio	7857	13772	75
Georgia	6779	12312	82	Oklahoma	7127	12651	78
Hawaii	8465	13647	61	Oregon	8076	13556	68
Idaho	7074	12882	74	Pennsylvania	7745	13529	75
Illinois	8870	14787	67	Rhode Island	7446	12995	75
Indiana	7703	13548	76	South Carolina	6293	11796	87
Iowa	7856	13544	72	South Dakota	6585	11864	80
Kansas	7847	13451	71	Tennessee	6561	12014	83
Kentucky	6605	12921	96	Texas	7746	13470	74
Louisiana	6738	12801	90	Utah	6594	12110	84
Maine	6308	11288	79	Vermont	6602	11651	76
Maryland	8348	14213	70	Virginia	7721	13425	74
Massachusetts	7926	13353	68	Washington	8553	14247	67
Michigan	8487	14441	70	West Virginia	6629	13085	97
Minnesota	7904	13587	72	Wisconsin	7532	13007	73
Mississippi	5582	10937	96	Wyoming	8687	14390	66
Missouri	7287	12744	75				

Source: U.S. News & World Report, Dec. 22, 1980.

Table VI   Durable Goods Expenditures in the United States
(in Billions of Dollars)

Year	1st Qtr.	2nd Qtr.	3rd Qtr.	4th Qtr.	Total
1963	1.51	1.88	1.88	2.25	7.53
1964	1.86	2.29	2.27	2.86	9.28
1965	2.24	2.77	2.89	3.60	11.50
1966	2.88	3.50	3.46	4.21	14.06
1967	3.14	3.56	3.40	3.96	14.06
1968	3.06	3.36	3.54	4.16	14.12
1969	3.38	3.98	4.03	4.59	15.96
1970	3.59	4.08	3.87	4.26	15.80
1971	3.11	3.52	3.40	4.12	14.15
1972	3.29	3.71	3.86	4.77	15.64
1973	3.92	4.65	4.84	5.85	19.25
1974	4.74	5.59	5.65	6.64	22.62
1975	5.10	5.59	5.16	5.99	21.84
1976	4.78	5.61	6.02	7.27	23.68
1977	5.80	6.79	7.17	8.00	27.77
1978	6.36	7.79	7.97	9.53	31.66
1979	7.53	9.17	12.99	15.73	45.42
1980	12.54	14.29	14.99	17.09	58.91

Source: U.S. Department of Commerce.

Table VII   Cost-of-Living Data on 232 Cities from 2nd Quarter, 1985
Includes an overall index, and separate indexes for grocery items, housing, utilities, transportation, health care, and miscellaneous items.

City and State	All-Items Index	Grocery Items	Housing	Utilities	Transportation	Health Care	Misc. Goods and Svcs.
Anniston, AL	92.8	96.8	72.9	142.6	82.5	84.3	93.3
Birmingham, AL	102.2	100.0	93.8	128.1	100.7	99.5	101.2
Dothan, AL	92.6	99.4	88.5	97.1	99.5	77.0	90.7
Gadsden, AL	89.4	95.1	70.7	111.4	92.5	84.5	91.5
Huntsville, AL	96.0	99.0	97.0	79.6	106.3	89.5	96.8
Mobile, AL	98.7	101.2	86.5	118.5	105.5	86.6	98.9
Montgomery, AL	95.7	100.7	79.8	91.8	98.4	95.2	104.9
Anchorage, AK	139.2	134.0	174.4	93.6	118.0	183.4	132.1
Phoenix, AZ	105.7	97.3	114.0	101.4	111.3	114.5	101.6
Tucson, AZ	100.3	99.9	106.7	74.2	97.9	110.0	104.3
Yuma, AZ	100.3	101.1	90.0	113.5	107.2	97.2	100.3

Reference: American Chamber of Commerce Researchers Association.

Table VII Continued

City and State	All-Items Index	Grocery Items	Housing	Utilities	Transportation	Health Care	Misc. Goods and Svcs.
Fayetteville, AR	94.5	97.2	89.0	99.7	103.4	80.7	94.5
Fort Smith, AR	92.3	90.2	87.3	88.6	94.5	88.4	98.3
Jonesboro, AR	89.6	96.2	80.4	103.1	79.5	77.4	95.1
Blythe, CA	102.7	99.5	95.6	104.4	106.4	124.3	102.3
Chico, CA	109.5	103.6	128.0	97.3	106.2	134.7	99.2
Fresno, CA	105.5	104.0	101.1	90.3	108.2	119.3	110.9
Indio, CA	106.9	95.5	109.5	106.8	99.8	136.7	107.5
Palm Springs, CA	119.8	95.9	158.0	112.5	100.3	143.6	110.8
Riverside, CA	112.0	105.6	129.5	103.6	107.7	127.0	104.1
Sacramento, CA	106.4	103.5	115.4	69.0	115.9	111.5	109.9
San Bernardino, CA	101.9	96.2	104.2	85.8	109.9	119.8	101.5
San Diego, CA	117.6	93.9	158.5	81.5	132.6	134.8	103.8
San Francisco, CA	135.4	108.1	222.5	56.3	120.0	150.9	119.0
San Jose, CA	111.4	100.8	150.4	72.6	102.4	131.0	102.2
Visalia, CA	100.9	97.0	100.0	88.6	105.7	106.6	104.8
Boulder, CO	108.7	104.7	144.8	75.0	101.8	109.2	99.9
Colorado Springs, CO	99.6	110.5	105.8	63.4	99.3	105.9	100.8
Denver, CO	108.9	105.0	136.8	75.1	110.4	111.1	101.9
Fort Collins, CO	98.4	102.5	101.5	68.9	100.3	102.6	102.9
Greeley, CO	100.6	105.3	107.8	69.8	103.5	103.9	102.0
Pueblo, CO	89.8	100.9	73.2	69.9	92.6	113.9	96.0
Hartford, CT	112.4	103.7	126.4	128.9	103.8	104.3	106.5
New Haven, CT	111.4	120.7	113.3	122.4	100.0	125.5	102.3
Boca Raton, FL	115.3	97.6	147.9	104.4	104.8	108.0	111.7
Gainesville, FL	98.6	95.8	102.0	84.8	96.2	108.0	101.8
Jacksonville, FL	103.8	101.2	113.8	97.9	89.7	108.6	105.1
Lakeland, FL	99.6	97.1	91.4	100.8	98.8	108.1	105.0
Pensacola, FL	95.4	99.9	90.3	80.9	95.3	109.6	98.5
Sarasota, FL	99.9	95.5	105.8	109.8	101.9	98.3	94.0
Tallahassee, FL	99.2	98.7	91.9	113.0	94.1	106.2	100.6
Albany, GA	89.9	87.1	92.8	80.8	88.7	89.8	93.1
Americus, GA	98.0	97.6	94.3	105.1	97.7	77.1	103.4
Athens, GA	95.9	93.3	85.4	127.0	92.6	86.8	97.1
Atlanta, GA	106.1	96.6	110.6	128.1	101.4	109.8	101.2
Augusta, GA	99.2	93.7	102.0	122.2	91.5	84.7	98.5
Columbus, GA	95.1	97.5	97.0	103.9	88.4	79.9	95.4
Macon, GA	100.4	99.2	97.4	119.9	95.9	94.5	99.5
Twin Falls, ID	97.1	100.2	94.4	91.6	98.7	104.9	96.8

City and State	All-Items Index	Grocery Items	Housing	Utilities	Transportation	Health Care	Misc. Goods and Svcs.
Charleston, IL	97.8	97.8	101.5	108.9	92.0	78.6	98.1
Decatur, IL	95.6	92.2	81.9	108.2	106.8	93.7	98.6
Peoria, IL	96.2	98.1	78.1	115.5	104.4	90.7	99.0
Rockford, IL	103.8	98.8	100.6	118.9	99.8	103.1	105.2
Springfield, IL	104.3	96.0	109.0	116.6	106.5	104.2	100.1
Anderson, IN	93.2	95.4	87.5	96.0	99.9	88.1	93.3
Bloomington, IN	93.6	102.9	88.3	97.9	91.4	82.7	94.0
Evansville, IN	98.7	107.3	96.9	88.2	94.4	96.1	101.3
Fort Wayne, IN	92.5	97.6	90.6	94.5	91.8	83.7	92.7
Indianapolis, IN	97.5	94.2	96.4	96.5	111.5	95.0	94.9
South Bend, IN	91.4	92.2	89.4	97.3	94.7	85.9	90.2
Warsaw, IN	98.1	101.5	93.0	112.1	100.3	103.8	92.3
Cedar Rapids, IA	99.6	92.6	109.9	83.9	107.9	93.0	99.6
Clarinda, IA	91.3	100.7	75.2	110.7	83.7	81.6	96.3
Des Moines, IA	102.4	93.2	119.1	101.9	107.4	87.0	96.9
Fort Dodge, IA	94.3	96.1	88.1	98.1	104.8	80.8	95.1
Marshalltown, IA	90.8	89.3	85.0	93.6	102.7	82.5	91.6
Mason City, IA	96.6	84.7	99.5	100.4	102.1	95.8	97.5
Sioux City, IA	96.2	92.9	93.1	96.8	96.5	94.2	100.3
Garden City, KS	97.1	97.2	85.2	113.1	96.3	96.0	100.5
Great Bend, KS	95.6	95.4	94.3	97.1	97.3	87.0	97.4
Manhattan, KS	102.1	107.9	94.9	103.5	99.3	99.0	105.5
Bowling Green, KY	94.1	103.1	89.8	83.6	102.3	94.3	92.5
Henderson, KY	92.8	101.7	79.3	100.3	96.8	90.9	93.7
Lexington, KY	99.9	101.2	109.1	95.2	99.2	87.7	97.3
Louisville, KY	96.6	100.4	86.9	107.3	99.0	110.8	93.2
Madisonville, KY	94.0	102.3	81.5	99.0	97.0	99.2	94.2
Murray, KY	90.6	105.5	73.2	104.4	88.1	88.5	91.6
Somerset, KY	90.0	105.0	80.2	100.1	86.2	89.0	86.7
Baton Rouge, LA	102.1	97.5	97.8	120.7	100.6	98.5	102.6
Lafayette, LA	104.0	105.0	108.3	116.4	102.9	91.1	99.3
Lake Charles, LA	99.6	91.1	95.2	120.7	107.8	100.0	96.3
Monroe, LA	101.6	97.0	92.8	110.8	106.8	105.9	103.9
New Orleans, LA	96.1	96.9	95.7	94.5	97.9	94.3	96.2
Lewiston, ME	103.5	99.3	109.2	121.8	92.3	94.9	101.9
Baltimore, MD	105.5	100.7	110.5	95.6	108.9	108.7	105.8

Table VII   Continued

City and State	All-Items Index	Grocery Items	Housing	Utilities	Transportation	Health Care	Misc. Goods and Svcs.
Fall River, MA	102.5	105.0	111.0	107.2	92.0	94.6	99.5
Worcester, MA	107.2	99.8	133.5	98.9	94.9	114.2	99.0
Adrian, MI	101.8	98.8	98.9	110.3	104.4	94.3	103.3
Benton Harbor–St. Joseph, MI	100.1	98.6	96.8	99.8	103.0	99.3	102.3
Jackson, MI	96.5	98.1	82.5	99.9	97.3	94.6	104.6
Kalamazoo, MI	105.0	97.2	113.4	100.3	106.9	117.8	101.2
Lansing, MI	104.9	98.6	106.7	90.2	113.9	121.9	104.5
Marquette, MI	96.0	100.2	78.5	97.2	100.0	122.7	98.1
Royal Oak, MI	106.8	104.4	96.8	134.8	115.1	112.7	100.1
Traverse City, MI	104.9	100.6	114.0	92.6	103.2	104.0	106.2
Duluth, MN	93.3	99.6	76.3	81.3	03.2	106.6	99.1
Fergus Falls, MN	94.3	98.7	80.3	113.5	98.3	93.9	93.4
Marshall, MN	95.7	95.8	95.9	90.1	99.6	82.0	98.9
Rochester, MN	102.1	100.0	104.1	93.9	102.3	118.4	100.8
St. Cloud, MN	97.5	99.5	84.3	104.5	99.6	106.1	100.7
St. Paul, MN	104.1	92.3	118.1	95.2	117.3	109.2	97.0
Clinton, MO	91.2	90.4	84.5	101.9	93.2	76.4	95.4
Columbia, MO	94.9	93.5	90.2	109.0	96.9	90.9	94.1
Jefferson City, MO	92.8	94.7	90.9	86.9	85.4	84.3	100.4
Joplin, MO	89.4	90.1	90.1	75.6	92.5	92.2	91.6
Kansas City, MO–Kansas City, KS	102.7	106.8	97.6	119.4	97.9	108.6	98.6
St. Joseph, MO	93.7	94.9	88.4	91.1	95.7	90.0	97.7
St. Louis, MO	98.7	95.9	102.0	91.1	98.7	104.5	99.2
Billings, MT	105.5	110.5	119.0	85.2	96.1	113.9	102.5
Great Falls, MT	98.7	106.0	89.6	85.7	101.6	104.1	103.4
Havre, MT	100.1	113.7	96.4	95.3	91.6	104.9	99.4
Missoula, MT	96.0	106.9	80.7	70.5	94.6	115.7	106.6
Hastings, NE	92.2	96.5	80.7	97.5	94.3	89.5	96.0
Holdrege, NE	96.8	105.4	91.0	90.9	89.3	91.6	103.0
Lincoln, NE	95.1	91.7	96.9	85.3	102.6	85.6	98.3
Omaha, NE	95.7	94.3	92.8	96.5	93.6	90.3	100.4
Las Vegas, NV	104.4	97.6	112.2	71.8	113.2	113.1	108.5
Reno–Sparks, NV	107.8	105.2	125.6	87.8	94.6	119.4	106.5
Newark–Elizabeth, NJ	122.7	108.6	148.5	130.9	110.4	132.5	111.9
Alamogordo, NM	102.5	106.1	105.5	97.4	109.6	108.0	95.9
Albuquerque, NM	101.0	101.1	109.8	71.6	106.6	100.3	103.1

City and State	All-Items Index	Grocery Items	Housing	Utilities	Transportation	Health Care	Misc. Goods and Svcs.
Los Alamos, NM	116.5	109.5	148.5	75.9	116.3	127.4	109.6
Roswell, NM	98.6	107.0	101.3	83.1	109.9	99.5	92.4
Binghamton, NY	99.3	97.2	102.2	103.8	93.8	101.6	98.4
Buffalo, NY	97.3	104.5	83.0	118.1	106.9	88.5	93.8
Elmira, NY	98.9	101.5	86.7	117.2	91.0	93.4	104.5
Glens Falls, NY	96.9	101.1	86.1	117.6	106.2	76.8	95.6
New York, NY	137.3	106.3	179.3	175.3	115.0	159.7	!14.6
Orange County, NY	110.0	03.4	115.2	143.6	98.0	116.8	101.1
Syracuse, NY	94.5	02.0	84.6	109.2	93.7	93.7	92.8
Asheville, NC	92.2	94.5	97.0	95.2	77.8	86.6	93.9
Chapel Hill, NC	101.9	92.5	124.7	91.1	97.5	103.3	96.1
Charlotte, NC	98.5	99.0	103.9	92.6	97.2	98.7	96.8
Concord, NC	94.9	94.6	102.1	88.6	94.5	87.2	93.9
Durham, NC	99.0	94.3	103.2	91.8	101.5	103.2	99.3
Greensboro, NC	95.2	95.1	105.1	92.0	90.1	88.5	92.8
Greenville, NC	95.8	94.4	92.9	93.2	92.4	97.1	100.8
Hickory, NC	95.4	90.3	94.1	92.1	107.7	84.9	97.4
Marion, NC	94.0	92.7	97.2	94.3	90.6	77.3	97.6
Raleigh, NC	102.7	94.7	124.6	99.9	97.2	101.5	94.8
Roanoke Rapids, NC	92.7	92.9	95.6	94.5	98.3	88.2	88.5
Winston–Salem, NC	95.7	92.7	99.2	92.0	92.7	89.8	98.9
Akron, OH	97.1	88.6	91.7	122.6	94.8	105.0	95.6
Bucyrus, OH	96.1	105.4	83.3	117.1	95.3	72.3	98.6
Canton, OH	91.1	87.6	93.4	99.9	91.0	90.0	88.6
Cincinnati, OH	102.9	100.0	96.9	125.2	108.2	93.9	100.4
Cleveland, OH	102.1	102.1	97.8	103.2	101.4	112.1	102.9
Columbus, OH	103.7	103.6	100.8	119.8	107.7	102.9	98.6
Lorain, OH	100.5	105.5	98.3	110.1	90.0	110.2	98.0
Mt. Vernon, OH	98.1	109.1	87.3	108.6	92.4	90.7	100.1
Newark, OH	100.8	105.1	101.4	98.0	94.4	98.1	102.4
Youngstown, OH	94.2	98.5	97.1	109.5	83.5	93.9	88.8
McAlester, OK	99.7	112.6	84.3	100.6	107.7	98.8	100.1
Norman, OK	104.0	104.3	102.8	104.1	104.7	94.5	106.5
Oklahoma City, OK	97.6	107.0	92.2	102.9	94.5	95.4	96.2
Tulsa, OK	102.5	105.9	101.7	102.2	98.2	100.7	103.5
Medford, OR	99.3	105.3	93.2	81.6	99.4	110.6	104.2
Portland, OR	103.8	115.4	99.2	69.0	116.0	129.1	102.3
Salem, OR	95.8	105.0	76.5	79.9	97.6	122.1	103.5

Table VII   Continued

City and State	All-Items Index	Grocery Items	Housing	Utilities	Transportation	Health Care	Misc. Goods and Svcs.
Altoona, PA	96.8	94.0	90.5	109.5	92.1	90.7	102.0
Erie, PA	98.0	98.1	84.3	101.2	107.5	96.1	103.1
Harrisburg, PA	103.6	95.0	99.9	107.7	106.6	106.9	107.7
Lancaster, PA	99.5	102.7	84.1	108.6	105.9	88.4	105.6
Philadelphia, PA	115.8	107.6	115.9	151.5	115.6	122.1	105.8
Reading, PA	102.6	105.7	100.4	124.4	98.9	85.5	100.2
Scranton, PA	97.4	97.8	86.5	132.4	87.9	94.0	97.3
Waynesboro, PA	96.5	99.2	104.3	93.5	92.9	87.7	93.9
York, PA	99.5	94.9	107.1	93.1	95.0	96.1	101.6
Columbia, SC	103.7	98.0	98.8	125.1	103.6	100.7	103.3
Greenville, SC	96.2	95.1	92.2	94.5	97.4	85.5	102.5
Spartanburg, SC	97.1	96.6	97.4	94.3	101.9	88.3	98.1
Aberdeen, SD	93.2	99.5	84.5	117.0	90.7	80.2	91.4
Rapid City, SD	96.1	105.6	91.0	86.0	97.5	110.8	94.2
Vermillion, SD	93.9	94.7	82.6	91.5	92.8	96.7	102.5
Chattanooga, TN	93.7	96.2	89.5	88.9	94.5	82.2	99.4
Cookeville, TN	89.2	98.6	82.7	91.0	96.8	71.4	88.9
Dyersburg, TN	90.1	101.5	78.3	103.9	82.8	67.1	95.8
Jackson, TN	91.7	103.1	79.7	82.5	93.6	80.8	99.2
Knoxville, TN	97.8	96.7	84.3	115.2	102.6	94.3	100.8
Memphis, TN	99.9	97.1	102.0	96.2	110.9	97.5	97.0
Morristown, TN	94.9	96.3	82.7	115.9	98.6	84.7	96.2
Nashville–Davidson, TN	100.7	100.3	101.2	103.9	110.6	89.4	97.8
Paris, TN	90.0	106.1	75.9	80.9	98.3	73.6	94.9
Abilene, TX	100.9	108.6	91.9	111.0	103.1	101.3	98.4
Amarillo, TX	98.7	102.0	108.2	85.9	93.4	94.4	97.8
Austin, TX	107.2	104.2	125.7	86.0	104.4	108.7	103.9
Fort Worth, TX	102.1	103.8	103.0	100.7	105.4	89.5	102.6
Harlingen, TX	99.5	97.8	99.5	99.5	112.0	98.8	95.3
Houston, TX	107.9	103.2	100.2	125.6	111.6	107.1	108.3
Kerrville, TX	102.3	103.7	108.0	95.1	102.9	93.9	101.8
Killeen, TX	95.0	99.4	92.1	96.3	95.9	88.5	95.4
Lubbock, TX	100.4	97.8	91.9	103.4	101.4	100.1	106.5
Mcallen, TX	101.0	100.3	93.1	112.2	101.5	90.6	105.3
Nacogdoches, TX	100.0	99.7	100.1	102.5	94.7	90.8	103.7
Odessa, TX	103.1	105.0	99.2	92.7	108.4	100.4	107.2
Plainview, TX	100.5	100.8	96.2	127.6	101.2	89.1	95.7
Port Arthur, TX	106.6	109.5	97.2	130.5	95.6	100.9	109.1
San Antonio, TX	99.2	99.3	99.6	109.7	104.1	93.3	94.3

City and State	All-Items Index	Grocery Items	Housing	Utilities	Transportation	Health Care	Misc. Goods and Svcs.
Sherman, TX	96.1	95.7	100.2	102.8	92.3	91.6	93.4
Temple, TX	93.7	99.3	91.9	94.0	90.2	86.0	94.9
Texarkana, TX–AR	92.0	96.2	95.8	80.5	96.8	85.1	90.7
Tyler, TX	105.0	108.1	100.1	102.3	105.8	100.5	108.5
Victoria, TX	102.0	103.6	106.8	97.5	106.9	91.3	99.7
Waco, TX	99.2	97.7	94.2	113.0	94.6	102.5	100.1
Wichita Falls, TX	104.3	106.5	97.5	125.9	107.5	99.1	100.0
Salt Lake City, UT	101.7	100.6	97.9	95.3	102.2	103.2	107.1
Barre, VT	99.4	103.3	105.8	95.5	94.9	83.6	99.5
St. Thomas, VI	129.9	142.5	138.3	148.2	102.1	127.0	122.7
Hampton Roads/SE, VA	100.6	97.7	104.8	98.2	96.8	93.0	103.6
Martinsville, VA	96.1	94.7	100.1	99.2	94.3	94.5	93.9
Richmond, VA	102.1	99.1	101.9	104.7	97.6	113.5	102.3
Roanoke, VA	95.4	99.9	100.5	78.8	103.6	82.6	94.7
Renton, WA	112.3	104.9	116.7	110.8	104.0	145.4	109.6
Richland–Kennewick, WA	94.5	99.7	80.0	75.7	94.0	133.5	100.1
Seattle, WA	109.5	110.6	104.8	90.2	116.3	133.0	111.0
Spokane, WA	104.0	105.1	101.5	85.7	98.1	129.8	108.5
Tacoma, WA	102.0	98.9	109.9	52.5	96.9	137.2	110.0
Wenatchee–East Wenatchee, WA	98.9	103.8	92.9	59.5	109.6	107.4	108.5
Yakima, WA	101.2	100.0	93.7	92.1	114.3	127.5	98.9
Charleston, WV	99.0	106.7	98.3	89.0	97.7	98.0	99.7
Appleton, WI	96.4	88.8	102.6	103.5	94.2	90.4	96.0
Fond Du Lac, WI	99.9	94.9	105.8	101.7	107.0	93.8	96.2
Fort Atkinson, WI	94.8	93.3	93.1	106.7	90.6	81.7	97.3
Green Bay, WI	97.3	96.7	100.2	94.9	100.7	87.4	97.4
Janesville, WI	90.0	94.6	87.0	86.7	79.5	87.9	95.7
La Crosse, WI	96.3	97.1	96.2	87.8	104.8	95.1	95.6
Marinette, WI	96.3	94.4	93.6	93.9	110.6	87.7	95.9
New London, WI	93.1	91.3	87.1	111.2	91.6	92.3	92.8
Oshkosh, WI	97.1	89.6	110.5	95.0	97.0	84.5	95.2
Wausau, WI	93.9	95.1	84.8	109.8	93.0	89.7	95.3
Casper, WY	101.5	104.7	91.1	96.3	98.2	112.6	108.0
Evanston, WY	104.8	104.6	107.7	91.6	100.1	105.6	109.4

Table VIII Stock Price Data from 1978 to 1981 (209 Weekly Observations)
Includes data on Revlon, a drug product index, a cosmetics product index, and a market index. Also lists weekly percentage changes for each of these.

Week	REV	COS	DRUG	CMPS	REVPC	COSPC	DRUGPC	CMPSPC
1	42.875	58.990	148.300	93.520	1.564	2.331	0.256	1.551
2	40.750	56.970	142.500	89.740	−4.746	−3.424	−3.911	−4.042
3	41.750	57.300	146.700	90.560	2.454	0.579	2.947	0.914
4	41.500	56.700	147.400	89.390	−0.599	−1.047	0.477	−1.292
5	41.875	56.710	149.900	89.930	0.904	0.018	1.696	0.604
6	41.625	56.950	149.400	90.830	−0.597	0.423	−0.334	1.001
7	41.000	55.980	146.200	88.830	−1.502	−1.703	−2.142	−2.202
8	41.375	56.060	141.600	87.560	0.915	0.143	−3.146	−1.430
9	39.375	55.730	140.700	87.190	−4.834	−0.589	−0.636	−0.423
10	39.750	56.110	141.600	87.840	0.952	0.682	0.640	0.745
11	40.000	57.000	145.300	89.120	0.629	1.586	2.613	1.457
12	39.000	56.680	145.300	89.470	−2.500	−0.561	0.000	0.393
13	39.000	57.060	144.700	89.640	0.000	0.670	−0.413	0.190
14	39.500	57.000	143.900	89.640	1.282	−0.105	−0.553	0.000
15	39.625	57.580	144.300	90.110	0.316	1.018	0.278	0.524
16	43.125	61.380	150.000	93.860	8.833	6.600	3.950	4.162
17	44.500	61.690	156.200	96.820	3.188	0.505	4.133	3.154
18	46.000	64.760	158.800	96.260	3.371	4.977	1.665	−0.578
19	45.250	64.540	157.100	95.920	−1.630	−0.340	−1.071	−0.353
20	48.000	67.060	165.800	99.600	6.077	3.905	5.538	3.837
21	46.375	65.670	162.000	97.080	−3.385	−2.073	−2.292	−2.530
22	47.250	65.380	163.100	97.240	1.887	−0.442	0.679	0.165
23	49.125	69.120	174.000	100.100	3.968	5.720	6.683	2.941
24	48.750	67.460	170.700	99.480	−0.763	−2.402	−1.897	−0.619
25	47.375	64.960	163.200	101.600	−2.821	−3.706	−4.394	2.131
26	48.250	65.610	161.800	95.400	1.847	1.001	−0.858	−6.102
27	47.000	64.630	160.200	94.270	−2.591	−1.494	−0.989	−1.184
28	48.000	66.960	166.500	96.240	2.128	3.605	3.933	2.090
29	50.125	67.940	171.600	98.120	4.427	1.464	3.063	1.953
30	50.000	68.970	170.900	99.080	−0.249	1.516	−0.408	0.978
31	54.000	72.610	178.200	102.900	8.000	5.278	4.272	3.855
32	56.625	75.560	180.400	104.500	4.861	4.063	1.235	1.555

Legend: REV: Price of Revlon stock.
COS: Index of cosmetic stocks.
DRUG: Index of drug stocks.
CMPS: Composite market index.
REVPC: Percentage change in REV from previous week.
COSPC: Percentage change in COS from previous week.
DRUGPC: Percentage change in DRUG from previous week.
CMPSPC: Percentage change in CMPS from previous week.

Week	REV	COS	DRUG	CMPS	REVPC	COSPC	DRUGPC	CMPSPC
33	51.000	74.680	178.000	104.700	− 9.934	− 1.165	− 1.330	0.191
34	56.500	74.310	175.700	104.900	10.784	− 0.495	− 1.292	0.191
35	56.125	72.530	173.600	103.500	− 0.664	− 2.395	− 1.195	− 1.335
36	56.375	74.340	177.900	105.400	0.445	2.496	2.477	1.836
37	56.000	73.040	177.500	106.300	− 0.665	− 1.749	− 0.225	0.854
38	52.250	68.600	167.900	101.700	− 6.696	− 6.079	− 5.408	− 4.327
39	52.375	68.050	166.500	101.700	0.239	− 0.802	− 0.834	0.000
40	53.000	68.590	168.300	103.100	1.193	0.794	1.081	1.377
41	54.000	71.700	168.600	105.400	1.887	4.534	0.178	2.231
42	51.875	68.190	160.600	100.500	− 3.935	− 4.895	− 4.745	− 4.649
43	49.375	65.040	154.000	97.310	− 4.819	− 4.619	− 4.110	− 3.174
44	50.000	67.330	159.300	96.850	1.266	3.521	3.442	− 0.473
45	50.375	65.950	153.500	94.450	0.750	− 2.050	− 3.641	− 2.478
46	50.500	64.290	151.700	92.710	0.248	− 2.517	− 1.173	− 1.842
47	52.625	65.500	155.900	95.480	4.208	1.882	2.769	2.988
48	50.500	64.320	153.200	93.750	− 4.038	− 1.802	− 1.732	− 1.812
49	54.750	68.450	162.200	97.490	8.416	6.421	5.875	3.989
50	52.625	66.170	158.400	96.060	− 3.881	− 3.331	− 2.343	− 1.467
51	50.250	64.210	158.400	94.680	− 4.513	− 2.962	0.000	− 1.437
52	51.500	66.270	163.700	96.660	2.488	3.208	3.346	2.091
53	52.375	66.080	164.800	97.800	1.699	− 0.287	0.672	1.179
54	52.625	65.870	164.700	98.770	0.477	− 0.318	− 0.061	0.992
55	53.000	66.750	167.100	99.480	0.713	1.336	1.457	0.719
56	53.625	67.440	165.800	100.200	1.179	1.034	− 0.778	0.724
57	50.250	65.630	164.300	99.930	− 6.294	− 2.684	− 0.905	− 0.269
58	49.750	62.620	158.400	97.160	− 0.995	− 4.586	− 3.591	− 2.772
59	50.500	62.840	161.800	98.870	1.508	0.351	2.146	1.760
60	49.875	62.110	160.700	99.070	− 1.238	− 1.162	− 0.680	0.202
61	47.625	60.270	157.300	96.280	− 4.511	− 2.962	− 2.116	− 2.816
62	49.375	61.650	161.800	98.440	3.675	2.290	2.861	2.243
63	49.500	61.680	162.500	99.710	0.253	0.049	0.433	1.290
64	47.625	60.970	164.100	101.300	− 3.788	− 1.151	0.985	1.595
65	49.250	61.370	165.200	102.100	3.412	0.656	0.670	0.790
66	49.500	61.820	165.400	102.700	0.508	0.733	0.121	0.588
67	48.000	60.900	164.100	102.300	− 3.030	− 1.488	− 0.786	− 0.389
68	47.875	60.380	165.100	101.700	− 0.260	− 0.854	0.609	− 0.587
69	47.250	61.690	165.700	102.500	− 1.305	2.170	0.363	0.787
70	45.750	60.950	163.600	101.700	− 3.175	− 1.200	− 1.267	− 0.780

Table VIII Continued

Week	REV	COS	DRUG	CMPS	REVPC	COSPC	DRUGPC	CMPSPC
71	45.250	58.830	157.600	99.460	−1.093	−3.478	−3.667	−2.203
72	45.125	58.020	156.200	98.420	−0.276	−1.377	−0.888	−1.046
73	46.000	58.850	159.800	99.890	1.939	1.431	2.305	1.494
74	45.375	58.340	157.000	99.110	−1.359	−0.867	−1.752	−0.781
75	46.500	59.180	162.400	101.300	2.479	1.440	3.439	2.210
76	47.375	60.330	165.400	102.300	1.882	1.943	1.847	0.987
77	46.750	59.480	164.100	101.600	−1.319	−1.409	−0.786	−0.684
78	47.250	60.380	161.200	102.300	1.070	1.513	−1.767	0.689
79	45.625	59.360	161.500	102.100	−3.439	−1.689	0.186	−0.196
80	48.000	60.310	164.900	103.600	5.205	1.600	2.105	1.469
81	46.625	59.550	160.700	101.700	−2.865	−1.260	−2.547	−1.834
82	46.875	59.730	162.400	103.100	0.536	0.302	1.058	1.377
83	47.500	60.480	164.500	104.200	1.333	1.256	1.293	1.067
84	50.625	64.270	170.300	106.000	6.579	6.267	3.526	1.727
85	54.000	66.700	176.200	108.300	6.667	3.781	3.464	2.170
86	54.625	66.490	175.200	109.000	1.157	−0.315	−0.568	0.646
87	53.250	66.350	173.700	109.000	−2.517	−0.211	−0.856	0.000
88	50.500	63.670	171.000	110.000	−5.164	−4.039	−1.554	0.917
89	50.250	63.150	170.500	107.800	−0.495	−0.817	−0.292	−2.000
90	51.000	63.880	171.200	108.300	1.493	1.156	0.411	0.464
91	52.000	64.470	174.500	110.000	1.961	0.924	1.928	1.570
92	51.000	63.460	175.600	109.600	−1.923	−1.567	0.630	−0.364
93	48.750	60.540	167.300	105.300	−4.412	−4.601	−4.727	−3.923
94	48.125	58.920	166.100	103.400	−1.282	−2.676	−0.717	−1.804
95	46.125	55.130	163.500	100.400	−4.156	−6.432	−1.565	−2.901
96	44.375	55.420	167.000	101.800	−3.794	0.526	2.141	1.394
97	44.375	54.600	163.700	99.870	0.000	−1.480	−1.976	−1.896
98	47.375	56.170	174.000	103.400	6.761	2.875	6.292	3.535
99	44.625	53.730	175.700	103.900	−5.805	−4.344	0.977	0.484
100	46.375	55.290	183.100	106.700	3.922	2.903	4.212	2.695
101	48.125	54.960	183.100	107.300	3.774	−0.597	0.000	0.562
102	45.500	54.560	182.200	107.500	−5.455	−0.728	−0.492	0.186
103	45.000	54.950	181.600	108.200	−1.099	0.715	−0.329	0.651
104	45.000	54.640	181.000	107.800	0.000	−0.564	−0.330	−0.370
105	44.125	53.310	176.900	105.800	−1.944	−2.434	−2.265	−1.855
106	44.875	53.930	184.300	109.100	1.700	1.163	4.183	3.119
107	41.125	51.790	180.100	111.100	−8.357	−3.968	−2.279	1.833
108	42.250	53.030	180.400	113.400	2.736	2.394	0.167	2.070
109	42.625	52.220	179.100	115.200	0.888	−1.527	−0.721	1.587
110	41.500	50.710	174.800	115.700	−2.639	−2.892	−2.401	0.434

Week	REV	COS	DRUG	CMPS	REVPC	COSPC	DRUGPC	CMPSPC
111	41.000	49.340	174.700	118.400	−1.205	−2.702	−0.057	2.334
112	39.250	49.370	173.800	116.500	−4.268	0.061	−0.515	−1.605
113	38.750	48.320	164.000	112.400	−1.274	−2.127	−5.639	−3.519
114	37.875	46.900	159.400	111.100	−2.258	−2.939	−2.805	−1.157
115	36.375	45.550	159.300	106.900	−3.960	−2.878	−0.063	−3.780
116	36.625	46.590	157.200	104.300	0.687	2.283	−1.318	−2.432
117	36.375	45.620	153.200	98.680	−0.683	−2.082	−2.545	−5.388
118	38.875	49.460	167.600	102.700	6.873	8.417	9.399	4.074
119	40.375	49.820	167.100	103.100	3.859	0.728	−0.298	0.389
120	40.250	48.430	162.300	101.500	−0.310	−2.790	−2.873	−1.552
121	41.500	50.620	165.700	103.700	3.106	4.522	2.095	2.167
122	42.750	51.770	169.600	106.300	3.012	2.272	2.354	2.507
123	43.875	54.730	174.600	107.200	2.632	5.718	2.948	0.847
124	45.375	55.270	176.500	106.900	3.419	0.987	1.088	−0.280
125	47.125	56.120	179.400	107.700	3.857	1.538	1.643	0.748
126	47.125	56.550	181.500	112.100	0.000	0.766	1.171	4.085
127	47.500	55.890	182.600	112.600	0.796	−1.167	0.606	0.446
128	47.875	56.200	185.800	116.000	0.789	0.555	1.752	3.020
129	47.000	56.000	184.400	116.300	−1.828	−0.356	−0.754	0.259
130	47.125	55.860	184.800	116.700	0.266	−0.250	0.217	0.344
131	45.000	54.530	182.500	115.700	−4.509	−2.381	−1.245	−0.857
132	47.875	55.300	184.800	118.000	6.389	1.412	1.260	1.988
133	50.250	58.160	187.100	119.600	4.961	5.172	1.245	1.356
134	50.125	58.970	190.500	121.900	−0.249	1.393	1.817	1.923
135	50.125	60.420	192.800	122.200	0.000	2.459	1.207	0.246
136	49.875	60.090	195.400	121.600	−0.499	−0.546	1.349	−0.491
137	52.125	60.670	198.700	123.300	4.511	0.965	1.689	1.398
138	51.125	59.580	197.000	123.800	−1.918	−1.797	−0.856	0.406
139	51.875	59.100	196.000	123.500	1.467	−0.806	−0.508	−0.242
140	51.250	59.490	198.600	126.100	−1.205	0.660	1.327	2.105
141	49.000	58.670	195.600	124.800	−4.390	−1.378	−1.511	−1.031
142	51.000	59.920	205.300	128.900	4.082	2.131	4.959	3.285
143	50.375	60.130	205.300	130.400	−1.225	0.350	0.000	1.164
144	48.625	57.530	199.000	127.100	−3.474	−4.324	−3.069	−2.531
145	49.250	58.370	200.100	131.700	1.285	1.460	0.553	3.619
146	48.625	57.590	199.600	133.700	−1.269	−1.336	−0.250	1.519
147	48.875	55.750	194.800	131.900	0.514	−3.195	−2.405	−1.346
148	45.875	55.110	192.000	127.900	−6.138	−1.148	−1.437	−3.033
149	47.750	55.530	196.300	131.300	4.087	0.762	2.240	2.658
150	47.625	55.670	199.700	134.600	−0.262	0.252	1.732	2.513

Table VIII   Continued

Week	REV	COS	DRUG	CMPS	REVPC	COSPC	DRUGPC	CMPSPC
151	48.750	56.710	206.000	139.100	2.362	1.868	3.155	3.343
152	48.000	55.710	205.100	140.200	−1.538	−1.763	−0.437	0.791
153	46.375	56.210	201.500	136.700	−3.385	0.898	−1.755	−2.496
154	43.000	53.190	191.300	128.300	−7.278	−5.373	−5.062	−6.145
155	43.625	52.730	197.000	132.900	1.453	−0.865	2.980	3.585
156	47.875	55.830	208.200	135.900	9.742	5.879	5.685	2.257
157	48.000	56.000	217.700	135.800	0.261	0.305	4.563	−0.074
158	50.750	57.890	219.400	135.100	5.729	3.375	0.781	−0.515
159	48.750	57.050	218.200	133.500	−3.941	−1.451	−0.547	−1.184
160	44.875	55.490	211.900	131.400	−7.949	−2.734	−2.887	−1.573
161	46.000	56.200	214.500	130.300	2.507	1.280	1.227	−0.837
162	44.000	55.720	210.400	128.600	−4.348	−0.854	−1.911	−1.305
163	44.000	55.820	210.000	128.200	0.000	0.179	−0.190	−0.311
164	44.000	55.650	210.900	128.500	0.000	−0.305	0.429	0.234
165	43.375	55.670	212.400	128.500	−1.420	0.036	0.711	0.000
166	43.250	56.500	217.800	130.900	−0.288	1.491	2.542	1.868
167	42.000	55.710	216.300	130.000	−2.890	−1.398	−0.689	−0.688
168	43.500	57.540	221.900	134.200	3.571	3.285	2.589	3.231
169	43.875	58.650	228.100	137.700	0.862	1.929	2.794	2.608
170	45.750	59.180	228.700	136.600	4.274	0.904	0.263	−0.799
171	44.750	58.400	228.600	134.300	−2.186	−1.318	−0.044	−1.684
172	45.500	60.790	230.100	134.200	1.676	4.092	0.656	−0.074
173	46.500	62.650	234.500	134.100	2.198	3.060	1.912	−0.075
174	43.125	59.780	231.600	133.100	−7.258	−4.581	−1.237	−0.746
175	43.750	58.120	223.900	130.800	1.449	−2.777	−3.325	−1.728
176	42.750	57.760	224.300	130.600	−2.286	−0.619	0.179	−0.153
177	42.250	56.780	226.300	132.000	−1.170	−1.697	0.892	1.072
178	41.750	58.150	229.900	133.800	−1.183	2.413	1.591	1.364
179	43.125	59.520	237.400	130.700	3.293	2.356	3.262	−2.317
180	44.875	60.760	236.000	132.300	4.058	2.083	−0.590	1.224
181	45.000	61.040	233.100	133.300	0.279	0.461	−1.229	0.756
182	42.125	58.530	228.600	132.700	−6.389	−4.112	−1.931	−0.450
183	41.875	57.690	217.800	129.800	−0.593	−1.435	−4.724	−2.185
184	42.375	57.170	212.400	128.300	1.194	−0.901	−2.479	−1.156
185	41.750	56.960	215.000	130.200	−1.475	−0.367	1.224	1.481
186	39.875	55.410	207.800	127.100	−4.491	−2.721	−3.349	−2.381
187	38.875	54.100	209.200	129.200	−2.508	−2.364	0.674	1.652
188	39.250	55.350	209.900	132.700	0.965	2.311	0.335	2.709
189	38.250	55.480	210.600	133.400	−2.548	0.235	0.334	0.528
190	38.250	54.630	207.100	130.500	0.000	−1.532	−1.662	−2.174

Week	REV	COS	DRUG	CMPS	REVPC	COSPC	DRUGPC	CMPSPC
191	38.625	54.660	202.600	125.000	0.980	0.055	−2.173	−4.215
192	36.750	53.360	200.100	123.500	−4.854	−2.378	−1.234	−1.200
193	35.500	50.950	194.100	118.400	−3.401	−4.516	−2.999	−4.130
194	34.750	51.220	194.300	118.900	−2.113	0.530	0.103	0.422
195	33.625	50.480	194.400	115.700	−3.237	−1.445	0.051	−2.691
196	34.125	50.630	195.400	116.200	1.487	0.297	0.514	0.432
197	37.000	53.010	202.100	121.300	8.425	4.701	3.429	4.389
198	35.750	52.920	200.400	118.800	−3.378	−0.170	−0.841	−2.061
199	38.125	53.200	203.800	120.100	6.643	0.529	1.697	1.094
200	29.000	50.030	205.300	119.500	−23.934	−5.959	0.736	−0.500
201	29.875	51.140	210.700	124.700	3.017	2.219	2.630	4.351
202	27.750	49.050	206.900	122.900	−7.113	−4.087	−1.804	−1.443
203	26.875	48.970	204.100	120.300	−3.153	−0.163	−1.353	−2.116
204	29.000	48.960	210.100	124.100	7.907	−0.020	2.940	3.159
205	31.375	50.360	212.400	124.700	8.190	2.859	1.095	0.483
206	30.000	50.090	214.300	125.500	−4.382	−0.536	0.895	0.642
207	29.750	48.160	211.000	122.400	−0.833	−3.853	−1.540	−2.470
208	29.750	47.590	211.600	122.300	0.000	−1.184	0.284	−0.082
209	30.500	47.220	213.300	122.300	2.521	−0.777	0.803	0.000

Table IX   Data on United States Cities

City	CHEMP	INC	TAX	UNEMP	POP80	POP70	W1	W2	HOUSE	UTIL	HS39	CRIME	FWAY	EDUC
Akron, OH	14.17	23682	791	9.1	660328	679239	0	1	55750	896	38.4	419.3	93	1541
Atlantic City, NJ	15.31	23525	1728	7.2	194119	175045	1	0	52228	945	42.6	650.1	19	1657
Baton Rouge, LA	34.80	25310	282	5.4	493973	375628	0	0	47114	867	14.1	788.2	24	1365
Bridgeport, CT	16.87	33518	1708	6.0	395455	401752	1	0	58107	834	38.1	352.4	59	1474
Buffalo, NY	7.83	23749	2507	8.7	1242573	1349211	0	1	64292	645	53.2	496.1	133	2098
Chattanooga, TN	28.52	23479	616	7.8	426540	370857	0	1	48927	1091	26.8	474.7	55	1168
Denver, CO	40.25	30545	1054	6.0	1619921	1239545	0	0	78112	593	21.9	609.3	160	1944
El Paso, TX	28.21	18411	885	10.0	479899	359291	1	0	48147	694	18.6	519.2	39	1056
Gary, IN	18.75	26668	828	10.2	642781	633367	0	0	48434	850	33.5	641.4	40	1402
Green Bay, WI	25.59	23614	929	6.7	175280	158244	0	0	51897	869	34.0	85.2	29	1670
Houston, TX	40.12	32565	723	4.4	2905350	1999316	0	0	65738	994	12.4	673.5	312	1332
Jacksonville, FL	21.74	23428	521	5.5	737519	621827	0	1	50605	894	18.6	799.9	94	1486
Kalamazoo, MI	23.09	25434	1298	9.2	279192	257723	0	1	48278	842	39.2	708.9	27	1617
Las Vegas, NV	55.64	30526	1005	7.4	461816	273288	0	1	79204	940	2.3	1024.4	33	1513
Little Rock, AR	21.62	24303	499	5.7	393494	323296	0	0	46252	772	21.5	781.0	84	1142
Macon, GA	13.60	21157	546	6.2	254623	226782	0	0	42325	860	22.8	440.7	23	1247
Milwaukee, WI	17.69	27929	2474	6.4	1397143	1403884	0	0	78810	807	41.0	277.2	150	1757
Nashville, TN	31.99	25032	527	5.3	850505	699271	1	0	51720	1033	27.2	518.0	102	1324
Omaha, NE	14.92	24546	1127	5.6	570399	542646	0	0	53936	924	38.9	440.2	51	1823
Peoria, IL	20.80	30563	1256	8.4	365864	341979	0	0	63480	1221	37.6	676.3	32	1470
Phoenix, AZ	36.69	27975	952	6.0	1508030	971228	0	1	65240	1145	7.4	673.9	92	1776
Portland, ME	24.99	23906	1436	6.3	183625	173381	0	0	56780	643	49.1	342.5	21	1408
Richmond, VA	22.86	28671	918	3.6	632015	547542	0	1	58869	1156	22.7	481.0	103	1471
Sacramento, CA	24.56	26438	1414	7.5	1014002	803793	0	1	77702	506	12.4	724.7	92	1783
San Antonio, TX	22.78	21819	752	6.8	1071954	888179	0	0	40878	825	22.0	446.3	156	1185
Santa Barbara, CA	26.30	28858	1982	5.1	298660	264324	1	0	136709	459	17.6	414.8	27	1888
Scranton, PE	10.83	21886	1540	9.8	640396	621882	0	1	50516	960	72.5	123.4	60	1538
Tacoma, WA	20.83	25449	1178	8.5	485643	412344	1	0	78564	762	26.2	494.5	40	1885
Wheeling, WV	24.38	24370	336	8.9	185566	181954	1	0	51748	908	66.1	162.7	34	1513
Wilmington, DE	24.73	21060	1196	6.5	524108	499493	1	0	75248	896	31.1	482.3	49	1792

Legend: CHEMP: Predicted percentage increase in employment from 1980 to 1990.
   INC: Average household income.
   TAX: Average sum of state, sales, and property taxes.
   UNEMP: Unemployment percentage.
   POP80: 1980 population.
   POP70: 1970 population.
   W1: 1 if city's weather is rated in top third of all large cities, 0 otherwise.
   W2: 1 if city's weather is rated in middle third of all large cities, 0 otherwise.
   HOUSE: Average market value of all houses.
   UTIL: Average yearly utility bill.
   HS39: Percentage of city's houses built before 1939.
   CRIME: Number of violent crimes per 100,000 people.
   FWAY: Number of freeway miles within city.
   EDUC: Average amount spent per student in grades K–12.

Source   *Places Rated Almanac,* 1982.

Solutions to Odd-Numbered Problems

Note: Many of the problems, especially those with large data sets, have been solved by the computer software package that accompanies this book. This may lead to slight differences from solutions found by hand or hand calculator.

Solutions for Chapter 2

1. With ten categories, frequencies are 7, 11, 8, 11, 6, 6, 2, 4, 2, and 3. With five categories, frequencies are 18, 19, 12, 6, and 5. The histogram with five categories is less bumpy (or irregular).

3. **a.** The over-50 histogram is slightly flatter and has a higher relative frequency for the over-$1000 category. The under-50 histogram has higher relative frequencies for the lower-dollar categories.
   b. Under-50 group: 2, 11, 34, 71, 151, 220, 276, 319, 355, 387, 402, 424, 446, 481; over-50 group: 0, 4, 15, 36, 79, 113, 142, 173, 202, 231, 241, 251, 270, 324   **c.** Same basic conclusions as in part (a)

5. **a.** 20%   **b.** $29.99, $15   **7. a.** 7%   **b.** Graph

9. Cumulative percentages for combined group: 25.2, 41.8, 50.8, 58.0, 79.6, 90.2, 95.4, 99.6, 100.0

11. Peaks in summer months, lowest sales in winter months, slight upward trend

13. Negative relationship between seniority and number of days absent

15. Slight upward trend until 1969, then a larger upward trend until 1974, then a much larger upward trend through 1980

17. **a.** $19,572, $17,118, $25,642   **b.** $20,272   **c.** $30.27

19. Any number between 49 and 52; any number between 58 and 59; any number between 72 and 73; any number between 82 and 83; any number between 89 and 91

21. First 24: $s = \$160.902$; last 36: $s = \$168.385$; combined: $s = \$164.129$ (slight round-off from value in text)

23. Cov = 6; Corr = .616, supported by positive relationship in scattergram

25. Any number between $21,150 and $21,189; any number between $66,720 and $66,882; median = $37,563

27. **a.** Graph   **b.** Median = $125; 25th percentile = $100; 75th percentile is any number between $145 and $150

29. $\overline{X} = \$33,720$, $s = \$25,865$

31. Under-50 group: $\overline{X} = \$420.21$; over-50 group: $\overline{X} = \$523.06$; combined group: $\overline{X} = \$461.61$ **33.** 9.96 kilometer/liter

35. $\bar{X} = 1.85$, $s = 2.01$, median $= 1$ **37. a.** $\bar{X} = \$381.50$, $s = \$370.30$ **b.** $\bar{X} = \$383.33$, $s = \$367.74$

39. a. Faculty: 6.85; graduate students: 5.83; undergraduates: 2.17   **b.** Combined: 4.69

41. a. $\bar{X} = \$128.5$, median $= \$125$, $s = \$36.54$
   b. Range $= \$145$, interdecile range $= \$100$, interquartile range $= \$47.50$, MAD $= \$29.18$

43. $\bar{X} = .4696$, $s^2 = .0980$; frequencies: 16, 11, 11, 9, 13

45. Large values in the right-hand tail pull average up, so $\bar{X}$ is larger than median; most likely values are in the lower half of the data set, so median is larger than mode.

47. a. Definite positive relationship   **b.** Cov $= 151.81$, Corr $= .716$; yes, it supports a positive relationship

49. a. Graph   **b.** 1940: 1.96%; 1985: 4.91%   **51. a.** Graph   **b.** $\bar{X} = \$157$ **53. a.** 65%   **b.** $\bar{X} = 77.4\%$

55. a. $\bar{X} = \$63.67$; $s = \$24.65$ **b.** From \$8.55 to \$118.79

57. a. True, because of Rule 2.1 with $k = 2$ **b.** True, because of Rule 2.2 with $k = 2$
   c. False; from Rule 2.2 with $k = 1$ we would expect about 28 or 29 observations in this range.

59. It is reasonable because of Rule 2.2. It should be good when the assumptions in Rule 2.2 hold; otherwise, it might be bad. For Problem 27, range $= 145$, $s = 36.54$. Then $145/4 = 36.25$ is excellent, but $145/6 = 24.17$ is not good.

61. Total of X's in group i is $n_i\bar{X}_i$, so $\Sigma\, n_i\bar{X}_i$ is sum of all X's. Then divide this by total sample size to obtain average of all X's.

63. a. Graph   **b.** $\bar{X} = \$35,533$, $s = \$26,009$
   c. For $k = 2$, at least 75% of observations should be between \$0 and \$87,551; only 2 out of 42 are outside this range. For $k = 3$, at least 89% should be between \$0 and \$113,560; only 1 out of 42 is outside this range.
   d. Rule 2.2 predicts $.95(42) = 39.9$ and at least $.99(42) = 41.6$, we observe 40 and 41, so Rule 2.2 predicts accurately in spite of skewness.

65. $s = 30.28$, MAD $= 25$. We expect s to be larger because it is based on squared deviations from the mean.

67. a. Downward trend   **b.** Corr $= -.89$ **69. a.** Mean $= 0$; st. dev. $= 1$ **b.** Confirms part (a)

71. 1975: NE, \$26,863; NC, \$26,610; S, \$23,453; W, \$26,465; 1981: NE, \$26,973; NC, \$26,070; S, \$24,228; W, \$27,538

73. For \$100: frequencies are 12, 16, 23, 8, 2, 12, 11, 4, 2, 2, 2, 8; for \$25: frequencies are 50, 23, 19, 4, 11, 11, 8, 4, 4, 4, 2, 6. We would expect a smaller discount (on average) needed for a smaller purchase amount, as supported by the graph; right-most category represents those who would prefer to purchase with credit card even with a 7% discount.

Solutions for Chapter 3

1. 7 to 3 against   **3.** $\frac{1}{7}$, $\frac{5}{17}$, $\frac{3}{11}$, .29   **5. a.** $\frac{36}{44}$ **b.** $\frac{39}{44}$ **c.** $\frac{18}{44}$

7. Typical outcome tells the number of batteries still functioning after 30 hours and lists the times of failure of the others.

9. a. Typical outcome tells which team wins and how many games are played.
   b. Typical outcome lists the sequence of winners of the games played.

11. Typical outcome lists the number (out of 250) in each of the four categories (the favorite network or "don't watch") and the number (out of 250) that do not respond.

13. a. E: at least 11,667 sold; F: at least 2,000 sold   **b.** E or F: at least \$20,000 profit   **c.** E and F: at least \$55,000 profit
   d. No; $\bar{E}$ and $\bar{F}$ (less than \$35,000 from first type and less than \$20,000 from second type) can occur.

15. a. Each company has at least 10% women or 5% blacks or both (or, no company has less than 10% women *and* less than 5% blacks).   **b.** At least one company has at least 10% women *and* at least 5% blacks.

17. No; it does not include (for example) an outcome where at least one person paid over \$50 and the average price paid is less than \$28.

19. a. Top row: $\frac{26}{190}$, $\frac{49}{190}$; bottom row: $\frac{53}{190}$, $\frac{62}{190}$ **b.** (a) .584 (b) .395 (c) .674 (d) .279

21. a. No greater than .38   **b.** at least .62   **23. a.** .09   **b.** .32   **c.** .88

25. a. If there are 0 total, there must be 0 in the shorter line. However, if there are 8 or more total, there *could* be 0 in the shorter line; it just turned out that this never happened.   **b.** .744
   c. P (at least 8 total and at least 3 in each line) $= .336$, so he may want to add a third counter.

27. a. .315 **b.** .093 **c.** .047 **d.** .148

e. In part (c) the sample space consists of all roads; in part (d) we restrict the sample space to the roads that are not dry.

29. a. .444, .527 **b.** .476, .572

c. Yes, probabilities above are larger for white-collar workers than for blue-collar workers.

31. a. .417 **b.** .219 **c.** .549 **33.** .8

35. P(at least one win) $= .0062$; P(no wins) $= .9938$; outcomes of separate contests should not affect one another, so independence is reasonable.

37. Top row: .12, .28; bottom row: .18, .42 **39.** 336 ways **41.** .00139

43. P(no aces) $= .3038$ **45.** .0154 **47.** .291

49. a. Approximately 1.378×10^{11} **b.** 46,558,512 **c.** .00361 **d.** .1708

51. a. .9458, probability of 3 or fewer A's when sampling 5 items with replacement from a population of 200 A's, 400 B's

b. .9648, probability of 6 or fewer A's when sampling 8 items with replacement from a population that is half A's, half B's

c. .9231, probability of 1, 2, or 3 A's when sampling 4 items without replacement from a population with 8 A's, 7 B's

d. .999964, probability of 2 or 3 A's when sampling 3 items without replacement from a population with 996 A's, 4 B's

53. P(no accident) $= .923$, P(accident, less than \$200 damage) $= .015$, P(accident, more than \$200 damage) $= .062$, so odds in favor of having no accident are less than 20 to 1 (more like 12 to 1)

55. a. A_1 or A_2 or A_3 **b.** Complement of (B_1 and B_2 and B_3)

c. (A_1 and B_2 and C_3) or (A_1 and B_3 and C_2) or (A_2 and B_1 and C_3) or (A_2 and B_3 and C_1) or (A_3 and B_1 and C_2) or (A_3 and B_2 and C_1)

57. a. .75 **b.** .91 **c.** .2 **59.** .30

61. a. It depends on whether you believe players have (short-run) hot streaks and slumps.

b. (1) .00157 (2) .2003 (3) .7997 (4) .0974

63. a. .1035 **b.** .2035 **c.** .307 **d.** No, because $P(F|E)$ and $P(F|\overline{E})$ are not equal.

65. a. .0059 **b.** .0041 **c.** .0077, .0178

67. a. $P(E|F) = 2P(E|\overline{F})$ **b.** Cannot conclude $P(E \text{ and } F) = 2P(E \text{ and } \overline{F})$ because $P(F)$ may not equal $P(\overline{F})$

c. No, $P(E \text{ and } F) = 6P(E \text{ and } F)$

69. a. False; for example, choose E to be the sample space S. **b.** True, because of the additive rule

c. True, from part (b) and multiplicative rule for probability of intersections

d. True: write $P(F_1|E) = P(E \text{ and } F_1)/P(E)$; now rewrite the numerator by using the multiplicative rule for intersections, and rewrite the denominator as in part (c).

71. .113 **73. a.** .2640 **b.** .2642

75. a. $\binom{3000}{31}\binom{7000}{69}/\binom{10,000}{100} \times \binom{3000}{25}\binom{7000}{75}/\binom{10,000}{100}$

b. $\left[\sum\limits_{k=35}^{100} \binom{3000}{k}\binom{7000}{100-k}/\binom{10,000}{100}\right] \times \left[\sum\limits_{k=0}^{25} \binom{3000}{k}\binom{7000}{100-k}/\binom{10,000}{100}\right]$

c. $\binom{100}{31}(.3)^{31}(.7)^{69} \times \binom{100}{25}(.3)^{25}(.7)^{75}$; $\left[\sum\limits_{k=35}^{100} \binom{100}{k}(.3)^k(.7)^{100-k}\right] \times \left[\sum\limits_{k=0}^{25} \binom{100}{k}(.3)^k(.7)^{100-k}\right]$; should be accurate, because only 1% of the population is sampled

77. a. Only column sums must be 100, because different columns represent different subpopulations **b.** .17, .531 **c.** .301

79. a. p_1 through p_8 are .0599, .1021, .0884, .0476, .1716, .0924, .1621, .2759

b. .539, .456 **c.** Probably the probabilities from part (b)

Solutions for Chapter 4

1. $P(X = 0) = \frac{1}{4}$, $P(X = 1) = \frac{1}{2}$, $P(X = 2) = \frac{1}{4}$

3. a. $P(X = 0) = \frac{39}{130}$, $P(X = 1) = \frac{45}{130}$, $P(X = 2) = \frac{32}{130}$, $P(X = 3) = \frac{10}{130}$, $P(X = 4) = \frac{4}{130}$ **b.** $\frac{116}{130}$

5. a. $P(X = 3) = .1$, $P(X = 3.5) = .2$, $P(X = 4) = .4$, $P(X = 4.5) = .3$ **b.** .3 **7. a.** .3 **b.** .45

9. .05, .5625   **11. a.** .59   **b.** Between .41 and .78

13. $P(X \leq 0) = .502, P(X \leq 1) = .876, P(X \leq 2) = .983, P(X \leq 3) = .997, P(X \leq 4) = 1$

15. a. .22, probability that no more than 2% are defective   **b.** .98, probability that at least 1% are defective
    c. .68, probability that between 2% and 4% are defective

17. a. .50, .50   **b.** .42   **c.** .40   **19.** .55

21. a. For example, $P(P = 25) = .20$, but $P(P = 25|D = 15,000) = .05/.43 \neq .20$ **b.** .57   **c.** .50

23. a. No, for example, $P(X_1 = 0) = .10$, but $P(X_1 = 0|X_2 = 0) = .01/.19 \neq .10$
    b. First row (with X_1 along the top): $\frac{1}{19}$, $\frac{3}{19}$, $\frac{6}{19}$, $\frac{9}{19}$; second row: $\frac{2}{29}$, $\frac{6}{29}$, $\frac{12}{29}$, $\frac{9}{29}$; third row: $\frac{3}{30}$, $\frac{12}{30}$, $\frac{6}{30}$, $\frac{9}{30}$;
    fourth row: $\frac{4}{22}$, $\frac{9}{22}$, $\frac{6}{22}$, $\frac{3}{22}$
    c. First row (again with X_1 along the top): .1, .1, .2, .3; second row: .2, .2, .4, .3; third row: .3, .4, .2, .3;
    fourth row: .4, .3, .2, .1
    d. Yes; for example, from the table in part (b), X_1 tends to be larger when X_2 is small than when X_2 is large

25. Because X_1 equals $500 - X_2$; that is, X_1 is known for certain when X_2 is given

27. a. First row (with X_1 along the top): $\frac{25}{50}$, $\frac{15}{50}$, $\frac{7}{50}$, $\frac{3}{50}$; second row: $\frac{40}{70}$, $\frac{20}{70}$, $\frac{8}{70}$, $\frac{2}{70}$; third row: $\frac{20}{30}$, $\frac{8}{30}$, $\frac{1}{30}$, $\frac{1}{30}$
    b. No; X_1 is more likely to be small when X_2 is large than when X_2 is small

29. a. Because the four tires are on different cars   **b.** .284, .269   **31. a.** 1, 1.5, 1.225   **b.** $15, 337.5, $18.37

33. 1.192, 1.094, 1.046   **35. a.** .6, .48   **b.** .6, .46   **37.** $27.50, 15,850, $435,725, Cov = -150

39. $E(Y_1) = $4.50, E(Y_2) = $5.43, \text{Var}(Y_1) = 6, \text{Var}(Y_2) = 1.308, \text{Cov}(Y_1, Y_2) = -2.625, \text{Corr}(Y_1, Y_2) = -.296$

41. One car: $\mu = .76, \sigma = .907$; two cars: $\mu = .60, \sigma = .800$; three cars: $\mu = .433, \sigma = .715$

43. a. 5.2, 1.56, 1.249   **b.** 15.6, 4.68, 2.163
    c. Probably not; successive litter sizes for a given dog are probably positively correlated

45. $270, $58.31   **47.** $-$3.70, $24 73; game has a negative expected value, so it is best not to play

49. a. Graph   **b.** .9375   **c.** .03125

51. a. $1 - F(1000) = .6, F(3000) = .9, F(2000) - F(500) = .7$
    b. (1) False, because $F(1000) = .4$; (2) True, because $F(500)$ must be between 0 and .2; (3) True, because $F(2000)$ must be
    at least .7

53. $P(X_1 = 0, X_2 = 2) = .25, P(X_1 = 1, X_2 = 2) = .25, P(X_1 = 2, X_2 = 0) = .25, P(X_1 = 2, X_2 = 1) = .25$, all other
probabilities are zero

55. a. .358   **b.** .149   **c.** .642

57. $P(X_1 = 0, X_2 = 2) = .36, P(X_1 = 1, X_2 = 1) = .48, P(X_1 = 2, X_2 = 0) = .16$, all other probabilities are zero.
    $\text{Corr}(X_1, X_2) = -1$ because $X_1 = 1 - X_2$; that is, there is a perfect negative relationship between X_1 and X_2.

59. a. $715   **b.** $680   **c.** $715, $715

61. $P(X = 0) = .4, P(X = 50) = .4, P(X = 100) = .2; P(Y = 150) = .1, P(Y = 200) = .9$

63. $P(X = 0) = .03, P(X = 1) = .09, P(X = 2) = .13, P(X = 3) = .15, P(X = 4) = .19, P(X = 5) = .16,$
    $P(X = 6) = .12, P(X = 7) = .07, P(X = 8) = .04, P(X = 9) = .02$

65. a. First row (with X_1 along the top): .15, .20, .10, .05; second row: .12, .16, .08, .04; third row: .03, .04, .02, .01
    b. .16   **c.** .35

67. .00165   **69.** 1.47, .35, $134.15

71. a. 105, 11.23   **b.** Yes, because $P(|X - \mu| < 1.34\sigma)$ is at least .443 from Rule 4.1

73. a. .752, .805, .836, .862, .946; yearly survival rate keeps increasing
    b. $E(X)$ is greater than this value; no bound possible because of the open-ended category

---

Solutions for Chapter 5

1. a. .75, .5, $-$.75   **b.** 2.475, $-$.849, $-$.707   **c.** $-$.8, $-$.2, 1.1   **d.** 1.732, $-$2.309, $-$1.732

3. a. .7257   **b.** .6914   **c.** .3342   **d.** .2812

5. a. .1587   **b.** .6736   **c.** .8186   **d.** .1711   **e.** .4986   **f.** .2908

7. a. -1.751 to 1.751 **b.** -4.645 to -1.355 **c.** -9.599 to 29.599 **d.** 9.268 to 20.732 **e.** -14.145 to 2.145
f. 94.818 to 105.183
9. $-1.068, -.566, -.180, .180, .566, 1.068$ **11.** 1.824 **13. a.** $.5987, .1057$ **b.** \$1.122 to \$1.278
15. a. $.0686$ **b.** $.5537$ **17. a.** 78.81% **b.** 6.37% **19. a.** 74 **b.** 189 (or 188)
21. a. \$908 **b.** \$324, \$2676 **23. a.** \$1309.75, \$9.711 **b.** $.842$ **c.** \$1325.72
25. a. $.2007$ **b.** $.0308$ **c.** $.3826$ **d.** $.1224$
27. a. $.0126$, probability of 4 A's when $n = 10$, $p = .763$ **b.** $.2659$, probability of 2 A's when $n = 25$, $p = .1$
c. $.9511$, probability of 10 A's when $n = 10$, $p = .995$ **d.** $.0450$, probability of 1 A when $n = 40$, $p = \frac{1}{9}$
e. $.0050$, probability of 8 A's when $n = 10$, $p = .989$
29. a. $.1789$ **b.** $.1643$ **c.** $.9924$ **d.** $.7625$
31. a. $P(0) = .1681$, $P(1) = .3602$, $P(2) = .3087$, $P(3) = .1323$, $P(4) = .0284$, $P(5) = .0024$
b. 1 **c.** Yes, because the same weather affects all runways
33. a. $.9427, .9992$ **b.** $30, 3.464$ **c.** Approximately from 27 to 33
35. a. $3, 1.55$ **b.** Exact: $.669$, approximate: $.68$
37. a. Hypergeometric: $P(0) = .3100$, $P(1) = .4305$, $P(2) = .2123$, $P(3) = .0440$, $P(4) = .0032$; binomial: $P(0) = .3164$,
$P(1) = .4219$, $P(2) = .2109$, $P(3) = .0469$, $P(4) = .0039$
b. Hypergeometric: $\mu = 1$, $\sigma^2 = .727$; binomial: $\mu = 1$, $\sigma^2 = .75$
39. a. $440, 15.70$ **b.** For X_2: $\mu = 480$, $\sigma = 15.80$; for X_3: $\mu = 80$, $\sigma = 8.58$
c. From Rule 4.1, probability is at least $.846$; from Rule 4.2, probability is between $.95$ and $.99$
41. a. $.677$ (binomial), $.645$ (normal) **b.** $.367, .373$ **c.** $.921, .934$ **d.** $.112, .111$
43. a. $.499$ **b.** $np(1 - p) = 2.58$, so it is not appropriate; approximation is $.459$ **45.** $.0003, .1001$
47. a. $.1755$, probability of $X = 4$ when $\lambda = 5$ **b.** $.0758$, probability of $X = 2$ when $\lambda = \frac{1}{2}$
c. $.7787$, probability of $0 \le X \le 3$ when $\lambda = 2.4$ **d.** $.3908$, probability of $6 \le X \le 9$ when $\lambda = 10$
49. Binomial: $P(0) = .5438$, $P(1) = .3364$, $P(2) = .0988$, $P(3) = .0183$; Poisson ($\lambda = .6$): $P(0) = .5488$, $P(1) = .3293$,
$P(2) = .0988$, $P(3) = .0198$
51. a. $.2202$ **b.** $.3032$ **c.** 14
53. 0 to 57.30, 57.30 to 62.89, 62.89 to 67.71, 67.71 to 73.30, above 73.30
55. a. No, there is not a single value of p **b.** $.962$ **57.** $.595$ **59. a.** 57.98 **b.** 60.27 **c.** $\mu = 58.91$, $\sigma = 4.34$
61. a. $.678$ **b.** P(between 700 and 900) $= .948$ (not quite 95% certain) **63. a.** $.9928$ **b.** 4
65. a. $.127, .648$ **b.** $\mu = 21.75$, $\sigma = 1.682$ **67. a.** $\mu = 4$, $\sigma = 1.549$ **b.** $.264$ **69. a.** $.077$ **b.** $.261$
71. a. Sampling is done with replacement, but a small percentage of the population is being sampled.
b. $.06\%$, $.28\%$, $.69\%$; percentage error increases because approximation is based on sample size being small compared to
population size
73. a. $.353$ **b.** $.689$
75. a. Multiply out the right-hand side to see that it is equal to the general expression for $P(k)$.
b. Starting with $P(0) = .0217$, use formula to obtain $P(1) = .1162$, $P(2) = .2597$, $P(3) = .3096$, $P(4) = .2076$,
$P(5) = .0742$, $P(6) = .0111$
77. a. $.282, .179, .013$ **b.** $.026$ (very low) **79. a.** $.248$ **b.** $.056$ **81.** $.180$
83. $.675$; because $P(-.675 < Z < .675) = P(\mu - .675\sigma < X < \mu + .675\sigma) = .50$ for any μ and σ when X is $N(\mu, \sigma^2)$
85. a. $.344$ **b.** $.0988$
87. a. P(at least $100{,}000$ responses) is practically 1.0 when $p = .505$, $.996$ when $p = .503$, and $.814$ when $p = .501$
b. $.992, .663$

Solutions for Chapter 6

1. $.007$ **3.** $.132$ **5.** $.214, .038$ **7. a.** $.432$ **b.** $\hat{p} \le .452$, $P(\hat{p} \le .452) = .406$ **9. a.** $.276$ **b.** $.836$
11. a. $.086, .012$ **b.** $P(\overline{X} \le 4.1) = .034$; fairly unlikely to see such a small $\overline{X}$ **13.** $.808$
15. $.103$; calculation is valid because population is normally distributed **17.** $.094$ **19.** $.032$

21. a. .006   **b.** 74.91   **c.** 15.81   **23. a.** .850   **b.** .850

25. a. 1.75, 1.043   **b.** 1.75, .1204   **c.** .797; Central Limit Theorem allows use of normal distribution

27. a. .253   **b.** 16.694   **29. a.** .212   **b.** .227   **31. a.** .838   **b.** .590   **33.** .427   **35.** Approximately 1.0

37. a. Approximately 0   **b.** .002   **39.** .697   **41.** .364   **43.** 18   **45.** .028

47. .425; Central Limit Theorem allows use of normal distribution for $\overline{X}$ even though parent distribution is exponential
   b. 3.64 to 6.36

49. a. .923   **b.** .313, approximately 1.0; these are different because variance of $\overline{X}$ is much smaller

51. a. \$472.50, \$45.50   **b.** .713   **c.** .572

53. a. True, because $n\hat{p}_1$ is binomially distributed   **b.** False, because variance is $p_2(1 - p_2)/n$
   c. False, because $\hat{p}_1$ and $\hat{p}_3$ are not independent (so the variance is wrong)
   d. True, because $\hat{p}_1 + \hat{p}_2$ is a sample proportion and $p_3(1 - p_3) = (1 - p_1 - p_2)(p_1 + p_2)$, so the variance term is correct
   e. False, because this sum is 1 with certainty

55. a. $P(\hat{p} \geq .27) = .162$ **b.** $P(\hat{p} \leq .27) = .133$ **57.** .431   **59.** .159

61. For whites, from .043 to .103; for blacks, from .119 to .203

Solutions for Chapter 7

1. No, because of possible sampling variation

3. $\hat{\mu}_1$ is preferred because its expected value is μ and because it varies less. But with a single sample, we could get unlucky and have a larger error with $\hat{\mu}_1$ than with $\hat{\mu}_2$.

5. a. Bias = 0, variance = $.36\sigma^2$ **b.** Bias = 0, variance = $4.5\sigma^2$
   c. Bias = $-\mu/31$, variance = $.312\sigma^2$ **d.** Bias = 0, variance = $.375\sigma^2$

7. Follows from rules of expected values (Chapter 4) and the fact that the coefficients of the X's (for each of the $\hat{\mu}$'s) sum to 1.

9. No, $\overline{X}$ is always unbiased; because of the rules of expected values and the fact that $n(1/n) = 1$

11. $\alpha = .90$, $n = 100$ goes with .520 to .680 because it must produce the shortest interval; $\alpha = .95$, $n = 70$ goes with .485 to .715 because it must produce the longest interval; $\alpha = .95$, $n = 100$ must therefore go with .504 to .696.

13. He gains preciseness in the sense that he is more certain that the statement he makes is correct. But he loses preciseness in the sense that his confidence interval will be relatively wide.   **15.** 38.28 to 45.72 quarts   **17.** 14.7 to 19.3 cents

19. 35.77% to 38.23%   **21.** −.34 to 2.54 hours

23. \$30.18 to \$40.62; because we are dealing with a single population of differences

25. −.052 to .212 gallons; no, because this interval includes 0   **27.** 96 (or 97)   **29.** −.355 to −.105

31. a. .317 to .387
   b. .613 to .683; it is the "complement" of the interval in part (a) since $1 - .317 = .683$ and $1 - .387 = .613$

33. a. 5074   **b.** .145 to .161, length .016

35. a. 9604
   b. .4002 to .4198; length is less than .02 because sample size formula is conservative (may be more than is needed)

37. a. 542   **b.** 769
   c. 90%: −.0964 to −.0016; 95%: −.0964 to −.0016; these are the same because the sample sizes have been adjusted to give the same length intervals

39. 99%: .73587 to .73603; 95%: .73589 to .73601; 90%: .73590 to .73600   **41.** 437

43. Both are unbiased because their coefficients sum to 1. Their variances are $\sigma^2/3$ and $.12\sigma^2$, as compared to the variance of $\overline{X}$, $.1\sigma^2$. Intuitively, $\overline{X}$ is better because it uses all of the observations.

45. a. .026 to .374   **b.** \$19,635 to \$22,689   **c.** 63 more   **47. a.** 11.855 to 11.871 ounces   **b.** 624 more

49. a. 201 (or 202) more   **b.** \$260.2 to \$285.8

51. Approximate: .1752 to .2248; exact: .1763 to .2259; they have the same length, but the exact interval is not centered at $\hat{p}$

53. a. Because θ may not be the mean of $\hat{\theta}$; that is, $\hat{\theta}$ may be biased

b. $(\hat{\theta} - \theta)^2 = [(\hat{\theta} - \mu_{\hat{\theta}}) + (\mu_{\hat{\theta}} - \theta)]^2 = (\hat{\theta} - \mu_{\hat{\theta}})^2 + 2(\hat{\theta} - \mu_{\hat{\theta}})(\mu_{\hat{\theta}} - \theta) + (\mu_{\hat{\theta}} - \theta)^2$. Now take expected values. The expected value of the middle expression is 0 because the expected value of $\hat{\theta}$ is $\mu_{\hat{\theta}}$ and $(\mu_{\hat{\theta}} - \theta)$ is a constant.

c. First term on the right is the variance of $\hat{\theta}$; second is the square of the bias of $\hat{\theta}$

55. 3.206 to 3.682 minutes

57. (α, n) pairs: (.10, 1083), (.09, 1151), (.08, 1227), (.07, 1314), (.06, 1416), (.05, 1537), (.04, 1686), (.03, 1882), (.02, 2164), (.01, 2655), (.005, 3148)

59. No, the relevant sample size is only 3, and sample means based on $n = 3$ may be very nonnormal.   **61.** At least 824

63. Statement 1: .123 to .177; statement 2: .023 to .097; statement 3: .199 to .321; statement 4: $-.089$ to .049; statement 5: .008 to .092

65. .521 to .727

Solutions for Chapter 8

1. a. -1.782, 1.782   **b.** -2.060, 2.060   **c.** -3.747, 3.747

3. a. 2.086   **b.** 1.706   **c.** Approximately 2.2   **d.** Approximately 1.75   **e.** Approximately 1.45
f. Approximately 1.48

5. a. ± 2.776 **b.** ± 2.160 **c.** ± 2.064

7. a. $\overline{X} = 41.4$, $s = 14.23$, $t = -1.24$, $P(t < -1.24)$ is slightly greater than .10   **b.** $31,221 to $51,579

9. $t = 2.23$, $P(t > 2.23)$ is approximately .02, so mean has probably increased   **11.** 23.62% to 30.78%; 25% is included

13. a. $t = -2.79$, $P(t < -2.79)$ is less than .01, so it is abnormally small   **b.** 30.28 to 34.72

15. a. .00118   **b.** 4.8 to 9.2 cents   **17.** -41.17 to -2.69 **19.** $-.31$ to 1.71 hours

21. a. 3.247, 20.483   **b.** 18.493, 50.892   **c.** .554, 12.833   **d.** 82.358, 118.498

23. a. 34.170   **b.** 2.558   **c.** Approximately 152.2   **d.** Approximately 19   **e.** Approximately 12.5
f. Approximately 176.3

25. 338.41, 326.6, 115.6; no way to tell which is most accurate for this particular sample   **27.** 4.69, 17.29

29. a. Between .95 and .975   **b.** Greater than .99   **c.** Much greater than .99   **31.** Less than .01

33. 95%: 88.67 to 157.98; 90%: 92.19 to 149.50

35. a. 2.98   **b.** 5.69   **c.** Approximately 1.6   **d.** Approximately 2.11   **e.** 4.85   **f.** Between 5.32 and 7.57

37. $P(s_1^2/s_2^2 \geq 2)$ is between .05 and .10, $P(s_2^2/s_1^2 \geq 2)$ is greater than .10, so the second is more likely.

39. $P(F_{15,24} \geq 1.44)$ is greater than .10, so it is not conclusive evidence   **41.** Between .11 and .12

43. a. 5.807   **b.** 2.269   **c.** Between .02 and .05   **45.** Equal variances: .197 to 4.269; unequal variances: .160 to 4.305

47. a. Approximately .09   **b.** .129
c. Part (a) uses the sample standard deviation, part (b) uses the population standard deviation; they do not contradict each other.

49. $t = .683$, $P(t > .683)$ is approximately .25

51. a. -3.67 to 9.87
b. .361 to 2.22; since this interval includes the value 1, we have reason to believe that σ_1^2 and σ_2^2 are equal

53. a. In the expression for s_p, the $(n-1)$'s cancel, giving $s_p = \sqrt{(s_1^2 + s_2^2)/2}$, so $s_{\overline{X}_1 - \overline{X}_2} = s_p\sqrt{2/n} = \sqrt{s_1^2/n + s_2^2/n}$
b. The expression for $\overline{n}$ reduces to $(n-1)(4s^4/n^2)/(2s^4/n^2) = 2(n-1) = n + n - 2$

55. a. .995   **b.** Greater than .99   **57. a.** 288   **b.** Approximately 60   **59.** 14.52, 11.80

61. a. $(X_i - \mu)^2 = X_i^2 - 2\mu X_i + \mu^2$; now sum each of the terms, using $\sum X_i = n\overline{X}$ and $\sum \mu^2 = n\mu^2$
b. $(X_i - \overline{X})^2 = X_i^2 - 2X_i\overline{X} + \overline{X}^2$; now sum each of the terms, and note that $\sum (-2X_i\overline{X}) = -2\overline{X}(\sum X_i) = -2n\overline{X}^2$ and $\sum \overline{X}^2 = n\overline{X}^2$, so that $-2n\overline{X}^2 + n\overline{X}^2 = -n\overline{X}^2$

63. 20 or 21   **65.** For mean: $8165 to $8531; for standard deviation: $176 to $467

67. a. For mean: 96.01 to 106.55; for standard deviation: 23.6 to 31.3
   b. $E(s^2) = 100$ is included, $\text{StdDev}(s^2) = 26.26$ is also included
69. For mean: .1406 to .1418; for standard deviation: .0030 to .0039

Solutions for Chapter 9

1. No, α is a conditional probability given H_0 is true, whereas β is a conditional probability given H_a is true
3. Yes, we know that $z > z_{.05}$, and this implies that $z > z_{.075}$ **5.** No, a type I error cannot be made because H_0 is not true
7. Type I error: send an innocent person to jail, $\alpha = .02$; type II error: set a guilty person free, $\beta = .20$
9. Even though $z < z_{.05}$ when $n = 40$, it might be greater than $z_{.05}$ when $n > 40$, because $z = \sqrt{n}\,(\overline{X} - 10)/s$ increases as n increases when $\overline{X}$ and s are fixed.
11. a. $\overline{X} > 102.781$ **b.** .095
    c. $n = 100$: $\overline{X} > 101.645$, $P(\text{type II}) = .0004$; $n = 250$: $\overline{X} > 101.040$, $P(\text{type II})$ is approximately 0
13. a. .0548 to .0612   **b.** Yes, because $z = 2.44$ ($z_{.025} = 1.96$)   **15.** Yes, because $z = -3.21$ ($z_{.05} = 1.645$)
17. a. 6.42 to 7.98   **b.** Reject H_0 unless μ_0 is between 6.42 and 7.98   **19.** $\overline{X} < 9.935$; $\overline{X} < 9.954$
21. a. Reject H_0 if $\overline{X}$ is not between 138.84 and 153.16   **b.** .870, .624   **23.** No, because z is only .65 ($z_{.05} = 1.645$)
25. a. .520 to .689   **b.** Yes, because .75 is not between .520 and .689
    c. No, because a type II error can be made only when H_0 is *not* rejected
27. a. .684 to .822   **b.** Cannot reject H_0 because z is only .909 ($z_{.05} = 1.645$); p-value is .182
29. a. .071 to .097   **b.** Any p_0 not between .071 and .097
31. a. No, because z is only 1.131 ($z_{.05} = 1.645$)   **b.** At least 243
33. No, z is only -1.45 ($z_{.05} = 1.645$); p-value is .147   **35.** No, z is only -1.06 ($z_{.025} = 1.96$); p-value is .145
37. In first city, $z = 1.6$, not quite significant; in second city, $z = 2.53$, significant ($z_{.05} = 1.645$); a given $\hat{p}$ is more likely to be significant when sample size is large
39. Yes, $z = 1.70$ ($z_{.05} = 1.645$)
41. No, test statistic (z or t) is only .929 ($z_{.05} = 1.645$)
43. a. 2.98 to 4.58   **b.** p-value is between .025 and .05 (approximately .04), so reject H_0 for any $\alpha \geq .04$
45. Yes, test statistic (t or z) is 9.7 ($z_{.01} = 2.326$)   **47.** Yes, $z = 2.0$ ($z_{.05} = 1.645$); p-value is .023
49. $\alpha = .59$ (very weak support for H_a)
51. Because $\hat{p}$ is a reasonable estimate of the common proportion when $p_1 = p_2$, but is not relevant (as an estimate of p_1 or p_2) when $p_1 \neq p_2$. When $p_1 \neq p_2$, use $\hat{p}_1(1 - \hat{p}_1)/n_1 + \hat{p}_2(1 - \hat{p}_2)/n_2$ as the variance estimate.
53. a. $\sigma_0^2 > 2.44$ **b.** $\sigma_0^2 > 1.84$ (approximately)   **55.** No, F is only 2.04 ($F_{.025,9,9} = 4.03$)
57. No, χ^2 is only 19.21 ($\chi^2_{.05,14} = 23.68$); p-value is greater than .10
59. No, F is only 1.586 ($F_{.10,20,24} = 1.73$); F test is appropriate because neither day's true variance is known
61. a. H_0: $\mu_D \leq 0$ versus H_a: $\mu_D > 0$, where μ_D is the mean of the differences; reject H_0 because $t = 2.77$ ($t_{.05,7} = 1.895$)
    b. Because there is (extraneous) variation between cars
63. a. Because there is (extraneous) variation between different couples' incomes
    b. Test 6A: $t = .519$ ($t_{.05,18} = 1.734$), do not reject H_0; matched pairs test: $t = 1.33$ ($t_{.05,9} = 1.833$), do not reject H_0 (but now closer to rejecting)   **c.** $\mu_0 < \$95.39$
65. a. Cannot accept this (alternative) hypothesis because t is only .595 ($t_{.05,14} = 1.761$)
    b. Because the sample sizes are not the same
67. a. H_0: $p \geq .5$ versus H_a: $p < .5$, where p is the proportion of votes for him
    b. $\hat{p} < .448$ (or less than 112 out of 250 are for him)
    c. Occurs when he would lose ($p < .5$) but sample does not convince him of this
69. $s_p = 3688$; do not reject H_0 when $s_p > 3688$

71. a. Do not reject H_0, because F is only 1.328 ($F_{.05,11,11} = 2.82$)   **b.** Reject H_0, because $t = 1.925$ ($t_{.10,22} = 1.321$)

73. a. $\alpha \leq .012$ **b.** P(type II) $= .616$, occurs when $\hat{p} \geq .9247$ (at least 185 out of 200 meet specifications)

75. $n = 500$ is too small because P(type II) $= .266$ when $n = 500$

77. $\hat{p}_1$ and $\hat{p}_2$ are not independent; a matched-pairs type of test is needed

79. a. .0265 to .0473 inches

b. Yes, because $\chi^2 = 41.04$ ($\chi^2_{.05,24} = 36.415$); part (a) is not applicable because this is a one-tailed test

81. $k > 1.51$

83. a. For 1975, reject H_0 because $z = 4.51$ ($z_{.05} = 1.645$); for 1981, same conclusion because $z = 4.55$

b. For men, cannot reject H_0 because z is only .725 ($z_{.05} = 1.645$); for women, reject H_0 because z is 4.11

c. For men, cannot reject H_0 because z is only .662 ($z_{.025} = 1.96$); for women, same conclusion because z is only 1.27

85. For A, $s_p < .643$; for B, $s_p < .056$

87. a. Because of the difference between companies   **b.** For 5% level, $s_D < 31.62$ days; for 10% level, $s_D < 40.58$ days

89. Only the fourth statement, z values are 1.01, $-.13$, .51, 4.57, -1.37 ($z_{.025} = 1.96$)

91. a. $\overline{X} > 8.144$ years   **b.** $\overline{X} > 8.078$ years, P(type II) $= .633$

Solutions for Chapter 10

1. They are random variables because their values are not known until we observe the sample data. E(MSTr) is larger than E(MSE) (so that F is large) unless the equal means hypothesis is true.

3. We are only accepting the alternative that not all the means are equal. The example given is one of many possibilities.

5. a. $F = 7.30$ ($F_{.10,2,12} = 2.81$) so reject the hypothesis of equal means.

b. $\mu_1 - \mu_2$: $-.013$ to .097; $\mu_1 - \mu_3$: .033 to .143; $\mu_2 - \mu_3$: $-.009$ to .101. Only μ_1 and μ_3 are significantly different, because the interval for $\mu_1 - \mu_3$ does not include 0.

7. a. Type 1: $\overline{X}_1 = 102.25$, $s_1 = 3.99$; type 2: $\overline{X}_2 = 104.25$, $s_2 = 5.12$; type 3: $\overline{X}_3 = 111.25$, $s_3 = 3.49$. The differences between the $\overline{X}$'s, especially between $\overline{X}_3$ and the other two, are fairly large in comparison to the standard deviations.

b. $F = 9.86$ ($F_{.01,2,21} = 5.78$) so reject the equal-means hypothesis

9. a. Visa: $\overline{X}_1 = \$69.42$, $s_1 = \$3.82$; Mastercard: $\overline{X}_2 = \$77.39$, $s_2 = \$4.95$; American Express: $\overline{X}_3 = \$84.89$, $s_3 = \$5.42$; other: $\overline{X}_4 = \$69.69$, $s_4 = \$4.85$. Looks like differences between $\overline{X}$'s may be significant.

b. $F = 12.81$ ($F_{.10,3,18} = 2.42$) so reject the equal-means hypothesis

c. $\mu_1 - \mu_2$: $-\$15.87$ to $-\$.07$; $\mu_1 - \mu_3$: $-\$23.37$ to $-\$7.57$; $\mu_1 - \mu_4$: $-\$8.52$ to \$7.98; $\mu_2 - \mu_3$: $-\$15.03$ to \$.03; $\mu_2 - \mu_4$: $-\$.20$ to \$15.60; $\mu_3 - \mu_4$: \$7.30 to \$23.10

11. a. Because of the difference in sales levels across department stores (the blocking variable)

b. F for treatments is 3.45 ($F_{.10,1,9} = 3.36$) so reject the equal-means hypothesis

c. $t = 1.858$ ($t_{.05,9} = 1.833$), leads to the same conclusion; $1.858^2 = 3.45$

13. a. Different golfers differ widely in their distance; one-way ANOVA would not control for this.

b. F for treatments is 5.74 ($F_{.05,3,18} = 3.16$) so reject the equal-means hypothesis

c. The F value for blocks is huge, 85.0.

15. a. Different people (the blocking variable) take different lengths of time to go to sleep.

b. F for treatments is 6.01 ($F_{.01,4,36} = 3.9$) so reject the equal-means hypothesis.

17. F for corn varieties is 4.32 ($F_{.05,3,24} = 3.01$), F for fertilizers is 26.0 ($F_{.05,2,24} = 3.40$), F for interaction is 6.87 ($F_{.05,6,24} = 2.51$). All are significant. The farmer knows that these two factors make a difference and that certain fertilizers may work better (or worse) with certain corn varieties; table of means indicates best combinations.

19. a. First row (single-level homes) means: 136.1, 153.3; second row means: 165.7, 174.8. Graph does not indicate strong interactions, but there could be main effects.

b. F for type of home is 9.97 ($F_{.05,1,16} = 4.49$), F for type of heating is 2.65 (same tabulated F), F for interaction is .25 (same tabulated F), so only main effect for type of home is significant

21. Means for winter: 7.43, 6.16, 5.59; means for spring: 7.90, 6.95, 6.66: means for summer: 8.78, 8.26, 7.76; means for fall: 8.32, 8.48, 6.04. F for season is 25.15 ($F_{.01,3,24} = 4.72$), F for type of store is 35.15 ($F_{.01,2,24} = 5.61$), F for interaction is 3.87 ($F_{.01,6,24} = 3.67$). The main conclusion is that turnover differs widely across seasons and across types of stores.

23. a. Because we know nothing about the variation within the individual cells

    b. The row means indicate that experience definitely makes a difference. The column means indicate that the terminal degree makes some difference, but it may not be significant. A graph of the individual cell means indicates that the interaction effect is probably not significant.

25. $F = 38.50$ ($F_{.05,3,228} = 2.60$) so we can definitely reject the equal-means hypothesis

27. If each statement has probability α of being wrong, the probability that at least one of the statements is wrong is greater than α.

29. Probably a block design, with people being the blocking variable, because different people like coffee to different extents and different people probably interpret the scale differently.

31. a. $F = .513$ ($F_{.10,2,12} = 2.81$) so we cannot reject the equal-means hypothesis

    b. Sales might differ greatly from one week to the next, so the weeks could be the blocking variable.

    c. F for treatments is 28.5 ($F_{.10,2,8} = 3.11$) so now we can reject the equal-means hypothesis. Blocking is useful because the F value for blocks is huge, 165.

33. The type I error probability is larger than we want it to be.

35. a. Brand 1: $\overline{X}_1 = 8.32$, $s_1 = .70$; brand 2: $\overline{X}_2 = 7.02$, $s_2 = .83$; $\overline{X}_3 = 7.46$, $s_3 = .77$. Differences between $\overline{X}$'s are fairly large relative to size of s's.

    b. F is 7.42 ($F_{.10,2,27} = 2.51$) so reject the equal-means hypothesis

37. a. Type AA means: 8.03, 7.53, 8.35; type C means: 8.83, 8.33, 10.48. There appear to be significant differences among type of batteries (AA or C); differences among brands are questionable.

    b. Graph indicates that interaction effects are minimal.

    c. F for type of battery (AA or C) is 20.30 ($F_{.05,1,30} = 4.17$), F for brands is 9.95 ($F_{.05,2,30} = 3.32$), F for interactions is 2.59 ($F_{.05,2,30} = 3.32$), so main effects are both significant, interaction is not.

39. a. $F = 4.55$ ($F_{.05,4,45} = 2.59$) so we can reject the equal-means hypothesis

    b. $\mu_1 - \mu_2$: -30.9 to 1.7; $\mu_1 - \mu_3$: -36.9 to -4.3; $\mu_1 - \mu_4$: -29.1 to 3.5; $\mu_1 - \mu_5$: -31.4 to 1.2; $\mu_2 - \mu_3$: -22.3 to 10.3; $\mu_2 - \mu_4$: -14.5 to 18.1; $\mu_2 - \mu_5$: -16.8 to 15.8; $\mu_3 - \mu_4$: -8.5 to 24.1; $\mu_3 - \mu_5$: -10.8 to 21.8; $\mu_4 - \mu_5$: -18.6 to 14.0. Only the $\mu_1 - \mu_3$ difference is significantly nonzero.

    c. μ_1 appears to be lower than the others, but the only significant difference is between μ_1 and μ_3.

41. a. Buy the third; it has the smallest mean time.   **b.** Probably a one-way design, because no matching has been attempted

    c. $F = 1.85$ ($F_{.05,2,15} = 3.68$) so the means are not significantly different

43. Graph of cell means indicates that interaction effects are minimal.

Solutions for Chapter 11

1. They should cluster around an imaginary line that rises from left to right.

3. a. Unlikely; relationship is nonlinear   **b.** Relationship is linear, but line is flat (so Y does not depend on X)

    c. Likely, relationship is negative and linear except for a couple outliers

5. Because salaries probably vary more as workers have more years of experience

7. a. Car with larger engine expected to get 2 mpg less

    b. Probably none, because no engine size is anywhere near 0 cubic inches

9. a. Graduated income tax schedule, tax shelters used mostly by those with large incomes

    b. β_1 is the expected amount of tax on an extra dollar earned; value would probably be between .2 and .4

    c. People with larger incomes probably have a larger variation in taxes paid.

11. a. Graph indicates a good linear fit, with β_1 positive

   b. $SS_{XX} = 3735.71$, $SS_{YY} = 5021.43$, $SS_{XY} = 3792.86$, $\hat{\beta}_0 = 32.658$, $\hat{\beta}_1 = 1.015$ **c.** Graph indicates a good fit

13. SSE = 1170.54, $s_e^2 = 234.09$, $s_e = 15.30$

15. a. Graph   **b.** $-.724$; seems right because points in scattergram decrease from left to right

17. $\hat{Y}$'s: 351.79, 356.29, 369.80, 306.75, 401.32, 360.79, 329.27, 369.80, 338.28, 324.77, 347.28, 365.30, 405.82, 297.75;

   SST = 24,160.4, SSE = 11,465.9, SSR = 12,694.5

19. $\pm.876$; it could be positive or negative

21. MSE; it is an estimate of the error variance σ^2

23. a. $\hat{\beta}_0 = 4.229$, $\hat{\beta}_1 = 4.116$ **b.** $\hat{\beta}_0 = -35.63$, $\hat{\beta}_1 = 6.564$

25. Because s_Y would be the standard error of the residuals if we used a horizontal line (at height $\overline{Y}$) as the regression line, and we can do better than this; s_e is the square root of MSE, and s_Y is the square root of $[SST/(n-1)]$.

27. a. $-.887$ **b.** $\hat{\beta}_0 = 98.397$, $\hat{\beta}_1 = -1.991$ **c.** $F = 29.4$ ($F_{.05,1,8} = 5.32$) so there is a significant fit   **d.** .786

29. a. $\hat{\beta}_0 = 581.16$, $\hat{\beta}_1 = 18.17$ **b.** $F = 145.6$ ($F_{.05,1,16} = 4.49$) so there is definitely a significant fit

   c. 90.1%, .949; $.949^2 = .901$

31. a. .574   **b.** $\hat{\beta}_0 = .127$, $\hat{\beta}_1 = .528$

   c. .022; this is a measure of how far off we are likely to be when we predict a batter's average next year from his average this year

33. a. Graph   **b.** Graph

   c. $\hat{Y} = -.2241 + .1098X$; $\hat{Z} = .0891 + .000447X$; the r^2 value is much larger with the first (.361 versus .005), so it probably gives the better fit

35. a. Graph supports a linear fit rising to the right.   **b.** $\hat{\beta}_0 = 16.184$, $\hat{\beta}_1 = .4977$

   c. $F = 13.1$ ($F_{.05,1,12} = 4.75$) so there is a significant fit; $s_e = 3.412$

37. a. 7.24 to 28.78   **b.** No, $t = -.609$ ($t_{.10,12} = 1.356$)

39. a. $\overline{Y} = 7.329$ **b.** 5.469 to 9.189   **c.** 7.111   **d.** 4.712 to 9.510

41. a. $\hat{\beta}_0 = 4826.97$, $\hat{\beta}_1 = -360.83$ **b.** $-.947$

   c. $F = 68.8$ ($F_{.05,1,8} = 5.32$, $F_{.01,1,8} = 11.26$) so there is definitely a significant fit

   d. -461.14 to -260.52 **e.** -23.70 to 1378.58

43. a. For β_1: 14.98 to 21.36; for β_0: 540.92 to 621.40   **b.** $P(Y < 750) = .021$

45. a. $\hat{\beta}_0 = 11.081$, $\hat{\beta}_1 = .5803$ **b.** .044 to 4.598 (in \$1000s)

47. a. $t = -2.26$ ($t_{.05,13} = 1.771$) so we can reject H_0; it is reasonable to expect two players with a certain batting average difference in one year to have the same difference the next year.

49. a. If one stretch averages 1 mph faster than another, we expect it to have about 4.3 more accidents per year; the fit is fairly good (r^2 is high); the estimate of β_1 is fairly good (its standard error is small).

   b. H_0: $\beta_1 \le 0$ versus H_a: $\beta_1 > 0$; $t = 3.07$ ($t_{.01,23} = 2.50$) so the answer is yes, we can reject H_0.

51. a. $t = 1.53$ ($t_{.05,13} = 1.771$) so we cannot reject H_0; confidence interval is $-.00106$ to .01424 (includes 0)

   b. .390   **c.** The points tend to rise from left to right, but they do not cluster tightly around any straight line.

53. Yes, because the confidence interval for β_1 does not include 0.

55. OLS estimates: $\hat{\alpha}_0 = -10.226$, $\hat{\alpha}_1 = .902$; estimates found by solving for X in terms of Y: $-\hat{\beta}_0/\hat{\beta}_1 = -15.068$, $1/\hat{\beta}_1 = 1.048$. The OLS estimates are found by minimizing the squared *horizontal* distances from points to the line, whereas the $\hat{\beta}$'s were found by minimizing vertical distances.

57. Estimated coefficients for (U, V) equation: $\hat{\beta}_0 = 0$ (except for round-off), $\hat{\beta}_1 = .919$ (the correlation between X's and Y's)

59. a. \$1,557, \$315   **b.** \$1,688, \$175, $\hat{\beta}_0 = .0571$, $\hat{\beta}_1 = .1032$

61. a. Because the marginal increase in sales from adding one more salesperson might decrease as the company has more salespeople.

   b. $\hat{\beta}_0 = -9.321$, $\hat{\beta}_1 = 21.647$

   c. Increase by 2.550; increase by 4.830; this is the effect explained in part (a).

   d. $r^2 = .564$ (practically no change); $s_e = 4.585$ (was 4.583, so almost no change)

63. a. It is more nearly linear except for two notable outliers.   **b.** $\hat{\beta}_0 = 30.392$, $\hat{\beta}_1 = -78.402$

c. $F = 8.45$ ($F_{.10,1,8} = 3.46$) so there is a significant fit, although previous F value (13.1) was larger; s_e is now 3.779, was 3.412. The two outliers appear to make this fit less good than the previous fit.

65. a. From the graph it is not clear whether there is a significant linear fit. **b.** $\hat{\beta}_0 = 113.536$, $\hat{\beta}_1 = .1078$, $r = .228$

c. Eliminate (197, 116) and (90, 142); $\hat{\beta}_0 = 74.172$, $\hat{\beta}_1 = .3809$, $r^2 = .643^2 = .413$

d. Although the equation in part (c) indicates a better fit (higher r^2), it may not be valid to throw away the two observations that "look" like they do not belong.

Solutions for Chapter 12

1. Graphs do not indicate any striking nonlinearities; they indicate that a linear fit is very likely.

3. The relationship between individual independent variables and the dependent variable can be nonlinear, even though the linear fit between the dependent variable and all independent variables as a group is very good. No, there is no foolproof way without estimating the multiple regression equation.

5. Because the value of the coefficient of any independent variable can depend on which other independent variables are included in the equation; one equation includes X_1, X_2, X_4, and X_5, the other includes only X_1 and X_2; β's are probably not the same.

7. a. Each gives the effect on the dependent variable if that independent variable increases by one unit and the other independent variables remain constant. **b.** Expected change in Y is $2\beta_1 + .3\beta_3$

c. Expected change in Y is $2\beta_1 + 2000\beta_2 + .3\beta_3$

9. Principles are the same (minimizing squared residuals), computations are more burdensome.

11. Letting $Y = $ BILL, $X_1 = $ THERM, $X_2 = $ SQFT, sums are $\Sigma Y_i = 2116.05$, $\Sigma Y_i^2 = 302,936.9$, $\Sigma X_{1i} = 1040$, $\Sigma X_{1i}^2 = 72,150$, $\Sigma X_{2i} = 23,499$, $\Sigma X_{2i}^2 = 37,309,581$, $\Sigma X_{1i}X_{2i} = 1,632,024$, $\Sigma X_{1i}Y_i = 147,072.9$, $\Sigma X_{2i}Y_i = 3,348,994$; equations are $\hat{\beta}_0 + 69.333\hat{\beta}_1 + 1566.6\hat{\beta}_2 = 141.07$, $1040\hat{\beta}_0 + 72,150\hat{\beta}_1 + 1,632,024\hat{\beta}_2 = 147,072.9$, and $23,499\hat{\beta}_0 + 1,632.024\hat{\beta}_1 + 37,309,581\hat{\beta}_2 = 3,348,994$

13. a. $\widehat{\text{BILL}} = -385.88 + 6.6706\text{THERM} + .01665\text{SQFT} + 1.8364\text{INCOME}$

b. These are estimated coefficients if all variables were standardized first; appears that THERM is most important (largest coefficient) **c.** Because independent variables are expressed in different units.

15. a. 8.46; indicates typical error in estimating Y

b. .822; 82.2% of the variation in the Y's is explained by the regression equation

c. $F = 16.94$ (p-value is .0002); means that the regression equation provides a good fit

d. For INCOME: StdErr $= .955$, confidence interval, $-.266$ to 3.939; for THERM: StdErr $= 1.626$, confidence interval, 3.092 to 10.249; for SQFT: StdErr $= .018$, confidence interval, $-.022$ to .055. Numbers in SIG T column are p-values; small p-value means that variable by itself is capable of explaining a significant amount of the variation of the dependent variable.

e. Correlations between THERM and SQFT and between INCOME and SQFT are fairly large, could cause problems in estimating β's accurately

17. a. X_1 enters first (largest correlation), probably X_3 next (because X_2 is correlated highly with X_1)

b. No, only magnitudes of correlations are relevant for this question

19. Correlation between this variable and dependent variable could be large, but this variable may be explaining the same thing that is already being explained by another independent variable

21. Numerator of s_e^2 (SSE) necessarily decreases, but so does the denominator ($n - k - 1$). Ratio could increase if decrease in numerator is small enough.

23. Almost any two variables could have a significant relationship (just by chance), especially if the sample size is large enough, but it might be meaningless in a practical sense.

25. a. For RC: people with a given IQ tend to read about 105 words per minute faster after a speed-reading course. For IQ: an extra IQ point means about 13.6 extra words per minute, whether or not people have had a speed-reading course.

b. 377.5, 272.2

c. Because no one in the sample has an IQ anywhere near 0 (so the intercept term has no practical meaning)

27. a. Rock members average 7.73 records per year more than country-western members, classical members average 1.41 records per year less than country-western members, given that they have all been in the club the same amount of time. The longer members are in the club, the more records they buy (coefficient of MONTHS is positive).

b. 15.02, 26.89 (rounded to 15, 27)

29. First equation: prediction is 192.98, standard error is 25.86; second equation: 185.01, 20.03; third equation: 188.65, 22.64. Based on these, second is probably most accurate.

31. a. Without: $\widehat{\text{SPEED}} = -1132.9 + 12.32\text{IQ}$; with: $\widehat{\text{SPEED}} = -1025.5 + 14.02\text{IQ}$ **b.** 160.7, 446.6

c. For people without a speed-reading course, relevant coefficient of IQ is 12.32; for those with a speed-reading course, it is $12.32 + 1.7 = 14.02$

33. a. 1.428 hours/day; since $s_e = .75$, the probability of this prediction being off by more than 1 hour is fairly small (approximately .1) **b.** $F = 11.76$ ($F_{.05,3,21} = 3.07$, $F_{.01,3,21} = 4.87$) so it is significant at both levels

c. Confidence interval: $-.027$ to $.107$; $t = 1.25$ ($t_{.025,21} = 2.08$), not significant; could tell it is not significant because confidence interval includes 0

d. Unmarried senior citizens watch about 1.2 hours less per day than those married (other variables being equal)

35. Nonlinear because of $\beta_1\beta_2$ term; could not estimate coefficients by OLS

37. Because RT and LT are extremely correlated; yes, standard errors will be large, but predictions should be accurate because either variable (RT or LT) is probably highly correlated with height.

39. Because it is impossible to separate the individual effects of the independent variables on the dependent variable

41. a. Unequal error variance (use logarithm of Y instead of Y as dependent variable)

b. Nonlinearity appears to be present (use a quadratic term)

c. Three separate groups of points (use a couple dummy variables)

43. Useful for detecting autocorrelation, especially for time series data; close to 0 or close to 4 means problems

45. Comparing first to second, $F = 6.48$ ($F_{.10,1,73} = 2.78$) so second is significantly better than first; comparing third to second, $F = 1.60$ ($F_{.10,4,69} = 2.03$) so third is not significantly better than second.

47. a. The change in the stock price is less than the change in the market or the change in the cosmetic industry (coefficients are less than 1).

b. Probably not, since changes in the cosmetic industry could cause changes in the market, and vice versa.

c. Expected change in the stock's price, given that the market index and the cosmetic index do not change; probably near 0

49. a. df's: 5, 14, 19; MS's: 340.82, 25.91; $F = 13.15$ is significant at just about any level, so overall fit is good; p-value (listed under "Significance") is much less than .01 **b.** 82.4%

c. No, its effect may be accounted for by another independent variable. **d.** 59.65, approximately .05

e. Yes, particularly because YRS, AGE, and SEN are probably highly correlated; causes difficulty in estimating individual regression coefficients (large standard errors)

51. There are really two separate equations relating YRS to EFF, one for those over 50 (DAGE $= 1$) and one for those under 50 (DAGE $= 0$). Fit is good (high R^2).

53. a. Yes, because correlations between JOBEFF and independent variables are fairly high; possible problems of multicollinearity because of high correlations between independent variables

b. $\widehat{\text{JOBEFF}} = -57.45 + .6097\text{TEST1} + .4294\text{TEST2} - .6130\text{TEST3} + 1.2223\text{TEST4}$. Confidence intervals: TEST1, .378 to .841; TEST2, .132 to .727; TEST3: $-.974$ to $-.252$; TEST4: .826 to 1.619. Problem of multicollinearity probably caused coefficient of TEST3 to be negative. **c.** Yes, $F = 33.73$ is very large. **d.** 79.20, 6.20

55. TEST4 is most important and explains $.6923^2$ (or 47.9%) of variation by itself. Other variables enter in order TEST1, then TEST3, then TEST2. R^2 increases to .8522 (72.6%), then $.8780^2$ (77.1%), then $.9185^2$ (84.4%), so each variable makes a substantial contribution. This is also seen by successive decreases in s_e.

57. a. $\widehat{\text{INC}} = 9.347 - .6080\text{AGRPCT} + .6340\text{EDUC}$

b. For AGRPCT: -1.035 to $-.181$; for EDUC: .145 to 1.123. Can reject these H_0's because neither confidence interval includes 0. **c.** $F = 8.04$ ($F_{.01,2,11} = 7.21$) so there is a significant overall fit.

59. a. Only possibly unexpected sign is between PRICE and COMPET, but this correlation is small in magnitude.

b. Expect DEMAND to decrease by 1.775 **c.** $t_{.025,16} = 2.12$, so each of the t's is significant

61. Residuals are 3.82, 2.04, −4.28, −1.27, −.27, 1.41, 2.73, −4.69, 2.23, −1.21, 2.48, .34, −1.09, 2.23, −1.50, 1.57, −1.64, −4.28, .49, .93; scattergram of residuals indicates no violations of assumptions.

63. a. Three estimated sales: $21,065, $19,442, $14,943; location 1 appears most promising.
   b. s_e is approximately $760, so it appears unlikely that the true sales for location 1 could be lower than the other two.

65. a. For FERT: $t = 2.55$ ($t_{.05,12} = 1.782$), significant; for INSECT, $t = 1.47$, not significant.   **b.** .8
   c. Probably not, because FERT and INSECT are not going to be near 0.
   d. s_{ind} is approximately $s_e = 4.81$; s_{mean} is approximately $s_e/\sqrt{n} = 1.24$

67. a. Economists in securities and investment industry earn more on average ($\hat{\beta}_5$ is positive), those in nonprofit research earn less on average ($\hat{\beta}_6$ is negative).   **b.** All signs are probably as expected.
   c. Confidence intervals: .222 to .226, .0166 to .0213, .0410 to .0570, .133 to .247, .172 to .318, −.276 to −.084, −.352 to −.210, −.333 to −.199, .024 to .110, .023 to .133, and .069 to .175. None include 0, which means we are fairly certain they have the correct signs.

69. 3,107.94 ($3,107,940), 2,689.79 ($2,689,790); the change is affected by the interaction term with age and years as CEO.

71. a. Because X_j is then correlated with the other independent variables (so it could be explained well by these other variables).
   b. As R_j^2 increases, the denominator decreases, so the ratio increases.
   c. When the X's are correlated with each other, it is difficult to separate their individual effects on the dependent variable.

73. Researchers' hypothesis may hold, because coefficients for two equations are not the same (especially those for work and supervision). Large standard errors relative to magnitudes of regression coefficients indicate that some of the estimated signs could be wrong.

Solutions for Chapter 13

1. No, $\chi^2 = 5.065$ ($\chi^2_{.10,4} = 7.779$)

3. a. First row: 10.076, 26.565, 15.573, 7.786; second row: 6.718, 17.710, 10.382, 5.191; third row: 5.206, 13.725, 8.046, 4.023   **b.** Yes, there are several fairly large difference between E's and O's.
   c. $\chi^2 = 10.983$ ($\chi^2_{.10,6} = 10.645$), independence can be rejected

5. $\chi^2 = 23.001$ ($\chi^2_{.10,9} = 14.684$), reject equal proportions

7. $\chi^2 = 122.34$ ($\chi^2_{.01,9} = 21.666$), reject null hypothesis that there has been no shift

9. $\chi^2 = 7.83$ ($\chi^2_{.10,4} = 7.779$, $\chi^2_{.05,4} = 9.488$), reject at 10% level, do not reject at the 5% level

11. a. $\chi^2 = 2.571$ ($\chi^2_{.05,1} = 3.841$), difference is not significant
   b. $z = 1.603$ ($z_{.025} = 1.96$), again cannot accept two-tailed alternative. One-tailed test is probably appropriate because we expect the sleeping pills to be more effective; $z_{.05} = 1.645$, now H_0 still cannot be rejected, but it is very close.

13. $\chi^2 = 14.40$ ($\chi^2_{.10,12} = 18.549$), cannot reject independence, although several cells have fairly large $(E − O)^2/E$'s

15. $\chi^2 = 80.39$ ($\chi^2_{.05,8} = 15.507$), a very significant shift

17. With 200 MBAs: $\chi^2 = 6.67$ ($\chi^2_{.05,8} = 15.51$), not a significant difference. With 600 MBAs: $\chi^2 = 20.02$ ($\chi^2_{.05,8} = 15.51$), now a significant difference. These results partially support the conclusion of the article (but other types of shifts are also occurring).

19. $\chi^2 = 5.35$ ($\chi^2_{.10,4} = 7.779$), not significant evidence

⁌. a. First row: .375, .3, .2, .125; second row: .167, .45, .217, .167; third row: .233, .4, .2, .167
   b. $\chi^2 = 6.00$ ($\chi^2_{.05,6} = 12.592$), differences are not significant
   ⁌nk sum test does not require normal populations. Rank sum test is not as powerful, and the two populations should have the ⁌ shape. The t test requires normally-shaped populations.
   ⁌ = .853 ($z_{.025} = 1.96$), differences not significant
   ⁌ores the magnitudes of the differences; in these data the differences with +'s are larger in magnitude than those with

   ⁌_{.05} = 1.645), difference is not significant

29. a. 1275 and 6275; 2850 and 8475　　**b.** $W < 3362.4$ or $W > 4187.6$; $W < 5224.8$ or $W > 6100.2$

31. a. Housewives' rankings: 12.5, 16.5, 8.5, 16.5, 8.5, 12.5, 5, 12.5, 16.5, 19.5; working wives' rankings: 8.5, 2.5, 21.5, 12.5, 2.5, 19.5, 5, 16.5, 1, 5, 21.5, 8.5. Ties are common because there are so few possible ratings.

　　b. $z = .89$ ($z_{.025} = 1.96$), difference is not significant

33. Sign test: $z = 2.31$, p-value $= .021$; t test: $t = 3.76$, p-value is less than .01. The t test is preferred because its assumptions are not grossly violated (if at all) and it is more powerful.

35. a. $z = 1.81$ ($z_{.025} = 1.96$), difference is not significant, p-value is .07

　　b. $z = 2.21$ ($z_{.025} = 1.96$), difference is now significant, p-value is approximately .027

37. a. Because the observations are matched across days, and particular days probably have different sales levels

　　b. $z = -1.96$ ($z_{.05} = 1.645$), difference is significant

39. a. $H = 3.873$ ($\chi^2_{.10,2} = 4.605$), differences are not quite significant

　　b. $F = 3.028$ ($F_{.10,2,16} = 2.67$), differences are now significant

　　c. Probably the ANOVA test, because it is more powerful and there are no obvious violations of its assumptions

41. $H = 6.935$ ($\chi^2_{.05,2} = 5.991$), differences are significant

43. a. .720, tells us that ratings are highly (positively) correlated　　**b.** .738, tells us about the same thing

45. a. 19, looks fairly random, no obvious patterns　　**b.** $z = -1.02$ ($z_{.05} = 1.645$), nonrandomness not significant

47. $R = 24$, less than expected ($ER = 27.89$); $z = -1.14$ ($z_{.05} = 1.645$), nonrandomness not significant

49. Because the sampling distribution of the χ^2 test statistic is not known unless the null hypothesis is true, that is, we do not know what to expect of χ^2 if the alternative is true.

51. a. .0198　　**b.** .3679, .3716, .1839, .0766

　　c. 36.79, 37.16, 18.39, 7.66; $\chi^2 = 12.51$ ($\chi^2_{.05,2} = 5.991$), differences are significant; only 2 degrees of freedom because p had to be estimated.

53. $\chi^2 = 2.496$ ($\chi^2_{.05,4} = 9.488$), cannot reject Poisson fit.

55. $\chi^2 = 6.033$ ($\chi^2_{.10,9} = 14.684$), differences are not significant. Population consists of rental data from all airports, we sampled only 4 airports.

57. a. 82.74, 89.88, 95.22, 100, 104.78, 110.12, 117.26　　**b.** 75.33, 84.45, 92.13, 100, 107.87, 115.55, 124.67

　　c. All we need are several well-defined categories, although the first (categories with equal probabilities) is probably preferred.

59. a. Label the proportions in the first row as p_1 and $1 - p_1$, those in the second row as p_2 and $1 - p_2$. Then each test is testing H_0: $p_1 = p_2$ versus a two-tailed alternative.

　　b. z for Chapter 9 test is -2.215, so $z^2 = 4.904$, approximately equal to the χ^2 value from Problem 10. Also, $z^2_{.025} = 1.96^2 = 3.842$, and $\chi^2_{.05,1} = 3.841$, so they are the same except for round-off.

61. a. Because a parametric test is more powerful when its assumptions hold, as here.

　　b. Approximately .108　　**c.** Approximately 470 above the mean

63. a. 1830, 0　　**b.** Above 1138 or below 692

65. $V = 25.5$, between V_0 for $\alpha = .10$ and V_0 for $\alpha = .05$, so difference is significant at 10% level, not at 5% level; same conclusion as in Problem 37

67. a. .661, means reactions to pollen and molds are positively correlated

　　b. Concordance means if one patient reacts more to pollen than another, then this patient also reacts more to molds; discordance is the opposite; $\tau = .467$

69. With 2 A's, 3 B's: $P(2) = .2$, $P(3) = .3$, $P(4) = .4$, $P(5) = .1$; with 1 A, 4 B's: $P(2) = .4$, $P(3) = .6$

71. For antiperspirants: $\chi^2 = 147.69$ ($\chi^2_{.05,2} = 5.991$), differences are extremely significant; for pet food, $\chi^2 = 76.15$, also extremely significant; for skin lotions, $\chi^2 = 16.70$, still significant; for prepared foods, $\chi^2 = 6.63$, just barely significant. Researchers' hypotheses are confirmed.

73. a. $\chi^2 = 5.731$ ($\chi^2_{.05,3} = 7.815$), differences are not significant.

　　b. $F = 3.729$ for main effect of prior letter ($F_{.05,1,796} = 3.84$), $F = .864$ for main effect of color, $F = 1.151$ for interaction between prior letter and color, none are significant; same conclusion as in part (a)

75. $\chi^2 = 21.55$ ($\chi^2_{.05,3} = 7.815$), differences are significant.

Solutions for Chapter 14

1. Seasonal is more regular and is a pattern that occurs within a year; cyclical is irregular and generally occurs over a period of several years.

3. **a.** Seasonal, definitely cyclic, a long-run upward trend   **b.** Seasonal, definitely cyclic   **c.** Seasonal only
   d. Long-run upward trend, but cyclic ups and downs

5. **a.** Graph indicates a very good linear fit   **b.** $\hat{\beta}_0 = 290.10$, $\hat{\beta}_1 = 31.629$ **c.** \$796.16, \$827.79, \$859.42

7. $Y_t - Y_{t-1}$: 23, 19, 30, 24, 18, 39, 34, 35, 22, 53, 29, 32, 42, 38; Y_t/Y_{t-1}: 1.07, 1.05, 1.08, 1.06, 1.04, 1.08, 1.07, 1.07, 1.04, 1.09, 1.05, 1.05, 1.06, 1.05. The ratios are more constant than the differences, so an exponential fit should be better.
   b. From Problem 5: 23.27, 14.64, 2.01, .38, -7.25, -20.88, -13.50, -11.13, -7.76, -17.39, 3.98, 1.35, 1.72, 12.10, 18.47, SSE = 2425. From Problem 6: -2.06, $-.27$, -3.77, 2.35, 1.02, -7.87, 2.61, 6.34, 9.22, -2.86, 13.98, 4.61, -4.11, -5.31, -13.16, SSE = 662. Exponential fit is much better in terms of SSE.

9. **a.** Graph indicates a very good linear fit   **b.** $\hat{\beta}_0 = 106.68$, $\hat{\beta}_1 = 5.293$ **c.** 170.20, 175.49, 180.78 (in millions)

11. $\hat{\beta}_0 = 1.864$, $\hat{\beta}_1 = .0426$, or $\hat{Y}_t = 6.449(1.044)^t$; hazardous because rates changed significantly in early 1980s

13. **a.** $\hat{\beta}_0 = 9.052$, $\hat{\beta}_1 = .1108$, or $\hat{Y}_t = 8536(1.117)^t$
   b. C_t's: 1.080, 1.025, .946, .973, 1.008, 1.040, .963, .867, .973, 1.051, 1.092, 1.095, .936
   c. Graph indicates several ups and downs

15. **a.** Seasonal factors (beginning third quarter, 1973): .990, 1.122, .887, 1.004, .996, 1.141, .898, 1.010, .972, 1.101, .886, .984, 1.012, 1.116, .874, 1.002, 1.028, 1.104, .856, 1.105, .983, 1.144, .834, .895   **b.** .873

17. Slight upward trend, obvious seasonal variation, because more Coca-Cola consumed during summer

19. Deseasonalized data: 135.33, 133.36, 138.13, 126.22, 145.89, 124.71, 146.88, 119.56, 127.89, 121.00, 156.75, 121.56. This series is still not smooth, but it is smoother than the original series.

21. **a.** Smoothed data (starting with L_1): 25.04, 25.246, 25.401, 25.611, 25.820, 25.918, 25.966, 26.070, 26.113, 25.701, 25.281, 24.943, 24.739, 24.665   **b.** Graph is smoother; this is the purpose of exponential smoothing.

23. L_t is a weighted average of an estimate of the current level ($L_{t-1} + T_{t-1}$) and the current deseasonalized observation; T_t is a weighted average of the previous T and the difference between the two most recent levels (L's); S_t is a weighted average of the S from one year ago and an estimate of the current seasonal factor (Y_t/L_t).

25. **a.** There is an upward trend of approximately 10 units per quarter; there is a seasonal pattern with quarters 1 and 4 low and quarters 2 and 3 high; and the current level is approximately 760.   **b.** 693, 936, 948, 560

27. **a.** Possibly, graph indicates that $\hat{\epsilon}$'s are negative, then positive, then negative; $r_1 = .473$

29. Errors show a definite pattern: negative for quarters 1 and 4, positive for quarters 2 and 3.

31. **a.** There is a pattern: errors are positive, then negative, then positive, then negative.
   b. $r_1 = .531$; positive value indicates errors tend to come in streaks of positives, then negatives, and so on.

33. $r_1 > 0$, $r_6 < 0$, $r_{12} > 0$, because gas consumption does not vary much from one month to the next, months separated by half a year usually have quite different weather, but those separated by a whole year are similar.

35. If quantities change radically from one period to the next, the price index keeps measuring the prices of different "shopping carts" of goods.

37. 115.75, 131.85, 148.03; could be a useful measure even though all four costs receive the same weight.

39. Laspeyres: 103.37, 106.79, 109.94, 114.60; fixed-weights: 103.31, 106.81, 110.17, 114.95 (very similar to Laspeyres)

41. Graph indicates exponential fit is probably better, although neither is really good.

43. **a.** Customers at a popular new restaurant; sales of a new product that catches on quickly, then tapers off
   b. $\hat{\beta}_0 = 150.36$, $\hat{\beta}_1 = 24.903$

45. Seasonal components (starting with third quarter, 1977): .999, 1.077, .895, 1.021, .997, 1.079, .916, 1.008, .996, 1.087, .933, .978

47. Adding this term knocks off September 1982 and adds on September 1983, which is just what we need. This saves adding 12 numbers for each average.

27. a. Rock members average 7.73 records per year more than country-western members, classical members average 1.41 records per year less than country-western members, given that they have all been in the club the same amount of time. The longer members are in the club, the more records they buy (coefficient of MONTHS is positive).

    b. 15.02, 26.89 (rounded to 15, 27)

29. First equation: prediction is 192.98, standard error is 25.86; second equation: 185.01, 20.03; third equation: 188.65, 22.64. Based on these, second is probably most accurate.

31. a. Without: $\widehat{\text{SPEED}} = -1132.9 + 12.32\text{IQ}$; with: $\widehat{\text{SPEED}} = -1025.5 + 14.02\text{IQ}$ **b.** 160.7, 446.6

    c. For people without a speed-reading course, relevant coefficient of IQ is 12.32; for those with a speed-reading course, it is $12.32 + 1.7 = 14.02$

33. a. 1.428 hours/day; since $s_e = .75$, the probability of this prediction being off by more than 1 hour is fairly small (approximately .1)   **b.** $F = 11.76$ ($F_{.05,3,21} = 3.07$, $F_{.01,3,21} = 4.87$) so it is significant at both levels

    c. Confidence interval: $-.027$ to $.107$; $t = 1.25$ ($t_{.025,21} = 2.08$), not significant; could tell it is not significant because confidence interval includes 0

    d. Unmarried senior citizens watch about 1.2 hours less per day than those married (other variables being equal)

35. Nonlinear because of $\beta_1\beta_2$ term; could not estimate coefficients by OLS

37. Because RT and LT are extremely correlated; yes, standard errors will be large, but predictions should be accurate because either variable (RT or LT) is probably highly correlated with height.

39. Because it is impossible to separate the individual effects of the independent variables on the dependent variable

41. a. Unequal error variance (use logarithm of Y instead of Y as dependent variable)

    b. Nonlinearity appears to be present (use a quadratic term)

    c. Three separate groups of points (use a couple dummy variables)

43. Useful for detecting autocorrelation, especially for time series data; close to 0 or close to 4 means problems

45. Comparing first to second, $F = 6.48$ ($F_{.10,1,73} = 2.78$) so second is significantly better than first; comparing third to second, $F = 1.60$ ($F_{.10,4,69} = 2.03$) so third is not significantly better than second.

47. a. The change in the stock price is less than the change in the market or the change in the cosmetic industry (coefficients are less than 1).

    b. Probably not, since changes in the cosmetic industry could cause changes in the market, and vice versa.

    c. Expected change in the stock's price, given that the market index and the cosmetic index do not change; probably near 0

49. a. df's: 5, 14, 19; MS's: 340.82, 25.91; $F = 13.15$ is significant at just about any level, so overall fit is good; p-value (listed under "Significance") is much less than .01   **b.** 82.4%

    c. No, its effect may be accounted for by another independent variable.   **d.** 59.65, approximately .05

    e. Yes, particularly because YRS, AGE, and SEN are probably highly correlated; causes difficulty in estimating individual regression coefficients (large standard errors)

51. There are really two separate equations relating YRS to EFF, one for those over 50 (DAGE = 1) and one for those under 50 (DAGE = 0). Fit is good (high R^2).

53. a. Yes, because correlations between JOBEFF and independent variables are fairly high; possible problems of multicollinearity because of high correlations between independent variables

    b. $\widehat{\text{JOBEFF}} = -57.45 + .6097\text{TEST1} + .4294\text{TEST2} - .6130\text{TEST3} + 1.2223\text{TEST4}$. Confidence intervals: TEST1, .378 to .841; TEST2, .132 to .727; TEST3: $-.974$ to $-.252$; TEST4: .826 to 1.619. Problem of multicollinearity probably caused coefficient of TEST3 to be negative.   **c.** Yes, $F = 33.73$ is very large.   **d.** 79.20, 6.20

55. TEST4 is most important and explains $.6923^2$ (or 47.9%) of variation by itself. Other variables enter in order TEST1, then TEST3, then TEST2. R^2 increases to .8522 (72.6%), then $.8780^2$ (77.1%), then $.9185^2$ (84.4%), so each variable makes a substantial contribution. This is also seen by successive decreases in s_e.

57. a. $\widehat{\text{INC}} = 9.347 - .6080\text{AGRPCT} + .6340\text{EDUC}$

    b. For AGRPCT: -1.035 to $-.181$; for EDUC: .145 to 1.123. Can reject these H_0's because neither confidence interval includes 0.   **c.** $F = 8.04$ ($F_{.01,2,11} = 7.21$) so there is a significant overall fit.

59. a. Only possibly unexpected sign is between PRICE and COMPET, but this correlation is small in magnitude.

    b. Expect DEMAND to decrease by 1.775   **c.** $t_{.025,16} = 2.12$, so each of the t's is significant

61. Residuals are 3.82, 2.04, -4.28, -1.27, $-.27$, 1.41, 2.73, -4.69, 2.23, -1.21, 2.48, .34, -1.09, 2.23, -1.50, 1.57, -1.64, -4.28, .49, .93; scattergram of residuals indicates no violations of assumptions.

63. a. Three estimated sales: \$21,065, \$19,442, \$14,943; location 1 appears most promising.
    b. s_e is approximately \$760, so it appears unlikely that the true sales for location 1 could be lower than the other two.

65. a. For FERT: $t = 2.55$ ($t_{.05,12} = 1.782$), significant; for INSECT, $t = 1.47$, not significant.   **b.** .8
    c. Probably not, because FERT and INSECT are not going to be near 0.
    d. s_{ind} is approximately $s_e = 4.81$; s_{mean} is approximately $s_e/\sqrt{n} = 1.24$

67. a. Economists in securities and investment industry earn more on average ($\hat{\beta}_5$ is positive), those in nonprofit research earn less on average ($\hat{\beta}_6$ is negative).   **b.** All signs are probably as expected.
    c. Confidence intervals: .222 to .226, .0166 to .0213, .0410 to .0570, .133 to .247, .172 to .318, $-.276$ to $-.084$, $-.352$ to $-.210$, $-.333$ to $-.199$, .024 to .110, .023 to .133, and .069 to .175. None include 0, which means we are fairly certain they have the correct signs.

69. 3,107.94 (\$3,107,940), 2,689.79 (\$2,689,790); the change is affected by the interaction term with age and years as CEO.

71. a. Because X_j is then correlated with the other independent variables (so it could be explained well by these other variables).
    b. As R_j^2 increases, the denominator decreases, so the ratio increases.
    c. When the X's are correlated with each other, it is difficult to separate their individual effects on the dependent variable.

73. Researchers' hypothesis may hold, because coefficients for two equations are not the same (especially those for work and supervision). Large standard errors relative to magnitudes of regression coefficients indicate that some of the estimated signs could be wrong.

Solutions for Chapter 13

1. No, $\chi^2 = 5.065$ ($\chi^2_{.10,4} = 7.779$)

3. a. First row: 10.076, 26.565, 15.573, 7.786; second row: 6.718, 17.710, 10.382, 5.191; third row: 5.206, 13.725, 8.046, 4.023   **b.** Yes, there are several fairly large difference between E's and O's.
    c. $\chi^2 = 10.983$ ($\chi^2_{.10,6} = 10.645$), independence can be rejected

5. $\chi^2 = 23.001$ ($\chi^2_{.10,9} = 14.684$), reject equal proportions

7. $\chi^2 = 122.34$ ($\chi^2_{.01,9} = 21.666$), reject null hypothesis that there has been no shift

9. $\chi^2 = 7.83$ ($\chi^2_{.10,4} = 7.779$, $\chi^2_{.05,4} = 9.488$), reject at 10% level, do not reject at the 5% level

11. a. $\chi^2 = 2.571$ ($\chi^2_{.05,1} = 3.841$), difference is not significant
    b. $z = 1.603$ ($z_{.025} = 1.96$), again cannot accept two-tailed alternative. One-tailed test is probably appropriate because we expect the sleeping pills to be more effective; $z_{.05} = 1.645$, now H_0 still cannot be rejected, but it is very close.

13. $\chi^2 = 14.40$ ($\chi^2_{.10,12} = 18.549$), cannot reject independence, although several cells have fairly large $(E - O)^2/E$'s

15. $\chi^2 = 80.39$ ($\chi^2_{.05,8} = 15.507$), a very significant shift

17. With 200 MBAs: $\chi^2 = 6.67$ ($\chi^2_{.05,8} = 15.51$), not a significant difference. With 600 MBAs: $\chi^2 = 20.02$ ($\chi^2_{.05,8} = 15.51$), now a significant difference. These results partially support the conclusion of the article (but other types of shifts are also occurring).

19. $\chi^2 = 5.35$ ($\chi^2_{.10,4} = 7.779$), not significant evidence

21. a. First row: .375, .3, .2, .125; second row: .167, .45, .217, .167; third row: .233, .4, .2, .167
    b. $\chi^2 = 6.00$ ($\chi^2_{.05,6} = 12.592$), differences are not significant

23. Rank sum test does not require normal populations. Rank sum test is not as powerful, and the two populations should have the same shape. The t test requires normally-shaped populations.

25. a. $z = .853$ ($z_{.025} = 1.96$), differences not significant
    b. It ignores the magnitudes of the differences; in these data the differences with $+$'s are larger in magnitude than those with $-$'s.

27. $z = -.98$ ($z_{.05} = 1.645$), difference is not significant

49. a. Just keep plugging in; each time there is another $1 - \alpha$ factor.

b. For $\alpha = .1$: .09, .081, .0729, .0656, .0590; for $\alpha = .5$: .25, .125, .0625, .0313, .0156; for $\alpha = .8$: .16, .032, .0064, .0013, .0003   **c.** From part (a), coefficient of Y_{t-k} keeps getting smaller as k gets larger, especially when α is large.

51. a. F's (starting with F_1): 425, 450.08, 475.52, 506.96, 558.62, 623.15, 693.97, 768.91, 853.62, 957.44

b. Forecasts lag behind; the trend is nonlinear, and this method evidently cannot track a nonlinear trend well.

53. $r_1 = .776$; yes, and this can also be seen by the pattern of residuals (first positive, then negative, then positive)

55. 104.54, 105.86, 108.94; meaningful because they all refer to the same Q's; could be misleading if the Q's change radically after the base year, but here it did not make much difference (as compared to Paasche index from Problem 54).

57. $\hat{\beta}_0 = 1.6781$, $\hat{\beta}_1 = .1067$, or $\hat{Y}_t = 5.355(1.1126)^t$; estimate for 1987 is 526.4

Solutions for Chapter 15

1. For each decision and each outcome, a payoff is given. The costs are the negatives of payoffs. For each outcome the opportunity loss for a decision is the difference between that payoff and the payoff from the best decision. Opportunity losses: first row: 30, 15, 40, 0; second row: 55, 0, 30, 40; third row: 0, 65, 0, 90

3. No dominated decisions, so it is not obvious which decision is best

5. Example is cost table with first row: 10, 20, 30; second row: 15, 15, 40

7. d_4, d_2, tie between d_2 and d_3, d_3, d_3. Optimal decision is sensitive to p because it changes as p changes.

9. Optimal EMV is still 25, from decisions d_2 and d_3.

11. a. First row (neither product): 0, 0, 0; second row (product 1): 160, 40, -30; third row (product 2): 135, 40, -20; fourth row (both products): 245, 30, -65

b. Introduce both products, with EMV $= \$75,500$; would be indifferent between getting $\$75,500$ for sure and taking risk of introducing both products

13. Optimal EMV is still $\$70,800$, from 1 backup.

15. Optimal EMV is $\$5.49$, from decision 2; not dependent on C because this cost occurs for both pricing policies.

17. a. Has disease (D) or does not (ND); $P(D) = .1$, $P(ND) = .9$ **b.** Positive ($+$) or negative ($-$) response.

c. $P(+|ND) = .05$, $P(-|D) = .07$, $P(-|ND) = .95$, $P(+|D) = .93$

d. $P(+) = .138$ **e.** $P(D|+) = .674$ **f.** $P(ND|-) = .992$

19. a. .462, .197   **b.** $-\$1,060$, so do not drill   **21.** .563   **23.** .017

25. Most company would pay for survey is $\$10,393$. If survey cost is less than $\$10,393$, company should publish only if survey indicates moderate success or very successful.

27. a. $\$180,000$, $\$150,000$ **b.** $\$106,000$, $\$96,000$ **29. a.** $\$397.50$ **b.** At least $\frac{1}{9}$

31. a. Regardless of sample outcome, go with Monopolize; EMV $= \$102,000$

b. EVSI $= 0$, because same decision is made regardless of sample outcome

33. Perform test, market only if test is favorable; optimal EU is .1293.

35. a. A is best, optimal EMV $= \$86,250$ **b.** A is still best, optimal $EU = -40,573$

37. a. d_3, optimal $EU = 109.3$ **b.** $E\hat{U} = a + bEU$ for any decision, with $b > 0$, so if EU is maximized, so is $E\hat{U}$

39. Best decision is to go with A, $E(\text{loss}) = \$72$. $E(\text{loss})$ is the expected amount forgone by (unluckily) not choosing the decision that turns out to be best.

41. If $E(X)$ is expected profit from putting all $\$5,000$ in safe stock and $E(Y)$ is defined similarly for risky stock, expected profit from diversifying is $.5E(X) + .5E(Y)$, which is necessarily no greater than the larger of $E(X)$ and $E(Y)$ since it is halfway between $E(X)$ and $E(Y)$.

43. Irrigate now, EMV $= \$90$ **45.** Approximately $\$185$

47. Reject current offer, $E(\text{profit}) = \$66,220$ **49. a.** .9   **b.** .85   **c.** 60%

51. Accept order now, say sorry if it cannot be completed in time; EMV $= \$500$ **53.** Accept Smith's offer now

55. Unsuccessful at 3: P(at 1) = .441, P(at 2) = .294, P(at 3) = .118, P(at 4) = .147; unsuccessful at 1: P(at 1) = .079,
  P(at 2) = .263, P(at 3) = .526, P(at 4) = .132; unsuccessful at 2: P(at 1) = .357, P(at 2) = .048, P(at 3) = .476,
  P(at 4) = .119; unsuccessful at 4: P(at 1) = .326, P(at 2) = .217, P(at 3) = .435, P(at 4) = .022

57. First at 3 (.4 largest), then at 1 (.441 largest), then at 2 (.454 largest)

59. a. $U(580) = 5$, $U(280) = 2.5$, $U(180) = 1.67$, $U(135) = 1.25$
  b. Yes, for each gamble in II he needs more EMV than in I to be willing to gamble.   **c.** Y must be at least $133.33.

Solutions for Chapter 16

1. All single-family dwelling within city limits; frame must include assessed valuation for each of these; sampling units are single-family dwellings.

3. (A, B, C), (A, B, D), (A, B, E), (A, C, D), (A, C, E), (A, D, E), (B, C, D), (B, C, E), (B, D, E), (C, D, E); each should have probability .1

5. Families selected: 36, 7, 20, 10, 33, 2, 27, 40, 17, 15

7. Error is difference between true mean and estimate of it; error is very likely to be less than this bound; magnitude of bound is half-length of confidence interval.

9. $\overline{X} = \$28,182$, confidence interval, \$21,812 to \$34,552; $\hat{p} = .4$, confidence interval, .128 to .672.

11. a. 1519   **b.** 1321 more   **13.** 95% of them; this is the meaning of a 95% confidence interval.

15. Because rates within these strata might be fairly homogeneous, resulting in a lower overall standard error.

17. Use frames from each of the strata to select four simple random samples, as in Section 16.3

19. $\hat{p} = .469$, confidence interval, .433 to .505

21. $n_1 = 103$, $n_2 = 80$, $n_3 = 69$, $n_4 = 34$; confidence interval could be significantly shorter than specified.

23. For simple random sampling: $\text{StdErr}(\overline{X}) = 1.09$; for stratified sampling: $\text{StdErr}(\overline{X}) = .708$

25. Stratum 1: $\overline{X}_1 = 25.7$, confidence interval, 22.56 to 28.84; stratum 2: $\overline{X}_2 = 32.5$, confidence interval, 31.84 to 33.16; stratum 3: $\overline{X}_3 = 40.3$, confidence interval, 40.14 to 40.46; total population: $\overline{X} = 36.89$, confidence interval, 36.52 to 37.26

27. .444, .132

29. a. $\hat{p} = .56$, confidence interval, .466 to .654
  b. $\hat{p} = .56$, confidence interval, .466 to .654 [same as in part (a), by coincidence]

31. $\hat{p} = .721$, confidence interval, .684 to .758   **33.** $\hat{p} = .149$, confidence interval, .138 to .161

35. Because a census is taken in each sampled cluster, so no errors arise

37. Probably that it is physically easier and cheaper. It is probably a good idea, because individual counties possess same type of behavior as state as a whole.

39. Numbers of samples: 10 ($n = 1$), 45 ($n = 2$), 120 ($n = 3$), 210 ($n = 4$), 252 ($n = 5$), 210 ($n = 6$), 120 ($n = 7$), 45 ($n = 8$), 10 ($n = 9$), 1 ($n = 10$)

41. Because the population sizes for individual strata are generally unequal; it is a true average only when these are equal; we do not use the usual average because we want to give larger weights to strata with larger population sizes.

43. a. For 150: $\hat{p} = \frac{8}{15}$, confidence interval, .287 to .779; for 300: $\hat{p} = \frac{8}{15}$, confidence interval, .281 to .785   **b.** 110, 172

45. $\overline{X} = \$3.70$, confidence interval, \$3.61 to \$3.79   **47.** $\hat{p} = .500$, confidence interval, .350 to .650, half-length is exactly .15

49. Error bound is .098, $\hat{p} = .488$; confidence interval, .390 to .586; means confidence interval half-length is .098, slightly less than .10

51. a. 4.836, .539   **b.** .656, .070   **53.** $\overline{X} = \$52,835$, confidence interval, \$47,801 to \$57,869

55. Simple random sample of clusters is first chosen, using random number table; then a census of each sampled cluster is taken.

Index

Table III   Percentiles of the *t* Distribution

This table gives values with specified probabilities to the right of them for the specified *t* distributions.

Degrees of freedom v	Right-hand tail probability α			
	.10	.05	.025	.01
1	3.078	6.314	12.706	31.821
2	1.886	2.920	4.303	6.965
3	1.638	2.353	3.182	4.541
4	1.533	2.132	2.776	3.747
5	1.476	2.015	2.571	3.365
6	1.440	1.943	2.447	3.143
7	1.415	1.895	2.365	2.998
8	1.397	1.860	2.306	2.896
9	1.383	1.833	2.262	2.821
10	1.372	1.812	2.228	2.764
11	1.363	1.796	2.201	2.718
12	1.356	1.782	2.179	2.681
13	1.350	1.771	2.160	2.650
14	1.345	1.761	2.145	2.624
15	1.341	1.753	2.131	2.602
16	1.337	1.746	2.120	2.583
17	1.333	1.740	2.110	2.567
18	1.330	1.734	2.101	2.552
19	1.328	1.729	2.093	2.539
20	1.325	1.725	2.086	2.528
21	1.323	1.721	2.080	2.518
22	1.321	1.717	2.074	2.508
23	1.319	1.714	2.069	2.500
24	1.318	1.711	2.064	2.492
25	1.316	1.708	2.060	2.485
26	1.315	1.706	2.056	2.479
27	1.314	1.703	2.052	2.473
28	1.313	1.701	2.048	2.467
29	1.311	1.699	2.045	2.462
30	1.310	1.697	2.042	2.457
40	1.303	1.684	2.021	2.423
60	1.296	1.671	2.000	2.390
120	1.289	1.658	1.980	2.358
z_α	1.282	1.645	1.960	2.326

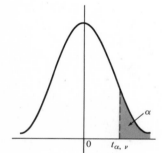

Example: For a *t* distribution with 20 degrees of freedom, the probability of being greater than 1.725 is .05. By symmetry, the probability of being to the left of -1.725 is also .05.

Source: E. S. Pearson and H. O. Hartley, *Biometrika Tables for Statisticians,* Vol. I. London: Cambridge University Press, 1966. Reproduced by permission of the *Biometrika* Trustees. Partly derived from Table III of Fisher and Yates, *Statistical Tables for Biological, Agricultural and Medical Research,* published by Longman Group Ltd., London (previously published by Oliver & Boyd, Edinburgh, 1963).